Hicks

Jackie Hicks
2nd Yr
734-0228

$2795

Managing Career Systems

Channeling the Flow of Executive Careers

The Irwin Series in Management and The Behavioral Sciences
L. L. Cummings and E. Kirby Warren, *Consulting Editors*
John F. Mee, *Advisory Editor*

Managing Career Systems

Channeling the Flow of Executive Careers

Jeffrey A. Sonnenfeld
Graduate School of Business Administration
Harvard University

 1984

RICHARD D. IRWIN, INC.
Homewood, Illinois   60430

ISBN 0-256-03143-6
Library of Congress Catalog Card No. 83–83331
Printed in the United States of America

1 2 3 4 5 6 7 8 9 0 K 1 0 9 8 7 6 5 4

This book is dedicated to my parents Rochelle and Burton Sonnenfeld and my brother Marc Sonnenfeld. Their inspiration, compassion, encouragement and societal concern have enormously influenced this volume on careers, let alone my own career.

Preface

Some resources, such as iron ore, lie idle and submerged, awaiting discovery. Other resources, such as water, are mobile, endowed with motion independent of our discovery. By understanding the natural flow of water, we have learned to channel it towards improving the quality of life through such activities as the production of hydropower, the prevention of diseased, stagnant drinking water, the provision of transportation across great stretches of land, and the flood control measures which check the dangers of overflow. In the course of their lives, people flow through work organizations. They gain entry, they gain membership, they advance, and they depart. Organizations try to channel this flow in ways which best release energy, prevent stagnation, and control outflow. In this book, we shall look at how firms can understand and control this natural flow of human resources. In particular, we will look at firms' ability to channel the flow of executive careers.

Unlike the management of other resources, where we are concerned primarily with efficient exploitation and renewal of supply, the proper management of *human* resources requires the participation and the development of the resource. Employees are not passive fuel to be consumed by the engines of work. Instead the employees, while critical resources, are also partners in the work process. Along with the company owners, employees are stakeholders in the success of the work process. Thus, as employees pass through the work organization, they both shape it and are shaped by it.

This two-way interaction is greater in the career development of managers than that of other workers. Managers tend to have more influence than others on the general patterns of their careers as well as upon the destiny of others. This is one reason why this book emphasizes executive development. A second reason is because the development of executive careers is a particularly complex and mystical process. While it may not be easy, at all times, to develop a skillful welder, a proficient assembler, an expert financial analyst, or an insightful engineer, it is far more clear how to manage such careers. Functional job expertise is developed through careful selection, specific training, and thoughtful patterns of assignments.

The needed skills, required sequence of experiences, criteria of excellence, and vision of one's next career moves are far more hazy for managers than for other workers.

This look at the management of corporate systems examines how certain personnel practices can be coordinated to develop needed executive talent. It is intended for study by general managers and human resource experts concerned about developing managerial talent but is especially targeted towards graduate students in management. Special emphasis is given to the impact of four sets of dynamics: (1) the interactions of career systems; and (4) the impact of soci-individual life stages upon career systems; (3) the impact of company life stages upon career systems, and (4) the impact of societal changes upon career systems. The cases cover a broad range of companies from small entrepreneurial firms to worldwide industrial giants. Traditional heavy manufacturing firms, high technology suppliers, and changing service industries are all studied.

In each of these settings, what is managed is not merely the energy and dreams of workers nor the needs and accomplishments of companies. Rather these concerns, whether personal or organizational, are managed relative to time—a nonrenewable resource. The great historian Daniel J. Boorstin recently wrote in *The Discoverers*:

> The first grand discovery was time—the landscape of experience. Only by the marking of months, weeks, and years, days and hours, minutes and seconds, would mankind be liberated from the cyclical monotony of nature. The flow of shadows, sand, and water, and time itself translated into a clock's staccato became a useful measure of man's movements across the planet. (Boorstin, 1983, p. 1).

Time, like oceans, continents, and planets,

exists independent of our discovery. Humankind's realization of the passage of time allows us to chart and plan the best use of this limited and precious resource. Career management, on the personal level and the company level, is the intelligent planning of the time which is consumed by our work lives.

Acknowledgments

Obviously a book this large and global, both in its volume and in its intended range of management topics, represents more influences than those solely of its author. The conceptual frameworks, the development of the cases, and the production of this publication have all benefited from the wise insights of many colleagues, several close friends, over 300 executives from the companies who assisted in the case profiles, at least 10 staff members of the Harvard Business School, and my family. This team shares in my satisfaction in completing this book, and I want to acknowledge their assistance.

Looking first at my immediate colleagues, the person who springs immediately to mind, and without rival, is Professor John Kotter from the Harvard Business School. John's enthusiastic endorsement and continuous interest has given me the courage to tamper with his pioneering work on introducing career issues to the classroom. My course, Career Management, is actually a later-life stage of his Self Assessment and Career Development course, which was a success since its infancy. The course now places equal emphasis on the organizational perspective through the career systems materials contained in this book and the personal perspective contained in John's materials. Other immediate colleagues who have served as career guides and advisors include Professors Paul R. Lawrence, Jay Lorsch, Richard Walton, Chris Argyris, Robert Miles, Michael Beer, D. Quinn Mills, Len Schlesinger, Howard Stevenson, John Gabarro, Richard Tedlow, and Calvin Pava. Paul Lawrence and Jay Lorsch initially attracted me to this sort of a career itself through their demonstrated commitment to making contributions on the frontiers of knowledge. They served as important early mentors in steering me towards the topic of careers. Quinn Mills, Dick Walton, and Mike Beer have each contributed through their ready embrace of career management as a critical element of human resource management. Quinn and Dick have helped me to appreciate the power of career development interventions as potent management levers, while Mike has convinced many of us of the value of tracking the flow of human resources through the organization. Chris Argyris and Bob Miles have served as consistently dedicated and thoughtful readers of a staggering portion of my writings. These two scholars are noted for their editorial judgment and breadth of behavioral insight. I was never in doubt of that opinion, and I remain much in debt to them. Finally, my colleagues Len Schlesinger, Jack Gabarro, Howard Stevenson, Richard Tedlow, and Cal Pava have generously served as sounding boards for many key brainstorming sessions on case development. I would also like to thank Dean John H. McArthur of the Harvard Business School for his consistent encouragement of this line of inquiry.

There are many scholars outside of this campus whom I must thank for their influence on this project. Professors David Riesman, George Homans, and Roger Brown of the Harvard Sociology and Psychology departments inspired me as an undergraduate to strive towards social contribution through the application of behavioral science to human problems. They convinced me of the importance of the Business School's field work and have remained trusted intellectual advisors for a dozen years. Professors Edgar H. Schein of the Sloan School at MIT, Douglas T. Hall of Boston University, Fernando Bartolomé of Bentley College, Anthony Athos of Boston College, Michael Arthur of Suffolk University, Barbara Lawrence of UCLA, Arvind Bhambri of the University of Southern California, Mary Ann von Glinow of the University of Southern California, James Clawson of the Darden School at the University of Virginia, John Davis of the University of Southern California, Victor Faux of the University of Hartford, and Thomas Gutteridge of the University of Southern Illinois have each shown an interest in the conceptual underpinnings of this book. They have recognized the importance of moving beyond a strictly personal or individual perspective on careers to consider the wide-ranging career demands a firm must address. In particular, I am grateful for the unique suggestions and thoughtful feedback of Ed Schein, Tim Hall, Arvind Bhambri, Tony Athos, and Fernando Bartolomé, which often served as basic conceptual building blocks.

In turning to the cases, I must of course thank the contributing authors for their efforts. I have listed each in the table of contents, yet I would like to especially thank those who have served as collaborators with me on several of these cases. They include James Dowd of the Harvard Business School, Peter Blanck of the Stanford Law School, Liora Katzenstein of the Jerusalem Institute of Management, David Fisher of the Irish Development Bank, Marylou Balbaky and Pamela Posey of the Harvard Business School, and Alice Morgan of the Cambridge Research Institute. I would also like to thank Dr. Fred Jacobs, Provost of the John Jay School of Criminal Justice, and Professors Wickham Skinner, Earl Sasser, John Gabarro, Len Schlesinger, and Thomas Raymond of the Harvard Business School for the use of some of their case materials. The truly unsung heroes of this case development effort are of course the executives who assisted from the participating companies. While they are too numerous to name, I would like to mention the following particularly generous managers: Charles Brazik of Hartmarx; Geri Kurlander of Union Carbide; Stephen Wall of Union Carbide; Jan Blakslee of the American Hospital Supply Corporation; Robert Goldfarb of Eastern Public Radio; Adam Aron of Pan American World Airways; Patrick Rich of Alcan Canada (CEO); Jerry Giordano, an independent consultant; Donald Feddersen of Applicon (CEO); Paul Mosher of Data Resources Incorporated; James Baughman of General Electric; Chester Siver of Conval Inc. (CEO); Richard Dunington, formerly of IBM and now an independent consultant; Bruce Henderson of the Boston Consulting Group (formerly CEO); Charles Francis Adams III of Raytheon (formerly CEO); Robert Lear, formerly of F. M. Schaefer Brewing (CEO); Thomas Carroll, formerly of Lever Brothers (CEO); John Fery of Boise Cascade (CEO); James McSwiney of the Mead Corporation (formerly CEO); and George Weyerhauser of the Weyerhauser Corporation (CEO).

These cases were also dependent upon the support of the Harvard Graduate School of Business Administration. The generous funding and thoughtful suggestions of the Division of Research at the Harvard Business School was perhaps the most central single ingredient making this volume a possibility. In particular, I want to express my gratitude to its Director, Professor E. Raymond Corey, Associate Director Joanne Se-

gal, and Assistant Director, Kathryn May. Other vital assistance from the School came from Rose Giacobbe and her crew of miracle workers of the School's word processing center, Marion Malkasian, Jean Burleson, Norman Descoteaux, Erna Manning, Audrey Barrett of HBS Case Services, and Dolores Mullin of the Audio Visual Center. My secretary and friend Gloria Buffonge labored with great dedication, speed, and tact in processing the endless array of tasks related to case development and preparation.

Beyond the conceptual development, the case writing, and the manuscript preparation are the contributions of a few very close friends and my family. Their genuine concern through the emotional ups and downs of this project as well as their insightful editorship deserves a deep thanks. Each of the following people faithfully assisted in the resolution of many of the minor crises which erupted during the course of this project: Linda Hill, Professor Niki Steckler, and Professor Michael Rukstad of the Harvard Business School, Joan Hornig and Diana Krumholz of Columbia University, George Hornig of the First Boston Corporation, Diane Hessan of the Forum Corporation, Dede Trefts of the Saddlebrook Corporation, Adam Aron of Pan American World Airways, Paula Carlson of the Boston Consulting Group, and John Lechner of Kidder Peabody. My parents Rochelle and Burton Sonnenfeld and my brother Marc Sonnenfeld certainly contributed emotional support, but it is far too antiseptically stated as merely that. They provided the needed caring, the humor, the sense of adventure, the perspective on the preciousness of time, and the optimism about societal progress which motivated me to even attempt such an undertaking as this, let alone a career in this field.

Finally, the motivation, the resources, and the support offered by each of the above individuals provided more than enough force to drive this project through to completion. Nonetheless, one individual's intense loyalty to the project ensured that the needed momentum would be maintained so that the book would meet its final deadlines. James Dowd, my research assistant, not only dutifully and tenaciously followed up on each of the several hundred exchanges needed to secure reprint permissions and the many other tedious but vital administrative tasks, but he also assumed a sense of pride and interest in the project which gave him the courage to question the author on fundamental conceptual schemes, case selections, and arrangement of materials and to give a scrupulous inspection of each written word of text.

Jeffery A. Sonnenfeld

Contents

    Introduction. Creation and Start-Up. Maturation and
    Transformation. Decline and Termination. The Cases. The
    Readings.

An Introduction to the Management of Career Systems

The Return to Work

The workplace is once again in the spotlight of national attention. In the 1960s, domestic crises surrounding family life, civil rights, urban affairs, the divisiveness of Vietnam, and campus unrest nudged the workplace from the center stage of discussion. In the 1970s, managerial and general public concern over alienation in the factories not only reinvigorated the nearly dormant interest in the quality of work life but also sparked a return of focus on the workplace. In recent years, the desire for improved rewards and enhanced settings for one's labors has swept the land from the shop floor to the executive suite. This renewal of attention toward work has been fueled by several major discontinuities in our society, such as a decline in international competitiveness, demographic crowding, new informaton technologies, shifts in economic sectors from manufacturing to service, and a transformation in work values. The swelling preoccupation with one's occupation is not merely focused on the static qualities of one's immediate job. The full career—the lifelong sequences of work-related events, roles, and experiences—has become the preferred style for discussing one's work life. The terms career goals, career paths, career mobility, career switches, career advancement, career crises, and the like are new but already familiar additions to the lexicon of everyday life.

This career consciousness is demonstrated in many ways, including social attitudes, school enrollment, publication, and company programs. Survey researchers, such as Daniel Yankelovich, report a "new breed" of American workers who demonstrate a great commitment to work coupled with strong aspirations for personal fulfillment at work.[1] Ends and means are experiencing a modest reversal for some as the career itself assumes a meaning far beyond the mere provision of the means for attaining off-the-job pleasures and necessities. The new career consciousness emphasizes life satisfactions, self-respect, social standing, achievement, challenge, and the sense of contribution gained through work. The fastest-growing sections of book stores and libraries are the career development shelves. New titles surge forward each week while old standards continue to ride the crests.

---

[1] Daniel Yankelovich, "Work Values and the New Breed," in *Work in America: The Decade Ahead*, ed. Clark Kerr and Jerome M. Rosow (New York: Van Nostrand Reinhold, 1979).

For example, Richard N. Bolles's famous *What Color Is Your Parachute?* has sold roughly 2 million copies.[2] Some 30 popular periodicals provide regular emphasis to career issues while many professional and trade journals provide frequent career tips to their readers.

In schools this new career fascination is reflected in reported dramatic shifts in undergraduate majors. For example, only 5 percent of undergraduates now receive degrees in English, down from 12 percent a decade ago.[3] The career-oriented emphasis in education is best evidenced by the increase in business school graduates—from 21,000 in 1970 to more than 50,000 in 1980.[4] Over 20 percent of these schools even have courses which are devoted to the study of career issues.[5] Evening courses and corporate-sponsored career planning programs abound. Companies use workbooks, lectures, counseling, training sessions, appraisals, and other techniques to introduce career management to the workforce.

Academic research and theory about careers has accompanied this increased societal awareness of career needs. Initially, researchers presumed that occupations were largely prescribed by one's social class at birth, and that individual traits leading to occupational success were determined in early childhood. In the last 20 years, researchers have come to appreciate the dynamism of the career environment and the developmental capacities of adults.[6] Instead of

viewing the individual as a passive and reactive accommodator to a set character and a limited array of career opportunities, we have begun to learn how individuals formulate career goals, make choices, develop new skills, and shape their environments.

The Organizational Perspective

Despite this intense interest in career issues, much of the discussion examines only the personal perspective on careers. The organization's perspective has been largely neglected. Critical career issues face employers as well as employees. Company executives must concern themselves not only with their own careers but with the careers of their workers and colleagues. Occasionally we hear a manager complain, "I don't like playing big brother or playing fortune-teller. Hard work and intelligence are the only type of career planning necessary." Unfortunately, the context of careers makes such a perspective dangerously naive. Performance and energy are important but more is required. Changing company needs, the need for appropriate sequential learning and experience to attain certain jobs, and the company political savvy needed to gain access to important career information are some of the reasons why career planning is important. It is true that one cannot successfully predict a career trajectory; luck, unexpected events, and changes in life circumstances can cause individuals and organizations to change their goals. Both the organization and the individual can take advantage of new opportunities only if the individual is prepared. As Louis Pasteur advised, "Chance favors the mind which is prepared."

Accordingly, managers must be prepared to accommodate the career needs of employees in ways consistent with the human

---

[2] Jeffrey Sonnenfeld and John Kotter, "The Maturation of Career Theory," *Human Relations* 35, no. 1 (1982), pp. 19–46.

[3] "Liberal Arts Lower in Popularity," *The Wall Street Journal*, September 1, 1983, p. 1.

[4] Richard N. Bolles, *What Color Is Your Parachute?* (Berkeley, Calif.: Ten Speed Press, 1974).

[5] Chris Welles, "Who Will Make Money in the 1980s?" *Esquire*, September 1982, p. 22.

[6] Jeffrey Sonnenfeld, "Editor's Note," *The Career Forum* 2, no. 2 (1983), p. 2.

resource needs of their firm. Frequently managers hold new job opportunities close to their vests, unwilling to notify others around the firm for fear of being flooded with unfamiliar candidates. Even more common are the managers who refuse to promote or further develop a cherished employee because of their fear of losing a highly talented and presumedly irreplaceable worker. Companies are unable to plan for future needs, and individuals cannot find the required form of human growth, if managers think of workers as merely job-holders instead of as career members of the organization. As long as 45 years ago, Chester Barnard pointed out in his classic book, *The Functions of the Executive,* that the primary management tasks are to "maintain a cooperative social system" by securing: (1) its collective adaptation to the environment, and (2) the satisfaction of the personal objectives of its members.[7] Managing the career implications of organization life provides the impetus for corporate development as well as for individual development.

The Urgency of Career Issues for Management

In the years subsequent to Barnard, this managerial mission has become both more difficult and more important. Organizations require certain constellations of talent, experience, and commitment. Managers must decide whether the needed human resources are to be acquired from the outside or be developed from within the organization. Staff surpluses and staff shortages have to be anticipated to be managed effectively. The balance between personal inter-

ests and work opportunities is in a state of continual flux. People's values shift and their skills become obsolete. Some jobs may be enhanced and others may be degraded.

The specific forces of change in our "post-industrial society" that add a sense of urgency to the understanding of the dynamics of career systems include new technologies, legislation (as that in financial services which changes the definition of industries), and patterns of industrial maturation leading to profound shifts between sectors of the economy. Last year, for the first time, the majority of the nation was employed in service, rather than manufacturing, industries. Already as many as 15 million people work primarily with information technology, and as many as 45 million jobs are likely to experience significant change as a result of this technology. Meanwhile, the powerful impact of the World War II baby boom generation is beginning to be felt. The head of the generation is in its late 30s and early 40s, while the tail of the generation is in its early 20s. The median age has already increased to 30 from 28 a decade earlier and is creeping towards age 38. Over the past decade there has been a 35 percent increase in the number of 25- to 44-year-olds. This has already intensified job search competition. This age bracket will have increased by 55 percent between 1975 and 1990. Many companies have willingly taken advantage of this large selection pool of new recruits. What will happen as this pool of new recruits later shrinks by 10 percent? What will happen as the bulge generation settles into the traditional lowered mobility and lessened opportunity available at mid-life?[8] As this generation jams into the crowded and antiquated career pipelines in corporations,

---

[7] Chester Barnard, *The Functions of the Executive* (Cambridge, Mass.: Harvard University Press, 1938).

[8] Jeffrey Sonnenfeld, "Dealing with an Aging Work Force," *Harvard Business Review* 56, no. 4 (November–December 1978).

pressures are bound to result that are reminiscent of the campus unrest of the recent past.

These issues have already been recognized by segments of the workforce. Demands for retraining have come from such diverse groups as displaced steelworkers and autoworkers, employed telephone operators and linespeople, community leaders in depressed regions, chemical engineers, oil and chemical engineers, and bank executives. Groups representing the work interests of women, minorities, and older people have begun to focus on such issues as plateauing of careers and the shrinkage of middle-management opportunities.[9] Effective management of career systems can do more than keep the organization responsive to such worker concerns. It also can provide the following benefits to the organization:

1. An inventory of worker skills and career goals ready for company use for relocation, reassignment, or retraining needs.
2. A better process for identifying future human resource needs.
3. The improvement of organizational change processes by a richer understanding of the micro or individual level of change.
4. A smoother and more successful facilitation of individual changes to new assignments and responsibilities by involving people in their own development plans.
5. The improved ability to anticipate the various stages of development for the variety of occupations and professions within a firm.
6. A policy for explicitly surfacing previously unrealized and hidden employee expectations.

7. A means of energizing and retraining endangered segments of the work force.

Defining Career Systems

It is now appropriate to define more specifically this concept of a career system. Systems involve the coordination of interdependent parts working toward some common goals. Examples include physiological systems, such as digestion or respiration, and social systems, such as families, neighborhoods, communities, and nations. Biologist L. J. Henderson and organization researchers Elton Mayo, Fritz Roethlisberger, and George Homans applied these concepts to work systems more than 50 years ago.[10] The workplace, as was argued, was more than a production system with a flow of work; it was also a social system with a flow of people.[11] Since that time, theorists have come to appreciate the workplace as an open system which is involved in exchanges with the external environment. An open system is described by the input of resources from the outside, the internal development and use of these resources, and the return or output of these transformed resources into products. The company acts as a career system in that it

[9] Albert S. Glickman, ed., *The Changing Composition of the Workforce* (New York: Plenum, 1982).

[10] Emile Durkheim, *Division of Labor in Society* (Glencoe, Ill.: Free Press, first published in French in 1893); Elton Mayo, *The Human Problems of an Industrial Civilization* (New York: Macmillan, 1933); L. J. Henderson, *Pareto's General Sociology* (Cambridge, Mass.: Harvard University Press, 1935); Fritz J. Roethlisberger and William J. Dickson, *Management and the Worker* (Cambridge, Mass.: Harvard University Press, 1937); George C. Homans, *The Human Group* (New York: Harcourt Brace Jovanovich, 1939).

[11] Jeffrey Sonnenfeld, "Hawthorne Hoopla in Perspective: Critical Illusions and Contextual Illumination" (Working Paper, Harvard Graduate School of Business Administration, 1981).

attracts people from the outside pool of labor (through assignments and training, and so on) and it releases them (through retirements, firings, layoffs, and resignations).

This flow of people through the firm from entry, development, and utilization through exit need not be mechanistic or exploitive. Not only can individuals receive a fair return during their career within a firm through payment, learning, and friendships, they also may gain intrinsic rewards through their involvement in shaping the firm. Organizations are not defined by their buildings, their logos, or their machines. Organizations are defined through their membership. The culture, strategy, and formal organizational structure of firms are determined by the most dominant members of the firm or by what theorist James D. Thompson called "the dominant coalition."[12] Career researcher John Kotter has suggested that the career policies of firms are empowering practices—whether intentional or inadvertent. Career policies determine which individuals gain exposure to which products, who develops expertise in certain processes, and who gains recognition or exposure on the outside.[13] The dynamic shaping and reshaping of the firm is a specialized property of such a system. Through its human resource policies, a firm, unlike the physiological system of a living being, has the capacity to be infinitely regenerative. It is the career system that allows for the repopulation and redirection necessary for the firm to succeed its founding generation. Naturally a firm with a vibrant career system cannot survive unless its market strategy, financial structure, and legal posture also are healthy. The ca-

[12] James D. Thompson, *Organizations in Action* (New York: McGraw-Hill, 1967).

[13] John P. Kotter, *The General Manager* (New York: Free Press, 1982).

reer system, however, is no less important a business concern than these other areas. New ideas about how to position, how to organize, and how to run a business come from people. The preparation, adaptiveness, and awareness of the executive team and the necessary training of the workforce could be provided through an effective career system.

Career Systems and Human Resource Management

Career systems capture the more dynamic nature of human resource management policies. The most cross-sectional concerns of human resource management, such as: *stakeholder relations*—including labor relations, government legislation, and community relations; *rewards systems*—including compensation, benefits, promotions, appraisal; and *work design*—including job task design, quality of work life, social-technological interfaces, and work conditions, are not the core ingredients of the career system. Instead, the *career system* is composed of the longitudinal and dynamic issues outlined on Figure 1–1. As the figure shows, activities include recruitment, selection, entry, socialization, training, assignments, promotions, and exit (retirement, layoff, resignation, firings). Thus, career systems is the fourth leg of the field of human resources with stakeholder relations, measurement and reward systems, and work design as the other three. Figure 1–1 also indicates that there is more to the study of careers than the human resource dimension captured by career systems. Just as there are other aspects of human resources than career systems, there are also other aspects of the study of careers than career systems. In addition to career systems, other dimen-

Figure 1–1 Career Management Components

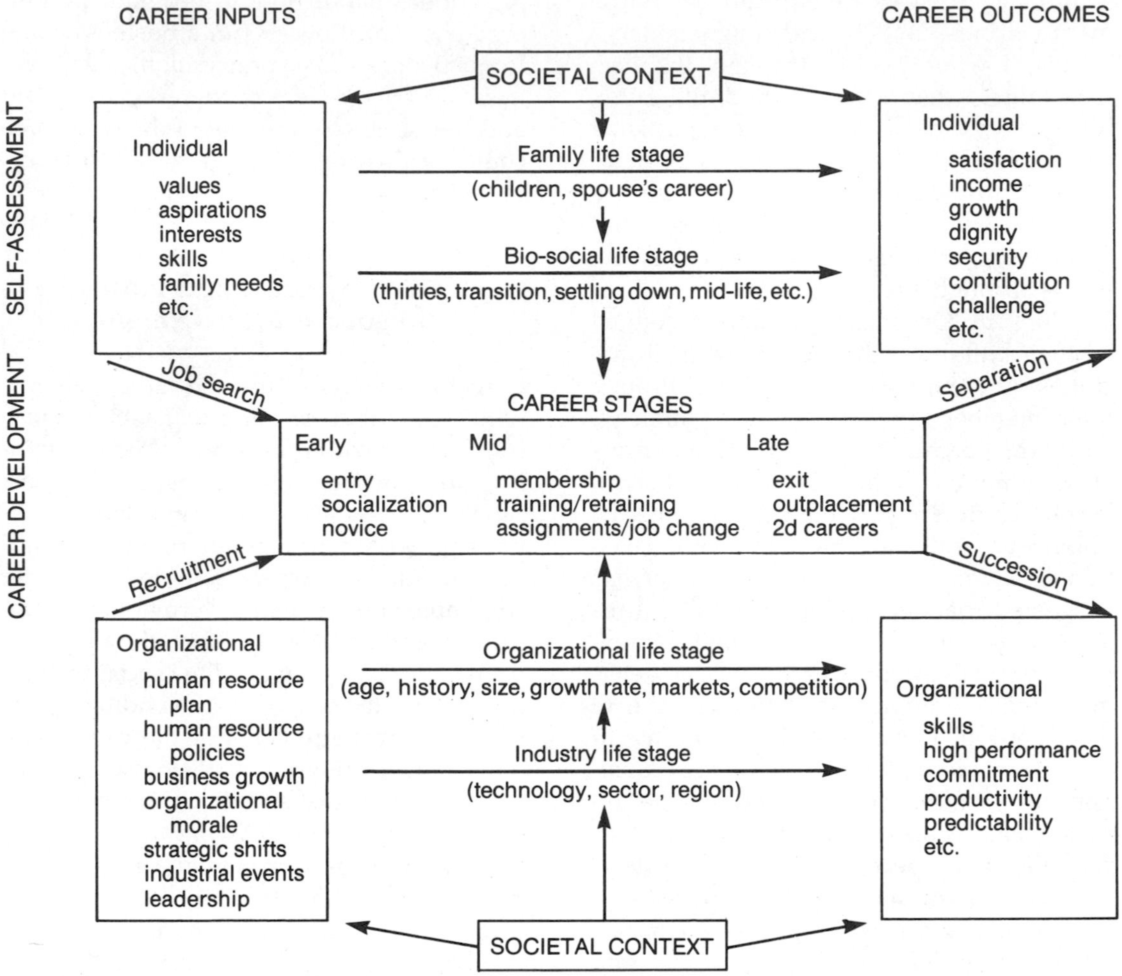

CAREER INPUTS   CAREER OUTCOMES

SELF-ASSESSMENT

CAREER DEVELOPMENT

SOCIETAL CONTEXT

Individual

values
aspirations
interests
skills
family needs
etc.

Family life stage

(children, spouse's career)

Bio-social life stage

(thirties, transition, settling down, mid-life, etc.)

Individual

satisfaction
income
growth
dignity
security
contribution
challenge
etc.

Job search

Recruitment

CAREER STAGES

Early	Mid	Late
entry	membership	exit
socialization	training/retraining	outplacement
novice	assignments/job change	2d careers

Separation

Succession

Organizational

human resource
plan
human resource
policies
business growth
organizational
morale
strategic shifts
industrial events
leadership

Organizational life stage

(age, history, size, growth rate, markets, competition)

Industry life stage

(technology, sector, region)

Organizational

skills
high performance
commitment
productivity
predictability
etc.

SOCIETAL CONTEXT

sions which enrich our knowledge of career events include the more individual self-assessment and career development concerns which appear on this model. While individual influences, industrial influences, and societal influences also affect one's career experience as registered in the dimension labeled career development, these forces are only indirect influences of the career system. This book will therefore consider these forces to the extent that they affect each of the elements of the career system.

Examining the Components of Career Systems

Many career systems are the product more often of evolution than of conscious design. The different emphasis placed on such various activities as planning, recruitment, training, assignment, succession, and exit programs may well be the result of a stream of unrelated internal factors. Such determining factors include: (1) the shift of major events in the company history (e.g., lawsuits, labor surpluses, or labor shortages); (2) corporate politics (e.g., executive preferences or departmental influences); (3) attributes of corporate culture (e.g., leadership priorities, commitment to internal personnel development; or (4) different patterns of needs by decentralized divisions. People are often hired to fill vacant positions instead of hired to begin careers within a firm.

Accordingly, companies' formal human resource policies deal with the flow of talent through the firm in a far more fragmentary manner than the way other policies channel the flow of products, finances, or management information through the firm. Consider the following situation:

A manager of an expanding specialty paper plant of a large paper company was transformed overnight from being seen as the local hero in a southern county, to the local villain in the area. He had refused to absorb any of the 350 workers laid off from the closing of a folding carton plant owned by the same company which operated in a neighboring town. The plant manager of this specialty paper plant complained: "The local press, the union, and even the company has made me out to be a demon. I just went out and recruited people from as far away as 168 miles, trained them—many were completely unskilled—to fill the urgent need for help we had six months ago. What do they want me to do, fire these new hires? I'd have loved to have experienced locals; but no one ever told me that they'd be laying off over at the carton plant." The former manager of the carton plant defended himself by claiming: "I didn't know that they'd be hiring over at the specialty paper plant until they made offers. We work

in completely different divisions. Furthermore, they seemed to be in a hurry to staff-up over there. I didn't have time to worry about sending people over there. We weren't sure what we were going to do here, we were trying to keep this place running."

Some consequences of this confusion were: the distrust of the company by its workforce, the suspicion of age bias by the union leaders, the loss of talented and well-trained workers, and the great personal hardship faced by the laid-off workers and their families. Decentralized, weak personnel staffs and short-term human resource thinking characterize many company career systems. Line managers, strategic planners, and human resource specialists have little direct interaction over common areas of concern. In this particular case, the company's industrial relations staff was reactively called upon to work out a plan to appease the unions and the town. The displaced workers were supported for six weeks of limited study on a local community college campus for retraining in health care and in welding, but few were able to secure employment nearby, even with such credentials.

In this example, we can see the distressing costs to companies and to individuals of the fragmentary and reactive approach to staffing an organization. Other common examples might include: (1) recruitment programs with high early career turnover; (2) an obsolete workforce whose skills are atrophying due to mutually inconsistent human resource programs; (3) the flight of experienced, trained, and valuable executives; (4) the assignment of high-potential new recruits to deadend jobs; (5) poorly allocated training dollars, which serve to entertain rather than to educate workers; and (6) the lack of opportunity for those seeking to bypass blocked career paths at mid-career. This list could continue for pages, but these illustrations are intended to convey the range of activities which companies can mismanage through a poorly functioning career system. We shall now look more carefully at each of the major components of the career system.

Recruitment and Selection

The relationship between the individual worker and the employing organization begins with the recruitment and selection process. While either the job candidate or the potential employer may initiate the search and selection, the firm's method of handling this process may greatly affect the later job performance and satisfaction of workers.[14] *Recruitment* is the means of gathering a pool of appropriate candidates for hire, while *selection* is the means of evaluating the qualifications and suitability of these candidates. These sets of activities are so closely related that they are frequently managed together. Therefore, they will be examined jointly in this section.

The first set of considerations in the process has to do with the assessment of the *human resource requirements*. The firm must decide what sort of workers will be needed to support current and future strategic directions. Into what new markets will the firm move? How will the technologies change? For example, firms will vary in their needs for technological expertise and for general management skill. Some firms may intend to acquire needed highly skilled technicians by purchasing companies which are well staffed. Other firms may intend to develop new technologies internally and then must either develop or hire the technical talent which they need. Firms where the

strategy features certain product lines and where the structure of the firms highlights functional arrangements may recruit along functional lines with fairly standardized criteria. Firms with more diversified and multiproduct emphasis or firms decentralized by region may require general management talent with more variation in recruitment criteria.

The firm can look at its internal supply of human resources after this consideration of strategy and organizational structure. The firm can identify internal shortages and surpluses through this effort which provide them with some direction before looking at the external labor market. When the firm does consider external employment conditions for access and availability, it can turn to several sources. These sources include the publications of the U.S. Department of Labor and many state labor departments, research centers, such as the Conference Board, and trade journals, personnel journals, and the general business press.

Firms differ, furthermore, in the amount of experience and expertise which they desire in new recruits. They may impatiently need fast help or they may be interested in developing people more slowly to fit within a strong company culture. Experienced executives not only offer a richer set of job skills but they may also offer more realistic expectations about work life and greater commitment. Less-experienced campus recruits, by contrast, offer less expertise but are attractive—in that they are easier to locate and may be more willing to learn new job skills and cultural norms. They may be also more flexible about relocation.

Having decided on the human resource requirements which inform their recruitment campaign, the firm can next consider which executives should be involved in the *selection process* within the firm. Recruitment

---

[14] J. P. Wanous, *Organizational Entry: Recruitment, Selection, and Socialization of Newcomers* (Reading, Mass.: Addison-Wesley Publishing, 1980).

policies may be set by senior management guidelines, by human resource staff department suggestions, by the discretion of line management, or by joint line/staff deliberation. Recruitment committees can resemble college admissions boards. Frequently, chief executives and line managers get involved in the specification of personnel needs and in visits to campuses. They tend not to perform the initial screening interviews of candidates. The probable initial supervisor is often involved in the final selection. The use of recent hires, line executives, and senior management varies by industry; the initial phases, however, are generally guided by professional recruiters. These recruiters act as gatekeepers to the firm, in that they disseminate information about the firm and manage the contact and the follow-through. The better informed the recruiters are about organizational needs, the better the recruitment decision quality.[15] Research has highlighted company image as being an especially difficult aspect of the process which recruiters must manage.[16] The prior reputation of the firm and the industry must be addressed through company literature as well as through the management of the recruitment process. Candidates evaluate their interactions with the firm as cultural indices. Abrasiveness, arrogance, confusing or lost materials, and missed deadlines can convey disinterest or disorganization.

Firms must then decide on their recruitment *methods*. The means of reaching recruits naturally depends on the location of the target population. One large survey found that 35 percent of the firms responding found newspapers to be the most effective method of recruiting managers. This method is quite inexpensive and yields a large pool of applicants. In this same survey, 27 percent of the firms found private employment agencies to be the most effective while 17 percent found search firms to be the most effective means of recruiting. Colleges and universities were rated as the most effective by only 2 percent of the respondents. Trade associations and professional groups, also used frequently, received moderate ratings on effectiveness.[17]

Such consideration of effectiveness, however, depends on the type of recruit that is desired. Executive search firms are used most often when more senior positions are to be filled and the labor market is tighter. Experienced managers, one of the most common targets of recruiters, are unlikely to be found in university campus placement offices. Technical experts are most effectively located through word-of-mouth channels and professional associations where similar oriented professionals can appraise the quality of work and availability of various executives. Technical specialists who work in information systems have also been located through computer matching systems, such as the Department of Labor's LINCS, the GRAD system, the IRIS systems, and such private companies as Connexions and Job/Net. These systems match firms with engineers, scientists, and technical managers through résumé life profiles of job seekers and through employer job descriptions. This process is generally so designed that job seekers are protected from discovery by their current employers.

Less formal procedures have been sup-

---

[15] Y. Weiner and M. S. Schneiderman, "Use of Job Information as a Criterion in Employment Decisions of Interviewers," *Journal of Applied Psychology* 59 (1974), pp. 699–704.

[16] William F. Glueck, *Personnel: A Diagnostic Approach* (Plano, Tex.: Business Publications, 1974).

[17] Bureau of National Affairs, *Recruiting Policies and Practices* (Washington, D.C.: Bureau of National Affairs, 1979).

ported as well. A recent review of recruitment literature concluded that new recruits were most likely to remain with their employers if they were referred through other employees.[18] This may be particularly effective for nonexecutive labor.

After a pool of candidates has been recruited, a *final selection* must be made. Sophisticated procedures, such as assessment centers, are sometimes used further downstream in the hiring process. Such techniques of selection grew out of the work of Henry Murray and other psychologists, who, in the 1930s, helped the Office of Strategic Services (the forerunner of the Central Intelligence Agency) develop methods of assessment. Such techniques include leaderless groups and in-basket exercises. Several firms, such as financial service firms, put new recruits in offices and simulate high-pressure work conditions. It is generally agreed that such situations are particularly valuable for developmental purposes, but the selection value varies greatly. Depending on the relevance to the job, other techniques include application, employment tests, reference tests, and physical examinations.

More common procedures for selection, however, include follow-on interviews with department heads, peers, and likely bosses. These interviews may be broken into various categories (e.g., informational, screening, and final evaluation). The use of company personnel in these different types of interviews should be thoughtfully considered in advance. Candidates often become the innocent victims of feuding between company officials who are anxious to assert their respective influence. Some firms, such

as insurance firms, banks, and industrial manufacturers, regularly begin with professional interviewers from the human resource function. Other firms, such as advertising companies, retailers, CPA firms, and consumer marketing firms, and smaller companies frequently use top management. Investment banks, real estate firms, consulting firms, and many other professional service firms make heavy use of lower-level managers and of recently hired executives. Regardless of who conducts the interviews, the company personnel should be trained to ask questions and overcome biases from self-fulfilling prophecies, derived from initial impressions (e.g., candidate attractiveness, sex, race, religion), and poor listening skills.[19]

Interviews in the final stage often blend into *early socialization* programs, through efforts to provide the candidates with "realistic job previews." Meetings with current employees, site visits, job descriptions, and the intelligent use of company literature on its history, performance, and career paths can supplement the more costly and more time-consuming interview process.

Assignments and Promotion

Once new recruits are oriented, they eagerly struggle for acceptance from established members of the organizations. The new recruits demonstrate their ability under the close scrutiny of co-workers. Overchallenging assignments and underchallenging assignments may not provide an opportu-

[18] Donald P. Schwab, "Recruiting and Organizational Participation," in *Human Resource Management*, K. Rowland and G. Ferris, eds. (Boston: Allyn & Bacon, 1982).

[19] Christopher Orpen, "The Effects of Race of Applicant and Type of Job on Hiring Decisions," *Journal of Social Psychology* 118 (1982), pp. 279–80; Robert L. Dipboye, "Self-Fulfilling Prophecies in the Selection-Recruitment Interview," *Academy of Management Review* 7 (1982), pp. 579–86; Terry A. Beehr and David C. Gilmore, "Applicant Attractiveness as a Perceived Job-Relevant Variable in Selection of Management Trainees," *Academy of Management Journal* 25 no. 3, (1982), pp. 607–17.

nity for the recruit to demonstrate his or her best effort. Research has suggested that initial job assignments have a substantial impact on a manager's later career.[20]

The link between the early assignments and later career success is, in part, attributed to a smoother adjustment to the realities of the workplace, a richer socialization to the new culture, and the self-fulfilling perception of appearing successful. In addition, it has been suggested that the competition for promotion begins early and follows through a filtering process much like the decreasing pools of competitors in a tennis tournament. Those who fail early are not likely to be included in later contests.[21] While the losers of promotion contests may not travel on much further, they may still face peer-level contests in new rounds of a tournament. As managers continue to struggle to maintain the same position, they may begin to feel stagnation or plateauing or other similar frustrations with mobility.

This stalled mobility results from more than merely a lack of competence for the next position. Although the perspective of humorist Lawrence J. Peter is that people are promoted until they surpass their level of competence, problems with one's career mobility are likely to be a mixture of changing personal aspirations, changing family circumstances, and changing job conditions.[22] We will outline some of these changing job conditions.

People will often withdraw from the competitive tournament for promotion because of the amount of lateral movement and relocation required along the way. Greater numbers of dual-career couples are finding it difficult and costly to try continually to readjust two careers, child day-care routines, community involvements, and home lives in an effort to satisfy traditional company beliefs that frequent movement is an important part of executive development.

A second common problem with one's mobility occurs when the organization does not have a thoughtful program for developing internal talent. Individuals in such situations often negotiate a plan for development with a particular boss. When this boss is moved, fired, or quits, the plan may die. The organization frequently will deny having made any commitment on mobility. Thus, those who follow the clichéd advice of "hitching their wagon to a rising star," may find that their star has become a shooting star. Commitments must be broadly anchored in the firm.

A third common problem which stalls managerial careers is when individuals inadvertently choose deadend tracks within a firm. Even those entering positions of high status or pay and with titles of "analyst" and "assistant to" can find it difficult to secure satisfactory next assignments. These individuals may work at high level, but without a staff, they have difficulty proving their ability to manage others. Furthermore, their staff position may suggest that such individuals possess information and contacts which can intimidate their next superior. Will there be channels of communication that challenge the chain of command?

A fourth common way by which the mobility of workers is hampered is when employers blindly assign them to losing causes—products or divisions which are in

---

[20] D. W. Bray, R. J. Campbell, and D. L. Grant, *The Management Recruit: Formative Years in Business* (New York: John Wiley & Sons, 1973); John P. Kotter, "The Psychological Contract: Managing the Joining-Up Process," *California Management Review* 15, no. 3 (1973), pp. 91–99.

[21] J. E. Rosenbaum, "Tournament Mobility: Career Patterns in a Corporation," *Administrative Science Quarterly* 24 (1979), pp. 220–41.

[22] Laurence J. Peter and Raymond Hull, *The Peter Principle* (New York: Morrow, 1969).

a state of decline. While such settings may be more flexible, chaotic, and challenging, the experience might greatly develop the executive in ways that elude those more detached from the scene. Unless companies maintain contact with executives dispatched to "turn around" situations, bright and hardworking executives may find their reputations tarnished by having been associated with failure. Naturally, if the mission succeeds, reputations will only be enhanced. In the case of failure, however, managers may become frustrated with their lack of career progress and their lack of accomplishment. They may then be attracted by opportunities elsewhere. Worse still, they may be mistakenly washed out the door in an overly zealous effort to clean out those responsible for the business difficulty. Finally, they may remain on the job, but their skills may atrophy from lack of development. At the same time, their spirit may die through the exhaustion of tedious, unrewarding assignments.

Companies can minimize these dangers by actively *monitoring* the direction and pace of individual career mobility. This direction and pace are the components of one's career path. Companies are now beginning to assume responsibility for continued development of managers through the routing of career paths rather than merely through hiring the best people available from the outside for each job vacancy. Companies can move people either through lateral transfers from job to job and across departments, or they can move people vertically through promotions and demotions. The pattern and speed of these job assignments can account for a good deal of the comprehension of the total business which a manager acquires. Furthermore, such patterns of movement affect a manager's breadth of exposure and influence within the organiza-

tion. Those being groomed for promotion will often have a broad array of job assignments.

Companies prefer to promote internally developed talent for several reasons. First, there is better performance data on those from within the firm, compared to those on the outside where performance reports are hard to check or interpret. Second, downtime and the training costs associated with orienting someone to the job and to the company are likely to be greatly reduced. Third, morale is generally aided through internal promotions, because senior management may be seen as attempting to recognize internal achievement and commitment.

Firms vary markedly in their actual reliance upon *internal promotion*. Some firms share talent across departments and share information through open exchanges, such as job posting and assistance in making lateral transfers. Other firms may heavily rely upon outside hiring, because of an inability either to share or to develop human resources companywide. At such firms, people may be hired to fill job vacancies rather than to begin career paths. Talented managers may be "hoarded" by their bosses, who claim to be protecting the employee from "raiders" from around the firm. This may not reflect a poor climate of trust within the firm, but rather may accurately reflect the inability of the company, at large, to develop the necessary pool of labor for sharing to be effective.

Companies also vary in the meaning they attach to someone's *career momentum* or pace. The expected speed of job changes with a utility will tend to be far lower than that within a fast-growing high technology firm. Both the corporate culture and the firm's strategy influence the appearance of being "on schedule," "ahead of schedule" (fast track), or "behind schedule" (plateaucd).[23] The growth rate and the goals of a company will effect the pressures and the opportunities for career growth. Several large companies believe that it is good to continually break up work groups and circulate people through different locations and tasks. Other firms seek to protect work teams that have formed. Employees at IBM have long joked that the company initials stand for "I've Been Moved," a reference to the frequent transfers necessary to support their full employment (no layoff) policy. To maximize their flexibility in making assignments at IBM, people are often given jobs with titles which make it unclear for months whether or not the job was actually a promotion, a demotion, or a lateral transfer.

Companies can best manage this job assignment process by linking it with other career development activities. What are the needs of those recently recruited? How will various assignments effect someone's development? Workers are frequently informed that a particularly unpleasant task will be good for their development. A more critical examination of how high-performing figures reached their positions within a firm may confirm or challenge such statements. Common paths for various jobs and families of related jobs may indicate key decision points and ladders or preparatory sequences.

Such monitoring and development of managerial careers is increasingly becoming an accepted responsibility of senior management committees. Even at firms as large and varied as General Electric, Exxon, and Citibank, senior management allows time each month to monitor the progress of the top 200 to 500 executives. In this way, succession planning for key positions is en-

riched far beyond a simple matching of individuals with jobs. Backup candidates can be easily located from across the organization—helping the firm to prepare for various changes in direction and allowing the individual to avoid being boxed in along a single linear path. Performance estimates can be so separated from mobility that valuable workers with slow-moving careers ("solid citizens") can be distinguished from low-performing workers with slow career movement ("deadwood").[24]

Finally, it should be noted that different individuals will seek different types of mobility. It has been recognized that preferences for different career paths can be identified by their degree of consistency in direction (e.g., linear, transitory, spiral, or steady-state)[25] or by the character of the desired tasks (referred to by Schein as anchors, encompassing such task environments as managerial, technical, entrepreneurial, secure, autonomous, socially constructive, and the like).[26] Career mobility will have different meanings to people in different life/career stages. Younger, early career workers may be disappointed with lateral movement while older workers may prefer lateral moves to hierarchical moves that would require relocating one's home.[27] In the next section, we will consider how companies can assist people in discovering their own career expectations.

[24] T. P. Ference, J. A. F. Stoner, and E. K. Warren, "Managing the Career Plateau," *Academy of Management Review* 2 (1977), pp. 602–12.

[25] Michael Driver, "Career Concepts and Career Management in Organizations," in *Behavior Problems in Organizations* (London: Prentice-Hall International, 1979).

[26] Edgar H. Schein, *Career Dynamics: Matching Individual and Organizational Needs* (Reading, Mass.: Addison-Wesley Publishing, 1978).

[27] John F. Veiga, "Mobility Influences During Managerial Career Stages," *Academy of Management Journal* 26 (1983), pp. 64–85.

[23] Barbara Steinberg Lawrence, "The Age Grading of Managerial Careers in Work Organizations" (Ph.D. diss., Massachusetts Institute of Technology, 1983).

Career Development Programs

Once the new recruit begins a job within a firm, he or she also begins a journey along a career path with the firm. In the next chapter we will consider the socialization of the new recruit to the culture of the firm. Here we will consider the role of the organization in planning the future career experiences of the individual. While it is naturally impossible for organizations or individuals to gaze into a crystal ball and see the many changes in opportunities and personal goals which will affect career outcomes in the future, it is possible to maintain the process of matching individual needs and organizational needs that began in the recruitment and selection stage of the career system.

The advantages cited by firms which offer formal career development programs include an improved ability to meet the psychological expectations of the individual and savings in the way of reduced personnel replacement costs and enhanced worker commitment. Firms have found there are many advantages to reducing the total control held by superiors over subordinates' careers. Companywide efforts to share information about training, job opportunities, and other similar career assistance have: (1) minimized the hoarding of managerial talent, (2) reduced drifts towards obsolescence, and (3) improved the provision of equal opportunities to women and minorities in firms.[28] A large study of firms which provide career-planning activities found that 80 percent of the firms claimed that the improved ability to develop and promote managers from within was a major reason to provide career planning.[29]

These career development programs tend to be more person-centered than position-centered in their orientation. This orientation is suggested through self-assessment programs and career planning programs where the individual takes the initiative for articulating his or her career needs. Individuals are guided through some degree of introspection, with lectures, workshops, films, and workbooks. In addition, a manager's superior frequently may become involved through the performance appraisal process. After a performance review, a superior and a subordinate will typically discuss short-term career development implications of the review. Separate career development meetings with one's superior are generally more effective than when such feedback is mixed with the emotional and short-term-oriented performance discussion.

Superiors often resent these additional special career development sessions, because they often feel inadequately prepared to assume the responsibility of advising people on their careers. They may also wonder why they should spend money out of their budget to develop and train someone who will only be stolen away by another department that has not paid for such training. Finally, superiors may feel a sense of rivalry with an employee whose career may accelerate past them despite a perceived lack of experience.

This resistance by superiors is obviously reduced by greater delivery of career information through central corporate services,

---

[28] R. B. Robinson, Jr., and W. F. Glueck, "Career Development and Organizational Effectiveness: An Analysis of the Literature" (Paper presented at the annual meeting of the Southern Management Association, New Orleans, November 1980); Manuel London and Stephen A. Stumpf, *Managing Careers* (Reading, Mass.: Addison-Wesley Publishing, 1982).

[29] James W. Walker and Thomas G. Gutteridge, *Career Planning Practices: An AMA Survey Report* (New York: AMACOM, 1979).

such as professional counseling, corporate human resource development programs, and company literature. Superiors' resistance is also reduced through training that equips them with knowledge about adult development, career paths, and changing company human resource needs. Finally, their resistance is also reduced if the career development of subordinates is officially treated as part of one's formal job responsibilities. Thus, employee development would be included with other measures of job performance in a supervisor's own appraisal and be considered worthy of reward. In this way, the immediate supervisor can be a valuable career guide and an important ally in the career development process.

This discussion of the ways of involving supervisors in employee career development raises an even larger issue. The issue is the need for the company to do more than to rely on individual employee initiative. For career development programs to succeed, it is important that the process not begin and end with employee self-assessment alone. Companies must seize the initiative first and do an assessment of themselves. Companies must discover the following characteristics about themselves first:

1. What are the changing human resource needs of the company?
2. What are the various paths likely to be followed by those who will fill the positions needed in the future (e.g., sequences of job experiences, skills, credentials, and so on)?
3. What are the current normal patterns of mobility from various jobs (e.g., high turnover, stagnation, crowding, and the like)?
4. How do employee career expectations vary within the firm?

5. What career paths should be rerouted to better serve company and worker interests?
6. How does this information reach workers?

Training and Development

While a career development program assists the continued balancing of individual and organizational expectations by clarifying the interests and by planning the steps needed for improved fulfillment of these expectations, it is largely through patterns of assignments and training that plans become realities. Executives' constellation of knowledge and skills, like that of all other workers, is not adequate indefinitely. Interests change, skills become obsolete, and company needs change as well. New job assignments and career opportunities frequently require more systematic learning than is available through on-the-job experience. The appreciation of existing levels of performance, the need for high morale, and the commitment to long-service employees are further reasons why companies create training programs. They help stabilize and upgrade the workforce.

Companies, thus, use training and education programs for many purposes. Most generally these programs can serve as key interventions in large organizational development efforts designed to change the full organization, or as individual development efforts designed to improve the immediate performance or longer term preparedness of particular workers. Some examples of training programs as components of organizational change efforts include: teaching new techniques, explaining new products, improving the inter-personal climate through the learning of conflict resolution, and the adjustment to new organizational structures. Some examples of individual development programs include: company orientation for new employees, entry level and advanced skills training in functional areas, midcareer development and general management training, late career enrichment, and preparation for retirement and outplacement.

After an *assessment* of the organization's training goals and the individual's training requirements (which are referred to as a "needs analysis") a curriculum is planned.

This curriculum may include:

1. Basic remedial skills (fundamentals of written and oral communication, mathematics, foreign languages, and so on).
2. Functional/technical expertise (accounting, financial reporting, sales and marketing, production, engineering, new products, and the like).
3. General management (leadership, developing subordinates, and so on).
4. Individual social development, such as listenership, assertiveness, time management.
5. Personal enhancement (retirement planning, second career preparation, recreation—photography, literature, and so on).
6. Company-specific information, such as orientation and new systems.

In addition to variations in subject matter, company training programs vary in their time frame. Some programs are designed to provide job task learning for immediate application while other programs provide preparation for more long-term career development and future responsibilities.

A wide variety of *pedagogical* techniques are used in management education. Information about well-established procedures and products can be conveyed through a mixture of self-study workbooks, video, or lecture. More behavioral (i.e., less cognitive) material tends to be better taught through class discussions, case examples, experiential simulation, and video. Information about new company products or expert insight into particular topics is well presented through lecture formats. Frequently, fairly dry class material will be presented in an atmosphere where various techniques, such as individual contests and group competition, have been used to energize the learning process. The more threatening the learning is, the more the trainees must understand the purpose of the new activities or products. How will their work lives and careers be affected? The atmosphere should allow trainees to ask all questions, since trainers will have difficulty following up on the job.

The selection of *instructors* is another key issue. Some firms rely upon a large pool of internal professional trainers. This approach improves the firm's ability to be able to rely on skilled teaching, but it increases the likelihood of biased diagnosis of need (teachers will teach what they know), credibility problems with more senior management, and lack of currency in latest developments in a field. Some firms rely on rotational shifts of line managers into training for temporary assignments in developments in their own areas. This approach may help establish business credibility with managerial audiences but does not guarantee the instructors will be effective or well-informed teachers. Finally, some firms rely heavily on outside sources for instructors, such as commercial vendors and universities. This approach might allow for more currency and expertise in subject matter as well as in teaching skill. It suffers, however, from unreliable quality and greater abstraction from company specific concerns. A firm must consider the special needs of the audience and plan on appropriate consideration of expertise, status, flexibility, currency, company specific sophistication, and cost.

Finally, the firm must *evaluate* the success of its training efforts. Education and training activities tend to fail when they are not integrated into a consistent career system. All too often, we find incidents where individuals were trained for products or technologies which are disappearing, while skill shortages for emerging technologies are virtually ignored. The topics taught may represent those most familiar to the trainers and managers rather than those most needed by the company at that moment. Workers often receive mixed signals from companies about the hidden meaning behind an invitation to participate in a training program. Is it remedial—and symbolically punitive for poor performance? Is it a development and selection experience where they must prove themselves? Is it a signal of an impending promotion already in the works? Is it a rare opportunity to have some fun meeting with people from other parts of the company? Managers with limited funds for training and pushed for immediate performance results may only consider training that offers instant results. Company training staffs can play critical roles as educational brokers or intermediaries among general managers, staff strategic and human resource planners, functional managers, trainees, and the various types of suppliers.

Organizational Exit

The timing, emotional quality, and situational characteristics of resignations, retirements, layoffs, and dismissals vary greatly, but collectively they represent a type of career event which companies manage most poorly—organizational exit. To most managers, the handling of this separation is one of the most difficult aspects of the job. It is made difficult especially when the reasons causing the job loss are beyond his or her control (e.g., international competition and business declines). Certainly organizations should be allowed to determine their own membership, providing the criteria for membership are fair and just. Companies may need to prune back from time to time because of changes in the business context and because of poor planning earlier in the corporate career system. People may have become hopelessly obsolete in their jobs. The wrong sort of workers may have been recruited. The company may have over-hired during a boom period. The company may not have foreseen some bottlenecks in career paths. An antiquated facility may close, idling its workers. Individuals' health and energy may deteriorate as they age. Finally, individuals may leave a firm for better opportunities elsewhere. While the logic behind such separations from the organization is often quite acceptable, the processes are often unnecessarily destructive to the departing individual and to the organization they leave behind.

As much as people may joke about their desire for life without work, *job loss* has been found to have a devastating impact upon people's emotional and physical health, as well as upon their pocketbooks. As immediate cash and long-run economic security may become less certain, the adjustment to the traumatic event of losing one's work identity can be equally costly. People's friendships, reference groups, sense of accomplishment, daily goals, and general life patterns are largely oriented around their work lives. The change in employment status means more than just a change in the workplace. The change spills over into all other life sectors. There has been a good deal of research into the psychological and physical effects of job loss on workers and their families.[30] Work serves as a major organizing principle in one's life. The loss of a work identity often shatters one's self-confidence in dealing with future challenges.

This personal suffering through job loss is often induced as much through the way the event transpired as through its actual occurrence. Awkward and brutal company separation practices can be damaging in themselves. Through unfair and discriminatory applications, these practices can inflict particular hardship on specific groups. The reasons for the separation are often quite murky and ambiguous, leaving room for a great deal of self-doubt and community speculation. Finally, the news of the separation is often delivered in an abrupt and angry fashion.

Looking at each of these ways by which companies inadvertently exacerbate the difficulty of managing organizational exit, we should first consider the lack of just and fair criteria for dismissal and layoff. Studies have found that, in some work settings, both minority and white coworkers have higher standards of performance for minorities than for nonminorities, so that mediocrity may "... be a special privilege of the white male."[31] In less overt ways, through seniority rules which respect "last in and first out" tenets, layoffs may hit women and minorities more severely if they tended to be more heavily represented among recent

recruits as part of newer affirmative action programs for equal employment opportunity compliance. Due to age bias, older workers often find job search to be much more difficult. Those over 50 tend to be unemployed three times as long as those under that age.[32] Many early retirement programs that coax out older workers dump them on an unwelcoming job market. Firms regularly waste valuable skilled workers because they allowed the skills of older workers to atrophy. Biases become self-fulfilling prophecies as older workers are denied opportunity for challenging assignments or chances to be retrained for new procedures and products.[33] Finally, through the many recent challenges to the traditional doctrine of "employment-at-will," courts and legislatures are requiring employers to justify dismissals of even nonunion workers to be certain that the right to free speech was not violated in the firing of a dissident or "whistle-blowing" employee.[34]

After considering why people leave, we should next consider how they leave. The management of the exit process is hampered by the reliance upon ambiguous messages and upon the anger and the abruptness of the act. Executives often find that they are taken off the circulation list for key office memos—so they appear uninformed and foolish in meetings. They are later cut off from meetings and denied planned promotions, without explanation. They are

---

[30] M. H. Brenner, *Mental Illness and the Economy* (Cambridge, Mass.: Harvard University Press, 1973).

[31] John P. Fernandez, *Racism and Sexism in Corporate Life* (Lexington, Mass.: Lexington Books, 1981).

[32] Joanne S. Lublin, "The Age Barrier: Older Jobless Workers Seeking a New Position Find Years Hurt Them," *The Wall Street Journal*, August 2, 1983, p. 1.

[33] Jeffrey A. Sonnenfeld, "Dealing with the Aging Work Force," *Harvard Business Review*, November–December 1978.

[34] David W. Ewing, *"Do It My Way or You're Fired": Employee Rights and the Changing Role of Management Prerogatives* (New York: John Wiley & Sons, 1983).

moved to undesirable office locations and denied support services. They are asked if they intend to relocate along with the rest of the company in office moves, and then are informed that new bosses have elected to bring in their own management team. Managers who lack the courage to address the facts surrounding the firing of a subordinate allow a cloud of suspicion about one's honesty or competence to haunt an executive upon dismissal. The lack of directness, the anger, and the abruptness may reflect a manager's fear of reprisal from loyalists of the deposed executive. Such behavior may also reflect a manager's own feelings of guilt. They may react impulsively and become enraged at the victim when it is actually that they themselves feel that they are doing something wrong.[35]

Such poor management of organizational exit not only damages the lives and careers of those departing but also damages the internal culture of the firm. The way a firm deals with members who leave serves as an index of the firm's appreciation of the past contribution of workers and respect for their human dignity. Frequently workers may leave and maintain a valuable sense of loyalty and commitment to the firm. This allows present workers to have trust in the integrity and fairness of the firm. It also allows the firm to draw upon the loyalty of those who leave. The ability of firms to draw upon retirees for grass-roots lobbying or to attract business from those who join other firms are examples of the value of such continued good rapport.

Thus, in summary, to effectively manage the process of organizational exit firms must first understand the *reason* for workers' de-

parture. High turnover may be symptomatic of underlying pathological organizational problems.[36] Exit interviews and research on resignations may be fruitful efforts. When the cause of separation is dismissal rather than resignation, firms must learn whether the firing was fair, appropriate, and necessary. Were the employees consistently receiving honest performance feedback? Older workers are frequently judged more generously by their bosses on formal evaluations and more harshly informally while they await an impending retirement. When the worker with satisfactory performance reviews is later pushed out of the firm, it is understandable that they may be stunned and seek redress in the courts.

Firms must also be certain which workers they are better off losing and which are hard to replace. Companies that use "open window" plans, which induce long-service workers to leave, often lose some of their most valuable employees though the lavish inducements offered. Those unable to find other work on the outside and those seeking less risk may decline such offers, while the talented and energetic experienced workers may be the first to leave. At the same time, those who are less satisfied and less work absorbed will leave eagerly, while those who are more involved in their work may find it more difficult to leave. Firms can anticipate these reactions in the programs which they design. Through salary cuts, reduced hours, job redesign, and the like, jobs can be saved during periods of economic slump. Through retraining, experienced and motivated personnel may eagerly learn to become more effective.

Firms can also better manage the exit pro-

---

[35] Judson Gooding, "The Art of Firing an Executive," *Fortune*, October 1972.

[36] James L. Price, *The Study of Turnover* (Ames: Iowa State University Press, 1971).

cess by easing the *transition*. Through out-placement counseling and retirement planning,[37] individual workers can prepare for their disengagement from the firm. Workers displaced through technology, those laid off because of economic downturns, those whose performance is no longer adequate for the job, or those who reach the retirement age can all benefit from advance notice of their termination. If the explanation for the termination is clear and assistance is genuine, the likelihood of retaliation and sabotage is not any greater than for any other source of disgruntlement. Programs for flextime, job sharing, part-time employment, and phased retirement allow the worker to learn to become increasingly involved on the outside.

Purpose of This Book

The first section of the book, "Designing Career Systems," will examine the basic properties of the career system. The various elements will be described individually and their linkage into an interactive system will be explored. The cases will feature various problematic and constructive aspects of these systems which appear in actual firms. The notes which follow will talk about new developments that may help to guide the design and implementation of these systems.

The next section of the book, "Career Systems and Individual Life Stages," looks at how the various components of the career system have differential impact upon workers whose ages and experiences vary. The cases look at early, mid, and later career stages, which require different types of responses by the firm. For example, differences in recruiting younger people versus recruiting experienced people will be considered. Rewards, mobility, career risk-taking, and approaches to learning vary dramatically with age and experience.

The cases will provide examples of young, workers who are being poorly developed, mid-career workers who are plateaued or who have switched careers, and older workers facing questions about their future. The readings will discuss successful policies for managing early career issues, such as entry and joining up, mid-career issues, such as mentoring, plateauing, and promotion, and late-career issues, such as disengagement or rejuvenation.

The third section, "Career Systems and Company Life Stages," again adds change to the career context. Here, instead of looking at the aging, the growth, and the experience of the individual, we look at the tailoring of the career system to the life changes of the firm. The cases look at new companies and old companies. Firms experiencing high growth as well as firms facing merger, maturation, and retrenchment are discussed. The readings examine the special concerns of fast-growth firms, the basic stages of growth in the life of a firm, the difference between professional service and other firms, and the various new approaches developed to assist displaced workers.

The fourth section, "Career Systems in Social Context," considers how the impact of changes in the institutional environment and the general public arena affect the internal career policies of a firm. Changes in laws, the assertion of ethical principles to ensure socially responsible behavior, the struggle to overcome sexual and career barriers erected through minority discrimina-

---

[37] Dane Henriksen, "Outplacement: Program Guidelines that Ensure Success," *Personnel Journal* 61, no. 8 (1980), pp. 583–89.

tion, and the lifestyle and family pattern expectations are the types of issues which are explored in the cases and the readings. The cases show the system-induced tension between conformity and risk-taking. This section is intended to provoke some thought about the societal impact of internal company career policies. The career policies of a firm guide an individual's work role. The worker role, however, induces a good deal of spillover into other life roles. Company career policies can enhance or damage a worker's ability to act as a parent, a community member, and so on. Furthermore, people enter the firm's career system accompanied by their external status and responsibilities. The materials in this section consider the legal, moral, and practical incentives for firms to anticipate and respond to these broader societal influences.

A Summary and Overview

Overall, the mission of this book is to give the reader a comprehensive overview of company career practices as a social system. After the basic components are profiled, we will look at the dynamics introduced through individual change, organizational change, and societal change. Career systems in firms will exist whether they are consciously and intelligently designed or whether they developed in seemingly accidental reactive ways. Like the processes of swallowing, breathing, and digestion, they are too vital to survival to happen only by deliberate choice. Consciousness of how the system interacts internally and externally, however, will improve its effectiveness. An organization which is aware of its own career policies and events can determine what works and what must be improved. Firms share many common problems in managing career systems. The cases describe real and generally undisguised human resource problems which have had a major impact on firms. The readings discuss the practical implications of current theory and research on these contemporary challenges to industrial society. Mystical approaches to hiring, development, and release of workers should appear in the pages of Charles Dickens, Franz Kafka, and George Orwell rather than in current company statements of career policies.

Designing
Career Systems

In this section, we will be looking at the different components of career systems and the links among them. The topics which are raised in the cases and in the readings include recruitment, selection, career path planning, assignments, promotion, and training and development. The materials highlight the interrelatedness of staffing decisions. The cases present a wide variety of settings—from heavy manufacturing to service industries, from high technology to medium technology, and from large mega-corporations to small enterprises. Despite their vastly different activities and purposes, each of these firms has confronted common problems of staffing an organization.

The Cases

The first case, *Investech*, describes the problems facing a young software firm as its tremendous growth and success begin to slow. Changes in the marketplace are made more difficult to overcome by the firm's continuing inattention to career management concerns of various employee groups. The case shows the problems Investech has with recruiting, selecting, placing, and developing

managers and technical employees with skills in great demand.

With this example established, the next two cases describe highly sophisticated human resources systems in two very large corporations. Both cases take broad view of human resource planning and of monitoring the development of careers within the firm. The Honeywell cases show a recent effort to develop a system for centralized human resource planning within a large decentralized organization. The (A) case presents the system and explains how information is acquired about the flow of people, the training needs, and other career development concerns across divisions. The (B) and (C) case sequels show the use of this planning process in two Honeywell divisions.

The American Hospital Supply case also addresses the difficulty of gaining divisional acceptance and credibility of a corporate-wide plan. The (A) case presents an interesting comparison of approach to the Honeywell cases. The (B) case highlights some of the difficulties of implementing this centralized system within a highly decentralized company.

The Hart, Schaffner & Marx case bridges

recruitment and development. It presents a large older clothing manufacturer and retailer questioning its purpose and method regarding campus recruiting. The case examines the MBAs recruited and the initial assignments which they receive.

The next case, C. Edward Acker, looks at recruitment of senior executives. In its darkest days, Pan Am turned to external sourcing for a new chief executive; Mr. Acker was selected to lead the troubled airline back to good health. The case raises questions about the sorts of methods and criteria to be used in assigning later-career executives to job opportunities.

The AT&T case looks at the next stage of selection by presenting the firm's formal approach to employee assessment for promotion. The (A) case explains the history and the use of assessment centers. The (B) and (B) cases provide the results for two employees who participated in the assessment process. They raise issues about the criteria and use of this process.

The Sundown Motels case, by contrast, presents a far less formal approach to assessment. The specific problem concerns the difficulties in changing someone's assignment when performance appraisal information is inadequate.

The next two cases profile two corporate approaches to guiding the careers of employees. The General Electric case discusses the dynamics of how a large firm maintains a crisp awareness of the career development of its top managers. The target group of executives is older and more experienced than the population studied in the Hart, Schaffner & Marx case, which focused on young new recruits. In the General Electric case, we also see a more formal system than was presented in the Hart, Schaffner & Marx case. The cases on the Wane Division of the American Instrument Corporation explore the creation and use of a more "bottom-up" approach to career development and planning than was presented in the General Electric case. It also presents a contrast to the more top/down approaches in the Honeywell and American Hospital Supply cases. The (A) case describes the background of the program. The (B) case examines the implementation of this program in a setting where the managers have not been previously exposed to such career planning concepts. This case raises specific questions about the means of integrating career planning with other human resource activities.

The Flowtrol case is similar to the Investech case in that we look at the role of job assignment promotion and succession planning in the development of executives. In the Flowtrol case we see a company's effort to recruit externally and select a successor for a chief executive and founder. The (A) case reports on the rationale behind the search process and describes the available internal candidates along with resumes of the externally recruited candidates. The (B) case looks at the later difficulties which developed between the intended successor and the incumbent executive during the grooming of this executive. This case also raises questions about dismissal. When does a manager assume the responsibility to develop a subordinate? And when does a manager replace a subordinate with someone better suited for the job?

The Union Carbide case shifts our attention to management development through training as well as through work assignments. It provides a view of how a firm follows up on its identification of needed career development. The management of the Africa Middle East Division felt that the division required greater depth in its international management. The case describes the "needs analysis," which was conducted and a plan of action developed to address those needs.

The Rawson Company case examines another aspect of corporate education and training. While the Union Carbide case presented the diagnosis and design of training programs, the Rawson case asks about the designer. The Rawson case offers the opportunity to consider who should provide training, develop materials, and evaluate the programs. One option is to rely upon internal trainers. Another option is suggested in the A University-Employer Collaboration: The University of Pennsylvania and INA case. This case looks at the evolution of employer/university collaboration between the Insurance Company of North America and the liberal arts program of a nearby university.

Thus, through these cases, we have covered a wide range of human resource activities that guide the entry, development, and exit of workers.

The Readings

The readings provide further discussion of the issues and examples of other sites. The Tichy, Fombrun, and Devanna piece places such managerial activities as selection, promotion, placement, and management development within the context of different company market strategies. They argue that the varied missions of firms require that they will have different human resource needs. When the strategic needs are not recognized, human resource practices tend to work at cross-purposes. The "Note on Career Development Programs" by Dowd and Sonnenfeld discusses the purposes and approaches taken by firms in guiding the careers of employees. The article entitled "The Tricky Task of Picking the Heir Apparent" looks at an especially complex sort of pro-

motion problem—the development of succession plans for top executives. The "Note on Executive Search and Placement" by Kenny, Katzenstein, and Sonnenfeld discusses the role of intermediaries in the job marketplace for experienced managers. The "Note on Education and Training in Industry" by Balbaky and Sonnenfeld describes how companies approach formal classroom management development activities. The piece highlights the costs and purposes of such programs.

CASE 1
INVESTECH
Jeffrey A. Sonnenfeld

In the dim light of dusk, David Mahoney, the chief executive of Investech, packed up his attaché case with work for the Labor Day weekend. The extra large load represented the plans for a new client service and the related needs profiles of two new clients. Realizing that he would not be able to fit in all the materials that he needed, Mahoney began to search for an old portfolio hidden in the back of a closet. Just then, the end of the week quiet was broken by the slam of Denise Haltom's door at the other end of the corridor. As Mahoney rushed towards the door, it reopened. Denise flushed in surprise at Mahoney's appearance:

> Dave! I thought everyone was gone for the week. In fact, thanks to Sarah, my staff may be gone for more than the week. Dave, I probably shouldn't mention this to you now, but I sometimes wonder whether there aren't places where I can act as a manager and not a mudwrestler!

At this Mahoney chuckled with surprise and started to back out of Denise's doorway. Sensing a lack of interest, Denise responded,

> Well I'm sure that this is not the way you wanted to start your weekend.

Dave nodded in agreement and said:

> Investech relies on your contribution as manager of product development, but I'm sorry we can't talk now. I'm supposed to be on Martha's Vineyard for a date with some Centrobanc execs and their families. You know what they mean to us. How about dinner next week?

Denise said that this would be fine but looked dissatisfied and mildly embarrassed. Mahoney left wondering whether he should have gotten a bit more information before leaving the office, but he thought he had a working knowledge of the basic situation and that it posed no particular urgency.

Company Founding

Investech was founded in 1972 by Melvin Levitsky and David Mahoney in a recently renovated Hartford warehouse that had been converted to offices. Levitsky had served as the vice president of information systems for a large insurance company in Hartford. He had fled Poland as a child with his family. He attended the City College of New York, graduating with a BS in actuarial sciences. He later obtained an MBA from the Wharton School of the University of Pennsylvania. He had worked for the same insurance company since graduation. At age 59, he was five years from retirement when approached with the idea of Investech.

David Mahoney's background was quite different from Levitsky's. Mahoney was 31 at the time of Investech's founding. He had grown up in South Boston and got his BA from Boston College and an MBA from the Harvard Business School. Before Harvard,

Mahoney had worked as a stockbroker for a large New York securities firm. It was in this capacity where his relationship with Levitsky began. Levitsky became an early and important client for Mahoney. They became good friends despite the age gap and maintained contact through Mahoney's two years spent working on his master's degree. Mahoney had, in fact, applied to Harvard at Levitsky's suggestion. Mahoney had performed well as a stockbroker but was afraid that he was approaching complete exhaustion after four years. He graduated with his MBA at age 29 and began work as an industry analyst for a large investment bank. His industry specialty was financial services; in particular, he focused on insurance companies. While he enjoyed the industry knowledge, research skills, and personal contacts which he gained from the job, he realized that the job was not what he termed "sufficiently entrepreneurial."

After attending a trade conference on the promise of new information technology for the insurance industry, Mahoney decided that the transformation of the insurance industry presented just the entrepreneurial opportunity which he sought. Mahoney contacted Levitsky who had attended the same industry conference. Levitsky agreed that the timing was right, not just for the industry, but also in his life. He felt that he had been passed over for a third time for a senior vice presidency. He was convinced that his age, his ethnic and religious heritage, and his technical background worked against his further advancement in the insurance firm. Levitsky had marketed insurance and served as an actuary, but most of his 30-year career had been spent in data processing. Now, he felt, was the time to make his move.

The plan Mahoney and Levitsky developed for Investech was for a firm which provided programming expertise and software systems for insurance companies. They had hoped to provide a wide range of software products including such routine areas as claims processing in commercial casualty lines to the highly sophisticated analysis of investment options for insurance companies. They had expected that personnel payroll systems and similar, more standard items would help to provide the funds for other types of development. Mahoney was designated president and Levitsky as chairman. The firm was privately held with Mahoney and Levitsky each owning 40 percent of the equity and an outside venture capitalist controlling 20 percent.

Development of the Business and the Organization

Many outside observers felt that Investech was both undercapitalized and overly optimistic. As the figures in Exhibit 1 show,

Exhibit 1   Investech—Financial Performance
($ thousands)

Year	Revenues	Profits
1972	0	(500)
1973	1,000	(30)
1974	2,000	100
1975	3,000	200
1976	4,000	400
1977	6,400	800
1978	8,900	1,000
1979	10,200	1,500
1980	12,400	800
1981	12,800	460
1982	13,400	48

the firm nonetheless enjoyed steady growth to revenues of over $13.5 million. Many of the nation's 3,000 insurance companies turned out to be far less resistant to new technologies than had been expected. In fact, several firms seemed very close to the frontier of current knowledge about information technology.

It was also expected that Mahoney and Levitsky would not work well as a team. In actuality, the partners functioned well together as each complemented the skills of the other. Levitsky took charge of product development and software engineering concerns. He managed the programmers, systems design projects, documentation activities for developing products, installation, and system maintenance. Mahoney took responsibility for marketing, finance, and administration. In particular, he managed the sales staffs, the accountants, and the administrative staff.

In addition to this business complementarity, each partner enjoyed the personal friendship of the other. Mahoney described Levitsky as a ". . . brilliant intellectual man with a dry wit, a calming manner, and a loyal soul." Levitsky described Mahoney as ". . . a perpetually youthful and energetic spirit who thrived on the company of others as they fell victim to his charm." This was consistent with the comment of one long-term employee, "Where one could excite us into doing almost anything in crisis, including panic, the other gave us the calm confidence to think through our priorities."

The problem-free management team began to disintegrate, however, by the end of the fifth year. Levitsky's wife had become quite ill, and he told Mahoney that he planned to retire by his 66th birthday in August 1979. Mahoney was saddened by this news, but he was anxious to show that he did not depend on Levitsky to manage the business. They began to plan for a smooth transition. Mahoney was named chief executive, and he purchased 15 percent of the equity back from Levitsky so that he would own 55 percent of the stock. Levitsky and Mahoney felt that the product line developed by Levitsky still met the current needs of clients so they did not appoint a vice president for development. Dan Sickles, an engineer who had been with the company for four years, was named vice president of software engineering with responsibility for systems maintenance and installation. Sickles had two technical degrees from the Massachusetts Institute of Technology and had worked for two years at another software house. Mahoney retained marketing responsibilities but hired Ken Frick as vice president for finance. Frick was formerly a vice president at a prominent econometric and technology consulting firm.

These appointments seemed like appropriate choices, but they each became problem-plagued decisions. Sickles, the engineering vice president, was more of an individual contributor than a group leader. His implementation teams were so poor that loyal customers began to solicit presentations and bids from Investech's competitors. The engineering teams became embroiled in circular, finger-pointing efforts, losing a sense of shared responsibility for problem solving. Sickles began to show signs of intense stress. A former drinking problem returned and became so bad that he would just leave work at noon, two to three afternoons a week. Sickles refused to discuss his schedule with his subordinates or clients. As client problems intensified, he began to attack regional sales managers for trying to make software engineering look bad in an effort to hide their own slipping performance.

Given his performance, Mahoney felt he had to replace Sickles. Sickles was fired in 1981, a year and a half after Levitsky retired. This time Mahoney located an experienced vice president of software engineering through an executive search firm. The new executive, Robert Myers, had previously worked for eight years at a firm which designed software for general accounting and bookkeeping systems.

Ken Frick, the vice president of finance, also became a problem for Mahoney soon after his appointment. Five months into the job, Frick began to raise questions of equity, suggesting that he was expecting 10 percent by the end of the year. Mahoney was distressed and turned to Levitsky for advice. Levitsky had taken a two-month leave of absence for foreign travel. Upon his return, Levitsky explained that he felt too detached to be of much help. He suggested that Mahoney delay any equity decisions for a year or so to gain more data on individual character and performance of key executives.

When Mahoney relayed this position to Frick, Frick erupted with indignation, "Do you mean that the last seven months do not demonstrate any skill or contribution?" Mahoney replied, "Ken, I assumed a great deal of risk and sacrificed a lot to create this business. If I am going to give any of it away, I want to know the recipient intimately." Ken, who had been hired at a salary of $80,000, said that he had accepted the job with the understanding that his salary would be enhanced through a generous stock allotment.

Mahoney felt that it seemed strange for Frick to raise this dissatisfaction over compensation now, but he agreed to consider the issue further. Over the next six months, Frick continued to work hard and assumed additional functions so that he now had responsibility for financial accounting, cost control, the treasury, the corporate secretary, billings, facilities, personnel, and internal information systems. Each unit performed so well that Mahoney rewarded Frick with a $20,000 end-of-the-year bonus.

Frick seemed satisfied with this award. However, late in 1981, Mahoney learned through three old clients that Frick and the West Coast sales director, Noel Clifford, were plotting to take over the business. Mahoney fired Frick and Clifford in the fall of 1981 after buying out the remainder of their contracts. Carl Myamoto, the northeast sales director, was made national sales director. Stan Friedman was lured away from a small San Francisco area maker of computer peripherals to serve as vice president of finance. As the sales force continued to raise the need for substantial fine tuning and customer tailoring, a product development group was added which reported to Carl Myamoto. Denise Haltom was hired for this job. Haltom had an MBA from Harvard and had worked at IBM and Chemical Bank.

The Current Climate within the Firm

In the last year, the senior management positions had been fairly stable. Despite this prior management tension, the company continued to grow through the late 1970s. Although the firm grew in revenues, it did not grow in worker talent. Three types of professionals were in short supply due to constant turnover. The professionals were installation engineers, programmers, and the MBA-trained sales staff. The programmers complained that they did not feel that their efforts were well coordinated and that innovation was not encouraged. The installation engineers complained that systems capabilities were being oversold by the sales force. Finally, the sales force complained that the existing systems were no longer adequate to meet client needs and that the installation was regularly sloppy. Mahoney felt that the 28 percent annual turnover in these areas was normal for high technology, but he was deeply perturbed by the problems in quality service delivery. He was

aware of the slipping support of customers who complained of lost time and data.

Mahoney was also concerned about the flattening of sales in the last two years. He had fired three regional sales managers in this period for what he saw as ". . . laziness, pure and simple" as well as two ". . . completely incompetent" managers in the installation area. An additional concern was the crowding in the market. When he and Levitsky created the company a decade earlier, they had one direct competitor; this had grown to 14, 11 of whom were on the East Coast. Although Mahoney had led the company into other segments of the financial services industry, most notably commercial bank portfolios and securities firms, these products lagged far behind the impact of the insurance company products. In particular, the systems development for the securities industry had many program bugs and intense competition. The materials for commercial banks were almost fully developed when several of the initial clients, middle-sized banks, delayed their actual purchase of systems, given impending mergers which may warrant new systems design. These new business materials on other industries were generated from a new business development group which reported directly to Mahoney.

The Installation Task Force

Mahoney decided that he wanted to pull together a team to work on the continuing problem in systems installation in insurance, the bread and butter of the firm. Sarah Cashion, a manager of market analysis, was given the assignment of pulling this team together. Mahoney chose Sarah because he thought that it would be a good idea to bring in someone more objective, less directly involved in the situation. Myamoto,

Friedman, and Myers agreed with this idea: Sarah Cashion was thought to be the perfect candidate. She had been hired from a consulting firm a year and a half earlier. Cashion had an MBA from Stanford. Initially, she reported to Mahoney as an assistant to the president. After eight months, she was assigned to report to a recently hired vice president of marketing. The vice president of marketing, Ron Tordella, delayed joining the firm full time as he was finishing off some prior business commitments which he had from a personal consulting practice. Cashion felt that she was in limbo for four months and recently complained about her lack of career direction. She considered Tordella's style to be too "impressionistic and anecdotal."

In just eight months, Cashion had developed a reputation for hard work and an abrasive temperament. She had generally worked on individual assignments. Mahoney thought that some experience closer to the line would help her managerial development. He also believed that Cashion's direct, confrontive style would be an advantage in that she would ask difficult and direct questions. This fresh probing was what Mahoney felt Investech needed.

One of Sarah's first acts was to choose a staff. She picked Larry Weinberg, a very charismatic technical trainer, Ben Worthington, a soft-spoken and experienced project engineer, and Leslie Monroe, a product development specialist. Mahoney, Myamoto, and Myers endorsed these decisions. Cashion was then told to obtain the consent of the immediate superior of each potential appointee.

This consent was easily obtained from two of the three superiors of these workers. Leslie Monroe's boss, Denise Haltom, however, was very disturbed by the whole task force. Haltom, although eight years youn-

ger than Cashion, had been at Investech for 19 months longer than Cashion. Their levels in the company structure were quite comparable. It was acknowledged widely that Haltom was one of the most knowledgeable experts on product capabilities within the firm, including Mahoney. She also had an effective, dependable style for which clients commended her.

Haltom was disappointed that this knowledge base was seemingly ignored in the creation of the Installation Task Force. When Myamoto had mentioned the possible creation of the task force months before it came about, she had assumed she had been told so that she would be prepared to take charge. She also knew that she would soon be finishing a major project for a brokerage house. This would allow her the time to make a smooth transition into the task force.

After the brokerage project was successfully concluded, Haltom had taken a long-overdue two-week vacation to South America. Upon her return, she found Mahoney's official memorandum announcing Sarah's appointment to the task force waiting for her on her desk. Two handwritten notes were attached. One from Myamoto said, "Sorry but it would have been a real hassle for you anyway." The other, which was from David Mahoney, read, "See me as soon as you return."

She called Myamoto at once for further background on this event. He welcomed her back but directed her to speak with Mahoney first. When she went to Mahoney's office, she was told that he would be tied up in meetings for the next two days and would get back as soon as he was free. With Mahoney's travel schedule and meetings, Mahoney and Haltom did not get to meet for a month after her return. By the time they met, Haltom's anger had dissipated, but her disappointment remained. She was certain that if she had been in town when this decision had been made, she would have been named to the task force. Mahoney tried to assure her that this was the best decision for all involved and was not merely a case of "a squeaky wheel getting greased."

Choosing a Team

Cashion's request to borrow Leslie Monroe for two to three months inflamed the situation all over again. Leslie Monroe graduated from Columbia with an MBA a year ago and had been hired directly in Investech by Haltom. They met at a campus interview and liked each other instantly. When she visited the firm for a second interview, Monroe was virtually ready to begin work on the spot. Haltom had been forced to return to campuses on a job search after she lost two valuable workers within three months. One, Kevin Hoffman, had left because he felt that he did not see any career opportunity for him at Investech relative to the deal offered by a large computer maker. Haltom was disappointed because she had invested a good deal of time and training into Hoffman. At the same time she told him that she could understand his temptation to leave.

The other worker, Kate Carlson, had quit with great reluctance. Carlson had worked for Haltom for four months and had come to feel very close to her. When Mahoney reassigned Carlson to work with Sickles, the former vice president of engineering, Carlson protested to Haltom. Carlson pleaded with Haltom to intercede and allow her to continue working for Haltom in product development. Sickles had acquired the

reputation of an abusive superior with a particular problem managing women. Although Sickles was later fired, Mahoney bristled when Haltom raised the issue of Carlson's assignment. He exclaimed,

> Look Denise, this is a small company. Kate just has to learn that she can't always work with her favorite girlfriends. There is work to be done around here which requires that she learn to work with different types of people.

Carlson quit promptly after hearing this message delivered through Haltom. She was immediately hired by a competitor firm at a position comparable to Haltom's.

Now, with Cashion's request, Haltom felt that once again, well-developed talent was about to be forced out the door of Investech needlessly. Cashion approached Haltom, claiming that the decision to remove Monroe had already been made and that the request was merely *pro forma*. Cashion said that she just wanted to inform Haltom in advance of the general announcement to the firm. Haltom responded, "Well, you certainly know how to flatter me. Say, did you think of mentioning this to your new employee, Leslie Monroe?" Cashion then said that Haltom was not to mention the plan to Monroe yet until Myamoto formally did so, given the political sensitivity of the task force. Haltom replied that she would rather have been told nothing than to receive this sort of briefing.

That night she entertained her project development team at her home. Each time she glanced in the direction of Monroe, she felt deceitful for not warning Leslie.

The next morning she called Myamoto for a meeting. She asked why she had not been consulted earlier. Denise explained that there were three reasons why she had

Exhibit 2 Investech Organizational Chart

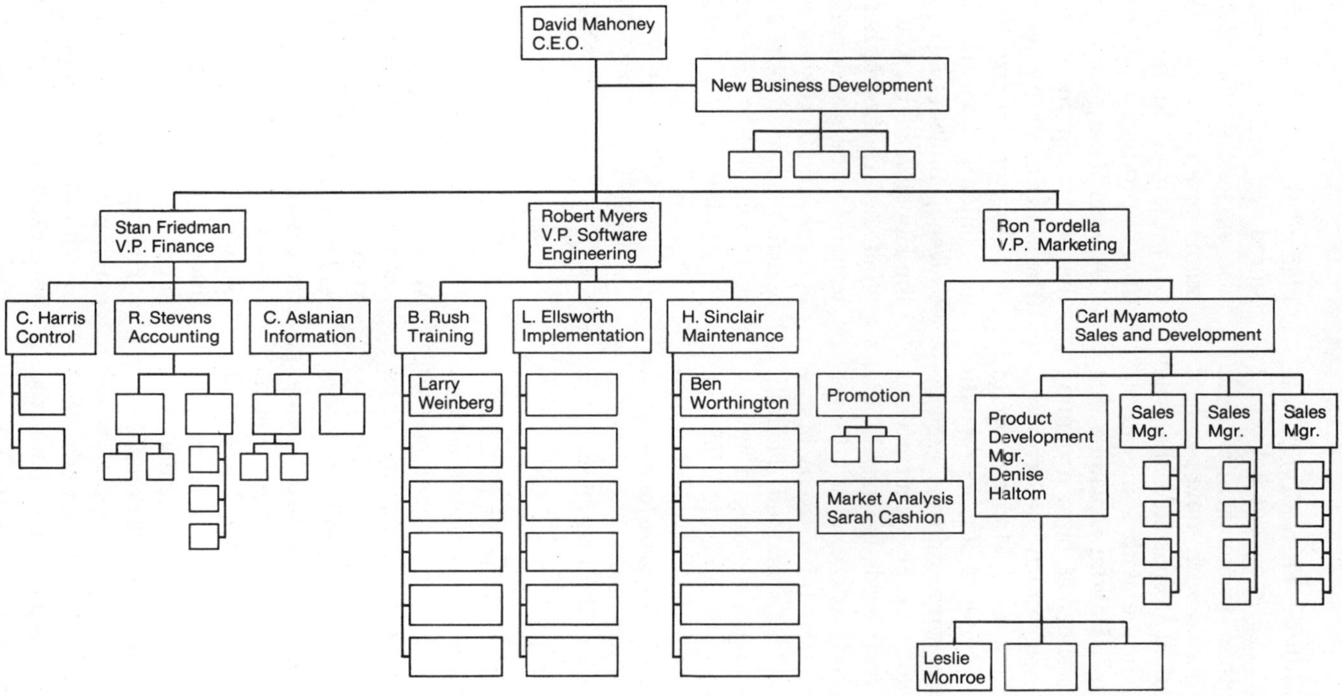

hoped to retain Monroe. First, Monroe was in the midst of a small-scale but important project for another brokerage. Second, Monroe was distressed with some personal family difficulties. Haltom stated that she was providing Monroe with some advice and support. Third, Haltom explained that she thought that she had been grooming Monroe for a job very much like her own.

Myamoto replied that Monroe would benefit from the experience of working with a new and perhaps more difficult supervisor. He explained, "Leslie won't always have a manager who holds her hand." He added that a good worker like Monroe would help to ensure the success of the Cashion project. He reminded Haltom, "You know Sarah hasn't managed anyone before, Denise, and we can't afford for this project not to work." Haltom asked, "Well what about Leslie's own goals for her own development?" Myamoto acknowledged, "Well, that's a good point. I mentioned it to Mahoney, and he said, 'This isn't IBM—we can't afford to be grooming layers and layers of extra talent.' " Halton asked, "Could I at least tell Leslie about this plan; I feel disloyal talking about her future behind her back." Myamoto agreed that this would be acceptable.

When Haltom returned to her office, she found Monroe slumped in a chair waiting. In halting, accusatory tones, Monroe said, "Carl Myamoto just called me. I feel a bit betrayed. How would you have known about it over dinner and not mention it to me? You know Sarah is like Eva Peron! I had to respond to Carl with no preparation for this shock." Haltom was angry that Myamoto had misunderstood about the need to inform Monroe promptly. She did not realize that Myamoto would beat her in reaching Monroe. Over lunch Haltom explained the whole chain of events and restored her credibility with Monroe. Haltom also suggested that the exposure, in fact, might provide greater breadth of knowledge than could be provided with more time in product development.

A week later, Monroe reluctantly began the new assignment with Sarah Cashion. The assignment involved a good deal of travel. Through August, the first month of the assignment, they traveled to New York, Chicago, Philadelphia, and Houston. On the Houston flight, Cashion asked Monroe what she expected of her career in the short term. Monroe was surprised by this interest and replied, "I'd like to be a manager within a year or so with some substantial responsibility for product development."

Cashion coldly warned,

> Look dear, it should be clear to you that this place is not growing that fast these days and you're a little too young to manage anything. I'd advise you to try to manage your marriage and not expect a promotion for several years.

Upon her return, at the end of August, Monroe called Haltom at her office. Monroe related her conversation with Cashion. Monroe claimed that in general, Cashion had been vindictive and disorganized. Monroe closed the conversation saying that she would be handing in her resignation on Monday and was planning to accept a job offered by Kate Carlson, Haltom's former subordinate.

Haltom asked her to wait a week before making any final decisions. After hanging up with Monroe, Haltom slammed her door and exclaimed, "This place is managed worse than a chicken coop." She reopened her door to see Mahoney standing there grinning.

CASE 2
HONEYWELL: HUMAN RESOURCES PLANNING (A)
C. Wickham Skinner

In March 1980, C. E. Brown, vice president, employee relations, felt three years' planning effort in employee relations and human resources was beginning to produce results. The major problem he and the company faced he had described in a speech a few months before in 1979 to members of The Human Resource Association:

> The number one problem facing Employee Relations directors is how best to relate their performance goals to those of the total corporation. The line's perception is that too often personnel directors set their annual MBO goals with little real knowledge of the long-range strategic and management goals they should be supporting.

Honeywell's effort began at a 1977 conference on employee relations and human resource planning that brought together some 50 general managers from the operating divisions and their counterparts from the personnel staff. The conference was third in a company series to discuss problems and opportunities between staff and line organizations. Brown later reported the participants challenged some assumptions and defined major areas of human resource effort:

> It was obvious, from conference, that both line and staff people finally understood that we had to start planning our people requirements. The assumption of always having enough people to fill our slots, so-called "ready availability," no longer is true.
>
> Five major areas for human resource work came out of that conference. First, we had to

start helping the divisions get the right people available at the right time. Second, we had to work on smoothing out the cyclical nature of some of our people flows. Third, the cost effectiveness of various skill levels and employee types had to be examined. Fourth, the coordination of recruiting had to be increased on a corporate-wide basis. Finally, the training of the technically skilled people needed in most of our divisions had to be done more effectively—possibly through corporate institutes and technical centers.

From this conference and these visits the need for a formal human resources planning system became apparent. As Brown further said:

> We needed information at the corporate level in order to be of some service to the divisions. We had to know what they thought their people requirements were and then build a consensus around that . . . numbers and types of people had to be documented, "how many of what kind" became an important question . . . to do this we needed to start some type of planning system.

During 1978, P. R. Elsen, a member of Brown's staff, worked on defining and developing what this type of human resource planning might consist of for Honeywell. In January 1979, a bulletin of Human Resource Planning (HRP) was written and released to all divisions. This bulletin stressed HRP's ties to organizational goals (see Appendix A).

Elsen and Brown knew that the drafting of a bulletin was not in itself likely to bring action and compliance by the various divisions. They were faced with some interesting problems: how would a strategy for the implementation of this plan might be devised? Given the decentralized and diverse

Exhibit 1   **Corporate Structure** (simplified)

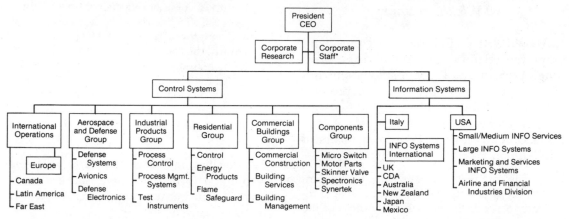

* Administration, legal, financial, employee relations, public affairs, field marketing, field administration, communications and public relations, planning, and business development.

nature of Honeywell's divisions (Exhibits 1 and 2), it was an open question as to how useful HRP might be to the various divisions.

In March of 1979, Brown, pondering over these issues, wrote a memo to himself summarizing his thoughts on HRP (Exhibit 3). Later that year, when he spoke at the con-

Exhibit 2   **Five-Year Financial Summary** ($ millions)

	1979	1978	1977	1976	1975
Revenue:					
Environmental systems and controls............	$1,013.2	$ 886.5	$ 779.6	$ 690.9	$ 590.6
Industrial systems and controls	912.5	711.5	553.9	461.9	427.2
Aerospace and defense........................	831.2	656.2	540.7	428.7	418.0
Information systems	1,452.6	1,293.6	1,036.9	913.8	856.1
	$4,209.5	$3,547.8	$2,911.1	$2,495.3	$2,291.9
Operating profit:					
Environmental systems and controls............	$ 142.2	$ 132.4	$ 115.2	$ 91.7	$ 64.2
Industrial systems and controls	138.4	107.0	75.3	47.7	29.1
Aerospace and defense........................	45.1	43.1	38.4	41.0	33.4
Information systems	152.4	105.7	79.4	41.4	40.4
	$ 478.1	$ 388.2	$ 308.3	$ 221.8	$ 167.1
Net income after taxes and other charges	$ 260.5	$ 201.4	$ 145.1	$ 113.1	$ 77.8
Net income per share	11.89	9.41	6.90	5.50	3.96
Dividends per share............................	2.40	2.05	1.75	1.50	1.40

Exhibit 3

March 5, 1979   F.U. _____

File

C. E. Brown

Corporate Employee Relations

LONG-RANGE HUMAN RESOURCE PLANNING—
OUTLINE FOR DISCUSSION WITH GROUP
VICE PRESIDENTS, GENERAL MANAGERS, ETC.

1. *Objective*
   (a) Primary objective is to increase the company's productivity by planning for the people we need and having them available and qualified when needed.
   (b) To be effective the long-range human resource planning process should be a part of the company's regular planning/reporting process—interwoven into financial planning, facilities planning, etc.

2. We need additional top level attention to the subject, as well as bottoms-up effort by the operating divisions.
   (a) Include on high level meeting agendas—Renier's and Spangle's staff, EERC, etc.
   (b) Our strategic planning policy statements and related matters should include human resource planning.
   (c) How about including in mid-year reviews?

3. Consider both short- and long-term plans.

4. Develop some examples to illustrate the benefits of planning.
   (a) Integrated circuit design requirements.

5. Determine the degree of involvement which our employee relations people have in overall business planning as well as involvement of the General Manager in human resource planning.

6. Consider some divisions as possibly being in a lead position on planning—DSD, PMSD, TID.

CEB/mmr

---

ference of The Human Resource Association on the problem of relating performance goals to those of the total corporation, he included these remarks:

Other common problems we all face are falling or stagnating productivity, technological obsolescence, unwanted turnover, excessive payroll costs, and faltering motivation, etc. The question was asked, what should we do about these many systemic problems which prevent us from achieving the high productivity which we might expect from the costly human inputs into our total management systems?

This process of introspection and self-audit in our personnel functions has continued. When we looked hard at our performance and capabilities, we found that we handle most of the traditional personnel functions quite effectively. Problem solving, crisis management, policy implementation were our strong suits—in fact, we handled fairly well all those tasks necessary to support an operational plan. On the other hand, the deficiencies we saw were in areas that require creative, thoughtful, useful input: to management planning and strategic planning—those processes that have a longer than one year time horizon.

To start this process of renewal, we have decided to concentrate efforts on these key steps that have proved successful in the management of other input resources:

—forecasting needs
—planning for timely resource procurement
—inventorying the resources already on hand
—adding value to new and existing resources
—controlling quality
—seeking and measuring employee feedback

I would like to share with you my thoughts on these planning steps and comment on some of the subsystems we have already in place.

Consider, for example, the process used to forecast future people needs. Typically, this process has been confined to estimating the need for replacement employees or those required to meet increased operating levels. But to be truly useful, human resource forecasting needs to cover in detail such other factors as future skills required, grades-level needed, cost of such employees, availability and source of candidates and induction training needed. These forecasts must cover a three- to five-year time frame so that we have adequate lead time to plan.

Human resource planning, if done thoroughly, can do much to support operating goals for production, service, or profitability. Such planning involves the translation of company operating goals into human resource requirements of all types, not just the number of needed employees but the skills at preplanned cost and time. Such planning involves appraising the current performance of individual employees and the prediction of their future performance. It should provide planned career paths for many individuals and include a system for matching employee skills with job requirement.

Human resource planning should ultimately address everything that involves or concerns people at work. This includes such factors as cost, morale, leadership, development, productivity, compensation and conservation of the resource. Human resource planning, when fully implemented, involves the total human input required by the firm and it assures a planned return for this special investment.

During the summer of 1979 Brown reorganized the corporate employee relations staff to include a broader-gauged and more fully developed human resources department. This move, which brought together the existing human resource skills of several corporate Minneapolis staff departments, was an acknowledgement that the problems of attracting, developing and satisfying employees had grown increasingly important to a technology-oriented company like Honeywell, and that these same problems could have a make-or-break impact on the company's growth plans for the 1980s.

F. A. Boyle, former director of employee

relations for the residential group and Minneapolis operations, was named director of the new department. He was made responsible for such people-oriented functions as EEO; recruiting and placement; executive, managerial and professional development; employee education and training; and human resource research and planning (see Exhibit 4).

To help guide the organization and management of his department, Boyle formulated a set of preliminary mission and objective statements (see Exhibits 5 and 6), that included a list of seven "givens."

As one of its first undertakings in October 1979, the HRD conducted a study following a conference of the control systems groups in the corporation on needs. The HRD gathered executive opinions as to the human resource activities most needed by control systems groups and where in the organization (corporate versus divisional locations)

these activities should be best performed (see Exhibits 7 and 8).

This conference was set up by the executive vice president of control systems, Dr. James Renie. He described the tasks ahead:

The corporate Human Resource department (which is proposing an increase in budget from \$2 to \$3½ million) will never be understood or get off the ground unless they have your support. Further, they probably will not get your support unless you understand their program and have the opportunity to provide them with the objectives that we must achieve. Frankly, although I understand their desire to enhance the program, I have no appreciation of what they have proposed since they really don't know what we need or want. We haven't told them in a satisfactory manner.

When one looks at the staggering number of people that we will be hiring in the next long-range period, and the change in mix that we must achieve, we must have objec-

Exhibit 4   Employee Relations Organization

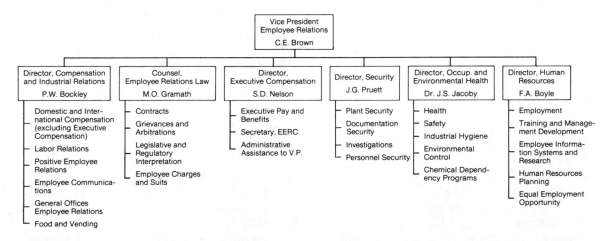

Exhibit 5 Human Resources
Department—Preliminary Mission Statement

MISSION: To insure the Corporation has Human Resource systems in place that provide a competent, trained, and productive workforce.

GIVENS:

1. We will operate in a decentralized manner. Therefore, we will operate primarily in a consultative role.
2. It is better to have a few good people than several average ones.
3. We will work on "live" problems, be able to change priorities and be flexible.
4. We will have a "can do" attitude—Not, "I will fit it into my schedule, but I will have it for you."
5. We will work on new problems each year (should be 50 percent) rather than run special Corporate programs.
6. We will try to challenge the divisions to do a better job.
7. Have an R&D mentality—How to do things better should be the programs on which we work.

---

tives and strategy that will minimize the number and achieve the proper mix.

One result of the conference and study was the preparation by the corporate group of a formal report on Honeywell people needs 1980 to 1985, which concluded with six propositions (see Exhibit 9).

The most significant result, however, of this activity throughout Honeywell management was increased human resource plan-

ning at several of the operating divisions. For example, Warde Wheaton, vice president of the aerospace and defense systems group (ADG) asked his divisions to submit human resource plans by the end of the first quarter of 1980. Two of these plans were well along the way in February and were expected to be completed on time. Brown felt that ADG was considerably ahead of the rest of the corporation in HRP. Nevertheless, the Information Systems Group had recently begun human resource planning, on a more centralized basis, at its headquarters in Waltham, Massachusetts. In contrast to previous efforts, the development of this human resource planning system was to be driven directly by the strategic issues identified in the I.S. Long-Range Business Plans.

Another result was the increased awareness of the need for comprehensive employee information systems, validated selection systems, automated tracking systems and planning and forecasting models that could be used by human resource planning groups throughout the company. The responsibility for providing these systems was assigned by F. A. Boyle to G. W. Bennington's systems and planning section (see Exhibit 10).

Current Issues and Concerns

In March 1980, Brown and his staff, while encouraged at the progress being made in HRP in several divisions were nevertheless concerned over the following issues. They cited the following:

1. Progress is being made but it is still far too slow to meet the company's real needs.
2. HRP needs to be done from the bottom up but guided and coordinated from the

Exhibit 6   Human Resources Department—Preliminary Objectives

OBJECTIVES:

1. To establish an effective advisory board to guide our efforts.
2. To strive to provide leadership for the Human Resource function.
3. To provide proactive research in the Human Resource field.
4. To develop the Human Resources of the Corporation—
   —On the Job
   —In the Classroom
5. To be consultants, integrators, auditors, forward thinkers, pushers.
6. To be pragmatic and operate programs that are in the mainstream of managing the business.
7. To provide one or more significant chair assignments in our department.
8. To provide leadership and development programs for the Employee Relations function.
9. To be creative in our work—provide ideas and present alternatives.
10. To develop a Human Resource Planning Model and assist the division in implementing such a model.
11. To provide a *strategy* for our Management Development Programs.
12. To develop new Management Development Programs.
13. To develop an EIS function that supports our other Employee Relations and the Divisions.
14. To develop an expanded employment function at the Corporate level—
    • Executive Recruiting
    • University Relations
    • Sourcing Expertise
    • Advertising Coordination
    • In-house Referral
    • Interviewing Skills
15. To develop broad-based validated selection techniques.
16. To develop programs that encompass a "how to" implementation strategy.
17. To develop a consulting function—
    —In House
    —Outside
18. To develop an effective mobility system that enhances meaningful transfers between divisions.
19. To develop development systems that "spot the stars" in their 30s.
20. To develop career paths/career planning systems.
21. To develop the capability to understand and apply Human Resource Principles/Behavioral Science Techniques to the new workforces of the 1980s.
22. To be able to successfully "merchandise" our development programs.
23. To provide Professional Development expertise to our professional workforce.
24. To develop a Performance Appraisal strategy for the Corporation that supports and enhances our Human Resource Planning and Development programs.
25. To continue to expand our Attitude Survey capability.
26. To provide an effective plant location acquisition capability.
27. To publish the Personal Benefits Statement annually for each Division.
28. To support and enhance the Production Team Program Capability.
29. To continue our effective EEO programs.
30. To develop more effective Talent Review and Executive Mobility Programs.
31. To develop a competent, responsive special projects capability.
32. To develop Organizational Planning capability.

Exhibit 7 **Population Growth/Replacement Projections** (controls systems)

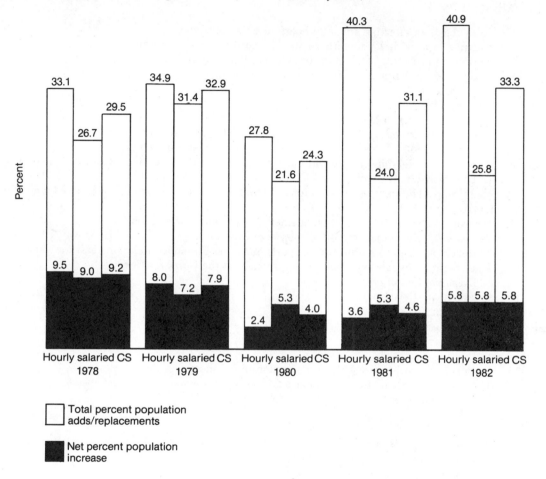

top down. It already needs more consistency now in the divisions where it's started by divisional impetus. We in corporate haven't been definite and specific enough yet. While divisional enthusiasm exists, it tends to take HRP and run with it after planning in a far less than complete way. The whole thing could get away from us and get uncoordinated and sloppy. We have to stay ahead of it all.

3. The divisions tend to focus on numbers since the division managers are driven by head counts as a control mechanism. They do not get concerned with demographics nor with changes in the kinds

Exhibit 8   Systems/Planning

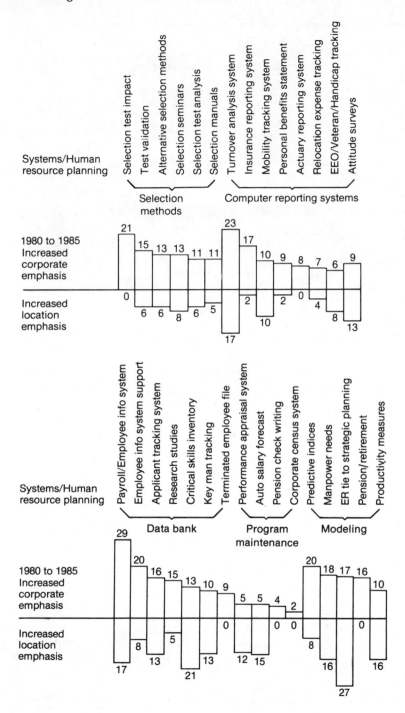

Exhibit 8 (*concluded*)

Conclusions/Recommendations

Increased corporate emphasis
* Selection testing
  —Validate test methods.
  —Determine long-range impact.
* Turnover analysis
  —Develop better data base.
  —Need predictive model.
* Corporate payroll/Employee info system (EIS)
  —Critical need for early implementation.
  —Will help in modeling and forecasting.
* Predictive indices
  —Corporate take the lead; provide more indicators to division.
* Manpower Modeling
  —Computer program needed; necessity for the 80s.

Increased location emphasis
* Employee relations tie to strategic planning
  —Employee Relations needs to be in business planning cycle.
* Critical skills inventory
  —Long-range need, particularly in special technical skills.

Maintain existing corporate/location balance

* Selection methods
* Selection test analysis/Validation
* Selection seminars
* Selection manuals
* Terminated employee file
* Key man tracking
* Research studies

* Applicant tracking
* Performance appraisals
* Attitude surveys
* Insurance, actuary reporting
* Mobility tracking
* EEO/Veteran/Handicap tracking
* Relocation expenses

* Personal benefits statement
* Pension/Retirement models
* Productivity measures
* Corporate census
* Auto salary forecasting
* Pension check writing

Corporate Headcount Recommendations

Present	*Proposed*
4	6

* Need to increase Corporate effort in developing models and establishing responsive data retrieval system.

Exhibit 9 Honeywell People Needs

Proposition I—

MANAGING HONEYWELL IN '85 WILL BE
TWICE AS DIFFICULT AS MANAGING IT IN '80

CHANGES   CONSEQUENCES/NEEDS

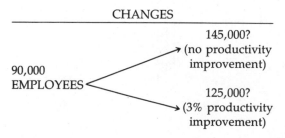

"HALF AGAIN"—PRESENT PEOPLE, SPACE,
DESKS, MACHINES, FILES, PAPERWORK,
MEETINGS, TRAVEL

90,000
EMPLOYEES

145,000?
(no productivity
improvement)

125,000?
(3% productivity
improvement)

Exhibit 9 (*continued*)

CHANGES	CONSEQUENCES/NEEDS
25 STRATEGIC BUSINESS ⟶ 40 UNITS	"DOUBLE THE MANAGERS"—PRESENT 8088 → 13000 (PLUS TURNOVER) MASSIVE TRAINING AND DEVELOPMENT EFFORT?
9 GROUPS ⟶ 14	"DOUBLE THE EXECUTIVES"? (CAN EXECUTIVE PRODUCTIVITY BE INCREASED?)

Proposition II—

INTERNAL BUSINESS CHANGES WILL DICTATE A DRAMATIC CHANGE IN PEOPLE NEEDS

CHANGES	CONSEQUENCES/NEEDS
• TECHNOLOGY REVOLUTION (Chips–bubbles–lasers–microprocessors)	• TECHNICAL & MANAGERIAL OBSOLESCENCE • NEED FOR IN-HOUSE TECHNICAL SCHOOLS
• MARKETING SEGMENTS	• RECONFIGURED WORKFORCE TO MATCH SEGMENTS
• HARDWARE → SOFTWARE	• "PEOPLE-LIMITED" GROWTH
• MFG → ASSY	• DISRUPTIONS, PER PRESSURES
• PRODUCTS → SERVICE	• LOWERED PRODUCTIVITY
• AUTOMATION	• LOWER SKILL NEED vs HIGHER REWARD EXPECTATION
• SYSTEMS	• PRODUCTIVITY?—PROFITABILITY?
• MAKE → BUY	• PURCHASING BECOMES A CRITICAL FUNCTION
• ONSHORE → OFFSHORE	• COMPLEXITY, COORDINATION?
• CONVERGENCE ON SOLID STATE PRODUCTS	• NEED FOR SYNERGISM, STANDARDIZATION
• HUMAN FACTORS	• NEW AWARENESS, SKILLS NEEDED

Proposition III—

WE MIGHT HAVE TO MODIFY OUR ORGANIZATIONS TO FIT THE AVAILABLE TECHNICAL EMPLOYEES RATHER THAN VICE VERSA

SITUATION	CONSEQUENCES/NEEDS
• ELECTRONIC INDUSTRY GROWING AT COMPOUNDED 17%/YEAR	

Exhibit 9 (*continued*)

SITUATION	CONSEQUENCES/NEEDS
• TOTAL ENGINEERING BASE GROWING AT 5% PER YEAR • CAMPUS ENGINEERING DEMAND GROWING AT 30%/YEAR • NO OVERALL GROWTH IN EE'S AVAILABLE, 1980 to 1985 • EMPLOYEES LESS MOBILE • SILICON VALLEY SYNDROME	{ COMPANY GROWTH IS POSSIBLE PROVIDING WE DEVELOP A SUPERIOR TECHNICAL WORKFORCE IN THE FACE OF NEGATIVE SUPPLY CONDITIONS

POSSIBLE STRATEGIES

1. RECRUIT MORE THAN OUR SHARE—COST?
2. INCREASE COLLEGE RECRUITING EFFORT
3. USE MORE COOPS AND INTERNS
4. USE MORE PARA-PROFESSIONALS, TECHS
5. USE TECHNICAL CONSULTANTS, "LEASED" ENGINEERS
6. TRAIN—RETRAIN—ENGINEERS, NONENGINEERS, UPGRADE TECHS.
7. UP PRODUCTIVITY BY CADAM, OTHER COMPUTERIZATION.
8. ACQUIRE COMPANIES WITH STRONG TECHNICAL DEPARTMENTS
9. LOCATE IN ATTRACTIVE CITIES
10. ORGANIZE AROUND "PRECIOUS FEW"—MOVE WORK TO PEOPLE

Proposition IV—

TURNOVER MAY BECOME THE CRITICAL FACTOR IN THE EQUATION OF THE '80s

DATA	CONSEQUENCES/NEEDS

TOTAL HIRES TO '85—150,000
⅔ OF HIRING TO COVER TURNOVER
15% OVERALL—BUT RANGES FROM 5–50%
MIDDLE MANAGEMENT RATE 5–10%
TURNOVER HI FOR SOME KEY JOB FAMILIES
PROBABLY WILL WORSEN
  • Energy shortage
  • Immovable employees
  • Silicon Valley syndrome
  • Prof. vs. Co. loyalty
	"CHOKING" ON NEWCOMERS? (150,000 CHANCES TO IMPROVE)
	COSTS-CONFUSION—EMPTY CHAIRS—LOWERED PRODUCTIVITY PERCEIVED AS "NOT TOO BAD"
	STAGNATION—BLOCKING HIPOTS
	LOST SALES, MISSED DATES, HI COSTS
	COSTS UP—NEED FOR BETTER PRACTICES, SUPERVISION

Exhibit 9 (*continued*)

POSSIBLE STRATEGY

USE
"MANAGED" — TO——→
TURNOVER

- CHANGE SKILL MIX
- LOWER AVERAGE GRADE
- REDUCE (MAINTAIN) PAYROLL COSTS
- MAKE EEO GOALS
- REVITALIZE WORKFORCE

Proposition V—

CHANGING PEOPLE-MANAGEMENT METHODS WILL BE A KEY EXECUTIVE CONCERN FROM NOW TO '85

CHANGES	CONSEQUENCES
EMPLOYEES DEMAND "RIGHTS"	MANAGEMENT MUST:
• Job security	Listen
• Participation	Encourage participation
• Medical care	Adjust
• Adequate income	Allow for costs
• Dual ladders	
QUALITY OF LIFE EXPECTATIONS	
• Fulfilling work	More attention to job design
• Experiences versus things	Increased employee participation in decisions
• Diversity of lifestyles	Flexible hours, assignments
	New forms of employee "ownership" of Corp.
NEW FORMS OF WORK PATTERNS	
• Working women, special hours	Increased EEO pressure
• Dual careers	Confusion, lowered productivity?
• Second careers	Increased career guidance
• Part-timers?	Training costs? Loyalty?
INTEREST GROUPS	
• Legitimized roles	More disclosure of company information.
• Cover all subjects	New methods to handle?
• Media-conscious	

Proposition VI—

OUR PLANNING FOR PEOPLE WILL HAVE TO BE AS EFFECTIVE AS OUR PLANNING FOR MONEY

SITUATION	CONSEQUENCES/NEEDS
INCREASING IMPORTANCE OF "PEOPLE LEAD TIME"	

Exhibit 9 (*concluded*)

SITUATION	CONSEQUENCES/NEEDS
• 20 YEARS TO DEVELOP A GENERAL MANAGER • 10 YEARS TO DEVELOP A DEPARTMENT MANAGER • 3–5 YEARS TO DEVELOP A DESIGN ENGINEER • 12–15 WEEKS TO FILL A SOFTWARE REQ. • 12 MONTHS NEEDED FOR COLLEGE REQS. FOR CONTACTS, NEGOTIATION, VISITS	NEED A PEOPLE FORECASTING/ PLANNING/DEVELOPMENT SYSTEM WHICH PROVIDES LONG LEAD TIME FOR CRITICAL, TIGHT-AVAILABILITY SPOTS
OUR "INVENTORY" OF HIPOTS IN ENGINEERING, SALES, AND MANAGEMENT MAY BE INADEQUATE TO SUPPORT RAPID GROWTH	NEED MORE INPUT OF HIPOTS, CAREER PATH PROGRAMS, DEVELOPMENTAL ASSIGNMENTS, MORE "MENTORING"

of skills or attitudes or traditional sources of people.

4. The staff members in Brown's group stated that the focus of planning numbers, based on needs versus "inventory," should be changed to analyzing key jobs and developing a better idea of abilities and skills needed in the future. "We are too bound to conventional job descriptions," G. W. Bennington stated.

5. Brown respected the opinions of the staff and their professional bias toward a good data base and "doing things right," but he felt that years of time and hundreds of thousands of dollars could be saved by "a division manager spending one full day with his people on human resource planning just getting down to business problems and listing problems and issues, clustering those issues into general areas and seeing the impact on people requirements."

6. People requirements always seem to be based on sales forecasts. Growth is high, yet forecasts are usually understated. Personnel plans are the slaves of forecasts.

7. A major problem is that HRPs are perceived by managements as appendages to the strategic business plan. This results in shallow, short-focused human resource planning documents, which don't get used for decision making.

8. There are already many planning mechanisms that produce MBO objectives, critical tasks and indeed training requirements. Some division managers feel they are already doing HRP and do not see it as a critical new need.

9. Formal, well-established EEO/AAP planning done in the division has not been integrated into the broader human resource planning process.

Exhibit 10 Functions of Structure

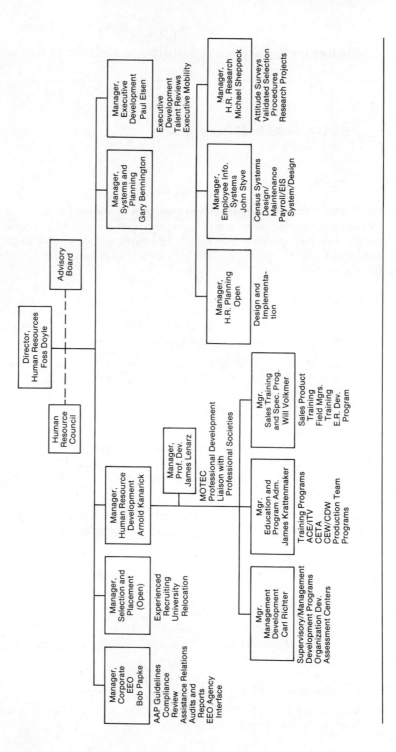

Appendix A
Honeywell Corporate Employee Relations Bulletin

Revised

SUBJECT: HUMAN RESOURCE PLANNING   Date: January 22, 1979
ISSUED BY: Paul R. Elsen   No: 167

GENERAL SUMMARY

Our continued concern for boosting employee productivity coupled with our increasing need for highly qualified professional, technical and managerial personnel calls for improved, comprehensive human resource management. Effective, long-range planning can significantly improve the management of our human resources. This bulletin provides general guidelines for developing such a planning process.

APPLICATION AND USER

This bulletin is applicable to all Honeywell locations. It should be used by location management as a guideline for developing a human resource planning process.

The completed plan should be a fundamental document used by the line managers to run the business, akin to the financial operating plan.

HUMAN RESOURCE SYSTEM DEFINED

The human resource system in Honeywell can be visualized as a continuous process of modifying the work force by means of employment, deployment, separations, training and development, so that optimum results are attained by both the organization and the individuals involved. An effective system should have the right people at the right place, at the right time, performing in a highly productive and satisfying manner.

To attain this goal, the line management of each operating unit, with staff input, should develop an appropriate process for planning and managing its human resources on a continuous and long-range basis.

File in Section _____

Suggested Index Entry: Human Resource Plan
                                      Planning, Work Force
                                      Personnel Plans

APPLICATIONS OF HUMAN RESOURCE PLANNING PROCESSES

There is a wide range of applications for an effective human resource planning process. It should provide management with a useful means to:

- Learn more about the overall configuration and composition of the organization's human resources.
- Determine how to meet affirmative action commitments.
- Identify areas for potential career development and training.
- Control actual staffing and personnel expense by relating them to budgeted staffing and expense.
- Adapt the available human resources to expected needs more gradually, based on anticipated changes in business needs.
- Identify problem areas within the human resource pool in terms of present or future shortages or surpluses.
- Recruit scarce skills more efficiently and effectively by providing longer recruiting lead time based on a better prediction of future business and technology requirements.
- Facilitate succession planning for key positions of leadership.

Each Honeywell division/operation should develop and implement a thorough human resource planning system as an integral part of its overall management system.

HUMAN RESOURCE PLANNING—COMMON ELEMENTS

Most human resource planning processes have the following elements in common (Figure 1):

   I.   Organizational Goals.
  II.   Human Resource Needs Forecast.
 III.   Employee Information.
  IV.   Human Resource Availability Projections.
   V.   Analysis and Evaluation of Gaps.
  VI.   Generating and Testing Alternatives.
 VII.   Implementation of Overall Program.
VIII.   Monitoring of Results.

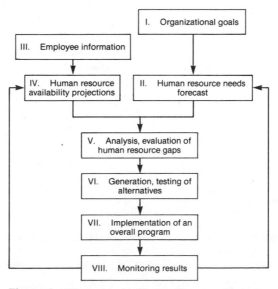

Figure 1   Elements of a Human Resource Plan

I. Organizational Goals

To be relevant, a human resource planning system needs to be clearly tied to the organization's business objectives. The plan must rest on a solid foundation of information about sales forecasts, market trends, technology advances and major changes in processes or productivity. Considerable effort needs to be devoted to the identification of reliable data on business trends and needs, as the basic input which will "drive" the human resource plan in terms of quantity and quality of needed labor content.

II. Human Resource Needs Forecast

A second element in the planning process is the forecasting of human resource needs based on the business objectives and production plans and the various indicators of changes in technology or operating methods. This is usually accomplished utilizing historical data and reliable ratios (i.e., indirect/direct labor), adjusting them for productivity trends. The result of this forecast is a spread sheet of employees needed to accomplish the organization's goals in terms of numbers, mix, cost, new skills or job categories, and numbers and levels of managers. Experience has shown that producing this forecast is the most challenging part of the planning process since it requires creative and highly participative approaches to dealing with business and technical uncertainties several years in the future.

III. Employee Information

A third element of the planning process is accurate information concerning the composition, configuration and capabilities of the current work force. This includes information about job classifications, ages, sex, minority status, organization levels, salaries, and functions. Employee information may also include resume data such as skills, educational and training data, and career interests. Much of the data needed for human resource planning currently exists in other personnel systems (i.e., payroll, talent review or professional development data).

IV. Human Resource Availability Projections

The fourth element of the planning process is to calculate what current human resources could be or will be available in terms of skills, numbers, age, deployment, etc., into the future. By projecting past data about the size, configuration and composition of the work force and data about the flows of the human resources (turnover, aging, hiring) one can determine the probable availability at a specific future time. The result of this kind of activity is a picture of what human resources an organization currently has and how they will evolve over time due to turnover, retirement, obsolescence, etc.

V. Analysis and Evaluation of Human Resource Gaps

The fifth element of the planning process is to compare what is needed with what is available in terms of numbers, mix, skills, and technologies. This permits a determination of the gaps and evaluation of where the most serious mismatches occur. Such analysis should help the organization address issues such as:

- Are there imbalances developing between human resource needs and projected availability?
- What is the effect of current productivity trends and pay levels on manpower levels and costs?
- Do turnover problems exist in certain jobs or age levels?
- Are there problems of career blockage and obsolescence?

- Are there sufficient high-potential managers to fulfill future needs?
- Are we short any critical skills?

This analysis of gaps will lead to the development of specific plans on a long-range basis for recruiting, hiring, training, transferring, and retraining of appropriate numbers and types of employees.

VI. Generating, Testing of Alternatives

The analysis of the human resource system should have impacts on a wide range of policies and practices such as: staffing plans; promotion practices and policies, EEO plans; organizational design; training and development programs; salary planning and career management systems. This phase of the process explores those implications and generates alternatives. Some more comprehensive human resource planning systems permit modeling the configuration and composition of human resources that would result from specific changes in staffing strategies or other personnel policies. This allows evaluation and testing alternatives. If not performed by a computer model, an equivalent manual testing of anticipated consequences should be utilized.

VII. Implementation of Overall Human Resource Program

Once the best alternatives have been chosen to address the organization's human resource issues they need to become operational programs with specific plans, target dates, schedules, resource commitments, etc.

The analytical steps above should shape an organization's staffing plan, EEO plan, training and development activities, mobility plans, productivity programs, bargaining strategies, and compensation programs.

VIII. Monitoring Results

The final element of a human resource planning process is to provide a means for management to monitor results of the overall program. This step would address such questions as:

- How well is the plan working?
- Is it cost effective?
- What is the actual versus planned impact on work force?
- Where are the weak areas?
- What changes will be needed during the next "cycle?"

HONEYWELL: HUMAN RESOURCES PLANNING (B)— THE AVIONICS DIVISION
C. Wickham Skinner

In March 1980, the Avionics Division of Honeywell was completing its first human re-

sources plan (HRP). Aerospace and Defense Group Vice President Warde Wheaton had asked the division manager to submit such a plan by the end of the first quarter.

The plan was being developed largely by a group working under Ken LaPorte, director of administration for the division. His department included personnel, electronic data processing, and long-range planning for the division.

The Avionics Division had its headquarters in Minneapolis, where it had extensive production, development, and laboratory facilities. In addition, a large production and laboratory operation was located in St. Petersburg, Florida.

The Avionics Division sold flight control, guidance, navigation instruments and systems, engine control, and air data and fuel management systems, militarized digital computers, communication and control systems, and devices for spacecraft, ships, missiles, and aircraft. A large field service engineering group provided on-site repair, maintenance, and technical assistance at or near customer facilities throughout the world. Current sales were approximately $250MM and were growing in constant dollars at a rate of about 7 percent annually. Customers included various agencies of the DOD, NASA, foreign governments, prime contractors, first-tier subcontractors, and commercial airline and airfare companies.

The Avionics Division was organized in six business areas, as follows:

Area	Total Sales (Percent)	Annual Growth Forecast (Percent)
Commercial aviation	9	41
Components	22	10
Guidance navigation	10	23
Military avionics	18	6
Space and strategic systems	24	6
Test equipment	27	14

Each business area had, of course, developed its own strategic plans for expanding its market share, penetrating new markets, and gaining competitive advantages. While these plans are necessarily proprietary, they can be characterized as depending heavily on developing new products, achieving technological superiority in state-of-the-art engineering, upgrading product reliability, increasir., overall cost effectiveness, and, in several products, becoming the lowest-cost producer.

The Human Resource Planning Process

Ken LaPorte described the origins of the group's approach as follows:

After the rapid growth 18 months ago, top officers laid down some challenges about HRP. We needed to spend more time on people planning. In the divisions there's no one single approach. We decided to plan on a global or entire division basis, top down in effect. We had already developed a modest data base showing numbers of people in 300 job skill codes over the past five years.

We looked at history, developed ratios, and made predictions. That sounds simple but it was more complicated. With our data base we ran regressions to find valid correlations between sales, key engineering head counts in the six business areas, ditto for production control, quality control, accounting, etc. We broke the numbers down by different functions such as production, research, development, proposals, etc. And then with the sales and various business forecasts we were able to predict numbers of people in total and by the various key skills we'd need using the models developed by computer analysis.

We gave this data to our managers for them to apply judgment. One problem was that the forecast came out 900 people less than the bottom-up forecast done by the managers, department by department. This had to be resolved, of course. But when the director of Engineering saw that new data, he gobbled it up and asked for more. In fact, most of our key managers felt that this was a tool for looking ahead that they'd never had before. Next time, using this data we'll give each manager a bogey or target to shoot for in planning people requirements. Head counts and analysis of that data serve to surface other issues such as causes for shortages, the kinds of skills and mix of skills needed, and basic personnel problems.

The data base and predictive models were proving useful in other ways, according to LaPorte. They helped his group to study salary compression and its effects, turnover, engineering obsolescence, and validate selection policies and practices.

LaPorte offered two pieces of advice for other divisions planning HRP operations: "(1) It must be systematic but not too automatic or mechanized, (2) it must be developed by division people so as to provide their 'ownership'. If you hire outside or cor-porate people to do your HRP, it will gather dust. Beware of the 'Personnel Department plan syndrome'. HRP must be woven into everyday management and everyday planning. Our top division management has now become very interested."

Key output elements of the Avionics HRP are summarized in the exhibits as follows:

Exhibit 1—Introduction to the HRP.
Exhibit 2—External Environment.
Exhibit 3—Work Force, Current and Projected.
Exhibit 4—Hiring Requirements.
Exhibit 5—Issues Surfaced by the Human Resources Plan.
Exhibit 6—Human Resource Objectives and Shortages for 1980.

Exhibit 1 The Avionics Division—Introduction to the Human Resource Plan

A management team was named early in 1979 to establish the HRP process and considerable effort was directed to the development of a plan for the Avionics Division. Representatives included managers from Finance, Engineering, Production, Business Systems, and Personnel. The team's effort was directed by the Deputy to the General Manager. The following objectives were established for the plan development:

- It is to be a general management tool (not a Personnel Department plan).
- It will be an integral part of the division's total planning process.
- It will serve as the basis for establishing both short-term and long-term human resource objectives (divisionally, and in each major department).
- It will predict manpower levels through the use of automated modeling techniques based on historical indices.
- It will provide for a comprehensive review of source data by divisional and departmental personnel to assure an orderly establishment of human resource objectives.

A significant portion of the team's time was devoted to establishing an effective means of predicting manpower levels. The lack of this capability has inhibited objective setting or problem identification in the past. The approach used involved an in-depth examination of past employment levels and their relationship to sales, B&P/I.D. funds, burden and material costs. As a result, a predictive modeling capability exists, which will facilitate meaningful forecasting and permit "what if" capabilities.

The manpower forecast data, coupled with management review and assessment, has yielded the following major goals for 1979:

a. Implement a plan to assure proper staffing levels for 1980 given the somewhat stable level of business.

Exhibit 1 (*concluded*)

b. Recruit designated key technical skills in the microwave, laser, digital design, and ATE software areas.
c. Establish means to make better use of workforce data to establish more meaningful goal setting on human resource issues.
d. Refine the data modeling techniques for application in other areas of planning (i.e., manpower budgeting and floor space planning).
e. Implement education programs to assure employee understanding of compensation programs.
f. Tailor departmental and customized training programs to meet technological and professional development of employees.
g. Take major steps to improve representation of minorities and females in management positions.
h. Develop an employee communication plan that ensures the upward and downward free flow of information.

While the effort during 1979 has provided a sound basis for problem identification and objective setting, two major challenges exist for 1980 which we must meet to make Human Resource Planning a truly general management business planning tool. They are (1) refinement of our predictive modeling technique in order to establish it as the most effective means of predicting manpower and in order to apply it to other areas of business management (i.e., budgets, floor space planning), and (2) incorporating the HRP process into the development of the business plan such that it is truly a part of the total planning process.

Finally, it has become apparent that the more sophisticated use of data on both the business and work force will permit better planning in the future. While key issues were developed in predicting manpower levels, there remains a great deal of work to do in data profiling the present work force. The new automated Employee Information System will provide the data necessary to better understand "today's" problems and manage accordingly as well as predict problems of the future.

Source: Company documents.

Exhibit 2 The Avionics Division—External Environment

- **17 Percent Growth Rate in Electronics Industry**

  Continued breakthroughs in technology are anticipated as substantiated by many economists. This being the case, continued growth is anticipated which will continue the tight supply of experienced engineering talent. (Growth in the 1980s, Kiplinger)

- **Campus Demand for Engineers Growing at 30 Percent per Year**

  Projections between 1980 and 1985 show no overall growth in students seeking EE degrees and, therefore, the new graduate picture will continue to be extremely competitive. (College Placement Council, Summer 1979) (National Center for Education Statistics)

- **Energy Concerns, High Interest Rates**

  Mobility of employees, particularly from Southern California and New England, will make recruiting outside the current facility locations increasingly more difficult.

Exhibit 2 (*concluded*)

- **Nonengineering Market Largely Local**

  For most job families no problems have been witnessed in recruiting with the minor exceptions of electronics technicians, grinders and technical writers. Modifications to recruitment techniques and special outside education programs are expected to resolve these staffing problems.

- **Modified Work Ethic Witnessed**

  Particularly in hourly areas it will be necessary to overcome higher turnover rates by introduction of new selection and development techniques in order to utilize effectively the work force of the future.

- **Competition for People**

  Employers of people similar to those we need are doing nothing distinctly unusual to attract, retain or motivate their employees. We must remain tuned in to change, however, so our policies can be modified if appropriate.

- **Challenge of the 1980s**

  On balance, our challenge will be to obtain and retain the necessary engineering talent from an overall lower supply of technical candidates while retaining an atmosphere conducive to obtaining and retaining other employees.

Source: Company documents.

Exhibit 3 Human Resource Plan—Workforce: Current and Projected (Avionics Division, December 1979)

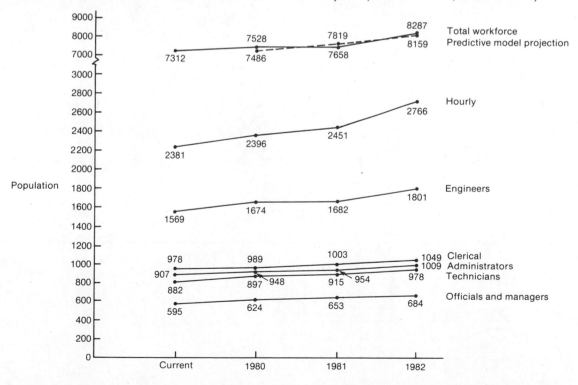

Exhibit 4 The Avionics Division Hiring Requirements

1980

	St. Petersburg		Minneapolis	
	Attrition	*Growth*	*Attrition*	*Growth*
O&M	9	8	10	22
Engineering	22	20	110	75
Administrative	13	8	53	13
Clerical	17	1	57	3
Technicians	27	12	42	12
Hourly	47	27	492	—
Total	135	76	764	125

Grand total = 1,100

1981

	St. Petersburg		Minneapolis	
	Attrition	*Growth*	*Attrition*	*Growth*
O&M	13	15	10	4
Engineering	52	16	92	21
Administrative	14	4	43	17
Clerical	15	39	58	12
Technicians	27	22	44	19
Hourly	49	52	495	36
Total	170	148	742	109

Grand total = 1,169

1982

	St. Petersburg		Minneapolis	
	Attrition	*Growth*	*Attrition*	*Growth*
O&M	11	7	12	19
Engineering	57	26	126	60
Administrative	14	4	35	8
Clerical	18	14	65	18
Technicians	28	23	49	21
Hourly	50	36	505	248
Total	178	110	792	374

Grand total = 1,454

Exhibit 5   The Avionics Division—Issues Surfaced by the Human Resource Plan

ISSUE	WHY

STAFFING

- HRP process points out that our planning process lacks refinement

    — Low correlation between traditional planning output and predictive model output

- Shortage of specific technical specialties

    — Critical skills which are in low supply nationally

  Engineering:
  — Systems engineers
  — Laser designers
  — RF designers
  — Reliability engineers
  — LSIC design

    — Captive technology in high growth business area
    — Short market supply
    — No glamour
    — Critical technology with short market supply

  Production:
  — ATE software
  — Digital

    — No glamour

- Special needs

    — Saudi Arabia assignment
    — Classified program assignment
    — Geophysical assignment
    — Service Center expansion

- Shortage supervisors, managers, and program managers

    — Accelerated growth of past couple years
    — Lack of depth

COMPENSATION

- Negative pay perceptions

    — Compression from new hires
    — Inflation
    — Wage and price guidelines

TRAINING & DEVELOPMENT

- Need for training in technologies of:

  Enginering:
  — Systems engineering
  — RF design
  — Integrated circuit
     design and applications
  — Laser design

    — Twenty-five percent of AvD workforce will be new during this plan period.
    — New technologies (MRP, ICs, etc.)
    — Job assignment changes

  Production:
  — ATLAS & ELAN programming
  — Micro-processor application
  Interpersonal
  Administrative
  — Material requirements planning
  — Integrated financial planning

EQUAL EMPLOYMENT OPPORTUNITY

- Female and minority representation

    — Shortage in workforce
    — High turnover (meaningful assignments)
    — Divisional climate

Exhibit 5   (*concluded*)

MISCELLANEOUS

- Communications

- Productivity

- Floor space:
  Insufficient/Surplus

— Perceived lack of timely, accurate and
  appropriate information.
— Need to perform on current business
— Enhance competitive posture
— Crowded working conditions
— Predicted employment levels don't justify
  expansion

Exhibit 6   The Avionics Division—Human Resource Objectives and Shortages for 1980

HUMAN RESOURCE OBJECTIVES	HUMAN RESOURCE STRATEGIES
• *STAFFING* *Professional:* To implement a recruiting plan designed to staff professional employees with the appropriate educational and experiential backgrounds (at an average cost not-to-exceed $4,000) within 90 days of the receipt of the requisition. Those primary skills are systems, microwave, laser physics, digital design, ATE, and software. *Managerial:* Implement a management identification and development process which will assure the appropriate number of individuals are available as job openings occur.	• *STAFFING* Analyze historical recruiting data to determine areas of successes so that a detailed recruiting plan can be developed around those areas and methods of success.
• *COMPENSATION* Implement an employee education program designed to help the employees better understand current compensation programs.	• *COMPENSATION* Develop audiovisual programs/pamphlets and other hard-copy material for distribution to employees.
• *TRAINING AND DEVELOPMENT* Develop and implement departmentally customized programs to meet the needs of the technology interpersonal or administrative developmental requirements of the employees.	• *TRAINING AND DEVELOPMENT* Meet with selected representatives from each department to determine specific training and development needs. Develop or purchase programs in response to those needs.

Exhibit 6 (*concluded*)

HUMAN RESOURCE OBJECTIVES	HUMAN RESOURCE STRATEGIES

- *EQUAL EMPLOYMENT OPPORTUNITY*
  To recruit minorities/females to meet the divisional AAP, and to implement a program designed to enhance upward mobility of minorities, females, and handicapped.

- *EQUAL EMPLOYMENT OPPORTUNITY*
  Determine causes of the lack of upward mobility of minorities and women.
  Effectively utilize the Black Caucus and women's organizations to determine current constraints on acquiring minority and female employees and limitations on upward mobility.

- *COMMUNICATIONS*
  Develop and implement a total divisional communications approach which will assure the upward and downward flow of information to all organizational levels.

- *COMMUNICATIONS*
  Publish a formal divisional communication policy and meet with each department head to establish individual departmental plans.

- *HUMAN RESOURCE PLANNING*
  Devise and introduce during 1980 a better and more reliable method of predicting manpower for use in budgeting and other divisional planning.
  Design and implement a process for forecasting the organizational structure on a three-year, forward-look basis.

- *HUMAN RESOURCE PLANNING*
  Investigate alternative correlations in the existing data base.
  Expand mechanization to support departments.
  Refine current historical indices.

HONEYWELL: HUMAN RESOURCES PLANNING (C)— THE SYSTEMS AND RESEARCH CENTER
C. Wickham Skinner

On March 11, 1980 managers of the Honeywell Systems and Research Center (S&RC) presented their first human resources plan (HRP). The presentation was made to Warde Wheaton, group vice president of the Aerospace and Defense Group, who had requested such a plan of each of his three divisions and the S&RC.

The Systems and Research Center employed 369 persons at the end of 1979, with an additional 102 student aides. Its work consisted of funded contracts to DOD, NASA and military-focused commercial firms (75 percent) and company-sponsored research and development work (25 percent). The development work was performed in 10 technology areas (such as microelectronics, computer systems, lasers, optical components, etc.) and five systems programs (such as space systems, combat systems integration, etc.). The largest share of sales in any one technology area was 17 percent and in one systems program 12 percent, hence there existed a wide range of focus and activities in the center. The S&RC head count had been growing by 5 percent

Exhibit 1 The Systems and Research Center Organization

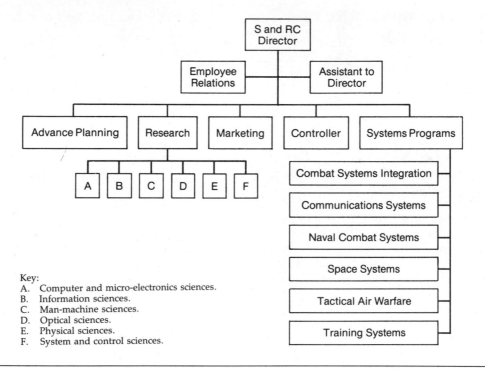

Key:
A. Computer and micro-electronics sciences.
B. Information sciences.
C. Man-machine sciences.
D. Optical sciences.
E. Physical sciences.
F. System and control sciences.

to 6 percent per year for several years, and this was expected to continue for the next three years. The organizational structure of S&RC is shown in Exhibit 1. The S&RC was expected to make a modest profit on funded contracts, but this profit was heavily outweighed in balance by S&RC's company-sponsored internal research and development work.

Human Resource Planning

The HRP for the S&RC had been developed in the latter half of 1979 by the joint efforts of Assistant to the Director A. P. Kizilos, and Employee Relations Manager R.

E. Overstreet. Essentially their approach consisted of the following steps and processes:

1. A statement of the business and technology.
2. Description of the external environment (Exhibit 2).
3. Description of the internal environment (Exhibit 2).
4. Develop an Organizational Unit Profile (OUP) for each section of the project (Exhibit 3).
5. Identify human resource issues and causes (Exhibit 4, Part B).
6. Identify HRP objectives and strategies for the future (Exhibit 5).

Exhibit 2   The Systems and Research Center External and Internal Environment

A.   External Environment

This section provides a brief assessment of the human resource market characteristics. Information included ranges from defense and capital equipment spending projections to lifestyle changes and competitor employment strategies.

Defense Spending

- The current Strategic Arms Limitation Treaty is perceived to be dead. The Pentagon claims it will need an extra $3 billion a year (4.1 percent increase in annual outlays). The 1985 annual outlays could reach $224.8 billion (*The Wall Street Journal*).

- Perceived change of public mood in favor of increased defense spending in the wake of the Iranian affair and the Soviet invasion of Afghanistan was credited by securities analysts in New York as having altered the political climate in the United States enough so that politicians in Washington are likely to support increased spending for defense in years to come (*Aviation Week and Space Technology*).

Inventories and Capital Expenditures

- In anticipation of further contracts, Westinghouse Electric is building inventories of electronic parts and is planning higher capital expenditures for 1980 (*The Wall Street Journal*).

Competitive Market for Scientific Talent

- The shortage of skilled workers will worsen as companies receive defense contracts and go searching in the market. Defense contractors are expected to implement proactive recruiting/ staffing programs in anticipation of additional contracts. GTE and Westinghouse have already implemented such programs (*The Wall Street Journal*).

Market for Research Personnel

- Six major markets exist for experienced research personnel. They include Seattle, Los Angeles, Dallas, Boston, Washington, D.C., and Minneapolis.

New Graduate Compensation

- High-technology specialists, such as optical scientists, are receiving high salary offers with little or no experience (new PhD: $30–42K per year—University of Arizona Placement Office). Rochester and Arizona Universities are the main recognized schools for optical scientists.

- College PhD graduate average salary offers have increased by 17 and 14 percent in 1978 and 1979, respectively. This trend is expected to continue (*College Placement Council*).

Future Availability of Engineering Personnel

- Projections in engineering fields for the years 1980–86 show continued increases in earned degrees at the bachelors and masters levels, but steady decreases are predicted for PhDs from a high in 1979 to a low in 1989 (*National Center for Educational Statistics*).

Increased Recruiting Activity

- Meteoric rise in recruiting has been experienced by technical college placement offices. Hughes Aircraft and General Dynamics have visited college campuses making "on-the-spot" job offers (*The Wall Street Journal*).

Corporate Sponsorship

- Advanced research labs such as those for microelectronics at Yale and Cal Tech, and information processing at MIT are supported with equipment and funding from such competitors as General

---

Exhibit 2 (*continued*)

Dynamics and IBM. MS and PhD candidates are contacted and tracked several years prior to graduation.

Equal Employment Opportunity
- Minorities and females represented only 10.4 percent of all engineering graduates in 1977. Projections for 1980 yield no major increase in availability (Honeywell Corporate Equal Opportunity Department).

Employment of Foreign Nationals
- A large number of technical degrees are conferred upon foreign students each year. Approximately 30 percent of all MS and PhD college graduates are foreign nationals (Institute of International Education and National Center for Education Statistics).
- Employment of aliens requires complex and costly legal assistance along with additional security clearance precautions and technology transfer concerns. Only two major corporations visiting the University of Washington in 1978 processed visa applications (University of Washington Placement Office).

Administrative/Marketing Professionals
- Administrative professionals are abundant in the Twin Cities metropolitan area. Marketing candidates are found in the military complex or correspond to markets for research personnel. Clerical talent, while currently available, is decreasing in quality and this trend is expected to continue along with availability decline.

Conflict-of-Interest Compliance
- Government conflict-of-interest policies have complicated the employment process. Recruitment of junior military officers and government service employees at senior levels requires attention to delicate legal issues.
- Management will have to contend with an employee who is better educated, who has higher expectations than his predecessors, and who is less loyal to his company, but more dedicated to his occupation or profession (*American Management Association Management Review*).

Mobility
- Mobility of job candidates has been limited by high interest rates and mortgage availability. An increasing number of dual-career families has complicated the recruiting/staffing process. Weather and high cost-of-living are concerns expressed by applicants.

Work Life Issues
- Some of the conclusions from an extensive study of the forces that will influence future work life in America are that inflation and high unemployment with the overwhelming need for jobs overshadow all other considerations; but, a growing undercurrent of greater cultural expectations about work can be identified; concern with meaning and quality of life by means of work, and a concern with individual rights and power will also influence the work environment (*Daedalus*, Winter 1978).

B. Internal Environment

The internal environment of SRC is continually monitored through the efforts of the line supervision, employee relations, and the organizational integrator. Attitude surveys, sensing sessions,

Exhibit 2   (*continued*)

and team building sessions are among the methods used to promote communications resulting in positive employee relations.

Diversity and Complexity of Technology
- The Center's charter requires that state-of-the-art technology be maintained in many disciplines which require the meshing of diverse technical skills. The center has managed to respond to these needs through effective teamwork and concerted team development efforts.

Matrix Structure
- A matrix structure aligning research, programs, marketing, controller, employee relations, and other support department functions exists. Some conflict and confrontation is encouraged as a means of improving the quality of the decision-making process.

Company Benefits
- Increased emphasis is being placed on personal and company benefits by all professional job families. Examples include desire for more leisure time (vacation), improved corporate retirement/investment programs, educational leaves of absence, professional recognition, technical equipment, and flexible work schedules.

Employee Attitudes
- Feedback sessions with Center employees yielded strong interest in pay policy and practices, career development, recognition of professional achievement, employee communications, capital equipment, and IR&D investment decisions (Attitude Survey Feedback Sessions—August 1979).

Work Environment
- Work environment traits valued most by first-line supervision include the people-oriented climate, informal communication encouraging feelings and opinions, flexibility of working hours and style, participation in management decisions, balance between technology advancement and divisional application as well as experimentation with personal, interpersonal, and management development programs (SRC Survey—January 1980).
- Desired improvements include additional emphasis on new technology, less control of discretionary funds, more career planning/development focusing on interdivisional and ADG opportunities, and establishment of better working relationships with other Honeywell locations through training and exposure (SRC Survey—January 1980).
- Applicants are amazed that capital equipment is not comparable to college/university facilities.

Turnover Analysis
- SRC employee attrition for 1979 was 17.7 percent. Over half of this amount represented transfers to other Honeywell divisions and centers.

New Supervision and Nonsupervisory Personnel
- Technology infusion and transfer goals along with steady growth during the late 1970s has resulted in a new, inexperienced workforce. Replacement has typically been from promotion within the Center. Backup candidates for supervisory and critical talent individuals are thin.

Technical Expertise
- Sixty-five percent of the engineering scientists have completed advanced technical degrees. Approximately one third have PhDs.

Exhibit 2 (*concluded*)

Word Processing
- Thirty-eight of the 43 SRC secretaries have voluntarily completed or enrolled in the Multics word processing training program. This will provide efficiencies in the areas of work output, time management, and communication.

Student Aide Program
- Approximately 20 percent of the SRC work force is composed of students at any given time. The student aide program provides college students with an opportunity to gain professional experience on a temporary, part-time basis and earn an attractive wage while completing degree requirements. The Center benefits through reduced labor costs, assessment of employment qualifications, and exchange of new ideas and technical concepts.
- Student aides range from undergraduate to doctoral degree candidates. Most participants attend the University of Minnesota, and specialize in technical disciplines though students from other nationally renowned schools are recruited. Approximately 16 percent of the student aides enrolled during the 1973–79 timeframe have been converted to permanent positions. Coordination takes place with other Honeywell divisions to identify student talent available for permanent positions.

Exhibit 3   **The Systems and Research Center: Organization Unit Profile** (OUP)

1. • Employee data
   — Demographics
   — Assignment plans
   — Training needs
   — Career goals
   — Availability indexes
2. • Staffing/Recruiting plan
3. • EEO/AAP
4. • Training and development plan
5. • Organizational issues/Plans
6. • Approvals
7. • Addenda

Note: Items 1 and 4 were completed on every employee.

Exhibit 4   **The Systems and Research Center Introduction to the Human Resource Plan**

A. **Design Criteria**

Based on the findings of the literature search, consultations with external consultants and other Honeywell Aerospace and Defense Group (ADG) human resource teams, data requests from management, and a thorough understanding of center business plans and work environment, the following criteria were established:

1. Integration of business and human resource plans affecting the entire planning process.
2. The first-line supervisor is the primary client of the HRP.
3. The plan is individualistic in that biographical data, job assignments, training plans, career planning, and availability indices are developed for each employee. Individual data is used to produce resource inventories.

Exhibit 4 (*continued*)

4. The plan is participative, utilizing inputs from all levels of the organization.
5. The plan is expandable and flexible. Additional human resource and business subsystems will be included in future revisions.

B. **Major Issues**

In order to obtain the objective of greater organizational effectiveness by matching business and employee goals, it was determined that the following major issues must be successfully addressed:

- *Staffing and Recruiting in a matrix organization:*
  Multiple manpower plans.
  Ownership shared by first-line supervision.
  Technical "skill mix."
- *Attrition:*
  Unexpected attrition to non-Honeywell organizations.
  High rate of employee transfer/promotion to other Honeywell organizations.
- *Multiple business/HRPs and subsystems:*
  Lack of focus on human resource related activities.
  Increased administrative demands on first-line supervision.

C. **Action**

1. *Staffing and Recruiting:*
   Develop a single manpower plan based on financial marketing plans and manpower availability to address center needs.
   Assure ownership by first-line supervision of future project funding, availability of existing employee resources, and manpower plans through a formal approval process.
   Identify future "skill mix" requirements through assessment of future business plans, and current and projected human resource availabilities to develop more accurate staffing requirements.

2. *Attrition:*
   Identify potential attrition to nonHoneywell organizations through proactive solicitation of employee concerns, and development of action plans.
   Continue to facilitate transfer/promotion of qualified employees to other Honeywell locations utilizing the SRC mobility policy with emphasis on career planning.

3. *Multiple business/HRPs and subsystems:*
   Coordinate existing and future business/human resource subsystems using the HRP to achieve a common focus.
   Provide a tool for first-line supervision that organizes administrative duties such as performance appraisal, job assignment, and training plans that will result in better business and human resource decisions.

D. **Elements**

The Organizational Unit Profile consists of the following sections:

— Biographical data and availability indices.
— Summary staffing/recruiting plan.
— Equal Opportunity/Affirmative Action plan.

Exhibit 4 (*continued*)

— Training and development.
— Organizational issues/plans.
— Approvals.
— Addenda.

E. Implementation/Upgrade

Efforts will continue to make the HRP an integral part of the total planning process. Initial implementation includes the engineering nonsupervisory job family with expansion to other SRC employees during April 1980. The 1980 HRP is designed to be flexible and expandable. These are important features, because there are several improvements which are planned for the 1981 HRP. These include:

• Computerization of data and updating of projections.
• Computer model for prediction of long-range manpower needs.
• Mobility policy inclusion in the HRP.
• Skill code definition and utilization.
• Expansion of the HRP to all employees of SRC.
• Inclusion of talent reviews.
• Inventory of training and development activities.

• *Computerization of data*

The data derived from the various work units by first-line supervision will be entered into existing computer programs.

Information on possible mobility actions, recruiting information, inventory of skills available and needed, training needs assessment, and other pertinent data will be readily accessible. Computerization and more frequent updating of department budgets will allow more closely monitored staffing/recruiting actions and correction of deviations from the plan.

Though the basic data will continue to be gathered by the first-line supervisor, and decisions affecting the human resources will be made by him or her, the process will be enhanced by automation.

• *Historical data*

Attrition, recruiting sources, and main technical disciplines will be gathered and applied to a computer model with predictive value. The statistically small sample that SRC provides makes the design of a meaningful model difficult. The definition of skill codes, newly derived department budgets, better historical data, and experience with the HRP will reduce the uncertainty and a useful model may be devised.

• *Skill codes*

The present HRP includes a section on main technical disciplines. Upon review of the 1980 results, it will be possible to define several disciplines which will account for the expertise of all SRC employees. It will be possible to have a skill code for each employee thus facilitating the identification of experts needed to work on various tasks.

• *Mobility policy*

An SRC mobility policy was formulated by a management committee in 1979, and was approved by the center director. The policy is based on broad guidelines established by the

Exhibit 4 (*concluded*)

Minneapolis Operations Technical Council (MOTEC). It provides for a procedure for increasing mobility which is beneficial to Honeywell and its employees.

The SRC policy will be incorporated into the HRP in 1980, and implemented by the first-line supervision. Computerization of the data will facilitate monitoring adherence to the policy and reporting on it to MOTEC as planned. Employee Relations will report semiannually on accomplishment versus plan to center management.

- *Expansion of HRP to all employees*

    Initial implementation addressed the engineering job families which make up the largest portion (46%) of employees at SRC. The plan will be expanded during April 1980, to include all professional employees. Subsequent plans will include all SRC employees.

- *Talent reviews*

    Management and technical talent are two of the most valuable resources of any research and development organization. Assurance of an adequate number of qualified and well-trained employees has been the goal of the Talent Reviews. Because of the sensitivity of this human resource element, it was decided not to include it in the HRP. However, data collected for the plan will be invaluable in the development of future Talent Reviews.

- *Inventory of employee training and development activity*

    An inventory of formal training and development activities attended prior to 1980 by employees does not exist. The current training and development records supplied in the HRP and transfer of computerization of data will reduce the difficulty of producing an up-to-date inventory. Such a record of training activities will increase our ability to plan for future training needs, improve the quality of training, cut costs through consolidation of efforts, and evaluate training effectiveness through questionnaires to past trainees in various courses.

Source: Company documents (abridged).

Exhibit 5   **The Systems and Research Center: Objectives and Strategies**

Staffing

Objective	Strategy
• Proactive recruiting/Staffing	• Establish *one* manpower plan • Ownership by first-line supervision
• Reduce unanticipated attrition	• Identify potential attrition and develop action plans • Sensing sessions/performance appraisals/career development
• Transfer/promotion to Honeywell divisions	• Implement mobility policy; emphasize training and career development
• Aggressive college recruiting	• Identify target schools, intern programs, alumni contacts, faculty visits, presentations
• Establish backup capabilities for key positions	• Appraisal/career development • Talent review

Exhibit 5 (*concluded*)

Compensation

Objective	*Strategy*
• Reduce/eliminate salary inequities	• Supervisory compensation training/manual • Implement HAY compensation system • Salary increase recommendation and appraisal forms (nonexempts)
• Communicate pay-for-performance concept	• Employee compensation manual • Update job descriptions • Establish and communicate promotional criteria (discriminators)

EEO/AAP

Objective	*Strategy*
• Assure EEO/AAP compliance	• Hire student aides (minority/female/handicapped) • Establish community/college contacts • Minority employment agencies • Utilize EEO funds

Training and Development

Objective	*Strategy*
• Functional training for supervisors	• Identify needs • Develop two-day workshop
• Training for nonsupervisors	• Identify needs and plan actions (HRP) • Inventory training accomplishments • Utilize need–growth funds

Positive Employee Relations

Objective	*Strategy*
• Improve self-image of administrative *nonexempt* and *technician* job families	• Reduce peak workloads—planning • Business area briefings • Organizational problem solving: timely intervention • Performance appraisal/salary forms • Committee assignments

Miscellaneous

Objective	*Strategy*
• Acquire necessary floor space	• Move Sotas (10,000 ft^2) • Expand within Ridgway Facility (10,000 ft^2)
• Improve tech lab equipment • Eliminate safety hazards	• Continue repair/purchase of capital equipment • Revise and publish safety procedures • Utilize Avionics safety specialist

The process was based on five key "design criteria" summarized in Exhibit 4, Part A, Introduction to the HRP Report. A key criterion was that the first-line supervisor is "the primary client of the HRP." This meant that before the OUP and statements on issues and objectives were considered completed, each first-line supervisor's agreement was necessary.

The OUP was considered the "heart of the program." For every section forms were filled out covering seven major areas which in total attempted to identify both section and individual needs and problems and to develop plans accordingly.

The group finished its HRP and prepared to present it to the group vice president with a general feeling of enthusiasm and accomplishment.

CASE 3
AMERICAN HOSPITAL SUPPLY CORPORATION (A)
Ann Pigneri and C. Wickham Skinner

The American Hospital Supply Corporation (American) developed and implemented a Personnel Planning System (PPS) in 1975. By 1979 PPS was considered a virtual necessity by many in top management as the corporation had rapidly grown from a firm where everyone knew everyone else to the current size of $2 billion in sales, 26 divisions, and 30,700 employees. In spite of the widespread use of PPS throughout the corporation, Jan Blakslee, director of management planning and development, felt that some changes were needed if it were to reach its full potential.

In 1979 American celebrated its 26th year

of consecutive growth in sales and earnings. Exhibit 1 shows the corporation's financial comparison for selected years from 1969 to 1979. American was characterized by its many diversified activities. American's markets and a partial list of their divisions is given in Exhibit 2. A financial breakdown of each of these market segments is shown in Exhibit 3.

Markets and Marketing Practices

The corporation's 1979 Annual Report included the following remarks in its markets and marketing practices description:

> American's product line of more than 133,000 items . . . is the broadest in the industry. This allows cost-conscious hospitals, laboratories and purchasing groups to achieve economy by consolidating many of their purchases with a single supplier.
>
> American's distribution divisions deliver products to U.S. customers through their network of 90 local and regional distribution centers, nine of which opened in 1979.
>
> In 1979, American's customers were served by 2,800 sales representatives. These people provide—in addition to products—"materials-management" systems that help customers control their total supply-related costs.

American planned to invest $40 million in research in 1980, up 15 percent over 1979. The company also planned capital investments of more than $80 million, to increase manufacturing strength, to continue developing its network of distribution facilities and computerized inventory and product-delivery systems. American expected to maintain sales and earnings growth at a midteens percentage rate in 1980.

American had a relatively young top management, about 90 percent of whom had come up through the ranks. Karl Bays,

Exhibit 1   **Financial Comparison** ($ and shares in thousands except per share amounts)

	1979	1978	1973	1969
Operating Statistics:				
Net sales	$2,039,380	$1,744,803	$851,406	$466,695
Increase in sales	16.9%	17.1%	21.1%	15.6%
Gross profit as % of sales	33.0%	33.2%	32.6%	34.7%
Operating expenses as % of sales	24.4%	24.2%	23.4%	23.7%
Operating earnings as % of sales	8.6%	9.0%	9.2%	11.1%
Pretax earnings	$ 156,895	$ 147,935	$ 78,047	$ 53,405
Pretax earnings as percent of sales	7.7%	8.5%	9.2%	11.4%
Effective income tax rate	30.2%	37.4%	45.6%	52.8%
Net earnings	$ 109,442	$ 92,551	$ 42,443	$ 25,211
Net earnings as % of sales	5.4%	5.3%	5.0%	5.4%
Increase in net earnings	18.3%	18.5%	15.7%	15.3%
Dividends—as % of net earnings on common stock	26.3%	26.2%	23.1%	29.2%
Depreciation	$ 35,940	$ 30,423	$ 11,534	$ 6,775
Asset Statistics:				
Working capital	$ 540,445	$ 479,655	$231,080	$208,288
Working capital as % of sales	26.5%	27.5%	27.1%	44.5%
Current ratio	2.9	2.7	2.8	4.3
Accounts receivable days	59	60	64	76
Inventory days	110	115	107	124
Capital expenditures	$ 74,169	$ 73,905	$ 45,558	$ 27,246
Capital structure statistics:				
Total debt	$ 256,109	$ 289,861	$ 45,398	$ 27,296
Total debt as % of total capital	26.0%	30.9%	10.6%	9.1%
Shareholders' investment	$ 730,728	$ 647,510	$383,728	$271,504
Return on average shareholders' investment	15.9%	15.1%	11.6%	10.7%
Common share statistics:				
Earnings per share	$ 2.78	$ 2.37	$ 1.14	$ .72
Dividends per share	$ .77	$ .65	$ .28	$ .225
Book value per share	$ 19.44	$ 17.29	$ 10.27	$ 7.45
Avg. number of common shares outstanding and equivalents	40,120	40,025	37,346	35,240
Common shares outstanding at year-end	37,587	37,459	37,368	36,446
Miscellaneous statistics:				
No. of employees at year-end	30,700	29,900	22,400	14,700
No. of shareholders at year-end	35,600	38,000	44,100	50,400
Sales per employee in dollars	$ 66,000	$ 58,000	$ 38,000	$ 32,000

Source: American Hospital Supply Corporation's 1979 Annual Report.

45, had been chairman since 1971 and chief executive officer since 1974. The newly appointed chief financial officer was 34 years old. Some division presidents were as young as 31. The organization chart for American is shown in Exhibit 4.

Personnel Data and Procedures

Turnover and promotion data for 1979 is given in Exhibit 5, and targeted exempt turnover for 1980 to 1982 is given in Exhibit 6. Costs of turnover are shown in Exhibits 7

Exhibit 2   **American's Markets and Divisions** ($ millions)

Market	Partial List of Divisions	Net Sales for 1979
Hospital market	Convertors Division	$883.3
	Dietary Products Division	
	Pharmaceutical Business	175.1
	McGraw Laboratories Division	
	Arnar-Stone Laboratories Division	
	Hamilton	
	Moore-Perk	
Medical/dental specialties market	Medical Market	213.2
	U. Mueller	
	Edwards Laboratories	
	Heyer-Schulte	
	Dental Market	
	American Midwest Division	
	Denticon Division	
	Ormco Division	
Laboratory market	Science Business	549.8
	Dade Products	
	Scientific Products	
International market	American has wholly owned operations in 16 countries.	319.1

Note: American has a total of 26 divisions.
Source: American's 1979 Annual Report.

and 8. Breakdown of American's employees by minorities and sex is in Exhibit 9.

American's benefits package included an incentive investment plan; medical, dental and life insurance; long-term disability protection; stock purchase plan; retirement plan; educational assistance plan; and a credit union.

In hiring new employees, American used nine behaviorally defined selection criteria. A three-day interview training program given to 700 to 800 managers explained corporate selection criteria and offered the use of exercises in developing managers' techniques in selection.

History of the Personnel Planning System (PPS)

Jan Blakslee reviewed the history of the PPS as follows:

In 1971 Karl D. Bays was appointed as CEO of American Hospital Supply Corporation. At that time the company was $500 million in sales. Mr. Bays realized we had to do a better job of building from the bottom and promoting from within, which had always been a corporate philosophy. At that point we were organized into nine operating groups and approximately 30 divisions. The only way that people could move across divisions, across functions, was to be identified through an intercorporate transfer system. The use of psychological assessments and the personal knowledge of the top officers of the company, especially the corporate vice president of personnel were the main determinants of the promotion from within system.

Between 1974 and 1980 the corporate staff dramatically increased in all areas. In 1974 there were six exempt people in the corpo-

Exhibit 3   Net Sales and Operating Earnings by Market

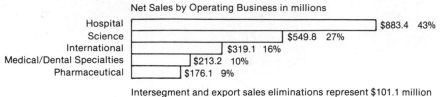

Net Sales by Operating Business in millions

Hospital	$883.4	43%
Science	$549.8	27%
International	$319.1	16%
Medical/Dental Specialties	$213.2	10%
Pharmaceutical	$176.1	9%

Intersegment and export sales eliminations represent $101.1 million or 5 percent of net sales.

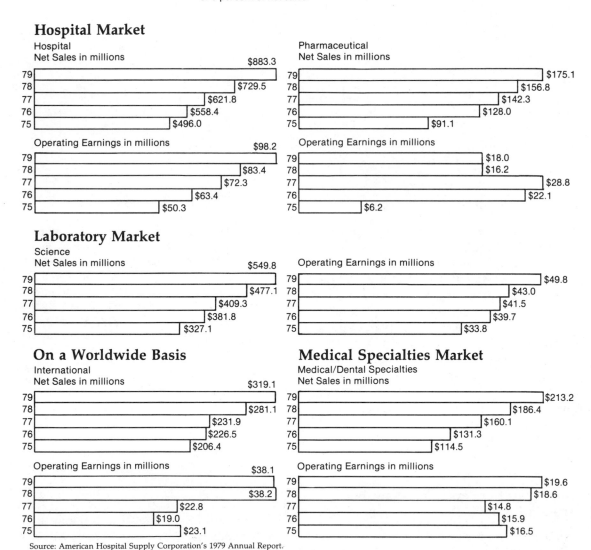

Hospital Market

Hospital
Net Sales in millions — $883.3

79	$883.3
78	$729.5
77	$621.8
76	$558.4
75	$496.0

Operating Earnings in millions — $98.2

79	$98.2
78	$83.4
77	$72.3
76	$63.4
75	$50.3

Pharmaceutical
Net Sales in millions

79	$175.1
78	$156.8
77	$142.3
76	$128.0
75	$91.1

Operating Earnings in millions

79	$18.0
78	$16.2
77	$28.8
76	$22.1
75	$6.2

Laboratory Market

Science
Net Sales in millions — $549.8

79	$549.8
78	$477.1
77	$409.3
76	$381.8
75	$327.1

Operating Earnings in millions

79	$49.8
78	$43.0
77	$41.5
76	$39.7
75	$33.8

On a Worldwide Basis

International
Net Sales in millions — $319.1

79	$319.1
78	$281.1
77	$231.9
76	$226.5
75	$206.4

Operating Earnings in millions — $38.1

79	$38.1
78	$38.2
77	$22.8
76	$19.0
75	$23.1

Medical Specialties Market

Medical/Dental Specialties
Net Sales in millions

79	$213.2
78	$186.4
77	$160.1
76	$131.3
75	$114.5

Operating Earnings in millions

79	$19.6
78	$18.6
77	$14.8
76	$15.9
75	$16.5

Source: American Hospital Supply Corporation's 1979 Annual Report.

rate personnel staff including the corporate vice president. In 1979, there were approximately 50 people, 30 of whom were professional.

Blakslee discussed the system that they implemented during this period:

> In the time frame 1974 to 1978 we installed the following systems: equal employment and affirmative action planning program, a Management/Professional Job Evaluation System, a salary planning system, a preventive labor relations program, an entire corporate training and development function, and a computerized personnel information system. We decertified a number of unions and we completely revised and upgraded our benefits programs. We went from hiring 50 people off the college campuses in 1975 to hiring approximately 450 people in 1979 off the college campuses, 25 percent of whom have advanced degrees, most of those being MBAs.

Instead of going to a consultant to develop and install the PPS, AHSC hired six people during 1975 to join their staff. These individuals included psychologists and development/training people. This constituted the management planning and development function.

The Personnel Planning System

The personnel plan was a formal way for the businesses and divisions to analyze their current human resource strengths and weaknesses and to plan for future needs. A personnel plan was completed for each operating division, stand-alone business center, staff group and for the corporation as a whole. Exhibit 10 shows the subject areas included in the personnel plan.

The following forms were used for documentation in the Personnel Planning System:

CMP-1 (Employee's Individual Experience Records)—an inventory of employee education, work history (detailed) continuing education, training, honors, proficiencies.

CMP-2 (Performance Evaluation and Career Development Summary)—annual employee and supervisor appraisal of performance, career interests, and readiness for advancement (Appendix A).

CMP-3 (Department Summary and Individual Career Forecast)—documentation by department of employees, ratings of performance, potential, and readiness for advancement (Appendix B).

CMP-4 (Organization and Staffing Plan)— organizational structure, backup strength and management succession plan (Appendix C).

Manpower Forecast (Schedule 11, Appendix D).

Turnover Analysis, Form A (Appendix E).

Annually, each division of the corporation was required to prepare a personnel plan that addressed the issues contained in Exhibit 10. Personnel plans were reviewed and discussed in the same manner as strategic and operating plans by the next higher level of management. A divisional vice president and personnel director submitted and presented their plan to one of the corporate executive vice presidents (EVP). The EVPs in turn prepare personnel plans, which are reviewed and presented to the CEO, COO, corporate vice president–personnel, director of management planning and development. Corporate vice presidents also prepare and review personnel plans in the same manner.

Exhibit 4   Organization Chart

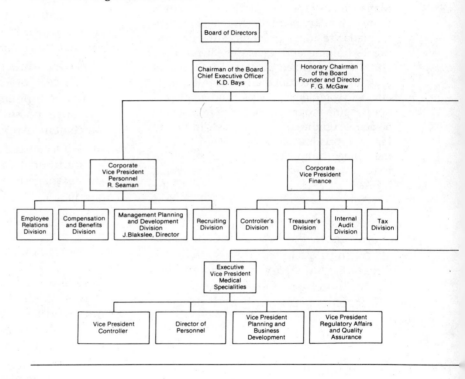

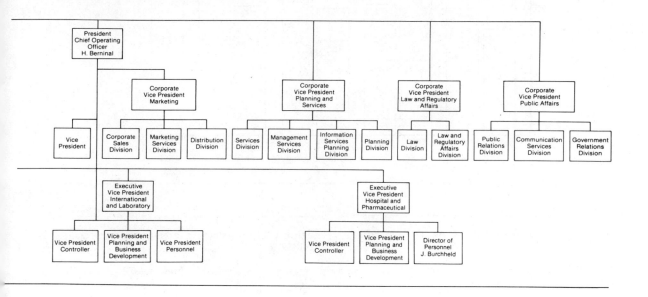

Exhibit 5   1979 Turnover and Promotions

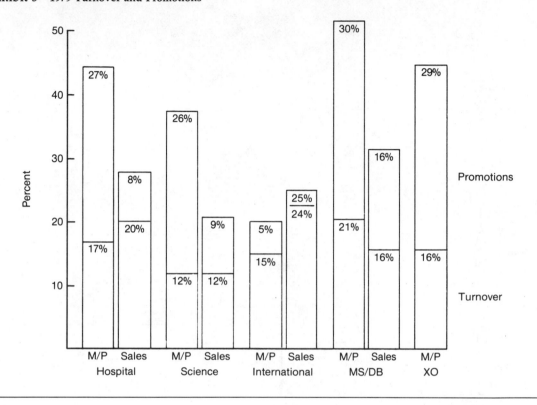

Exhibit 6   Targeted Exempt Turnover Rates 1980 to 1982

Year	Rate
1980...........	16%
1981...........	14
1982...........	12

Source: American Hospital Supply Corporation.

Exhibit 7   Corporate Nonexempt Turnover 1978 and 1979

	1978	1979
Office/technical...............	24.7%	27.9%
Hourly	37.4%	34.5%
Average cost per nonexempt hire		$400
Number of turnovers in 1979		4,727
1979 hiring cost due to turnover.................		$1,890,800

Source: American Hospital Supply Corporation.

Exhibit 8 Projected Cost of Exempt Turnover by Business 1980 to 1982

	Cost of Turnover at 1979 Rate (Total $ 000,000)	Cost of Turnover at Targeted Rate (Total $ 000,000)	Savings (Net $ 000,000)
Hospital/pharmaceutical:			
1980	7.0	6.2	0.4
1981	8.3	6.4	0.9
1982	9.7	6.5	1.6
Medical specialties/dental specialties:			
1980	2.8	2.2	0.3
1981	3.3	2.3	0.5
1982	3.9	2.3	0.8
Science specialties:			
1980	2.3	Presently at target	
1981	2.8	Presently at target	
1982	3.2	Presently at target	
International:			
1980	2.7	2.1	0.3
1981	3.2	2.2	0.5
1982	3.7	2.2	0.7
Corporatewide totals:			
1980	14.8	10.5	1.0
1981	17.6	10.9	1.9
1982	20.5	11.0	3.1

Source: American Hospital Supply Corporation.

Exhibit 9 U.S. Minority and Female Employees, 1978 and 1979 (as of December 31)

Category	Percent Minorities 1979	Percent Minorities 1978	Percent Females 1979	Percent Females 1978
Officials and managers	10.3	10.0	18.4	18.5
Professionals	17.5	15.8	36.7	29.1
Technicians	21.6	20.5	52.8	53.0
Sales	6.3	6.6	14.6	14.0
All other	37.7	39.0	62.7	62.6
Total	28.4	29.0	49.9	49.3

Source: American Hospital Supply Corporation.

Early Problems with PPS

Blakslee reviewed problems and criticisms identified by managers when PPS was first implemented in 1975:

1. Many managers did not completely understand the system and its objectives.
2. Many of the operating units felt "personnel" should take care of these matters. The operating units' primary role

Exhibit 10 Personnel Plan

Section Title	Objective	Items Included

Analysis and action plan summary	Report on previous Personnel Plan achievements, proposed actions, and outline of planning process	Narrative Review
		— achievement against previous year's plan (a review of 1979 Personnel Planning activity)
		— objectives not achieved
		Action Plan Summary (Executive Summary of important 1980 personnel strategies and actions)
		— key actions committed to for achievement by next planning period include:
		  . . . action
		  . . . responsibility
		  . . . timing
		— how will this plan be implemented?

Organization structure	Analyze current and future organization structure	Current Organization Charts for GO and functional areas (dated)
		— include:
		  . . . position/title
		  . . . current incumbent
		Narrative Analysis (subheadings)
		— current organization
		— strengths

Backups	Identify strengths, weaknesses, and readiness of backups for key management positions	CMP-4 followed by CMP-3
		— one for each for:
		  . . top level management
		  . . each functional area
		— all exempt employees must be reflected on these forms
		Narrative Analysis
		— overall assessment of quantity and quality of current backups by level and function
		— identification of positions currently without backups
		— action plans
		  . . for positions without current backup
		  . . for developing necessary strength
		— career progression paths
		  . . . within functional areas
		  . . . across functional areas
		— identify grooming positions currently blocked (no further advancement for incumbent)

Individual action plans	Identify and develop action plan for individual personnel issues	High Potentials (i.e., all those receiving potential ratings of 1 or 2) — identification (names) — next move — preparation (development plan) for that move

Section	Description	Outline

		Underutilized
		— identification (who?)
		— action plan
		Minority/Females
		— narrative analysis
		  . . . significant issues (turnover, recruiting problems, pay)
		  . . . significant movement
		  . . . development plans
		Marginal
		— identification (who?)
		— action plan

Management Development	Outline training and development plan and means to achieve it	Needs Analysis Summary
		— Organization Needs (principal internal barriers which may hinder the business in accomplishing its objectives)
		— Training Needs (knowledge and skills needed to improve performance in present jobs and to prepare for future positions)*
		Development and Training Objectives
		Action Plans
		— what?
		— when?
		— for whom?
		— conducted by whom? (if applicable)
		Budget Summary
		— total allocation
		  . . program costs
		  . . total costs

Forecast and Recruitment	Provide a quantitative statement of manpower needs and action plans to source them.	Schedule 11 (from operating plan) Narrative Analysis — discuss recruitment strategies — covers relevant issues not addressed in section on Organization Structure

Turnover	To identify trends in turnover solely from employees quitting or being terminated and the present action plans designed to address the causes of these trends	Form A (Numbers, Percents and degrees of change over previous year).
		— exempt (M/P)
		— sales
		— nonexempt
		  . . . salaried
		  . . . hourly
		Narrative Analysis
		— trends
		— causes
		— action plans

* List the participants not previously cited.
Source: American Hospital Supply Corporation's Personnel Planning Manual.

Exhibit 11 Calendar—1980—Personnel Planning Process

Operating Divisions*

Action	Timing
Division Personnel Plans prepared	March
Division Plans submitted to businesst	March 30
Business reviews division plans to formulate questions/critique	April
Divisions present plan and respond to questions/critique in face-to-face session with Business Executive Vice President (EVP) and Business Personnel Director	April
Division plans finalized and resubmitted to Business and XO Personnel Planning Department	April 30

Businesses

Action	Timing
Business Personnel Plans prepared	May
Business plans submitted to Corporate Vice President Personnel/Chief Executive Officer (CEO) Chief Operating Officer (COO)	May 30
Business plans reviewed, critiqued and questions formulated	June
EVP presents Business Personnel Plan to CEO/COO/Corporate VP Personnel and responds to critique and questions	June

XO Staff Groups

Action	Timing
Staff Group Personnel Plans prepared	May
Plans submitted to Corporate VP Personnel/CEO/COO	May 30
Plans reviewed, critiqued and questions formulated	June
Staff Group President presents Personnel Plan to CEO/COO/Corporate VP Personnel and responds to critique and questions	July 1–15

Corporate Personnel Plan

Action	Timing
Corporate Personnel Plan prepared and submitted to CEO/COO for approval	October 31

* Division as used here means existing operating division and stand-alone business center.
† At the discretion of the Business EVP, a company plan may be prepared.
Source: American Hospital Supply Corporation, 1980 Personnel Planning Manual.

---

was to make money and to sell and market product. By promoting the PPS, corporate was asking them to take time away from their very reasons for existence.

3. Many felt that the company promoted from within, so the units don't need all this paraphernalia.

Blakslee went on to say:

1. PPS was considered by some to be idealistic and unrealistic.
2. In some instances the plan was oversold—employees believed this was going to be their ticket to promotion.
3. Line/staff friction existed.

A series of regional workshops were conducted in 1976 for division personnel directors, in an effort to help combat these problems. Areas discussed included requirements of the system and the personnel directors' responsibilities in implementation.

Blakslee discussed the changes needed in the PPS in its early years:

In our personnel plans we have to concentrate more on building ownership on the part of the line managers than on the plan itself.

Second, we need to do a better job of tying

Exhibit 12   **Discussion of the Forms for the Personnel Planning System**

The CMP-1 form, which is a detailed record of the employee's education, work history, etc., is initially completed at the time of hire. It is reviewed and updated annually by the employee to ensure an accurate and current record. This may be done in conjunction with the CMP-2 review.

The CMP-2 form is completed separately by the employee and his/her supervisor. After completion of the forms, the supervisor and employee discuss them. The employee copy of the CMP-2 form is shown in Appendix A. The supervisor's form is identical to the employee's form except for inclusion of comments concerning the discussion.

The CMP-3 form (see Appendix B) is completed annually at the time of personnel planning by the department heads. The purpose of the CMP-3 form is:

> To review the current status of individuals within a work group and document in quantitative terms the data needed for career pathing and succession planning, including ratings of performance, readiness for advancement, and long-term potential.*

The CMP-4 (see Appendix C) form documents and identifies current strengths, readiness, and availability of backups for key managerial positions. The form lists backups for the manager's job and is completed by each member of a division's president's staff, division presidents, and executive vice presidents on an annual basis. The CMP-3 form supplies the necessary information to complete the CMP-4. Backups identified must be within the respective business center, division, or business.

Appendix D, the "Forecast Number of Employees" (Schedule 11) is the next form completed. The purpose of this form is to determine by functional area how many employees will be hired in each of the three plan years. This form is also used in the operating plan.

The last form in completing the personnel plan involves turnover and is documented in Form A (Appendix E). The purpose of this form is:

> To document turnover trends in the organization, and to provide a uniform reporting procedure for such data.†

* American Hospital Supply Corporation's Personnel Planning Manual.
† Ibid.

the Personnel Planning System into the business planning system. We need to integrate strategic, operating, and human resource planning into a common system which does not overlap.

Finally, the ability of our line managers to perform the tasks that these systems require was not there. Hence, we needed to spend time building their skills. In the instance of personnel directors who had direct responsibility for implementing personnel plans in the divisions, we ended up in the period of the mid to late 1970s replacing the majority of our personnel directors and upgrading the quality of division personnel staff. At that point the personnel function had evolved from one of essentially personnel administration to one of human resource management.

In 1978, instead of having the regional workshops, Blakslee and his staff spent a full day in one-on-one discussions with each division personnel director. As a result of these meetings:

1. The review format and review process for the personnel plans were redesigned to parallel immediately those used for strategic and operating plans.
2. The manpower forecast of employees was made identical to that forecast in the operating plan.

In 1976 American computerized each employee's work history, education and other demographic data. Certain information from the PPS was recorded on the computer and included: (1) ratings of management potential, (2) employee readiness for advancement, and (3) job performance. According to Blakslee:

We do not share ratings of potential with an employee unless they specifically request it. An employee has direct access on the CMP-2 form to the rating of performance, and to the rating of readiness.

There is some discontent in the organization that we only promote high potentials, "high pots," who are rated 1 or 2. We've started to study the distribution of ratings by function, by division, and by group. One of the ways that we control the distribution of ratings is to give managers and divisions feedback on how their rating distributions compare with corporate averages. We intend to build some controls in at the local (division) level so that there is a two-over-one approval process to all those ratings. An employee's performance will be reviewed by at least two levels of management above him: his boss and his boss's boss.

Blakslee elaborated upon one of the problems created by the PPS:

In one of these workshops I conducted, I was talking about how the system can be better utilized in a strategic sense within an operating unit. It can become a way for a personnel director to leverage power, to get things done, and to bring issues to the forefront. It's a tool that allows you to surface some of your own agenda, and to legitimate that in the eyes of the organization. While I never got the feedback directly, some of the division personnel directors felt: "Boy, he sure is naive. This planning system is a pain; it's something that I do to satisfy corporate. Yeah, it works, but he's really crazy if he believes that we can leverage power off a personnel plan."

On the other hand, I come back in my own thinking, and am critical of that personnel director and say: "If you don't use personnel planning in a strategic way you'll never accomplish the objectives that you've established." How do you get them to own the system when it is essentially a top-down system?

How do you get them to use it and buy in, given the inevitable conflict between line and staff? I'm saying, "You haven't got the vision which you need to really make this thing work for you." He's coming back and saying: "You've got all vision but no practical sense of what it is really like out here."

Appendix A

American	**CMP-2**	**Employee**	**Confidential**
Hospital Supply	**Performance**	**Copy**	
Corporation	**Evaluation and**		
	Career Development		
	Summary		

Name_____   Date_____
          Last   First   Initial   Month   Day   Year
Job Title_____   Date Entered Present Position
Division/Unit_____   _____
                                                              Month   Day   Year

I.   Self Evaluation—Results

List significant accomplishments since your last review. These may be objectives, goals, MBOs, or tasks from the job description that have been agreed upon by you and your supervisor. There are several ways you may review your accomplishments (results). You can list the agreed-upon objectives or tasks and comment upon the completion of each. Or you may list your accomplishments in order of priority and then comment on items not completely accomplished. You and your supervisor should discuss this and agree upon a format that will serve both your needs. In completing this section be specific and include a representative list of accomplishments from the entire review period.

II.   Performance Summary

Summarize your overall performance. Comment in general terms on significant results, difficulties encountered and overcome, the resulting impact of your performance on your department or division, and areas where improvement is needed. Again, be specific, complete, and representative.

III.   Performance Rating

The performance rating is assigned to indicate the level at which you feel you performed during the review period. This is an overall rating and should be based solely on an evaluation of your success in achieving the results, goals, or objectives of your position as expressed in your performance summary. Indicate your evaluation of your performance by placing a check in the appropriate boxes below:

☐ **1.   Distinguished**
Performance of this caliber is extremely rare. It is a rating that should be reserved for those who clearly and consistently demonstrate extraordinary and exceptional accomplishments in *all* major areas of responsibility. Those who perform at this level are easily recognized by others outside their own group or division, as well as those in related areas. It is a level of performance that is seldom equaled by others who hold positions of comparable scope and responsibility.

☐ **2.   Outstanding**
This is a rating that best describes a level of accomplishment that goes well beyond reasonable but demanding standards of performance, especially in the key critical areas of major responsibilities. The individual consistently demonstrates truly outstanding achievements in terms of quality and quantity of output. As an overall rating, this level of performance should describe those who number among the best.

☐ **3.   Competent**
A rating of competent should be assigned to those whose demonstrated performance clearly meets all the requirements of the position in terms of quality and quantity of output. It is good, solid performance normally expected of those who have the necessary education, training, and relevant experience to enable them to effectively perform in a consistently reliable and professional manner. Although minor deviations may occasionally occur, the overall level of performance meets or may slightly exceed major job requirements.

☐ **4.   Acceptable**
This is performance that does not fully meet job requirements in all areas of major responsibilities. The individual may demonstrate the ability to complete most assignments; however, the need for further development and improvement is clearly recognized. This individual needs coaching and counseling to achieve a fully competent level of performance.

☐ **5.   Marginal**
This is the lowest performance category. It includes the noticeably less than acceptable performance of those whose work in terms of quality and quantity of output is obviously below minimum job requirements, even when close supervision has been provided. This category describes a level of performance which should significantly improve within a reasonable period if the individual is to remain in the position.

☐ **6.   Too New To Evaluate**
This category should only be used for employees with six months or less in their current position.
Optional—This number may be further refined by circling either the plus (+) or minus (−) below:
+   Indicates somewhat higher performance than designated by the number checked above.
−   Indicates somewhat lower performance than designated by the number checked above.

IV.   Self-Evaluation—Skills and Abilities
Effectiveness on the job is influenced by your knowledge, skills, and abilities, and your analysis of these helps determine realistic career goals. Describe your strengths and developmental needs in relation to current performance and potential for advancement. Comment on (1) technical knowl-

edge and, (2) managerial and interpersonal skills. Listing just your traits, skills or areas of technical knowledge is not adequate; try to describe how you manifest these skills and abilities on the job.

A. Strengths

B. Developmental Needs
Indicate nature and significance of each:

V. Developmental Plans
Based on the areas identified above, indicate actions you intend to take over the next year to improve your skills. These can include a variety of actions, such as special assignments, formal training, or supplemental reading. You carry the major responsibility for implementing these plans and you should remember that there are generally no quick or single solutions that work for everyone. Be specific about your role and the role of your manager and be as realistic as possible.

VI. Short-Term Career Objectives and Timing
To facilitate your career planning, indicate your short-term career objectives and your expectations regarding their timing: these may include your current job, lateral transfers, or promotions. Be as specific as possible. Include geographic considerations.

Employee Signature_____

Source: American Hospital Supply Corporation's 1980 Personnel Planning Manual.

Appendix B

American
Hospital Supply
Corporation

CMP-3
Department Summary
and Individual
Career Forecast

Division _____ Functional Area _____

List All Exempt Employees In Your Work Group In Order Of Descending M/P Points:

Name Last _____ First _____ Initial __	MP Points	Position Title	

* Date Entered Current Position   ** Do not enter performance rating from this form.

Submitted By _____ Date _____
Position Title _____

Source: American Hospital Supply Corporation's 1980 Personnel Planning Manual.

_____ Department _____

Date* in Job	PDS 101 Poten- tial	PDS 103 Readi- ness	Perfor- mance**	Next Assignment	Social Security Number

Revised 10/80
Printed in U.S.A.

Purpose

To review the current status of individuals within a work group and document in quantitative terms the data needed for career pathing and succession planning, including ratings of performance, readiness for advancement, and long term potential.

Instructions

1. To be completed once each year at the time of Personnel Planning preparation for all exempt employees.
2. The information necessary to complete this form will be generated from the CMP-2 discussions of performance and readiness for advancement, as well as a rating of potential.
3. Department heads will ultimately be responsible for evaluating the potential of employees in their units. It is suggested, and most realistic, that a department head will seek guidance and input from individual managers, personnel staffs, or others who have direct knowledge about an individual being evaluated. This rating will be shown to an employee *only upon request.*
4. The information contained on this form must receive one-over-one approval.
5. This form should be completed within each functional area (i.e., personnel, finance, operations, sales, etc.), and individuals should be listed in order of descending M/P points.
6. Upon request, the individual may review his/her data as documented on this form. Candid CMP-2 discussions regarding performance and career goals should ensure that the quantitative documentation of performance and readiness for advancement come as no surprise to the employee. Under no circumstances should employees be shown CMP-3 information about anyone other than themselves.

Definitions of Ratings

Rating of Management Potential

Rating management potential is an essential part of personnel planning at American. It is used as an indicator of an employee's long term promotability. The rating of potential has a corporate-wide focus and should not be determined on the basis of opportunity only within a specific division or business.

Given further business exposure and developmental opportunities, what is the individual's long term potential to perform successfully in management:

1. **Very High** This individual has very high potential, and can ultimately perform successfully in top management positions, i.e., corporate CEO or COO. Executive Vice President, Company or Division President, or Corporate Staff Vice President.
2. **High** This individual has high potential, and can ultimately perform successfully in upper level management or staff positions. This category would include those positions reporting directly to an Executive Vice President, Company or Division President, or Corporate Staff Vice President.
3. **Good** This individual has good potential, and can ultimately perform successfully in management or staff positions reporting directly to a Division Vice President level, Business Vice President/Director or XO Staff Director.
4. **Moderate** This individual has moderate potential, and can ultimately perform successfully in management or staff positions immediately above first level managerial positions.
5. **Well Placed** This individual is well placed in his/her current position and is unlikely to move beyond that position.
6. **Too new to Evaluate** This category should be used only for employees with six months or less in their current position.

Rating of Readiness for Career Movement

The rating of readiness for career movement is a time sensitive indicator of when the employee will be ready for next assignment. This rating should not be influenced by the availability of job openings or backups. The following guidelines have been established:

1. Immediately ready.
2. Ready in six to eighteen months. Needs some preparation.
3. Not ready within eighteen months/not interested in career move at this time.

Rating of Performance

The performance rating is assigned to include the level at which the individual is currently performing. This is an overall rating and should be based solely on an evaluation of success in achieving the results, goals or objectives of the position.

1. **Distinguished** Performance of this caliber is extremely rare. It is a rating that should be reserved for those who clearly and consistently demonstrate extraordinary and exceptional accomplishments in *all* major areas of responsibility. Those who perform at this level are easily recognized by others outside their own group or division, as well as those in related areas. It is a level of performance that is seldom equaled by others who hold positions of comparable scope and responsibility.
2. **Outstanding** This is a rating that best describes a level of accomplishment that goes well beyond reasonable but demanding standards of performance, especially in the key, critical areas of major responsibilities. The

individual consistently demonstrates truly outstanding achievements in terms of quality and quantity of output. As an overall rating, this level of performance should describe those who number among the best.

3. Competent A rating of competent should be assigned to those whose demonstrated performance clearly meets all the requirements of the position in terms of quality and quantity of output. It is good solid performance normally expected of those who have the necessary education, training and relevant experience to enable them to effectively perform in a consistently reliable and professional manner. Although minor deviations may occasionally occur, the overall level of performance meets or may slightly exceed major job requirements.

4. Acceptable This is performance that does not fully meet job requirements in all areas of major responsibilities. The individual may demonstrate the ability to complete most assignments; however, the need for further development and improvement is clearly recognized. This individual needs coaching and counseling to achieve a fully competent level of performance.

5. Marginal This is the lowest performance category. It includes the noticeably less than acceptable performance of those whose work, in terms of quality and quantity of output, is obviously below minimum job requirements, even when close supervision has been provided. This category describes a level of performance which should significantly improve within a reasonable period if the individual is to remain in the position.

6. Too new to Evaluate This category must be used only for employees with six months or less in their current position.

Optional This number may be further refined by adding either a plus or minus:

\+ Indicates somewhat higher performance than designated by the number above.

\- Indicates somewhat lower performance than designated by the number above.

Source: American Hospital Supply Corporation's 1980 Personnel Planning Manual.

Appendix C

Purpose

To document and identify current strengths, readiness, and availability of backups for key managerial positions.

Definition

A backup is defined as an individual who would be qualified to assume the target position within eighteen months.

Instructions

1. The CMP-4 is completed by all executive vice presidents and their staffs, all corporate vice presidents and their staffs, all company and division presidents and their staffs, on an annual basis.
2. It is prepared after the CMP-3 has been completed by each manager. The CMP-3 will supply the data needed to complete the CMP-4.
3. Backups who are identified must be within the respective business center, division, company or business. For XO staff, backups may be identified corporatewide.
4. Under no circumstances should employees see CMP-4 information concerning anyone but themselves.

Source: American Hospital Supply Corporation's 1980 Personnel Planning Manual.

Appendix D
Forecast—Number of Employees

PURPOSE: The purpose of "Forecast-Number of Employees" is to specify by functional area how many employees will be hired in each of the three plan years and what employment source will be used. This Schedule 11 is the same document used in the operating plan.

INSTRUCTIONS:

1. Lines 1–12 are used to record the exempt staffing requirements by functional area.
2. Lines 14–15 are used to record the overall non-exempt staffing requirements.
3. (a) columns are used to record the anticipated turnover within the unit for each of the three years. Turnover is defined as personnel losses within the unit due to transfer or promotion out of the unit, quits, terminations and retirements.
4. (b) columns are used to record the anticipated number of hires within the unit in light of turnover and growth.
5. (c) columns indicate what the staffing levels will be at the end of the plan year.
6. Columns d–g are an indication of where the number of hires will be sourced (i.e., where will these people be hired from?). The numbers added in each of the four sourcing categories (per plan year) may not equal the number of hires (column b) in the plan year. That is, the sum of the figures in column d through g will exceed the total number of hires (column b) by the number of individuals hired to replace promotions within the division (column f).

EXEMPT POSITIONS TO BE ADDED DURING FIRST PLAN YEAR (Optional)

1. _____   7. _____
2. _____   8. _____
3. _____   9. _____
4. _____   10. _____
5. _____   11. _____
6. _____   12. _____

Source: American Hospital Supply Corporation's 1980 Personnel Planning Manual.

Forecast—Number of Employees

AHSC OPERATING PLAN _____ 19___
UNIT _____

EXEMPTS — Functional Area	Prior year actual 19___	First Year Plan 19___ — Estimated Employees — Turnover*	Number of hires	Staffing level end of plan yr.	College Recruiting	Outside hire	Promote inside division	Promote inside AHSC	Second Year Plan 19___ — Estimated Employees — Turnover*	Number of hires	Staffing level end of plan yr.	College Recruiting	Outside hire	Promote inside division	Promote inside AHSC	Third Year Plan 19___ — Estimated Employees — Turnover*	Number of hires	Staffing level end of plan yr.	College Recruiting	Outside hire	Promote inside division	Promote inside AHSC	
Business Planning																							1
EDP																							2
Finance																							3
Manufacturing (Mfg. Eng. Prod. Contrl., Purch.)																							4
Marketing																							5
Operations/Distrib.																							6
Personnel																							7
QA/QC																							8
RA																							9
R&D																							10
Sales																							11
Other (Specify)																							12
EXEMPT TOTAL																							13
NON-EXEMPTS																							
Clerical																							14
Production																							15
NON-EXEMPT TOTAL																							16
TOTAL EMPLOYEES																							17
	a	a	b	c	d	e	f	g	a	b	c	d	e	f	g	a	b	c	d	e	f	g	

* Turnover. The turnover figures should include personnel losses within the unit due to transfer or promotion out of the organizational unit.

Appendix E

American Hospital Supply Corporation

Form A
Voluntary and
Involuntary Turnover

Division/Unit _____

Employee Category	1978			1979					1980				
	Number Employees	Number Turnover	% Total Turnover	Number Employees	Number Turnover Vol.	Invol.	% Total Turnover	% Inc. (Dec.)	Number Employees	Number Turnover Vol.	Invol.	% Total Turnover	% Inc. (Dec.)
M/P													
Sales													
Non-Exempt/ Salaried													
Non-Exempt/ Hourly													
Total													

Instructions:

1. Turnover data should be reported for the preceding three years. These figures should exclude turnover due to promotions, transfer, leave of absence, reduction in work force, death and retirement. (Note that for purposes of this form turnover is defined differently than in Schedule 11—Forecast.)
The date required for completing this form is available from PDS report HR 305-05'(Quarterly Turnover Report).

2. The "number of employees" reported for each year is calculated by taking the average of the number of full-time employees on the first and last day of the year.

3. The percentage increase or decrease in turnover should be calculated by subtracting the previous year's percentage from the succeeding year's percentage.

4. The number of individual turning over in 1979 and 1980 should be broken out into two categories: voluntary and involuntary. The number of voluntary terminations should exclude all individuals who took the option of resigning prior to being formally terminated.

Revised 10/80

Printed in U.S.A.

AMERICAN HOSPITAL SUPPLY CORPORATION (B) AMERICAN CONVERTORS DIVISION

Ann Pigneri and C. Wickham Skinner

American Convertors Division (ACD) of American Hospital Supply Corporation began to use the Personnel Planning System (PPS) in 1976. In 1980 division managers

Copyright © 1980 by the President and Fellows of Harvard College. Harvard Business School case 1-681-039.

identified problems with this system as "timing," "confidentiality," and "lack of understanding by employees." These problems are discussed following a description of the division and its activities.

American Convertors was founded in 1958 as Ruby Products and manufactured the first nonwoven disposable surgical packs. American Hospital Supply Corporation acquired Ruby in 1961. At that time, the company was trying to "convert" the medical world from the use of linens to single-use throw-away products. For this reason, the name was changed to Convertors.

Exhibit 1   Convertors Division: Organization Chart—Executive Department

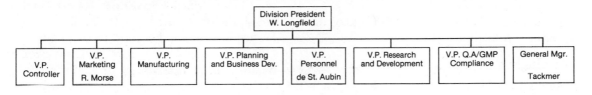

American Convertors maintained 10 regional sales offices plus one in Canada to handle international sales. The administrative office was located in Evanston, Illinois, a short distance from corporate headquarters.

The president, vice president–marketing, vice president–research and development, vice president–controller, vice president–business planning, and vice president–personnel, along with their staff (for a total of 57 employees) were located in the administrative offices. The vice president–manufacturing and the vice president–quality assurance and their staff were located in the El Paso manufacturing facility. The organizational chart is shown in Exhibit 1.

American Convertors' sales had been growing at a rate of 25 percent a year. Planned sales for 1980 were $100 million and the projected number of employees was 2,725.

Products and Services

American Convertors manufactured and marketed single-use products primarily designed for use in a hospital's operating or obstetrical departments. These products included: draping packs and components, surgical gowns, face masks, caps, shoe covers, and towels. In addition, the division had a comprehensive line of other apparel and bedding for use in intensive and cardiac care centers, emergency departments, isolation wards, pediatrics, and patient rooms.

Traditionally, these products were made of cloth, and were intended for repeated use. It was an axiom that "a wet drape is a contaminated drape." Since cloth is inherently absorbent, it is prone to contamination in the operating room, where quantities of fluids are always present. Also, great care had to be taken in laundering, sterilizing, and packaging of reusables to prevent the risk of cross-infection from patient to patient. American Convertors single-use products were made of a unique, nonwoven material which offered many advantages to the hospital and patient. Unlike cloth, it was liquid-resistant. This helped create an effective barrier to protect against bacterial migration and cross-infection. The fabric was strong yet lightweight, and air-permeable for greater comfort.

There were 350 products in the American Convertors' line. Three hundred of these were manufactured by the division.

American Convertors also made available many no-cost services for hospitals. These included feasibility studies, implementation programs, and an in-service nurse consultant program. Their full-time staff of professional operating room nurse consultants was available to assist hospitals with in-service training and program implementation.

Production. Table 1 shows the size of the production facilities.

Table 1 Facilities and Staff

Plant	Square Feet	Number of Employees
El Paso, Texas	496,000	275
Juarez, Mexico	138,000	1,800
Chihuahua, Mexico	25,000	400

The El Paso plant received raw materials from approximately 35 suppliers. The major operation at this plant involved spreading material, cutting from patterns, palletizing, and shipping across the border to the Juarez plant. Activities at the Juarez plant included sewing, folding, gluing, and packaging products to be shipped back to the El Paso plant for sterilization and stocking. Finished goods were delivered to distribution centers by American Convertors, AHSC, or common-carrier truck fleets. Each week approximately 200 border crossings were made, requiring proper documentation and customs release.

Marketing. In the hospital business segment, American Convertors was the market-share leader.

A second market for the American Convertors Division was the industrial business. Products for this market were developed and sold to customers in the electronics, clean room, and packaging activities. American Convertors entered this market in 1978 and ranked third in market share by 1980.

American Convertors' third market segment was the international market. The division's nonwoven products were exported for health-care purposes throughout the world. American Convertors was the market-share leader in Canada, Holland, and France, and ranked second in Germany.

Table 2 shows the percent of Convertors' business broken down by market segment.

Table 2 Percent of Convertors' Business by Market

Market Segment	Percent of Total Business
Hospital	91
Industrial	3
International	6

Turnover. According to Donna de St. Aubin, vice president–personnel for the American Convertors Division, turnover was not high when compared with the averages in respective areas.

Usually in excess of 20 percent is considered normal in sales, and we were at 18 percent in 1979. For management turnover, usually 15 to 20 percent is considered average, and American Convertors was only 10 percent. Our nonexempt turnover is high. Most of our nonexempt work force is in El Paso, Texas. Turnover in this category was 25 percent for office/technical and 33.9 percent for hourly workers. When compared with our less than 10 percent average in our Mexican operations, this seems quite high.

We are the second largest manufacturer in the city of Juarez. Turnover there is not a problem, mainly due to the high unemployment rate in Mexico and the lack of welfare benefits. This, coupled with our hiring standards and compensation practices, contributes to low turnover.

Hiring Practices. The corporation emphasized internal promotion for its manage-

Exhibit 2   Convertors Division Selection Interview Summary

(use ink—press hard—print clearly)

DIVISION _____

APPLICANT NAME _____

POSITION CONSIDERED FOR _____

DECISION: _____ HIRE _____ REJECT _____

REJECT BUT REFER TO XO FOR FURTHER CONSIDERATION

CRITICAL BEHAVIORS	CHARACTERISTICS	OBSERVATIONS	(circle one) RATING		
			LOW		HIGH
Intelligence	Conceptual ability, breadth of knowledge, verbal expression, depth of response, analytical thought process		1	2	3
Decisiveness	Nonambivalent, i.e., willingness to commit self, when asked makes definite choices, lets you know where he/she stands on issues, not tentative		1	2	3
Energy/ enthusiasm	Quantity as opposed to quality, animated, positive, spontaneous, fast paced throughout		1	2	3
Results— orientation	Responses revolve around task accomplishment, gets to point, emphasizes achievement, provides information relevant to interview objectives		1	2	3
Maturity	Acceptance of responsibility for one's actions, poise, self-confidence, dress, general demeanor, relaxed, ability to reflect on experiences		1	2	3
Assertiveness	Responds in a forceful manner and takes charge of the interview, speaks in a convincing tone, persuasive, good at selling self and ideas		1	2	3
Sensitivity	Sincere, friendly, tactful, responsive, not aloof, listens as well as speaks		1	2	3

Exhibit 2   (concluded)

Openness	Discusses shortcomings as well as strengths, isn't preoccupied with saying the right thing, consistent responsiveness regardless of content	1	2	3
Tough-/ mindedness	Stands up to interviewer when there's disagreement, discusses persons and events critically, doesn't allow emotions to cloud perceptions	1	2	3

COMMENTS: _____
_____
_____
_____
_____

INTERVIEWED BY: _____ DATE: _____

Source: American Hospital Supply Corporation literature.

ment talent. Filling entry-level through mid-level management positions was typically the responsibility of the division personnel function. When a manager was looking for a new management/professional employee, he contacted de St. Aubin, the division's vice president of personnel. For positions at mid-level management she would then contact John Burchfield, personnel director for the hospital/pharmaceutical business. His responsibility was to identify a slate of qualified internal candidates from other divisions. If a higher-level executive was sought, then de St. Aubin contacted Jan Blakslee, director of management planning and development at the corporate level.

Information generated in the respective division personnel plans was the data base for candidate slates—at division, business, and corporate level. Management succession and backup plans developed by every division (part of the personnel plan) was the starting point for identifying candidates for interdivision promotions. Ms. de St. Aubin stated that before the personnel planning system was implemented, a personnel manager having an open position would call other division personnel managers for assistance.

Recruiting Sources and Plans. Exhibit 4 discusses each of the functional areas in relation to recruiting. The percentage of total hires for the Convertors Division, broken down by source, is given in Table 3.

Table 3   Percent of Hires by Source

Source	Percent of Total Hires
College recruiting	20%
Agencies	25
Employee referrals	15
Newspaper ads	35
Interdivisional transfers	5

Exhibit 3 Convertors Division Forecast—Number of Employees

AHSC OPERATING PLAN
UNIT __Convertors__ 19 _79_

Column codes for each plan year: a = Turnover*, b = Number of hires, c = Staffing level end of plan yr., d = College Recruiting (Sourcing), e = Outside hire (Sourcing), f = Promote inside division (Sourcing), g = Promote inside AHSC (Sourcing)

	Prior year actual 19 78	First Year Plan 19 79 a	b	c	d	e	f	g	Second Year Plan 19 80 a	b	c	d	e	f	g	Third Year Plan 19 81 a	b	c	d	e	f	g	#
EXEMPTS																							
Business Planning	8	1	3	10	1	1	0	1	1	2	11	0	1		1	1	3	13	1	1		1	1
EDP																							2
Finance	10	1	5	14	1	2	1	1	1	1	14	1				1	1	14				1	3
Manufacturing (Mfg. Eng. Prod. Contrl., Purch.)	25	2	12	35	2	8		2	4	6	37	2	3	1		4	6	39	2	2	1	1	4
Marketing	6	1	3	8	1	1	1	1	1	2	9	1		1	1	1	2	10	1		1		5
Operations/Distrib.																							6
Personnel	3	1	2	4	1	1		1	1	1	4	1			1	1	1	4	1			1	7
QA/QC	8	1	3	10	1	1	1		1	2	11			1	1	1	3	13	2	1			8
RA																							9
R&D	7	1	16	22	2	10		4	2	13	33	2	10		1	3	23	53	4	17		2	10
Sales	82	8	9	83	2	6		1	8	9	84	3	5		1	8	9	85	2	6		1	11
Other (Specify)																							12
EXEMPT TOTAL																							13
NON-EXEMPTS																							
Clerical	66	6	19	79		6			7	14	86		14			8	16	94		16			14
Production	1875	18	42	1899		18			18	209	2090		209			20	231	2301		231			15
NON-EXEMPT TOTAL																							16
TOTAL EMPLOYEES																							17

Exhibit 4   Convertors Division: Recruiting

Sales/Marketing

We have experienced extremely high recruit-ing activities within the sales/marketing group over the past year. Much of this recruiting was a direct result of forced turnover. This turnover should be considerably lower in 1979–1980, but the normal attrition rate and increasing size of our sales force will continue to place a burden on the recruiting function.

R&D

R&D has placed additional pressures on the recruiting efforts at Convertors. In late 1978 we formed an internal R&D function and began staffing that department. This type of recruiting is relatively foreign to Convertors. Our tradi-tional sources such as college campuses and re-ferrals proved ineffective in finding the science and research technicians required. If we face any major recruiting challenge in 1979–1980 it will be a direct result of the expansion of this depart-ment.

Production

The last area of concern for recruiting is with the production supervision team in El Paso. We have traditionally promoted from within for that group. This policy, however, will not provide high potential, college-trained production man-agers. Our goal must be to "seed" the produc-tion staff with this type of recruit. This change will therefore require an expansion of our college recruiting activities. We must expand to include the recruitment of MEs, IE, and production man-agement managers along with our traditional sales/marketing and finance recruiting.

Career Paths

No recruiting program is successful if the fol-low-up positions from entry level are not pro-vided for the high potentials. There will have to be a career path developed in El Paso that will include the entry-level assignments as well as development positions beyond that. This does not necessarily mean an automatic progression system but rather a plan to orient the trainee to all phases of production management.

Source: Convertors Division, "Forecast and Recruiting Plans."

According to ACD's "Forecast and Re-cruiting Plans," the college recruiting pro-gram was primarily devoted to sales/mar-keting trainees. However, all accounting and staff accountants had also been hired from the campus for the past two years. The plan stated:

> We wish to expand this recruiting source to include the entry-level production man-agers, entry-level R&D positions, and engi-neering. This will necessitate the visiting of more schools, along with the expansion of the business schools presently visited.

ACD awarded $100 for personal referrals,

and the plan stated that this amount may increase in the future.

In selecting management/professionals, American Convertors Division used the nine salary criteria established by corporate headquarters (see Exhibit 2).

Of the current 26 division presidents, de St. Aubin believed not one was hired from the outside and thought 90 percent of the vice presidents also were promoted from within. She stated that only when searching for employees with special skills, such as the top corporate legal executive, had the corporation searched externally.

Use of the Personnel Planning System.
Ms. de St. Aubin and the human resource
manager interviewed each of the department heads regarding the key elements of
the information (i.e., organization structure, backups, etc.). This was drafted for
their review and edit before being consolidated into the final draft.

Each manager who had exempt employees reporting to him or her was asked to fill
out the CMP-3 (performance, readiness,
and promotability) and return it to the personnel department. These ratings were reviewed with the department heads and appropriate changes were made to readiness
or potential ratings and returned to the appropriate managers for review.

After the plan had been reviewed and
edited by the department heads, the president and the vice president–personnel,
mini-plans were returned to the departments.

On a quarterly basis, this information was
reviewed as a group to determine progress
toward goals and objectives stated in the
plan.

Two parts of the personnel plan that
needed to be done every year were the assessment of division needs and the critical
assessment of last year's progress.

The Personnel Plan Itself

American Convertors Division prepared
its fourth personnel plan in March 1979. Exhibit 3 shows the forecast of the number of
employees for 1979 to 1981. The division's
recruiting needs were developed from this
and other data.

ACD's forecast was passed up to the Hos-
pital/Pharmaceutical Business (HPB). This
business received personnel plans from
nine operating divisions. These plans were
then consolidated by the HPB personnel director and his executive vice president into a
personnel plan for the business.

Evaluation of the PPS

Comments concerning the PPS were obtained from the vice president–personnel,
the vice president–marketing, and from the
president of the Convertors Division.

Vice President–Personnel. When PPS
was first implemented, Donna de St. Aubin
was the employment manager for the Hospital Supply Division. Subsequently she
was promoted to director of personnel for a
small division (American Ormco) before she
assumed the position of vice president–personnel for the American Convertors Division in May 1979. Donna de St. Aubin discussed the value of the PPS:

> It has strengthened our abilities to de-
> velop clear-cut career paths for employees.
> We tend to see on a regular basis that people
> have taken the time to put additional infor-
> mation on paper, so it has been thought out.

A problem Donna de St. Aubin identified
with the PPS was timing:

> We do two other forms of planning in the
> organization: the strategic plan and the op-
> erating plan. The strategic plan begins in
> April or May, and the operating plan starts
> in right after the strategic plan is completed.
> It seems the personnel plan should run off
> the strategic plan and the operating plan.
> The personnel plan is starting the planning
> cycle rather than ending with the other two.
> So much of the plan really doesn't change,
> because the organization does not change
> drastically in a year. For example, the orga-
> nization structure should only need to be
> redone every two years. Two parts of the
> personnel plan that need to be done every
> year are assessing division needs and re-
> porting progress against last year's plan.

Donna de St. Aubin felt that the major problem with the PPS was that people were afraid to use the evaluation system critically for rating potential, readiness, and performance. Supervisors are afraid that they may block someone's career chances by rating them too low. She felt that this happened most often with the 2 rating being given instead of a 3.

Another problem of concern to de St. Aubin is that line people who are not in top management do not know anything about the system, except that it exists. They also do not understand how it links with the total business planning system.

Vice President–Marketing. Rich Morse, 31, vice president–marketing for the Convertors Division, had been with American Hospital Supply Corporation for over eight years.

Morse identified some good points of the PPS. He felt that the system did a successful job of identifying outstanding performance, marginal performers, and underutilized employees. Morris believed that it also formalized the communication between a manager and his or her subordinates.

> The system still forced the manager to sit down and say, "You are seen as promotable. You may not be the first in line, but you should know that this corporation thinks highly of you, and you have a good chance for advancing further in management."

He also noted several ways to improve the benefits of the PPS:

> I think it could work better if we put more time into its construction each year. We rather hastily make our list, especially in the marginal people area. There is not much joint teamwork in the plan preparation by the personnel director and the respective department heads, myself included. Down the line it doesn't get as well utilized as it should be. The employees who are one or two steps below the department head are not as involved in the personnel planning system as they should be.

Morse also commented about management development programs:

> I also think we do a terrible job of developing people once they are hired. . . . We do a decent job of training the sales reps we hire. Within the division we have a three-step system that we've instituted over the last 12 months. The first step is to be taken within the initial 30 days of employment; the second is taken within six months; and the third is taken after one year. We do nothing for the sales rep who is identified as a potential manager—we don't do anything to prepare him or her for the management spot. Or once he or she becomes a manager, we don't do anything to help with the transition. We also don't help a sales rep who becomes a product manager. We promote a rep to a product manager or a sales training manager to a sales management position, and we don't help the person make that transition by providing courses that would strengthen his or her skills.

Morse believed that employees were not being promoted as rapidly as in the past. At one time, he said, employees were promoted every six months when the company was growing rapidly. But now the corporation was slowing to a steady, consistent rate. Since the corporation was not acquiring as many companies, Morse noted, "the demand for new management at all levels is not as strong as it was previously."

Regarding promotion decisions, Morse stated that almost always the company promoted from within. "It's corporate policy that we promote from within and we always look to do that first and go outside only if we have failed to build adequate backups."

President. Bill Longfield, 41, assumed the presidency of the American Convertors Division in April 1974. He had some favorable opinions of the PPS:

> I think the thing I like best about the personnel planning system, from my position, is the fact that it formalizes the need for us on a periodic basis to look at our organization; to evaluate whether we have the proper people to continue our growth.

Longfield also identified some problems of the system. He felt the major problem was the inconsistency of the ratings. For example, a person one individual interpreted as a high achiever may have a totally different rating from another's point of view. Another problem was protecting the confidentiality of the personnel data system. Most of the information was on the computer. Longfield stated:

> It's very easy to access and we've had occasion where those computer reports haven't been dealt with internally as confidentially as they should be. As a result, people have gotten to know what others' salaries are, which has created some problems. But it's really not part of the planning system, it's more a byproduct of that system.

Concerning attitudes toward the PPS, Mr. Longfield stated:

> I think most managers don't like to do it because the paperwork is time consuming and it also exposes them in some area. If we've got a manager and we force him to rate his people, then he has to admit he's got some failures, some people who aren't performing. He knows it's going to be put on a piece of paper and it's going to get wide circulation. So, we get some manager resistance.

According to Longfield, personnel staff members seemed to be playing a bigger and bigger role in assisting the departments in completing their required forms. "It almost comes to filling in the blanks for some managers. . . ."

Appendix A
American Hospital Supply Corporation (D)—Convertors Division

EMPLOYEE COPY

AMERICAN HOSPITAL SUPPLY CORPORATION   CMP–2
Performance Evaluation and Career Development Summary   CONFIDENTIAL
(To be Completed by the Employee)

NAME _____   DATE _____
       (Last)   *(First)*   *(Middle)*   *(Month)*   *(Day)*   *(Year)*

JOB TITLE _____   DATE ENTERED PRESENT POSITION:

DIVISION/LOCATION _____ _____   _____
                                           (Month)   *(Year)*

I. SELF-EVALUATION RESULTS: List significant accomplishments since your last review. These may be objectives, goals, MBOs, or tasks from the job description that have been agreed upon by you and your supervisor. There are several ways you may review your accomplishments (results). You can list the agreed-upon objectives or tasks and comment upon the completion of each. Or you may list your accomplishments in order of priority and then comment on items not completely accomplished. You and your supervisor should discuss this and agree upon a format that will serve both your needs.

II. PERFORMANCE SUMMARY: (Summarize your overall performance. Comment in general terms on significant results and areas where improvement is needed.)

III. PERFORMANCE RATING: The performance rating is assigned to indicate the level at which you feel you are currently performing. This is an overall rating and should be based solely on an evaluation of your success in achieving the results, goals, or objectives of your position. Indicate your evaluation of your current performance by placing a check in the appropriate box below:

☐ #1 Distinguished:
Performance of this caliber is extremely rare. It is a rating that should be reserved for those who clearly and consistently demonstrate extraordinary and exceptional accomplishments in *all* major areas of responsibility. Those who perform at this level are easily recognized by others outside their own group or division, as well as those in related areas. It is a level of performance that is seldom equaled by others who hold positions of comparable scope and responsibility.

☐ #2 Outstanding:
This is a rating that best describes a level of accomplishment that goes well beyond reasonable but demanding standards of performance, especially in the key, critical areas of major responsibilities. The individual consistently demonstrates truly outstanding achievements in terms of quality and quantity of output. As an overall rating, this level of performance should describe those who number among the best.

☐ #3 Competent:
A rating of competent should be assigned to those whose demonstrated performance clearly meets all the requirements of the position in terms of quality and quantity of output. It is good, solid performance normally expected of those who have the necessary education, training, and relevant experience to enable them to effectively perform in a consistently reliable and professional manner. Although minor deviations may occasionally occur, the overall level of performance meets or may slightly exceed major job requirements.

☐ #4 Acceptable:
This is performance that does not fully meet job requirements in all areas of major responsibilities. The individual may demonstrate the ability to complete most assignments; however, the need for further development and improvement is clearly recognized. This individual needs coaching and counseling to achieve a fully competent level of performance.

☐ #5 Marginal:
This is the lowest performance category. It includes the noticeably less than acceptable performance of those whose work in terms of quality and quantity of output is obviously below minimum job requirements, even when close supervision has been provided. This category describes a level of performance which should significantly improve within a reasonable period if the individual is to remain in the position.

☐ #6 Too New to Evaluate:
This category should only be used for employees with six months or less in their current position.

OPTIONAL—This number may be further refined by circling either the plus (+) or minus (−) below:

+ Indicates somewhat higher performance than designated by the number checked above.

− Indicates somewhat lower performance than designated by the number checked.

IV. SELF-EVALUATION—SKILLS AND ABILITIES (Describe your strengths and shortcomings in relation to current performance and potential for advancement; comment on (1) technical knowledge and, (2) managerial and interpersonal skills):

A. STRENGTHS:

B. SHORTCOMINGS   (indicate nature and significance of each):

V. DEVELOPMENT PLANS (indicate actions you intend to take over the next year to improve your skills; be as objective and realistic as possible):

VI.   SHORT-TERM OBJECTIVES (indicate your short-term career objectives; be as specific as possible; include geographic considerations):

VII. RATINGS OF READINESS FOR ADVANCEMENT: The rating of readiness for advancement is a time sensitive indicator of when you feel you will be ready for your next assignment. The following guidelines have been established (check one):

☐ #1 Immediately Promotable.

☐ #2 Promotable in 6 to 18 months. Needs some preparation.

☐ #3 Not ready for promotion within 18 months.

COMMENTS:

SIGNATURE _____
                        (Employee)   *(Date)*

Source: American Hospital Supply Corporation's 1980 Personnel Planning Manual.

CASE 4
HART, SCHAFFNER & MARX

Liora Katzenstein and
Jeffrey A. Sonnenfeld

With still five to six months remaining before the onset of the spring campus recruiting season, Chuck Brazik began to wonder whether he needed to revise his firm's plan to attract and develop new MBA holders. Chuck was the Director of Management Development and Training at Hart, Schaffner & Marx, a major manufacturer and retailer of high-quality men's and women's apparel. Chuck's recent concern was stimulated by

Copyright © 1981 by the President and Fellows of Harvard College. Harvard Business School case 9-482-026.

some major changes in the corporation this year which underscored the future need for managerial talent. In January a new chairman and president were appointed. In March, the company's executive offices were united in a brand new Chicago office building. Following such changes as well as a renewed attention towards acquisition strategies, and the need for some collaborative efforts across the largely autonomous company divisions, the firm's complete organizational structure had been redesigned. To assess the future staffing needs of the company, Chuck had recently introduced the concept of formal executive succession planning. The divisions were seemingly receptive to this innovation.

Such internal events, in addition to the changes in the firm's competitive environment and the available production technologies, have stirred the interests of top company officers in securing fresh management talent. Chuck had entered Hart, Schaffner & Marx in 1978 with the creation of the corporate Human Resources Department in 1977. The company's new chairman and chief executive officer was a strong believer in active recruiting to strengthen the firm's executive ranks and encouraged Chuck to seek top quality MBA graduates.

Despite such senior level support for MBA recruiting, Chuck was concerned about the need to sell the credibility of such well educated, but often inexperienced outsiders to long tenured middle level company executives. Furthermore, Chuck was worried about the ability of Hart, Schaffner & Marx to meet the salary and advancement expectations of many graduates from the "high prestige" programs. Chuck was persuaded by some points made by Bob Mayer, his Manager of College Relations and Executive Recruitment, which favored focusing on strong regional schools in the Midwest. Bob suggested that such students were better acquainted with the firm and the region. Furthermore, the traveling required was less costly and the firm was able to build on its well established relationships from college level recruiting at these schools. At the same time, the "prestige" schools seemed to offer a larger pool of the "self-starters" which senior management felt the firm needed.

A commonly held view within the firm was that Hart, Schaffner & Marx offered real opportunity for growth and for responsibility within a pleasant, stable work environment. Far less clear than this message about the firm were questions of to whom the message should be sent and how it should be delivered.

The Company—A Brief History

The firm that describes itself as ". . . America's leading maker and retailer of quality apparel"[1] was founded in 1872, when 21-year-old Harry Hart and his 18-year-old brother, Max, opened a small tailor shop on Chicago's State Street, just six months after the city's great fire. In 1879, a brother-in-law, Marcus Marx, joined them. Eight years later Joseph Schaffner, a cousin, entered the firm and Hart, Schaffner & Marx came into existence.

At its beginnings the company concentrated on the manufacturing and retailing of better quality men's clothes. Or as Hart's report puts it, "Since the company's inception quality has been the keystone of its operation. Quality fabrics, quality styling and quality tailoring, all backed by solid technological and marketing expertise."[2]

The company, still very strong on the retail side, soon began venturing into wholesale distribution. According to the company's report[3] the transition from retail to wholesale began when a neighboring retailer placed an order for several garments. The Hart brothers saw in it an opportunity for expansion, which soon made them into major wholesalers as well. This strategy enabled Hart's to become one of the most successful examples of dual distribution in men's wear, selling the output of its manufacturing operations both to independent retailers and through its own retail stores.

Hart, Schaffner & Marx's emphasis on a quality product encouraged the company to embark on a constant search for new ap-

---

[1] 1981 *Midyear Report*, Hart, Schaffner & Marx, Chicago, Illinois, cover page.

[2] From the company's publication, *Careers with Hart, Schaffner & Marx*, 1981 edition, p. 3.

[3] Ibid.

proaches, both in the manufacturing as well as in the retailing end of their operations. The following are examples of some of the firm's innovative techniques.[4]

The concept of "One just price, and just one price," for all buyers, large or small.

At the turn of the century HS&M pioneered a new style of promotion by engaging world-famous artists to illustrate several series of advertisements in *The Saturday Evening Post*, thus starting an era of magazine illustration.

Later, the company introduced "proportional fit," scientifically proportioned sizes that insured better fitting clothing. HS&M also tailored the first Dacron, polyester, and wool suits.

The company has a history of commitment and social responsibilities in its dealings with its various community and union relations.

Through a dynamic acquisition policy over the last two decades, the company developed into both the largest retailer and manufacturer of tailored clothing, thus assuming the role of the unrivaled leader of the men's apparel industry.

Through skillful management the company survived the unhealthy market of the 1970s which disabled such other well-known tailored clothing manufacturers as Botany, Hammonton Park, and Eagle.

Recently the company introduced the use of licensing agreements to offer product lines which carry labels of well-known fashion designers (e.g., Christian Dior and Pierre Cardin) to extend the traditional image into high style items.

Hart, Schaffner & Marx was one of the first apparel companies in the country to introduce professional management practices, introducing formal business planning, marketing research, and human resource management in the mid-70s.

Since then, the company has developed into one of the country's top 10 apparel manufacturers (see Appendixes 1 and 2) with total sales approaching $800 million and with its stock trading on the New York Stock Exchange. It is ranked as number 400 in the *Fortune* 500 listing of companies. Hart's currently operates 32 plants and approximately 300 retail stores, thus positioning itself as the largest quality apparel manufacturer and retail clothing company in the United States. It has also diversified into various clothing segments such as sportswear and women's apparel. Emphasis on quality remains the company's main strategy, as its chairman, Jerome S. Gore, declared: "There's a greater interest than ever before in quality because nowadays quality means value. Value no longer means buying something at a low price that will last one season and then you throw it away."[5] The company has six divisions, four manufacturing men's clothing, one manufacturing women's clothing, and a retail division.

Manufacturing[6]

The company's major manufacturing division is Hart, Schaffner & Marx, which is also its major brand name. In addition, the division manufactures Christian Dior Clothing for men, Jack Nicklaus Sportswear, Society Brand, Austin Reed of Regent Street and Graham & Gunn, Ltd. The company also includes Gleneagles—the subdivision which manufactures men's rainwear, sports, and outerwear under its own name as well as the Hart, Schaffner & Marx,

---

[4] Ibid., p. 4.

[5] *Forbes*, January 8, 1979, p. 153.

[6] This information is based on Hart's publication, *Careers with Hart, Schaffner & Marx*, 1981 edition, p. 2.

Christian Dior Monsieur, Jack Nicklaus, and Nino Cerruti labels. Fashionaire, another subdivision of Hart, Schaffner & Marx Clothes Division, manufactures career apparel and uniforms for both men and women. Its customers include major airlines, car rental agencies, banks, savings and loan institutions, and fast food chains. Hart's Jaymar-Ruby Division is America's largest manufacturer of men's quality slacks. Jaymar, Sansabelt, Cary Middlecoff, and Pierre Cardin are its principal slacks brands. The division also markets sportswear bearing the name Jaymar, Nino Cerruti Sport, and Cesarani.

Hickey-Freeman, another division, enjoys a long-standing reputation for the superior quality of its hand-tailored clothing, produced under the Hickey-Freeman name and that of its companion brand, Walter Morton.

One of the company's fastest growing divisions—representing Hart's efforts to expand into the medium-priced men's suit and sport coat market—is M. Wile & Company, which produces the very successful Nino Cerruti designer line, the Pierre Cardin, Allyn St. George, and Johnny Carson lines.

Since the early 1970s the company has been trying to expand its client base by developing a moderate price line of men's apparel. This effort resulted in the repositioning of the Johnny Carson line. In addition, HS&M acquired in August, 1980, Country Miss, Inc., a New York maker of medium-priced women's sportswear, suits and dresses—the company's first venture into women's wear manufacturing. Certain analysts have been describing this new strategy as "a fight to expand from class to markets."[7]

Retail

The company is represented nationwide by retail chains or independent stores, each carrying its own name and functioning as independent profit centers. These retail outlets vary, not only in name but also in the clientele they are trying to attract—which accounts for the variety of layouts and atmospheres of the different company stores.

The nationwide coverage of HS&M retail stores division includes: on the East Coast, Wallachs, Tripler, Roots, Field Bros.; in the South and Southwest, Leopold Price & Rolle, Jas K. Wilson, Wolf Bros.; in the West, Silverwoods, Hastings; in the Midwest, corporate headquarters, Chas. A. Stevens, Baskin. Another 130 company-owned stores, each part of smaller regional groups, are positioned throughout the country.[8]

Another important and expanding part of Hart, Schaffner & Marx's retail business is in the area of women's wear. The company operates over 30 women's specialty stores, including Chas. S. Stevens, and Chas in the Chicago area, J. P. Allen in Atlanta, and de Jong's in Evansville, Ind. In addition, approximately half of the firm's men's stores have opened women's departments. According to Mr. Jerome S. Gore, the company's chief executive officer and chairman,[9] "Women represent a new and expanding market for the company. Of the approximately $400 million in retail sales volume achieved by the company in the 1980 fiscal year, women's wear accounted for 25 percent." He added, "It's going to be an important part of our business. We're very interested in acquiring women's retailing stores." The earlier mentioned acquisition of Country Miss, a company with proven

[7] *Business Week*, October 20, 1980, p. 74.

[8] Ibid., p. 4.

[9] *New York Times*, January 17, 1981, p. B–31.

expertise in women's wear, seems to confirm the company's determination to invest in this new field. According to the *New York Times*,[10] another sign of commitment to women's wear can be found in the naming in January 1981, of Bernard Zindler, former president and chief executive officer of the Union Company in Columbus, Ohio, to vice president of Hart's women's operations for the retail stores division.

The company is planning to expand its retail outlets through internal development and through the acquisition of existing outlets. The company has recently cleared its position in connection with an antitrust action filed against HS&M in 1969, after the company had gone on an acquisition spree, buying 40 men's stores in only four years. The Department of Justice then forced a divestiture of some of the company's stores and prohibited similar acquisitions. On June 30, 1980, however, the ban on new acquisition came to an end. The company reacted on September 25, 1980 by purchasing Bishop's, a men's store in Salem, Oregon, which was melded into the company's Klopfenstein's chain, based in Seattle. According to the company's chairman, the company was also looking at several opportunities to buy single stores or chains in the South, Southwest, or West Coast.

Company Culture

Through its history, the company has developed an amiable and conservative culture. Its products remain the quality leaders of the industry. The company's financial practices display conservative accounting methods and a reliance on internally funded growth. Finally, careers have tended to be slow-moving, with most executives traditionally developing through the ranks. Reputations and friendships tend to become strong in this fairly stable culture. One by-product is that retail operations and manufacturing operations tended to grow in different directions with separate organizations, career paths, and subcultures. Chuck commented that this has affected his placement efforts because the movement between retail and manufacturing can be difficult. Furthermore, "the divisions vary in their receptivity. Some executives think you need to have worsted in your blood. We hope that through the placement of our MBAs, we can show that these folks can contribute to our business without having necessarily been weaned on apparel and worked up from our plant floors and store counters."

The year 1981 brought some major changes to HS&M. In January 1981, the company's chairman, John D. Gray, announced his retirement, ending a 36-year career with the company. Jerome S. Gore, who had been chief executive and president since 1975, was named chairman. At the same occasion other major restructuring of top-level management was approved in an effort to revitalize the company's management. Among these changes was the establishment of the new posts of vice chairman and chief operating officer. John R. Meinert, 53, an executive vice president, was named vice chairman, and Richard P. Hamilton, 49, a former chief executive of Florsheim Shoes, who joined HS&M in 1978 as chairman of the retail stores group, was named president and chief operating officer.[11] Industry analysts welcomed this change, saying: "It took a change in management in the retail division to get things moving," and they claimed "it had nothing to do with manu-

---

[10] Ibid.

[11] *New York Times*, January 17, 1981, p. B–3.

facturing and they were smart to maintain their own name and reputation of quality. They just needed some new blood."[12] Other changes such as regionalization of the retail stores divisions and the addition of the Men's Apparel Group occurred in 1981.

Chuck offered this example of how the new management's increasing openness to recruiting and development is spreading throughout the organization:

> When I went to the general manager and president of one of our manufacturing divisions and asked if he needed any MBAs, he said, "No: I don't need any for two years and I can't afford any for months. I don't even want to consider it until June." We hear that a lot. Hiring becomes a priority for folks in June when it's too late. I went back and asked this fellow how he'd have the trained talent when he needed it in two years. It was amazing how he conceded, saying, "Yeah, I see what you're saying. I guess I have to bite the bullet in lean times so I have what I need later." That's a new way of thinking around here. A few years ago his answer would have been "No—not now" with no thought of the future. This fellow is a pretty rugged individualist but he's just recently come and told me, "Chuck, you need to do a study of where the high performance people are in this organization." For him to ask that of us shows a real change.

HS&M: Human Resources Department

In 1976, Hart, Schaffner & Marx created a Corporate Human Resources Department, following outside expert advice and the president's concern for better personnel management. The department, headed by Sherman Rosen, vice president of human resources, has eight professional staff mem-

bers and reports directly to the chairman and chief executive officer.

Chuck Brazik, corporate director of management development and training, who joined the company in 1978, has developed a series of human resources management instruments, including performance and potential appraisal formats, a succession plan guide, and a system for early identification of high potential executives. These programs were strongly supported by the company's upper management. The process, however, was implemented in a noncoercive manner, due to the company's divisions. Chuck's innovative ideas soon gained credibility within the company, and were widely accepted in the firm's various divisions. The retail units seemed particularly receptive to these new corporate efforts. Furthermore, awareness of the importance of human resources planning seemed to have been reaching the ranks of middle management, where the resistance to the early planning for the recruitment of new talent had been more pronounced.

The Company's Recruiting Strategy

Hart's college recruiting strategies were revamped in 1978, and have recently been updated with the encouragement of the company's new chairman, Jerome S. Gore. This effort is represented by the booklet, *Careers with Hart, Schaffner & Marx*, first published in 1980. This document presents interested students with an overall view of the firm, its history, and its place within the apparel industry. It then proceeds to describe various career opportunities with HS&M, in the areas of retailing, and/or manufacturing in specialties such as marketing and sales, merchandising, finance, store management, and lately also strategic planning. This colorful publication of 12 pages is handed out

---

[12] Ibid., p. B–31.

to anybody interviewing with the company (mostly undergraduates, however). Chuck Brazik explained, "We hire 20 to 30 BAs a year for management positions. We use the career brochure and I try to get in a class or two to discuss HS&M."

A direct effort at recruiting MBAs can be found in the so-called Hart's Scholar Program (see Appendix 3) started in 1981, in which the company finances graduate business education for "one or two outstanding liberal arts degreed students, who will attend Northwestern University's J.L. Kellogg Graduate School of Management Evening MBA Manager's Program."[13]

The company started formally recruiting MBAs directly from school in 1968. All graduates started in careers in the company's HS&M Clothes Division and some were personally mentored by the corporate president, Mr. Gore. By 1981, six of the eight recruits were in responsible management positions. Between 1974 and 1978, however, the firm hired only a few MBAs, mostly out of other companies. In 1978 the interest in MBA hiring was heightened. In 1979 three MBAs were hired and in 1980 another two were added, all from Midwestern business schools. In 1981, the firm did no MBA hiring out of school, hoping to capitalize on its Hart's scholar program. Chuck commented on this strategy of drawing from various pools of management talent.

> Last year we didn't hire any MBAs. It was a mistake. I thought we'd try a Hart's scholar program one year, and an MBA the next year and keep alternating every other year. I forgot that it takes longer to get an MBA if you are working part-time. We started the Hart's scholar program because we wanted to attract some bright, interesting people who would not naturally think of

this industry. We think BAs in liberal arts are well rounded and refreshing. I'm not interest in a lockstep, narrow approach to recruiting. I like multiple sources.

As of 1981, the company had 35 persons with MBA or equivalent degrees in its operations. In the academic year 1981–82, the company intends to hire two to four MBAs. This approach reflects the company's philosophy of "keeping the demand high and the supply low" (within the firm), thus guaranteeing each new recruit the maximum of attention and visibility.

The Company's Training Program (see Appendix 4)

During the 15 months of the training program the trainees work on various project assignments determined by each function, such as site selection for finance and administration group of the retail division. The goal of the program is, according to Chuck Brazik, "to get them familiar with the different corporate environments." He added, "If we hire them to fill specific jobs, they probably would all be placed in line operations, but they would lack the company overview we provide them through the rotation program." Human resources directors closely supervise the new recruits, meeting with them on a monthly basis to discuss their career choice within the company upon completion. The program is designed on a rotation basis between the three major areas of the company: retailing, manufacturing, and corporate. It is open-ended in its nature and doesn't require specialization. The choice of assignment after the training program is done through an open-bidding process within the company.

All five MBAs recruited in 1979 and 1980 currently hold positions especially created for them, including: assistant to the VP of

---

[13] From the company's document on the "Hart's Scholar Program," p. 1.

finance; industry planning analyst—Retail Division; assistant to the chairman—Clothing Division; and special projects manager—assistant to the president of a clothing manufacturing unit. Chuck seemed disappointed at this outcome. "I wanted them to leave our training program and move directly to responsible operating positions. I don't want to play big brother with their careers, following them through the organization until they reach such positions." He added, "If we find that these MBAs who were placed in specially created staff positions a couple of years ago are still not being moved into more responsible operating jobs, we'll have to change the program. If we scrap the program, whereby we recruit directly from schools, and begin to recruit MBAs who have been out of school in other companies for a few years, we might be able to solve the problem."

Opportunities for MBAs with Hart, Schaffer & Marx

Of the approximately 450 to 500 middle and upper-level managers there are 35 MBAs.[14] One such executive, Bill McNally, executive vice president of the Men's Apparel Group, a graduate of a well-known Eastern business school, commented on MBA opportunities with the company:

> I think there are excellent opportunities for MBAs within the two industries we serve generally and within our company specifically.
>
> The apparel industry is a big one—$60 billion in 1980. Retailing is also a big industry, employing as many people as all domestic manufacturing industries combined.
>
> Historically, apparel manufacturing and retailing companies have been dominated

by entrepreneurs. The strength of these entrepreneurs has been to create and develop companies. As the companies they created become larger and more complicated, they require professional management; but, unfortunately, it is the rare entrepreneur who has attracted professional managers. Today the entrepreneur of many apparel and retail companies in the industry are nearing retirement age and there is a dearth of professional management in the industry to replace them. The trend toward concentration and acquisitions in apparel and retail companies portends even greater opportunities in these industries for MBAs.

The industries are mature in terms of volume and are steeped in tradition; they may not be glamorous to an MBA who likes structured environments and advancement opportunities stemming from growth. But the industries are changing and companies in them are faced with many difficult problems of the sort MBAs are trained to solve. Moreover, an MBA will generally not face the kind of peer competition he or she will find in a packaged goods company or a consulting firm.

In our own company, while we have the strongest management in our segment of the industry, there is a shortage of management talent. During the past two years, we created eight brand manager positions in our manufacturing group and six regional manager positions in our retail group, and some of them are still open for lack of qualified candidates. In addition, there are no backups to some of our key executives. Moreover, other companies look to our company for management, so in the future we can project a number of positions to be filled, even though we are growing only at about the rate of the general economy.

But I don't want to draw an overly bright picture. Things can be quite frustrating in these industries, especially at the outset. In my own situation, I was quite frustrated for the first few years in HS&M. There were many times I thought about quitting. But I

[14] The company has a grand total of 21,000 employees.

really liked my boss and the people here and felt I was making a real contribution, so I stayed. And things have turned out very well.

Recruiting from the "Prestige" Schools

Chuck Brazik presented his experiences of recruiting at well-known business schools in the following discussion:

When we recruited MBAs from prestige schools we found some of them to be arrogant. They wanted more money than our plant managers and consistently wanted to know when they would become president. This attitude doesn't surface as much at Indiana, Illinois, or Michigan State as it does at Harvard, Chicago, Stanford, Wharton, and Northwestern.

Added Bob Mayer, manager of college relations:

This year we will be going to Chicago and Northwestern, but we don't expect to find someone there as readily as at the less-prestigious schools. We also planned on recruiting at Harvard, because if you are running what you consider to be a quality business, the Harvard name is always mentioned. But we couldn't get a schedule listing until mid-April and that's too late. It is really competitive to get on the schedules at these schools, for both the companies and the students.

Another major consideration to the company has to do with the cost of hiring MBAs from prestige schools. Said Bob Mayer: "We saw last year's figures for Harvard, and we have a difficult time justifying that in our company." To the suggestion to try and "sell" Chicago and the company culture to interesting, self-starter-type MBAs, as a compensation for lower salary levels, Bob responded:

We don't believe in the cocktail party approach to recruiting. We think it puts unfair pressure on the students' schedules and too much stress on them once they're there.

Added Chuck Brazik:

I believe in informing them realistically about the company. If I try to sell the company to them, we'll simply end up suffering high turnover. We never discuss salary until later stages, but we do keep it competitive to high for the industry. We believe in paying all trainees the same wage since they are doing the same work. In fact, all the way through management we pay for the job and not for the individual. My gut feeling is, however, that sometimes you can go to a prestige school and hire a good quality person at not so much more than a second-tier school. Another difference is that in the top business schools people are, on the average, older and have had several years of business experience.

Maggy Siegel, one of the two MBAs who joined the firm in 1980, added another dimension to the discussion:

Another problem we face in recruiting is that a lot of people don't know what we're about. Either they know we're in the retailing business, but don't know what stores we own, or they think we just manufacture suits. Our stores all have different names and we make several suit lines other than what's labeled "Hart, Schaffner & Marx."

What Should HS&M Do?

In discussing the different strategies for MBA hiring and for their effective use within the firm, the following opinions emerged:

Bob Mayer:

If we decide we need these people, we will have to come up with a means to pay for them. But that is not the main problem. I don't think that we need the very top of the class, but rather someone who knows how to ask questions, is a self-starter, and who would dare try new ways. Possessing "street smarts" is very important in this business.

Bill McNally proposed a different approach for the company:

I think that the MBAs we want to hire are definitely the self-starter types, but maybe we would be better off with those who have been out of school for a few years and have had a reality test. We should wait until those folks whose expectations are too high learn that they have to carry out mundane assignments, have their ideas fall on deaf ears, do their own Xeroxing, and learn they're not going to get promoted to a meaningful job in their first few months. These malcontents could be a good resource for us. They are still very bright and ambitious but by now they have become realistic about their expectations.

Chuck Brazik, in response to this suggestion, warned:

We must be cautious in who we hire, for internal acceptance of these folk who have been here for years is hard to get. The MBAs represent the corporate function, in some sense, as ambassadors. That's why I'd rather have folks grow with us. You cannot enter here without certain specific skills and expect to be handed high-level responsibility.

Maggy Siegel's (Indiana University MBA '80) Career with HS&M—A Typical Example?

When Maggy Siegel was about to graduate from Indiana University's MBA program, she knew she wanted to be in the retail or apparel industry. Hart, Schaffner & Marx was one of the few retail companies to

interview at IU that offered a training program designed just for MBAs. As spots on the interview schedule were extremely competitive, she had to wait all night in front of the placement office to guarantee her an opportunity to interview with the company. Her efforts paid off and she was hired by Chuck Brazik for a special 15-month rotation program designed according to her personal needs and the needs of the company.

The casewriters met with Maggy for a brief discussion:

Q: Could you give us your perspective on the one year you have been with Hart's?

A: I am quite pleased with my experiences in my first year at Hart's. My first rotation was in retail planning working on the division's five-year plan. This assignment enabled me to work closely with the company's financial statements, learn about the types of information collected at corporate level, familiarize myself with our accounting procedures, and gain an overall picture of the division's past, present, and future.

My second rotation was at Chas. A. Stevens, our largest women's specialty store with 27 locations all over Chicago. I spent six weeks as a "floating manager" between three locations. I was opening and closing the store, counting cash, selling, arranging merchandise, and, in general, running the store. It was especially crazy while I was there as it was right before Christmas. I also spent three weeks with a divisional merchandise manager, and two weeks in the promotion department. All in all, it was a great opportunity and one that has been extremely helpful in my current position.

From there I went into manufacturing division and fell into a great project. We had just purchased an existing plant in Winchester, Kentucky. I was assigned to acquaint the newly hired personnel manager with Hart's procedures and policies and to make his transition from the former company to our company as painless as possible.

In May, 1981, a regular position opened up with my first boss as a planning analyst with the Retail Division. I left the training program after nine months and have since worked on a variety of projects ranging from strategic planning to analyzing some of our problem stores. I report directly to the vice president of retail planning.

Q: You said you advanced fast. What does "fast" mean for you in this company?

A: Although I was hired for a 15-month training program, I was offered the opportunity to assume a regular position after nine months. I could have prolonged my training and taken another rotation with a different department or division, but I felt this was a worthwhile experience which I didn't want to pass us.

Q: Where do you see yourself going in the coming five years?

A: In accepting this position in planning, the thought occurred to me that I might have been entering a staff function too soon, especially in retailing. You really have to prove yourself at an operational level before being promoted to a responsible position at the corporate level. Fortunately, I'm situated so that I have a lot of visibility with senior management and I'm working towards my next position at the operational level. By gaining a broad exposure to the many components of Hart, Schaffner & Marx, I am sure that I'll be able to rapidly assume general management responsibilities in the future. Right now I feel I am in a unique position in the Retail Division and that I'm very much in control of my future with Hart, Schaffner & Marx.

Appendix 1

Apparel
Yardsticks of Management Performance

| | Profitability | | | | | | | Growth | | | |
| | Return on Equity | | | Debt/ Equity Ratio | Return on Total Capital | | | Net Profit Margin | Sales | | Earnings per Share | |
Company	5-Year Average	5-Year Rank	Latest 12 Months		Latest 12 Months	5-Year Rank	5-Year Average		5-Year Average	5-Year Rank	5-Year Average	5-Year Rank
Apparel:												
Levi Strauss	31.0%	1	29.5%	0.2	25.8%	1	25.7%	8.4%	24.2%	1	37.7%	1
Blue Bell	24.0	2	19.7	0.2	16.5	2	19.7	6.1	19.0	2	27.1	2
VF Corp	16.7	3	15.7	0.2	13.2	3	14.3	6.3	10.2	5	11.6	4
Interco	14.5	4	13.7	0.2	12.3	4	13.5	4.9	11.2	4	8.6	5
Hanes	12.1	5	16.9	0.4	12.8	5	9.9	5.0	12.3	3	17.2	3
Kellwood	11.9	6	13.9	0.9	9.4	6	8.9	2.0	8.6	7	3.8	7
Hart, Schaff & Marx	7.6	7	9.4	0.3	8.1	7	6.8	2.9	6.1	10	0.0	8
Cluett, Peabody	6.9	8	11.1	0.2	9.4	8	6.4	3.4	2.1	13	−1.6	9
Manhattan Industries	6.0	9	13.7	0.3	9.8	9	5.3	2.2	7.2	8	−7.3	10
Jonathan Logan	5.5	10	5.8	0.3	5.0	10	4.9	2.6	3.9	11	−10.3	11
Rapid-American	2.3	11	24.3	2.8	8.5	11	4.6	1.8	0.3	14	−12.8	13
Phillips-Van Heusen	1.4	12	1.8	0.6	1.9	12	1.9	0.4	3.8	12	−27.2	12
Warnaco	def	13	10.4	0.7	7.2	13	1.5	1.8	7.0	9	P–D	14
Genesco	def	14	def	1.7	4.1	14	def	0.3	−3.4	15	P–D	14
Oxford Industries	**		10.2	0.4	9.3		**	3.0	9.3	6	5.4††	6
Medians	7.3		13.7	0.3	9.4		6.6	2.9	7.2		3.8	

Appendix 1 (concluded)

Apparel
Yardsticks of Management Performance

Company	Profitability								Growth			
	Return on Equity			Debt/ Equity Ratio	Return on Total Capital			Net Profit Margin	Sales		Earnings per Share	
	5-Year Average	5-Year Rank	Latest 12 Months		Latest 12 Months	5-Year Rank	5-Year Average		5-Year Average	5-Year Rank	5-Year Average	5-Year Rank
Textiles:												
Cone Mills	16.4%	1	16.6%	0.2	15.0%	1	14.1%	6.1%	11.5%	3	36.4%	1
Riegel Textile	14.0	2	13.0	0.3	9.7	4	10.0	4.4	10.0	5	25.5	3
Graniteville	13.6	3	5.4	0.2	4.9	2	11.4	2.0	13.7	1	19.6	5
Collins & Aikman	12.0	4	13.7	0.1	11.6	5	9.9	4.2	9.8	6	1.3	12
Fieldcrest Mills	11.9	5	17.8	0.6	12.2	7	8.4	4.6	9.0	8	7.9	8
Reeves Brothers	11.7	6	14.8	0.3	11.9	3	10.0	4.4	6.4	12	10.7	7
West Point-Pepperell	11.0	7	12.1	0.4	9.4	6	9.5	3.7	12.1	2	18.7	6
Burlington Inds	8.9	8	7.0	0.4	5.8	8	7.0	2.9	4.3	13	3.6	11
J P Stevens	8.2	9	7.4	0.6	5.8	11	6.6	2.2	7.5	9	20.5	4
Avondale Mills	7.2	10	6.6	0.0	6.3	9	7.0	2.2	9.6	7	-0.1	13
Cannon Mills	7.0	11	8.3	0.0	8.3	10	6.9	4.3	6.7	11	4.9	9
Spring Mills	4.8	12	5.6	0.2	5.0	12	4.3	2.5	10.3	4	4.2	10
Dan River	4.7	13	6.9	0.5	5.4	13	4.1	2.1	6.8	10	28.2	2
M Lowenstein & Sons	0.0	14	4.5	0.7	4.4	14	1.7	1.0	3.9	14	P-D	14
United Merch & Mfrs	def	15	13.3	5.3	2.4	15	def	0.9	2.1	15	P-D	14
Medians	8.9		8.3	0.3	6.3		7.0	2.9	9.0		7.9	
Shoes:												
Melville	26.4%	1	27.5%	0.2	25.9%	1	24.0%	4.9%	17.8%	1	17.5%	2
SCOA Industries	20.5	2	22.6	0.8	13.7	3	12.7	2.1	13.6	2	50.7	1
McDonough	17.3	3	17.2	0.7	14.9	2	13.9	5.0	9.1	5	16.3	3
United States Shoe	15.3	4	17.9	0.5	13.6	4	11.7	3.9	10.8	3	10.8	4
Brown Group	10.9	5	14.3	0.4	11.4	5	8.9	3.4	10.3	4	1.8	5

Medians	17.3	17.9	0.4	13.7	12.7	3.9	10.8	16.3
Industry Medians	11.0	13.3	0.3	9.4	8.7	3.0	9.1	5.4
All-industry Medians	13.9	15.4	0.4	10.5	10.2	5.0	12.9	12.6

Note: †Three-year growth. P-D Profit to deficit. def Deficit. **Not available; not ranked.

Reprinted by permission, FORBES Magazine, January 8, 1979, p. 152.

Appendix 2

Apparel
Yardsticks of Management Performance

	Profitability								Growth			
	Return on Equity				Return on Total Capital				Sales		Earnings per Share	
Company	5-Year Average	5-Year Rank	Latest 12 Months	Debt/ Equity Ratio	Latest 12 Months	5-Year Rank	5-Year Average	Net Profit Margin	5-Year Average	5-Year Rank	5-Year Average	5-Year Rank
Clothing:												
Levi Strauss	34.3%	1	31.4%	0.2	27.7%	1	29.3%	8.2%	21.6%	1	38.5%	1
Blue Bell	25.5	2	19.0	0.1	17.2	2	21.5	4.9	18.1	2	27.6	2
VF Corp	16.7	3	19.3	0.1	16.5	3	14.3	7.0	8.4	4	9.2	5
Interco	14.8	4	14.5	0.2	12.0	4	13.3	5.3	10.7	3	9.3	4
Rapid-American	12.9	5	7.8	2.7	6.5	8	6.4	1.0	0.1	12	D–P	
Kellwood	12.1	6	6.6	0.9	5.5	5	8.8	0.9	8.3	5	6.8	7
Cluett, Peabody	10.3	7	9.0	0.4	7.2	6	8.7	2.5	3.7	10	23.2	3
Hart, Schaff & Marx	9.4	8	10.4	0.3	9.2	7	8.2	3.4	6.0	5	8.7	6
Phillips-Van Heusen	5.6	9	6.1	0.7	5.3	10	4.7	1.4	3.5	11	5.4	6
Warnaco	5.2	10	16.9	0.5	11.9	9	5.0	3.3	6.9	7	−11.4	9
Manhattan Industries	def	11	def	1.1	def	11	3.1	def	8.3	6	P–D	10
Jonathan Logan	def	12	def	0.3	def	13	def	def	4.7	9	P–D	10
Genesco	def	13	2.0	1.4	4.2	12	def	0.6	−4.9	13	D–D	12
Medians	10.3		9.0	0.4	7.2		8.2	2.5	6.9		7.8	

Textiles:

	(value)	(rank)	(value)	(rank)	(value)	(value)	(rank)	(value)	(rank)	(value)	(value)	(rank)	(value)	(rank)
Cone Mills	18.1%	1	18.3%	1	0.1	16.8%	1	15.9%	1	7.2%	11.2%	2	27.1%	2
Fieldcrest Mills	15.8	2	11.9	2	0.5	8.9	3	11.2	3	3.4	10.6	3	20.3	3
Riegel Textile	14.9	3	15.2	3	0.3	11.0	4	10.8	4	4.2	9.8	6	18.0	4
Reeves Brothers	14.5	4	13.8	4	0.2	11.7	2	12.1	2	5.0	9.3	9	16.7	5
Collins & Aikman	11.8	5	7.3	5	0.3	5.6	5	9.8	5	2.3	10.4	4	5.2	11
West Point-Pepperell	11.7	6	14.6	6	0.4	11.1	6	9.6	6	3.4	14.7	1	14.7	7
Dan River	9.7	7	11.7	7	0.4	8.4	10	7.0	10	3.5	6.8	12	39.4	1
Graniteville	9.3	8	11.7	8	0.3	9.2	8	7.9	8	3.6	10.2	5	1.4	12
Cannon Mills	8.9	9	9.2	9	0.0	9.1	7	8.8	7	4.6	8.5	11	11.7	9
JP Stevens	8.8	10	8.3	10	0.6	6.7	9	7.0	9	2.3	9.4	7	16.4	6
Burlington Inds	8.6	11	7.7	11	0.4	6.4	10	7.0	10	2.8	5.0	13	5.5	10
Springs Mills	7.7	12	9.3	12	0.2	7.6	12	6.6	12	3.5	9.3	8	13.9	8
Avondale Mills	6.5	13	8.1	13	0.0	7.8	13	6.3	13	2.3	9.1	10	-1.9	13
M Lowenstein	1.6	14	0.5	14	0.6	2.5	14	2.8	14	0.1	3.5	14	-9.4	14
United Merch & Mfrs	def	15	def	15	4.0	def	15	def	15	def	-3.7	15	P–D	15
Medians	9.3		9.3		0.3	8.4		7.9		3.4	9.3		13.9	

Shoes:

	(value)	(rank)	(value)	(rank)	(value)	(value)	(rank)	(value)	(rank)	(value)	(value)	(rank)	(value)	(rank)
SCOA Industries	29.4%	1	28.6%	1	1.0	16.5%	2	17.3%	2	3.3%	15.1%	2	64.3%	1
Melville	28.7	2	25.0	2	0.2	23.7	1	26.9	1	4.8	19.8	1	22.2	2
United States Shoe	17.6	3	18.3	3	0.3	14.5	4	13.5	4	4.0	12.5	3	16.6	3
McDonough	16.4	4	11.4	4	0.1	10.5	3	14.1	3	3.7	9.4	5	13.0	4
Brown Group	14.4	5	16.0	5	0.4	12.7	5	11.5	5	3.6	9.7	4	11.6	5
Medians	17.6		18.3		0.3	14.5		14.1		3.7	12.5		16.6	
Industry medians	11.7		11.4		0.3	9.1		8.8		3.4	9.3		11.7	
All industry medians	15.8		16.1		0.4	11.0		11.1		5.0	14.3		13.9	

Note: Explanation of Yardsticks calculations on page 49.   P–D: profit to deficit.   D–D: deficit to deficit.   D–P: deficit to profit; not ranked   def: deficit.

Appendix 3
Hart's Scholar Program

Overall Objective

To recruit, hire, and develop one or two outstanding liberal arts degreed students who will attend Northwestern University's J.L. Kellogg Graduate School of Management Evening MBA Managers Program and participate concurrently in the Hart, Schaffner & Marx MBA Training Program.

Overall Purpose

As an alternative to our graduate MBA Development Program, these students will become part of HS&M management reserve and later will be placed by way of the company's succession planning process.

Eligibility

Men and women holding a bachelor's degree from an accredited college or university are eligible for consideration. Prior study in business or economics is not a requirement for admission. Social sciences and humanities are typical backgrounds. It is up to the student to gain admission to Northwestern University. Final admission to the Hart's Scholar Program is contingent upon Northwestern University's acceptance to their program.

Tuition, Books, and Fees

Hart, Schaffner & Marx will provide all tuition, fees, and books for course requirements for the MBA degree program and reimbursement for application to the J. L. Kellogg Graduate School Managers Program.

Hart's Scholar and MBA Training Program Objectives

The objective of the HS&M MBA Training Program and the Hart's Scholar Program is to develop individuals for future positions of responsibility within the organization. After 18 months' participation in the training program and during the educational process, the training program will terminate and participants will be assigned to a regular position in the Chicago area so that the completion of the MBA degree will not be affected. The training program completion will be achieved by orienting participants to all facets of company operations through rotating assignments in each of the following sections (not necessarily in this order):

- Men's specialty store (Baskin)
- Women's specialty store (Chas. A. Stevens)
- Retail Division
- Manufacturing (Clothes Division, Jaymar-Ruby, M. Wile)
- Corporate business planning
- Corporate human resources
- Special projects

Most assignments will vary in length from 3–9 months and the overall program will not exceed 18 months. It will entail certain learning activities, highlighted in more detail in the MBA Program Manual. Participants will work as "assistants" to the "head" of each training unit.

The program has been designed to sharpen management skills while learning the technical aspects of the job. Since managers are "on their own" when it comes to determining daily objectives and achievements, scheduling their own hours, determining what work needs to be completed, and analyzing their own success through the results they achieve, participants will also be "on their own."

During the program, participants will be required to complete a number of projects designed to introduce them to various aspects of our industry; completing them will enhance their management capabilities. The effort put forth in each assignment and the standard of excellence set for the participant will determine how much is learned. In many cases, each participant will be exposed to the basics of an area and then be required to apply this knowledge or skill to another project. It is important at this stage to be watchful for similarities of procedures; this will help reduce development and training during the learning process.

Another vitally important aspect that must be kept in mind is learning what motivates people to perform well. As a future executive, each participant will be responsible for assuring that each person under his or her supervision does excellent work. Knowledge of what encourages or discourages productivity will lead to optimum results.

The area assignments should be considered a "living laboratory" in which the participant conducts "experiments" leading to learning. Sponsors are not responsible for supervising the daily activities of each participant; however, they will want to review the schedule at the start of each week to point out learning objectives that may coincide. Use of the sponsor's and other company executives' experience and working knowledge aids the participants in the completion of their projects.

Admission, Registration, and Financial Information

Along with this document the Northwestern University J.L. Kellogg Graduate School of Management Managers Program for 1980–81 is available through your college's placement director and should be read thoroughly by each applicant to this program.

Admission. Admissions may be granted for a student to begin studies in any term. Applications are processed on a continuous basis in order of receipt and should be submitted as early as possible. Applications will be coordinated through the corporate manager–training of Hart, Schaffner & Marx.

Criteria for Admission. In the selection process, the admissions committee attempts to identify the applicant's scholastic ability, qualities of character and motivation, evidence of leadership, and administrative promise. Both the applicant and the school are best served by an admission policy that seeks reasonable assurance in scholastic competence and promise of effective management performance. The admissions committee carefully appraises the following:

1. *Academic Record.* Undergraduate and any other collegiate record reflected in the official transcripts of all colleges and universities previously attended are examined not only for the overall grade average, but also for trends of grades in areas of particular scholastic strengths. The committee recognizes the differences in the scholastic maturity of the applicant and variations of the mastering of a difficult subject matter. Final transcripts of the total undergraduate credit and any advance study are required of all admitted students.

2. *Graduate Management Admission Test* (formerly Admission Test for Graduate Study in Business). All applicants, including students from other countries, are requested to take the GMAT, which is given in test centers throughout the United States and in some foreign countries. Complete information can be obtained from the Educational Testing Service, Princeton, New Jersey 08540. Applications to take the test must reach the Educational Testing Service at least two weeks before the desired test date. Scores are used as part of the evidence of academic ability.

3. *References.* At least two letters of reference are requested. Ordinarily the applicant should obtain these from faculty or administrative staff members from his or her undergraduate school. References from associates, business, or military which serve the mutual interest of the applicants and the school may be substituted or added.

4. *Provisional Admission.* Applicants who have not had an opportunity to take the GMAT may be permitted, in some cases, to register on a provisional basis. The strength of all of the other credentials must be outstanding and, in these cases, the applicant is required to take the test the next time it is given.

5. *Interview.* Whenever possible a personal interview with a representative of the school is helpful. With respect to the Hart's Scholar Program, an interview with Dean Don P. Jacobs, dean of the Graduate School of Management, Northwestern University, would be required. An interview may be arranged by telephoning the corporate manager–training of Hart, Schaffner & Marx at 312/372-6300.

6. *Transfer of Credit.* Students who are transferred to the Chicago area after having completed coursework at an AACSB-accredited graduate school of management or business may receive credit toward the degree for up to a total of four courses. Courses presented for transfer of credit must be similar in content to those offered at Northwestern.

7. *Full-time Study.* There is no provision for full-time study in the program described in this procedure or in the Northwestern University bulletin. A student ordinarily is not permitted to enroll for more than 2 courses a quarter or to complete the degree requirement in less than 10 quarters of study. The Hart's Scholar Program will follow this 10-quarter program of evening study.

The Manager's Program, Northwestern University J.L. Kellogg Graduate School of Management, 1980–81, booklet is available in the student placement office through the placement director and should be reviewed prior to considering employment with Hart, Schaffner & Marx for the Hart's Scholar Program. Students will be interviewed by the corporate manager–training; corporate director, management development and training; and the corporate director, human resources; as well as the dean of J.L. Kellogg Graduate School of Management, Northwestern University. Upon completion of all eligibility requirements (see flow chart, p. 6) and selection by Hart, Schaffner & Marx, students will then be afforded the opportunity to participate in this program.

Continued participation in the Hart's Scholar Program requires participants maintain academic standards of the school and acceptable job performance.

Appendix 4
Hart, Schaffner & Marx
MBA Training Program: Objectives and Orientation

The objective of the Hart, Schaffner & Marx MBA training program is to train you for future positions of responsibility within the organization.

This will be achieved by exposing you to all facets of company operation through rotating assignments in each of the following sections (not necessarily in this order):

- Men's specialty store (Baskin)
- Women's specialty store (Chas. A. Stevens)
- Retail Division
- Manufacturing (Clothes Division)
- Corporate business planning
- Corporate human resources

Each assignment will last approximately three to six months and entail certain learning activities, which are explained in greater detail in the sections that follow. You will be "assistants to" the head of each training unit.

The program has been designed to sharpen your management skills while you are learning the technical aspects of the job. Since managers are "on their own" when it comes to determining daily objectives and achievements, you will be responsible for scheduling your hours, determining what work needs to be completed on a given day, and analyzing your success through the results.

During the program you will be required to complete a number of projects designed to introduce you to the various aspects of our industry; completing them will enhance your management capabilities. The effort you put into each assignment and the standards of excellence you set for yourself will determine how much you learn. In many cases you will be exposed to the basics of an area and then be required to apply this knowledge or skill to another project. Always be watchful for similarities in procedures; this will help reduce your training time and expedite the learning process.

Another vitally important thing you must learn is what motivates people to perform well. As a future executive, you will be responsible for ensuring that your people do excellent work. Knowledge of what encourages or discourages production will lead to optimum results.

Your training period should be considered a "living laboratory" in which you conduct "experiments" leading to learning.

Your sponsors are not responsible for supervising your daily activities; however, they will want to review your planned schedule at the start of each week to point out learning experiences that may coincide. Use your sponsor's or company executive's experience and working knowledge to aid you in your projects. Repay them for their efforts and valuable time by providing high-quality work and an example of industriousness.

Appendix 5
Investment News & Views*

Pierre Cardin to Johnny Carson

New Lines Help Hart, Schaffner & Marx Fashion Smart Gains

Edited by Steven S. Anreder

Hart, Schaffner & Marx, the men's clothing manufacturer and retailer, seems well suited to score smart sales and earnings gains this fiscal year (ending November 30, 1981). Among the things going for it: a new acquisition marking its first entry into women's tailored wear; new, more modern production facilities; broader offerings, particularly in lower-priced lines; and a solid market position.

In fiscal 1980, HS&M posted 7 percent gains in both sales and earnings—gross ahead to $674.9 million, from $630.7 million, and net rising to $2.63 a share, from $2.45—marking the company's fifth straight year of profits growth.

This year should be No. 6. Hart, Schaffner's retail outlets experienced a flat first half, but have snapped back smartly with sales gains of 13% in the second quarter and like advances in both June and July. Moreover, thanks to strong unit volume, dollar sales on the manufacturing side are running 10 percent above year-ago levels.

At the half-year mark, Hart, Schaffner's sales were ahead 20 percent to $392 million and earnings had gained 13 percent to $13.8 million, or $1.60 a share. (Included in this year's figures are results of a recent acquisition, Country Miss, a women's apparel firm, which chipped in 7 cents a share to first half net. When the books are closed on November 30, HS&M Chairman Jerome S. Gore expects sales totaling $800 million, up 19 percent over fiscal 1980, and earnings of $25–$26 million or $2.95–$3 a share, a gain of better than 12 percent.

The key to Hart, Schaffner & Marx's performance is the matchup of its own quality reputation with major designer labels and famous-name labels, from the Johnny Carson and Playboy lines on the lower end to Austin Reed and Pierre Cardin in the center to Hickey-Freeman at the top.

Hart, Schaffner & Marx boasts a strong position in the $300–$500 suit market and a lesser but still respectable one in the $175–$250 area, Gore points out. However, though roughly one third of men's suits sold industry-wide retail for less than $100, the company has no position to speak of in the low end. HS&M last year did add a Playboy line of clothing, pushing into the $100–$150 retail market, which is directed more at the youth market than other lines. And the Johnny Carson line this fall will offer a three-piece suit that will carry a $135 price tag. Nonetheless, Gore stresses that it would be a mistake to brand those moves as a shift in strategy.

"Any attempt on our part to establish a position in the $100–$150 market for suits is only that—an attempt to establish a position—and not in any way an attempt to lessen our thrust of our determination to retain our position as a very important manufacturer and retailer of quality men's apparel," he says.

The Playboy and Johnny Carson lines, plus house-label clothes for retailers, are produced at the company's new Whiteville, North Carolina, plant. That facility, designed for efficiency and technology more than traditional handwork, will be used for the low-priced end of the company's line.

Gore maintains that such clothing still includes good, tailored suits, but they boast less overall quality than the higher-priced garments.

On the upper end, a new facility is being added this year to handle cutting for clothing carrying the Hart, Schaffner & Marx label. Located near the division's distribution center, close to Chicago's O'Hare International Airport, it is expected to provide important savings compared with the outmoded downtown headquarters building, where operations were conducted on several floors and necessitated constant shifting of goods. That building has been sold, and corporate offices already have been moved to another downtown Chicago location.

Funding new plants is not difficult for Hart, Schaffner. Long-term debt at the end of the last fiscal year was $54 million, just 19 percent of capitalization, including capital leases. Investment in fixed assets this year will be in the $28–$30 million range—roughly twice the $14.7 million spent in fiscal 1980. In addition, proceeds from sale of the Chicago building are expected to be in excess of the $2 million at which it was carried on the books. Together with $8 million realized from floating an industrial-revenue bond (at a floating rate that is roughly three quarters of prime), HS&M will have more than sufficient funds to pay for equipping the new facility and making the move.

Solid returns on those investments are likely. HS&M customers are less prone to layoffs, giving the firm a stable sales base. At the same time, sharp growth seems to lie ahead, as the baby boom ages. Males aged 35–54 represent "the backbone of our customers," Gore points out, adding that the group is expected to expand 28 percent during the 1980s—versus a 4 percent gain in the last decade.

To make sure it gets its share, HS&M is broadening its lines. Thus, HS&M Clothes include both designer and branded labels, such as the Grande Lux line of suits, retailing for $350–$400, which this fall will carry both the Christian Dior and the Hart, Schaffner & Marx labels. Last fall, the company introduced the Christian Dior label in a line that doesn't carry the HS&M badge—pricing those in the $225–$275 retail range. The more moderately priced Christian Dior Monsieur line is carving out a growing niche, with sales of suits and sport coats expected to reach 200,000 per year by the end of 1983.

The Johnny Carson line similarly is being widened. Besides offering a new $135 suit, the line this year also will sport its first $300 garment. The Carson label traditionally sold in the $150–$250 range. Orders are up 50 percent for Carson this fall, reflecting the new $135-suit line, and strong interest already is apparent for next spring, Gore says.

Also holding promise of smart growth is the new Country Miss, Inc. subsidiary, added to HS&M in January. The purchase of 80 percent of the firm—three top execs own the other 20 percent—brought Hart, Schaffner & Marx into the women's apparel market as a manufacturer for the first time. Country Miss earned $2.6 million in 1980 on sales of $41 million, and was acquired for $12 million in cash. Its earnings would have added $1 million to HS&M net, after interest deductions, and would have boosted earnings per share to $2.75 from $2.63 had the subsidiary been acquired at the start of fiscal 1980.

In the 11 months that Country Miss will be on the books this fiscal year, sales are expected to be $50 million; they are expected to grow to $100 million in 1985, Gore forecasts. Country Miss, which, as noted, added 7 cents per share to first-half earnings, is likely to make at least the same contribution in the second half.

Women's sportswear, including a variety of outfits that can be classified as office apparel, represents a major growth field. Similar to the men's suits market, the big buyers of such clothing are in the 25–50 age group, a group that is expected to grow in the '80s, Gore says. Country Miss is poised to cash in, with more than 5,000 retailer accounts across the U.S. The firm's new Weathervane collection of sportswear, introduced last year, is gaining ready acceptance among those customers.

Hart, Schaffner & Marx sells its line to independent retailers and department store chains as well as via its own outlets. Retailing operations contributed $403.7 million in sales in fiscal 1980, about 60 percent of the corporate total, but yielded only 43 percent of pretax operating earnings.

Company-owned retailers include Wallachs in the East, Zachry in the South, Baskin in the Midwest, and Silverwoods in the West. In all, HS&M operates more than 275 company-owned retail stores in 66 metropolitan areas.

In order to improve the return on its retail investment, control was put in the hands of five regional vice presidents; previously, each group of stores had a president who reported to the retail division. The parent also combined some small store groups, in some cases changing the names of the stores, to take advantage of advertising and buying economies. HS&M plans to open 20 outlets this year, closing two or three, Gore says. Last year, 14 stores were opened and 13 closed.

Profitability will be stressed, rather than sales, in expanding retail operations, according to Gore. The company's bonus plan is being geared in that direction also, rewarding higher returns on assets for divisional executives and return on equity for corporate officers.

In 1969, after a series of retail expansions, the Justice Department filed an antitrust action against Hart, Schaffner that resulted in some divestitures and a prohibition against acquisitions. When the consent decree expired last year, HS&M's Klopfenstein retail chain purchased Bishop's, a men's store in Salem, Oregon. Gore says he doesn't believe future acquisition activities would trigger antitrust problems.

Gore believes that the regional executive approach and consolidation efforts will help boost the performance of its retail outlets. Last year, the division posted only a 9 percent return on investment—an improvement but still less than the 12 percent return for the manufacturing division.

Also adding strength, he says, is a new management team that took over when Gore moved from president and CEO to chairman and CEO upon the retirement of John D. Gray in April. A key goal for the new team is to improve return on equity. With some drag from retailing, the return was 10.3 percent in 1980. Gore looks for an 11 percent return this year, and 12 percent in fiscal 1982.

—MICHAEL ROSENBAUM

CASE 5
C. EDWARD ACKER*
Gregory Kenny and
Jeffrey A. Sonnenfeld

On August 27, 1981, Edward Acker stunned a meeting of New York security analysts by

announcing that he was quitting as chairman of Air Florida to take another job. "I talked to Cunard Lines and told them I was interested in a job as captain of the Titanic," Acker quipped. "They informed me that I was 50 years too late. Not having that challenge available, I decided to try to find one comparable to that. And so, I am accepting the chairmanship of a company called Pan American World Airways."[1] When asked why he would leave a strong carrier of his own shaping for a foundering line, Acker said, "I've always thought of Pan Am as the epitome of the business, and that its chairman would have an exciting job in good times or in bad; now that times are so bad, I guess that is especially true."[2] Over the last decade, indeed over its entire history, America's flag carrier to the world has had its share of color and turbulence in the executive suite and periods of enormous economic difficulties.

Company Culture, Its Chairmen, and Operation

The early years of the company were strongly influenced by the personality of its founder, Juan Trippe. Trippe was noted for his tremendous drive, by his demand that the impossible be accomplished, and by his penchant for assigning short deadlines.[3] Trippe's enormous presence was felt even when he had been pushed out of the chairmanship in favor of banker Cornelius Vanderbilt Whitney in 1939. Following his removal, the unhappy Trippe was assigned to a small office not far from his former suite now occupied by Whitney. From this vantage point, Trippe took note of which of his former subordinates visited Whitney and

---

[1] *Newsweek*, September 7, 1981, p. 62.

[2] *New York Times*, August 27, 1981, p. 1.

[3] Robert Daley, *An American Saga; Juan Trippe and His Pan AM Empire* (New York: Random House, 1980).

the frequency of their visits. Trippe carried his intimidating tactics into corporate meeting rooms. He would take a seat at the other end of the table from Whitney and observe a self-imposed stony silence. Other members of the corporate team found themselves unable to be responsive to Whitney under Trippe's stare. In desperation, Whitney turned to an outside board member, Thomas Morgan, for help in breaking the impasse with Trippe. Morgan was to assume an active role in running the company on Whitney's behalf. However, he was no more successful than Whitney, as he found company records, historical commitments, and future obligations often locked safely in Trippe's head. Without Trippe's cooperation, Morgan, like Whitney, found that even the smallest problem could not be solved. After eight and one-half frustrating months, Morgan summarized the situation by noting that "Juan had everything so snarled up, nobody could ever untangle it. He had the company in his pocket."[4] After 10½ months, at Morgan's behest and with Whitney's acquiescence, Trippe returned as chief operating officer. As Trippe consolidated power, people who had supported Whitney too enthusiastically were punished. This usually meant depriving these individuals from further access to Trippe.[5]

By 1964, Trippe was presiding over a $1 billion conglomerate. This not only included what was widely recognized as the most prestigious airline in the world but also a business jet division, missile-range operations, hotels, and real estate. But according to one expert on Pan Am's history, "The airline was so vast, that Trippe had become isolated; no one could reach him that he did not want to see. He was not easily accessible even to his closest subordinates—they sometimes waited days or even weeks to see him—and when the meeting took place, it was to discuss Trippe's agenda, not theirs. 'Divide and rule' was the method by which many chief executives operated—Trippe, too, at the beginning, but from the middle years on, Trippe ruled without any question at all."

Trippe was particularly sticky on salaries. The subject of raises irritated him and, consequently, remuneration lagged far behind other industries. For many, it must have been a labor of love, as management turnover was practically nil. (Note: a large number of Pan Am managers were ex-WWII pilots who "grew up" with the airline.) Trippe rewarded his loyal and hard-working employees with bonuses, which sometimes were as little as $300 on the lowest levels. The unfailing devotion of his employees to the company and the aviation field enabled Trippe to run a vast and successful corporation with minimum overhead.

Trippe has been described as having ruled almost like a king with nobles grouped tightly around him and their various ranks in the hierarchy ordained, often not so subtly, by him alone. Vice presidents were reported to have learned to study the roster of officers every time a company report was published. Trippe was said to have moved his 10 or more VPs as the whim struck him. Those closest to the top—closest to Trippe's own name—had his favor, and in exactly the order they appeared. Vice presidents also became keen students of seating arrangements at company dinners, as they knew that Trippe entered banquet rooms a few minutes early to put the place cards exactly where he wanted them. The men beside Trippe were being rewarded and the men farthest away punished—in public.[6]

[4] Ibid., pp. 253–54.
[5] Ibid.

[6] Ibid., pp. 427–29.

In 1968, at age 68, Trippe stepped down as chairman and CEO of Pan Am. In 1969, things began to go wrong for the airline; increased foreign flag carrier competition, unfilled seats in the just-introduced 747, and a monumental debt of $600 million to pay for them, plus a lack of domestic routes, set a difficult course for the new president, Harold Grey. Grey, an engineer, hated politics and public relations. He once stated to one of his VPs, "All we have to do is be good, and people will recognize it." Grey lasted 18 months and was succeeded by Najeeb Halaby. Halaby, somewhat of a Renaissance man, came to Pan Am with high-level government experience, but knew little of the airline business. In 1971, as losses mounted, Halaby changed 17 of the company's 23 top officers.[7] Although he called this "pumping in new blood," others saw it as a blood bath—"a series of actions without cause," was the way one executive described it. In Halaby's opinion, Pan Am was woefully lacking in management depth—the result of decades of one-man rule by founder Trippe.[8]

Halaby's infusion of new management did not work out, as he later admitted: "We never really did have a team, we didn't even have unity born of fear as Trippe had inspired."[9] In April 1972, Halaby, after 27 months as chief executive, was replaced by former Air Force Brigadier General William Seawell. Halaby, who had unsuccessfully tried to curb charter competition and get domestic routes, left with the parting shot: "Without total self-help, which is under way, and the government correcting the regulatory errors of the past, Pan Am is in deep, deep trouble."[10]

Seawell had been hired by Halaby four months earlier to handle the day-to-day operations of the airline. Halaby's demise and Seawell's appointment came under pressure from major creditors from whom Pan Am was trying to renew a $270 million dollar line of bank credit.

At the time of his appointment, Seawell announced that trimming the payroll would be a major factor in his cost-cutting program. In addition, he felt that the airline in the past had been bogged down by a widespread, loosely integrated layer of vice presidents and other officials, which had been allowed to build up over the previous five years. Seawell planned a large-scale elimination of fringe positions and cuts in officer salaries. Seawell's concept of management called for a closely knit management team that communicated on all phases of the airline's activities to permit fast action in coping with changing conditions and fluctuating markets throughout a global route structure.[11]

Seawell managed to stem Pan Am losses, which totaled $350 million between 1969 and 1975, and produced three years of back-to-back profits.[12] His success was attributed to the abandonment of unprofitable routes—all of the Caribbean, for instance—and route swaps with TWA to give each carrier exclusivity in certain markets, and drastic personnel cuts.

In 1979, Pan Am began to court National stockholders in hopes of acquiring the airline. This was accomplished on January 7, 1980, at a cost of $393.7 million. After 34 years of unsuccessfully trying to get a domestic route system, Pan Am, for the first time, was able to attract traffic originating abroad destined for interior U.S. points,

---

[7] Ibid., pp. 440–47.

[8] *Newsweek*, April 3, 1972, p. 67.

[9] Robert Daley, *An American Saga*, p. 447.

[10] *Newsweek*, April 3, 1972, p. 67.

[11] *Aviation Week and Space Technology*, March 27, 1972, pp. 23–25.

[12] *Fortune*, August 27, 1979, p. 13.

and was able to attract National's domestic traffic destined for overseas points. In its original planning for the merger, Pan Am had hoped to grow rapidly beyond the combined revenues of about $3.2 billion annually. In effecting this, the planners had two choices: they could have kept two airlines, each reporting to a holding company with a small staff of long-range planners and financial executives, or they could merge operations as fast as possible with National's name disappearing. By going the speedy merger route, Pan Am raised the spectre in some minds on Wall Street of the ill-famed merger between the Pennsylvania and New York Central railroads. By trying to combine operations speedily, the Penn Central Transportation Company faced problems it never did solve. There was another harrowing similarity. Like Pan Am and National, the two railroads were confronted with the huge startup costs of a merger in a rapidly falling economy.

In 1979, Pan Am projected a 10 percent capacity increase for 1980. The poor economy later caused planners to revise targets for 1980 to include no capacity increase. Without growth, Pan Am officials knew that there would be redundant layers of management as the two companies came together. With airline jobs hard to come by elsewhere, Pan Am officials also knew that they couldn't rely on the usual attrition to reduce the ranks of management.[13] (Today, there are only two former National employees in senior ranks.)

The merger also proved to be a labor relations nightmare. Organized workers battled each other for better jobs and with management for new contracts combining the best features of the two old accords.[14] William F. Genoese, chairman of the Teamster negoti-

ating committee, attacked former managers of National involved in the merger, saying that they were trying to stick to the National Airlines tradition of "beating the hell out of the unions" and that former National managers were afraid to give in on anything and risk appearing weak to their new Pan Am superiors. Genoese also said management officials of the merged company regularly "pass the buck," blaming other departments for the lack of progress in the merger.[15]

The difficult decisions on the National merger and questions regarding the future of the airline led to increased quarreling between Seawell and Dan Colussy, the president. It got so bitter at one point that the two reportedly stopped speaking to each other for a few days. On November 4, 1980, Colussy abruptly left the company. Colussy's men were reportedly put on a hit list. This was only one of many problems that surfaced in the period immediately after the merger. In addition to the president's departure, at least eight vice presidents were fired. Scores of other managers were let go, took early retirement or quit.[16] Many of these were National managers who found that their informal style did not mesh with the more bureaucratic Pan Am organization. "If we had a problem," according to one National manager, "we used to walk into a guy's office and settle it in five minutes; but at Pan Am, we had to set up a committee and study it for months. It took forever and you never got a decision." A member of the board, James Maloon, a former top executive of the airline, was forced to resign in a dispute with Seawell. One analyst described Pan Am management as "so busy fighting with each other,

---

[13] *Business Week,* January 21, 1980, p. 56.
[14] Ibid.

[15] *Aviation Week and Space Technology,* April 21, 1980, p. 26.
[16] *The Wall Street Journal,* August 3, 1981, p. 1.

that they haven't been able to fight the air-line's problems which are enormous." In 1980, and the first quarter of 1981, the air-line had losses of $336 million dollars. This was offset by the sale of the Pan Am build-ing. Some industry analysts joked that the company should have kept the building and sold the airline. Critics say that the losses were foreshadowed by corporate instability created by Mr. Seawell. Some blamed it on Seawell's legendary temper and on political maneuvers which he learned as an Air Force general. Others say that Seawell, wary of sharing power, deliberately kept other exec-utives off balance.[17] *The Wall Street Journal* pointed to the creation of a shadow organi-zation alongside the regular Pan Am man-agement, as a factor in keeping executives off balance. As an example, they cited Henry Golightly, president of a firm special-izing in both executive recruiting and man-agement consulting. As a recruiter, Go-lightly reportedly helped Seawell win Pan Am's presidency in 1971. As a management consultant, Golighty was accused of having subsequently pushed through one reorgani-zation of Pan Am's management after an-other.

"He's reorganized this company to death," said one Pan Am officer. One exam-ple cited is the field-marketing organization, whose job is to help devise strategies for promoting travel on Pan Am. A few years ago, it was decentralized with key officials located in a few key cities around the globe to increase sales. Recently, according to *The Wall Street Journal* sources, Golightly spur-red an effort to centralize it, and many offi-cials were brought back to New York head-quarters. A former Pan Am official said that Golighty made "pablum out of the field-marketing organization just when we needed the revenue it was generating." At

one time, James Maloon, then executive VP for finance, fired Mr. Golightly's firm. Within weeks, Golightly was back on the payroll apparently by Seawell's orders.[18]

The constant reorganizations led some Pan Am executives to adopt the saying, "If you don't like your present job, just wait six months and it will change." One executive said "People have been moving from city to city, from country to country and continent to continent at blinding speed, and the dis-ruption has hurt us."[19]

After Colussy's departure, William Waltrip, an executive VP, was approached with the possibility of becoming the number two man to Seawell. As executive vice presi-dent, Waltrip was in charge of marketing and planning, including pricing and sched-ules. Prior to that, Waltrip was in charge of services and reservations. From December 1976 to 1978, he was executive VP directing operations (including flight and mainte-nance). Waltrip joined Pan Am as staff vice president for schedule planning in 1972. Prior to that, Waltrip had held various fi-nancial and economic posts at Eastern Air-lines, American Airlines, and the Air Trans-port Association.[20] Having seen the friction between Messrs. Seawell and Colussy, Waltrip was apparently reluctant to take the job.[21] As a solution, Jack Parker, former vice chairman of General Electric Company, and brought to the Pan Am Board by Seawell, began to push for an early replacement for his benefactor who planned to retire soon anyway. If that search failed, the directors' intention was to offer Waltrip clear-cut au-thority to run the airline reporting essen-tially to the Board. Among those ap-proached for the top Pan Am job, was Al

---

[17] Ibid.

[18] Ibid.
[19] Ibid.
[20] *The Wall Street Journal,* July 8, 1981, p. 21.
[21] *The Wall Street Journal,* July 6, 1981, p. 23.

Feldman, chairman of Continental Airlines, Los Angeles. Feldman had previously turned around Frontier Airlines and was enormously popular with Continental employees. One source said that "Continental was losing money; Frank Lorenzo, chairman of Texas International Airlines, was beating Feldman over the head (attempting to take over Continental) and the theory was that Feldman might consider coming to Pan Am."[22] Feldman stayed on at Continental and fought Texas International's takeover bid by supporting a plan to make Continental the country's largest employee-controlled company. Feldman committed suicide three days after the Civil Aeronautics Board approved Texas International's purchase plans. In a suicide note, Feldman was said to have described his depression over the death of his wife a year earlier. There was speculation that fatigue, and the lengthy battle for control of the corporation which, according to a Continental spokesman, "was his whole existence," might have contributed to his despondency.[23]

Another man approached for the Pan Am job was Edwin Colodny, who is chairman of U.S. Air, a successful regional carrier. Colodny didn't take the Pan Am offer, either. The focus returned to Waltrip, who was offered the job as acting CEO of the airline division reporting to the board.[24] He accepted and Seawell announced retirement plans. In announcing, he issued a statement saying, "I have served Pan Am as chief executive officer since 1972. During that time, we succeeded in bringing the airline through a period as difficult as we face today, and we succeeded in acquiring a domestic system by merger with National Air-

lines. With these developments, and the changing conditions surrounding the business, we approach the time when a new chief executive should assume these changed responsibilities."[25]

Waltrip, in his new role, immediately launched an intensified drive to cut labor costs. Pan Am's labor force had been one of the most costly in the industry. He also contemplated continued route restructuring and looked for a way to protect his profit margins given the price wars that ensued from airline deregulation and the concomitant rise of low-cost, no-frills carriers as a strong market force. As Waltrip faced some very tough tasks, Seawell continued to linger in the background.

During the summer, an executive recruiter approached Acker as a possible replacement for William Seawell.

C. Edward Acker

Born in Dallas on April 7, 1929, Mr. Acker received his BAs in economics and psychology from Southern Methodist University in 1950. It is said that he has been using his twin degrees ever since. According to Acker, "The key to success in the airline business is determining what customers want in each different market and how to give it to them." Acker joined the founding Air Florida in 1977 as chairman, bringing with him cash from a group of investors who were prepared to bet he could turn the airline around. Previously, he had worked in investment counseling and finance for a variety of Dallas companies between 1952 and 1965. He joined Braniff Airways, where he quickly gained the reputation of being one of the most shrewd financial executives in the airline industry. Acker rose to the presidency in 1970, a post he held for five years,

---

[22] Ibid.

[23] *New York Times*, August 11, 1981, p. D1.

[24] *The Wall Street Journal*, July 6, 1981, p. 23.

[25] *New York Times*, July 8, 1981, p. D7.

and was noted for his promotional flair and his popularity with employees. Although there was no direct tie to Acker, he nonetheless left Braniff in 1975 on the heels of a federal investigation of Braniff officials for illegally distributing airline tickets worth $1 million to travel agents in Latin America. Some of the proceeds were said to have been contributed to President Nixon's 1972 election campaign. After his departure, he worked as an executive of a financial holding company until joining Air Florida. Acker converted Air Florida from an obscure intrastate carrier into what many consider to be the most innovative and fastest-growing airline in the nation. His techniques became the talk of the industry. However, "his reach never exceeded his grasp," said one analyst. "He was always able to combine ambitious growth with the financial controls to pull it off."

Acker's tenure at Air Florida included unusual marketing techniques such as "Free Rides for a Kiss"—a promotion that gave customers a free trip if they kissed an airline employee, and his "Sunshine Sparkler"—an orange juice and champagne elixir served to early morning passengers. But most of all it was Acker's "Sweet and Simple" low-cost unrestricted fares that made Air Florida competitive with the more established carriers.[26]

Acker indicated that he may be taking a pay cut to accept the Pan Am challenge. He said his Air Florida income this year would have been about $500,000, but that he wanted his remuneration from Pan Am to be based on his performance in the months ahead.[27] Acker is separated from his wife and said that he would use his Westport, Connecticut, vacation home as a base for himself, two grown sons, and a daughter, while he looks for something closer to Pan Am's Manhattan office.[28] In a November 16, 1981, interview with *Barron's*, Acker noted that "New York is not one of the more desirable places to live."

Since accepting the Pan Am job, Acker has attracted quite a lot of press attention, which has greatly helped his October and November bookings. Some of his early statements:

> October 23, 1981:
> Pan Am has decided to move out of its headquarters building in New York, and the odds are 50-50 that the company will relocate in South Florida.

Acker's decision will partially be based on inducements offered by South Florida to move and by New York City to stay. Space in their New York headquarters leases for five times what it would cost in Florida. Acker is Florida's reigning businessman of the year—an honorary post.[29]

> October 29, 1981:
> I am not sure we need freighters at all. I doubt it. If anyone wanted to buy them I'd sell them all right quick. We do need to carefully study the freighter issue.[30]

Pan Am has not been making a satisfactory return on its all-freighter service. The interest charges on the equipment are significantly higher than the rate of return. In addition, some analysts feel that freighter loads could be more profitably diverted to the "bellies" of Pan Am's passenger aircrafts.

In a recent *Barron's* inverview:

> We've got an excellent balance sheet. We're just running our business poorly. We've let

---

[26] *New York Times*, August 28, 1981, p. D2.

[27] *Newsweek*, September 7, 1981, p. 62.

[28] *New York Times*, August 28, 1981, p. D2.

[29] *Miami Herald*, October 24, 1981, pp. 1A, 19A.

[30] *Journal of Commerce*, October 30, 1981.

our expenses get out of control, and we have way too much waste. . . . you have to get an operating plan and stick to it.

In the same interview he discussed the National merger:

They could have acquired those routes the same way Air Florida got them—just by applying for them. Deregulation had arrived, and you could get routes and fly them. If you merge, the cost of all the people becomes the same. We just took National's costs and automatically raised them 30 percent. I am opposed to mergers. At Air Florida, when we were talking about acquiring control of Western, we said that we could not merge those two carriers because that would have meant that Air Florida's costs would have gone up to Western's costs. We said we would operate it and run it separately. Pan Am could have done that with National.

When asked by the *Barron's* reporter if he suffered any culture shock moving from a smaller carrier like Air Florida to giant Pan Am and were the problems the same, Acker replied:

In some cases you have fewer problems, and in many cases, you have more problems. At the larger carrier, there is a larger staff, which means that a lot of things that you would have to do yourself in a smaller company, you can now delegate and get done. But the most difficult part is the decision-making process. The more people you have, and, of course, the more every one of them has to analyze, the longer it takes to make a decision which otherwise you could make by sitting around a table for 5 or 10 minutes. We're getting around that now. We are making decisions on a timely basis. There are still some decisions that are going too slow, but I think we'll be able to cut through that. The next area is in control. I like to control the quality and price of my product a little more closely than I'm able to right now at Pan Am.[31]

A message to 700 employees attending a Management Club meeting in New York:

Pan Am can only cut costs and retrench so far, before losing its ability to function effectively. Now the company is looking to its personnel for far greater productivity. In effect, "with our recent cutbacks, we're now asking for more for less."

My partner Bill Waltrip and I, as well as our top officers, will provide the leadership, guidance, and direction we require to get the job done. But the rest is up to you. All of you. Pan Am's future is in your hands.

On his approach to each day:

One philosophy I came upon the first day I was here is this: try to make some progress every day. I believe that this has happened. Each day we have come up with something that would add to the balance sheet, add to the marketing effort, add to the employees' relations efforts and so on. The first 100 days that I am around here we will have 100 positive things happen. Then we will be well on the road to financial recovery, growth in revenue, a return to black ink.[32]

CASE 6
ASSESSING MANAGERIAL TALENT AT AT&T (A)*
Emily Stein, Bert Spector, and Michael Beer

On August 21, 1978, Walt Jackson and Donna Lawrence boarded airplanes bound

---

[31] *Barron's*, November 16, 1981, pp. 4, 16.

[32] *Pan Am Clipper Magazine*, September–October, 1981, pp. 1, 5, 7.

for Atlanta, Georgia. For 3½ days, beginning that Monday evening, these (AT&T) middle managers were to participate in the company's first Advanced Management Potential Assessment Program (AMPA). Walt Jackson and Donna Lawrence, like the other participants, had been nominated to attend by their telephone company based on the belief of their supervisor and VP–personnel that they had the potential to advance to higher levels in the company. The program was designed to investigate their individual potential for top management positions. Before heading for Atlanta, Walt and Donna were each briefed by their own phone company's personnel vice president about the purpose and process of AMPA. Each individual, however, was somewhat unsure about exactly what the assessment technique would entail. Both hoped for a positive experience and were concerned about performing well as the assessment results would most likely have a major impact on their futures in the Bell System.

Background of Participants

Walt Jackson graduated from high school and went to work as an errand boy for a large machinery manufacturing organization. After several years he enlisted in the Navy, served for four years, and then returned to his original employer. He continued to work for that company for 20 years. During that time he completed a college degree, got married, and had a family. He joined the Bell System in 1968. Since coming to the phone company he has had three different middle-management positions. All have been district manager positions within the network operating department. Exhibit 1 provides his last performance appraisal before going to the assessment center.

Walt was recommended for assessment

by his vice president of personnel because "he is an intelligent, articulate manager who had demonstrated the ability to learn and perform in several areas of business."

Donna Lawrence came to work for the Bell System after graduating from college with a BA in engineering in 1970. Since joining the company she has had four different management jobs, each as an engineer in the network department. Each job has represented a step up the management hierarchy. In 1978 her title was District Staff Supervisor of Budgets and Results. This is a middle-management position (third level). Exhibit 2 provides her last performance appraisal before going to the assessment center.

Donna was recommended for assessment by her VP–personnel because "she has intelligence, drive, and desire to advance in the business. She is quick to learn and has proven her ability to take on new assignments, learn quickly, and make a contribution by effectively supervising her subordinates."

The AT&T Organization

American Telephone & Telegraph is the parent company of 23 operating telephone companies which provide service to the continental United States. AT&T has a majority of full ownership in these companies and sets standard policy according to governmental regulations in a variety of areas. However, each of the companies has its own board of directors and, within the boundaries of corporate policy, operates quite autonomously. According to Joel Moses, manager of human resource development at corporate, "This relationship between corporate and the independent companies is an interesting one. We [at corporate, located in Basking Ridge, New

Exhibit 1   **Assessment of Walt Jackson**

Management Performance Appraisal System

Performance Summary

Employee's Name   Walt Jackson _____   Title   District Manager—Plant _____

Area _____   Department _____

Supervisor's Name _____   Title   Division Manager—Plant _____

Date   10-24-77 _____   Date of Last Performance Summary   3-23-77 _____

Reviewed by _____   Title _____
      (Appraiser's Supervisor)

Performance—Keeping in mind the individual's major objectives, how well did he/she perform? Support your appraisal by citing specific instances of outstanding or deficient performance.

This year has been an unusual one for Walt Jackson, in that consolidation of the Dorman and Peabody Plant districts caused him to be reassigned three times. He started the year as district manager in Peabody. On June 1, after the decision to consolidate was made and after he was selected to be the manager of the new district, he was transferred to Dorman. Following two months of becoming familiar with Dorman, the consolidation was announced and he was appointed district manager–plant–Peabody/Dorman. Then, as part of the corporate reorganization, Walt and his district were reassigned to South Area on October 24.

Because of these changes, it would be difficult, and perhaps unfair, to attempt an evaluation of technical performance after June 1. An outline of performance during the first five months of the year at Peabody follows:

Maintenance:

Peabody's performance in the Exchange Maintenance Service Results index was especially strong through April, and continued the fine improving trend of the last two years. The Records Quality component averaged 98.9, or well above the 97.5 objective. The Report Rate component averaged 98.6, reflecting the substantial reduction of 13.7 percent in the customer report rate over the comparable period in 1976.

Subsequent Reports, Found-OKs, and the PBX Report Rate, also were improved over 1976 performance and well ahead of their respective objectives. The Public Coin rate, while slightly worse than objective, was one of the lowest in the Operations.

Repeated Reports proved to be a serious problem, as scoring accuracy improved and the absolute number of "Repeats" was not significantly reduced. Total Upkeep productivity ran some 0.8 percent behind the annual commitment through May.

Installation:

Customer Installation Service Results performance was uneven through the first five months of the year, with a monthly low of 91.8 recorded in January and a high of 97.8 in February. The Customer Service Comments and Requests Not Complied With components of the index were

---

Exhibit 1 (*continued*)

troublesome during this period, but missed appointments (Not Met) were the major problem. A special effort to reduce "Plant Other" misses eventually arrested a poor trend in this result.

Despite a great deal of attention to Outward Movement Control, Peabody had disappointing results in "Telephone Sets Removed on the Disconnect rate." Through May, the result was 54.2 percent, or roughly three quarters of the objective. Total C, X, and M productivity also proved difficult through the period, with performance at 9.05 work units per hour, or well behind the 9.76 objective. Two components of this result looked weak through the month of May:

Straight-line performance was 6.6 percent under objective, and had not met the objective in any month.

Assignment was 10.0 percent under objective.

Installation Sales continued to be Peabody's real claim to fame. While another district won the President's Plaque in the first quarter, Peabody was easily the top district in the Company in consistency through the first five months.

General:

The last five months surely have been difficult for Walt, and yet, he never let frustration show in public. Managing "around" the preparations for the consolidation and deciding on a myriad of detailed questions were special burdens. When morale problems developed after the consolidation was announced, he worked with them directly. Later, when the corporate reorganization raised tough questions from management people, as well as craft, Walt chose to work on a personal basis again. In both instances, he was most effective: his people were not necessarily happy, but adjusted to the changed conditions.

Overall, Walt Jackson has made a substantial contribution to the business this year. He should take pride in a job well done under adverse conditions.

He is familiar with the Affirmative Action objectives of the company, and has actively taken part in their implementation this year. In a recent internal compliance review, he made it quite clear to his subordinates that he supports the corporate commitment to EEO.

Management Methods—Describe the management techniques used by this employee in achieving his or her objectives.

Walt Jackson is an especially mature individual, who uses his experience to good advantage. He is thoughtful and deliberate, and evaluates as many aspects of a problem as possible, before taking action.

He is very sensitive to "people problems," and has confidence that he can work effectively with them.

During the last year or two Walt has become much more of a "field manager," in the sense that he spends much of his time asking questions, following-up, analyzing details and observing work operations first-hand. In the process, he has become increasingly well grounded in the fundamental aspects of the Plant job.

Strengths—In what way is this manager especially competent?

Walt is a highly competent communicator, both orally and in written form.

He has a very broad background in the business, and is seldom surprised when some "new"

Exhibit 1 (*concluded*)

problem turns up. He tracks a large number of operating results, and challenges his subordinates when poor trends develop.

Areas Requiring Improvement—What aspects of the job performance should receive attention?

He must continue to be alert to subordinates with "pat answers" and "quick solutions."

Development Needs—List specific action that should be taken to aid this manager's growth.

The newly consolidated district he is managing should be sufficiently challenging to continue to develop Walt's management skills over the near-term future.

Employee Response—How does the employee feel about the performance summary?

I appreciate the balanced perspective reflected in this performance summary. It is always gratifying when real understanding of one's efforts is displayed.

The problem areas discussed are, with one or two exceptions, less of a problem now than at the five-month mark. Of particular note is Total CXM productivity where substantial gains have been made. This, I think, is a tribute to the people working in the district and their will to try.

I shall continue to put forth my best effort to become all that a field third-level manager should be.

Employee's Initials   W. J.

Date   11/7/77

Jersey] manage cooperatively, not coercively. Yet, operations across companies are quite consistent."

AT&T and its 23 companies are organized similarly. Each is comprised of six major functional units including business, residential, network (operations), finance regulatory, and another department which includes a diverse group of functions including personnel. At the independent company level, these departments are divided geographically into divisions which are subdivided into districts.

Management structure at AT&T follows a 10-level pyramid pattern which applies both to corporate and each of the telephone companies. Each level represents a distinct step towards increased managerial responsibil-

ity. Titles are one tool used to differentiate between levels. Although they differ across departments, typically foremen are considered level 1 managers, supervisors are level 2, and district managers level 3. It should be noted that the company considers level 3 "middle management."

Division heads are level 4 and department heads are level 5. Level 5 individuals represent the bottom rung of top management and are considered primarily responsible for business operations. Level 6 employees are vice presidents and are viewed as policymakers. AT&T's highest level of top management, company presidents and the very top executives at corporate, are between level 7 and 10. Of the management personnel in the Bell System, 138,000 are at level 1;

Exhibit 2   **Assessment of Donna Lawrence**

Management Performance Appraisal System

Performance Summary

Employee's Name   Donna Lawrence   Title   District Manager—Switching Services

Area _____   Department   Switching Services

Supervisor's Name _____   Title   Division Manager—Switching Services

Date   2-4-77 _____   Date of Last Performance   9-75 _____

Reviewed by _____   Title   General Manager—Switching Services

(Appraiser's Supervisor)

Performance—Keeping in mind the individual's major objectives, how well did he/she perform? Support your appraisal by citing specific instances of outstanding or deficient performance.

For approximately the first three quarters of 1976, Mrs. Lawrence was responsible for all switching maintenance and dial administration operations in the Southwest District. Her productivity and service performance during that period was as follows:

C.O. Service Index

Bev XB		Por XB		Pro XB		Pul XB		Sou XB		Bev ESS		Pul ESS		Por ESS	
Obj.	*Act.*	*Obj.*	*Act.*	*Obj.*	*Act.*	*Obj.*	*Act.*	*Obj.*	*Act.*	*Obj.*	*Act.*	*Obj.*	*Act.*	*Obj.*	*Act.*
				97.1	96.6			93.3	94.4						
98.5	98.6	97.4	96.5	97.2	95.9	98.2	98.6	96.6	96.6	97.3	97.5	97.3	97.8	96.7	96.7
				96.5	96.6										

District Productivity

	17R	47R	77R	Tot R	603-04	Upkeep	M	Mtce
Obj.	25.88	7.35	14.00	9.78	34.26	11.386	7.95	10.838
Act.	30.49	7.63	15.83	10.21	37.17	12.020	8.53	11.542

All service objectives with the exception of Por XB and Pro #1 XB were met or exceeded. Of particular note is the outstanding accomplishment in productivity increases. The actual productivity achieved in every code not only greatly exceeded objectives, but were high in comparison with productivities achieved anywhere in the company for like codes and/or work unit composition.

During 1976, ESS operations presented Mrs. Lawrence with a particularly difficult set of problems: With three small offices she was forced to curtail the size of her work force to just eight craftsmen to meet her stringent productivity objectives; she had just three ESS foremen, two of whom split their time for nearly the entire year between ESS class at BSCTE and field operations, to cover the three offices and the SCC (this left her with effectively less than two foremen). Yet, in

Exhibit 2 (*continued*)

spite of these two fundamental handicaps, she met both her service and productivity goals, while reorganizing her ESS operations to the full SCC mode.

On October 1, 1976, the responsibilities of the District Switching Managers in North/South Division were realigned, with the result that Mrs. Lawrence assumed responsibility for all ESS switching maintenance, Sanborn and Portland XB maintenance, the Sanborn, South Cincinnati, and all succeeding cutovers, the implementation of the TASC and ATA systems and the creation of the EM-SCC.

This combination of duties represents an unusually heavy assignment requiring not only exten-sive and detailed follow-through, but the development of new procedures, methods, and organi-zational interfaces and arrangements.

Many difficulties in connection with ESS maintenance and cutover operations were encoun-tered and overcome during the year: A severely compacted schedule of growth and change jobs in the three control groups (including a major trunk frame rearrangement preparatory to the San-born cutover) to be done with a force barely adequate for normal maintenance; a continuing series of frustrating, time-consuming, and penalizing delays and errors by the Western Electric forces; despite an exceeding shortage of people, the Sanborn scrub is complete and the South Cincinnati scrub is proceeding in excellent fashion; with an inexperienced (but intelligent and well-moti-vated) switching manager responsible for cutovers, she has been involved in the development of exhaustive, detailed cutover planning, including interfacing with many peers and second-level managers in other groups on a most intensive scale to win their concerned involvement and successful assistance. As a result of her personal effort, all projects have been completed, or are proceeding, successfully on schedule.

Crossbar operations have also proceeded under difficult circumstances. Sanborn XB was re-duced to 9 craftsmen in 1976 (from 14 in 1975) with two foremen, and is presently operating with 6 craftsmen and one foreman (meanwhile service continues at a high level). Portland has shown decided improvement in both service and productivity.

The TASC project has been faced with delays in preparation of space for the computer (there-fore, delivery of the computer), and errors and delays in both Western Electric wiring and circuit design. Nevertheless, while the project is behind original schedule due to these WECO and building delays, the exceedingly detailed preparations necessary for implementation, which re-quired creating and training an entirely new group, are proceeding excellently.

Typical of Mrs. Lawrence's work is her approach to the Sanborn scurb. She located a Western Electric mechanized scrub program (TES) which could take the FRA output and perform a com-plete scrub on all but about 6,000 lines, and automatically assigns the lines in accordance with established balance and short jumper parameters. In addition, it will provide stick-on labels for Repair line cards. The process also produced direct savings of $20,000 over any other scrub methods. Furthermore, her search for a mechanized scrub method which would interface with FRA led the BIS people to uncover the DENS system, which has since been accepted for a trial in Cincinnati and Suburban Switching and promises to produce a 50% reduction in dial administra-tion clerical forces.

Mrs. Lawrence is familiar with Affirmative Action goals and rigorously implements them.

Management Methods—Describe the management techniques used by this employee in achieving his/her objectives.

Mrs. Lawrence learns the work and in intimately acquainted with its progress, plans with great

Exhibit 2 (*concluded*)

thoroughness, analyzes problems and conditions extensively, interacts intensively with subordinates and coordinates, develops new methods to deal with problems, confronts all problems (machines, methods, and people) forthrightly and positively.

Strengths—In what way is this manager especially competent?

She is quick to adapt to new situations and learn new technologies; very adept at analyzing problems and coming up with creative solutions. She is quietly determined in her dealings with others, yet completely flexible to alternate options that will produce comparable results. She is highly achievement motivated, completely comfortable in an open and forthright relationship with her colleagues and subordinates, with a streak of genuine compassion toward others.

Areas Requiring Improvement—What aspects of the job performance should receive attention?

Donna has been learning the need to develop a certain degree of wariness and toughness in her dealings with others. She has managed to develop these characteristics remarkably during the past year and apply them as needed with no loss of her excellent trust-building ability.

Development Needs—List specific action that should be taken to aid this manager's growth.

Continue in her present assignment.

Employee Response—How does the employee feel about the performance summary?

Employee's Initials _____

Date 9/5/77 _____

51,000 at level 2; 12,000 at level 3; 3,100 at level 4; 1,100 at level 5. Four hundred people hold managerial positions at levels 6 and 7. Approximately 9,300 people considered managers hold level-unspecified positions.

There is a great deal of interaction between AT&T and its phone companies, particularly in the area of personnel. Middle and top-level managers from the various companies rotate into corporate for several years of service and are sent back to their home organizations for the balance of their careers. This aids management development and increases communications between the parent and independent compa-

nies. Lower-level managers are both selected and trained by the companies themselves.

Manpower Planning and Development at AT&T

Manpower planning and development is a high corporate priority at AT&T. The human resources department at headquarters in Basking Ridge has been responsible for conducting research which aids the corporation in analyzing specific manpower needs, and developing and implementing programs designed to meet these needs. One major tool the human resource function has supplied is the assessment center technique. At AT&T this method has been used for the past 20 years as one tool in predicting management potential and identifying the strengths and weaknesses of individual employees.

Assessment Centers. The history of assessment centers can be traced back to World War II. The Office of Strategic Services (OSS) of the United States government had a great need to select capable individuals for hazardous and unusual assignments. After recruiting a large number of people who turned out to be "misfits," the OSS sought professional assistance in designing a more effective and reliable selection process. A group of psychologists hired by OSS designed and, by late 1943, had implemented the first assessment center employed in the U.S.

The center required its "assessees" to enact a variety of on-the-job situations. As a result, the OSS was able to select personnel who performed more effectively than those previously selected. The element which seemed to account for the success of the new method was the behavioral element of the design. Essentially, performance during simulated "spy-type" assignments allowed OSS to predict, with some accuracy, on-the-job ability. Once the OSS experience was publicized, an interest in the assessment center technique began to develop in the American business community. American Telephone & Telegraph was the first organization to research and actually apply the technique to personnel practice.

In 1956 AT&T launched a longitudinal management research study. Specifically, their research effort was designed to find characteristics which were associated with upward mobility in management or which

were developed as a result of movement up the management ladder. The company utilized a "tailor-made" assessment center as a major measurement tool for the study. Managers were assessed for three days when the study began, and again eight years later. Research findings to date, available in *Formative Years in Business* (Bray, Campbell, and Grant, 1974), indicate the method's validity and reliability over time as an aid in management selection.

Across the Bell System, many managers, who participated in the study early on, expressed an interest in adapting assessment centers for practical, as opposed to research, purposes. In 1958, AT&T developed such a center to aid in selecting first-line supervisors from the hourly ranks. Subsequently, other large organizations began to utilize the assessment technique not only as a selection tool but also as a tool for promotion and development decisions. Companies which adopted the method include Standard Oil of Ohio, Sears, IBM, and General Electric. As of 1977, at least 30,000 individuals are assessed yearly in well over 1,000 organizations.

The set of qualities or dimensions which are measured at any assessment center is a vital element of the entire technique. The center's validity greatly depends upon the degree in which the dimensions are representative of what is required for the position or level in question.

AT&T's Advanced Management Assessment Program (AMPA) contains several elements common to most successful assessment centers:

A series of exercises or simulations is a standard part of any assessment center. Although the nature of the exercises will vary according to the objectives and dimensions inherent in the center, certain types of exercises are used in most working centers.

Such simulations include group exercises, "in-baskets," individual problem-solving exercises, work simulations, interviews, and individual exercises. Each exercise or simulation stimulates behavior relevant to several assessment dimensions. Paper-and-pencil tests may also be used in an assessment center.

The assessment staff coordinates, administers, supervises, and carries out the assessment process itself. To function effectively the staff, comprised of one director and several assessors, who are often managers in the organization, must be well trained in the process of assessment.

Typically, assessment directors are trained professionals working out of the human resources area who may themselves have been involved in the development and design of their centers. Specifically, a director must manage a center's facilities, assessors, participants, and process. He or she generally supervises assessor training, administers exercises, chairs assessor discussions, writes up the final assessment report and recommendations, and carries out or delegates the feedback process. Organizations utilize directors either on a full-time or special-assignment basis.

One facet of the director's job is to supervise assessor training. To assure accurate, objective participant assessment while providing a truly developmental experience for assessors, a substantive staff training program must be included in the design and process of any assessment center.

A preestablished evaluation technique which includes a standardized rating scale is an essential part of any assessment center regardless of objectives, dimensions, or exercises employed. Such a technique is important because when it is understood and used correctly it assures the reliability and validity of the evaluations.

A feedback session and report is extremely valuable for the assessee's "back-home" manager, but can be especially valuable for the participants themselves.

The data collected by means of the assessment process describe an individual's strengths and deficiencies and can be quite useful as an aid in the selection of candidates for promotion. Because the process provides managers with a detailed and objective picture of the assessee, managers can also utilize this picture to understand developmental needs, and coach subordinates to establish appropriate training programs or job progression plans.

Assessment centers can be a valuable training method for managers acting as assessors. Observational and evaluation skills are required of these assessors. Managers who participate as assessors are asked to identify assessee strengths and weaknesses, understand the way these characteristics contribute to job success, and integrate observations about individuals and established job requirements in developing recommendations for promotion and development experiences. Assessors are trained, during the week preceding the assessment center, to observe behavior in assessment exercises carefully, relate observed behavior to the appropriate dimension, and select the behavioral anchor on each scale which most closely describes the observed behavior. According to Joel Moses, when assessors scrutinize participants, rate characteristics, and make developmental recommendations, they improve their own evaluation and interpersonal management skills.

Assessment at AT&T. AT&T's first assessment program, initiated in 1958, was directed at hourly workers with 10 to 12 years of company experience, and was used to identify individuals for level 1 managerial assignments. Since its inception approximately 100,000 individuals, representing 18 Bell System companies have participated in this two-day program. In 1968 AT&T instituted a second program, also two days long, which was used with level 1 personnel to assess potential for level 2 and level 3 positions.

Assessment programs at AT&T are typically designed by corporate staff and made available to the independent companies. Each company participates voluntarily. Apparently, the two assessment programs described are widely accepted across the organization as valid and reliable tools for decisions about management's development and promotion, although the results are used differently by different companies and managers. According to Joel Moses, AT&T maintains a constant and growing interest in the assessment process as evidenced by increasing numbers of program participants. Also, according to Moses:

> We have been very successful at meeting our organizational needs for low-level managers. In recent years, however, our needs have shifted. There is a real concern here now to identify talent for succession purposes. We need to be sure we are preparing people early in their careers for higher level management positions, now more than ever before.

AMPA Preparation and Implementation

AT&T conducted the first AMPA during July and August of 1978. Seven programs took place that summer. They accommodated a total of 77 level 3 participants who usually came in groups of 12. Fifteen assessors, level 5 managers, served the center for three to five weeks at a time in groups of six.

On board permanently in Atlanta were the center director, Joel Moses, three part-time clinical psychologists, and two secretaries.

Since 1976 formal efforts had been made to design an assessment tool which would look at promotability and developmental needs of level 3 managers for level 5 assignments. Extensive research was conducted and, by the spring of 1978, the program design was established (see Exhibit 3).

Having designed the program, Moses set out to manage the process of recruiting participants. On May 3 and 4 he held a meeting with the assistant vice presidents of personnel from interested Bell System companies. At this session he explained the intent of the program, its content, and the desired participant population. He explained that the company was interested in assessing third-level individuals who had been in-grade for a couple of years and who were considered likely candidates for promotion by back-home companies. (Most company personnel departments kept promotable lists so there was no problem in identifying capable people.)

By the end of June, phone company personnel vice presidents had identified candidates for AMPA, contacted them, filled out nomination forms on their behalf, and supplied AMPA applications to be completed by candidates themselves. By the end of June the 77 participants had been selected. Simultaneously, Moses was devoting energy to the process of selecting and training assessors. Assessors were drawn from the population of fifth-level managers in the seven Bell companies which elected to participate in AMPA that year. Once assessors and assessees were selected, care was taken to mix the participants according to sex, location, and functional area, and to mix assessors and participants so assessors would not have to assess individuals they knew.

Exhibit 3   AMPA Program Design

Monday	P.M.	Candidates arrive for social hour, orientation, meeting, and discussion.
Tuesday	A.M.	Group exercise (Business Game—explanation to follow). The candidates were divided into two groups of six. Each group was observed by three assessors who took notes on the total activity and two individual participants.
	P.M.	1. Individual interview with clinical psychologist. 2. Psychological testing with candidates for assessment information and research purposes. Free evening.
Wednesday	A.M.	Individual exercise (In-Basket).
	P.M.	1. Interview regarding In-Basket performance. 2. Additional testing. 3. Group exercise (Riverview).
Thursday	A.M.	1. Continuation of Riverview. 2. Problem-Solving exercise.
	P.M.	Free time to complete unfinished testing or interviewing, "decompression," "debriefing" and "re-entry" work. Assessees leave.
	Evening	Assessors work on writing two- to three-page narrative report based on observations of participants.
Friday		Assessors meet in teams of three with a psychologist to rate and evaluate participants and prepare developmental recommendations.
Post-program		Feedback given to at-home officer and candidate (to be explained in depth subsequently).

On July 10, 1978, about one week before AMPA began, the 15 fifth-level managers came to Atlanta to participate in a six-day assessor training program. The training included long hours of explanation meetings, observing simulations of exercises with local graduate students acting as assessees, rating their behavior according to established dimensions, and report-writing and critique feedback sessions. The training program was demanding but was devoted to preparing assessors to be as knowledgeable about the process and competent with their tasks as possible. It was characterized by two major design elements for this purpose, including: (1) extensive practice in actually rating behavior; (2) feedback and critique from very experienced assessors from AT&T's corporate human resources staff.

Walt Jackson and Donna Lawrence began their AMPA program by attending an orientation meeting conducted by the center director. In this session the goals of the program and the various elements of the 3½-day assessment process were explained. Specifically, AMPA was designed (*a*) to identify individuals for placement in a pool as potential officers of the company; (*b*) to examine the individuals in existing pools as potential officers of the company; (*c*) to identify individual developmental needs; and (*d*) to closely examine managers to understand more clearly the company's human resource strengths and weaknesses. Specifically, these goals were to be met by putting candidates through a series of exercises and tests, during which time assessors would observe participants, take careful notes, and later rate the behavior according to a set of dimensions which were associated with high-level management behavior.

Walt and Donna spent the next three days going through the six major assessment tools that were used at AMPA and which had been designed specifically for the program. Those tools involved two group exercises (Riverview and Investment Problem), and four individual activities (In-basket, Problem-Solving Exercise, Personnel Interview, and Paper-and-Pencil Tests).

Each exercise is described below, with sections of the assessment reports on Walt and Donna presented in italics.

Group Discussion (Riverview).   In this exercise, six participants role-play members of the Riverview city council. They are meeting to decide how to allocate a three million dollar federal grant to improve various services in their city. Each participant represents an elected member of the council for a different district, and is trying to obtain a portion of the grant to improve their district. Being an election year, there is considerable pressure to represent the needs of their districts in allocating the money.

This is a complex exercise, with a considerable amount of back-up information and data which candidates must sift through in arguing their proposals. The exercise consists of a one-hour preparation period, a one-hour oral presentation phase, and a 1½-hour group discussion phase. It is a primary source of information for evaluating interpersonal and communication skills.

Walt Jackson's Performance.   *Walt began his seven-minute presentation by assuming a standing position near the map. He used the map effectively as he acknowledged the previous proposals, recognizing overlap and potential conflict. At this time he appealed to the group with the question, "How much is life worth?" This emotional plea seemed to be his theme as he proceeded to describe his proposed traffic study.*

During his presentation he spoke slowly and clearly. His voice was solid and he effectively used inflections as he made his key points. He had good audience eye contact and seemed to hold the group's attention well throughout. He used a prepared chart as he discussed proposal components. He had no distracting mannerisms.

In summary, Walt delivered an interesting, convincing proposal. His use of visual aids, speaking technique, and little dependency on notes added to his effectiveness.

Walt's group worked at dividing the funds allocated on a "top-down" basis with little attention paid to specifics or what the money could do. Compromise was involved.

Most of the participants had prepared handouts before the exercise but none were used. Coalitions were formed during the hour but they were passing in nature and seemed to be more self-serving than cooperative efforts.

Walt was an energetic and confident member of the group. He had done his homework and was prepared to fight for his proposal.

He suggested a strategy for disseminating the funds by using a top-down approach. This was made after a number of participants made presentations which were self-serving and indicated an unwillingness to compromise. Walt seemed to be able to size up the group and was able to develop a strategy for compromise. Instead of attacking an individual's idea he helped the group focus its actions on its overall task of distributing funds.

Walt was quite active and took on a directive role, clarifying issues, questioning members, challenging ideas and probing for compromise. He was able to elicit good cooperation from a group of individuals who were basically unwilling to compromise.

He sensed that a number of coalitions had formed and obtained agreement from members before attacking another idea. He went to the easel and directed the group's attention to his summarization of the distribution of funds. Although not given the title, he clearly was the chairman of this group.

Donna Lawrence's Performance. Donna Lawrence participated consistently throughout this exercise although she lacked skill during both oral and discussion periods. She seemed to have spent a lot of time preparing her case and demonstrated a good grasp of the problem. She interacted with others in the group in a supportive manner, a challenging manner, and a consoling manner when appropriate. During the discussion period she was challenged by the group but eventually got what she asked for. She ranked herself the second-best performer and gave herself a very good rating.

Donna was the last member of her group to make a presentation. She made a brief presentation using the city map (premarked to indicate dams and flood areas) as an aid. She was very soft-spoken and had minimal eye contact with the group because she frequently referred to her hand-held notes. At several points she actually read her presentation. She presented numerical data verbally without using the easel or handouts. She included pertinent facts in her presen-

tation but it was brief. She did not seem very poised or self-assured when making her presentation.

Donna asked one question of each ''council member'' during the oral defense phase. During her own defense she made little or no reference to notes and seemed more sure of herself and less tense than she had during the presentation.

Donna was the first to speak up during the group discussion. She used the easel and showed how the previous days' requests were well over the allotted funds. She proposed cutting her own request as a means of achieving her goal within the stated budget. She also summarized each candidate's proposal. Each member of this group had also prepared a compromise and she was asked to post these. She did so while continuing to actively participate in the discussion.

While presenting her summary of overnight work, she relied heavily on notes and spoke so rapidly that she lost the group's attention at times. She did speak extemporaneously in pleasant conversational style during parts of the summary and made references to comments made by others. On two occasions she encouraged the group to discuss a subject she wanted discussed. As noted, she was able to get the funds she requested for her project.

In summary, while an active participant, Donna's role was to summarize others' positions. While able to get her project funds, she did not challenge others, nor did she really attempt to lead the group to accomplish its tasks.

Complex Business Game (Investment Problem).   Six participants work as the board of directors of the Ajax Fund, a small mutual fund investment company, in this 2½-hour exercise. During four trading periods, the directors buy and sell stocks based upon price quotations which change every five minutes during the period. A news ticker indicates ''developments'' which may affect certain stocks, and there are advisory services available for purchase which provide timely information about stock trends. Scheduled "breaks" for board of director meetings allow participants to negotiate and renegotiate strategies. The participants' objective is to maximize profits of the Ajax Fund (which starts with $10,000) through careful planning and trading of stock. Like the Riverview exercise, the Investment Problem is a primary source of information on interpersonal skills.

Walt Jackson's Performance. Walt's group made an effort to establish direction early in the exercise by immediately discussing objectives, ideas, and approaches. Most candidates participated in the initial discussion but no leader emerged. After several minutes of floundering conversation, the group sensed a need for structure, and role assignment was attempted. Roles were accepted but did not restrict out-of-role behavior. During the exercise candidates were reluctant to fully support the position of any one participant and, as a result, did not agree on much. Candidates did not listen well or respond to each other's suggestions.

Walt jumped into this exercise early, attempting to assume a leader role, and stayed highly verbal. He attempted throughout to delegate work to others. He was persistent in his opinions and equally persistent in his approach. He never actively sought collaboration or compromise.

Walt remained active throughout. He made numerous suggestions to purchase and sell various stocks. On a number of occasions, he persistently argued for his point of view and was able to sell his ideas. As noted, this was a competitive group with little support for individual ideas. Jackson was able to get his recommendations accepted more often than others. In part, this was a function of his persistence. In part, it was his good sense of timing. In part, it was his desire to win. All contributed to his performance here.

Donna Lawrence's Performance. Donna's group began with an attempt to organize themselves which was not very effective. They began to discuss what to buy, how much to invest, and whether to be risk or dividend oriented. Everyone participated and generally two or more candidates were always talking at once. Throughout the exercise the group was friendly and social, frequently laughing as they handled their task.

After a period of initial discussion the group unknowingly divided itself into two groups: one group stayed at the table, the other moved toward the ticker. Finally, one member called the group back together successfully and began to emerge as chairman of the group. The group remained disorganized and independent. However, they were able to realize a moderate profit. In summary, this disorganized, talkative group remained cooperative with a mutual desire to "win the game."

From the beginning, Donna did not contribute very much to this group. Although many opportunities arose, she offered only infrequent suggestions but instead kept records of news releases and stock purchases. When she did contribute verbally, her comments seemed calculated and very well thought out. In general, Lawrence was a quiet, attentive observer. Her substantive contributions were sparse. Regarding her own performance, she commented "[I had] some suggestions with a conservative outlook" and that "[my] contribution would have been greater given the time to plan and analyze. I tend to be more confident of decisions with thought behind them but will take a risk if there is justification." This final comment seems to capture her performance during this exercise. Donna ranked herself the third-best performer (out of six) and rated herself "very good."

In-Basket. This is a three-hour exercise where participants role-play an assistant vice president–traffic generation and operations for the Midland Central Railroad Company. The Midland Central has four divisions covering much of the central United States, and is a close affiliate of two other railroad companies with which it coordinates long-distance service. The AVP position has responsibility for a number of functional areas, including transportation, sales, marketing, industrial development, and public relations and interacts with peers responsible for finance, personnel, physical plant, and legal. The participant must work through a substantial amount of letters, memos, reports, and other written materials, making decisions on a variety of complex issues. The materials represent a mixture of short-term problems as well as longer-term concerns which require effective planning, and analytical and administrative skills.

After completing the exercise, participants are interviewed by a staff member who role-plays the incumbents' supervisor, the vice president. During this interview, the participant has an opportunity to review the decisions made and explain the rationale behind the action taken. The In-Basket is the primary source of information for administrative skills.

Walt Jackson's Performance. *Walt began the In-Basket problem by reviewing his material package. He studied the organization and oriented himself to superiors, peers, and subordinates. He then, in sequence, scanned each item for critical dates and key players in various problems. At this point he spent approximately 1½ hours reading the material in greater detail and relating common issue items. He then "prioritized" the items for action based on urgency and importance. All items were effectively related and prioritized.*

Walt felt a major time constraint during this exercise as evidenced by the fact that he finished only half of the items. He had a good understanding of all issues and good recall of facts for those

items where action was not taken. He felt a need for additional information for most items and planned to get that by requesting investigations. His overall view of the In-Basket was that it was tough, demanding, and comprehensive. If he had the opportunity to repeat the problem, he would allocate more time for taking action and would write out thought processes instead of letters.

In summary, Walt understood the content of the In-Basket well. His written actions were thorough and complete. Although he deferred most final decisions, the material was well organized, related, and prioritized but use of time was a deterrent. When given some additional time by this assessor, he described intended actions and solutions clearly. His written output did not capture his total understanding and, given the opportunity to discuss items during the interview, he demonstrated a good grasp of the materials and his strategy for action.

Donna Lawrence's Performance. *Donna began this exercise by looking for information to orient herself to the organization, its functions, and its territory. She reviewed all items, looking for those requiring special attention, and then proceeded to work on them in their existing sequence. She skimmed items and then reread those which seemed to require more attention. All items were not read, however.*

Because she did not at the outset organize the In-Basket items in terms of their potential interrelationships, Donna was on more than one occasion unaware of the impact of unread items on the issues she chose to address. In one instance, an important item which could substantially alter the company's relations with a major client was overlooked. She did state that she would approach the In-Basket by searching for "themes" were she to go through the exercise again. Nevertheless, Lawrence did do a thorough job on a number of items, attempting to tie in relevant background information and additional items where she saw fit.

Donna felt a definite time constraint and deferred two issues of lesser importance. The easiest matter for her to handle was one that had to be referred back to a subordinate. The most difficult item was one characterized by a multitude of related problems. The most important items were viewed this way because of their close time deadlines.

Donna appeared to be a bit nervous during the first few minutes of the interview and on the few occasions where she realized that she had overlooked a key piece of information, but otherwise was calm yet quick to respond. She was able to answer all questions asked and had good recall of the items, including some which she had not read in detail.

Problem-Solving Exercise. This exercise involves selecting, analyzing, and recommending a program of stress management in order to meet an objective set by the company president. Participants must work through and arrive at a solution to this problem by gathering facts from written material and questioning a staff analyst, and then analyzing the information obtained and presenting the recommended course of action to the president. There is no one "best" solution; participants are required to select from several possible options and to defend their decisions.

The exercise takes three hours to administer, and consists of four major parts: an initial preparation period; a fact-finding interview; a final preparation period; and an oral presentation, discussion, and defense period. It is a primary source of information for the analytical skills.

Walt Jackson's Performance. *Walt began his interview by stating the purpose of his visit and that he had eight questions that were applicable to each of the three possible options. He said he wanted to cover these questions and then he*

might have additional questions. He was very organized. He controlled the interview and did not let the assessor delay on items that he did not consider important. He remained calm throughout even when he thought assessor-given information was meaningless.

Although he followed a general plan, he did not hesitate to do additional probing when necessary. He accomplished his plan within the time allotted. In summary, Walt was poised, well organized, and in control at all times. Essentially, he got all important information. All questions were probing, open, and logical.

Walt began his presentation by revealing an easel with a thorough outline concerning the three possible programs to deal with stress. He covered each in detail but did not waste time on the two programs he did not recommend. He had sufficient notes but did not seem to need them. He used a pointer as he discussed information on the easel. He maintained a good pace and enunciated well. He reached his recommendations within the allotted time.

Walt presented his recommendations in a clear, concise manner following an outline depicted in a second chart. He outlined his program's positive points and defended it with solid evidence.

When challenged by the assessor, Walt argued well. He responded to direct questions logically. He went directly from a defensive to an offensive position restating the benefits of the program he recommended.

In summary, Walt had prepared well. His presentation was logical; he had integrated material well. He spoke clearly and used easel and notes effectively but not in excess. He seemed at ease and was not disturbed by challenges. He met time requirements.

Donna Lawrence's Performance. *Donna seemed very relaxed in her information-gathering role. She was able to obtain information on each of the three possible programs. She pressed the* *individual she was interviewing for facts, and for his opinions, but accepted his unwillingness to give them. All of her questions were stated clearly and a great many were open-ended. She was able to generate many questions and seemed adept at keeping the interviewer talking.*

Donna began her presentation in an almost apologetic tone. She claimed that she had limited information to work with but proceeded to review each of the three programs being considered. She asked the assessor his opinion concerning which program he wanted and seemed unable to give her own recommendations or conclusions. She frequently sought his reaction to what she had said.

Her presentation was not organized and was delivered in a monotone. She frequently spoke so softly that she was difficult to hear. She gave the impression that she really did not want to recommend anything but instead wanted the recommendations and decisions to be made by the president.

In summary, Donna gathered data effectively but seemed almost apologetic when asked to defend her position.

Personal Interview. The personal interview is designed to provide information on a number of career-orientation variables, as well as several personal characteristics. It is the only formal opportunity during the assessment week for the participants to discuss themselves, their experiences, and their careers with a member of the staff. The interview briefly covers their general background and early academic and work experience, and then progressively probes in greater depth the participant's feelings about his or her Bell System career—major assignments, career progress, career orientation, financial concerns, and major problems. The final portion covers the participant's perceptions on a number of self-development related areas—hobbies, interest, plans (short- and long-term goals), strengths, and weaknesses.

The interview takes a little over one hour, and is conducted by a clinical psychologist.

Walt Jackson's Interview. The psychologist who conducted this interview reported, "Walt is an extremely pleasant and self-assured individual who is in touch with his feelings and at ease with himself. He appears self-confident and happy. He is quite articulate."

Born in the South, Walt worked while attending high school to help support his family. (Walt's father died when Walt was in elementary school.) Hard work and achievement are dominant themes in this man's life. He has always worked hard and is proud of his accomplishments. He is a self-reliant individual.

Today, Walt is not as achievement oriented as in the past. Because he is in his mid-40s he feels that his opportunities for promotion are limited. He feels that he could possibly get one more promotion but doubts whether he can advance beyond that.

Walt has some very active outside interests. He owns and manages a 10-unit apartment building. This takes 10 to 15 hours per week. He has studied real estate and reads related books for pleasure. He used to be very active in the community and has earned 12 credits towards his master's degree. In 1970 he was hospitalized and now has tried to slow down. He plans to take early retirement in 15 years. He has no major goals for advancement but would like to have a different job within the next few years in personnel or labor relations.

Overall, Walt is an ordered and planned individual. He is pleased with his accomplishments, family-oriented, well adjusted, and satisfied with himself.

Donna Lawrence's Interview. Donna was interviewed by one of the center's clinical psychologists, who submitted the following report:

Donna is 29 years old, has been married eight years and has no children by choice. While growing up, Donna attended 12 schools in 12 years as her family moved a great deal. Donna reports that this experience helped her learn how to meet people, become involved in activities quickly, and how to be self-reliant.

After graduating from college she was pleasantly surprised to find a job she liked which offered good money and that was future-oriented. She had expected that she would marry, have kids, and publish scientific articles in between housewifely duties. She came to Bell with hopes that she would have the opportunity to use her math skills and be with people. In terms of her career at Bell, she enjoyed her jobs as manager and district manager between 1974 and 1976 most, because in those positions she had the opportunity to learn about the company and learn how to supervise. She was least excited about her job between 1970 and 1974, as plant engineer, which she found repetitive and boring.

To date, Donna is satisfied with her own career growth and has progressed faster than both male and female peers. She expects her next promotion to come within two years but if that does not materialize she will be patient for a while. She hopes future assignments will move her out of technical assignments and into supervision.

Donna wants very much to work with people but she is somewhat reserved and feels that maintaining personal privacy is very important. Typically, she will work through lunch and does not have a lot of friends now. She misses "grapevine information" this way and admits to being unaware of certain aspects of company politics. She is logical, tenacious, works hard, and has a desire to succeed but is unsure about whether, as a manager, she can convey a success feeling to subordinates.

Paper-and-Pencil Tests. In addition to the set of exercises just described, a series of tests are administered to participants during the 3½-day program. These tests are much less significant as assessment tools than are the exercises described previously. They are used only if they support behavioral data based on performance during the exercises. If they do not support such data they are ignored. Two kinds of tests are used, including:

A. Projective tools
  1. Sentence completion tests. A sentence completion test consists of a few words which are presented to the assessee to stimulate the formation of a sentence.
  2. Thematic Apperception Test. In the Thematic Apperception Test (TAT) the candidate is shown a series of pictures and asked to write a story about what is happening in the picture, what led up to the events described, and what the outcomes will be.
B. Bell System Qualifying Test (BSQT). This is an in-house instrument, developed by Educational Testing Service for the Bell System, which measures mental ability.

Walt Jackson's Performance. *The psychologist's report of Walt's Projective tests indicated that he is an open, realistic, down-to-earth kind of person. He is neither "driven" nor complacent but instead has established a comfortable balance between these two characteristics. Doing his best and living up to his potential are important to him. He is comfortable with competition but not highly competitive himself. He seems to prefer a cooperative approach but can be competitive on occasion. He likes people, is friendly and optimistic. He is accepting of people, values them for their individual qualities but is not a "do-gooder." He has a healthy interest in knowing himself better and working towards self-improvement. He views failure as an opportunity for* *growth. He doesn't expect to win every time but does want to always do his best. He is optimistic about his future, although in the past he has had family and monetary problems. Money is important to him now. He regrets having gotten a late or slow start in his career. In general, he takes a sensible, realistic approach to life, work, and interactions with others.*

On the Bell System Qualifying Test Walt received much higher percentile scores on verbal (78) than quantitative (10).

Donna Lawrence's Performance. *The psychologist's report of Donna's Projective tests indicated that she is an independent thinker, is very analytical in her approach to problem solving, organizes and plans actions carefully. She is not afraid to state opinions which are positive or negative but relies heavily on others for support. She tends to be a perfectionist who values excellence in herself and others and consequently is seldom satisfied with an end product. She gets great satisfaction from performing well but can be somewhat intolerant and impatient.*

Donna values honest, hard work, and "people relationships." She relates effectively to authority. She enjoys excitement, challenge, and even potentially threatening situations. She reacts well to stress and sees herself at her best when under pressure.

Donna has a good self-concept and self-respect. She works hard to increase her competence and increase working opportunities. At work she seeks support, acceptance, and recognition. She seems to relate easily to people and treats them as individuals. She is a relatively open person with a sense of humor. Her view of herself seems fairly objective and relatively accurate.

Donna likes to minimize boss/subordinate roles and prefers a more equal relationship. She is uncomfortable "bossing" and "being bossed" because she feels that is overbearing and demeaning. Since she is her own worst critic she resents further criticism. She feels she is regarded as a self-starting, energetic, bright, and competent person.

On the Bell System Qualifying Test, Donna scored in the 95th percentile in verbal, the 97th percentile in quantitive, for a total score in the 96th percentile.

Evaluation and Feedback

Following the 3½-day period, assessors were divided into two teams to evaluate candidates' performances. Teams were headed by the center director or one of the psychologists. Each evaluation took approximately two hours and was divided into three phases: (1) dimension ratings, (2) overall rating and (3) developmental recommendations. In preparation for the evaluation meetings, assessors wrote one- or two-page descriptive narrative reports about the candidates' behavior during each assessment activity. In the meeting their reports were read aloud and then they proceeded to individually rate 24 dimensions of behavior divided into six categories (see Exhibit 4 for a sample form).

To rate candidates, assessors assign a number between 1 and 5 for performance on each dimension. Each number is assigned a meaning which is behaviorally anchored and described clearly in an assessor manual. A behaviorally anchored rating scale is one in which each numerical point on the scale is explicitly defined by a description of the behavior an individual must display to receive that numerical score. Such scales are generally acknowledged to increase the reliability (consistency over time) of ratings and therefore their predictive validity and validity of the assessment.

A rating of 1 indicates a low amount of a behavior was observed and a 5 indicates that a high amount of that behavior was observed. Thus, 1 generally indicates poor

Exhibit 4 Variable Rating Form—Individual* (AMPA)

Code No. _____
Date _____
Staff Member _____

Personal Qualities:
1. Energy . . . . _____
2. Self-objectivity . . . . _____
3. Tolerance of uncertainty . . . . _____
4. Resistance to stress . . . . _____
5. Range of interests . . . . _____
6. Scholastic aptitude . . . . _____

Communication skills:
7. Oral presentation . . . . _____
8. Oral defense . . . . _____
9. Written communication . . . . _____

Interpersonal skills:
10. Leadership . . . . _____
11. Impact . . . . _____
12. Behavior flexibility . . . . _____
13. Awareness of social environment . . . . _____
14. Autonomy . . . . _____

Administrative skills:
15. Decision making . . . . _____
16. Decisiveness . . . . _____
17. Organizing and planning . . . . _____

Analytical skills:
18. Fact-finding . . . . _____
19. Interpreting information . . . . _____
20. Problem solving . . . . _____

Career orientation:
21. Inner work standards . . . . _____
22. Goal orientation . . . . _____
23. Need advancement . . . . _____
24. Development orientation . . . . _____

Overall rating: Indication of potential to perform effectively at fifth
level is:
Excellent _____
Good _____
Moderate _____
Low _____

* Each quality or skill is rated by assessors on a five-point scale with each point on the scale
illustrated by a descriptive statement which defines the extent to which the person demonstrated
the behavior.

performance and 5 indicates excellence. When rating candidates on various dimensions such as energy, decisiveness, or problem solving, assessors do this in relation to their extensive knowledge of other Bell System executives. That is, individual ratings are done in the context of Bell System executives in general, not just other assessment center participants. This is thought to increase their objectivity.

During evaluation meetings assessors do differ in their rating of a candidate on given dimensions. When ratings with a one-point spread are given, they are recorded without much discussion. The rating most often given is the final assigned rating. For instance, if three assessors assign a 4 to the fact-finding dimension and the fourth assigns a 5, a 4 is the final rating given. In the event of a tie the team leader makes the final decision. If, however, there is a two-point spread, discussion is required to eliminate the spread. After all of the dimensions are rated, then and only then are overall ratings assigned. Candidates receive an excellent, good, moderate, or low rating to indicate level of assessed promotability. These scores are based on performance during the exercises but are also influenced by assessor understanding of what is required in a top management job.

After arriving at an overall rating, assessors make developmental recommendations which are based upon all pertinent information gathered during the 3½-day period, the back-home personnel vice president's nomination form, and the candidate's application. These recommendations are shared with the personnel vice president and the candidate as feedback.

Two specific feedback mechanisms were employed by the center. The first was a written report to be sent to the vice president of personnel of each candidate's Bell System company (company coordinator) prepared by the center director. The report, which might be used by the vice president for staffing decisions, consisted of (a) an overall rating of potential; (b) a description of candidate performance; (c) an overview of strengths and weaknesses in each dimension area (personal characteristics, communication skills, interpersonal skills, administrative skills, analytical skills, and career orientation); and (d) suggested developmental assignments and activities. The vice president of personnel was the only recipient of this report. It was stored in a private personnel file and was not part of the individual's general personnel record.

Assessment center performance makes up only part of a promotional decision. One personnel vice president spoke for his own company and some of his peers in other companies when he commented upon how the AMPA results are considered:

> At lower levels, if we are confident an individual is promotable, we may put aside or ignore negative recommendations. However, at higher levels competition is greater and, I suppose, it would be difficult to promote someone who did poorly at AMPA. Still, AMPA results just can't be the only tool. They shouldn't wipe out an individual's future. As I said before we *do* take results seriously, and we *certainly* take developmental recommendations seriously. . . . But if our own perceptions are not confirmed we owe it to ourselves and the individual we sent to think twice.

The second feedback mechanism was a one-to-one meeting between an AT&T staff psychologist and the candidate. Wherever possible, this meeting was scheduled within two weeks of the actual assessment. The meeting consisted of an in-depth discussion of performance, self-perceptions, and developmental needs as discovered during the assessment process.

Although many candidates leave Atlanta already having learned a great deal about themselves, the feedback provides an objective view of performance and an additional opportunity for increased self-understanding and career or personal counseling.

When the assessors for AMPA 1978 met to evaluate Walt and Donna, they had a tough job ahead of them. Both candidates demonstrated a variety of strengths and weaknesses. They were viewed positively by some and negatively by others. As the assessors began their meeting they knew lively discussion would follow.

Leaving AMPA

Walt and Donna left AMPA with mixed feelings. They were in some ways relieved it was over. In other ways they were excited about the experience. Both were curious about the way in which they performed, looked forward to the feedback they would receive, and wondered about the impact such feedback would have on their careers.

ASSESSING MANAGERIAL TALENT AT AT&T (B) WALTER JACKSON'S RESULTS
Emily Stein and Michael Beer

Walter Jackson first came to the Bell System in 1970 on an exchange program from Western Electric. His first job was a level 3 line position in the plant department. Eighteen months later he was transferred to a similar position in marketing. Subsequently he was transferred back to the plant as district manager, the position he held when he was sent to AMPA. Five months after participating in the assessment program Jackson was promoted to general personnel supervisor, a level 4 staff position. According to Jackson the promotion was, at least in part, due to

the overall *good rating* he received in Atlanta. Walt Jackson discussed his feelings before, during, and after AMPA and his opinions about the entire assessment process:

For some time I've been familiar with the assessment process. When I heard I was nominated, I was flattered but didn't think much about it. I heard from my boss that I'd be going about three weeks before the program, put it on my calendar, and that was it. I was confident in myself. I thought it would be some kind of challenge but wasn't at all uncomfortable. I figured that the results of the process would either support data about me that had already been acquired from my on-the-job performance or would raise some questions. I wasn't expecting a promotion and wasn't really striving for one, so for me it was no big event.

Once I got to Atlanta, though, my feelings changed a bit. It was stressful. There were people in my group who were also being assessed who were very anxious. They felt it could make or break them. It was a very competitive situation. There was some camaraderie but overall, it was competitive. As we got involved in the exercises it became very obvious that everyone was there to do well for themselves. The exercises were stimulating and I think they were valid measures of certain skills. The people there, assessors and assessees, were top-notch.

The group exercises were challenging. The investment problem was a good one for me. I felt I performed well on that one. I wasn't pleased with my performance, however, on the Riverview exercise. I struggled with whether to say what I thought they wanted me to say or whether to say what I wanted to say. I tried to do a little of both and as a result it was a muddled mess. One thing I didn't like was all those paper-and-pencil and psychological tests. While doing those I got the feeling that this was an experiment for my level of management and that I was a guinea pig being observed every step of the way. During that part of it I kept thinking that, if I had a choice, I wouldn't go through with it. There was no choice, though, and I was there to participate so I did. I'm not convinced that those kinds of tests have much value.

After the program, on my very own, although I tried not to, I couldn't help but evaluate my own performance. I thought at that time I'd done pretty well. However, my feelings of confidence came and went. Even though I thought I'd done well, I wasn't quite sure I knew what the assessors had been looking for. I picked up signals from the people in my group and from some of the assessors that I had done well, but I really wasn't sure. I really had no idea about the kind of feedback I'd receive. Two weeks later when the psychologist from Atlanta came to give me feedback he said that, in fact, I had done well. He told me that the *good rating* was second from the top and that not too many people had earned such a high rating. Needless to say I was pleased. He said, on the positive side, that I seemed very aware and well-read. He also said I seemed to have high interpersonal skills. On the negative side he said I came across with very little motivation for advancement, and if my other strengths hadn't been there that I wouldn't have gotten such a good rating because of this. To tell the truth that surprised me a bit. But, I know myself pretty well, and when I thought about it I realized that at this point in my life, I'm 45, promotion wasn't that important to me. I work hard but I don't need a promotion to let me know I'm good. I have a lot of outside interests, some real estate, for instance, and I get a lot of gratification there. My job with the Bell System is only one part of my life. The psychologist also said, on the negative side, that I'm too demanding of myself and of others sometimes and ought to let up. He also said that I tend to be too cautious when making decisions and suggested I try to be more spontaneous. He didn't really have specific developmental recommendations for me. He said that I should just behave like I always behave because it seems to be working pretty well. After that meeting I felt pretty good. I didn't think a promotion was imminent but I definitely felt I was in the running.

On the whole I feel that AMPA is a pretty good measure of certain skills, but I'm not convinced that it really can predict how you do on the job in the day-to-day work environment. I don't think any assessment process can measure or predict that. In my company I feel that assessment is just one tool used to make decisions about promotions and that's good. But in other companies it seems to have more weight—I think that is wrong. There were people in my program for instance who I found out didn't do well at all. Maybe it's because they weren't capable, but maybe it's because they were so wound up about it they couldn't do well, or really didn't want to be there. For those people, negative assessment results were devastating. They felt as if their value as individuals was diminished. As we left, some people were very depressed and were talking about resigning. That's just not right. From my understanding, everyone who was sent to AMPA was viewed as competent on the job. If the assessment process ruins a career or someone's self-image, that's just not right.

ASSESSING MANAGERIAL TALENT AT AT&T (C) DONNA LAWRENCE'S RESULTS
Emily Stein and Michael Beer

When Donna Lawrence graduated from college in 1970 with an engineering degree she joined AT&T as a level 1 engineer in the network department. Subsequently she was promoted to a level 2 engineer and was responsible for long-range planning and cost analysis. When she was sent to AMPA she held a level 3 district-level manager position. Donna discussed her feelings about participating in the assessment program, her experiences at AMPA and her feelings about her feedback and the *"moderate" rating* she received:

When I heard my boss had nominated me to attend AMPA I was flattered and anxious. Several years ago I had attended a lower level assessment program and knew basically what to expect. Although I had done very well there and was promoted, I was still very anxious about AMPA. I was sure my competition would be much tougher. I envisioned polished MBA types with enthusiasm, energy, and real management potential. I was certain it was a do or die situation. I learned I'd be going to Atlanta about one month before I went; my anxiety built up steadily during that month.

When I got to Atlanta my fears were confirmed. The first night a bunch of the assessees went to dinner and I distinctly remember one woman in our group who set the tone by talking about what a cut-throat experience we'd be going through, and she wanted us all to know she wasn't planning on giving anyone any support and suggested that we all look out for ourselves. She stunned a lot of us and intimidated me, but finally a couple of us told her we didn't think it had to be a backbiting session but if she were going to backbite us we'd be sure to backbite her. That sort of set the tone for our group. It turned out to be very competitive and there was little camaraderie. There were subgroups formed of people who had similar reactions to that first encounter with "backbiter." I was with a group of about six who met for drinks and dinner and shared experiences, albeit reservedly under the theory that mutual support was as appropriate at AMPA as it is in life. That added to my anxiety. As anxious as I was, though, I wasn't as bad as some. Some people were afraid that if they didn't "pass" they'd have to quit their job because they couldn't bear the embarrassment of having gone through

assessment without a promotion. To be honest I guess I did feel some of that pressure, too. . . . During the program I really had no idea of how I was doing. On some exercises I thought I'd done very well when in fact I didn't do well at all. In other aspects of the program I was sure I'd done poorly but in fact, I'd done well. On the group exercises specifically I could feel I didn't participate enough. When I did speak I wasn't speaking clearly, intelligibly. I was disorganized, distracted, and still very anxious. Maybe that was because the backbiter was in my group. She really did intimidate me. I think I performed better on the paper-and-pencil tests. I guess I felt less anxious on those activities than during the group exercises themselves.

As I left the center I was exhausted, relieved, numb, and had grave doubts about how I'd done. I finally got feedback at an off-site meeting with a psychologist from Atlanta. True, he was very skillful in the way he presented it. He started out by telling me the good things, then the bad things, then he gave me the bottom line overall rating. That was clever of him because if he'd given me the rating first I probably wouldn't have heard the rest. Anyway, he told me I was intelligent and very charming. He really stressed the intelligence aspect and that was great. Then he mentioned that my written communication skills were poor and that I was lacking in administrative abilities. He recommended I get an MBA to build up my areas of weakness or at least take some kind of English composition course. At the time I felt that the feedback was odd. Part of my job involves writing letters for my boss. I've never had any complaints about them, they always go through. That made me think that part of the assessment was inaccurate. No one has ever complained about my writing before so I was surprised by that part of the feedback. The psychologist also told me that I have received a *moderate rating*. He explained that the rating was one of the higher ones given in my group. I felt very upbeat when I left that meeting. It took me several weeks to get over how intelligent I was!

When I look back on the assessment experience, in a way, I feel intruded upon. In one sense, I think in my case, the program measured how I reacted to anxiety rather than how capable I might be as a level 5 manager. In all my years working, I have never been put in as pressure-filled a situation as I had been in Atlanta. I also felt the group exercises were more game-playing than anything else. When you are in a work environment you know who you're dealing with; why they are there; and for the most part, you are all working for a common goal. At work, people are more concerned about their reputations as fair and honest people. At the assessment center it's a group of short-term strategists, with diverse motives; that just isn't like work. I don't think the exercises meant that much. For me the paper-and-pencil tests were more constructive than the exercises. When I think about how I did personally I can't help but think that the program put unrealistic time limits on me which just muddled my thinking. Also the back-stabber really intimidated me. That really made me too anxious to perform the way I really can perform. One other thing, when I think of the feedback I got I question their conclusions. No other source in my life had given me the kind of feedback they did, so I can't help but question it. I have some real questions too about the developmental recommendations. They make me feel intruded upon more than anything else. I'm too busy to take a course or get an MBA right now. To be honest I just don't want to now. I wonder what that will mean for my future here.

CASE 7
SUNDOWN MOTELS
Frederic Jacobs

Shutting his eyes, Doug DiMichi could hear Ralph Polk, his former teacher and faculty ad-

viser at the Harvard Business School, say: "There is a mine field out there and it's not marketing strategy or financial management or competition. Plainly and simply, it's the personnel function *that can blow you up, blow you up and destroy you, even if your product is a good one, and the company is strong. Personnel is a morass, and presidents can never be heros if they get involved; they just get their legs blown off!" DiMichi opened his eyes and shook his head from side to side wondering how he had gotten into this mess. After 11 years of steady growth and generally well-respected leadership, Sundown Consolidated Companies was facing a serious problem, and DiMichi's own credibility and effectiveness was in jeopardy.*

A Company's Growth

When Doug DiMichi graduated from the Harvard Business School in 1956, he began working for Traveler's Friend Motels (TFM), a company with approximately 30 motels mostly in the Southeast and Mid-Atlantic states. DiMichi was hired as assistant vice president for marketing, and he was responsible for "multi-unit sales," working with companies to encourage their employees, usually sales people, to stay at Traveler's Friend motels. DiMichi developed a reasonably successful discount plan and, in 1958, introduced an "incentive" bonus plan through which both employees and employers would receive S&H "green stamps." The incentive plan caused a minor revolution in marketing motels to commercial users, and Dimichi was, before he was 30, a well established and wealthy hotel executive. By 1962 he had become executive vice president at TFM, and one of its principal stockholders.

In 1963, partly on a hunch, and partly because he believed that Eisenhower's signing of the Interstate Highway Act in 1954 would eventually transform the society, he added "Sundown Centers" at 10 TF motels. These centers provided recreational arcades for children, supervised activities such as swimming, baseball and basketball, and "pubs" and restaurants for adults. The Sundown Centers were so successful that, by 1966, TFM began changing the name of its 58 motels (now operating in 11 states, still predominantly in the Southeast and Mid-Atlantic states) to "Sundown Inns." In 1968, the president of the company retired, and he and the board of directors offered DiMichi the position of president and chairman of the board. DiMichi accepted, and began a corporate reorganization which was completed in mid-1969, and the new entity was named Sundown Inns–USA (SI–USA).

DiMichi believed that SI–USA could be the foundation on which he would construct a network of restaurants, motels, recreation centers, and other leisure services in response to the increasing mobility and discretionary income of the American public. Through his hard work, aggressive marketing, and strategic assessments of emerging trends, he had transformed TFM into an important competitor in the motel industry, and the company had grown and prospered. In taking over a motel industry company with income of under $10 million, DiMichi had two short-term goals:

1. To double the income of SI–USA by 1975, and double it again by 1980.
2. To diversify SI–USA into other segments of the travel, recreation, and leisure markets.

The first opportunity for diversification came in 1970 when a small British-owned chain of hotels in the Bahamas and British Virgin Islands was offered for sale. DiMichi set up "Sundown Carib, Ltd.," and immediately offered "points" to anyone who stayed at an SI–USA facility; these "points" could be accumulated and used to discount prices at the Caribbean facilities owned by DiMichi's company. Within 18 months the new venture was so successful that DiMichi had to charter planes to transport guests to the Caribbean facilities.

Ever alert for new opportunities, DiMichi, disgruntled over bad-quality food when he traveled, offered to establish a franchise food operation for Nassau Air and Air Caribbean, the two principal carriers his company used. In its first year of operation (1972), Sundown Airport Services showed a considerable profit, and DiMichi was able to acquire franchises with several domestic carriers and secured a license to operate terminal cocktail lounges, restaurants, and snack bars at the airports in Memphis and Nashville.

These three corporate operations were very successful, and, somewhat to his own surprise, DiMichi noted that income had doubled in four years, and that the profits were, indeed, respectable. He made a decision to move ahead somewhat more slowly for the next year or two, but in late November 1973, DiMichi was presented with an opportunity "he couldn't refuse." The opportunity involved a comprehensive franchise package to develop transportation, housing, and eating facilities at eight sites in the Northeast for downhill and cross-country skiing.

With four separate and flourishing enterprises, DiMichi sought to create an umbrella organization and, thus, in 1974, Sundown Consolidated Companies (SCC) was established. (Exhibit 1 provides a financial summary of SCC and its components, 1969–80; Exhibit 2 shows the organization chart for SCC and its components, 1980.)

Exhibit 1   Financial Summary—Sundown Consolidated Companies (SCC)

Year	Total Income ($000s)	Total Expense ($000s)	Growth Over Previous Year (Percent)	Profit (Loss) ($000s)	Profit (Loss) (Percent)
1969	9,136	8,654	N/A	482	5.57
1970	11,840	10,960	22.8	880	7.43
1971	14,336	12,471	17.4	1865	13.0
1972	18,734	17,190	23.4	1544	8.24
1973	21,934	19,817	14.6	2117	9.65
1974	26,811	24,209	18.2	2602	9.7
1975	29,146	26,747	8.0	2399	8.2
1976	32,504	29,183	10.3	3321	10.2
1977	36,381	33,168	8.8	3213	8.8
1978	40,036	38,155	9.1	1881	4.7
1979	42,682	40,404	6.2	2278	5.3
1980	45,987	43,184	7.2	2803	6.1

Organizational Structure and Policies at SCC

Although pleased with the growth of his company, DiMichi was determined not to permit too wide a span of authority. The organizational structure he devised gave autonomy to the four directors (Sundown Motels—USA, Sundown Airport Services, Sundown Carib, Ltd., and Sundown RecResorts) who reported to a group vice president (Operations). But, many of the routine operations of SCC were channeled through the operations of the two senior operating offices of the company—the executive vice president and the financial vice president. One key element of the organizational structure was the Internal Auditing and Purchasing Department, which authorized and monitored all purchases and expenditures. As his two senior executives, DiMichi appointed two long-time associates, Schyler Dempe, hired in 1974, to be financial vice president, and Bruce Perkins, hired in 1977 as executive vice president. (Exhibit 3 identifies the principal persons in the case study.)

Dempe had spent his entire career at TFM and SCC, and, in fact, had started working there the same month as DiMichi. He was, in every sense, a "company man," loyal, persevering, and conservative. A competitor once said that Dempe was "ideal" at financial policy implementation and control. "No one is better in that area," he said, "but he is without any perspective whatsoever about creative leadership." Perkins, on the other hand, while equally loyal to DiMichi and SCC, was a task-oriented person who had a reputation for being crafty and shrewd. A former, disgruntled employee said: "Perkins is ruthless and, therefore, a lousy friend. But, he'd be a worse enemy!" Perkins and Dempe worked well together, and DiMichi relied on them to keep a relatively tight rein on the organization. Dempe accomplished this by careful development of procedures, and Perkins achieved this by being abrasive and aggressive when necessary. Prior to becoming executive vice president, Perkins had been manager of Sundown Inns–USA, and felt that, because he had come "from the ranks," he understood

Exhibit 2 Organization Chart for Sundown Consolidated Companies (SCC) (1980)

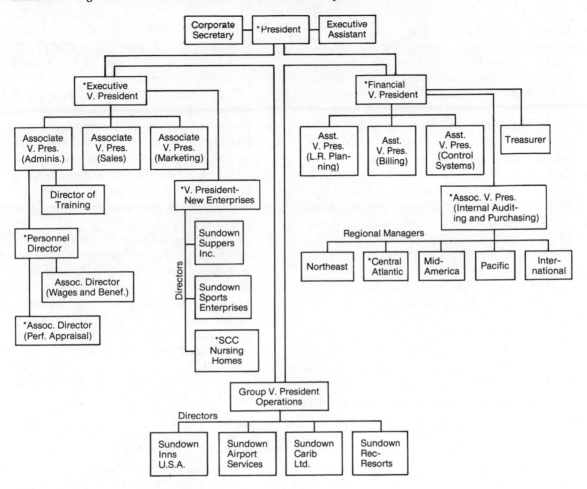

* Denotes person identified in case.

Exhibit 3 Principal Persons in SCC Case Study

Doug DiMichi	— President
Bruce Perkins	— Executive Vice President
Schyler Dempe	— Financial Vice President
Jonathan Henry	— Associate Vice President (Internal Auditing and Purchasing)
Gwen Laker	— Personnel Director
Frank Blessing	— Regional Manager (Internal Auditing and Purchasing)—Central Atlantic
Margaret-Ann Flandell	— Director—SCC Nursing Homes, Inc.
Morris Landers	— Associate Director (Performance Appraisal)
Timothy Edwards	— Vice President: New Enterprises

how to exercise appropriate control and restraint.

One personnel aspect of the company had always been something of a problem. SCC was often characterized by two descriptions: "acquisitive" and "aggressive." As an acquisitive organization, SCC "inherited" a number of employees whose long service (and, occasionally, age) made it difficult to terminate them; as an aggressive company, SCC had a number of young, ambitious, technically trained people who were on a "fast track." On occasion, these groups clashed, not in overt ways, but in manifestations of different values and perspectives.

There were four related policies in the area of personnel and salary:

1. Annual increments, for the most part, were linked to corporate profits, and, in most years, the median increment was within 1 percent of the percent of profit. (See Exhibit 4, Economic Indicators and Financial Information Re: SCC.)

2. "Merit" raises were limited to a small group, usually upper management.

3. Profit sharing, which extended to all line managers and senior staff and management, was calculated through a complex formula which skewed both to long-term and "fast-track" employees. (See Exhibit 5, Explanation of the Profit Sharing Plan at SCC.)

4. As a consequence of the above, *salary* decisions and *performance* appraisals were separate from one another in most instances. That is, while performance appraisals did take place, the "intensely systematized" policies regarding salary occurred independently of the evaluation procedures.

Exhibit 4   **Economic Indicators and Financial Information Re: SCC**

Year	National Inflation Rate (Percent)	SCC Profit (Percent)	SCC Median Employee Increase (Percent)	Special Note
1970	5.4%	7.43%	8%	First year of operation: Sundown Carib, Ltd.
1971	4.3	13.0	11	
1972	3.3	8.24	7	First year of operation: Sundown Airport Services
1973	6.2	9.65	8	First year of operation: Sundown RecResorts
1974	11.0	9.7	11	
1975	9.1	8.2	9	First year of operation: Sundown Sports Enterprises
1976	5.8	10.2	8	First year of operation: Sundown Suppers, Inc.
1977	6.5	8.8	7.5	
1978	7.7	4.7	5	First year of operation: SCC Nursing Homes
1979	11.3	5.3	5	
1980	13.5	6.1	8	

Exhibit 5 The Profit-Sharing Plan at SCC

Profit sharing is based on determining the number of Equity Shares (ES) for each eligible employee, and using that as a basis for calculating the unit value (UV) of each ES. There are two formulas used:

I. *Determining Number of Equity Shares (ES)*

$$ES = \frac{(.005\ S)(x)(1.y)}{10}$$

S = Annual salary
x = .1 per year of employment
y = merit increment range = 1.0 to 3.0)

Examples of I:

(1) Employee @ $25,000 for 12 years
Recently upgraded: merit increment is .3
$$ES = \frac{(125)(1.2)(1.3)}{10} = 19.5$$

(2) Employee @ $46,000 for two years
Recently promoted for 2d time in 18 months; merit increment is .9
$$ES = \frac{(230)(.2)(1.9)}{10} = 8.7$$

(3) Employee @ $39,000 for three years
Named regional V.P.; merit increment is 1.7
$$ES = \frac{(190)(.3)(2.7)}{10} = 15.4$$

(4) Employee @ $40,000 for six years
Exceeded sales quota: merit increment is .75
$$ES = \frac{(200)(.6)(1.75)}{10} = 21.$$

(5) Employee @ $32,000 for four years
No merit increment assigned
$$ES = (160)(.4)(1.) = 6.4$$

II. *Determining Unit Value (UV) of Equity Shares*

$$UV = \frac{AD}{N}$$

AD = Amount distributed ($)
N = Total of equity shares

Examples of II:

$$UV = \frac{\$36,000}{71.0}\ \text{(Amount approved by directors for distribution)}\\ \text{(Total of equity shares)}$$

$$UV = \$507$$

Example	Annual Salary	No. of Equity Shares @ $507	Dollar Amount of Profit Sharing	Percent of Salary
1	$25,000	19.5	9,886	39.5%
2	46,000	8.7	4,411	9.6
3	39,000	15.4	7,808	20.0
4	40,000	21.	10,647	26.6
5	32,000	6.4	3,245	10.1
		71.0	$35,997	

To a considerable extent, this situation reflected the mutual influence of Dempe and Perkins. The former wanted the rigors of an established process; the latter wanted the flexibility "to get the job done." Together, they created a situation and system which was accepted passively because, while company profits were high, so, too, were annual raises. And, furthermore, most employees understood that the "mechanically perfect" evaluation system had little impact on salaries or promotion. In short, it was administered, but not used.

Personnel Policy and Performance Appraisal at SCC

The personnel function at SCC had three components (see Exhibit 2):

- Training.
- Wages and benefits.
- Performance appraisal.

All of these function areas reported to the associate vice president (Administration). Gwen Laker, the personnel director, was primarily responsible for corporate hiring and for establishing hiring policies among the various corporate units. She published quarterly reports on "equity groups" and "salary steps" which were used by various directors and managers. In practice, deviations of up to 15 percent were routinely approved by Laker.

Morris Landers, associate director of personnel for performance appraisal, reported to Gwen Laker, but, in reality, worked very independently. Trained as a social psychologist, Landers had been brought to SCC in 1972 when the third corporate entity (Sundown Airport Services) had been acquired. Landers's job consisted of two principal tasks:

1. Reviewing the job and performance history of SCC employees acquired through merger and consolidation.
2. Developing a performance appraisal system which included information on perceived role and performance, interaction between employee and supervisor, potential for different or additional assignments.

To accomplish this, Landers developed a Standard Questionnaire (See Exhibit 6) which was used each year as part of the Annual Performance Review (APR). The APR consisted of the questionnaire, filled out by employee and supervisor, a review of attendance, and a comparison of salary steps and equity groups which was undertaken by Gwen Laker and her staff. Finally, if the employee was eligible for profit sharing, a merit factor was assigned by his or her immediate supervisor; in other instances, recommendations for merit or bonus increments were forwarded to the executive vice president for review and approval. The APR took place within one month of the anniversary of the start of employment. Salary changes were made on either January or July 1. Thus, for an employee who began work in March, the APR and salary change dates might be three months apart.

Landers believed that the system he devised had several unique features. First of all, he was convinced that the opportunity for *mutual* feedback was invaluable, and that it provided opportunities for candor and constructive criticism. Second, it protected long time employees of "acquired" units from capricious behavior by new supervisors by making *explicit* the requirements and expectations of the job. Finally, its standardization throughout SCC made it "inconspicuous" that any one person was being singled out for scrutiny.

Exhibit 6   Performance Appraisal System at SCC (Standard Questionnaire)

NOTE: Supervisor and Employee
            fill out identical forms

Annual Performance Apprisal for SCC Staff

Staff Member:_____   Date:_____

Department:_____   Job Title:_____

_____
_____

Section I
1. Please list the three most important responsibilities in this position, and rate the staff member's performance accordingly:

Unsatisfactory——Satisfactory
1   2   3   4   5

    _____
    _____
    _____

Section II
1. Please describe the staff member's major strengths in performing the job:
    _____
    _____
    _____

2. Are there special skills or knowledge required for the job which the staff member could obtain in order to perform the work satisfactorily now? In the future? _____ Yes _____ No (If yes, please elaborate.)
    _____
    _____
    _____

3. If the staff member has been employed for over a year, have there been performance changes since the last evaluation _____ Yes _____ No _____ Not applicable (If, yes, please discuss.)
    _____
    _____
    _____

4. Does the attached job description for this position adequately correspond with current duties and responsibilities? _____ Yes _____ No (If no, how does it differ?)
    _____
    _____
    _____

Exhibit 6 (*continued*)

Section III
Please rate performance in the following categories by checking the most appropriate description:

1. *Knowledge of job*
   a. ___ Excellent grasp of job content, displays initiative in learning new tasks and/or acquiring additional information
   b. ___ Good grasp of job duties, requires very little in further instruction
   c. ___ Adequate grasp of job, but still requires some assistance
   d. ___ Poor, limited job knowledge
   If appropriate, please indicate how performance could be improved.

2. *Organization*
   a. ___ Very well organized, methodical in follow-through
   b. ___ Good organization of work
   c. ___ Adequate organization of work, but improvement possible
   d. ___ Unsatisfactory organization of work
   If appropriate, please indicate how performance could be improved.

3. *Quality of work*
   (do not consider
   quantity here)
   a. ___ Work is always complete and of high quality, with few (if any errors)
   b. ___ Work is generally complete with minimal errors
   c. ___ Adequate work, but improvement possible
   d. ___ Work is generally incomplete and/or contains many errors
   If appropriate, please indicate how performance could be improved.

4. *Quantity of work*
   (volume)
   a. ___ Productivity consistently surpasses expectations
   b. ___ Productivity meets job standards and sometimes exceeds them
   c. ___ Productivity meets minimal standards
   d. ___ Work is not completed in reasonable amount of time
   If appropriate, please indicate how performance could be improved.

5. *Supervision needed*
   a. ___ Individual knows what to do and accomplishes it without supervision or specific direction
   b. ___ Minimal supervision and/or direction needed
   c. ___ Periodic supervision and some explicit direction needed
   d. ___ Close supervision and much direction required on a regular basis
   If appropriate, please indicate how performance could be improved.

6. *Cooperation/Attitude*
   (interpersonal skills)
   a. ___ Extremely positive attitude, consistently very cooperative with others
   b. ___ Good work attitude, cooperates well with others in most instances
   c. ___ Adequate work attitude, but improvement possible
   d. ___ Unsatisfactory work attitude, frequently uncooperative
   If appropriate, please indicate how performance could be improved.

7. *Punctuality/Attendance*
   a. ___ Rarely late or absent; responsible about calling in and making extra effort to "catch up" on work
   b. ___ Occasional absences or tardiness; careful to call in

Exhibit 6 (*concluded*)

        c. __ Late or absent more than desirable; occasionally may be careless about calling in

        d. __ Absences/tardiness are of such magnitude that office operations are negatively affected; careless about calling in

If appropriate, please indicate how performance could be improved.

Section IV
Summary:
   The results of this evaluation and the staff member's self-evaluation are intended to be shared, with comments noted below.

Staff Member:

_____
_____
_____
_____

Supervisor:

_____
_____
_____
_____

Signature: *Signature:*
Staff Member:_____   Supervisor:_____

Date:_____   Date:_____

RETURN COMPLETED FORM(S) TO SCC PERSONNEL OFFICE

December
1980

Adherence to the system was very high, and, although some questionnaires were tardy, there was an annual response rate of 95+ percent. Even Perkins and Dempe filled out questionnaires, working with DiMichi. In writing his annual report in 1977 after working at SCC for five years, Landers said:

> There are two flaws in the present system which I hope we can improve upon over time. First, the system does not provide for enough differentiation among units within SCC. For example, sluggish units, or newly acquired ones, may need more flexibility and a greater range of salaries, responsibilities, and descriptions than we presently have. Our system has the advantage of even-handedness, but it may lack incentive jolts. Second, we have linked salary and performance in a manner in which suggests that performance is rewarded only or exclusively through salary. Good or exemplary performance should lead to other rewards,

such as additional training, in order to prepare for new responsibilities.

In general, however, the APR worked well, and there was little complaint about it. Landers knew that, at the extremes, the APR did not work well. He knew, for example, that some marginal employees were "carried" despite inferior performance, and he was occasionally surprised to find that an individual who rose rapidly within SCC had received an average APR a year before. For the most part, however, the system seemed based on sound principles, and appeared to be administered effectively, and was well received.

Further Growth, Economic Stagnation, and Low Morale

From 1975 to 1978, SCC acquired three additional units, all of which were new developments rather than acquisitions. These were:

- *Sundown Sports Enterprises* (1975): a series of tennis, squash, and racketball clubs.
- *Sundown Suppers, Inc.* (1976): prepared meals for the elderly and for shut-ins, under contract with government agencies, charities, and religious groups and civic organizations.
- *SCC Nursing Homes* (1978): a chain of residential facilities for elderly people requiring minimal supervision and medical care.

DiMichi and his colleagues believed that these new enterprises would, over time, become important profit centers for SCC. Some were close to the break-even point after only a year of operation, but all needed close scrutiny and careful organizational support in their formative period. Because they were new entities, rather than acquisitions, they were staffed by existing SCC employees or by "new hires." In every instance, new skills were needed, either in marketing, product development, or technical support. This, in turn, put new and unprecedented demands on corporate resources, in terms of staff support and organizational structure.

In the first instance, the training area of SCC had to develop programs in four areas:

- *Technical training* to support the specialized equipment used, for example, in preparing and storing food, and in "making snow."
- *Marketing and sales* to equip SCC personnel to work in new—and highly competitive and segmented—markets.
- *Support services training* to assist in the increasingly complex operations of SCC, and in response to rapid changes in office technology, such as word processing.
- *Management development* to provide managers and supervisors for an increasingly diversified and far-flung corporation. Training, which had been a relatively small component until 1975, now became a busy—and crucial—operation.

In the latter instance. DiMichi knew that these fledgling operations could not coexist with the existing corporate entities. He modified the organizational structure to accommodate "New Enterprises" through the leadership of a vice president. While ultimately responsible to the executive vice president, these new enterprises were expected to utilize and rely on the resources of the Operations units; for example, billing, purchasing, and internal auditing were still done by offices which reported to the financial vice president. Although the potential for friction was present, in practice the system worked well. A manager for Sundown Suppers, Inc., put it this way: "It may not have been a logical system, but it was a natural one, and there was little apprehension about it."

This continued growth and expansion had made Sundown a profitable company, and consistent with its early practice, good profits were reflected in generous annual increments and profit sharing. In sum, SCC paid its employees well, rewarded its managers and executives generously, and had training and performance appraisal systems which worked effectively and unobtrusively. DiMichi said in his 1978 Annual Report:

> The condition of the company is sound, and our prospects for the future are quite good, indeed. I look to some further expansion, to new acquisitions and new markets and products, but, for the most part, I see us building on the existing network and increasing our share of the markets we are now in.
>
> While I am concerned about high interest rates and inflation, I doubt that we will be adversely affected because we are not in a capital growth posture at this time. Inflation will affect us somewhat, but we need not fret about it.

He soon came to regret those words and that optimism. The rate of inflation rapidly began to influence both operations and income, and the company's rate of growth and rate of profits began to stabilize (see Exhibits 1 and 4). As a result, within a short period of time, morale was low because for three successive years (1978–80) the median annual increase was less than the inflation rate. For the first time in the history of the organization, people began to complain about the *discrepancy* between performance appraisal and salary. A senior person in the marketing division left for a competitor firm. She said: "My salary did not reflect my work or its quality. I could have done half as much for the same raise. I'd much rather be

paid on a commission basis, under the circumstances."

DiMichi, Dempe, and Perkins were aware of the low morale and agreed that, as soon as possible, annual increases would be changed to exceed the inflation rate. As a gesture of concern and support, the amount of profit sharing was reduced by 50 percent from its 1976 high.

Blessing at Sundown

As Doug DiMichi later said: "The setting was ripe for an 'incident' and it would have taken little to precipitate a personnel crisis." The "incident" involved four people: Margaret-Ann Flandell, director, SCC Nursing Homes, Inc.; Jonathan Henry, associate vice president (Internal Auditing and Purchasing); Frank Blessing, regional manager (Internal Auditing and Purchasing)—Central Atlantic; and Timothy Edwards, vice president: New Enterprises.

In May 1980, after several months of frustration, anger, and increasingly acrimonious letters between Flandell and Blessing, Flandell wrote to Edwards, with copies to Henry, Perkins, and Dempe. She said, in part, that "those responsible for the new business units, such as SCC Nursing Homes, need more flexibility than established procedures permit." She went on to say that Blessing, in addition to being hostile and unreceptive, "actually impeded her work."

Previously, she had spoken informally to Jonathan Henry, Blessing's supervisor. He reviewed Blessing's job description with her, and said that he could find "no overt evidence" of either insubordination or overstepping his authority in areas of purchasing and internal auditing. Privately, he believed that Blessing, a long-time employee of Traveler's Friend, had "peaked," and was both tired and resentful. He was tired of being in the same job for 11 years (since it was created), and resentful of "fast-track" people who were clearly marked for success. Blessing, at 54, was six years away from even early retirement, and was neither inept nor incapable. His performance appraisals were adequate, even satisfactory, and Henry believed it unlikely that he would ever be involuntarily terminated. Yet, Henry had had other complaints about Blessing in the past, but none so detailed and adamant as Flandell's. He felt trapped because Blessing was, in his opinion, only marginally effective, but he had no choice but to defend him.

Subsequent to Flandell's letter, a meeting was held in Perkins's office, attended by Perkins, Dempe, and Henry. "It's simple," Perkins said. "We need to get rid of that guy. He's stopping Margaret from getting her work done. I think we should dump him." Henry fidgeted uneasily, and said, "But we have no basis for such drastic action. Frank has been a competent and loyal employee. He's done his job *to the letter*, and he's been told in his APRs that he was acceptable. To 'dump him' would be, would be . . . wrong."

"It wouldn't be *wrong*, Jonathan, it would be an act of treachery to Blessing, and an act of organizational self-destruction," Dempe said in an angry tone. He looked at Perkins and said:

> Bruce, I'm not going to argue on the grounds of humanity, or even on the grounds of haste and impulse. But there are some things more important than getting the job done. You are proposing that we trample our performance appraisal system, and replace it with random, irrational acts. I'd rather keep our systems intact, and deal with the consequences for our individual units, one by one.

Perkins replied: "Our job is to get the job done. We expect to invest $5 million over the next three years in SCC Nursing Homes, and no one person should stand in the way of the flexibility and opportunities we need. The hell with his APRs. Buy him off, fire him, promote him, for God's sake, but get rid of him!"

Tensions—and tempers—were rising, and the room became uncomfortably silent. Finally, Dempe said: "I believe in our present performance appraisal system, not because it's ideal, but because we have institutionalized it, and used it for eight years. At Sundown, Blessing is entitled to his job because we have never indicated dissatisfaction with his work."

"Blessing at Sundown is a curse," Perkins exploded, "and you will bury us in the antics of the personnel people until we move from our desks to the unemployment lines. I don't give a damn what the forms say—if Blessing is an obstacle, he goes, even if he got an 'A' on his silly report card."

Dempe rose and said, rather formally, that he would make a written recommendation to DiMichi. Dempe and Perkins, who normally met six or eight times each day, shook hands and parted without further words. Walking back to his office, Dempe was accompanied by Jonathan Henry, who said: "If we get rid of Blessing, it will make a mockery of the APR; it may be insubordination, but I'd never complete another one."

In Perkins's office, Tim Edwards said: "There's a hell of a lot at stake here; Margaret is pushing like crazy to make SCC Nursing Homes go, and she expects you and me to give her the space and resources to do that. This Blessing incident may get blown out of proportion and cause a real morale problem throughout the New Enterprises division."

Separately, Dempe and Perkins concluded that a storm was brewing, and that DiMichi needed to be involved. Two separate phone calls to him resulted in two separate meetings; and then, a day after the confrontation in Perkins's office, the three men sat down in DiMichi's conference room. They reviewed the events, the specifics, the general issues, and the ramifications of various acts. Finally, DiMichi said: "Guys, I'm beat. This has really jolted me, and I need some time to think this through. Let's meet again in the morning."

DiMichi drummed his fingers on the desk. "I wish I could get some outside, objective help," he thought. Suddenly, he thought about Ralph Polk and the help he had given him over the years. He buzzed his secretary and said: "Get Ralph Polk on the phone, right away."

CASE 8
GENERAL ELECTRIC COMPANY: THE EXECUTIVE MANPOWER OPERATION
David C. Rikert and C. Wickham Skinner

No action—such as interviewing a potential candidate, requesting such an interview, or "informally" discussing an opening with a potential candidate—may be taken prior to obtaining written approval of the candidate slate.

GE Corporate Policy

The General Electric Company had established a Corporate Executive Manpower Staff in 1967 and charged it with the primary responsibility of ensuring the development and timely availability of broadly experienced, competent, and proven general

managers for the company's top positions, including that of CEO. With its charter formally based in corporate policy and informally based in corporate culture, the staff reported directly to the corporate executive office and consisted of three complementary operations believed to be intimately connected: Executive Manpower, Organization Planning, and Executive Compensation.

A major responsibility of the Executive Manpower Operation was the preparation of candidate slates from which an executive was constrained to choose in making appointments to positions at the department echelon and above. Slate development was an interactive process. It was supported by an elaborate annual manpower review and by a corporate management inventory, and it drew upon both the experience of line managers and the extensive, in-depth knowledge of the Executive Manpower Consultants (EMC).

David Orselet was one of five EMCs in 1979. Forty-nine, and with 23 years of experience in GE's Relations function, Orselet was assigned to Sector Executive Jack Welch and the consumer products and services sector. As Welch said, "Successful management is having good people in key places where they can make things happen." Orselet, with professional skills and a corporate-wide perspective, was deeply involved both in helping those "good people" to develop and in matching those "good people" with "key places." By all accounts, he brought a very high level of ability and interest to what was universally acknowledged to be a demanding and highly sensitive role.

General Electric Company

With 1978 sales of $20.1 billion, net earnings of $1.2 billion, and assets of $15 billion,

Exhibit 1   General Electric Company Organization Chart, June 1, 1978

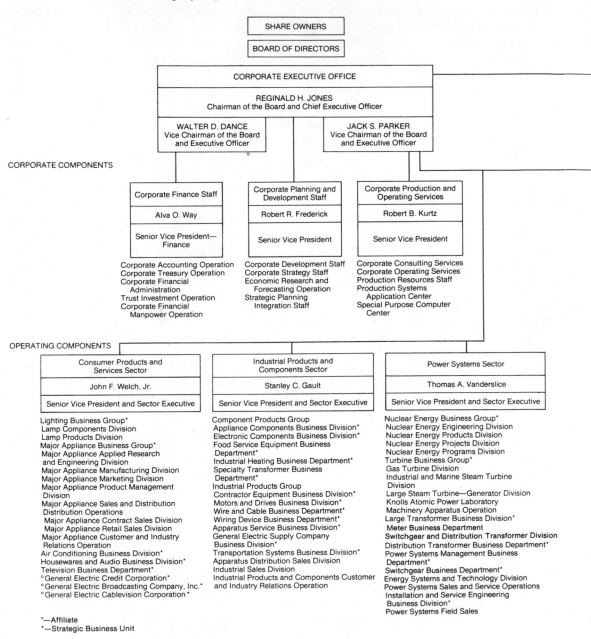

SHARE OWNERS

BOARD OF DIRECTORS

CORPORATE EXECUTIVE OFFICE

REGINALD H. JONES
Chairman of the Board and Chief Executive Officer

WALTER D. DANCE
Vice Chairman of the Board
and Executive Officer

JACK S. PARKER
Vice Chairman of the Board
and Executive Officer

CORPORATE COMPONENTS

Corporate Finance Staff

Alva O. Way

Senior Vice President—
Finance

Corporate Accounting Operation
Corporate Treasury Operation
Corporate Financial
  Administration
Trust Investment Operation
Corporate Financial
  Manpower Operation

Corporate Planning and
Development Staff

Robert R. Frederick

Senior Vice President

Corporate Development Staff
Corporate Strategy Staff
Economic Research and
  Forecasting Operation
Strategic Planning
  Integration Staff

Corporate Production and
Operating Services

Robert B. Kurtz

Senior Vice President

Corporate Consulting Services
Corporate Operating Services
Production Resources Staff
Production Systems
  Application Center
Special Purpose Computer
  Center

OPERATING COMPONENTS

Consumer Products and
Services Sector

John F. Welch, Jr.

Senior Vice President and Sector Executive

Lighting Business Group*
Lamp Components Division
Lamp Products Division
Major Appliance Business Group*
Major Appliance Applied Research
  and Engineering Division
Major Appliance Manufacturing Division
Major Appliance Marketing Division
Major Appliance Product Management
  Division
Major Appliance Sales and Distribution
  Distribution Operations
  Major Appliance Contract Sales Division
  Major Appliance Retail Sales Division
Major Appliance Customer and Industry
  Relations Operation
Air Conditioning Business Division*
Housewares and Audio Business Division*
Television Business Department*
°General Electric Credit Corporation*
°General Electric Broadcasting Company, Inc.*
°General Electric Cablevision Corporation*

Industrial Products and
Components Sector

Stanley C. Gault

Senior Vice President and Sector Executive

Component Products Group
Appliance Components Business Division*
Electronic Components Business Division*
Food Service Equipment Business
  Department*
Industrial Heating Business Department*
Specialty Transformer Business
  Department*
Industrial Products Group
Contractor Equipment Business Division*
Motors and Drives Business Division*
Wire and Cable Business Department*
Wiring Device Business Department*
Apparatus Service Business Division*
General Electric Supply Company
  Business Division*
Transportation Systems Business Division*
Apparatus Distribution Sales Division
Industrial Sales Division
Industrial Products and Components Customer
  and Industry Relations Operation

Power Systems Sector

Thomas A. Vanderslice

Senior Vice President and Sector Executive

Nuclear Energy Business Group*
Nuclear Energy Engineering Division
Nuclear Energy Products Division
Nuclear Energy Projects Division
Nuclear Energy Programs Division
Turbine Business Group*
Gas Turbine Division
Industrial and Marine Steam Turbine
  Division
Large Steam Turbine—Generator Division
Knolls Atomic Power Laboratory
Machinery Apparatus Operation
Large Transformer Business Division*
Meter Business Department
Switchgear and Distribution Transformer Division
Distribution Transformer Business Department*
Power Systems Management Business
  Department*
Switchgear Business Department*
Energy Systems and Technology Division
Power Systems Sales and Service Operations
Installation and Service Engineering
  Business Division*
Power Systems Field Sales

°—Affiliate
*—Strategic Business Unit

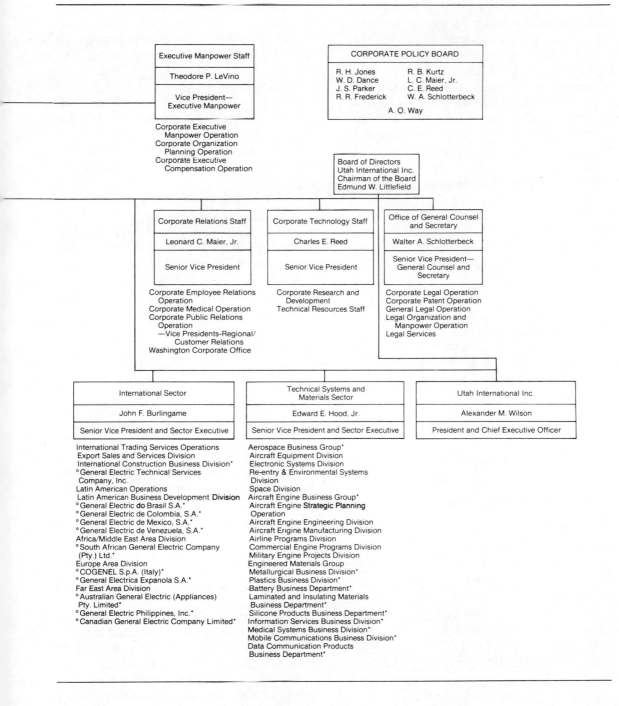

Executive Manpower Staff

Theodore P. LeVino

Vice President—
Executive Manpower

Corporate Executive
  Manpower Operation
Corporate Organization
  Planning Operation
Corporate Executive
  Compensation Operation

CORPORATE POLICY BOARD

R. H. Jones	R. B. Kurtz
W. D. Dance	L. C. Maier, Jr.
J. S. Parker	C. E. Reed
R. R. Frederick	W. A. Schlotterbeck

A. O. Way

Board of Directors
Utah International Inc.
Chairman of the Board
Edmund W. Littlefield

Corporate Relations Staff

Leonard C. Maier, Jr.

Senior Vice President

Corporate Employee Relations
  Operation
Corporate Medical Operation
Corporate Public Relations
  Operation
  —Vice Presidents-Regional/
    Customer Relations
Washington Corporate Office

Corporate Technology Staff

Charles E. Reed

Senior Vice President

Corporate Research and
  Development
Technical Resources Staff

Office of General Counsel
and Secretary

Walter A. Schlotterbeck

Senior Vice President—
General Counsel and
Secretary

Corporate Legal Operation
Corporate Patent Operation
General Legal Operation
Legal Organization and
  Manpower Operation
Legal Services

International Sector

John F. Burlingame

Senior Vice President and Sector Executive

International Trading Services Operations
Export Sales and Services Division
International Construction Business Division*
° General Electric Technical Services
  Company, Inc.
Latin American Operations
Latin American Business Development **Division**
° General Electric **do** Brasil S.A.*
° General Electric de Colombia, S.A.*
° General Electric de Mexico, S.A.*
° General Electric de Venezuela, S.A.*
Africa/Middle East Area Division
° South African General Electric Company
  (Pty.) Ltd.*
Europe Area Division
° COGENEL S.p.A. (Italy)*
° General Electrica Expanola S.A.*
Far East Area Division
° Australian General Electric (Appliances)
  Pty. Limited*
° General Electric Philippines, Inc.*
° Canadian General Electric Company Limited*

Technical Systems and
Materials Sector

Edward E. Hood, Jr.

Senior Vice President and Sector Executive

Aerospace Business Group*
Aircraft Equipment Division
Electronic Systems Division
Re-entry & Environmental Systems
  Division
Space Division
Aircraft Engine Business Group*
Aircraft Engine **Strategic Planning**
  Operation
Aircraft Engine Engineering Division
Aircraft Engine Manufacturing Division
Airline Programs Division
Commercial Engine Programs Division
Military Engine Projects Division
Engineered Materials Group
Metallurgical Business Division*
Plastics Business Division*
-Battery Business Department*
Laminated and Insulating Materials
  Business Department*
Silicone Products Business Department*
Information Services Business Division*
Medical Systems Business Division*
Mobile Communications Business Division*
Data Communication Products
  Business Department*

Utah International Inc.

Alexander M. Wilson

President and Chief Executive Officer

General Electric was a major U.S. corporation. Headquartered in Fairfield, Connecticut, the company's operations spanned the world. Products ranged from miniature light bulbs to huge turbine-generators, from household appliances to commercial jet engines. World-wide, employees totaled 401,000; domestically, they numbered 284,000, of whom the top 2 percent were the direct focus of the Executive Manpower Operation.

General Electric was highly decentralized, with 229 discrete units carrying *P&L* responsibility. In the words of Ralph Cordiner, CEO in the 1950s who had been the architect of the structure and articulator of the philosophy for which it stood:[1]

> In General Electric, decentralization is a way of preserving and enhancing the contributions of the large enterprise, and at the same time achieving the flexibility and the "human touch" that are popularly associated with—though not always attained by—small organizations.
>
> Under this concept, we have undertaken decentralization not only according to products, geography, and functional types of work. The most important aspect of the Company's philosophy is thorough decentralization of the responsibility and authority for making business decisions.

Structurally, GE's operating facilities such as plants were grouped by product or market into departments. Depending upon size, departments might be brought together into a division, and divisions might be combined into a group. For example, reporting to Sector Executive Welch were the general managers of the Lighting Business Group, the Air Conditioning Business Division, and the Television Business Department. The designation "business" in a com-

ponent title indicated that it was a Strategic Business Unit (SBU), the "basic business entity" of GE within which strategic plans for a given market or market segment were developed and implemented. GE had designated 49 SBUs.

The philosophy of decentralization developed by Cordiner sought to place decision making authority as close to the point of action as feasible and to establish the concept of real delegation of both authority and responsibility. "A result," one executive noted, "is that we give people general management experience fairly low in the organization. And that underscores our need to identify those individuals who have real general management ability and help them to develop it."

A General Electric organization chart and summary financial and employee data are presented as Exhibits 1 and 2, respectively.

An Overview of the Relations Function in General Electric

The personnel function in GE was broadly known as Employee Relations (ER), or simply, Relations. Specific procedures and reporting relationships varied among the operating units, depending upon factors such as the style of the top executive, the culture of the unit, and the relative importance of hourly and professional people to the unit. For illustrative purposes, the Relations function within the Lighting Business Group and the Consumer Products and Services Sector is described in this case (see Exhibit 3).

At the plant (or section) level, a plant employee relations manager reported directly to the plant manager and, in a dotted-line fashion, to the department ER manager. Primarily an implementer, rather than conceiver, of Relations practices, the plant ER

---

[1] *New Frontiers for Professional Managers,* Ralph J. Cordiner, McKinsey Foundation Lecture Series, p. 47.

Exhibit 2   Summary Financial and Employee Data ($ millions)

General Electric Company

	1978	1977	1976	1975	1974
Revenue	$20,073	$17,909	$15,972	$14,279	$14,125
Net earnings	1,230	1,088	931	689	705
Assets	15,036	13,697	12,050	9,764	9,369
Total capital invested	$ 8,692	$ 8,131	$ 7,305	$ 6,628	$ 6,317
Worldwide employees	401,000	384,000	380,000	380,000	409,000

**Consumer Products
and Services Sector**
(Percent of company totals)

	1978	1977	1976
Revenue	$4,788 (23.8%)	$4,148 (23.2%)	$3,453 (21.6%)
Net earnings	300 (24.4%)	256 (23.5%)	204 (21.9%)
Assets	$2,019 (13.4%)	$1,792 (13.1%)	$1,644 (13.6%)
Employees	110,849 (27.6%)	99,609 (25.9%)	91,795 (24.2%)

Source: General Electric annual reports and company personnel.

manager was responsible for all Relations activities in the plant community—"a crackerjack job, super for an individual's development," according to one Relations executive. As the operating unit became larger (department, division, group), this pattern of an ER manager reporting directly to a line manager, with a dotted-line relationship to a higher level Relations functional manager, continued. At the group level, Jack Hamilton, ER manager for the Lighting Business Group, said:

> In essence, I am the vice president of Employee Relations for an independent company. The Corporate Relations Office develops basic guidelines—for example, policies on wage management plans, the standardized company exempt compensation and benefit plans, basic parameters for union negotiations—but within these, I have a great deal of latitude. For example, we have developed a group incentive pay plan in one of our plants. We believe it is right for us and have fit it within the guidelines. We also have done a number of things

on our own with training programs at all levels.

Within Hamilton's staff, there were two distinct groups. One, Employee Relations, was largely concerned with nonexempt and hourly employees (85 percent of the group's 23,000 employees). Union relations, for example, was the responsibility of this group. The second, Organization & Manpower (O&M), focused on managerial and professional employees. Peter Mercer, Lighting O&M manager, explained:

> O&M is growing in stature now. Ten years ago, the "best and brightest" went to union relations; now we have a better balance. Part of this arises because Jack Welch has used David Orselet a great deal and encourages his managers to use their O&M people. And those managers are finding us a very useful tool. For example, they are finding that salary decisions really can help discriminate among different levels of performance, that the candidate slate process does produce better appointments. We are

Exhibit 3   Overview of Relations Function

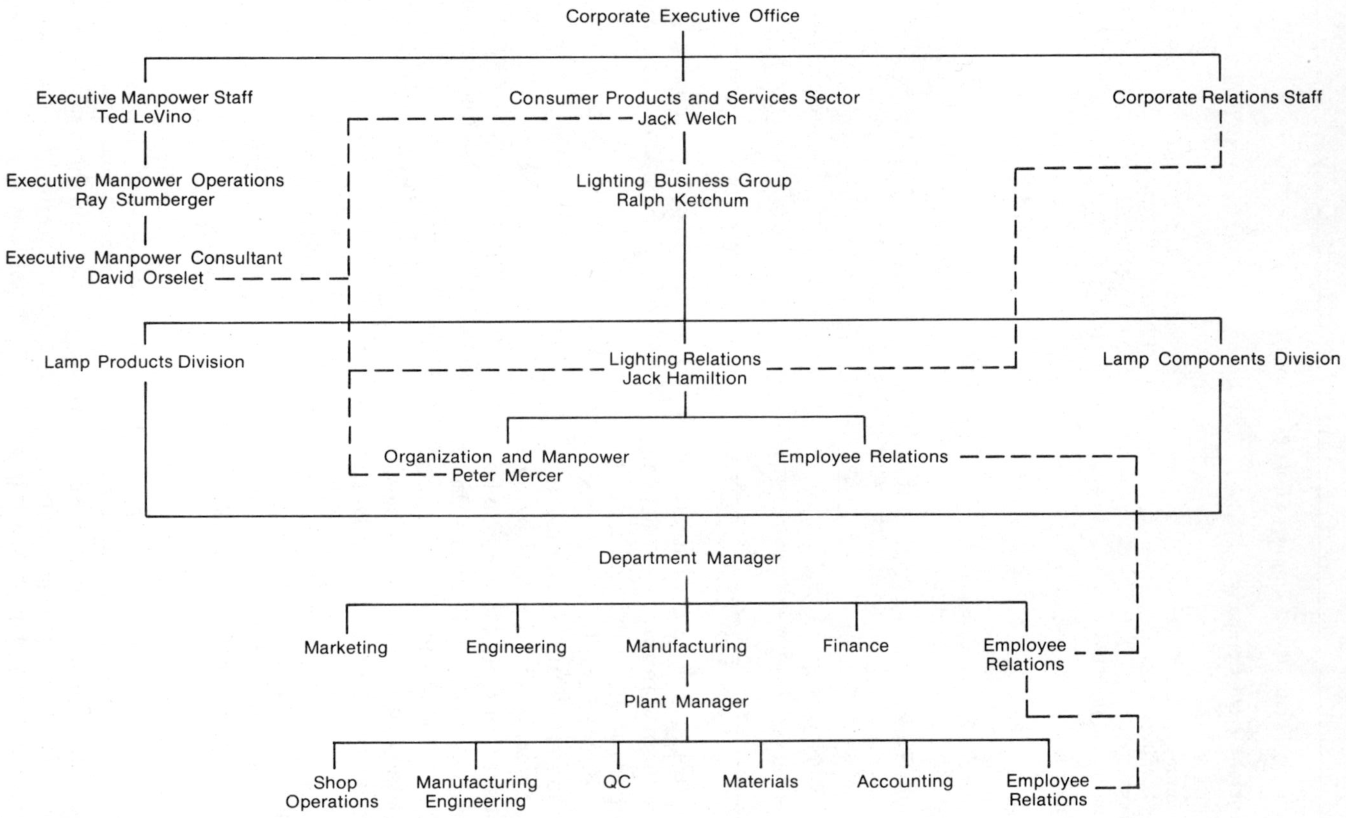

Note: Simplified diagram—many functional and operating groups are not shown.
Source: Company personnel.

increasingly assuming a counseling/advising role to the group and division executives, too. In all of this, the first interactions and appointments were critical, and our continuing role is very delicate. We have to be professional or we just won't have the credibility we need.

Mercer was responsible for candidate slate preparation for section-level managers and was in frequent contact with Orselet and the relevant functional consultant on the Executive Manpower staff.[2] He was deeply involved in the managerial manpower review process, and, as "human resource" issues increasingly became incorporated into the group's strategic planning, was involved in them.[3] Four managers reported to Mercer; one assigned to each of the two major divisions within the group (and responsible for "managerial staffing, manpower planning, organization planning and development, career counseling, and management consulting), one assigned to professional relations, and one to exempt compensation.

When the sector organization level had been established in late 1977, it had been decided that the sector executive's direct-report staff should not include a Relations position. While an executive manpower consultant had been assigned to each sector, the consultant continued to report to the Executive Manpower staff to ensure the independence from the line and contact among

---

[2] The slate process was not mandated by corporate policy below the department echelon. However, Executive Manpower staff has the capability to respond if requested by operating management to slate requests for section-level functional positions.

[3] For example, with domestic unit sales of the group forecast to be relatively flat, Mercer noted that two manpower issues had been explicitly raised: How can productivity be raised in an environment in which there is not a growing amount of unit volume? How can the sense of career opportunity for managers be kept alive?

the consultants upon which the truly corporate-wide perspective on executive talent was based. This decision was grounded in the belief that the overall relations function was best managed at the SBU level (group level and below, with overall guidance from the Corporate Employee Relations Office). In addition, it was believed that there would not be sufficiently challenging work for such a sector level position, especially with the availability of the executive manpower consultant to act as a conduit for information among corporate, sector, and group levels. Orselet noted:

> This leads to a grey area. Being accessible and visible, Relations questions, as well as a wide variety of complaints received by the sector and executive officers, are frequently referred to me. I will usually try to find out what is going on, and then solicit advice from our Relations experts or hand the matter over to them to handle. Of course, I have grown up with many of the executives in Relations, and we have a good feel for the sensitivities involved in any given situation.

The Executive Manpower Staff

By the 1960s, GE had developed a very strong Industrial Relations department under the leadership of Lem Boulware and Virg Day, "a real competitive advantage," one executive noted. At that time, Jack Parker, head of the Aerospace & Defense Group (which employed perhaps 50 percent of the engineering and other professional people in GE), hired a "talent scout" to work within the group to identify promising managers. As Parker's program developed, CEO Fred Borch urged the other groups to look at it. As one executive said, "Borch was dissatisfied with management succession within GE. He felt general manager appointments were being made too much on a 'knowledge of the hiring manager' basis, and that GE would be stronger if this critical pool of executives were developed and utilized across the whole corporation." By 1967, the Corporate Executive Manpower staff had been established. It reported directly to the chairman.

Over the years, three primary activities have been consolidated under the staff: the Executive Manpower Operation, responsible for managing the company's upper level manpower system; the Organization Planning Operation, responsible for studying and recommending changes in the company organization structure; and the Executive Compensation Operation, responsible for executive pay and benefit guidelines and plans. Ted LeVino, vice president–Executive Manpower, explained that these three shared two characteristics that necessitated their independent-from-the-line and administered-by-one-staff status:

> These are sensitive areas, requiring a high level of confidentiality, and an executive MUST have a high degree of trust in the staff working with him. We believe that this organization can provide that professionalism. A second, and major, reason is that we often utilize organization structure and compensation in creative packages to provide developmental assignments for promising general managers. Thus these groups have to be in close contact.

Executive Development at GE

At the executive level within GE, training and development were believed to occur more through on-the-job experience than through formal course work. As one executive said, "At that level, an executive needs the more intangible attributes, such as judgment, a strategic sense, and interpersonal competence, that are hard to 'teach.' So we use job assignments to broaden and deepen

an executive's experience, and we give him solid feedback on his performance."

Consistent with the decentralized organization and the emphasis upon on-the-job development, a strong "one-over-one" chain of command had developed. One executive explained:

> Our managers have a great deal of authority to make decisions. These decisions will be reviewed by a manager's superior (the one-over-one principle), but will seldom be reversed. However, a manager is accountable—responsibility definitely accompanies authority.
>
> Within GE, we have a strong culture, based on pride in the whole company, integrity, and very high standards. This has been established over the years by example, policy, reward, and audit. Managers who aren't comfortable operating within that culture usually end up leaving us. To tie this together, for example, if a manager deals with subordinates in a manner that doesn't fit our culture ("be tough on standards, not on people"), he may get by for a while, but more than likely will get scragged downstream.

GE maintains primarily a promote-from-within policy, with 95 percent of the top 600 positions so filled. "We must," LeVino noted, "make GE a good place to work so that people will stay; and we must do all we can to help those people develop—for their own motivation and for competitive Company reasons."

The Executive Manpower Operation

The Executive Manpower Operation, headed by Ray Stumberger, drew its charter directly from corporate policy. This policy, one of only 35, mandated that appointments to department echelon and higher positions be made from slates of candidates prepared by the Executive Manpower staff (see Exhibit 4 for excerpts from the policy).

Exhibit 4   Excerpt from Corporate Policy

Company Procedure for Approval of Staffing Changes

A consistent procedure for approving high-level changes in staffing can realize the greatest positive impact from such changes, and also help prevent misunderstandings. To achieve these benefits, the procedures outlined on the next pages are to be followed in presenting and securing approval for staffing changes in positions at the echelons indicated.

Corporate officers, general managers, and managers authorized to initiate and approve the changes described in the procedure are responsible for seeing that those individuals in their components who are directly concerned both understand and follow these procedures.

Candidate Slates.   Procedures and responsibilities for developing and obtaining approval of candidate slates for department-echelon and higher positions are shown in Table 2. The necessary requests, recommendations, and approvals must be documented. No action—such as interviewing a potential candidate, requesting such an interview, or "informally" discussing an opening with a potential candidate—may be taken prior to obtaining written approval of the candidate slate.

Table 2
Candidate Slates

1. General rule for approval of candidate slates is "one-over-one" (e.g., the echelon above the Manager to whom the position being filled reports). Exceptions to this general rule are:

Position Being Filled	Candidate Slate Approved by
Vice President—Regional Relations; Group Executive	Chairman (after review by CEO)
Division General Manager; intermediate-echelon General Manager reporting to Group Executive	Vice Chairman (after review by CEO)
	Vice Chairman
Department General Manager; intermediate-echelon General Manager reporting to Division General Manager	
Positions reporting to Senior Vice President in Corporate Staff; or to Officer who reports to the Chairman	Vice Chairman or Chairman (after review by CEO)

2. Department-echelon positions and higher: Executive Manpower Staff recommends/concurs on all candidate slates.

3. Additional concurrence on certain candidate slates is required as follows:

Exhibit 4 (*concluded*)

Position	Additional Required Concurrence
Manager—Finance	Senior Vice President—Finance
Counsel—Sector/Group/Division	Senior Vice President—General Counsel and Secretary
Manager—Strategic Planning and/or Review	Senior Vice President—Corporate Planning and Development
Manager—Employee Relations (Section level and higher)	Manager—Corporate Employee Relations
Manager—Organization and Manpower (Sector/Group/Division)	Vice President—Executive Manpower

Source: Company document

Stumberger commented: "The hiring manager, of course, is deeply involved and makes the final selection, as he should, but the slate provides an element of formal, corporate control over a process that is key in our growth-occurs-on-the-job program of executive development, and that assures a corporate-wide look for the best person available."

Reporting to Stumberger were six Executive Manpower consultants (one assigned to each of the five sectors and one to corporate components), three Management Manpower consultants (assigned to the finance/strategic planning, engineering/manufacturing, and marketing functions), and the manager of the Manpower Data System. Stumberger noted:

> Working in the sector yet reporting to Executive Manpower, the executive consultant position is one of the key Relations positions within GE. It is a challenging, high-risk job, demanding extraordinary sensitivity, integrity, and professionalism, as well as the ability to assess people well and to face difficult situations.

In addition to the preparation of candidate slates, the EMC's activities include participation in the annual manpower review, in-depth assessments of executives, assistance with salary planning, and various special projects. Some of this role is mandated, but much develops as the consultant becomes the "trusted sidekick" of the sector executive. Thus the actual role of the consultant will vary quite a bit from sector to sector, depending on the consultant, the executive, and other factors such as the nature of the business. For example, Consumer Products is growing rapidly so that there is a lot of change in the air, while Power Systems operates on a much longer time frame with less change.

I see about 80 percent of the work of the consultants and, of course, I talk with the sector executives. In evaluating a consultant, I ask questions such as: Is he good at assessing people? Has he shown courage in dealing with difficult situations? Were his slates both good and developmental?

The Executive Manpower Consultant—David Orselet

David Orselet had joined GE in 1956 with a college major in industrial relations. He had started in the corporate-wide Relations Training Program, and, over the years, had worked in a variety of relations jobs. In 1970, he had been appointed manager of professional relations for the Switchgear Business Division; in 1972, organization and manpower manager for the Consumer Products Group; and, in 1974, Executive Manpower Consultant.

In describing his job, Orselet said:

Basically, I provide a professional input into the sector's executive manpower activities, and work closely with Jack Welch. I spend about 25 percent of my time attending business review meetings, product assessments, manpower reviews, and so forth in order to watch the executives doing their thing in their own environments. I am actively involved with perhaps 50 or 60, and get to know them well. My background in several of our businesses is helpful here, too, since I have known some of them for a number of years and have seen them in a variety of positions. I also keep an eye out for younger people on the way up.

Another 20 percent of my time goes to the candidate slate development process, in which I work closely with Jack, the consultants responsible for the other sectors, and Ray Stumberger. I spend about 15 percent of my time on salary and organization planning with Jack, and another 15 percent on special projects for him, such as surveying the people side of an acquisition or working on some of the problems of a disposition. The remaining 25 percent of my time goes to interviewing and recruiting, both in-house and outside. For example, last year I talked with almost 50 managers from other sectors or from lower down in Consumer Products who came to me to introduce and sell themselves, to find out how they stacked up or to seek career counseling. And, in another vein, I was up at Harvard talking with MBAs in February.

I'm on the road about 40 percent of the time and my weeks average 60–70 hours. I love the job. It is extremely important work because it is the process through which we develop the individuals who will lead this company in the coming years. It is exciting because I interact with people across the whole organization structure. It is meaningful to me because it gives me an opportunity to influence the direction of a business, through the selection process. I get a good deal of psychic income when both the individual and the business succeed. And I really enjoy the opportunity to talk about so much more than just manpower. For example, I participate freely in the discussion of business strategy or manufacturing problems, and am not just pigeon-holed in personnel.

Several aspects of Orselet's job as Executive Manpower Consultant are described in more detail in the following paragraphs.

Candidate Slates. Orselet was responsible for generating slates for level 19–21 positions and for providing input to higher level slates.[4] He typically worked on 40–50 slates per year. The process consisted of the following steps:

1. Orselet "spec'd" the job with the executive to whom the position reported to determine the skills and experiences needed at that point in time. It was explicitly recognized that a particular job

---

[4] All GE exempt jobs were classified by position level (PL), with PL1 the lowest and PL29 the highest (CEO). PL19 was Department echelon, PL23 Division, PL25 Group, and PL27 Sector.

might require different skills at different times.

2. Orselet gathered a list of possible candidates from his own knowledge of executives, from fellow consultants, from line managers, and from the corporate management inventory.[5] He noted that the practice of an executive (or an EMC) "keeping a good person in his pocket" was minimized since the EMCs were measured in part on the amount of movement across division/group/sector lines.

3. He pared that list down to the formal slate, usually from two to five people, with no check for their availability. It was at this stage that the business needs of the organization and the development needs of the individual were balanced. This process was interactive, and detailed personal knowledge of candidates, based on direct observation, discussion, and reference, supplemented the written reviews of the formal record.

4. The slate was presented to the appropriate executives for written approval, as specified in the policy.

5. When the slate had been approved, Orselet tested the availability of the candidates, with the rule of thumb being that an executive was "fair game" after two years in a position (and occasionally af-

ter 1 or 1½). If a manager did not want to let a subordinate go, the decision was referred up the chain of command, to the chairman if necessary. One executive noted that availability was seldom a problem and that blocking a subordinate's move, except for very specific reasons, was rarely done.

6. The executive with the position to fill interviewed the candidates and selected one. Orselet was often asked by the executive to interview a candidate at this point, especially one from another sector whom he did not personally know. If the hiring manager found none of the candidates to be acceptable, the slate was refused, and the process began again. Orselet noted that few slates were, in fact, rejected: "The process is really very interactive, within executive manpower and with the line executives, so that problems are identified and resolved earlier in the process. But that option exists."

LeVino estimated that 25 percent of the appointments were made from outside the sector, and noted the importance of this movement to the development of broadly experienced executives. He also estimated that 60 percent of the hiring managers would say that candidate slates helped the selection process. "A conflict can arise," he noted, "if a manager tends to have his mind set on one person, especially when that person is not on the slate. It is in such situations that the judicious use of power all around is needed."

As an example of the impact of the candidate slate process, several executives cited a change within the Lighting Business Group. Historically, it had been a very independent group within General Electric, with Lighting executives all grown within the group.

---

[5] Experience, skill, and performance data on "promotable" managers from PL13–14 and from all managers from PL15+ were carried in a corporate management inventory. Included in 1978 were (approximately) 3,450 PL13&14s, 2,150 PL15–18s, and 600 PL19+s. In addition, the Executive Manpower staff maintained a finance manpower inventory of all exempt PL10+ managers (5,000), and a relations manpower inventory of all exempt PL5+ managers (1,400). Orselet noted that the inventory was most useful for PL18 and below managers since, above that level, the consultant knew most all of the executives in the sector personally.

In the early 1970s, as a position within the group opened up, slates had been presented with no internal candidates on them. Executives reported initial heavy resistance to the outsiders, but by 1979, with a series of very successful appointments, the resistance had faded and the group was in the mainstream of management talent flow across the company.

The Annual Manpower Review Process. In the words of one executive, the annual manpower review, known as Session C, was "the process by which the company takes a regular, organized look at executive staffing." The review had evolved in the late 1960s under the leadership of Cordiner, although it had not been formalized in corporate policy as the candidate slate procedures had. It was explicitly kept separate

from the annual performance review, which a manager held with each subordinate, and from the annual salary review.

A five-month process when completed, the review began with the subordinates of a department echelon manager filling out one side of the *Evaluation and Development Summary* form (Exhibit 5), which had sections entitled "career interests," "self-evaluation," and "development actions and plans." The manager then completed the other side (see below),[6] which had sections entitled "evaluation of performance and qualifications" and "development and career recommendations." The manager and subordinate then met face-to-face to discuss their responses—"an important and dis-

[6] Exhibits 5–9 contain these forms for five different managers.

Exhibit 5

Strictly Private

EVALUATION AND DEVELOPMENT SUMMARY
(This side to be completed by employee)

NAME Marketing Section Manager_____ SOCIAL SECURITY NO. _____
         (last)   (first)   (initial)

I. CAREER INTERESTS (Show your specific preferences and alternatives including position title, type business, product or service industry, etc., plus desired timing.)

   A. NEXT
      • Manager of product department
      • Manager of new business venture
      • Staff position—strategic planning

Exhibit 5 (*continued*)

    B. LONGER RANGE

- P&L responsibility of multifunction organization with broad product scope (general management)

II. SELF EVALUATION (Describe technical, interpersonal, managerial qualifications etc., and comment on the areas in which you feel you need further development.)

    A. STRENGTHS

- Business acumen
- Cross-functional integration ability
- People management—team coordination
- Broad perspective, handling great variety of multifunction activities
- Profit orientation
- Intelligent
- Versatile
- Goal-oriented
- Risk-decision making

    B. DEVELOPMENT NEEDS

- "Rounding out" in Marketing Manager position
- Continued attention to developing the Marketing interface with related organization of Sales, Product Service, and International

III. DEVELOPMENT ACTIONS AND PLANS

    A. ACTIONS (Taken in last 12–18 months to enhance skills, knowledge, experience, etc.)

- Attended Executive Development Course
- Increased interface with sales and key dealer personnel getting closer to the pulse of the market
- Increased interface with sister organization to broaden perspective to Division-level considerations

    B. PLANS

- Continue actions in A above
- Offshore trips to broaden total market knowledge and plant interface
- Work closely with other organizations in Division to strengthen strategic positioning and broaden personal contribution
- Increase activities to better understand our ultimate customer—the consumer

Signed_____

Date forwarded to Manager _____

Exhibit 5 (*continued*)

EVALUATION AND DEVELOPMENT SUMMARY
(This side to be completed by immediate manager)

IV. EVALUATION OF PERFORMANCE AND QUALIFICATIONS

A. PERFORMANCE (Describe individual's overall performance on present assignment in terms of major objectives. Describe special accomplishments. Indicate performance trend.)

Continues as the strong leader providing Marketing direction to this business. His business breadth utilizing our modified matrix structure enables him to become involved and a contributor in many non-Marketing aspects of our business. He has directed three considerable different businesses very effectively and has been a significant contributor to the great 1978 business results of the Department.

B. QUALIFICATIONS (Describe technical, interpersonal, managerial qualifications, etc.)

1. STRENGTHS

- Strong manager/team leader
- Strong balanced business judgment
- Integrates well with other business functions
- Handles many tasks/large volumes of work well

- Intelligent
- Analytical
- Logical
- Persistent
- Work-a-holic

2. DEVELOPMENT NEEDS

- Should become a "student" of push versus pull Marketing strategies
- Should continue to maximize his exposure to sales and distribution and key customers
- Care should be taken not to let his persistent quality come through as "dogmatic"

V. DEVELOPMENT AND CAREER RECOMMENDATIONS

A. DEVELOPMENT RECOMMENDATIONS (Specify development plans for the next 12 months which are responsive to identified needs.)

- Accelerate involvement/exposure to Marketing both for assisting and personal education purposes
- Press BBD&O in the areas of "pull" evaluations/tests/alternatives, etc.

Exhibit 5 (*concluded*)

B.   NEXT ASSIGNMENT (Consider alternatives)

Position Title	Organization Layer	Timing
General Manager	Product Department	Now
General Manager	Functional Department (Marketing)	Now
Manager, Oper./Strategic Planning	Department	Now

C.   CAREER ROUTE AND GOALS (How realistic are the individual's career goals and are they compatible with your views? Make a clear statement with respect to long-range development needs and recommendations for future positions and training.)

A strong, dedicated individual. He is ready now for a General Manager challenge but an added year in his current position would not be time wasted.

Completed by _____ Date _____ Date Discussed with Reviewing Manager _____

Date Discussed with Employee _____

Exhibit 6

Strictly Private

EVALUATION AND DEVELOPMENT SUMMARY
(This side to be completed by employee)

NAME   Multifunctional General Manager   SOCIAL SECURITY NO.   _____
          (last)   (first)   (initial)

I.   CAREER INTERESTS (Show your specific preferences and alternatives including position title, type business, product or service industry, etc., plus desired timing.)

Exhibit 6 (*continued*)

    A. NEXT

        Division General Manager—Multifunctional business—e.g., ACBD—1 year

    B. LONGER RANGE

        Group Executive

II. SELF EVALUATION (Describe technical, interpersonal, managerial qualifications, etc., and comment on the areas in which you feel you need further development.)

    A. STRENGTHS

        Experienced in managing diverse, multifunctional business. Profit-oriented. Analytical, conceptual, and independent thinker. Able to deal with complex business problems and make difficult decisions. Competent in selection, training, and motivation of employees. Effective at goal setting, planning, meeting deadlines, and implementation. Able to work with people whether employees, peers, managers, or outside the Company.

    B. DEVELOPMENT NEEDS

        Continuing experience as multifunctional general manager. Exposure to Sector and Corporate issues through task force assignment or similar experience.

III. DEVELOPMENT ACTIONS AND PLANS

    A. ACTIONS (Taken in last 12–18 months to enhance skills, knowledge, experience, etc.)

        Have gained significant experience and new knowledge serving in two multifunctional, general manager assignments. Both businesses were in turn-around situations. Developed long-term strategies while maximizing current period operating results.

    B. PLANS

        Continue in present assignment leading the final development and initial implementation of a new strategy for my current business.

Date forwarded

Signed _____ to Manager _____

Exhibit 6 (*continued*)

Strictly Private

EVALUATION AND DEVELOPMENT SUMMARY
(This side to be completed by immediate manager)

IV. EVALUATION OF PERFORMANCE AND QUALIFICATIONS

A. PERFORMANCE (Describe individual's overall performance on present assignment in terms of major objectives. Describe special accomplishments. Indicate performance trend.)

Moved into his current position with the specific assignment to develop an overall business strategy focusing especially on product-line fixes. With his team, a new strategy has been developed and outstanding new product concepts have been developed, approved and put into motion. Has developed a "win" spirit not seen in years. Through excellent merchandising plans, share has improved dramatically. Margin, however, has eroded and represents a real challenge.

B. QUALIFICATIONS (Describe technical, interpersonal, managerial qualifications, etc.)

1. STRENGTHS

- Decisive, results-oriented
- Strategic thinker
- Well organized
- "Take charge" leader
- Intelligent, adaptable, and resourceful
- Broad business interests and talent
- Sets high standards
- Can create team spirit and effort

2. DEVELOPMENT NEEDS

- Must monitor his personal needs to be sure not in conflict with business needs.
- Must increase support of Group while being an advocate for his business.

V. DEVELOPMENT AND CAREER RECOMMENDATIONS

A. DEVELOPMENT RECOMMENDATIONS (Specify development plans for the next 12 months which are responsive to identified needs.)

Concentrate on maintaining a "win" team attitude. More participation in Group issues.

Exhibit 6 (*concluded*)

    B.   NEXT ASSIGNMENT (Consider alternatives)

Position Title	Organization Layer	Timing
General Manager	Division	1 year

    C.   CAREER ROUTE AND GOALS (How realistic are the individual's career goals and are they compatible with your views? Make a clear statement with respect to long-range development needs and recommendations for future positions and training.)

    Goal to become a Division Manager is clearly realistic. His longer-term goal to become a Group Executive will depend on successfully broadening himself in a Division assignment.

Completed by _____ Date _____ Date Discussed with Reviewing Manager _____

Date Discussed with Employee _____

Exhibit 7

Strictly Private

EVALUATION AND DEVELOPMENT SUMMARY
(This side to be completed by employee)

NAME Functional General Manager   SOCIAL SECURITY NO. _____
          (last)   (first)   (initial)

    I.   CAREER INTERESTS (Show your specific preferences and alternatives including position title, type business, product or service industry, etc., plus desired timing.)

    A.   NEXT

    (1) In current position, contribute effectively as Product Board member and through leadership of the Manufacturing Department to the planning and decisioning required to successfully reach important and challenging productivity and quality improvement goals and a new level of profitability in our several product lines, plus identifying the priority issues facing the business and applying broad business thinking and bringing resolution; (2) Move to General Manager position in a larger manufacturing department or expand the scope of the current assignment by adding component plant(s) to this department.

Exhibit 7 (*continued*)

    B. LONGER RANGE

       Manager—Manufacturing Management and Quality Control Consulting, CCS

II. SELF—EVALUATION (Describe technical, interpersonal, managerial qualifications, etc., and comment on the areas in which you feel you need further development.)

    A. STRENGTHS

       Ability to conduct objective and constructive evaluations of operations and programs/problems, and generate alternative plans. Ability to recognize and foster development of potential in personnel. Ability to organize and integrate multi-functional effort to achieve complex bus·ness objectives. Ability to provide logical and useful counsel on functional, organizational and personnel matters.

    B. DEVELOPMENT NEEDS

       Assist in Product Board issue identification and resolution by bringing concepts and alternatives into Product Board deliberations which extend well beyond functional perspectives. Support alternatives with sound feasibility determinations.

III. DEVELOPMENT ACTIONS AND PLANS

    A. ACTIONS (Taken in last 12–18 months to enhance skills, knowledge, experience, etc.)

       Updated personal knowledge of state of the art in process technology, CAM, and automation in areas where productivity and quality improvement is critical to meeting business objectives. Visits have been made to four European manufacturing plants, two auto manufacturing plants, GE Brockport housewares plant plus CCS and CR&D and Pemco among other actions to accomplish this update. Continued as Chairman of Board of Trustees of sixth-class city.

    B. PLANS

       Continue extension of personal knowledge of new technology and alternate methods and sources that hold potential for significant improvements in product cost, process yield levels, employee productivity, more productive investment expenditures and improvement in prioritization of resource application.

Signed _____ Date forwarded to Manager _____

Exhibit 7 (*continued*)

EVALUATION AND DEVELOPMENT SUMMARY
(This side to be completed by immediate manager)

IV. EVALUATION OF PERFORMANCE AND QUALIFICATIONS

    A.   PERFORMANCE (Describe individual's overall performance on present assignment in terms of major objectives. Describe special accomplishments. Indicate performance trend.)

       Performed in a fully satisfactory manner in 1978. He continues to do well in balancing his role as a Board member and functional Department manager. He has picked up on the technology thrust and is actively pushing this area in a number of significant projects. His performance trend continues to be favorable. He has built an excellent manufacturing organization staffed with high caliber people. He can improve his contribution to this business by continuing his work on differentiating his approach to problem analysis. He has a large capacity for detail and on occasion can get overly involved. He needs to also continue to drive himself and his people to aggressively pursue key areas of cost and productivity.

    B.   QUALIFICATIONS (Describe technical, interpersonal, managerial qualifications, etc.)

       1.   STRENGTHS

          Excellent problem analysis skills, logical thinker, good coach and counselor. Good and interested listener. High level of integrity. Appropriately flexible. Tenacious and thorough. Always considers alternates.

       2.   DEVELOPMENT NEEDS

          Needs to continue to work on differentiating between problems which can be scoped and those requiring detailed analysis so as to better utilize his time. He needs to speed up his decision-making process; needs to pursue critical evaluation of some of the manufacturing related business problems; should work at more aggressive questioning of alternates.

V. DEVELOPMENT AND CAREER RECOMMENDATIONS

    A.   DEVELOPMENT RECOMMENDATIONS (Specify development plans for the next 12 months which are responsive to identified needs.)

Exhibit 7 (*concluded*)

I intend to assign one of the pooled plants to him. Also, any swap of General Managers among business would involve him.

B. NEXT ASSIGNMENT (Consider alternatives)

Position Title	Organization Layer	Timing
Mfg. & Eng. Consulting, CCS	Department	1979

C. CAREER ROUTE AND GOALS (How realistic are the individual's career goals and are they compatible with your views? Make a clear statement with respect to long-range development needs and recommendations for future positions and training.)

Goals are realistic. He can perform quite well on a higher level Manufacturing Department assignment and would be excellent in a role in CCS. I consider him as a viable Purchasing back-up. He would be outstanding in a role in Corporate Production and Operating Services.

Completed by _____ Date _____ Date Discussed with Reviewing Manager _____

Date Discussed with Employee _____

Exhibit 8

Strictly Private

EVALUATION AND DEVELOPMENT SUMMARY
(This side to be completed by employee)

NAME   Manufacturing Section Manager   SOCIAL SECURITY NO.   _____
       (last)   (first)   (initial)

I. CAREER INTERESTS (Show your specific preferences and alternatives including position title, type business, product or service industry, etc., plus desired timing.)

Exhibit 8 (*continued*)

A. NEXT

In the next one to three years, I would like to become a multifunctional Department General Manager. Specific options to achieve this goal that are of interest to me would include:

- Manager of a business section with multifunctional responsibilities
- Manager of manufacturing in a business which is closer to the consumer market place
- Manager of Strategic or Operational Planning
- General Manager of multifunctional department

B. LONGER RANGE

My longer range goal is to progress to higher levels of operating responsibility. For example, a Division General Manager of a business where my strengths in manufacturing management and materials processing would be of value. Alternatives along this career path for strategic planning and other staff assignments would be considered to round out my experience base.

II. SELF-EVALUATION (Describe technical, interpersonal, managerial qualifications, etc., and comment on the areas in which you feel you need further development.)

A. STRENGTHS

I am highly achievement motivated with a healthy disrespect for the status quo. I'm a strong believer in and user of goals and measurement systems to insure optimum use of resources. I have an extensive background in materials and materials processing with a good understanding of business finance and strategy. I have good oral and written communication skills. I enjoy working with people and helping them reach their full potential as employees.

B. DEVELOPMENT NEEDS

In order to reach my career objectives, I need to develop a better understanding of market/customer/business interfaces and to become more familiar with marketing strategies and concepts. I need more non-GE customer contact and exposure. I also need to continue to gain experience with multifunctional business and operational planning activities.

III. DEVELOPMENT ACTIONS AND PLANS

A. ACTIONS (Taken in last 12–18 months to enhance skills, knowledge, experience, etc.)

- Attended Business Management Course, Crotonville, February 1978
- Led Explorer Scout Sales Team
- Attended Product/Market Strategy Development Seminar

Exhibit 8 (*continued*)

B. PLANS

- Attend Advanced Marketing Manpower Seminar during 1979
- Continue to demonstrate performance in my current job while gaining more customer exposure
- Seek job opportunities which would provide more market/customer exposure

Signed _____

Date forwarded to Manager _____

Strictly Private

EVALUATION AND DEVELOPMENT SUMMARY
(This side to be completed by immediate manager)

IV. EVALUATION OF PERFORMANCE AND QUALIFICATIONS

A. PERFORMANCE (Describe individual's overall performance on present assignment in terms of major objectives. Describe special accomplishments. Indicate performance trend.)

Improved percent plant margin by 2.1 percent over 1977. Exceeded P&E budget by 4.8 percent, Versus sales increase of 20.2 percent (3 percent price), reduced exempt employment by 3.8 percent and non-exempt by 7.6 percent versus 1977. In spite of extensive overtime, held absenteeism to 2.4 percent. Overall accident rate dropped to 5.4 from 5.8. Maintained excellent quality record with customer returns under 0.8 percent of sales. Supported Syn-Cronamics cost reduction study with target of $860K savings. Savings verified and Chemical Products to be accomplished in 1979. Overall, achieved a tighter control of operations and improved rate of accomplishment over 1977.

B. QUALIFICATIONS (Describe technical, interpersonal, managerial qualifications, etc.)

1. STRENGTHS

Detail planning, technical comprehension, interpersonal relationships, communication, team player, responsive, paternalistic.

Exhibit 8   (*concluded*)

2. DEVELOPMENT NEEDS

Greater knowledge of total business and planning for given financial result. Customer exposure. Harder line with subordinates over failures/nonresponsiveness. Challenge by numerically larger organization where scope of work requires greater delegation. Challenge by an assignment outside of manufacturing.

V. DEVELOPMENT AND CAREER RECOMMENDATIONS

A. DEVELOPMENT RECOMMENDATIONS (Specify development plans for the next 12 months which are responsive to identified needs.)

Attend AMMS. Involve in customer relations. Involve more in total department financial planning. Assign leadership in total business planning. Actively pursue a promotional assignment to address development needs identified above.

B. NEXT ASSIGNMENT (Consider alternatives)

Position Title	Organization Layer	Timing
Business Section or Venture Mgr.	Section	Now
Manufacturing Mgr. (large dept.)	Section	Now
Strategic Planner	Division	Now

C. CAREER ROUTE AND GOALS (How realistic are the individual's career goals and are they compatible with your views? Make a clear statement with respect to long-range development needs and recommendations for future positions and training.)

Expectation of Dept. General Manager is probably realistic and a Manufacturing General Manager would be most readily achieved. To achieve this, an assignment such as a strategic planner or a venture manager would be helpful. A longer-term division manager goal is contingent mostly on getting a department manager position and demonstrating really superior performance and achievements.

Completed by _____ Date _____ Date Discussed with Reviewing Manager _____

Date Discussed with Employee _____

Exhibit 9

Strictly Private

EVALUATION AND DEVELOPMENT SUMMARY
(This side to be completed by employee)

NAME   Staff Section Manager   SOCIAL SECURITY NO.   _____
     (last)   (first)   (initial)

I. CAREER INTERESTS (Show your specific preferences and alternatives including position title, type business, product or service industry, etc., plus desired timing.)

A. NEXT

By mid-1980, general manager of a small, off-shore affiliate operation to demonstrate business and people management skills, to leverage successful prior experience in foreign environments and cultures, and to parlay prior training and preparation for operating in the international business arena.

B. LONGER RANGE

Line general management in domestic and international organizations of increasing size, scope, and complexity in GE's consumer, durable-goods based businesses. At least one significant corporate staff assignment in the area of strategic planning probably around sixth or seventh year of service. Goal: Division-level executive in 10 years.

II. SELF-EVALUATION (Describe technical, interpersonal, managerial qualifications, etc., and comment on the areas in which you feel you need further development.)

A. STRENGTHS

- Record of successful management of human and financial resources toward agreed-upon goals and objectives; a highly motivated team player.
- Strong interpersonal skills; ability to build confidence and to get commitment from others.
- Sound judgment; fact-based/analytical orientation; broad business perspective.
- Strong oral and written communication skills.

B. DEVELOPMENT NEEDS

Greater tolerance of individual differences in skill, motivation and ability to deliver results; must learn to work with the best each has to offer rather than always gravitating to the "super stars" who will deliver. Become less matter-of-fact/rigid when others don't see things my way. Could be more flexible without fear of compromising desired results. Learn to say "no" rather than overcommit (but difficult with high-task completion needs).

Exhibit 9 (*continued*)

III. DEVELOPMENT ACTIONS AND PLANS

A. ACTIONS (Taken in last 12–18 months to enhance skills, knowledge, experience, etc.)

- Engagement Management Training Program. One-week workshop in Switzerland (5/77) to reinforce approaches to managing people *and* ideas.
- Video Communications Workshop. Three-day workshop in NYC (10/77) to fine-tune oral presentation skills.
- Business Development (10/78) and Strategic Planning (11/78) Workshops to enhance overall effectiveness in current planning position

B. PLANS ·

- Through Strategic Planning/LRF cycle, develop deeper understanding of this business, its opportunities, vulnerabilities and economics to validate hypothesis of where I can make greatest personal and professional contribution to the short term
- Attend BMC—9/79

Signed _____

Date forwarded
to Manager _____

Strictly Private

EVALUATION AND DEVELOPMENT SUMMARY
(This side to be completed by immediate manager)

IV. EVALUATION OF PERFORMANCE AND QUALIFICATIONS

A. PERFORMANCE (Describe individual's overall performance on present assignment in terms of major objectives. Describe special accomplishments. Indicate performance trend.)

He has done an outstanding job in raising the level of planning for the Division. He has dramatically improved the level of strategic thinking in all of the Division's departments. In addition, he has contributed to the strategic planning effort of the Group by providing analyses of competitors and their strategic thrust as well as those Division portions of the Group strategic plan. The unsolicited demand for his services by the Division Departments is growing daily to the point where in just six months on the job significant priority setting is required. He is off to an excellent start in the General Electric Company.

Exhibit 9   (*concluded*)

B. QUALIFICATIONS (Describe technical, interpersonal, managerial qualifications, etc.)

1. STRENGTHS

Good analyst. Goal-oriented. Good with people, Good communicator.

2. DEVELOPMENT NEEDS

Needs to establish a General Electric track record by obtaining an opportunity to manage a GE line organization of some type. A product section or a foreign affiliate might fill this bill.

V. DEVELOPMENT AND CAREER RECOMMENDATIONS

A. DEVELOPMENT RECOMMENDATIONS (Specify development plans for the next 12 months which are responsive to identified needs.)

Enroll in appropriate Company courses to get broader experience and exposure in the Company, e.g., he is attending BMC in 1979. Try to find Group and/or Company task force or study assignments which would accomplish a similar end.

B. NEXT ASSIGNMENT (Consider alternatives.)

Position Title	Organization Layer	Timing
Manager, Marketing	Section	1 year
Manager, Product Section or Affiliate	Section	1 year

C. CAREER ROUTE AND GOALS (How realistic are the individual's career goals and are they compatible with your views? Make a clear statement with respect to long-range development needs and recommendations for future positions and training.)

His objective of managing a product section or a small affiliate some time in the next 12 to 24 months is realistic and probably an excellent way for him to demonstrate his longer range potential. Assuming a satisfactory performance in such a position, he appears to have the tools to function as a line General Manager in the Company. It is too early to comment on his long-term goal of Division level within 10 years.

Completed by _____ Date _____ Date Discussed with Reviewing Manager _____

Date Discussed with Employee _____

tinctively General Electric process," one executive noted.

As the next step, the manager completed the *Individual Career Forecast* form (Exhibit 10) in which he or she rated these subordinates on a scale ranging from "high potential—can move to the next higher organization layer with potential to move at least another organization layer later" to "unsatisfactory performance" and estimated when they would be ready for promotion. In addition, the manager completed the *Organization and Staffing Plan* (Exhibit 11) in which the three best replacements for each subordinate, and the manager, had to be identified—in essence, a succession plan.

At that point, the manager presented the evaluations, career forecasts, and succession plan to his or her superior in a formal review meeting. Discussion focused on individuals rated "high potential" and "unsatisfactory," upon the succession plan (with at least 40 percent of the meeting devoted to it), and upon special concerns such as the identification of able minorities. This process was repeated at each organization layer up to the chairman. At appropriate levels, O&M managers, such as Mercer, and EMCs, such as Orselet, sat in on the review presentations. Orselet explained:

> I take a very active role in these meetings, sometimes as advocate, sometimes as adversary. They are a great opportunity to bring several viewpoints to bear on how an executive is doing, and they can be quite lively.
>
> Of course, many managers fall somewhere between "high potential" and "unsatisfactory," and many have reached a level of responsibility at which they would like to remain. While this process doesn't focus on these managers, we do very much expect them to actively keep up with their field from year to year as well as, of course, to do the job well.

Data from the *Evaluations* and *Career Forecasts*, as well as from *Individual Experience* forms, were placed in the corporate management inventory. This file was maintained by the Executive Manpower staff and utilized by the consultants and by O&M managers to help identify prospective candidates for positions.

The Accomplishment Analysis. This was an in-depth look at the strengths and weaknesses of a manager 10–15 years down a career track (and so in a reasonably stable pattern) along such dimensions as knowledge, strategy, decision making, leadership, and relationships. Orselet gathered data from long interviews with the manager and his or her superiors and from the annual reviews. He discussed his analysis thoroughly with the manager, who could suggest changes. The analysis was used for developmental purposes by the company and the individual. Stumberger noted that, "It is really quite intensive and generates enriched data that goes well beyond an operating manager's annual performance review." An accomplishment analysis was very time consuming; each consultant was given an ongoing objective of completing six per year.

Perspectives

As Orselet reflected upon his job, he questioned:

> Are we "kingmakers" in executive manpower? While some in the company may occasionally see us this way, I believe that there are sufficient checks and balances to minimize that role, for us or for anyone, really. In any organization, certain values and skills will be rewarded and certain groups or individuals will do the rewarding. At GE, we have chosen to make this process

Exhibit 10

INDIVIDUAL CAREER FORECAST

1979

Year _____

(Identify Component and Parent Organizations through Group Layer)

NAME			Position Level	Position Title	Months in Position	FORECAST*			
Last	First	Initial				Code	Timing	Comments	
			14	Manager, Accounting Operations	23	3	Now	Accounting Operations or Administration	
			15	Manager, Operations Analysis and Financial Planning	15	1	2–3 yrs.		
			14	Manager, Information Systems	24	2	Now	Division Management— Information Systems	
			12	Manager, Auditing	17	3	2–3 yrs.		
			15	Manager, Manufacturing and Engineering Oper. Analysis	37	2	Now	Finance Section or Division Cost Operation	
			13	Manager, Marketing Operations Analysis	22	2	2 yrs.		

15	Manager, Financial Operations Component Products Section	32	2	Now	Capable of full finance operation

* Forecast Instructions:

List *all* employees reporting to the Manager of the Component and indicate for each a current career forecast using *one* of the codes below. Also forecast timing (now or number of years) for next move.

1. *High Potential* Can move to the next higher organization layer with potential to move at least another organization layer later.

2. *Promotable* to the next higher organization layer.

3. *Advanceable* to a higher position level within current organization layer.

4. *More time needed* before designation as promotable or advanceable.

5. *Not advanceable* but has satisfactory performance.

6. *Unsatisfactory* performance.

(Submitted by) _____ _____
                                              Date

Exhibit 11*

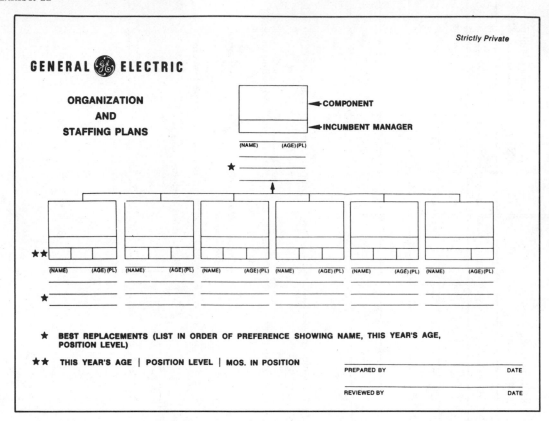

* Casewriter's note: the form presented here has been excerpted from the larger and more detailed company form.

quite explicit and above-board, with line management and executive manpower both interactively involved.

A key, and difficult, element in this process is talking straight, or negative feedback. And a good deal of this falls in my lap, or in the lap of a Pete Mercer or Jack Hamilton, for line managers often find it hard to do. When someone isn't selected from a slate, or doesn't make a slate, or isn't getting good reviews, we try to let them know the major things that, in other people's as well as our own perspective, are holding them back, and to work with them on identifying ways to improve. If a manager is not meeting his

numbers, he knows that and it is easy to address. But it is much more difficult to explain to a manager, who may be meeting his numbers, that he is perceived by the people evaluating him as weak in the softer areas of management, such as style, leadership or interpersonal relations. This feedback is important; and so, too, are opportunities, such as the movement of individuals into new units to which they will have to adapt, for managers to gain experience in these softer yet essential aspects of successful management.

I think that most criticisms of executive manpower boil down to a feeling that we infringe upon what a manager may have blocked out as his territory, such as a completely free hand in the selection of his own people and building his own organization. A manager he wants to promote, for example, may be a good manager, yet, when compared across the whole Company, he might only be the 5th best for that position. We try to provide that corporate-wide perspective.

Lighting Business Group Executive Ralph Ketchum had worked in Parker's Aerospace Group in the 1960s and had been one of the early "outsiders" in the Lighting Group. Having compiled an excellent record there, he had been appointed group executive in 1979. He discussed the Executive Manpower operation from his perspective:

> I am excited by the work we are doing to develop executives within GE as a whole and here in Lighting. We're providing great opportunities for promising managers and, as I view the progress here in this group, doing good things for the company. I am so excited by the annual manpower review process, for example, that I plan to take it down another layer or two in my organization this coming year, and will personally sit in on all the presentations, about five or six days of my time.
>
> Besides the corporate-wide exposure and movement the candidate slates provide, I think they generate fairer and more objective assessments of managers. I've heard some people question the fact that Orselet is involved: "How does he know me and the work that I'm doing? He's not a line manager," and so forth. But I believe that David does have a good basis for judgment. He actively participates in the Session C meetings, continually observes managers in their own settings, constantly talks with me, for example, about how people are doing; he's a real professional.
>
> The annual manpower review is very effective, but hard, for it forces us to evaluate and make judgments. That is easy with a top-notch subordinate, but harder with someone who isn't doing well, particularly in the face-to-face meeting. One of David's roles is to filter through the protective praise (and unfair criticism) that sometimes results. In a sense, he is a part of a system of checks and balances on executives. He has a key role, with respect and confidentiality critical.
>
> While these processes are implemented corporate-wide now, I think there is still quite a difference in *how* they are used. In one group, for example, their use is still quite perfunctory and I'd guess we are three years ahead of them. I want to keep working the process hard here to get good people— in no way are we yet inundated with good general managers. But I wonder about the future. As I look through our officer ranks now, there are many of us who came through Parker's group and moved on to find new challenges. As we now grow good managers across the company, will we continue to have the positions and challenges for these people?

CASE 9
THE WANE DIVISION OF THE AMERICAN INSTRUMENTS CORPORATION (A)
Peter D. Blanck and Jeffrey A. Sonnenfeld

The familiar sounds of "Auld Lang Syne" had special meaning for many at Wane's 1982 New Year's Eve party. As of January 1, 1982, a number of changes, which resulted in a major reorganization at Wane, became effective. Foremost among these changes was that Richard Sneider was to succeed Thomas Leonard as president of the Wane Division of the American Instruments Corporation.

Richard Sneider received an industrial engineering degree from MIT and started with Wane as a product director for industrial gas waste in 1957. Sneider became general manager of Wane's waste treatment systems in 1968. In 1974, Sneider was appointed a senior vice president at Wane with responsibility for waste treatment products and equipment. As a member of Leonard's staff, Sneider was responsible for various human resource policies.

Concern over the continued life of one such human resource effort, the Wane Career Management Programs, distracted Sneider from the holiday festivities. In three short years, beginning in 1978, Sneider and Leonard had each helped to develop and shape a new wave of managerial philosophy concerning career management programs at Wane. But now the division had encountered tough economic times and Leonard, a powerful program advocate, was leaving the division.

Sneider wondered what would happen to a large group of employees, some celebrating right before him, who might face layoffs. Furthermore, he wondered how to fend off criticism from corporate headquarters over additional expenditures for career management programs. Sneider questioned if he had needlessly raised the expectations of employees hoping to advance on the corporate ladder, and how to further centralize many of the fragmented employee programs already in place.

Sneider knew that during this particular new year he would have to redirect the focus and thrust of career management programs at Wane. As Sneider looked at his staff sitting at the table, he knew that they faced the task of generating enthusiasm and support for career management programs in the difficult economic times ahead.

The Wane Division of the American Instruments Corporation

In 1896 the American Instruments Corporation was founded in Rochester, New York. During the early 1900s American manufactured gauges, valves, pumps, and other such equipment for process industries. By the end of the Second World War, American had begun developing industrial equipment for the oil and chemical industry as well as for utilities.

In 1960, American Instruments acquired the Wane Corporation, which manufactured various types of pollution control equipment for monitoring emissions and effluents, waste treatment, and abatement equipment, such as scrubbers, cooling towers, and settling tanks. By 1981, American had posted sales of $7.1 billion and had total assets of $7.7 billion, with over 80,000 employees around the world. In 1981, Wane became the largest division in the American Corporation, with over 15,000 employees representing over $1.7 billion in sales worldwide.

Over the years, as Wane products had diversified, more and more brand names were used to promote individual products. This trend fragmented any attempts by Wane to present a single image to both the marketplace and Wane employees. At the same time the nature of the business began to shift to serve various equipment needs of energy-producing firms, Wane developed what was termed by management as an "identity crisis" due to this internal and external cloudiness.

In 1981, Wane management adopted a new logo as a symbol of the division's effort at a new image. As the new Wane logo was evolving, so was a new program for Wane's senior management, "Positioning for Excellence," which brought new direction to Wane's career management efforts. The Positioning for Excellence program, one of Tom Leonard's last initiatives as president of Wane, consisted of new management strategies for innovation, teamwork, and individual and corporate success. Beyond the "identity crisis" was a current economic crisis. Major customers in steel, automobile, and forest products had drastically cut investments in pollution control equipment.

Career Management at Wane: Before 1978

Since the early 1960s, career management programs had been in place at Wane. A placement staff of three full-time professionals was available to the 4,000 exempt employees and annually placed approximately 10 percent of these employees laterally and upwardly in the company. These placement officials responded to the initiative of senior management. Prior to 1978 and the Positioning for Excellence programs, Wane career management systems were defined within the framework of the American Instruments Management System (AIMS). AIMS was designed to ensure all American employees the opportunity to discuss and establish a career development plan with their supervisors. The Wane placement staff supervised AIMS.

The cornerstone of AIMS was the employees' Annual Performance Appraisal (APA). The APA process is used by the manager to evaluate a subordinate's overall performance and improvement in performance based on actual results since the last appraisal. The results of the APA interview are used by the manager in making decisions about compensation, management development, and management resource

planning. Appendixes 1 and 2 illustrate AIMS and APA.

American senior management believed the APA process benefited the manager, subordinate, and company in a number of ways. American viewed the benefits to the manager of conducting APAs as aiding in the accurate documentation of the subordinate's performance, enhancing communication between manager and subordinate, relating specific job standards to the subordinate, and motivating and developing the subordinate's performance. Management perceived the benefits of the APA process to the subordinate as providing formal feedback on both effective and deficient performance, clarifying job standards, and providing general career guidance. Finally, the APA process was perceived to benefit the company by detecting and correcting performance problems, improving the linkage of organizational rewards to employee performance, standardizing personnel decisions, and providing a systematic review of employee performance and development.

AIMS and APA did benefit the American Corporation, managers, and subordinates in many of these ways. However, in early 1978, Leonard and Sneider were convinced by department managers that a centralized and cohesive career management program, which was specifically relevant to Wane's divisional needs, was still lacking. AIMS had yet to be applied to Wane's long-range and strategic planning for human resources, the development of employees, and strategic hiring policies which greatly fluctuated with the nature of the economy. In short, by January of 1978, Leonard and Sneider believed that AIMS was not alone sufficient for developing and shaping new career management programs at Wane.

Career Management at Wane: 1978–1982

In February of 1978, a year after Thomas Leonard became the president of the Wane Division, Leonard was concerned about the identity crisis at Wane. Leonard subsequently requested his staff to assess the corporate culture and career management policies at Wane. The answers were vague and uninformative. Responding to Leonard's concern, the corporate management of American and of the Wane Division met in a company house in Atlanta for five days. During these five days, there were debates about who was responsible for career planning and development in Wane. The group discussed Wane's goals and the division's strengths and weaknesses. While many areas covered by AIMS such as salary administration were thought to be strong, other personnel practices were weak. In the areas where Wane was obviously weak, it was evident that management development and career planning practices came into focus. The group questioned whether career development was the responsibility of the Wane divisional staff or the corporate staff.

In Atlanta, the Wane Division's management agreed that the culture tended to criticize more than praise employee efforts, did not reward employee risk-taking and innovation, and lacked clear reward systems for high-potential and high-performing employees. The group further conceded that career management programs in Wane lacked a central focus and philosophy, and needed senior-level management support to survive in the good and bad economic times.

Upon the group's return from Atlanta, Leonard and Sneider began to shape a new corporate and divisional philosophy toward career management programs at Wane. One of Leonard's and Sneider's first actions was to delegate staff accountability for career management programs to Simon Burke. Burke had recently been appointed director of administration at Wane and was a member of Leonard's personal staff.

In June of 1978, Leonard, Sneider, and Burke further extended line accountability for career management programs by organizing a career management task force. This task force was comprised of the eight major line managers within the Wane organization. The task force of line managers was made responsible for the communication and advertising of career management programs to their subordinates.

By December of 1978, Leonard and Sneider began to search for a full-time employee relations professional to serve as coordinator and manager of the career management programs at Wane. In January of 1979, Wendy Kislik was hired to "pull together a good solid career management and development program." Kislik reported directly to Burke and was a member of his personal staff. She also was responsible for coordinating the career management task force.

From 1979 to 1982, the annual budget for career management programs at Wane rose from $50,000 to $300,000. During this period, Burke was responsible for the career management budget. Burke's budget included Kislik's staff expenses and material costs. At Leonard's request, the budget also included consulting fees to the Career Systems Corporation. Leonard believed that Career Systems could deliver training programs which would support his Positioning for Excellence programs. These programs included managerial training in career planning, budgeting, forecasting, and decision-making processes.

By January of 1982, Leonard had left Wane to become an executive vice president in the American Corporation and the economy had taken a sharp decline. Sneider, now the president of Wane, knew he had either to reduce dramatically the career management budget or postpone the entire process.

Burke and Kislik suggested that the $300,000 budget could be reduced by eliminating Career Systems' consulting fees. Kislik convinced Sneider that she could utilize Wane's and American's internal resources in customizing career management programs to meet Wane's immediate needs.

In March of 1982, Kislik presented Sneider a new budget of $75,000 for the career management programs. This budget included $50,000 for materials such as manuals, video tapes, and printing costs, and $25,000 for travel and staff expenses. Sneider accepted Kislik's new budget but, because of fiscal constraints, limited the scope of the programs to exempt employees who had been with the company for one year.

Hoping to further ease the economic strain, in June of 1982 Sneider reorganized the employee relations budgetary process. Up to now, Burke had allocated the employee relations budget. As of June 1982, each of the members of the career management task force was responsible for establishing career management budgets for their subordinates. Kislik was designated to serve as the coordinator and consultant of this new budgetary process. In September of 1982, each of the eight department managers separately submitted and negotiated career management budgets. All managers were responsible for communicating the scope of their new career management programs and resources to their subordinates. The career management programs included Career Development Labs, Career Development Self-Exploration Guides, Career Action Planning Guides, specialized Career Training Programs, and Career Counseling workshops for managers.

The first department in Wane actually to utilize the new career management programs was the Research and Development Facility in Torrington, Connecticut. At Burke's request, in July of 1981 Kislik met with Alberto Diaz. Diaz was the director of administration at the Torrington research facility. The Torrington facility was chosen as the first test case of these new programs because it was the largest single department within Wane, employing 3,000 exempt employees. Over the next year Kislik and Diaz reorganized the career management programs at Torrington.

The remainder of the case describes Burke's, Kislik's, and Diaz's views of the career management programs at Wane. All three perspectives comprise Sneider's 1982 personal staff reports of the strengths and weaknesses of the career management programs. The generic components of the programs are described, the results of the career management programs at Torrington are provided, and the dimensions of the economic strains facing Wane are discussed. Based on these staff reports, Sneider realized that he had to minimize the administrative costs of the career management programs while demonstrating continued corporate and divisional commitment to the current programs. By October of 1982, Sneider was committed to redirecting the focus of the career management programs, and Wane budget meetings were to begin next month.

Simon Burke: The Corporate Perspective

Career with Wane. Simon Burke is currently the director of administration and an officer of Wane. Burke, Sneider, four group vice presidents, and a director of operations constitute the senior management group at Wane.

Burke's previous company assignments were in sales, marketing, and line management. He had managed business areas with profit responsibility for plants, sales, marketing, and engineering products. Four years ago, in 1978, when the employee relations director for Wane retired, senior management thought that it would be a good time to move someone from a line organization, who is a generalist, and place him in the employee relations slot. Senior management hoped to bring a business manager's experience to employee relations activities.

Early Experiences and Problems as Director of Administration.

When Burke began as director of administration, many employee relations and career management programs (for example AIMS and APA) had been well established. But Burke found that Wane was lacking a centralized office which could coordinate the company-wide career management programs. Burke also noted that there were no quality controls on the career management programs already in place and in the field. Finally, Burke observed that the corporate emphasis on career management programs fluctuated with the nature of the economy. Burke remarked:

> We hire like crazy when times are good, we are out there with the "Oilies" trying to get every engineer. When times are bad, we are out there making excuses to the colleges why we will not be recruiting this year but we know we will next year.

> What we lacked was somebody who was managing our management development and managing our young people as they come in to make sure we are tracking their career properly.

> We had all these professional things going on and they were going well, but we were not pulling together a good management development program, a good career system, a ladder that people could look at and see where do I go from here and what are my opportunities. We worried about that stuff.

Before the 1982 changes in the budgetary process, Burke decided the extent to which career management programs would either be centralized or discretionary. That is, whether Wane would offer basic generic career management programs throughout the division, or alternatively, allow departmental managers discretion in determining the career management programs.

By 1979, Burke proposed that the role of the career management office was to inform the division about career management training related to the American Instruments Management Systems (AIMS). Further, generic AIMS programs such as "interpersonal communications skills" and "developing listening and feedback skills," were to be considered corporate-wide programs. Before 1982, these generic programs were included in Burke's career development budget.

Burke also decided that the utilization of other career management programs would be discretionary. For example, time management training, relevant technical training, and work-group skills were considered discretionary programs. Discretionary programs were also cheaper to conduct at the departmental level. Before 1982, discretionary programs were included in every department manager's career developing budget.

Coping with Corporate Pressures to Justify Career Management Programs. By 1979, Burke realized that it was difficult to demonstrate to the Wane senior management group that career management programs were cost justified. Leonard and the members of the senior management group wanted to see the tangible results of these programs. Burke noted:

> Once this year's program is not replaced by next year's program, you start to build credibility. Management must come to understand that these programs are not tied to specific business strategies. This is not something that business needed right then.

In 1979, Burke began to record the outplacement and inplacement statistics for Wane in order to help justify the career management programs in his budget. Burke recorded turnover rates in the various departments utilizing career management programs and also examined the exit interviews of exempt employees. Burke found that departments using career management programs showed a 20 percent decrease in the number of employees who left the company specifically because of a lack of career opportunities.

Building Support and Credibility for Career Management Programs. According to Burke, career management programs do not start in the trenches and work their way up the corporate ladder. In building and sustaining the credibility of career management programs, Burke believed that he had to continually convince senior management of the merit of these programs and convince the line manager that what he wanted to do with the manager's immediate group had long-term effectiveness. Burke remarked:

> If you don't get top-management's support right from the start, you are going to

fight the battle longer to build credibility. You may get there because the product is good; but if you get the top dog to agree that it is good, it will go down a lot better through the organization and people are going to listen.

Burke had observed several cases in American where career management programs had failed because of the lack of ownership by a senior management group. In particular, Burke and the Wane management were recently aware of a failure of a career management program in the American Business Systems Division. In Business Systems, the development of career ladders, career feedback sessions, and training in career management was performed by an outside consulting group. Senior and line management provided no input into the developmental process of the program. In the eyes of senior management, this very expensive program was of no practical use to the division. Senior and line management did not develop a sense of ownership and responsibility for the programs. The credibility of the program quickly declined and the program manuals sat on the divisional president's shelf.

In order to combat credibility problems which were associated with career management programs, Burke worked with Wane senior management in the development and pilot testing of the programs, advertised the successful programs in Wane to other divisions in American, and allocated funds in his employee relations budget for program development and research.

Finding Support in Good and in Bad Economic Times. By September 1982, Burke realized that it was going to take a year or more to get the career management programs established and create credibility so that people don't say, "Times are tough and those are great programs, but we really ought to wait until times are better and we can afford the stuff." Burke believed, however, that in bad economic times the emphasis could be directed toward program development, and with improvements in the economic situation, the emphasis could be redirected toward manager training and individual development programs.

> I think it is up to us through bad times and good times to get these programs established to where you may not go quite as fast sometimes, but you certainly do not come to a dead stop and lose momentum in a good management development program.

Burke was aware of the economic strains facing Wane. Burke knew that in 1982 Wane profit growth declined, a voluntary retirement program was put in place, work weeks were shortened in a few Wane plants in order to reduce the need for layoffs, and a hiring freeze was in place. Burke realized that in the current economic times it would be difficult to keep many of the career management programs in place. Burke remarked:

> With the economy as it is now, and it is very tough for us because we are heavily related to the steel industry, times are going to be bad for a while. We are going to be struggling with line managers to keep these programs alive and well.

Wendy Kislik: The Coordinator's Perspective

Career with Wane. In 1979, Burke hired Wendy Kislik to serve as coordinator and manager of the career management programs at Wane. Kislik had recently received a graduate degree from New York University in the area of labor relations and had been conducting counseling workshops and specialized management training programs for the Wane organization. Kislik was highly regarded by Burke and the American corporate staff. She was seen as a strong and innovative leader.

Kislik's new role was to manage the career management programs. Kislik explains:

> The role of facilitator here is a very key one in this organization because the power structure was divided among so many people and it was not always productive the way they resolved conflict. It required a strong personality to run it. You just couldn't pick up somebody who had some good OB skills and run it as a typical process because this organization had been through a lot of different problems.

Early Experiences as Manager of Career Management. After meetings with the eight members of the career management task force, Kislik discovered that the Wane line managers had received minimal formal training in career management or career counseling. Kislik believed that it was more important to have the managers trained to understand career management issues than it was to send employees off to expensive programmed workshops. Kislik decided that the focus of the new career management programs had to be geared toward line managers.

> It is my feeling that the people who submerge and kill a new program are not the tough guys and it's not the average employee, it's the lower level supervisor or manager who is always cut from the real information flow. He never knows what the strategic plan is, never knows why the things are going the way they are. They tend to be the ones that are the most resistant to career management programs.

Kislik believed that line managers needed to develop an understanding of employee problems, take increased responsibility for the career path of their employees, and be sensitized to emotional and often painful confrontations when talking with employees about career development.

In one of their meetings, Kislik suggested to the task force members that if, for example, a manager runs into a career development problem that is related to stress in the workplace, the manager can take several steps in counseling the employee. First the manager can identify the problem and discuss the problem in terms of work-related behavior. Next, the manager can offer to get the employee some help or convince the employee that she or he needs help. Finally, the manager should not attempt to "psychoanalyze" the employee.

Kislik explained to the task force members that the line manager who is trained in career management and career counseling realized that (1) she or he is not totally powerless, (2) there are many corporate services available for career counseling, (3) helping a subordinate in various phases of his or her career is just as important as the APA process, and (4) career management advice is part of the job as a manager of people.

By 1982, Kislik realized that it was going to be increasingly difficult to retain the task force members' interest in and involvement in the career management programs. Task force members complained that with the recent business slowdowns and the 10 percent downturn in gross revenues, the number of positions were greatly reduced, and when there were job openings they were not allowed to be filled. Secondly, task force members did not appreciate the long-term rather than short-term aspects of career management. Kislik explained to the task force members that the long-term goals of the career management programs included the long-term matching of skilled personnel

in the organization to the requirements of the business needs in the future and providing future leadership. The short-term goals of the career management programs included providing employees with information about their own career development and filling immediate job slots in the organization. Kislik also explained that these long- and short-term needs had to be integrated into the career management strategies already in place in Wane.

The Career Management Resources at Wane. There are currently five potential career management resources available to all exempt employees at Wane. These resources may be used individually or in combination as part of a manager's overall career management strategy in working with an employee. The five resources include: (1) a Developmental Lab, which analyzes managerial skills; (2) a Career Development and Self-Exploration Guide; (3) a Career Review Discussion and Career Action Planning Guide; (4) several Training Options, including training in corporate management development and technical training; and finally, (5) Career Counseling Workshops for Managers.

The Developmental Lab for analyzing managerial skills is an intensive two-day workshop conducted at the center for managerial development in Houston. The lab provides the employee personal assessments, feedback, and training in managerial styles of interaction with others, specific managerial skills as an input to career choices and actions, and career development action plans. Participants are provided the opportunity to experiment with different managerial styles in a safe environment, and then receive feedback on these approaches. The results of the lab serve as one input in deciding, for example, whether a manager wants to move in a technical or managerial ladder. Department managers contract with the Developmental Lab through Kislik's career management office, but as of October 1982 lab fees are allocated from departmental career management budgets. There is no allotment per Wane employee for developmental labs.

The Career Development and Self-Exploration Guide was developed by Kislik in 1979. The Self-Exploration Guide is a pencil-and-paper self-assessment exercise which helps employees set career priorities. The guide helps employees assess career strengths, weaknesses, desires, and directions. Employees also systematically assess where they have been and set priorities for the future. Finally, the guide prepares employees for career review discussions with the manager. Copies of the guide can be obtained from the department manager. Appendix 3 illustrates the self-exploration model.

Kislik suggested that employees who would benefit most from the completion of the Self-Exploration Guide would be (1) employees who have a few years of work experience, but are at the "early" stages in their careers and desire to make systematic choices in future career management, (2) employees at "mature" stages in their careers who wish to confirm or re-assess career choices and/or evaluate possible new alternatives, and (3) employees in "transition" who are changing career directions for either organizational or personal reasons.

The Career Review Discussion and the Career Action Planning Guide was also developed by Kislik in 1979 and was designed to assist managers and employees in preparing for a career discussion. The guide describes how managers can be helpful to employees at different career stages, such as "Entry," "Settling in," "Full membership," "Mid-career," and "Late-career concerns." "Entry" concerns include providing subordinates detailed feedback on performance and providing opportunities to demonstrate one's skills. "Settling in" concerns include keeping employees informed of department plans and career opportunities. "Full membership" concerns include focusing on employee career paths and discussing future opportunities inside and outside of the company. "Mid-career" concerns include aiding the employee to fit "career dreams" to the corporate reality, and balancing life and work needs. Finally, "Late-career" concerns would include demonstrating to the employee that their contribution is still valuable to the organization, and assigning old members to serve as mentors for younger members.

The Career Discussion Guide also provides recommendations for conducting the career discussions and tips for managers in responding to typical employee questions and concerns. Appendixes 4 and 5 illustrate recommendations for career discussions.

The Career Discussion Guide also describes the point at which an employee might be ready to discuss career aspirations and directions with the manager, and when an employee might need to realistically appraise career objectives. Additionally, the guide helps employees and managers to share and discuss expectations about the employee's career, and to jointly establish a career development action plan for the employee. A career review may take place anytime during the year. Copies of the guide are available to all managers.

The American corporate career management staff also offers several Training Options to all divisional managers and supervisors. Costs for the training programs are allocated through the individual departments. American offers two basic training options. The first training option is the corporate management development program. These programs are utilized when the employee needs to (1) understand and use AIMS tools for the self-management of a career, (2) develop specific skill-building in managing skills, and (3) develop specific skill-building in professional development skills. The second training option is the technical training option. These programs are utilized when the employee needs to (1) develop knowledge and skill-building in technical data processing skill areas, (2) understand new technologies, and (3) develop American Instruments specific skills in project design and management. In Wane there is also technical training available within departments.

The final career management resource available to Wane employees is the Career Counseling Workshop for Managers. The Counseling Workshop was developed by Kislik in 1979 and designed to provide managers with the skills and information necessary to assist employees in their career development. The workshop is an intensive one-day session conducted by Kislik for Wane managers. Departments contract with the Wane career management office to send managers to the workshops.

There are three basic objectives of the workshops. First, to help participants better understand career planning in the context of personal history and the stages of adult development. Edgar H. Schein's *Career Anchors Inventory* is employed to aid managers in developing this life-stage approach to career planning. The second objective of the workshop is to help managers use career ladders, department or position descriptions, measures of performance, and annual performance appraisals as aids in providing career counseling to employees. The final objective of the workshop is to aid man-

agers in conducting career counseling discussions and developing career plans with employees. To meet this objective, role-playing exercises are performed and analyzed.

Career Management Needs in the Future. Reflecting on her past three years as manager of career management at Wane, Kislik suggested that the term "career management" essentially provides an umbrella statement for describing the various career ladders, workshops, training programs, and self-assessment exercises available to Wane employees.

Kislik stated that career management programs should be a joint effort involving the organization, the manager, and the employee. The role of the organization is to provide a structure and climate that encourages career planning and development. This includes providing career ladders and career planning processes that are integrated with the APA and salary systems. The role of the manager is to provide appropriate resources, assignments, information, coaching, and counseling to assist employees in the realistic planning and attainment of career objectives. This role includes realistically appraising employee career objectives, identifying skill development, and facilitating career movement. Finally, the role of the employee in the career management process is to maintain primary responsibility for managing his or her own career plan. That is, it is the responsibility of the employee to seek out career planning resources, access organizational resources for growth, identify long-term and personal career objectives, and manage the total career process.

For Kislik, the Torrington career management program was a first step toward the integration of career management activities within Wane. Kislik had involved the organization, the managers, and the employees in this effort. As Kislik was waiting to receive the survey results of the career management programs at Torrington in September of 1982, she knew that the future success of career management programs throughout the various departments of Wane was dependent, to a large extent, on the results of the Torrington project. Before committing time and money to new career management programs, the other departments were waiting to see the results of the Torrington program.

Alberto Diaz: Torrington's Perspective of Career Management

Career with Wane.   Alberto Diaz, an engineer with an MBA, had been with Wane for over 15 years. In 1976 he became the director of administration and operations at the Wane research and development facility in Torrington, Connecticut.

Diaz had experience in technical work and technical management. He had no formal training in career management programs. Diaz stated, "Almost all of my thinking about career planning comes from the viewpoint of the practitioner."

Career Management History and Problems in Torrington.   The Torrington plant, with 3,000 exempt employees, was Wane's research and development support center. Wane's research and development, technology, and health, safety, and environmental affairs programs were all designed in Torrington. The majority of exempt employees at Torrington were professionals—engineers, chemists, physicists—with advanced degrees.

In the past, Torrington had paid minimal attention to career management issues. Be-

cause the Torrington facility was Wane's major research and development plant, all of the employees worked in the same plant location. Typically, when an employee changed jobs at Torrington, she or he moved his or her office down the hall. The physical work environment at Torrington was, by objective standards, a very closed and self-sufficient system.

But there was a deeper personnel problem at Torrington. Before 1975, the Torrington plant had operated in a closed managerial environment. That is, almost no personnel and employee relations information seemed to get passed down below the vice presidential level. Kislik remarked:

> At Torrington things were sort of done in secret and almost anyone you talked to, regardless of level, would tell you that. The kind of career management we were offering could never have gotten off the ground against that kind of backdrop. They got very little information about how things were really done and how personnel decisions were made.

In the middle of 1977, the technical employment at Torrington reached its all-time peak. Several major business ventures in the environmental protection area were in place. The major resources of these ventures were technical personnel, as opposed to capital goods or raw materials.

Toward the end of 1977, the environmental protection ventures began to be affected by the government's withdrawal of funds from this market. These withdrawals began a business cycle which Wane was still feeling in 1982. As a result, staff had to be reduced. The reduction was accomplished mainly through attrition and recruitment cutbacks, but almost 10 percent of the exempt employees were asked to leave for performance reasons.

During this period, Diaz began to notice a

"downbeat" atmosphere among the younger staff at Torrington. Diaz recalled:

> We had a lot of people leave the company on their own accord, people who we were not happy to see go under any circumstances. We asked these people why they left. What began to surface was that a lot of our younger people were leaving the company because they felt, and rightfully so, that they did not have a sense of the career paths in the company. They felt that nobody was paying attention to them as long-term career employees and there was no continuity established for them as far as career development and growth was concerned.

This uncomfortable and downbeat feeling by the younger employees when coupled with the recent business cutbacks sent a clear message to many of the younger employees: "Maybe it's time to look for another job." This atmosphere also sent a clear message to Diaz.

Two years after becoming the director of administration at Torrington, Diaz realized that there were obvious weaknesses in communication between middle management and supervisory first-line managers, in career management programs for young and high-potential employees, and in career planning and development procedures. Diaz interviewed the line managers at Torrington and found that many employees did not seem to profit effectively from their first five years of association with the company, and employee concerns about their career development distracted their learning processes and productivity. Finally, it was plainly becoming too expensive for Wane to retrain large numbers of skilled employees at approximately $25,000 to $30,000 per employee.

Career Management at Torrington: 1978– 1981. Diaz's concerns about the downbeat atmosphere at Torrington led him to form a local Personnel Advisory Committee (PAC) late in 1978. Diaz was the chair of the committee. PAC had senior level manager representatives drawn from each of the major departments at Torrington. Diaz remembered:

> PAC quickly got to work on this question of what we chose to call "personnel development." We adopted a broad approach to the problem and felt that career management is something that you cannot develop in a vacuum. We couldn't look at career management in the context of career planning exclusively because we were talking about something that had roots in the environment in which we were operating. And so we felt that the environment that we were maintaining, and its degree of professionalism, was just as important in a personnel development sense as a formal career management process.

Diaz and PAC soon developed their own model for conceptualizing career management activities at Torrington. The model consisted of four related, but separate, areas of activity—Career Development, Career Planning, Professional Development, and Job Enrichment. The Career Development program was aimed at developing all high-potential exempt employees in the proper career direction. The program was limited to those employees whose APA performance was judged as superior and whose potential in the long run was judged as outstanding. The Career Planning program was aimed at properly placing all employees in the career path most likely to lead to maximum performance. Establishing the proper path was thought to be a logical consequence of the APA process. The Professional Development program dealt with developing an employee's expertise within a given profession. The technical training was conducted within the Torrington facility and generally related to engineering and manufacturing professional development. Finally, the Job Enrichment program was aimed at insuring that there was "fun" in the job content. Individual supervisors were responsible for maximizing the attractiveness and positive aspects of the job.

By 1980, all employees at Torrington were aware of PAC and the new career management activities. However, Diaz still believed that his career management activities were not integrated into the overall career management strategies of Wane. In July of 1981, Burke contacted Diaz and recommended that the Torrington facility, Wane's largest department, be the first test case for Kislik's new career management programs.

The Torrington Career Management Program: 1982. From July 1981 to July 1982, Kislik integrated Diaz's and PAC's earlier work on career planning with Wane's career management programs. Torrington supervisors and managers at all levels were trained in career counseling techniques and were all familiarized with the various career management programs offered by Wane. An employee information package was compiled and delivered to all exempt Torrington employees. The information packet contained the Torrington career ladders, the qualifications for key career paths, department functional descriptions, and Torrington organizational charts.

Kislik and Diaz also formed three career management training committees. The Management Skills Committee conducted a needs analysis to determine the appropriate management skills training offerings. The Professional Skills Committee also performed a needs analysis to determine the appropriate professional and technical training offerings. Finally, a Personal Skills

Committee was formed to determine the topics of interest of the general Torrington population which related to career activities. All three committees were comprised of department managers.

Kislik and Diaz further decided that there would be associate director, or third-level, accountability for the career management of all exempts. Kislik and Diaz authorized each associate director of Torrington to summarize the career development action planned for his organization and made him accountable to follow through on the plans. Kislik believed that this accountability would provide clear vehicles for employees to have input in the career management process because the associate director level is "high" enough to have organizational impact, yet "low" enough to be familiar with particular employee needs. Finally, Kislik and Diaz continued to support the work of the PAC committee as a sponsor of much of the career management activities.

By July, all supervisors and managers had been trained for their role in the career management program. In September of 1982, Kislik conducted a program evaluation survey of the project. Of the 132 evaluations received, 80 percent felt that the program "Exceeded" or "Greatly Exceeded" their expectations, 99 percent felt that the concepts and subject matter were "Good" to "Excellent," and finally, 94 percent felt that the concepts and skills taught in the program would be helpful back on the job to "a good amount" or "a great deal." Appendix 6 provides additional data on the participants' attitudes toward the career management programs.

In October of 1982, Kislik and Diaz began the career management implementation. First, a letter was mailed home to all exempt employees informing them of the existence of the Torrington Career Management Program. It was explained that participation was voluntary and their supervisors would soon formally introduce the career management programs. Second, supervisors received employee information packages for each of their exempt employees with suggested guidelines on how to conduct a career management meeting. Third, associate directors were notified that they were to collect relevant career development plans and to provide a summary of these plans to the Torrington senior management by this December. Finally, Kislik planned to measure the overall program effectiveness and acceptance in July of 1983. The evaluations would include measures of promotions, lateral moves, program attendance, and associate director's fulfillment of career development plans. Additionally, employee and supervisor perceptions of the programs would be collected.

Kislik and Diaz also planned other career management efforts. First, they hope to establish a program for "Early Career Management." This program would provide job orientation and training for selected new hires and high-potential employees. Second, a "Torrington Orientation Program" is planned. This program is designed to orient all new exempt hires to Torrington, Wane, and its senior management.

Richard Sneider: The Future of Career Management at Wane

Toward the end of his first year as president of Wane, Richard Sneider evaluated Burke's, Kislik's, and Diaz's comments on the implementation and history of career management programs at Wane.

Sneider realized that Wane had made a long-term commitment to career management and development, but now the programs had to be approached on a more modified basis. With a predicted economic decline in 1983, more layoffs would be likely. Sneider also did not want to send a mixed message to Wane employees by simultaneously supporting career management activities for some employees and laying off others. As memories of last New Year's party faded, Sneider reflected on his first year as president of Wane; he realized certain trade-offs would have to be made.

Appendix 1
American Instruments Management System*

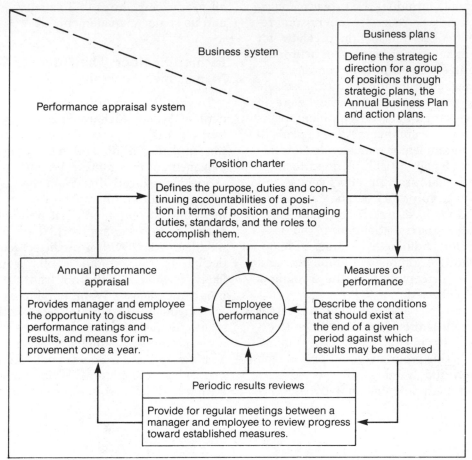

* This is a simplified depiction of the many subsystems which, together, comprise the AIMS.

Appendix 2
AIMS: Annual Performance Appraisal*

ANNUAL PERFORMANCE APPRAISAL	
Employee Name	Division or General Department
Position	Appraiser Name
Date Entered Job / /	Appraisal Period / / to / /

Instructions

Please do not complete this form without reading the Performance Appraisal System Manager's Manual.

Performance Level: Choose the most appropriate rating to appraise position, management and overall performance.

1. Performance is exceptional.
2. Performance is substantially beyond that accepted as normal for performing the full job.
3. Performance meets or exceeds the normal requirements for performing the full job.
4. Performance improvement is necessary to satisfy the requirements of the full job; a performance improvement plan is required.
5. Performance is that of an individual new to the job. (This rating should not be used beyond the appropriate learning period.)

To choose the appropriate performance level, consider the results attained during the appraisal period against agreed-upon position and management duties, standards and measures.

In developing the overall rating, the appraiser should take into account both position and management ratings and the relative importance of management results and position results in the job.

In developing each rating, the appraiser must also take into account the difficulty of measures; the relative importance among measures; the quality of results achieved; the extent to which external factors affected results achieved; and the effect of performance on the results of others.

Summarize the considerations that led to each rating in the spaces provided. If additional space is required to complete pages 1–3, use the back of page 3.

I. PERFORMANCE LEVEL
Enter performance rating and comment upon those results and other factors significant in arriving at the rating.

A. Appraisal of performance against position measures of importance.   Rating:

Comments: (Please describe the basis for this rating.)

B. Appraisal of performance against management
standards and measures of performance.   Rating:

Comments: (Please describe the basis for this rating.)

C. Appraisal of overall performance against both   Rating:
position and management measures of performance.

Comments: (Please describe the basis for this rating.)

II. IMPROVEMENT IN PERFORMANCE: This evaluation requires a review of the annual appraisal rating for the previous year. An appropriate explanatory or clarifying statement should be included in the comments section. Indicate your evaluation of the change in overall performance level since the previous appraisal.

___1. Outstanding ___2. Substantial ___3. Noticeable ___4. Stabilized ___5. Decreased

Comments: (Please describe the basis for this rating.)

III. ANNUAL APPRAISAL INTERVIEW; DEVELOPMENTAL PLANNING FOR CURRENT JOB: Discuss the employee's performance during the appraisal period, performance improvement planning, and present or current job-related development needs.

A. Discuss 1. Performance against measures of performance.
            2. Improvement in performance.
            3. Relationship between performance and compensation.
            4. Specific results improvement and/or skill development needed to maintain or improve performance in the present job.

Record specific development actions to be taken during the next year. Please be sure to include all commitments.

B. Additional comments: e.g., manager/employee reaction to discussion, development plans, contingent actions, etc.

Appraisal interviews conducted by: Signature_____Date_____
Appraisal content reviewed by: Signature_____Date_____

IV. PROMOTABILITY
Indicate your assessment of this individual's current readiness for advancement to the next level by checking the appropriate statement below. In the comments section include explanatory information as to the basis for this assessment.

___1. Ready now
___2. Ready within 1–2 years

___3. Ready within 3–4 years
___4. Possible
___5. Unlikely

Comments:

V. PLACEMENT
Considering the employee's needs, the Corporation's objectives, and the above assessment of promotability, indicate which action should be considered for this individual during the next year. In recommending specific positions for which the employee could be considered, include positions outside your own organization.

___1. Promote
___2. Remain in present position.
___3. Move laterally for developmental experience.
___4. Move laterally into a position better utilizing abilities.
___5. Move downward into a position where performance can be satisfactory.

Comments:

VI. CAREER DIRECTION
Describe and comment as appropriate upon the employee's career objectives and general career direction.

* This is a simplified version of APA.

Appendix 3
Career Planning Self-Exploration Model

Where I've been   Where I am now   Where I want to go   How I can get there   What I will do

| Work history → Critical projects | Skill/ Knowledge inventory → Needs/ Values | | Ideal job → | Organizational support/ constraint → | Action plan |

Appendix 4
Recommendations for Career Discussions

Avoid	*Try*
Raising false hopes about promotion	To set realistic expectations for the discussion
Interrupting	To insure privacy and set aside plenty of time for reflection and continuity of thinking
Insinuating that the only good future is up the managerial ladder	To focus on growth in the present assignment and how it can be made more meaningful.
Evaluating employee's future for him or her as you see it	To ask for his or her thoughts and offer information and additional suggestions regarding his or her future
Criticizing employee's evaluation of his or her future	To find out why he or she feels that way about the future and add information
Discouraging a stated ambition	To discover why he or she has a stated ambition and suggest alternatives, ways to learn more about it, and ways to test interest and aptitude for it
Evaluating employee's readiness for the career he or she wants	To ask him or her to evaluate his or her competitive position
Making unrealistic commitments; you may not be able to keep them	To focus discussion about the future on matters within your control and the employee's control
Ending with analysis	To ask the employee to translate his or her ideas into specific action plans

Avoid	*Try*
Displaying a negative, uninterested attitude	To give him or her exposure to those who make promotion decisions, and help him or her prepare for his or her exposure
Doing too much for the employee so that his or her own abilities aren't tested	To exhibit a positive attitude; be the employee's sponsor or campaign manager
Solving his or her career problems	To provide information while letting him or her manage his or her own career
Fixing a goal rigidly; it may be needlessly limiting	To look at alternative goals; provide for some flexibility
Looking too far into the future	To focus attention on actions during the next year or two
Recording information the employee doesn't know about or want in the record	To agree on what should be recorded

Appendix 5
Tips for Managers: How to Respond to
Typical Employee Questions/Concerns

Typical Employee Question about Roles	*Helpful Responses*
"How can I manage my career plan when I don't have control over position openings?"	Career planning is a joint effort between the employee and the manager. The action plan established reflects not only U/A reached between the parties, but also outlines specific steps for which the manager and the employee are responsible. It's true that employees don't have "control" over openings, but they do have control over identifying for managers their goals, aspirations, preferences and personal/ professional developmental activities. With this data, managers are better able to match employee career objectives with job availabilities.
"I always thought my manager was supposed to tell me what development I needed as well as what my next assignment will be."	It is the *manager's responsibility* to help identify developmental or improvement needs as well as to identify for employees the kind of positions for which he or she is a qualified candidate. It is also the *employee's responsibility* to identify for himself or herself development/improvement needs, initiate plans and learn about generic job requirements by referencing any

Typical Employee Question about Roles	*Helpful Responses*
	available career development information, job descriptions or other resources. Employees should put just as much thought and energy into their own career development as their managers do.
"Some current incumbents don't have all the 'requirements' listed for jobs on the career ladders. Why should I have to attain more stringent requirements to be considered for those jobs than the people already there?"	The typical requirements listed for each job on a ladder reflect what is currently needed on the job today as well as the requirements management sees as likely in the future. Specific job requirements change according to the direction, depth, breadth and complexity of the changing business needs. If a vacancy were to occur, management would most likely look for candidates who are qualified to meet the changing requirements of the job.
"Do the arrows on the job ladders identify the *only* lines of progression?"	No. The arrows depict the *typical or most likely* patterns of movement. Moving between any two positions requires looking not only at the transferability of skills from job to job, but also at the set of skills, experience, knowledge that is unique to each employee.
"Why doesn't each organization have its own career ladders?"	The ladders purposely ignore organizational reporting lines to demonstrate the commonality and transferability of skill *across* department lines. This serves to provide the employee with a wider range of job possibilities.
Questions about Pay and Promotion	*Typical Responses*
"I hear that managers make more money than technical employees at the same level"	Not true. For equivalent salary grades, the possible salary range is the *same* regardless of type of *job* (management versus technical) *function* (data processing, finance, production, sales, etc.) or *division*. Difference in pay within a salary grade are made according to *employee performance*.

Questions about Pay and Promotion

Typical Responses

"If an employee has done his or her best and performed well, don't you think he/she is *owed* a promotion?

No. American Instruments owes its employees equitable *pay for performance.* Promotions are not *owed* to employees.

"If an employee can demonstrate all the requirements for a higher rated job, shouldn't the organization raise him or her to the next higher grade?"

No. Demonstrating all the requirements for the next level job makes the employee a *candidate* for the job when an opening occurs. It does not guarantee the employee the job. *Jobs are created in response to justified business needs.* Jobs are not created (or salary grades elevated) because the employee is "ready" or because he or she has been in the present grade for a long time. *Within the context of meeting business needs,* managers try to match qualified candidates with job vacancies.

"Why does management encourage lateral broadening for employees who want to be managers?"

As business needs become more complex in the future, the organization will need managers who have been "broadened" in more than one discipline. This does not mean that all employees need to broaden laterally. For employees who are considering management jobs, however, it is suggested that they get experience in more than one area.

Appendix 6
Participant Comments—Content Analysis

The following is a summary of the areas highlighted by 132 Torrington participants in their comments about (I) the *workshop* and *concepts* of career development, and (II) *management support* for implementation. The numbers in parentheses ( ), indicate the number of times a particular comment was made.

I. *About the Workshop, Content, and Philosophy of Career Development Program*

    A. Participants *liked* and found the following areas *helpful:*   (Frequency)

        1. The formalized, structural approach and process for conducting career counseling.   (58)

        2. Philosophy, assumptions, concepts presented in the program (phases of career development, employee responsibility, honest communication, voluntary participation, etc.).   (27)

(Frequency)

3. Forms, tools, and aids for the manager (prework form, career anchors, typical tough questions, etc.).   (25)
4. Opportunity to interact, exchange ideas, and discuss concepts with other managers in workshop.   (23)
5. Information presented in the Employee Information Package.   (22)
6. Opportunity to practice concepts and approach (Application role-play exercise).   (22)

B. Participants found the following areas not helpful:
Application role-play exercise (not enough time, artificial, unrealistic, etc.).   (15)
Videotape (too short, unrealistic).   (8)

C. Participants wanted *more* of the following:
Practice.   (4)
Discussion on particular employee types, tough situations.   (3)
Reading materials (adult development, career anchors, etc.).   (3)
Information (on specific position requirements, on other Wane areas).   (4)

II. *About Management Support, Next-Step Implementation, and Evaluation*

A. Participants were *pleased* about the following:
Providing the course itself for all Torrington management signals management's real support for the program.   (14)
Finally! It's about time! This has been long overdue!   (12)
Providing information and more responsibility to individual employees.   (6)

B. Participants had *concerns* about the following:
Will management really make the feedback loop work? How do we know whether the employee's input ever really gets factored into personnel placement decisions?   (7)
Individual employees don't have enough "clout" to really make their development plans work. Supervisors may not be able to deliver what's been agreed to.   (5)
Supervisors and managers don't have enough skills. Would like more short, one-day "how-to" workshops on appraisals, handling performance problems, etc.   (4)
How will management follow up to make sure it's working? Will it die after the training program?   (4)
Don't raise expectations. Don't oversell.   (2)

THE WANE DIVISION OF THE AMERICAN INSTRUMENTS CORPORATION (B)
Peter D. Blanck and Jeffrey A. Sonnenfeld

In January of 1983, Richard Sneider completed his first year as president of the Wane Division of the American Instruments Corporation. During 1982, Sneider, along with Simon Burke and Wendy Kislik, directed the design and implementation of a career management package at Wane's research and development facility in Torrington. All 150 managers at Torrington had been through the Career Counseling Workshop for Managers. Torrington's exempt employees had received their Career Development Employee Information Packages and had developed Career Management Action Plans. Sneider knew that, despite the impact which the 1982 business climate had on the Torrington population, Torrington management had perceived the career management activities as successful (see Appendix 6 in the Wane Division of the American Instruments Corporation (A)).

A Systematic Approach to Career Management

In late January of 1983, Sneider and the Career Development Task Force met to discuss the development of a division-wide plan for the implementation of career management programs at Wane. Sneider and Kislik defined the group's task as deciding the key populations, time frame, and project accountability for the career management programs in Wane.

In its discussions, the group decided to

limit the career management programs to all exempt employees. With the predicted improvement of financial conditions, the group eventually hoped to expand the program to include nonexempts. Within the exempt population, several groups of employees were given priority in the career development process. First, managers were assigned the highest priority in receiving the career management programs. Managers were assigned the highest priority in order to ensure that all exempt personnel would be provided with career development tools and information, and provided the opportunity for career discussions and a career development plan with their supervisors. All managers needed to be provided with both the "back to basics" American Instruments Management System (AIMS) refresher course and the career counseling training session. The group decided that all managers would receive the one-day AIMS refresher course and the one-day counseling workshop for managers.

The next subset of the exempt employee population to receive the career management programs would be the "fast-track employees." For this population, the objectives were to develop employee profiles (using AIMS) and plan and monitor developmental activities (e.g., promotions, training). Sneider and Kislik also learned from the Torrington experience that it was essential to provide early management development training to fast-track employees to foster a sense of advancement. To meet these goals, the group decided to discuss, at the vice presidential and presidential staff meetings in the spring and fall, the progress of all fast-track employees. Additionally, fast-track employees were to be offered the corporate-sponsored "Exceptional Management Practices" workshop.

Finally, the relatively few "new hires"

were also thought to be a key subset of the exempt employee population for career management opportunities. Sneider and the group decided to require the development of orientation programs in all Wane departments. The Torrington group that was headed by Alberto Diaz, for example, was directed by Sneider to begin the development and discussion of a new six-month orientation program to career management and career opportunities at the research and development facility. Kislik was to coordinate the development of the orientation programs.

Sneider next turned the discussion to the time frame for career development activities. Kislik's experience at Torrington had illustrated the need for about 18 months in the development and implementation of a career management program. Within this general time frame, the group developed a generic "eight-step process" for the planning of career management programs in Wane.

A *first step* in the process would be to perform a needs analysis. Typically, 10–20 managers and employees at all levels in the organization would be randomly selected to be interviewed. This group would be presented with questions designed to assess the training and career needs of the department, and the understanding of the career programs already in place. The needs analysis would be carried out by Kislik and her staff, and all responses would be held in confidence.

The *next step*, during the second month of the process, would be for Kislik to develop a summary proposal for the career management. In such a proposal, the strengths and weaknesses of the department would be discussed. This proposal would be sent to Sneider and the Career Development Task Force for comments, suggestions, and budgetary analyses.

Kislik and the Career Development Task Force would next establish a departmental career development task force, comprised of managers and employees. This departmental group would be responsible for establishing and charting career ladders, and reviewing the process for integrating AIMS and career development. The departmental task force would report directly to Sneider and the Career Development Task Force at the career development staff meetings in the spring and fall. The departmental group was required to submit the recommendations for the career management plan by the third month of the process.

During *step 4*, Kislik and her staff would design, develop, and customize the career management materials to meet the needs of specific departments. Input from the departmental task force would guide this development. The career management materials were planned to be developed and revised by the sixth month of this process, thereby leaving one year for the training and implementation of the program.

Step 5 would actually involve the training of the managers. The AIMS and career counseling workshops would be employed during these next six months. *Step 6* would next entail the actual implementation of the career program to the specific populations. The final six months would be allotted for this implementation phase.

The follow-up phase, documented by *step 7*, would establish organizational feedback loops to ensure program accountability. For example, at Torrington the associate director was made accountable for the career management programs of all exempts. At Torrington, this accountability was designed to provide clear vehicles for employees to have both input in and feedback from the career management process. It was thought that the associate director level was "high" enough to have organizational impact, yet "low" enough to be familiar with specific employee needs. The main function of accountability and organizational feedback loops were to allow relevant information to flow to higher levels of management. In this regard, Sneider and the Career Development Task Force specifically decided that each department would require managers at the associate director level to serve as liaisons for the career programs. Associate directors would be responsible for communicating program specifications and updates to employees, and employee concerns to management.

An eighth and *final step* in the career management process was included to provide an evaluation or follow-up of the impact of the program. Sneider and the Career Development Task Force decided that, after a program had been in place for one year, Kislik and her staff would conduct surveys and interviews to assess the immediate impact and success of the program. A one-year follow-up was designed to provide employees and managers with feedback on the career program strengths and weaknesses for the next appraisal year. The follow-up measures would additionally include behavioral measures, such as the rate of turnover and promotions in key employee populations both before and after program implementation. The report of the follow-up would be written by Kislik and presented to Sneider, the Career Development Task Force, and departmental management for review and discussion. The Torrington program will enter this phase late in 1983.

At the January meeting, Sneider and the career development task force further proposed a tentative plan for the implementation of the career management programs across the various Wane departments. It was decided that two basic criteria would be used in determining the order of implementation of the career programs in the Wane

departments. The first criterion, "career needs," would be assessed by examining both manager and employee career needs. Departmental managers would be interviewed to assess their commitment to, and willingness to support, the career programs. Employees would also be surveyed to determine the immediate career development needs in the various departments. Special attention would be given to departments in which key employee populations demonstrated a need for the career programs.

The second general criterion to be used in determining the implementation of career management programs would be a department's proportion of the total business. Higher priorities were to be assigned to the larger and more profitable departments. Additionally, the departments which were considered to be "people resource centers," such as the Marketing Department, rather than departments which were considered to be "technical resource centers," such as the newer high-technology production departments, were given priority in the career management process.

Sneider also explained that, although Torrington was a research and development facility, it had been chosen as the first test site for the career management program because the facility provided Kislik with a relatively homogeneous employee population, all working in the same plant location. All the other Wane departments were spread out across the entire United States, thereby making program implementation more difficult.

With these criteria in mind, Sneider and the group outlined the tentative order for the implementation of the career programs in the remaining Wane departments. The Marketing Department had previously been determined to be the next department after Torrington to receive the career management programs. The Marketing Department was Wane's largest people resource center, and its needs analysis had demonstrated the clearest need for career management programs and training. The order of the remaining departments was determined to be the Production Department, the Financial Control Department, the Pollution Equipment Department, the Energy Systems Department, and the Employee Relations and Staffing Departments.

The remainder of this case documents the planning, development, and implementation of the career management program in the Marketing Department. This was to be the next step in career development at Wane. One of Kislik's first actions in this regard was to contact and interview Louis Hart, the director of marketing at Wane.

Louis Hart: Career Management in the Marketing Department

Career Management History and Problems in the Marketing Department. Louis Hart, the director of marketing at Wane, had been with Wane in the sales and marketing area since 1954. As the director of marketing, Hart reported through a vice president to Sneider. Hart had previously been a regional sales representative, an assistant regional sales manager, and a regional marketing manager in various parts of the United States. Hart recalled the early "career development" practices at Wane:

> When I started, people did not even use career development in their vocabulary. If we were talked about, or the managers had any grand plan, it was never publicized or known. We were different from the young people today. In those days we did what we were told and did not question. If the management said "Get on a train, we need you

in Flint, Michigan," well, you went right home and got your toothbrush.

When Hart became a sales manager in the early 1960s, he remembered informally getting together with his managers and "going over people." Hart described this kind of people management as the "state-of-the-art" in terms of career development in the Marketing Department in the 1960s. Later, as a regional manager in the late 1970s, Hart was bothered by the fact that his younger managers believed that no formal career discussions ever took place in the Marketing Department.

By 1978, Hart and Sneider were convinced that the competition was doing more in terms of career management than Wane in the marketing area. Hart was also aware that turnover had significantly risen to 15 percent among marketing employees in their first five years of service. This was the highest turnover rate in the Marketing Department since the early 1960s. Hart repeatedly received comments from outgoing employees about the lack of concern about career issues at Wane.

Because of these concerns, Hart hired Robert Abrams in 1978 to formalize and coordinate training and career development in the Marketing Department. Abrams had previously worked for the Production Department for two years in the area of training but had received no formal training in the area of career development. Hart envisioned that Abrams could coordinate human resource planning, training, recruiting, and career practices in the Marketing Department. By 1979, however, Hart realized that, while Abrams had all the tools for leading a human resource effort, he did not understand the marketing business. Abrams had trouble adapting his human resource policies to meet the needs of the

Marketing Department. Hart and other marketing managers also complained that Abrams did not travel to the field to learn of the regional needs of the marketing employees. By mid-1979, the turnover rate in the Marketing Department had not declined and was still close to 15 percent among employees in their first five years of service. Hart believed that Abrams was not improving this situation. Abrams was removed from his assignment in early 1980.

From 1980 to 1982 the Marketing Department had no integrated career management program. In May of 1982, Simon Burke, who was a friend of Hart's and former marketing executive, recommended that Hart contact Wendy Kislik to discuss the development of a career management program in the Marketing Department. Kislik and Hart discussed the eight-step process for the planning of an integrated career management program in the Marketing Department, and agreed to begin a program in July 1982.

In their subsequent talks, Hart emphasized to Kislik his need for "bringing career development out of the closet." Hart wanted to publicize and formalize the procedures. Hart believed that he could combat employee turnover and career frustration by making employees aware that career practices did exist in Wane.

Early in this process, Hart received some initial resistance to the idea of resurrecting a human resource effort. One of Hart's regional managers expressed the concerns of many older employees in the marketing department when he wrote:

> Under recommendations for training development and strategic human resource development, I would agree that we certainly need work done here. That's motherhood; but I am concerned that we become so tied up in doing this sort of thing that the real work of the Marketing Department—selling the product in a way that both satisfies our customers and makes some money for Wane—somehow gets short shrift in the exchanges that take place. I would also be concerned that we might become a little ossified by such strategies and this might cause too much concentration on the wrong things. We don't want this to be another Skills Inventory, where we went around collecting career data on everybody and then just filed it away.

Despite these warning calls, by June 1982 Hart was convinced that the Marketing Department needed these programs. Hart was also aware of the apparent success of these programs in the Torrington Research and Development facility. Hart told Kislik to begin the process in July 1982.

Developing a Career Management Program: Steps 1–4. As a first step in the developmental process, Kislik performed a needs analysis of the Wane Marketing Department exempt population. Specifically, a survey of AIMS (which is comprised of Measures of Performance (MOPS), Periodic Results Reviews (PRRs), and the Annual Performance Appraisal (APA)), and the career development use and practices was conducted during July of 1982. It happened that 375 of the 481 employees surveyed responded, for a response rate of 78 percent. (For a review of AIMS see Appendix 1 in the Wane Division of the American Instruments Corporation (A).)

The needs analysis yielded data on the use of AIMS and career development tools in the marketing department. In relation to MOPS, 91 percent of the survey respondents had received MOPS for the year 1981. Specifically, 76 percent indicated that their MOPS had been jointly established with their managers; 14 percent had established their own MOPS and 8 percent had their MOPS dictated to them. The participants also commented on MOPS, and among the most frequent themes were: (1) MOPS should be more specific and objective, and (2) MOPS were a useful way to plan business and career objectives, and to set standards for evaluation, compensation, and career goals. The results clearly indicated that approximately one quarter of the employees who were surveyed believed that there was room for improvement in how MOPS were established, understood, and used as a basis for evaluation.

The survey next yielded results on the use of PRRs. Only 52 percent of the respondents had a PRR or similar opportunity to review progress in attaining their MOPS and career objectives anytime prior to the APA. Participants most often commented that PRRs: (1) were perceived to be nonexistent, and the feedback on career issues often comes too late; (2) should happen more frequently to provide opportunities for constructive feedback on performance and career progress; and (3) should be taken more seriously by management. These results indicated that PRRs were being used by only half of the Marketing Department. Additionally, only about half the new hires reported receiving six-month reviews of their performance and career progress. Participant comments strongly suggested a desire for more feedback from management on work and career objectives during the year.

The survey also yielded results on APA, the last component of AIMS. Here, 85 percent of the survey respondents indicated that they had a formal performance appraisal in 1982. Concerning their perceptions of managers, 85 percent indicated that their managers regarded the review as an opportunity for a frank and informative discussion of performance and career develop-

ment during the year. Eleven percent believed that their managers conducted the review mainly because it was required. Overall, 69 percent indicated that the appraisal and discussion had been "very beneficial" or "beneficial" to them, while 26 percent felt that it had been only "somewhat beneficial" or "not at all beneficial." Among the most frequent comments of APA and AIMS were: (1) managers were unable to give real guidance on both improving performance and career direction; (2) job classifications and career ladders were unclear and secretive; (3) there was a need for more precision in defining skills, experience, and responsibility for jobs; and (4) AIMS was properly formatted and could be an effective tool for people development. In their view, effectiveness was seen as dependent on the interpersonal competence of the managers administering the system.

The survey results of APA seemed to indicate that the performance appraisal was in place, and that there was a general understanding of what the appraisal was designed to do. The results also indicated misunderstandings and several demotivating aspects of the appraisals, such as managers' lack of skill in providing meaningful feedback in the career development process, and in the relationship between job, career path, performance, and future career growth. There was a strong indication that managers needed more education and training in understanding and articulating performance and career issues.

Finally, training and career development needs were assessed by the survey. Only 28 percent of the survey respondents indicated that their managers had suggested participation in training programs during their last appraisal, while 65 percent indicated that their managers had not suggested any training. When asked what further training would be helpful to them in their current assignment or in preparation for future career opportunities, 30 percent indicated a desire for managerial training skills and only 31 percent indicated a desire for continued professional and career development training. Several recurring themes emerged when participants were asked to comment on managerial and career development training needs. These themes included needs for (1) basic preparatory training for management positions prior to becoming managers; (2) training on how to motivate, lead, and manage human resources; (3) communication and interpersonal skills training; (4) career development training; (5) a better and more publicized system for determining advancement opportunities and individual career paths; (6) meaningful career discussion guides; and (7) understanding the relationship between the AIMS process and career advancement.

In sum, survey respondents indicated a perceived deficiency in the current practice of identifying, developing, and advancing employees. Respondents believed that there was no integrated system in place which identified people for upcoming opportunities, elicited employee input on career goals, and established career plans.

In August 1982, Kislik sent a summary proposal and career development recommendations, based on the survey of the marketing department, to Sneider and the career development task force. From August to September of 1982, Kislik, Sneider, and a newly developed "Marketing Career Task Force," headed by Hart, debated the career development plan and recommendations. During these months—steps 3 and 4 of the career development process—the group developed the general guidelines for the Marketing Department's career management program.

In relation to MOPS, marketing management decided to reinforce the importance of establishing MOPS for all employees through a face-to-face discussion with managers. This process was to be "standard operating procedure" for all marketing managers. The Marketing Department would also continue to provide the AIMS refresher course to all current and new managers within their first year in management capacity.

Second, in relation to PRRs, the marketing management mandated that all employees would receive at least one PRR during the year. "New hires" would additionally receive a six-month review of their performance and career development. All managers would also be provided the one-day PRR workshop to learn how to conduct a PRR, understand the relationships of PRR to MOPS, APA, and career management, and be provided practice in coaching skills. Finally, on a needs basis, managers would be provided the corporate sponsored three-day "Interpersonal Skills Workshop" for intensive skill building and practice in providing constructive criticism, responsive listening, and coaching and handling career conflicts.

Next, in relation to APA, the marketing management decided to establish as standard operating procedure that all employees would receive a formal APA. All managers would also receive the one-day "APA Refresher Course." Further, the group decided that a general career plan for *each* employee would be discussed during the last part of the appraisal process. A detailed career discussion of the employee's strengths, weaknesses, and a *specific developmental plan* would also be arranged for a separate time for at least one to two hours, at the employee's request.

The group similarly developed several

guidelines for career management policies in the Marketing Department. The Marketing Career Management Task Force was formally appointed with Louis Hart as its chairman. The task force was comprised of Hart, three of the seven regional marketing managers on a rotating basis, and an employee relations staff member. The task force was required to systematically investigate and design actions in (1) the identification of strategic human resource needs (e.g., the resources or skills required in the future to meet the Marketing Department's commitment in each strategic business plan), (2) the establishment of the skills and experience required at each job level (see Appendix 1 for an example of a regional marketing career ladder in Wane), (3) the assessment of the inventory level of professional, managerial, and career capabilities of the employees, and (4) the design of training and career development programs to improve the current capabilities. All of the actions were deemed necessary for providing a long-term perspective, and an integrated approach to human resource management. Special attention was to be given to "key employee populations" in all of these areas. In accordance with these goals, Sneider assigned a $150,000 budget to the Marketing Department for career management activities for 1983.

In October of 1982, Kislik and the Marketing Task Force began to customize the AIMS and career management materials to meet the needs of the Marketing Department. This was step 4 of the career management process. From October to December 1982, this group drafted and revised the marketing training and career development curriculum. In customizing the materials, Kislik utilized the results of the needs analysis to understand both the types of training and career development systems already in

place, and the operating culture in the Marketing Department. Kislik realized, for example, that the Marketing Department culture stressed minimal paperwork, creativity, and innovativeness in marketing. Kislik believed that it was essential, therefore, in customizing the marketing materials to develop concise and eye-catching manuals. Additionally, unlike Torrington, the Marketing Department was spread out over the entire United States—creating a very heterogeneous group of managers. The materials had to reach a wide range of managers with different social and ethnic backgrounds.

By December of 1982, a marketing career management plan had been established and sent to the field managers for comments. A training and career development curriculum was established, which (1) provided for all the basic formal training and other job developmental experiences required to enable an employee to assume a territory assignment, (2) provided for continuous formal training and job-development experiences for all marketing personnel, and (3) provided a set of "tools" for managers to use when setting MOPS, providing career and performance feedback through PRRs and other informal counseling sessions; evaluating performance, development, and areas of growth through APA; and conducting career discussions and establishing a joint career development plan.

The scope of the program specifically included the following elements: (1) *training courses,* in which formal training courses in sales and sales management were offered; (2) *developmental sequences tied to job requirements,* which established guidelines for sequencing training so that employees received training in the most appropriate subject at the optimal time in their career; (3) *diagnostic pre/post measures of learning,* which would provide management with information regarding the level of knowledge and experience of the employee before training and after training; (4) *reinforcement*, provided by post-course counseling sessions with the manager to insure that the learning can be applied to job demands; (5) *sponsors programs*, where each region had a designated "sponsor" who provided focus counseling to employees; sponsors were to be specially selected and trained by the marketing task force; and (6) *periodic evaluations*, which would assess whether the training provided was meeting the needs of the participants, marketing management, and the primary business clients.

Training the Western Region: An Example of Steps 5–8. From January to March 1983, Kislik trained marketing managers in the seven United States regions. During these three months, Kislik implemented step 5 of the career program. This section describes the experiences of the western regional marketing managers at a three-day training session on AIMS and career management.

Before the training sessions began, several of the attending managers discussed their perceptions of AIMS and career management at Wane.

Dave Tannen, the western regional marketing manager for the last 15 years, described how the recent emphasis on career management had evolved:

> We ran into a lot of recruiting problems in the mid-1970s. I used to recruit at Stanford, and the questions the young people asked were things like "tell me what my job is," "describe my job fully," "tell me where I could be in five years." I was having a lot of trouble answering these questions, and that was just the way it was.

Steve McGuire, the western region marketing manager for Pollution Control Equip-

ment for the last six years, described the need for integrating AIMS and the career management process:

> A formal career system has to start with some classification of jobs and identification of skills, all of which I am totally unaware. I am not prepared to give MOPS, PRRs, and APAs. I need this information to answer my employees' questions like "where do I go from here?", "am I doing a good job?", "I want to aspire to this, how can I get there?". I cannot think of anything more demotivating than having your boss, a guy like me, not give appropriate answers to these questions. I just don't know the answers to these questions. How can I discuss career development when I can't properly evaluate employee performance, or don't have a knowledge of the career opportunities which exist in my own department?

Harry Asher, a western regional marketing manager in the area of administration for the last 28 years, described the career concerns of employees over the years:

> When I started back in 1954 there was never any such thing as career development. It really hasn't been until the last 10 years that any formal effort has been made in the area of career development. In fact, I can remember that 10 years ago, after I had been with Wane for 18 years, was the first opportunity that I ever had to sit down with my boss and hear from him how I was doing and where my career could go. As a manager myself, the only "career counseling" that I ever attempted was in answering the informal career questions during the APA.

During the first day of the course, Kislik encouraged the managers to express their concerns and confusions about AIMS and career management. The most obvious concern related to the lack of integration between performance, performance appraisal, and career development. The concerns were consistent with the findings of the needs analysis. Kislik next provided an overview of AIMS (for a review of the basic concepts of AIMS see Appendixes 1 and 2 in the Wane Division of the American Instruments Corporation (A)). Kislik stressed the link between AIMS, which was designed to help managers appraise people resources, and the career management programs.

In the afternoon of the first day, the managers role-played the development and execution of MOPS, PRRs, and APA from both the employees' and managers' perspectives. A videotape of the appraisal process was also presented. Finally, the managers discussed how the appraisal process might be structured for different employee populations (e.g., for new hires, older employees nearing retirement, and fast-track employees).

Day 2 of the course focused on interpersonal skills. While the emphasis during day 1 was on the management system, the emphasis during day 2 focused on the tools that managers needed in interacting with employees. Day 2 was designed to teach the managers how to sensitively and effectively relate and articulate career and performance issues.

During day 2, Kislik discussed several general approaches for improving manager/subordinate relationships. In particular, Kislik stressed that (1) employees need a clear understanding of the work they are expected to do (e.g., as reflected in MOPs and PRRs), (2) guidance and coaching on how to do the work is valuable, and (3) employees should have the opportunity to grow in their jobs (e.g., by utilizing the career discussion and career guide materials) and to advance in the organization (e.g., by understanding the career paths and training opportunities in Wane). Kislik also had the managers role-play five basic interpersonal skills. These skills included positive reinforcement, responsive listening, constructive criticism, developing ideas, and handling conflicts.

In the afternoon of day 2, Kislik described the specific guidelines for conducting manager/subordinate performance and career development discussions. Premeeting techniques included planning the interview, gathering background information, arranging for a comfortable meeting place, giving the employee sufficient notice for the meeting, and rehearsal strategies. During the interview process, Kislik stressed that the manager confirm the purpose of the meeting, discuss the problem or issue at hand, identify improvement or career growth areas, and discuss a mutual career action plan. Post-interview issues included the development of a follow-up plan for monitoring the employee's progress.

The final topic discussed during day 2 was the distinction between managerial coaching and managerial counseling. Coaching was described as the one-on-one activity a manager does to guide an employee's career growth and development. Coaching usually takes place on the job and involves evaluating the employee's strengths and weaknesses, and offering guidance on how to achieve performance and career goals. Coaching was described as most effective when utilized in conjunction with AIMS, in particular during the PRR.

Career counseling, which is closely related to coaching, was described as a one-on-one activity in which a manager and employee discuss an employee's career planning and career pathing, or the resolution of personal problems affecting work performance (see Appendix 2 for a description of coaching and counseling guidelines).

The final day was devoted to the career management practices at Wane (for a review of the career management practices at Wane see Appendices 4–6 in the Wane Division of the American Instruments Corporation (A)). Kislik discussed the Career Development and Self-Exploration Guide, the Career Review Discussion, the Career Action Planning Guide, phases of adult development, and career anchors. Throughout the morning, Kislik stressed that career management was the process by which a manager *and* employee explore the employee's career in the context of the business needs and constraints, and the employee's personal history, needs, aspirations, and values (e.g., as assessed by the career exploration guide).

During the afternoon of day 3, Kislik and the group discussed the Marketing Department's career ladders and job descriptions which had been developed by the Marketing Task Force. The requirements for advancement in the various ladders were discussed. Finally, each manager was supplied with information about a fictitious employee and asked to role-play a career discussion with this employee. The career discussion was to be conducted within the framework of AIMS (day 1 of the course), and to employ the interpersonal skills and one-to-one meeting skills discussed earlier (day 2 of the course). At the conclusion of day 3, managers were presented a videotape of actors role-playing a similar career discussion. In closing, Kislik emphasized that the managers needed to take advantage of the variety of information sources which were available for aiding in career management practices. Appendix 3 summarizes the career management roles and responsibilities at Wane.

All 12 managers attending the course filled out post-course questionnaires. One hundred percent of the managers reported that the AIMS, interpersonal skills, and career development programs "exceeded" their expectations. One hundred percent of the managers also reported that the con-

cepts and skills presented in the program would be a "great deal" or a "good deal" of help to them back on the job. Many of the managers commented that they still needed more skills-practice before they would feel comfortable in their dealings with employees.

The three managers who had discussed their concerns before the course now discussed their learnings from the course.

Steve McGuire commented:

> This course sure took a lot of the intuition out of the management process. We now have a framework for understanding AIMS, interpersonal skills, meeting procedures, and the applications of these areas in the career management process. Of course, each manager still has to personalize the process, but now we have a common framework for operating.

Harry Asher remarked:

> I am excited to bring these materials home to reread, and let the concepts sink in. The framework and the concepts are very helpful. Just understanding that an employee is in mid-career and the problems that go along with this stage, or what another employee's career anchor may be, is helpful for me in understanding his problems and needs. I never thought of employees in this way, and now, if I get in trouble, I have a place that I can look.

Dave Tannen described his next steps:

> My MOPS are going to be to involve myself more in the appraisals and career management of people. Another MOP will be to make sure my managers follow through with these programs. If we don't follow through, these programs will just raise everyone's expectations and then nothing will happen. Our people won't stand for that.

Career Management in the Marketing Department in the Future. By June of 1983, Kislik hoped that all the marketing managers would have implemented a career counseling discussion and PRR with all their exempt employees. This would complete step 6 of the plan. A meeting of program "sponsors" was set for August 1983 to document the progress of the implementation process (step 7 of the process). Finally, a follow-up survey of all exempt marketing employees was planned for September 1983 (step 8 of the process). Kislik believed that the total program could be in place for the 1984 appraisal process.

In March of 1983, Richard Sneider was enthusiastic about Kislik's plan for the Marketing Department. He believed that, at last, a comprehensive program was ready for a de-partment-by-department introduction to career planning. Nonetheless he was reluctant to publicize the success of either the pilot program at Torrington or the initial training programs in the Marketing Department. He was concerned about what might happen at a later stage in the Torrington program. In particular, Sneider realized that the results were based only on the exposure of managers to career issues, and not on the application of these issues to subordinates' careers. Sneider was also anxious about the possible effects of a major layoff at Torrington which could affect several hundred employees.

Appendix 1
An Example of a Regional Marketing Ladder in Wane

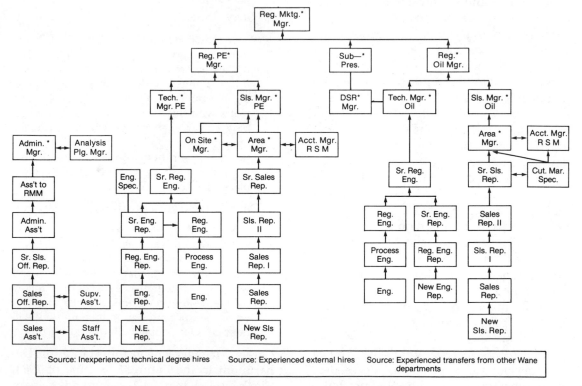

* These managers attended the Western Region Training Session.

Appendix 2
AIMS: Managing One-on-One Meetings with Subordinates

Coaching Analysis (What Is Influencing Unsatisfactory Performance?)

In analyzing a performance problem, the coach may find it helpful to go through the following question/decision process:

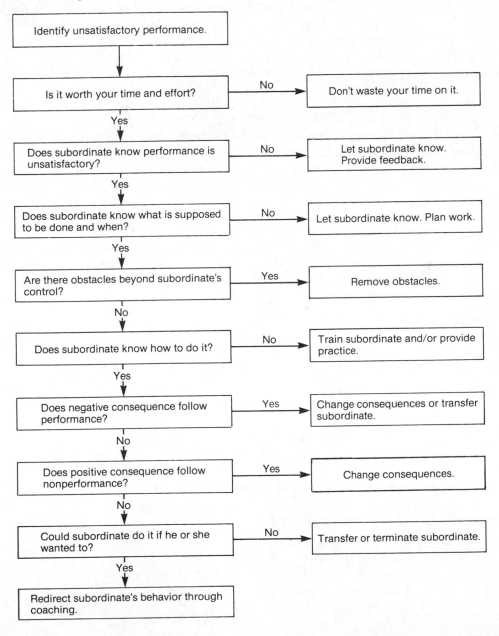

Identify unsatisfactory performance.

Is it worth your time and effort? — No → Don't waste your time on it.

Yes ↓

Does subordinate know performance is unsatisfactory? — No → Let subordinate know. Provide feedback.

Yes ↓

Does subordinate know what is supposed to be done and when? — No → Let subordinate know. Plan work.

Yes ↓

Are there obstacles beyond subordinate's control? — Yes → Remove obstacles.

No ↓

Does subordinate know how to do it? — No → Train subordinate and/or provide practice.

Yes ↓

Does negative consequence follow performance? — Yes → Change consequences or transfer subordinate.

No ↓

Does positive consequence follow nonperformance? — Yes → Change consequences.

No ↓

Could subordinate do it if he or she wanted to? — No → Transfer or terminate subordinate.

Yes ↓

Redirect subordinate's behavior through coaching.

Counseling Guidelines

Some key guidelines for effective counseling are:

1. *Accentuate the positive.* Compliment unusual accomplishments, being specific. If there is an area in which the subordinate needs help, it can be compared effectively to one of his or her strengths.
2. *Provide timely feedback.* The sooner it is given after an event, the more effective it will be. Be prepared to document any statements you make about his or her work, particularly in areas where you feel improvement is needed.
3. *Do not argue.* If the two of you have a disagreement that can't be resolved in this session, suggest an adjournment to think it over. Be sure to schedule another meeting to reconsider the point.
4. *Ask skilled questions.* They should be open-ended, rather than questions that can be answered "yes" or "no."
5. *Be a good listener.* Encourage the subordinate to talk about his or her work, standards of performance, goals, ambitions, and plans for improvement.
6. *Respect the subordinate.* His or her perceptions of an event must be listened to, honored, and appreciated. You must understand the subordinate's viewpoint before you can explore together possible solutions.
7. *Reflect the subordinate's feelings.* Focus on the subordinate's attitudes and feelings instead of giving advice.
8. *Concentrate comments on behavior that the subordinate is capable of changing.* Stress performance and avoid a frontal approach to discussing personality traits.
9. *Be alert for signs that the subordinate is willing to make a commitment to change.* Once he or she assumes responsibility for improving, your job is on the way to a successful outcome.

Counseling skills are particularly useful during Annual Performance Appraisals with regard to career counseling and work-related family and attitude problems.

APPENDIX 3
THE WANE DIVISION OF THE
AMERICAN INSTRUMENTS CORPORATION (B)

Career Management Roles/Responsibilities at Wane

Organization: *Provide Structure and Climate*

- Establish career ladders.
- Establish interlocking personnel committees.
- Establish a process tied to AIMS, etc.
- Make it part of a manager's job (MOPS).

Manager: *Provide Support, Opportunities, Info, Coaching, to Assist the Employee*

- Set MOPS, conduct PRRs/APAs.
- Identify development/improvement needs.
- Realistically appraise employee aspirations against opportunities/realities.
- Access formal channels (committees, etc.) and informal networks to assist employees.

Employee: *Maintain Responsibility for Managing Own Career Plan*

- Understand/perform current job.
- Identify improvement/development needs and initiate plans.
- Seek out "mentors" and resources who can help.
- Get feedback from others.
- Integrate career with family and life plans.
- Self-manage the plan.

CASE 10
FLOWTROL, INCORPORATED (A)
Alice B. Morgan and
Jeffrey A. Sonnenfeld

Hal Walton, chairman of the board, president, and CEO of Flowtrol, Inc., reached for his ringing telephone.

"Hi, Hal, it's Alvin Perold. I'm calling to fill you in on the response to our ad in *The Wall Street Journal*. It appeared about a month ago, and you would not believe the number of résumés and letters I've received. At last count there were over 700!"

"Incredible. I hope you're still willing to go through them for me."

"Oh, sure, but it will take a while before I send you the ones that look most promising. Reading all these materials is a huge job, even with the clear guidelines you and I worked out before we placed the ad. I don't really know when I will be finished, and résumés are still arriving daily."

"Well, I appreciate all your work, Al. I'm not in a hurry, and I don't want to put undue pressure on you or our staff. Just proceed as rapidly as you can, and if you want to send me some of the replies before you've checked them over, go right ahead. After all, Flowtrol is the one looking for a new president!"

Hal replaced the telephone, then after a moment picked it up and dialed his wife, Flowtrol's corporate secretary, who had until about a year previously been the corporation's comptroller.

"Helen," he said, "you know that ad we placed? Al just called to tell me he has over 700 replies already, and they're still coming! What does that suggest about American industry? Here we have a very small company looking for a top executive, and hundreds of people in powerful positions in very large corporations are anxious to apply for the job. Frankly, I'm amazed."

The ad to which Alvin and Hal referred had run in *The Wall Street Journal* on Tuesday, April 27, 1982. (It appears as Exhibit 1.) In the end, over 1,000 responses were received from men and women living all over

Exhibit 1

This ad appeared in *The Wall Street Journal* of April 27, 1982, and in the *National Business Employment Weekly* of May 2, 1982.

PRESIDENT

Outstanding Opportunity

Our privately held company, well capitalized and highly profitable, requires C.E.O. to assume the operating duties of retirement aged Owner-Chairman. This metal cutting manufacturer of proprietary product lines has experienced significant growth over the past several years under the direction of the Chairman-President, and is located in an appealing rural Southern New England community.

Forward your qualifications, in confidence, to:

Box ES-593, *The Wall Street Journal*

(handwritten in left margin:) Great ad. Who won't apply? No spec's

the United States and even abroad, with backgrounds ranging from marketing to finance, who held positions in small, medium, and large corporations.

Flowtrol, Inc.

Flowtrol manufactured and sold globe and check valves for use in utilities plants (both fossil fuel and nuclear), chemical plants, oil and gas wellheads, and other applications where tight seal under high pressure was critical. The patented FLOWSEAL mechanism, developed by Hal Walton in 1962, provided a valve with very few components, that was fairly light for its capabilities, and that could be serviced without removal from its place of installation. Flowtrol produced the valve in various sizes and configurations, and marketed it via manufacturers' representatives throughout the United States and in several foreign nations as well. The company's headquarters and manufacturing facility were located in Williams, Rhode Island. (A partial organization chart appears in Exhibit 2.) In 1982 the company had 76 employees and sales of just over $5 million.

Hal Walton had invented the FLOWSEAL valve after founding his own firm, Walton Engineering Company, in 1962. Walton already held more than 20 patents for designs

Exhibit 2   Flowtrol Corporate Organizational Structure

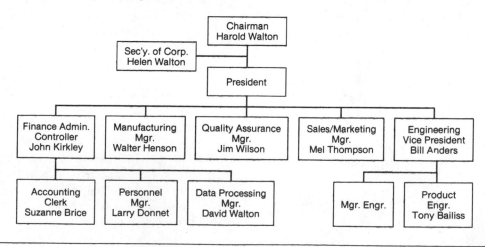

which he licensed to various manufacturing companies. He planned to produce the FLOWSEAL valve himself, however, and began to investigate appropriate technology. His design called for four electron-beam welds, and he knew that Hamilton Standard, a division of United Technologies Corp., manufactured and sold electron-beam welders. Walton took his pilot model to Hamilton Standard and asked that the required welds be made. If they could be done successfully, he intended to buy the necessary machinery from Hamilton Standard for his own firm. Recalling the events that followed, Hal Walton explained:

> They said they'd be happy to weld the parts to demonstrate that their machine could do it. When I went back to pick up the parts, I was told the vice president would like to see me, so I went directly from the lobby to the vice president's office. He said, "Well, there's no use beating around the bush; we'll get right to the point. We're greatly impressed with your product line and we'd like to have an exclusive license."

Shortly thereafter, Hal Walton signed a favorable licensing agreement with United Technologies, and joined the firm as program manager for his valve. Over the following three years, the product line was established and thoroughly tested both in the laboratory and on-site at a steam power plant. By 1964, an advertising campaign had begun, and rep organizations had been established all over the country. Then in 1965, United Technologies drastically revised its corporate strategy, emphasizing jet engines and aerospace, and divesting much of its industrial products business. The company sought a sublicensee for the valve product line, but after two years, had still not found one. In 1968, Hal Walton bought all the relevant tools, jigs, dies, fixtures, and inventory, and founded Flowtrol to produce his

valve as he had originally planned to do six years previously.

Walton had thus been Flowtrol's central figure since he established the company in 1968. He owned the land and buildings used by Flowtrol, as well as all but 14 percent of the stock. (That portion had been bought by the firm's original vice president of sales.) He had designed the product line, and had overseen every phase of production and sales from the beginning.

Hal had originally hoped that his oldest son would become Flowtrol's chief officer. Tragically, however, his son had died in an airplane accident in 1974. Hal had looked hard for people who might be capable of growing into the job, and had carefully considered applicants generated by search firms, as well as individuals who were already serving Flowtrol in various managerial capacities. He had in fact hired a manager of operations who seemed promising, only to find that the man "just seemed to be retired. He came in late and left early, and he had no programs at all, so I terminated him in a hurry." A subsequent operations manager had become terminally ill.

Within Flowtrol there were currently three especially promising candidates for executive responsibility. Mel Thompson, the sales manager, had worked as an engineer at nuclear power plants, and before that he had been a manufacturer's representative in a firm partly owned by his father. He had served in the Navy and had an MBA from the University of Connecticut. His experience in sales was still somewhat limited, and he had done no general management. Hal believed Thompson was a good decision maker, but was not yet ready to take on wider responsibilities.

Walter Henson, the company's manager of operations, had good experience in manufacturing control, but lacked exposure to the financial and sales functions. Hal believed Henson's personality led to conflict; he had lost his two previous jobs. He would have to demonstrate that he could hold a job successfully before Hal was willing to consider him a candidate for advancement.

The third internal possibility was John Kirkley, the comptroller. He had served Rhode Island Bank and Trust as vice president, and before that had been comptroller at Fallon Brothers. He had been in the Navy and then gone to Harvard Business School for an MBA, and thus had no background in manufacturing, sales, or engineering. Hal believed Kirkley needed more time before he could advance into broader responsibilities. All three of these men were in their early 40s.

Even younger than these three, and more specialized in his training and experience, was Hal's second son, David. David, a soft-spoken technically-oriented 33-year-old, was Flowtrol's director of data processing. David had majored in computer science at Purdue University, and then spent the next six years in Indianapolis. He had worked first for the city, and had subsequently become a systems programmer at Lane Bryant. David believed it was important for him to have business experiences in settings other than Flowtrol, to prove his worth both to himself and to his father. Moreover, his chosen field was still too costly for Flowtrol during the 1970s: it was only as computer expenses dropped while Flowtrol's sales rose that data processing for Flowtrol became cost-effective. David knew that he would have to choose, within the next few years, whether he wanted to continue on a strictly technical path, or whether he wanted to make the switch into general management. His current project, introducing Material Requirements Planning at Flowtrol, currently absorbed all his time, but once the MRP arrangements had been implemented, he would have the opportunity to gain ex-

posure in other areas. Both he and his parents hoped, therefore, that a new executive at Flowtrol would be capable of and interested in providing appropriate guidance for David's development.

Hal, now 70 years old, was determined to develop a viable plan of succession. He sought to turn over some of the day-to-day operating responsibilities to someone who might eventually step into full executive responsibility as well. His wife, Helen Walton, had retired not long before as Flowtrol's comptroller after 10 years in that position, and both she and he enjoyed making sales trips in Flowtrol's recently purchased motor home. Hal believed such trips were especially important now, because Flowtrol had resolved some production bottlenecks, and could meet greater demand than it was currently experiencing. Hal's profound knowledge of the product line made him the company's most effective salesman, and he had some ideas about how to generate increased purchases and new customers that he was eager to try out.

Hal had often discussed with Flowtrol's board of directors his efforts to find a new COO and president, and he did so again in early 1982. Joel Bannon, a Harvard Business School professor and member of the board, suggested to Hal that he run an ad, and, with the assistance of Bannon and Alvin Perold, Hal drafted the one that appeared in *The Wall Street Journal* in late April. Alvin, Flowtrol's auditor, agreed to place the ad and to receive the replies, thus helping to keep the process confidential. Alvin was screening the résumés in accordance with several criteria that Hal had developed—a slow process, since there were so many responses.

Harold M. Walton

Hal Walton's history showed him to be versatile, self-reliant, and creative.

In 1930 my parents sent me $75 so I could come home from college for Christmas. That was the last money I had from them. From then on, I was on my own.

Hal attended the University of Wisconsin for a year before entering the Naval Academy, from which he graduated in 1934. He proceeded to MIT for a master's degree in mechanical engineering, after which he became a development engineer with Linde Air Products, a division of Union Carbide. In 1940, the Navy recalled him to active duty as commanding officer of a small patrol ship. In early 1941 he was transferred to the Brooklyn Navy Yard and then to the staff of the Commander Service Forces, Pacific, in June 1945.

Three months later, Hal was able to leave active service, and he enrolled that September in Harvard's eighth Advanced Management Program. After graduating from the program, Hal worked for several manufacturing concerns in engineering, marketing, and general management positions. These included Union Carbide, Rockwell International, and Black, Sivalls & Bryson, as well as Chapman Valve, his last employer before going into business for himself and developing the FLOWSEAL valve. Although he made the decision to form his own firm in 1962, being an entrepreneur was not a long-time goal. As a result, joining United Technologies seemed a perfectly acceptable step, and it was only when that company failed to bring the valve to market that Hal again felt moved to establish his own company, now named Flowtrol. During the years between 1965 when he had ceased working for United Technologies and 1968 when production started at Flowtrol, Hal supported himself by playing the stock market. He commented:

> When I started this business, I had a lot of soul-searching to do, because I had generated enough funds so that I didn't have to

work. With the gamble on Flowtrol, I was putting everything on the line. But I thought it would be much better to be doing something for industry and society instead of just living off the stock market. And I had these patents which were no good if they weren't working, so I decided to start the company. I was fortunate in that I was able to handle the financing myself, so that I didn't have to give up much of the business.

Since its founding, Flowtrol had prospered. In the past three years, sales had gone from $2.5 million to more than twice that sum. Growth was financed conservatively, and by 1982 Flowtrol had no long-term debt. Sales in 1980 were 44 percent higher than those of 1979, and 1981's sales were up 47 percent over those of 1980. In 1982, however, sales were essentially flat. Flowtrol's profitability had been notable throughout its history, and the early 1980s brought no change in this regard. (Exhibit 3 provides some unit and dollars sales information.)

In 1982, when Hal Walton and Alvin Perold planned the ad that appeared in *The Wall Street Journal,* Hal was Flowtrol's president and CEO. All department heads reported to him, and his long familiarity with every aspect of the business made him capable of, and interested in, every type of activity, from metal cutting on the shop floor, through selling across the nation. He routinely examined reports on every level, reports which, in most cases, he had himself designed. Hal was thus able to participate in decisions on all topics being made at all levels of the firm. In 1980, Flowtrol had purchased a motor home. Since that time, Hal and his wife had used it for his frequent trips, as he put it, "from chimney to chimney"—that is, to various parts of the country to visit manufacturers' representatives and users. Hal's familiarity with the product line made him an expert salesman: he was

Exhibit 3

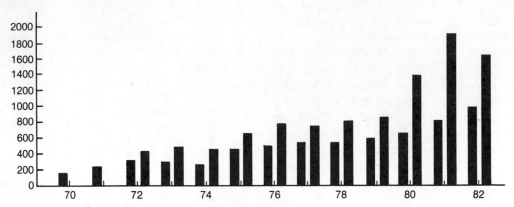

Left bar: Sales orders/year
Right bar: Invoices/year

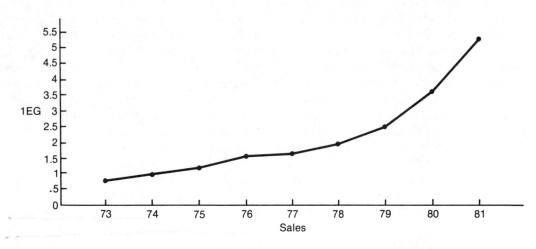

1EG

Sales

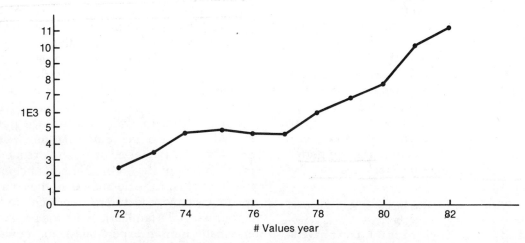

1E3

Values year

often able to see potential applications that were obscure both to the representative and to the plant manager or parts purchaser as well. Similarly, new product ideas, versions of the valve that might have additional applications, had been developed by Hal as a result of discussions with users of current products. Such discussions had led to the development of a gate valve for Du Pont, a product which Flowtrol was now planning to manufacture and market as an addition to its present product line.

Looking for a New President

In seeking to share the responsibility of managing Flowtrol, Hal Walton was not looking for an immediate replacement. He had no desire to stop working, or even to work fewer hours per day, or for only part of the year. He planned to retain his post as chairman of the board, and to continue as Flowtrol's CEO. The new employee would function as president and chief operating officer. All department heads would report to him, and he would implement new strategies, as well as maintain present operating levels. Hal had no wish to sell his business, despite numerous offers from individuals and from other firms, so an equity position was not available unless the new president could convince the man who owned 14 percent of Flowtrol to sell some or all of his holdings.

When asked about the criteria he and Alvin Perold had used to evaluate the résumés they received, Hal noted, "It was more a set of negatives than of positives—more a matter of ways in which people didn't qualify."

Given the nature of Flowtrol's business, Hal hoped to find good candidates with strong engineering backgrounds, who were involved in manufacturing operations. He tended to rule out those with financial, accounting, or marketing backgrounds exclu-

sively. The successful individual, he believed, would have to have functioned in a decision-making capacity, so anyone who did not appear interested in being a "number one man" was eliminated. Hal looked for a career progression from narrow areas of responsibility to larger ones, and for a present position of considerable supervisory stature.

Hal looked as well at the candidates' current job settings. He believed that someone who had spent all his or her working life in a large corporation would not function effectively in a firm like Flowtrol,

> I had to have the impression this person could operate in a small business. So many were used to having such large staffs that I felt they'd be lost here. At Flowtrol they'd have to be able to treat everything on a very detailed level, which doesn't happen in a big firm.

In addition to criteria relating to the individual's educational and work experience, Hal had a fairly rigid age criterion, and was consciously looking for someone who would fit in well with his present managerial staff.

> I've got a number of excellent people here, department heads. I've got a sales manager, I've got a comptroller, an operations manager, a senior engineer. These are very able individuals, and somebody coming in as chief operating officer has to be acceptable to the department heads.

Hal determined this matter of acceptability himself, and an important element in his determination was age.

> Our department heads are all in the 41-, 42-year-old bracket. I wanted somebody in the 55-, 56-year-old bracket.

An older candidate would probably be less threatening to current managers, and would leave open the possibility that one of them might ultimately move up further in the executive hierarchy.

The Elimination Process.   As Alvin Perold read through the résumés, he set aside those he thought most promising, and eventually sent them on to Hal. Hal reviewed them, using a numerical code to indicate his reactions: he assigned them numbers from one to five, with five the most appealing. In late May he got in touch with Janet (Jan) Wolff, a professional recruiter based in Boston, who had been recommended by one of the members of Flowtrol's board. Jan and Hal reviewed the résumés marked "5" and some of the others as well, and Jan was given the task of following up on these by telephone. She was to check with each candidate to see if he was still interested in the position, and to ask some additional questions about each individual's career, current situation, and interests for the future. Jan noted:

> I often explained some details about Flowtrol, to be sure candidates understood the size and type of business we were talking about. I had to be careful, however, that I did not reveal so much detail that the firm could be identified. Hal had not yet told his employees what he was doing—in fact, on the two or three occasions when I went down there I was introduced as a friend of his wife's.

Jan felt that Hal had very clear views on the kind of person he was looking for:

> Hal looked first of all for an appropriate background—one in operations, preferably in metalworking. And he wanted to see a straightforward career progression, with clear evidence that the individual would be able to lead others. I knew from the way that Hal had financed Flowtrol, using his own and internally generated funds, that he didn't want someone who would rush into

heavy borrowing to underwrite dramatic expansion. He wanted someone who would fit with his own managerial style, and with the company, its workers, and the local community. I called people all over the United States, but I knew that only someone really happy with the idea of living in Rhode Island was a likely choice. The transition would be hard enough without an unhappy family situation contributing to the difficulties.

Jan spoke by phone with about 40 candidates. There were a few who were in the running to whom she did not speak, because Hal had begun his own follow-up before she had started to assist him. One of these was Brooks Carswell, who had been the president of Cranston Equipment Corporation, a Rhode Island manufacturer of plastics and packaging machinery. Hal mentioned Brooks to Jan; he had had lunch with him, and was expecting to confirm a golf date in the following week. Despite this promising lead, Hal was anxious to pursue the 40–50 people whose résumés had survived his scrutiny. Jan reached most of these people during the month of June, telephoning them at home in the evening and on weekends, to maintain the confidentiality that many of their letters had requested. A critical question dealt with the reasons for seeking a change of position. Why, Hal wanted to know, did these successful individuals find the idea of running a small company so interesting? Jan commented:

> I found that many people really were intrigued by the thought of being the true boss, of running their own show. Some, of course, were just in need of a job, rather than of this particular type of job. And many of those I called wanted *more* control than the Flowtrol position offered: several, for example, were willing to consider the opportunity only if they could participate in the equity, which in this case was not possible.

The Final Selection. As a result of Jan's efforts and the contacts Hal himself had made earlier, by July the choice had narrowed considerably. After reading Jan's comments and talking with her about them, Hal himself called 15 people, arranging to see about 8 of them. (Résumés and Jan's written commentary for four of these appear as Exhibits 4 through 7.) Brooks continued to be a strong candidate. Apparently almost equally strong was another relatively local man, Lester Ellwers, who had begun in marketing and engineering, and had become vice president of manufacturing for a privately held company making capital equipment. (See Exhibit 4 for his letter and résumé.) His background in metal cutting, and his functional experience in engineering, sales, and operations, were just what Hal was seeking. Moreover, he had risen to

---

Exhibit 4

Lester T. Ellwers
Swan Lane
Port Judith, Rhode Island 09464

May 4, 1982

Box ES-593
The Wall Street Journal
22 Cortland Street
New York, New York 10007

Gentlemen:

The enclosed resume is forwarded in response to your advertisement in the *National Business Employment Weekly* issue of May 2, 1982.

I am an experienced metal cutting executive with a background in Marketing and Engineering. In these areas my experience has been with a privately held company which grew from 15 to 100 million in sales in my 18 years of service. Initially, I spent 10 years with a large power equipment manufacturer in service and design work. I moved to a small company and started as an Outside Sales Engineer, working up to Regional Manager before transferring to the manufacturing side of the business and progressing to Vice President of Manufacturing. So, I consider myself the beneficiary of a well rounded business education and feel that my experience is a great asset to the position described in your advertisement.

I would like to discuss this opportunity with you and am available at your convenience.

Sincerely,

Lester T. Ellwers

Exhibit 4 (*continued*)

Lester T. Ellwers
Swan Lane
Port Judith, Rhode Island 09464

CONFIDENTIAL RÉSUMÉ

Background   Over ten years in direction and management of entire manufacturing operations for international multiplant capital equipment supplier. Experienced in computerized factory control systems, modern NC machinery, purchasing, manufacturing engineering and maintenance. Previous decade with same company in sales and sales management rounded education with understanding of customers, salesmen and their needs. Initial decade spent in field service and power industry engineering has given insight to details and field problems.

Employment   *Phillips Compressor Company*
History   Vacuum Pumps & Compressor Manufacturer
             1975–1981—Vice President—Manufacturing
             1973–1975—Director—Manufacturing
             1971–1973—Assistant Director—Manufacturing

             Responsible for entire manufacturing operation of two United States plants, a Canadian and a Belgian plant and manufacturing liaison with British and Brazilian subsidiaries as well as Swedish, Finnish, Australian, and South African licensees. Exercised direct control of 300 plus people utilizing machinery up to 100″ boring mills, fabrication and testing. Directed plant design and equipment modernization program to increase productivity and reduce energy consumption. Installed MRP in production control along with computerized work-in-progress, manpower utilization and efficiency controls. Evolved computerized ability to review costs in all plants and subsidiaries to spot problems and facilitate smart sourcing. Instigated computer aided manufacturing for tooling and fixture design as part of CAD system. Developed alternate material sources for plants in countries with import restrictions and interplant part sales based on lowest unit cost. Conceived design and directed building of two efficient teletype controlled satellite machining-assembly plants utilizing direct labor only, with all overhead remaining in home office. Developed Pattern Shop utilizing plastic pattern copies for worldwide consumption to insure casting interchangeability.

             1969–1971—District Sales Manager—St. Louis
             1966–1969—Regional Sales Engineer
             1962–1966—Sales Engineer

Exhibit 4 (*continued*)

> Directed and trained Midwestern sales force in sale of vacuum pumps and systems to chemical and power industry and operated factory repair center. As Regional Engineer, trained commission sales agents and resolved their technical problems.
>
> Initially worked as Sales Engineer in New Jersey industrial corridor where broad experience was gained from diversity of customers' applications.
>
> 1953–1962—*Brown-Boveri Corporation*
> Heavy Industrial Equipment Manufacturer
>
> Started as Field Service Engineer with start-up and service on power plant and windtunnel projects, primarily pump and compressor situations, moved to Condenser Department in 1958 as Project Engineer on Power Plants and Shipboard Nuclear Navy. Dealt with design to specification, sale by bid, manufacturing and start-up.

Education
> United States Merchant Marine Academy—1953—BSME
> Cornell Executive Development Program—1973
> Attended numerous seminars on computerized production and inventory control; OSHA and Manufacturing—Industrial Site Selection, Productivity, and Automation.

Personal
> Birthdate—December 29, 1931
> Married—four children
> Health—Excellent
> Veteran

Jan Wolff's Comments:

Lester T. Ellwers
Port Judith, Rhode Island

Lester Ellwers worked until last summer for Phillips Compressor Company. As he described it, the company was involved in building a new plant over the existing one. All operations were to continue during the building period. He would normally have been in charge of the building project but because of the complexity of the task and the need to continue normal plant operation, an assistant was put in charge and directed to report to the Board on a weekly basis. Elwers said that he did not involve himself in the project because he felt he was explicitly directed to concern himself only with maintaining plant operations. About two thirds of the way through the construction, it became apparent that the assistant had made c. $1/2 million change orders which had never been authorized by the Board, despite the weekly meetings which were held. Ellwers was asked to resign.

Exhibit 4   (*continued*)

Mr. Ellwers describes himself as "not a completely structured person, open, somewhat demanding of his assistant . . . one who listens, doesn't believe in running off at the mouth . . . doesn't like to interfere but does have a habit of wandering through the plant once or twice a day just so that he can check to see that things are proceeding smoothly . . . tends to rely heavily on financial people and not second guess them but, because he's an engineer, may tend to second guess engineers . . . not too demanding, but people usually know where they stand . . . tries to give praise when he feels it's due and if they need their tail kicked in he will kick it in. . . ."

Mr. Ellwers earned $66K at Phillips.

Exhibit 5

> 60 Lakeside Drive
> Ridgefield
> Rhode Island 09144
>
> May 8, 1982

The Advertiser,
Box ES-593,
The Wall Street Journal,
22 Cortlandt St.,
New York,
N.Y. 10007.

Dear Sir,

I have read with interest your advertisement in the "Wall Street Journal" dated April 27, 1982, for a President of a privately held company, and wish to apply for this position.

Attached is a résumé of my career and qualifications covering the past 25 years. The experience I obtained during this period was through a progressive climb in the management ladder from Department Head to Managing Director (President). I acquired knowledge and skills in a variety of industries and in every aspect of company control and activity, being responsible for Department/Divisions in Sales, Marketing, Manufacturing, Design/Engineering, Quality, Labor Relations etc.

Exhibit 5 (*continued*)

I am English by birth and qualified with Permanent residence status of the United States. I reside with my wife in Ridgefield and our daughter is at present attending the New England Conservatory of Music. There are no other dependents and no family ties in the United Kingdom which would interfere with re-location within the United States.

I trust the foregoing and attachments will be of interest to you.

Yours faithfully,

LIONEL NEWMAN

Lionel Newman
60 Lakeside Drive, Ridgefield, Rhode Island 09144

AGE:	52 years.
DATE OF BIRTH:	6.7.29.
PLACE OF BIRTH:	Brighton, England.
NEXT OF KIN:	Wife—Mary Newman
CHILDREN:	One daughter, aged 22 years.
QUALIFICATIONS:	Associate Membership of the Institute of Production Engineers, Sussex University, England.
	Associate Membership Institute of Works Managers.
	Member British Institute of Management.
	Executive Management Development Course, Cornell University.

Exhibit 5   (*continued*)

<u>Lionel Newman</u>

SUMMARY

A business and planning executive with extensive experience in general management, strategic planning and corporate growth. Emphasis has been in industrial and specialist businesses.

PRESENT COMPANY

VICE PRESIDENT CORPORATE PLANNING

(1981—Present)

Responsibilities include operations and long range strategic planning for the Corporation.

Produce and monitor strategic plan for Parent company and subsidiaries, including utilisation of physical, financial and human resources.

Responsible for performance, growth and profit of British subsidiary.

Chairman of quality improvement program.

Responsible for trademark, licencee and other legal matters.

(1975–1980)

MANAGING DIRECTOR (PRESIDENT)

Responsible with full autonomy for management and direction of United Kingdom subsidiary.

Reporting to me were division directors responsible for manufacture, sales/service, finance, production services including management information systems, design/engineering, production control/purchasing and industrial relations.

Because of achievements with regard to profit (increased tenfold in first year and maintained at an average of 10.4 percent after tax for five years) and growth (increased 300 percent during five years, 200 percent in real terms), I was invited to join the parent company as Vice President Corporate Planning.

STRUTHERS
(MACHINE TOOLS)
LTD. Division of
Skinner Machine
Tools.

MANAGING DIRECTOR (PRESIDENT)

Manufacturers of heavy duty and special machine tools.

Exhibit 5 (*continued*)

<u>Lionel Newman</u>

(1970–1975)	I had complete autonomy for the management and direction of the company, reporting to the Chairman of the Parent company.
	Responsible for growth and profit through five division directors.

WORTHINGTON LTD.   WORKS DIRECTOR (Responsible for three divisions).

Valve and Pressure Gauge manufacture.

(1966–1970)

General responsibilities included:

Sales
Production control—purchasing
Manufacture
Industrial relations
Training
Engineering—design
Quality assurance
Methods engineering and tooling
Foundry producing ferrous and nonferrous castings.

WARD PATENTS LTD.   FACTORY MANAGER

(1964–1966)

Automotive accessory manufacturers.

Responsible to Group manufacturing director for:

Production—labor relations
Engineering—quality control/quality assurance
Methods, tooling, production services.

TURNER VALVE CO. LTD.   WORKS MANAGER

(1959–1964)

Valve manufacturer for Petrochemical, Oil Refinery, Industrial markets.

Responsible for:

Forecasting, production control.
Manufacturing, engineering.
Labor negotiations.

Exhibit 5   (*concluded*)

HEMPHILL PRECISION ENGINEERS LTD.	PRODUCTION CONTROLLER
(1958–1959)	Aerospace sub-contract machining and assembly.
	Production planning, scheduling, expediting and progress of batch production and one-off special requirements for guided missile and aero-engine components.
(1956–1958)	CHIEF JIG AND TOOL DESIGNER
	Responsible to managing director for tool design and manufacture.

Jan Wolff's Comments:

Lionel Newman
Ridgefield, Rhode Island

Lionel Newman works for Patterson Pumps, a $100 million, 1500 employee American Company which makes pumps and compressors. Mr. Newman was brought over to this country because he was so successful in running a British subsidiary. At the moment, he is very disillusioned with the company. From abroad he had no idea that the company was so poorly managed. He feels that they have been successful more through good fortune than good management and that the company executives have no idea how to cope in a downturn economy.

Mr. Newman is looking around for another opportunity, although he has not really done any serious looking to date. What had appealed to him about the ad was the potential to be a chief executive in an industry with which he is very familiar. He ran a machine tool shop for 5 years and has been CEO for 11 and feels that he has had excellent experience in turn-around situations. He feels he has an ability to communicate with people, utilize them to mutually good advantage. He feels that people like to be busy and productive and given proper direction will enjoy their work and do it well. He took a company which was in the doldrums from 1.5 million pounds sales to 6 million pounds without any increase in personnel. He feels he can lead people. He misses line management responsibilities, the pressures, the decision making. He is not entirely sure he would be interested in a company of the described size, but he wouldn't want to rule it out at this point because a lot would depend on salary, benefits, possible profit sharing.

His salary this year is $72K plus a possible bonus up to 40 percent.

Exhibit 6

Stephen P. Walonizk
7272 Ambler Rd.
Fort Washington, PA 19007

May 8, 1982

Box ES-593
The Wall Street Journal
22 Cortlandt St.
NY, NY 10007

SITUATION: President

The enclosed résumé will indicate that my qualifications and expertise meet your requirements. My résumé was formulated in anticipation of a possible change in management, when Narco Avionics was put up for sale. The inevitable happened.

Since the beginning of '82, I have been working as consultant for an aviation firm in Bakersfield, California. The company manufactures altimeters, air speed indicators, and pressure transducers for the general, commercial, and military aviation markets.

My directive is to: (a) establish a marketing organization and program
                     (b) institute a product development program
                     (c) reduce inventory
                     (d) be profitable.

By nature I am more comfortable in an environment where I can implement my recommendations and be responsible for the results.

I appreciate your consideration and would gladly agree to a mutually arranged interview. I can be reached by telephone at   , or write to me confidentially, at the following address:

Aero Dynamics Corp.
60 Fallon Drive
Bakersfield, CA 91403

Sincerely yours,

S. P. Walonizk

Encl: 1

Exhibit 6 (*continued*)

RÉSUMÉ

STEPHEN P. WALONIZK

7272 Ambler Rd.
Fort Washington, PA 19007

SITUATION

President/or
General Manager

OBJECTIVE:

Senior Management Position in a progressive company where leadership of the management team will provide the direction to meet profit and growth goals.

SUMMARY OF QUALIFICATONS:

A managing executive officer with over sixteen years of successful P & L experience in companies manufacturing electronic/mechanical products for the aviation and medical markets; and process and power plant equipment for the industrial market.

Highlights of experience include all aspects of management in a manufacturing environment:

Market planning and sales organization
Financial control
Long range planning
International experience
Product development
Labor negotiations (U.A.W.)
Company acquisitions and divestitures

A demonstrated record of success in establishing two foreign subsidiaries. A proven capability in turning around three financially troubled companies to a profitable position.

Exhibit 6   (*continued*)

BUSINESS EXPERIENCE:

PRESIDENT AND GENERAL MANAGER—July 1979—September 1981

Air-Tech, Div. of Shields & Foster, Inc.   Valley Forge, PA 19035

An eighteen (18) million dollar company manufacturing navigation and communications equipment for general aviation, and emergency locating beacons for marine use.

Replaced entire staff and slimmed middle management positions.

Restructured business to be profitable at 20% lower sales caused by a shrinking marketplace.

Formalized product planning program with definite cost and introduction targets.

Introduced new digital product line on target, time and cost wise.

Reduced sales effort, inventory by 20% and service costs by eliminating slow-moving, obsolete and unprofitable products above.

Lowered warranty cost and reject rate by locating on-site technicians.

Maintained morale and viability of division during lengthy corporate divestiture.

CORPORATE GROUP DIRECTOR—June 1978—July 1979

Shields & Foster, Inc.   Valley Forge, PA 19035

Windsor Div.—1.5 million dollar manufacturer of dental analgesia equipment and compressors.

Atlee Div.—4.2 million dollar manufacturer of gyroscopic and flight instrumentation.

Ballard Div.—3.2 million dollar manufacturer of winches and other sail handling equipment.

Foster Div.—3.8 million dollar manufacturer of navigation and communications equipment for pleasure and work boats.

Provided guidance to the General Managers of these divisions in planning and meeting their corporate goals.

Smoothed the management transition in Ireland (Air-Tech Europe).

Acquired a vacuum pump manufacturer to complement the Windsor product line.

Headed divestiture teams on Ballard and Foster Divisions.

Exhibit 6 (*continued*)

VICE PRESIDENT AND GENERAL MANAGER—November 1976—June 1978

Air-Tech/Europe, Div. of Shields & Foster, Inc.   Dublin, Ireland

Managed a 1.8 million dollar company manufacturing hospital equipment for infant care and anesthesiology.

  Instituted employee training and R & D programs funded by government grants.

  Vertically integrated by installing metal and plastic fabrication.

  Re-established quality image of Irish built products.

  Penetrated Eastern European and Black African markets.

  Negotiated with European approval authorities to meet their standards.

  Achieved highest percent profit for entire corporation—award for best corporate performance.

VICE PRESIDENT AND GENERAL MANAGER—May 1974—November 1976

Atlee, Div. of Shields & Foster, Inc.   Dallas, Texas

Turned around a 4.2 million dollar company manufacturing vacuum and electric gyroscopic flight instrumentation.

  Installed a standard cost system.

  Reduced overdue backlog by cancelling unprofitable orders.

  Revitalized MRP system, which improved deliveries and reduced inventory.

  Built a sales organization and instituted new marketing concepts.

  Instituted a product development program.

VICE PRESIDENT—MANUFACTURING MANAGER—August 1971—May 1974

Sullivan Systems   Camden, N.J.

Sixteen (16) million dollar manufacturer of high pressure nuclear and power plant valves, industrial jet equipment, desuperheaters, heat transfer equipment, condensers and vacuum pumps, rotameters and flow indicators, sold to the process and power industries.

  Reduced overdue backlog from two (2) million dollars to $200,000 in two years.

  Instrumental in obtaining an "N" stamp from the Atomic Energy Commission.

Exhibit 6 (*continued*)

Installed an MRP system.

Revised order entry system so stock items were shipped in 24 hours.

Started a vendor evaluation program.

Handled union contract negotiations.

VICE PRESIDENT AND MANAGING DIRECTOR—January 1970—August 1971

Sullivan Systems U.K.   Lavenham, England

Sales volume of one (1) million dollars with products similar to the parent company, except for the Valve line. Break even achieved at time of transfer to U.S.A. under new owner.

Located plant and hired personnel.

Purchased machinery and tooling.

Instituted accounting procedures and order entry systems.

Set up production and inventory control procedures.

Established sales organization.

GENERAL MANAGER AND DIRECTOR—December 1966—December 1969

Sullivan Systems Canada   Vancouver, B.C., Canada

Start-up with duties similar to those above. Started with sales of $115,000 (loss of $20,000) in '66, increasing to $600,000 (profit of $62,000) in '69.

VARIOUS POSITIONS—June 1952—December 1965

Sullivan Systems   Camden, N.J.

Diversified experience, with increasing responsibility as:

Industrial Engineer

Cost Manager

Purchasing Agent

Production Manager

Plant Manager

Exhibit 6   (*continued*)

EDUCATION:

Manhattan Technical Institute
   Certificate, Drafting & Machine Design
Villanova University
   B.S. Economics
Temple Graduate School
   M.S. Industrial Engineering
Drexel Institute of Technology
   Courses, M-B-O, Communication and Behavioral Science
IBM, Endicott, New York
   Certificate, Executive Training on Computer in Industry
Irish Management Institute
   Financing with Foreign Currencies

BUSINESS REFERENCES:

Roger Domenick, Chairman and C.E.O.
SHIELDS & FOSTER, INC.
970 Williams Ave.
Valley Forge, PA 19035

Harris Neal, Senior Vice President and General Manager
SULLIVAN SYSTEMS, INC.
32 Fisher St.
Camden, N.J. 08904

Paul V. Sullivan (Former owner, SULLIVAN SYSTEMS, INC.)
46 Laurel Lane
Arbor, PA 18943

Edward Warwick, President and Owner
WARWICK INDUSTRIES, INC.
Welsh Road
Fox Chase, PA 19040

Jan Wolff's Comment:

Stephen Walonizk
Fort Washington, Pennsylvania
(currently on assignment in California)

Mr. Walonizk describes himself in terms such as "people oriented . . . always look to the quality of the staff in a company and judge that . . . then feel it's up to me to manage and direct . . . not bureaucratic . . . run staff meetings that are open . . . take recommendations of staff . . . will make a decision if it

Exhibit 6   (*concluded*)

hasn't been made below me, but would prefer not to . . . like to develop people who are working for me . . . don't like bureaucracy . . . you have to take chances sometimes, and that can be difficult in a bureaucracy. . . ."

He returns to Pennsylvania about once a month.

Exhibit 7

April 30, 1982

The Wall Street Journal
Box ES-593
22 Cortlandt St.
NY, NY 10007

Gentlemen . . . ,

Your advertisement for President in the April 27 Wall Street Journal truly intrigues me.

Here is my "just prepared" résumé, since I have not been seeking a career change. You will note I have been President and Chief Operating Officer of Cranston Equipment Corporation for the past 10 years and feel extremely well-qualified to become a Chief Executive Officer.

Nearly all my experience has been with metal cutting manufacturers, and much of my experience has been spent in the Sales and Marketing area.

The Company for which I presently work is proprietor operated and I have a very good understanding and liking of this management style.

Would you please call or write so I may meet with you.

Thank you,

Brooks M. Carswell

BAW/ib

Enc.

Exhibit 7   (*continued*)

BROOKS M. CARSWELL

CAREER OBJECTIVE:

• Chief Executive Officer or Chief Operating Officer of a Manufacturing company

• Profit responsibility for a major Division

EMPLOYMENT HISTORY:

1964 to Present: Cranston Equipment Corporation, Ames, Massachusetts. Manufacturers of plastics and packaging machinery—6 plant locations, Last Year's Sales—$58,000,000.

    1972 to Present: President, Chief Operating Officer, and Board Member

          Primarily responsible for annual profit. All Corporate Marketing and Sales, Manufacturing, Product Engineering, Data Processing, Administration, Computer Operations, and Personnel report to me.

          I achieved particular success in finding and buying unprofitable companies, then quickly making these acquisitions highly profitable.

    1967 to 1972:   Executive Vice President

          Responsible for total Company Marketing, Sales, and Engineering.

    1965 to 1967:   Vice President of Engineering

          Responsible for Product and R & D Engineering as well as Manufacturing Engineering.

1958–1964:   Brookpark, Inc., Cleveland, Ohio
           Manufacturers of Melmac plastic dinnerware—800 employees

           My first responsibility was Manufacturing Manager for multiplant sites, then two years as Vice President—Corporate Planning.

1954–1958:   Hydraulic Press Manufacturing Company, Mount Gilead, Ohio. Producers of plastics and metalworking machinery—1,200 employees.

           Was Divisional Sales Manager and then Chief Engineer.

Exhibit 7 (*continued*)

1951–1954: Lewis Welding & Engineering Company, Cleveland, Ohio. Designers and builders of special plastics machinery—700 employees.

Worked as Design Engineer and Sales Engineer.

EDUCATIONAL HISTORY:

Ohio State University
    Bachelor Mechanical Engineering— 1951
    Master of Science—Machine Design Major—1951

Harvard University
Graduate School of Business Administration
Advanced Management Program—1969.

June 22, 1982

The reason for this letter is to provide you additional details concerning my background. The original brief résumé—together with our interesting conversations—did not cover a number of pertinent highlights.

You know for the past 10 years, I have been President and Chief Operating Officer of Cranston Equipment Corporation—$58,000,000 in sales and 900 employees. As President, I was responsible for all Sales, Manufacturing, Product Engineering, Personnel, and Administration. Here are some of my major achievements:

PROFITS: Produced operating profits of 12% of sales over 10 years in highly competitive mature capital goods industry—20% of volume exported.

ACQUISITIONS: Bought four small companies in past six years at bargain prices—three losing money. Within two years, all were made very profitable. Each of these divisions now has 50–100 employees with sales volume to $6,000,000. I have been directly responsible for their operations.

PRODUCT LINE STRATEGY: Built Packaging Division from $6.5 million (1972) to $24,000,000 last year. This was accomplished by rebuilding and motivating the field sales force, engineering new products, and constructing a highly efficient 80,000 square feet factory in the Southeast.

ADMINISTRATION: Defined effective controls as company expanded from one site to six sites. A major factor was development of a low-cost (1% of sales) user intensive Data Processing and MIS.

Exhibit 7 (*concluded*)

For the 8 years at Cranston Equipment Corporation before becoming President, I was Vice President of Engineering, then Executive Vice President. As Vice President of Engineering all Research & Development, Product, and Manufacturing Engineering reported to me. Upon becoming Executive Vice President, Marketing and Sales responsibility was added to my Engineering role.

For 13 years prior to PMC, I had hands-on experience as a Manufacturing Manager, Sales Manager, and Chief Engineer. Most of this experience was in the metalworking/machinery industry.

H. M. Walton —2— June 22, 1982

I was born in 1927 and received two engineering degrees from Ohio State University—a Bachelor of Mechanical Engineering and Master of Science with a major in Machine Design. In 1969 I completed the Advanced Management Program at Harvard University. Subsequently, time has been spent at Harvard University, AMA, and IBM to keep me updated in manufacturing systems and computer usage. I am a Registered Professional Engineer in Ohio and Massachusetts.

Community activities have been a rewarding and broadening experience. These have been my principal interests:

President: Greater Northwood United Way
Trustee: American International College, Northwood, MA
Director: Associated Industries of Massachusetts
Committee Member: Bay State Hospitals
Chairman, Computer Committee: Town of Ames, MA
Board of Trustees: United Church of Christ

My management approach has emphasized personal leadership together with operational know-how so people are motivated to willingly work *with* me. Employees have responded well to this method and it has been the basis of my managerial success since college.

Hal, perhaps this additional information added to our conversations will give you a more complete picture of my background, achievements, and style. I believe my references are outstanding, so please contact anyone who knows me for personal or professional recommendations. Let me know should you like names and phone numbers of key references.

Working in your Company would be most appealing to me, since my most rewarding experience and success have been managing Cranston's Divisions—comparable in size to your company. I am confident our association would be a long-term productive and happy situation for both of us.

Sincerely,

Brooks M. Carswell

BMW/ib

a vice presidency, thus demonstrating his managerial capabilities. But when Hal met with him, the result was disappointment. Hal found him rigid and uncompromising, lacking in insight as to why he had recently lost his position, and "immature in response to authority when he is threatened by his feeling of need to compete." Hal's notes concluded: "Not a number one executive."

Another strong candidate who turned out better was an Englishman who was at that time vice president of corporate planning for a Rhode Island company making pumps and compressors. (See Exhibit 5 for his letter and résumé.) Lionel Newman was considering leaving because of differences with management over proper planning for a downturning economy. He had served as president of the company's British subsidiary, had extensive experience in machine tool manufacturing, and found the possibility of running a well-managed small firm very attractive. His response to the ad was a very early step in his job search, and he was not sure that Flowtrol was large enough, or that the possible remuneration would be sufficient to tempt him. He and Hal Walton found they had a great deal in common, and in the end he was of some assistance to Hal in providing information about local applicants. Newman himself decided that this was not the right opportunity for him, and withdrew from the competition.

Another strong candidate had recently left an avionics division that was sold to another company. (See Exhibit 6 for his letter and résumé.) Stephen Walonizk had been the division's president, and had had substantial general management experience in this division and in other parts of the parent company. He had also worked as manufacturing manager for a valve company, and had an engineering degree. Although he

was currently consulting for a firm in California, Walonizk was happy at the thought of resettling in Rhode Island. (He was living in Pennsylvania, the site of his previous job.) Flowtrol appealed to him because it provided a chance at senior management, and because he found that as a consultant he missed the challenge of implementing his suggestions and being accountable for the results.

With these men, as with Brooks, Hal spent some time, took notes, and even snapped a photo to aid his recollection. He discussed his reactions with his wife. He was still following up on his interviews with Brooks Carswell, who had left Cranston Equipment earlier in the year. (See Exhibit 7 for Brooks Carswell's letter and résumé.) Brooks had extensive metal cutting manufacturing experience, had been involved in sales and marketing, and had been president and COO of Cranston for 10 years. At $60 million in sales, Cranston Equipment was about 10 times the size of Flowtrol, but Brooks had worked with much smaller units of the firm. In fact, Brooks had planned and carried out several acquisitions of firms very much Flowtrol's size, which had then become divisions of Cranston. He had an engineering degree and had started with Cranston as vice president of engineering; he had served in the Navy. He worked and lived just over the Massachusetts border, quite near to Flowtrol. There would thus be no relocation involved if he were to take the job.

Naturally, one of Hal's chief concerns was why Brooks had left Cranston. Brooks explained that, in the current economic downturn, Cranston was shrinking. The company's chairman together with his family owned 55 percent of the stock, and, as it did not seem necessary to retain two powerful executives, it was Brooks who left.

Hal was determined to choose Flowtrol's new president before the summer was too far advanced. By July he had followed up the most promising leads, and had interviewed everyone he thought worth seeing. He was ready to make his decision.

FLOWTROL, INCORPORATED (B)
Alice B. Morgan and
Jeffrey A. Sonnenfeld

Hal Walton, founder, president, CEO, and chairman of the board of Flowtrol, Incorporated, a valve manufacturer in Rhode Island, had spent the past several months choosing a new president and chief operating officer for his company. (For company background and information about Hal Walton, see Flowtrol, Inc. (A).) He had placed an ad in *The Wall Street Journal* on April 28, 1982, and, with the assistance of Flowtrol's auditor and a recruiting firm in Boston, had culled from the more than 1,000 responses some 40 individuals who seemed especially well suited to the position. Hal had eventually interviewed about eight of these final candidates, and after review and discussions with his wife and with Jan Wolff, the recruiter, he had made his choice. He decided to offer the job to Brooks Carswell, who had recently left his post as president of Cranston Equipment Corporation, a company that made plastics and packaging machinery. For details about Brooks and other candidates for the position, see Flowtrol, Inc. (A). Hal commented:

> Brooks not only had engineering background, he had a master's degree in Manufacturing Engineering—Machine Design. He was a Navy man, had been through Har-

vard's AMP, and had held responsible managerial positions. He was in the right age bracket. He had no ambition to acquire equity—so many of the candidates were understandably ambitious for aggressive control and that was not what I wanted. And there he was in Ames. I didn't want the responsibility of taking someone away from a job and moving him here and having him not turn out. There were also plenty of candidates who were unemployed but would have required moving, although I didn't talk to any that seemed to fit. I opted for the easy way out.

Before making Brooks an official offer, Hal arranged for him to meet with Phil Denton, an industrial psychologist whom Hal had previously consulted on another matter. Brooks and Phil spent about three hours together, and Brooks came away feeling that, if the interview and the few written tests he had been given had gone well, the job was his. His intuition on this point was correct, and in mid-July Hal asked Brooks if he would become Flowtrol's president. Hal had recently sent Jan Wolff a note, which read as follows:

> Brooks has checked out amazingly well. I think I should settle on him. He has a good technical background, sales experience, is a good administrator, has handled acquisitions, and has been stable in employment and lifestyle.

Brooks's Acceptance

Brooks had left Cranston Equipment with generous severance pay, and was in no hurry to find a job. On the other hand, the more he learned about Flowtrol, the more he liked the sound of it. He wanted a position which entailed responsibility; he was interested in running operations. He liked the fact that the firm was nearby. He had dealt with divisions of Cranston, which, like Flowtrol, were in the $6 million range: in fact, Brooks had planned and carried out several acquisitions of firms very much Flowtrol's size, which had then become divisions of Cranston Equipment. As a result, he did not think the transition from a $60 million company like Cranston to one about one 10th as large would be too difficult. And he and Hal seemed to get along well, which was clearly a critical factor. Brooks commented:

> When I had this opportunity with Flowtrol, I also had an opportunity to become president of a Textron division doing $60 million in the Minneapolis area. I thought it over and I really liked the idea of a small company. Everybody says, "You took Flowtrol because you didn't have to relocate." That was a small factor really. We had relocated before and it was not that much of a problem. It was really the job content that made the difference. Flowtrol is just a beautiful company.

Brooks found the idea of working with Hal Walton appealing, although he realized that it might be difficult at times. Hal had, after all, been not only top man, but a major contributor to all facets of the business, and might have trouble relaxing his control over the firm's operations. But he was impressed with Hal's willingness to allow Flowtrol to change. And he felt the selection process, particularly the final interview with Phil Denton, the industrial psychologist, had been extremely well handled.

> I think it was a pretty enlightened thing for Hal to do. I would recommend it to any one-man-dominated company. Hal had a lot of faith in Phil, and really it's obvious that if you come to work at Flowtrol and you aren't going to get along with Hal Walton, you may as well save your time and energy and do something else. So this way Hal would get an objective reading.

Brooks Carswell became president and COO of Flowtrol on August 18, 1982.

Hal had discussed the addition of Brooks with each of the department heads, privately, before Brooks started work. Hal wanted to be sure the move would not alienate members of a smoothly working team. The rest of the organization learned about the search only when Brooks arrived on the scene. Reactions in the company were strongly supportive: a second in command was clearly desirable, and Brooks's age (56) meant that the younger department heads still had opportunities for growth within Flowtrol.

In early October, Hal and his wife left on a selling trip to New Jersey and points south. They spent seven weeks on the road, using the Flowtrol mobile home as well as occasional air transport, and went as far as the southern tip of Florida. Brooks commented:

> I felt very good about that, because Hal was willing to leave when I had only been here about two months. I thought it was a vote of confidence, based on very little evidence.

While he was away, Hal had called in regularly two or three times a week, and Brooks was able to reach him if any pressing questions arose. Hal's trip was a success, and Brooks was able to guide Flowtrol during his absence without undue difficulty.

To ease the process of transition, Hal and Brooks consulted Phil Denton, the industrial psychologist. Phil had been helpful in the decision to choose Brooks, and after Brooks started work, Phil met with him again. Brooks explained:

> There are certain things, I'm sure, that displease Hal about me, and there are certain things that he does that sort of bother me. Each of us talked to Phil, and then Phil in turn got back to us. It did help. For example, Hal has a habit of starting to talk, then

pausing. I've always been in what you might call a verbally combative situation, so when he'd pause, I would interrupt. He told Phil, "It really bothers me to have Brooks do that." Great. Phil told me about it, and now I'm careful to be sure Hal is finished before I start to respond. I found it very valuable to have this kind of assistance.

Brooks's First Few Months

When Brooks began his tenure as Flowtrol's president and COO, he knew he had a lot to learn:

> At first I wondered what the devil I could contribute—I was sure I would never know as much as Hal about valves and about the company.

But Brooks did have marketing and strategic planning experience that he believed would be useful to Flowtrol, and he soon realized that his background in general management was also of value in his new position. He found that Hal had been Flowtrol's major force for so long that many of his subordinates were essentially task-oriented, accustomed to moving from task to task under Hal's close supervision. Brooks planned to try to make the staff more self-actuating. At the same time, Brooks himself often shared the tendency toward task orientation:

> I have to admit even I am doing a fair amount of it, partly because I am new and don't want to go off in some direction that makes no sense. I am also still trying to determine exactly what Hal wants me to do, and what he would like to do for himself.

Brooks's Managerial Role. Officially, Brooks was Flowtrol's chief operating officer. He reported to Hal and nearly everyone else reported to him. There were only two exceptions to this rule. Mrs. Helen Walton,

the corporation's secretary, also reported to her husband. In addition, one man, the first Hal had hired for Flowtrol, still reported to him. This individual had been a designer and technical consultant for Flowtrol since its founding, and was responsible, with Hal, for the development and production of all company's products. He had little formal training, and, although he held the title vice president of engineering, in fact he did no supervision. Hal viewed him as temperamentally unsuited to management, but felt a strong sense of loyalty toward him for his many years of devotion to Flowtrol. As a result, he served as a kind of roving consultant, and reported only nominally to Brooks.

Apart from these two, other functions reported to Brooks. Decisions on policy were made by Hal, Brooks, and the manager whose function was involved. Thus, although Brooks had only made two sales calls by early December, he and the sales manager and Hal worked together to develop Flowtrol's first marketing plan.

Hal's role as president had been mostly that of monitoring, checking to see that operations or engineering was running smoothly, rather than actively participating in those functions. Brooks was surprised to learn that Hal's monitoring was often at a very detailed level. He might want to know why a particular man was chosen to work the first shift, and another the second.

> Hal looked at every invoice; he had his hands on everything.

Brooks did not plan to emulate Hal's management style, although he was intending to utilize some parts of it. He found, for example, that he enjoyed dealing with problems directly, rather than through those reporting to him. Instead of talking about manufacturing issues in an office, he reviewed them on the shop floor. Implementation could be easily monitored, and Brooks could check out new policies in action by walking only a short distance from his office. Brooks found Flowtrol's intimacy exhilarating:

At Cranston, I used to wake up at 4:00 in the morning, and wonder if I really had any impact on the larger company. I didn't see much of it—maybe 2 percent—but through policy and strategy decisions I hoped I was having an effect. But I really wondered. Here there is no question: you can see everything. I probably work more hours here, but there is not as much anxiety, because I am more in control of what is going on. As long as you can see what is going wrong, you can do something to make it right. When you are dealing through three layers of people, everything is much more remote, and there is really a lot of anxiety.

At the same time, Brooks sometimes experienced a sense of near-claustrophobia. He missed his frequent travel, both in the U.S. and abroad. He was dealing with a few products that came in a few sizes, rather than with several diverse product lines. He could easily identify the company's market, which was nearly all domestic or Canadian. In these respects, the world of Flowtrol differed greatly from that of Cranston Equipment.

Business Development at Flowtrol

In order to better assess the potential for Flowtrol, Brooks had familiarized himself with its market position and that of its competitors. He estimated that the company's market segment was about $25 million a year, and that it might be shrinking because construction of new utility plants had slowed. The MRO or maintenance and repair orders were still strong, however. Flowtrol currently held about 20 percent of the market. As Brooks noted:

You can go from 1 percent to 2 percent of a market a lot easier than you can go from 10 percent to 20 percent. If we grow much more, we are suddenly going to become visible, especially as the overall market is probably shrinking a little. In my experience, nothing arouses the interest of your competitors as much as loss of market share.

Brooks believed that if Flowtrol began to invade its competitor's share of the market, there would be immediate response. Some firms would decide to get out without challenging Flowtrol. Others, however, would stay and fight, probably by reducing prices. In Brooks' view, it would be difficult to compete with Flowtrol on price:

Flowtrol is a very low-cost producer. I come from a company where at the end of 10 years you had three weeks vacation, and after 20 years you had six. There were 14 paid holidays, sick leaves, and so on. This company has three weeks vacation at the end of 15 years—and so far there is only one person eligible! There are eight paid holidays, and none of the fringes you get in the larger metalworking operations. Our biggest competitor is Rockwell International. I have known other divisions of big companies, and I can't believe that Rockwell is a low-cost producer. But Flowtrol is, and that will help.

Of course Brooks realized that Rockwell, with its huge capitalization, might attack Flowtrol's position by accepting very low margins on its valves. But on the whole he had faith that Flowtrol could increase its sales and its market share.

Morever, there were other strategies for growth which Brooks considered appropriate for Flowtrol. He would have to determine, with Hal, how these strategies fit into Hal's vision of the company's future, and what level of risk Hal was willing to contemplate in order to implement them. Brooks noted:

> If, say, the absolute goal is to quadruple the company in five years, you have to take all sorts of huge risks.

Flowtrol had been financed very conservatively, and Brooks was not sure what financing alternatives Hal would be willing to consider.

One means of increasing Flowtrol's size was through acquisition, a route with which Brooks was quite familiar. Flowtrol could double right away by acquiring another company of about the same size:

> With our balance sheet that would be easily accomplished. We have to decide about that. And we need to consider other types of development as well. Do we want to get into a completely new product that takes a new kind of sales force and new manufacturing? All these things are possible, but we have not yet addressed the issues specifically.

Brooks believed that because Flowtrol had been so successful, there had not been much motivation to consider alternative strategies. Now, however, he expected that some strategic decisions would need to be made. Expansion or growth seemed easy to attain:

> Hal has built an organization, frankly, that is capable of doing a lot more. If we grew, everyone would just move up. Hal has managed to develop or hire people within the last couple of years who have the potential to run a much larger operation, keeping up with Flowtrol as it grows.

Seven Months after Brooks's Arrival

By March of 1983, Brooks had settled into his new job. Some major strategic decisions had been made, and Flowtrol was gearing up to expand its sales, leaving such matters as new products or acquisitions for the fu-

ture. Mel Thompson, the sales manager, planned a sales conference for March 10–11, at which Flowtrol's representatives met each other and discussed how best to sell the product. Hal had taken another trip of several weeks' duration, and was convinced that additional sales effort would increase the company's current backlog, enabling Flowtrol to use all its new capacity and to continue to grow.

Brooks accepted this strategic decision, and was doing his best to become thoroughly familiar with Flowtrol's product line and with the details of running the company. He had not encountered any unexpected difficulties but he did feel that it was taking longer than he had anticipated to master these details, since they required attention to matters that were not part of a COO's concerns in a larger organization. The management style he had used previously had to be modified for his new position:

> As president of another company, I had management techniques where I did not have to know a great deal about the intimate details of the company. Here I must know not just that we sell valves or what kinds of valves but what particular material goes into every piece of each valve.

Brooks believed he was making good progress in this area, and he praised Hal's capacity as a trainer. He also expressed gratitude that he had been given considerable freedom to make important decisions on marketing, personnel, and manufacturing policies. Brooks accepted the idea that one of his roles was to give David Walton the training and support he would need if he were eventually to step into an executive position at Flowtrol. He remarked:

> One of the considerations, I think, in my being hired at the age I am, is that this company has some very good people for its size. They still have plenty of time to develop

over the coming years. I always consider it part of my job to develop a successor, and while I haven't yet had much time to work on this, I certainly view it as a priority. Both the sales manager and the comptroller have great potential, but they need multidiscipline experience. I hope to help them get it. Both men were captains in the Navy, so they both know how to take command.

Brooks had several immediate objectives. Because the overall market for valves was not expanding, growth for Flowtrol would have to come from increased market share. Brooks believed that greater brand name recognition was essential, and that marketing and advertising were the routes to this end. From a production standpoint, the critical issue was to remain the low-cost producer. Flowtrol planned to purchase additional computer controlled lathes to help keep costs low. There was at present no formal cost-accounting system at Flowtrol, and Brooks and Hal had discussed Hal's desire to introduce a modified cost-accounting production-control system tailored to Flowtrol's needs. Brooks noted:

> For a small company like this, the system has to be unique because textbook systems are really too expensive. They tell you more than you can afford to know in a small company. We have to tailor a system to our needs, using our judgment as to what will pay off and what we can really do without.

Planning for David's MRP and shop-scheduling system was well under way. A DEC PDP computer and IMS software package had been acquired and Dave and the comptroller were working on a simple management information system to help Flowtrol keep track of its business.

When asked about personal goals, Brooks expressed a desire to go into the field to sell Flowtrol's products:

> There are two reasons for that. One is that we have a very "thin" sales force and I could

provide backup where needed. The second is that it's difficult to determine a complete policy for a company if you don't understand the sales and marketing aspect. This is something, of course, that you'd never do in a larger company.

In summary, Brooks believed that he was already in a position to make a contribution to Flowtrol, although he was not yet in full control of all the details he needed to know. He agreed with Hal about the company's direction, and had some ideas about how to achieve the greater sales that were essential for growth. He had encountered only cooperation from the men who reported to him, and he had a very high opinion of their capabilities. Brooks's agenda included extensive training of key personnel, including David Walton, and implementation of control systems to keep Flowtrol a low-cost producer.

> I feel that where the company is today, I can make a substantial contribution. That might not have been true when the company was starting—I'm just not an entrepreneur. I view myself more as a business manager, and the company has grown to the point where it needs some fairly sophisticated things to happen.

Hal Walton's Perspective. Hal's goal in seeking a president for Flowtrol was to remove himself from day-to-day responsibilities, so that he could "look over the shoulders of others and see what needs strengthening." He wanted to spend more time in the field, making clearer to the manufacturers' representatives the advantages Flowtrol's products provided and how best to sell them. Hal intended no immediate retirement from active functioning as Flowtrol's CEO; he wanted a president and COO with whom he could work harmoniously, but who would be able to take over should it become necessary. In March 1983, Hal was beginning to have some doubts.

> At this point, I don't know if Brooks is going to satisfy the requirements of the job or not. He has not sold me completely yet.

One problem Hal encountered in working with Brooks centered on communication. Hal worried that Brooks did not always really listen to what he was being told, and saw an incident that occurred during the selection process as possibly characteristic. The Waltons had arranged to meet Brooks at a restaurant whose name was very similar to that of another local eating place. Because of the possibility of confusion, Hal had been particularly explicit in making the appointment. Nonetheless, Brooks had gone to the wrong restaurant.

> We've talked about the need for good communication. That's one of the reasons I asked Phil Denton to meet with Brooks. But I'm still not sure he really hears what I'm saying. And he himself has a tendency to verbalize the obvious, rather than getting to a more profound level of discussion.

Hal, like Brooks, was conscious that Flowtrol required a different managerial style from the one Brooks had used at Cranston Equipment.

> Brooks has not been involved in detail. At Cranston, he relied on others to give him reports, and he did not have the hands-on type of experience which I feel is necessary at Flowtrol. It's been a case of his having to learn to do the job.

Hal wondered if Brooks would be able to pay attention to all the details essential to running the company.

More important, in Hal's view, Brooks too often acted merely as a conduit, transmitting material from others without giving it added value. Hal recalled in particular the analysis Brooks had sent him concerning a new machine which Flowtrol was considering buying. The machine costs were outlined in detail, but no information on the labor costs associated with the machine were included. When Hal realized this and asked about it, he was told that the report was only preliminary. In his view, this made very little sense. He was not prepared to act on a preliminary report, and he naturally assumed that the material he received was based on a complete analysis. Brooks, Hal believed, had merely passed along the information he had been given, without doing any further exploration and without reaching any decision. "I'm afraid he may be too much of a pass-through individual—not resolute and decisive enough."

There were occasions where Brooks did take action: for example, he had taken out a substantial business insurance policy without consulting Hal. Hal felt, however, that this decision actually came from Flowtrol's comptroller, and that Brooks had simply accepted it.

> I think Brooks is dedicated, hard-working, interested, and animated. . . . But I'm not sure he has the ability to sit down and resolve. There's a big question mark: is he going to be an executive? Does he have the ability to analyze ways and consider action? I may have made a mistake.

CASE 11
UNION CARBIDE CORPORATION: CAREER DEVELOPMENT IN AFRICA AND THE MIDDLE EAST
James J. Dowd and
Jeffrey A. Sonnenfeld

Early in 1976, Union Carbide started producing flashlight batteries in Khartoum, Sudan, at the confluence of the Blue and White Niles. The managing director was an American, with experience in other parts of Africa, Latin America, and the Far East. The treasurer was a Greek, trained in Greece and the United States. The sales manager and the assistant engineer were both Indians. The plant engineer was a Chinese from Singapore who had worked most recently in Indonesia. And the assistant plant manager was a Kenyan of Indian origin who was trained in Kenya and the United States. These people will return home or go on to other international assignments as Sudanese employees—the vast majority of the Khartoum workforce—are trained and develop the skills necessary to fill these key positions.

The Khartoum operation demonstrates Union Carbide's commitment to develop and deploy its people so that they achieve their full potential. This required training programs at almost every location and for every occupational level. It requires a management system that stresses individual performance which is measured against challenging but achievable objectives. And it requires an increasing flexibility that permits individuals to transfer to other corporate businesses, functions, and locations where they can develop to their full potential and be most effective in their jobs.

> Annual Report, 1976
> Union Carbide Corporation

For Union Carbide–Africa and Middle East, 1981 had been a difficult year. Due largely to the worldwide recession, both sales and profits were down from the previous year. While concerned with the year's operating results, UCAME Chairman Boris Sokoloff, Jr., was pleased with his company's progress in managing career development. Responding to sweeping changes both in the market and in the corporation, Mr. Sokoloff and his staff had requested help from Mr. Stephen Wall, manager of Union Carbide's Corporate Management Development department, in improving UCAME's management development pro-grams. Mr. Wall had therefore spent much time in 1981 in helping the area company, identifying training and development needs, formulating action plans to address immediate problems, and designing and implementing an ongoing system for managing career development in UCAME. Now six months into the action timetable recommended by Mr. Wall, Mr. Sokoloff and his senior managers believed that the progress they had made was impressive, but they wondered how they might gain a better understanding of ways to evaluate more formally the work they had done.

Union Carbide History and Background

By any standard, Union Carbide Corporation was one of the world's industrial giants in 1981. In that year Union Carbide employed over 110,000 people worldwide and posted $10.1 billion in sales, one third of which resulted from international operations. Its vast resources were allocated among five industry segments: chemicals and plastics, gases and related products, metals and carbons, batteries and home/automotive products, and specialty products. While the majority of its sales were to industrial users—a major customer was the U.S. steel industry—almost all Americans were familiar with some Union Carbide products; Simonize car wax, Prestone antifreeze, Glad bags, and Eveready–Energizer batteries were the most prominent of the company's well-known brand names. As an integrated domestic producer, Union Carbide doubly enjoyed its retail sales leadership in antifreeze and plastic bags, because it led also in industrial sales of the basic raw material, polyethylene and ethylene oxide/glycol. Other chemicals and metal markets in which Union Carbide held major positions included urethane foam, nitrogen, oxygen, tungsten, vanadium, and uranium.[1]

The corporation could trace its origins back to 1886, to the founding of a small carbon products company in Cleveland, Ohio, which produced the world's first commercial dry cell battery and sold it under the trademark "Eveready." But although the carbon business was historically regarded as the foundation of the corporation, Union Carbide and Carbon Corporation (the name was shortened later) was actually created in 1917 when the carbon company was merged with a Chicago chemical company and three other manufacturing firms. This combined entity, with strong industrial bases in metallurgy, chemicals, and gases, with early overseas operations, was the real beginning of the modern Union Carbide Corporation. It grew rapidly and expanded into related products by capitalizing on new applications of its technology. In the early twenties, for example, Union Carbide became one of the first companies to make petrochemicals.

Over the next 50 years, Union Carbide continued to grow through acquisition and internal product development, expanding its product lines and its market coverage around the world. The task of managing this multiproduct multinational corporation grew likewise more complex, requiring the planning and control of billions of dollars in assets among increasingly diverse businesses in some 35 countries. And external pressures, including government regulation, increased international competition, and global economic instability, posed serious challenges to management's goal of achieving Union Carbide's full potential in growth and profitability as the corporation moved into the 1970s.

A New Management System

Accordingly, in 1971, top management launched a program to develop "a unified global management system placing greater emphasis on training key personnel to become professional managers." This program "to improve all elements of personnel and business management" had four principal objectives:[2]

Strengthen the assignment of individual responsibilities and accountabilities, with emphasis on performance standards and compensation commensurate with achievement in meeting goals.

Strengthen business management methods, with emphasis on long-range strategic planning, worldwide.

Allocate resources selectively to the corporation's better business opportunities.

Practice good corporate citizenship at home and abroad.

The resulting Union Carbide Management System (UCMS) represented a major shift in the way the corporation managed and evaluated its resources, both financial and managerial. One subsystem of UCMS, the Business System, addressed the development and implementation of budgetary, strategic, and operating plans, decisions and procedures, while another subsystem, the Performance Appraisal System, defined "the structure of the organization—the way jobs are designed, the authority, accountability, and role relationships, and the way progress toward goal attainment is evaluated."[3] As described in the 1976 Annual Report:

Basic to this subsystem is the establishment of a position charter through interac-

---

[1] *Everybody's Business, An Almanac: The Irreverent Guide to Corporate America* (San Francisco: Harper & Row, 1980), p. 610.

[2] Excerpted from Union Carbide Corporation Annual Report, 1974.

[3] From company publication, "Quick Reference Guide to the Performance Appraisal System," 1981.

tion between the employee and his or her manager, with the standards of performance and the results expected carefully defined. This is followed by regular review of actual performance relative to the charter, salary actions that align the individual's compensation with performance, and a personal development program that assists the individual in matching his or her career objectives with the needs of the corporation.

Under UCMS, several new management techniques and concepts were introduced: strategic planning units and an integrated long-range planning system; resource allocation based on competitive position, growth rate of markets, past and present financial performance, and consistency with corporate objectives; and formalized procedures (and a corporate department) for new business development. These were described in the 1974 Annual Report as "The New Fundamentals of Union Carbide"; in fact, UCMS was mentioned prominently in all annual reports from 1971 through 1976.

Accompanying these changes in management systems were several changes in management itself. In 1972, three men were appointed to the new position of executive vice president; each assumed responsibility for certain domestic businesses and one or more geographical areas outside the United States. Three years later, they switched jobs. In 1975, each was assigned responsibility for business lines and geographical areas different from those with which he had worked before. The Annual Report for 1976 explained, "This move was consistent with Union Carbide's policy of exposing its management personnel to a wide range of assignments—an important aspect of the corporation's personnel planning and development process." The same report announced the retirement of Chairman F. Perry Wilson; he was to be replaced by President William S. Sneath, who would in turn be succeeded by Executive Vice President Warren M. Anderson.

A New Strategic Direction

William Sneath seemed the ideal person to lead Union Carbide through the next decade. After receiving his MBA degree from Harvard Business School in 1950, Sneath went to work for Union Carbide, his father's employer. Twenty years later, at age 45 an executive vice president and Union Carbide's chief financial officer, Sneath was appointed president and chief operating officer. He worked closely with Chairman Wilson through the early 1970s and assumed full control of Union Carbide in 1977.

His leadership over the next five years reshaped the Union Carbide Corporation, symbolically represented by the headquarters relocation from New York City to rural grounds in Danbury, Connecticut. The new strategy focused on the *profitability* of Union Carbide's *core businesses.* Rather than seek growth in revenues, Sneath strove to increase profits; rather than make heavy cash investments in new high-growth prospects, Sneath chose first to support the company's fundamental businesses in plastics, industrial gases, lightweight carbon fibers, and batteries.[4]

The execution of this strategy: from 1977 to 1981 Union Carbide divested itself of about $1 billion in assets. It withdrew from 27 "infant businesses" and from 12 "established Carbide businesses" because of unacceptable returns. Among the newer ventures dropped were Indonesian shrimp fisheries and brain scanners. Chief among the established operations discontinued was the European plastics and chemicals unit with annual revenues of over $300 million, sold to its prime supplier, British Pe-

---

[4] *The Wall Street Journal,* May 4, 1982, p. 10, "Carbide Plans to Shed Business in Nuclear Arms."

troleum, for $200 million in cash and BP's assumption of about $200 million in Union Carbide debt.[5]

Naturally these business decisions had major impact on the Union Carbide organization, but the organization itself was also being consciously reshaped. Executive staff shrank by 1,000 managers through early retirements; two executive vice presidents retired and Sneath did not replace them. He disbanded the corporate New Business Development Group. And in staff offices throughout Union Carbide, he increased the awareness of the costs of administration.

In 1980's Annual Report, management introduced its review of operations with a single page, which read:

> Because of the diversity of its operations and its strengths in research and technology, Union Carbide has always been presented with a wealth of business opportunities. Management's focus during the past few years has been on selecting those businesses and business strategies which most clearly deserve support. Since 1977, we have been redeploying assets into a uniquely diversified portfolio of businesses which enjoy strong competitive positions and good prospects for either earnings growth or cash generation. While we may make some further adjustments, we believe our portfolio is now essentially where it should be. Our main task over the next several years will be to develop our businesses along the strategic lines we have laid out for them.

On January 1, 1982, William Sneath retired as chairman, serving from then on only as a director. The 1981 Annual Report recognized his many contributions in 31 years with the corporation, and especially noted his "wise leadership during an important period of transition in the corporation's business strategy." The same report brought disappointing news of operating results: with worldwide recession, a slump in the U.S. housing and automotive markets, and high interest rates, Union Carbide had had a difficult year just staying about even with 1980's results. Yet management was confident for its future. On a dark page before its Review of Operations, management had printed the following in white letters:

> After an intensive period of self-assessment, Union Carbide has focused its energies, its ingenuity, and its technical know-how on a group of core businesses in which the company enjoys special competitive advantages. We are putting technology to work in order to strengthen these businesses, a strategy that has proved its worth in the year just ended and one we believe will prove even more effective in the years to come.

Union Carbide Africa and Middle East

Union Carbide managed its international operations through seven area companies. The smallest of these, Union Carbide Africa and Middle East, Inc. (UCAME), was also the youngest; Union Carbide did not operate there until after World War II. In 1981 the UCAME organization included affiliates in Egypt, Ghana, the Ivory Coast, Kenya, Nigeria, Saudi Arabia, Sudan, and Dubai; it employed about 2,500 people and reported $124 million in sales. Although its sales were historically at about 1 percent of total company sales, UCAME's prospects for growth were excellent. Its major product line was batteries, and new battery plants had begun production in Egypt and Nigeria in 1980, in anticipation of battery market growth in that part of the world.

---

[5] *Forbes*, April 28, 1980, pp. 97 and 101, "Union Carbide's Well-Laid Plans."

UCAME's chairman and president was Boris Sokoloff, Jr. His career with Union Carbide spanned the evolution of the corporation's international business, from foreign departments to a division, to an international company, and then to area companies. Mr. Sokoloff had worked for Union Carbide–Eastern in Singapore and for UCAME in Athens—living overseas for almost 13 years—when he returned to corporate headquarters as vice chairman, Union Carbide–Eastern, in 1977. This was the job from which he was promoted to chairman of UCAME in 1979.

Reporting to the chairman were two staff functions—employee relations and finance and administration—and two area vice presidents. The staff and the chairman worked in Danbury, while the area vice presidents managed from Athens.

One of the area vice presidents, Mr. N. J. Moden, had responsibility for the Battery Products organization. This included all UCAME production facilities and the sales force for batteries. The other area vice president, Mr. J. P. Lykidis, had no responsibility for manufacturing at all; accordingly, his organization, Industrial Products, employed far fewer people than did Battery Products. All products sold under Mr. Lykidis's direction were sourced from other Carbide units. Reporting to him were two general managers, one each for Africa and for the Middle East, and product managers for each of Union Carbide's larger divisions: Linde, Carbon, Agricultural Products, Polyolefins, and Chemicals and Plastics.

Management Development Needs in UCAME

UCAME's major undertaking in 1981 to analyze its management training needs derived in part from problems in the field. The two plant start-ups in 1980 had problems management attributed to a lack of trained supervisors; a new sales force had been established in Dubai and needed instruction. These were two examples where "training" seemed the obvious solution to an obvious problem.

But Mr. Sokoloff and his director of employee relations, Richard McClurg, sensed that UCAME needed to do more than just address those two particular troubles. Corporate, technological, competitive, political, and employee pressures called for a more broad-based analysis and an overall plan for management development in UCAME.

Its international operations and workforce imposed special requirements on the organization's thinking about career development. UCAME managers were drawn from different countries and had disparate backgrounds, yet working for Union Carbide's purposes, they had to be able to "speak the same language of management." And due to the distance between local units and between Africa and Connecticut, it seemed especially difficult to achieve and sustain the identification with Union Carbide overall which effective coordination of local businesses required.

Local governments exerted pressure, and so did local nationals, for the replacement of expatriate managers with local nationals. At the same time, some reduction in the number of international assignees (IAs) might have been welcome news at headquarters; they were extremely expensive employees, and they were getting harder and harder to find. Dual-career marriages, unattractive locations, or lack of adventure, whatever the cause, young managers were noticeably reluctant to accept IA positions in Africa and the Middle East.

Within UCAME itself, Mr. Sokoloff had noticed for some time an increasing number

Employee needs

of employees requesting training or other developmental assignments. Through the UCMS system, employees were assured of an opportunity for formal discussion with supervisors about career development; more employees seemed to be taking this opportunity more seriously. Younger employees seemed concerned about "moving with the world" and fearing obsolescence, as Mr. Sokoloff put it, they were asking the company, "I want to improve myself. I want to do something for myself. Help me be a better manager." Other employees were interested in training in the United States largely for the status they believed that selection would confer.

There was yet another kind of request for training; it came from managers and salesmen who knew they needed help. The competitive atmosphere had changed dramatically in that part of the world; Union Carbide had instituted its new management system in part to respond to the new competitiveness in its markets. But for the employee caught between the changing market and the changing management system, career anxiety could be extreme. As Mr. Sokoloff explained:

Old mgrs new needs

Taking the example of Africa, traditionally there have been expatriates, French and English people, running very profitable little businesses in an extraordinarily relaxed and parochial manner. And suddenly appear on the scene Americans and Japanese and Germans, and all hell breaks loose. And so the individual suddenly finds out that just knowing somebody in Paris or having gone to the right school isn't enough. And so he will then tend to ask his management: Tell me more about certain things I should know.

The other side of the coin is that the corporate management techniques have been exposed to the same kind of pressures. Again, many years ago, I understand that one of our larger divisions, which accounted for around 50 percent of the business, had three salesmen, and most of the business was done once a year—a trip to Paris, or it so happened that heads of different industries might have been there at the same time and you'd sort of chat and say, "Incidentally, don't forget it, you know, about next year's requirement," or something like that. This is not the situation today.

Mgr goals

We expect more of our managers. We expect them to be much more alert and much better equipped in many different areas: in human relations skills, in management skills, in understanding financial statements, and coping with a whole series of things. And so then we felt over and over again, particularly at these performance reviews, that we perhaps had not done something for the employee.

In other words, with many of the old-timers we got into a situation of saying, "Look, you really are not doing your job according to today's requirements . . . you're just saying you've got sales from the top customers is not enough. We want to have a breakdown by product, with analysis of ROAs, ROIs, and ROEs." We'd say all of this . . . and then he'd say, "Well, why didn't you tell me before? You know I've been with the company for 28 years, and now you're telling me that I don't have the basic knowledge of managing or motivating, or whatever."

I think this is why we finally decided that we really have to have an organized program.

The catalyst for action came with a corporate request for job vacancy projections one, two, and three years out. As Mr. McClurg prepared these reports, he conferred with Mr. Stephen Wall, a colleague from Corporate Management Development. Then, reporting back to Mr. Sokoloff, he and the chairman decided to request help formally from Mr. Wall in addressing an issue they agreed was growing in importance. Mr. Sokoloff described his reasoning this way:

> It was the desire to ensure objectivity in our self-analysis and in our analysis of the needs of this organization. I think it's a general concern about being either too parochial, or too inner-oriented; or perhaps you have thousands of years of experience, having been around and whatnot, and you say "Maybe I know everything." But it's really worth the investment to have an outsider, a knowledgeable outsider, come in and tell us how he sees the situation.
>
> Many of us had actual information on how this could be handled, but I think all of us realized that the organization does change and what one person feels is the right way may not be the right way from the corporate standpoint . . . therefore, we went to a professional group and said, "Here's our problem. Help us. Help us develop a program."

A Formal Needs Analysis

Stephen Wall, the man to whom UCAME turned for help, was manager of the corporate Management Development Department. His organization was responsible for the corporate-wide maintenance of UCMS, for management and supervisory training, and for human resources management consultation. CMD staff provided consulting and training services to all domestic and international divisions of Union Carbide. Mr. Wall had worked at Union Carbide for seven years; in 1973 he came to the corporation from AT&T's Management Selection and Development Department, with two master's degrees in psychology.

From the first, Mr. Wall was aware of the problem as it was seen by UCAME top management. In several early discussions, Mr. Sokoloff and Mr. McClurg identified four critical concerns:

1. Need to enhance managerial skills of a number of individuals with a view toward . . . replacement from within.
2. Need to upgrade the skill levels of many supervisors.
3. Need to develop selling skills of salesmen to facilitate professional development.
4. Need for some development activities to facilitate the replacement of IAs with local nationals.

Such were the problems as UCAME saw them. But one benefit they sought from this consultation was the objective, but informed, opinion of an outsider, someone to check this understanding of the situation. Therefore, they felt strongly that, to provide real help, Mr. Wall had to go and see UCAME people and plants overseas.

And so after reading and studying UCAME's structure, history, financial controls, business plans, and performance, Mr. Wall went to Africa. He stayed in the field for 18 days, visiting plants and sales offices in Alexandria and Cairo in Egypt, in Dubai, in Nairobi and Nakuru in Kenya, and in the Sudan. In addition to conducting some 25 interviews, he also administered a standard, commercially available job analysis instrument/questionnaire ("PDQ") to supervisors, salesmen, and managers in these facilities, as well as to the area management in Athens. Specifically, information about position responsibilities, critical job skills, and current perceived training needs was gathered through observation, interviews, and the questionnaire. Employees were asked about their own jobs and then asked to describe others' jobs as well.

On returning to corporate headquarters, Mr. Wall tabulated and analyzed the reported information by computer. Sample results of this process are presented in Exhibits 4 and 5. Exhibit 4 shows the data provided by interviews for one location, describing frequent problems, skills and experience required, and perceived training needs for three positions. Exhibit 5 presents summary results of the position analysis for all positions in all locations across the nine dimensions measured by the PDQ.

Based on his field observations and his analysis of questionnaire and interview data, Mr. Wall concluded that there was a "need to improve the existing system used for managerial resource planning and development." His report to top management in UCAME in April 1981 stressed that need and recommended a series of meetings of management groups to address it. At the same time, his report also recommended specific training programs for certain groups to resolve immediate career issues.

These recommendations were presented as three interlocking action plans, one each for Battery Products and Industrial Products, and one for the UCAME organization overall. Both Battery and Industrial Products were advised to review UCMS; each area vice president was to meet with his direct reports and work to improve the effectiveness of UCMS. Then, with a clear understanding of UCMS, these direct reports would meet with their direct reports, and so on.

But for Industrial Products alone, Mr. Wall recommended training for salespeople. This training would be aimed at both the process of selling—"how the salesman conveys to the customer the basic features, advantages, and benefits of Union Carbide products"—and at "selling skills"—"effective influence and communication." Mr. Wall further suggested that such training be "customized" for UCAME use by Union Carbide's Personnel Development Laboratory (PDL) in Tarrytown. PDL had already prepared specialized sales training pro-

grams for Union Carbide Pan American and two other area companies. Two salespeople from Industrial Products would travel to PDL and help tailor the program to UCAME; these two would then return home and train the other salesmen.

For Battery Products only, Mr. Wall recommended supervisory training on both "the job of supervision" and on communication skills for problem solving; but he recommended a slightly different training program for each plant, as he understood its special requirements. For example, this describes the supervisory training recommended for one plant:

> the basic skills of the supervisors are quite good. However, supervisors in this plant need a better understanding of how their jobs mesh with the rest of the organization. Thus, a one-day UCMS overview for all supervisors in [this] plant is recommended. Several managers stated, "We need a program that familiarizes us with the Carbide System." This will be particularly helpful in assisting supervisors to clarify accountabilities and goals. Furthermore, it was found that supervisors in [this] plant have difficulty in solving problems on a face-to-face level with their subordinates—particularly because of the need to maintain the self-esteem of the worker. Therefore, training in face-to-face problem solving is recommended for this plant's supervisors.

And at the overall UCAME level, the recommendations focused on the steps necessary to install a system for managerial resource planning and development. Mr. Wall's model required information of two types: data about the individual (performance, promotability, and placement preferences), and data about the organization (jobs and skills requirements, succession plans tied to strategic plans, and identified candidates for development). As he described this overall system in his report, it would rely on the functioning of several "key personnel systems":

> Position duty analysis for determining skill requirements for selection, placement, succession and development planning.
> Establishment of objectives and standards . . . for assessment of performance and promotability.
> Manager-subordinate appraisal of performance for determining and identifying career interests and possibilities. In other words, the personnel subsystems of UCMS.

Accordingly, much of Mr. Wall's approach aimed at improving the effectiveness of UCMS, specifically its subsystem in performance appraisal, to get at the question of management planning for UCAME. His conception of the series of steps needed to reach that goal is presented in the timeline in Exhibit 6. The timetable projected management actions out through a top-management meeting to be held in January 1982.

Reviewing Progress to Date

In interviews conducted in July 1982, Messrs. Sokoloff, McClurg, and Wall discussed the progress of their efforts. They admitted to being about six months behind schedule; the meeting scheduled for January had actually been conducted in late June. The implementation problems were due largely to the logistics of arranging group meetings. As Mr. Sokoloff said,

> one may sit here and say we're going to have a meeting. . . . Let's go to Cairo, or let's go to Kuwait. Three weeks later somebody comes in and says, "Well, you know our employees with the Iranian passes will not be able to travel there . . ." and also the Ghanaians cannot get their exit visas and the Kenyans cannot get currency—and so many

things get postponed because of the complexity of operations.

But despite the scheduling problems, Mr. Wall pointed out that the steps he recommended were still being followed in sequence and results were beginning to be seen. At the management review session held that summer, all management personnel's performance appraisals and career plans were reviewed and discussed. When a sufficient number of managers were believed to share a common training need a program would be offered locally; a course in managerial finance and accounting was to be offered in Dubai, for example. When one or two managers shared a need for training, they could be sent to a course in Europe, or to the United States if necessary. But overall, it was important to recognize that only about one fifth of the individual development plan activities were actually "training" per se; Mr. Wall estimated that about 80 percent of these activities were temporary assignments, additional responsibilities, attendance at meetings or conferences, and the like.

The forum at which human resource planning took place "manager by manager, position by position" was a meeting of the operating committee of UCAME. In these sessions the chairman, the area vice presidents, and the staff directors (and, for the summer of 1982, Mr. Wall) reviewed performance data and individuals' career plans three levels down from the chairman. From these sessions the organization would maintain a continuing awareness of its management inventory and also generate the actual plans for training programs, given the needs identified in the session across UCAME. Mr. Wall felt strongly about the importance of those face-to-face discussions about people and jobs. He said,

Part of what makes these management development review sessions work well is all the various perspectives and information and history that Boris and each of his people bring to that table. And what goes on there is a very complex set of problem solving, and sharing of information, and then problem-solving activities. Testing each other's viewpoints and perspectives . . . both in terms of the business itself . . . and the perspective on people you know.

I've often been impressed with Boris reaching back and saying, "Seventeen years ago we said this about this guy" or "We made this promise to this fellow." And a lot of the glue that holds this stuff together, the cultural elements, is carried in people's heads . . . you can't model it.

Mr. Sokoloff and Mr. McClurg were certain that the work done by Mr. Wall had been helpful to them, and they believed that UCAME was on the right track in developing its managerial resource planning and development system. They admitted that evaluations of their efforts would not be easy to make, however. When asked how to appraise the success of a program like theirs, Mr. Sokoloff said:

Well, again I guess you get to the performance appraisals, and, of course, we have exit interviews and things of that sort, and if you try to keep an ear to the ground . . . there should be a general feeling among

managers that there is a system and it works.

And Mr. McClurg added:

You can add up the number of supervisors who have gone through supervisory training and say, good, we've gotten 85 percent of our people through, that's wonderful. But whether that has helped your production, whether it's made your labor relations situation better—you know, it's pretty hard to put them together.

If we have set a plan with a pretty high performer . . . this guy has been a salesman, so we want to put him into a situation where he's got to deal with production in order for him to advance, and then get him a little bit of accounting, a little bit of finance, send him through assignments . . . you get the playback from different people: the finance guy says, "Boy, this guy's a real dodo. This guy doesn't know anything about numbers." Well, then, our plan didn't work too well. On the other hand, if everything goes well, and the guy seems to go in and have the capability to do his new job, something's happened and the chances are that in that instance, you can say, "without those exposures he would not have done it as well."

But to ever have it down on a piece of paper which I can sign and give to Boris, and say "therefore the system works"—I don't think that will happen.

Exhibit 1   **Selected Financial Data** ($ millions, except per share figures)

	1981	1980	1979	1978	1977
From the income statement:					
Net sales	$10,168	$9,994	$9,177	$7,870	$7,036
Cost of sales	7,431	7,186	6,491	5,580	4,930
Research and development expense	207	166	161	156	156
Selling, administrative, and other expenses	1,221	1,152	1,053	943	860
Depreciation	386	326	470	417	359
Interest on long-term and short-term debt	171	153	161	159	149

Exhibit 1   (*concluded*)

	1981	1980	1979	1978	1977
Other income (expense)—net	164	41	(42)	12	13
Income before provision for income taxes	916	1,052	799	627	595
Provision for income taxes	258	360	251	205	179
Minority share of income	47	49	25	33	32
UCC share of income of companies carried at equity	38	30	33	5	1
Income before cumulative effect of change in accounting principle	649	673	556	394	385
Cumulative effect of change in accounting principle for ITC...	—	217	—	—	—
Net income..	649	890	556	394	385
Income per share before cumulative effect of change in accounting principle..............................	9.56	10.08	8.47	6.09	6.05
Cumulative effect per share of change in accounting principle for ITC...................................	—	3.28	—	—	—
Net income per share	9.56	13.36	8.47	6.09	6.05
Pro forma net income with 1980 change in accounting principle for ITC applied retroactively..................			573	448	431
Pro forma net income per share			8.73	6.92	6.78
From the balance sheet (at year-end):					
Working capital......................................	$ 2,147	$2,124	$2,070	$1,621	$1,645
Total assets..	10,423	9,659	8,803	7,866	7,423
Long-term debt.....................................	2,101	1,859	1,773	1,483	1,601
Total capitalization	8,018	7,282	6,317	5,794	5,603
UCC stockholders' equity............................	5,263	4,776	4,042	3,639	3,407
UCC stockholders' equity per share	76.74	70.90	61.06	55.92	52.79
Other data:					
Funds from operations	$ 1,172	$1,211	$1,114	$ 924	$ 877
Dividends..	224	206	190	181	178
Dividends per share.................................	3.30	3.10	2.90	2.80	2.80
Shares outstanding (thousands at year-end)	68,582	67,367	66,206	65,065	64,533
Market price per share—high	62⅛	52½	44½	43¼	62⅜
Market price per share—low..........................	45¼	35¼	34	33⅝	40
Capital expenditures	1,186	1,129	831	688	805
Number of employees (at year-end)	110,255	116,105	117,031	113,371	113,669
Selected financial ratios:					
Current ratio (at year-end)	2.2	2.2	2.2	2.0	2.2
Total debt/total capitalization (at year-end)	30.3%	29.9%	31.4%	32.3%	34.5%
Net income/sales....................................	6.4	6.7*	6.1	5.0	5.5
Net income/average UCC stockholders' equity	12.9	15.3*	14.5	11.2	11.9
Net income + minority share of income/average total capitalization	9.1	10.6*	9.6	7.5	7.8
Dividends/net income	34.5	30.6*	34.2	46.0	46.3
Dividends/funds from operations......................	19.1	17.0	17.1	19.6	20.3

* Net income excludes the non-recurring credit for the cumulative effect of the change in accounting principle for the investment tax credit. (See page 22.) Pro forma net income data are restated on a pro forma basis to reflect the change in accounting principle for the ITC. (See Note 2, "1980 Accounting Changes," on page 31.) Net income per share is based on weighted average number of shares outstanding during the year. Funds from operations include net income and non-cash charges (credits) to net income. (See Consolidated Statement of Changes in Financial Position.) Total debt consists of short-term debt, long-term debt, and current installments of long-term debt. Total capitalization consists of total debt plus minority stockholders' equity in consolidated subsidiaries and UCC stockholders' equity.

Exhibit 2   Operating Units

Union Carbide Corporation's business worldwide is conducted through the divisions and subsidiaries listed in boldface type below. Major affiliates owned by the Corporation as of March 1, 1982 which were actively producing during 1981, or which were scheduled as of March 1, 1982 to begin production during 1982, are listed beneath the division or subsidiary having management responsibility for them. Subsidiaries and affiliates are 100% owned by the Corporation unless otherwise indicated.

Agricultural Products Division
Union Carbide Agricultural Products Company, Inc.

Battery Products Division

Carbon Products Division

Coatings Materials Division

Electronics Division

Engineering and Hydrocarbons Division
Gulf Coast Olefins Company

Engineering Products Division

Linde Division

Ethylene Oxide Derivatives Division

Ethylene Oxide/Glycol Division

Films-Packaging Division

Home and Automotive Products Division

Medical Products Division

Metals Division

Nuclear Division
Operates facilities by the U.S. Government

Union Carbide Africa and Middle East, Inc.
EGYPT
Union Carbide Egypt S.A.E.—75%
GHANA
Union Carbide Ghana Limited—66.67%
IVORY COAST
Union Carbide Cote d'Ivoire
KENYA
Union Carbide Kenya Limited—65%
NIGERIA
Union Carbide Nigeria Limited—60%
SAUDI ARABIA
Carbide Hashim Industrial Gases Company—25%
SUDAN
Union Carbide Sudan Limited—84%

Union Carbide Canada Limited—74.72%

Union Carbide Eastern, Inc.
AUSTRALIA
Chemos Industries Pty. Limited—60.02%
Union Carbide Australia Limited—60.02%
HONG KONG
Sonca Industries Limited
Union Carbide Asia Limited
INDIA
Union Carbide India Limited—50.9%
INDONESIA
P. T. Agrocarb Indonesia—70.7%
P. T. Union Carbide Indonesia
JAPAN
Nippon Unicar Company Limited—50%
Union Showa K.K.—50%
Sony-Eveready, Inc.—50%
Union Carbide Services Eastern Limited
KOREA
Union Gas Company Limited—86.15%
MALAYSIA
Union Carbide Malaysia Sdn. Bhd.—80%
Union Polymers Sdn. Bhd.—60%
NEW ZEALAND
Union Carbide New Zealand Limited—60.02%

GERMANY (WEST)
Ucar Batterien G.m.b.H.
Union Carbide Deutschland G.m.b.H.
Union Carbide Industriegase G.m.b.H.
GREECE
Union Carbide Hellas Industrial and Commercial S.A.
ITALY
Elettrografite Meridionale S.p.A.
Uniliq S.p.A.
Union Carbide Italia S.p.A.
SPAIN
Argon, S.A.—50%
Union Carbide Iberica, S.A.
Union Carbide Navarra, S. A.
SWEDEN
Unifos Kemi AB—50%
Union Carbide Norden AB
SWITZERLAND
Union Carbide Europe S.A.
UNITED KINGDOM
Union Carbide U.K. Limited
Viskase Limited—50%

Union Carbide Pan America, Inc.
ARGENTINA
Union Carbide Argentina S.A.I.C.S.—99.99%
BRAZIL
Eletro Manganes Ltda.—55%
Tungstenio do Brasil Minerios e Metais Ltda.
S.A. White Martins—50.14%
S.A. White Martins Nordeste—50.14%
Union Carbide do Brasil Ltda.
COLOMBIA
Union Carbide Colombia, S.A.
COSTA RICA
Union Carbide Centro Americana, S.A.
ECUADOR
Union Carbide Ecuador C.A.
MEXICO
Union Carbide Mexicana, S.A. de C.V.—45.70%
VENEZUELA
Union Carbide de Venezuela, C.A.

Union Carbide Puerto Rico, Inc.
Union Carbide Caribe Inc.
Union Carbide Films—Packaging, Inc.
Union Carbide Grafito, Inc.

Exhibit 2   (*concluded*)

Polyolefins Division	PHILIPPINES	**Union Carbide Southern Africa,**
	Union Carbide Philippines, Inc.	**Inc.**
Silicones and Urethane	REPUBLIC OF SRI LANKA	REPUBLIC OF SOUTH AFRICA
Intermediates Division	*Union Carbide Ceylon Limited—60%*	*Elektrode Maatskappy Van Suid Afrika*
	SINGAPORE	*(Eiendoms) Beperk—50%*
Solvents and Intermediates	*Metals and Ores Pte. Limited*	*Tubatse Ferrochrome (Proprietary)*
Division	*Union Carbide Singapore Pte. Limited*	*Limited—49%*
	THAILAND	*Ucar Chrome Company (S.A.)*
Specialty Chemicals	*Union Carbide Thailand Limited*	*(Proprietary) Limited*
and Plastics Division		*Ucar Minerals Corporation*
	Union Carbide Europe, Inc.	ZIMBABWE
	BELGIUM	Unconsolidated subsidiaries
	Union Carbide Benelux N.V.	*Zimbabwe Mining and Smelting*
	Indugas, N.V.—50%	*Company (Private) Limited*
	FRANCE	*Union Carbide Zimbabwe (Private)*
	La Littorale S.A.—99.95%	*Limited*
	Union Carbide France S.A.	
	Viscora, S.A.—50%	

Exhibit 3   Union Carbide Financial Data by Geographical Area

	1981	1980	1979	1978	1977
Africa and Middle East:					
Sales*	124	126	105	85	75
Operating profit	5	17	13	10	9
Identifiable assets	155	164	124	107	90
Canada:					
Sales	671	609	531	426	366
Operating profit	41	89	74	30	58
Identifiable assets	722	690	615	566	520
Europe:					
Sales	925	1,060	959	1,011	929
Operating profit	83	100	108	67	15
Identifiable assets	831	922	833	726	1,096
Far East:					
Sales	755	709	597	478	406
Operating profit	80	95	82	60	45
Identifiable assets	604	518	459	372	271
Latin America:					
Sales	714	645	590	534	471
Operating profit	116	122	41	75	84
Identifiable assets	678	588	486	471	385

Exhibit 3 (*concluded*)

	1981	1980	1979	1978	1977
United States and Puerto Rico:					
Sales	6,979	6,845	6,395	5,336	4,789
Operating profit	852	869	754	626	619
Identifiable assets	7,115	6,542	5,884	5,344	4,770
All International operations:					
Sales	3,189	3,149	2,782	2,534	2,247
Operating profit	325	423	318	242	211
Identifiable assets	2,990	2,882	2,517	2,242	2,362
Total UCC Consolidated:					
Sales	10,168	9,994	9,177	7,870	7,036
Operating profit	1,177	1,292	1,072	868	830
Identifiable assets†	9,904	9,180	8,196	7,408	6,964

* All figures represent millions of dollars.
† Totals do not add, due to intersegment eliminations.
N.B.: Data reported for "Africa and Middle East" include financial results of Union Carbide Southern Africa, Inc., *not* under UCAME management. As such, this information cannot be interpreted to represent UCAME performance, but is presented only for purposes of comparison to other geographical area results.

Exhibit 4   Interview Results Analysis

Position	Described by	Frequent Problems	Skills/Experience Required	Training Needs
Salesman	General manager	Operating through agents Many markets to sell in	Selling Planning	Selling
Salesman	Resident mgr. (Industrial Products)	Lack of career planning Selling Coverage and service Measures of performance	Technical knowledge Selling skills Negotiating	Selling skills Product knowledge
Treasurer	Treasurer	Need a strong financial team Keep overhead low Training Finance Pricing	Aware of corporate policy Culture Arab-speaking	Financial Supervisory
Salesman	Salesman	Planning Control	Organizing Selling	Selling
Marketing manager	Marketing manager	Time differences Many distributors Scheduling	Problem solving Planning	Performance review Selling skills

Exhibit 5 PDQ Score by Position, Function, and Country*

	Strategic Planning	Product and Services	Controlling	Monitoring Business Indicators	Supervising	Coordinating	Customer Relations Marketing	External Contacts	Consulting	Level	Function	Title
Greece (Athens):												
1	1.40	.80	3.29	3.57	3.00	1.57	1.13	2.21	.80	Officer	B & C	Mg. director
2	0.00	0.00	1.14	0.00	3.14	3.14	0.00	1.00	2.40	MSE	B & C	ER manager
3	.80	1.20	2.57	1.14	3.00	2.43	0.00	1.00	3.00	M of M	AF/B & C	Mg. fin./adm.
4	.60	1.20	2.14	3.29	3.29	1.57	2.50	.14	0.00	M of M	B & C	Prod. dir.
5	1.00	2.60	1.43	2.86	4.00	4.00	2.50	.57	3.90	M of M	AF	Mgr. Poly.
6	2.00	3.00	2.00	2.86	3.71	3.71	2.88	1.29	3.20	M of M	B & C	Prod. dir.
7	1.60	2.00	2.57	3.29	2.86	1.14	3.13	.79	1.60	M of M	S & M	Gen. mgr.
8	2.60	3.00	3.86	3.14	3.71	3.43	3.13	1.50	3.80	Officer	B & C	GM UCMEL
9	2.40	0.00	3.43	1.17	3.14	2.71	.50	.71	3.60	M of M	Af	Mgr. fin./adm.
10	0.00	0.00	2.71	2.86	3.43	2.57	2.00	.07	0.00	M of M	B & C	Gen. manager
Kenya:												
1	.80	2.80	2.14	3.00	2.57	2.29	3.75	1.71	2.60	MSE	S & M	Mgr. ind/chem
2	.60	0.00	1.57	.29	2.00	4.00	0.00	2.43	3.20	Officer	AD & GEN	Mgr. ind/rel.
3	2.60	3.60	3.71	3.57	4.00	3.29	2.50	2.36	3.60	M of M	S & M	Mgr. mktg.
4	1.80	1.40	3.14	3.71	2.57	1.00	1.13	1.00	1.80	Officer	B & C	Director
5	2.40	1.60	3.29	3.86	4.00	3.29	.25	1.07	3.60	MSE	AF	Treasurer
Sudan:												
1	.20	.40	3.29	0.00	2.43	1.57	0.00	.21	1.60	MSE	AD & GEN	Plt. manager
2	2.20	1.60	2.71	4.00	2.71	2.00	.25	2.29		Officer	B & C	Director
3	1.00	.20	3.29	.57	3.00	.71	0.00	.54	1.20	M of M	S & M	Plt. manager
4	0.00	0.00	3.43	1.43	3.86	2.29	1.25	1.50	2.20	MSE	ACC/FIN	Treasurer
Egypt:												
1	2.00	3.00	4.00	1.71	2.86	2.43	1.63	.64	1.60	M of M	S & M	Director
2	0.00	0.00	0.00	0.00	2.43	2.29	0.00	0.00	0.00	MSE	Prod.	QC manager
3	0.00	0.00	3.00	0.00	3.43	2.71	0.00	.21	1.20	MSE	Tech.	Engineer
4	0.00	1.60	.50	0.00	0.00	4.00	0.00	.36	1.40	MSE	AMG	ER manager
Dubai												
1	2.60	3.00	3.00	4.00	3.00	2.43	2.63	2.00	2.20	MSE	S & M	Branch mgr.

* Key:

0– .99   not a part of the positions
1.00–1.99   a minor part of the positions
2.00–2.99   a moderate part of the positions
3.00–3.99   a substantial part of the positions
4.00–4.99   a crucial and most significant part of the positions

Exhibit 6 Potential UCAME Timelines 1981–1982

	June 1	July 30	August 15	September	October	November	Early 1982
UCAME proper and admin.	Area VPs and chairman meet individually with CMD consultant • Establish MRP* for UCAME	VPs meet with area chairman • Develop UCAME plan and policies for MRP • Monitor 81–82—Plan for training and development of managers					VPs meet with CMD consultant (Jan. 1982) • Specifics of a Human Resource Development System finalized • Review 81–82 MRP plan • Review personnel
Industrial products		Area VP meets with product directors and general managers • UCMS overview • Discuss management resources planning issues • Enhance "Lateral" coordination and decision making	Sales trainer (Training) • For selling performance	General managers meet with resident managers • UCMS overview • Discuss results of previous meeting and establish plans	Salesmen in field trained • Selling skill development		

Battery
products

Area VP meets with general managers and managing director	Subordinate managers meet individually with their general manager or managing director	Pro 1s meet individually with their subordinates	Supervisors training (train by plant)	"Country Company" managers meet with their staff
• UCMS overview • Management resource Planning issues • Plan for system application	• UCMS overview • Position charters and MOP review • U&A confirmed • Specify supervisory training needs by plant	• Establish position charter and MOPs • Communicate plans	• Supervisory orientation • Communication skills for problem solving	• UCMS overview • Delineate areas of accountability • Monitor MRP plan and progress

* Management Resource Planning & Development (MRP).

CASE 12
RAWSON COMPANY, INC.
Pamela A. Posey and
Jeffrey A. Sonnenfeld

David Parker, director of Management Education Programs at Rawson Company, Inc., was concerned about the management development issues his company must consider as it faced new demands generated by continued internal growth and growing external pressures. Increasing diversification and internalization of the company placed heavy demands on an already overburdened development staff. And external demographic and regulatory changes emphasized the need to train managers to be responsive to the impact of external events on the company.

Founded in 1925, Rawson had expanded rapidly to become a major industrial force in the international marketplace. Strong financial growth had been accompanied by expansion of the workforce to a record high of 200,000 employees worldwide in 1980. Two thirds were employed domestically, and one quarter of the workforce was considered professional (supervisory level or above). Traditional centralized management systems had given way to a decentralized operating mode in the postwar era: the sheer size of the company demanded the more flexible and responsive management system gained through decentralization.

Management Education Programs: Operations

The concept of management development as an integral function of effective op-

erations was a guiding principle at Rawson, where commitment to professional management was well known: education was one of a number of methods utilized for professional development. Corporate goals for education were tied to the corporate policy of developing managerial talent internally and the desire to broaden and strengthen the available management talent pool. It was estimated that 8 percent of the total workforce was involved in management education programs in 1980 at a cost of nearly $6 million.

The educational experience was designed to enhance the functional skill knowledge needed for continued operational success. Prior to 1970, education programs were available at headquarters only for top-level managers: division managers were trained within their own units. In the 1970s, however, it became apparent that central programs would be useful for division personnel, and courses were developed for them at the headquarters level. By 1980, education programs were available from three sources: (1) offerings at the division level designed there to meet unique unit needs, (2) offerings from outside agencies such as universities and consulting firms, and (3) offerings from corporate headquarters education staff.

The cost of education was a direct expense to the operating divisions based on use, which forced operating managers to evaluate its potential merit relative to other methods of development. Because of this cost structure, managers could not be required to offer education to their professional employees. Even so, support for educational activities remained strong, and education became an important vehicle for accelerating professional and management career development.

Demand for Education Programs

Educational programs were discretionary at Rawson for employees as well as the operating divisions, but the corporate culture appeared to value internal corporate development programs. Course progress was tracked on page 1 of the employee evaluation forms, although there were no direct inducements for participation. There were, however, corporate regulations concerning selection procedures for education. At the executive education level, headquarters made the decision about which managers received internal versus external training. Below the division general manager level, the unit retained the authority to select internal or external programs for lower-level managers. Corporate policy dictated that middle managers at division level were not to be trained outside the company: their needs were viewed as too company-specific for external programs to be of value.

Because of the diversity of training and development needs, it was difficult to retain an internal staff capable of handling the entire training workload, yet Rawson had continued its policy of maintaining an internal faculty core. The company demanded educational activities designed to teach skills central to its operations. Circumstances and issues grounded in the company's operating methods and culture were addressed in educational programs; internal professional faculty were more conversant with organizationally based methods of approaching these issues.

The desire for an internal faculty core posed a problem for individual development within the company. There were only three job levels within the education section, and once a faculty member reached the top level there was no further option for promotion. They had no functional experience with Rawson and found it difficult to make lateral moves into operating areas. Corporate policy dictated that an individual did not move into operations without direct company functional experience, and this experience was usually gained early in the career before the person became eligible for promotion to a management position. This situation raised serious questions for an organization committed to advancing its professional employees.

In addition, the expanding size of the workforce and the desire at the executive education level for nationally recognized expertise and fresh perspectives from outside the company generated pressure to increase use of outside faculty and programs. The demands on management education programs at Rawson were greater than ever before.

David Parker defined his problem as essentially a make-or-buy decision, and was considering several alternatives which had been suggested to him. First, he could increase the in-house faculty from its current core size of 18 to a level which could deal more effectively with the demand. Yet, this would do little to alleviate the career development problems already faced by the faculty and the company. Second, on-leave faculty from academic institutions could be hired for short-term (one-year) contract periods; they could be rotated in and out of the company on a regular basis. While this would meet some of the staffing needs, it could create difficulties with continuity of courses, staff turnover, and lack of company-specific knowledge in the teaching corps. Third, Rawson could contract out educational needs as packages, dealing on an institution-to-institution basis and reducing the cost spread associated with individual faculty to institution negotiation. Again, however, company-specific information would be lacking.

The situation was becoming critical, and any changes would take time to implement. A means of meeting the increased demand for educational services at Rawson would have to be found.

CASE 13
A UNIVERSITY-EMPLOYER COLLABORATION: THE UNIVERSITY OF PENNSYLVANIA AND INA*
Frederic Jacobs and James Honan

Ed Gallagher, director of Management Development at INA, arrived in his office somewhat earlier than usual. He wanted to review his notes and files so that the meeting could move efficiently from a discussion of current operations to issues of long-range planning. The purpose of the meeting was to review the second year of operation of the collaboration between INA and the University of Pennsylvania's College of General Studies. Along with several INA colleagues, Gallagher would be meeting with Polly Jenning, vice-dean at CGS, Alyce Mead, the program coordinator, and others from Penn.

Gallagher was convinced of two things as he envisioned the meeting: first, the operations to date had been smoothly and effectively administered; and, second, the program was too new and too small to be able to make any broad generalizations. Thus, he felt inclined toward continuing the collaboration. Indeed, the "press" was good within INA and throughout the business community, and there were no "storm clouds" on the horizon. But, Gallagher believed that broader policy issues for the future needed to be addressed. He felt some frustration because, of the

* Author's note: The writing of this case was funded by the Office of Adult Learning Services at the College Entrance Examination Board.

literally hundreds of requests for information he had received, almost all of the them dealt with questions of "start up" and "implementation." "How did you do it?" was the most frequent question he was asked to answer.

As he heard the knock on his door indicating that the others were ready to begin, he was determined to focus this meeting on the important, but frequently overlooked, policy issues for the future.

Background

Polly Jenning, vice dean of the College of General Studies (CGS) at the University of Pennsylvania, is responsible for maintaining and expanding services to nontraditional students by designing and implementing programs for CGS consistent with the university's overall mission. Over a period of years, she instituted several noncredit outreach courses, including one for senior citizens.

The idea for a university-employer collaborative program evolved as Jenning became aware of the financial barriers and burdens described by various CGS students and potential students. In her work in CGS, Jenning had had little previous experience or contact with corporations; talking with students and potential students, however, she realized that tuition benefits from employers were a common means by which working adults financed their studies. As she described it: "I was seeing *some* students eligible for tuition reimbursement from their employers, but why wasn't I seeing many more such students? What was keeping them from coming?" She continued to wonder how effectively tuition benefit programs were utilized, and decided to seek advice from the National Institute for Work and Learning (NIWL). NIWL had conducted several studies on the use of employee tuition benefit programs.

Those studies identified two significant barriers which appear to prevent more widespread utilization of employee tuition benefit programs: (1) a relatively small proportion of employees know about tuition benefit programs for which they are eligible, and (2) a significant number of eligible employees would not attend college courses unless they are readily accessible.

With the barriers identified in the NIWL studies in mind, Jenning reflected on the role that Penn's College of General Studies could play in addressing the problem. Jenning and her colleagues at Penn concluded that a jointly sponsored program offered *on-site* at neighboring corporations would both help to alleviate the barriers to participation and would be consistent with CGS's mission. She contacted the Philadelphia Chamber of Commerce to request information about the city's major employers. As a result of the information she obtained from NIWL, her own observations and data from the chamber of commerce, she conceived the idea for a collaborative program with a corporation in the Philadelphia area with a large group of potential program participants. Jenning believed that Penn's College of General Studies was in a unique position to be the educational partner in a university-employer collaboration.

Founded in 1740 by Benjamin Franklin, the University of Pennsylvania is a prestigious ivy-league institution located several miles from "Center City," Philadelphia's downtown business district. The University's College of General Studies was established in 1894 as the "Liberal Arts division for students who wish to continue their education primarily in the evening on a full-time or part-time basis." Courses in all fields of the arts and sciences are offered for credit, and are taught by members of the University of Pennsylvania faculty. Unlike most continuing education divisions at other universities, CGS offers courses and grants degrees that are equivalent to those in the undergraduate day school. Although CGS serves nontraditional students of all ages, its primary focus is on working adults in the 20 to 35 age group. In 1975, CGS was incorporated into the university's Faculty of Arts and Sciences. Penn is widely regarded as the city's most well-respected educational institution, and many of the city's most influential leaders are Penn graduates.

Jenning's interest began to focus on a single corporation: INA. With more than 4,000 employees in Center City, INA appeared to be an ideal potential partner since it offered its employees an extensive tuition benefits package, and about 30 percent of its workforce had little or no college background. INA Corporation is one of the nation's largest financial services organizations, with worldwide operations in property-casualty insurance, life insurance, employee benefits, health care, and investment management. The company ranks eighth in *Fortune*'s listing of diversified companies in the United States and has one of the largest workforces in the Philadelphia metropolitan area.

Moreover, INA has long been committed to training and development programs for its employees. It was one of the first companies to establish a formal training program for new employees, and offers an extensive array of training programs for upper-level managers. In 1980, INA opened a $17 million training facility and conference center in nearby Montgomery County.

Bernard Gold, chairman and chief executive officer of INA since 1975, is a strong believer in liberal education. Gold wrote: "Education in the liberal arts plays an important role in developing managers. It provides a vital perspective on the interrelationship and growing complexity of business and society."

Jenning took the initiative and wrote directly to Gold. She was unaware at the time that he was a member of Penn's board of trustees. Gold referred her to William Jackson, INA's vice president for operations. In May 1980, Jenning met with Jackson and Tom Walsh, the company's vice president for human resources, and proposed offering a liberal arts degree program to INA employees at its downtown headquarters. Jackson and Walsh were both enthusiastic and approved the idea that day. Walsh was particularly supportive of the program's liberal arts focus: "A liberal arts degree develops critical skills and gives a better perspective on work," he said.

Another participant in the preliminary planning meetings pointed out that an insurance/financial services company is well suited to a collaborative effort in the liberal arts. He said: "We don't manufacture products or machines. . . . It's very *people* intensive, and this kind of program is consistent with the emphasis at INA on training and developing people."

Thus, in the spring of 1980, after a series of meetings between INA administrators and Jenning, a joint decision to create the University of Pennsylvania/INA Division was announced. Beginning in the fall of 1981, Penn would offer courses in the humanities, social sciences, and natural sciences *on-site* at INA headquarters. Participants could earn either an associate or bachelor of arts degree; the degrees would be the same as those offered for on-campus study at CGS.

In retrospect, Jenning was surprised by the enthusiasm and by the minimal "bureaucratic hassles." "I always pictured big corporations as being hard to deal with," she said, "but everyone seemed eager to get going once a decision was made."

The Initial Agreement and the First Year

The agreement creating the Penn/INA joint degree program called for courses to be taught by Penn faculty four days a week in classrooms at INA's downtown headquarters. The academic calendar for the program consists of two 14-week semesters (fall and spring) and one 12-week summer session. Several (4–6) courses per semester would be offered with each meeting one day per week. Degree requirements and academic regulations for the INA program are the same as those for Penn's on-campus programs. The program was designed so that an employee could earn a bachelor's degree in liberal arts in five and a half years.

The program is administered by a coordinator who reports to Jenning at Penn and Walsh at INA. In addition to serving as administrator for the program, the coordinator serves as an advisor to students, handling such matters as admissions procedures, course registration, and textbook sales. The coordinator's work day is generally split between Penn and INA, although this varies depending on program needs.

According to the terms of the joint agreement, INA assumed costs for tuition, half of a program coordinator's salary, plus other miscellaneous administrative and support items (see Exhibit 1). Penn assumed costs for faculty salaries, the remaining half of the program coordinator's salary, and some miscellaneous administrative expenses. Instead of *reimbursing* students for tuition, INA paid the full tuition for each participant directly to the university; students paid only a $15 application fee, and the cost of textbooks. Prior to the joint program with Penn, INA offered its employees a relatively traditional tuition reimbursement package, for job-related courses, reimbursing the employee for 50 percent tuition upon enroll-

Exhibit 1   **Costs to INA** (Academic year 1981–1982; fall, spring, summer semesters)

Tuition:

(75–125 course units	Fall 1981	$ 37,540.00
per semester)	Spring 1982	34,490.00
	Summer 1982	21,900.00
Total tuition charges		93,930.00

Administrative and other support costs:

Coordinator's salary (½)	8,000.00
Benefits	1,896.00
Support salary	2,500.00
Benefits	112.00
Communications	775.00
(mailings, duplication, etc.)	
Faculty travel stipends	5,100.00
(17 × $300)	
Curriculum development	1,500.00
Tutorial support and special workshops	3,100.00
Total administrative and other costs	22,883.00
Total cost to INA	$116,813.00

University of Pennsylvania assumes cost of faculty salaries, remaining half of coordinator's salary, plus other miscellaneous administrative expenses.

For 1982–83, INA has agreed to begin building a program library, including copies of all required texts. The expense is expected to be several hundred dollars per semester; however, curriculum development and special workshop fees were one-time start-up expenditures. Hence the 1982–83 budget estimate is $115,000.00, despite a rise in tuition fees, and the expectation is that program cost in future years will remain in the $115,000–$130,000 range. Programs in other corporations with approximately the same number of students (100–125) might reasonably be expected to incur similar costs.

ment and for the remaining 50 percent upon successful course completion (a grade of C or better for course-work, and a grade of B or better for graduate). In 1980–81, the year prior to the establishment of the Penn/INA Division, approximately 3,000 INA employees utilized these benefits annually; this benefit continued to be available to all INA employees even after the Penn/INA program was instituted.

Once the logistical and organizational aspects of the program were finalized, INA and Penn made an effort to publicize the program broadly. Program publicity focused on such slogans as:

"WHY NOT COMMUTE TO COLLEGE BY ELEVATOR? EARN A B.A. AT INA."

INA informed employees of the newly created degree program by enclosing information in every paycheck (see Exhibit 2). In addition, a series of briefing sessions led by Jenning and Walsh were held to further publicize the program. Approximately 800 INA employees attended one of 16 meetings where they were informed of application procedures, degree requirements, and course offerings.

Two hundred and forty INA employees applied for admission to the program for

---

Exhibit 2

UNIVERSITY OF PENNSYLVANIA AT INA
Take the Elevator to the Ivy League
Earn a Penn Degree Where You Work

What is it?

A liberal arts, A.A. or B.A., degree program taught by University of Pennsylvania faculty in classrooms on the 11th floor of the INA Tower building. Classes meet once a week, from 4:30 to 7:10, for two 14-week (fall and spring) and one 12-week (summer) session. Courses offered range from English Composition to Economics, from Sociology to the History of Philosophy—a complete selection of liberal arts courses leading to a degree with a major in social science. Students accepted into the program may also take courses on Penn's campus if they choose to, and they have all the rights and privileges of regular Penn students.

How do I get in?

Interested employees may contact the Penn/INA Coordinator, 11 Tower, 241-2638, for an application form and an interview. Applicants must submit transcripts from high school and any college previously attended. Admissions decisions are based on grades and test scores, with consideration given to relevant work and life experience.

How much does it cost?

Nothing to you, except the $15 application fee. INA pays all tuition bills, up front. You do have to buy your own books, however, and these are sold at the beginning of each semester on 11 Tower.

But I never expected to go to college. I'm scared. Can I really do it while working full time and maintaining my family and personal life?

College classes *are* difficult, and the decision to go to Penn is a serious one; attending college requires time, energy, and discipline. But many INA employees have found the process to be especially rewarding—and, even though they had never planned to go to college, they are now committed and enthusiastic students. Because the program is small, students receive a great deal of personal attention, and the coordinator is always available for counselling and referrals—to ease the transition to college and to make the experience a positive one. Call for further information or to arrange an appointment to talk about your educational plans.

Fall 1981. Each applicant was interviewed by Jenning or another CGS representative; all admissions decisions were made by the University. One hundred and one students were admitted; an additional 45 employees were given a "deferred" status and were encouraged to attend a university-sponsored English workshop or another college. Twenty of a total of 28 students who enrolled in the workshop were admitted to the degree program for the following semester. When classes actually began in the fall, 80 INA employees enrolled in the program. A large majority of the students were clerical/secretarial employees; approximately 80 percent were women.

In May 1982, at the end of the program's first year of operation, Jenning hired Lucy Roth, an educational consultant, to conduct an evaluation of the Penn/INA Division (see Exhibit 3). The evaluation revealed that overall, both INA and Penn were generally satisfied with the program's initial year. Alyce Mead, the program coordinator, expressed her satisfaction with the partnership, stating: "INA's financial and programmatic commitment to this B.A. program is an indication of their belief in the value of nonbusiness education and development. Our partnership is thus a very special one, and is exciting for all of us involved."

INA employees cited the possibility for career development and promotion and life enhancement as two major motivating factors for participating in the Penn/INA program. Although INA officials caution that there is no "guarantee" of career mobility for those who participate in the program, they point out that enrollment in the program "doesn't hurt" one's chances for promotion.

The "life enhancement" benefits of program participation are more easily examined. Mead points out that the Penn/INA program is "totally changing the lives of

**Evaluation of the Penn/INA Program—First Year
Methodology**

The evaluation was conducted between May 24 and June 22, 1982. Interviews were held at INA with 18 students, 9 of their bosses, and 3 executives who were involved in initiating the program. Telephone interviews were conducted with 5 faculty members and the administrator. Students and faculty members who were interviewed were selected by the administrator to represent a broad range of opinions and attitudes toward the program. All interviewees were assured anonymity, except for the program administrator.

Responses from each category of interviewees (students, faculty, bosses, executives, administrator) are reported separately in the five sections which follow. Summaries:
1. Penn/INA students.
2. Penn/INA faculty.
3. Program administrator.
4. Students' supervisors/managers.
5. Top management of INA.

Penn/INA Students

Eighteen students were asked to respond to 25 questions about their decision to enroll in the program, their instructors, the choice of courses, advising and counseling, administrative procedures, and the relationship between school and work. Students cited the desire to go to college, the convenient schedule and location of the program, and fully prepaid tuition rather than reimbursement as major reasons for deciding to enroll in the program. Approximately half of the students interviewed indicated that their greatest concern when they began the program was that they were fearful of their ability to handle the academic requirements. Most students reported that their initial fears disappeared after the courses began and that no new fears have been generated.

some people." One student highlighted the personal benefits from being enrolled: "I believe that program is a marvelous opportunity for me. I have been in the program from the outset, and I feel we are a unique, elite group at INA. The liberal arts course is not the thing in education today. However, I'm in it for the sake of learning and the enrichment it offers. I am the envy of most of my friends—they are absolutely amazed."

The Second Year and Beyond

In June 1982, Tom Walsh, who had worked with the program in the planning stages and during its first year of operation, was promoted to be vice president for human resource planning and development for CIGNA Corporation, the "parent" company emerging from the January 1982 merger between INA and Connecticut General. Although the merger itself did not result in any major changes in the Penn/INA program, Walsh's promotion did. Responsibility for the program shifted to Ed Gallagher, INA's director of management development.

Under Gallagher's supervision, the second year proceeded with few changes from the first. Enrollments remained constant (Exhibits 4 and 5 show the enrollment history). Gallagher was interested in a more detailed and comprehensive program evaluation; he hoped to identify possible correlations between participation in the program and job performance. Also, he was interested in examining the effect of the program on job satisfaction, and on the degree to which the program affected employee turnover rates (which were typically high for secretarial/clerical employees in the insurance industry). INA officials believed that it would take several years to establish a sufficient data base for such an examination.

In addition to wanting a more detailed "impact study" and program evaluation, Gallagher and his colleagues wanted to examine the Penn program in the context of two other initiatives now under consideration. First, plans were being formulated for an in-house Career Development Center; the center would assist all INA employees, including participants in the Penn/INA program, in discussing and assessing opportunities for career advance-

Exhibit 4   Enrollments in Penn/INA Program

	Fall 1981		Spring 1982		Summer 1982		Fall 1982		Spring 1983	
	People	C.U.'s	People	C.U.'s	People	C.U.'s	People	C.U.'s	People	C.U.'s
Semester student entered program:										
Fall 1981	78	100	54	75	37	41	39	48	39	48
Spring 1982			21	27	11	11	16	18	17	20
Summer 1982					2	2	1	1	1	1
Fall 1982							12	16	10	16
Spring 1983									4	4
Total	78	100	75	102	50	54	68	83	71	89

Exhibit 5   Semesters and C.U.'s Completed

	Semester Entered		Number of Students			
	Fall 1981	Spring 1982	Summer 1982	Fall 1982	Spring 1983	Totals
No. of semesters attended:						
1	16	2	1	2	4	25
2	15	1		10		26
3	12	11	1			24
4	11	7				18
5	24					24
Total no. of C.U.'s carried:						
1	14	1	1	1	4	21
2	12	2		5		19
3	12	9	1	3		25
4	10	5		3		18
5	10	2				12
6	8	1				9
7	5					5
8	1	1				2
9	4					4
10	1					1
11	1					1
Totals	312	76	4	32	4	428

ment and promotion within the company. Potentially, the center could help balance the raised expectations resulting from participation in the program with the realities for mobility within INA. Second, some people with INA wanted to expand the Penn model to company offices in other cities. In fact, Tom Walsh had met with administrators and faculty members from Delaware Community College to discuss that possibility. Unfortunately, there was insufficient support from college officials, and negotiations stopped.

After two years of operation, courses had been offered in a variety of areas, taught by some of Penn's most respected and effective faculty. (Exhibit 6 summarizes the course offerings.)

Exhibit 6   Course Offerings, Fall 1981–Spring 1983

Courses offered include introductory courses appropriate for beginning students as well as more advanced courses to meet the needs of students with several years of college experience. Courses meet university distributional requirements and requirements for the social science major, an interdepartmental, broad-based curriculum including economics, political science, history, anthropology, sociology, and American civilization. All classes, except foreign language courses, meet once a week, 4:30–7:10, in the main headquarters of INA. Language classes meet twice weekly, 4:30 to 6:30. Approximately six courses are offered each semester.

College preparatory workshops:

English	(2 sections)
Math	(1 section)

Freshman seminars:

English 1—Craft of Prose	(4 sections)
English 6—Short Fiction	(2 sections)
English 8—Drama	(2 sections)
English 9—Literature and Human Values:	(2 sections)
"The Possibilities of Female Heroism,"	
"The American Dream"	

Foreign languages:
French 1, 2, and 3
Spanish 1, 2, and 3

Humanities:
English 84—Major American Writers since 1900
Philosophy 1—Introduction to Philosophy

Social sciences:
Sociology 1—Introduction to Sociology
History 15b—Europe, 1789–present
History 20b—History of American Democracy, 1860–present
American Civilization 229—American Popular Culture
Economics 1a and 1b—Introductory Economics (Micro and Macro)

Natural sciences:
Psychology 1—Introduction to Experimental Psychology
Anthropology 3—Physical Anthropology

Faculty members have included some of the University of Pennsylvania's most distinguished teachers and scholars from all rank levels: graduate student lecturer to full professor and department chair. Many have been winners of university teaching awards; all have demonstrated a commitment to, and competence in, the instruction of nontraditional students.

Issues for the Future

Generally, INA is optimistic about the future of the Penn/INA collaboration. As Tom Walsh points out: the program "positions the company as a leader in employee education and development." INA Chairman Bernard Gold echoes those sentiments. He sees special benefits of a collaboration which emphasizes the liberal arts. He said:

> As a multinational company doing business in 145 countries around the globe, INA recognizes the need to understand not only our own business, but also the diverse and complex social, political, economic, and cultural environments we work in. It is no longer enough for managers to be well trained; they must be well educated. The demands of business and society require them to explore and act on dynamic and wholly new concepts that accept no traditional solutions. For that they will need to know the best that has been thought and said by generations before them, and that is the benefit of a liberal arts education for business decision makers and leaders.

It will be several years before there is sufficient longitudinal data on program participants to be able to measure efficiency and effectiveness. For the present, both the university and INA must view the program as an experiment; both institutions have benefited from the favorable publicity and from actually implementing a program, even if only on a small scale. Larger issues remain, however. Among those areas which require further consideration and scrutiny are the following:

1. *Program structure.* To what extent can the program be made more efficient, both financially and in terms of opportunities for students? How can INA employees be integrated into the overall CGS program? How can INA provide the full array of student services available to those who study on campus?

2. *Program administration and cost effectiveness.* How do the costs of this program compare with other INA education programs? Is the model efficient and are these efficiencies of scale? Are there administrative problems in running the program? Do the two organizations work well together? To what extent was the program's success dependent on the vitality and effectiveness of its administrator, Alyce Mead?

3. *Individual impact.* To what extent has participation in the program increased satisfaction and reduced turnover? What are the principal obstacles to beginning the program and to remaining in it? What are the key determinants in getting individuals to participate?

4. *Financial issues.* Where does the money for this program come from *within INA*? What are the *tradeoffs* of committing resources to the Penn program instead of pursuing other options? What *measurable* criteria can be used to justify the costs of this program?

5. *Policy considerations.* What are the advantages and disadvantages of a collaboration between a university and employer? What are the advantages and disadvantages of a broader tuition benefit program? Can an employer offer both types of education programs simultaneously? With what consequences?

There was a pause in the discussion. As he had anticipated, the initial part of the meeting dealt with present operations and with some "tinkering" with budgets and logistics. Now, Gallagher was ready to shift the focus of the meeting. He began to speak: "Can we turn our attention to a discussion of this collaboration and its long-term consequences?"

READING 1
STRATEGIC HUMAN RESOURCE MANAGEMENT
Noel M. Tichy, University of Michigan
Charles J. Fombrun,
University of Pennsylvania
Mary Anne Devanna,
Columbia University

Technological, economic, and demographic changes are pressuring organizations to use more effective human resource management. While sagging productivity and worker alienation have popularized management tools, such as quality circles and profit-sharing plans, the long-run competitiveness of American industry will require considerably more sophisticated approaches to the human resource input that deal with its strategic role in organizational performance.

Recent attacks on American business have stressed the short-run financial outlook of its management and its distinctly callous treatment of workers. The Japanese organization, on the other hand, is seen as the prototype of the future, as its planning systems center on worker loyalty.

This article, however, argues that we should not evaluate the Japanese organization per se. Rather, we should focus on human resource management in terms of its strategic role in both the formulation and the implementation of long-run plans. The strategic human resource concepts and tools needed are fundamentally different from the stock in trade of traditional personnel administration. This article, therefore, stresses the strategic level of human resource management at the expense of some

of the operational concerns of the standard personnel organization. Several companies are described as examples of sophisticated American organizations that have instituted strategic human resource management as an integral component of their management process. Specifically, this article presents a framework for conceptualizing human resource management; links human resource management to general strategic management; and describes some current applications of human resource management as a strategic tool in achieving corporate objectives.

Strategic Management

Three core elements are necessary for firms to function effectively:

1. Mission and Strategy. The organization has to have a reason for being, a means for using money, material, information, and people to carry out the mission.

2. Organization Structure. People are organized to carry out the mission of the organization and to do the necessary tasks.

3. Human Resource Management. People are recruited into the organization to do the jobs defined by the division of labor. Performance must be monitored, and rewards must be given to keep individuals productive.

Figure 1 presents these basic elements as interrelated systems that are embedded in the work environment. In the past, human resource management has been largely missing from the general strategic management process. Thus, our aim here is to help make human resource management an integral part of the strategic arena in organizations.

Figure 1   Strategic Management and
Environmental Pressures

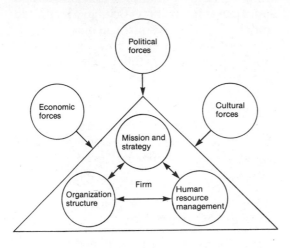

Strategy is defined as a process through which the basic mission and objectives of the organization are set and a process through which the organization uses its resources to achieve its objectives. In turn, structure reflects "the organization of work into roles such as production, finance, marketing, and so on; the recombining of the roles into departments or divisions around functions, products, regions, or markets, and the distribution of power across this role structure."[1] The structure of the organization embodies the fundamental division of labor, describes the basic nature of the jobs to be done, and aggregates them into groups, functions, or businesses. It also defines the degree of centralized control that top management holds over the operating units.

Strategy Follows Structure

In his historical study of American industry, Chandler provided a convincing argument that the structure of an organization follows from its strategy.[2] He identified four major strategies that resulted in structural or organizational design changes. They are: (1) expansion of volume; (2) geographic dispersion; (3) vertical integration; and (4) product diversification. Each of these strategies is followed by a structural transformation from function through to product forms. But while Chandler's work focused attention on the structural supports needed to drive a strategy and on the use of the organization's formal design in the implementation of a strategy, he did not discuss the role of the human resource systems in the implementation process.

Strategy, Structure, and Human Resource Management

The addition of human resource management to the strategic arena was presented by Galbraith and Nathanson, who expanded on Chandler's analysis.[3] They focused on such issues as fitting performance measures to the strategy and structure as well as to rewards, career paths, and leadership styles. Table 1 modifies and expands upon their work to illustrate how strategy, structure, and human resource management systems fit together: the fundamental strategic management problem is to keep the strategy, structure, and human resource dimensions of the organization in direct alignment. In the rest of this article, we will discuss some of the human resource man-

---

[1] See A. Chandler, *Strategy and Structure: Chapters in the History of American Industrial Enterprise* (Cambridge, Mass.: MIT Press, 1962).

[2] Ibid.

[3] See J. Galbraith and D. Nathanson, *Strategy Implementation: The Role of Structure and Process* (St. Paul, Minn.: West Publishing, 1978).

Table 1   Human Resource Management Links to Strategy and Structure

Strategy	Structure	Human Resource Management			
		Selection	Appraisal	Rewards	Development
1. Single product	Functional	Functionally oriented: subjective criteria used	Subjective: measure via personal contact	Unsystematic and allocated in a paternalistic manner	Unsystematic largely through job experiences: single-function focus
2. Single product (vertically integrated)	Functional	Functionally oriented: standardized criteria used	Impersonal: based on cost and productivity data	Related to performance and productivity	Functional specialists with some generalists: largely through job rotation
3. Growth by acquisition (holding company) of unrelated businesses	Separate self-contained businesses	Functionally oriented, but varies from business to business in terms of how systematic	Impersonal: based on return on investment and profitability	Formula-based and includes return on investment and profitability	Cross-functional but not cross-business
4. Related diversification of product lines through internal growth and acquisition	Multidivisional	Functionally and generalist oriented: systematic criteria used	Impersonal: based on return on investment, productivity, and subjective assessment of contribution to overall company	Large bonuses: based on profitability and subjective assessment of contribution to overall company	Cross-functional, cross-divisional, and cross-corporate/divisional: formal
5. Multiple products in multiple countries	Global organization (geographic center and worldwide)	Functionally and generalist oriented: systematic criteria used	Impersonal: based on multiple goals such as return on investment, profit tailored to product and country	Bonuses: based on multiple planned goals with moderate top-management discretion	Cross-divisional and cross-subsidiary to corporate: formal and systematic

Table adapted from J. Galbraith and D. Nathanson, *Strategy Implementation: The Role of Structure and Process* (St. Paul, Minn.: West Publishing, 1978).

agement concepts and tools that are needed to describe completely the strategic management role.

Human Resource Policies: A Context. A number of fundamental organizational policies provide the context for considering human resource management. These policies vary from organization to organization and tend to limit or constrain the actual design of a human resource system. While they are not the focus of this article, they are identified as important contextual issues that organizations must consider along the way. These policies are:

1. Management Philosophy. A basic policy that influences the overall design of a human resource system is the organization's management philosophy, i.e., its "psychological contract" with employees. An organization typically specifies the nature of the exchange with its employees. On one end of the spectrum is "a fair day's work for a fair day's pay," a purely extrinsic *quid pro quo* contract. Many U.S. blue-collar jobs fit this description. At the other extreme is the contract that stresses "challenging, meaningful work in return for a loyal, committed, and self-motivated employee," an intrinsically oriented contract. Some of the Scandinavian companies committed to quality of work life are positioned at this end of the spectrum. Such organizations typically develop people from within and seldom go to the external labor market to fill job openings.

A second policy decision involving management philosophy is the extent to which the organization is "top-down" or "bottom-up" driven. In a top-down organization, the human resource system centralizes all key selection, appraisal, and reward and development decisions. A bottom-up system encourages widespread participation in all activities.

2. Reliance on Development or Selection. Organizations vary in the degree to which they weight the impact of these two factors of performance. Some companies do almost no training or development. Other companies, such as AT&T, invest heavily in development. A company such as GE ascribes to a management philosophy that stresses both careful selection and development.

3. Group versus Individual Performance. The human resource systems can be geared toward collective, group-based performance or individual performance, or toward some mixture of the two. When the emphasis is on group performance, the selection must take into account social compatibility; the appraisal system must be group focused; and rewards must provide incentives for the work group.

The Human Resource Cycle

In light of these policies, we may now focus on four generic processes or functions that are performed by a human resource system in all organizations—selection, appraisal, rewards, and development. These four processes reflect sequential managerial tasks. Figure 2 represents them in terms of a human resource cycle. Clearly the dependent variable in Figure 2 is performance: the human resource elements are designed to impact performance at both the individual and the organizational levels.

Performance, in other words, is a function of all the human resource components: selecting people who are best able to perform the jobs defined by the structure; motivating employees by rewarding them judiciously; training and developing employees

Figure 2   The Human Resource Cycle

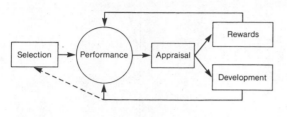

for future performance; and appraising employees in order to justify the rewards. In addition, performance is a function of the organizational context and resources surrounding the individual. Thus, strategy and structure also impact performance through the ways jobs are designed, through how the organization is structured, and through how well services or products are planned to meet environmental threats and opportunities.

In order to put these functions in the various contexts of the organization, we rely upon Robert Anthony's distinction among the three levels of managerial work: the strategic level, the managerial level, and the operational level.[4]

The strategic level deals with policy formulation and overall goal setting: its objective is to position effectively the organization in its environment. The managerial level is concerned with the availability and allocation of resources to carry out the strategic plan. To be in the business(es) specified by the strategic plan, the company must decide what its capital, informational, and human resource needs are. At the operational level, the day-to-day management of the organization is carried out. (Operational

activities are ideally carried out under the umbrella of the managerial plan.)

Table 2 illustrates the kinds of activities associated with these three levels for each generic component of the human resource cycle. For example, in the selection/placement area, operational level activities include the annual staffing and recruitment plans. Managerial selection is more concerned with manpower planning for the intermediate future. For instance, a company that is about to open two plants in different parts of the country would want to know the kinds of people the company will need and how it should go about finding the people to run the plants. Strategic selection is concerned with identifying who can best run the business(es) in the long run.

Selection, Promotion, and Placement Process

The selection, promotion, and placement process includes all those activities related to the internal movement of people across positions and to the external hiring into the organization. The essential process is one of matching available human resources to jobs in the organization. It entails defining the organization's human needs for particular positions and assessing the available pool of people to determine the best fit.

Three strategic selection concerns are particularly salient. The first involves devising an organization-wide selection and promotion system that supports the organization's business strategy. For example, if a company will be diversifying over a 10-year period, it is most likely that the types of people needed to run the new business will be different than they had been in the past. Thus, a redesign in the selection process will be required. This process is taking place in the

---

[4] See R. Anthony, *Planning and Control Systems: A Framework for Analysis* (Boston: Division of Research, Graduate School of Business Administration, Harvard University, 1965).

Table 2 Human Resource Activities

Management Level	Selection	Appraisal	Rewards (Compensation and Fringe Benefits)	Development
Strategic	Specify characteristics of people needed to run business in long term Alter internal and external systems to reflect future	In long term, what should be valued? Develop means to appraise future dimensions Early identification of potential	In world as it might be in long term, how will work force be rewarded? Link to the long-term business strategy	Plan developmental experiences for people running business of the future Systems with flexibility to adjust to change Develop long-term career paths
Managerial	Longitudinal validation of selection criteria Development of recruitment marketing plan New markets	Validated systems linking current and future potential Assessment centers for development	Five-year compensation plans for individuals Cafeteria-style fringe packages	General management development programs Organization development Foster self-development
Operational	Staffing plans Recruitment plans Day-to-day monitoring systems	Annual or more frequent appraisal system(s) Day-to-day control systems	Wage and salary administration Benefit packages	Specific job skill training On-the-job training

oil industry as it launches its 20-year diversification effort.

The second strategic concern requires creating internal flows of people that match the business strategy. Companies that diversify or change their strategic direction need to alter traditional promotional patterns in order to move new types of people into key positions. AT&T's move into the competitive electronic communication and knowledge business has necessitated their developing internal promotion systems for profit-driven people who are able to innovate and deal with competitive markets. This is a major change from the regulated telephone monopoly that was service-oriented, that was low on innovation, and that was not managed competitively where profit was regulated.

The third strategic concern is matching key executives to the business's strategy. There is a growing interest in meshing strategic planning with executive skills. This is especially true in companies that are using a product portfolio analysis approach to strategic management. The Boston Consulting Group's (BCG's) portfolio matrix is the most common and simplest formulation. Using the BCG approach, there is a set of prescribed business practices for managing each type of business. Several examples of companies already committed to using senior executive selection as a strategic management tool are presented below:

General Electric.   GE uses a more complex portfolio matrix with nine cells. Yet the underlying concepts are based on the same product life-cycle notions represented in the BCG matrix. GE defines its products in terms of the kinds of management practices required for success. Thus, its products are defined as "growers" for wildcats, "defenders" for stars, "harvesters" for cash cows, and "undertakers" for dogs:

> Its [GE] general managers are being classified by personal style or orientation as "growers," "caretakers," and "undertakers." . . . They [GE] have a shortage of growers but they are making a great effort to remove the undertaker types who are heading up growth businesses. The lighting business is mainly mature but we [GE] just designated international operations as a growth area to our five year forecast. . . . John D. Hamilton, the manager responsible for manpower planning, says he and the executive manpower staff at corporate headquarters looked at the whole pool of corporate talent. They decided to move in a manager who had an industrial rather than a lighting background, but who seemed to show entrepreneurial flair.[5]

Corning Glass Company.   At Corning, an extensive effort is under way to assess the company's top 100 executives for such qualities as entrepreneurial flair. The goal is to have a clearer profile of the organization's pool of executive talent specified in terms of capabilities for managing different parts of the BCG matrix. An example of this process occurred in December 1979:

> Corning reshaped its electronic strategy, deciding that the market was starting to expand again, and that it needed a growth oriented manager. It placed a manufacturing specialist who had shown a great deal of flair in working with customers in the top marketing slot for electronics, and, says Shafer, "It looks like he's turning it around."[6]

Chase Manhattan Bank.   During the period between 1975 and 1980, the bank underwent major managerial changes. A key

---

[5] See *Business Week*, February 25, 1980, p. 173.
[6] Ibid., p. 166.

to the bank's successful turnaround from a troubled bank in the mid-70s was its careful strategic level selection and placement of executives. Historically, at Chase, as is the case with banking in general, senior level positions were filled based on the historical precedent: the old boy networks played a major role. Furthermore, the tradition was to reward those with banker skills and not those with managerial skills, which were implicitly considered to be of less importance. But under the stress of serious performance problems, Chase Manhattan Bank had to reexamine these practices. As a result, a very systematic effort was launched to strategically manage senior selection and placement decisions. For example, "When the trust manager retired, corporate management decided that the department, whose operation had been essentially stable, should focus on a more aggressive growth strategy. Instead of seeking a veteran banker, Chase hired a man whose experience had been with IBM" because it was felt that he would bring a strong marketing orientation to the trust department, which the new strategy required.[7]

Texas Instruments. At TI, there is an explicit attempt to match management style to product life cycles. "As a product moves through different phases of its life cycle, different kinds of management skills become dominant."[8] The mismatch of managerial style to the product life cycle can be quite serious. For example, a risk-taking entrepreneurial manager who is in charge of a cash cow business is likely to reduce the profitability of the business by trying to "grow" the business and take risks. On the other hand, putting a cost-cutting, efficiency-oriented manager in charge of a growth business can stifle innovation and prevent the business from acquiring market share. TI feels that, in the past, it did not pay adequate attention to the match between product life cycle and managerial style. As a result, TI feels it lost its early lead in integrated circuits. During the growth stage, TI had a "cash cow manager in charge rather than a grower or entrepreneurial type."[9] The result was that "tighter controls were introduced, but TI failed to recognize that a research orientation was really what the Integrated Department needed at the growth stage. TI has since redoubled its efforts to match management orientation with job needs. Bucy, now president, personally reviews the records of the top TI managers."[10]

Reward Processes

Performance follows the selection process. Once people are in their jobs, they need to be rewarded for good performance. The list of rewards that exist in organizational settings is surprisingly long. The following is a partial list of potential rewards:

—Pay in its various forms: salary, bonuses, stock options, benefits, and perquisites.
—Promotion: both upward mobility and lateral transfers into desirable positions.
—Management praise.
—Career opportunities: a long-term chance for growth and development.
—Appreciation from customers and/or clients of the organization.
—Personal sense of well-being: feeling good about oneself for accomplishing objectives.
—Opportunity to learn: a chance to expand one's skills and knowledge base.

---

[7] Ibid., p. 166.
[8] Ibid., p. 168.

[9] Ibid., p. 168.
[10] Ibid., p. 168.

—Security: a sense of job and financial security.

—Responsibility: providing individuals with a sense of organizational responsibility.

—Respect from co-workers.

—Friendship from co-workers.

Most organizations, however, do not do a very good job of managing these rewards to produce desired organizational behaviors. As a result, the reward system is one of the most underutilized and mishandled managerial tools for driving organizational performance. As can be seen from the human resource cycle in Figure 2, rewards are a major factor in influencing performance. Assuming that the organization can appraise performance, which is not always a good assumption, the organization then has a rationale for allocating rewards based on how well people perform. Many times organizations think of rewards only in terms of managing pay.

Thus, a major strategic issue concerning the reward system is how to use it to overcome the tendency toward short-sighted management. The rewards for this year's profits generally turn out to be both financial incentives and promotions. Motivation of senior executives toward long-term strategic goals is difficult, given that the reward system often encourages short-term achievement at the expense of long-term goals. The following excerpt is a statement made in the *New York Times*:

> Though bonuses based on achieving sales or earnings goals have long been common, the emphasis on long term is a new element. Top corporate executives, under pressure from Wall Street, and stockholders have been rewarded with bonuses and stock options when immediate profits spurt. The auto industry, for example, is notable for its short-term rewards.[11]

It is unreasonable and unwise to recommend that managers be rewarded only for long-term strategic goals, as businesses must perform in the present to succeed in the future. Thus, the reward system should provide balanced support to short-term and long-term strategic goals.

Balancing Long- and Short-Term Goals

Texas Instruments. TI has thought long and hard about the use of its reward system for driving the company's short- and long-term goals.

One major part of TI's strategy since the early 1960s has been to adhere rigidly to the "learning curve theory." Simply put, it states that "manufacturing costs can be brought down by a fixed percentage, depending on the product, each time cumulative volume is doubled."[12] The strategy involves constant redesign improvement of the product and of the processes of production so that prices can drop as fast as possible. This strategy was implemented by organizing Product Customer Centers (PCCs), which are decentralized profit centers that could be closely monitored for cost performance. The reward system was closely tied to the PCCs so that managers worked hard to make the learning curve theory operative. However, there were some problems.

The Product Customer Centers and associated reward systems worked against another organizational strategy—the development of innovations for future products. The rewards were structured to drive managers to be overly concerned with short-run

[11] See *New York Times*, April 24, 1980.
[12] See *Business Week*, September 18, 1978, p. 68.

efficiencies and not with long-term strategic goals.

The solution to this dilemma was to design a new organization and to drape it over the existing PCC structure. The new organization, which was called Objectives, Strategies, and Tactics (OST), was created to supplement the PCCs, which remained intact. The OST structure was used for the formulation and implementation of strategic long-range plans, and it consisted of the same managers as that of the PCC organization.

Thus, the top managers at TI wear two hats. Wearing one hat, they are bottom line, efficiency-focused managers who work to drive the PCC system and who are rewarded and evaluated for accomplishing the efficiency objectives. Wearing the other hat, the OST one, the managers are involved in working toward a strategic objective that may have a 10- to 20-year time horizon. Separate monitoring and appraisal systems tied to the OST organization are used to drive performance in the long-term strategic area. For example, a manager may be responsible for PCC efficiency, while, at the same time, he may work in the OST structure toward a strategic objective in the development of products in the computerized auto industry of the future. If 60 percent of his time was allocated to the PCCs and 40 percent of his time to OST, then his compensation would be split to reflect the short- and long-term aspects of the job.

TI also used the reward system to encourage another set of desired strategic behaviors when it discovered that managers tend to set low-risk objectives in order to enhance their chances of receiving a bigger bonus, and thereby stifling their creativity and innovativeness. TI altered the reward system through a "wild hare" program that provided funding for more speculative programs. Under this program, managers were asked to rank speculative projects on a separate basis. The bonus system was then tied into this process.

Another strategic reward mechanism for fostering organizational innovation is to provide any organization member(s) with a chance to obtain a grant from a pool containing several million dollars to fund innovative projects. The result has been the emergence of informal groups who apply for grants from the innovation pool, called IDEA; these groups then attempt to turn these ideas into viable products.

Management Development

Activities designed to insure that individuals are properly equipped with skills and knowledge to carry out their jobs fall into the management development category. These activities range from simple job training for lower-level employees to long-term development of senior executives. The three major areas of the developmental process are: (1) job improvement: the development of specific job skills and competencies; (2) career planning: a longitudinal focus on individual growth and development in relation to organizational opportunities; and (3) succession planning: the organizational focus on insuring an adequate supply of human resource talent for projected needs in the future based on strategic plans.

At the long-term strategic level, the developmental process includes such activities as management education, job assignments, and the use of mentor relationships. Some of the strategic level developmental concerns are discussed briefly.

Insuring that the organization has an adequate supply of human resource talent at all levels is no easy task, especially when the organization is undergoing rapid strategic changes. The key to this concern is to have a human resource planning system that makes accurate forecasts of needs and of resources available to meet those needs. Such systems, however, are not easily built, and even though most large companies have manpower planning systems, they are often very inadequate as a result of two basic flaws.

The first flaw is that data about people that are fed into the system are very unreliable because managers generally do not appraise employees well. As it now stands, the appraisal process that provides this data is the weakest link in the human resource cycle. Thus, planning systems that are built on these data are also inadequate. In order to plan for the future, it is necessary to have an inventory of current human resources that includes both an assessment of current performance and of the future potential of key individuals.

The second basic flaw is that there is a missing link between human resource planning systems and business strategy. Although many organizations have given lip service to this missing link, the reality is that it has been treated as an afterthought that has usually been delegated to the human resource staff without any line management involvement. As a result, the human resource plan is a paper exercise that is not utilized by the strategic decision makers.

There is a handful of U.S. companies that have strategically managed the development of senior executive talent. Among these companies are General Motors, Exxon, General Electric, Texas Instruments, IBM, and Procter & Gamble. The emphasis has been on carefully developing managers by following such principles as:

1. Sustained interest in and support for management development and succes-

sion planning on the part of top management.
2. Efforts to identify young professionals deemed to have potential for top-level management positions.
3. Comprehensive and systematic rewards used for managerial performance.
4. The appraisal includes data from multiple sources and is used in making decisions about management development.
5. Special recruiting efforts to provide appropriate raw materials for general managers of the future.
6. Opportunities for capable young professionals to develop managerial skills early in their careers.
7. Compensation policies and salary administration to help stimulate management development and retain key personnel.
8. Clear developmental objectives and career plans for managers at all levels.
9. Effective coaching from personnel's superiors.
10. Stressing results in the performance appraisal process.

Some companies have been very strategic in developing managers. For example:

Exxon. The Compensation and Executive Development (COED) system at Exxon is designed to insure a disciplined approach to the development of managerial talent for the company. The system is directed from the top, where the COED committee is headed by the CEO, Clifford Garvin, and is made up of members of Exxon's board. The committee is in charge of reviewing the development and placement of the top 250 Exxon executives. Meeting nearly every Monday, the COED committee carefully reviews the performance of executives and examines their developmental needs. To insure that there is a continual flow of managerial talent for the company and that all positions have back-up candidates, the committee then compares the performances of all the executives and makes decisions according to their future developmental needs.

There is also a COED system within each of the Exxon subsidiaries, where the president of each subsidiary has his or her own COED committee, which is similar to the one Mr. Garvin heads. Each subsidiary also has a senior level staff for the COED committee; this enables the COED system to reach the top 2,000 or so managers at Exxon.

In discussions with senior Exxon managers, it is rather striking to hear the universal acclaim given the system. Most agree that the system accounts for Exxon's overall success and that it is an excellent system for developing managers.

General Motors. General Motors is another company with an equally strong tradition of management development that dates back to Alfred Sloan.

> At General Motors, the supreme court of executive review in recent years included the top six executives in the company. . . . During the week-long sessions in the board room of Detroit headquarters each February and July, they spend long days and nights listening to analyses of more than 600 managers from each of GM's 10 vice presidents and group executives. . . . A variety of questions are covered to get an accurate picture of where the individual stands in his career development. . . . We don't have jobs at GM, we have careers. Along with performance, the probing is centered on just what kind of potential the executive may have. Here are some examples. Does the executive seem to be developing at the rate expected? What is the job contributing to the

person's ability? Is it rounding out the person as we intended? What should be the next job for this executive? Should it be in another division or involve greater responsibility? If so, who would we put in this executive's place?[13]

Chase Manhattan Bank.   A more targeted use of management development took place at Chase Manhattan Bank. A management development program was designed to support the company's first formal strategic planning process. The two-week program for the top officers of the bank focused on awareness and frameworks needed to support the new strategic planning process. The program had the involvement of the then chairman, David Rockefeller, and the then president, Willard Butcher. Both symbolically and substantively, the program strongly reinforced the importance of the new strategic planning process.

Appraisal Process

Perhaps the least liked managerial activity is doing the annual performance appraisal. The activity is often only a perfunctory paper exercise. Performance appraisals are like seat belts: everyone agrees that they are important and that they save lives, yet no one uses them. Similarly, the problem with appraisal systems includes poorly designed procedures, a psychological resistance of managers to give negative evaluations, and a perceived invalidity. The appraisal system, nonetheless, is central to the human resource cycle. It contributes to three essential processes:

1. Rewards can be allocated in relation to performance only through the use of an appraisal system by which performance

---

[13] See *New York Times*, September 4, 1980.

can be measured. Such appraisal systems range from subjective personal evaluations to impersonal criteria based on profitability, return on investment, market share, and other quantitative measures.

2. Human resource planning relies on valid appraisals. A current inventory of talent can be made only through a valid appraisal process that shows those who have been performing well and those who have not. In addition, future human resource projections must be based on an assessment of the potential of the employees, which is indicated by the appraisal process. Without the data provided by a valid appraisal, such forecasting is impossible, as there is no basis for making predictions.

3. The development process is also built on the appraisal process. Based on an assessment of an individual's performance and potential, both the individual and the organization can plan for future training and development. A weak data base leads to a hit-or-miss training program and retards the development process.

Relationship to Strategy.   A strategic concern for companies is to develop appraisal processes that are supportive of the business strategy. A study by Lorsch and Allen indicated that such a link influences total performance.[14] In this study, the authors compared the appraisal systems in diversified companies to those in integrated companies. They found that the diversified companies placed more emphasis on objective and result measures, such as productivity, profit, volume, etc. The integrated

_____

[14] See J. Lorsch and S. Allen, *Managing Diversity and Interdependence* (Boston: Division of Research, Harvard Business School, 1973).

firms, however, tended to rely more on operating and intermediate measures, as well as on more subjective evaluation of abilities, such as "planning," "controlling," "organizing," and "leadership." The diversified appraisal system worked better because the divisions were more self-contained, having little interdivisional or corporate contact. The integrated companies, on the other hand, had greater interdivisional contact and greater sharing of resources, which made it hard for them to decide who exactly was responsible for how much of the end results. These two simple examples underscore some of the strategic issues involved in matching an appraisal process to the business strategy.

The key to an effective appraisal system at the strategic level is the commitment of quality managerial time to systematic examination and evaluation of executive talent. The descriptions of the Exxon and GM development systems, which were discussed earlier, are in part descriptions of their appraisal systems as the two systems are interrelated. But perhaps the company with the best strategic appraisal system is General Electric, where much time and staff work go into appraising the top 600 executives.

General Electric.   The diversification of GE makes the appraisal of managers more complex than that of most other companies. Unlike GM or Exxon who have one major line of business, GE has more than 240 businesses. As a result, GE has developed elaborate approaches to handling the appraisal of key managers.

An example of this is the slate system. The top 600 positions at GE are carefully managed and monitored by the chairman. A special human resource staff that is under the direction of a senior vice president reviews these key executives. This staff works with line managers to develop slates of acceptable candidates for key managerial positions in the company. Positions must be filled from among those on the approved slate; that is, a business head cannot select his own vice president of marketing unless the individual is among those on the official slate list for the position. Although a manager may select an individual who is not on the slate, the decision must ultimately be kicked up the hierarchy at GE to the chairman. However, this kind of selection is frowned upon and thus very few people who are not on the slate are selected for key managerial positions.

One of the services that the human resource staff provides in developing the data base for the slate system is an in-depth executive review of key managers. Highly trained personnel spend several weeks preparing a report on a single executive. The process involves interviews with subordinates, peers, bosses, and even customers of GE to get a composite picture of the individual's strengths, weaknesses, accomplishments, failures, and potentials. These reviews estimate the expected future progress of the individual at GE and give extensive suggestions for further development. The completed report is then reviewed by the individual, who can voice disagreement. It then becomes part of the individual's file. (Only 40 of these reviews are conducted in a year.)

Implementing Strategic Human Resource Management

In another article, we discussed a methodology for moving a human resource function into the strategic arena.[15] The approach is based on a human resource audit that

provides the organization with data on the internal capacity of the human resource function and data from the line concerning the kind of services the organization needs at the operational, managerial, and strategic levels. As a result of our conducting these audits in several large companies, we developed the following suggestions for making the human resource function more strategic:

The Internal Organization of the Human Resource Function. The first area of focus is on how to properly organize, staff, and manage the human resource function. This involves:

—Step 1. Identify the portfolio of human resource tasks at the strategic, managerial, and operational level for each human resource element.

—Step 2. Reorganize the human resource function to reflect the operational, managerial, and strategic needs of the business. The *operational level* is best served by a traditional functional personnel department where there are separate units carrying out recruitment, compensation, development, etc. The *managerial level* must be organized to cut across the subfunctions identified at the operational level (recruitment, development, compensation, etc.) by using such design tools as liaison managers, teams, or, under limited conditions, a matrix organizational design. The *strategic level* activities require an elite senior human resource management (individual or team, depending on the size of the organization) that is supported by strong managerial human resource services.

—Step 3. The human resource staff must be trained in the more strategically focused organization. At the operational level, the function must be staffed with technically focused professional personnel and/or with MBAs who are starting out in their

15 See M. Haire, "A New Look at Human Resources," *Industrial Management Review* (now *Sloan Management Review*), Winter 1970, pp. 17–23.

careers and who need to learn the nuts and bolts of personnel. At the managerial level, individuals who possess a more general managerial orientation and background either through actual work experience or through an MBE degree should be selected from the operational level. Finally, at the strategic level, staffing should be based on selecting human resource executives who have political skills, a broad business orientation, and a broad human resource management background. A proactive stance toward the strategic future of the organization is also required.

—Step 4. The reward and control systems must be altered to support the strategic human resource function. The rewards and controls should reflect specific tasks at each of the three levels. Most personnel reward and control systems are geared toward operational level activities; these should be expanded to reward and control people in terms of the new strategic and managerial level activities.

Linking the Human Resource Function to the Line Organization.   Major changes are also required to link the human resource function to the user organization. Most personnel functions are linked to the operational business activities. With the addition of new managerial and strategic activities, new linking mechanisms will be required:

—Step 1. Provide the business with good human resource data bases. These include environmental scanning of labor markets and social and economic issues that impact the long-term human resource context of the organization. In addition, data on the internal labor pool are required in both a present and a future context. Internal marketing data on the human resource needs of various user

groups in the organization are especially helpful.

—Step 2. Alter the senior management role when it comes to human resource management issues so that these concerns receive quality attention. The managers need to be committed to weighing human resource issues with the same level of attention as that of other functions, such as finance, marketing, and production.

—Step 3. The line organization must alter its incentive and control systems so that the overall human resource function is managed. It will also be necessary for the organization to have ways of measuring the overall performance of the human resource function at the strategic, managerial, and operational levels. This will entail ongoing audits of the human resource function to determine how well it is doing in providing services to its clients. Also, adjustments must be made in budgeting for human resource services, as some of these adjustments will require new sources of corporate funding.

These steps are illustrative of what is involved in developing a more strategic human resource function. Obviously, every organization must develop its own answers and a tailored strategic stance in terms of its human resources.

Summary and Conclusions

Human resource management is a major force in driving organizational performance. Thus, when business is castigated and when American industry is unfavorably compared to that of Japan or West Germany, two major factors are underscored: (1) our lack of a long-term perspective in management; and (2) our lack of skill in managing people. Both of these factors can be changed only with a concomitant change in the human resource activities inside our organizations; that is, it requires changes in the way people think and behave. In the final analysis, three concluding points should be made about human resource management:

1. Human resource activities have a major impact on individual performance and, hence, on productivity and organizational performance.
2. The cycle of human resource activities is highly interdependent. The human resource system is therefore only as strong as its weakest link.
3. Effective strategic management requires effective human resource management.

Additional Readings

M. A. Devanna, C. Fombrun, and N. Tichy. "Human Resource Management: A Strategic Approach." *Organizational Dynamics*, Winter 1981.

J. Galbraith and D. Nathanson. *Strategy Implementation: The Role of Structure and Process.* St. Paul, Minn.: West Publishing, 1978, p. 118.

B. Henderson. *Henderson on Corporate Strategy.* Cambridge, Mass.: Abt Books, 1979.

C. Hofer and D. Schendel, *Strategy Formulation: Analytical Concepts.* St. Paul, Minn.: West Publishing, 1978, p. 42.

T. Peters. "Putting Excellence into Management." *Business Week*, July 21, 1980.

READING 2
A NOTE ON CAREER PROGRAMS IN INDUSTRY
James J. Dowd and
Jeffrey A. Sonnenfeld

That individuals with ambition, drive, and foresight try to plan their own career advancement is not new. The works of writers from Machiavelli to the Earl of Chesterfield have found readers eager for advice on how to reach career goals of power, position, and prestige. In the same way, the popularity of self-help career books today reflects a continuing hunger for information and assistance in answering the age-old question: What can I do to get ahead?

What is new is the increasing organizational involvement in career planning. Traditionally, aspiring managers in this country looked to hard work, performance results, and a little bit of luck to achieve their career goals. American values of self-reliance and rugged individualism encouraged a faith in corporate meritocracy: career success came to those who earned it on their own. Help from the organization was neither sought nor expected.

Over the past 15 years, however, American companies have become more active in managing employee careers. In 1973 just over 100 companies were operating employee assessment and development centers; by 1981 that number had grown to more than 2,000.[1] A 1982 study of career development programs in 40 corporations found that more than 80 percent had been created since 1970.[2] Another recent study reported significant budget increases for career programs in more than half of the firms studied.[3] While the actual practices of American corporations may not be quite so extensive as these findings might suggest, there is no doubt that organizations have

---

[1] Leland C. Nichols and Joseph Hudson, "Dual-role Assessment Centers and Development," *Personnel Journal*, May 1981, p. 380.

[2] Thomas C. Gutteridge and Fred L. Otte, "Organizational Career Development: State of the Practice;" unpublished monograph, October, 1982.

[3] Marilyn A. Morgan, Douglas T. Hall, and Alison Martier, "Career Development Strategies in Industry: Where Are We and Where Should We Be?", *Personnel*, March–April 1979.

taken on a larger role in the planning and development of individuals' careers.

Why has business chosen to assume more responsibility in this area? What benefits do organizations hope to gain from career programs? What kinds of programs have been designed to achieve those benefits, and how successful have they been? What problems are encountered by organizations attempting these new practices, and what direction are these programs likely to take in the future?

To answer these questions this note will draw primarily on the results of three recent studies. The first was undertaken by James W. Walker and Thomas G. Gutteridge in 1979 for the American Management Association. Walker and Gutteridge surveyed 225 companies to ascertain the pervasiveness of career development activities in American industry, the factors influencing the establishment of these programs, their general features, and their effectiveness.[4] The second, conducted by Marilyn A. Morgan, Douglas T. Hall, and Alison Martier, surveyed 56 companies in metropolitan Chicago in 1979, with research goals similar to those of the AMA study.[5] Third, a study by Thomas G. Gutteridge and Fred L. Otte in 1981 focused on the details of career development practices in 40 firms, primarily large industrial corporations known to have established career programs.[6]

Why Establish Career Programs?

Manpower Inventories. One reason seems primary: to ensure that an internal

[4] James W. Walker and Thomas G. Gutteridge, "Career Planning Practices: An AMA Report," AMACOM, 1979.

[5] Morgan, Hall, and Martier, "Career Development Strategies."

[6] Gutteridge and Otte, *Organizational Career Development.*

supply of managerial, technical, and professional talent is maintained, and that it is sufficient to meet the strategic needs of the organization for as far into the future as those needs can be projected. That impetus comes from the top of organization: Gutteridge and Otte report that pressure from top management was the single most frequently mentioned reason for the creation of corporate career programs. Management has come to appreciate employees as a critical factor in the successful accomplishment of strategic goals. Staff specialists are directed to review strategic plans from that perspective: if we are going to increase international sales by 30 percent over the next 20 years, how many salespersons are we going to need, and with what skills and what background? How many electronic engineers do we need to compete in this rapidly growing industry, and where are we going to get them? What kinds of exposures to our various businesses should future senior managers have had in order to manage the entire corporation, and how can we provide them with that?

Staffing from Within. Career programs spring from such concerns, and they are nourished by the widespread organizational preference to develop and promote employees from within. Over 80 percent of the 225 firms surveyed in the AMA report named that desire as a major factor in the creation of their programs. Rather than spend money to locate and recruit the talent they need, organizations seek to become more self-reliant in meeting their human resource needs. In a sense, this is a classic make/buy decision. The savings in fees not paid to executive search firms are complemented by avoidance of less tangible organizational costs: "imported" talent takes longer, in a new job in a new company, to "get up to speed" and to make a productive contribution to the business; morale is adversely affected when employees see "obvious" internal candidates passed over in favor of an outsider; and executives new to the firm are likely to be less dedicated, less personally identified with the firm's continued success. For these reasons, some firms regard external executive sourcing as evidence of organizational failure to select and develop the best possible executive talent from within. Repeated failure to staff from within has led many companies to establish career development programs; 63 percent of the AMA survey respondents reported "a shortage of promotable talent" as a major reason to establish formal career programs.

Current Staffing Problems. Career development programs may also be established to address immediate personnel problems. Organizations troubled by *high turnover* may discover in exit interviews that employees leave the firm discouraged by a perceived lack of career opportunities or guidance within the company. *Recruiting* specialists may report that talented candidates prefer employers with extensive, formal programs aimed at employee development and career advancement. *Affirmative action* goals and timetables frequently required special efforts in counseling and training. Concerns such as these were mentioned by over 70 percent of the respondents in the AMA study.

Employee Interest. Career development programs may also develop in response to increasing employee requests for assistance in industrial career planning. At least four factors account for this increased reliance on the organization for help in what was formerly a strictly personal concern.

First, employees are seeking more from their work than pay and security. Today's workforce, more highly educated than in the past, has higher expectations for career success. Employees now consciously look to their work to meet their psychological needs for growth, achievement, and competence. They expect the organization to provide them with the information and assistance they require to meet these needs.

Second, there are more aspiring managers today than ever before. The sheer size of the baby boom generation makes it impossible for everyone to achieve their career goals. The resulting competition for limited advancement opportunities engenders anxiety and frustration in employees' working lives. Employees look to the organization to help avoid or alleviate those work-related problems.

Third, employees today face a rapidly changing organizational environment which threatens the achievement of their career goals. New industries with unfamiliar skill requirements appear and grow, while more familiar, mature industries shrink in decline. Middle-management positions require knowledge of office automation technology only now being included in high school and college curricula. Many employees rightly fear that technological advances will eliminate their positions, and realize that, at the least, they must learn to master the new technology to survive. Here again they turn to the organization for assistance in training and education.

Finally, extensive media coverage of the topic has certainly increased public awareness of the importance of career planning. Popular magazines offer articles on job search strategies, special career problems of minorities and women, mid-career changes, mentors, and so on. Bookstores devote entire shelves, even sections, of the store to "careers" publications. Employees exposed to such materials learn what other companies do to help individuals' career planning, and they come to expect the same, if not more, from their own companies.

All of these factors, singly or in combination, may lead to the establishment of career programs in a company. They define the program objectives, which, in turn, influence the choice of techniques and practices used to achieve them.[7]

What Kinds of Career Programs Exist?

Thus far the term *career programs* has served as a catch phrase to cover all activities involving the organization in planning and developing individual careers. At their most elaborate, career programs are comprised of many smaller programs, systems, and subsystems involving all aspects of the management of human resources. Morgan, Hall, and Martier describe 7 categories of career programs; Gutteridge and Otte list 10.

For simplicity's sake we shall speak of career programs in two general groupings: those which primarily serve the needs of the *organization,* and those which primarily serve the needs of *employees.* That this distinction is a crude one is admitted from the start; most programs serve both. Nonetheless, for ease of description and understanding, we present the programs as being in one category or the other. We urge the reader to remember, however, that our distinction is of little practical value.

Two further caveats are necessary here. First, what follows is a description of career programs in industry, not in any one corporation. It is unlikely that many corporations—if any—employ *all* practices, techniques, and tools listed here. Although we

will speak of "a company," our discussion is descriptive and fictional, neither normative nor real.

Finally, within that context, the program descriptions are general and conceptual. Details of actual practice differ from one company to the next. Career programs may vary significantly in three major respects: formality, administration, and scope.

Formality: One company may employ staff psychologists to provide formal employee counseling, while another may train supervisors to perform that role. Both would report the existence of career counseling programs in their firms.

Administration: Responsibility for program administration may fall primarily on the human resources department in one organization, primarily on line managers in another, and in another the responsibility may be shared equally. Morgan, Hall, and Martier found each approach equally represented in their study sample.

Scope: Participation in a given career program may be limited to employees of certain geographical locations, skills and qualifications, career stages, job grades, or other criteria.

Differences along these dimensions are too extensive to consider in detail in this paper; accordingly, we again urge the reader to keep in mind the general and conceptual nature of this discussion.

Career Programs to Meet Organizational Needs

Organizational Human Resources Planning. Top management determines the strategic direction of the firm, sets objectives, and then plans their implementation. Along with capital requirements, the need for human talent is considered: what kinds

---

[7] Ibid., p. 11.

of people do we need to reach our goals? Staff specialists draw up forecasts that detail the number of employees needed in any of several functions—research and development, sales, project management, manufacturing, and so on. Their analysis results in a list of employee types, with estimated numbers required of each type. *Succession planning* for key management positions is a common example of this practice. Although most often conducted independent of strategic plan analysis, succession planning aims to meet the same need—to ensure that the organization has qualified replacements ready to assume critical responsibilities, in order that the firm may outlive its senior managers of today.

Career Pathing. With future needs determined, the organization analyzes the skill requirements for these positions: what kinds of job-related knowledge and experience must those employees have? That analysis leads to position specifications for years of education and specific work experiences necessary to perform the jobs. In this way career paths (or career ladders) are developed specifying alternative sequences of positions which provide required on-the-job training for higher-level jobs.

Workforce Analysis. Now the organization looks to its current workforce: what kinds of employees do we have here? Such information is usually already recorded in personnel files—job applications, résumés, performance appraisals, and ratings of potential. Corporations sometimes attempt to program this data into computerized information systems called *"skills inventories"*. The goal of these systems is to allow for rapid internal searches for qualified candidates to fill vacant or new positions. Other corporations seeking such information may establish *assessment centers* to examine individual employees more closely. Teams of specialists interview high-potential employees and run them through a series of "tests" (leaderless group discussions, in-basket exercises) to arrive at more substantive and defensible evaluations of their strengths, weaknesses, and potential for advancement. Another technique is a formal *needs analysis* conducted by training specialists. Through questionnaires and structured interviews, employees are asked to tell management which formal educational or training programs they feel would better enable them to perform their jobs and prepare them for future responsibilities. The results of this sampling are reported to management as a formal assessment of workforce capabilities and limitations.

Developmental Programs. Having identified its needs and its resources, the organization then seeks to bridge the gap between them, if any. Given a preference for staffing from within, what can we do to develop the employees we have today into the workforce we need for tomorrow? To achieve that goal a number of programs may be established:

Orientation programs for new hires, explaining career paths and opportunities for advancement within the firm.

Mentoring and "buddy" systems to allow for more formal monitoring of progress in the early career of high-potential employees

"Fast-track" programs for specially recruited and selected employees, providing rapid and intensive exposure in accelerated career paths

Formal in-house training courses in technical, supervisory or managerial skills.

Tuition reimbursement plans for job-related

coursework undertaken by individuals on approval of supervisors of staff counsel. Participation in on-campus university programs for advanced management education.

Through four types of career programs—organizational human resources planning, career pathing, workforce analysis, and developmental programs—organizations meet the primary goals of strategic human resource management. They may establish other career programs in response to pressures from the government (e.g., affirmative action plan-mandated training for protected employee classes) or from society at large (e.g., outplacement programs for employees affected by plant closings). And, as already stated, career programs may be developed in direct response to employee calls for assistance in planning individual careers.

Career Programs to Meet Employee Needs

To plan a career in an organization, individuals must assess their skills and interests, determine career goals, investigate opportunities in the firm, and finally develop action plans to achieve those goals. Employees look for two kinds of help from the organization to complete this process: *assistance* in self-assessment, goal setting, and action planning, and *information* on career opportunities in the company. Organizations develop programs of both types to meet individuals' needs for support in the career planning process.

Assistance in Self-Assessment, Goal Setting, and Action Planning. What skills, abilities, and potential do I bring to my work? What are my interests, values and preferences? Answering those questions does not require organizational involvement but, because

the process can be extremely difficult, help is offered through four types of programs.

Workbooks and self-help materials. Organizations can distribute written materials covering the basic concepts of career planning to employees wishing to plan their careers. The workbooks are self-explanatory, and employees are expected to complete them on their own time without formal assistance. Some companies purchase workbooks generally available in bookstores, while others design and develop materials geared specifically to employee groups within their own firm. Upon completion of the workbooks, employees can turn to their supervisors or to personnel department staff for feedback and assistance in implementing their career plans.

Career planning workshops. Employee peer groups meet in classroom settings with career specialists to discuss the career planning process. Workshops are designed to cover the basics, but they may also be tailored to address specific issues: interviewing skills, retirement planning, dual-career problems, and so on. Support from, and interaction with, peers are two strengths of workshop programs.

Assessment and testing. The same programs established primarily to identify high-potential employees also may be used to assist employees seeking formal evaluations for personal planning purposes. In assessment centers or in consultation with human resources staff, individuals take psychological tests, participate in task simulation exercises, or interview with psychologists to obtain more current, standardized assessments of their potential for advancement. Such techniques and instruments give employees valuable feedback on their analytical, interpersonal, communication, and leadership skills, and assess intelligence, value orientations, occupational interests, and cognitive style.

Career counseling. Employees frequently wish to go over their personal career plans or self-assessment results on a personal basis for reactions and criticisms from trained career counselors. Counseling programs may structure open discussions of career plans with human resources staff, but supervisors, outside counseling services, and in-house psychologists often play important roles in some organizations.

Information Services. Even with completed self-assessments and clearly defined career goals, individuals cannot plan their careers without knowing the opportunities and the developmental programs offered in the firm. Information essential to career planning may be included in employee handbooks, in career workshops and workbooks, or in company newsletters; it may be shared through supervisors and managers; or, as in some companies, career resources centers may be established to serve as central information clearing houses for all career-related information. However the information is communicated, employees seek information of four types.

Staffing policies. Knowing the details of the methods by which the firm selects, trains, and promotes employees is essential for employee career plans to conform with corporate policies and procedures.

Job posting. Listings of vacant or new positions are commonly seen in unionized plants, where employees are guaranteed by their contracts the right to bid for open jobs in the bargaining unit. This practice is extended in some companies to include positions up to the executive level, where more complex selection procedures are typically employed, or where confidentiality is critical.

Career paths. The results of organizational career pathing programs are sometimes shared with employees to clarify management expectations for candidate qualifications for certain positions. A career path or "ladder" may state progression through a functional area so explicitly as to constitute in itself a career plan, complete with end goal, intermediate steps, and estimated timetables for reaching the final objective.

Employee evaluations. Individuals often seek to obtain the formal performance evaluations and ratings of potential on record in their own personnel files. Many organizations traditionally have regarded this information as confidential, refusing to release it even to the employee evaluated. But the value of this information for individual career planning is obvious. No career plan can be achieved without the support of the organization, and employees want to know where they stand in the organization's eyes before developing a detailed career plan the company might regard as impossible to support and, therefore, impossible to achieve.

Are Career Programs Effective?

We have stated several reasons that might prompt an organization to establish career programs, and we have shown that there are many types of programs organizations may choose to establish to meet those needs. Once a firm has committed itself to a career program, how can it know if its efforts are worthwhile?

To the extent that the programs have been established to address current staffing problems, organizations may use traditional personnel measures to evaluate program effectiveness: turnover rates, the number of external over internal hiring decisions made for executive positions, analysis of exit interviews, the results of EEOC audits, and the like. Some companies attempt to prove the effectiveness of their programs by pointing to increases in sales and profits, though such measures are related remotely if at all to career programs.

Gutteridge and Otte described *formal evaluation systems* which rely on course evaluations for workshop participants, questionnaires generating feedback on workbook helpfulness, telephone contacts with program participants and their supervisors, and periodic followup interviews with participants to gauge the longer-range impact of the programs on job performance, satisfaction, and attitude. They also found *informal evaluation systems*, which rely mainly on feedback voluntarily offered to program administrators by employee participants.[8]

For the most part, it seems little is done to systematically and formally evaluate program effectiveness in most firms today. Gutteridge and Otte's sample of 40 corporations with programs found only 15 with formal systems of evaluation, 8 with informal methods, and the rest attempting no program evaluation whatsoever.[9] These companies seem to share the attitudes expressed by two respondents to the study conducted by Morgan, Hall, and Martier, who stated: "We don't try to evaluate our programs," and "we just have faith in them."[10]

Evaluating the effectiveness of career programs is difficult for at least three reasons.

First, in trying to determine whether or not they contribute substantially to improving current staffing problems, one must assign and prove causal relationships. One must first determine what causes turnover, for example, and then disentangle the effects of the many variables to prove that declining turnover rates can be viewed as the effects of additional career programs. Second, in the case of long-term goals, costly and complex longitudinal studies are required to show any relationships between career programs and improvements in strategic human resources management; and more of the same is needed to show the relationships between strategic human resource management and improved organizational functioning. And finally, such variables as employee morale, job satisfaction, and career satisfaction are difficult to define and measure. Given these obstacles, it is not so hard to see why many human resources specialists and their managers are willing to rely on faith alone as justification for continued expenditures and efforts in career programs.

In a more positive light, an interesting approach was taken by Gary Hart and Paul Thompson in 1976. They compared employee assessments of their managers along several dimensions, including fairness, attentiveness to employee concerns, communication, and feedback for good performance. They found that managers who had attended career programs were rated higher by their subordinates in each of those dimensions than were managers who had not attended the programs.[11] Nonetheless, even this evidence cannot be taken as proof of the value of career programs in a corporation. Until further research identifies better ways

---

[8] Ibid., p. 23.

[9] Ibid., p. 23.

[10] Morgan, Hall, and Martier, "Career Development Strategies," p. 249.

[11] Gary L. Hart and Paul H. Thompson, "Assessment Centers: For Selection or Development?" *Organizational Dynamics*, Spring 1976, p. 73.

to evaluate program effectiveness, corporations will have to stand on unsubstantiated belief in the value of the programs to justify offering them.

The Problems with Career Programs

An inability to evaluate the effectiveness of career programs is one problem with career programs, but organizations seem to avoid it by ignoring it. At least three other drawbacks, however, are not so easily sidestepped.

First, there is the question of employee expectations once these programs are offered. Companies seem willing to offer some information and assistance to individuals who wish to plan their careers, but they cannot assume full responsibility for planning the careers of everyone in the organization. Management fears that employees will become overly dependent on the organization for counseling and advice. Or, in some cases, once employees have established their career plans, the organization fears that they will become impatient for advancement. Participants in career workshops, special training programs, or management assessment centers cannot be left with the belief that promotions are the inevitable and imminent outcomes of career programs. Managing employee expectations of the organization's role in their career planning and in their career advancement is a major concern of organizations implementing career programs today.[12]

Second, organizations must carefully define the limits of such programs within the firm. Which programs will be universal, offered to all employees, and which will be limited to certain groups? On what basis will these decisions be made? Organizations fear that employee demand for career programs will far outstrip their willingness to fund and their ability to implement them.

And perhaps most important, organizations must consider the costs of such programs, and the many resources required to establish and maintain career programs. In addition to budget allocations and the time that these programs demand, like any other organizational initiative, human resources are needed as well. In particular, most programs rely heavily on the effective support of supervisors to succeed. In both the AMA study and the study conducted by Morgan, Hall, and Martier, respondents stated that the supervisor is the most important counselor in career planning programs. Yet, the AMA study reported the following disturbing findings:[13] (a) 63% of supervisors perceived career planning as an increased burden; (b) 58% of supervisors felt that career planning for subordinates is *not* part of their jobs; and (c) 87% of supervisors felt that few were equipped to help with career planning and employee counseling.

Such widespread resistance to career programs by supervisors will necessarily hamper organizational efforts to implement effective programs. No matter how many human resources specialists may be hired at the staff level, there can be no substitute for the support and participation of first-line supervisors in the career planning process. Until supervisors perceive that their time and effort in this area is required and rewarded by the organization, and until they are trained in the skills and concepts of career management, they will fail to provide the critical input on which the success of career programs depends.

---

[12] James W. Walker, "Does Career Planning Rock the Boat?" *Human Resource Management* 17, no. 1 (Spring 1978), pp. 2–7.

[13] Walker and Gutteridge, "Career Planning Practices," p. 12.

Future Directions for Career Programs

Organizational involvement in individual career planning is increasingly common; but because it is a relatively new activity in most companies, much work remains to be done before career programs fully meet the needs of organizations and of individuals. Walker and Gutteridge concluded their 1979 study with the following observation:[14]

> The results suggest that career planning programs for salaried personnel are not nearly as common or as advanced as might be thought. While there is widespread support for career planning as a *concept,* there is a wide gap between the ideal and the reality of current practices.

Morgan, Hall, and Martier supported that conclusion in their finding that most career programs they studied were still experimental and informal.[15]

Based on these early attempts to make the ideals of career management in organizations a reality, American corporations should work for improvements in four areas.

First, organizations must more clearly define the *goals* of careers programs in terms of specific results expected from them. Much of the difficulty in evaluating program effectiveness is due to unclear management expectations of what these programs are intended to achieve. Likewise, employee expectations may be exaggerated partly because management has not made the roles and limitations of its involvement clear to them.

Second, organizations should test and improve the *techniques* employed in each type of career program offered. Much work can be done to improve the ways in which man-

power planning is linked to strategic planning, the instruments used to assess employee potential, and the computer systems employed in establishing and maintaining an accurate inventory of employee skills. All of the career programs described in this paper rely on techniques and procedures still being developed, and most are as yet unproven on their effectiveness and efficiency. More experimentation and evaluation is needed to ensure that organizational goals are being met in the best possible way.

Third, organizations must train their managers and supervisors in the concepts and goals of career planning in organizations. We have already stressed the importance of these individuals in making career programs successful; the most sophisticated and advanced techniques will be useless in the hands of managers and supervisors who do not understand or support the rationale for increased organizational involvement in the field. They must be shown how career management benefits the organization as well as the individual; they must be convinced that the increased demands on their time and effort are of real significance to the organization; they must accept the fact that career management *is* a part of their jobs. This will require a considerable effort on the part of organizations to train their managerial and supervisory personnel; it will take time, primarily because it requires changing a state of mind.

And finally, organizations must prepare their employees for the new organizational involvement in planning and managing their careers. Companies must clarify their purposes and their practices in career management if they are not to face widespread employee dissatisfaction with their efforts. Career planning does not mean promotions for everyone; it does not mean individualized career counseling on demand; it does

---

[14] Ibid., p. 1.

[15] Morgan, Hall, and Martier, "Career Development Strategies," p. 250.

not allow employees to fall back in passive reliance on the organization to tell them what they want from their work and then to give it to them. Organizations must instead communicate the goals, the programs, and the practices of career management in the firm which will allow each individual to take personal responsibility for planning and developing their own careers.

Career management is a relatively new and powerful concept in American corporations, one which is gaining strength and visibility as it results in a proliferation of programs and practices which show promise of meeting fundamental organizational and individual needs. The organization has a basic need to assemble a staff competent to meet the challenges inherent in its business; the individual has a basic need for economic security and psychological success in his or her work. Career programs, with time and experience, will enable both organization and individual to achieve their respective goals.

READING 3
NOTE ON EXECUTIVE SEARCH, CAREER COUNSELING, AND OTHER PLACEMENT SERVICES
Gregory Kenny, David Fisher, Liora Katzenstein, and Jeffrey A. Sonnenfeld

Executive search firms ("headhunters"), career counseling firms, employment agencies, and outplacement services are the topic of this note. Executive search and career counseling firms can be distinguished from each other in that executive search firms are under contract with corporations and nonprofit organizations to find candi-

dates for specific jobs; career counseling firms provide, as the name suggests, career counseling services to private individuals for a fee. Employment agencies can be divided into private employment agencies and government employment services. The former charge a fee, while the latter operate as a public service. Outplacement services provide help to those people who have been terminated by their company. Outplacement services can be either external or internal to the firm. Except for the very large corporation, it is usually the former. The rest of this note will describe each of these services in more detail.

A. EXECUTIVE SEARCH

Historical Overview

The modern executive search industry grew out of recommendations made by general management consultants in the 1950s. As client companies were urged to reorganize, positions were created that couldn't always be filled internally. This required an outside search for talent, something that consultants naturally developed as an adjunct to their established business. Annual gross search billings during the 1950s were on the order of $500,000 for the entire industry.

During the 1970s there was a dramatic increase in the use of search firms principally attributed to the decline in the use of the "old boy" or "patronage" system to fill jobs. In addition, high inflation rates and an uncertain global environment led to an increased demand for "quality" managers often possessing "special" or "unique" talents.

During the last four years the search industry has grown by 74 percent led by a 110 percent growth rate for the "Big Six".[1] The

[1] *Fortune*, September 3, 1981, p. 65.

Big Six dominate the search business and individually bill on an annual basis in the $15–$35 million range. These firms are Korn/Ferry International, Heidrick and Struggles, Spencer Stuart and Associates, Russell Reynolds Associates, Egon Zehnder International, and Boyden Associates. In spite of the growth rate of the larger firms, the industry is still dominated by one- to three-person firms (often split off from the Big Six). Industry observers estimate that there are probably 1,700 search firms of varying size doing business in the United States.

While the larger firms have gained notoriety for their occasional and, after completion, well-publicized searches for chief executive officers (CEOs) and board members (in 1980 "executives such as Richard W. Hanselman, Genesco Inc's new president; Clarence W. Spangle, Memorex Corp.'s new chief executive officer; Thomas D. Barrow, CEO for Kennecott Copper Corp.; and James H. Maloon, Itel Corp.'s CEO, found their positions through search firms"),[2] the bulk of executive recruiting is done in the middle and upper-middle management levels, for jobs generally paying $40,000 to $120,000 annually.

Firms can be broken down by those who are generalists and those who specialize in specific industries, functional areas, or geographic locations.

Why Companies Engage Search Firms

In a corporate address entitled "Ten Principles of Development of Key Professional Personnel," J. Stanford Smith, then chairman and chief executive officer at International Paper, said: "Executive recruiting can be a great stimulus to high-level perfor-

mance and is the surest way of gauging whether performance and compensation are mutually competitive."[3]

Industry observers[4] and practitioners cite several additional reasons for using search firms, among them:

The growing belief that human resources are the key to profitability in highly competitive markets.

The notion of half-life effectiveness of executives (creative energy early on is displaced by status-quo-seeking later in career).

Emphasis on bringing in new blood; firms are no longer womb to tomb.

Increased competition for executives in the 40 to 60 age group. Supply has been reduced due to low depression area birthrates, coupled with heavy casualties in WW II.

Corporate boards are increasingly dominated by outsiders accustomed to looking externally for talent.

Companies will call in a search firm when they are in need of a quick solution to a tough placement problem.

Internal politics often dictates the use of a well-known search firm to lend credibility to highly visible searches; consultants can bring objectivity.

Smaller firms requiring two or three executive searches a year can't justify the hiring of additional personnel staff.

Search firms have done a good marketing job and have gained acceptance in top management.

International expansion by American companies and corporate affirmative action programs added pressure for specially tailored searches.

---

[2] *Business Week*, May 5, 1980, p. 66.

[3] *California Management Review* 20, no. 4 (Summer 1978), p. 80.

[4] See for example, ibid., p. 79.

How to Choose the Right Executive Search Firm

Sixty-two search firms, including most of the major ones, are members of the Association of Executive Recruiting Consultants, Inc. (AERC). AERC members subscribe to a *Code of Ethics and Professional Practice Guidelines*,[5] which serves to define the relationship between a search firm and its client. According to John Conzelman, executive director of the AERC, this is "a form of self-regulation and the guidelines are part of an evolutionary process." The association also publishes *A Company's Guide to Executive Recruiting*;[6] it contains information about the executive recruiting process, how to select and work with a recruiting consultant, and information about fees and about the association's regulatory role.

A human resources director or corporate manager who is deciding on the use of a search firm should consider the following:

A. *Type of job to be filled.* Most search firms, while maintaining generalist capability, have well-known track records in certain areas. Some examples:[7]

Russell Reynolds / finance.

Lamalie Associates, Inc. / manufacturing.

William H. Clark Associates, Inc. / legal issues.

Bartholdi and Co. / small companies.

Witt Dolan / hospital administration.

Heidrick and Struggles / corporate presidencies.

Korn/Ferry / total service concept (mid-level recruitment through CEO).

Spencer Stuart / top management; strong international experience.

Except for the search arms of accounting firms, such as Peat, Marwick, Mitchell & Co., and for some general consulting firms, most search firms are not publicly held. As a result, factoring the size of a search firm into the choice criteria may be suspect since they all use varying accounting procedures. Korn/Ferry reports the largest annual billings and has a long-standing offer to go public with its audit if the competition will do the same.

B. *Engagement and fees.* Competition among search firms has gotten quite sharp. Headhunters are increasingly engaged in "shootouts," where several firms are called in to make an offer on a particular job. Some firms refuse to engage in such price wars and feel that they have no business doing a search if the potential client is "arguing over a couple of thousand dollars." As one search V.P. put it, "Fees are always a matter of judgment."

Traditionally, firms have generally charged about 30 percent of the starting salary to perform a search. Currently, the range seems to be between 20–60 percent, depending upon how difficult the search is expected to be and how well acquainted the search firm is with the client's structure and requirements. Repeat business is generally considered to be easier and more profitable. Many firms even go so far as to measure their performance on the basis of percentage of repeat business.[8] One recruiter stated that a New York-based search has a floor cost of around $15,000 due to high overhead, and billing charges that are

---

[5] *Code of Ethics and Professional Practice Guidelines.* Effective July 1977, by John F. Schlueter, Executive Director, Association of Executive Recruiting Consultants, Inc. (8 pp.).

[6] *A Company's Guide to Executive Recruiting*, copyright 1971, revised edition 1977 (12 pp.).

[7] *Business Week*, May 5, 1980, p. 66; and *Dunn & Bradstreet* Reports, January/February 1981.

[8] *California Management Review*, 20, no. 4 (Summer 1978), p. 83.

approximately $175 per hour for the principal, $100 for associates, $85 for research assistants, and $48 to $68 for secretarial help. This firm usually bids on a project (cost constructive) basis. Pricing policies have not been within the purview of the AERC.

C. *Raiding.* In order for a recruiting firm to do a good search for a client, it must learn about the client's organizational structure and personality. To do so requires that the headhunter become familiar with the executives within the client company. This familiarity could prove beneficial for the headhunter as they need to continue to expand and develop their "talent base" in order to meet future search requirements for different clients. The practice of courting the executives of former clients in industry jargon is known as "raiding." Traditionally, search firms would put former clients "off limits" to talent raids for the two years following a search, during which they are considered "active clients."

This greatly limited the growth potential of the industry and led to a lot of spinoffs. These smaller firms were able to sidestep self-imposed two-year rules since they were new entities. The larger firms with client bases sometimes exceeding 2,000 increasingly saw the two-year rule as a real barrier to growth. When Roger H. Morley, for example,[9] left the presidency of American Express Co., the numerous firms that have had Amex as a client could not recruit him. Many of the major corporations would hire each of the Big Six for a relatively low-level search in order to provide insurance against future raiding. Today guidelines are established on an individual basis during initial negotiations. Large multinationals generally will receive protection only for the division for

which the search is being conducted. Norms concerning raiding seem to be a matter of negotiation and conscience.

When choosing a search firm, industry sources have underscored the importance of getting client references, checking the firm's search competition rate (have they followed through expeditiously or let a search drag along), and, once engaged, getting involved in the process.

How the Search Process Works

When a client retains a search firm it is generally with the expectation that there will be a "quality placement" within a reasonable length of time (60–120 days) and handled in a professional and confidential manner. To accomplish the aforementioned, search firms generally proceed in the following manner:[10]

1. *Definition of Client's Need*

    A study is made of the client's organizational structure, management style, and place in the industry. Interviews are held with key people within the organization to assess the demands of the position and the type of individual that would offer the best fit. When a consensus has been reached on position requirements and candidate qualifications, the "headhunter" then draws up a job specification. With the criteria now in writing, the search for the right person begins in earnest.

2. *Sourcing*

    The searcher begins to generate prospective candidates by:

    a. Running an in-house computer search. Most firms find unsolicited

[9] *Business Week*, May 5, 1980, p. 66.

[10] This information is partially drawn from the company brochures of Korn/Ferry International and Russell Reynolds Associates, as well as the November 1979 issue of *The Executive*, which did a cover story on Richard M. Ferry of Korn/Ferry International.

résumés to be out of date in about 6 months and are thus hesitant to enter these individuals into their computers. Timeliness of data entries is a problem, and for this reason the major firms have been slow to implement the use of computers. Competitors do cite Russell Reynolds as an innovator in this area as they do frequent data updates and have executives categorized by function, type of industry, salary level, geography and age. Industrywide, however, only 1 in 20 candidates are generated from existing files.

b. Review of directories and professional journals. If an executive's name shows up in *Fortune* or the like, that person will probably be approached by headhunters in the near future.

c. Headhunters use working papers from past searches as lead sources (an executive who previously was an unsuccessful finalist for a finance position should not despair as there is a good chance that this executive will be approached again when a similar placement comes up).

d. Consultation with industry sources. This is where most candidates come from. Some firms send letters to CEOs and other top officers asking them to recommend people. Others charge that this is just clever advertising and are loathe to bother top people at this stage of the process. Most firms will wait until they have a few finalists and then ask top management for their judgment. All recruiters place a high premium on developing a network of industry contacts who play a key role in candidate identification and verification.

3. *Prescreening*

For senior positions, between 5 and 20 people will be interviewed by the recruiter. Headhunters say that a good personal chemistry between the interviewer and interviewee is the most important factor in the advancement to finalist status. In addition, candidates who have done some preliminary research on the client organization's structure and industry position frequently have the edge over their competitors.

4. *Submission of Finalists to Client*

A written report discussing each candidate's current job, responsibilities, relevant experience, accomplishments and background is presented to the client along with a subjective evaluation by the recruiter. The client then selects the individuals with whom they wish to conduct a personal interview. At this point the search firm will do a discreet reference check to corroborate their judgment.

5. *Negotiation and Closing*

Once the client has selected the person they want, it is then up to the recruiter to act as a mediator and help set the stage for final negotiations. Compensation and relocation issues need to be narrowed. This requires continuous communication by the recruiter with the candidate and client. Once the candidate is placed, the recruiter will try to closely monitor the developing relationship in order to smooth the transition period.

How to Get Noticed by a Search Firm

Thomas Aquinas once said, "Goodness is diffusive of itself." Translating this into the language of the executive placement firm, it means that people with strong track records in a particular area will be noticed and sought out. A good industrywide reputation in a functional area seems to be the most conspicuous avenue to the recruiter's lunch table. In today's tough economy, proven, operating and financial managers are reported to be in strongest demand. The MBA with a few years experience should not despair as search firms are increasingly handling middle management assignments. An effective way to bring one's availability to the attention of a headhunter is to have an article published in one of today's numerous industry magazines or through a personal introduction by an executive of a client company. In addition, most search firms publish a prospectus which includes biographic information on staff members.[11] A person sharing a common university affiliation can be a good résumé target. Lacking a contact, the aspirant might send their résumé to a number of search firms with a short cover note describing the type of position they seek and their functional area of interest. If the candidate has a varied background, this interest bracketing will be of particular importance. Search firms generally reply to this kind of inquiry with a short note stating that nothing is available now that matches the candidates professional qualifications but they will keep the résumé on file should an appropriate client situation develop. Then again, there may be that luncheon invitation. . . .

Executive Search as a Career

"Headhunters" can perhaps be described as a combination of entrepreneurs, behaviorists, and salesmen. Most firms experi-

ence very high turnover (20–25 percent per year) due to low entry costs (all you need is a telephone), growth limits for the larger firms, and high rewards. Mergers and splits are more the rule than the exception. The industry is still in a shakeout period and this will insure a good measure of uncertainty for those who choose search as a career. For example,[12] more than a fifth of Heidrick and Struggles's U.S. based professionals walked out in spring '81, pocketing their annual bonuses.

A. Hiring. Search firms have traditionally drawn candidates from three major areas:

1. Industry (people who have established a good line or staff reputation in a particular specialty area);
2. Human resource managers (who usually have become acquainted with the recruiting firm in a client capacity);
3. Other search firms (there is a lot of mobility within the industry; everyone seems to know each other).

Some firms, such as Korn/Ferry and Russell Reynolds, have hired people out of the better MBA programs, usually with three to five years experience. Good listening skills and a problem-solving orientation are underscored as key ingredients to a successful recruiting career.[13]

B. Compensation. Compensation in the industry has historically been tied to performance. Partners who brought in a lot of business did quite well. Many firms have found that highly competitive compensation structures have hurt intracompany co-

---

[11] See for example, *Russell Reynold Associates, Inc.,* Corporate Profile, 1981.

[12] *Fortune*, September 3, 1981, p. 67.

[13] See for example *California Management Review* 20, no. 4 (Summer 1978), p. 79.

operation and overall search quality. Increasingly, recruiters are being evaluated in part on how well they contribute to total performance. Handy Associates, for example, pays their executives a straight salary and a year-end bonus tied to company profitability. J. Gerald Simmons, president of Handy, notes that this structure removes artificial barriers to good search by downplaying competition between recruiters.

In general, a good practitioner with a few years of recruiting experience who is associated with a larger firm will earn around $120,000 to $140,000 per annum. Entry level positions offer between $30,000 and $50,000 per year depending on experience. Experts feel that it usually takes three years for the novice to learn the craft and become a full-fledged recruiter. A recruiter must be mobile, and willing to meet with candidates after hours.

The Future—Problems and Prospects

A flat world economy and a proliferation of search firms has led to increased competition within the industry. As a consequence, firms are looking for new ways to enlarge the pie. Many have begun to invest more effort into the international side of the business. Multinational corporations have helped headhunters catch on overseas. Spencer Stuart does 60 percent of its business abroad through an extensive network of locally staffed offices. Many of its competitors are headed in the same direction. Worldwide talent searches are becoming more common especially in the energy and financial fields. This area will continue to grow as headhunters become more practiced in this type of global search.[14]

Search firms are also headed into middle-management ranks in an attempt to broaden their base. Korn/Ferry, for example, is positioning itself to handle all the middle and top-management searches required by a client. To encourage this type of loyalty, Korn/Ferry maintains continuous contact with client companies in a human resource advisory capacity. Concurrent with their role as resource advisors, search firms are devoting more time to the publication of newsletters, surveys, opinion journals, and alike. These activities keep search consultants in the public eye (they are heavily quoted, for example, in *The Wall Street Journal*'s Tuesday "Labor Letter") and are a way of providing more value to their clients. The development of specialist expertise and a strong emphasis on "value added" will be key criteria for the future success of the search industry. This is especially important as headhunters have watched a growing trend by client companies to use in-house recruiters[15] (usually personnel departments). Human relations staffs are credited with becoming more sophisticated and discerning and are often cheaper to use than outside services.

Accounting firms with search arms have long battled with the problem of not being able to recruit from their SEC audit clients. Large consulting firms with search practices have found similar conflict of interest problems. Recently Booz-Allen dropped its profitable 50-year-old search practice, reportedly because they found it awkward to seek job candidates from the firm's 3,000-plus consulting clients.[16]

Despite some problems, search executives feel that the good firms will survive and prosper by providing quality services to clients that must compete for management

---

[14] *Fortune*, September 3, 1981, p. 65.

[15] *Business Week*, September 24, 1979, p. 62.

[16] *Business Week*, May 5, 1981, p. 66.

talent in a world where executive organizational loyalty has diminished and opportunism abounds.

B. CAREER COUNSELING FIRMS

Career counseling firms are different from executive placement firms in that they enter into a client-customer relationship with you. The leading firms are Haldane, Franklin and Robert Jameson Associates. They emphasize that they are not employment agencies, but provide career counseling. The types of service they provide are as follows:

1. Company executives spend time with each client providing career counseling.
2. They assess the marketability of the client and construct a marketing strategy for him. (Some career counseling firms refuse to take on people they feel are unmarketable.)
3. They help in writing résumés, cover letters, thank you letters, etc.
4. They make available computer listings of job opportunities.
5. They help to identify, generate and reach key contacts in various industries, by developing the client's sophistication in letter writing, conducting interviews, screening newspaper advertisements, and the like.
6. They provide guidance in negotiating and evaluating job offers.
7. Some firms provide access to positions not publicly listed (an area of increasing controversy, discussed below).

Fees Charged for These Services

Career counseling firms charge large fees for their services. The fee scale varies, but is usually related in some manner to the salary level expected. For example, some firms charge 10 percent of the salary level desired. Thus, if you are seeking a job with a salary of \$35,000, the fee you would pay would be \$3,500. These fees are usually paid up front or in installments over the career counseling period. Some firms only market clients to companies who are prepared to reimburse these clients for any fees incurred. Other firms provide varying refund guarantees if a suitable position is not obtained by the client, but it is important to note that a lot of money is payable up front.

Recent Controversy Concerning Career Counseling Firms

Over the last few years, a lot of accusations have been made against career counseling firms. These complaints usually center around the fact that the firms do not provide the results they promise in their advertisements. This is especially true with regard to the hidden job market (i.e., those positions not publicly advertised). People have complained that such "access" consisted only of being provided a long list of companies to which résumés could be sent. Career counseling firms reject these complaints, saying that all they promise to provide in their advertisements is knowledge of techniques to seek out and acquire jobs which are not normally publicly advertised.

The Usefulness of Services Provided by Career Counseling Firms

The services provided by career counseling firms appear to be most useful to the following type of person:

a. A person who feels that he or she has reached a plateau of their career and is seeking to give it a new direction.

b. A person who has lost his or her job for any reason and is seeking a new position.

C. EMPLOYMENT AGENCIES

As mentioned in the introduction, employment agencies can be divided into private employment agencies and government employment services. Each is discussed in turn.

Private Employment Agencies

The distinguishing feature about private employment agencies is that they charge a fee. The amount of the fee varies, as does whether it is paid by the employer or the employee. Services to employers may include the advertising of vacancies so that the employer's identity is not revealed, screening applications, conducting initial interviews and other services. Employment agencies may also be of help in providing temporary staff during summer periods. For the prospective employee, the employment agency can provide a source of job listings. In addition, services may include counseling and help in writing résumés. Employment agencies cover a wider range of people than executive placement firms, including people with technical skills, clerical skills, and so on. They are also less exact in their minimum requirements for taking on people.

Government Employment Services

In order to qualify for unemployment assistance a person is required to register for work with his or her employment service and be willing to accept any suitable work offered. For this purpose, public employment offices are maintained around the country, although their services are not restricted only to these people. They are state administered but subject to federal control, since states receive financial support from federal tax rebates. The service identifies for employers people who are unemployed and seeking work. In addition to supplying job applicants, the services of some state agencies include assisting employers in performing employment testing, job analysis and evaluation, community wage surveys, and the like. The services provided vary from state to state.

The state employment agencies do not charge for their services. Unfortunately, many employers tend to think that well qualified employees find work through other channels, so they only look to the government employment services for less skilled labor. Thus, well qualified people do not bother looking there, with the result that a vicious cycle begins.

Overall, employment agencies, both private and public, provide a useful service. They would appear to be most useful for employers and employees seeking to fill/obtain positions in middle to lower grade levels.

D. OUTPLACEMENT

Outplacement as a service grew out of the 1973–75 economic slowdown when many companies were forced to pare management ranks.[17] Recent increases in the number of mergers, acquisitions, plant closings, and worker displacement due to technology change or import substitution have also spurred the demand for mechanisms to handle dismissed employees. Today three fourths of the nation's largest corporations as well as a number of governmental institutions provide either in-house outplacement

---

[17] *U.S. News and World Report,* September 24, 1979, p. 77.

or engage the services of an outside contractor.

Leading firms are Career Management Associates, Performance Dynamics International, and T.H.I.N.C., Inc. The services provided by outplacement firms differ, but basically they provide counseling and job search help to employees who have been dismissed by a company. The typical outplacement program is usually made up of the following:

1. *Severance package:* Before a worker is fired a severance package is designed (Today discharged workers are getting triple the severance pay of five years ago. Now the average is about three month's pay. Companies are also extending the post-termination coverage period of insurance policies and other noncash benefits).[18]
2. *Supervisor coaching:* Most managers put off the unpleasant task of firing an employee. The outplacement firm tries to get managers to face the problem and to handle it in the best possible manner.
3. *Employee self-appraisal, confidence building, packaging, and contact assessment:* Terminated workers will be coached in the discovery of strengths/weaknesses, past accomplishments, skills transferability, areas of interest and opportunity. Help is offered in developing a positive sales pitch, a résumé, and a job search strategy. The development of a worker's personal contacts plays an important part in the process.

It differs among companies, but the employee is usually kept on for a period of time either on a full or part time basis while the outplacement program is being given. The use of a phone, office, and so on is provided. This helps the dismissed employee in the job search in that the employee may not have to come forward directly and say he or she has been fired. In addition, the fees of the outplacement firm are usually paid for by the former employer (usually 10 to 15 percent of the fired worker's annual salary, plus expenses).[19]

In recent years, outplacement companies have begun looking at placing dismissed employees in different areas of the same organization. It may be that the employee who did not meet the job requirements of one division, section or function, may have talents which are compatible with positions in other areas of the organization. There are many advantages to this practice. The main one is a cost consideration. Between severance pay, executive search fees, and the like, it can cost a company a lot of money to fire and replace an executive. If an executive can be successfully relocated in another part of the organization, a lot of these costs can be saved. In addition, cross-placed employees tend to retain loyalty to the company. They also have the benefit of knowing the company and how it works, which makes them productive a lot more quickly than a new employee.

In another development, many firms have begun outplacement counseling for discharged blue collar workers. Union contracts have made plant closings and work force cutbacks very expensive. If workers can be gotten off severance benefits and onto the payroll of a new company, then outplacement can pay for itself.

Outplacement firms have had good results in teaching assertiveness and job hunt skills to blue collar employees in spite of being hampered by the general unwillingness of non-management employees to pull up roots and move.

---

[18] *The Wall Street Journal,* October 13, 1981, p. 1.

[19] *U.S. News and World Report,* September 24, 1979, p. 78.

If outplacement programs at the lower level succeed on a pilot basis, it could, in the words of James C. Lindsey, president of a local United Rubber Workers chapter, "become a standard demand in contract talks."[20]

Companies who provide an outplacement service, either through the employment of an outside company or through in-house capability, say that the service they provide is successful. Besides helping dismissed employees get over the trauma of the dismissal and helping them to find new employment, it also usually has a beneficial effect on company morale. Employees tend to feel that the company is concerned with their welfare. David Switkin, the industrial psychologist who runs Citibank's outplacement service, says that direct employer help gives more undivided counseling and gives visible evidence to people who stay that the company cares.[21] Charles Klensch, assistant vice president of Citibank, adds that it is absurd to say it, but people in the program actually feel good about it.[22] Finally, it also helps to retain the loyalty of dismissed employees who otherwise, through either frustration or bitterness, reveal confidential or compromising information to people outside the firm.

READING 4
NOTE ON TRAINING AND EDUCATION IN BUSINESS*
E. Mary Lou Balbaky and Jeffrey A. Sonnenfeld

The training and development of employees are and have been significant parts of modern business. Business is no less a segment of the nation's educational system than colleges and universities, technical institutes, and other schools. A company cannot run effectively and efficiently today without a skilled and committed workforce, no matter how good its business strategies. An increasingly salient question is: whose responsibility is it to ensure a well-prepared and responsive workforce? Technological advances and other factors that affect the labor market profoundly are posing problems of training and retraining of the workforce that are unparalleled in history. From management's point of view, continuing education of blue-collar, white-collar, and professional employees is a matter of survival. From the societal perspective, unless training and retraining programs are provided the livelihoods of hundreds of thousands of people are likely to be affected in the next decade with widespread social repercussions.[1]

Many business executives are critical of the performance of the nation's schools and colleges in preparing people for work. Some charge that public education has not done an adequate job of teaching people even basic mathematical and communications skills, and has had little concern with fitting education to meet industry's needs.[2]

Companies have always done some in-house, on-the-job training of employees. Formal training programs were established in the late 19th century with "corporation schools" which enabled industry to meet its need for skilled labor when vocational education programs were too few to meet the demand. Following World War II, as business and industry became increasingly large

---

[20] *Business Week*, February 4, 1980, p. 88.

[21] *The Wall Street Journal*, November 10, 1980, p. 32.

[22] Ibid.

---

[1] "Changing 45 Million Jobs," *Business Week*, August 3, 1981.

[2] Sally Reed, "The Basic Skills, Company Style," *New York Times*, August 30, 1981, Section 12, p. 20.

and complex, a shortage of managerial talent made it necessary for companies to establish their own developmental programs for supervisory, managerial, and executive personnel as well.[3]

Yet, the extent of business involvement in education and training is still expanding significantly, according to a special report by the *New York Times* in August 1981. Business enterprises are taking ever-increasing responsibility for the education and training of their employees and have become leading competitors of schools and colleges at all levels, from the provision of remedial reading and math courses to postdoctoral training.

Although the scope of education and training in business is extremely broad and clearly expanding, good quantitative data on the number and type of training programs which exist and the costs of this investment in human capital are very sparse. The total scope or dimensions of corporate education and training activities are only dimly perceived. No one has yet defined or described the full dimensions of education in business in the detail that is needed and little is known about the total training structure in the United States, or even within very large companies, because training activities are so diffuse.

Pilot feasibility studies of training in business and industry were done in 1968 and 1971 by the Bureau of Labor Statistics and the University of Wisconsin Center for Studies in Vocational and Technical Education. A survey was also done by the Bureau of National Affairs in 1969. These studies yielded some indicative data but concluded that their mail survey methods were inadequate.[4]

The most extensive study done in the 1970s was a survey by the Conference Board in 1974–75 of almost 2,800 companies, which yielded 610 completed, usable questionnaires. The study was limited to inquiries about formal, off-the-job training programs by companies with over 500 employees.[5]

Indications

The surveys to date indicate that only medium-size and large firms (over 500 employees) have significant training programs, and most firms with large training programs are in manufacturing and service industries. Although training is very extensive, company records on training lack detail and uniformity and are frequently unavailable.

An estimate made in 1971 suggested that "in the early 1970s training programs (of all kinds) probably included $2/3$ of all workers."[6] The 1969 Bureau of National Affairs survey found that three-fourths of the 286 firms studied had both formal and informal training programs for rank-and-file employees. This figure doesn't include orientation, general education, and management development courses.

The Conference Board study concluded that approximately 4.3 million employees of big business—better than one in eight—took formal courses offered by their companies, most during working hours. The study also reported that 75 percent of all companies provided some in-house courses for their employees; 89 percent had tuition aid or refund programs; 75 percent authorized some of their employees, mostly managers and professionals, to take outside courses

---

[3] William R. Tracy, "Training and Development in the 1970s and 1980s," in *Managing Training and Development Systems*, AMACOM, 1974, p. 4.

[4] Ibid., pp. 6–9.

[5] Seymour Lusterman, *Education in Industry* (New York: The Conference Board, 1977).

[6] Tracy, "Training," p. 7.

during working hours at the company's expense.[7]

Costs

The most elusive aspect of education and training in business is costs. Detailed records of costs are often nonexistent. The training activities in a company are frequently spread through many different departments and costs are buried in individual budgets. Some firms consider training as an expense; other capitalize it as the cost of a product and carry training expenses as subaccounts of major accounts. Only one-third of 240 firms surveyed in 1969 had a separate budget for training activities.[8]

Various estimates of overall costs of education and training by business enterprises in the United States have been attempted in spite of the sparse data which exists. A report in 1971 estimated that expenditures for education by businesses in the late 60s totaled almost $20 billion annually. In 1974, W. R. Tracy estimated that the total expenditure in the U.S. was around $27 billion, assuming that two out of three employees received some kind of training.[9]

In 1981, the estimated total business corporation outlay for educational activities was $30 billion, according to the American Society for Training and Development.[10] This amount is almost as much as the annual expenditure on education in all publicly financed colleges and universities.

The Conference Board survey made a much lower but still substantial estimate of total annual costs for 1974–75. They estimated that companies spent about $2 billion on direct costs alone for formal, off-the-job educational courses.[11]

AT&T has been frequently described as a fascinating example of the extent and costs of education in the workplace. To maintain its skilled workforce of over 1 million employees, AT&T provides more education and training than any university in the world. In 1977, AT&T reportedly spent $700 million on its programs. In comparison, MIT's 1977 budget was only $222 million.[12] The AT&T cost figures for 1977 may actually be low. Among other problems in gathering cost data, the definition of what constituted "training" varied within the company. Current cost figures are reportedly more accurate. According to the *New York Times* report, in August 1981 AT&T invested $1.1 billion a year on developing courses, paying instructors, and providing facilities for its extensive training system. Of the total AT&T workforce, 30,000, or about 3 percent, attend classes on any given day.

Types of Training and Educational Courses

The range of skills and subjects taught in corporations is very large, ranging from high school remedial courses to postdoctoral-level programs. Remedial courses have been necessary in part to comply with federal affirmative action guidelines that require hiring minorities with sometimes inadequate educational backgrounds. At AT&T all courses conducted and funded by the company must directly prepare employees for doing their jobs. However, this has not always been the case. In the mid 50s, AT&T provided many of its upper and mid-

---

[7] Lusterman, *Education in Industry*, p. 2, 11.

[8] Tracy, "Training," p. 10.

[9] Ibid., p. 11.

[10] Gene I. Maeroff, "Business Is Cutting into the Market," *New York Times*, August 30, 1981, Section 12, p. 1.

[11] Lusterman, *Education in Industry*, p. 12.

[12] Stan Luxenberg, "Education at AT&T," *Change*, December–January 1978/79, p. 27.

dle-level managers with fine graduate programs and courses in the humanities. Other companies vary in the extent to which they require education and training, paid for by the company, to be directly job oriented.[13]

Companies use various mixtures of outside and inside resources, of during and after-hour study, of on-site and off-site special seminars and institutes. Exhibit 1 gives a list of the most common types of training and education courses offered in business and industry today.

Retraining programs for employees displaced by automation are increasing but adequate statistics are not available. In 1969, the Bureau of National Affairs reported that already about 15 percent of the companies surveyed had retraining programs for employees displaced by automation and about 30 percent had systematic upgrading programs to prepare first-line supervisors and rank-and-file employees for job advancement.[14]

One of the most important areas in training and education has been the identification and development of managerial talent. Common programs include:

1. Presupervisory training programs that usually focus on the development of supervisory, human relations, and leadership skills.
2. Middle-management development programs that focus on management theory, decision making, and problem solving. They make use of such techniques as assessment centers, case problems, critical incidents, discussion, simulation, in-basket exercises, and business games. They may involve rotational job assignments, participation in committees and junior boards, and at-

---

[13] Ibid., p. 33.
[14] Tracy, "Training," p. 9.

Exhibit 1 Types of Training Programs Widely Used in Business and Industry

1. *Companywide training programs*, which include orientation courses for new employees, tuition aid or remission programs to enable employees to improve job-related skills or to acquire new skills, voluntary general education programs designed to further personal development, safety training, human relations training, training programs covering specialized enterprise functions and processes, and correspondence study for field employees.

2. *Manufacturing and production training programs*, which include apprenticeship training to develop needed production and manufacturing skills, formal entry-level semiskills and skills programs to develop beginning-level job proficiency, formal advanced-level skills and technical training, on-the-job training, both entry level and advanced, and cooperative work-study programs, in which assignments are alternated between the company and a cooperating school or college.

3. *Engineering and scientific training programs*, nondegree in-house programs designed to update and upgrade the knowledge and skills of engineers and scientists, on-site degree programs to enable engineers and scientists to pursue advanced degrees, resident university programs designed to permit employees to acquire advanced degrees, part-time campus degree programs, and engineering or scientific management programs designed to update the skills of employees responsible for managing highly technical and scientific functions.

4. *Marketing and sales training programs*, of varying lengths and degrees of complexity, sales engineering training, service engineering training, customer training, and dealer training.

Source: William R. Tracy, *Managing Training and Development Systems*, AMACOM, 1974, p. 8.

tendance at outside seminars and conferences. Study at colleges and universities may also be included.

3. Executive development programs that usually involve on-the-job coaching. Formal in-house training may include discussions, simulation role playing, and grid seminars. Sensitivity training and university courses also may be promoted.

Many firms pay particular attention to identifying "high potential" employees making long-range plans for their development and training.

Why Do Companies Educate?

Education and training are the most basic means to ensure that a company has the skilled manpower that it requires. The need to teach new employees about their jobs or to train present employees and to take on new responsibilities seems self-evident. What is less evident is that a major portion of education and training in business is undertaken because there is no alternative. Most large companies require some special kinds of expertise which are not found in the general labor market, and many companies' needs for highly skilled people far outstrip the supply produced by our uncoordinated and dispirited public educational and vocational training systems. The rapid technological changes which are occurring in the highly competitive worldwide market are a dramatic example of pressures which compel large corporations to set up or expand their internal training and retraining systems.

In addition, a large part of company-sponsored education and training is seen by management as an "investment in human capital." Education and training programs are widely regarded as ways of engendering occupational vitality and commitment to work, particularly among professionals and managers. Company-sponsored education encourages individual growth without loss to the company of essential personnel and with the possibility of a "return on investment" of increased competence, productivity, or innovativeness.

Training programs at all levels are seen as methods of stabilizing employment—of building on and making use of the available knowledge and experience of people in the company while reducing turnover and enhancing morale.[15] Education and training opportunities, and the implicit promise of advancement which they hold out, increase the attractiveness of a firm and can sometimes be traded for lower wages. But there is an inherent tension in programs which develop personnel. Unless actual advancement follows the successful completion of a training program, the program itself may breed frustration and discontent and increase turnover. One company in the Conference Board survey which supported employees in obtaining college degrees found that 12 percent of new degree winners who were not promoted quit the company within a year.

Training programs may also reflect a commitment on the part of top management to meet in good faith the legal and moral requirements of increasing opportunities for racial and ethnic minorities, women, and older employees.

But there are also irrational reasons why companies maintain extensive training programs, including the attraction of new management fads, tradition, and inertia. Training programs can proliferate and become well-entrenched systems which are difficult to evaluate and difficult to dislodge.

---

[15] Lusterman, *Education in Industry*, p. 6.

Trends and Challenges

There are a number of forces gaining momentum in society which lead observers to predict a "training crisis" for businesses and for the educational system as a whole. To what extent the crisis is real and how dramatic its impact will be is yet to be determined. We can, however, list the areas of significant change which will require awareness and response from business management. Factors include rapid changes in technology and automation of work processes, changes in the makeup of the population and the workforce, intensified foreign competition, economic pressures including inflation and high unemployment, changing attitudes and expectations toward work and careers, and continuing government regulation of employment practices.

Technological Change. *Business Week* in August 1981 reported that:

> Scholars of automation . . . expect a radical restructuring of work including a devaluation of current work skills and the creation of new ones at an ever increasing rate. . . . These changes will require employers to retrain huge numbers of workers. Ultimately the nation's educational system will have to prepare future workers for functioning in an electronic society. . . . There are no reliable statistics on how many companies retrain workers for new technology but most experts feel that such programs are few—or at least underdeveloped—compared to what will soon be required.[16]

Changes in the Workforce and Population. The population of the United States is slowly growing older on the average, in part due to increasing longevity. Expectations for second careers and longer working

lives may have to be met requiring extensive retraining. Increasing numbers of women are entering the workforce with different needs, motivations, and expectations. There is more demand from racial and ethnic minorities for higher-status jobs and opportunities.

Foreign Competition. Economic competition from other countries becomes more vigorous every year. American industry is having to consider other, possibly more effective forms of work organization and new ways of creating motivation and commitment on the part of employees.

Economic Pressures and High Unemployment. Inflation and recession economics put pressures on management for better cost controls, including reducing turnover rates and providing other work incentives besides wage increases. There is serious threat of high unemployment and labor imbalances stemming from increasing automation and the lack of any coordinated, flexible public/private adult education and job information systems.

Changing Attitudes and Expectations Toward Work and Careers. Although there are increasingly greater extremes in educational attainment in the population, the average educational level has been rising, bringing with it different values and attitudes toward work.

Direct production, clerical, and service jobs are declining while the demand for "knowledge workers"—engineers, accountants, computer personnel, managers—is increasing.

Among highly educated workers there are greater demands that work be meaningful both to the individual and to society. Education is considered as a lifelong experi-

---

[16] "Changing 45 Million Jobs," *Business Week*, August 3, 1981.

ence not limited to a single phase of the life cycle. There is a greater questioning of the authority of status and position, more demand for involvement in decision making, and much higher valuation of personal growth and opportunities for training.

READING 5
THE TRICKY TASK OF PICKING AN HEIR APPARENT*
Roy Rowan
Katharena Leanne Zanders, research associate

Picking a successor, say chief executives, is the most important decision they and their directors will make. It also may be the toughest and one of the worst. "You see the wrong guy selected a lot," says J. Peter Grace, 69, the longest-reigning chief executive of a Fortune "500" company, who is reluctantly beginning to think about replacing himself at W. R. Grace & Co. Within the next three years, 35 of the 100 biggest corporations among the 500 are due to change leaders.

To explore the selection process, *Fortune* recently interviewed 25 reigning and former chief executives. Clearly it's a sensitive subject. The boss doesn't relish talking about that near or distant day when he will abdicate power, nor does he want to tip his hand. "Obviously I don't go around talking about who should succeed me," says Edward Jefferson, 61, chairman of Du Pont. And an ex-chief executive is loath to give away secrets about a company that he probably still serves in an advisory capacity.

Departing bosses and their boards will talk in general terms about the kind of replacement they want, and how this up-and-

coming leader should be groomed. They identify the most sought-after qualities as integrity, self-confidence, physical and mental fitness, the ability to think strategically, and a facility for communicating ideas. They also expect the new chief to be homegrown—either cultivated in the headquarters greenhouse or farmed out to a major division until he's ripe. Directors stress the importance of an orderly transition, or "no surprises," as they say.

But surprises persist. This is a dangerous time for men at the top. Increasingly the freshly picked chief gets fired or quits in a huff, and headhunter rushes to the rescue. RCA has become a revolving door for chairmen and presidents, having survived a total of eight in the past eight years (see box, page 345). ITT stumbled dramatically trying to fill Chairman Harold Geneen's giant shoes. His first successor, Lyman C. Hamilton, Jr., lasted a mere 17 months.

Sometimes it's the Job-patient heirs apparent who are passed over with stunning suddenness. Just this year two long-serving presidents, David Judelson of Gulf & Western and Ronald Fidler of Black & Decker, watched their executive vice presidents catapult into the chief's seat. Then there are those widely heralded hired-gun successors, who sometimes get sacked before they succeed—a not entirely unexpected happening if they've entered the employ of such hardy perennials as William Paley, 82, of CBS—who finally yielded up the chief executive's title to Thomas Wyman—or Armand Hammer, 84, of Occidental Petroleum.

"Not enough thought is given to the psychological fit of a chairman or president to his role," says Harry Levinson, publisher of a Cambridge, Massachusetts, management newsletter that frequently dwells on succes-

Braking the Revolving Door at RCA

RCA is a prime example of what can happen to a company when the successors don't succeed and the selection process breaks down. Four chief executives plus assorted presidents and subsidiary chiefs whirled in and out of RCA's revolving door in just six years. By 1981 profits were down by 83 percent and the company had become "the laughingstock of Wall Street," as Chairman Thornton Bradshaw puts it. The board finally took control by firing Chairman Edgar Griffiths and putting Bradshaw, president of Atlantic Richfield and an RCA director since 1972, in his place. "This was a very troubled corporation," says another director, Champion International Chairman Andrew Sigler. "It was much more complicated than what the analysts were saying—just sell off a couple of subsidiaries and everything will be all right."

The board gave Bradshaw a five-year contract and three goals to accomplish before it runs out in 1986: find a way to stabilize the dissension-torn company; find out what kind of company it should be; find a replacement. The urbane doctor of commercial science (he once taught at Harvard), known as Brad, signed up Gerard R. Roche, the chairman of the Heidrick & Struggles search firm, to mount an exhaustive hunt. As Bradshaw explains: "The problem was how to conduct a wide external search and still keep it quiet. We didn't want people at RCA to get upset, though it was apparent that there was no suitable successor within the organization." Bradshaw had used Roche once before to find a director for RCA. "I knew he had a tremendous file," Bradshaw says. "More important, I knew he could keep a secret."

Roche produced an initial list of 75 names. "Mature, experienced, low-key, nonflamboyant, but with a high energy level: those were the characteristics we were looking for," says Roche. "We didn't want some star-fire executive with a big ego who would knock down the structure Brad was working hard to build." But few executives possessing those traits also had the desired "mirror image," as Roche called the matching experience in broadcasting, electronics, aerospace, international sales, and finance that the candidate needed to run RCA.

Brad and Gerry huddled frequently, while the chairman kept the board apprised of progress. Very quickly they cut the list to a dozen. "All of them were gainfully employed," recalls Bradshaw, "and, we assumed, happy with what they were doing." Roche contacted each man. Some said they didn't want to be considered, but would talk. Others sounded interested. Bradshaw invited each to lunch—most often at his New York apartment. "If they showed up at RCA," he says, "somebody would have surely asked, 'What in hell's he doing here?'"

One by one the list of names shrank. "There were only three or four who were really outstanding," says Bradshaw. By then the finalists were being subjected to "intensive reviews" by the board's executive committee, consisting of Sigler; Peter G. Peterson, chairman of Lehman Brothers Kuhn Loeb; John Petty, president of Marine Midland Bank; Robert Cizik, president of Cooper Industries; and Donald Smiley, former chairman of R.H. Macy & Co. "We were asked by Brad to use our references to discreetly check them out," says Peterson. "When the board brought Brad in, we said we wanted quality and we got it. The same went for his heir apparent. We couldn't afford a mistake." Sigler is even blunter: "I don't think Brad could have picked somebody we didn't want."

Last September Bradshaw and the executive committee made their choice: Robert R. Frederick, 57, executive vice president of General Electric.

The mirror image Roche was so anxious to attain seemed almost perfect. Formerly chief of corporate planning and development at GE, Frederick had also headed GE's international operations, GE Credit Corp.—a subsidiary similar to RCA's CIT Financial—and the consumer products group, which included appliances and GE's TV and radio stations.

Frederick did not immediately accept. Roche sized up the problem this way: "Here was this man who could replace Bradshaw, but there was one important profit center—NBC—that would not be reporting to him." In one of his first moves, Bradshaw had fired NBC President Fred Silverman and brought in Grant Tinker, who still reports directly to him.

Frederick claims Tinker's independence was not the problem. "I knew GE wasn't going to promote me," he says. "That was my top-out job. But the issue was: do I leave a company that had been good to me for 34 years for a company that had, you might say, an uneven performance and a reputation for chewing up management?" The decision was made even harder because the security blackout imposed by Bradshaw meant Frederick couldn't talk it over with pals and business associates. But he liked Brad. "He seemed open, supportive, and looking for leadership," says Frederick. "It was not a situation where he'd want to hang on."

Bradshaw plans to remain chairman for three more years. "When Bob will become C.E.O. is still open," he says. "When he has his feet on the ground," he adds professorially. What are Bob's plans? "I told the executives here that my goal is never to go outside for a president again." Then he adds, "But I can't commit to that."

sion problems. He cites International Harvester's appointment of Archie McCardell as chief executive in 1978 as a flagrant case of a company "failing to put together a behavioral job description before bringing in a new chief." Though few blame Harvester's problems entirely on McCardell, he was fired four years later after a long and largely fruitless battle with the United Auto Workers and much criticism of his generous compensation arrangements.

A sagging economy can also alter the specs on chief executives. In boom times budget, production, and marketing miscalculations are easier to cover over. "Today the tightfisted bottom-line manager is the guy everybody's looking for," says David F. Smith, New York director of Korn/Ferry International, the largest executive search firm. But he claims companies know only what kind of chief executive they want at a particular moment. "Obviously it's a longer-reaching decision," he says. Smith believes that in a year or two the bottom-liners may be out of fashion and the "strong marketers" back in vogue.

In the best of times, selecting a new boss is an impressionistic process. Much of it is unspoken and intuitive. A glance or a nod at a board meeting may carry more weight than words when the choice is being made. So in many cases the deciding factors are never known. Headhunters believe that selection committees frequently feel frustrated because they are searching for a composite—a mythical executive who combines all the best traits of the candidates being considered. "Often they're looking for the impossible dream," says Russell S. Reynolds Jr., chairman of the search firm that bears his name.

Although his firm's computerized retrieval system keeps tabs on 15,000 executives, Reynolds concedes, "The best C.E.O.s tend to come from within." The inside appointment, he says, is better understood and less of a shock. "Companies do not respond well to shocks," he adds. "It takes a boat a long time to stop rocking."

E. Pendleton James, President Reagan's former White House personnel director and a headhunter who specializes in recruiting directors and chairmen, lays a lot of the blame for succession problems on cronyism among directors. "I'm negative on boards as they're now constituted," he says. "They're ossified and incestuous." Many directors, he feels, "stay too long at the fair" and serve on too many boards. "After reading this," he adds, "no one will want to retain me."

When a board is willing to look outside the company, James sees a new tendency to look outside the industry as well. He points to CBS's Wyman, recruited from Pillsbury; Burlington Northern's new chairman, Richard Bressler, brought in from Atlantic Richfield; and former Secretary of Transportation Drew Lewis, hired to head Warner Amex Cable Communications. "They came after Lewis because he was a man with great leadership and management skills, not because he was a transportation expert," observes James.

Only paltry statistics have been kept that bear on the success and failure of the chief executive selection process, and most of the figures are buried in headhunters' computers. Carl Menk, president of Boyden Associates, a search firm based in New York City, reports that during the three years beginning in 1976, 62 Fortune 500 companies changed chief executives, an average of 21 a year. During the four years starting with 1979, the average jumped to 36, an increase of 80%. During both periods slightly more than a quarter of the new bosses were recruited from outside the company.

Eugene Jennings, professor of business administration at Michigan State University, says that 22.5 percent of the two top officers of a sampling of major companies either resign or get fired before reaching retirement age, compared with 5% in 1969. His "mobility auditing program" lumps together the records of the No. 1 and No. 2 executives at 480 corporations—a list that he claims is roughly comparable to the Fortune 500. "Almost a third of those now leaving early have got caught up in some kind of palace revolt," reports Jennings, who spends more time advising chief executives than he does teaching. Conflict over the strategic direction of the enterprise can trigger early departure. "Disagreement over where the company is going and how it should get there takes its toll," Jennings says.

Big companies have no standard procedures for picking the people to run them. A standing nominating committee that the board uses to get new directors frequently takes on the task. If he's especially strong, the outgoing chief will take the lead. Lately, however, boards have become more independent. "More and more you see the selection committee of the board picking their own person and derailing the chief executive's candidate," says Jennings.

Some companies mark the finalists well before a winner is declared. General Electric named three vice chairmen in 1979 and a year later made one of them, John F. Welch Jr., chief executive. Many big firms use formal "leadership identification" programs. Some even color-code personnel records to indicate an executive's potential—red for "not promotable," yellow for "take another look," and green for "promotable."

Prime Candidates for Change at the Top

Fortune 500 Rank	Chief Executive and Company	Age	Years on Top	What Security Analysts Say
Chief executives past customary retirement age:				
50	**J. Peter Grace,** W. R. Grace	69	38	He gave up the president's title to Carl Graf and made his cousin Charles Erhart a vice chairman. But nobody wants to guess when Grace will retire.
15	**Armand Hammer,** Occidental Petroleum	84	26	President Robert Abboud is ready and waiting, but Hammer isn't quitting. Major stockholder David Murdock will probably end up the real boss.
80	**William C. Norris,** Control Data	71	26	The visionary founder is in no hurry, but when Norris does quit, analysts expect less idiosyncratic management under engineer Robert Price.
99	**Dean A. McGee,** Kerr-McGee	79	20	Heir apparent to the founding partner is President Frank McPherson, up through the ranks since 1957, who is not expected to change much.
28	**Fred L. Hartley,** Union Oil of California	66	19	Hartley probably will not leave until the shale oil project—his real interest—is on its feet. No clear successor is visible from outside.
46	**David S. Lewis,** General Dynamics	65	13	Oliver Boileau came from Boeing in 1980 as heir apparent. But Lewis may take another look now that his contract has been extended for two years.
26	**Walter A. Fallon,** Eastman Kodak	65	11	Fallon's still unannounced retirement is slated for July. President Colby Chandler is next in line, continuing Kodak's tradition of homegrown bosses.
25	**J. Paul Sticht,** R.J. Reynolds Industries	65	4	Sticht delayed retiring and there's a shootout among four candidates. Wall Street gives an edge to Hicks Waldron, head of new subsidiary Heublein.
76	**John W. Culligan,** American Home Products	66	2	He was already 64 when he took over as an interim chief executive; his predecessor left at age 67. President John Stafford, 45, is being groomed.
One year or less away from customary retirement age:				
10	**John E. Swearingen,** Standard Oil (Indiana)	64	23	After 23 years, Swearingen is scheduled to step down in September. President Richard Morrow is the choice of nearly everyone, including Swearingen.
94	**William B. Johnson,** I C Industries	64	15	Competition is between Vice Chairman Robert Schnoes and Executive Vice President Robert Stewart. Either would continue to diversify.
83	**John V. James,** Dresser Industries	64	13	Early favorite John Murphy, who is president, may be losing ground. A dark horse would come from the company's Texas old-boy network.
31	**Robert E. Kirby,** Westinghouse Electric	64	8	Douglas Danforth will take over in December in a preplanned, preannounced transition. The only question is why no No. 2 was named.

73	**Donald D. Lennox,** International Harvester	64	5 mos.	This is no time to be worrying about a successor at troubled Harvester.

Two years or less away from customary retirement age:

20	**Harry J. Gray,** United Technologies	63	11	He lost Ed Hennessy to Allied and Al Haig to the State Department, so Gray is due to pick a new heir. But he'll probably stay on top for a few more years.
32	**George Weissman,** Philip Morris	63	5	Too early to tell. But analysts think Weissman ought to make something out of his disappointing Seven-Up acquisition before choosing a new chief.
5	**Philip Caldwell,** Ford Motor	63	4	In this giant bureaucracy it's hard for outsiders to see the rankings. But everybody noticed when Harold "Red" Poling was brought back from Europe.
17	**William C. Douce,** Phillips Petroleum	63	3	President C. J. "Pete" Silas will move up just as Douce did two years ago in a company that prizes orderly transitions.
91	**Edwin A. Gee,** International Paper	63	3	Current favorite is President John Georges, who like his boss came to the company after a career at Du Pont.
4	**John K. McKinley,** Texaco	63	3	President Alfred DeCrane and Vice Chairman James Kinnear are both qualified, but analysts have noticed that Kinnear has the larger office.

Some of the chief executives on the list above—drawn from the 100 largest companies on the Fortune 500—seem oblivious to any sort of retirement age. Others are bound by tradition or company policy to step aside by their 65th birthday for a younger manager. Tradition is the stronger force. Boards of directors can make exceptions to the rules—as General Dynamics did last fall. But that action is rare where precedent has been long established. Founder-leaders often stay on and on.

Change at the top can be especially unsettling when the boss has been a dominant figure for many years. It is less so where professional managers have made transition in the leadership more a process and less an event. Fortune talked to more than 50 Wall Street analysts who follow the various companies. The comments above are compiled from their expectations of what will happen after the changing of the guard.

But no fail-safe system prevents a candidate colored green throughout his company career from bombing as boss. On today's fast track the highest-octane performer "may be burned out by the time he sinks into the chief executive's chair," says Robert W. Lear, former chairman of the E. & M. Schaefer Corp. and a visiting professor at the Columbia University Graduate School of Business. Or he may have been judged too much on efficiency, rather than on less tangible character traits. "Chief executives can fail or succeed depending on whether they attract the trust of their colleagues," says Kenneth R. Andrews, editor of the *Harvard Business Review* and a director of Xerox. "It's a rather slippery thought, but it's important, especially with all the hoopla about the failure of the American manager because he's too short-term oriented and not concerned about the development of people."

From the chief executives' vantage, choosing a successor is a complex task that requires as much help as he can get. "I don't think any CEO sits in his office and comes up with a name," says Du Pont's Jefferson. "I have an exchange of views with members of the board and former chief executives, including Irv Shapiro, Charles McCoy, and Crawford Greenewalt. The other thing I do is make sure that the senior members of management get plenty of exposure—reviewing plans at board meetings, and under more informal circumstances. That way all the directors have a pretty good understanding of the merits of the people who could be candidates when we finally get down to a replacement.''

The $33-billion-a-year corporation has one executive committee for traditional Du Pont operations and another for Conoco, acquired in 1981. ''Both report into the office of the chairman,'' Jefferson explains. ''Three of us are there—myself, Dick Heckert, who's vice chairman for the traditional business, and Ralph Bailey, who's vice chairman for the Conoco division. In the course of the deliberations of those committees you get quite a reading on people, and what they accomplish.''

Like many chief executives, Jefferson believes that new directions taken by the company will help determine who succeeds him. ''Where you're trying to go,'' he says, ''is part and parcel of the decisions on people. I've got to emphasize, though, that there are many ways of skinning a cat and many ways of running a business. Different people bring different things. But then you're asking me to comment on something I haven't done yet and will only do once.''

Jefferson's mentor and predecessor, Irving Shapiro, 67, admits that in a big corporation with the executive depth of Du Pont there were several potential chief executives to pick from. ''It's a close call,'' he says. ''You're looking for that indefinable extra quality—wisdom in all its aspects. Besides, I think that fellow has fire in his belly.''

Now a partner in the Wilmington office of the law firm Skadden Arps Slate Meagher & Flom, Shapiro began reviewing his thinking

about a successor with the board a year before the vote. ''It's like dealing with a family,'' he says. ''You know whatever your successor does well is going to reflect on you. That feeling is part pro-enterprise and part selfish.''

Another succession, just as carefully orchestrated, is about to occur. On May 1, James Evans, 62, will turn over the Union Pacific throttle to William Cook, who will be 61 in September. The two men have worked together for 14 years, and although their ages are close, Evans insists he ''wants to give Cook the stripes for a few years.'' Evans, however, will retain the chairmanship and concentrate on long-range strategy for the diversified rail and energy company, whose assets swelled to $10 billion after a merger with Missouri Pacific last December.

''A guy burns himself out,'' admits Evans, who has been the boss since 1977. ''It's better for the company if I turn over control to Bill. That'll give him four years.'' Evans sees several possible future chief executives in the 50- to 55-year-old age bracket. ''We have a group of executives who are keen for the job,'' he says. ''But I'd always go with the guy 55 over the guy 45. He's had 10 more years' experience and has been roughed up in the fray. Also, he's more willing to listen to others and not make too many unilateral decisions. People do get wiser, you know.''

One corporation where the crown may not be lifted from its present head and placed on another without fuss is W. R. Grace. Chairman Peter Grace has been undisputed boss of the chemical and natural resources conglomerate (1982 sales: $6.1 billion) for 38 years. Has a succession plan been worked out? ''Since I don't want to retire, I haven't addressed myself to that question," he replies crustily, though clearly he has given it considerable thought. Two years ago he picked Carl Graf, 57, as president and chief operating officer, and Charles Erhart Jr., 57, his cousin and a great-grandson of founder W. R. Grace, as vice chairman and chief administrative officer. "These are the only two in a position to succeed," says Peter, who quips: "Unless Graf changes the *f* to *ce*, the next chief executive won't be named Grace."

A member of the Grace family—by birth or marriage—has always run the company, which became publicly owned in 1953. In 1945 Peter's father suffered a stroke and telephoned orders from his sickbed to install his son in his place. "I got the job without any right to it," admits Peter, who says his selection caused "quite a bit of fighting, and things couldn't be worked out for two weeks."

Last month Peter again discussed succession plans with the board: "I said we think Graf and Erhart are the two best people to get the training, and the board agreed." Although Grace says he would be "appalled" if the board went outside for the next chief executive, he prefers to deal with outside directors. "When I first became president, the board was dominated by inside directors," he says, "I found out quickly how dangerous that situation is. Because the chief executive is superior to these people for 29 days a month, you find them sticking it to you on the 30th day. Two or three might even close ranks and say, 'We don't like the way he's pushing us around.'"

For filling lower-ranking slots, Grace holds a high regard for headhunters. "I used to dislike them intensely," he says. "They'd come in and start tampering with our team. They have unbelievable antennae." But Grace thinks chief executive pickings are slim on the outside. "I serve on 10 boards, and I know exactly what's out there," he says. "Even when I'm not a director of a company in the process of picking a new chief executive, I think I know when they've picked a lemon. If the chief executive is imaginative and has good ideas, but isn't too well organized, his No. 2 man may be able to put the pieces together. But when No. 2 gets promoted, they discover he hasn't got the innovation or the drive, and his entire capability hinged on working alongside his old boss. I've seen this happen a number of times."

For 145 years Deere & Co. of Moline, Illinois, had similarly been run by a descendant of its founder, blacksmith John Deere, or by an in-law. Last September, when Chairman William A. Hewitt, 68 (husband of Deere's great-great-granddaughter), was named Ambassador to Jamaica, he broke the string by engineering the appointment of his No. 2, Robert Hanson, 49. "I talked only with the outside directors," says Hewitt, who was boss of the tractor company for 27 years. "It would have been futile to discuss this with the inside directors because they were all contenders."

A pothole-filled transition occurred at Greyhound Corp. By the time Gerald Trautman, 70, the curmudgeonly chairman for 16 years, retired to his tennis, golf, and stamp collecting, he had left a slew of No. 2's by the roadside. Just in the last five years the transportation and food conglomerate has tried out four heirs apparent. "We almost ended up suing Booz Allen because of the way they conducted the search," Trautman says. "They kept pushing five or six different candidates." Booz Allen declines comment.

The carnage started in 1978 when James Kerrigan, head of Greyhound Lines Inc. and Trautman's presumed successor, was fired. Now chairman of Trailways, Kerrigan told a reporter: "Nobody's going to have a different view on anything in the Greyhound Corp. than Gerry Trautman." In 1980 Robert Swanson, recruited from General Mills as heir apparent, resigned after eight months. Ralph Batastini was named president briefly and then kicked upstairs to vice chairman. Finally, in October 1981 John W. Teets, 49, who was back at Greyhound after a nine-year hiatus, was made chief executive. (He got the chairman's title from Trautman just eight months ago.) Says Teets: "It's interesting to see the failures in picking C.E.O.s, especially when the board goes outside. Generally, it's the chemistry that doesn't work. Or the rank and file may not accept the new leadership."

The close Teets-Trautman relationship was unusual, considering Teets's defection from Greyhound. "But he was a good learner and knew when to ask questions," says Trautman, who kept in touch with Teets all the time he was away. Adds Teets: "There was a feeling of camaraderie, and I knew he was interested in me as a person. He made it very easy for me to come back."

But in business the two men functioned very differently. "I knew my style of management was not a bit like his," says Teets, who was initially put in charge of the problem-plagued Armour division and thought it only remotely possible that he would end up as chief executive. "I was more meeting-oriented, and had more interacton with people. Gerry reviewed everything and didn't get personally involved. I asked if he'd like me to change my style. He said no. Instead he gave me a longer tether."

Trautman continues to serve as a consultant. "He's been very helpful," says Teets politely. "You don't always find that to be the case when a man's been as dominant as he has." But then the tireless Trautman is not relaxing his grip completely. "I will remain on the board of Greyhound, and on the boards of all major subsidiaries," he proudly declares.

Another old war-horse pushing 70 and still pulling hard is Ben W. Heineman, chairman of Northwest Industries. He's had four careers: attorney, railroader, conglomerator—and, for a spell three years ago, interim boss of the First National Bank of Chicago. As an outside director he stepped in to keep the bank running after A. Robert Abboud, the abrasive chairman who had cleaned out some 200 executives in the ranks below, was himself dismissed. "There was a vacuum from top to bottom," reports Heineman, whose hurry-up task was to find a new chief executive. He turned to headhunter Russell Reynolds. "Call me every hour if you have to," he told Reynolds. "It would be impossible for you to overcommunicate with me." By the time Barry Sullivan was brought in from Chase Manhattan, Reynolds says, "every member of my family knew Ben Heineman's voice."

Ben Heineman is adamant that a company should never hesitate to go outside for a new chief executive. He says, "At Northwest Industries we operate a number of large companies and I have not always taken the recommendation of the retiring chief executive. I thought I knew better. And I had to live with the decision. Besides, chief executives tend to replicate themselves and pick people in their own image. But what might have been right in the past may not be right for the future. The world changes. Business changes. On the other hand, if it turns out the board has to choose between two or three very fine inside candidates—well, that's a very high class problem."

To uncover those hot inside candidates, management consultants advocate switching the executives among difficult slots to see how they perform under pressure. Richard Beaumont, president of Organization Resources Counselors Inc., headquartered in New York City, calls this "playing the Parcheesi game." He says: "You have to make spaces available to move candidate X out and candidate Y in, if for no other reason than to provide experience and exposure."

One company trying that is Texaco. "We're so big," says Chairman and Chief Executive John K. McKinley, 63, "that four of our divisions would be in the top 100 companies. One way of developing new leadership is to give the best men the responsibility for those divisions." Texaco set up a succession contest. Last month the board elevated two division chiefs, James W. Kinnear, 55, and Alfred C. DeCrane Jr., 52, to vice chairman and president, making them the front-runners in the race for McKinley's job. "The board," he says, "expects me to make a recommendation. I would be surprised if it didn't give that recommendation a high priority."

But this is not the way Richard M. Furlaud, 60, chairman of Squibb Corp., is playing the succession game. "Even ten years from retirement," Furlaud says, "the chief executive should advise the board who is most likely to succeed him. That way rivalries won't consume the company." In 1978 he picked Dennis C. Fill, 53, the former executive vice president for operations, to be president and clear heir apparent. Like Teets of Greyhound, Fill had left the company; he was living in Asia, serving Squibb

as a consultant. Furlaud lured him back. "We had worked closely together," says the chairman. "That's the real test of a protégé." However, Furlaud leaves himself an out. "If a mistake is made, it can be corrected,' he says. "But it's a shame to go outside. Being chief executive is the ultimate prize."

Because executive talent windfalls are always possible, Chairman Forrest N. Shumway, 56, of the Signal Companies dislikes the idea of giving the board a succession plan years in advance. "All of a sudden some whiz-kid vice president comes along and your plan is shot," he says. Also, he claims the outside directors don't have enough contact with the candidates. "They meet them on a legal deal or on a financial deal," says Shumway, "but they don't know who can stand up at a stockholders' meeting and take the kind of pounding you get there, or if a candidate is going to blow up every time he talks to the press."

Early this year when Signal, a builder of petrochemical plants, aircraft equipment, and trucks, acquired Wheelabrator-Frye, an environmental, energy, and engineering concern, Shumway felt that one of the biggest prizes he had won was his eventual successor, Michael D. Dingman, 51. But to make room for Dingman, who had been Wheelabrator-Frye's chairman, Shumway had to demote Signal's president. "We haven't changed our opinion of our guy one iota," says Shumway. "But obviously the head of Wheelabrator had a lot more experience and stature." As for setting up a horse race between them, Shumway adds: "That way you waste two years and lose two guys while you're wrecking the company."

What does it take to succeed at the top? Professor Jennings calls that "the biggest guessing game in business." As he says, it's always been a gamble and always will be, "because there's no rung on the way up the corporate ladder that prepares you for the last one." From one rule of thumb, however, occupants of the lower rungs may take comfort. Academicians, headhunters, and the men who have actually perched at the top agree that it helps to have been knocked down a couple of times during your upward climb.

Career Systems and Individual Life Stages

3

Introduction

For corporate human resource policies to succeed, they must satisfy not only corporate needs but also the needs of the individual workers for whom the policies were designed. In the last chapter we examined the basic design of career systems. Each of the processes within this system dramatically affects the shape of people's lives. At the same time, the reverse is true as well. People's own human development and life situation guides their reaction to company human resource initiatives. Each of us has a unique constellation of needs, fears, joys, goals, worries, and values. Moreover, these personal characteristics are not static but change through one's life. One of the most effective ways of looking at both the commonalities across individuals and the changes is to look at lives longitudinally. The chronology of people's careers and biosocial patterns follow remarkably similar stages.

These stages must be considered in managing career systems. A recruiting approach for inexperienced college seniors would probably be wholly inappropriate for attracting middle-aged executives. A training program designed for new job entrants would not serve as an appropriate model for retraining older workers. Assignments which require patient judgment and cautious negotiating savvy might be valuable adventures for an older worker while a younger worker might feel trapped in quicksand. Long hours and chaotic conditions might challenge a younger worker and exacerbate burnout in an older worker.

Biosocial Stages

We will consider these life and career stages further by looking at how people's psyches and life situations change with age. In adulthood, as in childhood, individuals pass through various biosocial stages as they age.[1] In the late teens and early 20s they begin young adulthood, which is characterized by leaving one's childhood family and by the establishment of an independent identity. In the mid-20s, they gain entry into the adult world, having acquired an adult identity. They begin to explore adult roles

---

[1] Erik Erickson, *Childhood and Society*, 2d ed. (New York: W. W. Norton, 1963); Daniel Levinson, *The Seasons of a Man's Life* (New York: Alfred A. Knopf, 1978); and George E. Vaillant, *Adaptation to Life* (Boston: Little, Brown, 1977).

through commitments, memberships, and relationships. In the 30s, individuals go through a transitional period where they question those life structures which were just recently created. During this period, people often question their life dreams and aspirations, based on their new perspectives and disappointments with the realities they now perceive. They may reformulate goals for adult life, based upon the experiences of adulthood rather than upon childhood. In the mid-30s, people go through a period of consolidation or of settling down into more stable roles. The period is characterized by a search for order, security, and control. Many people deepen commitments and invest more of themselves in pursuing central values. In this period, people frequently develop influential relationships with more-senior colleagues who serve as mentors, whether formal or informal in nature.

These relationships tend to decline in the late 30s as people struggle to break free from any authority which seems to confound the effort to become one's own boss. Organizational commitments and rigid mentor relationships are strained. This break from authority diminishes by the early to mid-40s as people enter a turning point in life through a mid-life transition. This is hastened by a haunting sense of their own physical deterioration and the reality of their own mortality. This general rethinking of life may be further precipitated by the disillusionment of a persistent gap between personal aspirations and actual achievements. In the mid-to late-40s, people enter a new period of stabilization and revitalization. This spirit can last as long as they feel connected and generative. When people lose their friends, their influence, their social involvement, and their physical health late in life, they can allow themselves to disengage from the community. The pervading and depressing feeling that all of life's excitement is part of the past rather than the present can become debilitating to work life, as well as life in general. Through a continued sense of contribution, such psychological withdrawal may be greatly reduced.

Career Stages

In parallel sequence to these biosocial life stages, people also pass through career stages.[2] These stages are a product of one's changing occupational and organizational identity. A person generally enters the world of work as a novice with a low level of craft of professional skills. As they go through an apprenticeship, training, and developmental assignments, they eventually become independent masters of their trade.

At the same time, they enter as outsiders to an organizational culture. As they advance up the company hierarchy, many will stop short of reaching the heights which they sought, but some will surpass their wildest dreams. Some may discover unrealized interests and talents. Others will plateau because of a lack of opportunity. Some may reach limits to their potential in certain fields. Some may become obsolete with changes in the marketplace or the technologies of work. Many, however, will lead happy and productive lives—with a readiness to steer the course of their careers to avoid disaster and to seek adventure in each job. By late career, some people begin to

---

[2] Edgar H. Schein, *Career Dynamics: Matching Individual and Organizational Needs* (Reading, Mass: Addison-Wesley, 1978); Douglas T. Hall, *Careers in Organizations* (Pacific Palisades, Calif.: Goodyear, 1976); and Paul H. Thompson and Gene W. Dalton, "Are R&D Organizations Obsolete?" *Harvard Business Review* 54 (November/December 1975), pp. 105–16.

look to retirement early, while others avoid the thought of it. In some cases, people retire to escape dreaded work, and in other cases, many enjoy their work and still retire, by mandate or choice. Retirement is eased for those executives who have opportunities for gradual transition to either second careers or to a life without work through part-time work or phased retirement. Those with more outside interests, greater material comfort, clear post-retirement plans, and an accumulated sense of contribution at work retire with more grace than those who lack such assets.

Overall, early to mid-career issues and mid to late-career issues differ in several fundamental respects. While the new entrant may be interested in becoming an established member (i.e., through competence, acceptance, direction, and so on), late-career workers tend to be already established members. They are thus often more interested in sustained contribution and career maintenance. The tasks here may involve: *(a)* learning to accept mentoring responsibilities; *(b)* the anticipation of the threats of obsolescence; *(c)* the mastery of the frustration of diminished opportunity and eventual departure. The mid to late-career transitions may require assessment, planning, and retraining to ensure continued growth and contribution. We will consider ways that organizations can anticipate such differences in the workforce in the cases and readings to follow.

The Cases

In the cases, we look more deeply into the dynamics of these individual life/career stages. In the Brian Nelson case, we trace a graduating MBA student through his job search, his job choice, and critical socializa-tion to his new job. We are given rich insight into Brian's prior expectations and the realities of his eventual work situation. After two years, Brian is at a crossroads, in that he is considering now how best to manage his disappointments to accelerate a possibly stalling career. The cases raise questions for a manager about how best to use early career assignments, and for a supervisor about how best to develop a new worker. In the Adam Aron case, we again consider the best use of a young manager. In this situation we learn about the opportunities facing a strong fast-track performer in a crisis-filled organization. These cases encourage some consideration of the career enticements needed to retain a valuable early career worker who is attracting tempting outside offers through his outstanding performance.

The next three case situations illustrate careers that have hit snags earlier on due to performance problems instead of performance successes. In each of these cases, the role of the young manager's immediate superior and the relationship between these people are important for an understanding of the dynamics of performance in such a workplace. In the Roger Clarke case we are presented with a newly entering 25-year-old computer market specialist who has advanced quickly through the good relationship which he developed with a senior executive. Unfortunately, Roger developed a poor relationship with his immediate superior. A worsening superior/subordinate relationship is complicated through the discovery of exaggerated and deceptive sales forecasts.

In the Robert Goldfarb case, we see a young broadcaster enter a new job in a new radio station and begin to define his mission immediately. Before understanding his board of directors and his constituents, this talented radio station manager began to implement changes which triggered a major community controversy.

The Karen Harper case highlights a young woman who, after receiving her MBA, began a powerful relationship with a devoted mentor. Although she has achieved a great deal of mobility from her formal clerical employment, she is not happy with her present attainment and dependence. The case looks at her career development and need to set new goals.

In the next six cases, we move further along the life span and consider the career issues which surface as workers approach mid-life. In the Frank Mason case series, we follow the rough early career history of a young MBA and watch his difficulty in learning from his mistakes. The specific focus is on his third job after losing his two prior positions because of poor search strategies and joining-up behaviors. In the case, we see Frank's troubled relationship with a difficult boss as it leads to a disastrous company situation. At the same time, we can trace the dynamics of his relationships with his various co-workers which contribute greatly to the complex scenario.

The next case, Gerald Stanton, presents a set of mid-career issues very different from those confronting Frank Mason. Like Frank Mason, Gerald Stanton is just beginning to anticipate the approach of mid-life. Unlike Frank Mason, however, Gerald Stanton has been highly successful. His dilemma is whether to take a difficult assignment as vice president of sales with a great deal of responsibility and the challenge of working directly with colleagues many years senior to him in age and experience.

While the Mason and Stanton cases look at individuals approaching mid-life and mid-career, the next three cases profile individuals who have decisively crossed the

mid-career transition. The David Connolly case presents the successful pathway of a creative executive. Various turnaround general management triumphs are described. The case provides comments of subordinates, peers, and officers in Connolly's firm on David as a manager. David Connolly also offers his own view on his career advancement and satisfactions along the way.

The Biography of an Executive similarly provides a description of the successes and disappointments of a mid-career manager. Not only are many details of his work events and career progress presented, but a rich feeling for the spillover of work life and nonwork life developments is illustrated. The critical events in the family life cycle are outlined and the views of the executive's wife are examined.

The Case of the Plateaued Performer differs from these two cases in that we see an executive with a more difficult adjustment to mid-career. The lack of mobility, intergenerational age tensions, and conflicting loyalties of workers provide much of the richness of the background context for this vivid management dilemma.

Finally, the last two cases of this section turn our attention toward late career. In the Patrick Rich case, we see a senior executive questioning whether he has accomplished what he had hoped in life or whether he would like to try a second career in his 50s. The case looks at how an assessment of the executive's interests and values was conducted and then presents several career possibilities. The Abboud case presents later career crises with the dismissal of a prominent chief executive. The case entitled "Chucking It," by contrast, highlights the thinking of a late-career executive who decides to opt out of the continual corporate trials of executive life. The case provides some insight into when and how someone can decide that he or she has had enough. It presents a very different perspective on retirement from the Flowtrol cases, which were included in the previous chapter of this book. In the Flowtrol cases, we saw an entrepreneur who was very reluctant to retire from his growing business. In Chucking It, we meet Ken Mason, a chief executive who has decided that there is more which he hopes to extract from life than he can through his present work commitments.

The Readings

The readings parallel the early, mid-, and late-career stage perspectives of these cases. In the article entitled "The Psychological Contract: Managing the Joining-Up Process," John Kotter discusses the role of employee expectations in the transition from classroom life to work life. Implications for programs which manage entry to the work organization are suggested, with special attention to such activities as recruiting, first assignments, early supervision, training, and rewards programs.

In Daniel Feldman's piece, "A Practical Program for Employee Socialization," we are given a model of the key stages of orientation and early training. He focuses on the mutual influences between workers and organizations on such events as "getting in," "breaking in," and "settling in." These stages involve the formulation of role definitions and the resolution of conflicting influences upon socialization.

Ross Webber's discussion of "The Career Problems of Young Managers" diagrams the sources of common difficulties of early career workers, such as conflicting expectations, generational battles, political naiveté, and poor supervisors. Employee passivity, loyalty, and ethics are presented as special

challenges, the handling of which can exacerbate or ameliorate early career difficulties.

The next two articles serve as a helpful transition to the next career stage as the authors address both early career and mid-career executives. Lloyd Baird and Kathy Kram's "Career Dynamics: Managing the Superior/Subordinate Relationship" considers the career stage needs of both mentors and protégés. They provide guidelines on how each party can identify the needs of the other.

Manfred F. R. Kets de Vries's article, "Managers Can Drive Their Subordinates Mad," provides an important warning to a dangerous characteristic of leadership patterns called folie à deux. Through rich descriptions, he defines the problem of subordinates' inability to recognize the pathological effects of their dependence upon an irrationally behaving manager. Kets de Vries suggests aspects of the individuals and the context which help to define and control such a problem.

The last three articles focus more directly on the mid- to late-career dynamics.

Harry Levinson's article entitled "On Being a Middle-Aged Manager" provides insight into the feelings of decline, deterioration, and disillusionment which grow as people approach their 40s and beyond. While currently at one of life's peaks, organizations and individuals must prepare for mid-career disappointments. Levinson suggests ways by which companies can turn one's career crisis into a career renaissance. In the next article, Levinson looks at the debilitating impact of career exhaustion rather than mid-life disillusionment; "When Executives Burn Out" considers the insidious ways in which work assignments can catch up with executives and exhaust them by surprise. Even self-proclaimed workaholics can become victims of excessively challenging and unrewarding jobs which offer no hope for escape. This article suggests inexpensive ways by which companies can identify burnout-prone positions and control the personal and organizational damage which they can cause.

Finally, Leland Bradford's article, which asks "Can You Survive Your Retirement?" presents the difficulties of withdrawal from active work life without disengaging from society. Bradford profiles the impact of the loss of a work identity and purpose upon one's self-concept and interpersonal relations. The article discusses the need to adjust to reduced influence, radically altered family roles, confining societal attitudes, and an ambiguous personal mission. Bradford identifies key stages in the adjustment to retired life and suggests important ingredients for company workshops, training programs, and retirement policies to smooth the exit process.

CASE 1
BRIAN NELSON (A)
Mark P. Kriger and James G. Clawson

Introduction

Brian Nelson, a second-year student in the MBA program at a major metropolitan business school, was only two weeks away from his last final exam. He had just made a decision along with his fiancée to accept a job in marketing at a data processing and computer manufacturing firm, Binary Systems Corporation (BSC). Having made that decision, Brian was in the process of planning the period between accepting the offer from BSC and beginning to work there. In that period, Brian planned to get married,

move to a new apartment, go on a two-week honeymoon in Europe, graduate from business school, celebrate his 30th birthday, and begin his career at BSC. Both Brian and his wife-to-be were aware of the number of changes and events they were about to live through in a short time. In addition, Brian wanted the joining up with his new job to proceed smoothly. In preparation he had begun to consider how he could best manage the varied tasks and events before him.

Background

Brian Nelson's grandparents were born in Scandinavia and emigrated to Kansas. As a result both his parents were born and grew up near one another in a small town of 200 people, children of the Depression, the dust bowl years, and Roosevelt's conservation programs. Whereas his father was able to finish only the eighth grade, his mother received the luxury of a high school education. During World War II Brian's parents moved to the Los Angeles, California, area where Brian was born shortly after the war.

Brian did very well in school, often getting all A's in honors classes. His counselor told him he had the aptitude to do almost anything he set his mind to. Of his two favorite options, either going into the ministry or becoming an aeronautical engineer, he "decided" upon the latter when he was accepted into the University of California at Los Angeles right away and did not hear from Pacific Theological Seminary until it was too late.

After four years Brian received his engineering degree and began a career in aeronautical engineering. A couple of successful projects and one year later, he was managing an engineering team of 13 men, most of whom were in their 40s and 50s. Several years of engineering team management followed, but a worsening recession and the beginning of boredom resulted in Brian applying to two prestigious MBA programs. Brian accepted the offer to attend a program on the East Coast.

In the fall term of the second year of his MBA program, Brian Nelson took a course in Self-Assessment and Career Development. Partly as a result of this course, he decided that the firm he worked for had to be either in New England or in the Seattle, Washington, area. The quality of the environment, clean air, low pollution, and the immediate setting of the firm were important to him. Ideally there would be trees and a rural setting. He had also decided that he wanted to sign on with a "quality" high-technology manufacturing firm, which Brian felt would offer high growth and commensurate possibilities for relatively rapid advancement into general management. Initially he was undecided as to whether he wanted to go into manufacturing or marketing.

Brian's Job Search Strategy

During the Christmas break, Brian called the head of the alumni business club for his school in Seattle to ask for some career leads. One of the people Brian was referred to was the chairman of the board of the largest bank in the Pacific Northwest. With a little effort Brian was able to get an interview with him and, although a job offer did not follow, Brian did receive some valuable referrals to other businessmen in the area.

Brian also went through his business school's Graduate Directory for Seattle. Brian said:

> I went through the entire list and picked out companies that I thought were contacts. I called them up and tried to talk to them. I was interviewing up until the day before Christmas. I was trying to get interviews on the day before Christmas Eve and nobody was there.

Nelson spoke with people from a total of 16 companies, including a medical electronics firm, a computer firm, a yacht outfitting company, a forest products company, a truck scale company, a construction firm, a telephone equipment company, and a jet aircraft manufacturing company. In retrospect, Brian said:

> Some places really were deadends. I tried to focus on technologically oriented companies. I figured that once I got out of aerospace and got an MBA degree, if I went back to aerospace I'd be branded for life. . . . I think what happened was that I wasn't really impressed by the quality of the jobs that I was finding out there. Salaries were very low.

As the second term began in the MBA program, Brian signed up for the most solid courses he could take. Brian's second-year schedule emphasized financial analysis. He also took two courses in marketing. Although he was concerned about "flunking out," he actively continued to research job opportunities.

Brian got a list of all the firms that were coming to interview on campus, went through the list, and checked off the ones that he thought he wanted to talk to. He obtained interviews with a total of 12 companies, all of which were in high technology.

Part of Brian's job search strategy was to acquire an offer from the manufacturing firm he had worked for the previous summer. He had little intention of accepting the offer since the company's plants were in places which Brian considered undesirable, but Brian felt that the offer would help him approach his other opportunities with a sense of security and some negotiating leverage. By February, however, Brian had not received a firm offer, and he began to worry.

During the spring Brian interviewed with the 12 companies. However, early in the job search process he developed *a clear sense of his two top choices,* before he had even interviewed with either of them. He gathered many impressions about these two companies, Binary Systems Corporation and Data Power, Inc., by talking to interviewers from the other 10 firms. Brian stated that this was a key tactic in his interviewing with recruiters. When the recruiter from a company would ask him with whom else he was interviewing, he clearly stated which ones the other companies were. He felt that this increased his status in the eyes of the recruiter. To his surprise and delight the recruiters freely gave their opinions of other companies.

Usually they made negative comments about the other companies. However, Brian was unable to get a negative comment or reaction from anyone from the other companies about one company: Binary Systems Corporation. In addition, a sales manager from one of BSC's primary competitors claimed that one of his personal goals was to get one of his own sales force hired away by BSC. The recruiter felt that when this happened he would feel very satisfied since this would indicate that his own sales team had come to equal or surpass the high quality demanded in personnel by BSC. As a result, before Brian had had the on-campus interview with BSC, it was clearly number one on his list. Brian stated:

> In preparation for the on-campus interviews I went over and used the Career Resources Center, but I found that that's the corporate propaganda that the companies want to put out. It is hard to find out what a company is really like.
>
> I did find out one thing about BSC—I found a list of where their facilities were located. I said to myself, "Hey, now if you

want to work for a company and have a nice lifestyle, this company is consistent with that because they are located in nice places," which is very much a part of their corporate philosophy. They are in places where people like to live. That was important to me. High technology was also important. What other people thought of the company was important. I just couldn't find anybody to say anything bad about the company.

> I also knew they had quality products. I knew they had a high-quality name. I also found out through a friend that engineering had more say than marketing over how products were designed.

Brian's On-Campus Interview with BSC

Brian's sole objective for his interview on campus with BSC was to get invited to a further interview. During the on-campus interview with BSC, which was the last of the 12, he spoke with the recruiter about cameras for the first 15 to 20 minutes of the half-hour. The interviewer, Mr. Tom Dancy, a division manager, was considering purchasing the same camera that Brian already owned, and *Brian decided that he was willing to let the BSC interviewer take the lead.* Brian said to the casewriter:

> My strategy in that interview was to be invited to a full day of interviews. I thought I'd get more information from that full day of interviews than I would out of that half-hour. I thought that it was a preliminary type of thing. I did make sure that I committed myself to working for the division of the guy I interviewed with. *He was the manager of the business systems division* which I was interested in working for. I told him that I was interested in his products, and I was interested in New England, and that was it.

At the end of the interview Brian was invited by Mr. Dancy to a cocktail party with

BSC the evening of the second day of the interviews. At the cocktail party both sides were trying to sell each other.

Two weeks passed and Brian had yet to receive word of a further interview. Brian said:

> I was getting a little bit antsy about it. I called up the corporate personnel department at BSC and said, "What's the process you're going through there? I haven't heard from anybody!"

The corporate personnel department explained that all the forms had to be sent to corporate personnel and then routed to the division that the people were interested in.

Finally, three weeks later, Brian received a form letter asking him to call up to arrange for an appointment for a day interview onsite at BSC division headquarters for business systems. Brian arranged for April 5 to be the date.

On April 4, Brian received a letter and a telephone call. The letter was from his previous summer's employer and contained an offer for a permanent position. The phone call was from Burke Wiley, a division manager at Data Power, Brian's number two choice. The manager was flying into town that evening and wanted Brian to meet him at the airport at 5:30 for dinner and an interview. Brian agreed, although he knew it would be difficult to leave his afternoon appointment with company three, Systems-Tech, in time to meet Wiley's plane.

That afternoon, as Brian was finishing his last appointment at Systems-Tech, Brian was asked to stay for another meeting with the personnel manager because they wanted to make him an offer. Brian agreed, and then tried to call his fiancée to have her meet Wiley. Brian charged the call to his home phone. When the operator checked, Brian's roommate told her to tell Brian that

Wiley's plane had been delayed by a storm and that he would not be in until after 7:00.

Relieved, Brian collected his offer at Systems-Tech and then drove to Wiley's hotel. Brian and Mr. Wiley established a quick rapport and continued talking and drinking until 3:00 A.M., when Wiley made Brian an offer.

Brian's Visit to BSC

After less than five hours of sleep Brian got up, dressed quickly, and drove to the BSC business systems office where he was to interview.

Brian arrived at BSC at 9:00 A.M., generally wiped out and, in his estimation, looking it. Brian said:

> I was a little bit anxious because these were probably the most important interviews. But basically I was just feeling tired because I had been up late the night before.

Brian was met by Fred Miller of the personnel department, who led Brian over to where John Lancaster worked. John was a graduate of Brian's school working in manufacturing scheduling. John's "office" was way in the back. His desk was one of many in a large open office area with a scenic view. Brian said:

> The job that John was talking about didn't really turn me on a lot. It didn't bother me to say to him, "I don't think that's what I want."
>
> John did tell me that if I joined BSC I should start working before July 1, because that was one of the two opportunities a year to apply for the substantial employee benefits package.

John took Brian to George Thompson, a marketing product manager, for the next interview. Brian described George as being personable, coordinated in his dress, an obvious star. We talked about the kind of product that he worked with. It seemed interesting. We started talking about ideas, ways to sell it. It turned out that a couple of things that I thought of were things that they had just finished trying.

I asked George for an organization chart and he hesitated. He gave me one which did not show the manufacturing portion of the company [see Exhibit 1]. It didn't really make a lot of sense to me. I thought, "How could manufacturing impact me? That's a whole different department." I just discounted the whole thing. I didn't think that it was important.

At about 11:00 A.M. George took Brian over to Robert Hill, the head of the marketing area. Hill was in the process of making some calculations on the financial advantages of buying a new house. Hill and Brian talked about net present value and house appreciation. At first, Brian disagreed with

Hill's formulation of the analysis, but he was eventually persuaded by Mr. Hill's point of view. Brian reflected that Mr. Hill never did outline the job for which Brian was interviewing.

After lunch in the company cafeteria, Brian met with Al Patterson, who worked in manufacturing engineering.

Al started the interview by pulling out a blueprint of an electronic schematic diagram and asking, "What is this?" Later I discovered that this was a favorite trick of his to catch people off guard. I said, "It beats me." He then said, "How the hell do you expect to work in manufacturing engineering if you can't read an electronic blueprint!" We then talked about things in general and how they manufactured things. He turned out to be a nice guy.

Brian next spoke with Tom Dancy, the division manager whom he had met and in-

---

Exhibit 1   The Organization Chart That Brian Received during his Company Visit

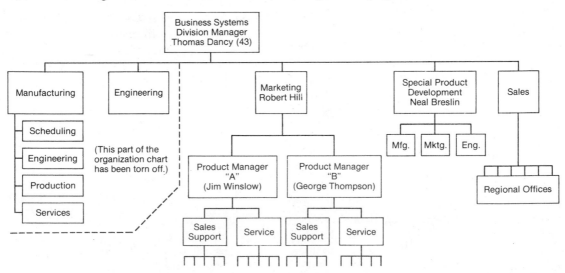

terviewed with on campus several weeks earlier.

> I talked to Tom about pay. I was trying to get clear about the employee benefits package, how it worked, what the employees contributed, what the company contributed.
>
> We also talked about particular products in the business systems division. He asked me about the different people I had talked to and what interest I had in each area. Also, who I felt I would enjoy working with.

Tom Dancy was the highest person in the BSC organization Brian spoke with that day. Although Brian did not realize it until much later, it was Tom who had the final say in the hiring decision.

At the end of the interview day, around 3:30 P.M., Brian met with John Lancaster again for a half-hour. Brian was given an opportunity to ask further questions and to recap the day. Brain left BSC feeling happy; the day had gone quite well in spite of his fatigue, and he felt sure he would get an offer. The pace of the last two days also made Brian's head swim a little; he had gone from no offers to three sure ones and a probable one in less than 48 hours.

Brian's Job Offers and Decision

Within a few days Brian received a written offer from a staff person at BSC to work as a marketing engineer under George Thompson on a particular computer product line. No statement of responsibilities or travel requirements was included. Although Brian was quite happy to receive the offer, he did not respond with an immediate acceptance.

By that time, Brian had five offers: two in manufacturing, two in marketing, and one in finance. He crossed off two of the five offers immediately because the plant locations were undesirable. He had kept one

company on the line until the BSC offer came in, but then he rejected that one as well. He was now down to two.

First, there was the offer from BSC. Then there was the offer from Burke Wiley of Data Power. That company was also a computer firm with a business products division, a competitor of BSC.

Both offers were attractive to Brian. In order to make his choice as carefully as he could, he took Ann to an inn over a weekend in April. He wanted to get away from the pressures of school so that they both could think more clearly. Brian brought a profile of himself developed from his self-assessment course composed of themes and implications (see Exhibit 2). In Brian's words: "But it was fairly cut and dried. We went down each criterion for BSC. Does this fit? Yeah, Does this? Yeah."

Brian called up George Thompson on Monday and said, "Hi, George, I've got some good news. I accept your offer."

Brian's Plans

Brian wanted to begin work before July 1 in order to take advantage of the company's employee benefit plan. Before learning of this deadline he had hoped to take a three–four week honeymoon after graduation; but if he were to begin work before July, he would have to halve his honeymoon period.

The period between May 1, when Brian made his final decision and his first day of work, was to be a busy one for Brian. His calendar looked like this:

May 1:   Final decision on job.
May 13: Last final exam in MBA program.
May 15: Brian and his wife-to-be, Ann, who had been living in a separate location, planned to rent a van and to move to a new apartment.

Exhibit 2   Life Themes

Theme	Number of Data Points from Written Interview
Dominant themes:	
Wants and needs to control his life	47
Wants and needs friends and friendships	32
Major themes:	
Philosophical about life	25
Family is important	21
Enjoys working hard	21
Needs an aesthetic environment	20
Willing and able to maneuver both himself and other people to his benefit	20
Sees the world in an aesthetic manner	19
Intermediate themes:	
Had a difficult relationship with his father	18
Fairly competent	18
Curious about the world and likes to learn	17
Wants to improve himself	17
Independent	15
Aggressive	13
Needs self-respect	13
Enjoys academics	13
Competitive	12
Wants to achieve	12
Likes an active life	12
Deals well with people	12
Used to be lonely	11
Proud of his father	11
Doesn't like a licentious life	11
Doesn't have a specific goal for his life	10
Likes responsibility	10
Has a strong relationship with his mother	10
Doesn't like to be inept	10
Subordinate themes:	
Doesn't like to have anyone infringe on his rights	9
Likes to be creative	8
Has strong emotions	8
Money is relatively unimportant	8
Has a quantitative ability	7
Likes to travel and see the world	6
Not proud of his father	5

Implications

I. **Job/career implications**
   (a) Related themes:
         Wants and needs to control his life
         Enjoys working hard
         Willing and able to maneuver both himself and other people to his benefit
         Needs an aesthetic environment
         Fairly competent
         Wants to improve himself
         Independent
         Aggressive

Exhibit 2 (*continued*)

Needs self-respect
Competitive
Wants to achieve
Deals well with people
Likes responsibility
Likes to be creative
Money is relatively unimportant
Has a quantitative ability
Likes to travel and see the world

(b) Implications:

(1) Would probably do better in a line position than a staff position (more control and has responsibility).

(2) Would do well in a position that requires interaction with a large number of people (maneuvers people and deals well with people).

(3) Should work for a company with a good growth rate (enjoys working hard, aggressive, wants to achieve).

(4) Would do well in a political environment (maneuvers people, deals well with people, likes to be creative, competitive).

(5) Should have a given area of responsibility (control of his life, likes responsibility, independent).

(6) Should work in a nice, clean environment (needs an aesthetic environment).

(7) The job should be located in an aesthetic locale, i.e., not densely urban, like New York (needs an aesthetic environment).

(8) The job should let him work as hard as he wants (control his life, enjoys working hard, aggressive).

(9) Some travel for the job would be okay (likes to travel).

(10) He might enjoy starting his own company (needs to control his life, fairly competent, wants to improve himself, independent, aggressive, competitive, wants to achieve, creative).

(11) Would do well in a technologically oriented company (quantitative ability, creative, needs self-respect).

(12) He might do well in an operations function (aesthetics, quantitative ability, maneuvers people, responsibility, money relatively unimportant).

(13) He should not have a direct sales job (needs to control his life, needs self-respect).

(14) He should not work in a position that relies on the profit motive for motivation (money relatively unimportant).

(15) He should work for a company which will allow him to move from position to position fairly easily (control his life, improve himself, creative, wants to achieve).

(16) He should not work for a company which would require him to move a lot (control his life, independent, aesthetic environment. Contradiction: likes to travel).

II. Lifestyle implications

(a) Related themes:

Needs to control his life
Needs friends and friendships
Family is important
Needs an aesthetic environment
Sees the world in an aesthetic manner
Curious about the world and likes to learn
Enjoys academics
Doesn't like a licentious life
Money is relatively unimportant
Likes to travel and see the world
Likes to be creative
Likes an active life

(b) Implications:

(17) Lifestyle, family, and friends are probably more important than his career (control his life, needs friends, family important, money relatively unimportant, and relative ranking of these themes).

Exhibit 2 (*concluded*)

    (18)   He should have free time for family, friends, and hobbies (family important, needs friends, needs aesthetic environment, creative, likes active life).

    (19)   He should live in an area where he could take night classes at a university (curious about the world, enjoys academics).

    (20)   He should not have a job that can *demand* a lot of his time continually (needs to control his life, family important, needs friends, likes active life).

    (21)   He should live someplace where it's good to raise kids (family important, doesn't like licentious life).

    (22)   He should be able to take trips and vacations when he wants to, within reasonable limits (control his life, likes to travel).

    (23)   He should not live in a densely urban environment, such as New York City (needs aesthetic environment).

III. **Implications relating to personal motivations and goals**
    (a) Related themes:
          Needs to control his life
          Philosophical about life
          Sees the world in an aesthetic manner
          Wants to improve himself
          Needs self-respect
          Wants to achieve
          Likes an active life
          Doesn't have a specific goal for his life
          Likes to be creative
          Money is relatively unimportant
    (b) Implications:
      (24)   He should have a career in which he can switch directions if he wants to (control his life, philosophical, sees world in aesthetic manner, no specific goal, wants to achieve).

      (25)   He should have a career that allows him to take time to think about how he likes his life (control his life, philosophical, needs self-respect).

      (26)   He should have a career that he finds intrinsically satisfying (needs self-respect, money relatively unimportant).

      (27)   He should strive to have a career that he finds stimulating and challenging (likes to achieve, likes an active life, needs self-respect, wants to improve himself, creative).

May 29:   Marriage and a small reception for 65 people. Relatives from the West Coast were to arrive May 26.

May 30:   Plans for a four-week honeymoon in Europe.

June 16: Graduation from business school as well as Brian's 30th birthday.

During the first two weeks in May, Brian spoke on the phone with George Thompson several times. They talked on a couple of occasions about having dinner together, but Brian's busy schedule had precluded that so far.

George seemed very interested in helping Brian to prepare for his first day on the job and gave him several things to read. Brian wrote down this list of things to do before joining BSC.

1.   Read technical specs of products.
2.   Review electrical engineering.
3.   Read business computer system text.
4.   Read copies of current memos.
5.   Study BSC organization chart.
6.   Read literature BSC gives to buyers.
7.   Read consulting report on BSC.
8.   Look through literature in current magazines concerning cost contain-

ment in computerized business systems.

9. Study report on demographic trends in the market area.
10. Study material on BSC's major product line.

Brian said to the casewriter concerning the above list:

> It wasn't a big deal if I did this stuff or didn't. You know it wasn't emphasized at all. But, I did have to let him know when I was going to start work.

BRIAN NELSON (B)
Mark P. Kriger and James G. Clawson

Brian decided to start work on June 20 in order to take advantage of the employee benefits options. Between May 1 and June 16, Brian Nelson took his final exams at business school, moved to a new apartment with his wife-to-be, hosted relatives from the West Coast, got married, and had a two-week honeymoon in Europe. On June 16, Brian graduated from business school with second-year honors. It was also his 30th birthday. (See Brian Nelson (A).)

Brian was to begin his first day of work at Binary Systems Corporation on June 20. In early May, Brian had been given by George Thompson, his future boss, some technical specs, current memos, a computer system text, reports on marketing, and assorted product literature. Brian had managed to read some of the reports and literature; however, since he had little spare time, he had been unable to read the copies of current memos, the textbook or to review electrical engineering. Brian had also been un-

able to take advantage of an offer from George to have dinner together before he started work.

An Important Telephone Call

At 4:00 P.M. on June 17, the Friday before his first day of work, Brian received a telephone call from George Thompson:

George: I'm calling to make sure that you're reporting for work on Monday.

Brian: Yes, I'm ready to start on Monday.

Some small talk then followed. Finally, as the conversation appeared to be coming to a close, George said: "By the by, you're not going to be working for me. You're going to be working for Jim Winslow rather than myself."

Brian: Who is Jim Winslow?

George: I thought you had interviewed with Jim when you were here.

Brian: No, I didn't. I don't think he was there that day.

George: Jim is a guy who has worked for BSC for many years. He has the other product line. Sorry he wasn't there the day that you interviewed.

George did not explain the situation much further. He said that he had just found out himself about the change at noon when he had decided to pursue other opportunities out in the sales force. He said he felt bad about it, but that he was sure that it would work out all right.

A Second Telephone Call

Immediately after speaking with George, Brian called his best friend, Mike, who was in the same MBA program.

> I just needed to talk to somebody about it. I described to Mike what had happened and then asked him, "Would you be worried?" And Mike said, "Yeah, I think I'd be wor-

ried. Are you worried?'' I said, "Well, kind of. Not too bad, but I wonder what the hell is going on that I don't know about!''

BRIAN NELSON (C)
Mark P. Kriger and James G. Clawson

Brian Nelson, having graduated from business school five days earlier, reported for his first day of work in the marketing department at Binary Systems Corporation (BSC) on June 20. He was dressed conservatively in a three-piece suit and felt a bit nervous as he entered the reception area at 9:00 A.M., in part because he was about to meet his new boss. Jim Winslow, for the first time.

Jim came out to the reception area to welcome Brian. They shook hands, exchanged "hellos" and Brian was taken to his desk, which was one of many in a large open office area.

Brian said to the casewriter:

> My first impression of Jim was that he looked like an overweight truck driver. Inwardly, I had a strong emotional reaction to seeing Jim because I had been overweight for many years . . . my reaction to Jim probably showed on my face. I felt like this was going to be a terrible situation.

Brian discovered that Jim was of Swedish descent and that Jim's business strength was his more than 20 years of experience in the field of business systems. Jim had been with another company for 13 years before BSC had bought him out. Jim stayed on and now had been with BSC for 12 years. Brian doubted whether he would have come to work for BSC if he had known Mr. Winslow was to be his first boss.

When Brian began with BSC he was the youngest of 16 people assigned to his product group.

His job required interpersonal and sales skills as well as knowledge of the product line and of marketing techniques. Brian found that he needed little or no knowledge of manufacturing policy, business policy, engineering, or net present value analysis. Brian felt that he had to travel one week in six in order to market and sell the product line.

After a few weeks it became even more clear that Jim Winslow did not see eye to eye with Brian. In an informal review Jim raised a number of criticisms and pet peeves:

1. Getting along with others: He needs to fit in better.
2. Too much numerical analysis: He uses his calculator too much and doesn't rely on or try to develop more "gut feel."
3. He doesn't know the products well enough.
4. He doesn't spend enough time in the field: I would like Brian to spend one week in four in the field, rather than one in six.
5. Brian doesn't focus enough on current sales situations.
6. Brian does not ask for advice often enough.

Three months after starting, Brian realized that he needed to loosen his style in order to fit in with his peers, so he started wearing golf shirts, occasionally, rather than a suit and tie. More than anything else Brian felt that this helped to improve his acceptability and image at the firm. Nonetheless, Jim's pet peeves continued to surface in subsequent reviews, as well as during more informal exchanges.

As Brian was with the company longer, he discovered at least part of the reason why George Thompson had torn off part of the organization chart and then left marketing so abruptly. BSC's marketing and manufacturing organizations were in a state of rapid change, and it had appeared that Thompson was about to be asked to work for an unpopular senior officer. Rather than do so, Thompson had decided to make a transfer. Subsequently, Brian was assigned to Mr. Winslow's product group.

Brian's Goals

When Brian joined BSC he had several professional and personal goals:

To do a good job at BSC and be recognized for it.

To become a Product Manager and triple sales for his product line.

To start a family.

To buy a home.

To be a division manager at BSC within 10 years.

To have talented people working for him.

Brian said he had no intention of becoming president of BSC since it would mean too much of a sacrifice in his personal life.

Brian Begins to Reassess His Job

After two years on the job, Brian felt somewhat better about his change in assignment.

In spite of our differences, for a time there, Jim was treating me like a son. In fact, as I look back I could have been really shafted if I had gone to work for George Thompson. If George had waited until I came on board to leave, then I would have been stuck working for this unpopular senior manager. Working for Jim has been a good thing because I've been able to learn some skills complementary to my analytical strengths.

Brian had learned, he said, not to contest Jim's gut feel but to support it with some harder analysis. Further, when Mr.

Winslow was out of the office, he left Brian in charge, an opportunity that pleased Brian greatly.

Brian's situation was not all good, however:

Jim does not believe in positive reviews. He gives everyone a "hard" review. Only two or three times in the past two years has he given me positive feedback. This is hard for me to accept.

Two weeks ago I got a call from a "head-hunter." I am being offered 50 percent more than I make now and a chance to be a product manager at a competing firm. They are still in this area, although the commute is more, about 45 minutes each way. It's a good company, but doesn't have the reputation BSC does. Also, some of its plants are in urban areas. I've heard, too, that the people there work long hours.

The fact that I found out last week that I was passed over for the product manager's job here (at BSC) makes the decision harder. I came to BSC because of the lifestyle the company offered me, but I also have these desires to advance. I thought when I joined that I could make product manager in a little over a year. In the last two years we have had three new marketing managers and only 3 of the 16 original people are still here. Nevertheless, my wife doesn't like the idea of my leaving BSC.

CASE 2
ADAM ARON (A)
David Fisher and Jeffrey A. Sonnenfeld

There are two things you can do when the ship is in danger of sinking. You can either try to patch the leak or you can run to the lifeboats. If you go to patch the leak, you had better do a good job, because the boats will be long gone. But if you love the ship, don't you try to patch it? And, who wants to be the first to jump ship?

This is one of the proudest companies in the history of aviation. Pan Am is the pioneer of transoceanic travel and has a worldwide reputation of great dignity. Yet, we are in serious trouble. Out of dedication and pride I would like to help save Pan Am. On the other hand, you have to be fair to yourself and consider other options. And right now, there are a lot of people in this organization looking at a lot of options.

With these words, Adam Aron mused over his future and whether he should remain at Pan American World Airways, Inc., the company which he had joined with such high hopes two years before. When he had joined Pan Am upon graduation from the Harvard Business School in 1979, it was with the hope and expectation of a long and successful career in a company he had wanted to join for many years. Now, in June of 1981, he was wondering whether he should leave. As he stared out of his window overlooking Manhattan, he reflected on his opportunities, his sense of loyalty to Pan Am, his travel benefits, and his uncertain future.

Adam Aron

Adam Aron was 27 and single. He was raised in Philadelphia and attended a large public high school, where he held a variety of offices. Upon graduation from high school, he was admitted into Harvard College.

He graduated from Harvard College in 1975 with a BA cum laude, in government. By the time he graduated from Harvard College, Adam had decided he wanted a career in business. More specifically, he wanted to work in the airline industry. This interest in the airline industry perhaps stemmed from trips and work abroad while an undergraduate student. Thanks to an international student organization which arranged short-term jobs for business students in foreign countries, he spent his college summers working for Holland's largest department store chain in The Hague, and Japan's central bank in Tokyo. It was also perhaps this interest in things international which aroused his interest in working for Pan Am. Pan Am had developed over the years as the "ex-officio" U.S. national flag carrier, with extensive routes all over the world.

The two years between his graduation from Harvard College and entrance into the Harvard Business School were spent abroad. He spent one year in Brussels working as the fourth-ranking officer of the international student organization he worked with in college. He was responsible for directing the association's 55 member-country chapters throughout the world. He also spent time working for Finnair (Finland's national airline) in Helsinki in its marketing department. His duties brought him in contact with Pan Am, and resulted in his getting to know many of the company's executives quite well.

Upon return to the United States, he entered the Harvard Business School and kept in close touch with Pan Am. Thus, when Adam was offered a job with Pan Am after graduation, he was in a sense joining a company which he knew very well before. He was also known to many of the senior people and had a good deal of visibility.

Since joining Pan Am, Adam has done well. In his first marketing position, he was perceived as thorough and competent. Seven months after joining Pan Am, he was promoted to manager, Market Analysis–Pacific. In this position, Adam helped to redesign Pan Am's Pacific schedules, served as the airline's forecaster of Pacific traffic flows, and constructed Pan Am's Operating

Plan in the Pacific for 1981. The operating plan forecasts traffic demands for each flight in significant detail, and was signed off by the company's board of directors.

Overall, Adam is held in high esteem, which is evidenced by the fact that he has been promoted a second time. His present position is director of Marketing Product Development. He serves as the liaison between the vice president of Passenger Services and the vice president of Marketing, and is one of the youngest directors in Pan Am.

In January of 1981, Adam received an offer to join the federal government from the Assistant Secretary of Transportation for Policy and International Affairs in the new administration. He would have been her sole special assistant. With the demise of the Civil Aeronautics Board, it was anticipated in Washington that the Department of Transportation would assume all remaining regulatory functions for the airline industry. However, Adam turned down this offer to remain in the private sector.

Pan American World Airways, Incorporated

Pan American World Airways, Inc. has had a long and proud history, opening aviation to much of the world. But this has sometimes been a checkered history, especially over the last 10 years. In the early 1970s, Pan Am was beseiged by overcapacity problems, caused by its ambitious plans for a "jumbo jet." Pan Am was the airline that first ordered and flew the Boeing 747. But as the new plane was more than double the size of the then largest existing airplane, there were a lot of seats that went unfilled. In October 1974 a group of top officers from Pan Am met with a specialty law firm in New York to get a briefing on the procedure for filing for bankruptcy. Pan Am had been

hit hard by the oil crisis, just as it was heading back to profitability from its overcapacity problems. At the time of that October meeting, Pan Am had only enough cash to last another three weeks. But on that occasion, the banks provided additional funds and the storm was weathered. Corrective action was taken through major route restructuring and a 40 percent cut in the size of the workforce. This resulted in the company returning to profitability in 1977,[1] but in the last 18 months, difficulties have been encountered once more.[2]

Like most other major airlines, Pan Am has been hit by a combination of steadily rising costs, especially aviation fuel, combined with a period of recession, which has affected demand. In addition, airline operations have been affected by high interest rates and deregulation in the industry. The latter has increased competition and has also created a downward pressure on airfares.

Traffic has held up fairly well on Pan Am's international routes, but at the expense of deeply discounted fares and increased commissions to travel agents. This, combined with increased costs, has had a strong negative affect on earnings.[3]

In addition, however, Pan Am has been hit by problems encountered in its takeover of National Airlines. Pan Am acquired extensive domestic routes for the first time in January 1980, with the purchase of National Airlines. This merger has not worked out as

---

[1] In fact, the Air Transport Association of America, the airline industry trade association, reported that Pan Am's earnings in 1979 were the third highest of the 30 major U.S. airlines. (*Air Transport 1980,* Air Transport Association of America, Washington, D.C., June 1980, pp. 6–7.)

[2] "Pan Am In the Black for Now," *Business Week,* September 5, 1977, pp. 52–56.

[3] "The Surgery Pan Am Hopes Will Save It," *Business Week,* June 15, 1981, pp. 36–37.

had been hoped and has contributed greatly to operating problems.

The result of all the above has been that Pan Am posted an operating loss of $129.6 million in 1980. In the first quarter of 1981, an operating loss—the worst in the company's history—of $114.5 million was reported. The second quarter promised to be equally bad. This outlook of a second quarter loss was made worse by the fact that the second and third quarters are usually the most profitable in the airline industry.[4]

A $294 million profit on the sale of its New York headquarters enabled Pan Am to report a net profit of $80 million in 1980. But the airline's problems remained. Since September 1980, Pan Am has laid off 3,500 employees, and nearly one fourth of its management positions have been eliminated. Routes were under careful review, and rumor was rampant throughout Pan Am and the industry that the top-management team was about to change. Other actions the company intended to take were a reduction in director's fees, and a request to employees to accept wage freezes and "voluntary" forfeiture of future raises.[5]

What effect these measures would have on the results of Pan Am had yet to be seen. Additional background information on Pan Am and its present position is given in Appendixes 1–3.

Discussions with Adam Aron on Pan Am and His Future Options

The rest of this case is taken up with excerpts from a discussion with Adam Aron, during which he talks about Pan Am, the position he feels he is in and the options that are available to him.

---

[4] Ibid.
[5] Ibid.

Why He Joined Pan Am

Because of its history. Because this company started the industry. Because this company is highly international. And as its lack of profitability now shows, operates one of the most complicated product delivery and marketing systems in the world. The challenge of making it whole is a great one, but the personal satisfaction is therefore great in return. And the personal benefits of being able to hop off to any point on the globe can't be overlooked. To do business in Nairobi, Tokyo, and Rio de Janeiro is kind of exciting. In addition, I had a personal career reason. I was well known inside the organization, and had more visibility going in to this company than most people have after many years in a large corporation. Furthermore, in 1978–1979 Pan Am looked to be in a state of financial recovery. The company's earning performance was excellent.

The Last Two Years and the President Position

Despite strong earnings in 1978 and 1979, Pan Am has been operationally unprofitable for the last 21 months. We merged, which is to say we bought a smaller company almost two years ago, and the two companies have had tremendous problems integrating. The respective unions have not come to terms, and a full 19 months after integration of the companies on paper the companies are not integrated in practice. Few of the anticipated synergies have come to pass.

Last fall, the president and COO of the company abruptly resigned. The executive shakeups have been pretty extensive. We've lost half of our officer corps in the last 12 months. Over 10 percent of the company's employees have been let go since September, and more deep cuts are expected soon. In a sense, these cuts were long overdue, but they point out the desperate state of the corporation. We've been hemorrhaging financially in the first five months of 1981, including a huge loss in the month of May, which is traditionally a fairly good month for the company in a transition to profitability. We are a very seasonal business. The first and fourth quarters are soft and the second and third quarters are usually very strong and, if the second quarter is a little weak, certainly the third quarter is strong. As you get later and later in the second quarter, you should see a strong surge of profitability— and it's not there this year. We're only halfway through June, but so far it's disastrous. As you start with the perception that the company is in real trouble, and that people are being fired left and right, it's logical to ask yourself, "Are you personally vulnerable?" And my answer to that question is "I'm not."

I am highly thought of, I think. In full performance assessments I've always come in at the top fifth. I've gotten virtually the highest allowable raises the corporation has authorized; I've been promoted twice in 17 months. I'm known to many in the officer corps and I am respected. Also, Pan Am has very few young managers and, if Pan Am does survive, I'm the type of person who will be needed for the future. I'll be in the last fifth or maybe the last quarter of employees to be fired, but there are two issues that are particularly disturbing. One is, it is possible that the last fifth will go after the first four fifths go. It is really possible that this multibillion dollar enterprise will go under. I'm not really that worried that we are going to go bankrupt per se. We have a lot of resources left, we have $600 million of book value left, we have two subsidiaries which are probably worth $500 million if we sold them on an auction block, so we can last. . . . We're "only" losing $250 million a year. So we can certainly last a while. There is time in which to change the structural problems of the company and its cost structure, and the scope of its products and their delivery. In my heart of hearts, I don't think Pan Am is going to die. But then there is a real chance that Pan Am could not survive, and since we are talking about a $4 billion

corporation—America's second largest airline—that's sobering.

What's more troubling is simply how much fun is it going to be to work in an organization that's in such a desperate condition? With dynamic leadership from the top, a turnaround could really be thrilling. You could rally round the flag a little bit and say, "Our backs are to the wall, we're going to fight our way out of it, we're going to be prouder than we were coming in. We will have saved a noble institution, with a very exciting past, and in a sense we'll be heroes because we kept a very troubled company from going belly-up." There is a certain sense of satisfaction that comes from that alone, but if you don't have confidence in the people who are going to lead what in effect almost becomes a crusade, it's pretty hard to march in step, rank and file. And it's tough to have confidence right now. The newspapers are filled with speculation that our most senior officers have lost the confidence of our board of directors. A change is very likely, but nobody knows who or when. There is no real sense in the company that our senior management team is stable as yet. There has been constant changing of jobs and responsibilities. And more changes at very senior level are probable.

So the question you have to ask yourself is, do you want to leave, or do you want to put up with all the tough times ahead? The tough times ahead may include what has been announced as a 10 percent pay cut for everyone in the management corps, from the chairman of the board on down, and while that's a nice gesture from us to Pan Am, does it really help you eat? New York is not an inexpensive town.

Other Options

At the same time in the industry there are some revolutionary things happening. In fact, they in part are the reason that this company has been dislocated as much as it has. There are a lot of new companies starting up, trying to siphon off very small segments of the market, but they're doing it quite effectively. Midway, New York Air, People Express, Air Florida—they are the darlings of Wall Street right now. They are finding it easy to raise equity capital. Companies with as little as $900,000 of partnership equity are raising $25 million on Wall Street, even before the first airplane flies. Not so incidentally, the partners founding these companies are turning their $900,000 of investment into as much as $10 million in book value. While blue-sky laws prohibit you from taking it all at once, it looks like for the next year or so there is tremendous money to be had. Instead of being a $35,000-a-year, knock-your-head-against-the-wall executive of a falling-apart company, you could decide to start one of the new sexy small upstarts that threaten to take over much of industry.

So in simple terms, there's a dilemma because you are in a company where your professional safety is relatively assured, but the safety of the organization is not. On the strength of your hopes for the company to succeed and of your loyalty to the organization, do you stay? Even if staying means severe personal stress as you see people around you getting cut down? Do you stay in light of great personal sacrifices, not only in terms of effort and stress and hard work, but a possible real drop in income? And the dilemma is that if you decide to stay, are you foregoing a chance to make millions, having already recognized that there is room in the industry for these little guys?''

Setting Up a New Airline

Among the options available to Adam was the prospect of participating in the formation of a new airline.

Business Week just ran a cover story on the new small carriers in formation. There was a line in the article that said whenever an ex-

ecutive leaves an airline, now, you look to see for the concurrent announcement that he's going to start a new airline. There are four in Texas that I know of, three in California, one in Chicago, one in Baltimore, one in Miami, and one in Atlanta being talked about.

I've given a lot of thought to this possibility and have pursued it fairly seriously. I've been in touch with several knowledgeable and respected people in the airline industry and the financial community with respect to a specific proposal. All have been positive. I have financial commitments of a million and a half dollars in partnership equity already if I choose to go further with the idea.

It really could be exciting to be involved in a start-up situation. The responsibilities would be all-encompassing; the team would be made up of people you like; and the satisfaction of accomplishment would be pretty immediate. In addition, there's the chance to make a small fortune and to gain high visibility in the industry.

At the same time, though, the risks of starting a new airline now are very real. With the number of start-ups underway, the skies may be a little crowded. If Pan Am can teach any lessons, it is that profitable airlines can become very unprofitable very quickly if they are subject to sustained overcapacity. Any day now, the media will start to pick up on the "sky war" between Southwest and Muse Air in Texas. The public may be happy about low fares, but don't kid yourself. Muse will have a very bloody battle on his hands. It may do well, but not without trauma, and not without great business skill and acumen.

I suppose my point is that my friends and advisers all say I have nothing to lose, and if I am ever going to roll the dice, now's the time. Well, I'm just not convinced it's all so easy to succeed in this industry. It's easy for others to recommend that I take the risk now because they are not the ones who'll have to work in a rat-trap office someplace sweating bullets on the low-seat factor on a Tuesday in February. And they won't have to be the ones worrying when United and Delta all announce they're going to drive this precocious little airline into the sea.

Joining Another Carrier

As you can tell, I like the airline business. It is challenging, fun, and you really have to use your wits because it's so hotly competitive. Should I leave Pan Am, and should I decide it's a little too risky to start an airline, or that I'm a little too green—after all, I've only been doing this for a couple of years—I could always seek out employment at another airline. There would be much less risk, and I think I could succeed in another career just as I have done at Pan Am. A drawback though, would be that any other airline would be much less international in scope than Pan Am.

I could look to join a current major carrier or I could go to one of the start-ups themselves. Right now, I am mulling over an offer from one of the more interesting smaller

airlines to be their third most senior marketing executive with a 50 percent raise. They have asked me for my response within a week. It's a very enticing offer but it all gets back to the central issue: should I stay with Pan Am?

The Decision

I went to see one of the most senior officers at Pan Am, whom I admire and respect greatly. He tried to convince me to stay, saying how noble it would be to be one of the people who helped turn Pan Am around. He further told me that if a turnaround could be accomplished, I'd be in an excellent position for serious career advancement at a very young age.

And loyalty is a quality I pride myself in. And now is the time that I am needed. On the other hand, a 50 percent raise is a 50 percent raise. And I am not through with the new airline idea, either. I have a meeting in three weeks with a man who wants to invest a million dollars. How's that for a choice? And it is getting to be decision time.

Appendix 1

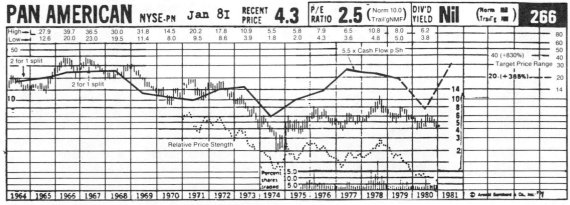

Reprinted by permission of the publisher. Copyright 1981, Value Line, Inc.

We look for the sale of Pan Am's New York headquarters building to be completed soon. The $290 million pretax profit ($2.90 a share aftertax) is included in our 1981 first quarter earnings estimate, accounting for the contraseasonal profit estimated for this period. The funds obtained from the sale of the building will probably be used to scale down outstanding indebtedness and to finance equipment purchases. Pan Am has subleased the National terminal at Kennedy airport to TWA, but has made no progress in disposing of its excess aircraft.

Pan Am has five DC-10s for sale. The profitable disposal of these relatively new aircraft was not accomplished last year; it is expected that the planes will be sold and/or leased on a long-term basis in 1981.

Pan Am is slated to resume service to China this month, the first scheduled air service between the U.S. and mainland China since 1949. Although the service will be limited to three flights weekly at first, it does provide Pan Am with an expanded Pacific market having considerable growth potential.

Pan Am continues to streamline its operations. Flight schedules have been reduced about 10% and the employee roster is now down to 32,000. Another major cost reduction program is planned in an effort to place flight operations in the black, now that the major expenses for the integration of National Airlines into Pan Am are over. The "new" Pan Am has emerged. The carrier is operating under a single identity even though pilots and flight attendants still have not reached a final seniority settlement. The financial benefits of the merger are still not apparent. In the current weak air travel market, the achievement of an operating profit may be delayed until 1982.

Pan Am has sizable 3- to 5-year appreciation potential. When the combined airline is fully consolidated, we look for much larger earnings to be reported. While the stock is of interest to risk-taking investors for the long pull, it probably will continue to be a poor market performer until its earning power is clearly demonstrated.

Appendix 2

Troubled Pan Am Trims Staff, Salaries in Cost-Cutting Step

By a WALL STREET JOURNAL *Staff Reporter*

NEW YORK—Financially beleaguered Pan American World Airways set about slashing its payroll costs by eliminating the jobs of 10 vice presidents, firing 112 management-level staffers, and reducing salaries of those remaining.

Union members, at present unaffected, also will be asked to tighten their belts when current contracts expire.

A Pan Am spokesman said six vice presidents were asked to resign. Three others who are retiring won't be replaced. And another resigned voluntarily. The 32 vice presidents retained will accept 10 percent cuts in pay, said the spokesman, James Arey. Other managers will make comparable sacrifices, he said.

William Waltrip, executive vice president for marketing and planning, said Pam Am's top management began work on the cost-cutting plan "after it became obvious in March that things were going to hell."

Pan Am posted a loss of $114.5 million for the first quarter of 1981, the largest quarterly deficit in its 53-year history. For 1980, it reported a record operating loss of $129.6 million, compared with an operating profit of $72.1 million in 1979.

However, profit from the sale of the Pan Am Building in Manhattan offset the adverse factors and produced full-year 1980 net income of $80.3 million, or $1.13 a share on a primary basis, up from 1979's net income of $76.1 million, or $1.07 a share.

One source said the move to cut costs was because Pan Am's second quarter this year may be even worse than the first quarter. "April and May were terrible" for Pan Am's results, the source said.

Like other airlines, Pan Am has been hit by spiraling fuel costs. Until recently, it complained that it was unable to obtain permission for fare increases from foreign governments to offset fuel costs. In addition to these problems, Pan Am also is trying to combine its operations with those of National Airlines, which it acquired in January 1980.

The 112 management-level workers who lost their jobs made up about 15 percent of Pan Am's headquarters staff. The vice presidents whose jobs were eliminated weren't identified. But it was reported that J. Howard Hamstra, vice president and general counsel and secretary, was among those asked to resign.

Sources also said that William Roy, a vice president who has been in charge of putting Pan Am and National operations together, was among those leaving the company. They also said that Walter Rauscher, a vice president in the marketing division was leaving. However, these reports couldn't be confirmed.

Efforts to contact them were unsuccessful.

In a letter to employees in which cooperation for the cost-cutting was sought, Mr. Seawell said that pay given up might later be recouped once Pan Am achieved a 5 percent operating profit on its airline activities. The cost-cutting doesn't involve Pan Am's subsidiary businesses, which, Mr. Waltrip said are "well organized and making money."

Pan Am Debt Rating on Some Issues Is Cut by Standard & Poor's

By a WALL STREET JOURNAL Staff Reporter

NEW YORK—Standard & Poor's Corp. lowered its ratings on about $422 million of Pan American World Airways debt securities, citing the airline's large losses during the past year.

Pan Am declined comment.

The lowered ratings involve some 38.5 percent of the $1.1 billion in debt that Pan Am owed at Dec. 31, the rating concern said. Included are $250 million of subordinated convertible debentures, which were lowered to triple-C from single-B-plus, as well as $52 million of equipment trust certificates and $120 million of guaranteed loan certificates, both of which were lowered to single-B from double-B.

The ratings reflect Standard & Poor's assessment of Pan Am's ability to pay interest on its debt and repay the principal.

Pan Am had posted a first quarter loss of $114.5 million, the largest quarterly deficit in its 53-year history. For all 1980, the airline reported a record operating loss of $129.6 million, compared with a year-earlier operating profit of $72.1 million.

The rater said Pan Am's losses probably won't turn around soon. "While profitable airline operations may be achieved during the normally strong summer season," it said, "attainment of satisfactory operating profits on a sustained basis appears unlikely" in the near term.

Pan Am's debt is likely to increase as capital programs in 1981 and 1982 are financed, Standard & Poor's said.

The rating service said many of Pan Am's financial troubles have been shared by other airlines facing rising fuel costs and fewer passengers. Making Pan Am's situation worse, it said, was the company's acquisition of National Airlines, which hurt its domestic operations. Savings there have been hard to realize, it said, due to difficulties in combining schedules, fleets and crews.

Pan Am's international operations lost money during the past year as the airline had trouble raising fares above those charged by international airlines backed by foreign governments.

Appendix 3

What the National Merger Did to Pan Am

A merger that once seemed made in heaven has turned into hell for Pan American World Airways, Inc. Its $394 million purchase of National Airlines, Inc., is largely responsible for the company's current woes. On June 10 Standard & Poor's Corp. cut its rating of Pan Am's senior debt to B from BB and knocked the rating on its subordinated debt to CCC from B. Still losing money at a prodigious rate, Pan Am is desperately trying to improve the terms of its loan agreements so that it does not have to yield any control to its lenders. Last year Pan Am avoided technical default only when its bankers granted a temporary waiver of one of its loan covenants. "We're now negotiating with the banks an agreement of about $475 million for an extended period and with covenant ratios that we think we can live with," says J. Kenneth Kilcarr, Pan Am's executive vice president for finance.

Pan Am has made money in only 3 of the past 10 years, and thus far 1981 has been a disaster. The National merger was supposed to solve a lot of Pan Am's problems—first, by buying a modern fleet at bargain prices, and second, by supplying instantly a domestic system to feed its international routes. Pan Am Chairman William T. Seawell evaluated the options and decided to go flat out to merge the two companies' operations: He knew a tough economic climate was coming and wanted to gain the strength of the combined carriers as soon as possible. But it has not worked out that way. Basically, four things were wrong from the beginning:

- National, with a route structure extending from the West Coast to Florida and from there up the East Coast to Washington and New York, could not give Pan Am enough traffic.
- In a bidding war with Texas International Airlines Inc. for National, Pan Am ended up paying too much.

- Integration of the two carriers is still not completed.
- Pan Am did not keep enough of National's management and staff to run the unfamiliar domestic operation.

Pan Am's tinkering with the old National route system, right up to the present, has made it difficult for the marketing department to do its job, since it never knows from one timetable to the next what the schedule will be. A prime example of the chaos caused by Pan Am's domestic inexperience is Savannah, Ga., which National had dropped some time before the merger because the service was no longer profitable. Nonetheless, in its effort to rally all the political support it could get for the merger, Pan Am promised the mayor of Savannah that if it won National, it would restore service to his city. The Pan Am scheduling department now has done the same arithmetic the old National people did and is about to pull out of Savannah again, much to the disgust of the mayor and the top Pan Am officers who had given him their word.

Ironically, though, Pan Am is starting New York–Phoenix service. The timing of this strikes most observers as curious, since the traffic in and out of Phoenix in summer is a fraction of the winter business.

During the pre-merger maneuverings, Seawell hammered at the theme that this was to be a merger of equals. But when the two airlines joined officially, on Jan. 1, 1980, "Pan Am people acted like conquering troops," according to a former Pan Am officer. "They flatly and explicitly ignored the National people's advice on how to operate a domestic airline." Only one National executive—John B. Andersen, senior vice-president for sales and service—is still with Pan Am.

Room at the top. Strong operations people are notably absent from Pan Am's upper echelon. Seawell, a former Air Force brigadier general, has gone through three chief operating officers in his 10-year tenure at Pan Am. The latest of them, Dan A. Colussy, left in November, and the company and its board have been actively seeking a replacement. Industry experts say Seawell's treatment of former COOs is part of the reason why the job is still vacant. One former

Pan Am executive theorizes that the board has already found a new chief for Pan Am—one who will not take the job until some housecleaning is done, which would include the early retirement of Seawell, who is 63.

Speculation and political intrigue are endemic at Pan Am. That environment is fostered by the chaos in the executive suite, now in the throes of this third consolidation in less than a year. Seawell has been the chief operating officer as well as the chief executive since Colussy's departure. "Even though he's an ex-aviator himself and once was the operations v-p at another airline [American Airlines Inc.], he doesn't have the operating sense that we need in top management," says one Pan Am co-pilot. Adds Robert J. Joedicke, first vice-president of Lehman Bros. Kuhn Loeb, Inc.: "A lot of the ability to get the airline operation back on track depends on getting a good strong chief operating officer."

Perhaps the biggest problem with the National merger was that it so preoccupied Pan Am's management that the company failed to pay sufficient attention to industrywide problems created by soaring fuel costs and sagging traffic. "They just didn't get a fast enough jump on the situation," says L. John Eichner, executive vice-president of aviation consultants Simat, Helliesen & Eichner, Inc. "Seawell focused on the runner on second base—National—when all else were focusing on first base—the fuel crisis, the need to become more efficient." One former Pan Am executive sees plain bad luck as part of Pan Am's problem: "If you could pick and choose your timing to go through the trauma and enormous extra expense of a merger, you probably wouldn't want to do it just as the economy was heading into a recession and the prime lending rate was heading to 20 percent."

Nor did management monitor service levels. Seawell found out just how bad they had become on Pan Am's inaugural flight to China in December: The airline lost his son's and daughter-in-law's luggage on the outbound flight, and back at New York's Kennedy Airport he waited an hour for his own bags. He decided to take over supervision of operations himself.

"Obsolete species." Pan Am has special problems stemming from its long history as a strictly international carrier. Nearly 70 percent of Pan Am's traffic is still overseas, and there the reve-

Pan Am's Dismal Decade

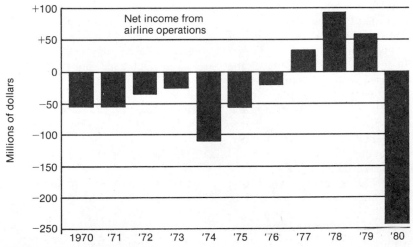

Data: Pan American World Airways, Inc.

nue per passenger mile, known in the industry as yield, is rising much more slowly than the rate of inflation. Numerous attempts to acquire domestic routes before airline deregulation in 1978 had been futile, and the negotiation of more liberal bilaterals—agreements that govern international aviation—has created new competition for Pan Am, which must vie with foreign government-owned carriers (*BW*—Jan. 26). "Pan Am may be an obsolete species. It's questionable whether there is a place in today's international competition for an airline with neither strong feed nor government support," states Charles C. Tillinghast Jr., former chairman of Trans World Airlines Inc.

Pan Am's losses for the second quarter are expected to match the staggering $114.5 million deficit reported in the first quarter of this year. Its $80.3 million profit in 1980 was achieved because of the $294.4 million netted on the sale of its New York headquarters building. In short, Pan Am's situation is grave.

Even with a big boost from hefty amortization and depreciation, to the tune of $234 million last year, Pan Am's cash position is eroding fast. In the first quarter alone, working capital decreased by $206 million. Unable to generate needed cash, it tapped its virtually untouched credit lines for $152 million. Sources close to the company say the bankers are getting nervous. Before it sold its building last year, the relation between Pan Am's cash flow and fixed annual costs, such as interest expense, debt repayment, and lease obligations, would have fallen below the coverage ratio spelled out in its loan agreements if the bankers had not eased that provision for 1980. Pan Am is now within that ratio, but without profits to beef up both equity and working capital, it could well breach the covenants regarding both coverage and debt-to-equity ratios this year. To keep its bankers at bay, Pan Am is trying hard to renegotiate its current bank loans and come up with more favorable covenants. "We expect to complete that renegotiation by the end of June," says Kilcarr.

Seeking objectives. Kilcarr hopes to have that agreement for Pan Am's July 7 board meeting, which will also consider an operational restruc-

turing of the airline. Consultants McKinsey & Co. have been working since January on a strategic study of the airline's operations to determine "what the core objective of the airline should be," says a senior Pan Am official. Already aircraft schedulers are alerting Pan Am's international pilots to "a lot of changes coming up." Says the senior official: "The steps to be decided on in July are really aimed at 1982." But Pan Am cannot wait that long. It is already working on ways to pare fuel costs, including investing in ventures that could provide oil to trade for its own fuel needs.

. . . . On the personnel front, Pan Am on June 2 eliminated 10 vice-presidential slots and announced 112 other staff cuts (*BW*—June 15). Now it is trying to win worker agreement to an employee contribution program it says could save the company $200 million between Aug. 1 and the end of 1983. The key to the plan is union endorsement, without which no salary cuts can be made. And although teams of Pan Am managers are circulating among employees to sell the plan, it is doubtful whether they will succeed. The unions have not closed the door on aiding the company, however. Workers recall all too well that the pilots contributed 10% of their wages in 1974 and never got it back. Under the present plan, workers are asked to give up a portion of future wage increases, which they will get back only if the company generates a 5% profit on its operating revenues by 1986.

The Transport Workers Union, for one, objects to the 1986 deadline. "By the end of 1986, if you haven't got your money back, it's gone," says John Kerrigan, director of the TWU's airline division. "If they borrowed that money from a bank, they'd have to pay it back." And the TWU does not believe Pan Am can make a 5 percent return by 1986.

Generating cash. Pan Am needs productivity improvements as well as cash from its workers. Relative to other international airlines, Pan Am's cost structure stacks up fairly well. But among domestic airlines it is near the bottom of the list. "It was one thing to have all this nonproductivity when you were flying only 747s internationally and collecting big fares," says a former Pan Am officer. "But put that against a bunch of $99 tickets to Miami, and you can't play the game."

There will be resistance, but Pan Am stands a good chance of improving many of its rigid work rules. It is also working to better basic services and in the past few months has improved both on-time performance and its telephone reservation system.

Management is also "working on other things" to generate cash, says Kilcarr. It is trying to sell the five long-range DC-10s it got in the National merger, but it is not sanguine about a deal in the current depressed used-aircraft market. It does hope to lease out one of those planes soon, however, and it also has other planes for sale.

Pan Am does not have another nonairline asset as big as the building it sold last year. "You should have kept the building and sold the airline," shouted one shareholder at Pan Am's May 12 annual meeting. The sale of Pan Am's hotel division—which last year earned $41.6 million pretax on revenues of $273.6 million and lists, at cost, assets of $136 million—is a possibility.

Good money after bad. The biggest question, of course, is whether Pan Am will stay in the airline business. "It would be a mistake not to consider any and all alternatives," says the senior official. "We are a corporation and must face the issue of how best to manage our assets."

Some analysts strongly support a withdrawal from the airline business. "Pan Am's overriding problem is that on the international side it's not competing in the real world," says Michael R. Armellino, vice-president at Goldman, Sachs & Co. "That's been compounded by poor management and the National merger. The answer is to get out of the airline business. Stop throwing good money after bad. Do a bit of what TWA's done—begin to work down the airline and build up other businesses."

It is easier to talk of getting out of the airline business than to do it, however. In an earlier time, the corporation might have sold either specific routes or the entire airline. Today, deregulation has wiped out the resale value of its domestic routes. United Airlines, Inc., which wants Pacific routes badly, might buy those, and East-

ern Air Lines, Inc., would be interested in South America but has no cash. Probably no one would want Pan Am's brutally competitive system across the North Atlantic.

Even if it wanted to build other businesses, Pan Am would first need profits. Earning them will take a lot of skill and more than a little luck. Lower fuel prices and an expected economic pickup later this year would help. The company also stands a good chance of increasing its yields in the North Atlantic. The International Air Transport Assn. agreed in early June to ask governments for a 5 percent fare increase in that area. And in the Pacific heavy competition from government-owned carriers is showing signs of easing.

Into the fray. Seawell's job is to develop policies that will enable Pan Am to capitalize on its basic strength in international aviation and to become an efficient domestic competitor as well. And he must create more stability in the executive suite, even as he develops strong operations people and his own successor. He is a crisis manager who has steered not just Pan Am but American Airlines and Rolls-Royce as well through heavy turbulence.

Some officials and ex-Pan Am officers say managers fearful of displeasing the demanding Seawell do not always brief him fully on potential troubles. Others say he knows everything that goes on but is not a hands-on manager, which is what Pan Am needs most right now. "When you grow up in the military," says Joedicke, "you've got a predetermined echelon type of reporting. In the best airline operation, you've got to get right down in the field."

ADAM ARON (B)
James J. Dowd and
Jeffrey A. Sonnenfeld

Looking back over the past 14 months at Pan Am, Adam Aron, now director of frequent traveler marketing, seemed to have no regrets whatsoever about his decision to stay with the still-struggling airline. Thinking back to June of 1981 and recalling his options then, Adam explained his decision to stay:

> Why didn't I join the start-up? Things just didn't look like they were going to work out. The economy was in trouble, and the larger airlines became more determined to beat down the new entrants before they gained too much market share. In the end, it just didn't look like a good idea. And what's more, I didn't want to leave Pan Am.
>
> Why didn't I go with the regional carrier who was offering me so much money? Because I didn't want to leave. And besides, Uncle Sam takes half anyway.
>
> So why did I stay with Pan Am? If Pan Am had gone under and I wasn't there, I'd have felt like a heel. I did all the wrestling with my conscience and I just felt that as a major U.S. company of longstanding tradition, and glory, and heritage, Pan Am did not deserve to die. And I had the chance to help do something about that.
>
> The way I looked at it, if I stayed, and Pan Am went down, I wouldn't be scarred for life; but if I stayed and things worked out, it would mean tremendous opportunity for me. But either way, if I left, I would have felt guilty. I would have felt like I had deserted my post.

In July of 1981, Adam was promoted to director of agency marketing. He described his feelings about that promotion as follows:

> That was a very important job at Pan Am for two reasons. First, as it means responsibility for Pan Am's relationships with travel agents around the world, it plays a major role in about 75 percent of our worldwide sales. And second, the final stage of airline deregulation is the opening up of the distribution system. That suggests there are going to be major changes in the way airlines

sell tickets. The director of agency marketing of a major carrier like Pan Am has the potential to help shape those changes, and certainly the responsibility to manage the impact of those changes on Pan Am.

> But the job was important to me personally for two added reasons. All my previous positions with Pan Am had been highly quantitative; I had begun to get a reputation for being able "to juggle numbers." But this job with agency relationships was a pure people job. It gave me the opportunity to balance my image, to build a reputation as someone who can handle not only the hard quantitative issues but also deal just as well with people.
>
> And then second, the job entailed a great deal of visibility, both inside and outside the airline. When you hold a meeting with your 100 largest distributors/dealers/brokers, the most senior people in your company *have* to get involved. And when large agency syndicates get together and ask for a speaker from Pan Am, they get the chairman, or the president, or the senior vice president of marketing. These same men are also their contacts for questions and problems. As a result, frequent involvement with senior management was common.

Adam was responsible for Pan Am's participation at the annual convention of ASTA, the American Society of Travel Agents, held in Honolulu in August of 1981. Then one month later he organized and managed Pan Am's annual ITAAB conference, the International Travel Agents Advisory Board, representing the top 30 travel agencies from 15 countries. This four-day meeting involved Pan Am's highest-level executives, including the chairman, the president, the division vice presidents, the senior vice president of marketing, the vice president of sales, and the vice president of customer service. Both these conferences were extremely successful. As a result, the senior vice president of marketing asked

Adam to take on an additional special assignment working with him to develop relationships with a major worldwide hotel chain.

While Pan Am continued to lose money and executives, Adam's career continued to thrive; he really began to enjoy his job. In April he took a three-week tour through the Orient to build and enhance relationships with travel agents in that part of the world. He began to see his name mentioned in the trade press, as he was gaining knowledge of and exposure to the industry's most important people.

But in May of 1982, only 10 months after he had assumed his new position, he was promoted again—this time to a newly created position, the director of frequent traveler marketing.

The latest development in the highly competitive air travel market was the offering of substantially discounted, and sometimes free, tickets to travelers who accumulated a given number of miles flown with one airline. Examples of such programs were American Airlines' "Advantage" and United Airlines' "Mileage Plus."

In early 1982, American Airlines announced that its Advantage program would now include British Airways and offer discounts on overseas travel. This development posed a serious threat to Pan Am, as the mileage bonus concept spread to Pan Am's bread and butter—international travel. Pan Am knew it had to counter that move; a competitive program had to be designed and marketed, quickly.

So on May 12 (the day of the Braniff bankruptcy announcement) Adam Aron was named director of frequent traveler marketing, reporting directly to the vice president of sales. His charge: go to the market with a frequent travelers program. And, in the first week of July, he did. Direct mail pieces au-

tomatically enrolled all of Pan Am's best customers in the new program, WorldPass. Two-page spreads in the *New York Times, The Wall Street Journal, Time, Newsweek, Fortune, Business Week,* and other major newspapers and magazines announced the introduction of Pan Am's WorldPass Program. WorldPass was Adam's "baby," as he called it; succeed or fail, the responsibility would be his. Indeed, he would have some direct responsibility for the bottom line.

For Adam Aron, the 12 months from July 1981 to July 1982 have meant unqualified success. For Pan Am, however, the year was a disaster. And while Adam's career prospects looked very good, the future of Pan Am itself remained doubtful in the summer of 1982. Reflecting on the events of the past year, and looking to the future, Adam's spirits remained undaunted, and he proved himself once again to be Pan Am's greatest fan:

> It certainly has been exciting! As I had expected, we have a new management in charge who are really dedicated to reviving the company. We've got a new dynamic CEO in Ed Acker from Air Florida and a very strong team beneath him in Gerry Gitner from People Express, Stephen Wolf from American, and Marty Shugrue from within our own ranks at Pan Am. We've moving forward and making progress every day.
>
> I'm going to live through a major chapter in American business history, a dramatic turnaround or a bankruptcy.
>
> The biggest frustration of staying has been that you work so hard and you don't always see fruition. The third and fourth quarters of 1981 were disastrous, and the first quarter of 1982 was the worst in the entire history of Pan Am. We lost about $125 million, but still our stock went up a half point, because that's about $30 or $40 million better than Wall Street thought we'd do! In the second quarter of this year we've halved our loss

Exhibit 1

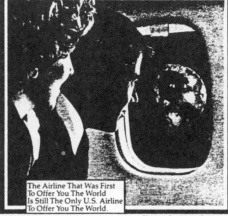

versus second quarter of last year, so maybe things are picking up.

The guys at Braniff saw the bankruptcy; I'd like to think we're going to see the turnaround. But it has not been a *fun* year. I've worked hours that make a consultant's life look like a summer vacation. You tell yourself, "Well, if there ever were a time to do this, *now* is when they really need it." But it's been "Now they really need it" for two straight years now with another one coming!

A lot of my colleagues have been through this once before, in 1974; I hope I only have to go through this once. I'm not really sure I have the stamina to go through this again—100-hour weeks, 14 weeks in a row. Yes, it's been challenging, and exciting—but not fun. A 90+ percent turnover in the officer corps, constant change in management staff, 20 percent overall company layoffs—that kind of thing is just not good for morale.

And yes, there are still outside opportunities. Two airlines have expressed some interest, a big one and a little one. And they've upped the price—I am passing up $20,000 to stay.

But I don't want money. I really want to save Pan Am. I believe it can be done. There are a lot of very talented executives in this company, and I believe we can do it. If WorldPass is as much of a success as I hope it will be, I think I can be one of the guys who helps.

CASE 3
ROGER CLARKE (A)
W. Earl Sasser

Six weeks after being promoted to advanced market development specialist, Roger Clarke realized that he was in trouble. The glowing reports and forecasts which had

provided the momentum for his predecessor's promotion to marketing manager were either overly optimistic or outright fabrications. There was no chance of Roger's meeting his 6-month or 12-month goals unless he continued the creative accounting and report writing so brilliantly engineered by Brad Carter, who was now his boss. In fact, as he reread a memorandum from Carter to Conrad Dawson, the group vice president, he was convinced that Carter was building up a case to fire him.

The Path to Advanced Market Development Specialist

Roger Clarke was born in 1948 in a small Midwestern town. Of modest financial means, he worked his way through Indiana State University, receiving a bachelor's degree in engineering management at the age of 22. His first job after college was in a sales capacity with IBM. Clarke compiled an outstanding sales record and was recruited to Universal Computers in March 1973 to assume a sales representative's position for the Securities Industry Group in the Chicago office. In Clarke's mind the opportunities to advance rapidly at Universal appeared outstanding.

In July 1973, Clarke made a well-received presentation to the national sales manager, Robert Simmons, and the group vice president, Conrad Dawson, during a regional meeting. Shortly after, during a four-week training program at group headquarters in New York, Clarke asked Conrad Dawson to promote him to market development specialist, stating that "most of the market development specialists are not qualified to carry my briefcase." At the end of a six-hour dinner, the group vice president gave Roger his blessing and promoted him to the position of advanced marketing development specialist assigned to the group's headquarters in New York City. The group's organizational structure is depicted in Exhibit 1. The promotion had been a double advancement because it normally took a marketing development specialist several years in the field to obtain the "advanced" status. All other market development specialists were in their early to mid-30s. The advanced market development specialist in the other region was 40 years old; Clarke was only 25. His salary was $27,000, a 50 percent improvement over his prior salary.

Clarke had direct responsibility for the three market development specialists in his region. They, in turn, had dotted line responsibility for the sales representatives in their districts. Clarke reported to Brad Carter, Securities Industry Group marketing manager. Carter had recently been promoted from the position Clarke assumed.

The First Month

After the promotion had become effective on September 10, Clarke had spent one week with his boss in New York, making a whirlwind tour of brokerage firm clients in New York City. The next week he had spent most of his time getting to know most of the Securities Industry Group's sales representatives in New York and making introductory sales calls with a few of the sales people. He had spent the next two weeks visiting brokerage firms in New York and visiting sales offices in Philadelphia, Baltimore, and Boston, where he had met both sales representatives and clients who were located in those cities. In addition, he participated, with the eight other marketing specialists and Brad Carter, in a Marketing Plan Review for 1974. Clarke recalled the hectic

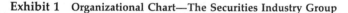

Exhibit 1   Organizational Chart—The Securities Industry Group

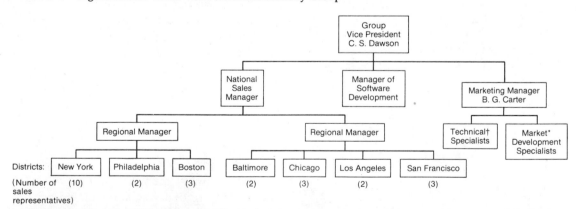

* There were two advanced market development specialists (one for each region) and seven market development specialists (one for each district). Roger Clarke was advanced market development specialist for the New York–Philadelphia–Boston region.
† There were seven technical specialists (one for each district).

nature of the first month in his new position: "besides meeting all the sales representatives and clients during this period, I was in the process of buying a house on Long Island, getting married [on September 21], and arranging to move my possessions from Chicago to Long Island."

A Meeting with the Marketing Manager; October 15, 1973

On October 15, Roger Clarke had met with Brad Carter for two hours discussing his performance to date. Quite to Clarke's surprise, Mr. Carter had prepared a list of problems he had with Clarke's performance in the first month on the job. The day after the meeting, Mr. Carter had written a memorandum to Conrad Dawson, the group vice president and the man who had promoted Clarke, outlining the points covered in the meeting; he had also sent a copy to Clarke (Exhibit 2).

Roger Clarke's Dilemma

After his promotion and marriage, Clarke had been in a state of euphoria. The meeting with Carter and subsequent memorandum came as quite a shock. However, in retrospect, Clarke believed that he should have seen it coming:

> I should have realized that trouble was brewing at the September 28 Marketing Plan Review meeting. At the meeting I was not as optimistic about the future as Carter thought I should be. However, everywhere I went, brokerage firm executives were complaining about excess computer capacity. At the meeting Carter assigned 1974 performance commitments for all market development

specialists. I expressed concern that my goals would be impossible to achieve. After the meeting Carter called me aside and gave me a pitch on the huge growth opportunities of our market. I nodded my head; but after two weeks visiting our customers, I had been more optimistic at the meeting than what I had seen made me want to be.

As he sat at his desk looking at the copy of Carter's memorandum, Clarke recalled the advice he had received from Dawson about his new position:

> Conrad Dawson warned me that I was entering a political situation. He told me that Carter was not exactly overjoyed with my promotion; he had wanted to promote a market development specialist to my position.
>
> If I have a sponsor in this organization, it has to be Conrad. He took a high risk promoting me despite Carter's objection. However, he told me that he expected my performance, and not our relationship, to be the key to my next advancement.

Clarke acknowledged that he had not been very concerned with politics when he assumed the new position; his only concern had been with understanding his new duties as quickly as possible. But what should he do now? Should he arrange a meeting with Dawson? Should he respond in writing? Should he not rock the boat and do exactly what Carter tells him even when he is convinced it is a waste of time? Should he try to move laterally to another group in Universal Computers? Should he send out his résumé to other firms? These were just a few of the questions on his mind after re-reading Carter's memorandum. Next week he, his wife, and belongings would settle into their new house on Long Island. He thought the fall would prove rather interesting.

Exhibit 2

October 19, 1973   <u>Personal and Confidential</u>

TO: C. S. DAWSON
      OFFICE

SUBJECT: <u>Roger Clarke's Performance</u>

Since Clarke's commencement as a Market Development Specialist on September 10, 1973, there have been a number of incidents which reflected unfavorably upon his performance. We had discussed most of these incidents as they occurred, but I felt it necessary to meet with him on October 15, 1973, to review all my displeasures with his performance and chart a positive course for the future. The following is a summary of our approximately two-hour discussion.

I told Roger I was not at all pleased with his performance to date and that we would be watching him closely over the next thirty days with the expectation of marked improvement. We reviewed a number of problems including the following:

1.   Reports of Roger being pompous and "smart ass." I indicated that I supported those descriptions. We discussed these impressions in some detail and how to change them.

2.   Not letting our office know where he is when plans are changed by him. Discussed the importance of his whereabouts and the fact that he is not free to drastically change his plans without my knowledge.
     Example: On October 12, Philadelphia office and I were looking for him. His itinerary said Philadelphia Office. At 3:00 pm he called from Boston and said he was there because "there was nothing to do in Philadelphia." He did not have two assignments ready for me that were due that day. He had left Philadelphia the evening of Oct. 11. In his behalf, he did leave a note at the Philadelphia office describing his plans.

3.   Trouble dealing with Small World Travel. The negative information here came from my secretary, Rena, in an incident on October 4, 1973. Roger was upset with certain travel arrangements made for him. He had called Small World to express his displeasure and they called Rena back to further determine Mr. Clarke's displeasure in that they had booked him on the flights we requested. Rena reports he grabbed the phone from her, complained more and hung up. We discussed the fact that we had never had any particular problems with this agency and valued our cooperative relationship. It was not his place to be so heavy handed in this situation. He said he preferred to use his own travel card in the future and not deal with a travel agent. I agreed, but will reverse my decision and advise him that my

Exhibit 2   (*continued*)

C. S. Dawson   —2—
October 19, 1973

signing of ticket advance forms is, in effect, my *required* approval of his travel plans. I know of no one else in marketing who does not work in this manner, so he is not being singled out.

4. Does not follow up on requested information. Several incidents here, but the major ones are as follows:

Example 1: On September 27, I asked him to check why Dean Witter had not purchased our equipment. Approximately three reminders got no good answer as of this day. A visit to Dean Witter now planned.

Example 2: Approximately September 20, requested the status of Merrill Lynch. Only answer I ever received was he would check into it next week.

Example 3: On September 27, I requested organizational charts for the operations function at several major brokerage houses. His reply at that time was that he "doesn't see the reason to have these." I told him they were important, explained why, and still never got them.

5. Perhaps playing devil's advocate, but very negative in September 28 Marketing Plan Review Meeting.

I would say that Roger accepted and discussed this criticism in a humble and constructive manner. Plans to alter or correct the previous five problems are as follows:

1. *Plan* constructive positive calls when dealing with field Market Development Specialists. Have the purpose and necessary sales aids to complete an objective. Do not make calls for the sake of meeting people.

2. Call office at least once per day, preferably twice.

3. Travel plans to be arranged like everyone else. I will tell Roger not to use air travel card as I had previously agreed.

Exhibit 2   *(concluded)*

C. S. Dawson   —3—
October 19, 1973

    4.   Roger now says he understands that my requests are not of a "jog the memory" type, but rather a request for information in my hands.

    5.   Says he will try to be more positive internally as well as continuing his positive external attitude.

Roger plans to move his wife and household goods to Long Island on October 26. Hopefully a more settled home life will improve his work performance. Roger and I will discuss his overall performance again in mid-November.

Brad G. Carter

Brad G. Carter
SECURITIES INDUSTRY MARKETING MANAGER

BGC:rps
CC: Roger Clarke

ROGER CLARKE (B)
W. Earl Sasser

In early February 1974, after five months in his position as advanced market development specialist, Roger Clarke described his feelings about the job to a close personal friend:

> My attitude and enthusiasm are terrible. My boss is trying to fire me. With the continued volume downturn in the stock market, the future for our group looks very limited. The only thing that keeps me going are conversations with several managers outside our group who say they understand the problem and advise me to stand firm.
>
> I have been working closely with the National Sales Manager and Manager of Software Development to develop a new sales program around improved applications. The only way for us to sell more computers is if we can convince brokerage firms to switch to ours because of our superior service and software. We have done all the easy applications. The next ones will take months to develop and will not provide significant results for several years. I spent most of November, December, and January working on such special projects while still openly conflicting with my boss on his projections and forecasts. He and I were almost ignoring each other while doing our best to destroy each

other. My strategy has been to disassociate myself from him.

Now he has written another memorandum [Exhibit 1] to Dawson after a meeting we had on January 28. This time I was not sent a copy but somehow a copy appeared on my desk. I don't know if a friend or enemy put it there.

I guess Carter's memorandum triggered this short note from Dawson [Exhibit 2]. I have drafted a response [Exhibit 3]. Is this what I want to say?

Exhibit 1

January 30, 1974   Personal and Confidential

TO: C. S. Dawson
     OFFICE

SUBJECT: Roger Clarke's Performance

On October 19, 1973, I wrote you a memo regarding my dissatisfaction with Roger's performance. Since that time, Roger has been diverted from his assigned Market Development task by marketing meetings and special projects. It is only recently that it has been totally fair to judge Roger in his job performance.

The week of January 21, 1974, Roger and I spent the week together making calls in New York on brokerage firms. On January 28, 1974, Roger and I had another rather lengthy discussion regarding his attitude, enthusiasm and job performance.

Attitude

Roger spends a disproportionate amount of time complaining about the problems of selling to the brokerage firms and not nearly enough time on positive marketing approaches. We have discussed the fact that he is getting paid to sell the accounts and not to agree with our clients about the negative attributes of our products and the present state of overcapacity in the securities industry.

Enthusiasm

In our January 28 discussion, I told Roger that while I believe he is a highly capable person, I do not believe he is putting forth anywhere near his maximum effort. I suggested that on a scale of "0–10", his enthusiasm rates a low "2." He agreed. I also stated that this is totally unacceptable and could quickly lead to our parting ways. Roger felt that all his actions were being dictated by me. It was at this point where perhaps we unrooted the problem. I asked if he felt I "dictated" to Joe Case, our other Advanced Market Development Specialist, to which he replied, "No." I inquired as to what new or even slightly imaginative marketing approaches he has put forth in the past 4 and a half months. Answer: "None." Why were you not in New York for the past 1 and a half months? Answer: "Sales meetings and special projects."

Exhibit 1 (*concluded*)

C. S. Dawson —2—
January 30, 1974

I told Roger that when I see no new targets, no imaginative marketing and no sales calls in New York over a period of time, I will become a dictator for his actions.

At this point, I retrieved a notebook of presentations and associated letters which Joe Case had used in his selling efforts. We paged through and Roger stated that all those letters with all those internal copies are purely political and not his style. Roger stated emphatically that he has been doing the same thing with handwritten notes to customers. I pointed out that our secretary does a fine typing job and copies of notes, letters or whatever are good politics and also prove to your boss that you are working . . . "something that remains doubtful in my mind in this case." I suggested we take a look at his letter-book. There were only one or more letters there to customers with no internal copies. Roger promised a continuous deluge of written communication and customer follow-up.

Summary

Roger agrees with shortcomings pointed out. He promises to greatly increase his written correspondence, develop unique marketing approaches, and spend more time with our customers.

I hope these promises materialize in the coming 30 days. If not, I recommend we find a replacement for Roger in this critical job.

Brad G. Carter

Brad G. Carter
SECURITIES INDUSTRY MARKETING MANAGER

BGC:rps

Exhibit 2

R. J. CLARKE   January 31, 1974

<u>OFFICE</u>

Roger:

  I have had a chance to get Brad Carter's perspective on your performance. Since I believe we are all earnestly attempting to improve a situation which did not get off on the best foot, I would like you to reduce to writing *your* perspective on your recent performance and your understanding of what specific areas *must* be improved.

  I will be most happy to review this in a discussion with you, but I should like the benefit of your thoughts reduced to writing first.

C. S. Dawson
C. S. Dawson

cc: B. G. Carter

Exhibit 3

February 1, 1974

C. S. Dawson
Office

Conrad:

<u>My Perspective:</u>

  Started super-enthusiastic, began to question, began to be hobbled, lost sight of objectives, became defensive.

I concur that we are all attempting to improve the situation. During my meeting with Brad on January 28, we uncovered the immediate day to day problem and my tensions dissolved.

Exhibit 3 (*concluded*)

Joe Case writes everything and copies everyone, and this is what Brad expects. It is my style to rely on the telephone and handwritten notes and to write formal letters only as necessary and then to copy only the affected persons. I assumed (should never assume) that Brad was automatically copied on the correspondence and reports that I did do.

Because he never saw any of my notes nor any of my cost analysis nor any of my letters, he thought I was doing nothing. The more he thought that, the harder he leaned on me, and the more perplexed and rebellious I became.

There is still the problem that I don't believe some of the things we are committed to. We can do the impossible half of the time, but the other half bothers me. It would be simple on my job to be unrealistically optimistic and to be gone when the reckoning comes. My attitude is not negative; instead, I define it as realistic.

Must Improvements:

- More formal letters, reports, and copies.
- If today's position and problems are understood, then we'll try to do the impossible all the time.
- Be positive.

Roger J. Clarke

Roger J. Clarke

RJC/la

ROGER CLARKE (C)
W. Earl Sasser

Brad Carter's most recent letter to Dawson convinced Roger Clarke that his position as advanced market development specialist was in jeopardy. He estimated that he only had two months to rectify the situation. The only solution as he saw it was to take the offensive against his boss, Brad Carter. So, he began a series of memorandums, reports, letters, and projections which began

to expose previous double counting and "creative forecasting."

On April 1, 1974, a marketing presentation was made to the group VP and national sales manager. Just prior to the meeting, rumors were rampant about the impending demise of Brad Carter. Roger Clarke explained the reason for the rumors:

> We were preparing a three-hour presentation for the April 1 meeting. Carter wanted it to come out positive; but after two days at a retreat preparing it, we came up with him on one side and me on the other, with the others supporting me.

On April 4, 1974, it was announced that Brad Carter was being moved laterally to an "undefined" special project. Roger Clarke was announced as the new marketing manager.

ROGER CLARKE (D)
W. Earl Sasser

On July 1, 1974, Roger Clarke announced that he was resigning from his position as marketing manager of the Securities Industry Group of Universal Computers to begin full-time studies for an MBA. He explained the decision as follows:

> I was not overjoyed at getting the promotion to marketing manager. I had been lobbying Dawson, and others in New York, to get into another part of the business because I knew the group would still do poorly compared to the growth of other segments of Universal's business. In fact, I was arguing for them to disband the group for many months.
>
> Upon assuming responsibility for the group, I began reducing the size of our staff by finding jobs for them in other groups. Those of us who remained began working on long-range conceptual development programs. This allowed us to make presentations on fancy topics without being tied to the poor short-term performance. The development programs would not generate business for 2–5 years, but they would provide conversation during the years.
>
> In retrospect, I think Carter moved out of the position knowing that I would be his replacement. He knew that I had made a lot of enemies in what seemed to be a move to push him out. By being relegated to the Securities Group and, as a result of the bad publicity of the six-month battle, I lost the war. There was no way to turn the situation around except to make the marketing group

leaner and develop for the future and even that would not get me promoted. My career at Universal had plateaued.

> Painfully, I learned some important lessons. Pick your job and manager carefully. I also believe that if I had perpetuated the myth as Carter had done when he saw the growth slowing, I probably would have slipped on through and kept on the fast track. Fighting with one's boss is not a winning situation, even if one wins the battle.

CASE 4
ROBERT GOLDFARB (A)
Joseph W. Chevarley, Jr., Liora Katzenstein, and Jeffrey A. Sonnenfeld

Robert Goldfarb finished the draft for the upcoming WFCR fund-raising campaign. As he wrote the date, September 20, 1980, he reflected on the events of the past year and wondered if, indeed, he was approaching his last month at this public radio station. He sat back and let his eyes roam from the "Station Manager" plate on his door to the map of Boston hanging prominently above his desk. He wondered whether he had been too forceful or not forceful enough in his actions. His recent handling of Spanish-language broadcasting had led to his threatened dismissal and a serious community challenge of the station's license.

Robert Goldfarb

Robert Goldfarb developed a strong attachment to radio at an early age. He got his first broadcasting job when he was 16. Soon he was actually on the air as host of a call-in talk show. He continued to work on the air through high school. As an undergraduate at Harvard College he worked for the campus radio station and eventually became its president. He also worked part-time at Boston-area commercial stations. After graduation, he took a job with a commercial classical music station in Boston. He left there three years later to attend Harvard Business School.

Following the completion of his MBA, Goldfarb went to Washington, D.C., where he took an administrative position as special assistant to the executive vice president of National Public Radio. A year later, the fall of 1979, anxious to get back to a station, Goldfarb applied and was hired to be station general manager at WFCR in Amherst, Massachusetts. When asked about his commitment to broadcasting, Goldfarb replied:

> I know what it is that excites me about broadcasting. I've come to value what radio can do to expose people to things that they might not seek out. Because radio is available to people at a flick of a dial, they don't have to buy a book or go to a movie to get what's on the radio. And so I think it can be a tremendous educational tool for people to come into contact with great music, great ideas, great words—poetry, prose—and that's why I'm interested in public radio, because that's what it does.

WMBC, University of Massachusetts, and WFCR

In 1953, four Pioneer Valley colleges—University of Massachusetts, Amherst, Smith, and Mt. Holyoke—formed the Western Massachusetts Educational Television Council to explore possibilities for establishing a public television station in the area. In 1957, broadening its interests to encompass public radio, the council changed its name to the Western Massachusetts Broadcasting Council (WMBC). It was not until 1961, though, that the WMBC arranged with Bos-

ton's well-known public station, WGBH, to operate a radio station in the four-college area. In effect, WGBH operated the station, WFCR, by rebroadcasting its own programming 12 hours per day. In 1967, in order to stimulate more local programming, the WMBC and WGBH agreed to transfer the license to the University of Massachusetts. Since then, WFCR has broadcast its programming not only to the now five-college area—with the opening of Hampshire College—but also throughout the Pioneer Valley, to Springfield, Hartford, and farther points.

As licensee, the University of Massachusetts has ultimate responsibility with the Federal Communications Commission for the station's operations. But the university typically defers most decisions to the WMBC in order to promote five-college collaboration. The WMBC acts very much like a board of directors. In the fall of 1979, it had 11 members—representatives from each of the five colleges, the executive director of the five-college consortium, and five members from the general public.

Que Tal Amigos?

"Que Tal Amigos?"—"How are you, friends?"—was a pioneering venture into Hispanic programming when it went on the air over WFCR in 1969. Julio Torres was involved in the program from the start. He and his wife, Sonia Vivas, soon took over its production. Their program quickly went from 30 to 60 minutes in length. Over the years, it was broadcast in different time slots. In the fall of 1979, "Que Tal Amigos?" was broadcast six nights per week—7:30 to 8:30 P.M., Mondays through Fridays, and 7:00 to 8:00 P.M. on Saturdays. The program mainly featured recorded popular Hispanic music; but it also broadcast, in Spanish, the news, weather, community announcements, and occasional interviews and poetry readings. Sonia Vivas explained that:

> This program has been the link among the Hispanic community in the Connecticut River Valley area for more than 10 years now, always presenting quality material: different varieties of music, of poetry, and information from Latin America and Spain. Our Hispanic community is made up of people from different countries. Our audience is not only Hispanic but also includes English-speaking people who are learning Spanish or are interested in Latin American music as well.[1]

Bob Goldfarb's Perspective[2]. Bob Goldfarb offered this account of his perception of the sequence of events:

> It all started on November 5, 1979, my first day on the job. Actually nothing happened then, but I knew early that Hispanic programming was a question at the station. I had seen a lot of radio schedules and I had never seen one that had six hours a week of Spanish-language programming on prime time.
>
> In my first weeks on the job I said that I wanted to meet with everybody on the station staff, which isn't all that many. There were about 14 full-time people and a few more part-timers. I didn't mention anything about my concerns about foreign-language programming until I met with the people who produced it, and I told them that one of my jobs was to assess programming and budgeting priorities for the station. I told them that it seemed to me that there were real questions about how high a priority their programming should be, how much it should receive in resources and in air time.
>
> Shortly after that I sent a memo to our

"Board of Directors," the Western Massachusetts Broadcasting Council (WMBC). I had decided to send them a memo about every month or so, telling them what was going on at the station. The last item in the November memo said something like: "The priorities have to be reassessed and if other things have a higher priority, it might be necessary to cancel foreign-language programs"—I said programs because there was also one in French—"to cancel the programs and to use the resources for something with a higher priority." Well, very quickly members of the public found out about it, mostly because the people who produced the programs told them. Since I had distributed my memo to the staff, believing as I do in open communications and not sending memos behind people's backs, they got a copy of it so there I was, on record, in writing, as having said that. Now, I had made no decision. I had just identified it as a trouble spot, but everyone assumed that I had made a decision.

Well, around that time, in order to help assess what priorities the station should have, I did several things. Aside from talking to the staff, I had announcements on the air where I asked people to write in and say what they liked or didn't like. After a few weeks, it was clear that a lot of people were writing in about foreign-language programming. Quite a number were defending it— as people will do in the case of an underdog program—but also a number of people did not like it. So I recorded a new set of announcements, which said that "the most controversial programs we seem to have are the foreign-language programs, so if you have an opinion about those, please be sure to write." That aggravated things further. Some people felt that I was being an "agent provocateur" in getting people upset about the whole issue.

In January I held an open house at the station, invited listeners from hither and yon to come to the station to meet the staff, and to talk with us about programming.

---

[1] *Eco Latino*, February 19, 1980, pp. 5. (Supplement to the University of Massachusetts *Collegian*.)

[2] See Exhibit 1 for an outline of the sequence of events, and see Exhibit 2 for a listing of key actors.

Exhibit 1 **Sequence of Events**

5 Nov 79	Robert Goldfarb takes over as station general manager at WFCR on standard one-year contract.
Mid-Nov 79	Goldfarb privately tells "Que Tal Amigos?" coproducers that he has real questions about how high a priority their program should be.
End Nov 79	In his first monthly memo to the Western Massachusetts Broadcasting Council (WMBC), Goldfarb explains that "it might be necessary to cancel [foreign-language] programs" if a reassessment shows that there are higher priorities. Goldfarb distributes copies of the memo to his staff.
Dec 79	Goldfarb solicits listener opinion about foreign language programming through on-the-air announcements over WFCR.
Dec 79	Julio Torres, coproducer of "Que Tal Amigos?", resigns over the uncertainty surrounding the program's future. The other coproducer, Sonia Vivas, announces her intent to resign at the end of June.
20 Jan 80	Opponents demonstrate in support of Hispanic programming at WFCR's Sunday open house.
1 Feb 80	At a Friday press conference Goldfarb announces his decision on "Que Tal Amigos?" Effective April 1, the hour-long program will be cut from six nights a week to two—Tuesdays and Thursdays—and moved from prime time to 11:00 P.M.
3 Feb 80	Goldfarb hosts a Sunday evening call-in program on WFCR to explain his decision.
26 Feb 80	Opponents demonstrate at WMBC meeting held at the University of Massachusetts and speak out against Goldfarb's decision. The WMBC votes unanimously to form an advisory committee to assist Goldfarb in determining how WFCR's programming can meet the needs of the Hispanic community. The committee is mandated to report its findings to the WMBC on May 10.
Mar 80	Opponents from Coalition for Public Involvement in Public Radio vow to challenge WFCR's Federal Communications Commission operating license when it comes up for review in December.
31 Mar 80	Opponents demonstrate at WFCR and then stage a sit-in in the office of the chancellor of the University of Massachusetts to protest Goldfarb's intent to carry out his earlier decision to cut back "Que Tal Amigos?" effective April 1.
2 Apr 80	Opponents end three-day sit-in after reaching a seven-point compromise agreement with the WMBC, meeting in emergency session. Key provision restores "Que Tal Amigos?" to prime time, four nights weekly through June 30.
7 May 80	Advisory Committee forwards to Goldfarb a statement of the mission of Spanish-language broadcasting as it envisions it.
Early June 80	Goldfarb informs the Advisory Committee and the WMBC that he wants to cut back Spanish-language programming to two hours per week, effective July 1.
17 June 80	Motion to suspend Golfarb is voted down at emergency WMBC meeting.
End June 80	Sonia Vivas, remaining coproducer of "Que Tal Amigos?" resigns.
5 Jul 80	Protestors demonstrate peacefully at WFCR as new Spanish program succeeds "Que Tal Amigos?"
28 Jul 80	In the face of strong Coalition pressure, the WMBC votes in executive session to recommend to the University of Massachusetts that Goldfarb's contract not be renewed.
1 Aug 80	The University of Massachusetts informs Goldfarb that his contract will not be renewed in November.
Aug 80	Goldfarb solicits Coalition and Advisory Committee help toward hiring a new producer for Spanish programming. A search committee is formed.
15 Sep 80	Supporters speak out for Goldfarb at WMBC meeting. The Council clarifies its earlier decision that Goldfarb's contract "might not be renewed."

There was an organized effort on the part of the Hispanic community—first in the form of a demonstration with picket signs. Eventually, a lot of the Hispanics and their sympathizers came into the station and struck up discussions with me, some staff members, and some members of the public. That brought another round of press attention to the issue, exacerbating it further.

Since this had become such a big issue, I held a press conference on February 1, the date by which I had promised a decision; I

Exhibit 2   Key Actors

Advisory Committee on Hispanic Programming
Formed in February by the council to advise Goldfarb; chaired by Woodward Wickham.

Coalition for Public Involvement in Public Radio
Formed by various community groups in March 1980 to oppose cutbacks of Hispanic programming on WFCR and to challenge the station's license when it comes up for renewal in December 1980.

Tony Crayton
One spokesperson for the Coalition; employed at the University of Massachusetts' Office of Third World Affairs.

Robert Goldfarb
Station general manager of WFCR.

Daniel Melley
Former chairperson of the Western Massachusetts Broadcasting Council; Goldfarb's superior at the university.

E. Jefferson "Pat" Murphy
Member of Western Massachusetts Broadcasting Council; negotiated with protestors during sit-in at

university chancellor's office; executive director, Five Colleges, Inc.

Julio Torres
Coproducer of "Que Tal Amigos?"; resigned in December.

University of Massachusetts
Holds FCC license for WFCR.

Sonia Vivas
Coproducer of "Que Tal Amigos?"; resigned in June.

Western Massachusetts Broadcasting Council
Acts as WFCR's board of directors.

Woodward Wickham
Member of Western Massachusetts Broadcasting Council; chairperson, Advisory Committee on Hispanic Programming; negotiated with protestors during sit-in at University of Massachusetts chancellor's office; executive assistant to the president of Hampshire College.

---

had decided to cut back "Que Tal Amigos?" from six hours per week to two and to move it from prime time to 11:00 P.M. The changes were to take effect on April 1. [See Exhibit

3.] The next evening I went on the air to explain my position. I also listened to listener comments through on-the-air phone calls. This, too, was an organized effort by

---

Exhibit 3

WFCR Radio to Curtail Spanish Program

By Alice Dembner

AMHERST—A new WFCR radio program schedule, which drastically cuts back the Spanish language programming and adds jazz and folk shows, was announced yesterday for five college public radio by general manager Robert Goldfarb.

The changes are a result of "internal scrutiny

Source: *Daily Hampshire Gazette*, February 2, 1980

of programming combined with the comments of listeners" and are not permanent, according to material distributed at a press conference yesterday.

"This schedule provides a base for planning our next six months of programming," Goldfarb said. "Things will change again in October."

Goldfarb cited a goal of replacing most or all of the station's syndicated programming with locally-produced shows. He also stressed a need for a local public-affairs magazine, more new, folk and "world" music, cross-cultural shows, and a better use of five college resources.

He talked at some length about the need for a

Exhibit 3 (*continued*)

Third World news program to present news that would be based on "different assumptions" than current news programs.

His announcement that the 10-year-old nationally recognized program, "Que Tal Amigos," would be cut back from six to two hours a week and those two hours scheduled at 11 P.M. Tuesday and Thursdays instead of the current 7:30 to 8:30 P.M. drew immediate criticism from show producer Sonia Vivas who attended the press conference.

"This decision is inhumane and irresponsible," she told reporters. "It's a way to cancel or eliminate the show. Workers, students and children who listen to the program are not awake from 11 to 12 P.M."

Ms. Vivas said she did not know how the local Hispanic community and the broader group of listeners would react to the program change, but said she would announce the situation over the air.

Two weeks ago, about 50 people picketed the WFCR offices after reports leaked out that Goldfarb was considering eliminating the show, along with a French show, "Tout en Francais." Members of the local Third World community have leveled charges of racism against Goldfarb.

"Tout en Français" was rescheduled from a half-hour Tuesday and Thursday from 6:30 to 7 to one hour Sunday at 6 P.M.

Subjective editorial judgment

In announcing the cutback of "Que Tal Amigos," Goldfarb said he made "a subjective editorial judgment" in response to complaints about the show.

"Everyone agreed the program is a good idea but felt it was on at the wrong time and too frequently," he said.

Goldfarb said he had received numerous comments about the show, the majority of which he said favored a cut-back in hours and time change. Ms. Vivas, who asked Goldfarb for copies of all letters pertaining to the Spanish language show, said the letters ran 10 to 1 in favor of continuation of the show at its current time.

Goldfarb admitted receiving a number of petitions in support of the foreign-language programs and their usefulness in language education. He said he "now believed that this questioning of the premise of the French and Spanish programs was probably too hasty."

The station manager emphasized that the station was still committed to foreign language programs, which he said would be expanded in the future.

But he challenged the concept of WFCR programming aimed at specific audiences.

"All of our programs should be geared towards sharing. If we aim a program specifically at Hispanic culture, we are abdicating our responsibility to share between cultures," he said.

Share between cultures

"The number of hours is not as important as the total mission, which we see expanding," he said. "A lesser number of hours will allow the program to focus on what it has done best—news, culture, and poetry, and not make it so necessary to play as many records."

Goldfarb said he felt the music aired on the program was "strictly popular music" which did not live up to WFCR's "art music" standards. Ms. Vivas objected, saying that popular music plays an important role in Latin American culture and said the lyrics of many well-known poets are currently being set to popular music by young musicians and thus given more widespread distribution.

By October, Goldfarb said he would like to reschedule one hour of "Que Tal Amigos" at "a better time."

Another reason cited by Goldfarb for the cutback of the show was the recent establishment of a commercial Spanish station in Hartford. He said WFCR's alternative focus should therefore switch to jazz and folk music, which he said were not being aired locally.

Ms. Vivas questioned the quality and educational value of the commercial program.

Goldfarb also said he felt a disproportionate amount of the station's staff worked on the

Exhibit 3 (*concluded*)

show, and said that had to be changed. According to him, two people produced "Que Tal Amigos" while eight remaining production people produced the remainder of the station's programming and managed the control room.

One of the Spanish program's full-time producers, Julio Torres, resigned recently due to the instability and controversy surrounding the continuation of the program. The remaining producer, Ms. Vivas, has resigned effective July 1, and Goldfarb said yesterday he would not replace either staff member.

The general manager announced he would pull together an "advisory group" of volunteers to put out the program. A similar group is now responsible for "Tout en Francais."

With the resignation of Torres and Ms. Vivas, as well as Jose Tolson, who produced a black classical music show called Bright Moments, the station will lose its entire Third World staff.

Staff reorganized

Questioned on that point, Goldfarb said the station would "redouble its efforts to attract qualified minorities" to apply for four positions currently open at WFCR.

He said elimination of the two paid "Que Tal Amigos" positions would free money to hire free-lance reporters and a news director and to allow more staff people to spend time outside the studios.

In talking about the need for more local programs, Goldfarb agreed that it was contradictory to cut back existing locally produced programs like "Que Tal Amigos," but he said "program content was currently a higher priority than localism."

Other program changes announced by Goldfarb include a half-hour earlier airing of the children's program, "The Spider's Web," followed daily at 7 P.M. with an hour of jazz and folk music. At 8 P.M., classical music from the New York Philharmonic, Chicago Symphony, and Library of Congress will be offered in addition to the WFCR production, "The Music Box," "The Vocal Scene," and concerts from the White Mountain Music Festival. The Philadelphia orchestra series will be discontinued.

The hour beginning at 10 P.M. will be devoted to the spoken word, followed by "Que Tal Amigos" Tuesdays and Thursdays and three new programs—historic recordings on "Collector's Item," vocal music on "The First Fifty Years," and folk music and humor on the "Midnight Special."

"Music for Night People" will begin at midnight.

The award-winning National Public Radio program "Jazz Alive" will be aired Saturdays at 6 P.M., followed by the Boston Symphony and Folk Festival USA.

On Sundays, a single topic will be explored from noon until 5 P.M. At 7, the Los Angeles Philharmonic concerts will be aired, followed by full length plays at 9.

"Mbarí Mbayo" moves to Wednesdays at 1 P.M.

The "Swing Session" series has been suspended while "Soundscript" will be revamped and revived in a few months, Goldfarb said. "Commonwealth Journal" will be heard as part of a new magazine program weekdays at 12:30 P.M. and "Options in Education" will switch to Saturdays at noon.

A complete list of changes will be included in the March program guide.

Hispanics to dominate the program—as indeed they did.

My going on the air generated quite a lot of listener response in the form of letters and phone calls. The letters mostly favored my decision, but the phone calls mostly favored what the Hispanics were pushing for.

Toward the end of February we had a meeting of the WMBC and it was held in a large meeting room at the University of Massachusetts. There was a demonstration before it and, I would say, 30 or so Hispanics and their sympathizers came into the meeting and sat there and registered in advance to speak during the public comment portion of the meeting. There were somewhere between 7 and 10 speeches given, all of them opposing my decision, all of them given by people of this organized group. It so happened that they were the only people requesting to speak. I think that's what usually happens when something is attacked. People who are on the defensive are the first to speak. The people who backed my decision felt no obligation either to go to the meeting or to speak.

Members of the audience carried placards, which said something like—I don't have the wording exactly in my mind—something like "Task Force on Jewish Education," a big Jewish star and "Que Tal Amigos?" The implication of it was that people who didn't know Hispanic culture, such as a Jewish station manager, should listen to the program before they condemn it. At that meeting, I gave what I thought was a conciliatory response, saying that I thought it was important for the station to reconsider its actions in the face of the strong community outcry. I said I thought it was important to work with people in the community to reach a solution. At this stage the WMBC authorized the creation of an Advisory Committee of people interested in Hispanic culture to advise us on how to proceed. [See Exhibit 4.]

The understanding was that this Advisory Committee would function primarily to advise the station on what should go into Spanish-language programs. I had made some statements about what I thought about the content of "Que Tal Amigos?" and this committee was supposed to provide expert advice on that. I didn't think it was a very good program. It was a mixture of music and talk; mostly it contained a succession of public service announcements from night to night, the same records over two or three week periods, very little musical variety, a little

news and weather forecasting in Spanish. I thought it was not a very useful program, not creative musically, not informative. It had once been much better, but it was just not very good programming.

There was another council meeting a month later in March, and that meeting was generally peaceful. I thought we were home free, but some people claimed that as a condition for the formation of an Advisory Committee we had agreed to suspend all change in the program schedule. [See Exhibit 5]. That was not true. So the issue suddenly came back. There was a demonstration announced for March 31, which was the last day before the change would go into effect. The demonstration first centered around the station. People were marching around the building in which we were located; but very quickly they went off to the student union, where they picked up another couple of dozen people and marched into the office of the chancellor of the university, who has legal responsibility for WFCR since the station is licensed to the university. They demanded to meet with him, to have him settle this problem. [See Exhibit 6.] He was new to the position and I hadn't met him before. He asked me to come over to talk with him—which I did— and he attempted to mediate the discussion. He thought this could be done relatively quickly. It was about one in the afternoon and he said "I really have to get out of here by 3:00 P.M."

It actually took three days to get the people out of the chancellor's office because the demonstrators quickly decided that negotiations were pointless: they were holding out not for a compromise but for 100 percent of their demands. As soon as they announced that they were staging a "sit-in," the chancellor immediately ordered coffee and donuts for everyone. Now, this began at one o'clock in the afternoon. I stayed until about 4:00 and it so happened that that was the first night of Passover, so I left and didn't come back until they were out of the building.

Exhibit 4

WFCR, Hispanics Agree to Panel

By Alice Dembner

AMHERST—Weeks of protesting by the members of the local Hispanic community and their supporters against the reduction of Spanish-language programming on the area public radio station paid off yesterday.

The Western Massachusetts Broadcasting Council, which oversees operation of Five College Public Radio, WFCR, established a committee of Hispanic residents to recommend programming that will serve the needs of Spanish-speaking people.

Though the committee will be advisory, members of the board said yesterday they expect station manager Robert Goldfarb to take heed of its suggestions, and Goldfarb said he expected to make some changes by July.

The board asked Woody Wickham, assistant to the Hampshire College president, to select the committee members and asked for a report by May 10. Wickham asked for nominations from faculty, students, and community members within the next week.

Protesters present

More than 70 people attended the afternoon meeting to show their support for "Que Tal Amigos?", the existing Spanish-language program, and to criticize Goldfarb's cutbacks of the show. Many of the supporters demonstrated on the University of Massachusetts campus prior to the meeting and carried signs in with them challenging Goldfarb and asserting that the station's call letters stood for Whites For Classist Radio.

Fourteen people spoke to the board for more than an hour on the importance of the music and public affairs show to the Hispanic community, to those learning Spanish, and to the university's affirmative action program by helping attract students to the school. Faculty, staff, and students from U Mass and the four colleges lauded the quality of the program and told the board the

show should be maintained six hours a week at a reasonable hour with full-time producers.

As part of a major change in programming to begin April 1, the new station manager recently announced "Que Tal Amigos?" would be cut to two hours a week, moved to 11 P.M. at night and produced by volunteers. Supporters said that amounted to eliminating the program.

In establishing the committee, the board admitted they had been remiss in not paying more attention to the issue.

"If you want to accuse us of not taking interest in this, you are probably right," council chairman and U Mass public relations director Dan Melley told the group. "Some decisions were made without the proper input."

After the meeting, Goldfarb told reporters that it was "clear the board feels something ought to be done," and said he took that "as a mandate."

Goldfarb said he would announce a time change for the program soon, but would wait for recommendations of the advisory committee before making any changes in content or amount of time the show is on. The time change will not take effect until July, he said, because of program and scheduling commitments already made by the station for the next 13-week period.

Another dispute brewing

The board did not address another controversy brewing over the rejection by Goldfarb of a locally produced show on contemporary classical music and social issues.

Producers and supporters of New Directions, a program aired on local college stations, picketed board member Horace Hewlett's South Amherst home yesterday morning to protest Goldfarb's rejection of the show for airing on WFCR.

Program executive director Mike Richards said the show was rejected because it tries to deal with issues of racism, sexism, and classism in music and because of personality conflicts with Goldfarb.

Goldfarb defends his decision not to air the show despite his commitment to more local and contemporary programming, saying the show isn't good enough for WFCR.

Source: *Daily Hampshire Gazette*, February 27, 1980.

Exhibit 5

Protest Group Forms over WFCR Programs

By Marcia Black and Alice Dembner

AMHERST—Members of the Five College public radio audience from Springfield to Northampton have formed a Coalition for Public Involvement in Public Radio in the latest response to the continued controversy over the cutback of Spanish-language programming at WFCR-FM.

At a press conference Tuesday the coalition criticized a committee now being formed to advise the WFCR governing board on the need for Spanish-language programming. The coalition also demands changes in the station's programming and operations, including more Hispanic air time, removal of the station manager, and the addition of minority members to the governing board.

Copies of the demands are being sent to the members of the Western Massachusetts Broadcasting Council, as the governing board is called, with copies to the University of Massachusetts trustees who are responsible to the Federal Communications Commission for WFCR's operations.

The coalition includes both Hispanic and white members of the Five College Community as well as listeners from Holyoke, Springfield, and other communities, and it is growing, according to spokesperson Marcel Ringawa, a University of Massachusetts student.

Peaceful dialogue

Despite the demands, Ringawa said the coalition is interested in "entering into peaceful dialogue with the station and the governing board." However, he suggested that "a breakdown in good faith" would lead the coalition to take other action including contacting the FCC, calling national attention to the controversy and asking listeners to withhold monetary support from the station.

One measure of "good faith" would be a statement meeting the groups' demands by April 1, Ringawa said. On that date the current Spanish language program, Que Tal Amigos?, is scheduled to be cut back from six to two hours a week and moved from prime time to late at night. By July 1, the program will also be produced entirely by volunteers instead of the two professionals who were responsible for 10 years of the show.

But station manager Robert Goldfarb has said previously that the program schedule for April 1 must stand because of previous commitments but that changes could be made by July. Council Chairman Daniel Melley told the *Gazette* the governing board "has no intention of changing any of the programming by April 1."

The coalition would also like to see minority members appointed to the council. The coalition Tuesday demanded at least two blacks and two Hispanics be added to the board.

At the last meeting of the council, Melley said the board would seriously consider affirmative action in seeking someone to fill the one empty seat on the board. Another board member, Woody Wickham, told the *Gazette* yesterday he agreed with coalition members that "one essential way to act in good faith is to add minority members to the board."

Want advisory committee

The coalition Tuesday criticized the council's efforts to establish a community committee to advise the general manager about the need and shape of Hispanic programming.

Coalition spokesperson Anaida Colon said that Hispanic people who wanted to volunteer to serve on the committee have been unable to reach Wickham who was named to organize it.

Wickham told the Gazette the committee is two-thirds formed, that he hopes it will begin meeting next week, and that the council will take the committee and its recommendations seriously. The committee was established by the council to report back by May 10 after concerned citizens protested the "Que Tal Amigos?" cutbacks.

Exhibit 5 (*concluded*)

Wickham attributed the delay in establishing the committee to his own "distractions" and to a "paucity of calls and inquiries" about it. He urged people interested in serving on the committee to contact him, and said he could be reached through the Hampshire College switchboard. He said he had only received two calls about the committee and had returned both calls.

Coalition member Luis Fuentes said the group believes that little can be gained if the board only has advisory power and if the program changes are not stopped before April 1.

Fuentes said the opposition to the committee was not expressed at the council meeting when it was established because "it took a little while to see through it." The UMass professor says general manager Robert Goldfarb's classification of that meeting as a "safety valve" in a recent memo to the council helped clarify the issue, as did the decision that the committee's work would not affect the April 1 decision.

Want Goldfarb suspended

The coalition is demanding that the governing board suspend Goldfarb and insist that "Que Tal Amigos?" remain at prime time, be increased to three hours daily, and continue to be produced by paid professionals. They insist that WFCR "cease to impose nonminority ideology and programming on minority producers."

Council chairman Dan Melley told the *Gazette* the board has "no intention of mandating hours or specifying what programs go on the air," a job which the council sees as the manager's. "The board has responsibility for the ultimate goals of the station which include a commitment to the Hispanic community. There will be some changes but that does not lessen our commitment."

Though "Que Tal Amigos?" is the current focal point of the coalition's actions, Ringawa said the group needs to move on to other issues concerning public involvement in WFCR.

Source: *Daily Hampshire Gazette*, March 20, 1980.

Because I was away for Passover, I was not directly involved in the negotiations. However, the Western Massachusetts Broadcasting Council negotiated, supposedly, on my behalf. The board was represented by two of its members, E. Jefferson Murphy, known as "Pat" Murphy, executive director of Five Colleges, Inc., the five-college consortium, and Woodward A. Wickham, executive assistant to the president of Hampshire College. They conducted the negotiations; but there was an emergency meeting of the entire council in the midst of this, too, so, in fact, everyone was involved. They ended up negotiating a seven-point settlement, which I was not advised of. [See Exhibit 7.] I was advised of the discussion of how many hours of programming should be on per week but any other

point was just between them and the demonstrators, the Coalition for Public Involvement in Public Radio. [See Exhibit 8.]

When I came back to Amherst, I was told to pick up a copy of the agreement, and was asked what I thought of it. Actually, it was read to me over the phone before I picked up the written copy, and I said, "I think this is unacceptable." This was in a discussion with my administrative superior in the university, Daniel Melley. And he said, "Don't jump to any conclusions. Read it over. Think about it." Which I did. Within the next few business days I met with him and with the two negotiators, Messrs. Wickham and Murphy, and told each of them why I thought it was unacceptable. And they said, "Well, this is only until June 30 and after that it is no longer binding." And I said that

---

Exhibit 6   Coalition for Public Broadcasting Press Release, March 31, 1980

FOR IMMEDIATE RELEASE:

STUDENTS' SIT-IN TO PROTEST WFCR'S RACIST TACTICS

Since his arrival at the Amherst campus, Robert Goldfarb, WFCR's station manager, has imposed policies affecting public broadcasting without community or staff input. These policies reflect racist and elitist attitudes which have disturbed all elements of the WFCR listening community, especially minority groups. These groups are outraged by the station manager's decision to reschedule and restrict the only Spanish language radio program—"Que Tal Amigos?" As a result of this action, all minority group producers at WFCR have either resigned or have been subjected to harassment at the station.

We have tried peacefully to resolve this situation. Using the following tactics listed in chronological order, we have tried to resolve the crisis: (1) letters and phone calls supporting "Que Tal Amigos?" Dec. 10, 1979; (2) Open House protest, January 20, 1980; (3) supportive telephone calls—"Let's talk to the Manager," February 3, 1980; (4) protest at Hills South campus, February 14, 1980; (5) Public Meeting with the Broadcasting Council, February 26, 1980; (6) meeting with Advisory Board, Wednesday, March 26, 1980; (7) meeting with the Broadcasting Council, Friday, March 28, 1980; (8) Protest Demonstration, Friday March 28, 1980.

We see the manager's actions supported by the Western Massachusetts Broadcasting Council and the University of Massachusetts administration as another racist attack on Hispanic and other minority groups in the area, since student monies are used by the University administration to support the station.

We demand that the University of Massachusetts administration:

1. formally suspend and evict W.F.C.R. from Hampshire House;
2. suspend Daniel Melley as the University's Public Affairs director for not providing leadership or a forum necessary to resolve this controversy;
3. suspend the radio station's manager Robert Goldfarb;
4. include at least two Hispanics, two Blacks, and student representatives as voting members of the Western Massachusetts Council;
5. impose a moratorium on programatic changes effective April 1st for "Que Tal Amigos?";
6. provide more hours (3 daily) for "Que Tal Amigos?";
7. insist that "Que Tal Amigos?" remain on prime time;
8. assure that producers of "Que Tal Amigos?" remain and are paid for their services;
9. maintain that WFCR public radio cease to impose non-minority ideology and programming on minority producers;
10. publicize the budget including: (a) all salaries, (b) expense accounts of all council members, manager and employees;
11. publicize the following: (a) the membership, function, bylaws and history of the council of

Exhibit 6   (*concluded*)

> directors, (b) all council policy and actions, (c) other council meetings, including the monthly public meeting, and (d) the council's decision making policies;
> 12. explain publicly all contract changes with accompanying justifications;
> 13. publicly accept responsibility for Robert Goldfarb's action and subsequent controversy, and seek appropriate solutions without the use of "buffers."
>
> Therefore, we've decided to stage a sit-in demonstration in the office of the Director of Public Affairs, Daniel Melley, to make the administration deal with this controversy. We ask Chancellor Koffler to meet and negotiate with us.

Exhibit 7   Seven-Point Settlement Negotiated between Council and Coalition, April 2, 1980

1. The Council pledges to take seriously its supervisory role with respect to the general manager, to evaluate his performance throughout the term of his contract, and to conduct a thorough evaluation at the conclusion of the first year of his service.

   In all of these activities, the Council will take into special account the concerns of the Coalition.

2. In light of the Council's recognition of the need that the membership of the Council be more representative of WFCR's diverse constituencies, the Council has expanded its size by two positions, making a total of three vacancies. The Council will fill at least these three vacancies in such a way as to ensure minority representation. The Council also invites the nomination of students. The Council will make every effort to fill all three vacancies by June 1.

3. The Council will restore "Que Tal Amigos?" to prime time (7–8 P.M.) four nights per week through June 30 while the special advisory committee considers present and future Hispanic programming policy.

4. The Council pledges that the WFCR budget will assure adequate funding for high-quality Hispanic programming, taking into account the advice of the special advisory committee.

5. The Council reaffirms the right of WFCR producers and other staff to exercise their creativity and professional judgement within the overall policies of the Council and WFCR. The Council will create a personnel committee before April 10 to consider employee grievances.

6. The Council recognizes the right of public access to published policies, budgets, and procedures of WFCR, and of timely notification to the public regarding meetings.

7. The Council reaffirms its long-standing commitment to Hispanic programming and recognizes that this commitment has not been satisfactorily exercised in the process by which decisions have been made regarding "Que Tal Amigos?" To ensure responsive programming the Council recognizes the integral importance of the special advisory committee to the decision-making process.

(Pending full implementation of these agreements, the Council will meet monthly with a committee of the Coalition to discuss progress to date.)

Exhibit 8

WFCR, Protesters on Same Frequency

By Megan O'Reilly and Alice Dembner

AMHERST—At 9 last night the sign on University of Massachusetts Chancellor Henry Koffler's office door reading "Welcome to Que Tal Amigos? Country" was yanked down, marking the end of the 55-hour occupation of his office by people protesting cuts in Spanish-language programming at public radio station WFCR.

The protesters, members of the Coalition for Public Involvement in Public Radio, left after reaching agreement with the Western Massachusetts Broadcasting Council, which governs WFCR. The settlement involved several days of negotiations and represented compromises from both sides.

Back on the air

The key element is the immediate restoration of the cultural affairs program Que Tal Amigos? to prime time, four nights weekly through June 30. The show, which was off the air this week, will be broadcast, beginning tonight, from 7–8 P.M. Monday through Thursday. This represents a cut from the five-hour weekly broadcast the coalition was asking for and from the previous six hours the show was aired.

The coalition will meet monthly with the council to monitor the agreement. In the interim, a special advisory committee established by the council will meet to make recommendations on the future of Hispanic programming.

The council also agreed to add two public members and to fill these and one vacant seat "in such a way as to ensure adequate representation." Students will be considered for these slots.

The council will establish a personnel committee before April 10 to consider employee grievances. No further resolution was reached on the issue of professional or volunteer procedures for the show beyond the June 30 deadline.

Negotiating for the Council yesterday were E.

Jefferson Murphy, Five College Coordinator, and Woodward A. Wickham, special assistant to the president of Hampshire College. Anaida Colon and Marcel Ringawa, both UMass students; Tony Crayton, director of the UMass Office of Third World Affairs and School of Education Prof. Luis Fuentes bargained for the coalition.

In answer to demands regarding actions of WFCR general manager Robert Goldfarb, who cutback Que Tal Amigos?, the council agreed to evaluate his performance and to "take seriously its supervisory role" over Goldfarb.

Chancellor Koffler, who skipped a UMass trustees meeting yesterday to participate in negotiations, said he was pleased with what he hoped would be a "fair and lasting agreement." He also said, "No punitive measures will be taken against those who peacefully sat in my office during the last two days," relieving the fears of some demonstrators.

Speaking for the coalition, Jamila Gaston emphasized that the members were still dissatisfied with the airtime. "We're going to fight the four hours," she said. "We are struggling for culturally sensitive programs all hours of the day."

After a massive office-cleaning effort, the 40–50 occupiers, most of whom were Hispanic students, faculty, and area residents, celebrated the final decision with a banquet at the chancellor's 25-foot conference table catered by Yvonne Jolon, the cook at The New Africa House Snack Bar.

During negotiations yesterday, coalition supporters paraded outside the Whitmore Administration building holding signs and chanting slogans, as they had throughout the two-day seige.

WFCR Sit-In Ends with Compromise

By Marisa Giannetti Union Correspondent

AMHERST—Members of the Hispanic community, including UMass students and faculty,

Source: *Daily Hampshire Gazette*, April 3, 1980.

Source: *The Morning Union*, April 3, 1980.

Exhibit 8 (*concluded*)

ended their three day occupation of administrative offices on campus Wednesday night after accepting compromise proposals over Spanish language radio programing on WFCR-FM.

According to Jamila Gaston, a spokesman for the Coalition for Public Involvement in Public Broadcasting, the protest group, the coalition feared punitive action from the university as a result of the occupation of an administrative suite of offices in the Whitmore Administration building.

"Our major concern is that students and faculty who have occupied these offices may be in jeopardy of losing tenure or financial aid. We want to prevent that," Gaston said.

Talks with Chancellor Henry Koffler on this issue Wednesday night assured protesters they had no fear of administrative reprisals, she said.

A final negotiation session with the Board of Trustees of public radio station WFCR-FM resulted in the acceptance of all compromise proposals by the coalition except the issue of programing hours for "Que Tal Amigo?", a Spanish language news and music program aired on WFCR.

Gaston said the coalition will continue to negotiate at a later date with the board on the exact number of hours the show will be aired, but she speculated the negotiations on both sides will settle soon on 4–5 hours per week in prime time for the show. The coalition had demanded six hours per week; the board Tuesday had proposed three hours per week.

In the meantime, the 35 protesters have left the offices.

Originally "Que Tal Amigos?" was scheduled to be cut back from six to two hours per week and shifted from prime time to a late night slot, by General Manager Robert Goldfarb. The occupation was sparked by this cutback in programming hours and scheduling changes.

The coalition had originally demanded the resignation of Goldfarb and Daniel Melley, chairman of the Board of Trustees. That demand was dropped when the board issued a resolution Tuesday night stating the "Que Tal Amigos?" cutbacks had been a grave mistake, said Gaston.

Other compromises the coalition and the board had agreed on Wednesday night include hiring two minority members to the Board of Trustees of WFCR; establishing a personnel committee for the radio station before April 10 to consider public grievances; publishing public access to board policy decisions and timely notification of board meetings to the public and creating a special advisory committee to help the board in programming.

I considered that essential because, if after June 30 I didn't have the latitude that was taken away from me as a result of these agreements, then there would be no point to my continuing at WFCR.

Several of the points were definitely unacceptable, because they went beyond the question of programming, although the programming point was unacceptable, too. All along I said that I would agree to a compromise in the programming under certain circumstances. But the agreement read—and I can remember the exact words—"The Council will restore 'Que Tal Amigos?' to prime time four nights per week." I said, "That is not the council's job. That is my job, and it is unacceptable to me that the council should interfere in making a scheduling decision, which is one of the prerogatives of management." They answered, "Gosh, wasn't it too bad we worded it that way; we didn't mean to." But in any event I decided to let that go, because I was assured of the June 30 end date.

Well, I took that very seriously and the next programming quarter began July 1. So, in early June I determined that I wanted to reduce Spanish-language programming time again. Now, I was duty-bound to consult with the advisory committee on this matter. The first person I talked to was the chairman of that committee, who was Woody Wickham, and he was appalled. He could not believe that I would do something so stupid as to cut back the programming after they'd had this building occupied. I replied that the merits to me did not seem related to the building occupation, and, furthermore, we had every reason to believe that the woman who was producing the program was going to leave in June. It was impossible for me to continue doing the programming without her because we had no one else. Incidentally, we did have a Spanish-speaking person on the staff who worked on a part-time basis as an engineer, and we thought that he might be able to do something on an interim basis.

Well, Wickham was appalled, as I say, and thought that I should keep this quiet until the council had time to deal with it. They called an emergency meeting and were all just very upset and were about to overrule me. At this point I let it be known that if they overruled me I would resign. It was a large public meeting at Smith College which was covered by a local TV station—to give you an idea of the charged atmosphere— and at the meeting I would say a half-dozen members of the station's staff spoke in my defense. There were also some people from the Hispanic community and their sympathizers who said that my decision was bad, although they primarily at that time hit the issue of consultation—they said they had not been consulted. I maintained that that was not my responsibility because the council had determined that it would consult with the Coalition for Public Involvement in

Radio and I had attempted to meet with the advisory committee but they had not invited me to meet with them. I agreed that there should have been consultation, but the council, I thought, didn't hold up its end, in keeping its commitment to consult with the coalition.

Well, there was an executive session toward the middle of that meeting, and the motion on the floor at the executive session, which I did not attend, was to suspend me as general manager. They voted that down.

The program schedule changed in July, seemingly without incident. The only slight incident was on July 5, which I think was Sunday, at the time when the new Spanish program succeeding "Que Tal Amigos?" went on: there was a relatively quiet demonstration outside the station. From that point things moved along largely behind the scenes. There were hasty discussions prior to consulting with the coalition, and I held a meeting with representatives of the coalition—which was at my instigation—and I thought it was a useful, constructive session. We didn't get that much done but we were talking. They made me a proposal and I agreed to make them a counterproposal. My proposal was eventually rebuffed, but, of course, I didn't know that right at this stage. I rather thought that I was making real steps toward meeting with the coalition. Meanwhile, I had also tried to meet with the advisory committee. None of them came— no one, zero. It was just me and Woody Wickham at a meeting for an hour, so that didn't work. But at least I felt that I had taken the appropriate steps.

Nonetheless, the July 28 meeting of the WMBC was extremely acrimonious. The chairman exercised no control whatever, and allowed Tony Crayton of the coalition to give two 45-minute tirades, which went far beyond the bounds of normal public comment at the meeting of a public broadcasting governing board. His charges are painful to

Exhibit 9

WFCR Board Hears Goldfarb Backers

by Alice Dembner

AMHERST—Robert Goldfarb's tenure as general manager of public radio station WFCR was the major topic for the station's governing council last night but no decision was reached about continuing his contract.

After hearing strong statements of support for Goldfarb's actions from members of the public, the Western Massachusetts Broadcasting Council went into closed session to discuss Goldfarb's position and other personnel matters.

After about 90 minutes, the council emerged with a statement admitting that the majority of the council present at the July meeting had voted to recommend to the University of Massachusetts chancellor that Goldfarb's contract "might not be renewed." The council also said last night that they had taken no further action on that matter.

Goldfarb was notified in early August by UMass that it did not intend to renew his contract when it runs out November 1. Though Goldfarb reports to the council, he is officially employed by UMass.

Goldfarb has told the Gazette he is looking into other job possibilities.

Offer support for Goldfarb

Six listeners, who spoke to the council at its meeting in Springfield last night, voiced strong support of Goldfarb though some said they disagreed with some of the changes he has made in the station's programming.

Members of the public also expressed annoyance that the decision was made in private with no hearing for public opinion, and that it seemed to be based on Goldfarb's actions concerning Spanish-language programming.

"It's my opinion that since Mr. Goldfarb has taken over, there have been a good many positive changes at the station including new folk,

jazz and chamber music programs and a lot more locally produced programming," said Thomas Babbin of Pelham.

"He has solicited public comment and has been trying to take those opinions and mold them into a cohesive program schedule. If despite this the board has decided not to renew his contract, then it must be over Spanish-language programming. Only one side of that issue has been heard and it is the obligation of the board to hear the other side. I urge you to reconsider or postpone your decision and to hold a public hearing."

Dr. Lewis W. Whiting of Springfield told the council he has "been listening to WFCR for as long as it has been on the air" and has "noticed an increase in the quality of the programming in the last few years."

"The only programs that have less than optimal interest are ethnic programs in foreign languages," he said. "They do nothing to make Americans out of people who've come here to live. The efforts of Mr. Goldfarb in trying to play down this sort of thing are all to the good."

Members of the Coalition for Public Involvement in Public Radio, who have supported Hispanic programming, had not signed up to speak prior to the meeting and were not allowed to comment. After the meeting, they said they wanted to speak in favor of Hispanic programming, in support of their actions in defense of that programming and against what they called the "racist remarks" of Dr. Whiting.

WFCR board asks: who should run the station?

AMHERST—The WFCR radio governing council learned last night that the newly appointed Hispanic member of the council had resigned, that the search for a producer of Spanish programming is beginning and that it will not be easy to rid the governing structure of the ambi-

Exhibit 9 *(concluded)*

guities that have caused problems in the last few
months.

Western Massachusetts Broadcasting Council
Chairman Kenneth Williamson announced that
Jose Santiago had resigned his seat on the council because of pressing obligations to his church.
The reverend attended his first council meeting
in late July and was quickly briefed by the local
Hispanic community about problems over Hispanic programming. In a letter to the council,
Santiago said his resignation was "in no way
connected with the problems faced by WFCR"
but was due to the opening of Bible school by his
Hartford church. He urged appointment of another member of the Hispanic community.

The council was also informed last night that
ads will be published this week seeking applicants for a producer of Spanish language programming. The deadline for applications is Oct.
10.

A large part of the council meeting was taken
up by a discussion of changes in the governing
structure for the station, including the matter of
who holds the license.

Currently, the University of Massachusetts
holds the license and contributes a substantial
amount of money to the station, but the council

is responsible for policy decisions about WFCR.
The council currently includes representatives of
UMass and Amherst, Smith, Mount Holyoke
and Hampshire colleges, along with several public members.

The complicated governance structure created
problems when people upset with changes in
Spanish-language programming occupied the office of the UMass chancellor last spring but the
chancellor could not unilaterally make decisions
about the issues concerning the occupiers.

Options under discussion by the council for
future governance range from turning the station
over to UMass entirely, to enlarging the power
of the council, to turning over the station to an
existing public radio or television station.

An extensive discussion of the issue will be
held at the council's next meeting Oct. 22 at 5:30
P.M. in Brattleboro, Vt.

The final decision will be made by the UMass
Trustees with opinions from the council, the four
college presidents and the UMass chancellor, according to council member and Five College Director E. Jefferson Murphy.

Source: *Daily Hampshire Gazette*, September 16, 1980.

recall, as they included almost everything
from bad faith to racism.

When the council went into executive session, I was asked not to be in the room, and I
didn't oppose their wishes. I was not told of
the outcome of that meeting until four days
later. This was a Monday night. The Friday
of that week I was told by Dan Melley that
the council had voted not to renew my contract. I informed a few members of the staff,
but generally kept it to myself.

In August I had my first meeting with the

Advisory Committee on Hispanic Programming. The discussion centered on how to
get a producer—a new producer for Spanish-language programming. I thought it was
a very good session, and we have since advertised for such a position. In the meantime
there has really been very little said by the
coalition. There was another meeting of the
council on Monday, September 15, 1980. At
that meeting, seven or eight members of the
public said that they had heard through a
newspaper article, which appeared in early

September, that my contract was not to be renewed, and they thought this was terrible. The council went into another executive session and spent an hour talking this same issue over and came up with a statement which said simply that the majority of the members of the council present and voting during the meeting of July 28 had said that my contract might not be renewed. And indeed the press statements by members of the council have tended to de-emphasize the finality of this decision. [See Exhibit 9.] Meanwhile the contract expires on November 1, 1980, and, barring any additional action, on November 2 I don't have a job.

ROBERT GOLDFARB (B)
Joseph W. Chevarley, Jr., and Jeffrey A. Sonnenfeld

When November 2 arrived, Robert Goldfarb found himself still station general manager at WFCR. His contract had been renewed, but only after protracted discussion and debate.

After the September meeting of the Western Massachusetts Broadcasting Council (WMBC), Goldfarb took the initiative and approached council members individually, some for the first time. He asked them what they thought he should do if he were to stay on at the station. He felt he received candid and useful counsel in these sessions.

At its October 22 meeting, the council decided to refer the whole matter to WFCR's Community Advisory Board (CAB), a group which had just been formed—independent

to the Hispanic programming controversy—in response to new Federal Communications Commission dictates. The CAB invited Goldfarb to attend its meeting five days later, but he declined because of an out-of-town commitment. In his absence, the CAB was unable to reach a decision: a move not to renew the contract failed by a five-to-four vote; a subsequent move to renew failed by the same margin. The WMBC then stepped in and voted in favor of renewing Goldfarb's contract for another year. The University of Massachusetts' chancellor, however, did not follow the WMBC's recommendation. He elected, instead, to offer Goldfarb a six-month contract. He then announced the appointment of a faculty mediator who would resolve the question of Hispanic programming on WFCR.

In the face of all this, Goldfarb himself has continued the search for a new producer for Hispanic programming, someone to put together two hour-long weekly programs—one that features interviews and discussion, and one that revolves around musical themes. This undertaking has been complicated by the need to follow university search committee rules and procedures. In the meanwhile, the Coalition for Public Involvement in Public Radio has officially notified the WMBC that it will file a petition to challenge WFCR's license.

Woodward A. Wickham, WMBC member and chairperson of the Advisory Committee on Hispanic Programming, offered the following perspectives on the Spanish-language programming controversy and Robert Goldfarb:

> Well, I feel that the council was insufficiently directive in the first contracts with Bob and other potential managers, and in its

work with Bob during the first several months of his contract with regard to—possibly many things—but certainly with regard to the importance of the sensitivity of Spanish-language broadcasting. On the other hand, I think there is evidence in the record that individual members of the council did say to Bob as to other candidates that Spanish-language broadcasting had a long history at the station, had done very well at times, and that we were very proud of it. And I think they made a case for the wisdom of not intruding—not changing—Spanish-language broadcasting very radically. But, since they couldn't anticipate what would happen, they didn't specifically say, "You shouldn't cut back from six hours to two."

Bob has essentially a different relationship with everyone on the council—that's natural—but I think he is also seen in different ways by members of the council. There are those who, I think, think that Bob has done a terrific job technically, that the staff morale is basically much better, and who want to support him and are insistent that a small group not dislodge him. There are those who think that he has done a very good job but feel that there is real question whether this whole problem's going to get resolved and whether this is not one in a series of difficulties that will arise because of the way that Bob handled it. And then there's a third group, I think, for whom the skill with which he's managed the station is not persuasive at all. They don't deny that he is technically skillful, but they feel it shouldn't be a factor. They feel that he is destructive of relationships between the station and the council, the station and the community, the council and the presidents of the five colleges, and between the station and the university.

Shorthand for it is that, perhaps, Bob's not political enough, that it's not enough to set out a very clear position, a principled position, clearly identified, moral, a consti-

tutionally good one that one is protecting and defending, because then the opposition simply reacts to that and sets up its competing positions.

By contrast, you can go to work aligning, wherever you can, people who have similar interests and some influence in all of this, so that you will end up with a solution that is perhaps not your ideal but still is as near as possible to your ideal. There has to be give as well as take, some erosion of one's opening position. This erosion may be necessary to the other parties' feeling that they have gained something. Now in building those alliances and marshalling support for a position, one needs to be able to divide the world not into those who are unalterably opposed and who are 100 percent in favor—but those who are flexible and those who are not. One should feel that one can draw from the opposition, that one can convert, can put deals together.

CASE 5
KAREN HARPER
John P. Kotter

I've got to know by tomorrow morning, Karen. I've got two MBAs from Harvard bugging me every 10 minutes on the phone about whether or not they're going to get the job. If you say no, it goes to one of them. Besides, I'm beginning to feel a little uncomfortable around Harry when I see him in the hall—if you leave Fund Management to come work in Investment Advisory, he'll be all over me. I can handle that, but I'd like to get things settled.

Those had been Steve Ackerman's words to Karen Harper this afternoon. As she rode home on the train she began once again to make a list of pros and cons.

The Last Six Years

Karen was 28 years old and had spent the last six years in the Fund Management Group at Hingham Investment Company. Like so many other English Lit grads, she had graduated from college with absolutely no career preparation. She moved from New England to Chicago without a job and into a crowded apartment with three roommates.

On the first day of her job search she registered with a personnel agency as a junior secretary. All she wanted was a job that promised a paycheck every week—she would think about a career or graduate school later. All that mattered was that she survive in Chicago. The agency sent her to Hingham Investment Company, a large, well-known investment management firm whose offices occupied a 20-story older building in the financial district. Karen was well-dressed, attractive, and articulate, and didn't think she'd have any trouble getting a job fast.

Her interview took 20 minutes. She was offered an entry-level marketing slot in the retail marketing department. Her boss (and interviewer) was Harry Rosenberg, the vice president and manager of the department. Harry, who had been with Hingham for the past five years, was a modishly dressed man in his early 50s. He had started the retail marketing department at Hingham, which was a departure from Hingham's traditional business of investment advisory services for large institutional and retail clients.

Karen and Harry liked each other right away. Karen saw Harry as a father-type figure who was very interested in her, both professionally and personally. He told her that she was selling herself short as a secretary and that the marketing slot was a great opportunity to learn the business. He was very concerned about her adjustment to Chicago and invited her to join him for dinner that evening. Karen was flattered and grateful. After pinching pennies for so long, it was great to go out in style. Harry talked a lot about the business and treated Karen like an old friend. Harry's general philosophy seemed to be that hard work really pays off, and, since Karen was bright and willing, the sky was the limit.

The next six years seemed to prove Harry's theory. Karen worked hard, often until nine in the evening. After two years in marketing, Harry promoted her to the most prestigious and highly paid area—securities acquisition. Until Karen assumed this role, Harry had done it himself. Karen was viewed by the other members of the department as Harry's favorite. This was undoubtedly true, since no one else spent as much time with Harry, nor did he brag to outsiders about anyone else. When Karen decided to get an MBA and was considering applying to Harvard and Stanford, Harry convinced her to remain in her job and get her MBA by doing evening course work at Northwestern, which the firm paid for. Karen's salary increased from $8,000 at her time of hiring to $40,000 plus a sizable bonus six years later. Harry told her she had it made.

At times Karen believed him. She made plenty of money to support herself in a comfortable apartment. No more roommates. Her job was lots of fun and was coveted by others in the department. Harry allowed her considerable fringe benefits—expense account, free cabs home after a late night at work, after a big project she was free to take a day off. But still she always felt vaguely uneasy—why was Harry doing all this for her? Was it all in her best interests? What did the rest of the firm think? Now she had an MBA—why weren't any other MBAs attracted to retail marketing—there were plenty of them in Investment Advisory.

Karen knew the answer to this last question—it was because of Harry. General opinion in Hingham was that Harry was a real eccentric. Karen had to agree that Harry had a rather unorthodox management style and didn't know the first thing about delegating authority. Harry had started retail marketing at Hingham and could do all of the functions better than anyone else in the department. He loved his work and had to get his hands in everything. Subsequently, no one in the department had much autonomy and the general feeling was that Harry was "on everybody's back" all the time. Karen found that her working relationship with Harry was smoothest when she didn't try to take over things, but instead checked every so often with Harry to keep him informed and ask his advice. Usually she didn't mind this, since it made for the most tranquil atmosphere; but sometimes she felt angry about having to ask Harry's advice on something she felt perfectly able to handle herself. Waiting to see Harry slowed things down considerably and often created problem situations.

The real zinger about Harry was that, in spite of all his yelling and meddling, he paid his people exceedingly well and always gave them a sizable bonus at the end of the year—much bigger than those given out in Investment Advisory to nonpartners. He was always ready to help out an employee in an emergency or problem situation—with either money or time off or whatever. Those who worked for him often said that "just as they were feeling real good about hating Harry for being such a tyrant, he'd go and do something really great out of the blue and totally screw up their heads."

The Investment Advisory Division

Karen's opportunity was to start out as an associate in the Investment Advisory Division. Providing investment management advisory services to clients had always been Hingham's main business. The associate position had been created in order to give young, talented individuals an introduction to money management by working closely with a variety of senior investment managers. Associates were considered to be part of a "resource pool" that was available for work on different projects as they came up. If a large pension fund, for example, requested Hingham to make a presentation on fixed-income management, a senior manager in the fixed-income area of Investment Advisory would select a group of fixed-income specialists and an associate from the "pool" to work on the presentation. Senior managers also called on associates to assist on day-to-day work with existing clients, which could involve gathering research on a particular industry or providing market information. After a year or so of being in the pool, the associate has the opportunity to indicate his or her preference for where he or she would like to be placed—whether it be fixed income, equities, foreign currency, research, and the like. If this preference coincides with the firm's needs, the associate moves into the desired area. After initial placement, an individual often decides that he or she would like to try another area. If he or she has developed a strong reputation, this movement is usually easy to accomplish.

At the present time, nearly all of the associates in the pool were recent graduates of top business schools. Investment management was generally regarded as a prestigious field, and the possibility of being made a partner lured many MBAs who were eager to earn big dollars over a period of time. Hingham had recruited at the top business schools for many years for the Investment Advisory Division. No MBA had ever been hired to enter any other area of the firm, including Fund Management.

Associates were expected to work long hours in the first few years. Most associates stayed until early evening at least and were often in the office on weekends. The hours one put in were viewed with a certain degree of pride and indicated how committed one was to the firm and to getting ahead. Associates were often called upon to travel with senior managers to clients' offices. Often this travel was on very short notice. You never really knew where you were going to be the next day.

The Retail Marketing Department

Retail marketing seemed to be viewed as an amusing curiosity by the rest of Hingham and the investment community. The product was portfolios of securities which were assembled and sold through a broker network to small individual investors and were subsequently not managed but were sold on the basis of providing steady income and safety through diversification. Its very nature was in contrast to Hingham's traditional business, which was to provide expert advisory service to very wealthy clients and institutions on managing their investment portfolios. By its design, retail marketing was a very profitable department for Hingham. Although other firms had tried to imitate the Hingham product, none had been as successful. Most observers attributed Hingham's success to their high-quality and long-standing reputation in the investment community and access to extensive brokerage sales networks. But Harry Rosenberg, the partner in charge of retail marketing, insisted that it was his genius that was responsible for the success and that he could do the same at several other firms.

Only about 40 people worked in the fund management department—of these, about 10 could be considered to be professionals, either in buying, marketing, or research. The majority of the staff had been there for several years—several had come to Hingham with Harry about 11 years ago when he had joined the firm. Hingham Investment Company employed close to 500 people, of whom about 100 were professionals and 28 were partners.

The major part of Karen's job was selecting securities for the "packaged pools" of securities that Hingham marketed. The purpose of the pools was to allow small investors to participate in the attractive yields offered to institutional investors without having to select their own individual portfolios. The product was very successful— popular with both investors and securities brokers and very profitable for Hingham. In fact, during the "bad times" of 1974–75, it was retail marketing which kept Hingham in the black.

Due to the fund's popularity, there was an almost constant need to accumulate more securities for the pools. Karen bought about $50 million each week. The process of buying securities involved following credit market rates, checking with the department's research team on the current creditworthiness of individual issuers, maintaining a balance of different types of issues in the portfolio, and most important, trying to get the best price on every security purchased. Karen bought stocks and bonds from a wide variety of brokerage firms; she had direct phone lines to eight of the largest firms. Every day involved taking phone calls from about 20 different bond salespeople—mostly aggressive, smooth-talking salesmen. These people worked on commission and had a vested interest in keeping Karen happy since she was such an important customer. They were continually offering theater tickets, dinners on the town, party invitations, and so on. Although they could be a nuisance, Karen enjoyed this part of her job a lot—most of them were reasonably bright and funny. She had to keep reminding herself, however, that their attentiveness was due solely to her buying power, not her personal charms.

Because of her close relationship with Harry, Karen was involved in all of the strategic decisions of the department, something which was not a strict function of her job. In the past Karen had helped develop new concepts for pools to expand on the theme. Harry valued Karen's opinions very highly and often designated her as his spokesman at meetings both inside and outside the company.

When Karen tried to analyze her feelings about the job, it boiled down to the old joke about "not wanting to join any club that would have me as a member." She suspected this might be silly, but she had

learned this job almost five years ago without any MBA or financial background—how difficult could it be? Harry made such a big deal about it; in moments of hyperbole he called her the "most important Wall Street-type woman anywhere." She really enjoyed the job itself, but she didn't feel that she was really "growing" any more, and, wasn't growth supposed to be essential? Karen's doubts were exacerbated by the fact that Hingham was practically unique in both the size and activity of its retail marketing department; no other firm offered a position similar to hers so there was no way of comparing herself with others. She got a lot of attention from salesmen, but nobody else really knew anything about the pools—it wasn't a well-known glamor position like Investment Advisory or investment banking. She was worried that she would become a high-priced but "illiquid" commodity. If something went really wrong with the department where would she go? To sum up, she felt like a very large fish in a very small pond.

The atmosphere in retail marketing could best be described as "chaotic." Harry Rosenberg's personality most definitely contributed to this situation. His moods seemed to determine the group mood. He involved himself in all areas of the department and delegated very little authority but much responsibility.

Harry Rosenberg

Harry usually arrived in the office at 10:00 or 11:00 in the morning after calling his secretary and key people at least once by phone from home. Everyone knew when he arrived and there was always a "mood check"—is he in a good or bad mood?—which would be verbally relayed throughout the department. Harry spent most of the day in meetings and on the phone and always left the office at 1:00 o'clock for a two-hour lunch. Since so little authority was delegated, workers in the department had to consult Harry before making important decisions, and this resulted in a line of people outside his office all day. Once you did get in to see him there were constant interruptions—phone calls, secretaries (three of them) walking in and out to extricate papers from his jumbled desk, urgent questions from underlings who didn't know what Harry wanted done about this or that. Harry liked to stay in the office late—often until 8:00 or so, and several people regularly stayed late in order to get to talk to him without the constant interruptions. Often Harry would take an employee out to dinner to continue these discussions. He expressed great disdain for "nine-to-five-ers" and commented that they would "never get ahead in his department."

Harry had a very controversial management style. If something or someone displeased him, he would let the offender know exactly how he felt. He had a violent temper which didn't last very long. He seemed to explode only with those workers from whom he expected a lot and who had disappointed him. In spite of all his noise, he had never fired anyone. There was a continual rumbling in retail marketing that Harry was "absolutely nuts" and that he was "driving everybody crazy." Key people would threaten to leave from time to time but actual turnover was very low.

Harry gave the impression of having absolute authority in his department and gave little indication that he was concerned about any hierarchy at Hingham that was above him. The partnership structure at Hingham was actually quite stratified, and Harry was several rungs down from the top of the partnership group. He found this structure exceedingly frustrating and was very critical of top management. The senior partners tended to stay away from retail marketing; it was not the mainstream of the firm's traditional business and, though it was extremely profitable, was not fully understood by many of the older partners. Most of the professional staff in retail marketing had had limited, if any, exposure to the partners above Harry's level.

Most sources attributed Harry's managerial autonomy to the profitability of the product. General sentiment was that "as long as Harry brings in the dollars, nobody's going to tell him what to do." Harry enjoyed running the department as a little profit center and did many things which were not "standard Hingham policy."

> I like to think of retail marketing as my little family and I'd do anything for my people. I pay them much more than they'd get anywhere else and they feel they're working for me, not Hingham and Company. Yeah, I know I don't do things by the book; but I don't want this place to be just a regular department of a stuffy, impersonal firm where everybody gives 50 percent of their energy and ability and gets a raise every year and a vacation. People here know that if they put out the maximum effort, they'll get rewarded—and that any job in the department, including mine, is open to anyone who shows me they can do it.

Karen's Dilemma

> I know Investment Advisory *seems* to be appealing to Karen, but it's dead wrong for her. She's got it made here if she'd just wise up and realize it. That's the trouble with young people in business today—they think they've got to keep moving all the time—get titles, etc. If they'd just plug away at something and be patient they'd be a lot better off. Look, I've been in business for 30-odd

years and I've seen just about all there is to see. If Karen just sticks with me and accepts the fact that I've got her best interest at heart and have the experience to know what's the best course for her, she'll be fine. She's a bright kid, but when she gets all this MBA-rhetoric in her head, she's dangerous. What happens if she goes to Investment Advisory? She'll be just one MBA in a sea of them—and they're all after the same thing—to be a partner. Well, the existing partners would have to be hit by the plague for spots to open up fast enough to please these kids. She'd be working her ass off for a whole bunch of people, none of whom would be able to give her the kind of close direction and support I can. I'm not going to be alive forever; I'm 57 years old—somebody's got to take my spot—and Karen's the obvious choice if she doesn't lose her head and do something stupid.

Karen had heard Harry's thinking a million times. She thought he was sincere, but seriously doubted that if she stayed in retail marketing a senior partnership would ever open up for her. The rumor mill had it that the senior partners were concerned about Harry's management style and were just waiting until he retired to put someone into that spot who was "one of them"—someone who could integrate retail marketing better into the Hingham mainstream. Karen felt sure that no matter how competent a manager she was, she would always be viewed as "Harry's girl" and would be considered suspect. She thought a lot about how she could stay in retail marketing and get more visibility with top management, but was at a loss as to how to accomplish this. Day-to-day business did not put her in much contact with the rest of the firm, and it was Harry who met with the partners at the weekly luncheon and planning sessions. She knew that he always spoke highly of her; but didn't know if that was a

positive or negative fact, given the partners' general reaction to Harry.

Maybe she should grab at the associate's spot while it was available. She had known Steve Ackerman, the junior partner in charge of the training program, for several years and they had always been cordial. After a particularly frustrating day last week, she had called him on an impulse and asked to meet him for lunch. She had guardedly confided her frustration in working with Harry to Steve. He seemed to understand completely and said that he, himself, could never work for someone like Harry. This made Karen wonder if there was something wrong with her—why was she putting up with this situation? The more she thought, the madder she got. Before lunch was over, Steve had offered her the chance to enter Investment Advisory as an associate. He warned her that initially it might seem like a step down—taking orders from everyone and doing grunt work after she had been largely on her own, not counting Harry's influence, for the past few years. The move would mean an initial pay cut of $5,000, which would still make her the most highly paid associate. Steve explained that this was the best he could do, since he didn't want the newly hired MBAs to think that someone doing the same job, although experienced in another area, was being paid $10,000 more than they. Besides, Steve had explained, the salary would increase over time and her chances of making a partnership were definitely enhanced.

Karen felt depressed and confused. The idea of entering the competitive world of an associate in Investment Advisory really didn't appeal to her. She felt she had proven her ability and didn't want to go through the initial stages of having to make a big impression again. Besides, Harry was her mentor, wasn't he? And from all she'd read about women in business, wasn't the mentor system supposed to be an essential ingredient in helping women move to the top? Was she looking a gift horse in the mouth and just being a spoiled brat? After all, without Harry's guidance and support, she might be still typing somewhere.

The flip side of this argument was that Karen felt that she was getting too old to be involved in the paternalistic relationship with Harry. If she didn't stand on her own now, when would she? She knew that some of the partners had definite opinions as to the nature of Harry and Karen's relationship. Even though Karen knew that their insinuations were unfounded, she still felt a little embarrassed. The rumor mill also postulated that the reason why Harry was so supportive of Karen was that she was a woman—and in Harry's macho mind that meant "nonthreatening." Why had Harry never taken a bright young *male* under his wing and pushed him along?

Karen knew she had to decide tonight. She didn't want to throw a great thing away—but she didn't want to get trapped in a childlike relationship, either.

CASE 6
FRANK MASON (A)
N. J. Norman and John J. Gabarro

"It was like stepping out of a steam bath into a cold shower," Frank Mason reflected as he recalled the day he left Great Pacific Paper Company. He now wondered if he would have left had he known what awaited him at the Abbot Business Supply Company. Frank sat in his office on Monday morning, September 14, and glanced

out his door, noting that Ed Nolan, president of Abbot, had not yet arrived. In recent months, working for Nolan had been the most difficult experience of his otherwise successful career. When Frank had joined the company in March as vice president for marketing and sales, Nolan seemed to be delightful, charming, almost charismatic. Nolan had given Frank a free hand in reorganizing the marketing area and had practically guaranteed that Frank would be president of Abbot within two years. But then, things began to go wrong. He and Nolan no longer got along, his autonomy had been severely limited, company sales were again declining, and things in general were rapidly deteriorating. To make things worse, Daryl Eismann, president of Houston Electronics, Abbot's parent company, would be flying in the following week to review the company's current situation.

The previous week, Frank had decided to take some action before Eismann arrived. It seemed that it was time to have a candid talk with Nolan to try to resolve their differences. Frank had thought that Nolan would surely want to talk these things out before Eismann's impending visit, but even after working for Nolan for six months, Frank still found him unpredictable. On Tuesday, Frank had asked Nolan to have drinks with him that afternoon, but Nolan declined. He also declined Frank's invitations for lunch on Wednesday and Thursday with no explanation. However, Frank noted that Nolan continued to have lunch with some of the other managers in the firm. Frank still felt that a candid discussion about their relationship and the problems of Abbot could no longer be delayed, and he was determined to see Nolan as soon as he arrived. Nolan usually arrived at 9:00 A.M., which gave Frank almost half an hour to review the situation and gather his thoughts.

Frank Mason

Frank was 35 years old, single, and a native of Peoria, Illinois. He received his BA in economics from Antioch College, served four years in the Navy, and earned his MBA from the Harvard Business School. He then joined the Great Pacific Paper Company in Spokane, one of the country's largest and most profitable manufacturers and marketers of consumer paper products. The company sold nationally advertised facial tissue, bathroom tissue, paper towels, paper napkins, and other paper products. It was primarily Great Pacific's good reputation in the consumer products field that had appealed to Frank. His success in the marketing division had been spectacular—product manager in two and a half years (a company record), and senior product manager in only six more months. His salary had more than doubled by the end of his fifth year at Great Pacific.

But Frank also recalled the sense of personal stagnation that was growing during his last months there. Establishing new products had lost its charm; it involved the same procedures again and again, and he felt that there was simply nothing new to learn there. Moreover, because of Great Pacific's strong hierarchical control, ever-present committee work, and endless rounds of required approval, he felt that he had not really tested himself. In fact, with such strong control and competent staff support, it would be difficult to fail. He also recalled Great Pacific's disastrous acquisition of a regional chemical company, which forced them into austerity measures and restriction of expansion and advancement.

For these reasons, Frank left Great Pacific and went to Gleason Pro Shops, a retail sporting goods chain based in Seattle, as VP for planning and marketing, receiving a 15

percent salary increase over his Great Pacific pay plus a bonus. The autonomy he had there was indeed like an exhilarating cold shower. But corporate financial problems seemed to follow him from Great Pacific, for Gleason fell into a severe cash flow bind a few months after his arrival. Being unable to afford Frank's salary, the company sent him on his second search for employment in less than 18 months.

As he thought back on the experience, there were two things about his 15 months at Gleason Pro Shops that still concerned Frank. First, although he did not consider himself a "job hopper," he found himself beginning to fit this unattractive mold. Second, none of his co-workers were college graduates, and they all used strong profanity, which seemed crude and unsophisticated to Frank. In retrospect, however, he suspected that he may have been too severe in his assessment of them, which may in turn have caused some of the personal animosities that had developed there.

After he left Gleason, Frank was contacted by an executive search agent, who told him of the job at Abbot Business Supply. The executive search firm had been engaged by Houston Electronics to find a vice president of marketing and sales for its Abbot subsidiary. Abbot had been a family-owned company with a very paternalistic style of management prior to its acquisition a year earlier by Houston Electronics, a producer of military avionics and space-tracking radar systems. Abbot was a regional manufacturer of stationery and other paper products, as well as a distributor of related business supply items. The company sold over 2,000 products with annual sales of about $10 million. In addition to stationery and business forms, the product line included envelopes, typewriter paper, machine rolls, folders, loose leaf sheets, pens, pencils, duplicating supplies, staplers, blotters, and stenography supplies. Stationery and business forms were Abbot's largest items, accounting for 45 percent of sales, and were produced and printed on Abbot presses. About 50 percent of their orders were received from stationery and business supply stores, 30 percent from businesses, and 20 percent from school systems and colleges. Abbot was located in San Francisco, with 70 percent of company sales in the Bay area, 20 percent in Los Angeles, and the remainder in Sacramento. School systems, colleges, and businesses were contacted by company salespeople on a regular basis, while stationery and business supply stores sent their orders directly to the sales department. The company had been urgently in need of a vice president of marketing and sales, and the agent offered Frank a salary 20 percent higher than his salary at Gleason Pro Shops plus a 25 percent bonus at the end of the year. Although not initially interested, Frank eventually agreed to a luncheon interview later that month with Ed Nolan, the president of Abbot.

Interviews with Ed Nolan

After a discouraging interview for an unattractive job in Burbank, Frank arrived in San Francisco on a beautiful, clear day in late February. It was at the Top of the Mark Restaurant in the Mark Hopkins Hotel that Frank first met Ed Nolan.

Nolan appeared to be in his mid-50s, about medium height, slightly overweight with large, heavy jowls, and a full head of gray hair. Nolan was originally an engineer and had spent much of his career in high-technology companies. He had impressed Frank with his excellent mind, which could accumulate, sort, and evaluate a large amount of information and reach a conclu-

sion in a very short time. Frank was also impressed with Nolan's personal charm, good sense of humor, and attentive interest, which made him seem, at least to Frank, almost benevolent. The one thing that Frank remembered most strongly about the meeting was that it seemed strangely unnecessary to "score points" with Nolan. It was as if Nolan was selling him on the job, rather than the other way around.

Frank also remembered his surprise when Nolan told him he was also president of another division within Houston Electronics, with $300 million in sales. But Nolan had explained that he was only acting as steward of Abbot until he could find an aggressive, intelligent, young manager to take his place there. It soon became apparent to Frank that the next VP for marketing and sales was very likely to become the next president of Abbot within two years. Frank expressed interest in the job and, without making any firm commitments, they left the restaurant and Frank took a cab back to the airport.

Ten days later, Nolan called Frank at his parents' home in San Diego and asked him if he was still interested. Since he was, they agreed on a date for Frank to fly up to San Francisco for a visit to the company plant and offices. Nolan told Frank he would pick him up at San Francisco International Airport on Monday morning, March 6. In thinking back to that March morning, Frank was a little amused at the comedy of errors that had occurred. Nolan had not shown up as expected, so Frank called his apartment. Nolan's wife explained that Ed had already left for the office, and a second call to Nolan's secretary revealed that he was not yet in but was expected shortly. Frank felt it would be a waste of time to wait at the airport, so he took a cab to the Abbot offices. Nolan greeted Frank warmly upon his ar-

rival and seemed genuinely sorry for the mixup. Nolan then discussed company operations with him for the rest of the morning. Frank had researched the company thoroughly and was able to conduct an intelligent, knowledgeable discussion. In fact, it had seemed to Frank that he was more prepared to discuss specifics than Nolan.

However, Nolan had some strong general opinions on how to run a business. He was a believer in management by objectives and stressed the importance of good communication among top management. But he was equally convinced that each manager should run his or her own area simply and without help from other functions. Nolan emphasized the importance of the controller as guardian of the company's assets, and he stressed the need for efficiency and tight inventory control in production. He then added, "But in this business, control and marketing are the most important functions." Frank got the impression that Nolan saw people as either competent or incompetent, with great contempt and distrust for the latter. Nolan also talked for quite some time about his experience at Houston Electronics and the importance of accurate cost estimates in calculating required margins for their government contracts. According to Nolan, there were no serious pressures from the parent company, even though Abbot's sales had been declining. Until things were turned around, Houston Electronics could make up any Abbot losses. Frank talked with Nolan until mid-afternoon and then flew back to San Diego.

Two things bothered Frank about his prospects at Abbot. First, Nolan had failed to introduce him to any of the other people in the company (see Exhibit 1), explaining that they were busy with the quarterly report. Second, the job was in industrial marketing, which lacked the excitement of surveys, mass advertising, packaging, and so on. However, Nolan had promised the autonomy that Frank wanted, and there seemed to be a very good chance that he might be president within two years. To Frank, the autonomy and challenge of making major marketing decisions seemed to greatly outweigh the less exciting marketing problems of a small, nonconsumer company such as Abbot. Additionally, he could live in the San Francisco area, which he had always liked. When Nolan offered him the job the following week, Frank accepted without hesitation.

A Talk with St. Clair

On March 22, Frank began his job as vice president for marketing and sales of Abbot Business Supply Company. He soon met Bob St. Clair, a consultant to Abbot, who was also a graduate of Harvard Business School, and had been a consultant to Great Pacific Paper Company. They quickly became good friends, and Frank asked St. Clair to talk with him about the company's background. One afternoon they met for lunch, and St. Clair explained that Nolan was apparently the protégé of Art Lincoln, executive vice president of Houston Electronics (see Exhibit 2). St. Clair was on good terms with Lincoln, since they had been college roommates. Nolan had been the only high-level manager in Houston Electronics who was in favor of acquiring Abbot. His influence with Lincoln and his record as a high performer had apparently outweighed objections to acquiring a company in such a different industry. Nolan was made president of Abbot and was put under heavy pressure from Eismann to improve its performance. St. Clair confided to Frank that Nolan had just told Lincoln that Abbot was in serious trouble. Lincoln had recom-

Exhibit 1   Partial Organization Chart—Abbot Business Supply Company, March 1

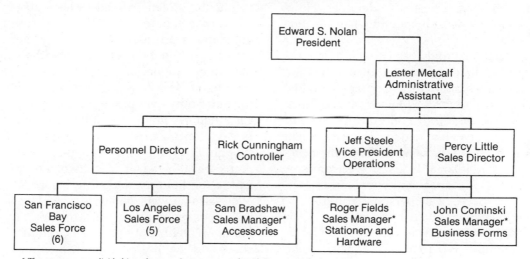

* The company was divided into three product groups, each with its own product manager:
- The Accessories Group included bulletin boards, rubber bands, paper clips, maps, and art supplies (18 percent of sales).
- The Stationery and Hardware Group included stationery and envelopes, appointment books, scratch pads, calendars, card indexes, stenography supplies, fasteners, and paper punchers (39 percent of sales).
- The Business Forms Group included business forms, business envelopes, machine rolls, typewriter paper, indexes, folders, and expanding envelopes (43 percent of sales).

Exhibit 2   Partial Organization Chart—Houston Electronics Corporation, March 1

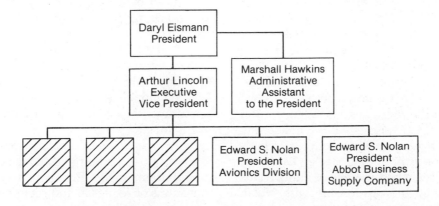

Nolan not honst

mended that Nolan spend all his time in San Francisco and leave his division in Houston in the hands of his capable deputies. However, Nolan was still spending half his time in Houston.

St. Clair also told Frank that, while most people seemed to have difficulty getting along with Nolan, Rick Cunningham, the controller, and Lester Metcalf, the administrative assistant, were on good terms with him. They usually had lunch with Nolan three or four days a week. Both men had worked for Nolan at Houston Electronics. A rumor had it that several years earlier Metcalf had been near personal bankruptcy, and Nolan had saved his career. St. Clair added that Metcalf was very loyal to Nolan. Cunningham was an accountant who strongly emphasized cost control but reportedly had no sympathy for salespeople's problems. He, too, was very loyal to Nolan, and they occasionally attended basketball games together. As far as St. Clair knew, these basketball games with Cunningham were Nolan's only social life.

St. Clair knew that Nolan considered Frank a possible candidate for the president's job. However, he warned Frank that Jeff Steele, VP for operations, also wanted to be president of the firm and that Frank could be in for a difficult time with him. As a final word of advice, St. Clair urged Frank to move into the vacant office next to Nolan's office, "before someone else tries to gain the favored position." Frank thanked St. Clair for the information and advice, and he returned to his office. The next day, he moved into the room next to Nolan's office, as St. Clair had suggested. At first Frank had been apprehensive about St. Clair's warning concerning Jeff Steele. Later on, however, Steele became one of Frank's best friends, while his relationship with Nolan became worse over the summer.

The First Three Months at Abbot

Initially, Nolan seemed to have absolute confidence in Frank's ability. Frank's recommendations on marketing strategy met no resistance, and he seemed to be the commanding influence on Nolan for his first few months at Abbot. Nolan had given Frank full autonomy over pricing, even though St. Clair had recommended that Nolan retain pricing control over very large orders. Although St. Clair also recommended that Frank be allowed at least two months to gain a foothold in marketing before taking over sales as well, Nolan wanted Frank to take responsibility for sales in early April. Frank was reluctant to take on too much too soon, but he hesitated for other reasons also.

When Frank first joined the company, Percy Little was in charge of sales. Frank saw Little as a highly regimented person who paid careful attention to detail but often could not see the whole picture. He thought that if Little had a personal motto it would be "everything to please the customer." Although Little had excellent relationships with the salespeople, he seemed to have little administrative ability. Nolan would often ask detailed, probing questions of Little, which he could rarely answer without checking his books or asking one of his salespeople. Little's failure to have the answers at his fingertips invariably angered Nolan, who made it clear to Frank that he thought Little was incompetent and should be fired immediately. Frank also recalled the attitude of the sales force at that time. They were mostly "old-timers," many of them having over 25 years of service with the company. In his initial contacts, Frank found them to be shy, responsive to his questions or requests, and seemingly frightened of him. This was not a situation Frank wished to become involved in at that time.

But Nolan was persistent, and Frank finally yielded and took charge of sales. He felt that he would have to manage the salespeople as best he could, dealing with them primarily through Little. Little proved to be loyal to Frank, even though he, too, was one of the company "old-timers." Little seemed to be relieved when Frank took charge of sales. After this change, the organizational chart for Abbot Business Supply was redrawn as shown in Exhibit 3.

In early May, the company had a visit

Exhibit 3   Partial Organization Chart—Abbot Business Supply Company, May 1

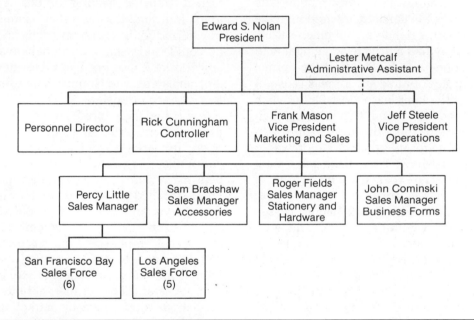

from Art Lincoln, executive vice president of Houston Electronics. The main purpose of his visit was to hear Frank present Abbot's business plan. When Nolan introduced Frank to him, Lincoln remarked, "So this is the guy who walks on water." Frank was somewhat surprised, but replied, "It depends on how deep it is." The presentation for Lincoln was a one-man show, and Frank was the star performer. Much of his presentation concerned a reorganization of the marketing function and its communica-

tion needs. He recalled that after his presentation everyone had been happy except him, because he knew that he now had to deliver.

In his first three months at Abbot, Frank had been faced with several difficult decisions. In late May, he found it necessary to release the entire Los Angeles sales force, since the volume for that region was not large enough to justify the operating costs involved. He contacted four large stationery stores and three distributors in the Los

Angeles area, which agreed to order exclusively from Abbot. Frank felt that this action would retain most of the volume in Los Angeles without the high operating costs of the salespeople. He appointed James Au, the Los Angeles warehouse manager, to watch over these accounts and to call on them at regular intervals. Although the salespeople were released because of financial considerations and not age, Frank still had mixed feelings about firing them. One salesman was 69 years old, even though the company had a policy of retirement at 65. He reportedly had a private agreement with Nolan to remain in his job past the normal retirement age. Frank felt a great sense of relief when he later learned that all of them had obtained jobs within two weeks of their severance from Abbot Business Supply. Another thing he found necessary to do was to fire Sam Bradshaw, one of the sales managers. Sam was 57 years old with 32 years of company service and was afflicted with Parkinson's disease. Frank had discussed firing Bradshaw with Percy Little, and, after a long and labored discussion, Little begrudgingly admitted that it probably wasn't necessary to keep Bradshaw. Although he did not find it easy, Frank eventually gave Bradshaw his notice.

As he began to get the feel of his new job, Frank also made friends with Roger Fields and John Cominski, his two sales managers, who seemed quite happy that Frank was taking the lead role in the company. Both of them also seemed to have considerable difficulty in dealing with Nolan. But Frank had dismissed any concerns they might have had about Nolan, believing that they were simply too unsophisticated to effectively deal with him.

In mid-May, Frank added Steve Lewis to his staff as a product manager. When Frank first met him, Lewis was working for Cun-

ningham in the controller's office. Frank and Lewis were both bachelors in their mid-30s, and they soon discovered that they were very similar in their lifestyles and sense of humor. One evening over drinks, Lewis expressed an interest in working for Frank. Frank had been impressed with Lewis's ability, and he remembered Cunningham commenting favorably on Lewis's competence. When Cunningham later returned from a meeting in Los Angeles, Frank indicated his interest in having Lewis transferred to the marketing division. While he could understand Cunningham's reluctance to let Lewis go, Frank was nevertheless persistent, and Cunningham eventually agreed to the transfer.

Frank had also hired Tony Buccini as a product manager in May. Although Buccini often appeared abrupt and stubborn, his enormous energy and his ability with numbers made him a good product manager. Frank recalled the day in mid-May when both Lewis and Buccini were officially assigned to marketing. He remembered how Nolan had emphasized that each manager should be able to run his own area without help from other functions. Therefore, he told Lewis and Buccini that, although their official functions were in marketing, they should keep themselves informed of other aspects of the company as well. The following week, Buccini approached Frank with what he saw as an impending problem in the company's cash position. They discussed it with Cunningham, who assured them that there was no problem with the projected cash flow. Neither Frank nor Buccini were convinced, and later that afternoon they met with Nolan to explain the problem. Nolan could see no problem either and, over their objections, dismissed the issue as unimportant. Frank remembered the staff meeting two days later in which Nolan had emphasized the soundness of the company's cash position and how it was not a subject of concern. In retrospect, Frank felt that this incident may have strained Buc-cini's relationship with Cunningham. Now that Lewis and Buccini were working for Frank, the company organizational chart was again redrawn, as shown in Exhibit 4.

Exhibit 4   Partial Organization Chart—Abbot Business Supply Company, May 25

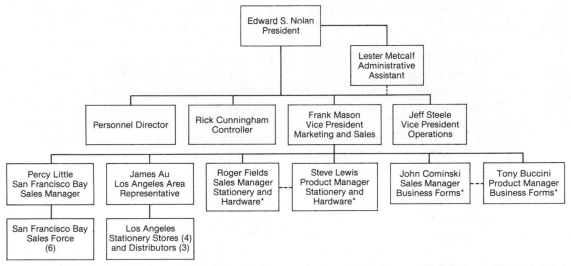

* The products in the Accessories Group were absorbed by the other two product groups. The Stationery and Hardware Groups (49 percent of sales) then included rubber bands, paper clips, and bulletin boards, and the Business Forms Group (51 percent of sales) included maps and art supplies.

After a short time, Frank began to have mixed feelings about his job at Abbot. After searching for greater and greater autonomy, he had suddenly found himself thinking that he almost had too much autonomy. While the Great Pacific Paper Company approach had been tight control, supplemented with strong staff support, the approach within Houston Electronics could be summed up as "self-sufficiency," or as Frank often put it, "parochial functionalism." For Frank, this meant doing his own control, budgeting, planning, and so on. Also, it seemed to Frank that he, not Nolan, was supplying the leadership for the company. The scope of his autonomy seemed a little frightening.

Problems with Nolan

During May and June, Frank began to see unexpected and unpleasant aspects of Nolan's personality. He recalled how volatile and unpredictable Nolan began to appear, particularly in the way he treated other people, such as Percy Little. Frank's tour in the Navy had taught him that when dealing with subordinates the rule was, "Praise in public, censure in private." Nolan seemed to take exactly the opposite view. It seemed to Frank that Nolan was a Theory X manager—"If something goes wrong, raise hell!" Also, during his frequent outbursts, Nolan would often use strong profanity, even during staff meetings, which Frank found distasteful and at times upsetting. He was shocked that a man of Nolan's stature would use such language at any time, but especially when conducting company business. At first, Frank had attributed such behavior to the other managers' ineptness in dealing with Nolan, but even so, he felt that Nolan's methods and language were unnecessary.

One particular incident stood out in Frank's memory. At a staff meeting in May, Nolan had wanted Jeff Steele to set up the warehouse like a supermarket in order to get away from the computer printouts they were using at that time in inventory control. "When I want to know what we have in inventory," he shouted, "I want to walk through the warehouse and see it with my own eyes!" Steele had argued that the computerized location system was efficient and reliable, and that there was no need to group and display their products in the warehouse like supermarket merchandise. Frank remembered how angry Nolan became during the conversation. Nolan apparently disliked computer printouts and believed that a good manager should have the relevant information in his head. What seemed quite strange to Frank was that Nolan seemed to look to him for assurance as he argued with Steele. Nolan even interrupted the meeting to ask Frank for advice on the matter. Frank responded that from his own perspective there would probably be no problems, but the real issue was whether or not the company would incur incremental costs by changing to the supermarket-type arrangement. The company

changed over to Nolan's system within a month.

In June, Frank began to notice that his relationship with Nolan was growing more tense. Nolan had become very concerned about Abbot's recent financial performance, especially the firm's low margin. The low margin was primarily the result of Frank's price-cutting strategy aimed at reversing Abbot's declining sales. Also, the price of paper had sharply increased shortly after Frank took over pricing, which further hurt performance. Although the company's performance was not good when compared to the business plan, Frank pointed out to Nolan that it was still an improvement over the February figures. But his reasoning had little impact on Nolan, who continued to complain about the poor margin.

Frank's relationship with Nolan grew more strained in July, and early in the month they had their first major argument. Frank had approved the sale of an order at below the break-even point. Since he believed that the customer would not pay a higher price, and since the firm was experiencing high inventory levels, he approved a price that at least covered variable costs and provided some contribution, rather than lose the order. Cunningham informed Nolan of Frank's decision, and Nolan became very upset with Frank, since his decision would further reduce the margin. After expressing his anger at Frank for several minutes, Nolan suddenly demanded to know the margin on a small order for desk pens. Since Frank regarded his role in the company as strategist, he left details such as this to his subordinates. When he told Nolan that he would have to check, Nolan became furious. During the next few minutes, Nolan also expressed his displeasure that the former owner of Abbot had somehow obtained some sensitive information about their operations in Los Angeles. He was sure that one of the marketing people had leaked this information, and he demanded to know what Frank was going to do about it. The entire discussion left Frank feeling very disturbed, confused, and angry, but he managed to tell Nolan that he would bring it up at his next staff meeting.

A few days later, Frank opened his staff meeting with a few words on the sensitivity of company information. He later informed Nolan of this action, but Nolan demanded to be present at the next meeting to see for himself. A week later, Frank presented the same information to his staff, as Nolan had instructed, while Nolan sat by the wall near the head of the table. When Frank finished his opening remarks, Nolan abruptly left the room, slammed the door, and did not return.

At Nolan's next staff meeting, he told Frank that he should send Percy Little to Los Angeles on Mondays to visit the major stationery stores there. Frank protested that there was no need to send Little to Los Angeles, and that he could be of more help in the home office. Nolan became visibly angry at Frank's response and instructed Frank that he wanted Little in Los Angeles on Mondays "even if all he does is sit there!" Then, without looking directly at Frank, he said, "When I tell someone to do something, I expect them to do it!"

Shortly after the incident over the break-even sale, Frank felt the need to talk with Nolan about how things were going. He spoke to Nolan one morning and expressed his frustration and confusion over what was expected of him. Nolan, however, responded that things were going fine and there was nothing to be overly concerned about. This discussion left Frank feeling very unsatisfied. It seemed to him that such a discussion should have had a more powerful impact on Nolan, but instead Nolan had been very calm and approving. Frank decided that it would be better to discuss the matter with Nolan during their trip to Los Angeles the following week.

Frank and Nolan arrived in Los Angeles on a hot, smoggy afternoon in late July. During the ride from the airport, Frank began to tell Nolan about the problems he saw at Abbot Business Supply. He said that since Nolan spent much of his time in Houston, there were communication problems, a lack of central focus, and a power vacuum in the company. Additionally, since Lester Metcalf, the administrative assistant, also went to Houston fairly often, no one was in charge of the company for long periods of time. Frank felt that Nolan needed to be at Abbot either all the time or not at all. Frank also felt that, if Nolan could not be there at all, then he should make some sort of power arrangement. After expressing these thoughts to Nolan, Frank suggested that a conference phone hookup from Houston might be feasible. Nolan listened to Frank and seemed to be very understanding of the problems and frustrations Frank was experiencing. He agreed with Frank's analysis and seemed appreciative of his candor; Frank began to feel optimistic, since Nolan seemed ready to make some needed changes.

The Construction Paper Incident

After their conversation, Nolan casually mentioned to Frank that the company ought to sell more school construction paper because of its current margins. Frank agreed and, upon his return to San Francisco, began to gear up for increased construction paper sales. One week later, Frank was surprised to discover that there was no construction paper in inventory. For an explanation, Frank went to Jeff Steele, who told him that Nolan had ordered him to stop purchasing construction paper a few days earlier. Frank then went to Nolan and expressed his distress that he had not been informed of this decision. Nolan remarked, "This is a small company. When I tell one guy something, he should tell the others." He had little else to say, so Frank returned to Steele's office and they discussed the matter for over an hour.

The following Tuesday, a salesperson from a major paper producer offered to sell 40,000 reams of construction paper to the company at a very good price. Frank talked to Steele and then to Nolan, explaining that the supplier would guarantee the order to the company's specifications and would allow Abbot to inspect the shipment before delivery. Nolan, however, didn't think it was a good idea. Although 40,000 reams was a small amount of construction paper, Nolan still said no, stating that "I don't want to go into it. I've talked to paper experts and they say we're too small to be hedging in the paper market." The next day, Steele asked Frank about the order and Frank told him of Nolan's decision. Steele responded, "I want to talk to Nolan," and went straight to the president's office. Twenty minutes later, Steele returned to say that Nolan had changed his mind and had decided to buy the 40,000 reams of construction paper. When Frank confronted Nolan about this reversal, Nolan explained, "For that amount, we can sell it. Besides, Frank," he continued, "you didn't give me all the facts about this deal. You never told me that we could reject the order at no cost to us, if it wasn't prepared to our specifications." When Frank pressed him, Nolan simply dismissed the issue, saying that Frank needn't be concerned about it. Frank left Nolan's office feeling angry and frustrated.

The New Pricing Scheme

In early August, Nolan took control of all pricing. The margin for July was as poor as that of May and June, and Nolan decided to remedy this problem with his own pricing scheme for Abbot's products. His pricing scheme was based on a required, overall company margin of 24 percent.[1] Since the cost of each item was known, Nolan could calculate a price for each of the company's products that would produce a margin within two or three percentage points of the required figure.

However, Frank felt that this scheme was far too simple. It treated every product the same, regardless of differences in demand, competitive situation, or unique qualities of each item. Also, it had the effect of lowering the price on high margin, low volume goods and raising the price on low-margin, high-volume goods. Since stationery stores often carried thousands of items, they could not absorb large orders and, therefore, would be unable to take immediate advantage of a lower price on the high-margin, low-volume items. Furthermore, if prices were raised on high-volume, low-margin items, which were typically price competitive, the company might lose those sales to lower-priced competitors. Although Frank voiced these objections, Nolan insisted on going ahead with his plan. When Frank saw the new price list, he protested that he couldn't possibly generate the volume at these prices. Nolan replied, "When did I expect you to worry about volume?"

---

[1] Margin, in percent, was calculated by dividing gross margin by sales revenue. Gross margin = Sales revenue − cost of goods sold.

As Frank had expected, Nolan's pricing scheme proved to be a complete failure, and the company's performance for August was even worse than it had been for May, June, and July. Nolan received the August performance results on September 4 and since that time had spoken to no one but Cunningham and Metcalf. Since Frank's autonomy was now very limited, and since Nolan was no longer speaking to most of his managers, it seemed to Frank there was no longer any leadership in the company.

Rick Cunningham

It occurred to Frank that his deteriorating relationship with Nolan was paralleled by his deteriorating relationship with Cunningham. During April and May, he and Cunningham got to know each other fairly well, and they would occasionally have drinks and dinner. Although they got along well after working hours, it seemed to Frank that Cunningham was a completely different person at the office. Frank felt that "apple-polisher" would be too kind a word for Cunningham, who blamed everyone else for any problems and always answered Nolan with "Yes, sir," "No, sir," and "Right away, sir." Cunningham also saw Percy Little as a major problem in the company because he was "giving the products away" with low prices and easy credit terms.

It seemed to Frank that Cunningham and Nolan were always on the same side of every issue. After Nolan's reprimand over the break-even sale, Frank discovered that Cunningham had informed Nolan of Frank's decision to approve the order. That afternoon, Frank had found Cunningham in the hall and had asked him why he had gone directly to Nolan without coming to him first. Frank made it clear that if Cunningham didn't have the decency to deal

with him directly instead of running to Nolan, then he, too, could play that game. In response, Cunningham demanded that Buccini mind his own business and accused Frank of letting Percy Little operate in his usual way, which was causing the company to lose money. After a short time both men calmed down and returned to their offices.

After this incident, Frank's relationship with Cunningham became more openly hostile. A few days later, Buccini drove to Sacramento and returned via San Rafael on company business but neglected to get receipts for the bridge tolls. The controller's office had recently established a new policy that specifically prohibited reimbursement of expenses for company business without a receipt, and Buccini's request for $2.35 was refused. Buccini explained the situation to Frank, who was amazed at the pettiness of the refusal. Frank was so angered by it that he went directly to the company clerk and complained. However, the clerk argued that he could not make the payment under the company's policy, and Buccini never received payment for this expense. A few days after this incident, Frank received a memo from Cunningham which said, essentially, "If you have a complaint, don't talk to my people, talk to me." To Frank, the note seemed to be the last straw. By the time he reached Cunningham's office, Frank was so angry that he simply crumpled up the note, dropped it in Cunningham's wastebasket, and told him, "I got your note."

The Current Situation

The most recent problem facing Frank involved Nolan's insistence that he dismiss James Au, the Los Angeles area representative. Frank had put Au in charge of the Los Angeles accounts after he had released the

Los Angeles sales force. He had felt that the volume of business there was large enough to warrant a company representative to service these accounts. It seemed to him that, without a local representative in Los Angeles, the company would probably lose these accounts to competitors. Nolan, however, felt that these accounts could be serviced equally well from San Francisco, and that Frank should dismiss Au to cut costs. Although Frank had recommended that no raises be given to himself, his product managers, or his sales managers in an effort to reduce costs, Nolan still insisted that Au be fired. Frank felt that this problem, as well as the pricing problem, had to be settled before Daryl Eismann arrived. The impending visit of the parent company's president gave an added sense of urgency to resolve these and other problems that had developed over the previous few months.

Over the weekend, Frank had even considered resigning from Abbot. At first the idea seemed appealing, under the circumstances, but the more he thought of it, the more distasteful it became. A resignation, to Frank, would be an admission of failure, and if he took another job it would be his third in less than two years. Additionally, he had recently purchased a house overlooking the Bay, and the prospect of being without income again for an undetermined period of time would strain his resources. Frank had invested most of his savings in the property, and he did not have enough cash to sustain a prolonged job search. Also, he liked the Bay area and did not look forward to leaving it, if he could not find a job nearby.

Frank leaned back in his chair and tried to put the last six months into perspective. He had taken a job with substantial autonomy, a good chance for advancement, and a very good relationship with the company president. But the relationship had deteriorated,

his autonomy had been severely curtailed, and his chances for advancement looked dim. Nevertheless, he felt that he could no longer continue with things as they were. Some immediate actions were needed to improve the situation with Nolan and Cunningham. Frank became lost in his thoughts for a few minutes until he heard the familiar sound of Nolan's heavy, purposeful footsteps down the hall. Frank looked up and stared at the president's door, waiting expectantly.

FRANK MASON (B)
N. J. Norman and John J. Gabarro

Nolan walked into his office and closed the door. Frank knocked, entered, and began by telling Nolan that the two of them needed to talk. He then launched into a description of his feelings of frustrations and the problems that existed as he saw them. As he became more excited, Frank heard himself saying, "What do you expect from me? I don't understand my role in the company. If Cunningham is your chief of staff, let me know." For each of his complaints, Frank provided detailed examples. Nolan was very quiet and nodded slowly as Frank reeled off point after point. Nolan finally broke his silence while Frank was discussing Cunningham. "I feel comfortable with Rick," Nolan interrupted. "I know him from our days in Houston Electronics. I communicate with him very often, and I probably shouldn't." Frank continued to complain that, as VP for marketing and sales, he should be involved in pricing. Nolan countered by stating that the new scheme was his own idea and he would run it himself. "Besides, Frank," he continued, "you let me down before. Try it my way now." Then Nolan became more active, complaining that Buccini was interfering with other areas. Frank defended him, stating that he believed Buccini was doing a fine job. Nolan suddenly demanded, "Why haven't you fired Little?" Frank explained that Little was his link to the salespeople, and firing him would be a mistake. They continued their discussion for about 20 minutes, and as Frank was about to leave, Nolan said, "Frank, you shouldn't feel that we have to get away from the office for us to talk. My door is always open; you can come in anytime."

Frank left Nolan's office feeling somewhat relieved. What had begun as a difficult, emotional argument had ended surprisingly well. Nolan seemed to understand the problem Frank was facing and indicated that he would try to be more reasonable. On the whole, it had gone better than Frank had expected, and he anticipated a better relationship with Nolan and a gradual return of his autonomy.

The next morning, it was as if they had not talked at all. Nolan began his staff meeting by criticizing Cunningham but looked at Frank as he did so. Then, Nolan began to complain loudly about the poor margin for the last four months. Although he was very active during the staff meeting, Nolan remained aloof and distant for the rest of the week, except for his lunches with Cunningham and Metcalf.

The following Monday, Daryl Eismann arrived and met with Nolan and his managers all day. Eismann asked many difficult and pointed questions, and Frank got the impression that Nolan and Cunningham were attempting to smooth over the problems at Abbot. After Eismann left, Frank drafted a letter to him but did not mail it. (See Exhibit 1.) Later in the week, Nolan

Exhibit 1 Frank's Unsent Letter to Daryl Eismann

Dear Daryl,

I enjoyed meeting you and found your comments helpful in moving the business ahead.

While you were exposed to many of our problems during your visit, there are others of which you may not be aware. I would like to speak with you further about these problems at your convenience.

Sincerely,

Frank Mason

had another staff meeting, announcing that Marshall Hawkins, Eismann's administrative assistant, would arrive at Abbot on Monday for additional meetings. Nolan's opening words were, "Eismann is sending his sleuth for a visit."

Hawkins arrived on Monday and talked with each of the top managers in Abbot. Frank believed that this was the time to state his position. He talked with Hawkins privately and candidly explained his view of the situation at Abbot. Frank also showed Hawkins the letter to Eismann he had drafted a week earlier. When Hawkins read it, he remarked, "It's a good thing you didn't send it." It seemed to Frank that Hawkins was sympathetic to his problems. Hawkins thanked him for his time and candor and left his office. Frank noted that Nolan and Cunningham were again attempting to smooth over the company's problems. The next day, Hawkins issued a list of six actions that he designated as high priority, three of which involved marketing. Hawkins left on the afternoon plane for

Houston, and Nolan left for Houston the following morning.

One of the priorities on Hawkins's list was to increase the prices on Abbot's line of desk calendars and appointment books. However, when Frank showed Metcalf the new price list, Metcalf refused to approve it. Frank reminded him of Hawkins's instructions, but Metcalf replied, "Hawkins is staff, not line. As long as Ed Nolan is president of this company, we sell these items at the lower price." Frank asked for a memo of his decision, but Metcalf remarked, "I'm sending a letter straight to Hawkins!"

Two weeks later, Steele received a call from Hawkins, who asked for his observations on the company's progress since his visit, expressing a particular interest in Frank's area. Steele informed Frank of the call, explaining that he had said a few encouraging words in general but had declined to discuss Frank, stating that he felt it inappropriate to evaluate a peer.

A few weeks after Hawkins called Steele, Metcalf invited Frank to lunch and explained that "some things are going on" that he could not divulge. After making sure that Frank was doing all he could to comply with Hawkins's instructions, Metcalf added, "If you have any problems, call me. I'll be in Palm Springs." A week later, Metcalf called Frank to see what progress he was making on Hawkins's instructions. Frank made a favorable report, adding that he had also completed James Au's severance papers as Nolan had wanted. During most of the following month, Frank worked to implement the priorities on Hawkins's list, as did most of the other managers at Abbot. Nolan was beginning to play a conspicuously small role in the management of the firm. Since Eismann's visit, Nolan had spent only about one day a week at Abbot and the rest in Houston.

Two months after his initial visit, Daryl Eismann returned to Abbot and informed the top-management group that Nolan had been relieved of his duties. He went on to add that, in his opinion, Abbot was in serious trouble and every member of top management was suspect. He also pointed out that an internal person would not be chosen to replace Nolan. Eismann concluded by promising them answers concerning their future in the company as soon as "circumstances" permitted.

A week later, Hawkins arrived at Abbot and informed Frank that he was fired. Hawkins explained that they were dismissing him because Houston Electronics had a policy of "cleaning house" whenever a division president was fired. "It's nothing against you," he added, "it's just company policy." Two weeks later, Frank called Buccini to inquire about the situation at Abbot. Buccini replied that Hawkins had taken over as acting president, but that no one else had been fired at that time.

CASE 7
GERALD STANTON
John P. Kotter

On January 10, 1978, Gerald Stanton, the manager of advertising and sales promotion in the Retail Division of Best Products, Inc. (see Exhibit 1 for an organization chart), was sitting in a routine meeting at Best's corporate headquarters in Dallas. At 10:30 Floyd LaPatta, Gerry's boss, interrupted the meeting and called him outside. LaPatta announced that he was being transferred to another division at Best Products and that he was going to recommend that Gerry take over his current job. For Stanton, this would

Copyright © 1979 by the President and Fellows of Harvard College. Harvard Business School case 9-480-015.

Exhibit 1

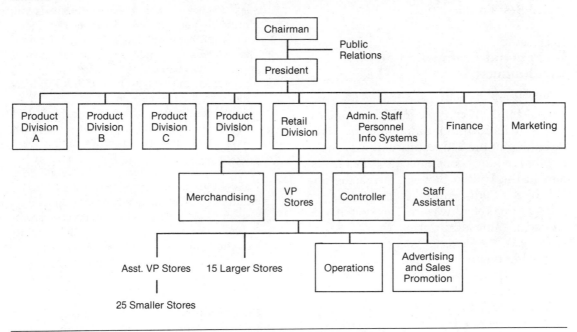

mean a sizable increase in responsibilities. Gerry currently supervised a dozen staff people. A promotion into LaPatta's job would mean that he would supervise approximately 600 people, that his budget responsibility would go up very significantly, and that he would be one of the two youngest vice presidents within Best Products. La-Patta told Stanton that if he had any reservations about such a move that he should make them clear within the next 24 hours before LaPatta made his recommendation to corporate management.

Background Information on Gerald Stanton

Gerald Stanton was born in the southwest part of the United States in 1945. He and his younger sister, Phyllis, were raised in a moderately large city by Herbert and Ellen Stanton. Herb Stanton was a lawyer whose parents had emigrated to the United States shortly before he was born.

Gerry generally did well in school; he finished in the top 20 percent in his high school and was a member of the National Honor Society. After high school Gerry went to college at a well-known university in the northwestern part of the United States. He concentrated in a prelaw curriculum that was mostly liberal arts. He was active in a variety of extracurricular activities and was president of his fraternity and of a theatre group. Academically, Gerry maintained a B average. Upon graduation he entered law school at the same university but, after one term, dropped out. After a series of part-time jobs that lasted approximately a year, Gerry enrolled in an MBA program at a school in Dallas. He finished the program doing moderately well academically and joined Best Products, Inc.

Background Information on Best Products

Best Products was founded in the early part of the 19th century in Philadelphia. It moved to its current location in Dallas at the beginning of the 20th century. It was one of the first modern consumer product companies in the United States. During the first half of the 20th century, it dominated the primary markets it was in. This domination eroded significantly during the 1960s and early 1970s, however.

In addition to four major product lines, Best also had a string of retail stores that were located in the Southwest. These 40 stores employed approximately 600 individuals and generated a yearly sales volume of approximately $100 million. The stores primarily sold products made in the other four Best divisions. The other divisions also sold their products through a number of different distribution channels beside the retail stores.

In commenting on Best Products, one industry analyst had the following to say:

> Best has been a highly successful company in the past, perhaps too successful for its own good. It dominated some of its markets to such an extent during the earlier part of this century that it never had to be a particularly aggressive or keen competitor. In the last 20 years this has hurt them. Although Best is still a very profitable and very important competitor, it is no longer the premier organization in its markets. Today there are quite a few companies that are more aggressive, that have more talented employees, that are quicker to bring out new products, and that are more profitable. Al-though the top management at Best has been trying to take corrective actions in the last five or six years, the company is still probably too centralized for its own good and it probably still has too many long-term employees who are not up to the current competitive battle.
>
> Perhaps the weakest part of Best Products today is their Retail Division. Many of us think that the retail group is probably breaking even or losing money, and we wonder why they haven't gotten out of the retail business. Of course the Retail Division is a very visible part of Best Products and it does allow for an important distribution channel, but its current management and operations seem to be having trouble making it profitable. They also seem to have difficulty attracting and retaining good young people.

Stanton's Career at Best

Gerry entered Best in a training program that lasted approximately six months. He was then placed as a department manager in one of Best's retail stores. A few years later he was promoted to store manager. At the time, he was less than 30 years old and was the youngest store manager in the history of the Retail Division at Best. Two years later, Gerry was promoted into a staff job at corporate headquarters, within the Retail Division. One year after that, he was made manager of advertising and sales promotions, reporting to the vice president of stores within the Retail Division.

Commenting upon Gerry's career at Best, one fellow employee had the following to say:

> Gerry's initial rise in the organization was unusually quick by our standards. I think he achieved such a fast track by establishing himself as a very bright, hard-working young man. He often spotted and solved problems that other people didn't even see.

Another employee had this to say:

> Gerry is a terribly bright young man. He's very goal-oriented, articulate. He's honest. He's a hard worker. He's good with numbers. He has a good sense of humor. He's a good problem solver and a good teacher. He's not particularly good at delegating, but I'm sure this will improve over time. He can also be a bit philosophical at times, but that doesn't get in his way of getting the job done.

A manager in one of Best's competitor's who knew Stanton had the following to say:

> Gerry stands out among Best employees at his level quite a bit. If you see him there at corporate headquarters, you notice immediately that he's younger, better looking, and a lot brighter than most of the people around him. He's a good man, and I, for one, have enjoyed knowing him very much.

The Vice President of Stores Position

The vice president of stores job reported to Joe Clark, the head of the Retail Divison (see Exhibit 1). Clark had been with Best Products for nearly 35 years, and had been head of the Retail Division for 10 years. Before taking over his present responsibilities, he was within the merchandising part of the business for 20 years. He began his career at Best in one of the retail stores. Since the early 1970s, Clark had been active outside the company in a number of industry associations. He traveled a good deal, and when he was away, the vice president, stores, was informally left in charge of the division.

Eighteen people reported to the vice president, stores, position. Most of them were managers of the larger stores. One person reporting to this position, the assistant vice president, stores, served as a second in command.

The job description for the vice president, stores, position listed numerous "duties" and concluded by saying that the vice president, stores, was "responsible for the overall well-being of the retail stores." The position was treated by accounting as an expense center (profitability was calculated for the division as a whole).

In commenting on the vice president, stores, job one employee at Best said the following:

> Because of the visibility of the stores, the vice president's, stores, job is a very visible position within Best Products. The biggest problem with the job that I see is that it reports to by far the least respected and least powerful of the division heads at Best. Joe Clark, the Retail Division head, is 62 years old and will be retiring soon. My impression is that he is not at all respected within the upper ranks at Best and that he has been allowed to remain on the job only because he's so close to retirement.

Another employee had this to say:

> The job has, at least in the recent past, been mainly one of firefighting. A million things can go wrong in the stores and it's the vice president's, stores, job to cope with all of those problems, to keep the stores running smoothly. But the job should be a lot more than that. The entire Retail Division does not have a clear strategy. The vice president, stores, should be thinking about broad, important, strategic issues. For example, should the company have 40 stores? Are they located in the right spot? Is the mix of merchandise we're putting in each store correct? Is the basic design of the stores appropriate? It seems to me these are very important questions.

Stanton's Decision

Gerry Stanton sat in his office on the afternoon of January 10, 1978, with mixed feelings. On the one hand, the opportunity that was being presented to him excited him very, very much. On the other hand, he wasn't entirely sure how to approach the vice president, stores, job and he did not want to take it if he thought his performance in the job would be any less excellent than his performance previously in the company. He knew he would have to give his boss a response the next morning. He wasn't quite sure what that response should be.

CASE 8
DAVID CONNOLLY
John P. Kotter

David Connolly was born in 1936 in a small town in Connecticut. He was the first of five children born to John and Cynthia Connolly. David grew up in a number of different cities in the United States and Europe, since his father was a manager and was transferred about every five years. David attended a prep school in New England before going to Yale as an undergraduate. He graduated from Yale magna cum laude, was married, and went to business school at the University of Pennsylvania (Wharton). He graduated from Wharton in the middle of his class academically, and took a financial job at the corporate headquarters of AX Industries, a large diversified corporation.

Connolly's Career at AX

Choosing the Job at AX.   When David began looking for a job in his second year of the MBA program, he targeted his search toward corporate finance within a particular industry. AX did not have any businesses in

that industry, and David had given no thought to interviewing the company until a fellow classmate told him of his experience at AX the previous summer. The classmate was very enthusiastic about AX, and that led David to schedule an interview with them:

> I was really impressed by the person who interviewed me on campus. When I was later asked to visit AX corporate, I jumped at the chance. That day at AX I talked with eight or ten people, and was completely snowed. I liked the place, the people, the climate. When I was offered a job a few weeks after that, I grabbed it immediately.

The First Five Years.   During the first five years at AX, David worked in the corporate Financial Analysis Group. This was a small group (five people) of MBAs that worked on various projects for the chief financial officer. Reflecting on these years, Connolly remarked:

> I learned a great deal, although, in retrospect, it was dull work. But at the time I enjoyed it a lot, and my work was received very well by the corporate officers. The projects eventually evolved into acquisition studies and the like. In the process I got to know a number of the law firms in town. I also got to know some investment bankers, and that was useful. And I began to learn about negotiation, about how one has to do one's homework on the other guy in order to succeed.

Just before David's fifth anniversary with AX, the chairman of AX retired and John Phillips, the general manager of one of AX's largest divisions, was promoted to succeed him. Three weeks later Phillips asked David to lunch:

> He told me he had read a study I had done on an industry we were thinking of going into. He had some background in that industry, and he thought my conclusions were right on. At the end of the lunch, he

asked me to start working for him, as an assistant to the chairman, immediately.

Working for the Chairman. As an assistant to the chairman, Connolly continued to do industry and business studies:

> Phillips wanted to clean up our current portfolio of businesses, as well as look for new possibilities. I made a list of things to look at and got to work. Eventually, I recommended we get out of a number of businesses, and we did. This had to be done with some tact, since the people responsible for these businesses were still around.
>
> I got along very well with the chairman. Our styles meshed. He's a no-nonsense guy, and I'm like that, too. I think he respected my doing the work, doing it well, and not playing games. We didn't develop a personal relationship, only a professional one. But it was a very good one. He learned to trust my judgment. I would come up with ideas that were different from what others suggested.
>
> For example, one of the businesses we had gotten into was a sleazy business. We should never have gotten into it. And we were not making money. The only reason we hadn't already pulled out was because we were going to have to take a large write-off. No one wanted to reduce this year's profits by that much. So I looked into the situation and found a way we could get out without having to write off a dime. It was very "creative." It was a long story and involves some intrigue. The chairman loved it. Some people were shocked, I think, not because we did anything illegal, but because it was bold and because they thought that ethically we were in a grey area. Anyway we did it. And it worked. We saved $10 million.

The Next Three Years. Connolly worked for Phillips for three years and then became an assistant to the financial vice president of AX. In this job he was given a $30 million portfolio to manage. He also continued to undertake projects for the chairman. More and more he began to take part in the managerial process at the top—attending planning meetings and the like:

> As assistant to the financial vice president, I began trading the portfolio I had, and made a goodly amount of money in the process for AX.
>
> After two years in that job, the chairman asked Bill Shannon and me to go to work for one of our group vice presidents as special assistants. Phillips was concerned about a number of his businesses, which included Zodiac Products, McAllister, Inc., and two others. These businesses were growing more rapidly than other parts of AX, but they were also experiencing many problems, too. Bill and I worked well together, and after about six months Phillips called me in one day and told me he wanted me to take over as the general manager of Zodiac. He said he was going to fire the current general manager.
>
> Zodiac was a small business, but it was losing money, and Phillips was not at all happy about the size of the investment he was being forced to make in the company.
>
> The job offer was given to me in a way that would have been difficult to turn down. But frankly, I wasn't at all sure that I wanted it. I was enjoying my work. I had a nice big office on the same floor as the chairman and president. I didn't have to worry about managing people. I always felt I could move a lot faster on a project if I did it alone. Taking the job at Zodiac meant moving away from the corporate womb into a dingy building, where there was no one to help me. And it meant moving into a business that was different from the core businesses at AX.

Zodiac Products, Inc.

Connolly was at Zodiac for three years. During that period of time, the company came out of the "red" and started making money. Labor productivity increased by over 200 percent and revenues went up substantially.

Commenting on his Zodiac years, Connolly said:

When I started to work at Zodiac I was scared to death. I had never supervised more than a few people before in my life. Zodiac had a few hundred employees. I had never had even the smallest general management job before, and here I was with a general management job in a company that was in trouble.

Just a few days after I started work I attended a party for a guy who was leaving. When I arrived I noticed immediately that the room had two groups of people in it. On one side were essentially the blue-collar workers and on the other side were the white-collar and managerial workers. I asked one of the employees that reported to me what was going on. He said that the blue-collar group was essentially the union leaders and that they were fairly upset because of a decision my predecessor had made before he left. He had decided to transfer one of the most-liked and highest-status members of the union into a job that was not very good. The union was furious about this and was seriously considering walking out. I walked over to this particular union employee and to the shop steward and introduced myself and asked them to step into a separate room with me. I told them that I had just taken over running the company and I wanted to know what was happening. The shop steward said that the former president of the division, my predecessor, had taken a move just before he left that was designed to humiliate this other union member. I asked a few questions and listened to them for about 5 or 10 minutes, and the story that the two of them told me sounded very plausible, made a lot of sense, and I believed it. So I told him that I would reverse the decision. We all walked back into the party and within five minutes the tension that was there beforehand was gone. The two groups of employees began to mingle and I was off to a good start with the union.

The rebuilding job at Zodiac was an incredible one. Essentially we had to reestablish relationships and our credibility with everyone, not just the union, but our other employees, customers, the local community we worked in, our suppliers, and, of course, top management at AX Industries. I spent most of my initial time at Zodiac trying to get a team of people together and trying to get them to agree on what was reasonable for us to do. We were fairly successful in this regard and began rather quickly to get things off dead center.

The next few years saw us making a lot of changes at Zodiac. It was an exciting time and one which ultimately worked well for Zodiac, the people that I worked with, and AX Industries.

After I had been at Zodiac for about three years, once again the chairman called me and asked me (or rather told me) that I would be taking over as general manager of a different AX division, one whose products were related to Zodiac's, and one which was losing money at the rate of a few hundred thousand dollars a month.

McAllister, Inc.

David started at McAllister, Inc., in September. Within the next six months, he fired five of the seven top officers of the company. Reflecting on this period, Connolly said:

It was very clear by the time that we let those people go that they simply were not performing. It was still difficult to do. Two of them were friends of mine. We brought in a different group of people, mostly from AX, to replace those that left. During the first six months or so I also restructured the organization and put a heavy emphasis on developing some type of written strategy for the division and on getting people to play team ball.

The success we've had at McAllister has been due to a variety of factors. We've managed to cut our unit costs significantly, and we've also been able to increase our revenues fairly significantly. This was due to better analysis, which was due in part to the better measurement systems we developed. It was also due to the better people we had on board, and I suppose to a bit of luck.

The year before Connolly took over at McAllister, the firm lost $5 million. Two years after he took over the firm earned over $10 million on about double the sales volume. David was 38 years old at the time. His salary and bonus were about $180,000.

Comments on Connolly

From others at AX

A former subordinate:

I must admit that I think that David is absolutely terrific. Working for him was a great learning experience and a pleasure. I can be a bit volatile at times and I used to storm into his office, screaming about something or other that had gone wrong, and wanting him to take immediate action on it. He'd typically listen very calmly and try to calm me down, and he'd say something along the lines of "Listen, you know more about this than I do, so why don't you just sit down, and nothing formal, spend a few minutes thinking out these options, and projecting them out a few years into the future, maybe with a few numbers, and then bring it back to me and we'll settle it." Anyway, I'd calm down and go off and do my little analysis, and usually half the time conclude that I was wrong and in the process I'd learn something about decision making. I also gained a lot of self-confidence after a while.

He's an extraordinarily competent person. He seems to have a lot of inner peace. He's also got good street sense. In the broader systems that he operates in he's very political, but in his own organization he's a team person and will not tolerate politics. He fosters trust and confidence.

He's also very, very smart. At least it seems that way to me. I think he's going to be the president of this corporation some day.

A peer at AX:

What impresses me most is his ability to grab hold of a very complex strategic situation and be able to understand and articulate what's going on. He's also very, very effective at getting things done. Some people even say he's ruthless, but I'm not sure if that's fair. He's a very demanding person and appears to be very straightforward, no bullshit. But I suspect, and I say this as a compliment, that he's a superb politician. He has a special rapport with the chairman, as you know, and that's important, too.

A subordinate:

David is a fix-it person. He knows how to fix things. He's very good at it. He's also a savvy businessman, a very effective manager, and he's very smart. He can make decisive decisions about people, which a lot of people can't. He delegates a lot, he doesn't get caught up in detail, and he's not easily conned by other people. He's also a very good strategic thinker. The combination of being willing to delegate and being a good strategic thinker means he'd really prefer spending most of his days sitting in his office with his feet up on his desk, thinking, and letting his subordinates do their jobs. And that's what he does to a large degree. And it is very successful.

A subordinate:

David gives feedback constantly, and he's very good at praising people and at trying to get them back on the right track. His normal way of saying something is bad is to say something like, "Well I'm glad you're working on that, but why don't you try it from this point of view?" He encourages people to take risks, and allows them to fail and to learn. He's done that with me and it's made a lot of difference. He's very generous in giving other people credit when they are due, and at making them visible to the top management at AX.

A top officer at AX:

David is one of the most promising younger managers. I suspect that there is a good chance that he will be running this company some day. He has matured a lot in his time here at AX, and he's continuing to mature. When he first came with us he was fairly arrogant and insensitive to people issues. He could be rather ruthless. I think he's mellowed a lot, especially in the last five years.

A subordinate:

David is very, very successful. That's what I think of first when I think of him. He's also not afraid to make hard decisions, like firing people. He's persistent. He has tremendous strength in financial areas. He's good at delegating, and willing to do it. He's very direct, no bullshit. He's accessible to his people. He has a terrific feeling for the use of management tools. And he's very good at picking people. I think that he has constructed, with AX top management's help, an incredibly strong management team here at McAllister.

A peer at AX:

I worked with David a number of years ago on an acquisition deal. For all practical purposes, he was the key element in making the deal work. The whole idea of the acquisition was at least partly his. In working with the key parties, which included the top management of AX and the top management at the firm we acquired, David demonstrated that he was a knowledgeable, solid citizen. He spoke only when he had something important to say, and very quickly he earned the respect of just about everybody. He developed a strong rapport with both the top management at AX, and the key parties of the firm we eventually acquired. He essentially used that credibility to bring the two parties together, and eventually get them to make a deal. He handled himself just beautifully throughout the entire negotiating period. He certainly earned my respect.

Another subordinate:

David has been the key ingredient in turning this division around. He has made most of the key pricing decisions and he's handled all the key personnel decisions. Internally he's set up the nuts and bolts of a good management system, characterized by rigorous financial analysis and systematic personnel management. He's worked very adroitly with top management at AX to make sure that they're comfortable with what we're doing, and he involved himself heavily in resolving tradeoffs, and resolving conflicts in our organization.

He's a very manipulative person. He gets things done when other people can't. His style is to say in that calm, even voice of his, "Listen, I'm not going to jam this down your throat," just as he's jamming it down your throat.

A top manager at AX:

I've known David for a number of years now; I knew him when he was a bright young person right out of business school. Back then he was a bit of a pain in the ass. I can still remember a time when he sat in my office telling me what a great deal he'd just structured for the corporation. He was patting himself on the back constantly while I was thinking what a bunch of bullshit the deal was. I very much supported the chairman's idea to put David in charge of Zodiac Products. The idea was to see what he could do. He's about as bright as you'll find. The question I had in my mind was could he really manage? Well, of course, it's incredible what he did. I mean, just incredible. He won the respect of everyone there, even the blue-collar workers, and he did it quickly.

David can be very tough. He can be unemotional about people decisions. He's one of the few people I've ever met that can be terribly objective about people.

I think David is a person that you could put into a CEO role in almost any division, and he'd do a good job.

A subordinate:

We have a terrific organization here. Good, intelligent, young people working well together. David gets the major credit for this. He's pulled together a management team and he's fostered the team approach to our business.

David is excellent at motivating people. He uses both positive and negative reinforcers. If you're doing a good job and he sees it, he'll tell you that he appreciates it, he'll compliment you on it in front of others, and he'll reflect your performance in salary. He'll even make sure that you get the deserved visibility in top management. But if you screw up badly, you'll be fired. There's no question about that. He'll tell you that you're doing badly, he'll be fair; but if you can't do it, you're out.

Two things about him that impressed me in particular. One is he's a very cool person. He doesn't overreact or get excited. He's fairly unemotional about things, and that can be very helpful. And two, it's not difficult to give him bad news, or to bring problems to him. He makes it rather easy. I personally have enjoyed working for him more than anyone else I've ever worked for.

A subordinate:

David believes very strongly in team work. He also believes in delegation. He's told me a dozen times, "Listen, this is your area, decisions in this area are yours," and then he follows through. He has great restraint. He lets me do my job. He also goes out of his way to try to make people strong, not to make them weak; to make people grow. It's terrific.

A top officer of AX:

David has developed good relationships with an awful lot of people within AX. He knows and is respected by people in almost all the corporate staff functions as well as his boss, his boss's boss, and of course the chairman. I suspect he spends time and effort nurturing those relationships and using them to help him do a good job at McAllister and to help out his own boss with various corporate projects.

From Connolly

I've seen quite a few management styles here at AX, and I've tried to pick and choose and put together something that works for me. The style I use today, or try to use, I would characterize with the words *team, mutual confidence, abhorrence of being blind-sided, informal, no personality cult, high involvement, loyalty,* and *straight/no politics.* I also like very much to work with aggressive people who take initiative, who I can delegate to.

I put in a pretty long week, although I'm spending more and more time these days with my family, too. I never used to take vacations, and was here at all hours, and was probably over-intense. That has changed. I suspect that contributed to my divorce. I'm spending more time with my new family and enjoying it a great deal, and I encourage others in my organization to do the same.

I see my job as essentially one of working with others to create a game plan (which we, of course, rework periodically), to make sure that everyone understands that game plan, to watch to see that we're operating by it, to discuss exceptions to it, and to maintain relationships with my subordinates by giving people a kick in the seat when they need it, and a pat on the back when they need it, by delegating as much as possible, to let them implement their part of their plan and by showing interest in people.

I like my job very much. It's very challenging. I'm in no hurry to move on. Ultimately I think I'd like to be one of the three or four people who have a chance to shape the strategy of the corporation as a whole. I am not interested in acquiring vast wealth. I'm making pretty good money right now, and am enjoying life very much.

CASE 9
BIOGRAPHY OF AN EXECUTIVE (A)
Paul L. Rosenberg and Jay W. Lorsch

This biographical case stems from information collected at three different times in Tony Roderick's life. The earlier material comes from a casewriting assignment in the Harvard Program for Management Development. Roderick chose to write about his career and was also interviewed about the issues he faced. That assignment was completed in 1968 when Roderick was 37 years old. Two years later, Roderick was again interviewed by an HBS casewriter and provided information on his early post-PMD years. The balance of the data is based on interviews which took place when Roderick was 48 years old.

In the account which follows, Roderick's observations will be labeled as based on "PMD," or "recent," interviews to distinguish among these three data-gathering periods.

Overview

Born in 1930 of Middle Eastern immigrant parents, Tony Roderick entered school at age four and, consequently, graduated from high school at the early age of 16. He then entered the California Institute of Technology, earning a BS, MS, and PhD by age 26.

During his final two years in graduate school, he was first an instructor and then an assistant professor. During graduate school, Roderick married Donna, whom he had known since high school. Tony and Donna have four children: Bill (23), Jane (21), John (18), and Kathy (7). Both of Roderick's parents are still alive, living in the same California community where Tony grew up.

Roderick left Cal Tech at age 26 and joined Alleron, a large, high-technology conglomerate. He remained at Alleron for 17 years, working in R&D as a research engineer, in the International Division, and then as a manager of research. At age 37 he left Alleron for 16 weeks to enter the Program for Management Development (PMD) at Harvard Business School. Returning to Alleron upon completion of PMD, Roderick remained with the company for five more years. In 1973 at age 43, Roderick left Alleron to join TMU Corporation, where he remained for two years, attempting to revitalize and manage an aging plant. In 1975, Roderick left TMU Corporation and joined Harrison Corporation, a large multinational conglomerate. Roderick became plant manager of a failing Harrison plant in Frankfort, Kentucky. After three year as plant manager and a successful turnaround, Roderick, at age 47, was promoted to vice president for operations of another division of Harrison Corporation. He remains in that position today.

The Move from Cal Tech to Alleron

In the PMD interviews, Roderick noted that he left Cal Tech because teaching and abstract research just were not his "cup of tea." He wanted to see the end result, and the right job in industry could provide the opportunity for highly visible results. Besides that, he felt a need to leave the West

Coast where parents and in-laws were nearby. He had seen the results within the family of too many generations living in one place. There was a very heavy emphasis on family relationships. Life centered on the ethnic group. People got mired down with the relatives and their problems, and it consumed a lot of time.

As Tony put it:

> Even now, when I go back and visit the family it still bothers me, although now I can at least kid my mother about it. But I still have to listen to all that gossip. They'll say things like, "Why did so-and-so marry an Italian? Italians are bad, but maybe this guy will come around. . . ." Donna's parents aren't Middle Eastern, but they also lived in the valley. Donna comes from strong Dutch stock—hard-working people, but it's the same closed-in situation. My friends knew they had to escape, and Donna and I did, too. In fact, not one of the top 25 students in my high school graduating class still lives in the community.

Roderick described the beginnings of his relationship with his wife, Donna:

> I'd known Donna in high school. When I was in college, Donna was dating my best friend. In fact, we used to double date quite a bit. But Donna is not Catholic and my best friend was, and so I knew nothing would develop between them. He dated her for a whole year, and I bided my time. Then we began dating. We got married in 1954 when I was in graduate school. By that time I was getting tired of asking her to marry me. One night I was busy running an experiment in the lab, and she walked in and said, "Isn't it about time we got married?" I said, "Don't bother me now, I've got to finish this experiment"—that's how it happened.

Roderick continued:

> I don't think I ever intended to make a career of teaching at Cal Tech. But I really enjoyed it there because of the people, and I

really hit the valley of depression after joining Alleron because I missed those people really stimulating and challenging me. But fundamental research just wasn't it for a lot of reasons. One reason was just taking a look at the caliber of people I had to compete with. I ended up in association with some guys I considered near geniuses and that's just the wrong ballpark for me. Plus during the two years on my doctoral thesis the stimulus of doing fundamental research just wasn't there.

> I enjoyed the couple of years on the faculty—teaching and all—but I don't think at any time there was any real effort and desire to make a career of it. Anyhow, the time came and the situation resolved itself, and it was time for me to leave and there was a very clear process in my mind of what I was going to do. One, I wanted to get into an industrial lab where there was clearly a measurable result—the company or lab wanted something done; something clear in mind and where the task would be concretely defined and you could clearly identify yourself with having done it or not done it. Short-term tasks. You know, you can work on fundamental research jobs forever. You're never, never finished. The other thing that I wanted was a situation where I was visible—where the product of my effort would move the system. In talking it over with my department head he said, "Just tell me where you want to interview and I'll set it up for you." He was in a position to do that. He suggested Du Pont and Dow and so on, and I said, "No." He was kind of hurt. He was a consultant for them. But I didn't want to go to one of those big places where I would not be visible and my efforts would not have a visible effect. I had to be seen. I didn't want to get lost. Finally, he suggested Bunch (later consolidated into Alleron) and the name Bob Jackson which I immediately recognized. Bob Jackson had just recently joined Bunch and was starting a research lab. I jumped at the opportunity to talk to Bob. I lined up some other interviews, but it was the first one, and I pretty much made

up my mind right there on the spot. Everything fit. I could be in on the ground floor in building an organization. But Bob Jackson was the key factor in my decision. He had gotten his PhD from Cal Tech about 15 or more years ahead of me. He was a guy I could learn from—a guy with unquestioned integrity. By integrity I mean not only that he never lied but also there was no undercutting. It's impossible for Bob to hurt anybody. He didn't use people. He dealt fairly with everyone and went to great lengths to make sure his people got credit for their contributions. There are, to me, a lot of similarities between Bob and my father. I've learned a lot observing Bob. He's a very reserved guy—no emotions, at least they never show. I really never had any social dealings with him because of the age gap, but I really missed him when he left the lab to become VP. I tried imitating him for a while. I forgot I was myself.

After talking to Bob, I gave some thought to cancelling the other interviews, but I didn't. I talked to my father and I talked to at least three guys who I thought could listen to what I had to say and the mental gyrations I was going through. The head of the department and two other profs—very close friends. They were in my wedding party. I knew even then that you do get emotionally wrapped up in things, and I needed at least the feedback on what other people heard me saying. Were there any flaws—any contradictions? I guess all of them came through and said, "Well, it's pretty clear. You ought to go to work there." That was it. I was putting my chips on Jackson. But it didn't bother me.

Interviewer: "What did your folks think about your career choice, leaving Cal Tech and going to Alleron?"

Roderick: The funny thing was I didn't want to go off to college. I guess I just wanted to get out and work. My dad ran a grocery store and I thought, "Man, we could make a lot of money. Buy up the corner, build a supermarket." I always wanted that, to be building something and to manage it. But I guess I didn't appreciate my dad's lack of interest in the grocery business. He must have shuddered internally at what I was saying. He started about the eleventh grade; he just used every subtle and nonsubtle means of trying to convince me that life would be better if I got a college education. He would get friends who were doctors and engineers to drop in on Sunday afternoons and inevitable I ended up in a chat with them. Finally, I struck up a deal with my dad. I'd go down to Cal Tech and take the entrance exam, and if I didn't get in, he'd stop his campaign. I think it's impossible for me to take an exam without seeing if I can score a hundred. So I went down and I was kind of scared. Here were all these veterans with "slip-sticks" and oh, boy! But after a week and a half I got a notice: "You're accepted." My dad really conned me. He knew me well enough to know that if he got me to that point . . . my dad couldn't afford it but somehow he got me through the first couple of years and after that I did various things to help out.

So my mother and dad were very happy with my choice of going off to college. My staying on to teach . . . my dad doesn't show that much emotion. I guess he was pleased with it. My mother—it was pretty obvious. Her chest puffed up. She went around and told everybody that her son was a professor. Even though she couldn't pronounce it. Being foreign, it came out "feffesor." But she was quite pleased even so. The decision to leave that and go and work for a company—in her eyes—was a comedown. In the old country you couldn't get a higher position or one with more prestige than a teacher. So why should I give this up and do routine and mundane work for a living? And she was quite broken up by my not staying in the area. I'm sure she had very strong feelings about it. My dad just doesn't show emotion. Once I had made a decision, he merely said, "That's your decision."

Alleron and the Move to PMD

Alleron turned out to be a good choice for Roderick. It was a conglomerate with annual sales nearing a billion dollars. Its several major divisions were engaged in state-of-the-art work in diverse technologies. The pace of technical progress was accelerating throughout the company. Tony had worked hard; he had learned a lot; he had built and molded a group of 60 competent R&D men into one of the top teams in the industry; and in the process he had achieved a solid reputation—not only in Alleron but industry-wide. Upon reaching his mid-30s, Tony's name was associated with some very solid technical advances. To achieve this success he had often put in as much as 18 hours a day, but it was fun. The problems in developing new concepts and reducing them to practice had been challenging and exciting. He had liked the job. He had a hell of an achievement need. He liked to accomplish things and he took a lot of pride when they were done—when he could say "I did that." Tony also needed some praise. The bosses or people who had been most effective with him were those who had astutely handed out praise for a job well done. He needed a challenge. He needed to solve problems. After almost ten years in research, however, the technical problems began to lose the element of challeng for him. Government contract R&D had become like a merry-go-around. You went through the same cycle over and over. The need for challenge had boiled over into a competitive thing.

He had often found himself in a verbal duel with people, particularly his oldest son Bill. This realization made him feel strongly that he had to do something about the situation. At about the same time, Tony also began to realize that, although he had been managing research, he was not a good manager. This was a shock to Tony, but many people pointed it out to him. This eventually led to the decision to enter PMD.

In a PMD interview in 1968, Tony spoke of events and feelings which culminated in the move to the PMD.

Roderick: About a year ago I was made aware of the fact that I was ignoring my family, and the shocking thing is that I didn't realize it. I went to Alleron in 1956, threw myself into the job, working up to 18 hours a day and having a hell of a lot of fun. Any time it came up as a question my answer was, "I'm doing it for my family." John Bowles, a behavioral scientist in our group, kept prodding me about this in a weekly session we were having. Finally, one day he got through my thick skull. I wasn't doing it for my family. I was doing it for me . . . because I like it. That realization started a chain of events. It was the first time I sat down and asked myself why I did anything. . . . It's been a slow, hard struggle to get my family, career, and job in perspective. I have three children, but I realized I didn't know my oldest son . . . I really didn't. And it was a shock to me.

The jolt came from a comment my dad made when we were visiting my parents. The kids were running around the house with my sister's kids. Christ, it was just bedlam! And my parents are getting to the age where they can't take much of that. So I started to chew Billy out, and, being kind of insensitive to this, I was chewing him out in front of his cousins. When it was all over my dad said, "How old is Billy?" He was 10 or 11 or something. Dad said, "Do you realize you've had him for half of all the time you're ever going to have him?" My dad is a phenomenally great man. I've never known a man like my father . . . just . . . no man can match him. His comment hit me like a sledgehammer.

You know, in retrospect, I can see that my father ran his grocery store unsuccessfully. But he didn't really care. He just did it to earn a living. The supermarkets after the Second World War ran the corner groceries out of business. Even I saw it coming. I saw it as a kid! A phenomenally scholarly guy, he was trained in the old country—both of my parents emigrated here—as a school teacher. When he came over he had a working knowledge of four languages. Unfortunately, when he landed here before the First World War, those opportunities weren't available to teach or make use of his training. But it didn't change him any. We had books and newspapers—at least four foreign-language newspapers around the house all the time. He never did find out what football, baseball, or Boy Scouts were all about. He just read and took great delight in discussions of economics and philosophy and relations with people of similar interests. It drives my mother wild. She doesn't understand why you have to have books on the economic conditions of South America. He's just tremendously stimulating to talk to. Like a lot of other people . . . well, I always went back to him for advice because he could get to the core of a problem very quickly. You know—"You're ducking the real issue"—that kind of thing. That example with my boy—"You're missing the point, Tony, with children." He was very good at that and still is.

Anyway, it was that piercing comment by him, at that point, that stimulated my concern for my son Bill. I realized that I didn't know him and I wasn't going to have him as a child for very long. Now, I'm more concerned about him. He's a good kid . . . he loves life . . . he lives every day to the hilt, and I haven't done that, so I don't know

how to approach a kid like that. We're worlds apart. I just don't know how to relate to him. I had been telling him things like, "Look ahead—plan for the future." Man, what a waste of time for a kid like that!

To bridge the gap, the thing I have to do is try the things that he likes just to find some common ground. I've at least got to try them and be honest with myself. If I try them and can't do them, I've got to admit it and not force myself because kids spot a phony pretty quick. He's pointed out to me a number of times where I haven't quite been . . . you know, where it's been phony. He's phenomenally disarming in that manner. And then I thought, "I've got to find ways to get him to try things that appeal to me." I read a lot, all sorts of books—to see if that was a common ground. I had to find ways to say "yes" rather than automatically saying "no" whenever he requested something of me.

You know my son has told me that I frighten him . . . that I come across as a big, overwhelming type of person, and that's not surprising. I guess he sees me at home . . . I can remember half a dozen times when he was small—three or four o'clock in the morning—I'd be working on a government contract proposal, and he'd stumble out of bed going to the bathroom and there's his father working away. It comes as a surprise to find out what your kid's image of you is, and I . . . I was kind of formidable, rather unapproachable.

You know, formidable is a word a number of people at Alleron applied to me as well. For instance, when I got promoted to department manager, I picked my successor—a guy that worked for me—to take over my section. A phenomenally good technical man, completely different from me in personality. He's an introvert, and I guess I'm pretty much an extrovert. I wanted him to succeed so badly that I didn't realize what I was doing to him, and I . . . I'm amazed that he stayed. There were weekly meetings where the section managers and I held a review of what had happened and what we were going to do, and without realizing it I was making him a whipping boy in those meetings. Then, in a separate private discussion with one of the other section managers, we were discussing some particularly tough problem and we weren't getting anywhere. Finally, this guy just blew up and said, "God damn it! You're not going to do to me what you're doing to Ralph Glass," who was the guy I picked. Then he stormed out of the office. Jesus! you know it was a bolt out of the blue. What the hell am I doing to Ralph Glass? So a couple of days later I went back and said, "What the hell! What are you talking about?" In the discussion that followed I realized that I wasn't being fair to Glass or to myself and I wasn't doing a very good job of managing either that meeting or those guys or anything else. I was being overbearing, and if a subordinate faltered, I'd take over and do the job myself. That's one example . . . and that guy eventually quit. Things like that . . . I . . . became aware that I didn't know diddly-bo about the whole business. I began to realize that I had grown strictly concerned with me. I thought I cared about the people working for me, but I didn't . . . not really concerned with their goals. I'd hire engineers and use them as technicians. Most of what they wrote I'd heavily reword and not worry about their feelings in the process. I didn't help them to rephrase things. I just rewrote them. I was the dominant person. I just overwhelmed the guys working for me. And I demanded a lot—a lot of loyalty to the job and to what I was trying to do. If I had difficulty with a guy I'd just cut him off. I wouldn't have any dealings with him. He'd become a nonperson as far as I was concerned. Of course, I couldn't do that with my boss Al Bosch, who succeeded Bob Jackson as head of the lab. So I'd stew like hell for three or four days until I just had to contact him.

Finally, as I got more responsibilities, I began to realize that no matter how hard driving I was, I just couldn't do it all. I was forced to try to give some of my men some real responsibility, and I found it was hard to do. They responded to a greater degree than my skill . . . and my boss, Al, was no help. He wasn't any better at managing than I was. I started to read and pretty much decided I needed training in the whole business of managing a business because the technical area just didn't light a fire in me any more. Solving a research problem, regardless of how technically difficult it was, just no longer interested me.

Another factor in the decision was money. Money is important. I can't ever remember not being interested in money. During the Depression, I was just a kid about four or five, and my father ran a little grocery store, and just two doors away was where the people lined up to get the handouts, the welfare lines. I can still remember my mother saying, "Look how terrible," or "shameful" . . . there's a real connotation of "bad" associated with being in that situation although I personally didn't experience it—being in those welfare lines. Some of my relatives and some of my neighbors were in those lines and there was a tremendous amount of shame. I can't ever remember not being interested in a buck. My salary in the last few years has far more than covered my needs, but, contrary to what I've read, I've never stopped being interested in money or making more. But I'm not sure how to assess this factor. Probably it's related to my desire for praise. . . .

So I decided to leave Alleron and go back to school on my own. I discussed it with my wife and surprisingly she was pleased, tremendously relieved—I sensed it. I had a hell of a lot of problems . . . I worked sleepless nights . . . difficulty getting things done . . . I had a boss . . . who's good, but . . . totally incapable of handling my kind of situation. His career objectives are just so totally different that he doesn't understand Tony Roderick's. He's 15 years older and the head of the R&D department, and he's realized his ambition. That's all he wants to be:

head of R&D. When the break finally came, he reacted like I wanted his job and that since I couldn't get it I was giving up—quitting. To this day he just doesn't understand. But anyhow, my wife . . . her reaction made a lasting impression and convinced me more and more that I came across to my family in a rather negative way. I realized then finally the extent to which I was weighing on her. She had tried in the past a couple of times to get involved . . . I have tended to kind of curl problems up inside on my own and I guess let them gnaw away at me. She's not one of those persons who I would pound out my company technical problems with, although I've hashed out other problems with her—things that concerned me. She's a great listener. Maybe I thought that technical problems were such an integral part of the problems I've felt that I just haven't exposed her to them. When I'd be having problems with my immediate boss, Al Bosch, she'd find me sitting up at 2:00 A.M. struggling with them. She'd say, "Why don't you quit?" But that wasn't the solution for me. There were some rough times. My stomach got all tied in knots and did flip-flops. I came home a real bear and was very short with my kids . . . and did not realize it. Literally, I had married the job. It sounds like textbook cases, doesn't it? But you just don't realize you're in it. . . .

When I went to Bob Jackson, who was the VP in charge of research, development, and engineering at that time, he finally realized the intensity of the problem although I had been talking to him about it for around a year. Bob realized that it wasn't just a case of 35-year-old restlessness. So, when the break came with R&D and I finally blew up with my boss, Bob talked me into going over into corporate planning and going for a shorter program than a two-year MBA because a lot of that would be superfluous because of the experience I had. I began working for a boss, the VP in planning, who had a much broader perspective and was much more aware of the problems that people like my-

self go through. He had been at Harvard in the AMP 10 years ago and was tremendously involved in the behavioral type of thing and was the first to bring on board the behavioral scientists here. In fact, as I found later . . . he saw a number of people in this organization committing career suicide. He had a list of those guys and my name was on that list!

Alleron after PMD

Roderick entered the Program for Management Development at age 37 and enjoyed the program. He felt that he had learned a considerable amount about managing an enterprise, and about managing people.

At age 40, several years after Roderick had left PMD and returned to Alleron, he made the following comments in the course of the "post-PMD" interviews:

You know, the quality of my life has changed. One of the ways that I can really experience this change—be reminded of it—is getting a kick or pleasure out of somebody else's win. Like—when I down in Savannah [Georgia] at NTL [National Training Laboratory] there was a guy in my T-group who was with a competitor of ours. He was personally very involved in their bid on a very large multimillion-dollar contract for the government. It meant a lot to him—we talked about it. Just recently, I saw in *The Wall Street Journal* that he had won it—I think over one of our divisions. But it really gave me a thrill to see that Bill had won. I wrote him a letter and sent him some materials I'd gotten from the lab and got a nice letter back from him. It felt good to see him win—I knew he really wanted it.

Another example—we've got a big meeting with a group of corporate VPs Monday to make a presentation on our response to technological change in the industry. My guys are doing the work, and I've made a couple of bad decisions that have put a couple of them in the pressure cooker. This thing is very important. Talk about visibility, man, it's going to be me, my guys, and a bunch of VPs all day. But I haven't jumped in and bailed people out. I'm going to just make some introductory remarks and hand 'em the ball. They're going to have to put in a lot of time this weekend—a lot of time—to be ready. I don't know, I may come in for a little while—maybe not. Last night I just cut the grass. I don't get those flip-flops in my stomach anymore when the deadline gets close.

I still have to struggle to keep on an even keel. I caught myself the other day debating with my youngest son over keeping the doors closed when the air conditioning is on. I had to send him away to get my bearings. "Now what are you doing?" I asked myself. But more often than not I am more aware of people and their feelings. My wife says, "You're getting better."

Ten years later, at age 48, Roderick described the return to Alleron. He had returned at age 39, and his first assignment pleased him greatly.

He became director of engineering for a division. It was managing engineering, not supervising research, and he began to put his developing skills into practice. Tony's goal was to become an operating manager, and within a year and a half he thought he had his chance.

Tony's boss, general manager of the division, was given the added responsibility of running a second division which had serious problems. To turn around a failing plant, his boss put an experienced plant manager, who was approaching retirement, in charge and asked Tony to go to the plant as the plant manager's technical adviser. As Tony recalls, his boss said, "You go out there and give the plant manager some help, and we'll send you in as assistant to the general manager. We'll make up some title, and in a year's time you'll take over as plant manager." Tony jumped at the chance. That's what it was all about! He was on his way! Except that his boss had never told the plant manager that Tony would eventually take over in a year's time. Tony walked into a hornet's nest and didn't know it:

When I arrived, the plant manager was awfully suspicious. He must have been thinking "What's the boss sending this guy down for?" It was an impossible situation, he didn't know what my function was, and all I could do was suggest and push and that kind of thing, and I couldn't give an order to anybody. The plant manager never knew I was supposed to eventually replace him. He just assumed I was a spy. I guess I was a little naive. Today, I'd recognize that situation.

At any rate, the new job meant moving my family, but my wife and I decided to wait until the end of the school year. After six months, I went to my boss and said, "Hey, Ken—ah, where do we stand, you know—it's been six months." Ken said, "Hey, get a house—I don't want a plant manager who doesn't live in the community. You've got to live down here." Okay, fine. I went down with my wife Donna, and we looked around for houses.

It may sound naive as hell, but it just never occurred to me that my boss didn't mean what he said when he told me to go down there. In June, after school was out, I went to him and asked him where we stood. I wanted to start planning ahead. He said, "Fine, get a house, start moving down. I don't understand why you haven't moved yet but start looking for a house—get ready to take over in a few months." But by September the thing came to a head. My boss called me and said, "Here's what we'd like you to do. We'd like you to go in as the engineering manager of this plant for another year. We want to replace so-and-so. We don't think he's doing the job. Would you go in under Clarkson as the engineering manager and we'll look at it again in another year." A real blow, but no way! I was naive in some areas, but I also knew what was going on in that plant. That plant had problems you couldn't begin to believe, and the losses were going to be in the millions.

But the guy who was helping to create some of the problems in that plant was Joe Clarkson, the plant manager—a personal friend of my boss. I was in a hell of a quandary, so I just said, "That doesn't fit my career path." That made me sound like a pompous ass, but I had no alternative. I just said, "No way am I going into that situation."

I would have been fired on the spot, but I had 15 good years at Alleron and had a reasonably good reputation in operations. I think Ken, the division manager, wanted to fire me, but Bob Jackson or someone convinced him not to. In any event, I was told "Get back to corporate headquarters." I sat there in an office doing nothing, like a pariah, for two months. And emotionally it just tore me apart because I wanted to be part of the organization, but I just couldn't do it.

His first shot as plant manager a shambles, Roderick was finally assigned to the International Division to work with some Japanese engineers on a joint venture to produce an Alleron offshore plant. That joint venture led to another and Roderick spent several years globetrotting, advising on the building of Alleron plants in a number of countries.

I was very heavily involved in the international operation, which I was reasonably happy doing except one thing came along that significantly changed my whole attitude and my whole life—my daughter Kathy was born.

You know, those long stays in Japan— you've got a choice of how you're going to handle yourself personally and, man, I'll tell you, after two or three weeks there, I couldn't wait to get back home and one of the consequences was Kathy.

When Donna found out she was pregnant—this is 11 years after our last child—it was traumatic, a tremendous emotional shock. And we discussed abortions at the time. I said, "Donna, if you want to have an abortion, all right." But if you knew my wife, she might think about it, but there's no way she would do it. She would consider it, she says, but I knew she would never do it; it's just not in her nature. So we decided to have the child, and people told us, "Hey, it's great to have a second family—keeps you young." Keeps you *tired* as far as I'm concerned.

When Kathy was born one of the things that I realized was that I had missed my three oldest kids; they had gotten away from me. I was so busy being whatever it is I wanted to be, that I really missed them growing up. And I just wasn't going to let that happen with this one. I was going to be around as much as I could with that child. She was born in '72, right in the middle of this Japanese deal. To people who haven't traveled much it sounds like, "Gee, overseas, that's exciting and wonderful." But let me tell you something—a motel in Milan is no different than a motel in Des Moines; the trouble is you don't speak the language and that makes it worse, and your work schedule is such that your time is consumed. You really don't have time to sightsee. But, most important, there's nobody to share it with you. You don't have your wife with you.

That international travel started to wear pretty thin. Kathy came along and I said, "Boy, you're not going to miss this one. You're just going to spend as much time with that child as you can. You missed it on the first ones." I don't recall spending very much time with my eldest son, Bill, when he was a child. That was factor number one that made me stop to think about to what extent I wanted to continue doing what I was doing.

At Kathy's birth Roderick faced another problem with the Japanese joint ventures. He became convinced that the plants they were building were designed to build a product which Roderick felt did not match the Japanese marketplace. Coming back from one of his trips in 1972, Roderick wrote a trip report. The plant project had reached the critical stage—they had to order equipment to produce a certain size product, and he was convinced it was the wrong product:

I wrote the report, handed it to my boss, and Mount Vesuvius was a little firecracker compared to his reaction. It just blew the roof because my boss considered himself the world's greatest marketer. I got called in and he said, "Who the hell do you think you are telling me what the market is? What do you know about marketing?" We argued back and forth until my boss said finally, "Look, we're behind schedule on this plant, place the orders on the equipment as planned." I said I couldn't in good conscience place those orders for equipment that I thought was the wrong equipment. We eventually got to the point where I said, "Here's what I'll do. I won't send my report to the normal distribution list; I'll send it just to you with one copy in my file and one copy elsewhere. But I won't cut those equipment orders." It was a Mexican standoff. So he went ahead and he ordered the equipment and, sure enough, they ended up missing the market, and I turned to other things.

If you take all that together, Kathy's coming along, she's about a year old at this point, I'm getting sick and tired of traveling overseas. And sitting down and thinking through, what am I doing? What am I doing? And what is my status in this company? And I concluded I had to leave Alleron. I concluded that my bosses thought very highly of me as a PhD in a research lab, but none of them could make that final step of making me a plant manager. Ten years later, now I see that part of it was a simple case of

"familiarity breeds contempt"—if you're too long in an organization you're stereotyped. No one in Alleron was ever going to listen to me about marketing or manufacturing because they could only see me as a PhD research scientist.

So I came to the conclusion that I had to leave Alleron, and it hurt. Alleron was almost like a family. I had grown up with that company. It was a little frightening—it's very safe if you're in one company, and you know the people and the power structure. I had never been with another company.

Eighteen months after leaving Alleron, Roderick was once again looking for a job as he emerged from a "disastrous" interlude with a company called TMU Corporation. He had joined TMU because they offered him what he had always wanted, the opportunity to manage a plant. The company, seeking to get into the machine tool business, had purchased an old steel foundry which had been shut down for several years. With Roderick's experience in materials, he seemed like a perfect fit to manage the foundry. They offered him the plant manager's position, and he jumped at the chance.

In my mind, what I couldn't get at Alleron I was going to get at TMU. It was a chance to manage the whole entity, and I wanted it so badly that I didn't bother to go look at the plant I was to take over. I called up a friend of mine, who knew the industry, and asked him to go take a look at the plant and give me his opinion. He came back and said, "Tony, it's a catastrophe. You aren't seriously thinking of taking this, are you?"

But I completely discarded his advice. He told me all the problems, but at that point I had mentally made the decision to leave Alleron, and here was an opportunity to get out and be a plant manager. To a certain extent, I wanted to show them at Alleron that they were wrong about me . . . well, the plant *was* a catastrophe: dirt floors, very low crane heights, still running on DC current—in 1973! Incredible! What was funny was that, as I realized later, I walked into exactly the same situation I had once criticized at Alleron, a complete mismatch of plant facilities for the product line and the marketplace.

Roderick rebuilt the plant's labor force, starting from scratch, learning a great deal about managing a plant in the process:

I learned that you make things happen out on a production floor, not in an office. You can have the world's greatest staff, and they won't do it for you. It's the people on the floor who get the stuff out the door. If you don't have their hearts and minds, if they're only doing it because of that paycheck, you're going to fail. I had to force myself to learn how to go out on that floor and talk to people and get a feel for what's going on. A second great thing that happened to me at TMU was that I was put under a superb division head—Jim Stanfield. You've heard of the fastest gun in the West, well Jim had to be the fastest mind in the United States—just click, click, click, and a problem is solved. I learned a hell of a lot from him, superfast mind and super great human being, and a technical guy to begin with! He always handled everything with a smile and a joke, even when he was demanding results he did it with a very soft touch.

Working with Stanfield, Roderick put together a multimillion-dollar capital development plan to build and upgrade facilities, and the TMU president approved it. Then everything began to turn sour. In a top-management shakeup, the company president was replaced and the new management cancelled the equipment orders for the new capital development program.

They just cut the legs out from under us. I was shocked. I went to Jim and said, "Jim, if we accept this, then it means that the whole basis on which we put together the overhaul of this division was wrong. It was a lie. We can't operate this way." I said, "Jim, there's no future here for me, I've got to leave." He said he understood and that he would help me find another company. And he wasn't bitter, and we're still friends. Jim never let operating problems interfere with his personal relations.

At this point Roderick was asked to compare Bob Jackson, his earlier mentor at Alleron, with Jim Stanfield at TMU Corporation.

Bob was independently wealthy, so no one could use the leverage on him of threatening to fire him, and he never had any desire to get out of the technical area. He represented a guy who could not be intimidated or bullied by the rest of the organization. I admired that. But Bob was not somebody you could ever get close to. He never had close friends—super-introverted kind of guy.

Jim is just the opposite about social things, very gregarious, always stepping out on the dance floor. But in mental capability they were alike—two of the fastest minds I've ever seen. But their managing styles were totally different, too. I never heard Bob Jackson say anything negative about anybody, while Jim has very clear-cut opinions on everyone. Jim could be ruthless. Once he made up his mind that a guy couldn't contribute, he'd cut his legs off. Bob Jackson would never do that. If he found that a guy didn't fit a position, he'd move heaven and earth to fit the guy in somewhere else. I guess I'm more like Jim. If I'm in a raft with 13 people and it only holds 12, I don't have any trouble throwing the 13th guy overboard, I really don't. Bob Jackson could find a way to inflate that raft to carry 13. I couldn't do that, and Jim Stanfield couldn't either. I guess you'd have to say I'm tough-minded. When I see a solution to a problem

I literally close my mind to other solutions and start working to implement the solution I have.

So Roderick left TMU, and two months later, April of 1975, became plant manager of the Frankfort, Kentucky, plant of a division of Harrison Corporation, a large multinational conglomerate.

Plant Manager

Harrison had been looking for a manager of its Frankfort plant for quite some time before they hired Roderick. The original Harrison family, who had built the company, were quite antiunion. Part of old Dr. Harrison's strategy was to locate his plants in out-of-the-way places where the unions could not get at them. Harrison would find a rural spot and pick a town where they could be the dominant industry. Frankfort was, at the time the plant was built, just such a location. One of Roderick's predecessors had been Joe Jones, an extremely outgoing man with excellent ties in the community and a good rapport with the workers on the shop floor. Under his leadership, the plant remained nonunion. When he left in 1972, union organizing at the plant began in earnest. Jones's successor was Gary Nelson, a good manager, but unskilled in interpersonal relations. A union was formed, racial tensions in the plant mounted, and a failure to reach agreement on a contract sent the plant out on its first strike. The strike soon exploded into violence—windows were broken, cars shotgunned, and Harrison reacted by going all out to keep the plant operating. They brought in supervisors from other plants, hired people off the street, and kept the plant in operation. But, in the process, anti-Harrison feeling in the community rose extraordinarily high. Eventually,

the strike was settled, the union decertified, and a new, more sensitive, plant manager hired, but bad feelings lingered.

It was into this environment that Roderick entered in 1973 and sought to turn the plant around. As he described it:

> The plant had been an assembly line making many small parts, but the current need was for huge, customized components, which required a job shop. If you get four of the same, it's a big production run. The plant was in transition, and they had orders galore, past due because of the strike and other reasons. Phil Harrison, president of Harrison, was getting phone calls from presidents of companies who had invested $200 to $300 million in capital equipment which couldn't run because we hadn't delivered two or three of our customized components. They couldn't order quickly from someone else, because of the quality requirements. So, Phil Harrison was getting these irate calls. And you can bet that if *he* had a $100 or $200 million investment sitting there idle, in *his* plant, he'd make some phone calls, too. That's what I walked into.
>
> But in spite of all that, the minute I walked into that plant it was like coming home. It was like walking into the old Alleron plant I'd been in. They even used the same green paint. I could sense the same noise, I could see the machines . . . and I said to myself, "Tony, this is a job you can do."
>
> When I was hired, they brought me to corporate headquarters, all the way up to talk to the corporate VP of personnel because they were so sensitive to union and personnel problems in Frankfort. I needed this VP's blessing before taking on such a sensitive job. But I remember him thinking I was presumptuous about the whole thing. Because, after walking into that plant, I knew I could handle it, and I didn't want to talk about the plant manager's job. I wanted to talk about my *next* assignment because I knew I could handle this first one. It was the

height of conceit, they told me that later, but I just felt very sure.

Well, everything came together for me at Frankfort, all the things that I ever learned at Alleron, at Harvard, at TMU. It crystallized all at once; it was just an extremely good combination of everything. There are eight or nine managers who report to the plant manager and, with two exceptions, they were all superb people. At first, I couldn't understand why they were having such trouble. The problem turned out to be very simple. Each of them was a great manager, but they were all going in different directions. Each one of those guys was honestly and conscientiously trying to respond to what he saw was the most pressing priority. And my predecessor was not a leader. His lack of leadership instilled in my mind the absolute importance of leadership in running any organization. A manufacturing plant is not a democracy. There's got to be one guy who says, "I am the leader, I'll lead you out of the wilderness."

Well, they responded beautifully. They said, "If Roderick's willing to take the heat, we'll give it to him." And things started to turn around immediately. When I came in April, we had $9 million of orders past due, a $30 million backlog, and we were shipping $0.75 million of orders per month. But by September, we were shipping at $2.4 million in one month.

The one poor manager I had when I started was my personnel manager, a crucial position. It's very hard to pass judgment on a guy; but within a few months I knew this was the wrong guy for the job, so I let him go and was fortunate to find a good replacement.

One of the keys to my success at Frankfort was the support I got from upper-level management. My boss was very supportive, and I was producing. Like corporate audits, for example. It seemed as though the plant was being audited every five minutes in those days, and one day two guys came in to audit the purchasing system. These guys were driving me nuts, and I physically threw them out of the building. These auditors reported in two levels higher than my boss's boss, at the group level, so you can imagine what my boss heard. But he took the guff—the orders were going out the door so he left me alone. He defined the result, not the activity, and I got him results.

I was working about 18 hours a day in the plant to get those results. My family wasn't around; we weren't going to move until after school let out. I was staying at a motel that wasn't more than 10 minutes from the plant. Hell, there wasn't anything to do, but be at the plant, and we were working three shifts trying to get all this backlog out. And I knew that, given the history that I learned about the workforce and the union and everything, that I had to get to that workforce, and I just spend all the time I could on that goddam floor, talking to everybody. I just went up and introduced myself, and I had a tough time.

In a sense I was preaching a sermon, "Hey, fellows, it's as important to you that we improve as it is to me." And we did a number of things. Like putting up big scoreboards showing every day's production versus plan, to let everyone know how we were doing because nobody ever knew. The first quarter that we went over the shipping target I said, "Hey, dinner is on me." I had this restaurant down the road come right into the plant, at all three shifts, and put on a tremendous spread of pork barbecue. All you can eat, and I'll tell you these guys can eat. Boy, did they fill up their plates. It was a spontaneous thing that I did that one time, but it really went over big. So after that, every quarter that we made budget, dinner was on me. Not it's almost a ritual. And while we were doing it we concluded that the guys really felt it was coming out of my pocket, and they figured, "Tony's with us." I felt I established my relationship with them on the basis that I was a fellow human being.

The most important thing to a guy on the

floor is his job. If he loses his job, he's in tough shape. So we instituted a program of quarterly talks on the state of the business for all the hourly workers. If there are tough times coming, they want to know it. They don't want to hear it by rumor. I can remember telling them, "Hey, you're going to hear rumors—baloney! Come and ask me before you repeat them. I'll tell you the truth."

In October of 1977, the vice president of operations of Roderick's division was promoted, and Tony became a candidate for the job. He was 46 years old. The new job would have meant leaving Frankfort and moving to California, not far from where he grew up, and where his parents still lived:

I discussed the move with my family. We had Thanksgiving dinner together and I brought up the subject indirectly. My oldest son Bill went through all of secondary school in one place, but Jane had to change schools in her senior year of high school. It was kind of traumatic. Both Bill and Jane were in college now, but there were still John and Kathy, and I concluded that it wasn't a good deal. I was never going to get a favorable response from my family.

But the family wasn't the only factor in the decision, I admit that. It was also that I didn't think I could get the kind of recognition I wanted in the new job. Harry [Roderick's boss] had done a superb job in overhauling the division, bringing it up to one of the most profitable divisions in the entire corporation. Well, one of the reasons I get a lot of visibility as plant manager in Frankfort is that when that Frankfort plant was in trouble, everyone in Harrison knew who the hell Tony Roderick was. Phil Harrison has to say, "Where the hell is that part?" and "Who's running that plant?" So you get visibility in that kind of situation. If I ended up getting Harry's job, I could go in and work my fanny off and improve profitability by maybe 1 percent, but who would know

it? It was a hard act to follow, combined with an unresponsive family situation. So I wrote a letter saying I didn't want to be a candidate for the job. But the family consideration wasn't that big. Actually, I would love to get back to California because my parents are old, and I would be close to them. And my wife's from there as well. But, it was more the nature of the job that decided it for me.

I thought for awhile that I could stay at Frankfort for the rest of my life. Everything was going great, the plant was a showpiece of the division; but about the time I turned down that chance to move up, I knew that I was getting bored. I was finding a hell of a lot of time to read, and I found myself looking at the stock market again. I didn't have time for either reading or the stock market before, so that was one sign. Also, there weren't really any new problems to tackle. I thought, "What the hell, this is a great life, and I'm reasonably well paid." But, like everybody else you know, inflation and so on, I'd started to think about that. I hadn't really decided what to do. Donna and I talked about it a few times. She's always willing to move. In fact, I kid her that she's happiest when she's leaving town. But I knew that if I moved up, I wouldn't have the contact with people on the floor that I had as a plant manager. I really needed to be down on that floor three or four times a day; it was like an addiction. If I got tied up in an all-day meeting, I'd call a coffee break and we would walk out on the floor, and I really enjoyed it. I started to second-guess myself, you know, what I want to do next. And I really hadn't come to any conclusion, but it was really stirring in my own mind. Sure this was the dream; this is what I wanted. I had gotten it, and I was reasonably successful at it. Now what? There were a lot of conflicting factors involved in it. One is the family. The other is, you know, why go on to the next job? If you enjoy doing this, why change? My own conclusion is that you grow or you die. It's like everything else in nature, if it doesn't grow, it dies.

So I stayed at the plant for another year, while Bill finished up college and Jane finished up her premed. And I was beginning to think twice about whether I wanted to move. I had become enchanted with the Frankfort area. But I concluded I would have to move on. Then, one day, I went up to corporate headquarters to talk with the head of the Roper Division. Roper was just the opposite of the division I was in. Roper Division was in deep trouble. They were getting plenty of attention from up top; they had all the visibility they wanted. The job offered was VP operations, and I came home and talked to Donna about it.

I had to think long and hard about it because again, timing wasn't quite right. It would have been better familywise if it had been a year later. Because then Bill would be out of school and Jane would be just about finished, John would be out of high school and would be going off to college somewhere. But you know, you have to take things as they come along; you can't really dictate time. But we finally concluded, or I concluded, I'd take it. And we would move in the summer. John would just have to live with moving in the senior year, and this time I actually discussed it with the two older kids.

"It isn't going to make much difference to us," Jane and Bill said. They were both living in apartments on campus, and they weren't spending any time at home. While they weren't enthusiastic, they weren't going to move with us anyway. They'd stay right here, and so I decided to take it.

Roderick began work as vice president of operations of the Roper Division of Harrison Corporation in February of 1978 at the age of 47. While he had planned to move his family to St. Paul, it quickly became apparent to Roderick that the key to salvaging the division's profitability lay in a large-scale move southward, the closing down of the division's huge antiquated facility in New York State, and a large-scale reduction of capacity. Roderick reported his recommendations and a couple of months later received indirect confirmation that his plan was being considered when he was told to "go slow on buying a house in St. Paul."

Roderick prepared a plan for relocation and new production facilities and began working to implement it. One part of this implementation involved closing the New York plant.

I would walk into the plant and here are these people who had worked there 30 years and came up through the ranks. Good, solid, skilled, first-class people. And you know you're shutting the plant down. It's not an easy thing to do, and it's not an easy thing to look those guys in the eye and know that you're the architect of a plan that, in effect, is going to shut this thing down. At one time there were 8,000 people working here, and it was a booming economy and so on. I personally found it tough to walk through that plant and look at those guys.

Roderick was asked by the casewriter in the current interviews to describe his children, and how they fit his changing career pattern.

Kathy was important and she still is important simply because I do with her what I think I didn't do with the other three children. It *is* possible to spoil children; but it is not possible to give them too much love, and there is a difference. As a child myself, I remember how often there was hugging and kissing by my grandparents and my parents, my mother, not my dad. I didn't do that with my first three children, but I sure as hell do it with my fourth one. It's almost a fetish that I'm constantly hugging and kissing her. The other thing that I've done with her is that I remember reading an article on Jackie Kennedy Onassis, a story on how she was raised. One of the things that the author pointed out was why Jackie seems to act the way she does, with a kind of beauty that is beyond her physical beauty. It's her self-confidence, which she got because her father told her constantly, "Jackie, you are a beautiful, brilliant, wonderful person." As a child he constantly told her that so she would believe it, and I tell the same thing constantly to Kathy.

Now my elder daughter, Jane, at 21 is really an exceptional person. Jane has got a first-class mind, really first-class, very sensitive to other people and very aware of what affects them, how she reacts to them, how they react to her. It was the realization that she had a first-class mind and, my God, this could all be wasted, that made a women's libber out of me. I never bothered with it until I thought, "I don't want this girl wasted. I want her to have all wonderful things in life to go with a first-class mind." And I have really literally pushed a lot of things at her, like ballet, art, painting, even some things I don't understand or appreciate fully because I want her to be exposed to them because she's got a mind that just sponges it all up. I think the relationship between Jane and me is very close. Donna has a very close relationship with all four kids. They talk to her on every subject. But she has always been open and she's got that, she's got what a lot of good mothers have, that ability to have a close relationship with each one of her children and they, I'm sure, share with her their most intimate thoughts, but not with me. On the other hand, Jane and I have a very close intellectual relationship. She just doesn't have time to read and learn everything she wants to, and when she is taking all these classes and she runs into some history, geography, or literature or anything else, she's got me as an infinite resource in that she can always come to me and get an open discussion on any subject. I can always be a sounding board. She can't get that out of her mother because her mother isn't technically trained or has not had that great an interest, until recently, in art, literature, and other stuff.

Now the two boys, that's different. Bill, my eldest son, is a completely independent guy. I don't know that he has a confidant anywhere. If he does, I don't know about it. My relationship with Bill really has changed only slightly since he was a child because I was really too busy to be at home. And it went astray, really went astray in junior high school and senior high school. . . .

I don't know what happened. I guess I hadn't paid any attention when it all started, but somewhere in high school he picked up the habit of smoking. That's nothing unusual, but he also picked up the marijuana habit. It never occurred to me, like a lot of parents, that he would even do that or that he would ever bring marijuana cigarettes into the house. Never even entered my mind until the day before his graduation from high school. They were having a night-before graduation celebration and he and three or four other kids were in a little Volkswagen driving around the neighborhood and they rolled that car over. It was a neighborhood very much like the one we live in now and it ended up on somebody's lawn and the boys were scattered all over the place and it was only a block away or half a block away from home and he came stumbling into the house screaming about his shoulder, and that he'd been in an accident. Well, I thought that he'd broken his shoulder or something so it was late at night and I had to get some clothes on. We jumped in the car and I was gonna take him to the hospital and we drove by the accident and as I drove by there was a policeman there. I said, "Hey, my son was involved in this and he appears to have been hurt. I'm gonna take him to the hospital and I'll be back." We took him to the hospital, they X-rayed him and found nothing was broken. Well, I took him home and the net result was that the police found marijuana in the car and he was still a juvenile. The police came and I'll tell you, that was a real blow. It's hard to describe that kind of a shock when something . . . you know . . I guess

I had it coming. I couldn't conceive of my son being involved with anything that had to do with marijuana. You have your own fictional vision of what your children are like, but if you don't deal with them you don't really know.

I went all through the range of emotions—sadness, anger, frustration, shock. It was incredible. I was angry, and I asked Bill and he said, "Yah, I did it." He didn't see anything wrong with it—"good stuff." To me, doing anything where you lose control of your ability to control yourself, it's just so obviously a stupid thing to do. We got a summons to go to juvenile court. Bill didn't have the least bit of regret, which added to my anger and frustration. Oh, he said, "Yah, I won't do it again, anymore," and all that kind of stuff, but lo and behold! the very night before we had to go to court he was out puffing away on marijuana which just . . . galled me. We ended up in juvenile court and they put Bill in front of the judge. I think the judge gave him the usual lecture and let him off with probation or some such thing. When we left there I completely fell apart. It all came in on me and I just broke down. It took me about an hour to recover. I cried, and the lawyer and Donna and Bill let me alone but it was . . it was hard to describe the hurt. You don't ever recover from that. And within a week Bill was back at marijuana and he wasn't about to change. I thought it was the end of the world, really. But it obviously wasn't.

It was a very awkward summer. There was just no way that Bill and I could even talk about it. In Bill's mind, it was just "good stuff." To me, you have to be a complete idiot to take any kind of drug because it's bad for your system. Who would want to lose control of his senses? Why the hell would you do that? Why would you ever put yourself in a position to be at the mercy of somebody else? In any event, we went through the summer and I just basically accustomed myself to the fact that there was no way I could stop him. He had already

been accepted to school up in Michigan and he went off to school and I thought I didn't know what other worse fate was going to befall me, but I had mentally prepared myself for the worst. He went off to school that fall and took the usual liberal arts. Grades were average, but, you know, I kind of had mentally given up on the kid. I was really exasperated with the whole damn thing and I didn't know if he was smoking marijuana or not, I really didn't. Then, in the second semester of his second year, two things happened that really changed the boy. He had to find an elective in the sciences to fill out his requirements, and somebody said, "Why don't you take geology because of the lab and it's a lot of fun, and you can get through it." Well, he took that course and that was it. That changed him completely. He found a field. I think he loved it because it allows him to be a Boy Scout for the rest of his life. I really believe that. But anyhow, he found a field or subject that really interested him. I tell you it was obvious when he came home at Easter that second semester he was a different person. He just bubbled over with enthusiasm and all he could talk about was geology. I just couldn't believe the difference. He quit acting like a boy and started acting, trying to act, like a man. I can't tell you how relieved I was. The other thing that happened is that one of the boys who was in his dorm or one of his roommates or something was killed in an automobile accident. I don't know whether the boy had been drinking or smoking dope or whatever it was, but he was alone in the car and it went off the road and Bill was very close to him, and it obviously had an impact on him. It really changed Bill, it really did. He was just so markedly different from one time to the next that it just stood out. To say that I was relieved is an understatement. Those were two rough years in terms of thinking about Bill; after that, it was a lot easier to talk to him. . . .

But Bill's attitude is totally different than mine when I was his age as a student. I worried about getting a job; I worried about earning money. In a sense, I envy him. If he does really worry or if he does have tensions, he sure doesn't show it. He either has supreme confidence in his ability or he's a fatalist. "What will happen will happen," and he doesn't get overly concerned about the things I would get concerned or upset about. I guess maybe my anger, when I show it as that, is really envy. I think very, very often that I wish to hell I could be like that, but I can't. For example, I can't get in an automobile and not know where I'm going. I've got to know exactly where I'm going. If I'm going to go to XYZ I've got to look at a map, I can't fly blind. In a sense that's reflective of the tremendous amount of effort I put in as an operating manager, planning ahead. I don't like surprises, I like to at least explore all the possibilities that I can think of, plan a course of action and, if something does happen, at least I thought about it in advance, and I'm prepared to deal with it. But my wife can get in the car and not know where she is going, and Bill is exactly the same way. I say, "Where are you going?" She says, "I'm going to blah, blah, blah."

"How do you get there?"

"I don't know."

"You don't know?"

"No."

"Well, how are you going to get there?"

"Well, we'll get there."

I mean, somebody will call her up and say, "Why don't you come over for coffee." And she answers, "Okay." She goes and gets in the car and she doesn't even know where the hell the friend lives, but somehow she gets there. I couldn't do that. And Bill doesn't do the kind of forward thinking that I think a guy ought to do. If he was me . . . I'm beginning to realize he isn't me and he isn't ever going to be me and that's very frustrating.

I think my wife Donna handles the frustrations a lot better than I do. When things were tough with Bill, with the court appear-

ance and all, Donna didn't show her emotion the way I did. She hid it, but I know she was supremely affected by it all. It is paradoxical because she can't watch a movie that has the slightest bit of emotion in it without gushing tears. But when it really counts, she keeps her emotions inside her. I'm sure the thing with Bill affected her, but I'll tell you frankly, I was so busy being hurt and feeling sorry for myself, just dealing with my own emotions, that I just didn't pay any attention to her during the worst part of the whole episode.

Donna's really incredible. I thank God for her. She is super-sensitive to my ups and downs when there's tension and pressure and frustration, and she has accommodated to it completely. When work is getting to me, I can come home and bitch and use her as a sounding board. She's a good listener and I get it all out of my system and tomorrow is another day. So my release in handling tension is to get it out, unload it on my wife, and once it's out, it's gone.

One of the real changes in Donna, and it's both a pleasure and a little frightening, has been since Kathy's gone to school. One of the things Kathy did is lengthen the time, as women will say, before Donna got out of "prison." I mean the time when the last child goes to school full time. Then the wife's day is her own. Up until that time, they're tied to the house. Kathy came along at the wrong time in terms of Donna getting out of "prison." But this year Kathy went to school full time. So, once Donna shoots her off to school in the morning, the rest of the day is hers until 3:00. It has not been that way for 25 years. And the change has been dramatic in Donna. It's both a joy for me to watch and a little frightening in the sense that you're losing something you're used to and you don't know what's coming. For example, Donna is basically, that I can see, the perfect mother and housewife. She just looked after those kids, she loves to sew, she hates all the washing, but she loves to sew, makes most of her own clothes and

Jane's and Kathy's. But now she's starting to become another person.

She's become involved with the local art museum. All the time, until a year ago, when we went overseas to visit, she just had a casual interest in the museums and all these other subjects. Now I mean I don't know whether it's a burden, but she's another person. The world is now open. I guess she feels she can now be what she was going to be. She's a college graduate and all that, and she's involved in art up to her eyeballs. I just found out the other day she's president of some garden club. She's a different person, I can see it. I can see it coming and I can see the pleasure she's got in it. I really take great joy in seeing that because, in a sense, she's becoming more fulfilled as a person. But it's a little frightening because what I'm used to, in the Donna I know, my wife, isn't going to be there anymore; it's just a few more years and then it's not the same. You can see it in small things, like there isn't always a shirt in the closet. Or it takes a little longer to get a button sewed on. Very small, subtle things, which really are a reflection of the fact that they are no longer number one priority. And I'm happy and at the same time a little, not concerned or afraid . . . . But everybody is uncomfortable with change. I guess that's it. Every time things change you're a little uncomfortable with it until the change is over. But she is changing.

Oh, I kid her about it. I tell her, "You know, you've got to get rid of that guy, I know he's around all right, I know his name, his name is Art." Art Museum, see? There's nothing to discuss, she's doing it, she's happy with it. I'm aware of the change, it's not a point of contention. I'm just expressing to you what I really haven't ever said to her, that I'm uncomfortable with change, but it's for the better. It is really for the better, and she's absolutely enjoying it. It's useless for me to call her in the afternoon, she's never home. I know she's gone. It is not a point of contention in any

shape or form. She is changing and it's good for her.

We're going to celebrate our 25th anniversary this summer. Just a week or two ago the two eldest kids said, "Jesus, 25 years! That's a long time. How do you stay married to each other for that long?" Now my parents have been married over 50 years and 25 seems like yesterday. How do you stay married? And I sometimes do wonder. If it's a successful marriage it's because of her, not because of me, because she's basically adjusted to everything. It sounds kind of mushy, but you fall in love with your wife many times during a marriage. It goes through a period when everything is so busy with the kids, or you take things for granted and suddenly, somewhere along the line, something happens or something is said and you suddenly see your wife in a different light and it's just like meeting her for the first time. You know, you just fall in love with her again, and it's great. Now that's happened two or three times during the 25 years. I can remember that it happened right after Kathy. . .

There's one other person in my life who's like Donna in that they serve as a great listener for me—someone who I can let it out to and bounce my ideas off. That's my father. When I really had tough problems, I went to my dad, and he listened. Confidants are usually good listeners, and I'm a robust talker. If I can talk, I can usually get enough out to solve my own problems. All I need is a good listener. My dad's perfect for that, and I usually don't share my personal problems with others. I have friends in the company, but we usually talk about operating problems. They're all really peripheral. My father and my wife are the real friends.

On the other hand, there aren't many people who I serve as listener to, the way my Dad and Donna listen to me. There are exceptions, of course. Like the guy who's plant manager now out in Nebraska. I talked to him this morning. He called me, said he wanted somebody to talk to. I don't attract a lot of people to be their confidant. The guys I do that with are the guys I have a reasonably close relationship within the day-to-day job. Other people are far better listeners for me than I am listener for them.

Roderick also spoke of his community life and recreational activities:

I read and read and read, and I enjoy it. I've tried a number of times to learn golf, but I just can't. It looks like it would be fun but I just can't get the enthusiasm for it. Currently, the kids are pushing me to learn tennis. I'm basically a lazy guy, I guess. I still enjoy swimming from time to time, only it's a little harder to do now. Both Donna and I enjoy foreign travel. It's ironic in that I detested it as part of my job because then I had nobody to share it with. Recently, I developed a strong desire to see where I'd come from. So we planned a trip for the entire family, including my parents, to the Middle East. My father was very excited about it, and practically led us up and down the mountains there. But my mother, to my disappointment, absolutely refused to go. I guess she preferred to preserve her memories of the place as they were when she left it as a child, but there was no way we could convince her to return. My kids, especially Bill and Jane, really loved this trip, but it struck me while we were there that, in a sense, I'm a schizophrenic. My parents are immigrants who have never become fully American, but my kids are completely American. I guess I have one foot in each world.

Roderick returned to a discussion of his career, and his future. As operations VP for the Roper Division, he has the sort of "turnaround" situation which he had initially faced at Frankfort. There is a lot of visibility and things *were* starting to turn around. His plans for consolidation and a move south had been approved, and he was now presiding over the execution of those plans.

For the next year, at least, Roderick felt committed to carrying out his consolidation plan. After that, the real doubts began:

I guess if someone came along and said we'd like you to run such and such a division, either my boss's job or the equivalent to his job, I'd sure as hell consider it and chances are I'd take it. Because so far I've never had a situation where sales organization reported to me as well as production. One of the problems is that the image I've got in this organization is of being antisales. I keep telling them, "I'm the most sales-oriented guy you've got. *You're* the undisciplined ones." That is a matter of personal pride that I'm very customer-oriented, I think, and I'd like to prove to myself that I could handle the profit and loss of an entire division. But, I'm not so sure anymore, not after spending a year at corporate headquarters, in a big building with a thousand people who produce no product but paper. I refer to it as a "funny farm." It's unreal because nobody there really appreciates the fact that their salary is the result of efforts by a bunch of guys on the production floor in little towns nobody's ever heard of. Some of them have never even seen the product. It's unreal that those people come to work every day and shuffle papers and really think they have accomplished something. It might be that I feel this way, as somebody once said, because I was not the kingpin there at corporate headquarters. And that may be right. I was just one of, Christ, there must be 50 vice presidents in that building. You're a dime a dozen. You run the Frankfort plant and you're the kingpin. I just felt no sense of accomplishment. Just seemed to wear me down. I often scheduled trips to the plant just to get out of there because I couldn't take it anymore. I wonder, in my own mind, how happy or fulfilling it would be to be a division manager. I really do. I don't know where the division managers get their fulfillment. They gotta get their kicks or pleasure of fulfillment out of getting the orders and getting the sales and building up the division into a bigger one. It seems to me that it would be very limiting for a person like me to try to operate that way. And I wonder not only how effective, but how happy I would be one level higher. I'm sure I'd like the money and the car and all the rest of the stuff that goes with it, but . . . I've actually been thinking about going completely out of Harrison and out of manufacturing management.

One thing has run through my mind, and it really at the moment is half-baked because I don't know if I could survive doing it. When I was at the Frankfort plant, I reached the point in the relationship with those hourly people where a number of the guys came to me or called me up and said, "Hey, I'd like to talk to you privately, it has nothing to do with the business." They had basically financial problems. Not, "I'm broke," but "What is Harrison stock, what is this stock business? Should I buy the insurance? What is it? How do you judge it?" Basic fundamental questions about how to handle their finances, how to make what you and I might take as the most elementary straightforward budgeting, financial, and monetary decisions. These people are struggling with them, and they don't have anywhere to turn and they don't trust anybody. He could go ask a broker what is Harrison stock or he could read any book if he could read, but you know, how do you ask the question without being embarrassed? Their problems were very real, and some of them had to do with, "There must be something wrong, I can't live on what I'm making, yet I know I should be able to." Or "You know I got a bright kid, how do I go about getting him into school?" A lot of these people don't know who to turn to. I put all this in the back of my mind, but it came out again recently when I got a call from a neighbor; you know the neighborhood I live in is pretty affluent, and this guy's a doctor. His father just died and left him and his sister a big chunk of stock and he didn't know what to do with it. He had to face a tax problem:

should he sell, shouldn't he sell? He had to pay inheritance tax and he just didn't know how to come to grips with how to evaluate the stock, what to do. He said, "Gee, you're obviously a successful businessman, you know all about these things." If he knew how I blew some things in the stock market he would never have asked me. He wanted my advice and help. There's probably a big wide-open field out there of people who need help on the basics. You can really feel a hell of a lot more satisfaction if you've helped somebody and you're involved with people you know on a real gut level. But as I say, it has been ticking around in my mind for the last couple of years and it came to a head here a few months ago with this doctor friend. It has a certain appeal to me because I think it's a real problem. It appeals to me because it's a one-on-one basis with some very real people. They're the salt of the earth. It allows my personal direct involvement. Right now, I'm two or three steps removed from people. You move up into a division management job and you're getting further and further removed from the people who make things happen. It's hard to put your finger on. Of course, it's a super high risk. As I say, it's only a thought and it's a pretty wild one, and I don't know that I'd ever end up doing it, but . . . I think about it.

BIOGRAPHY OF AN EXECUTIVE (B): THE SPOUSE'S PERSPECTIVE
Paul L. Rosenberg and Jay W. Lorsch

Case (A) traced the development of Tony Roderick, currently vice president of operations for a major division of a large multinational company. Case (A) attempted to explore Roderick's career, family life and future aspirations from his own perspective. This case presents Roderick's wife Donna's views on some of the same issues and events. It is based on interviews with Donna Roderick which took place when Tony Roderick was 48 years old.

Donna Roderick met her future husband Tony in 1948 when she was a high school student and he was in college. While Tony is of Middle Eastern parentage, Donna is of Dutch descent. They both lived in the same geographic area growing up. Donna's parents were divorced shortly after she graduated from college. As Donna describes it, "As I grew up and got into high school, they really should have been divorced, but they stayed together because of me until I finished college."

Donna and Tony were married in 1954 when he was still working on his PhD, and their first child was born in 1955. Donna spoke of the early days of their relationship:

> Meeting Tony was really the best thing that ever happened to me. He's always been sort of like my teacher; he's always known so much more than me, and he's always encouraged me to do whatever I want as far as learning was concerned. . . . He was a few years older, technically minded, and I was a home ec major. When we were married, I wanted to get away from my hometown and the family—especially Tony's. . . . I was an only child and Tony had a big, close-knit family—they liked to see each other often, and Tony's mother expected me to come and visit. I just didn't want my whole life to be involved with his family and not have a life of my own. So when we had the opportunity to move, I thought it was great.

Donna Roderick commented extensively on her relationship with her husband and on his character:

> Our relationship really hasn't changed that much over the years. Tony has always been a confidant and friend. . . . He's al-

ways encouraged me to grow. If we were talking about something and I said "Lord, I don't know anything about that," he'd say, "Why don't you find out about it?" We both like to travel, and he likes to plan his own itinerary and read about the countries beforehand. I don't do that nearly as much as he does, but now I'm finding I've really missed a lot by not doing my own reading. . . . Tony and I have gotten closer over time—sexually and emotionally. We've always talked, but I think I talk more now. I felt intimidated in our earlier years, and I don't feel that way anymore. I don't think Tony's aware that I was intimidated *or* that I no longer am. . . . But we talk about everything, including his work and his ambitions. We've always talked a lot about his work, and I appreciate that. There are so many wives who don't even know what their husbands do at work. And if he's in a bad mood, and I know there's a problem at work, I won't be worrying that it's something *I've* done that's put him in such a funk. . . . But we've certainly had our differences. For example, we would differ over the raising of the children. I allowed them to get away with more than he would. He'd come home and say: "Why did you allow them to do that?" But I wasn't a disciplinarian, and sometimes I felt guilty about not being strict enough. I felt really guilty when our oldest son, Bill, got in trouble with marijuana, and Tony felt guilty, too. . . . I don't think our marriage and homelife have changed much during the ups and downs that Tony's had in his career. Tony's moods might change, but it didn't interupt family activity very much.

Donna also spoke of her children and of Tony's relationship to them:

> When I had our first son, Bill, Tony was very happy because in his background boys were important. It was important to the family that I produced a boy as a first child. Originally we thought we wanted to have six children, but after two Tony decided that

was it. I persuaded him to have another child, and we did; but the children didn't get to see much of Tony while growing up because he was so involved in pursuing his career. I felt some resentment that he used to spend so much time at work and less with the family. He used to work Saturdays. He was a workaholic, although less so now that the kids are grown, except for Kathy. I guess family togetherness is not all it's cracked up to be. With three screaming kids back in those days, maybe he worked more to escape that. It sometimes seemed like the kids were happier if he *were* at work instead of at home—he intimidated them. . . . But I felt he should spend more time, especially with his eldest son. I think Tony realized that as they grew up; but by that time, the three oldest kids had reached a point where they didn't need him as much or didn't want to do something with their parents. At the time I spoke with Tony about spending more time with the kids, but I think he had the same philosophy that his father pursued. His father never played baseball with him or did anything that typical American fathers do. And he felt he grew up fine, and therefore he didn't really see the need for it. In earlier years, I think my relationship with Bill was better than Tony's was. Bill could come to me more easily than to his father if he had a problem. I was able to see both sides of a story, and it wasn't all black and white. With Tony in those days everything *was* black and white. . . . With John, our second son, Tony acted somewhat differently . . . he's trying not to go wrong with John the way he feels he went wrong with Bill. He said to me: "You're in charge of John; don't make me come home and be the ogre; you handle the situation because you're with him and I'm away so much." . . . Joan, our eldest daughter, has a completely different relationship with Tony. She's always been able to talk with him—they have a good rapport. If Joan ever felt Tony was doing something wrong, she'd tell

him. But the boys were different; they could not be critical—Tony just wouldn't stand it. . . . But as Tony has aged, his relations with his children are different, and I think our youngest child, Kathy, who's only seven, had a lot to do with it. Kathy's coming along has strengthened the bonds of our marriage. Everyone is grown up and gone, but *we* still have a young person at home. Tony's very affectionate toward Kathy. He never displayed as much affection with the other kids as with her. He's much more emotional and physical with Kathy than I am. I'm more restrained about such things. I think that Tony has realized that the youth of his three oldest children, their growing up, has escaped him, and with Kathy he's not going to let that happen again.

Donna Roderick also spoke of her husband's character and how she may or may not have influenced it:

Sometimes in Tony's work, people will see him as an ogre, but he's not that way at home. At work he demands perfection, and in a sense he treats his family the same way. He'll say, "These are the things that need to be done, and if you have anything to say about it, go ahead and say it, but makes sure they get done"—and he's usually right, which is very frustrating to me sometimes. . . . Tony's gotten more mellow as the years have gone by—he's more interested in talking things out than when we were first married. Then he was apt to be more dictatorial. I hope I've changed him a little but not by challenging him, more by unconsciously influencing him. I'm a lot more easy going than he is. I don't get upset the way he does, and that probably bothers him. All in all, I don't really think I've changed him that much.

As discussed on pages 465 and 466 of Case (A), Donna had recently begun to develop some outside interests, including volunteer work at a local art museum. She commented on this trend in her own life and its impact upon Tony:

> In earlier years raising three children who were close in age, I guess I was just so busy that I didn't have the time or need to fulfill myself as an individual. The way I did it at that time was by sewing. I could be creative doing that—sewing for myself and my children. . . . Kathy's birth extended that busy period where I really had to be at home. But Tony has encouraged me to do my thing, whatever it is. He's even suggested that I should take a job if I want to. I tell him I really don't want to work. Actually I'd like to work three days a week, but you can't find those jobs. I really feel that the mother should be in the home and should be there when their children need them. I don't think homemaking is a put-down job; I think it's very important, so I really haven't had any desire to work. Lately, though, I felt, "What if something should happen to my husband?" He keeps saying, "If I should die before I'm 65, you got it made; you don't have to work." But what if something happens afterwards and I would have to support myself? I would have to do something to prepare myself for that because I've never worked—I worked one year teaching school. I think about that a little, but I haven't pursued it. Perhaps when Kathy gets into junior high school or high school, I might consider taking a full-time job. . . . In the meantime, I *have* gotten involved as a part-time volunteer at the art museum, which I really enjoy. I'm surprised that Tony doesn't ask me what I'm doing with the art museum. He hasn't asked: "Are you enjoying it?" Maybe he's just so involved with his own work that he hasn't thought about it. He may see it as a change in me—there aren't always clean socks or a shirt to wear the next day. Those things have become less important to me—I'm no longer too concerned if there's some dust on the furniture.

> I think Tony's reactions to our daughter Joan's pursuit of a career are completely different. He's really encouraged her, even pushed her, to become a professional. I've encouraged her too—I mean why not use all of your mental abilities?—but I haven't encouraged her as much as Tony has.

Finally, Donna Roderick spoke of her husband's career, his changes of positions, and possibilities for the future:

> The hardest part about Tony's job changes and career has been the traveling and all that time away from home working. The weekends were rough—you can do a lot of things with other people and amuse yourself during weekdays, but weekends . . . well, most other women have their husbands home, and you feel like you are intruding if you participate in their activities. . . . That's changed now—Tony's always here on weekends. The only thing that I miss now is the social life that comes with being a plant manager. Since Tony's left the plant manager's job to commute to division headquarters, we just don't seem to have a lot of friends to do things with now. Tony doesn't have contacts here in town anymore because he doesn't have an office here. Everybody thinks of him as if he's moved, but we're still here. . . . I think Tony hated to leave the plant manager's job. I think he's questioning himself now saying: "Is all this extra work worth it—being away from home and family during the week?" I think he would have been content to remain here as plant manager for a few more years. It was a comfortable, emotionally rewarding job. He just doesn't *enjoy* life; he works too much; he can't sit and relax. We've talked about early retirement to do something like get into a business of his own, but I don't agree with early retirement unless we have enough money to live on—it's just too risky. . . . I guess when it comes right down to it, I just don't know what's going to happen.

CASE 10
CASE OF THE PLATEAUED
PERFORMER*
E. Kirby Warren, Thomas P. Ference,
and James A. F. Stoner

"Grow old along with me, the best is yet to be." When Robert Browning expressed this sentiment, he was not writing as a spokesman for business to promising young executives. Yet in the 19th century, while such poetry may have been out of place in business, the thought was very fitting.

In fact, until quite recently corporations have been able to reward capable employees with increased responsibilities and opportunities. Based on our recently completed research into nine companies, however, the more prevalent corporate sentiment might be, "Stay young along with me, or gone you well may be."

We found a large number of managers who, in the judgment of their organization, have "plateaued." That is, there is little or no likelihood that they will be promoted or receive substantial increases in duties and responsibilities. These long-service employees are being regarded with growing concern because plateauing is taking place more markedly, and frequently earlier, than in years past. Further, executives feel that plateauing is frequently accompanied by noticeable declines in both motivation and quality of performance.

While plateauing, like aging, is inevitable, in years past it was a more gradual process. For the most part, those who sought advancement in their managerial careers had ample opportunity to get it, within broad limits of ability, while those who did not

desire advancement (including competent individuals content with more modest levels of achievement and success) could be bypassed by colleagues still on the way up.

Today the situation has changed. Declining rates of corporate growth and an ever-increasing number of candidates have heightened the competition for managerial positions. The top of the pyramid is expanding much more slowly than the middle, and the managers who advanced rapidly during the growth boom of the 1960s are now at or just below the top. Their rate of career progress has necessarily slowed, and yet they are still many years from normal retirement and with many productive years to go. As these managers continue in their positions, the queue of younger, aggressive aspirants just below them is likely to grow longer, with spillover effects on opportunities and mobility rates throughout the organization.

This is precisely the dilemma confronting Benjamin Petersen, president and chairman of the board of Petersen Electronics.

Petersen founded the company in 1944, and it grew rapidly during the 1950s and 1960s, reaching sales of $200 million in 1968. Growth since then, though, has been uneven and at an average of less than 5 percent per year. However, 1974 was a good year, with sales and profits showing leaps of 12 percent and 18 percent, respectively.

Despite the good year, Benjamin Petersen, now 61 years old, is concerned about the company as he nears retirement. His major problem involves George Briggs, 53, vice-president of marketing, and Thomas Evans, national sales manager, who is 34 years old and one of Briggs's four subordinates. Nor have the implications of the situation between Briggs and Evans been lost on Victor Perkins, 39, vice-president of personnel.

Petersen's View of the Predicament

"When we started, a handful of people worked very hard and very closely to build something bigger than any of us. One of these people was George Briggs. George has been with me from the start, as have almost all of my vice-presidents and many of my key department heads.

"For the first five years, I did almost all the inventing and engineering work. Tom Carroll ran the plant and George Briggs knocked on doors and sold dreams as well as products for the company.

"As the company grew, we added people, and Briggs slowly worked his way up the sales organization. Eight years ago, when our vice-president of marketing retired, I put George in the job. He has market research, product management, sales service, and the field sales force (reporting through a national sales manager) under him, and he has really done a first-rate job all around.

"About 10 years ago we began bringing in more bright young engineers and MBAs and moved them along as fast as we could. Turnover has been high, and we have had some friction between our young Turks and the old guard.

"When business slowed in the early 70s, we also had a lot of competition among the newcomers. Those who stayed have continued to move up, and a few are now in or ready for top jobs. One of the best of this group is Tom Evans. He started with us nine years ago in the sales service area. Later, he spent three years in product management.

"George Briggs got him to move from head of the sales service department to assistant product manager. After one year, George Briggs named him manager of the product management group, and two years later, when the national sales manager retired, George named Evans to this post.

"That move both surprised and pleased me. I felt that Evans would make a good sales manager despite the fact that he had had little direct sales experience. I was afraid, however, that George would not want someone in that job who hadn't had years of field experience.

"I was even more surprised, though, when six months later (a month ago) George told me he was afraid Evans wasn't working out, and asked if I might be able to find a spot for him in the corporate personnel department. While I'm sure our recent upturn in sales is not solely Evans's doing, he certainly seems to be one of the keys. Despite his inexperience, he seems to have the field-sales organization behind him. He spends much of his time traveling with them, and from what I hear he has built a great team spirit.

"Despite this, George Briggs claims that he is in over his head and that it is just a matter of time before his inexperience gets him in trouble. I can't understand why George is so adamant. It's clearly not a personality clash, since they have always gotten along well in the past. In many ways, Briggs has been Evans's greatest booster until recently.

"Since George is going to need a replacement someday, I was hoping it would be Evans. If George doesn't retire before we have to move Evans again or lose him, I'd consider moving Evans to another area.

"When we were growing faster, I didn't worry about a new challenge opening up for our aggressive young managers—there were always new divisions, new lines—something to keep them stimulated and satisfied with their progress. Now I have less flexibility—my top people are several years from retirement. And yet I have some younger ones—like Evans, whom I would hate to lose—always pushing and expecting promotion.

"Evans is a good example of this; I could move him, but there are not that many *real* opportunities. He could go to personnel or engineering or even finance. Evans has the makings of a really fine general manager. But I'd hate to move him now. He really isn't ready for another shift—although he will be in a few years—and despite what George claims, I think he is stimulating teamwork and commitment in the sales organization as a result of his style.

"Finally, while I don't want to appear unduly critical of Briggs, I'm not sure he could get the job done in these competitive times without a bright young person like Evans to help him."

Briggs's Account of the Situation

"Before I say anything else, let me assure you there is nothing personal in my criticism of Evans.

"I like him. I have always liked him. I've done more for him than anyone else in the company. I've tried to coach him and bring him along just like a son.

"But the simple truth is that he's in way over his head and showing a side of his personality I've never seen before. I brought him along through sales service and product management and he was always eager to learn. While I couldn't give him a lot of help in those areas (frankly, there are aspects of them I don't yet fully understand), I still tried, and he paid attention and learned from others as well.

"The job of national sales manager, however, is a different story. In the other jobs Evans had—staff jobs—there was always time to consult, to consider, to get more data. In sales, however, all this participative stuff he uses takes too long. The national sales manager has to be able to make quick, intuitive decisions. What's more, like the captain of a ship, he has to inspire confidence in those below him. If the going gets rough, the only thing that keeps the sailors and junior officers from panicking is confidence in the skipper. I've been there and I know.

"Right now, with orders coming in strong, he can get away with all of his meetings and indecisiveness. The people in the field really like him and are trying to keep him out of trouble. In addition, I have been putting in sixty to seventy hours a week trying to do my job and also make sure he doesn't make any serious mistakes.

"I know he is feeling the pressure, too. Despite the fact that he has been his usual cheery self with others, when I call him in to question a decision he has made or is about to make, he gets very defensive. He was never that way with me before.

"I may have lost a little feel for what's going on in the field over the years, but I suspect I still know more about the customers and our sales people than Tom Evans will ever know. I've tried for the past seven months to get him to relax and let the old man help him, but it's no use. I'm convinced he's just not cut out for the job, and before we ruin him I want to transfer him somewhere else. He would probably make a fine personnel director someday. He's a very popular guy who seems genuinely interested in people and in helping them.

"I have talked with Ben Petersen about the move, and he has been stalling me. I understand his position. We have a lot of young comers like Evans in the company, and Ben has to worry about all of them. He told me that if anyone can bring Evans along I can, and he asked me to give it another try. I have, and things are getting worse.

"I hate to admit I made a mistake with Evans, but I plan on seeing Ben about this again tomorrow. We just can't keep putting it off. I'm sure he'll see it my way, and as soon as he approves the transfer, I'll have a heart-to-heart talk with Tom."

Evans's Side of the Story

"This has been a very hectic but rewarding period for me. I've never worked as hard in my life as I have during the last six months, but it's paying off. I'm learning more about sales each day, and more important, I'm building a first-rate sales team. My people are really enjoying the chance to share ideas and support each other.

"At first, particularly with our markets improving, it was hard to convince them to take time to meet with me and their subordinates. Gradually they have come to accept these sessions as an investment in team building. According to them, we've come up with more good ideas and ways to help each other than ever before.

"Fortunately, I also have experience in product management and sales service. Someday I hope to bring representatives from this department and market research into the meetings with regional and branch people, but that will take time. This kind of direct coordination and interaction doesn't fit with the thinking of some of the old-timers. I ran into objections when I tried this while I was working in the other departments.

"But I'm certain that in a year or so I'll be able to show, by results, that we should have more direct contact across department levels.

"My boss, George Briggs, will be one of the ones I will have to convince. He comes from the old school and is slow to give up what he knows used to work well.

"George likes me, though, and has given me a tremendous amount of help in the past. I was amazed when he told me he was giving me this job. Frankly, I didn't think I was ready yet, but he assured me I could handle it. I've gotten a big promotion every few years and I really like that—being challenged to learn new skills and getting more responsibility. I guess I have a real future here, although George won't be retiring for some years and I've gone as high as I can go until then.

"George is a very demanding person, but extremely fair, and he is always trying to help. I only hope I can justify the confidence he has shown in me. He stuck his neck out by giving me this chance, and I'm going to do all I can to succeed.

"Recently we have had a few run-ins. George Briggs works harder than anyone else around here, and perhaps the pressure of the last few years is getting to him. I wish he'd take a vacation this year and get away for a month or more and just relax. He hasn't taken more than a week off in the nine years I've been here, and for the last two years he hasn't taken any vacation.

"I can see the strain is taking its toll. Recently he has been on my back for all kinds of little things. He always was a worrier, but lately he has been testing me on numerous small issues. He keeps throwing out suggestions or second-guessing me on things that I've spent weeks working on with the field people.

"I try to assure him I'll be all right, and to please help me where I need it with the finance and production people who've had a tough time keeping up with our sales organization. It has been rough lately, but I'm sure it will work out. Sooner or later George will accept the fact that while I will never be able to run things the way he did, I can still get the job done for him.''

Perkins's Opinions

''I feel that George Briggs is threatened by Evans's seeming success with the field-sales people. I don't think he realizes it, but he is probably jealous of the speed with which Tom has taken charge. In all likelihood, he didn't expect Tom to be able to handle the field people as well as he has, as fast as he has.

''When George put Tom in the job, I have a feeling that he was looking forward to having him need much more help and advice from the old skipper. Tom does need help and advice, but he is getting most of what George would offer from his own subordinates and his peers. As a result, he has created a real team spirit below and around him, but he has upset George in the process.

''George not only has trouble seeing Tom depend so much on his subordinates, but I feel that he resents Tom's unwillingness to let him show him how he used to run the sales force.

''I may be wrong about this, of course. I am sure that George honestly believes that Tom's style will get him in trouble sooner or later. George is no doddering old fool who has to relive his past success in lower-level jobs. In the past, I'm told, he has shown real insight and interest in the big-picture aspects of the company.

''The trouble is he knows he has an outstanding sales manager, but I am not sure he has the same confidence in his ability as vice-president. I have seen this time and again, particularly in recent years. When a person begins to doubt his future, he sometimes drops back and begins to protect his past. With more competition from younger subordinates and the new methods that they often bring in, many of our experienced people find that doing their job the way they used to just isn't good enough anymore.

''Some reach out and seek new responsibilities to prove their worth. Others, however, return to the things they used to excel in and try to show that theirs is still the best way to do things. They don't even seem to realize that this puts them in direct competition with their subordinates.

''What do we do about this? I wish I knew! At lower levels, where you have more room to shift people around, you have more options. When the company is growing rapidly, the problem often takes care of itself.

''In this case, I am not sure what I will recommend if Ben Petersen asks my advice. Moving Tom to personnel at this time not only won't help me (I really don't have a spot for him), but it won't help Briggs or Evans either. Moving Evans now would be wasteful of the time and effort we've invested in his development. It may also reverse some important trends Tom has begun in team building within the sales force.

''If Briggs were seven or eight years older, we could wait it out. If the company were growing faster, we might be able to shift people. As things stand, however, I see only one approach as a possibility. And I'm not entirely sure it will work.

''I would recommend that we get busy refocusing Briggs's attention on the vice-president's job and get him to see that there is where he has to put his time and efforts. Perhaps the best thing would be to send him to one of the longer programs for senior executives. Don't forget he is a very bright and experienced person who still has a great deal to offer the company if we can figure out how to help him.''

What Would You Suggest?

Petersen has agreed to talk with Briggs about Evans tomorrow afternoon. As he thinks about the situation, he wonders what he can do that would be best for the company and everyone concerned. Should he go along with Briggs's recommendation that Evans be transferred to personnel? Or would it be preferable to do as Perkins has suggested and send Briggs to an executive program? As you consider the various perspectives, why do you think the impasse came to be and what do you think could be done to resolve it?

CASE 11
PATRICK J. J. RICH
Peter D. Blanck, James J. Dowd, and Jeffrey A. Sonnenfeld

There are certain times when a person has to think in a wider context about his life, his family, and the aspirations of each of its members. One has to ask oneself what really counts in life; one has to choose between worldly recognition and one's deepest needs as a person.

—Patrick Rich
Alcan Newsletter, 1981

For Patrick Jean Jacques Rich, the spring of 1982 was one of those times. Following a major reorganization at Alcan Aluminum Limited, he had made a decision which would dramatically affect both his career and his personal life: after six years at headquarters as an executive vice president and director, he had requested a transfer to the

position of field vice president:Europe, and simultaneously announced his decision not to seek reelection to Alcan's board.

Before assuming his new position in Geneva, however, Patrick Rich enjoyed a six-month leave from all his Alcan duties, studying and lecturing as an executive-in-residence at the Harvard Business School. During that time, he reflected on his career and his family life, past, present, and future. Working with members of the faculty, Patrick used several self-assessment instruments from the career management course to identify major themes in his life. Now 50 years old, he wished to gain new insight and direction from them as he began to plan the final stages in his career.

The Road to Montreal

In 1959, Pat Rich began his career with Alcan, the world's second-largest producer of aluminum, as finance director for a project in Guyana. Over the next 23 years, he and his family were relocated by the company 10 times. His international assignments took them successively to France, the U.K., Argentina, Spain, Italy, back to Argentina, and finally, to Alcan world headquarters in Montreal.

His career path included several positions in finance, including a time as chief financial officer for an Alcan company in Madrid. In 1971, he and his family moved to Argentina for the second time as he was named to head all operations in Latin America as area general manager. The Rich family remained in Argentina for five years.

Then, in 1976, Patrick was promoted to regional executive vice president for Continental Europe, the United Kingdom, Africa, and Latin America, stationed in Montreal and reporting directly to the president and CEO of Alcan Aluminum Limited. At the same time, he was appointed to Alcan's

board of directors. For his family, this
meant yet another move; however, his wife,
Louise, was particularly pleased with this
relocation. A native of Quebec, she welcomed the opportunity to return home and
expose her three children to their French-
Canadian roots.

Patrick's career continued to move upward, increasing in responsibility and in
scope. The company reorganized its regions
in 1977, and Patrick was named regional executive vice president for the Western Hemisphere. Of Alcan's three regions, this was
the largest in terms of production, sales
(1977: $2.5 billion), capital employed, and
number of employees. All area general
managers in the hemisphere reported to Patrick, who enjoyed full responsibility for all
operations in the region. Over the next four
years, he concentrated his efforts on three
critical issues: entry into the U.S. canning
business, improvement in labor relations,
and expansion of Alcan's natural resources
and energy base in Canada.

The Move to Geneva

In recognition of the increasingly complex
and expanding nature of Alcan's worldwide
operations, top management announced
in the final quarter of 1981 a major restructuring of the corporation. Philosophi-
cally geared toward decentralization, the
changes would greatly increase the autonomy of area vice presidents and general
managers in the field, while retaining responsibility for strategic decision making at
corporate headquarters.

The three world regions were divided
into seven areas, each to be headed by a
field vice president (FVP) located in that
area, not at headquarters. This effectively
eliminated the position of regional executive
vice president. Instead, the three incum-

bents were named senior vice presidents
(SVP) who, with the SVP-finance, would
constitute the office of the president. In
their new roles, the SVPs would be assigned
responsibilities for certain areas and corporate functions, "with a view to ensuring coordination and continuity of the management of the company, while providing flexibility to the CEO to shift these responsibilities as required."[1] Such responsibilities would be in the nature of dotted-
line reporting relationships, with the SVP
providing guidance and counsel to the assigned area or function.

As CEO and president David M. Culver
described it:[2]

> They will, as members of the office of the
> president, concentrate more on matters that
> may change the business rather than on run-
> ning it and will otherwise assist me in carry-
> ing out my role. In this context each will
> have designated geographical and func-
> tional contact responsibilities which will be
> interchangeable.

While he fully supported these management changes, Pat Rich found himself unable to accept the offered job of SVP. He
knew himself as one with "a need for human contact, for down-to-earth problems,
for crises and the rush of adrenalin they
bring."[3] As he would say later to Harvard
interviewers:

> I have to believe that one of my strengths
> has been leadership with autonomy, but one
> of my weaknesses is the fact that I am much
> more difficult to live with when I am not in

---

[1] From Alcan's Organizational Manual as reproduced in *Compass*, an Alcan publication, November
1981, p. 5.

[2] "New Year to Bring Management Changes," *Compass*, an Alcan publication, November 1981, p. 3.

[3] "Patrick Jean Jacques Rich Writes about His Return
to Europe," Alcan Newsletter, 1981.

the leadership position or when I have not got the autonomy.

That is in fact one of the reasons which has led me to my last decision, which, rather than become a senior vice president, a staff member of the president's office, to move back to the field as a field vice president, because I have difficulty without the driving wheel and that feeling of autonomy and accountability within a relatively defined field which I would selfishly describe as being mine.

* * * * *

The primary appeal was more not to get myself into a management setup where I would have been one of four senior vice presidents helping the president, being of a different generation—about eight or nine years' difference from my colleagues—and, therefore, having very often different opinions, and becoming probably a minority person.

Having decided then to turn down the SVP position, Patrick considered staying on in Montreal as field vice president:North America and Caribbean, but then made a surprise request: to be assigned to Geneva as FVP:Europe. He had two major reasons for this move.

First, he wanted a challenge. After six years of responsibility for North America and the Caribbean, Patrick felt that that area's strategic problems were relatively well under control; "in terms of intellectual excitement," he said, "the glamour . . . was gone." So despite the somewhat smaller scope of Alcan's European operations, that area was far more attractive because its problems were formidable: in 1981, Alcan: Europe had lost $71 million on sales of $1.4 billion. Given the increased autonomy of the position and the urgency of improving the area's financial performance, that

job would place Patrick where he would be happiest, "right in the line of fire."[4]

Second, and equally important, Pat wanted to go home. Now that his wife and children had solidified their sense of identity and belonging in French Canada, Patrick felt a similar need to show his children their European heritage as well. His oldest son Jean-Luc would remain in Montreal, but the two others would travel to Geneva with their parents. As Patrick said:

I could have stayed . . . but the opportunity to go back to Europe, it was the last moment where the kids, at least the two younger ones, were still at an age where they could look at Europe, get roots there— and that seemed to be an irresistible thing.

So Patrick Rich was named field vice president:Europe. Because he did not want to be the only FVP on the board of directors, he decided not to run for reelection in 1982. It was agreed that as FVP:Europe he would not report to the office of the president through one of the SVPs, his former peers, but would instead retain his direct reporting relationship to Alcan's president and CEO.

In the annual report for 1981, the following explanations of Patrick's unexpected reassignment were given:

The Chairman's message (excerpt):

Patrick Jean Jacques Rich will not be standing for reelection to the board at the annual meeting. Mr. Rich has served as a director since 1976 and it is gratifying that his expertise and sound counsel will remain available to Alcan from his new position as vice president:Europe. He is spending the first six months of the year at the Graduate School of Business Administration, Harvard University, as an "Executive in Residence."

---

[4] Ibid.

President's message (excerpt):

Patrick J. J. Rich, formerly an executive vice president, has, at his own request, given up his executive responsibilities in Montreal and is not standing for reelection as a director at the annual meeting. He will take up the post of vice president:Europe, in July this year.

Self-Assessment at Harvard Business School

Although Patrick Rich intended to devote his stay at Harvard primarily to the study of "the noneconomic—but essential—objectives of business enterprise,"[5] he spent a great deal of time studying himself. Working with faculty in organizational behavior, Patrick took several psychological tests and used other data-generating devices from the career management course to develop a greater understanding of the patterns and themes in his life. He subsequently identified six major life themes, which are presented with supporting evidence as Appendix A.

Next, Patrick discussed the themes and their implications in detail with members of the faculty. Based on those discussions, Pat set for himself a short-term agenda of five objectives, covering 1982–84. (See Exhibit 1.) Then, looking further into his future, Patrick decided that by 1984 he wanted to be prepared for his next major career decision. He foresaw three primary options:

1. Stay in Geneva a while longer, remaining as FVP:Europe.
2. Run for CEO:Alcan Aluminum Limited.
3. Take early retirement and teach, consult, and become a "professional director."

---

[5] Ibid.

Exhibit 1   Patrick Rich: Objectives 1982–1984

1. Turn Europe around.
2. Get financially independent.
3. Control the "beat the clock" by making time for mind and body.
4. Commit to: teaching time, sports time, outside boards time, family time. Need to go down to 50 hours per week in core business, by:
   Tightening up staff work.
   Proper decentralization.
   Improved time management.
5. Meditate with wife our "roots question." Get out all the facts, all the feelings:
   Family—ours, hers, mine.
   Life agenda/lifestyle.
   Location, friends, security.
6. Be prepared for next major career decision.

Appendix A
Notes on Patrick J. J. Rich's Themes, April 1982

The Themes

1. I want to make my environment predictable.
2. I want to get it all.
3. My life has paralleled that of my parents.
4. Importance of understanding and deepening family roots.
5. Beat the clock and the sense of mortality.
6. Need to influence my community.

Thematic Analysis

Theme 1.   I want to make my environment predictable.

Written Interview:

(At age 6–7) My world of friends changes: I know I am insecure, trying to break into a new circle: What an envy of this group of kids who are at ease with other! (1)[1]

It is 1938; my mother cries. Will Europe be at war? (2)

(As a child) I spell letters, playing-as a game . . . words come out . . . I can read!! (2)

(As a child) War in Spain; movies with the weekly news: screeching planes, little silhouettes collapsing. (2)

(As a child) Daddy is called up: Lieutenant in the Electricians Corps (Engineers). The war is announced. The adults cry. I do not understand. (2)

The prisoners came back from Auschwitz. Walking skeletons. An everlasting feeling of wounded, bent, damaged, humanity— soiled with the original sin of knowing its limits *now*. (4)

(At 26 years old) I develop an obsessive capacity to work and bulldoze my way through (officer's training school). (8)

(At 26) I discover war, death, fear, hatred, the somber business of torture, the inescapable ambiguities of the moral conscience—sophisms and truths all the same. (8)

I have formed an idea on management: very by-the-book but with that people dimension factored in (early career-12).

We get held up at gunpoint by three young toughs in our own house (midcareer). (18)

The new organization where I became

part of the group's top management at the age of 44, is a mess. (18)

By now, I see other advantages: being noncommitted in terms of decisions taken by the management committee from now on!, i.e., I remain a "virgin" (midcareer). (23)

I'm sure I will like my new job: it is right in the line of fire. (Alcan publication.)

24-Hour Diary:

Close adherence to time structure (continuous references to time-planning). Structure in diary is clear (finish—"The End"). "Assignment successfully completed. Now time has come for the daily chores: tidying up the rooms. . . ."

Rorschach Test:

Majority of "W" responses. Expression of a full appreciation of the environment.

Hand Test:

Total people and total environment responses are high, of approximately the same magnitude. Concern with both social and physical aspects of life.

Strong-Campbell:

Very high on adventure but also very low scores on more mechanical activities and office practices. May suggest a need for challenging activities, yet challenges that can be mastered and provide a sense of fulfillment. Profile scores also similar to that of an Army officer. Suggests some general need for order, predictability.

Learning Style Profile:

Active experimentation and abstract conceptualization high—control environ-

---

[1] Page references refer to the location of the data in Pat Rich's original written interview, and "Patrick Jean Jacques Rich Writes about His Return to Europe," Alcan publication. English is Pat Rich's second language.

ment through contingency analyses. Dominant learning style is the accommodation type—environmental planning, mediator and arbitrator qualities.

Lifestyle Representation:

Map of the world (carefully drawn) with arrows providing a sense of the direction of the emotions. Business presses (Alcan offices) located on the corners of the diagram and are in geometric form unlike the rest of the flowing diagram.

Career Anchors:

Managerial anchor rated the highest. Suggests a need both to integrate the efforts of others (as in theme 6), and to be fully accountable for total results, for *tying together* the different functions in an organization. $(Q)^2$

At Alcan liked the freedom of action but also liked the overall strategic guidance, support, and control. (I)

Developed my own network of associates and "followers" over the years at Alcan. (I)

Directive leadership style was emphasized by Pat. (I)

Would like to reorganize the family and plan joint activities. (Also see roots theme.) (I)

Projections and Dreams:

This is a big break away from the present. A jump into an environment almost unknown to the younger set . . . an environment in which Louise and I lived last 13 years ago—but in then relatively small style.

---

[2] Q = questionnaire part of *Career Anchors Exercise,* I = interview portion of *Career Anchors Exercise.*

Everything starts with "setting up shop." The shared pleasure of seeing things move in the right direction.

A life which leads, by more consulting and more boards and trading assignments, progressively to the *end* of business life.

Theme 2. I want to get it all.

Written Interview:

The thirst to express myself: the school is great—friends. (5)

Beautiful impression of discovery of foreign culture: the British morning tea ceremony. (6)

I discover museums, places, music, and jazz. It is picture time; the eye claims the place: films, drawings. (6)

Middle Class USA!! Commuting, the booze, sailing, dancing/necking weekends!! (7)

My first mentor . . . one of these amazingly well-balanced people who were the pride of Europe of the reconstruction! (9)

We enjoy music, theatre, opera, have two (successive) sailboats, a delightful house. (17)

Culture and physical needs are well balanced. (24)

Those who know me are aware that I like to consider problems intellectually. This character trait—a legacy of my European education, no doubt—has at times made me the object of teasing about "Cartesian logic." (Alcan publication)

Will I return to head office some day? I would like to reply with this approximate quote "The heart has reasons of which reason knows nothing." (Alcan publication)

24-Hour Diary:

Packed daily schedule from 6:00 A.M.–1:00 P.M. Continuous references to artistic interests (4 references to music, 2 references to literature).

Rorschach Test:

Majority of "W" responses. Sense of a need to take in the full environment. Quality of generalizations is in the grand manner.

Hand Test:

Active category high: interests in athletics and physical full life. Passive category low: interest is in influencing life outcomes.

Strong-Campbell:

High on adventure, music/dramatics, and art. Artistic theme is the highest. Very low scores on mechanical activities, science, and office practices. May suggest no interest in more mundane occupational interests.

Predisposition Test:

Tolerance for ambiguity is highest. May suggest mobile and flexible qualities.

AVL Study of Values:

All 6 values are relatively tightly grouped. There is a split—social, religious, and economic values are somewhat higher than theoretical, aesthetic, and political values. The holistic attainment theme (e.g., renaissance man values) is suggested by this split. Highest co-score is religious values, suggesting a value on spiritual fulfillment.

Lifestyle Representation:

Items on representation include social, athletic, artistic, business, family. Active full representations.

Career Anchors:

Variety is highly valued in terms of career orientation. This may suggest a value on intellectual challenges, new and varied tasks, in many different parts of the organization.   (Q)

Geographic security is not an issue; values excitement in world affairs.   (Q)

Autonomy is also valued in terms of organizational rules allowing a sense of freedom and mobility.   (Q)

Moved to next job as assignment became bureaucratic and static, needed a change.   (I)

Emphasis on personal freedom and financial independence.   (I)

Fear of sudden lack of mobility.   (I)

Fear of sudden shortening of vision and foresight.   (I)

Projections and Dreams:

We also know how its physical location looks (Geneva): the school on the other side of Geneva—university, the lake—are seen from the large garden of the house—my offices, penthouse view. What attractive settings.

The house, huge, a unit for common and individual activities. Music room, photo room, library, sauna, exercise room, the swimming pool—the individual rooms—everybody has his or her own private kingdom. An indoor-outdoor house where the kids play music, exercise, work, and think, receive their friends

. . . a house where people come to listen to music, to discuss politics, to eat . . .

Dinners, the box at the opera, theatre, so many ways to meet and invite people, to learn about their tastes, ideas, way of looking at life.

The rediscovery of medieval, Renaissance, 17th–18th century Europe.

Some teaching . . . to keep the mind sharp.

A very hectic, diverse life which gives us that diversity we have become addicted to.

Increasingly long vacations, more time visiting places while on business.

My team at the European head office is an interesting one, well-balanced, professional, cultured, and warm.

It looks like Switzerland would bring us the sophistication of European culture and surroundings, nature (sea and mountains) . . .

Theme 3. My life has paralleled that of my parents.

Written Interview:

I am at home lying under the piano (grand, grand piano) and father is playing. (1) (After merger) . . . in a fling of rage . . . back to France, with my parents. (13) . . . 1968, my mother is pathologically jealous of Louise. (13)

I have learned no longer to play "win or lose," but pace life and ambitions and dreams, and I have found the importance of challenge vs. status. (24)

24-Hour Diary:

Meanwhile I keep myself busy by writing a letter which needs to be done. (See vi-

deotaped interview for comparison to parents' tendency for "busy" lifestyle.)

AVL Study of Values:

Social value is high. May suggest a sense of unity in lifestyle patterns; parallel to parents' values and lifestyle.

Lifestyle Representation:

Picture of father playing the piano—self-interest in arts and music. (See also description of parents in videotaped interview.)

Career Anchors:

Like parents (mother) feel an urge for the international life. Excitement about foreign assignments. (I)

Being an only child—need to relate to other youngsters. Like being a part of a gang. (I)

Theme 4. Importance of understanding and deepening family roots.

Written Interview:

Louise and I love Spain and so do the kids; with the latter, we start to discover the problems of cultural and school adaptation. (13)

I finally decide to spend a lot of time with him (Son: Jean-Luc), realizing that I failed to help him (in school), I only criticize his performance instead of working with him to reestablish his self-esteem. I feel shame for my immature behavior. (17)

The family is a tight little unit, overcoming adversity. (19)

Meanwhile the family thrives. We are getting involved in a lot of social activities: hospital board, civic boards, etc. (2)

Mother dies on December 6, 1979. I live the last three weeks with her, sharing her death and helping my father. (21)

My reasons are complex (asking for a transfer): on the one hand, I want to find my roots which I have neglected so long and which our kids hardly know or understand. (21)

Family is a profound well of love and affection; my wife and I have developed inextricable roots of mutual trust and support and respect. (24)

We have no regrets whatever (leaving Montreal). My wife and children have been able to deepen their Quebec roots. (Alcan publication)

But the time has come—with the help of circumstance—for us to seek our other family roots: those of Europe, which my children hardly know. (Alcan publication)

24-Hour Diary:

Time has come to write letters I should have written one back to France.

Strong-Campbell:

Occupational scales high on social worker and minister. May suggest interest in interpersonal dynamics, perhaps family related. Concern with "existential" problems.

AVL Study of Values:

Social values high. May suggest concern for understanding social and familial roots.

Lifestyle Representation:

Family doing activities together. Hearts and flowers related to the love of the family. As a child watch father play the piano (related to theme 3).

Career Anchors:

One career change (to Montreal) help find wife's roots and give son (Jean-Luc) a new school environment. Leave Montreal as Louise has "cleaned up her roots problem." (I)

Family has had to fight for their share of my time. Emphasized nonoverlapping cycles of work and family. Work is now as important as family life. (I)

Projections and Dreams:

We are already working with a few "knowns" as a family: the realization that we will only be 4 instead of 5, Jean-Luc staying in Montreal . . .

Each morning early family wakeups.

The family looking inwards and outwards.

The pleasure of seeing things together all 4 (or 5 when Jean-Luc comes).

Helping the kids in becoming self-starters and living their own life, like Jean-Luc, who is the first test case.

Plus an ongoing dimension of intellectual challenge for all members of the family . . .

Theme 5. Beat the clock and the sense of mortality.

Written Interview:

I continue every year my reserve periods as a paratrooper reserve captain with the 11th choc: Probably in order to maintain a physical counterpart to business life. (14)

Personally, this is exciting: traveling

around, negotiating with governments, planning and doing living like a proconsul. (17)

I also travel a lot abroad: do some bullfighting in Spain at Don Pedro Domecq's domain in Jerez de la Frontera; Australia, Japan, Europe, North America. (17)

I have just turned 50 this year, and I feel that my life is entering a new phase. (Alcan publication)

There are certain times when a person has to think in a wider context about his life, his family and the aspirations of each of its members. (Alcan publication)

24-Hour Diary:

Don't forget to take the multivitamins.

Rorschach Test:

Majority of "W" responses. May suggest a concern for redirecting overall life plan. "D" responses are in the minority.

Hand Test:

Emphasis on active, social life—"living life to the fullest."

Strong-Campbell:

High on adventure. Low on more mundane activities (e.g., mechanical activities—see also theme 2).

Learning Style Inventory:

Active experimentation high—may suggest active/athletic needs in lifestyle.

Lifestyle Representation:

Continuous activity represented throughout. Skiing, sailing, travel, theatre, social activities.

"In the center (of the diagram): Flowers and hearts symbolization of the warm, carefree lifestyle."

Projections and Dreams:

Feeling time suspended for a while, unless the crew is more tempted by skiing, traveling through Europe or sitting lazily in the sun reading or playing backgammon and scrabble.

Waste time squandering . . .

A life where at times there is the self-imposed pause: life almost at metabolic level: our Quebec hideout in the Eastern mountains where we can disappear to for a week . . . to rearrange the basis for our intimacy, to walk through the forest, share thoughts and feelings which the other helps to clarify . . .

Or in the south of France where we "lose" time shopping for cheese in the local market, sitting for long moments at sidewalk cafes . . . remaining hapless and content . . .

That should do until my wife and I together make it 100 years! That would be a good full period of our lives! Living in the present every minute.

Theme 6. Need to influence my community.

Written Interview:

I became leader of another gang of children (at 7). (1)

I am aggressive, a little gang leader, and very playful. (3)

I seem to be an excellent pupil and I have lots of followers—but I am still at war with a gang led by the only boy I would really like to be friends with! (3)

I'm the leader, but I'm also top of my class. (4)

(At a summer camp) I talk to them (the children), organize things for them, knock one down every so often.   (6)

I have found the importance of challenge vs. status.   (24)

I have a need for human contact, for down-to-earth problems, for crises and the rush of adrenalin they bring on.   (Alcan publication)

For my part, I have tried to make a contribution to the building of Alcan and to the community that has welcomed me and my family.   (Alcan publication)

24-Hour Diary:

Emphasis on social interactions in diary (e.g., "fascinating conversations").

Hand Test:

People category is high and within the people category, affection, communication, and direction are all relatively high. Concern for relating, influencing, and leading people. A strong value in social exchanges.

Strong-Campbell:

High occupational themes: artistic, social, enterprising. An interest in self-expression, humanistic concerns, a verbal leader.

Very high on public speaking, law/politics. Profile similar to lawyer, public relations director, advertising executive, social worker, recreation leader, elected public official, personnel director, and public administrator.

Predisposition Test:

Solitude level is low, autonomy is moderate and tolerance for ambiguity is high.

Interest in a challenging and social lifestyle.

AVL Study of Values:

Highest score is social, suggesting a need to influence others and a need for human concern. Political score is the lowest, suggesting little concern for influence just for the sake of power.

Learning Style Profile:

High scores on active experimentation and abstract conceptualization. Learning style indicates an accommodating learning style. Relates to leadership and social skills.

Lifestyle Representation:

Picture of addressing a group, business or community meeting. Activities with friends and family. Several references to social activities in the description.

Career Anchors:

Sense of service/dedication to a cause rated as a primary value. Suggests a need to make the world a better place to live, improving the harmony among people. Interestingly, this is rated as the most essential career value, and would not be compromised or eliminated.   (Q)

Technical/functional anchors are considered to be nonessential to career and self-concept—this is too narrow a focus (also related to theme 2).   (Q)

In the Army liked leading people. Studied law and politics to satisfy the urge to lead. "I guess I have a gift for communication." "I like serving and leading."   (I)

(I am) a specialist in managing large numbers of people, large assets, and forecasting futures. Both a leadership urge and need for empathy and affiliation.   (I)

Ability to motivate employees rather than use coercion. An interest in human nature.   (I)

Projections and Dreams:

. . . (Discuss) how we can improve our communication with them (people).

. . . What a great pleasure to see the people, meet their families to understand them better.

(In the future) . . . we will draw our friends into a circle—more time for it!

Appendix B
Explanations of Data Sources in Appendix A

Written interview:

A written autobiography, from earliest childhood memories to the present. Described in John Kotter, Victor Faux, and Charles McArthur, *Self Assessment and Career Development* (Englewood Cliffs, N.J.: Prentice-Hall, 1978).

24-hour Diary:

A record of events, thoughts, and/or feelings over any 24-hour period. As described in Kotter, Faux, and McArthur.

Rorschach Test:

Four of Rorschach's famous "ink-blots" displayed for one minute each; subject records what he or she sees in the picture. Results scored as "W" ("whole") if description addresses entire blot, "D" if description addresses only a major portion (major detail), and "d" for minor details.

Hand Test:

Drawings of a single hand in various positions are shown to subjects, who are asked "What might this hand be doing?" Nine drawings and one blank sheet are displayed for one minute each. Responses are scored with regard to the description showing the hand as active or passive (e.g., grabbing versus resting) and interacting with people or with things (environment). Described in "The Hand Test," HBS Case Services, #9-476-010, Boston, 1975.

Strong-Campbell Interest Inventory:

Popular, reliable, and commercially available instrument for assessing occupational interests. Subjects respond to questions scored to evaluate their interests—not abilities—compared with test groups in dozens of fields. Owned by Stanford University and distributed through Interactive Scoring of Minneapolis, Minnesota.

Learning Style Inventory:

Test of cognitive style through forced-choice rankings of word groups. Styles include active experimentation, abstract conceptualization, reflective observation, and concrete experience. Profiles of learners are grouped into four clusters: convergers, divergers, accommodaters, and assimilators. This test by David Kolb is available through McBer and Co., Boston, Mass.

Lifestyle Representation:

Graphic depiction of lifestyle drawn by individual to represent self-perceived influences and priorities.

Career Anchors:

Test devised by Edgar H. Schein of MIT and Thomas Delong of Brigham Young University, for self-assessment purposes. Interview with partner and individual questionnaire results combined identify "core" occupational values such as: managerial, entrepreneurial, security, service/dedication to a cause, autonomy, variety, and technical/functional competence. The underlying premise is that analyzing the series of choices and career moves in one's past may reveal consistent preferences and direction of movement.

Predisposition Test:

Measures predispositions for solitude and autonomy, and tolerance for ambiguity. Developed by John W. Morse and J. W. Lorsch, *Organizations and their Members* (New York: Harper & Row, 1974).

AVL Study of Values:

Allport-Vernon-Lindsey study of values uses forced-choice rankings to rank-order values defined as: economic, political, social, religious, aesthetic, and theoretical. Available through Houghton-Mifflin Company, Boston, Massachusetts.

CASE 12
ROBERT ABBOUD
Liora Katzenstein and
Jeffrey A. Sonnenfeld

The Event

On Monday, April 28, 1980, The First Chicago Corporation, holding company for First National Bank of Chicago and one of the nation's leading banking organizations, dismissed its top-ranking officer, Chairman Robert Abboud. First Chicago also announced the immediate resignation of Harvey Kapnick, the second most powerful figure in the company. The bank announced

that Abboud would stay on until his successor was named.[1] The two executives were reported to have experienced a "short but stormy tenure together,"[2] which took its toll on the bank's earnings. The news about the departure of the two officers startled bankers around the country, who could not recollect a similar incident occurring at a leading bank. First Chicago Corporation, with assets of more than $30 billion, is the ninth largest banking organization in the United States.

A special meeting of the board of directors of the bank had been called to settle the dispute between Abboud and Kapnick over the division of duties between them. But according to Ben Heineman, Abboud's successor as chairman of First Chicago's Executive Committee, "the conflict between Abboud and Kapnick was irreconcilable and was beginning to permeate the entire organization."[3] Heineman explained that the essence of the issue was that Kapnick thought he was second in command on all matters. Abboud, however, contended that Kapnick was second only in certain areas, such as planning and information services, but not in banking matters.[4] Despite the efforts of the board of directors, the conflict caused both executives to leave.

Abboud

At 50 years of age, Abboud had acquired a reputation as a "pugnacious and controversial member of the banking fraternity."[5] He was once described by Gabriel Hauge, formerly chairman of the Manufacturers Hanover Trust Company, as "certainly a colorful, distinctive personality—a man of 90-degree angles rather than gentle

---

[1] *The Wall Street Journal*, April 29, 1980, p. 8.

[2] *Time*, May 12, 1980, p. 61.

[3] *Fortune*, June 2, 1980, p. 15.

[4] *New York Times*, April 29, 1980, p. D-11.

[5] Ibid.

curves."[6] In fact, *Fortune* magazine in its April 21, 1980, issue named Abboud "one of the 10 toughest bosses" in corporate America.[7]

It was reported[8] that Abboud's combativeness began in the streets of the working class Boston neighborhood where he grew up during the Great Depression. Abboud's growing years were characterized by scholastic achievement and leadership of an unbeatable high school football team. An athletic scholarship brought him to Harvard, from which he graduated in 1951. Soon thereafter he joined the Marines and was stationed in Korea where he earned a bronze star and a reputation for toughness. It is told that, "evacuating troops during one battle, Lieutenant Abboud exploded when the command post turned down his request for additional supplies. 'If you don't get those supplies up here on the double . . . , my last two rounds are going to be used on your position.' He got his supplies."[9]

After the war Abboud returned to Harvard, getting degrees both in law and in business administration. Gaylord Freeman, then First Chicago's chief executive officer, personally recruited Abboud to join the bank. Abboud was warned by his first boss to keep his sights modest given the obstacles facing a person of Lebanese descent in an Anglo-Saxon culture.[10] Nonetheless, Abboud enjoyed a meteoric rise. Within a decade after starting his career with First Chicago, he was in charge of the bank's international operations. In 1972 Abboud and four others were promoted to executive vice presidents. This was the setting for the

power struggle that Abboud was bound to win.

In 1975 Abboud succeeded Gaylord Freeman as CEO of First Chicago. Upon taking office he immediately set about paring down the proportion of high-risk REIT loans in the company's portfolio. The abruptness of this action was reported to have "shaken up the bank's management corps."[11] Executive perquisites such as free magazine subscriptions were dramatically curtailed. These actions exemplified Abboud's conservative style of management, which gained followers in the banking industry after the 1974–75 recession. It was reported[12] that Abboud applied the same harsh measures to the bank's corporate clients. When in the midst of the Lockheed payoff scandal, First Chicago was asked to participate in refinancing the company's half-billion dollar debt, Abboud conditioned his agreement on the removal of Lockheed's two top officers. He again got his way.

By the end of 1977 the bank's earnings had shown a steady rate of improvement, and some Wall Street analysts had begun to recommend First Chicago's stock again. By the fourth quarter of 1979, however, First Chicago posted a 47 percent drop in earnings.[13]

In other respects as well, Abboud's tenure was a mixed success. He was often regarded by his colleagues as abrasive. Reportedly "the tongue-lashing to which top executives were subjected, often in front of their colleagues, were the frequent subject of criticism from some of the more than 200 officers who left First Chicago during the first three years of Abboud's strong reign."[14]

---

[6] Ibid.

[7] *Fortune*, April 21, 1980, p. 65.

[8] *Time*, July 25, 1977, p. 63.

[9] Ibid.

[10] *Time*, August 21, 1978, p. 58.

[11] *New York Times*, April 29, 1980, p. D-11.

[12] *Time*, July 25, 1977, p. 63.

[13] *Business Week*, February 11, 1980, p. 33.

[14] *New York Times*, April 29, 1980, p. D-11.

Others[15] resented the fact that he expected everybody to conform to his own "I-made-it-the hard-way" workaholism. A *Fortune* survey described him as "bright, abrasive, aggressive, extremely ambitious, very tough on people and used to dressing down his peers as well as subordinates."[16] And Moody's Investors' Service mentioned personality conflicts within First Chicago as a major factor when it lowered the bank's ranking in February 1980.[17]

Abboud loyalists, however, contended[18] that many of the executives who left the bank after Abboud took office did so because their careers were linked to those of Abboud's rivals. Others claimed that Abboud's reputation for toughness had been greatly exaggerated. As his next employer, Occidental Petroleum's director, Arthur Groman, said: "Our indication is that people who are not competent find him difficult to work for. Competent people find him a pleasure."[19]

It was also noted that his conduct during the course of his dismissal from First Chicago won admiration, even from his adversaries. It was Abboud who called the directors to a special meeting of the board to discuss his conflict with Kapnick. He opened the meeting by turning to Heineman and saying, "Ben, I assume the discussion you intend to have will be easier if the inside directors remove themselves."[20] And at a press conference following the meeting he said, "Sometimes it is necessary for the coaches to select a new quarterback."[21]

Abboud's individualism has also been reflected in his staunch Democratic ties within a heavily Republican profession. First Chicago's $3.3 million personal loan to Bert Lance, the former Carter administration budget director, raised questions of impropriety. However, Abboud was totally cleared in a report by the United States comptroller of the currency, following an investigation of the issue.[22]

The Conflict

The Abboud-Yeo Conflict. In January 1980 Abboud found himself in a bitter clash with two of his highest ranking officers, President Richard L. Thomas and Chief Financial Officer Edwin H. Yeo III. Yeo was blamed within the bank as the source of a *New York Times* story which reported that Thomas was being stripped of most of his authority in an attempt at management restructuring.[23] This story, along with rumors that Abboud was working to get Yeo a seat on the board, was reported to have caused Abboud to sever his ties with Yeo and to side with Thomas.[24] Within days, Yeo, a former under secretary of the treasury, resigned and became Chicago Mayor Jane Bryne's chief financial officer.

Other accounts,[25] however, focussed on Yeo. They claim that Yeo had been forced to resign for incorrectly assessing the trend of interest rates—which contributed to the bank's major losses in the fourth quarter of 1979. Sources more familiar with First Chicago's internecine conflicts believed that it was Yeo's ego, reputed to be "large even by standards of the executive suite,"[26] that finally did him in.

[15] *Time*, August 21, 1978, p. 58.

[16] *Fortune*, April 21, 1980, p. 65.

[17] *The Wall Street Journal*, April 29, 1980, p. 8.

[18] *Fortune*, June 2, 1980, p. 15.

[19] *Fortune*, September 8, 1980, p. 48.

[20] *Fortune*, June 2, 1980, p. 15.

[21] Ibid.

[22] *New York Times*, April 29, 1980, p. D-11.

[23] *The Wall Street Journal*, January 23, 1980, p. 31.

[24] *Business Week*, February 11, 1980, p. 33.

[25] *Newsweek*, February 4, 1980, p. 67.

[26] Ibid.

This situation left Abboud and Thomas at the head of First Chicago, and they were reported to get along reasonably well. But even after this adjustment, the outward flow of high executive talent continued unabated; two executive vice presidents, two vice presidents and the president of a subsidiary quit, two senior vice presidents took early retirement, while a third took a leave of absence.[27] All this triggered suspicion as to how much longer Abboud himself would remain with the company. It was reported that some bank directors were quite upset about this last management crisis. Ben V. Heineman, a director of First Chicago and a long-time Abboud supporter, was quoted to be "getting a little dismayed"[28] by Abboud's actions.

Speculation began to rise as to who might take over Abboud's job, in the event of his dismissal. The two most frequently mentioned candidates were Harvey Kapnick, 54, the bank's new deputy chairman, and William McDonough, 45, an executive vice president who was elevated to Yeo's vacated position. The stage was set for the new conflict. This time it confronted Abboud with the no-less-abrasive Kapnick, in a clash that cost both men their positions with First Chicago.

The Abboud-Kapnick Conflict. The conflict between Abboud and Kapnick began in late 1979, almost as soon as Kapnick, former chairman of the Arthur Andersen accounting firm, joined the bank as second in command. Ironically it was Abboud who, against the will of several directors of the bank, solicited Kapnick to leave his $499,000-a-year job, following a policy dispute with his partners at Arthur Andersen. Abboud declared that he brought his old friend into the bank "to sharpen our administrative procedures."[29] But, Abboud did not view Kapnick as a banker, treating him instead as a mere administrator. Kapnick, who is said to possess a style "almost equally truculent"[30] as Abboud's, regarded himself as chief operations officer in charge of everything—especially banking. Kapnick claimed[31] not to be seeking Abboud's position, but only to be carrying out what he viewed as his own job. The struggle between the two was not an ordinary power play. It was claimed to have been "like putting two wild tigers in the same room."[32]

First Chicago's board concluded that the discord within the executive ranks had become a profitless exercise. It was reported[33] that the board took just an hour and a half to decide on dismissing Abboud. Executive Committee Chairman Heineman contended in his report to the press that "the board, to a man, has tremendous respect for Bob Abboud's integrity and banking ability. However," he continued, "at this particular time . . . it was desirable to find a new chief executive officer with Bob Abboud's integrity and banking skills, but perhaps with more people skills than Bob has been able to demonstrate."[34]

Although the decision was communicated to the press as having been "clean, simple and painful,"[35] there seems to exist more than one version concerning the ac-

---

[27] Ibid., p. 68.

[28] *Business Week*, February 11, 1980, p. 33.

[29] *Fortune*, June 2, 1980, p. 15.

[30] *Time*, May 12, 1980, p. 61.

[31] *Fortune*, June 2, 1980, p. 15.

[32] Ibid.

[33] *Time*, May 12, 1980, p. 61.

[34] *New York Times*, April 29, 1980, p. D-11.

[35] *Time*, May 12, 1980, p. 61.

tual circumstances of Abboud's departure. According to Abboud,[36] Kapnick came over to Abboud's house and delivered an ultimatum: Abboud could remain chief executive, but Kapnick would run the bank. Abboud did not intend to succumb to Kapnick's pressure, and the board, after deliberating the issue, decided to fire Kapnick. Abboud remained with the bank for another three months in order to supervise his own succession but professed to have been "mortally wounded in the encounter."[37]

Abboud's New Challenge. Robert Abboud was not out of work for long. He was fired from First Chicago in April 1980 and by late May 1980 was hired as president and chief operation officer of Occidental Petroleum Corp. Abboud was brought in by the 82-year-old Occidental founder and chairman, Dr. Armand Hammer, who had built Occidental from scratch into the nation's 12th largest oil company, with sales of $9.6 billion in 1979.[38]

Hammer himself is somewhat of a maverick in the nation's business community. A physician who never practiced medicine, he was reported to be "a sort of privateer out of the past, something of an anachronism in this day of organization charts and elaborate managerial theories.[39] On his long way to success, Hammer has anointed and then disposed of a number of heirs apparent. It was commonly presumed that Abboud's hiring was one more step in Hammer's long search for the "perfect" chief executive to succeed himself. Accordingly, Hammer acknowledged to reporters, "I expect to hear

that same old criticism that we have a revolving door executive suite. But I have to run this company the best way I know, and Abboud is the man for the job."[40] He added, "Now I can go to my grave and be sure Occidental will continue to grow."[41]

This, however, sounded conspicuously similar to Hammer's statement following the hiring of Abboud's predecessor, former Dow Chemical Chairman, Zoltan Merszei, 57, in April 1979, when he boasted that "Zoltan Merszei is the best acquisition I ever made."[42] A Hungarian who studied architecture in Switzerland but chose not to exercise his profession, Merszei was often described as "methodical, meticulous, and orderly to a fault,"[43] qualities that stood in sharp contrast to Hammer's impulsiveness and spontaneity.

According to *Fortune*, the "mutual attraction" between Hammer and Merszei "seems to lie in a shared and boundless optimism, . . . (both) see the world as a collection of large and succulent opportunities waiting to be speared."[44]

Hammer first met Abboud in the mid-60s, when Abboud headed First Chicago's Frankfurt office. "I have the highest regard for him as a banker and as an executive,"[45] Hammer said. "And imagine," he added, "Abboud has been with one company all these years, working his way up from assistant cashier. I like that."[46] Hammer also liked Abboud's loyalty. Although he offered Abboud the job with Occidental upon learn-

---

[36] *Forbes*, September 1, 1980, p. 35.

[37] Ibid.

[38] *Fortune*, September 8, 1980, p. 48.

[39] *Fortune*, November 19, 1980, p. 70.

[40] *The Wall Street Journal,* August 5, 1980, p. 29.

[41] Ibid.

[42] *Fortune*, November 19, 1980, p. 71.

[43] Ibid., p. 72.

[44] Ibid., p. 71.

[45] *The Wall Street Journal,* August 5, 1980, p. 29.

[46] Ibid.

ing the news of Abboud's dismissal from First Chicago, Abboud would not give him an answer until the day he actually left the bank. Hammer pointed out that "the fact that Abboud stayed with First Chicago those extra months and did not give a lot of interviews criticizing everybody shows a lot of character and integrity."[47]

Abboud's appointment came as a surprise to Wall Street analysts. A San Francisco analyst was quoted alleging that "Abboud knows nothing about the resources business and brings nothing that I can see to the company."[48] Another, a New York-based analyst, said that, "This is not going to build up investors' confidence."[49] Hammer, however, was heard to say that Abboud's lack of experience in the operations of an oil company would not hurt him on the job. "After all, what kind of experience did I have 25 years ago? And Abboud has some feel for the business, since a number of oil companies were his clients."[50] It was also argued that the new job was "tailored" for Abboud in many ways, especially since his nuts-and-bolts approach and close attention to detail would be complementary to Hammer's big-picture approach.[51]

It was hoped that his arrangement would not interfere with the responsibilities of Zoltan Merszei, who was to remain with Occidental in his prior position as vice chairman and director. He was also charged with overall strategic planning, an area in which Abboud is supposed to be weak.[52] But Merszei was to be removed from Occidental's center of operations. His new function as chief executive officer of the Hooker Chemicals and Plastics Corporation took him to Houston, Texas. There he had to face Hooker's poor earnings record and an even poorer reputation, due to the waste disposal problems at Love Canal in Niagara Falls, New York. Some analysts expressed doubts that Merszei, "a volatile, entrepreneurial manager with a reputation for wanting to be on the firing line, would enjoy being so far from the day-to-day operations of Occidental."[53]

When questioned about this issue, Abboud told reporters that he and Merszei had known each other for years and would not have any trouble working together. "Zoltan is very much like George Patton, and we are going to give him the Third Army to run across Europe and build up Hooker's international business."[54] In another interview he added, "Zoltan is a great industrial field commander. He really is. Would taking over Hooker be stepping down?"[55]

Zoltan Merszei, however, has not given up his ambition to run Occidental. "I intend one of these days to head this organization, or I would not be staying here,"[56] he told reporters. When the same question was posed to Abboud, he contended that "Dr. Hammer did not promise me the chief executive's title. If and when the day comes that a new chief executive is needed . . . , it is then going to take several people to run this far-flung diverse company."[57] He further denied having considered succeeding Dr. Hammer, proclaiming that "any notion that Armand Hammer is mortal should be discarded immediately."[58]

[47] Ibid.

[48] *New York Times*, August 5, 1980, p. D-1.

[49] Ibid.

[50] *The Wall Street Journal*, August 5, 1980, p. 29.

[51] Ibid.

[52] Ibid.

[53] *New York Times*, August 5, 1980, p. D-6.

[54] *The Wall Street Journal*, August 5, 1980, p. 29.

[55] *Forbes*, September 1, 1980, p. 35.

[56] *The Wall Street Journal*, August 5, 1980, p. 29.

[57] *Forbes*, September 1, 1980, p. 35.

[58] *The Wall Street Journal*, August 5, 1980, p. 29.

CASE 13
CHUCKING IT*
Myron Magnet

Ken Mason was president of Quaker Oats and headed for the top. At 57 he quit and moved to an island in the north woods "to reflect."

At 54, Ken Mason had it made. An advertising boy wonder in his 20s, partner at his own thriving ad agency in his 30s, advertising director and executive vice president of Quaker Oats in his 40s, he became in the fall of 1976 Quaker's president and chief operating officer. Thereafter success continued to smile. Company directors applauded his skill at plotting tactics thoughtfully linked to long-term strategy, and many considered him likely to succeed Chief Executive Robert D. Stuart, Jr., who turned 65 this spring.

Three years into his term as president, Ken Mason chucked it. Though incredulous directors pressed him to reconsider, he resigned the presidency, gave up his grand paneled duplex on Chicago's North Michigan Avenue, and transported himself and his wife—a successful businesswoman turned conservation lobbyist—to an island in a vast and remote lake in the north Minnesota iron country.

"Remote" is a mild way of describing pristine Pine Island. Bird calls punctuate the deep quiet, squirrels out of a Walt Disney movie tug your trouser cuffs to demand a peanut, dusk brings a deer across the expansive lawn of Mason's big stone lodge, built with rustic-luxurious stylishness by an oil tycoon in the Twenties.

A trauma on thin ice

In winter the remoteness deepens. Vacationers lock up their summer cottages, leav-

ing the Masons alone in a frozen lake, now perfectly still except for an occasional chain saw whining on shore or the nighttime howl of migrating wolves. Summer's pleasant half-hour boat ride to the mainland for groceries is now a snowmobile expedition in cold that can drop to 40 below. Once Mason and his machine fell through thin ice, and the three-mile trek home nearly cost him his feet. "It's the most thrilling feeling," says Mason, "to walk along that shoreline and think you're all alone here." Yet every night before bed he locks all his doors.

There is much to fill Mason's pastoral days, starting with the logistics of running a 120-acre estate with no help. His directorships—of Quaker Oats and of Rohm & Haas, the Philadelphia chemical company—also take time (and, with his pension, bring his annual income to $95,000, not counting investments). But primarily he sits in his study and reads and thinks, mostly about business. And, he confesses, "I'm frankly speculating on life, so there's some looking out the window." After a year and a half, he thinks he has "something meaningful to say," and he's planning a series of lectures. So far, many of his ideas seem half-formed and conventional. How much more he'll have to say he doesn't know: "I don't feel I have to write a book to justify what I've done."

Why did Ken Mason chuck it? It wasn't because he was pushed out or burnt out, and neither is he a hippie dropout camouflaged in pinstripes all those years. "He was," notes Chairman Stuart, "a button-down kind of businessman." Burt Manning, who handled the Quaker account for J. Walter Thompson–U.S.A. and is now CEO of that agency, says, "One can't exaggerate his rage for the bottom line." For his part, Mason says he sees corporations as the central institution of our age—"like what the Church must have been in the Middle Ages." And concerning Quaker Oats he declares: "That was my arena; I was really happy there."

Nevertheless, Mason had one ambition no corporation could satisfy, as he had in fact warned Quaker officials: "I had a strong desire to have time, before I got too old, to reflect on what my experiences had all been about and not be on a treadmill up to the last minute. It's almost embarrassing to say, but I'm a great believer that the examined life is much more worth living than the unexamined. In the back of my head I was always thinking about early retirement." (Socrates, who invented the examined life, examined his in the busyness of the marketplace.)

Mason has chucked it before. In 1951, at the age of 29, he abandoned his step-uncle Earle Ludgin's Chicago advertising agency to live in Mexico and write. In this too he succeeded, at least to the extent of selling well-constructed if mechanical stories to magazines like *Woman's Day* for then-handsome fees ranging from $600 to $1,200.

One of the stories he wrote in Mexico—30 years later he considers it his best—sheds light on the impulses that led him to walk away from business success at the end of his career as at its beginning. The story hardly has a plot; it's about a couple who, after seeing *High Noon*, try to figure out over ice cream at the drugstore the true nature of Gary Cooper's heroism. The story's main character identifies with this "great man . . . caught in a spot where he has to do something dangerous and important." What he responds to isn't just that Cooper takes on himself the duty of delivering a town from thugs who threaten it, but that Cooper does so even though not one townsman stands up to help. "Worse, he even has to fight the people who normally should be

on his side," but who instead "tell him to give up and go away." So Cooper—in a powerful American myth that reconciles the wish for independence with feelings of responsibility to society—has to stand alone against the community in order to save it.

A peculiar self-confidence

Mason's allegiance to both parts of the *High Noon* myth was nurtured in his adolescence by the Asheville School, a highly regarded North Carolina prep school. Mason was made more than usually impressionable to the stamp of that experience by his need for a father, his own having died of tuberculosis when Ken was six. Mason found a substitute in a strong-minded young English teacher, Charles M. Rice, and with more than a student's need for approval, Mason took to heart with special literalness the ethic of his school as Rice embodied it.

Rice, says Mason, "taught me morals without ever mentioning the word. He made you keep looking at what the difference between right action and wrong action was." What is right, according to this prep-school ethic, is not merely to excel but also to be of service to society; the children of a fortunate class have a special responsibility to work hard and give society something in return. At the same time, this ethic encourages a peculiar self-confidence. I you've developed all your faculties, it holds, and if you've taken to heart such gentlemanly virtues as truthfulness and courtesy, then you are everything you ought to be. There's no need to pose or to doubt yourself, and you needn't shrink from being an iconoclast. Rice means to praise when he notes that Mason "had a very sharp eye for artificiality and phony values." All in all, Rice judges, Mason "certainly is what we in the prep schools like to think of as what gets turned out."

The man who emerged from this boyhood discipline—urbane, gracious, witty, quick—has "the highest standards of any individual I've ever met," says Jack M. Young, president of Quaker's foods division. "He applies them to himself; he applies them in every direction—laterally, vertically, to his mother as well as to business." As a result, Burt Manning recalls, "people used to tremble when Mason came into a meeting. They just never knew if they were meeting his standards." This sounds like a demanding teacher coming into his classroom, and Mason's close relationships have something of that quality. "He wanted you to arrive at his conclusion because you saw the rightness of it," Manning says. "He put you through an almost Socratic process."

In a speech he made as president of Quaker not long before he resigned, Mason had a showdown of his own with enemies of the community. The issue at stake was children's television, which Mason had started pondering in the early 70s in response to complaints about commercials for kids. In Mason's view, children's TV is to our era what nursery legends were to Plato's Athenians—the means by which children's values are formed. By college age, Mason calculates, the average American has "spent more time in front of a television set than in school, in church, or in conversation or play with . . . parents." Worse, Mason thinks, the programming is dumb, false, and dead.

Gibberish about Quisp and Quake

In the speech—quoted approvingly by Ronald Reagan in a newspaper column—Mason sketched a remedy. The answer, he argued, isn't to ban TV commercials for children; that would be "big brotherism." The solution is to cluster commercials by product—toys or cereals, say—and introduce them with a lead-in identifying the ads as separate from the program and encouraging kids to think critically about the products. "It would force all of us to be more informational," says Mason, who thinks most of Quaker's commercials "explained the reason-for-being of the product as opposed to jumping up and down and singing nonsense." Mason speaks with rueful authority about ordinary kiddie commercials, having conceived the boffo Quaker campaign pitting a space creature named Quisp against a troglodyte called Quake—"sheer gibberish," he now thinks.

To upgrade children's programming, Mason urged the networks to divvy up Saturday mornings, each producing a third of the shows, and all three networks running the same programs simultaneously. With no fear that competitors would snatch viewers by pandering, the networks, he believes, would put on good programs.

Under Mason, Quaker tried to push things in that direction by developing *The Ancient Astronauts*, *Say Goodbye*, and other TV specials embodying wholesome values. Mason says they were "as effective on a recall basis as zany comedies or shows offering sexual innuendos."

During Mason's presidency, Quaker developed other children's programs, but the networks turned them down, and in these battles Quaker had few allies. For Mason the experience rankled. "TV," he now says, "looms very important in infecting this culture with the very diseases businessmen decry: a lack of values on the part of the workforce, loss of the work ethic, kids who don't have any ambition." And responsibility for this, he believes, rests on "the managers of *Fortune*'s 500. That's their work. They're saying to the country, 'Yeah, we don't mind that kind of programming; this is a good use of our money.' "

In his island retreat, Ken Mason is developing a critique of corporate management. Managers, he thinks, do not pay attention to long-term social consequences of actions, and the results have been contrary to business's best interest. For example, the fact that more than half the public now think ads are usually misleading indicates to Mason that management has dulled a valuable business tool. Labor relations, he notes, haven't imbued the workers with loyalty to their companies, identification with corporate objectives, pride in their jobs and products, or high productivity. When Mason outlined these views in an article in *Business Week,* Reagan had no comment, but enthusiastic praise came from Ralph Nader in his newspaper column.

Presbyterianism at Quaker Oats

"It's not that I want to do away with the free-enterprise system," Mason insists. "It's just that the people running it are asleep at the switch." He wants to wake them up, for he believes no invisible hand will pull the lever for them. "There are too many places where the invisible hand is invisible because it doesn't exist," he says. Thus he excoriates Milton Friedman's view that business's undeviating attention to the bottom line will inexorably promote the common weal. Only the moral and aesthetic as well as financial judgment of managers who explicitly take the good of the community into account can do that, Mason thinks. How can businessmen, he asks, "having had a gentle upbringing, like I had," fail to appreciate this?

Walter J. Salmon, who is a Harvard professor of retail marketing and Quaker director, counters, "There aren't many Harvard MBAs who would disagree with these principles." But he adds: "There aren't too many who would know how to act on them as frequently as Mason did while still making a respectable profit."

At Quaker Oats, a company still tinged (despite its name) with "the fundamental Presbyterian attitude" of its founding family, according to Executive Vice President Robert N. Thurston, "the environment is hospitable to that type of person." So why did Mason retire? Why not keep that high position and use it to change the business climate? "I think," says Manning, "that Mason had a continual edge of frustration about what he was doing because reality was constantly getting in the way of implementing the grand design." And for that Mason needed more power than his office afforded: "I'm not impressed with the power of a corporate president," he says. "I am impressed with the power of ideas. If you have sound ideas, they'll find their way whether you're sitting in the president's chair or off in a hut somewhere. Here I have a better chance of developing the theories that are needed than if I were doing the things presidents have to do."

And so in the fastness of northern Minnesota, working in his lighthouse overlooking the lake during the summer and through the freezing winters in one of his two guesthouses, where he sits draped against the cold in an electric blanket, Mason is playing his ultimate role—the determined loner committed to saving business in spite of itself, however thankless the task might be. Will he formulate an analysis significant enough to inspire change? Says Salmon, "I've been at the business school 25 years and seen faculty come and go. It's hard to predict who will do it, but you see minds that might, and Ken's one of those minds."

On the other hand, Terry Turner, an executive of the Chicago public broadcasting station whose board Mason sat on, remarks that Mason's "thinking patterns are advertising-agency-influenced"—that his true gift is to "take a large batch of material and condense it." This is a valuable mental discipline, but not all that Mason needs to achieve his ambition. And to serve the community, perhaps you have to remain inside it; after all, when Gary Cooper stood alone, he stood alone on Main Street.

READING 1
THE PSYCHOLOGICAL CONTRACT: MANAGING THE JOINING-UP PROCESS*
John Paul Kotter

A growing number of organizations in recent years have been reporting problems that center around getting the new man, often a recent college graduate, "on board." These problems take on many forms:

• Some organizations have reported as much as a 50 percent turnover rate of new men after their first year of work.
• Recently, some corporations have complained about a generation gap between new men and older managers which was putting a severe strain on their organization.
• Other companies complain about the loss of creativity, innovativeness, and energy in their new employees during their first few years (often labeled a "stifling of creativity").
• Managers have often complained about the naiveté of new employees. ("They come in with unrealistic expectations and then get mad when they don't come true!")
• Organizations have reported that it takes

* © 1973 by the Regents of the University of California. Reprinted from *California Management Review*, vol. XV, no. 3, pp. 91–99, by permission of the Regents.

some managerial and technical specialists two years or more to really get on board, while others have reported that it takes one half or one fourth that time.

This article is concerned with the process of assimilating new employees into an organization, which we call the "joining-up" process. All of the above incidents are symptomatic of problems in this process. It is the purpose of this article to present research that argues the following points:

1. Early experiences (the joining-up period) have a major effect on an individual's later career in an organization. Specifically, early experiences can significantly affect job satisfaction, employee attitude, productivity level, and turnover.

2. Efficient management of the joining-up process can save an organization a great deal of money by making employees more efficient faster, by increasing job satisfaction, morale, and productivity, by decreasing turnover, by increasing the amount of creativity, by decreasing counterproductive conflict and tension, and by increasing the number of truly effective members within the organization.

For an organization that hires 25 college graduates with bachelor's degrees each year, the difference between a well-managed and a mismanaged joining-up process is $200,000 a year at a minimum.

3. Due to a complex set of forces, most organizations do a poor job of managing the joining-up process. Often because of a problem of measurement, organizations either do not realize this problem exists or do not realize its magnitude.

This article will outline some recent research and present the results. To clarify the implications of the research, two case studies will be presented, followed by a summary and a set of conclusions.

The Research

Research was recently undertaken at MIT's Sloan School of Management to explore problems in the joining-up process and to try to understand how it can be better managed.[1] A simple model of the process was constructed and data was gathered with an eight-page questionnaire given to a randomly selected group of Sloan master's graduates and Sloan Fellows. These Sloan master's graduates had completed a two-year master's degree program in management somewhere between 1961 and 1969. Sloan Fellows are managers in their 30s and 40s who had just completed a one-year "master's" program. Ninety responses from middle managers ranging in age from 23 to 45 were eventually used in the data analysis.[2]

At the heart of the model was the concept of the "psychological contract," which was first introduced a decade ago by Chris Argyris[3] and Harry Levenson.[4] As it was defined for this research, the psychological contract is an implicit contract between an individual and his organization which specifies what each expects to give and receive from each other in their relationship.

When an individual joins an organization, he has expectations of what he expects to receive (such as advancement opportunities, salary, status, office space and decor, amount of challenging vs. dull work, and so on) as well as expectations of what he expects to give (such as technical skills, time and energy commitment, communication ability, supervisory skills, loyalty, and so on). The organization also has expectations of what it expects to receive from the new employee (examples of which are similar to what the employee expects to give) and expectations of what it expects to offer him in return (examples of which are similar to what the employee expects to receive).

These expectations can be the same, or they can be quite different. For example, a young chemical engineer from MIT may expect that he will be given his own office when he goes to work for a company. If the company also expects to give him an office of his own, then there is a "match." If they do not expect to give him his own office, there is a "mismatch." This mismatch can be small (they expect he will share an office with one other person) or large (they expect he won't be given an office, desk, or anything). These four sets of expectations and the matches and mismatches make up the "psychological contract."

This contract is very different from a legal or labor contract. It may have literally thousands of items in it (see Table 1 for an example of some categories used in the research) although the job seeker or new employee may consciously think of only a few. His expectations of the types of technical skills he will give may be very clear, while his expectation of how willing he is to take on company values may be very unclear. Likewise, the organization may have a clearer picture of some expectations than others. These expectations may be explicitly discussed during recruiting or with the first supervisor or they may not. The new recruit may have a deep, clear understanding of some, all or none of the company's expectations and vice versa. Finally, this contract changes as the individual's and the company's expectations alter.

---

[1] "The Psychological Contract: Expectations and the Joining-Up Process," an unpublished master's thesis by the author (Sloan, 1970).

[2] Data was collected during January and February 1970.

[3] Chris Argyris, *Understanding Organizational Behavior* (Homewood, Ill.: Dorsey Press, 1960).

[4] Harry Levenson, *Men, Management & Mental Health* (Cambridge, Mass.: Harvard University Press, 1962).

Table 1 Types of Expectations*

(a)

The following list of 13 items are examples of areas in which an individual has expectations of receiving and an organization has expectations of giving. That is, for each item in this list, the individual will have an expectation about what the organization will offer him or give him in that area. Likewise, the organization has an expectation about what it will offer or give the individual in that area.

1. A sense of meaning or purpose in the job.
2. Personal development opportunities.
3. The amount of interesting work (stimulates curiosity and induces excitement).
4. The challenge in the work.
5. The power and responsibility in the job.
6. Recognition and approval for good work.
7. The status and prestige in the job.
8. The friendliness of the people, the congeniality of the work group.
9. Salary.
10. The amount of structure in the environment (general practices, discipline, regimentation).
11. The amount of security in the job.
12. Advancement opportunities.
13. The amount and frequency of feedback and evaluation.

(b)

The following list of 17 items are examples of areas in which an individual has expectations of giving and the organization has expectations of receiving. That is, for each item in this list, the individual will have an expecta- tion about what he is willing or able to give or offer the organization in that area. Likewise, the organization has an expectation about what it will receive from the indi- vidual in that area.

1. The ability to perform nonsocial job-related tasks requiring some degree of technical knowledge and skill.
2. The ability to learn the various aspects of a position while on the job.
3. The ability to discover new methods of performing tasks; the ability to solve novel problems.
4. The ability to present a point of view effectively and convincingly.
5. The ability to work productively with groups of people.
6. The ability to make well-organized, clear presentations, both orally and written.
7. The ability to supervise and direct the work of others.
8. The ability to make responsible decisions well without assistance from others.
9. The ability to plan and organize work efforts for oneself or others.
10. The ability to utilize time and energy for the benefit of the company.
11. The ability to accept company demands which conflict with personal prerogatives.
12. Social relationships with other members of the company off the job.
13. Conforming to the folkways of the organization or work group on the job in areas not directly related to job performance.
14. Further education pursued off company time.
15. Maintaining a good public image of the company.
16. Taking on company values and goals as one's own.
17. The ability to see what should or must be done, and to initiate appropriate activity.

* These 30 types of expectations were adapted from earlier research by David E. Berlew and Douglas T. Hall, "The Socialization of Managers: Effects of Expectations on Performance," *An Administrative Science Quarterly* (September 1966), pp. 207–23.

Research Results. The research findings can be summarized in the following points:

1. The first finding confirmed the major research hypothesis that psychological con- tracts, which are made up primarily of matches in expectations, are related to greater job satisfaction, productivity, and reduced turnover than are other contracts

which have more mismatches and less matches. In other words, those people who established a contract that was comprised of more matches in expectations, had a more satisfying and productive first year and remained longer with the company than those people whose contract had fewer matches.

We have all observed personal examples of this phenomenon in its extreme. A number of the Sloan master's graduates reported that they took their first job with completely unrealistic expectations of how hard it would be to introduce new techniques into their companies. This expectation, although unrealistic, was an important one to each of them initially. They lasted in their first jobs on the average of one year.

The more subtle differences in job satisfaction or productivity resulting from a greater or lesser number of matches in the psychological contract are more difficult to observe. The pattern often looks like this: The contract formed during the joining-up period has mismatches, but neither the employee nor his boss really recognizes them or confronts them. After the first year the employee begins to "feel" those mismatches as disappointments, let-downs, and so on. Since he thinks the company has broken their contract, he reacts by slowly breaking his part of the bargain. He often "digs in" and becomes another moderately productive, uncreative, body.

2. The concept that showed a measurable relationship to productivity, satisfaction, and turnover was "matching," not getting more or less than was expected. Mismatches that gave more than one expected caused as many problems as those which gave less than one expected. In other words, organizations or individuals who approach the contract trying to get "the most," or "the best," instead of "a fit" or "a match," are missing the boat. Often we

don't have strong preferences for something, but we still plan for the future based on what we expect. For example, Warren, a 25-year-old bachelor working for a West Coast aeronautics firm, expected that he would be transferred East after one year of work. He really didn't care one way or the other, but based on his expectation he made elaborate plans for the move, which, when it didn't occur, left Warren very upset.

The sales department of a moderate-sized industrial products firm put on a strong recruiting campaign a few years ago to get the "best men possible for the money." Their strong recruiting effort did succeed in getting a remarkably strong group of new men. Unfortunately, the job did not require the skills many of these young men had. The contracts formed had many large mismatches in them (but mismatches which the company thought were in its "favor"). Within two years the company lost 60 percent of these men and only 10 percent (two men) were doing very well.

3. It was found that the clearer an individual understood his own expectation on an item, the higher was the probability of a match. Likewise, the clearer an expectation was to the organization, the higher the probability of a match.

It is fairly obvious what is happening in this case. Many times people do not explicitly think of all the areas in which they have expectations. Often a new employee out of college isn't consciously aware of what he wants and needs, or what he is capable and prepared to give. Unfortunately organizations also are not clear as to what they expect (in detail) either. As a result they don't talk about many areas or pay attention to them. Mismatches can occur by accident, out of neglect.

What is needed then is for the new man, the company, and his boss to carefully consider all areas of expectations in order to overcome the problem of clarity. One of the reasons this hasn't been done in the past is that people have not considered its importance.

4. If the new man explicitly discussed his expectations with a company representative, the two parties' mutual understanding of the other's expectations increased and so did the probability of matching.

There are a number of reasons why this doesn't happen more frequently. There often appear to be norms surrounding the interview and the initial work period which define some items as not legitimate to talk about. The fact that the new man often feels

powerless limits his ability to initiate such a discussion. His supervisor may be overworked and not rewarded for helping the new man and as a result doesn't initiate what could be a complex deep discussion.

These first four points are summarized in model form in Figure 1.

5. It was further discovered that clarity (point 3), discussion (point 5), and even some give and take were not enough to resolve some mismatches, which we called basic. In this situation, an individual and his organization, having clarified and discussed their expectations, find themselves unwilling or unable to find a commonality of expectations in an area which is important to

Figure 1

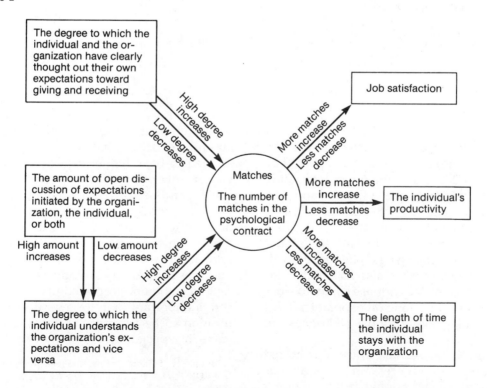

both of them. In some cases, this may mean that the employee should resign, a reality that some people and some organizations don't like to face.

It was also discovered that there were small but statistically significant differences—mismatches—between the expectations of all individuals as a group and all organizations as a group on some items (see Table 2).

Table 2   **Basic Mismatches***

	Expectation	Mean for Individual[a]	Mean for Organization[b]
1.	Personal development opportunities	4.54 (individual expects to receive)	4.20 (organization expects to give)[b]
2.	Security	2.30 (individual expects to receive)	2.94 (organization expects to give)[b]
3.	Taking on values and goals	2.80 (individual expects to give)	3.30 (organization expects to receive)[b]
4.	Ability to work with groups	3.75 (individual expects to give)	4.06 (organization expects to receive)[b]
5.	Conforming	2.19 (individual expects to give)	2.53 (organization expects to receive)[b]
6.	Interesting work	4.36 (individual expects to receive)	4.10 (organization expects to give)[b]
7.	Sense of meaning or purpose	4.24 (individual expects to receive)	3.98 (organization expects to give)[b]

* "The Psychological Contract."

Note: All differences are statistically significant at .05. The expectations are listed in decreasing order of statistically significant differences (from .0003 to .048).

   a.   As measured on a 1-to-5 scale (1 = not expected, 5 = strongly expected).

   b.   As perceived by the respondent.

As the reader can see, the individuals had higher expectations with respect to the personal development opportunities they would be offered, the amount of interesting work they would be offered, and the amount of meaning or purpose in their work. On the other hand, the organizations had higher expectations toward the amount of security that they would offer the individual. The organizations also had higher expectations of the individual's ability to work with groups, his taking on of organizational values and goals, and his willingness to conform.

Schein, in an earlier article, suggested that basic differences in expectations seemed to be developing between recent college graduates and industry.[5] In particular he reported that college graduates seemed to have higher expectations of advancement opportunities, increased responsibility, and personal growth opportunities. He also reported very different expectations on how to sell ideas and get things done, how important and practical "theoretical" knowledge was, and how ready the new man was for use. These findings are consistent with the ones reported in Table 2.

It is important then for a particular organization to be sensitive to growing differences in expectations between it and its new

---

[5] Edgar H. Schein, "How to Break in the College Graduate," *Harvard Business Review* (November–December 1964), pp. 68–76.

men. Resolving these basic differences can be a much more difficult task than resolving the other types of differences. In an extreme case, resolving this problem could require an organization to find a new labor pool or to undergo major internal changes in order to survive on a long-run basis.

6. Finally, for the particular sample used in this study (Sloan School graduates and Sloan Fellows), the nature of the conflict in the process looked something like this: the individual was most interested in exchanging non-people-related skills (technical knowledge, drive, writing ability, and so on) for exciting, challenging, meaningful work and development (and advancement) opportunities. The organization, however, expected to give the individual less of that which he expected most, and expected to receive in addition to skills, more on such items as conformity, loyalty and so on.

In summary, there are a number of general points that result from this research which are not usually found in "conventional wisdom." First, the initial period *is* very important, and as such is worth carefully managing. Second, what you don't know *can* hurt you. A clear understanding of one's own expectations and the other party's will help form better contracts. Third, the key in contract formulation is achieving a match or a fit, *not* getting more, or the best, or whatever. Fourth, if an organization and an individual have one or more very central, basic mismatches, it may be in their best interests to shake hands and part. Finally, if an organization's expectations get too far out of line with its labor pool, it can get into deep trouble.

In order to obtain a better feel for the implications of this research, let us look at a few examples of organizations who have tried to improve the management of their joining up process.

Applications: Case Study I. This first case involves a manufacturing plant of a large consumer product company, employing about 300 workers and 40 managers. In June, the plant hired three new college engineering graduates as junior managers. For their first three months they participated in a combined program of work and training. A senior manager at the plant was concerned that the plant could do a better job of getting the new employees on board. In particular his concerns were:

• He wanted the new men to get up to speed, to become "socialized" and to learn the plant's norms faster (in general to learn more about the plant, the people, and so on).
• The new men (almost through with training) would be getting their "first boss" soon. He wanted them to explore their expectations and to be prepared for negotiating a psychological contract with their new boss.
• He wanted to receive feedback from the new men on their three-month history with the company and to explore better methods for future training programs.
• In addition, he wanted some of the plant's top management to get a feel for what the new college graduates were like, and to explore management's implicit expectations of the new men.
• Finally he wanted to do some team building. He wanted to help the new men feel part of their management team.

To accomplish these goals, four senior managers, three supervisors, and the three trainees were invited to a 12-hour session, led by an outside consultant, spread out over three days during their shut-down period. Prior to the session the three trainees and three supervisors (who had been with the organization only one to two years) filled out questionnaires on their specific expectations of giving and receiving, and answered how clear each expectation was to them (see Table 1 for such a list of expectations). The senior managers filled out questionnaires on what the company expected to give and receive to each of the new employees. This exercise was designed to help the participants explore explicitly their expectations before the session.

The session began with a "contract setting" exercise for the 12-hour session. The participants were asked to state explicitly what they expected to give and to receive from this session and the consultant, as the workshop leader, did the same. A contract was then explicitly established among all the participants which included the goals of the session, the roles each person would assume, the schedule we would follow, and so on. This provided the group with a good start for the session and with some real-time experience concerning psychological contracts and contract setting.

The next input was a brief lecture on the joining-up process and the concept of the psychological contract. Following this, the group was divided into three homogeneous groups (new men, supervisors, senior managers) and given time to develop lists of "mismatches." The new men and young supervisors were told to identify mismatches from their own experiences, including the cause. The senior managers were told to develop a list of what mismatches they thought new men often have when they join the company.

It was interesting to note that all three lists were different. The mismatches the new men presently felt were different from those of the one to two year men. The senior managers' list reflected their own experiences and was also different. In a sense the three lists provided a chronological picture of the problems and concerns an employee faced as he grew up in this organization.

The three groups, one at a time, presented their lists, point by point, and the entire group discussed them. This discussion was one of information exchange, exploration, and confrontation. Information was candidly exchanged on subjects that were not normally discussed but which were important (performance criteria, dress, hair length, career paths in the company, money, company policy, and so on). Many misunderstandings and misperceptions (on the part of all three groups) were aired and resolved. One of the new men started asking some questions about how to get something done that he had been suppressing for weeks out of a fear of looking stupid. A major conflict that one of the supervisors faced was confronted (he was seriously considering leaving) and, after the session, resolved (he was transferred).

The session ended with some group problem solving on the issue, "what can we do better concerning our joining-up process." They developed several recommendations, including the use of similar sessions in the future. The participants' response to the session was enthusiastic and the senior manager who initiated it felt it had accomplished his five goals.

Case Study II. A much larger effort, which is in progress at this writing, involves an R&D division of a giant consumer products company. Some of the top management became concerned about the joining-up process in their division due to a number of factors, including a speech on socialization and joining-up by Ed Schein. They established a task force comprised of a diagonal slice of the organization, an internal organizational development specialist, and an external consultant.

The division contains about 400 people, 20 of whom had been with the company one and one-half years or less. The first task of the group was a diagnostic one, in which information was collected from various sources in and out of the organization. As a part of this effort, almost all of the new employees (two groups of eight) met for a one-day session designed to help them examine and articulate their brief experiences with the company. Questionnaires were given to all new people, their bosses, and their bosses' bosses. These inputs and others from other divisions, academia, and so on led to a diagnosis of critical variables that could be improved upon.

The most important factor turned out to be the skills of the new man's supervisor. The process was facilitated if the new man's supervisor had skills in the following areas: giving and receiving feedback, articulating expectations and performance criteria, explaining realistically decisions passed down from above, coaching and helping, communicating, understanding new people's problems, and so on. Other important factors included the selection of the first project, the selection of the first environment (including boss, peers, and section), formal and informal training, opportunities for quickly learning about the company and facilities, the clarity of key policies, the reward system, and so forth.

At this writing, the task force is planning and implementing changes in the organization based on their diagnosis and understanding of the joining-up process. The types of changes they have developed can help the reader to see what can be done to improve a joining-up process:

Creation of a training program for a new man's boss.—This program is designed to help him better understand the new man and the joining-up process and to help him develop better skills as a coach.

Creation of a criterion for project selection.—A more careful selection of first projects can speed up a new man's learning.

New formal training activities to replace old ones.—New formal training was created to replace the old based on new employee feedback on inefficiencies, usefulness, and so on.

Explicitly stated division policies.—Unclear policies in some key areas were causing false expectations in important areas. Top management is changing this.

Creation of a joining-up workshop.—This workshop is somewhat similar to the one described in the first case study, except that the new man's boss is present, and there is more emphasis on relationship building and contract setting.

Planning aid for supervisors who expect new man.—A number of devices have been created to help supervisors plan for their new man's arrival. These include help in setting training objectives, in meeting a wide range of new man needs, and so forth.

Creation of performance criteria.—Vague performance criteria have caused unreal expectations. Supervisors are now creating more explicit, but not mechanistic ones.

This effort, which is still in progress, will take about one and one-half years in total.

Summary and Conclusions

Early experiences in an organization can have a great effect on a person's career. The joining-up process, which determines these experiences, must be carefully managed. The quality of the management of the joining-up process will effect two major outcomes: the cost of getting new people on board and keeping them in the firm, and the level of productivity, commitment, innovativeness, and so on of people when they get on board.

Unfortunately in many organizations this process is mismanaged, or not managed at all. The costs of mismanagement are very high.

The concept of the psychological contract has proven to be a useful one in examining the joining-up process. Recent research has shown that if a new person's expectations are out of line with the company's this will show up in low production, low creativity, dissatisfaction, and turnover.

While it is not really useful to propose "cookbook" solutions for better management of the joining-up process beyond the conclusions drawn from the research, the following are key variables in most organizations' joining-up process.

(A) *Recruiting effort.* Does your recruiting effort allow both the recruitee and your organization to exchange accurate expectations? Does the recruitee get a fairly realistic picture of the challenges and problems in your organization? Do you carefully explore his expectations and try to get the best fits or matches or do you look for "good people"?

(B) *The first supervisor.* Do the managers who supervise new employees have the skills and knowledge to help create sound psychological contracts? Are they good coaches and teachers? Do they know enough about the organization to help someone else learn? Are they effective members themselves? Do you carefully select and train first supervisors? In many organizations this man is the key variable in this process.

(C) *Reward and control system.* Do the supervisors of new men perceive that they are being rewarded for efficient and effective management of a new man's joining-up process or do they think they are rewarded only for doing the "real work"?

(D) *First job environment.* Does the environment a new man is put into contribute or detract from his getting on board? Does it help reduce his initial anxieties and help make him a part of the group? Will his peers teach him what you want him to learn about his job and the organization? Careful selection of the first environment and activities outside of it can prove useful.

(E) *Performance criteria and training objectives.* Do the supervisor and the new man know what the reward system is for the new man? Are the performance criteria clear to both? Are training objectives clear to both? In other words, how clear are your expectations of new men?

(F) *Training.* Do the formal and informal training activities achieve the training objectives quickly and effectively or do they waste time, frustrate the new man, teach the wrong things and bore everyone? What assumptions do you make when you design the training activities? Do they come close to meeting the expectations of new men?

(G) *First Assignment.* How is the first assignment or project chosen? Does it provide an opportunity for the new employee to learn, meet people, grow, and so on. Is it clear to the new man why he was given that assignment, what he can get out of it, and what is expected of him?

Obviously this isn't an exhaustive list, and the importance of these items will vary from organization to organization, but it should give the reader a feeling of what can be adjusted for better results.

In the final analysis, the payoff for a particular organization will depend upon its awareness of the importance of this process, and upon the creativity with which it systematically examines its unique situation and derives solutions for better management of this process.

READING 2
A PRACTICAL PROGRAM FOR EMPLOYEE SOCIALIZATION*
Daniel C. Feldman

What is it about the ways organizations recruit, select, and develop employees that makes some new recruits feel competent and others helpless, makes some feel effective as good organization members and others feel isolated and rejected, makes some workers passive observers and others active contributors to organization success?

These are the basic questions in the study of organizational socialization, the study of the ways by which employees are transformed from total company outsiders to participating and effective corporate members. The success of the socialization process is critical for individuals, because the way their careers are managed by organizations influences both the quality of their work life and the quality of their outside lives. And as the success of organizations becomes increasingly dependent on the commitment of members rather than on traditional control systems, the questions posed here about organizational socialization become increasingly important to organizations as well.

* This research was part of a doctoral dissertation presented to Yale University Graduate School. The author wishes to thank J. Richard Hackman for helpful comments on this article. Richard Hackman, Clayton Alderfer, and Gerrit Wolf provided valuable assistance during the conduct of the research.

I recently conducted a large-scale study of the socialization process at a community hospital, using as a sample 118 employees—nurses, nurse's aides, radiology technologists, accounting clerks, and tradespeople (plumbers, electricians, and carpenters, for example). I interviewed each employee extensively, and each completed a questionnaire about his or her experiences in entering and adjusting to the organization. This article discusses the highlights of the research, which was addressed primarily to four sets of questions:

1.   What happens to individuals as they enter organizations and adjust to new work assignments? What are the indicators of good socialization experiences?

2.   What are the results, or consequences, of socialization programs? What aspects of socialization programs most influence these results? What are the differences in outcomes between the socialization experiences of professional, paraprofessional, and nonprofessional workers?

3.   What are the specific practices and policies that organizations can follow at each stage of socialization to make the process easier, quicker, and more effecitve for employees?

4.   What are the general implications of this research for the use and design of organizational socialization programs?

We'll consider each of these sets of questions separately.

There seem to be three distinct stages that employees go through as they adjust to new jobs in organizations.

Stage I: "Getting In"

The socialization process begins even before employees enter the organization. First of all, before they actually take jobs and enter the organization, they try to get a full picture of what life in the organization is really like. Second, they try to search for jobs for which they are "best suited"—in terms of making the best use of their talents, in terms of working with people whose company they would enjoy, or in terms of a variety of other reasons.

There are two indicators that the socialization process is going smoothly for people at this "getting in" stage. The more positive these indicators are for individuals, the more likely it is that the two later stages of socialization will go smoothly as well. These two indicators are:

1. *Realism*. The more realistically a person portrays himself to the organization, and the more realistically the organization portrays itself to the person, the more likely it is that the person will be hired for a job for which he is well suited and that he will receive the type and amount of training he needs. A study of appointments to West Point, for example, found that those who received a booklet realistically portraying life at the military academy were more likely to accept appointments to the academy and to survive the first year than were those who had received no booklet. Similarly, John Wanous found that realistic job previews for telephone operators resulted in higher job satisfaction and greater job survival without reducing the flow of qualified applicants.

In the community hospital situation, the behavior of both employees and supervisors during the selection process in the accounting department illustrates this relationship. Employees in the accounting department do mainly clerical work, such as billing, typing, and keypunching. A very important aspect of these jobs, however, lies in dealing with patients and lawyers, often hostile, who are trying to unravel payment problems or billing errors. This part of the job is often not communicated to new employees. Most employees who had not known that their jobs would entail so much interpersonal conflict often felt that they had unfortunately taken clerical jobs much less suited to their abilities than other, similar jobs available, while those who had been forewarned about the interpersonal conflict made a better adjustment. On the other hand, employees are generally made aware of the fact that the workload is heavy and that the jobs demand speed. Obviously, realism works both ways. Employees who either overestimated their own typing skills—a sincere misconception—or incorrectly pictured their abilities to their prospective supervisors were more likely to discover after being hired that their jobs were too much for them.

The case of Arthur, a relatively new tradesman in the hospital's engineering department, illustrates the problems that unrealistic expectations can create. Arthur, a licensed refrigeration expert, fully expected to be doing refrigeration repairs. But he was sent to the electrical shop, where he felt "like I was at a road with 10 forks, not knowing where to turn or even how to find out how to turn." Three months after the study, I learned that Arthur had quit his job after a period of great ill will with co-workers and supervisors.

2. *Congruence*. It is important, too, that people have the skills necessary to do the jobs that organizations need them to perform and that the jobs the organization provides can satisfy individual needs and preferences. If this congruence of individual needs and skills with organizational demands can be achieved, we can expect greater general satisfaction and work motivation on the part of individuals and longer job tenure for new recruits as well.

On the other hand, where the congruence between job requirements and individual needs is low, great job dissatisfaction is a likely result. Barbara, a nurse's aide, commented, "I don't respect what I'm doing. . . I have a good mind and I'm not using it." She was overqualified for her job and found coming to work unpleasant: "I don't say, 'Gee, I can't wait to get to work.' This job just has to be tolerated." Nancy, a radiology technologist trained to do sophisticated radiological tests, complained bitterly that she spent most of her time doing routine X-rays. When asked which direction she thought her career would take, she replied, "I didn't spend three years being trained to say, 'Hold it, now breathe,' and I don't expect to spend the next three years saying it, either."

Stage 2: "Breaking In"

During the second stage of the socialization process, the "breaking in" stage, the employee actually enters the organization and attempts to become a participating member of his own work group. There are four major activities of employees at this stage.

First, employees establish new relationships with co-workers and supervisors, both as they perform their jobs and as they relax with others during breaks and lunches. Second, employees learn new tasks that are needed to do their jobs; this involves not only learning new skills but also becoming acquainted with the operation and maintenance of equipment, learning the bureaucratic procedures associated with their jobs, and so on. Third, new employees clarify their roles in the organization. Since job descriptions are generally expressed in very global terms, employees often insert their own personalities into jobs, putting more emphasis on those tasks they particularly like to perform or feel competent to perform. During the first few weeks and months, employees try to define exactly what tasks they have to do, what the priorities among those tasks are to be, and how they are to allocate their work time among them. Fourth, employees not only evaluate their progress within the organization, but also try to come to some agreement with others in the work group about the overall quality of their work and about specific areas of strength and weakness in job performance.

In this "breaking in" stage, there are four indicators that the socialization process is still running smoothly—indicators that suggest the last stage of socialization will go smoothly as well:

1. *Acceptance.* The more accepted a new recruit feels, the more he will feel trusted and be trusted by other group members; he also will be more likely to receive evaluative and informal information that will help him both in doing his job and in interacting with other organization members. Both Dornbush, writing about the "union of sympathy" among recruits in a Coast Guard Academy, and Becker, writing about new medical students, indicate that work groups can serve as a defense against oppressive forces in the organization, as a source of emotional support, as a source of possible solutions for work problems, and as a source of referral for appropriate types of behavior.

Feelings of lack of acceptance at work impact heavily on an employee's sense of self-worth. One accounting clerk in the hospital, for example, commented that she "felt like an orphan, hoping someone would take me in," while another clerk reported she spent over $50 per month in long-distance phone calls to talk to friends near her former residence about her present problems with co-workers. Uneasiness at work influences performance as well. For instance, Bruce, a radiology technologist, was experiencing a good deal of difficulty in his relationships with workers: "I've been here two months, and even now I don't feel accepted. . . . I worry about my relationships with other workers all the time. . . . This worry drives out concern for patients, for work, for everything."

2. *Competence.* Employees need to feel self-confident and skilled, both to bolster self-esteem and to begin a "benign circle of development," writes M. B. Smith. "Launched on the right trajectory, the person is likely to accumulate successes that strengthen the effectiveness of his orientation toward the world, while at the same time he acquires the knowledge and skills that make his further success more probable. . . . Off to a bad start, on the other hand, he soon encounters failures that make him hesitant to try. . . . And he falls increasingly behind his fellows in acquiring the knowledge and skills that are needed for success on those occasions when he does try."

Joan, a billing clerk, was seen as truly competent by her co-workers. Assigned the clients whose last names began with the letters O through Z, she was affectionately known as the Wizard of Oz by peers, who constantly turned to her for help. Joan expected to stay in the organization and work her way up the hierarchy. In contrast, Carol, another clerk, reported feeling like "a little nothing, a very little cog in a very big wheel." Although she was unsuccessful in getting through training, her supervisors decided to keep her on after her probationary period. Now both Carol and her supervisors are regretting that decision and both are fearing the impact of termination.

3. *Role definition.* The more the individual employee can set his own priorities and allocate time the way he would like among the jobs he has to do, the more satisfied the employee will be. When supervisors are responsive to negotiating job descriptions and assignments with employees, employees report feeling more committed to doing high-quality work and having positive feelings about supervisors and co-workers. Moreover, as Edgar Schein points out, it is healthy for individuals to question some of the demands put on them during socialization. When an employee accepts all the behavioral demands and values of supervisors, he "curbs his creativity and thereby moves the organization toward a sterile form of bureaucracy." Organizations should demand that employees accept only those behaviors and values that are crucial to the accomplishment of organizational goals, and should allow employees some freedom to be independent and resourceful.

In the hospital, we see the impact of role definition most clearly in nursing service. Three-year diploma nurses tended to feel that the mark of a good nurse is the ability to keep on schedule, to handle all patients quickly and efficiently, and to be solicitous of the attending physician's demands. By contrast, four-year degree nurses tended to feel that the mark of quality nursing care is emphasis on the total individual patient, both his physical and his psychological needs, and that the nurse should share more fully in the diagnosis and treatment decisions made on the floor.

The 30 head nurses, too, differed in their philosophy of nursing, with some putting more emphasis on administration of nursing care and others on counseling. Those nurses who shared their head nurse's philosophy of nursing and defined their jobs accordingly also tended to feel more fairly and equitably evaluated on their job performance; those nurses who did not share their head nurse's idealization of the nurse's role—the bulk of the three-year nurses—experienced greater turnover and requested more internal transfers. In fact, most of the four-year diploma nurses request transfers to oncology or geriatrics, where counseling is a more accepted nursing activity and where head nurses with that attitude are more often assigned. As one nurse put it, "Some people put emphasis on patients, others on beds. We all have priorities—some of us are just lucky enough to get supervisors with the same ones!"

4. *Congruence of evaluation.* Employers and employees should also be able to come to some agreement over the individual employee's performance evaluation and his or her success in the organization. If an employee feels that he is progressing well, and a significant number of his peers agree with his evaluation, then the employee is likely to continue in his work with feelings of satisfaction and self-esteem. If, however, he feels that he was performed well, but others feel he has not, he will continue behaving in inappropriate ways and will be less likely to continue satisfactorily in his job. Unless the individual employee receives feedback soon to correct his perceptions and behaviors and/or gets additional help or training, his long-term prospects in the organization are poor.

Two main factors were most frequently cited as sources of friction over evaluation. Tony, a radiology technologist, stated that in her department "the standards are set so high that, no matter how well you perform, you still feel incompetent." Radiology technologists and nurses also reported that they got feedback only when they performed poorly, never when they performed well. This led one nurse to comment that "even a well-trained pigeon should be positively reinforced more than once every 365 days."

At times this resentment over failure to evaluate fairly or frequently leads to severe supervisor-subordinate interpersonal problems or even to sabotage of the workflow.

Stage 3: "Settling In"

Once an employee has entered an organization and come to some tentative resolution of adjustment problems in his or her own work group, he needs to resolve two types of conflicts. The first are *conflicts between work life and home life.* Work and home can come into conflict over the employee's schedule (for example, both the number of hours worked and when they are scheduled, vacation time, days off), the demands on the employee's family, and the effect of the job on the quality of home life (for example, amount of worry and preoccupation associated with work, demands on the family for emotional support, and so on). The second set of conflicts that the employee needs to deal with are *conflicts between his work group and other work groups in the organization.* Different groups in the organization—other departments or divisions, superiors further up the organization hierarchy, and so on—may have very different expectations of the employee from those his work group has of him.

There are two indicators of a successful "settling in" period:

1. *Resolution of outside life conflicts.* We have already observed that work life can influence one's outside life in terms of scheduling, demands on an employee's family, and the quality of life possible for an employee outside of work. Employees who do not resolve these conflicts may be forced to leave the organization at some point in their career or experience emotional withdrawal. These outside life conflicts are more common for women—and they are particularly severe for women with children at home. In the hospital, for example, Irene, a married accounting clerk with two children, reported that an hour before work closed, her mind became "like a pile of leaves blowing across the lawn—I start dwelling on the million errands I have to run for my children, and how I'm going to get them all done." Another employee reported feeling like a split person, "a hassled, grousing housewife masquerading as a chin-up professional nurse."

2. *Resolution of conflicting demands.* Members of other departments may disagree strongly with a new recruit's definition of his job and may have very different expectations of a new member of the work group. Employees who are continually upset by these work conflicts and who have not developed decision rules to deal with them will need to invest more energy and time in resolving each and every conflict and will, therefore, have less energy for dealing with their actual task demands. Nurse's aides, in particular, had a hard time dealing with all the conflicts that they experienced as they moved from department to department performing the tasks of nursing service. One aide commented, "In this hospital, everyone passes the crap down to the next lowest level, and we end up getting the most unrefined crap in the place." The aides' supervisors, and the aides themselves, acknowledged that the aides spent almost as much time in fighting with supervisors, fighting with people in other departments, and complaining to others as they spend in doing real work.

For example, nurse's aides do most of the transporting work of the floor—bringing patients down for X-rays, special treatments, and so on. Their supervisors instruct them simply to leave the patient off and come back to the floor to continue their work. X-ray and other departments, however, often demand that the nurse's aide remain with the patient until after the treatment so that the patients are not left hanging around their departments. If the aide leaves without the patient, he or she is reprimanded by auxiliary service; if the aide returns late to the floor, he or she is reprimanded by the head nurse. As a last-ditch attempt to solve the transport problem, nurse's aides met with nursing administrators and made the suggestion (which was accepted) that the aide would stay with the patient if and only if the auxiliary service supervisor obtained permission from the head nurse on the floor.

There are several ways in which we can evaluate the consequences of socialization programs for individuals: general satisfaction of workers, mutual influence, internal work motivation, and job involvement. Let's look at each of these outcomes a little more closely and examine what aspects of the socialization process influence them.

General Satisfaction

J. Richard Hackman and Greg Oldham define general satisfaction as the degree to which an employee is satisfied and happy in his or her work. Two types of organization outcomes are most frequently associated with the level of general employee satisfaction. The first of these outcomes is absenteeism and turnover. Research is convincing that the more satisfied a worker is, the longer he or she will stay on the job and the lower his or her absenteeism will be. The second of these outcomes is job performance. Evidence suggests that general satisfaction may be related, under some but by no means all circumstances, to a moderate increase in job performance.

My study showed four variables to be

positively associated with general satisfaction: congruence, role definition, resolution of conflicting demands, and resolution of outside life conflicts.

1. *Congruence.* Congruence is most strongly correlated with general satisfaction; the better the fit between an individual and his work, the more happy and satisfied he will be with his job situation. Where the fit is not good between the individual and the job—as in the cases of our overqualified nurse's aide and radiology technologist—the consequent dissatisfaction can cause individuals to think of leaving their jobs altogether.

2. *Role definition.* Role definition and general satisfaction are also positively related. Employees who could largely determine what tasks they would do and how they could allocate their time among those tasks expressed more positive attitudes about the nature of their work and their relationships with other members of their work group. We saw one good example of this relationship with nurses who held the same or different philosophies as their supervisors. In the former case, both the nurse and her superior shared the same definition of the job and general satisfaction was high, while in the latter case, differing job definitions led to conflicts and low satisfaction.

We found another example of this relationship in the engineering department. There are several short-term projects to which the tradespeople in the department may be assigned, ranging in desirability from jobs on a renovation crew to jobs like shoveling snow or cleaning up after a flood. Employees with latitude in accepting or rejecting short-term jobs enjoyed their work more and had more positive feelings about their supervisor.

This latitude in accepting or rejecting short-term jobs often depends on the supervisor's evaluation of the employee. If a supervisor feels particularly positive about an employee, the supervisor may give the worker more opportunities to learn new tasks and skills and may be more willing to let him dump unwanted chores on others. If the supervisor has a low evaluation of the employee, however, he or she may load all the simpler tasks on him or hold him back from doing more challenging tasks until the employee has mastered the tasks already assigned.

Role conflict stemming from demands from different departments serves as a constant irritant to some hospital employees, making the overall quality of the work experience less positive. We see this relationship in our example of the nurse's aides. We also see it frequently among the registered nurses. Hospitals have two hierarchies—a medical hierarchy from the chief of staff down to orderlies, which is responsible for medical care, and an administrative hierarchy from the chief administrator down to first-line supervisors, which is responsible for the operation of the entire hospital facility. The nurse's role is overloaded with responsibilities to both hierarchies. As part of the medical hierarchy, the staff nurse is the only employee allowed to give certain medical treatments and use certain medical equipment, and she is ultimately responsible for the medical services provided by all the staff under her. Simultaneously, as part of the administrative hierarchy, she acts as liaison between floor staff and auxiliary medical personnel, the chief person responsible for record keeping, and the employee responsible for scheduling the floor staff and for requesting and accounting for supplies.

3. *Resolution of conflicting work demands.* Nurses who are less upset by role conflicts—and such conflicts are inevitable—

have come up with some decision rules for handling them and thus are happier in their work situations. Their most common way of learning how to handle these role conflicts is by modeling the behavior of senior nurses on the floor. New nurses are generally not required to deal with external groups their first two weeks at work; during this time they have ample opportunity to learn which conflicts they will face most often and some of the best ways of dealing with them. For instance, a perceptive nurse will learn not to escalate a conflict with another department to a higher level in the organization; if a conflict must be escalated to be solved, that is the job of the head nurse. She may also learn which people in other departments are the most cooperative, so that conflicts can be avoided by requesting out-of-the-ordinary favors when receptive staff will be on duty. Nurses may also learn not to try to settle conflicts on night duty or weekends; there are too few staff members on duty to warrant making issues out of work hangups. If a nurse does not catch on to these rules by herself, generally she is explicitly told about them by her peers or by her head nurse at evaluation time.

4. *Resolution of outside life conflicts.* The positive relationship of this resolution to satisfaction raises some provocative issues for the role of the organization in the socialization process. The finding suggests that what happens to the employee outside of the workplace does indeed influence his or her satisfaction with the job, much as in the cases of our female accounting clerk and nurse, and that organizations, in fact, have little influence over one major determinant of job satisfaction.

There are some interesting differences between departments on general satisfaction, as shown by comparing registered nurses and tradespeople from the engineering department. See Figure 1.

Nurses rated lower than tradespeople on the four variables related to general satisfaction. While nurses and tradespeople both have jobs that suit their skills and abilities, nurses have a good deal of difficulty in defining their jobs because they have so many different tasks to perform, along with disagreements over assigning priorities to these tasks. Moreover, nurses have the severest role conflicts to handle—at work, managing the conflicting demands of medical and administrative duties and, at home, managing unusual scheduling problems and the effects of patients' problems on them. By contrast, tradespeople have fewer inconsistent demands put on them as they clarify their work roles. They have very little to do with the medical hierarchy at all and can pretty much go about their business without being bothered; rarely, if ever, do tradespeople have to work nights or weekends.

Mutual Influence

Mutual influence refers to the extent to which an employee feels some control or power over the way work is carried out in his or her department. One of the most frequently cited indicators of ineffective socialization is lack of influence. Indeed, John Van Maanen writes that "the socialization process is often deemed unsuccessful if it produces the overconforming member," while Robert Dubin refers to such overconformers as "institutional automatons." Although an employee must generally accept the legitimacy of influence attempts by the organization as a condition of employment, establishing a legitimate influence on his own part is likely to make him a much more

Figure 1   Tradespeople and Nurses on General Satisfaction and Its Correlates

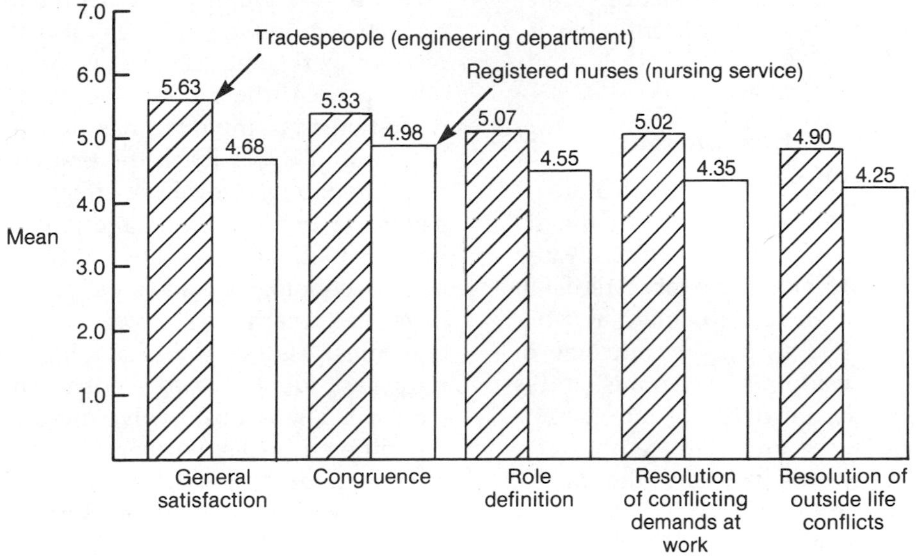

creative and participative member of his group.

Two variables at the "breaking in" stage—competence and congruence—are associated with mutual influence. Employees believe that until such time as they feel on top of their jobs, they would look foolish trying to suggest changes about work-related activities to co-workers or supervisors. Moreover, the employees studied felt that they needed to earn the right to make suggestions, and that the way to do this was to demonstrate competence. Carol, our accounting clerk who felt incompetent at her job, remarked, "Who will listen to my suggestions when I am blasted by my boss at least once a day for a major error?"

And, when employees feel they are evaluated fairly, they feel they have a good chance of getting at least an open hearing

from a superior on some suggestions. Joan, "the Wizard of Oz," was seen as competent by supervisors and felt fairly evaluated; as a result, she felt she had some power and control over the way things were done in her unit. By contrast, when employees feel that they are not appreciated or fairly evaluated, they doubt that their supervisors will appreciate and positively evaluate any of their suggestions. For instance, one radiology technologist at the hospital who felt unfairly evaluated also felt that the inequitable evaluation reflected her supervisor's lack of confidence in her and a negative evaluation of her contributions to the radiology group. When asked if she felt she could influence the way work was done in her department, she replied, "You can't make Tuesday Friday."

Most hospital procedures and operating

policies are mandated by law or determined at the very top levels of the organization; for these reasons, mutual influence scores across departments are consistently low.

Internal Work Motivation and Job Involvement

Internal work motivation refers to the degree to which an employee is *self*-motivated to perform effectively on the job. At least in the management literature, internal work motivation is cited as a likely outcome of training and development programs, and is most frequently related to job performance—that is, the greater the employee's motivation to work, the higher the quality of that employee's work.

Job involvement refers to the degree to which an employee is personally committed and involved in his work, in other words, the degree to which the total work situation is an important part of his or her life. It is often cited as a necessary condition if the individual is to fully accept the demands placed upon him by members of an organization.

It is important to note that *no* variable in this research is significantly and positively related either to internal work motivation or to job involvement. It is more likely that the *nature of the work itself* rather than the way one is recruited or trained at work makes a difference in increasing the levels of these two variables.

A number of studies, especially those by G. Richard Hackman and Edward Lawler and by Hackman and Greg Oldham, have shown that there are strong relationships betwen jobs with high "motivating potential scores" and high internal work motivation and job involvement. Five job charac-

teristics contribute to the motivating potential of jobs: variety of skills required to do a job, task identity (the degree to which the job requires completion of a "whole" piece of work), the significance of the job to other people, the amount of freedom and discretion the employee has at work, and the amount of feedback the employee gets from the job itself on how effectively he or she is performing. The three jobs with the highest motivating potential—nurse, radiology technologist, and tradesperson—also have the three highest scores on these two outcomes. All three jobs have high skill variety, task identity, and feedback from the job itself. These jobs involve the use of several different skills; workers do identifiable pieces of work; employees can tell right away—from patients, from films, or from equipment—whether they have performed effectively. In addition, nurses have high task significance and a good deal of autonomy as well.

In jobs with lower motivating potential—accounting clerk, for example, or nurse's aide—employees experience lower job involvement and internal work motivation. Their jobs require fewer skills, allow less autonomy, and are much less significant than the other jobs studied. Accounting clerks do not even have high task identity, because each clerk does only a small piece of work involved in billing a patient or in collecting payments. On internal work motivation, for example, nurses scored 6.03 (out of 7) while accounting clerks scored 5.53; on job involvement, nurses scored 3.57 while accounting clerks scored 2.87 (see Figures 2A and 2B).

The research provided some tentative ideas about ways in which socialization can be made more effective. Let's consider some of these ways.

Figure 2A   Scores for Total Sample and Job Categories on Internal Work Motivation

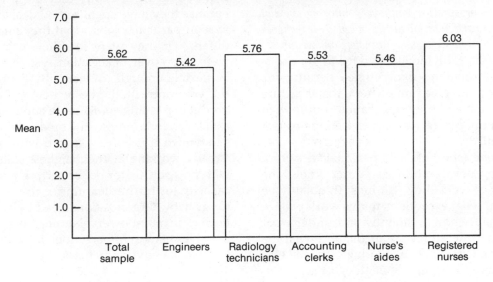

Figure 2B   Scores for Total Sample and Job Categories on Job Involvement

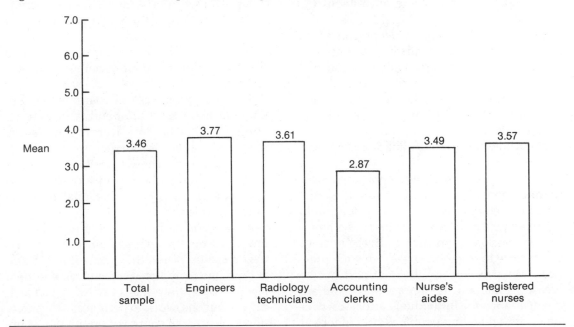

Stage 1: "Getting In"

Give prospective employees information not only on particular job duties but also on the work group, promotion and transfer opportunities, and so on. Individuals often fail to get realistic information—many times because it's distorted to give him or her a rosier picture of the job and the organization. But though it is unnecessary to trigger feelings of discontent by relaying to new recruits every negative aspect of every personality or work group, new employees *should* know the types of work they will most frequently be doing, what exceptions to this work pattern are made, how frequently and under what circumstances they are made, and what the general climate of the work group is like as well as something about the pattern of supervision in the work group. Is the particular supervisor relatively authoritarian or does he leave the individual plenty of leeway in the way he or she goes about the job?

Design selection and placement programs that:
1. Make more realistic assumptions about the relationships between personal characteristics and job performance.
2. Consider the needs and desires of job applicants as well as the demands of the organization.
3. Allow for more flexibility and growth in career paths.

We have discussed how important it is for organizations to accurately picture the organization to the individual and to put him in a job for which he is well suited. The literature is conclusive on the positive outcomes that accrue to organizations from such practices. What is not so obvious, and not so well documented, is the fact that there are changes in both individuals and jobs over time, so that having people tightly fit jobs at one point may not turn out to be the best

planning in the long run. There is evidence that people are the way they are precisely because they have spent a good deal of their lives in particular jobs—that they might be different if they were in different job settings. Moreover, a selection system should be flexible enough to deal with changes in the environment. If the technology of job production changes to a more sophisticated skill level, for example, the organization will be stymied if it is fully staffed with people already working at their highest skill level with no aptitude for better performance, no capacity for further learning, and no desire for growth. Organizations need to be more flexible in manpower planning to prevent massive changes in personnel or technology in unstable environments.

Stage 2: "Breaking In"

Carefully design orientation programs that:
1. Allow opportunities for new recruits to meet the rest of the employees upon, or soon after, their arrival.
2. Choose the key people involved in the orientation for their social skills as well as their technical skills.
3. Give the people in charge of the orientation extra time to spend with new recruits for informal task learning and social talk.
4. Do not put new recruits in the position of having to choose sides or be labeled as a participant in interpersonal or intergroup conflicts.

It is surprising how much impact the first few days in the organization can have on new recruits. When they come into a group and no one introduces them or makes them feel welcome, they start out having bad feelings about the work experience. The choice of people to take charge of orientation is important as well—they need to have social skills as well as technical skills, and they should be given extra time to spend with new recruits. They should also help to buffer new recruits from existing interpersonal conflict, which confuses new employees and keeps them from making friends or trusting others until they can understand the tensions involved.

Structure a training program that:

1. Identifies job-relevant skills and provides training geared to those skills.

2. Provides frequent feedback to employees on how they are performing.

3. Integrates formal training with informal training and orientation programs.

There is an abundance of training literature that conclusively demonstrates the need for job-relevant skill training and for frequent feedback. This research points out,

in addition, the need to integrate formal training with informal training and orientation. Many employees reported feeling that until such time as they become friendly with and could trust co-workers, they could not find out information essential to doing their jobs well. In nursing service, for instance, employees felt that some of the most important things to learn about their jobs were the preferences and personalities of the doctors with whom they worked—but only when they were trusted did they receive such information. The average length of time employees reported it took to feel accepted by others was 2.7 months, while the average time it took to feel competent was over twice as long, six months (see Figure 3). Only in radiology, where there is a great deal of hostility between graduates of the

Figure 3   Estimated Time to Feel Competent and Time to Feel Accepted for Total Sample and Job Categories

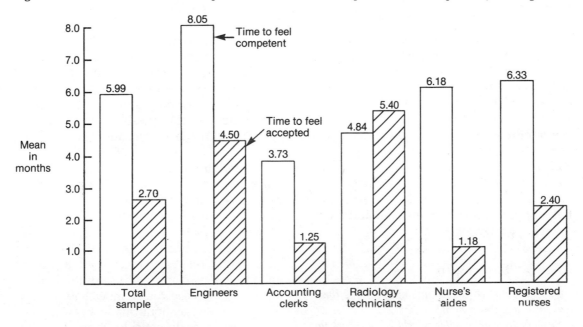

hospital's own school of radiology and graduates of other programs, does this relationship not hold.

Provide a performance evaluation system that:

1. Allows face-to-face meetings between employees and supervisors.

2. Has performance criteria that are as objective as possible.

3. Trains supervisors in how to give feedback.

Peter Drucker, George Odiorne, and other management-by-objectives authorities have all stressed the importance of the feedback process and the need for objective performance criteria, the setting of realistic goals, and competent supervisory handling of feedback meetings. My research adds to and reinforces this literature by pointing out the importance of the congruence of evaluation as well as the absolute level of evaluation, and the impact that lack of feedback has on employees.

Use the addition of new work group members as an opportunity to:

1. Reallocate tasks as much along individual preferences as possible.

2. Consider work redesign projects.

It is inevitable that employees will bring particular strengths and weaknesses to their jobs and have strong preferences for some assigned tasks over others. Instead of trying to avoid these individual differences, supervisors should try to reallocate tasks as much along individual preferences as possible and use the opportunity posed to change the boundaries of group membership in ways that will yield both more efficient and more satisfying group work designs.

Stage 3: "Settling In"

Provide counseling for employees to help them deal with work and home conflicts.

Be as flexible as possible in scheduling work for employees with particularly difficult outside life conflicts and in adjusting the work assignments of employees with particularly bad conflicts at work.

Recognize and deal with structural or interpersonal problems that generate conflicts at work.

This study demonstrated the impact that role conflicts can have on general job satisfaction and turnover among employees. As organizations become more and more complex, and as two-career families and new work patterns become more prominent, we can expect role conflicts to play an even greater part in determining the quality of the work life of employees. It is important for the organization to take as active a part as possible in dealing with role conflicts by providing structural changes in workflow or work assignments and by using social science interventions, such as third-party intervention or intergroup conflict resolution, wherever they seem appropriate.

Don't expect too much from socialization programs. A major implication of this research is that socialization programs are not appropriate for achieving some of the results most frequently expected from them. Managers often expect that socialization programs will help them motivate new workers and facilitate employee communication. Unfortunately, none of the variables commonly associated with the socialization process are significantly correlated in this study either with internal work motivation or with employee job involvement. What socialization programs *do* affect are the general satisfaction of workers and their feelings of autonomy and personal influence. These factors are important, because general satisfaction consistently relates to decreased turnover and absenteeism and because mutual influence may increase the number and quality of creative suggestions made by workers. Employers need to consider more carefully just what they want to accomplish in the development of individuals and tailor their programs more carefully to those ends.

Make sure that organizational efforts in the socialization process are continuous. Different organizations and different levels of organizations tend to focus on one phase of socialization as being particularly important, thus underemphasizing the other two phases. The two most common emphases in socialization programs are:

1. Concentration on the attraction and recruitment of workers. This is most frequent in organizations heavily staffed with professional workers—such as hospitals, universities, and law and accounting firms. The levels at which this strategy is most frequently used are the higher levels of the organization, where the cost of hiring the wrong applicant or the implications of choosing the wrong candidate are greatest.

2. Concentration on the training and development of workers. This is most often found in organizations heavily staffed with unskilled or low-skilled labor, such as production and manufacturing companies. The emphasis on socialization is also more common at the lowest levels in an organization (that is, nonsupervisory personnel). The rationale: since the jobs are unskilled, only minimal effort should be put into recruitment and much more effort into training and developing new employees.

When organizations concentrate only on recruitment and selection, they may prolong the time it takes workers to adjust to their jobs; when organizations concentrate only on training and development, they risk hiring an unnecessarily large percentage of people who are unsuited for the jobs involved and who will be hard to train. To most effectively socialize new employees, organizations must incorporate all three phases of the socialization process into their plans and actions.

Don't depend too heavily on occupational socialization in planning particular socialization programs. Even professional and technical employees have socialization needs beyond what's provided for in a professional or technical school. Workers need to learn how their particular job is practiced in a particular setting. They need to know whether their professional goals and personal needs can be met by a particular organization; they need to know what procedures and tools are used in the particular organization, what skills will be most utilized, and what activities will be required of them most frequently. They need to know not only what will be expected of them in terms of dealing with their co-workers and other work groups in the organization but also the impact this particular job will have on their outside lives. Organizations need to pay more attention to the variances in workers' behavior that may be attributable to the particular organization's socialization practices rather than merely to the differences between occupations.

READING 3
CAREER PROBLEMS OF
YOUNG MANAGERS*
Ross A. Webber

Drawing on interviews with more than 100 managers, discussions with several hundred more, and published literature, this article examines some of the common difficulties experienced by young specialists and managers and offers some advice on career management. Hopefully, no one is so un-

---

* ©1976 by the Regents of the University of California. Reprinted from *California Management Review*, vol. XVIII, no. 4, pp. 11–33, by permission of the Regents.

lucky as to confront them all, but knowledge forewarned is courage armed.

Early Frustration and Dissatisfaction

The early years of one's first permanent job can be difficult. The young college graduate's job expectations often exceed reality, eliciting feelings of underutilization that can result in departure.[1] The causes of this condition rest with the young person, organizational policy, and incompetent first supervisors.

Conflicting Expectations.   Business school graduates often are trained through cases to think like managers and to solve top level executive problems. If they enjoyed this perspective in college, they may expect real work to be similar and their actual authority to equal the synthetic authority in class. But this takes years to achieve, so they frequently experience difficulty in adapting to changed time horizons that accompany the transition from school to work. Many students have been accustomed to almost immediate gratification and to short time spans—this semester, next academic year, a few years to graduation. The passage of time and status changes are clearly signaled by changes in routine and frequent vacations.[2]

A permanent job is quite different. The time horizon is much longer, fewer events mark time passing, and it is a full year until a two-week vacation. Not surprisingly, some young employees attempt to perpetuate the school perspective by changing jobs frequently and taking off on unofficial vacations. However understandable the behavior, older managers perceive it as immature.

These older managers may also be at fault because they don't provide young specialists and managers with sufficient challenge. Large organizations tend to treat newly employed college graduates as all the same and to assign them to boring tasks that could be performed by people with less education. Management argues that young people's expectations are unrealistic and they must prove themselves before being assigned more important jobs.[3] But many young people detest being treated as "average" or as a

---

[1] Over 50 percent of all MBA's leave their first employer within five years. J. A. De Pasquale and R. A. Lange, "Job-Hopping and the MBA," *Harvard Business Review* (November–December 1971), p. 4ff. See also, J. A. De Pasquale, *The Young Executive: A Summary of the Career Paths of Young Executives in Business* (New York: MBA Enterprises, 1970); and G. F. Farris, "A Predictive Study of Turnover," *Personnel Psychology* (1971), pp. 311–28. When a young graduate joins an organization, a "psychological contract" is forged between individual and organization. If the organization doesn't live up to the individual's perception of the contract, he feels offended and leaves. Unfortunately, the specific terms of this implied contract are seldom discussed. J. P. Kotter, "The Psychological Contract: Managing the Joining-up Process," *California Management Review* (Spring 1973), pp. 91–99. The reasons why the relationship is initially vague lie in the implicit bargaining and selling that take place in the attraction and selection process. No one really wants to communicate "truth." See L. W. Porter, E. E. Lawler III, and J. R. Hackman, "Choice Processes: Individuals and Organizations Attracting and Selecting Each Other," in *Behavior in Organizations* (New York: McGraw-Hill, 1975), pp. 131–58.

[2] Lawler argues that expectation of immediate gratification means that management should shorten periods between evaluation and award frequent small raises rather than yearly. E. E. Lawler, "Compensating the New Life-style Worker," *Personnel* (1971), pp. 19–25. See also, T. F. Stroh, *Managing the New Generation in Business* (New York: McGraw-Hill, 1971).

[3] In general, the younger the managers, the higher the level they expect to reach in their careers. Thus, virtually all are disappointed at some time. M. L. Moore, E. Miller, and J. Fossum, "Predictors of Managerial Career Expectations," *Journal of Applied Psychology* (January 1974), pp. 90–92. Some executives are highly skeptical of MBA's in particular. Here is a portion of a letter written to the editors of *Columbia Journal of World Business* (May–June 1968), p. 5:

"I can't agree completely with Mr. [T. Vincent] Learson's statement (Jan.–Feb. 1968) that the salvation of the business world is the "scientifically trained man that comes from the ranks of the graduate schools." I

member of a category like everyone else. They want to be considered unique, if not special, because their culture stresses the individual.[4]

Corporate culture, however, emphasizes efficiency in handling large numbers of people identically until individuals have demonstrated their uniqueness. Paradoxically, management's attitudes and policies may promote the very "immature behavior" that is given as the reason for the policies in the first place. Obviously, patience and understanding are needed on both sides.

Before concluding that it is better to work for a small organization, one should realize that situations change. Beginning professional and managerial positions in small businesses are reported to be more challenging and satisfying than similar posts in large firms. Small companies can't afford to train young graduates on unproductive jobs, so they put them to work on important tasks immediately. Nonetheless, 5 to 10 years into careers, the views reverse: middle managers in large organizations report their jobs as more challenging and rewarding than those in small firms, who mention frustration and pressure for conformity. In

the large organizations, middle-level jobs apparently carry more autonomy and authority than do similar level positions in small firms where the top can dominate everything.[5]

Incompetent First Supervisor. A first boss plays a disproportionate role in a young person's career.[6] The impact of an incompetent first supervisor can be especially unfortunate because the early experience tends to be perpetuated. What operates is a kind of self-fulfilling prophecy. If a superior doesn't expect much of his young subordinates, he doesn't challenge them and many don't perform well.[7] Even worse, if the incompetent supervisor doesn't set high standards for himself, almost everyone's performance deteriorates.[8] The word spreads that other managers don't want people from the group; the young person can be stuck in a dead end.

Ambitious young specialists and managers want visibility and exposure—opportunity to show higher-level executives how well they can perform and to understand executive problems and objectives. A fearful intermediate supervisor, however, can

have found many of these people have no concept of the value of a dollar. They are theorists only and for the most part have no desire to learn the basic fundamentals of the business they are engaged in, but rather consider themselves above finding out the basic principles of the business by experience. They want everyone to hand them experience on a velvet pillow and are too concerned with taking over the presidency of an organization six months after they enter an organization. I do believe the scientifically trained graduate student does have his place in industry, but. . . ."

[4] A. G. Athos, "Is the Corporation Next to Fall?" *Harvard Business Review* (January–February 1970), pp. 49–60. For more on characteristics and expectation of young managers and specialists, see J. Gooding, "The Accelerated Generation Moves into Management," *Fortune* (March 1971), p. 101ff.; and L. B. Ward and A. G. Athos, *Student Expectations of Corporate Life* (Boston: Graduate School of Business Administration, Harvard University, 1972).

[5] L. M. Porter, "Where is the Organization Man?" *Harvard Business Review* (November–December 1963), pp. 53–61.

[6] J. A. Livingston, "Pygmalion in Management," *Harvard Business Review* (July–August 1969), pp. 81–89.

[7] D. E. Berlow and D. T. Hall, "The Socialization of Managers: Effects of Expectations on Performance," *Administrative Science Quarterly* (September 1966), pp. 207–223.

[8] In general, a superior's stringent personal standards are associated with higher subordinate performance than lower personal standards. The superior's personal standards also seem to exert more influence on subordinate performance than subordinate's personal standards. The best performance, however, is where both superior and subordinates have high personal standards. J. P. Campbell, M. D. Dunnette, E. E. Lawler, and K. E. Weick, *Managerial Behavior, Performance and Effectiveness* (New York: McGraw-Hill 1970), pp. 447–551.

block such opportunity by relaying all communications himself and not allowing his subordinates to see higher levels. Handing a report to your immediate boss with no opportunity to argue in its favor and never hearing what happens to it can be very disturbing (especially if you discover later that your name on the cover was replaced by your superior's).

Organizations should institute policies to ensure that young specialists and managers enjoy the opportunity to communicate with and be evaluated by several higher executives and not just by their immediate supervisors. And young managers should fight for the right to go along with reports.

Resignation may be the best answer to an untenable position under an incompetent supervisor, but short of this step, understanding the situation may allow an individual to set higher personal standards than the boss does. He or she may be able to perform better than others in a demoralized department—even only slightly better may bring the attention of other executives who are not blind to the difficulty of performing well in that setting. The organization, of course, would be better off if young graduates were assigned mainly to the best supervisors, and many firms do this.

Insensitivity and Passivity

All human organizations are political. This is neither condemnation nor praise, merely fact. For an organization to be effective, its managers must engage in the politics by which power is directed to problems and solutions implemented. Unfortunately, many young managers are insensitive to or even resentful of the political aspects of organizations.[9] This hurts them personally be-

cause they are passive about their careers, and it hurts the organization because it hinders development of power coalitions necessary for effective results.

Insensitivity to Political Environment. Managers who climb hierarchies rapidly tend to be protégés of successful higher executives.[10] These sponsor-protégé linkages move together because members come to respect and trust each other. They personalize organization life and make it more predictable. When a manager has a problem, he prefers to consult someone whom he knows, not just an anonymous occupant of a bureaucratic position. To be sure, the criteria for inclusion in the group are often arbitrary and undemocratic in devotion to old-school tie and proper religion, race, or sex, but they are important nonetheless.

The importance of political relationships to the organization is that they form the power coalitions necessary to make and implement decisions.[11] Very few organizations are autocratically ruled by one omnipotent person; even fewer are pure democracies

---

[9] For some case studies of sensitive and insensitive young managers, see W. R. Dill, T. L. Hilton, and W. R. Reitman, *The New Managers* (Englewood Cliffs, N.J.: Prentice-Hall, 1962).

[10] E. E. Jennings, *The Mobile Manager: A Study of the New Generation of Top Executives* (Ann Arbor: Graduate School of Business Administration, University of Michigan, 1967). For examples of the critical importance of sponsors or mentors for ambitious females, see Gail Sheehy, *Passages: Predictable Crises of Adult Life* (New York: E. P. Dutton, 1976) and J. Thompson, "Patrons, Rabbis, Mentors—Whatever You Call Them, Women Need Them, Too" *MBA* (February 1976), p. 26.

[11] On the importance of power, McMurry writes:
"The most important and unyielding necessity of organizational life is not better communications, human relations or employee participation, but power. . . . Without power there can be no authority; without authority there can be no discipline; without discipline there can be difficulty in maintaining order, system and productivity. An executive without power, is therefore, all too often a figurehead—or worse, headless. . . . If the executive owns the business, that fact may ensure his power. If he does not, and sometimes even when he does, his power must be acquired and held by means which are essentially political" R. N. McMurry, "Power and the Ambitious Executive," *Harvard Business Review* (November–December 1973), p. 140.

where the majority dominates. Most require a skillful minority coalition able to lead the majority through competent argument and common action. Without strong coalitions, power remains fractionated, actions are divisive, and the organization drifts willy-nilly.

A common complaint about young business school graduates is that they overemphasize analytical tools and rational decision making to the detriment of human understanding.[12] In spite of their desire to be treated as unique individuals, some observers note, they treat others as objects to be manipulated. Thus, the new graduates apparently are more Machiavellian in their managerial attitudes and more willing to use coercion than are practicing managers.[13] As one corporation vice president puts it, "It takes us a couple of years to show our business school graduates that an organization is composed of people with whom they must develop personal relationships."

Personal Passivity. Insensitivity to political environment is frequently accompanied by personal passivity and inadequate probing of the world around the young man-

ager.[14] Such a person fears what he may discover about himself or assumes that virtue guarantees reward, so that good intentions will ensure that people will think he is doing a fine job. One man's experience as committee chairman illustrates such a common career mishap. Dave Seymour was assistant administrative manager of a regional office of a large company. He reported to the regional administrative manager responsible for office operations. Shortly after Dave assumed the post, the regional vice president personally requested that he become chairman of a committee to find ways to improve office efficiency. The committee was composed of various junior managers whom the vice president appointed. Dave accepted the job with alacrity because he saw it as an opportunity to prove his managerial potential.

Unfortunately, two years passed and nothing happened except meetings and collection of hundreds of pages of data and recommendations. None were implemented by district or regional managers. Dave hadn't known what to do; the vice president never inquired and Dave couldn't make up his mind to raise the issue with him. Dave had been flattered to be appointed chairman and figured it was an opportunity to distinguish himself. Months later he found that he had made no impact. Details differ, but the pattern is common.

Dave's first mistake was that he accepted the assignment without analyzing his political position and the attitudes toward change among the executives who would actually implement any improvements. Second, he did not clarify his personal power or the committee's authority. What were they to

---

[12] J. S. Livingston, "Myth of the Well-educated Manager," *Harvard Business Review* (January–February 1971), pp. 79–88. In general, Livingston argues that there is no relation between managerial success and school performance and that schools don't develop important attributes. That "wisdom" is the neglected attribute is maintained by L. Urwick, "What Have the Universities Done for Business Management?" *Management of Personnel Quarterly* (Summer 1967), pp. 35–40.

[13] One survey indicates that MBA students express more authoritarian and Machiavellian views than do practicing managers, but that business school professors were more Machiavellian than either! J. P. Siegel, "Machiavellianism, MBA's and Managers: Leadership Correlates and Socialization Effects," *Academy of Management Journal* (September 1973), pp. 404–11. A similar finding is in R. J. Burke, "Effects of Organizational Experience on Managerial Attitudes and Beliefs: A Better Press of Managers," *Journal of Business Research* (Summer 1973), pp. 21–30.

[14] D. Moment and D. Fisher, "Managerial Career Development and the Generational Confrontation," *California Management Review* (Spring 1973), pp. 46–55. See also, D. Moment and D. Fisher, *Autonomy in Organizational Life* (Cambridge: Schenkman, 1975).

do? Issue orders directly to managers and try to persuade them to adopt the changes? Or just gather information in case anyone ever asked for it? The third mistake was that Dave did nothing to avoid his fate as time passed. He did not initiate action to modify the political environment or to better define his authority.

When accepting a delegated task, it is important that a subordinate try to clarify the nature of the delegation by asking certain questions:

• After I look into the problem, should I give you all the facts so that you can decide?
• Should I let you know the alternatives available with the advantages and disadvantages of each so you can decide which to select?
• Should I recommend a course of action for your approval?
• Should I select the alternative, let you know what I intend to do and wait for your approval?
• Should I take action, let you know what I did and keep you informed of results?
• Should I take action and communicate with you only if it is unsuccessful?

Dave did not ask these questions of his vice president. Worse, he didn't inform his superior that no changes were being made. No doubt this is one of the most difficult acts in management, but sometimes a subordinate must inform a superior that he (the subordinate) is powerless and that nothing will improve unless the superior acts. At times you must push your boss to make a decision.

It is often easier to drift with the times and hope things will work out for the best, but this is not a recipe for managerial success. The paradox is that the most promising young staff specialists may be the ones who find it easiest to drift. To be in demand is a mark of status and being busy gives a feeling of importance. Consequently, a good young person might allow himself to be dominated by other's desires, to be over-committed to a narrow specialty, and to remain in a staff position too long. If you think of the organization as a cone, the staff tends to be on the outer surface, while line management is closer to the central power axis.[15] In his or her 30s, a young person may find himself making too much money to accept the pay of a lower line position, which is farther away from the top but has a more direct route to it. Young managers should take time to explore and probe the organizational environment and to understand people's attitudes, develop relationships, and clarify their own positions.

Ignorance of Real Evaluative Criteria. A central rule for managerial success is "please your boss." Unfortunately, what pleases him or her is not always clear so that insensitive and passive young managers don't know the real criteria by which performance is being evaluated. Business is often less structured and more ambiguous than the authoritarian stereotype that many young people bring with them. Of course, managers highly value good performance, as measured by profits, sales, productivity, and so on. Subordinates who occupy positions where results can be easily measured in these terms tend to report greater satisfaction and autonomy in their jobs than those in posts where performance cannot be evaluated quantitatively.[16] People in positions measured only by subjective evaluation tend to be less satisfied and to feel greater pressure for conformity in dress,

---

[15] Three-dimensional cone model of organization from E. H. Schein, "The Individual, the Organization and the Career. A Conceptual Scheme," in D. A. Kolb, I. M. Rubin and J. M. McIntyre, *Organizational Psychology: A Book of Readings* (Englewood Cliffs, N.J.: Prentice-Hall, 1971), pp. 301–16.

[16] Porter, "Where Is the Organization Man?"

thought, and action. In the absence of other criteria, these people may be measured by how closely they fit the superior's prejudices rather than by actual results.

Most people are biased by their own successes or failures in making judgments. We like others to be like ourselves, especially successful others because they verify our own correctness. Superiors tend to rate more highly those subordinates who are like them in appearance and managerial style.[17] Hence, hair length, speech habits, and clothes do affect how personnel are evaluated, with some superiors seeing mustaches and mod suits as signs of immaturity and radicalism, while others perceive them as showing creativity and vitality.

The same is true for evaluation on the basis of managerial style. However, since the predominant style in the past has been authoritarian, many superiors more highly value subordinate managers who demonstrate authoritarian leadership. Even in the absence of corroborating performance data, authoritarian managers may be more highly rated than those who are participative or abdicative. One study indicated that a "permissive" manager whose division had good performance and much higher morale was rated as having no promotability, while a parallel authoritarian division manager with equal performance and lower morale was cited for excellent potential.[18]

A manager who desires to utilize a less directive style that is ill-suited to his superior's expectation is in a difficult position. If

---

[17] Campbell et al., *Managerial Behavior.*

[18] The study compared three regional managers of different styles—"authoritarian," "permissive," and "recessive" (*laissez-faire*). Objective measurements indicated no difference in regional performance, but higher management consistently rated the authoritarian as most effective and promotable. J. H. Mullen, *Personality and Productivity in Management* (New York: Temple University Publications, Columbia University Press, 1966).

his boss is a hard-driving authoritarian manager, he may expect good subordinate managers to be similar to himself. By asking frequent questions and demanding reports, he makes it difficult for the subordinate to be anything but authoritarian.

A courageous, tough, and independent manager in the middle may serve as a buffer between his superior and his subordinates. By absorbing the pressure coming from above and not passing it on immediately to his people, he allows them enough autonomy to proceed collaboratively. Such leadership requires demonstrable success to survive.

Tension between Older and Younger Managers. Tension between older and younger professionals and managers is very common. It may be exacerbated by individual personalities, but basically it stems from differences in life and career stages. A recently graduated specialist or manager understandably relies on what he or she knows best—academic knowledge. He or she is at least somewhat familiar with statistics, psychology, and economics, and these can be very valuable. Unfortunately, they can also hinder his working relationships with older managers.

Armed with an arsenal of analytical techniques, the young manager looks for problems to which they can be applied. But frequently the problems which the textbook solves are not the important ones. He may even talk to older personnel in the arcane vocabulary of "stochastic variables," "break-even points," and "self-actualizing opportunities." Such talk can be very threatening to an older person to whom it is unfamiliar. He may perceive the younger person as endeavoring to manipulate him.

In some cultures, older persons are automatically respected for age and assumed wisdom, but in the United States the young may respond to the older person's skepticism with veiled contempt. Because the older manager doesn't know the new techniques, the young specialist or manager erroneously infers that he is not as competent or important. But this can be a career-crippling mistake, because organizational contribution and influence have little to do with technical knowledge. An offended older executive can oppose the younger person's future advancement.

A young person should recognize that some older managers will see him or her as a threat (although the managers will deny it, even to themselves). The threat is not to position, but one of obsolescence and a reminder of human mortality.[19] Tension can arise even when the older person likes the younger. The young specialist should endeavor to show respect for the older, to frame his vocabulary appropriately, and to avoid condescension. As the young person comes to recognize the importance of political influence and intuitive judgment, he can develop the vertical coalitions helpful to both older and younger.

Loyalty Dilemmas

Loyalty is a popular but vague concept that is subject to both praise and scorn. There is little doubt, however, that most people in authority value subordinates' loyalty. But what is this quality? Some of the various unspoken views on loyalty that superiors expect of subordinates are: obey me; work hard; be successful whatever it takes; protect me and don't let me look bad; and tell me the truth. All of these concepts of loyalty are partially valid and contribute to organizational effectiveness. Unfortunately, all can also be distorted to the detriment of people and organization.

---

[19] H. Levinson, "On Being a Middle-Aged Manager," *Harvard Business Review* (July–August 1969), pp. 51–60.

Loyalty as Obedience. The superior can equate loyalty with subordinates doing what they are told. All managers have a right to expect general obedience, but excessive emphasis on it enshrines the "yes man" philosophy as organizational religion. It is understandable that a subordinate's willful disobedience would be construed as disloyalty, but equating loyalty and obedience assumes that authoritarian management is the only valid style while it ignores the possibility that loyalty may sometimes reside in not doing what the boss has ordered because disaster could follow.[20]

Loyalty as Effort. Young specialists and managers are rightly expected to work hard in the interest of the organization. Executives are skeptical of the intentions of young people who make a minimal commitment to their work. Yet when effort and hours worked are equated with loyalty, people will put in excessive hours without real effort or contribution. Consider the comments of some young managers in the home office of an insurance company:

"The officers are the first here in the morning and the last to leave at night; they are always here Saturdays and many Sundays."

---

[20] That not obeying may be loyalty is demonstrated by D. Wise in *The Politics of Lying* (New York: Random House, 1973). Newton Minow, appointed head of the Federal Communications Commission by President John F. Kennedy, is quoted as saying that in April 1962, after a story that was highly critical of the President was broadcast on the NBC "Huntley-Brinkley Report," Kennedy called Minow. As Minow recalls the conversation, it went like this:

JFK: "Did you see that goddamn thing in 'Huntley-Brinkley'?"

Minow: "Yes."

JFK: "I thought they were supposed to be our friends. I want you to do something about that."

Minow says he did not do anything except calling a Kennedy aide the next morning and asking him to tell the President he was lucky to have an FCC chairman who doesn't do what the President tells him.

"They set the pace and, at least implicitly, it is the pace we must accept and follow."

"If you want to get ahead this is the pattern you must accept. Contribution tends to be judged in terms of time spent in the office, not things accomplished."

"If you want to get ahead, you come in on Saturdays regardless of whether it is necessary or not. The cafeteria and offices are sometimes filled with people who just feel they can't afford not to come in on Saturday."

Thus, behavior can become a game to convince others that you are loyal even when it contributes nothing to organizational effectiveness.

Loyalty as Success. The superior can see loyalty as synonymous with reliability and successful performance whatever it takes (and don't bother him if it entails shady things he shouldn't know about). It is reasonable to expect honest effort; but this version of loyalty can be tough, because it adds a moral criterion to judgment of competence. Thus, not all young managers who miss deadlines are disloyal. The task may simply be impossible within legal or ethical limits. A superior who judges all people and performance from a loyalty perspective will discourage honest communication and encourage illicit managerial practice.

Loyalty as Protection. The superior expects the subordinate to protect him and the organization from ridicule or adverse evaluation by others. Subordinates who only follow their superior's instructions to the exact letter *are* disloyal if they don't exercise common sense and fill obvious gaps. This version of loyalty has particular relevance when the superior is a generalist over specialist subordinates who know more than he does in their areas of expertise. In return for subordinate concern and protection, he im-

plicitly promises to look out for their personal and political interests.

This loyalty concept sometimes includes an injunction to subordinates never to disagree with the superior in public when the boss's boss or outsiders are present. This makes sense, but it can become exaggerated when a sharp distinction is made between "us," to whom we owe loyalty, and "them," to whom we don't. The efforts of coalitions to conceal, contain, or cover up their mistakes reflect this view of loyalty. Violation through "leaks" and overly candid communication with outsiders is one of the most heinous organizational crimes because it threatens the security of the hierarchical system.[21] There is little that managers fear more than subordinates trying to make them look bad in order to get their positions. Unfortunately, an insecure superior will sometimes attribute this motivation to a young manager when it really doesn't exist.

Loyalty as Honesty. This view of loyalty exalts truth over harmony. The superior expects the subordinate to warn him of potential failure before the control system picks it up or others find out. This can be particularly hard on a young manager because it tells him to report his own mistakes. To do so is threatening because the bearer of bad tidings is sometimes confused with the tidings. The Turks have an old proverb that warns, "He who delivers bad news should have one foot in the stirrup." Most of us would prefer not to report impending failure in the hope that it will go away or that no news will be interpreted as good news. One of America's most dynamic companies fights this by pushing the dictum: "Don't let us be surprised by unpleasant news." Not

---

[21] For a disturbing example of the retribution heaped on a manager who reported his firm's shortcomings to the press, see K. Vandivier, "The Aircraft Brake Scandal," *Harper's Magazine* (April 1972), pp. 45–52.

reporting failure before it produces adverse results is worse than the failure itself.

The Dilemma. The young manager's problem is that sometimes he doesn't know what version of loyalty is expected by the organization or superior. He may even discover that a boss entertains several simultaneously contradictory views: that he expects strict obedience, but will be angry if obedience leads to poor performance; or that he interprets mistakes as disloyalty but still expects advance warning of impending failure. Loyalty expectations may violate the young manager's personal values if there is no excuse for failure and the hierarchy must be protected at all costs. Under such unhappy circumstances, the role-conflict-resolution tactics possible include conformity to power or authority, selectively ignoring what he can get away with, attempting to modify the superior's expectations, or departure.

Personal Anxiety

With time, promotions, and increased rewards, job satisfaction improves for most managers. The daily task becomes more challenging, yet new concerns crop up for many young managers—anxiety about personal integrity, organizational commitment, and dependence on others.

Anxiety about Integrity and Commitment. People admire different qualities at different stages of life. High school students place high value on independence as they struggle to become adults; college students stress individuality as they endeavor to find their uniqueness; older executives admire decisiveness that would allow them to bear the burdens of high office more easily. Young middle managers especially admire conviction and integrity in the person who remains his own man but believes in what

he or she is doing. As they are rewarded by the organization, many persons begin to question the fundamental value of their jobs.[22] As one young brand manager for a major food company put it, "I'm a success, I earn over $20,000 per year, and I get a big kick from my job and seeing the climbing sales chart, but sometimes I wonder if getting 'Colonel Zoom' cereal on every breakfast table is really that important!" (Especially since it is being attacked by nutritional experts as having little food value.)

This questioning can be difficult for a young manager to understand. After years of apprenticeship, he is reaping the rewards of effort—autonomy, discretionary authority, and opportunity to achieve. Job morale is high. But for some it is not enough, because questions nag. "Am I really selling out to the organization?" "Have I forgotten to ask the important question of what I'm contributing to society?" If he or she concludes that the answers are more affirmative than negative, the young manager is faced with a dilemma—what to do?

Open complaint about the organization's activities may cause others to view the complainer as disloyal, hindering present security and future promotability. Associates and superiors will subtly suggest to the displeased young manager that he keep quiet, work his way upward, and then change company policy if he desires to. This is not bad advice, but the young manager might find being an executive so satisfying that he forgets what it was that he wanted to change. He might alleviate his dissonance by changing his personal values to agree with the dominant view. This facilitates total commitment to the organization and pro-

---

[22] On changing career identities, see D. T. Hall, "A Theoretical Model of Career Subidentity Development in Organizational Settings," *Organizational Behavior and Human Performance* (January 1972), pp. 50–76; and J. F. Veiga, "The Mobile Manager at Mid-Career," *Harvard Business Review* (January–February 1973), p. 115ff.

motes the certainty that most of us desire. Such a solution may work for the individual, but it may ultimately harm society.

No entirely satisfactory answer exists for this dilemma. If the organization's mission and policy are in violent disagreement with personal values, the best course is resignation and perhaps a new career.[23] But premature departure can also be a cop-out, a flight from difficult moral choices. If the decision is to stay, the young manager should strive to keep his values alive, to apply them to small matters which he controls, and to remember them when he has the power to affect policy.

Attitudes toward commitment are ambivalent. A sense of certainty about career is desired because it simplifies one's life and stills the restlessness about whether one is in the right place. Nonetheless, many young people also fear commitment because it means closing doors and giving up the pleasant illusion that they can still do anything they wish. Yet maturity means facing reality and deepening interests. Therefore, a central facet of all careers is balancing commitment to the organization with maintaining a sense of independence.[24] Pure rebellion which rejects all or-

ganizational values and norms can end only in departure; pure conformity which accepts everything means loss of self. Creative individualism accepts pivotal values and norms, but searches for ways to have individual impact.

The occasion for loss of integrity is often a person's first failure. After a history of success in school and work, a young manager with a weak sense of identity can be overwhelmed by destruction of his illusions that he cannot fail, that he is immune to career crisis, and that he enjoys widespread social support. The current generation of young people may be especially vulnerable in this area because they are the progeny of prosperity. Success has grown, unchecked by fear of economic deprivation.[25]

Anxiety about Dependence. One aspect of the struggle for maturity is to declare psychological independence of home and parental authority while identifying oneself as an individual. Dependence on others is difficult to handle shortly after successfully establishing one's independence. Thus, undergraduate students tend to dislike team projects in which their grades can be lowered by others' mistakes. Nonetheless, total independence is impossible in real organizations. Superiors are dependent on subordinates' performance, subordinates are dependent on their superior's judgment and

[23] Hirschman suggests that economists will tend to exaggerate the power of leaving while political scientists and sociologists conversely underrate it. A. Hirschman, *Exit, Voice and Loyalty* (Cambridge, Mass.: Harvard University, 1970). On new careers see D. L. Hiestand, *Changing Careers After Thirty-Five* (New York: Columbia University Press, 1971). Connor and Fielder recommend that firms pay for the reeducation of unhappy managers who could then move on to other careers. S. R. Connor and J. S. Fielder, "Rx for Managerial Shelf Sitters," *Harvard Business Review* (November–December 1973), pp. 113–20. See also, R. F. Pearse and B. P. Pelzer, *Self-directed Change for the Mid-career Manager* (New York: Amacom, 1975).

[24] A. Zaleznik, G. W. Dalton, L. B. Barnes, and P. Laurin, *Orientation and Conflict in Career* (Boston: Graduate School of Business Administration, Harvard University, 1970). The authors suggest that many people never reconcile this conflict between personal identity and organizational values, yet those in conflict may be

more effective than those who are "oriented" toward the organization. See also, E. H. Schein, "Organizational Socialization and the Profession of Management," in Kolb et al., *Organizational Psychology: A Book of Readings*, pp. 1–16. Stoess reports a study indicating that managers are relatively more conforming than the general population. A. E. Stoess, "Conformity Behavior of Managers and Their Wives," *Academy of Management Journal* (September 1973), pp. 433–41.

[25] E. E. Jennings, *Executive Success: Stresses, Problems and Adjustments* (New York: Appleton-Century-Crofts, 1967); and E. E. Jennings, *The Executive in Crisis* (East Lansing: Graduate School of Business Administration, Michigan State University, 1965).

effective representation, and middle managers are dependent in both directions.

All of this dependence can provoke anxiety. For example, many junior military officers have suffered from psychosomatic illness because they bear the responsibility for their unit's safety and performance when they don't have as much experience or technical knowledge as their senior enlisted personnel. They cannot solve their problems by denying their dependence, but these problems can be reduced by learning the technical details of subordinates' duties. In the long run, however, young supervisors must recognize interdependence and strive to facilitate subordinate performance while representing their interests upward.

Most young adults are aware of their fear of being dependent on others, but they usually are not conscious of anxiety about having others dependent on them.[26] As they acquire spouse, family, job status, and community position, they receive increasing demands to give financial, temporal, and emotional support to more and more people and organizations. This sense of others' dependency can be gratifying, but time and energy are limited. Independent and self-reliant managers are sometimes disturbed to discover that they feel dominated by the needs of people dependent on them. If and when the burden becomes too great, they must establish life priorities that balance demands of family, organization, and community in a way that may fully satisfy none, but allows relations to continue with all.[27]

---

[26] E. Fromm, *The Art of Loving* (New York: Harper & Row, 1956).

[27] J. Steiner, "What Price Success," *Harvard Business Review* (March–April 1972), pp. 69–74. For optimistic advice on how open communication between husbands and wives can help to solve many of the conflicts at home caused by an executive's commitment to career, see E. J. Walker, " 'Til Business Us Do Part?" *Harvard Business Review* (January–February 1976), pp. 94–101.

Ethical Dilemmas

Few young people begin their careers with the strategic intention of being unethical as a means to success. And few managers are unethical as a matter of policy. Yet the majority share a problem of determining what is ethical or unethical when faced with unexpected dilemmas.[28] Many people believe that ethical means "what my feelings tell me is right." Unfortunately, feelings are very subjective phenomena, so one person may think that misleading advertising is all right while another believes it is wrong.

Others argue that ethical means religious beliefs or the golden rule, law and common behavior, or what contributes to the most people. Clearly, no single view of ethics is always correct or incorrect. A manager should assess his decisions from a variety of useful perspectives.[29]

Ethics as Economic Self-Interest.   When a young manager in a high-technology firm was offered a position by a competitor, his employer sought a court injunction to prevent his moving. On the witness stand it was suggested that there was a matter of loyalty and ethics involved in leaving with the knowledge and expertise he had derived from his employment. The young man's response was, "Loyalty and ethics

---

[28] The conceptions of ethics are from R. Baumhart, *Ethics in Business* (New York: Holt, Rinehart & Winston, 1968). See also S. H. Miller, "The Tangle of Ethics," *Harvard Business Review* (January–February 1960), pp. 59–62; J. W. Towle (ed.), *Ethics and Standards in American Business* (Boston: Houghton Mifflin, 1964); T. M. Garrett, *Business Ethics* (New York: Appleton-Century-Crofts, 1966); C. C. Walton, *Ethos and the Executive* (Englewood Cliffs, N.J.: Prentice-Hall, 1969).

[29] G. F. F. Lombard, "Relativism in Organizations," *Harvard Business Review* (March–April 1971), pp. 55–65; J. F. Fletcher, *Situation Ethics* (Philadelphia: Westminster Press, 1966); J. F. Fletcher, *Moral Responsibility: Situation Ethics at Work* (Philadelphia: Westminster Press, 1967).

have their price; as far as I am concerned, my new employer is paying the price."[30]

It is easy to criticize this manager for his ethics and choice of language, but he is expressing faith in the free market system— that scarce resources such as he should flow to the buyer who can utilize them most and who is willing to pay the highest price. Ability to pay theoretically reflects market demand and social interest, so he could best serve society by changing employers for more money.[31] In addition, his position reflects the temporary nature of his demand. Like the athlete, his technical skills are subject to obsolescence and he owes it to himself to gain the most from them while they last. Under this ethic, his only responsibility to his present employer is to give him the opportunity to match the offer.

Not everyone shares this faith in the free market system, however, because ability to pay could reflect raw monopoly power and not consumer wishes.[32] And even those who believe that the market should allocate resources in this way don't all agree that economic self-interest is a good criterion for ethical decisions at the individual level. Most people see no connection between "ethical" and "economic" or "self-interest."

Ethics as Law. When asked about kids' buying his pornographic magazines, a publisher and purveyor of "adult" material responded, "What's the matter, don't you like to look at pictures of naked pretty girls and boys? I keep within the law. My magazines aren't meant for kids, but I can't keep them from buying them. That's the government's problem."

For this businessman, law is the criterion for decision making. If society thinks what he is doing is unethical, it is government's responsibility to legislate. In the absence of prohibition, he does what is allowed. Certainly managers bear responsibility as citizens to obey the law.[33] The young marketing managers in the electrical equipment industry who secretly met to fix prices and allocate markets violated the law, and in their case the law was relatively clear.[34]

Sometimes the law is not clear, though. Even the managers in the electrical conspiracy argued that the law was vague because it required competition and prohibited collusion, yet they believed that cessation of "cooperation" would lead to dominance by the giant firms and decreased competition.

Most people feel that adherence to law is a necessary but insufficient basis for ethics. Behaving legally so you won't be punished is merely being prudent, not ethical. Law imposes demands from outside, while eth-

---

[30] M. S. Baram, "Trade Secrets: What Price Loyalty," *Harvard Business Review* (November–December, 1968), pp. 66–74. On various horror stories of managers who supposedly put profits over ethics, see F. J. Cook, *The Corrupted Land* (New York: Macmillan, 1966) and R. L. Heilbroner et al., *In the Name of Profit* (Garden City, N.Y.: Doubleday, 1972).

[31] M. Freedman, *Capitalism and Freedom* (Chicago: University of Chicago Press, 1962). Carr argues that it is dangerous to a manager's career to act purely upon personal beliefs, but he can help his organization if he can show how unethical policies actually harm economic performance. A. Z. Carr, "Can An Executive Afford a Conscience?" *Harvard Business Review* (July–August 1970), pp. 58–64. Thus, Carr is both pessimistic and optimistic—pessimistic that only economics guides business behavior, but optimistic that many dilemmas may be converted to economic terms where economics and public interest correspond. That good ethics is good economics and good business is argued by G. Gilman, "The Ethical Dimension in American Management," *California Management Review* (Fall 1964), pp. 45–52.

[32] J. K. Galbraith, *The New Industrial State* (Boston: Houghton Mifflin, 1967).

[33] A. Chayes, "The Modern Corporation and Rule of Law," in E. S. Mason (ed.), *The Corporation in Modern Society* (Cambridge, Mass.: Harvard University Press, 1959), p. 25ff.

[34] C. C. Walton and F. W. Cleveland, Jr., *Corporations on Trial: The Electrical Cases* (Belmont, Calif.: Wadsworth, 1967).

ics should come from inside.[35] Besides, if law constituted the only behavior limits, government and law enforcement would swell to overwhelming proportions. Big Brother would be everywhere and freedom to do either wrong or right would disappear.

Ethics as Religion. If government law is not sufficient, what about higher law? One business executive suggests that there should be no problem knowing what is proper: "If a man follows the Gospel he can't go wrong. Too many managers have let basic religious truth out of their sight. That's our trouble."

Most religions maintain that there are universal moral principles that should guide human behavior[36]—that in almost all times and places, thou shalt not lie, steal, or murder, for example. Thus, advertisements that deceive customers and industrial espionage to discover a competitor's secrets are clearly proscribed by common religious principles. Nonetheless, only a minority of managers think such principles are the basic ethical criteria for their managerial decisions. The

problem is that moral principles are often abstract and difficult to apply to specific cases.[37] To be sure, intentional lying is clearly wrong, but most businessmen sincerely believe they must hide information and distort public communication as protection against competitors or unions. And stealing seems wrong, but padding expense accounts or "borrowing" company tools doesn't seem so immoral when the employer knows and seemingly condones it (perhaps this is a form of supplemental compensation). Catholic theology holds that every employer has an obligation to pay at least a "living wage," but determining this is subject to debate. Perhaps it is just unrealistic to expect a guide to conduct developed in the Middle East 2000 years ago to have direct relevance to the complex conditions of modern managers.[38]

Pragmatists argue that religious teachings and the golden rule are not meant to apply to competitive business anyway, that management is more akin to a poker game than to the religious life.[39] If obfuscation and deception are part of the game and everyone knows it, then they are not sinful. Finally, many people subscribe to no religious beliefs and bitterly resent believers' attempts to impose their tenets on everyone. Clearly, religion as an ethical guide is helpful and

---

[35] A former chairman of the Chase Manhattan Bank writes about ethical problems:

"Government's response to the problem, characteristically, has been that 'there oughta be a law.' In the first session of this Congress, more than 20,000 bills and resolutions were introduced, 20 percent more than in the first session of the previous Congress. The same approach has been in evidence on the state and local levels. The objective seems to be to hold together our fractured moral structure by wrapping it in endless layers of new laws—a kind of LSD trip by legislation. Yet it should be clear by now, even to busy lawmakers, that the great lesson to be learned from our attempts to legislate morality is that it can't be done. For morality must come from the heart and the conscience of each individual." George Champion, "Our Moral Deficit," *The MBA* (October 1968), p. 39.

[36] H. L. Johnson, "Can the Businessman Apply Christianity?" *Harvard Business Review* (September–October 1957), pp. 68–76; J. W. Clark, *Religion and the Moral Standards of American Businessmen* (Cincinnati; South-Western, 1966).

---

[37] T. F. McMahon, "Moral Responsibility and Business Management," *Social Forces* (December 1963), pp. 5–17.

[38] See *Fortune* editorial in response to Pope Paul's encyclical "On the Development of Peoples" (May 1967), p. 115. The editors argue that the Church's view would hinder growth and harm the underdeveloped nations more than a few unethical companies do.

[39] A. Z. Carr, "Is Business Bluffing Ethical?" *Harvard Business Review* (January–February 1968), pp. 143–53. In a similar vein, Levitt argues that advertising is like art: it is not reality, but illusion and everyone knows it. Therefore, some distortion is acceptable. T. Levitt, "The Morality of Advertising," *Harvard Business Review* (July–August 1970), pp. 84–92.

good, but only to some people some of the time.

Ethics as Common Behavior. "But everyone does it" has been a popular guide and justification for behavior from time immemorial. Realists argue that if the majority engage in a certain activity, then it must be all right, regardless of what parents or policemen say. The young manager could make his judgments based upon the characteristic behavior of his boss and his organization or industry, not universal rules. Thus, the garment salesman argues that he couldn't possibly follow the strict custom against booze and sex as aids to selling computers. His industry accepts such inducements and buyers expect them, so he feels he couldn't compete without them. Similarly, managers in fiercely competitive industries argue that they can't be as open about costs and policies as a monopoly such as telephone communications.

Every young manager will experience the pressure of others' behavior as determinant of his own.[40] Yet we have a paradox: most agree that others' behavior is not the most elevated criterion for individual decisions yet still maintain that their superior's behavior is the major reason they behave unethically. It is the top that sets the ethical tone in most organizations and this is one of the gravest obligations of high-level executives. Their behavior will be emulated and converted into institutionalized custom by lower managers.[41]

A young person caught in such an unhappy situation pursues one of several courses: he adjusts his personal beliefs and stays happily; he stays, but with a guilty conscience (hopefully to change things when he gains power); or he departs.

Ethics as Impact on People. Upon being asked about unethical managers, a former president of General Electric observed that unethical people are not the problem: "What we must fear is the honest businessman who doesn't know what he is doing." Thus, most companies that have polluted the air and despoiled the land did so out of ignorance, not immorality. Knowledge may assist managers in making decisions based upon what is best for the greatest number of people.

This is what schools of business administration and management have striven for—to make management a profession whose primary concern is social contribution, not narrow self-interest.[42] By teaching prospective managers how business, economy, society, and environment interact, the hope is that their graduates will take the broader picture into account when making decisions. No intelligent executive in the last quarter of the 20th century can really believe

---

[40] Baumhart, *Ethics in Business.*

[41] On the difficulties of managers who are confronted with accepting questionable conduct of their superiors, see J. J. Fendrock, "Crisis in Conscience at Quasar," *Harvard Business Review* (March–April 1968), pp. 112–20. For reader response to the situation, see J. J. Fendrock, "Sequel to Quasar Stellar," *Harvard Business Review* (September–October 1968), pp. 14–22. Ninety-eight percent said it was wrong to keep quiet, but 64 percent admitted they would be tempted to.

[42] K. R. Andrews, "Toward Professionalism in Business Management," *Harvard Business Review* (March–April 1969), pp. 49–60. Some are skeptical about whether business schools really affect the ethics of their graduates. An executive observes, "They tend to get the notion up at Harvard that some things are more important than profits. But that doesn't affect them when they come here. They're not really contaminated. They're typical, intelligent, ambitious, greedy, grafting, ordinary American males." Quoted in S. Klaw, "Harvard's Degree in the Higher Materialism," *Esquire* (October 1965), p. 103. Schein argues that educational institutions tend to accept the values of the enterprises they prepare students for. E. H. Schein, "The Problems of Moral Education for the Business Manager," *Industrial Management Review* (Fall 1966), pp. 3–14.

that air and water are "free goods" to be used as he or she unilaterally deems most profitable for the firm. Even if the firm doesn't pay for them, his education should have shown him that society does.

No doubt ignorance has occasioned much apparently unethical behavior, and greater professional knowledge should be of great benefit to all. But unfortunately, some professionals who have taken the Hippocratic oath or sworn allegiance to the Constitution cheat clients, defraud the public, and rape the environment. It is naive to expect that education alone is a sufficient guide for ethical behavior. Besides, what contributes to the greatest number of people sometimes means exploitation of the few or even breaking laws. Some executives have violated various business laws in order to protect the jobs of employees on the grounds that no one is hurt by colluding with a competitor, but many would be out of work and collecting unemployment compensation if pure competition existed.

Beware of Cynicism. No single ethical criterion is sufficient. The young manager striving to be ethical should do more than depend on economic self-interest, obey the law, observe his religious principles, follow his superior, and obtain the greatest good for the most people. He will have to take all of these into account filtered through his subjective judgment of what is right. In making these judgments, however, he should guard against cynicism.

Many people attribute poorer motivation and more unethical behavior to others than themselves. Young people today seem to be very cynical about business ethics and managers. They tend to believe that practicing managers engage in more unethical behavior than they would and more than the managers themselves think they do. Thus, students attribute such activities as padding expense accounts, stealing trade secrets, and immoral cooperation to managers to a greater extent than the managers anonymously report that they do. Research suggests that the younger the person, the greater his cynicism about managers; the older the manager, however, the greater the optimism about others. Whether this reflects time or "the times" is unknown. Do people become less cynical as they become older and see that everyone isn't as unethical as they had once thought? If so, today's young people might become less cynical as they climb their organizational ladders. Or is today's cynicism actually justified because older managers forget what it is like at lower levels or delude themselves about actual practice?

Nonetheless, excessive cynicism encourages unethical behavior on the grounds that "I'd be a fool not to if everyone else is." Cynicism thus can be self-fulfilling prophecy. More likely, a young manager who believes everyone does it will discover that they don't and that if he does, his career may be ruined.

Advice on Career Management

Advising young people on how to manage their careers is a risky proposition. It depends upon the individual's objectives and his or her definition of success: Climbing to the top? Maintaining integrity? Keeping job and home separate? Happiness? These are not mutually exclusive goals, but they can be competitive.[43]

Assuming that a young manager's objective is to climb to higher managerial ranks,

---

[43] On different career perspectives, see H. O. Prudent, "The Upward Mobile, Indifferent and Ambivalent Typology of Managers," *Academy of Management Journal* (September 1973), pp. 454–464.

the following suggestions have been offered by various people:[44]

• Remember that good performance that pleases your superiors is the basic foundation of success, but recognize that not all good performance is easily measured. Determine the real criteria by which you are evaluated and be rigorously honest in evaluating your own performance against these criteria.

• Manage your career; be active in influencing decisions, because pure effort is not necessarily rewarded.

• Strive for positions that have high visibility and exposure where you can be a hero observed by higher officials. Check to see that the organization has a formal system of keeping track of young people. Remember that high-risk line jobs tend to offer more visibility than staff positions like corporate planning or personnel, but also that visibility can sometimes be achieved by off-job community activities.

• Develop relations with a mobile senior executive who can be your sponsor. Become a complementary crucial subordinate with different skills than your superior.

• Learn your job as quickly as possible and train a replacement so you can be available to move and broaden your background in different functions.

• Nominate yourself for other positions; modesty is not necessarily a virtue. However, change jobs for more power and influence, not primarily for status or pay. The latter could be a substitute for real opportunity to make things happen.

• Before taking a position, rigorously assess your strengths and weaknesses, what you like and don't like. Don't accept a promotion if it draws on your weaknesses and entails mainly activities that you don't like.

• Leave at your convenience, but on good terms without parting criticism of the organization. Do not stay under an immobile superior who is not promoted in three to five years.

• Don't be trapped by formal, narrow job descriptions. Move outside them and probe the limits of your influence.

• Accept that responsibility will always somewhat exceed authority and that organizational politics are inevitable. Establish alliances and fight necessary battles, minimizing upward ones to very important issues.

• Get out of management if you can't stand being dependent on others and having them dependent on you.

• Recognize that you will face ethical dilemmas no matter how moral you try to be. No evidence exists that unethical managers are more successful than ethical ones, but it may well be that those who move faster are less socially conscious.[45] Therefore, from time to time you must examine your personal values and question how much you will sacrifice for the organization.

• Don't automatically accept all tales of managerial perversity that you hear. Attributing others' success to unethical behavior is often an excuse for one's own personal inadequacies. Most of all, don't commit an act which you know to be wrong in the hope that your superior will see it as loyalty and reward you for it. Sometimes he will, but he may also sacrifice you when the organization is criticized.

---

[44] Career advice is summarized in E. E. Jennings, *Routes to the Executive Suite* (New York: McGraw-Hill, 1971). See also, R. H. Buskirk, *Your Career: How to Plan It, Manage It, Change It* (Boston: Cahners, 1976). A summary of books on career planning may be found in K. Feingold, "Information Sources on Life Style/Career Planning," *Harvard Business Review* (January–February 1976), p. 144ff.

---

[45] B. M. Bass and L. D. Eldridge, "Accelerated Managers: Objectives in Twelve Countries," *Industrial Relations* (May 1973), pp. 158–70.

Summary

Frustration and dissatisfaction in young graduates' early careers is widespread because of several factors: their job expectations are unrealistic; they find it difficult to change from school's short-range perspectives to work's long-range view; many employers assign them boring tasks that don't challenge them; and they may begin under an incompetent first supervisor. As a result, turnover from first positions is substantial.

Many young specialists and managers are insensitive to the organization's political aspects so that they needlessly offend older managers and fail to develop alliances necessary to concentrate power on important issues. To compound their problems, some are passive in not asking questions to clarify what is expected of them and what authority they possess. They let their careers drift under the control of others without even knowing the real criteria by which superiors evaluate their performance.

Loyalty presents one of the most difficult dilemmas for many young managers; everyone values it, but its meaning varies. For some superiors loyalty is subordinates doing exactly what they are told. For some it is subordinate success whatever the means. For still others it is subordinates who protect the executives and organization from looking bad. Finally, for a few it is subordinates who communicate honestly what is going on. All of these conceptions of loyalty are partially valid; an organization should value obedience, effectiveness, effort, reliability, and honesty, but all can distort behavior if carried to excess.

With time's passage and achievement, many still young managers experience anxiety about personal integrity, commitment, and dependence. They worry that they are losing track of their personal values while being rewarded for their contributions. They wonder if they are really doing something worthwhile that justifies the doors they have closed and the opportunities passed by. And some feel they are so interdependent with others that they are losing control of their lives.

The occasion for personal anxiety about integrity and commitment is when young managers are faced with ethical dilemmas. Most think they should be guided by personal feelings, but this is extremely subjective and other criteria should also be examined: economics and self-interest, regulations and laws, religious principles, others' customary behavior, and impact on people. All of these criteria can be helpful in making decisions, but none alone is sufficient all the time. In making decisions, however, be wary of cynicism that assumes the worst in everyone else. It can lead to improper and inappropriate behavior.

Career advice includes admonitions to perform well, be active in managing your career, strive for visibility and exposure, develop relations with senior sponsors, learn quickly and train a subordinate, nominate yourself for new positions, rigorously assess your strengths and weaknesses, don't be trapped by narrow job descriptions, recognize that organizational politics are inevitable, and be prepared for ethical dilemmas.

READING 4
CAREER DYNAMICS: MANAGING THE SUPERIOR/SUBORDINATE RELATIONSHIP*
Lloyd Baird and Kathy Kram

I don't know what's wrong with my boss. When we came to the data center together three years ago, we knew our job was to

* Reprinted by permission of the publisher from *Organizational Dynamics*, Spring 1983. © 1983 by AMACOM Periodicals Division, American Management Associations, New York. All rights reserved.

decentralize and over a two year period put ourselves out of a job. We used to work well together. We've done what we came to do, and we should be looking for new jobs. I have been thinking about switching from data processing to human resources. Trouble is, my boss is no help at all. I can't even get any leads from him or help in deciding what to do.

—Bill

When I joined the organization three months ago I had high hopes. I liked the group I'd be working with and I particularly liked the person I would be reporting to directly. He had been on the job only three months and had lots of enthusiasm and drive. He seemed like a fast-rising star that it would be good to link up with. But nothing has worked out. He just doesn't seem to have the time or interest to help me get established and learn this job.

—Sue

Most of us have, at some time, faced frustration and failure when working with a superior. No matter what we do, the relationship just doesn't work. Like Bill and Sue, we don't understand why it is not working and because we don't know how to manage the relationship, we give up and withdraw. Many times superior/subordinate relationships don't work right from the start because we don't recognize the different needs each of us brings to the relationship. Other times, relationships start well and then go sour as our needs change and the relationship doesn't change to match them.

In this article we draw from recent research on career development to develop a model for understanding what is happening in superior/subordinate relationships and how such relationships can be managed. We begin by reviewing how career stages affect the superior/subordinate relationship, make some comments and give some exam-

ples of how to manage the relationship, and then provide some suggestions on what people in organizations can do to improve the way in which superiors and subordinates work together.

How Career Stages Affect Personal Needs

A superior/subordinate relationship is affected by the particular needs that each person brings to it. To effectively manage the relationship, it is essential to understand not only these needs at any given point but also how they change over time. What each subordinate needs from his or her boss, and vice versa, is different now from what it will be next month, in two months, or next year. What each individual needs to get his or her work done, and what each needs as a person will change with time.

Research on the careers of engineers, scientists, and professional managers has found that what one wants and needs from a job will depend on the person's career stage—that is, the jobs they have held, their current position, and the direction in which they are moving. This research has also found that individuals progress through particular career stages, each of which is characterized by unique dilemmas, concerns, needs, and challenges. Because experience and maturing cause people to go through these career stages, and what they need from each other changes as they move through successive career stages, it is important that they maintain a dynamic perspective on their superior/subordinate relationships.

Career development research suggests that individuals generally go through an establishment stage, an advancement stage, a maintenance stage, and withdrawal stage. At each stage, a person will face characteristic psychological adjustments, work responsibilities, relationships and needs. Adult development research broadens this understanding by suggesting that other spheres of life will also affect an individual's concerns and dilemmas at each career stage and that to understand particular career stage needs, one must consider the person's broader life structure.

The Establishment Stage. During the establishment phase, at the outset of a career, people are most likely to need guidance and support to launch their careers. It is generally a period of great uncertainty about one's competence and performance potential. The person who is in the establishment phase is dependent on others for learning, support, and guidance, and at the same time is likely to resist dependence as attempts to establish competence are made. It is a period of building new roles both at work and in one's personal life. Questions about competence, whether to commit oneself to a particular organization, and what kind of family relationships to develop are primary concerns at this stage.

In *The Seasons of a Man's Life*[1] (Knopf, 1978), Daniel J. Levinson and his coauthors describe the major tasks of early adulthood as forming a dream, forming an occupational identity, forming intimacy, and forming a mentor relationship. This is the apprentice stage when the individual's primary role is learning, when she or he must confront and manage dependence, and when she or he is preparing to become an independent contributor. Sue is a good example of a person at this career stage. Having been with the organization for only three months, she faces the challenge of learning the ropes, proving her compe-

[1 Other studies of adult and career development are recommended in the Selected Bibliography at the end of this reading.]

tence, and building new relationships. She needs coaching, sponsorship, and opportunities to learn from her new boss.

The Advancement Stage. During the advancement stage, people become fully independent contributors. Needing less guidance, they know the ropes of organizational life and are most concerned with exposure and advancement through continued demonstration of competence. While people need close supervision and guidance when they're in the establishment stage, collegial and peer relationships become more important in the advancement stage. To learn to operate autonomously at this point in one's career is a major psychological adjustment. If an individual's career is launched in his or her 20s, then the advancement stage is likely to occur in the person's 30s, when concerns about self and family are related to settling down, building a family, and/or radically changing important aspects of the life structure. It is likely to be a period of making commitments—a period that is less prescribed than the establishment stage. A person in this stage is likely to be most concerned about advancing and about appropriate commitments at work and in the family. Thus, coaching and exposure are important aids to advancement, while counseling, role models, and friendship are important aids for resolving important dilemmas at this stage.

The Maintenance Stage. At the maintenance stage, people are likely to have achieved the greatest advancement opportunities of their careers, and they are now investing greater energies in helping and developing less-experienced subordinates. For those who feel satisfied with their organizational accomplishments, it becomes a period of guiding others and finding satisfaction in contributing to the development of human and organizational resources. For those who are dissatisfied with their accomplishments and/or face blocked opportunities, it can be a difficult period of coming to terms with disappointments and losses. The latter are likely to be ineffective supervisors and unable to help other people develop as long as they are plagued with personal dissatisfaction. The maintenance stage frequently commences with mid-life—a time when people also face concerns about the family structure's changing as children leave home, as well as the realities of aging and disappointment over what one has accomplished in contrast with earlier dreams and expectations. Concerns about self, career, and family are likely to stimulate a period of reassessment and redirection. Some of this reassessment may lead supervisors in this stage to devote greater effort to developing subordinates.

The Withdrawal Stage.   Eventually careers do end as people retire or move on to new careers. As they begin to anticipate leaving an organizational career, the withdrawal stage begins. At this stage one can still make contributions. The experienced worker has invaluable perspectives based on experience and history that can be shared with other organization members. Outside of work, concerns about self and family are likely to involve adjusting to greater leisure time and future retirement, and to the reality of aging and mortality. Letting go of a highly involving work identity is a major task of the withdrawal stage.

Other Concerns at Various Stages.   Career stages are affected by outside work concerns, as well as by particular features of the organizational context. Thus there are variations in how individuals progress through these major stages. It is not uncommon, for example, to see individuals launching new careers at mid-life, or individuals moving through the four stages several times during a lifetime. In other instances, the particular needs of the individual will be unique. The progression from advancement to maintenance and on to withdrawal identifies in general the concerns people have as they move through a career.

However, we must attend to the life circumstances and organizational circumstances involved to develop an accurate picture of the unique needs and concerns of a boss or a subordinate. Consider, for example, Mary, who is launching a new career in a manufacturing firm at mid-life. She has developed confidence and a sense of competence in other life endeavors, but comes to an organizational career with concerns about establishing herself in the new setting. At an older age, however, the experience of being an apprentice dependent on superiors for information, coaching, and support presents a challenge. In addition, her superior is much younger, and yet more knowledgeable and established in the profession. In this situation both Mary and her boss must adapt to a unique set of circumstances. How the boss feels about having an older subordinate and how the subordinate feels about being a novice will affect the quality of their relationship. These concerns evolve directly from previous life and career histories.

The organization can also affect the concerns people have at the various career stages. For example, John is an entry-level manager in a fast-growing, high-technology firm; movement and advancement are generally rapid. John will not have long to launch his career and get established before he will be moved to a new position with greater responsibility. The opportunity to build a supportive relationship with his boss is confined to a short period of time. Yet it is essential to build a good relationship so that he can learn as much as quickly as possible from the position. Not only will his career stages be compressed into a much shorter time, but the challenges in managing the relationship are greater because individuals and positions are changing so rapidly.

It is also true that individuals will go through the four stages on a minor scale with each new position. There are always periods of establishment, advancement, maintenance, and withdrawal as one begins a new job, experiences the learning curve, works easily as a result of completing the learning required to do the job effectively, and finally withdraws to move on to something new. So beyond understanding where an individual is in a broad career and life-cycle perspective, another source of insight can be found by looking at his or her tenure in a current position.

When assessing the needs each party brings to a superior/subordinate relationship, it is useful to begin with a look at each party's career stage. One can predict what concerns about self, career, and family are likely to be salient and how these concerns may be shaped by the current organizational context or the individual's particular life history. This diagnosis of needs based on career stage is a critical first step toward effectively managing a superior/subordinate relationship. Let's examine, respectively, what subordinates and their superiors need at each stage.

What Does the Subordinate Need from the Boss?

The subordinate will have both task and personal needs on the job that his or her boss can help fulfill. Task needs relate to accomplishing job responsibilities and personal needs relate to the person's own adjustment, coping, and learning. Let's look at how subordinates' needs from their bosses change as they progress through their careers.

Task Needs.   Accomplishing job responsibilities happens in three phases: deciding what is to be accomplished (the goal), how it is to be accomplished (activities), and how progress will be measured (evaluation and feedback). Subordinates need help from the boss in each of these phases.

The Objectives (Where Are We Going?).   In order to get the job done people need to know what their jobs are and what they are expected to accomplish. The boss has a key role in defining those expectations. He or she translates the organization's objectives into job responsibilities. The boss identifies not only the job responsibilities, but the constraints within which each subordinate works to accomplish them.

In the best case, the subordinate's responsibilities and objectives are clearly defined and understood by both boss and employee; moreover, they fit the boss's goals. In some cases, however, resources aren't available, or the organization's objectives aren't clear—or, if they are, they conflict with the superior's objectives. Subordinates need to know where the areas of conflict are and what resources are limited. They need to know what areas are flexible, what is uncertain, and what is likely to change.

The Plans (How Are We Going to Get There?).   To get the job done well, subordinates need help in determining appropriate activities. What should they do and how should they do it? They need the resources and assistance necessary to get the job done. To be motivated, they need challenging work that is properly directed towards the desired results.

Feedback (How Do You Know When You Have Arrived?). To change and improve, people need feedback on their accomplishments. This feedback will allow them to know what they have accomplished, how well they've done, and what adjustments are appropriate to improve future performance. They need coaching and counseling on how to proceed. Without it, there is no guidance. This feedback may come from the superior, or it may come from systems and procedures that are built into the job by the subordinate and the supervisor. Wherever feedback comes from, it must be related to performance on the job and as specific as possible.

These task-related needs remain fairly fixed, with some slight variations as people move through their careers. During the early stages people will need more attention to all the components, particularly setting goals and learning how to do the job. As they gain experience they will be able to develop realistic goals. They will know how to do the job and assess their own accomplishments. The superior will still be involved, but not nearly as much as at the beginning.

Personal Needs. Even though the task needs won't change much through the career stages—except to be reduced—personal needs really change. Personal needs arise from concerns about self, career, and family. Let's look at the four major career stages and consider how person-related needs change.

During the establishment stage, when people are newcomers to an organization, there are a variety of ways in which the boss

can help them learn the ropes of organizational life and develop competence and comfort in their new roles. During this period of building a professional identity in a new setting, people may have concerns about how to get the work done, who the players are, whether they are performing up to expectations, and whether they are building the required skills for future advancement. A boss can serve a critical function by providing on-the-job training, coaching, and feedback on performance. Ostensibly these are task-related functions that enable people to get the job done. At the same time, however, they are directly responsive to the developmental needs of the establishment stage.

In this early stage of a career, as people are learning a great deal about their competence, career interests, and potential in the organization, a boss can also serve as a role model—someone to emulate and to identify with as one searches for one's own professional niche. The boss can also provide protection in high-risk situations when people may be putting themselves in difficult situations unlike anything they've experienced before. Exposure to such situations can also have high payoffs. The boss's support in these contexts will enable the subordinate to gain from the exposure without risking his or her newly emerging reputation as a competent professional. Finally, because self-confidence may be tenuous during this stage of a career, ongoing acceptance and confirmation by the boss of the person in the new role can be critical. Consistent support and encouragement from a boss, while desirable at every career stage, is particularly important in the earliest years of a new career.

During the advancement stage of a new career, person-related needs are likely to shift somewhat. With their greater self-confidence and knowledge of the organization, people are more likely to be concerned about promotion, advancement, and growth than about basic competence and ability to get the work done. With a track record developing, they will be looking ahead with questions about whether to stay and advance, and how to balance promotional opportunities with outside work interests and responsibilities; they will be interested in clarifying the range of possible long-term options available.

The most useful thing a boss can offer at this stage is the opportunity to do challenging work that gives the person a chance to develop skills, to demonstrate potential, and to gain visibility in the organization. Challenging work alone, however, won't provide as much mileage without exposure to those who can judge the person's potential and will be making promotional decisions in the future. Thus, both *challenging work assignments* and *exposure and visibility* will be central to paving the way for advancement. Finally, *sponsorship* ensures that the person's hard work and competence will benefit him or her by creating actual opportunities for promotion. A boss can greatly facilitate career development during this stage by speaking highly of the person in places where it counts—to his or her own superior, for example.

While the primary concern during this stage is with advancement possibilities, career stage theory also clarifies concerns about self and family that coincide with these career-related concerns that are intimately intertwined with work experiences. The decision to accept a promotion and the possible costs to one's personal life are likely to be of concern. Whether to stay with the organization and become increasingly committed to it may also surface. What kind of relationships to nurture in the organiza-

tion with peers, superiors, and subordinates will also arise because the person is no longer a newcomer, but rather one with a history in the organization. The opportunity to discuss these concerns with a good listener and sounding board will greatly aid work on these concerns and free the person's energies for productive work. This *counseling* function is valuable at every career stage, but particularly important during the advancement stage.

By the time people reach the maintenance stage of their careers, many of their person-related needs of earlier career years have been addressed. They may no longer need coaching, protection, training, or frequent counselling, but as subordinates they are likely to need autonomy and the opportunity to develop younger subordinates. Passing on their own experience and knowledge to those in newcomer positions enhances self-esteem at mid-career. The opportunity to guide others will enrich their work life. Thus a boss who encourages autonomous action and rewards a subordinate's attempts to support less-experienced employees will be most supportive of career development in the maintenance stage.

Finally, as an individual approaches retirement and enters the stage of withdrawal, a boss will be most helpful by conveying the message that one's tenure and experience in the organization is still valued. The opportunity to continue to develop others and to serve in consultation to others counteracts any fears of becoming useless in one's work role. A boss who assigns consultative roles acknowledges the person's experience and provides a vehicle for utilizing the person's talents in productive ways—both as an individual and for the organization.

People's personal needs at each major career stage are summarized in Figure 1. Ide-

Figure 1   **What People Need from Their Bosses: A Checklist of Personal Needs**

Career Stage	Personal Needs
Establishment	Coaching
	Feedback
	Training
	Role-modeling
	Acceptance and confirmation
	Protection
Advancement	Exposure
	Challenging work
	Sponsorship
	Counseling
Maintenance	Autonomy
	Opportunities to develop others
Withdrawal	Consultative roles

ally, many of these functions would be provided by the boss. However, that likelihood depends on each person's ability to know what he or she needs and to negotiate for it, and on the boss's willingness and capacity to provide it. Assessment of one's own needs and assessment of one's boss's needs must be accomplished before successful negotiation can occur.

What Does the Boss Need from the Subordinate?

Any relationship is an exchange. Knowing the boss's career stage can greatly enhance the subordinate's ability to manage their relationship effectively. The better subordinates understand their superiors' concerns and needs that arise from a particular career stage, the better prepared they are to offer support in exchange for what the superior can provide. Because every relationship involves give and take, this understanding enables the subordinate to predict what he or she can offer to develop a mutually enhancing relationship. While it is difficult to know someone else's career

stage exactly, it is possible to make some educated guesses on the basis of the perspective offered in the previous sections.

When the boss is in the establishment stage, it is quite likely that she or he will be primarily concerned with demonstrating supervisory competence, with learning the ropes, and with developing a positive reputation in the organization. While it is unlikely that people in this stage will be bosses (because they are relative newcomers), that can happen in at least two types of situations. An individual may come from another organization or department, and although he or she may have been established in another job, in this new position establishment-stage concerns will surface. Alternatively, competent technicians who are assigned supervisory responsibilities may be well established in their technical competence but just beginning their supervisory careers.

While it is unlikely that a boss who is in the establishment stage will be assigned subordinates who are in either an establishment or advancement stage, such a situation is the most difficult for all concerned. Supervisors in the establishment stage themselves need guidance, support, visibility, and sponsorship, just as subordinates do. Because of their own uncertainties about their own performance and potential, such supervisors may not have the energy or inclination to provide support to subordinates. And they may also have competitive feelings that interfere with giving such support. What such a boss is likely to need from subordinates at this stage of his or her career is technical and psychological support. This is something that subordinates frequently don't think of, but it is something that can enable a boss to provide some of what subordinates need as well.

During the advancement stage of a boss's

career, what she or he will need most from subordinates is loyal followship that can reflect well on his or her competence as a boss. A subordinate who actively supports a boss by producing good work and by using his or her expertise to make the department and the boss look good will be valued. When a boss in the advancement stage is confident of this followship, she or he will be more likely to provide coaching, challenging work, sponsorship, and the other functions that subordinates may need.

It is not until the maintenance stage, however, that a boss is psychologically prepared to provide the range of support that subordinates need in their early career stages. It is at the stage that a boss is prepared and inclined to be a mentor to others, particularly if he or she is self-confident about his or her own accomplishments. Becoming a mentor to others can be intrinsically rewarding at mid-career. The superior needs a vehicle for redirecting creative energies away from rapid advancement concerns towards developing others. She or he can share valued wisdom and experience with less experienced subordinates. It is the individual at this stage who has the greatest potential to be the ideal boss for someone in the establishment or advancement stage.

Finally, a boss in the withdrawal stage needs, most of all, the opportunity to be in a consultative role to others. With a positive reputation in the organization, she or he can continue to provide a subordinate with sponsorship, exposure, coaching, and other functions needed through the advancement stage. However, because such a person is now looking toward retirement—most likely with some ambivalence—the opportunity to feel like a valued resource because of, rather than in spite of, his or her age and experience is critical at this late career stage. The subordinate who solicits such consulta-

tion and demonstrates respect for what is offered will find a receptive boss who can provide a variety of the type of help needed in earlier career stages.

From these descriptions it is obvious that there are matches of boss and subordinate that are likely to work better than others. The boss in an establishment stage will not be of great value to a subordinate in the advancement stage, for example. The reality is, however, that more often than not, a subordinate has no choice as to who his or her boss will be. The next best thing is for the subordinate to diagnose what the boss's situation is, and to make some assessment about what they can give each other. In this way, the subordinate increases the likelihood of developing an exchange that supports both parties. These assessments must extend beyond the normally considered task needs into personal needs. When only task-related needs are considered, it is likely that opportunities will be missed and problems created. Figure 2 presents a checklist of the boss's personal needs from subordinates.

Figure 2   What the Boss Needs from Subordinates: A Checklist of Personal Needs

Career Stage	Salient Personal Needs
Establishment	Technical support
	Psychological support
Advancement	Loyal followship
Maintenance	Opportunities to mentor
Withdrawal	Consultative roles

The Relationship as an Exchange

The relationship between a boss and a subordinate involves two people, each of whom is in a particular career stage characterized by unique challenges and psychological adjustments. In some instances there will be a good fit, and the needs of each will be complementary. In other instances there will be a mismatch, and their needs will conflict. In general a relationship is most effective, contributing to both productivity and individual development, when it responds to both individuals' most salient concerns; it becomes troublesome when it is unresponsive to one or both people.

For example, if the subordinate is in the establishment phase and the boss is in the maintenance stage, it is likely that needs will be complementary. (See Figure 3, Time 1.) At that point, the subordinate needs

Figure 3   **Career Dynamics** (Bill)

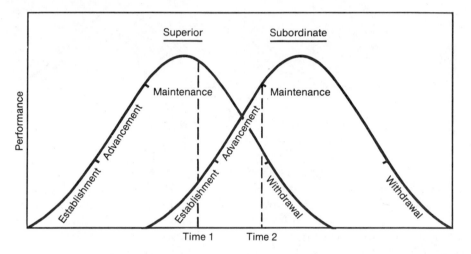

guidance, coaching, training, feedback, and protection in high-risk situations, and the boss is inclined to want to develop and support younger employees. Both will find satisfaction and support in the relationship. Either individual can initiate a useful exchange of resources that will be responsive to both individuals' needs. More often then not in this situation, the exchange emerges naturally; it is equally feasible for the subordinate to initiate the exchange by soliciting coaching and advice from his or her boss.

On the other hand, there are many situations when the fit is not good. For example, consider a case such as Sue's, which is represented graphically in Figure 4, Time 1. Here both superior and subordinate are in the early stages of their careers at the same time. It is not likely that the boss will be able to provide the kind of attention and guidance that the subordinate needs, and competition for advancement may interfere with potential collaboration and mutual assistance.

The most complex thing about the supe-

Figure 4 Career Dynamics (Sue)

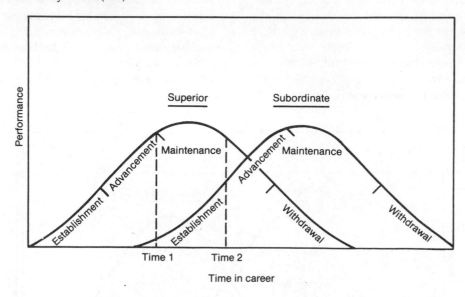

rior/subordinate relationship is that it changes. The needs of both boss and subordinate change as each moves to different stages of their careers. What was once a productive relationship may become unproductive unless adjustments are made. Similarly, unproductive relationships can become productive. Consider the examples in Figures 3 and 4. In a case like Bill's (represented in Figure 3) the relationship may have been productive early on (at Time 1), but as Bill begins to look for advancement and possibly a new career (Time 2), he finds that his boss doesn't have the time or the interest to provide guidance and assistance. A boss who is entering a declining period in his or her career is unlikely to be available to offer critical support.

On the other hand, relationships like Sue's may work in reverse, moving from bad to good. As her superior gains more

experience and security (Figure 4, Time 2), he should be better able to provide the support and sponsorship that Sue needs.

The moral of these shifts is clear. The boss can't provide everything, and whatever the relationship is now, it will change. It is a wise subordinate that recognizes his or her own needs, understands clearly what the boss can provide now and in the future, and finds and prepares alternatives to the boss's support.

How Do People Get What They Need?

We have identified what subordinates need to manage their jobs and themselves, how those needs change as they progress through their careers, and how they and their supervisors relate to each other. Here are some suggestions for both parties on how to manage the superior/subordinate relationship so it can be as productive as possible.

1. *Recognize that "the relationship" is an exchange.* Clarifying what each party needs from the other is a critical first step towards managing the relationship. Both parties must realize that this is a two-way process through which both parties try to meet their own personal objectives.

Most work relationships involve an exchange of technical, psychological, and/or organizational resources. For example, the boss can provide technical guidance and information, and support and encouragement, and/or she or he can open doors for advancement and success. Similarly, a subordinate can support his or her boss by producing quality work on a timely basis that supports departmental objectives, by listening to his or her concerns and frustrations, and by making the boss look good to other departments. By recognizing the relationship as an exchange, both parties improve the chances of getting what they need by fulfilling the other's needs.

2. *Clearly identify your own and the other party's needs.* It is critical that subordinates and bosses identify their own needs, as well as each other's needs, so they can ask for, and provide, the resources that will be most meaningful to both. We have identified two broad categories of needs: task needs and personal needs. The better that bosses and subordinates understand the needs that each has in these two categories, the more likely it is that they will cultivate a productive relationship.

Task needs are shaped by organizational objectives and constraints. Both bosses and subordinates have formal business objectives, and will need technical assistance, psychological support, and organizational support to further these objectives. So, for example, if a subordinate needs access to information at higher levels of the organization to complete a task, the boss may have to get it or the subordinate may need advice on how to get it on his or her own. The variety of possible task needs is very broad. Once they are identified and understood, it is possible to develop an exchange that is mutually beneficial.

As we've discussed, everyone has personal needs as well. These are shaped by life and career history, and current circumstances. Thus, in addition to considering task needs, bosses and subordinates must assess the personal needs they bring to the relationship.

Age and experience shape personal needs a great deal. A subordinate who is launching a career and attempting to learn the ropes of the organization is likely to need guidance, coaching, feedback, sponsorship, and support. It is not unusual to need and want these from one's supervisor; and knowing what is needed is a first step towards making them a part of the exchange of technical, psychological, and organizational resources.

At the same time, however, it is necessary to assess what personal needs the boss brings to the relationship. Boss and subordinate may have complementary needs; in which case they can work together to meet each other's needs. For example, a boss who is at mid-career and relatively satisfied with his or her accomplishments to date is likely to be willing to provide support, guidance, and opportunities for growth to a subordinate. In fact the opportunity to help a subordinate grow and develop is likely to meet the needs of a superior in mid-life and mid-career who wants to pass on his or her experience and wisdom.

On the other hand, the subordinate and the boss may have competitive needs—in which case both will have to learn how to work together and meet their needs from other sources. A boss who is launching a career, for example, may be so concerned by his or her own quest for knowledge and support that she or he may not be able to provide the resources the subordinate needs at the beginning of his or her career. Because both need support and guidance, maybe they can work together to find what they need.

Ultimately, it is likely that task and personal needs will never be entirely complementary because people are always changing. More often than not, in fact, some needs may be complementary while others are competitive. Because of the complexity of relationships it is necessary for people to periodically assess (1) when their needs are complementary (for instance, when the boss wants to be a mentor and the subordinate wants to be coached), (2) when the boss's and subordinate's needs are shared (for example, when both boss and subordinate are concerned about advancement and both want to produce a high quality departmental record), and (3) when their needs are competitive (for example, when a subordinate wants exposure while the boss wants to take all the credit for the department's good performance). When needs are shared or complementary, a positive exchange of technical, psychological, and organizational resources is possible. When needs conflict, it is most fruitful for the parties to recognize the conflict, not to expect mutual support, and to find ways of minimizing conflict by finding the resources they need elsewhere.

3. *Understand how the two of you fit together now and recognize that the relationship is likely to change.* It is unrealistic to expect that any relationship can provide a satisfactory exchange forever. Indeed, research on mentor relationships has indicated that most such relationships progress through predictable phases of initiation, cultivation, separation, and redefinition. During the initiation phase both individuals discover the value of relating to the other, and it is this discovery that sets the relationship in motion. During the cultivation phase, a broad exchange of resources is established and maintained as each person discovers what he or she has to offer and to gain from the relationship. During the separation phase, needs and/or organizational circumstances change, and the relationship established during the cultivation phase is disrupted. The individuals come to the painful realization that the relationship is no longer meeting their needs, and they begin to withdraw from each other. Finally, as new relationships are formed and needs are met elsewhere, the relationship reaches a point of redefinition that is generally characterized by a minimum expectation of resource exchanges beyond ongoing friendship and mutual respect.

These phases of a relationship apply to superior/subordinate relationships. During the initiation phase, both parties must discover what kinds of resource exchange will be mutually beneficial. During the cultivation phase, each can provide technical, psychological, and organizational resources that make it possible for both to attain individual and organizational goals. During the separation phase, a subordinate may simply move on to a new boss or may have to look to others for resources and support. Finally, at some time it is likely that both parties will no longer expect or need resources from each other, but because they have worked together some kind of ongoing friendship and mutual respect remains. The key then is to recognize that the relationship will change, that the needs of both parties vary, and that they must continually monitor the relationship and recognize changes in it.

One key to managing superior/subordinate relationships successfully would be for both parties to recognize their future needs and find and prepare the resources to fill them.

4. *Understand the constraints under which the boss operates.* Realism about what a boss can provide in terms of technical, psychological, and organizational resources is critical. Clearly there are constraints that make it impossible for the boss to provide all of the resources the subordinate needs. Once subordinates understand these constraints they can identify which resources the boss can provide. So, for example, the boss may not be able to allocate more technical recourses to the subordinate because of budget constraints, but he or she may be able to sponsor the subordinate in an effort to make a lateral move. While organizational constraints may prevent the subordinate's obtaining some important resources, the boss's personal needs may make it possible for him or her to give the subordinate other equally important resources. The time and attention that a boss spends helping the subordinate to learn may be far more important than the desk and office he or she can not provide. Not receiving resources because the boss can't provide them is truly frustrating. But it is even more frustrating when the subordinate focuses on the resources that the boss just can't provide rather than on those she or he can provide.

The cultivation phase of a relationship begins when task and personal needs have been clearly identified, and both boss and subordinate are exchanging resources. Actively managing the superior/subordinate relationship is an attempt to get the relationship to the cultivation phase as quickly as possible. This can happen when the subordinate has realistic expectations about the boss and him- or herself.

5. *Establish a feedback and evaluation sys-*tem for continuously assessing the relationship. Finally, to monitor the quality of the superior/subordinate relationship, periodic feedback is needed. As needs and organizational constraints change, it will be necessary to make adjustments; some resources may become less available; others may become more necessary. Periodic dialogue about the relationship provides an opportunity to renegotiate when necessary. Just as performance is reviewed regularly, so should the quality of the relationship between superior and subordinate be assessed so that it can be cultivated and maintained to the benefit of both parties. Figure 5 provides a list of questions for the subordinate to use in assessing the superior/subordinate relationship. These can be adapted so the supervisor can also assess the relationship.

Figure 5 Assessment of the Superior/Subordinate Relationship by the Subordinate

1. What is your current career stage? What will it be three to five years from now?
2. What is your boss's current stage? What will it be three to five years from now?
3. What job and career needs do you have now? What will you need in three to five years?
4. What job and career needs does your boss have now? What will he or she need in three to five years?
5. How do you and your boss fit together?
   a. What resources can your boss provide you?
   b. What resources can you provide to the boss?
   c. Which needs are complementary? Shared? Conflicting?
   d. At what stage is your relationship? Initiation? Cultivation? Separation? Redefinition? Where should it be?
6. What preparations can you make for your future job and career needs?
7. What alternative sources do you have for the needs that your boss can't fill? Can you help provide alternative sources for your boss for the needs that you can't fill?

Other Sources of Support

What if, in spite of all that the parties do, the relationship doesn't work? The last question in the assessment asks about other sources of support. There will be times when active management of the relationship does not result in a mutually satisfying exchange. Both personal and organizational factors can contribute to a situation in which it is not possible to achieve a productive relationship. If, after attempting to define goals, develop strategies for meeting goals, and design feedback systems, the subordinate finds that the boss is not providing the job and career resources that the subordinate needs, it is quite likely that the boss cannot do so.

Whether resources had been provided earlier and the relationship has moved into a separation phase or resources have never been provided—indicating failure to establish the relationship at all—this is a time for subordinates to consider other sources of support to help them meet their task and personal needs. The first step is for the subordinate to make sure he or she has clear goals, because that is the only way to determine if the relationship is working. Then he or she must determine what is needed from the relationship to make it productive. Certainly, it is preferable for the boss to be the subordinate's primary source of organizational resources, but if active management of the superior/subordinate relationship doesn't yield the appropriate results, it is time to seek other sources.

Relationships with other superiors and peers offer important alternatives. The immediate supervisor is not the only one who can provide critical resources. Others can coach, counsel, and provide exposure and sponsorship. By assessing one's own and one's co-workers' task and personal needs, it is possible to create mutually beneficial exchanges with a variety of people within the organization. By cultivating several relationships that provide a range of resources, each person is less likely to become dependent on any one relationship and may be able to establish a much wider resource base to draw on.

Peer relationships provide a unique opportunity to develop mutual problem-solving and counseling arrangements. Because it is likely that peers share common concerns and dilemmas, empathy and mutual understanding is relatively easy to achieve. Peers can learn from each other's experiences. Peer relationships are uniquely suited to foster growth and mutual support because neither party is responsible for evaluating the performance of the other. However, the competition inherent in organizational life often prevents people from realizing the full potential of peer relationships. Competition among peers tends to create barriers to effective sharing and mutual problem solving. It is possible, however, to compete and collaborate simultaneously. Actively managing peer relationships will identify areas in which mutual support is possible. So, for example, a person might decide to share strategies for managing work and family pressures with one peer, but not discuss a particular job opportunity to which both aspire. Here again, identifying shared and complementary needs as opposed to competitive needs is a crucial step in the process of forming a relationship—in this case, between peers.

The option of developing relationships with individuals who are not in the organization is another possibility. This alternative eliminates the competition inherent within the organization and provides an opportunity to gain from an outsider's perspective on an insider's dilemmas. When needs are not met by active management of the superior/subordinate relationship or other internal relationships, external relationships can prove valuable.

Because relationships are constantly changing, it is necessary for people to periodically review their current networks of relationships. Active management of these networks involves periodic assessment and renegotiation in the same way as managing the superior/subordinate relationship requires such attention.

If none of these approaches works, it may be time to think about moving on. There is nothing worse for a person than to get stuck in an absolutely unproductive position. Notice, however, that this may not happen as often as most people anticipate. People can actively manage relationships in such a way that what at first appeared unproductive may prove to be beneficial. The key is active management of the superior/subordinate relationship.

Summary

Superior/subordinate relationships often fail to work because both parties lack realistic expectations about what they can provide for each other. If people critically analyze and understand the needs of themselves, their bosses, and their subordinates, they will be in a much better position to take advantage of superior/subordinate relationships. Bosses can't provide everything. Many times their ability to provide resources is limited by the organization. They can, however, often provide such important personal needs as training, counseling, exposure, and sponsorship.

Two critical characteristics of a superior/subordinate relationship make managing it important. First, the relationship is an exchange. The subordinate gives the boss support and resources in the same way that he or she supports the subordinate. The relationship will be productive only if it is mutually beneficial. So, in analyzing and managing the relationship, both boss and subordinate must consider what they can do for each other. Second, inevitably this relationship will change. Both parties must anticipate and plan for the change and must actively manage the superior/subordinate relationship.

Selected Bibliography

The literature on adult and career development encouraged us to look at how life and/or career stages affect relationships with bosses and subordinates. Adult development perspectives suggest that individuals are likely to encounter characteristic concerns about self, career, and family at every life stage. For an in-depth look at a model of adult life stages, see *Seasons of A Man's Life* by Daniel Levinson et al. (New York: Alfred A. Knopf, 1978), and *Transformations: Growth and Change in Adult Life*, by R. Gould (New York: Simon & Schuster, 1978). Career development perspectives focus more specifically on the professional and personal concerns that are faced as one advances in a career. Several of these works illustrate how both career stage and life stage affect individuals' experiences in a work setting. The most prominent of these books include: *Careers In Organizations*, by Douglas T. Hall (Santa Monica, Calif.: Goodyear Publishing, 1976), and *Career Dynamics: Matching Individual and Organizational Needs*, by E. H. Schein (Reading, Mass.: Addison-Wesley Publishing, 1978).

Our particular interest in superior/subordinate relationships was supported by an important study of the careers of engineers and scientists reported in this journal several years ago. "The Four Stages of Professional Careers: A New Look At Performance By Professionals," by Gene W. Dalton et al. (in *Organizational Dynamics*, Summer 1977) highlighted the psychological adjustments, changes in role, and changes in relationships that one is likely to encounter at each major career stage. This work illustrated how the nature of relationships would shift significantly with career advancement, suggesting the need to further understand how superior/subordinate relationships are affected by the career stage of each individual. In addition, several works have emphasized the important role that supervisors play in the new careers of young managers. The most prominent are: "The Socialization of Managers: Effects of Expectations of Performance," by David E. Berlew and Douglas T. Hall (in *Administrative Sciences Quarterly*, November 1966), and "Pygmalion in Management" by J. S. Livingston (*Harvard Business Review*, July–August 1969).

Recent work on mentoring relationships has identified a range of developmental functions that are provided in this type of relationship to support career advancement and personal development. See "Mentoring In Managerial Careers" by James Clawson, in *Work, Family and Career*, edited by C. Brooklyn Derr (Praeger Publishers, 1980); "Much Ado About Mentors," by G. R. Roche (*Harvard Business Review*, January–February 1979); "Everyone Who Makes It Has a Mentor" by E. Collins and P. Scott, in *Harvard Business Review* (July–August 1978). Some studies also suggest that mentoring relationships are not readily available and that, when they do exist, they last only a

few years until the career stage of either individual changes or organizational circumstances change. These findings reinforce the importance of encouraging the boss to provide mentoring functions. For a comprehensive view of mentoring relationships and how they affect personal and professional development, see *Mentoring at Work*, at Kathy Kram, to be published by Scott, Foresman (Glenview, Ill.) in 1984.

There are a number of references on interpersonal communications that can provide practical guidance on the skills required to build supportive work relationships. For a review of the important concepts, see *Essays in Interpersonal Dynamics* by Warren Bennis et al. (Homewood, Ill.: Dorsey Press, 1979), and *Interpersonal Behavior* by A. G. Athos and J. J. Gabarro (Englewood Cliffs, N.J.: Prentice-Hall, 1978).

For a look at the more concrete skills needed to accomplish what we suggest in the article, see "Barriers and Gateways to Communication" by Carl Rogers and Fritz Roethlisberger, in *Harvard Business Review* (July–August 1952); "Active Listening" by Carl Rogers and R. Farson; and "Defensive Communication" by J. Gibb, both printed in *Organizational Psychology: A Book of Readings*, edited by David A. Kolb and James M. McIntyre et al. (Englewood Cliffs, N.J.: Prentice-Hall, 1979).

Finally, we recognize that boss/subordinate relationships are influenced by the organizational context in which they are imbedded. The structure, norms, and culture of an organization will affect which developmental functions are provided, and how a particular relationship evolves over time. To date there has not been much published on how organizations affect relationships. However, a very interesting case study of an organization that considers this in some depth is *Men and Women of the Corporation*, which was written by Rosabeth M. Kanter (New York: Basic Books, 1977).

Acknowledgements

We gratefully acknowledge the manager who talked with us about this topic, helping up to better understanding the challenges of managing a boss. In addition, we appreciate the feedback we received on an earlier draft from our colleague, Tim Hall, and the editorial assistance that we received from Carla Deford.

READING 5
MANAGERS CAN DRIVE THEIR SUBORDINATES MAD
Manfred F. R. Kets de Vries

When managers and subordinates become mutually dependent in an isolated environment, they may slip into folie à deux, or shared madness.

Managers, no less than other people, have personality quirks. Little things they do on occasion drive their subordinates "up the wall." In the main, however, subordinates tolerate their manager's quirks because for the most part the manager's style is acceptable and for many subordinates it is much more than that. But what happens to subordinates when a manager seems to be all quirks, when there is no in-between?

As an administrator, J. Edgar Hoover struck many as an erratic autocrat, banishing agents to Siberian posts for the most whimsical reasons and terrorizing them with so many rules and regulations that adherence to all of them would have been an impossibility.[1] Hoover viewed his direc-

Copyright © 1979 by the President and Fellows of Harvard College; all rights reserved. Reprinted by permission of *Harvard Business Review,* July–August 1979.

[1] "The Truth about Hoover," *Time,* December 22, 1975.

torship as infallible; subordinates soon learned that dissent equaled disloyalty. No whim of Hoover's was considered too insignificant to be ignored. For example, nonobedience to participation in an antiobesity program was likely to incur his wrath, and rumor had it that chauffeurs had to avoid making left turns while driving him (apparently his car had once got struck by another car when he was making a left turn).

If it originated from Hoover, a trivial and unimportant order changed in meaning. Even if the directive was unclear, subordinates would have to take some form of calculated action and, it was said, should expect trouble if they did not take the directive seriously. Nurtured by the organizational participants, these directives often assumed a life of their own. Only appearances of and actual slavish obedience to the rules, and statistical accomplishments such as monetary value of fines, number of convictions, or apprehended fugitives counted. And problems arose if the figures did not increase each year.

Naturally, those agents who embraced the concept of the director's omnipotence were more likely to succeed. To ensure compliance, inspectors would be sent out to field offices in search of violations (the breaking of some obscure rule or instruction). If a "contract was out" on the special agent in charge of the office, a "violation" would inevitably be found. Apparently, the inspector's own future at the FBI was at stake if no violations were discovered because then, in turn, a contract might be issued on *him.* If one wanted to survive in the organization, participation in many of these absurdities was often unavoidable. Many of these bizarre activities seem to have been treated as quite normal aspects of organizational life and were carried out with great conviction.

While Hoover at the FBI, Hitler in the days before the collapse of the Third Reich, and, even more recently, Jim Jones at the mass suicide in Guyana are newsworthy examples of what leaders can do to their subordinates when they lose touch with reality, the effects of dependence also occur in less heralded tales.

The president of a faltering company in the apparel industry seemed increasingly unwilling to face the declining profit position of his company. Even two months before the banks eventually took control, the president held meetings during which non-existent orders, the development of new revolutionary machinery, and the introduction of new innovative products were discussed. These new developments were supposed to turn the company around and dramatically change its position in the industry. The president ignored the dismal profit and loss picture, inefficiencies in production, and poor sales performance, attributing them to unfair industry practices by competitors, or even sabotage, and assured his managers that change was imminent and the company would be out of the red shortly.

Sadly enough, these glorious ideas were far removed from reality. While the president seemed to originate most of these fantasies, his close associates not only participated in them but also encouraged his irrational thoughts and actions. The rare subordinate who expressed his disbelief was looked on with contempt, found himself ostracized and threatened with dismissal. Among the small but increasingly isolated group of managers the belief persisted that everything was not lost. Miraculous developments were just around the corner. Only when the banks took control was the spell finally broken.

What is striking about both these anec-dotes is the shift of what appear as delusions and unusual behavior patterns from the originator of these activities to one or more others who are closely associated with him or her. These associates not only take an active part but also frequently enhance and elaborate on these delusions. The delusions seem to escalate in intensity when the people involved try to solve problems concerned with an already deteriorating situation. They inevitably aggravate the situation, make it worse, and become correspondingly more and more reluctant to face external reality. Feeling most comfortable in their own chosen, closed environment, they do not welcome the opinion of outsiders, seeing them as threatening the status quo and disturbing their tunnel vision.

Also noticeable in these two examples is just how contagious the behavior of a senior executive can be, and how devastating its effect on his subordinates and his organization. In Hoover's case, the reaction of his subordinates further encouraged him to continue in his dysfunctional behavior. Perhaps the particular mission of Hoover's organization may have contributed to the fact that very few subordinates were willing to refuse to participate in some of these bizarre activities. Regardless, many conformed to his wishes and some may actually have believed in the appropriateness and importance of his actions. In the second example, again the process of mental contagion is central.

In psychiatric literature, mental contagion is a recurring theme. This particular process of influence, which usually goes together with some form of break with reality occurring among groups of individuals, is generally known as *folie à deux*—that is, shared madness. Although folie à deux as a way of interaction has been limited to seriously disturbed relationships between two people, a broader definition of this particular psychological process may be helpful in understanding the interactions between leaders and followers in organizations.

One may gain insight into what is frequently described as an "eccentric" leadership style if one studies emotionally charged superior-subordinate relationships characterized by some kind of impaired ability to see things realistically within the context of folie á deux. One may discover that this phenomenon, with various degrees of intensity, is a regular occurrence in organi-

zations and can be considered one of the risks of leadership.

A senior executive should not underestimate the degree of influence he wields in his organization. Recognizing dependency—need for direction—as one of man's most universal characteristics, a manager should be aware that many of his subordinates will sacrifice reality for its sake, participating in even irrational decisions without mustering a critical stand and challenging what is happening. (For a better understanding of how strong dependency needs are, see the accompanying boxed insert.)

The Paradox of Dependency

Two French psychiatrists were the first to coin the term *folie à deux*. Other names given to this phenomenon have been *double insanity, mental catagion, collective insanity,* or *psychosis of association.* Folie á deux essentially involves the sharing of a delusional system by two or more individuals. This phenomenon has frequently been observed among family members living an isolated existence.

To better understand this psychological process, let us look for a moment at the early childhood development of a person responsible for instigating this form of mental contagion. One central theme in the origin of this disorder appears to be the degree of success or failure a person has in establishing feelings of basic trust with people (originally with the parents). Lack of basic trust due to the absence of sustained interpersonal care, accompanied by anxiety because of frustrating, humiliating, and disappointing experiences will contribute to a lack of cohesive sense of self, a sense of betrayal, and a perception of the environment as hostile and dangerous. The individual's personality will develop accordingly.

In his dealings with others, such a person will continually take precautions and be on his guard to be ready for any confirmation of his suspicions. In situations of power, as a reactive way of dealing with what he sees as a hostile environment, he will be highly susceptible to grandiose fantasies and prone to delusions.

Apart from suffering the emerging paranoid disposition, a person who lacks trust also suffers an absence of closeness and, consequently, has frustrated dependency needs. For such a person, the world becomes a dangerous place where only a few individuals can be trusted. If an opportunity arises to satisfy these dependency needs, the attachment this person makes to others can become extremely intense, frequently overpowering all other behavior patterns. Because this person's attachment is so important, he will do anything—even sacrifice reality—to preserve it.

The individual to whom this attachment is directed, and who is not without his own dependency needs (though perhaps not of such an intense nature), may enjoy the way the other person is taking care of him and giving him some form of direction and guidance in life. One outcome may be that he will strongly identify with those things for which the other person stands.

However, the price for these feelings of closeness becomes the acceptance of the behavior and actions of the domineering person, often without much concern for its base in reality.

This identification process appears to be of a special nature, and contains elements of the defense mechanism sometimes called *identification with the aggressor*. This is an unconscious process whereby a person takes for his own his image of a person who represents a source of frustration. Paradoxically enough, the process is gratifying because it becomes a way of overcoming a sense of inner weakness. Through identifying with the aggressor, the susceptible person neutralizes his own hostile and destructive wishes (which can be viewed as a reaction to feelings of helplessness and dependency on the dominant partner), and fear of retaliation about these wishes. At the same time he gains through the alliance and symbolic merger with the aggressor, rather than allowing himself to be the victim.

To preserve the dependency, both subordinates and superiors create closed communities, losing touch with the immediate reality of the organization's environment to the detriment of organizational functioning. When the reality is not abandoned completely, however, this phenomenon is often difficult to recognize. But in view of its damaging consequences, even in a limited form, it deserves serious attention. I will explore this aspect of leadership, hoping to help managers diagnose and prevent the incidence of its potentially disastrous effects.

Dynamics of Folie à Deux

We have seen that folie à deux is marked by contagious irrational behavior patterns, but how does it occur in organizations?

Suppose a senior executive under the strain of leadership, trying to cope with often disconcerting imagery around power and control in addition to the general pressures of the business environment, gradually loses touch with the organization's reality. Also, this individual's charismatic personality may once have attracted executives with highly ungratified dependency needs to the organization. Or it may have been the organizational climate itself which was conducive to a reawakening of these executives' dependency needs.

Whatever the reason, during their association with the organization these managers may have become dependent on the senior executive. Although strong, these needs do not at first completely overpower all other behavior patterns. What changes dependency needs into folie à deux? When both senior executive and subordinates become dependent on each other in a situation which offers few outside sources of gratification, their complete commitment to each other can be taken as symptomatic.

At some point, triggered by an event usually associated with a depriving experience of the past, the senior executive may become preoccupied with some delusionary ideas (and this is not necessarily a conscious process), one of which being that his subordinates are taking unfair advantage of him. As a result, he develops a certain amount of hostility. But, at the same time, since the subordinates' expressions of attachment finally fulfill his own dependency needs which have been ungratified for so long, he experiences guilt about this feeling of hostility.

In spite of lingering resentment, therefore, the senior executive is extremely reluctant to give up his relationships with his subordinates. They may be among the few close relationships he has been able to establish. Consequently, to defend himself against his own emerging hostility toward his subordinates, he externalizes it and attributes the hostility to others.

The senior executive absolves the closely associated executives of responsibility for these feelings; it is "the others" who are to blame. This blame can take many forms, eventually encapsulating everything that may be going wrong with the company. The senior executive, who has been the originator of this process, now needs his subordinates to support his delusionary ideas and actions. He needs that support not only because the ideas are his defense against hostility but also because he may lose his feelings of closeness with his subordinates if he does not get it. There seems to be only one option—namely, to induce his subordinates to participate.

If a subordinate resists, the senior executive will become overtly hostile, including him in his vision of "the other camp"—the enemy. Naturally, the subordinate's level of anxiety will rise. A double-bind situation develops for the subordinate; he will have to choose between the loss of gratification of his dependency needs and exposure to the wrath of the senior executive, on the one hand, and the loss of reality, on the other.

In many instances, the subordinate will solve this intrapsychic conflict by giving in to the psychological ultimatum, "identify with the aggressor." He thus satisfies his own dependency needs and deflects the hostility of the senior executive. Separation from the person who started this process is viewed as much more of a direct, tangible loss than the loss of reality.

Identifying with the aggressor usually implies participating in his or her persecutory fantasies. The shared delusions are usually kept well within the realms of possibility and are based on actual past events or certain common expectations. Because the ac-

cusations contain a bit of reality, this process is difficult to discern. Through participation in these fantasies, the subordinates maintain their source of gratification, lower their anxiety and guilt level, and express their anger in a deflected form by directing it toward others. The process is mirrorlike; the actions of the initiator of the process become reflected in those of the subordinates and vice versa and can be viewed as the outcome of an effort to save the alliance from breaking up.

Now let us look at some of these dynamics in greater detail.

Getting Trapped. In organizations, folie à deux can be one of the pitfalls of leadership. Often, however, this dimension of leadership is not seen for what it is, and contagious behavior patterns are more often than not accepted and rationalized as being merely side products of an eccentric or autocratic leadership style.

Take, for example, the behavior and actions of the first Henry Ford, who had been acclaimed not only a mechanical genius but also, after the announcement of the five-dollar day, as a philanthropist. Because of the darker sides of his actions, however, this image eventually changed. While the public merely ridiculed his escapades, for the employees of the Ford Motor Company the situation was not a laughing matter. His despotic one-man rule and his continuous search for enemies increasingly had repercussions in every function of the company. He began to view Wall Street bankers, labor unions, and Jews as his enemies, seeing each group as supposedly endangering his complete control over the company and obstructing him in his grandiose plans (e.g., the Peace Ship mission, his idea to stop the First World War, or his senatorial campaign).

At one point there may have been an element of reality to some of Ford's notions (i.e., the labor union movement), but over time what there was got lost. One can regard the relationship between the senior Henry Ford and his lieutenants Liebold, Sorensen, and, particularly, Bennett in the context of folie à deux. Using a system of intimidation, helped by a large number of Detroit underworld characters, Bennett spread terror in the organization, a process originally instigated by Henry Ford but perfected by Bennett and his henchmen.

Executives who did not participate in the idiosyncrasies of Henry Ford and his close associates were fired. The Model T, which carried the company to its original success, eventually became a burden. Regardless, reinforced in his behavior by his close subordinates, Henry Ford stuck to his original strategy of a cheap car for the masses, making even suggestions of modification taboo. Only in 1927, after the Model T had been in production for 19 years, and only after an incredible loss of market share to General Motors, was Henry Ford willing to make a model change.

This example illustrates how contagious a senior executive's behavior can be and how originally functional behavior can become increasingly damaging to the organization and even bring the company close to bankruptcy. Henry Ford's subordinates only encouraged his views, although it remains open to question which subordinates were only conforming and which were truly believing in their actions.

A more contemporary example involves the behavior of a manager of an isolated plant in a mining community who had developed the belief that the head office wanted to close down the production facility. The recent introduction by the head office of a new factory control system started

him in his belief, and regular visits by head office staff to implement the new control system only reinforced these ideas, which he communicated to his subordinates and which were widely accepted. Although the production figures were more than adequate, a collusion began to develop among plant personnel. Eventually the plant manager and his subordinates began to falsify information to show the plant in an even more favorable light. Only a spot check by the internal auditor of the head office brought these malpractices to light.

In many of these instances, however, a major question remains. How much of the behavior of the subordinates can be accurately described in the context of folie à deux, and how much is mere compliance to the eccentric leadership style of a senior executive? The latter situation is illustrated by this example:

The division head of a company in the machinery equipment industry would habitually mention the advanced product technology used in his plants to each visitor of the company and at talks at trade association meetings. On promotion trips abroad, he was always trying to obtain license arrangements for his technology. And occasionally he would be successful. But, in spite of the fact that the company was turning out a high-quality product, there was nothing unique about the technology. As a matter of fact, most competitors were using comparable or even more advanced technological processes. Although most of his subordinates were aware of the actual state of affairs, they were unwilling to confront the division head with the facts. Compliance seemed easier than confrontation.

It is worth noting that mere compliance, if continued long enough, can evolve into stronger alliances, possibly resulting in active participation in these irrational actions.

These examples also emphasize some of the characteristics of folie à deux; for example, the relative isolation of the actors, their closeness, the existence of a dominant partner, and the emergence of delusionary ideas.

The Search for Scapegoats. Interaction that contains elements of folie à deux can contribute to collusion among subgroups that fosters and maintains organizational myths and fantasies often only remotely related to the reality of the situation. In these instances, for some cliques, the organization's overall objectives and strategies become of lesser interest than tactical considerations. As concern for the maintenance of various irrational motions consumes more energy, there is less congruence between specific actions and available information.

It appears as if the members of these groups live in a polarized world that no longer includes compromise or the acceptance of differences. Everyone is pressured to choose sides. It is also a world where one continuously has to be on one's guard against being singled out as a target for unfriendly actions. In such an organization, scapegoating becomes a predominant activity directed not only toward individuals within the organization but also toward such groups as the government, labor unions, competitors, suppliers, customers, or consumer organizations. What may have been a well-thought-out program may become distorted. For instance, alertness to the environment, which at one time may have been an organizational strength, can turn into a watch for imminent attack—a caricature of its original purpose.

Because of structural arrangements, subgroups frequently overlap with departments or other units. When this happens, people jealously guard areas of responsibility; territorialism prevails. The determination of boundaries between departments can lead to disputes. Seeking or accepting help from other groups may be considered a weakness or even a betrayal.

For example, in a large electronics company a vice president of production development began to imagine that two of his colleagues, a vice president of R&D and a vice president of manufacturing, wanted to get rid of him. He perceived that his two colleagues were trying to reorganize his department out of existence and incorporate it into their own functional areas. At every available opportunity, he communicated his concern to his subordinates and expected them to confirm his own suspicions. Disagreement was not tolerated; resistance resulted in either dismissal or transfer to another department. Gradually, many of his executives began to believe in his statements and to develop a siege mentality which led to a strong sense of group cohesion.

Relationships between this group and members of other departments became strained. What were once minor interdepartmental skirmishes deteriorated into open warfare. Committee meetings with members of other departments became public accusation sessions about the withholding of information, inaccurate data, and intrusion into each other's territory. In addition, because of his recurring complaints about poor quality of delivered material and late deliveries, the vice president's contacts with some of his suppliers deteriorated. (A subsequent examination by a new vice president found that most of these accusations were unwarranted.)

Eventually, managers of other departments began to avoid contact with product development people, thereby confirming their suspicions. Over time, the rest of the company built up a number of separate, fairly informal information systems to avoid any dealings with the product development group. Finally, after the product development group made a number of budgetary mistakes because of distorted information, the president transferred the vice president and reorganized the department.

In this example one can see how excessive rivalry and suspicion can lead people to adopt a narrow perspective of organizational priorities and become defensive and controlling. Without integrating mechanisms to counterbalance their effect, these attitudes can fractionate an organization. Understandably, organizational participants will take refuge in policies and procedures, collusive activities, and other forms of organizational gamesmanship. Cooperation will disappear and priorities will become distorted.

Where elements of folie à deux seep into organizations, conflict becomes stifling, creativity is discouraged, and distrust becomes the prevailing attitude. Instead of taking realistic action, managers react to emergencies by withdrawing or scapegoating. Fear will be the undercurrent of the overall organizational climate. As ends and means become indistinguishable, the organization will drift along, losing touch with originally defined corporate goals and strategies.

Entrepreneurial Dangers

Because of the great intensity and closeness that develop in small isolated groups, entrepreneurial ventures tend to be particularly susceptible to folie à deux behavior patterns. In many instances the venture begins because the entrepreneur tries to overcome his or her feelings of dependency, helplessness, and rejection by adopting an opposite posture, a financial and psychological risk-taking style. In addition, the entrepreneur may have a strong need for achievement, control, and power, as well as an intense concern for autonomy.[2]

The relationship between entrepreneur and enterprise is usually an involved and conflict-ridden one in which the company has great emotional significance for the individual. Frequently, this type of attachment may lead to growth and succession crises, episodes aggravated by developments of a folie à deux nature, as the following example shows:

The president and founder of a medium-size electronics company often expressed concern about the need for more professional management in his company. He liked to state that the entrepreneurial phase had been passed and that the time had come to make organizational changes, prepare to go public, and plan for succession. To that end, he became personally involved in the recruitment of MBAs at various business schools. His charismatic appeal and his strong advocacy of professional management attracted a great number of MBAs. The MBA influx was balanced, however, by a steady exodus of many of the same MBAs who soon realized the difficulties in conforming to the president's demands.

Under the guise of being "a happy family," the founder felt he could intrude into the private family affairs of his subordinates. What he presented as the great deal of responsibility that he would delegate to the newcomers turned out to be poorly defined assignments without much authority, which frequently led to failure. A person's career advancement depended on his or her closeness to the president, compliance with his wishes, and willingness to participate in

---

[2] See my article, "The Entrepreneurial Personality: A Person at the Crossroads," *Journal of Management Studies*, 1977, 14(1), 34.

often irrational behavior patterns. Exile to various obscure sales offices became the price of resistance. Eventually, the company had to pay a toll for this leadership, but the president blamed the steady drop in sales and profits on government intervention, union activities, and sabotage by a number of singled out employees.

Hoarding of information, playing of favorites, inconsistent handling of company policies, and, generally, creating ambiguous situations constitute a common phenomenon in entrepreneurial companies. Because the company's survival does depend on the entrepreneur, many subordinates are easily drawn into supporting him even when what he does may be irrational. Those unwilling to participate leave, while conformers and ones susceptible to folie à deux relationships remain.

This phenomenon may explain why in so many entrepreneurial companies a strong layer of capable middle managers is missing. In situations of folie à deux-like behavior, those who remain will spend a great part of their energies on political infighting and supporting the irrational behavior and beliefs of the entrepreneur. These activities can become even more intense if members of the entrepreneur's family are employed in the company so that family and organizational dynamics become closely intertwined.

Management of Folie à Deux

Assuming a folie à deux pattern occurs in an organization, what can be done to cope with it? How can managers prevent getting stuck in this peculiar circular process? How can they recognize the symptoms?

Before outlining the steps managers can take, I want to stress that some aspects of what might look like folie à deux are not always organizationally undesirable. As I indicated earlier, in the initial phases interpersonal processes that could lead to folie à deux may be a source of strength contributing to team building, commitment to goals and strategies, or even the establishment of effective environmental scanning mechanisms. Unfortunately, in the long run, interpersonal relationships that in extreme form typify folie à deux may become a danger to the organization's operations and even its survival.

The first steps in the containment of folie à deux are recognizing those individual and organizational symptoms:

1. *Check out your managers.* Managers likely to initiate this type of behavior usually show specific personality characteristics. For example, they may appear to possess a lot of personal charm and seductiveness, qualities that may have been originally responsible for their personal attractiveness. A closer look, however, will reveal that this behavior is often a cover-up for attitudes of conceit, arrogance, demonstrative self-sufficiency and self-righteousness. Individuals prone to folie à deux find it extremely difficult to alter their concepts and ideas; their actions often contain a rigid quality.

Because of his need to dominate and control other people, this type of executive usually stands out. He will deeply resent any form or use of authority by others. He seems to be continually on his guard, prepared to fight suspected, often imagined, dangers. Hyperalertness, hypersensitivity, and suspiciousness of others tend to become ways of life. Frequently, he is preoccupied with people's hidden motives and searches for confirmation of his suspicions. He evinces a great concern about details, amplifying and elaborating on them. Not surprisingly, the creation and maintenance of a state of interpersonal tension in the organization will be one of the effects of such behavior.

Such an executive will easily feel slighted, wronged, or ignored. Lack of trust and confidence in others can make him extremely self-conscious, seclusive, reserved, and moody. Frequently, there is querulousness, insensitivity, and a lack of consideration of others. Dramatic mood swings can be observed. If an attitude of friendliness and companionship temporarily prevails, such behavior will be quickly shattered by the slightest provocation, after which the full force of hate, mistrust, and rage may break loose. A sense of playfulness and humor seems to be lacking.

When behavior of a folie à deux nature starts to spread, the influenced persons may show similar behavior patterns, but in most instances not of such an intensive nature. For all the participants in this form of mental contagion, a key problem remains the existence of highly ungratified dependency needs. It is exactly those needs that the instigators of this process fulfill. By being directive, self-assured, and willing to take complete control, these executives attract those followers who need to be treated this way.

2. *Look at their organizations.* The danger signals of folie à deux can also be detected by looking at possible peculiarities of the organization's culture and ways of operation. One symptom is unusual selection and promotion procedures that largely reflect a senior executive's idiosyncracies rather than a concern for a candidate's overall managerial capabilities. Strange, selective, and unsystematic decision-making patterns, erratic information systems, and excessive control and extreme secrecy can also often be taken as danger signs.

Other indications may be a department's preoccupation with details at the cost of overall company effectiveness, and excessive manifestation of various stress symptoms in the organization, such as a large turnover of executives and a high degree of absenteeism. One can also view frequent changes in organizational goals, and existence of grandiose, unrealistic plans, and insistence on supposed conspiracies, or the actual creation of the latter, as other signs.

Whatever the exact nature of the disturbing behavior pattern or process one notices, one should keep folie à deux processes in mind as a possible cause. Once symptoms are recognized, managers need to take corrective action, as well as to design systems and procedures that will counteract folie à deux:

1. *Establish a trusting relationship.* When folie à deux is in full swing the manager involved is beyond helping himself. For the person who started this process, the route back to reality is particularly difficult. A disposition toward delusional thinking can be difficult to overcome. Appeal to the manager's logic and reality does not help; on the contrary, it might evoke uncompromising, hostile, and aggressive reactions. Rather, in these instances, one has to establish some degree of trust and closeness with the affected manager to make him willing to entertain the possibility that his assumptions of the organizational environment are invalid.

This change in attitudes is not going to be arrived at easily, but without a change it will not be possible for an affected manager to make a realistic self-appraisal of inner strengths and weaknesses. Substituting reality for fantasies is likely to be a slow and difficult process involving reintegration and adjustment of many deeply ingrained behavior patterns. Because of the intensity of the delusions, in many instances these persons may need professional guidance.

The outlook for the affected followers is more positive and usually less dramatic. Frequently, merely the removal of the closeness with the affected senior executive will be sufficient to break the magic spell. Some form of disorientation may occur at the beginning, but proper guidance by other nonaffected executives will soon help to bring the managers back into more normal, reality-oriented behavior patterns.

2. *Monitor your own susceptibilities.* One way to make the occurrence of this behavior less likely is to be aware of your own susceptibility to it. Most people are to some extent vulnerable. We like to be taken care of at times and do not seriously object when others make decisions for us. It is sometimes easy to relax and not be responsible, to have someone to follow, to guide our behavior. Moreover, an activity such as scapegoating has its attractive sides; blaming others for things you may be afraid of but tempted to do yourself creates not only a sense of moral righteousness but also a sense of satisfaction about your own behavior. Furthermore, as long as the interpersonal interactions retain a firm base in reality, these behavior patterns are not disturbing or dangerous. Unfortunately, the slide into irrational action is easy.

To prevent yourself from entering into a folie à deux pattern you should periodically take a critical appraisal of your own values, actions, and interpersonal relationships. Because it is hard to recognize your own possible "blind spots" and irrational behavior patterns, you might consider getting help in this appraisal process from outside the organization. Also a certain amount of courage is needed to face these confrontations with yourself.

Nonetheless, the executives with the willingness to test and reevaluate reality will be the ones who in the end possess real freedom of choice, acting out of a sense of inner security. Ability for self-examination enhances a person's identity, fosters adaptation to change, and limits susceptibility to controlling influence. Because these qualities form the basis for mature working relationships, mutual reality-oriented problem solving, and a healthy organizational climate, they deter episodes of folie à deux.

3. *Solicit the help of interested parties.* Awareness of the occurrence of folie à deux is of limited help when the instigator is a powerful senior executive who happens to be a major shareholder. Occasionally, however, in such instances, the support of a countervailing power such as the government or a union may be necessary to guide the organization away from possible self-destructive adventures. Naturally, other possible interested parties who could blow the whistle are customers, suppliers, and bankers.

The situation becomes somewhat less problematic when the chief executive officer is not a major shareholder since the board of directors and the shareholders can play a more active monitoring role. One of their responsibilities will be to watch for possible danger signs. Naturally, the possibility always exists that board members will be drawn into the delusionary activities of a senior executive. Such an event is, of course, less likely to happen with a board of outside directors.

Regardless, because boards traditionally follow the directives of the CEO, the possibility of folie à deux indicates how important the selection of board members is. Important criteria in this selection process will be independence, a sense of identity, diversity of background, and reality orientation which can neutralize a folie à deux process.

4. *Reorient the work climate and structure.* Organizational solutions to folie à deux become more feasible when the instigator is not a senior executive officer. Then confrontation, transfer, or, in serious cases, dismissal will be sufficient to stop the process. Also important, however, are the systems and procedures in an organization. For instance, reward systems that promote irrational behavior also give it implicit approval. Thus it is crucial to foster a healthy climate where irrational processes cannot take root.

Supporting individual responsibility and independence of mind in the organization, as well as selecting and promoting managers who behave accordingly, can be a buffer against folie à deux. An organizational culture of mutual collaboration, delegation, open conflict resolution, and respect for individuality will expose a process of mental contagion before it can spread. Such organizational patterns will lessen dependency needs and force conflict into the open, thus counteracting the incidence of vicious circles in interpersonal behavior.

Objective information systems can also assist managers to focus on reality, as can using many different sources for information gathering and processing. Interdepartmental committees and formal control systems can fulfill a similar function.

Contemporary pressures toward participative management, or work democratization, are other ways of preventing, or at least limiting, the emergence or proliferation of folie à deux. These structural changes can reduce the power of senior executives and restrict the advantage they may take of their subordinates' dependency needs.

READING 6
ON BEING A
MIDDLE-AGED MANAGER*
Harry Levinson

For most men, attainment of executive rank coincides with the onset of middle age, that vast gulf which begins about 35 and endures until a man has come to terms with himself and his human fate (for no man matures until he has done so). It is the peak time of personal expansion, when a man lives most fully the combined multiple dimensions of his life. He has acquired the wisdom of experience and the perspective of maturity. His activity and productivity are in full flower; his career is well along toward its zenith. He is at the widest range of his travels and his contacts with others. He is firmly embedded in a context of family, society, career, and his own physical performance. His successes are models for emulation; his failures, the object lessons for others. He has become a link from the past to the future, from his family to the outside world, from those for whom he is organizationally responsible to those to whom he owes responsibility. In a word, he has it made.

And need it all come to a harsh and bitter end? *No.*

A man cannot alter his inevitable fate. But he can manage the way he comes to terms with it. If he does so, rather than simply letting events take their course, he can do much to prolong the richness of his life as well as his years.

Sophocles, who lived to be more than 90, wrote *Oedipus Rex* at 75 and *Oedipus at Co-*

lonus at 89. Titian completed his masterpiece, "The Battle of Lepanto," at 95; he began work on one of the most famous paintings in the world, "The Descent from the Cross," when he was 97. Benjamin Franklin invented bifocals at 78. Benjamin Duggar, Professor of Plant Physiology and Botanical Economics at the University of Wisconsin, was removed at age 70 by compulsory retirement; he then joined the research staff of Lederle Laboratories and several years later gave mankind Aureomycin. At 90, Pablo Casals still played the cello as no other man ever had. Santayana, the philosopher, wrote his first novel, *The Last Puritan*, at 72. Carl Sandburg wrote *Remembrance Rock* at 70. Freud's activities continued into his 80s.

These men are the exceptions, of course. But the fact that many people can mature creatively indicates that there is indeed hope for all of us who are closer to 35. In this article I propose to examine some of the experiences of middle age and suggest ways of maintaining creative potential.

First, however, permit me a brief qualification. I am not arbitrarily splitting businessmen into under 35 and over 35. That would be unrealistic. The figure 35 is not fixed. It will waver, because I am using it here in the sense of a stage of life, not a birthday.

Indexes of Health

Behind the flowering of middle age, a critical physical and psychological turnaround process is occurring. This is reflected in indexes of health. Statistics from Life Extension Examiners indicate that specific symptoms—such as extreme fatigue, indigestion, and chest pains—rise sharply among young executives just moving into top management. Only one third of the symptoms found in the 31- to 40-year-old management group can be traced to an organic cause, the examiners report.[1] They suggest that these problems come about because of both the manner in which the men live and the state of mind in which they work.

Psychological Factors

While some explanations for this increase in symptoms are no doubt a product of the aging process itself, there are more pressing psychological forces. The British psychoanalyst, Elliott Jaques, contends that a peak in the death rate between 35 and 40 is attributable to the shock which follows the realization that one is inevitably on a descending path.[2] This produces what for most men is a transitory period of depression. Depression increases a person's vulnerability to illness. There is much medical evidence to indicate that physical illness is likely to occur more frequently and more severely in people who feel depressed.

Lee Stockford of the California Institute of Technology reports from a survey of 1,100 men that about 5 out of 6 men in professional and managerial positions undergo a period of frustration in their middle 30s, and that 1 in 6 never fully recovers from it. Stockford attributes the crisis to a different kind of frustration: "This is the critical age—the mid 30s—when a man comes face to face with reality and finds that reality doesn't measure up to his dreams."[3]

A number of factors in executive work life

---

[1] "Clinical Health Age: 30–40," *Business Week,* March 3, 1956, p. 56.

[2] Elliott Jaques, "Death and the Mid-Life Crisis," *The International Journal of Psychoanalysis,* October 1965, p. 502.

[3] Unpublished.

contribute to the intensification of these feelings and the symptoms which result:

Increasing contraction of the hard work period. The average age at which men become company presidents is decreasing. As it does, the age span during which success can be achieved becomes narrower. The competitive pace therefore becomes more intense. It is further intensified by devices, such as management by objectives and performance appraisals, which give added impetus to the pressures for profit objectives.

Inseparability of life and career patterns. For managerial men in an intensely competitive career pattern, each year is a milepost. Time in job or level is a critical variable. If one does not move on time, he loses out on experience, position, and above all, the reputation for being a star. This means there necessarily must be repetitive subpeaks of anxiety around time dimensions.

Continuous threat of defeat. When both internal and external pressures for achievement are so high, the pain of defeat—always harsh—can be devastating, no matter how well a man seems to take it. Animal research indicates that when males are paired in combat, up to 80 percent of the defeated ones subsequently die, although their physical wounds are rarely severe enough to cause death. We cannot generalize from animals to humans, but we can get some suggestion of the physical cost of the experience of personal defeat. When we turn back to the management pyramid and the choices which have to be made, obviously many men experience defeat, and all must live with the threat.

Increase in dependency. To cope with competition, the executive, despite his misgivings, must depend on specialists whose word he has to accept because of his lack of specialized knowledge. In fact, John Kenneth Galbraith advanced the thesis in *The New Industrial State* that the technical infrastructure of an organization really makes the decisions, leaving only pro forma approval for the executive.[4]

The specialists have their own concepts, jargon, and motivation which often differ from those of the executive. Every executive wants to make good decisions. He is uneasy about decisions based on data he does not fully understand, gathered by people he does not fully understand, and presented in terms he does not fully understand. He is therefore often left to shudder at the specter of catastrophe beyond his control.

Denial of feelings. Commitment to executive career goals requires self-demand and self-sacrifice, and simultaneously inhibits close, affectionate relationships. One cannot allow himself to get close to those with whom he competes or about whom he must make decisions, or who are likely to make decisions about him. Often he bears a burden of guilt for the decisions he must make about others' careers.[5] No matter how strongly a man wants the achievement goals, he still has some feelings of anger, toward both himself and the organization which demands that sacrifice, for having to give up other desirable life goals. He must hold in tightly these feelings of anger together with the feelings of affection and guilt, if they are unacceptable to him or in his business culture. Repressed feelings must continuously be controlled, a process which requires hyper-alertness and therefore energy.

Constant state of defensiveness. The pursuit of executive success is like playing the children's game, "King of the Hill." In that

---

[4] Boston: Houghton Mifflin, 1967.

[5] See "Management by Guilt" (Chapter 18) in my book *Emotional Health: In the World of Work* (New York: Harper & Row, 1964).

game, each boy is vying for the place at the top of the stump, fence, barrel, or even, literally, the hill. All the others try to push the incumbent from his summit perch. Unlike the game, in executive life there is no respite. Given this stage of affairs, together with the other conditions to which I have just referred, one must be always "at the ready," as the military put it. To be at the ready psychologically means that one's whole body is in a continuing emergency state, with resulting greater internal wear and tear.

Shift in the prime-of-life concept. Western societies value youth. It is painfully disappointing to have attained a peak life stage at a time in history when that achievement is partially vitiated by worship of youth, when there is no longer as much respect for age or seniority. This is compounded by one's awareness of the decline of his physical capacities. Thus, at the height of a manager's attainment, he is likely to feel also that he has only partly made it, that he has already lost part of what he sought to win. Since only rarely can one have youth and achievement at the same time, there is something anticlimactic about middle-age success.

Subtle Changes

The issues having to do with health are only one facet of the middle-aging process. There are also subtle, but highly significant, changes in (1) work style, (2) point of view, (3) family relationships, and (4) personal goals. Let us look at each of these in turn.

1. Work Style. Both the mode and the content of the work of creative men differ in early adulthood, or the pre-35 stage, from that of mature adulthood, or the post-35 stage. Jaques pointed this out when he observed:

The creativity of the 20s and early 30s tends to be a hot-from-the-fire creativity. It is intense and spontaneous, and comes out ready-made. . . . Most of the work seems to go on unconsciously. The conscious production is rapid, the pace of creation often being dictated by the limits of the artist's capacity physically to record the words or music he is expressing. . . . By contrast, the creativity of the late 30s and after is sculptured creativity. The inspiration may be hot and intense. The unconscious work is no less than before. But there is a big step between the first effusion of inspiration and the finished creative product. The inspiration itself may come more slowly. Even if there are sudden bursts of inspiration they are only the beginning of the work process.[6]

Jaques adds that the inspiration for the older man is followed by a period of forming and fashioning the product, working and reworking the material, and acting and reacting to what has been formed. This is an experience which may go on for a period of years. The content of work changes, too, from a lyrical or descriptive content to one that is tragic and philosophical, followed by one that is serene. Jaques recalls that Shakespeare wrote his early historical plays and comedies before he was 35, his tragedies afterward.

Contrary to popular misconception, creativity does not cease at an early age. It is true that creative men have made major contributions before 40, but it is equally true that those who demonstrated such creativity continued to produce for many years thereafter. In fact, both in the arts and in the sciences, the highest output is in the 40s.

Executives have many of the same kinds of experiences as artists and scientists. Executives report the greatest self-confidence at 40. Though their instrumentality is the orga-

---

[6] Jaques, "Death and the Mid-Life Crisis," p. 503.

nization, younger and older men do different creative work with organizations. The younger man is more impulsive, flashy, and star-like with ideas; the older man is more often concerned with building and forming an organization. A conspicuous example is the hard-hitting company founder who, to the surprise of his organization, becomes less concerned with making money and more preoccupied with leaving an enduring company. Suddenly, he is talking about management development.

2. Point of View. Concurrent with the shift in work style or orientation is a shift in point of view. This occurs in political and social thinking as well as in business. It is a commonplace that most people become more conservative as they grow older. It is an unspoken commonplace that they are more bored.

True, many activities are intrinsically boring and become more so with repetition, but others no longer hold interest when one's point of view has changed.

Disillusionment. Some of the boredom results from disillusionment. Early idealism, the tendency toward action, and the conviction of the innate goodness in people are in part a denial of the inevitable. Young people in effect say, "The world can be rosy. I'll help make it that way. People can be good to each other if only someone will show them how or remove the conditions which cause their frustration."

But in mid-life it becomes clear that people are not always good to each other; that removing the conditions of frustration does not always lead to good, friendly, loving behavior; and that people have a capacity for being ugly and self-destructive as well as good. One evidence for the denial of disillusionment is the effort in so many companies to keep things "nice and quiet." Such com-panies are characterized by the inability to accept conflict as given and conflict resolution as a major part of the executive's job.

Obsolescence. Another factor in change in point of view has to do with the feeling of becoming increasingly obsolescent. The middle-ager feels himself to be in a world apart from the young—emotionally, socially, and occupationally. This is covered today by the cliché "generation gap." But there is something real to the distance because there is a tendency to feel that one cannot keep up with the world no matter how fast he runs. Thus the sense of incompetence, even helplessness, is magnified. Some of this is reflected in an attitude that middle-aged executives often take.

For example, I once addressed the 125 members of the upper management group of a large company. When I finished, I asked them to consider three questions in the discussion groups into which they were going to divide themselves:

1. Of what I had said, what was most relevant to their business?

2. Of what was most relevant, what order of priority ought to be established?

3. Once priority was established, who was to do what about the issues?

They handled the first question well when they reported back; none had difficulty specifying the relevant. They had a little more difficulty with the second. None touched the third; it was as if they felt they were not capable of taking the action with which they had been charged.

Vocational choice. This incident might be excused on a number of bases if it were not for other unrelated or corroborative evidence which reflects a third dimension in our consideration of change in point of view. Harvard psychologist Anne Roe did a series of studies on vocational choice in the adult years. In one study she was trying to find out how people make decisions about selecting jobs.

"The most impressive thing about these interviews," she reports, "was how few of our subjects thought of themselves as considering alternatives and making decisions based on thoughtful examination of the situation. . . . They seemed not to recognize their role as chooser or their responsibility for choices. It was, indeed, this last aspect we found most depressing. Even among the executives, we find stress on contingencies and external influences more often than not."[7]

Pain of rivalry. The sense of being more distant from the sources of change, from the more impulsive agents of change, and of not being a chooser of one's fate spawns feelings of helplessness and inadequacy. This sense of remoteness is further magnified, as I have already noted, by feelings of rivalry. For boys, playing "King of the Hill" may be fun. For men, the greater the stakes and the more intense the motivation to hold one's place, the more threatening the rivals become. Yet, in the midst of this competitive environment, one is required to prepare his rivals to succeed him and ultimately to give way. The very name of the game is "Prepare your Successor."

I recall a particular corporate situation in which the president had to decide who was to be executive vice president. When he made his choice, some of his subordinates were surprised because, they said, the man he picked was the hottest competitor for the president's job and usually such men were sabotaged. The surprising part of the event, as far as I was concerned, was not the choice, but the fact that the subordinates

themselves had so clearly seen what tends to happen to rivals for the executive suite. It is indeed difficult to tolerate a subordinate when the executive senses himself to be, in any respect, on a downward trail while the subordinate is obviously still on his way up and just as obviously is demanding his place in the corporate sun.

This phenomenon is one of the great undiscussed dilemmas of the managerial role. Repeatedly, in seminars on psychological aspects of management, cases refer to executives who cannot develop others, particularly men that have nothing to fear, in the sense that their future security is assured and they still have upward avenues open to them. What is not seen, let alone understood, in such cases is the terrible pain of rivalry in middle age in a competitive business context that places a premium on youth. This paragraph from Budd Schulberg's *Life* review of *Thalberg: Life and Legend* captures the rivalry issue in one pointed vignette:

> There was to be a dramatic coda to the Irving Thalberg Story: the inevitable power struggle between the benevolent but jealous L. B. Mayer and the protégé he 'loved like a son.' Bitter was the conflict between Father and Son fighting over the studio's Holy Ghost. They fought over artistic decisions. They fought over separation of authorities. They fought over their division of the spoils, merely a symbol of power, for by now both were multimillionaires. It was as if the old, tough, crafty beachmaster L. B. was determined to drive off the young, frail but stubborn challenger who dared ask Mayer for an equal piece of the billion-dollar action.[8]

In this case, the rivalry was evident in open conflict. It could be with men at that level and in that culture. However, in most cases,

----

[7] Anne Roe and Rhoda Baruch, "Occupational Changes in the Adult Years," *Personnel Administration,* July–August 1967, p. 32.

[8] *Life,* February 28, 1969, p. 6.

if the rivalry does not go on unconsciously, it is carefully disguised and rationalized. Executives are reluctant to admit such feelings even to themselves. Therefore, much of the rivalry is unconscious. The parties are less aware of why they are quarreling, or perhaps they are more aware of the fact that they never seem to settle their quarrels. Every executive can test such feelings in his own experience by reviewing how he felt when a successor took his place, even though he himself moved up, particularly when that successor changed some of his cherished innovations.

Thus it is difficult for each of us to see the unconscious battle he wages with subordinates, now wanting them to succeed, now damned if they will. Subordinates, however unable they are to see this phenomenon in themselves, can usually see it quite clearly in the behavior of the boss. But then there are few upward performance appraisals to help make such behavior conscious, and the behavior itself indicates to the subordinate that the rival would do well to keep his mouth shut.

Dose of anger. The change in point of view which throws such problems into relief and intensifies fear (though rarely do executives speak of fear) is compounded further by a significant dose of anger. It is easy to observe the anger of the middle-aged executive toward today's youth—who have more money, more opportunity, and more sex than was available yesterday. There is anger, too, that the youngsters are free to "do their thing" while today's executives, pressed by the experiences of the depression and the constraints of their positions, sometimes find it hard to do what they really want to do.

The anger with youth is most often expressed as resentment because "they want to start at the top" or "they aren't willing to wait their turn or get experience" or "they only want young ones around here now." It is further reflected in such simultaneously pejorative and admiring descriptive nouns as "whiz kids," "jets," and "stars." These mixed-feeling phrases bespeak self-criticism and betrayal.

Every time the middle-aged manager uses such a phrase, he seems also to be saying that he has not done as well or that he has been undercut. He who had to learn how to size up the market from firsthand contact with customers finds that knowledge now useless, replaced by a computer model constructed by a man who never canvassed a customer. He who thought business to be "practical" and "hardheaded" now finds that he must go back to school, become more intellectual, think ahead conceptually, or he is lost. The kids have outflanked him. They have it so good, handed to them on a platter, at his expense.

Older generations have always complained that the youth not only are unappreciative of their efforts, but take for granted what they have struggled so hard to achieve. Nevertheless, management has never taken seriously the impact of such feelings on executive behavior. The result is an expensive loss of talent as it becomes apparent to young people that managements promise them far more than companies deliver.

I am certain in my own mind that it is the combination of rivalry and anger which makes it so difficult to create challenging ways to use young people in management. (Certainly it is not the dearth of problems to be tackled.) That in turn accounts for much of the astronomical turnover of young college graduates in their first years in a company and also for much of their subsequent disillusionment with managerial careers.

3. Family Relationships. The same narrowing which occurs in the cycle of achievement in business has also been taking place within the family. People are marrying at earlier ages, children are being born earlier in the marriage and, therefore, leaving their parents earlier. In turn, the parents live alone with each other longer (according to latest census figures, an average of 16 years). This poses several problems which come to a head in middle life. By this point in time one usually has lost both his parents. Though he may have been independent for many years, nevertheless for the first time he feels psychologically alone.

Because an executive can less readily establish close friendships at work, and his mobility makes it difficult for him to sustain them in his off-work relationships, he tends to have greater attachment to his children. He therefore suffers greater loss when they leave home, and he usually does not compensate for these losses any more than he actively compensates for the loss of old friendships through death and distance.

His heavy commitment to his career and his wife's to the children tend to separate them from each other—a problem which is obscured while their joint focus is on the children. When the children leave home, he is left with the same conscious reasons for which he married her as the basis for the marriage (attractiveness, charm, liveliness) and often the same unconscious ones (a substitute for mother, anything but like mother, a guaranteed nonequal, and other, similarly unflattering, reasons).

But she is no longer the young girl he married. She has aged, too, and may no longer be her ideal sylph-like self of 20 years before. If, in addition, his unconscious reasons for marrying her are now no longer as important as they were earlier, there is little left for the marriage unless the couple has worked out another basis for mutual usefulness.

Meanwhile, for most couples there has been a general decrease in satisfaction with each other, less intimacy, a decline in frequency of sexual intercourse, and fewer shared activities. Wives become more preoccupied with their husbands' health because age compels them to unconsciously rehearse for widowhood. Husbands sense this concern and the reasons (which sometimes include a wish for widowhood) for it, and withdraw even more. This is part of what increases the sense of loneliness mentioned earlier, in the context of the need for greater closeness. These factors contribute to the relatively new phenomenon of the "20-year" divorce peak.

4. Personal Goals. Up to approximately age 45, creative executive effort is largely self-centered. That is, one is concerned with his achievement and his personal needs. After age 45, he turns gradually to matters outside himself. As psychologist Else Frenkel-Brunswik has shown, he becomes more concerned with ideals and causes, derived from religious or parental values.[9] He also becomes more concerned with finding purpose in life.

For example, a young executive, a "jet" in his company, became a subsidiary president early. And while in that role he became involved in resolving racial problems in his community. Although still president, and likely to be promoted to head the whole corporation, his heart is now in the resolution of community problems. Similarly, another executive has retired early to become involved in conservation. Still others leave

---

[9] "Adjustments and Reorientation in the Course of the Life Span," in *Middle Age and Aging*, edited by Bernice L. Neugarten (Chicago: University of Chicago Press, 1968), p. 81.

business for politics, and not a few have become Episcopal priests.

As part of this change (which goes on unconsciously), there are periods of restlessness and discomfort. There appears to be a peak in travel between the ages of 45 and 50, and also a transitory period of loneliness as one leaves old, long-standing moorings and seeks others.

The restlessness and discomfort have another source. When the middle-aged manager is shifting his direction, he must necessarily use psychological energy for that task. As a consequence, it is more difficult to keep ancient, repressed conflicts under control. This is particularly true when the manager has managed to keep certain conflicts in check by promising himself he would one day deal with them. As he begins to feel that time is running out and that he has not delivered on his promises to himself, he begins to experience intense internal frustration and pressure. Sometimes he will try to hide such conflicts under a contemporary slogan like "identity crisis."

Not long ago, a 42-year-old executive told me that, despite his age, his professional engineering training, and his good position, he was still having an identity problem. He said he really did not know what he wanted to do or be. A few questions quickly revealed that he would prefer to be in his own business. However, the moment we touched that topic, he was full of excuses and wanted to turn away from it. He did indeed know what he wanted to do; he was simply afraid to face it. He wanted to be independent, but he could not break away from the security of his company. He had maintained the fantasy that he might some day, but as the passing years made that less likely, his conflict increased in intensity.

Most men will come nowhere near doing all they want to do with their lives. All of us have some degree of difficulty and frustration as a result. We become even more angry with ourselves when the prospect arises that time will run out before we have sampled, let alone savored, much of what there is in the world. But most of us subtly turn our efforts to meeting those ideal requirements.

The important point in all this is that, as psychologist Charlotte Buhler points out, it relates directly to survival.[10] The evidence indicates that a person's assessment as to whether he did or did not reach fulfillment has more to do with his old-age adjustment than literal loss of physical capacities and insecurity. Put another way, if a man has met his own standards and expectations reasonably well, he adapts more successfully to the aging process. If not, the converse holds: while experiencing the debilitation of aging, he is also simultaneously angry with himself for not having done what he should have. Anger with self is the feeling of depression. We have already noted the implications of depression for physical illness.

Significant Implications

Up to this point, we have been looking at the critical physical and psychological symptoms of the aging process. Now let us turn to the personal and organizational implications in all this.

Facing the Crisis. First, all of us must face up to the fact that there is such an event in men's lives as middle-age crisis. It is commonplace; it need not be hidden or apologized for. It frequently takes the form of depressive feelings and psychosomatic

---

[10] Quoted in Raymond G. Kuhlen, "Developmental Changes in Motivation During the Adult Years," in Bernice L. Neugarten, *Middle Age and Aging,* p. 134.

symptoms as well as increased irritability and discontent, followed by declining interest in, and efforts toward, mastering the world.

There is a premature tendency to give in to fate, to feel that one can have no choice about what happens to him, and, in effect, to resign oneself to the vagaries of chance. This period is essentially a mourning experience: regret, sorrow, anger, disappointment for something which has been lost—one's precious youth—and with it the illusion of omnipotence and immortality. It is necessary to be free to talk about the loss, the pain, and the regret, and even to shed a tear, literally or figuratively. We do indeed die a bit each day; we have a right to be shaken by the realization when we can no longer deny it.

When a middle-aged manager begins to experience such feelings, and particularly if they begin to interfere with his work or his enjoyment of life, he should talk to someone else about them, preferably a good counselor. This kind of mourning is far better than increasing the intense pace of running in an effort to escape reality. In the process of talking, the wise man reworks his life experiences and his feelings until he is all mourned out and no longer afraid of being mortal.

When a manager can take his own life transitions and his feelings about them seriously, he has the makings of maturity. In the course of making wine, after the grapes are pressed, the resulting liquid is left to age. In a sense, it continues to work. In the process of aging, it acquires body, color, and bouquet—in short, its character.

Like wine, people who work over their feelings about the aging process acquire a certain character with age. They deepen their awareness of themselves and others. They see the world in sharper perspective and with greater tolerance. They acquire wisdom. They love more, exploit less. They accept their own imperfection and, therefore, their own contributions. As Jaques has put it, "The successful outcome of mature creative work lies thus in constructive resignation both to the imperfections of men and to shortcomings in one's work. It is this constructive resignation which then imparts serenity to life and work."[11]

The middle-aged manager who fails to take himself, his crises, and his feelings seriously keeps running, intensifies his exploitation of others, or gives up to exist on a plateau. Some managers bury themselves more deeply in their work, some run after their lost youth with vain cosmetic efforts, others by chasing women, and still others by pursuing more power. A man's failure to mature in this sense then becomes a disease that afflicts his organization. He loses his people, his grasp of the realities of his life, and can only look back on the way it used to be as the ideal.

The executive who denies his age in these ways also denies himself the opportunity to prepare for what is to come, following some of the suggestions I shall discuss in the next section. He who continues to deny and to run will ultimately have to face emptiness when he can no longer do either and must still live with himself. The wise man will come to terms with reality early: he will take seriously the fact that his time is limited.

Taking Constructive Action. Second, a man must act. Only he who acts on his own behalf is the master of himself and his environment. Too many people accept what is for what will be. They most often say, "I can't do anything about it." What they really mean is that they won't do anything.

---

[11] Jaques, "Death and the Mid-Life Crisis," p. 505.

Check your own experience. How often do you mean "won't" when you say "can't"? Much of psychotherapeutic effort is directed to helping people see how they have trapped themselves this way. There are indeed alternatives in most situations. Our traps are largely self-made.

There are a number of fruitful avenues for action in both personal and business life. In personal terms, the most important efforts are the renegotiation of the marriage and the negotiation of new friendships. Husband and wife might wisely talk out their accumulated differences, their disappointments and mutual frustrations as well as their wishes and aspirations. As they redefine their marriage contract, they clarify for themselves their interdependence or lack of it. If they remain silent with each other or attack in their frustration, they run the danger of falling apart in their anger at the expense of their need for each other.

In social terms, the executive must make a formal effort to find and cultivate new friends with a particular emphasis on developing companionship. We know from studies of concentration camp survivors and of the process of aging that those who have companions cope most effectively with the traumas of life. Those who do not almost literally die of their loneliness. As a man becomes less self-centered, he can devote more energy to cultivating others. When he individualizes and cultivates the next person, he creates the conditions for others' recognition of him as a person.

In public terms, the executive must become future oriented, but this time in conceptions that go beyond himself and his job. He invests himself in the future when he becomes actively involved in some ongoing activity of social value which has enduring purpose. Hundreds of schools, colleges, hospitals, and community projects—most of them obscure—await the capable man who gives a damn and wants that damn to matter. Most executives need not look more than a few blocks beyond their offices for such opportunities.

In business terms, the executive should recognize that at this point in time he ideally should be exercising a different kind of leadership and dealing with different organization problems. In middle age, the stage Erik Erikson has called "the period of generativity,"[12] if he opts for wisdom, he becomes an organizational resource for the development of others. His wisdom and judgment give body to the creative efforts of younger men. They help turn impulse into reality, and then to shape and reshape it into a thousand useful products and services. They offer those characteristics in an executive to be admired and emulated. He shifts from quarterback to coach, from day-to-day operations to long-range planning. He becomes more consciously concerned with what he is going to leave behind.

Organizing for Renaissance. Third, organizations must take the middle-age period seriously in their thinking, planning, and programming. I know of no organization—business, university, church, or hospital—which does. No one knows how much effectiveness is lost.

If one of the needs for coping with middle-age stress is the opportunity to talk about it, then part of every supervisory and appraisal counseling should be devoted to some of the issues and concerns of this state. Company physicians or medical examining centers should provide time for the patient to talk with the doctor about the psychological aspects of his age and his life.

---

[12] *Childhood and Society* (New York: W. W. Norton, 1964), p. 43.

Sessions devoted to examining how groups are working together should, if they are middle-aged groups, have this topic on the agenda. Company educational programs should inform both men and their wives about this period and its unique pressures. Personnel counselors should give explicit attention to this issue in their discussions.

Obviously, there should be a different slant to executive or managerial training programs for men over 35 than for those under 35. Pre-35 programs should be geared to keeping the younger men "loose." They should be encouraged to bubble, to tackle old problems afresh. This is not the time to indoctrinate men with rules and procedures, but rather to stimulate them toward their own horizons. Training challenges should be around tasks requiring sparkle, flashes of insight, and impulsive action.

Developmental programs for men over 35 should be concentrated largely on refreshment, keeping up, and conceptualization of problems and the organization. Tasks and problems requiring reorganization, reformulation, refining, and restructuring are tasks for men whose psychological time it is to rework. Brilliant innovative departures are unlikely to come from such men, except as they are the fruition of a lifetime of ferment, as was the *aggiornamento* of Pope John XXIII.

For them, instead, more attention should be given to frequent respites from daily organizational chores to get new views, to examine and digest them in work groups, and to think of their application to organizational problems and issues. When they move toward the future, they are likely to go in protected steps, like the man crawling on ice who pushes a plank before him. Pushing them hard to be free of the plank will tend to paralyze them into inaction. Rather, training programs should specifi-

cally include small experimental attempts to apply new skills and views with minimum risk.

Much of managerial training for these men should be focused on how to rear younger men. This means not only emphasis on coaching, counseling, teaching, and supporting, but also time and opportunity to talk about their feelings of rivalry and disappointment, to ventilate their anger at the young men who have it so good—the whole world at their feet and no place to go but up. Finally, it should include the opportunity for them to recognize, understand, and accept their uniquely human role. Instead of rejecting the younger men, they can then more comfortably place their bets and cheer their favorites on. In the youngsters' winning, they, too, can win.

For the executive, his subordinates, and the company, middle age can truly be a renaissance.

READING 7*
WHEN EXECUTIVES BURN OUT†
Harry Levinson

The military knows about burn-out—but calls it battle fatigue. To offset its devastating effects, the military routinely schedules its personnel for recreation and relaxation retreats, sends soldiers into combat in groups so they can support and help each other, and limits the number of flights that pilots fly. Managers are not soldiers but, according to this author and others who have researched the subject, they are prone to a similar exhaustion and sense of futility. Like

---

* *Author's note:* I am indebted to Dr. Kenneth Bradt for suggesting the need for this article.

† Reprinted by permission of *Harvard Business Review*, May–June 1981. Copyright © 1981 by the President and Fellows of Harvard College; all rights reserved.

other professionals, mental health workers, and policemen who work under severe pressure in people-oriented jobs for long periods of time—with little support and limited gains—managers are among the prime victims of burn-out. The author describes what burn-out is, discusses why he thinks that modern organizations are good breeding grounds for situations that lead to it, and offers some helpful ways top managers can combat it.

"I just can't seem to get going," the vice president said. He grimaced as he leaned back in his chair. "I can't get interested in what I'm supposed to do. I know I should get rolling. I know there's a tremendous amount of work to be done. That's why they brought me in and put me in this job, but I just can't seem to get going."

Eighteen months before making these comments, the vice president had transferred to company headquarters from a subsidiary. His new job was to revamp the company's control systems which, because of a reorganization, were in disarray. When the vice president reported to headquarters, however, top management immediately recruited him to serve as a key staff figure in its own reshuffling. Because he was not in competition with line executives, he was the only staff person who interviewed and consulted with both the line executives and the chief executive officer. And because the top managers regarded him as trustworthy, they gave his recommendations serious attention.

But his task was arduous. Not only did the long hours and the unremitting pressure of walking a tightrope among conflicting interests exhaust him, also they made it impossible for him to get at the control problems that needed attention. Furthermore, because his family could not move for six months until the school year was over, he commuted on weekends to his previous home 800 miles away. As he tried to perform the unwanted job that had been thrust on him and support the CEO who was counting heavily on his competence, he felt lonely, harassed, and burdened. Now that his task was coming to an end, he was in no psychological shape to take on his formal duties. In short, he had "burned out."

Like generalized stress, burn-out cuts across executive and managerial levels. While the phenomenon manifests itself in varying ways and to different degrees in different people, it appears, nonetheless, to have identifiable characteristics. For instance, in the next example, the individual changes but many of the features of the problem are the same:

A vice president of a large corporation who didn't receive an expected promotion left his company to become the CEO of a smaller, family-owned business, which was floundering and needed his skills. Although he had jumped at the opportunity to rescue the small company, once there he discovered an unimaginable morass of difficulties, among them continuous conflicts within the family. He felt he could not leave, but neither could he succeed. Trapped in a kind of psychological quicksand, he worked nights, days, and weekends for months trying to pull himself free. His wife protested, to no avail. Finally, he was hospitalized for exhaustion.

As in the previous example, the competence of the individual is not in question; today he is the chief executive of a major corporation.

Quite a different set of problems confronted another executive. This is how he tells his story:

> In March of 1963, I moved to a small town in Iowa with my wife and son of four weeks. I was an up-and-coming engineer with the

electric company—magic and respected words in those days.

Ten years later things had changed. When we went to social gatherings and talked to people, I ended up having to defend the electric company. At the time we were tying into a consortium, which was building a nuclear generating plant. The amount of negative criticism was immense, and it never really let up. Refusing to realize how important that generating plant was to a reliable flow of electricity, people continued to find fault.

Now, nearly 10 years later, we are under even greater attack. In my present role, I'm the guy who catches it all. I can't seem to get people to stand still and listen, and I can't continue to take all the hostility that goes with it—the crank calls, being woken up late at night and called names. I don't know how much longer I can last in this job.

Before looking in depth at what the burn-out phenomenon is, let's look at the experience of one more executive who is well on his way to burning out:

I have been with this company for nearly 15 years and have changed jobs every 2 to 3 years. Most of our managers are company men, like me. We have always been a high-technology company, but we have been doing less well in marketing than some of our competitors. Over the past 10 years we have been going through a continuous reorganization process. The organization charts keep changing, but the underlying philosophy, management techniques, and administrative trappings don't. The consequence is continuous frustration, disruption, resentment, and the undermining of 'change.' You don't take a company that has been operating with a certain perspective and turn it around overnight.

With these changes we are also being told what we must do and when. Before, we were much more flexible and free to follow our noses. These shifts create enormous pressures on an organization that is used to different ways of operating.

On top of that, a continuous corporate pruning goes on. I am a survivor, so I should feel good about it and believe what top management tells me, namely, that the unfit go and the worthy remain. But the old virtues—talent, initiative, and risk taking—are *not* being rewarded. Instead, acquiescence to corporate values and social skills that obliterate differences among individuals are the virtues that get attention. Also the reward process is more political than meritocratic.

I don't know if we're going to make it. And there are a lot of others around here who have the same feeling. We're all demoralized.

Burn-Out—a Slow Fizzle

What was happening to these executives? In exploring that question, let's first look at what characterized the situations. In one or more cases, they:

• Were repetitive or prolonged.

• Engendered enormous burdens on the managers.

• Promised great success but made attaining it nearly impossible.

• Exposed the managers to risk of attack for doing their jobs, without providing a way for them to fight back.

• Aroused deep emotions—sorrow, fear, despair, compassion, helplessness, pity, and rage. To survive, the managers would try to harden outer "shells" to contain their feelings and hide their anguish.

• Overwhelmed the managers with complex detail, conflicting forces, and problems against which they hurled themselves with increasing intensity—but without impact.

• Exploited the managers but provided them little to show for having been victimized.

• Aroused a painful, inescapable sense of inadequacy and often of guilt.

• Left the managers feeling that no one knew, let alone gave a damn about, what price they were paying, what contribution or sacrifice they were making, or what punishment they were absorbing.

• Caused the managers to raise the question "What for?"—as if they'd lost sight of the purpose of living.

Those who study cases like these agree that a special phenomenon occurs after people expend a great deal of effort, intense to the point of exhaustion, often without visible results. People in these situations feel angry, helpless, trapped, and depleted: they are burned out. This experience is more intense than what is ordinarily referred to as stress. The major defining characteristic of burn-out is that people can't or won't do again what they have been doing.

Dr. Herbert J. Freudenberger of New York evolved this definition of burn-out when he observed a special sort of fatigue among mental health workers.[1] Freudenberger observed that burn-out is followed by physiological signs such as the inability to shake colds and frequent headaches, as well as psychological symptoms like quickness to anger and a suspicious attitude about others.

Christina Maslach, who is a pioneer researcher on the subject at the University of California, Berkeley, says that burn-out "refers to a syndrome of emotional exhaustion and cynicism that frequently occurs among people who do 'people work'—who spend considerable time in close encounters."[2]

People suffering burn-out generally have identifiable characteristics: (1) chronic fatigue; (2) anger at those making demands; (3) self-criticism for putting up with the demands; (4) cynicism, negativism, and irritability; (5) a sense of being besieged; and (6) hair-trigger display of emotions.

Although it is not evident from these examples, frequently other destructive types of behavior accompany these feelings—including inappropriate anger at subordinates and family and sometimes withdrawal even from those whose support is most needed; walling off home and work completely from each other; diffuse physical symptoms; efforts to escape the source of pressure through illness, absenteeism, drugs or alcohol, or increased temporary psychological escape (meditation, biofeedback, and other forms of self-hypnosis); increasing rigidity of attitude; and cold, detached, and less emphatic behavior.

Most people, even reasonably effective managers, probably experience a near burn-out at some time in their careers. A 20-year study of a group of middle managers disclosed that many of them, now in their 40's and with few prospects of further promotions, were tolerating unhappy marriages, narrowing their focuses to their own jobs, and showing less consideration to other people.[3] Despite outward sociability, they were indifferent to friendships and were often hostile. They had become rigid, had short fuses, and were distant from their children.

Personality tests disclosed that these men had a higher need to do a job well for its own sake than did most of their peers, and they initially had a greater need for advancement as well (although this declined

---

[1] Herbert J. Freudenberger, "Staff Burn-Out," *Journal of Social Issues*, vol. 30, no. 1, 1974, p. 159; see also his recent book, *Burn-Out: The Melancholy of High Achievement* (New York: Doubleday, 1980).

[2] Christina Maslach, "Burn-Out," *Human Behavior*, September 1976, p. 16.

[3] Douglas W. Bray, Richard J. Campbell, and Donald L. Grant, *Formative Years in Business* (New York: John Wiley & Sons, 1974).

over time). They showed more motivation to dominate and lead and less to defer to authority than other managers. While they still could do a good day's work, they could no longer invest themselves in others and in the company.

When people who feel an intense need to achieve don't reach their goals, they can become hostile to themselves and others as well. They also tend to channel that hostility into more defined work tasks than before, limiting their efforts. If at times like these they do not increase their family involvement, they are likely to approach burn-out.

The Breeding Ground

Researchers have observed this exhaustion among many kinds of professionals. As the previous examples indicate, it is not unusual among executives and managers, and under very competitive conditions it is more likely to occur than in a stable market. Managerial jobs involve a lot of contact with other people. Often this contact is unpleasant but has to be tolerated because of the inherent demands of the job.

And one problem with managing people lies in the fact that such a focus creates unending stress for the manager. The manager must cope with the least capable among the employees, with the depressed, the suspicious, the rivalrous, the self-centered, and the generally unhappy. The manager must balance these conflicting personalities and create from them a motivated work group. He or she must define group purpose and organize people around that, must resolve conflicts, establish priorities, make decisions about other people, accept and deflect their hostility, and deal with the frustration that arises out of that continuing interaction. Managing people is the most difficult administrative task, and it has built-in frus-

tration. That frustration, carried to extremes beyond stress, can—and does—cause managers to burn out.

Many contemporary managerial situations also provide the perfect breeding ground for cases of burn-out.

Today's managers face increasing time pressures with little respite. Even though benefits such as flexible working hours and longer vacation periods offer some relief, for the most part the modern executive's workday is long and hard. Also, as more women join the work force, the support most men used to receive at home is lessening, and women at work get as little, if not less, than the men. To many managers, the time they spend with their families is precious. It is understandable if managers feel guilty about sacrificing this part of their life to the demands of work and also feel frustration at being unable to do anything about it.

Adding to the stress at work is the complexity of modern organizations. The bigger and more intricate organizations become, the longer it takes to get things done. Managers trying to get ahead may well feel enormous frustration as each person or office a project passes through adds more delays and more problems to unravel before a task is finished.

Along with the increase in complexity of organization goes an increase in the number of people that a manager has to deal with. Participative management, quality of worklife efforts, and matrix structures all result in a proliferation in the number of people that a manager confronts face to face. Building a plant, developing natural resources, or evolving new products can often mean that a manager has to go through lengthy, and sometimes angry and vitriolic, interaction with community groups. Executives involved in tasks that entail controversial issues can find themselves vilified.

As companies grow, merge with other companies, or go through reorganizations, some managers feel adrift. Sacrifices they have made on behalf of the organization may well turn out to have little enduring meaning. As an organization's values change, a manager's commitment and sense of support may also shift. Another aspect of change that can add to a person's feeling burned out is the threat of obsolescence. When a new job or assignment requires that managers who are already feeling taxed develop new capacities, they may feel overwhelmed.

These days change can also mean that managers have to trim jobs, cut back, and demote subordinates—and maybe even discharge them. Managers whose job it is to close a plant or go through painful labor negotiations may feel enraged at having to pay for the sins of their predecessors. Also, a fragmented marketplace can mean intense pressures on managers to come up with new products, innovative services, and novel marketing and financing schemes.

Finally, employees are making increasing demands for their rights. Managers may feel that they cannot satisfy those demands but have to respond to them.[4] And if inflation gets worse, so will these kinds of pressures.

Prevention Is the Best Cure

Top management can take steps to keep managers out of situations where they are likely to burn out. Of course, something as subtle as psychological exhaustion cannot be legislated against completely, but the following steps have been known to mitigate its occurrence:

---

[4] Opinion Research Corporation reports a recent survey that confirms this point.

A. First, as with all such phenomena, recognize that burn-out can, does, and will happen. The people in charge of orientation programs, management training courses, and discussions of managerial practice ought to acknowledge to employees that burn-out can occur and that people's vulnerability to it is something the organization recognizes and cares about. Personnel managers should be candid with new employees on the psychological nature of the work they are getting into, especially when that work involves intense effort of the kind I've described. The more people know, the less guilt they are likely to feel for their own perceived inadequacies when the pressures begin to mount.

Keep track of how long your subordinates are in certain jobs and rotate them out of potentially exhausting positions. Changes of pace, changes of demands, and shifts into situations that may not be so depleting enable people to replenish their energies and get new and more accurate perspectives on themselves and their roles.

Change also enables people to look forward to a time when they can get out of a binding job. Long recognizing this need, the military limits the number of combat missions Air Force personnel fly and the duration of tours ground personnel endure.

B. Time constraints on a job are crucial to preventing burn-out. Don't allow your people to work 18 hours a day, even on critical problems. Especially don't let the same people be the rescuers of troubled situations over and over again. Understandably, managers tend to rely on their best people; but best people are more vulnerable to becoming burned-out people.

Overconscientious people, in particular, need to take time off from the role and its demands and to spend that time in refreshing recreation. The military has long since learned this lesson, but for some reason management has not. One way to make sure people break from work would be to take a whole work group on a nominal business trip to a recreational site.

Some companies have set up regular formal retreats where people who work together under pressure can talk about what they are doing and how they are doing it, make long-range plans, relax and enjoy themselves, and, most important, get away from what they have to cope with every day. When managers talk together in a setting like this, they can make realistic assessments of the problems they are up against and their own responsibilities and limits.

I think, for example, of the extremely conscientious engineers in many of the small electronics companies on Route 128 in the Boston area, of those in the research triangle in North Carolina, or in the Palo Alto, California, area who have reported feeling that they simply are not developing new products fast enough. They are convinced they aren't living up to the extremely high standards that they set for themselves. Such people need to talk together, often with a group therapist or someone else who can help them relieve some of the irrational self-demands they frequently make on themselves as groups and as individuals.

C. Make sure your organization has a systematic way of letting people know that their contributions are important. People need information that supports their positive self-images, eases their consciences, and refuels them psychologically.

Many compensation and performance appraisal programs actually contribute to people's sense that their efforts will be unrecognized, no matter how well they do. Organizational structures and processes that inhibit timely attacks on problems and delay competitive actions actually produce

---

I Read the News Today . . .

A week before he suddenly quit as president of Pratt, Bruce Torell spoke, a little wearily, of "death throe competitions" which had become the norm, rather than the exception. (In earlier decades, engine makers might compete to determine what engine would launch a new jet; after that was decided, the business seemed assured for decades.)

"Almost as much effort was needed to deal with the critics as with the problems," said Torell in an interview on retirement.

Torell's retirement came as a surprise to most workers at the company. In an interview a week before, he had spoken of the ongoing challenges of his job. He put it this way: "This is a business where the risks are high, the stakes are high, and hopefully the rewards are high."

The week after those statements, the wind seemed to have gone out of him. He had, he said, no plans. "After eight years in a real tough environment, I won't be looking for anything quite so stressful."*

---

* *New England Business*, September 1, 1979, p. 11. Reprinted by permission.

---

much of the stress that people experience at work. If top executives fail to see that organizational factors can cause burn-out, their lack of understanding may perpetuate the problem.

It is also important that top managers review people's capacities, skills, and opportunities with their employees so that, armed with facts about themselves and the organization, they can make choices rather than feel trapped.

D. During World War II, the Army discovered that it was better to send soldiers overseas in groups rather than as single replacements. It may be equally effective for you to send groups of people from one organizational task to another rather than assemble teams of individually assigned people. When Clairol opened a new plant in California, it sent a group of Connecticut-based managers and their spouses, who were briefed on the new assignment, the new community, and the potential stresses they might encounter. They discussed together how they might help themselves and each other, as well as what support they needed from the organization.

Some construction companies also create teams of people before undertaking a new project. People who have worked together have already established various mutual support systems, ways to share knowledge informally, and friendly alliances. These can prevent or ameliorate potential burn-out that may occur in new, difficult, or threatening tasks.

E. Provide avenues through which people can express not only their anger but also their disappointment, helplessness, futility, defeat, and depression. Some employees, like salespeople, meet defeat every day. Others meet defeat in a crisis—when a major contract or competition is lost, when a product expected to succeed fails, when the competition outflanks them. When people in defeat deny their angry feelings, the denial of underlying, seething anger contributes to the sense of burn-out.

If top executives fail to see these problems as serious, they may worsen the situation. If the company offers only palliatives like mediation and relaxation methods—temporarily helpful though these may be—burn-out victims may become further enraged. The sufferers know their problem has to do with the nature of the job and not their capacity to handle it.

Those managers who are exposed to attack need to talk about the hostilities they anticipate and how to cope with them. Just as sailors at sea need to anticipate and cope with storms, so executives need to learn how to cope with the public's aggression. Under attack themselves, they need to evolve consensus, foster cohesion, and build trust rather than undermine themselves with counterattacks.

F. Another way to help is to defend publicly against outside attacks on the organization. In recent months a prominent chief executive raised the morale of all of his employees when he filed suit against a broadcast medium for false allegations about his company's products. Another publicly took on a newspaper that had implied his organization was not trustworthy. A visible, vigorous, and powerful leader does much to counteract people's sense of helplessness.

G. As technology changes, you need to retrain and upgrade your managers. But some people will be unable to rise to new levels of responsibility and are likely to feel defeated if they cannot succeed in the same job. Top management needs to retrain, refresh, and reinvigorate these managers as quickly as possible by getting them to seminars, workshops, and other activities away from the organization.

As Freudenberger commented after his early observations, however, introspection is not what the burned-out person requires; rather, he or she needs intense physical activity, not further mental strain and fatigue. Retreats, seminars, and workshops therefore should be oriented toward the cognitive and physical rather than the emotional. Physical exercise is helpful because it provides an outlet for angry feelings and pent-up energy.

H. Managers who are burning out need support from others from whom they can get psychological sustenance. Ideally, those others should be their bosses—people who value them as individuals and insist that they withdraw, get appropriate help, and place themselves first.

In times of unmitigated strain it is particularly important that you keep up personal interaction with your subordinates. To borrow from the military again, generals valued by their troops, like George Patton and James Gavin in World War II, make it a practice to be involved with their front-line soldiers.

Freudenberger points out that the burnout phenomenon often occurs when a leader or the leader's charisma is lost. He notes that people who join an organization still led by the founder or founding group frequently expect that person or group to be superhuman. They were, after all, the entrepreneurs with the foresight, vision, drive, and imagination to build the organization. "As they begin to disappoint us, we bad-rap them and the result, unless it is stopped, is psychic damage to the whole clinic," he comments.[5] The issue is the same whether it is a clinic, a hospital, a police department, or a business.

Executives who are idealized should take time to publicly remove their halos. They can do that by explaining their own struggles, disappointments, and defeats to their subordinates so that the latter can view them more accurately. They need also to help people to verbalize their disappointment with the "fallen" executive hero.

When the leader leaves, either through death or transfer, when a paternalistic, successful entrepreneur sells out, or when an imaginative inventor retires, it is important for the group that remains to have the opportunity to go through a process of discussing its loss and mourning it. The group needs to conduct a psychological wake and

consider for itself how it is going to replace the loss.

Frequently, the group will discover that, though the loss of the leader is indeed significant, it can carry on effectively and contribute to the success of the organization. Failing to realize its own strengths, a group can, like the Green Bay Packers after the death of coach Vince Lombardi, feel permanently handicapped. To my knowledge, few organizations effectively deal with the loss of a leader. Most respond with a depression or slump from which it takes years to recover. Also, and more crippling, is the way people in the organization keep yearning and searching for a new charismatic leader to rescue them. As part of a national organization, Americans have been doing this searching ever since the death of John Kennedy.

READING 8
CAN YOU SURVIVE
YOUR RETIREMENT?
Leland P. Bradford

Until they leave employment at the end of their lifelong work careers, many men and women are unaware of how much the organization means to them. The author of this article, the longtime head of a relatively small enterprise (Mr. Bradford was one of the three founders of the National Training Laboratories (NTL)—the pioneer in sensitivity training—in 1947) was delighted to escape the office, move to a warm climate, and rush to the golf course. "How wrong I was!" he writes. He experienced a tremendous sense of loss, futility, and uselessness. Moreover, he was soon bored and began having petty marital arguments. He learned

---

[5] Freudenberger, "Staff Burn-Out," p. 160.

that many retirees, apparently overcome by their feelings of emptiness, die not very long after they have supposedly entered the "promised land." How the author and his wife gained insight into their new situation, worked out their difficulties, and eventually made a comfortable transition into retirement is the basis of this article. Out of his research on the subject in the past few years, he provides guidance to managers and their organizations for surviving the emotional stress of this experience.

I was the chief executive of an organization I had helped found, as well as a professional behavioral scientist, and I should have known better. But I didn't. After 25 years of working under the strain of building an organization, of interweaving the ideas and needs of the key staff with a multiplicity of outside forces, I was ready for the beautiful promised land of retirement. I persuaded my wife to leave our lovely Georgetown home and move to North Carolina, where I could golf to my heart's content and enjoy relief from the stress of having to make daily decisions. I thought it would be just wonderful.

How wrong I was! The first year was awful. The organization moved on without me. Important decisions I had made were reversed. No one called for advice. As far as I could see, no one cared. I even felt that my professional reputation had vanished. It hurt.

At times I thought with empathy of a friend who had been president of a large multinational company. He had told me, before he retired, that he had everything planned carefully. A year after his retirement, some of his former vice presidents told me he came to the office at least twice a week seeking someone who was free to lunch with him.

I found that golf did not fill a day. The consultation and volunteer work I did was not satisfying. Other interests paled before the challenges I had faced. Life felt empty. I was not aged, just a little older. I had plenty of energy and I felt just as competent as I had been.

When for the umpteenth time I complained to my wife about the emptiness of my life, Martha exploded. "I've heard enough of your complaining! You dragged me away from the city and home I loved best. Do you know why I don't like it here? Do you know why I've gone to the hospital twice this year for checkups, only to find nothing wrong? It was because I'm unhappy. Did you consider my life in retirement when you retired?" I hadn't, though I thought we had talked everything over. Maybe I had just talked about *my* retirement. What she said woke me up, and I listened.

Then we talked for days, for weeks, it seemed like months—at breakfast, teatime, the cocktail hour, during evenings when there were no parties. We came to know each other's feelings and problems better. We asked ourselves if we were the only ones to react this way, so we looked about us and talked to many others on the golf course and at small parties. We found we weren't alone, although people usually covered up at first before acknowledging the empty hours they dreaded and their sense of futility and uselessness. (We learned later of a census study showing that many persons die four to five years after retirement, seemingly out of a sense of uselessness. And according to a famous French physician, people can indeed die of boredom.)

Only after we had talked through our own difficulties to our satisfaction did we begin to question why this transition period was so very difficult and so different from others we had negotiated. Was it because it marked an ending or were there other causes? Here are our conclusions.

What One Loses in Retirement

As we thought about what had happened to us and to others, we began to see how organizations inadvertently fulfill a number of basic psychological needs for people. The loss of these gratifications on retirement can be devastating unless effectively accommodated to or replaced.

Acceptance and socialization: The organization, for almost all positions, provides colleagues, work groups, teams, committees, units, or departments. Members perforce feel a sense of belonging that they share with others, whether the cohesive factor is task completion or antagonism within groups or the company. Conflict adequately handled is energizing. Task accomplishment is a mutual gain. Work provides the contacts vital for psychological well-being. Otherwise there are no correctives for perceptual distortion, no antidotes for loneliness.

I found all this out. I felt the alienation of no longer being a part of groups I had belonged to for 40 or more hours a week for more years than I cared to remember. Even in my childhood, when I had been temporarily ostracized by playmates, I had not felt so keenly excluded, bereft, outside, disposable.

I thought again of my friend who had returned hungrily to the office to seek the companionship of his past subordinates. What was different for him, and now for me, was the apparent lack of an arena offering equal challenges and companionship. I found it harder than I ever expected to say a permanent good-bye to a lifetime work career. It took time and suffering to find an adequate solution.

Goals, achievement, and affirmation: Organizations provide goals and tasks to be formulated and accomplished. During the middle years these are interwoven with personal financial aims and family responsibilities. Goals make achievement possible, sometimes with soul-warming results. Achievement brings affirmation from others and from one's self. Without this periodic affirmation, self-esteem and self-worth diminish. They are intricately interdependent and, oh, how important!

To be without goals is to be purposeless, to have no reason to arise in the morning; for some, even to live. I teetered on the brink of goallessness and it took Martha to awaken me. Also, a perceptive club member said to me, "Do you realize the purpose of our club is to keep useless people alive?" That helped wake me, too.

Not long ago I had lunch with a man whom I had known for years. Highly successful in the positions he had held, he was generous, sensitive to others, and a good companion. He had been retired for a couple of years. During the two hours of lunch, I don't think I got in three sentences. He didn't tell me what he was doing, because he wasn't doing anything to talk about, but he did talk about the well-known people who sought him out and the artists and musicians who wanted his company. I left our luncheon saddened. He who had achieved so much was now reduced to seeking affirmation from others in superficial ways. How had retirement so drastically stripped him of his sense of achievement?

Power and influence: Companies provide for most employees some degree of power and influence. For top executives, of course, the degree is great, though most would admit to various constraints. Power conveys importance to the person and aids the formation and perception of identity. Power increases the areas in which accomplishment can occur and leads to the gaining of more power.

For executives and others who have known considerable power, its sudden loss at retirement can be an acute deprivation. The shock for many is not only great but also bewildering. Events are less under one's control, and the importance in others' eyes that power gives has evaporated. Must the person who has lost power continue to vie for it, or can the individual find power and importance within himself?

On the board of directors of a local organization of not much significance sit some former executives of well-known companies. The board meets periodically for a stated two hours each meeting. For 8 to 10 minutes real work is accomplished. These executives, before retirement, would have ended a meeting in no more than 15 minutes. Now they are content to spend the two hours. Why? One might guess that, since they have little else to do, two hours fill a portion of a day. One might also hazard a guess that for those two hours power and influence are again theirs.

Support systems: Individuals need a variety of support systems for psychological and emotional health. Colleagues, friends, neighbors, clubs, community responsibilities, family, and others serve as support systems providing recognition, admiration, assurance of abilities, reality testing, feedback on behavior, and encouragement.

When retirement comes, and particularly if the couple moves away, many support systems disappear. I wish I had thought to list all my support systems before I retired, then crossed off those I would miss. I could then have gone on more than just intuitive feeling in deciding which ones were crucial to replace.

Routines and time: The busy executive with wide-ranging interests and multifaceted decisions to make seldom realizes the stabilizing force of set routines—regular staff meetings, daily agendas on the desk each morning, planned luncheon engagements, organized trips, prearranged social events.

When retirement comes, most of these routines stop. At first it seems heavenly: no clock ruling you, no secretary reminding you of your luncheon appointment, no hurried breakfast, no train to catch. So I found it; but not for long, because habit is strong. Besides, inasmuch as my day no longer had its ready-made structure, I was left with the aggravating necessity of making many small decisions. Therefore, routines need to be set; else why should one get out of bed at all? This is a small but significant change in the transition to retirement.

Where we now live there is no postal delivery. Sometime during the morning, everyone goes to the post office to meet friends, exchange gossip, make golf dates, and sometimes arrange parties. Gradually routines like this become established, but only if the person deliberately develops them; no longer does the organization create them.

Before retirement, the expenditure of time, like routine, is primarily under the control of the organization, and time spent on nonwork activities is fitted into the slots remaining. During the driving, challenging, responsible work years, time becomes a scarce and precious commodity: it is the duty of secretaries and assistants to ensure that this precious resource is effectively used.

In retirement the reverse is too frequently true. Time must be filled, somehow, to pass the day. Time can lead people into the dangerous wasteland of empty time, where no purpose is present to stir any interest or desire. If empty time recurs each day, the will and motivation to seek new interests dwindle. Boredom joins with apathy to reduce the joy of living and speed psychological if not physical deterioration.

In my early days of retirement I would become irritated on the links if a slow foursome in front held up our play. My partners, longer retired, would say, "What's your hurry? What else do you have to do today?"

For many of us, golf was followed by time at the bar, perhaps some bridge, more cocktails at home or at a party, followed by a dull evening. The intense preoccupation with work and community responsibilities had precluded leisurely reading in former years. Interests and new skills not developed before retirement were difficult to cultivate after retirement.

So the challenging hours of yesterday become empty hours today, often with disastrous consequences.

Problems of the Retired

The very different conditions of retirement create new problems stemming from existing situations. Two are sufficiently common and serious to be critical in a misery-free transition to retirement.

Marital Difficulties. Marriage, as a dynamic process, alters of course with changing conditions. The abrupt passage from work to retirement should require consideration of possible marital adjustments. There are a number of factors leading to this necessity.

The rights of each: I never realized that my work career, title, status, job responsibilities, office, secretary, even desk represented my turf, or territory, and thus largely defined my identity to others and to myself. When I thought of turf I thought of the way animals fight to secure or defend a bit of space. It was only at retirement, when all

aspects of my turf were given to another, that the dreadful realization of being turfless struck home. For an awful moment, I became uncertain of my identity. I knew who I had been, but I was not certain who I was. The sudden movement from "I am" to "I was" was difficult to adjust to.

I had always thought of the home as mine as well as Martha's. But now I found that it was her turf. It had been her territory to manage, where she had made and implemented decisions and dealt with a host of people. I had never thought of the time and knowledge she had put into managing the home.

It was not long before it occurred to me that I was intruding on her turf. I managed to be in the wrong place at the wrong time—for example, we kept bumping into each other in the kitchen. It was her domain and I was obviously curtailing her freedom of action. We talked it through and worked out accommodations that gave me some turf without depriving her and allowed us time alone as well as shared time.

We observed how turf-loss and intrusion problems beset other retired couples. Once we were looking at clothes in the downstairs section of a store. Sitting on the steps leading downstairs was a gray-haired man. A woman standing near us saw us glance at him and she felt impelled to speak. "Since he's retired he goes wherever I go. I can no longer shop in peace," she said, with a hostile look toward the stairs. "It's like having a child with you all day long. I don't know how long I can stand it!"

Then there is the extreme where intrusion means control. An acquaintance of ours had always been restless, but his nervous energy had fit well with the demands of his high-level corporate position. He did not slow up even in retirement. No sooner did he and his wife return from one cruise or plane trip, with stops at various cities, than he was planning another. His wife grew more weary with each trip.

Finally she spoke up, saying she couldn't take it any longer. He brushed her feelings aside. "Nonsense," he said. "Travel is broadening. It's good for you." That silenced her; she couldn't stand up to his strong (and insensitive) personality. But finally, for the first time, she complained openly and bitterly to her friends.

Unless the couple can undertake a conciliatory review of their turf-loss and intrusion problem and make adjustments to it, irritations will grow, bitterness will mount, and conflicts will continue. But such a marital review is not easy to make. Talking through the problem requires a sense of self-worth on the part of each so that feedback can be openly given and nondefensively received. It requires respect of each by the other and sufficient self-understanding so that each feels secure.

The turf-intrusion problem is typical of the mutually affecting strains that become especially stressful in retirement, when husband and wife find themselves spending much more time together. The turmoil that one of them experiences upsets the other. Unless each can share the problems and can accept help and support from the other, relations that before were calm become potentially explosive.

Sex role questions: Particularly for the man who has lost his turf, the fear of losing a masculine image is bothersome. He has had an identity as the family provider, the family head, the ultimate judge on major issues. Title and position in the eyes of others bolster one's self-image, and a man tries to project himself to others as a strong and competent person worthy of their respect.

Because a man cannot overtly assert his macho drives, he directs them into various innocent and socially acceptable channels. The individual may only be dimly aware of these drives, but they are strong.

Not long ago Martha and I attended a small dinner party with four other couples, all friends or acquaintances. The host had always appeared to us to be a quiet, unobtrusive man. That night, however, he was assertive and extremely aggressive toward his wife. If she broke in on his conversation, he told her to wait until he was finished talking. He corrected her and instructed her not to talk unless she knew what she was saying. She made no protest, out of good manners or perhaps for other reasons. The other guests looked as embarrassed as we were.

Martha and I talked the matter over when we arrived home. What we had seen was not the couple's normal pattern of relationship. One hypothesis stood out in our thinking: the husband, without realizing it, was endeavoring to show the other men at the party that, though long since retired, he was still a man and master of his home.

Growing apart: Over the years sharp differences in work responsibilities may have brought first imperceptible and then palpable differences in the levels of growth of the partners. Because so much of the day was spent apart, these differences may not have been important. But with the closer living of retirement, they become almost unbearable.

One man we know rose far in his company through sheer ability. His frequent new contacts, coupled with his absorbing mind, brought continual expansion of his interests. His wife stayed home and socialized with a tight circle of friends. Then he retired, and he suddenly found they had little in common and even less to communicate about. It seemed they had come out of different worlds, and there was nothing they could do but to live out their lives as best they could. My wife and I agreed that both were to blame—he because he had done nothing to help her grow, and she because she had insulated herself and had made no effort to develop.

So at retirement, couples need to undertake a marital review. Those who have negotiated this transition successfully probably made sensitive adjustments as needs arose without waiting for problems to become serious. But those who think that their relationship will remain the same and make no accommodations are in for trouble.

Societal Attitudes. Formerly individuals retired only when they were incapacitated or too old to work. The myth that this is so persists. To be retired, think many younger people, is to be aged. To be aged is somehow obscene; it is a disease to be avoided. Television advertising tells us so—advertising promotes products and devices to make people appear younger. One advertisement asks, "Why look as old as you are?"

A person who is retiring finds it very easy to accept this attitude and feel disposable, unneeded, and useless. It takes effort and will to reject that attitude and project the true picture—to oneself and others—that vast numbers of retired persons are still energetic and competent.

To counteract society's attitude, the individual must not only reject the concept of aging before the fact, he must also change his own attitudes about himself, recognizing the particular psychological and emotional needs which his work formerly satisfied but which he now (together with his partner) is obliged to satisfy himself. My wife and I agree: many years went into preparing us to enter the world of work but nothing was done to prepare us to leave it.

One day we were having a leisurely lunch with a couple who had been longtime

---

One Employer's Retirement Workshops

Dayton's Department Store, one of the first Minneapolis-St. Paul employers to institute a preretirement program, holds a series of workshops that is typical of the kind of efforts other companies have adopted. It started in 1976 and is updated annually.

Four sessions are presented in the spring and three in the fall. Each informal workshop is two hours long and includes a guest speaker, refreshments, extensive question and answer periods and a list of suggested readings. Spouses or friends of employees are invited.

The 1978 series went like this:

• At the first workshop, Etta Saloshin, an Austrian-born social worker and an expert in gerontology with the University of Minnesota, spoke to employees on the challenge of retirement. She concentrated on the psychological adjustments—the loneliness and depression that can accompany the loss of a productive job and the identity and self-esteem associated with it.

• The second and third sessions covered financial planning, considered by personnel directors to be the area of highest interest among employees. Included were lectures on Social Security and Dayton's retirement and saving and stock purchase plan, supplemental employment opportunities, and money management.

• The fourth workshop was entitled "Where to Live," and Dick Flesher, coordinator of services to the aging for Catholic Charities, discussed the pros and cons of staying here or moving to the Sun Belt, whether to sell a house or buy a condominium, or move into a residence for senior citizens.

• The fifth meeting was on health and safety, and employees were reminded of basic nutrition and the importance of physical activity. It recommended that they make safety changes in their homes, like installation of bannisters on all staircases, and bathrooms on all floors, to prepare for their elderly years. Lecturers were David Rodosevich and Joyce Jensen, both of the Public Health Center.

• The sixth workshop, covering legal affairs and consumer protection, was led by Gary Flakne, former Hennepin County attorney, and Richard Putnam, director of the Senior Citizen Assistance Program. They talked about making up wills, estate planning, consumer protection, and commercial and tax advantages available to the elderly.

• Robert Gagne, Minneapolis director of senior services, lectured on the use of leisure time at the final workshop. He emphasized that activity—whether it be volunteer work or a hobby, a part-time job or travel—is essential to happiness and longevity.

Reprinted with permission from the *Minneapolis Star*, September 2, 1979. Written by staff writer Josephine Marcotty.

friends of ours. He was retiring soon from a key executive post, so Martha and I asked them what they had done in anticipation of that event. He replied that lawyers had worked out family trusts and special accounts for his wife. We pursued the point. She added that they were already looking for the right place to live. We pursued again. They looked puzzled. We explained some of the emotional problems and their causes that we had encountered. They were surprised; they hadn't thought of those.

What Can Be Done

There is no cookbook recipe for retiring. Some may find it a release from hated work and strain; others, whose focus has been the job, may find it a deprivation. Personalities and needs differ. The answer to successful retirement seems to lie in self-understanding, a feeling of self-worth, and the will and ability to survive emotionally.

Census studies indicate that persons reaching 65 can expect, on the average, 15 more years of life—almost one fifth of the total life span. That is too big a chunk to waste or to endure without purpose or meaning.

Today, well over 400 companies reportedly hold preretirement training programs, compared with only a few dozen five or six years ago. Unfortunately, few of these programs deal seriously, if at all, with emotional problems; they merely stress the importance of remaining active and maintaining a healthy outlook. But some enterprising companies are expanding their traditional preretirement sessions to include extra dimensions. The boxed insert outlines what one employer is doing. Here is a sample of other programs:

Connecticut General Insurance Company conducts a program over an eight-week period offering a package developed by the American Association for Retired Persons and called AIM (Action for Independent Maturity). Among other aspects, it deals with marital difficulties and emotional problems. The program's focus is new-career planning, whether that means sitting in a rocking chair or embarking on a different type of job.

This insurance concern offers its 13,000 employees a flexible arrangement by which a person can retire as early as age 55 (or leave as early as 45 with vested pension benefits). The employee can participate in the preretirement sessions up to five years before scheduled retirement.

Moog, Inc., which employs 2,500, has taken the initiative to expand its program covering the "classic" matters of health and safety, finances, legal issues, and recreation. For the last two years, this manufacturer of electrohydraulic controls has conducted a pilot program examining emotional adjustments that retirees and their spouses must make. Each group includes about a dozen employees plus their spouses. Some of the sessions are group affairs, and some involve only a single couple.

The participants are in their last year before leaving employment. To help workers make a smoother transition, Moog management plans eventually to start the program for employees in the 50-to-55 age range. The company will encourage "refresher courses" when the employee reaches age 60 and each year thereafter until he or she retires.

Exxon Corporation's giant U.S. affiliate (40,000 employees) recently launched a pilot program in Houston; the first participants were employees retiring in 1979 or early 1980. The company plans to continue the sessions, scheduled for about two dozen persons at a time, and modify them as experience dictates. Each session starts one evening and lasts the next three days.

Exxon's previous preretirement program had stressed the economic factors and—to an extent—physiological factors of retirement. The new program covers psychological elements, particularly how the person can replace the satisfactions and rewards formerly provided by his work. Developing and sustaining relationships with others is a focus of the program (spouses are invited to join the group in this portion).

As the Connecticut General program stresses, retirement can be the beginning of a new career, and the employer can aid the individual in planning and preparing for it. The reward from a new career need not be money; it can be satisfaction, self-affirmation, and achievement of meaningful goals.

Recent research on adult development stresses that growth and learning can continue throughout the life span. The tremendous increase in continuing education courses offered by colleges, community organizations, and high schools is based on this premise. Acceptance of the concept of a new career, increasingly supported by organizational and societal expectations, makes retirement merely a time when careers change. A career, lest the word seem pretentious, can be any sustained activity whose purpose or goal is meaningful to the person, where motivation is maintained, and where achievement brings affirmation from self or others.

Steps to Take

There is much that organizations can do to help employees to make the transition from the organization to a new kind of life in retirement:

1. Employees can be encouraged to widen personal interests that can be carried on in later years and to develop the skills necessary for a second or third career, which need not be for monetary gain. A physician friend, for example, had taught woodworking at night while going through medical school. Today, long retired, he joyously spends his time as an expert cabinetmaker for the benefit of relatives and friends.

2. Training programs can be conducted through the early and middle years of employment for persons who have settled in at the organization. Particularly if such training stresses greater self-awareness and self-acceptance, this can help prepare them for retirement. Many companies offer training programs designed to help each person look backward at accomplishments, assess himself, and look forward to his future life.

3. Preretirement programs, one to two years ahead of the event, should be the focal point of the organization's efforts. It is very important that spouses attend, particularly during sessions dealing with emotional and marital issues. These sessions can be designed in such a way to permit husband and wife to discover gradually for themselves the problems that may be encountered, test some solutions in small groups, and then reach their own decisions in private. Carefully designed sessions permit the person who is retiring to treat realistically the problems of empty time, loneliness, and feeling useless—then to formulate and discuss practical rather than impossible solutions.

But ultimately the development of a successful retirement plan lies with the individual or couple, whether the retiree is a chief executive or a clerk. The will and initiative to seek new activities and socialization patterns—and awareness that saying "I can't" is a way of saying "I choose not to"—are imperatives for the major achievement of the retired: emotional survival.

Career Systems and Company Life Stages

4

Introduction

In this chapter, we will consider another set of dynamic influences on corporate career systems. In the last chapter we investigated the ways career systems can be designed to anticipate the special circumstances presented by changing workforce needs that are prompted by individual career and life-stage changes. The effectiveness of company career systems is also influenced by a second set of life-stage dynamics. Not only does the company's workforce change with age and experience, but so does the entire character of the organization as a whole. Thus, we must consider the impact of company life stages upon the career system. Just as various policies for recruitment, promotion, training, and the like differ in appropriateness depending on the age and experience of the workforce, they differ in appropriateness depending on the age and the experience of the firm as an entity. A young—that is, newly created—organization has a vastly different set of human resource priorities than an older, more mature firm.

A firm does not live in the sense that a true organism lives. It does not literally eat, breathe, rest, or reproduce, nor must it eventually die. In a more general and metaphoric sense, however, we do see that firms are born through the actions of creators. The grow, they age, they change through acquired experience, and they can cease to exist. Researchers have increasingly begun to appreciate the value of a longitudinal understanding of the culture and the actions taken by an organization.[1] The company life cycle has been crudely clustered by researchers into three general stages, which are similar to the early, mid, and late career stages of individuals. These stages are: (1) the firm's creation, (2) the firm's maturation and transformation, and (3) the firm's decline and termination.

Creation and Start-Up

The first of these life stages, creation, has been studied along several key dimensions,

[1] J. R. Kimberly and R. H. Miles, *The Organizational Life Cycle* (San Francisco: Jossey-Bass, 1978).

597

including: the creator or the entrepreneur,[2] the external entrepreneurial environment,[3] and the internal climate of the entrepreneurial firm.[4] The career system in the young entrepreneurial firm must accommodate the needs imposed by these key dimensions. First looking at the entrepreneur, the firm must be staffed in a way which enhances the skills of the entrepreneur and which compensates for his or her weaknesses. We must consider the entrepreneur's background to assess such important qualities as: technical expertise; industry-specific competence; external credibility to investors, creditors, customers, and suppliers; personal initiative, creativity, conflict resolution, decision-making ability, and the motivational strength of one's charisma. While partners generally share work values and a sense of mission for the business, their skills should be complementary rather than redundant.

The pace and the care which goes into this staffing of the entrepreneurial organization is greatly influenced by the pressures from the external entrepreneurial environ-

ment. Such outside factors include: the certainty and clarity of the business context (e.g., Are the competitors well identified? Do the customers understand the new services offered?); the degree of turbulence (e.g., Do suppliers come and go each month, or are they a stable group?); the scarcity of resources (e.g., How tight is the labor supply of appropriately skilled workers? How available are venture capital funds and debt financing sources?). The configuration of these outside factors may determine when a firm can seize rare opportunities and staff quickly, and when recruiting must be foregone resulting in very stretched workers.

The internal entrepreneurial climate is produced through these contextual pressures, the personal style of the entrepreneur, as well as by the character of these individuals who join the organization. Co-workers are often total strangers to one another. Given that these people must work closely with each other under highly pressured and intensive work situations, their lack of familiarity with each other can become a troublesome concern. Co-workers in the new firm must learn about one another's style, competence, and integrity to build a team which values trust and effective communication.

Even when the various parties are familiar with each other through prior relationships, the new work roles associated with the start-up are likely to complicate old roles. Former classmates, former work colleagues, and family members frequently join forces to launch a new business. While they may have the advantage of understanding each other's strengths and weaknesses, lingering tensions from these relationships will haunt the parties in the new enterprise. The prior interpersonal dynamics and spillover from more recent,

---

[2] J. R. Kimberly, "The Life Cycle Analogy and the Study of Organizations," in Kimberly and Miles, *The Organizational Life Cycle*, pp. 1–33; E. H. Schein, "The Role of the Founder in Creating Corporate Culture," *Organizational Dynamics*, Summer 1983, pp. 13–29; A. C. Filley, R. J. House, and S. Kerr, *Managerial Process and Organizational Behavior*, 2d ed. (Glenview, Ill.: Scott, Foresman, 1976); D. S. McClelland, "Need Achievement and Entrepreneurship—A Longitudinal Study," *Journal of Personality and Social Psychology* 1 (1965), pp. 387–92.

[3] J. M. Pennings, "Environmental Influences on the Creation Process," in Kimberly and Miles, *The Organizational Life Cycle*, pp. 134–64; H. E. Aldrich, *Organizations and Environments* (Englewood Cliffs, N.J.: Prentice-Hall, 1979).

[4] R. H. Miles and W. A. Randolph, "Influence of Organizational Learning Style on Early Development," in Kimberly and Miles, *The Organizational Life Cycle*, pp. 44–83; A. Van de Ven, "Early Planning, Implementation and Performance of New Organizations," in Kimberly and Miles, pp. 83–134.

even current, off-the-job crises will color the picture of the new work relationships. As the parties make new demands of each other, altered status, changed expectations of each other, and startlingly new character revelations may add stress to the prior relationships.

Thus far, we have highlighted the recruitment and selection processes in the entrepreneurial firm. Because these organizations are small and new, most human resource policies are informal and highly individualistic. Therefore, the components of the career systems are so highly interrelated that it is almost impossible to distinguish one from the other. Nonetheless, each component is very much involved in the success of the firm.

First, recapping recruitment, the firm's search is driven by such criteria as complementary skills, trustworthiness, and flexibility. The lack of predictability of customer support, production processes, and the like, guarantees substantial uncertainty in work routines. The minimum of slack in resources also suggests that the firm will hire reactively rather than in anticipation of overload. The recruiting techniques generally favor a reliance upon informal networks, where backgrounds can be checked through professional association and through friendships.

Rather than train workers to meet changing needs, the entrepreneurial firm will use this recruiting process to "raid" dominant firms with workers skilled in related fields. The training investment tends to be quite low because the small entrepreneur is unable to assume the risk of heavily investing in the development of talent which they are likely to lose to a competitor's predatory recruitment. At the same time, there are still immense needs for management development and functional training. Given the lack

of funds and the changing nature of the entrepreneurial firm, individuals will frequently be underprepared for the demanding jobs they acquire. Much of the learning takes place through advice from outsiders with greater experience and through the lessons of personal mistakes.

Given this learning-through-experience avenue for development, the method of job assignments is very important. Assignments are generally allocated informally on the basis of preference and prior experience. People often trade tasks, thereby enabling individuals to cover for each other during absence as well as maximizing the informed perspectives on the lessons of mistakes. A common problem with assignment processes in entrepreneurial firms is the inability of some entrepreneurs to surrender any important authority to subordinates. Entrepreneurs often think that each of their own ideas is the best way to manage the business. The perceived danger in delegating key decisions to the experts hired is the fear that one costly mistake may have a disastrous impact upon the struggling firm. Both internally oriented activities, such as product development, and externally oriented activities, such as sales and marketing and financial reporting, are closely guarded by entrepreneurs despite their differently focused and time-consuming nature.

Finally turning to organizational exit, we again come across qualities unique to the entrepreneurial firm. For example, consider the following examples.

1. The young creator of an advertising firm enticed a needed, more-experienced partner through a generous offer to share equity in a successful new business. Eight months into the partnership, the creator learned through a loyal customer that his partner was forming a

rival business practice through the diversion of business from this advertising firm to one being created. As the creator tried to sue his partner and fire him, he was stymied by the substantial equity owned by his partner, who sued for mismanagement.

2. A promising new publishing house found that its books were just not selling as expected, although they were well written, expertly edited, attractively bound, and on topics of high public salience. It was not for a year that two of the three founding partners discovered that their third partner had a substantial drinking problem and had failed to follow through on any of the vital marketing plans. They tried to squeeze out this third partner and quickly hire a new marketing executive. The third partner reacted angrily to this lack of support from his old friends, and as a major shareholder, he sued his colleagues.

3. The owner of a large chain of cafe/gourmet shops found that his hardworking senior managers were regularly over their heads in managing a multistore operation and approached them with a lavish severance arrangement, which was intended to facilitate an amiable separation. Despite the generosity of the plan, the announcement of the turnover of management led to a mass walkout of subordinates who were disillusioned by the violence done to a congenial company culture.

Through such examples, we can appreciate the complexity which complicates the processes of organizational exit in entrepreneurial firms. Family relationships are damaged—if not destroyed—as family members split as partners. Shattered loyalties lead to bitterness between friends and formerly dedicated workers. Financial entanglements due to equity control blur the crispness of exit. The violation of implied commitments by quitting workers or bosses handing out dismissals is accompanied by emotional trauma.

Maturation and Transformation

As firms age and mature, they enter a period of dramatic transformation into stable organizations. The research literature on this area has focused on the organization's gradual institutionalization of the entrepreneur's charisma or legitimacy,[5] the drifts in company values and purpose,[6] and strategic adaptation to a changing environment. The forces which bring about these dimensions of organizational transformation involve the aging and experiences of the management, the increased size of the business, the rate of growth, the increasingly complex product marketplace, and changes in the control of ownership.[7]

Looking at each of these forces, the aging and changing experiences produce an alter-

---

[5] T. Parsons, *Structure and Process in Modern Societies* (New York: Free Press, 1960); P. Selznick, *Leadership in Administration* (New York: Harper & Row, 1957); M. Weber, *The Theory of Social and Economic Organization* (London: Oxford University Press, 1947, in German, 1895).

[6] T. M. Lodahl and S. M. Mitchell, "Drift in the Development of Innovative Organizations," in Kimberly and Miles, *The Organizational Life Cycle*, pp. 184–208; R. K. Merton, *Social Theory and Social Structure* (New York: Free Press, 1968); L. E. Greiner, "Evolution and Revolution as Organizations Grow," *Harvard Business Review* 50 (1972), pp. 37–46; C. Perrow, *Organizational Analysis* (Belmont, Calif.: Wadsworth, 1970).

[7] P. R. Lawrence and D. Dyer, *Renewing American Industry* (New York: Free Press, 1983; R. H. Miles, *Macro Organizational Behavior* (Santa Monica, Calif.: Goodyear, 1980); P. R. Lawrence and J. W. Lorsch, *Organization and Environment* (Cambridge, Mass.: Harvard Graduate School of Business Administration, 1967); J. D. Thompson, *Organizations in Action* (New York: McGraw-Hill, 1967).

ation in the career values of the managers. Some may become burned-out and lose ambition, while others may be energized through successes and decide to pursue even greater challenges. This might cause executive turnover and restaffing of the organization. The increased size of the firm may lead to a drive for standardization and efficiency in operations, more uniformity in costing and measurement, and established procedures for pay and promotions. A rapid rate of growth may necessitate the need for socializing and training and influx of new people, as well as a continual effort to locate badly needed talent. The growing complexity in the marketplace through new products, new competitors, and growing customer sophistication introduces the need for greater management responsiveness through delegation and decentralization of authority. Careers are altered by increased responsibility and relocation. Finally, changes in ownership occur through the need for capital expansion to remain in business. New product development, market research, larger facilities, improved marketing, and investments in more efficient production equipment all require a greater need for funds. As firms go public on the stock market, they gain outside control as well as outside money. The outsiders frequently understand very little about the acquired business and are often disappointed with the realities they meet after the purchase. A 1982 study of 537 large companies found that these large buyers were disappointed with more than 40 percent of the acquisitions which they had made during the previous years.[8] Anxious to recoup mistakes, they often attempt to change man-

agement positions to improve efficiency or add synergy with other activities of the parent company.

Once again, the unique business pressures of company life stage thus have a powerful influence on each of the components of the career system. Recruitment tends to continue in importance but is likely to become more formal than in the creation phase of corporate existence. Particular specialized functional skills are likely to have been identified as company priorities. To avoid duplication of effort and to ensure equity in hiring practices and consistency in presentation of the firm's identity, the recruitment campaign becomes a planned activity.

The nature of training activity changes as well. Firms now discover that they are frequently unable to locate the mix of skills which they badly need. They have grown large enough that they begin to feel more confident about their ability to retain the talent which they develop by offering stimulating career tracks. Because of rapid growth, many firms cannot expect that new entrants can learn the company cultural norms and job skills by informal on-the-job learning. The large influx of outsiders which continues to flow into the growing firm suggests that many co-workers will be novices themselves. Hence, more formal training programs begin to take shape.

Similarly, assignment patterns begin to be the product of career planning. Company needs for functional expertise and general management sophistication along with the career aspirations of larger numbers of workers render the old ad hoc practices as obsolete. Frequently, the thoughtless manner of handling the career needs of employees in the aftermath of major transformations, such as mergers, leads to a mass exodus of the talent which was largely responsible for the present success of an en-

---

[8] T. Mitz, "Merger Expert Has 7 'Don'ts' in Acquisitions," *The Wall Street Journal,* August 8, 1983, p. 19. The study cited was conducted by Acquisitions Horizons, Inc., of Columbus, Ohio. Also cited was work by Cox Lloyd, Ltd.

terprise.[9] People fear for job security in the acquired firm and wonder about the realistic possibilities for advancement within the parent company, just to name a few of the many problems which accompany the traumatic effect of merger upon a company.

Finally, the nature of organizational exit is changed in the organization approaching maturity. While the emotional aspects of job loss remain intense, company severance practices are introduced by firms in this stage in an effort to smooth the roughness of separation. Generous income bonuses, such as the infamous "golden parachutes," and practical assistance through outplacement are offered to reassure executives that they do not jeopardize long-term security by remaining employed in a firm undergoing transformation.[10] Should they lose their job in the commotion, they will still be provided employment assistance.

Decline and Termination

The final phase of organizational life—decline and termination—is not a necessary step in the firm's development. Companies can often sense their own deterioration and take the necessary steps to ensure their reju-

venation. This stage often reflects the emergence of long-dormant pathological traits of the organization. The research literature on this final life stage has focused on: the periods of vulnerability and the loss of legitimacy of the firm by constituents,[11] the key failures in the firm's process of learning and adaptation,[12] and the lack of fit with a radically altered business environment.[13] While increased age presents special challenges to a firm's ability to adjust to changing internal and external conditions, most firms actually die in their infancy rather than in their old age. A firm may go bankrupt due to insufficient revenues as consumer support changes to other suppliers. Loss of support from other constituencies, such as creditors' faith, shareholder confidence, or employee commitment, can also inflict fatal wounds upon the firm. Changes in the marketplace, the relevant technological frontier, and societal expectations (e.g., regulation over product safety or pollution control) may reflect changes in the business environment which surpass the company's ability to adapt.

Firms experiencing the pains of deteriorating health may respond in many ways. They may attempt to defend their old turf better, or become more prospecting and analytic in their strategy.[14] If crisis is imminent

---

[9] Lawrence Ingrassia, "Employees at Acquired Firms Find White Often Unfriendly," *The Wall Street Journal,* July 7, 1982, p. 23; George Getshow, "People Problems, Loss of Expert Talent Impedes Oil Finding by New Tenneco Unit: Employees of Acquired Firm, Disdaining Bureaucracy, Strike Off on Their Own," *The Wall Street Journal,* February 9, 1982, p. 1; Lydia Chavez, "The Acquisitions That Haven't Paid Off," *New York Times,* March 28, 1982, Section 3–1; "Golden Parachutes May Go the Way of the Dodo," *Business Week,* January 9, 1984, p. 34.

[10] Ann M. Morrison, "Those Executive Bailout Deals," *Fortune,* December 13, 1982, pp. 82–87; Frederick C. Klein, "A Golden Parachute Protects but Does It Hinder or Foster Takeovers?" *The Wall Street Journal,* December 8, 1982, p. 56; Tamar Lewin, "Using Golden Parachutes," *New York Times,* November 30, 1982, p. D–2.

[11] David A. Whelton, "Sources, Responses, and Effects of Organizational Decline," in Kimberly and Miles, *The Organizational Life Cycle,* pp. 342–375. Todd D. Jick, "Threatened Jobs and Threatened Careers in Budgetary Hard Times," Paper presented at the Academy of Management Annual Meetings, Dallas, August 14–17, 1983.

[12] Chris Argyris and Donald A. Schon, *Organizational Learning: A Theory of Action Perspective* (Reading, Mass.: Addison-Wesley Publishing, 1978).

[13] Howard E. Aldrich, *Organizations and Environments* (Englewood Cliffs, N.J.: Prentice-Hall, 1979).

[14] Ray E. Miles and Charles C. Snow, *Organizational Strategy, Structure, and Process* (New York: McGraw-Hill, 1978).

they can enter into a Chapter 11 bankruptcy, which buys them time and shields them from dismemberment by angry creditors. The struggle to survive may involve a deep retrenchment of peripheral production, services, and personnel management. Through divestiture, the firm may pare away net drags on company resources. Plant and office facilities may be shut down as operations are consolidated in triage-like cost-saving efforts. Formerly treasured assets, such as headquarters buildings, may be sold off for quick cash. Through legally enforceable commitments to workers and communities, as well as through salvage efforts to draw upon the strength of past loyalties, workers at all levels of the corporate hierarchy may undergo fundamental retraining to master new technologies and job skills. Mass layoffs and relocation may assist the company in an effort to scale down its exposure to external threats.

The unique business pressures of this company life stage tend to deemphasize certain components of the firm's career system and highlight others. Recruiting, for example, is used in a far more selective way. Firms will frequently issue broad across-the-board freezes on hiring and on advancement. Outside executives may be imported, but on a limited basis. These executives will frequently be turnaround experts with established reputations as saviors.

Career mobility continues in importance as well. Workers may have to accept great changes in job tasks, transfers to new functions, vastly expanded ranges of responsibilities, and relocation to different work sites—and even to different regions of the country. Assignment issues are critical at this stage, because the clarity and the security of career paths in the midst of crises are essential if the firm intends to hold onto the valuable managers required for survival.

Sometimes a very capable and effective manager is promoted into a problem-plagued division only to be inadvertently pushed out the door in subsequent cost-cutting retrenchment efforts which phase out this division. At other times, key players, worried about their futures, will jump at enticing offers dangled by executive search recruiters who raid an endangered firm. On still other occasions, some firms, particularly conglomerates, which cannot turn a profit on acquisition, may divest money-losing operations and sell them to ambitious insiders who can thrive in that unit but not in the parent company.[15] Companies can signal to executives through career-planning programs whether or not it makes sense for them to stay through troubled times. Companies such as Ford Motor Company and Union Carbide have instituted such programs successfully.

While many ancillary human resource functions are pared back, only some training programs are likely to be sacrificed. Certain types of education which provide more personal enhancement and remedial assistance will be curtailed while other types of education, such as sales training and skills retraining for improved efficiency, as well as adjustments to new technologies, become a top corporate priority. It is through such updating and realignment that individuals can see their membership in the firm renewed. Otherwise, they become obsolete and marginal to the firm in time of crisis.

Finally, company exit policies may be the most trying of all aspects of the career system. Whatever sophistication which the firm may have acquired for assisting departure from work life, the heavy usage of

---

[15] Leslie Wayne, "Joys of Fleeing the Corporate Stable," *New York Times*, November 15, 1981, p. 3–4; Lawrence Freeny, "Park Sausages is Back for More," *New York Times*, December 20, 1981, p. F–4.

these channels may tax them beyond their ability. Corporate commitments to displaced workers, which may be felt by many responsible firms, are often inadequately fulfilled despite good intentions. Retraining for other occupations and outplacement job search assistance may be a tremendous boost for reentry into the labor market. These efforts, however, may fall far short of expectations of all parties in regions of the country which suffer from harsh economic distress. Incentive programs that offer large cash allotments to older workers in an effort to entice some to leave voluntarily often assist the company in preventing the personally traumatic and culturally destructive act of forced exit. At the same time, many of the most talented workers may accept the terms of such a "buy-out," while those less valuable to the firm may remain, fearing their inability to obtain employment elsewhere. Furthermore, such programs may begin with the false premise that older workers are the firm's most expendable resource. Other exit programs which respect seniority may have very different implied biases. For example, last-in/first-out programs may excessively punish more recently hired segments of the workforce, such as minorities. Dismissals, even when prompted by the appearance of a financial crisis, must still be supported by well-documented performance data and by easily demonstrated economic hardship to ensure the compliance with fair labor standards.

The Cases

Each of these three stages in the life history of organizations is illustrated in the cases which appear in this section. The Jim Heavner cases bring us a close look at a successful entrepreneur and the risks and rewards of life within the entrepreneurial firm for others. The case provides rich detail about the early days of the firm, with special emphasis on the dynamics of the relationship between the founder Jim Heavner and his right-hand man Roger Jennings. The (A) case conveys the spirit and climate which characterized the rewards and development offered. The (B) case takes a later look at the explanations for difficulties suffered by the firm and the new career questions faced by the founder.

While this case looks at a mini-conglomerate, the People Express case provides a view of a more-focused enterprise, a new start-up airline. Again we see the role of the entrepreneur in shaping the key components of the career system. The founder Don Burr, explains his approach to keeping close to his workers as the firm grows. The special problems of rapid growth are demonstrated as stress and morale issues surface in reaction to understaffing.

In the PDI case we see a firm moving from its creation phase to its transformation into a stable work organization. The firm has begun to install new promotion policies as it matures. This case provides a perspective on some of the special problems of career development within a professional service firm as Dick Harbour, a consultant, contemplates his required hurdles for advancement.

In the Transcom cases we see another firm's progress towards a more mature situation. In an effort to acquire the needed capital for expansion, the first outside professional manager running a new high-technology equipment manufacturer agreed to merge into a much larger firm in an unrelated industry. The (A) case presents the situation faced by the chief executive in advance of the merger while the (B) case reports on his initial actions following the merger. Questions about executive succession, integration of career systems into a larger parent company, and management retention follow from this examination of the merger process.

In The Split, we are given a detailed chronology of the creation, transformation, and eventual break-up of one of the country's major law firms, Jones, Day, Reavis, and Pogue. The influence of promotion policies and executive succession are presented as key ingredients in the firm's dismemberment.

The case entitled The Weston Corporation: Amherst Plant presents a doomed plant within a firm which is radically changing its production technologies. Tom Newton, the plant manager, was uncertain over how to respond to the distress of his aging workforce within the plant.

The Weymouth Steel Corporation case presents another company struggling with the career implications of decline. Because of foreign competition, the firm is embarking upon a major retrenchment, which may involve plant closings, a loss of overtime, potential layoffs, and an early retirement program.

Finally the Webster Industries cases provide a particularly rich description of the background leading up to the layoff of 43 of 289 managers. The (A) case presents the search for criteria to use in making the separation decisions. The (B) case describes how the reduction in the managerial workforce was actually accomplished. The personal stress of the decision maker, the ethical responsibility of the firm, and human costs are highlighted in this case on exit policies.

The Readings

The readings provide some research and practical implications of these company life stages. Each article describes alternative ways of managing the dilemmas presented by each period. The article entitled "Evolution and Revolution as Organizations Grow," by Larry Greiner, looks at changes in management focus, organization structure, top-management style, control systems, and rewards policies within firms over five phases of growth. He concludes with a discussion of the lessons of history in managing the smooth developmental trends and abrupt transitions over time.

The article by John Kotter and Vijay Sathe, "Problems of Human Resource Management in Rapidly Growing Companies," highlights the special pressures placed upon such components of the career system as recruitment and training, given the stresses of fast change and swelling numbers of new co-workers.

The relationship of company strategy to career systems is illustrated in David Maister's article, entitled "Balancing the Professional Service Firm." This article graphically demonstrates how a professional service firm must develop a career system with recruitment and development policies that support the firm's unique reliance upon skill, hard work, industry expertise, and the nature of the client relationship. The market for professional labor, the firm's organizational structure, the market for the firm's services, and the firm's economic structure are presented as interrelated characteristics.

The article by J. Gerald Simmons, on "What Merged Employees Need to Know," outlines the career risks of mergers to workers in the aftermath. A checklist for employee preparation is presented.

Finally, the last reading provides a broad scan of the types of successful approaches firms facing retrenchment have taken to assist displaced workers. Although entitled "Canada's Good Example with Displaced

Workers," the author, William Batt, describes the key elements of this difficult exit process which have helped companies and workers in several settings.

CASE 1
THE JIM HEAVNER STORY (A)
Robert H. Miles

Sitting across the table from Roger Jennings, executive vice president of The Village Companies, I could not help noticing that he seemed much older and grayer than I remembered. As he smiled the corners of his eyes formed deep crevices that weren't there a decade earlier when The Village Companies was just WCHL, a local radio station. His face seemed to reveal all the experiences which had transformed this small radio station into a multi-divisional, geographically dispersed company (Exhibit 1).

Roger was one of the first persons hired by Jim Heavner. Starting as a sales person for the radio station, he had emerged as the most solid citizen in what was to become Heavner's core group. In the space of less than a decade, Roger had moved through the roles of sales manager, division manager, and general manager of the company's first major out-of-town acquisition, and now he was back in the home office having tendered his resignation. He seemed much wiser now and he looked tired.[1] At the ripe age of 36, Roger was through with The Village Companies and with Jim Heavner. He was going out on his own.

The Birth of WCHL

The Village Broadcasting Company, or what local citizens and university students knew as simply "WCHL," was formed in Chapel Hill, North Carolina, in 1953 by Sandy McClamroch and a partner. It began as a small AM "daytimer" (it went on the air at daybreak and off again at sunset), and was situated in a community known to many as "the village" and to more than a few as "the southern part of Heaven."

Despite dramatic growth, Chapel Hill retains its village atmosphere. The almost complete merger of town and gown (the University of North Carolina is located in the village) is one reason for its enduring character. Growth in the community was caused not only by enrollment increases at the university but also by the desirability of living in the village perceived by nearby Duke University faculty and by scientists, executives, and other professionals drawn to the area by work assignments in "The Research Triangle Park" (a large tract of land joining the cities of Chapel Hill, Durham, and Raleigh and zoned for corporate headquarters and research laboratories).

Recent growth statistics for Chapel Hill reveal the expansion in size and affluence of WCHL's radio audience. For instance, the number of households increased by 125 percent from 1960 to 1978. During the same period, permanent residents increased by 180 percent and student enrollment by 136 percent. Influenced in part by the relocation into Chapel Hill of a major Southeastern bank, bank deposits soared by 15,352 percent between 1960 and 1978. But this growth was managed carefully by an active town government that, for example, placed severe limits on commercial developments like apartment complexes and high-rise projects (only the bell tower at UNC would extend above the trees).

It is not clear, however, that Sandy and his partner fully appreciated the bonanza that was to come when they made the

[1] Observation of the casewriter.

Exhibit 1   **The Evolution of The Village Companies: 1953–1979**

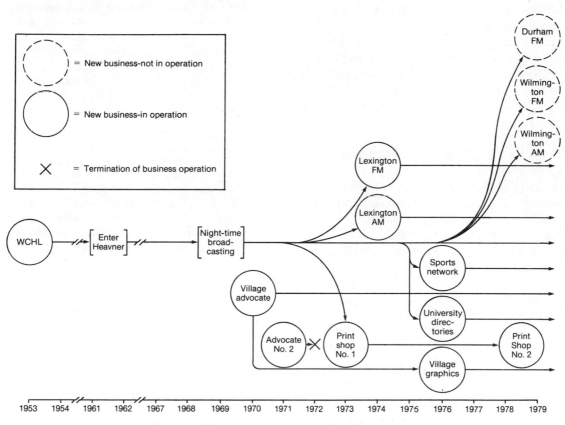

WCHL purchase decision. What is known is that Sandy's father was a professor at UNC, where Sandy had graduated with a degree in commerce, and that his roots in Chapel Hill were deep. So when he learned of the opportunity to start this little daytimer, for approximately $20,000, Sandy left his job selling farm equipment and went into business in the village.

In time, WCHL began to turn a small profit and Sandy bought out his partner. Sandy had many community interests and, by then, he had become active in local affairs and politics. He also was involved in

other real estate and business ventures that profited from Chapel Hill's explosive growth. But things at WCHL did not really take off until Sandy decided to hire Jim Heavner, then in his early 20s, to handle the day-to-day activities of selling and programming.

Jim and the Mayor

Jim Heavner came from a small town in rural North Carolina. He recalls that at the age of 10 he was pushed by his parents to develop writing skills and to enter "speech contests." And he often refers to the series of "marvelous accidents" that he believed had been an important part of his exciting and rewarding career. For example, Jim had broken his arm while trying out for a junior varsity basketball team in high school. As a consequence of not being able to play, he began scoring the games and announcing the plays over the P.A. system. These activities led him to write sports stories for a local newspaper.

By the time Jim reached the university at Chapel Hill, he was an experienced announcer and he had been involved in all aspects of radio programming and copy writing. As Jim recalls, "When I hit Chapel Hill I was just enough ahead of the pack to get a job as an announcer at WUNC (the university's radio station)." By the end of his first year, Jim was working part time at WCHL. He left six months later to take a job as an announcer at a nearby television station. That led to a central role as sports announcer in a weekly television bowling show which lasted about a year. As Jim recalls,

> that was an incredible experience. . . . It meant that for 60 minutes every Sunday afternoon the only voice that was heard, with the exception of one break for a national commercial, was mine.

As the bowling show was winding down, Sandy phoned to see if Jim would be interested in returning to WCHL. Sandy, who is 15 years Jim's senior, provided this account of his decision to hire young Heavner:

> All I can remember is that I was going to be Mayor [of Chapel Hill] and that Ty Boyd [WCHL's only radio personality] was going to leave [to become the "morning man" at a much larger station in Charlotte]. Jim had worked for us as an announcer while he was in school and had left to do a bowling show

on TV. And in just the short experience where I had gotten to know him, he was the only one I knew who had the capabilities, in my estimation, to take over the selling job *and* the programming job. I had no real knowledge of the programming myself. I had been selling since the beginning of the station and watching the dollars primarily. . . . Even back then, at 20 years old, you could tell that Jim could sell.

From Jim's recollection, the offer from Sandy came something like this:

> Sandy called and asked me to come over. (I already had the news that Ty was leaving.) I shot down the boulevard and wandered into the little concrete block building at the foot of the Hill which contained the radio station. And Sandy began by saying, "You know, Ty is going to Charlotte and I'd like you to take his job." I said, "Fine Sandy, I'll be here in two weeks." And he says, "Well, wait a minute. I want to tell you how much you're going to make. Let me tell you about the job. Let me tell you what your duties are, your responsibilities. . . ." And I said, "Sandy, if it's Ty's job and if you're my boss, that will be fair." He went on to say, "Well, we're going to pay you $125 a week." And then he said, "Ty had done a great job here. He has built the radio station up to the point that selling now is," and I am confident that I'm quoting, "it's pretty much an order taking job now." . . . I got a car. It was a 1949 Ford whose axle was going to break within the next 90 days.
>
> So all of those things were just marvelous, marvelous, marvelous. It may be one of the last times of my life when I experienced totally unexpurgated joy at the prospect of something new. I knew I could work for Sandy. I knew that I liked him. I think I had an intuitive sense that he was supportive and interested in outcomes and that I was very active and interested in creating the solutions; and I sensed that we had a match.

Jim also recalls that Sandy said, "Someday, if this thing goes well, if you want to stay here, and if you do a good job, I might let you buy some stock in it." Jim's reaction: "Mmmm. . . . Heavy. That was a heavy idea." So, Jim cancelled plans to continue studies at the university. At the age of 20, he felt his was "a rare opportunity" and everyone he consulted tended to agree. Even before he assumed his new duties, however, another of his "marvelous accidents" occurred:

> Sure enough, Sandy was elected Mayor about 10 days before I came to work. Being a mayor was something Sandy liked a lot. So he started spending a lot of time at Town Hall. The town manager retired and they had to go through the laborious process of hiring his replacement. And then, if you remember, in 1960, '61, '62, and '63, social issues began heating up. Kennedy was elected in 1960. We began to have the crisis of rising expectations and the civil rights advocates began taking to the streets somewhere in the early 1960s, and Chapel Hill was highly vulnerable to this kind of thing.

These events took Sandy out of the day-to-day operations of the radio station. He remained in the office of the mayor for eight years of the most tumultuous times the village had ever witnessed.

Building WCHL

Jim Heavner described what he found when he arrived for work at WCHL:

> WCHL was what I would call a single-cell amoeba, a *very* simple operation. I was sales manager, program director and "morning man." . . . The early work was principally week to week. We had no forecasting system and, of course, I had no formal business training. . . . We didn't draw a budget for seven or eight years. Advertising spots were being sold for $1 and total annual sales ap-

proximated $60,000. Most of the time I would just ask Sandy how things were going and, if our collections were running behind, he would say, "Not so good. We need to collect some money," and I would say, "Oh? Who owes us?" And he would tell me and I would hit the street and try to collect some money. Because Sandy was so highly respected, I would attempt to delegate that to him. But Sandy really did not like to carry unpleasant news, so he was not a super collector. Interestingly enough, however, when the bank balance got low enough, Sandy became a great collector. He had a really clear picture. He had a feeling that if you've got more money in the bank than I have, then dammit you ought to pay me. But if I'm sitting here with more money in the bank than you have, and you owe me some, then I won't bug you. . . . It was my observation that Sandy could really be tough if he wanted.

Out of this modest beginning, Heavner began to fashion a business strategy that would eventually lead to local respectability and financial success for WCHL. His early priorities were to build up sales and improve programming. His little station fortunately operated in an "unrated" market, where listenership statistics were not available to customers. Nevertheless, the broadcasting power of WCHL barely reached the fringes of Chapel Hill, while bigger stations in nearby Durham and Raleigh were powerful enough to reach the village audience.

Heavner's overall strategy was, first, to cater to village interests and politics in programming and, second, to demonstrate that WCHL could serve Chapel Hill clients better than the competition.

On the sales side, Heavner wanted local retailers and other business people to feel that WCHL was working *hard* for them. He viewed sales people at the larger stations as account managers and order takers. In many cases they managed longer term accounts with regional and national advertisers, who often provided the copy they wanted on the air. They also tended to view local accounts as fillers.

He built his marketing approach around the slogan "WCHL *Works*," and he hoped to make the double meaning obvious to his clients. Early on, Jim developed a quarter-hour diary in order to help him maximize his contact with clients. He tailored creative copy to the particular image of each customer, often taking different recordings of an advertising spot to customers for preview before selecting the one to broadcast. He sent out mailers to WCHL clients extolling the virtues of WCHL staff or reporting WCHL's involvement in community projects, ". . . a lot of shirtsleeves pictures." With time, the strategy paid off and sales began to mount.

On the programming side, Jim gradually evolved music format changes to cater to the growing student and young adult population. More important than these programming changes were his innovations geared toward becoming more closely identified with the community. Political debates involving town matters were frequently aired on WCHL. The station became involved in numerous community events like "Hot Diggity Day," the "Halloween Carnival," and "Apple Chill Fair." They were all big affairs in the life of the village and soon they became institutionalized in the town culture and calendar. Thus, on the positive side, Heavner observed that, "The radio station had done a good job of establishing itself as a worthy community citizen, but we turned everybody over to our competitors at sundown because we had to sign off."

So, Heavner emerged from this first phase in the development of WCHL with both an expanded and stable local client base and the respect and identification with the radio station of this unusual community. Moreover, Jim felt that all this hard work, together with the good vibes from being a part of the community, had a very positive effect of the morale and motivation of his staff.

There was personal reinforcement for Jim, too. Not only did he emerge as a highly visible young man on the move, but the national Radio Advertising Bureau picked up his act. Billing Jim as "the world's largest one-man sales staff," RAB invited Heavner, then 25, to speak at their national management conferences. As Jim explains, "There were a lot of little ideas coming out of WCHL . . . we were an idea station." But a comment made repeatedly from these audiences eventually triggered the next stage in the development of both Jim Heavner and WCHL:

> they would nearly always say, "If you're so smart, why aren't you hiring some other guy to be doing this with you? Why are you a one-man sales staff?" My answer came to be, "I will hire another salesperson when the station's resources are enough that I can afford someone who has the potential to be more competent than I am. I will teach him all I know and expect him to bring his own intellectual resources to it, and then I will learn from him and we will move ahead together." And I was really committed to that idea.

By now, Sandy had begun to let Jim participate more and more in the ownership of the company. Moreover, Jim had always received both an increase in base pay and a bonus each year:

> each year Sandy would give me a bonus check which, in every case, I felt was more than fair. I never felt underpaid. It was always just a little more than I thought I had coming and that was a nice feeling. And to

the extent that we can do that today in our bonus plans, we attempt to execute that now. That takes some careful management.

Roger Jennings and the Developing Salesforce Concepts

By 1967, the resources of the company had grown to the point that Heavner had already made a bad mistake in hiring his first salesperson. Jim remembers that, "I didn't want to have a typical small-town radio time peddler working for me." So he hired a young banker who had been president of the Durham Jaycees and local Man of the Year. "I failed to comprehend, however, how difficult it would be for someone without a media background . . . and someone who couldn't write." One day, about three months later, the guy called from a bank in Virginia and informed Jim that he wouldn't be returning to WCHL.

At about that time, Heavner remembered a conversation he had had with Roger Jennings, a graduate student at UNC in radio, television, and motion pictures. Roger had come to him, offering to "take over the thirty worst accounts in the radio station and sell them" to demonstrate that he was worthy of a position at WCHL. When asked what his goals were, Roger told Jim that he eventually wanted to be an ETV director and hoped to be earning about $15,000 by the time he was 35.

> Not a bad strategy. I had thanked him but said, "No thanks." But I remembered that Roger had written me a couple of letters. His syntax was pretty good and he had paragraphs that seemed to flow with nice transitional phrases. I remembered that. And I learned that he had finished his course work for his master's and was working as director at the university's television station.

Roger was hired, with Jim's promise of "a

chance to grow," and this event marked the beginning of a long, close relationship. As Jim recalls,

> I'd had that failure and Roger, by God, was not gonna fail. He and I got in the trenches together. I was there and he was there, night after night after night.

Roger was carefully coached in all aspects of selling that Jim had perfected during his first half decade at WCHL. But Heavner's approach to Roger's development extended beyond training. "Something I believe deeply," said Heavner, "is that of equal value to the training is the commitment the trainer must make to the trainee for his or her success. The coach has to be willing to say I'm going to win or lose with you."

Roger described those early months at WCHL as follows:

> There was a great feeling of community in the place because it was so small; and, certainly, Jim and I had a very personal kind of business relationship—a very one-on-one kind of situation. There were not a lot of systematic approaches to things at that point, although Jim had developed a few. It was still a "fly by the seat of your pants" kind of operation; and the more formal approaches to things that have worked so well for us really evolved over a period of time.
>
> I'm just embarrassed to say we had no method of projecting sales. We just went out and sold all we could and hoped we beat last year's performance. Then Jim attended a seminar one summer at Harvard, and came back with this plan on how you project sales and try to exercise a lot more control over what you are going to do. It was this kind of thing, the little seminars and special kinds of training sessions and reading a lot of books, I think, that got us into a more business-like approach.

During this first year together, Jim and Roger refined the company's marketing strategy and developed systems for managing and motivating the growing salesforce.

Heavner's marketing maxim became, "In unmeasured radio markets, great selling can rescue poor programming, absolutely; but great programming can never rescue poor selling." Therefore, Jim placed most of his emphasis on the sales side. Given the nature of the market, he concentrated on what he referred to as the "humpability factor" in his salesforce. "We were successful in dealing with retailers because we would just outwork the other guy."

George McCall, a college friend of Roger's, joined the sales staff in 1968. At that time, Roger became sales manager and Jim assumed the duties of general manager. George quickly came to understand the meaning of the "humpability factor."

> We had to leave at nine and be back at five, and you did *not* show your face back here 'til five o'clock. . . . I was scared. I mean I realized that this was something I had to do to succeed.

With Roger, Jim developed an intensive sales training and development program that was applied to all newcomers in sales and which was still in place in 1978. There were three basic components in Heavner's salesforce training and development program: (1) bottoms-up goal setting, (2) high teacher-pupil ratio, and (3) collaboration based on a team bonus plan.

Although Jim had become convinced that "if you are looking after the best interests of the individual who's working for you, he or she will tend to look after yours," the Harvard program provided him with the process to link individual and company goals.

> What I had not thought of before, was that you could lock that individual goal into a highly detailed planning process in which you analyzed monthly what you were doing on an account-by-account basis, from A to

Z, plan a strategy for every one of those accounts, and assign responsibility for it. Then you had a much higher chance for success and it increased the purposefulness of the people doing the selling. And it really did work. . . . It's the sweet spot. If I'm right, it's the most important thing we do. If I'm wrong, it's the most expensive.

As Roger recalled, the monthly goal-setting and review process was "very detailed. It was not enough for a person to come in and say, 'I'm going to do $100,000 in sales next year.' That person had to show how he or she was going to do it."

Jim placed the monthly goal-setting process in a team framework. His emphasis was on developing new sales people, and the record of the approach reveals that he has never had a failure at WCHL. Collaboration rather than competition was Heavner's overall approach. He emphasized that,

> I think I can increase their "humpability rate" fairly significantly with a highly competitive situation. I could give away individual prizes and incentives and I think that would hype up productivity for the short term. In time though, there will have to be winners and losers . . . and you would have high turnover. . . . My observation has been that in companies where you have high turnover in the sales area you also have very unpredictable sales curves.

He set up a reward system for the salesforce with the joint objectives of maximizing both the success rates of new sales people and the development of general management talent. As he explains:

> If you create a situation in which you have five motivated teachers working on one student, it seems to me that you cinch the learning situation. . . . So what I do is tie the compensation of the veteran members of the sales team to the performance of the new person. That way, the newcomer gets a lot

of training. Also, each salesperson personally must approve the hiring of each new member. The payoff is twofold. First, you increase the probability that the new person will learn and succeed. Second, you are conditioning future managers to get comfortable with the idea that they are going to be dependent on the performance of others for their success.

New sales people had to earn their way into the sales team. For example, they might start at a $10,000 annual base salary.

> We give them a grub stake of $3–4000 a month in the business which, if it's done right, is picked to be a little bit of everything. People who love us and will just die for us, and some people who need to be sold a little bit. We want them to get some successes. They're paid half-commission on that business. They're then given a full commission on all the new business they bring in.
>
> When the newcomer's commission reaches a level at which total compensation exceeds base pay, he or she is paid an override each month. When the newcomer's total compensation reaches or exceeds $1,000 a month for three consecutive months, he or she is converted to a minimum guarantee of $12,000 per year, given a car, and accorded full membership in the team process. At that time the initiate and all members in the team are paid the same way on a team bonus at the end of the year.
>
> . . . if it goes as we design, when he or she is knocking on the $20,000 door, we want to have created an opportunity for that person to be a sales manager.

The reports of two sales trainees who became senior vice presidents of The Village Companies attest to the effectiveness of Heavner's motivational concepts.

Kay Allison:

> I literally fainted on the day I was supposed to go out to begin selling. I was scared to death; you know, the whole nine yards.

But I had received good coaching from Roger Jennings and I went out and was successful, or at least he made me believe that.

George McCall:

> I had just been fired from another job, and that will *flat* get your attention! But with Roger, I was a miracle worker! Four months from when I started I was commissionable. [George's commissions had exceeded his starting base salary for three consecutive months.]

Not long after these salesforce concepts had been implemented, the FCC granted Heavner's petition for nighttime broadcasting. Gone were the frustrations of heliotropism. By 1969, Heavner's growing sales team was primed under the leadership of Roger Jennings to make the most of the nighttime air space.

With the growth and development of the salesforce and the expansion in air time, the company began to pile up the resources which led to its expansion into other businesses. As Jim recalls,

> We had to expand. We had established an internal intrinsic need to grow. Moreover, the tax structure requires you to grow or die. You don't have any choice but to grow. . . . Suddenly in 1969, we were paying 50¢ to Uncle Sam on every dollar that came in the door. That's the year we started our profit sharing plan and all kinds of things to shelter money. It was in that environment that we started *The Village Advocate*.

At about this time, Jim approached Sandy about the issue of ownership. Although Jim was satisfied with his increasing share of WCHL, his focus was on future developments in the company. As a result of these discussions, they agreed that Jim could put up half the money for each new venture and that they would share ownership 50-50 in all new businesses.

The Village Advocate

The idea for a "penny saver" newspaper came from Roger, who, in turn, had been persuaded by a client who told him, "They just make more money than God!" The paper would contain advertisements and feature local color stories. It would be delivered free to every Chapel Hill resident. Revenues would be generated from the sale of advertising space alone. As Sandy McCalmroch explains:

> Jim had great ambition to expand, but we found that, at the time, it was hard to get the money to start in the radio field. We found that we could start *The Village Advocate* on a lot less money.

Jim added that a court decision, involving a Boston newspaper, also tempered his decision to avoid new radio station acquisitions during this time. According to Jim, this decision by the FCC to revoke the license of the newspaper's television subsidiary, in response to a campaign mounted by a public interest group, created a lot of uncertainty among members of the radio industry about the risks inherent in a broadcasting license.

In addition to these concerns, the Chapel Hill market looked right for a "shopper." The village had a thrice-weekly newspaper that reached less than 50 percent of the local households. Jim and Sandy thought that their professional sales approach would enable them to compete effectively with the local paper.

But the decision to initiate this new venture, particularly this *kind* of business, was not an easy one. Would a "throw-away" paper damage the image of WCHL in the community? Jim reflected on this difficult choice:

> The thing we felt we really risked in that thing was our reputation. It was one of the few times in my adult life when, professionally, I've experienced anything I could really call terror . . . in deciding to crank up that thing in our home town and stake our reputations on the line with the idea that it might not make it, and go absolutely nose to nose against a 50 year old local newspaper. . . . Except for local introductions, we never allowed a WCHL salesperson to make a single sales call for *The Village Advocate*.

Jim discovered that the National Association of Advertising Publishers served as a clearing house on "shoppers." So, for a $150 membership, WCHL was inundated with information. Jim attended the NAAP national conference where, by asking everyone he met who the smartest shopping guide publisher was, he identified a husband and wife team in Des Moines. He spent a week following the duo around Des Moines.

> I came back feeling that I knew everything there was to know . . . I spent 18 hours a day with them . . . they physically would lay out each page . . . and I went with them to the printer and everything, including sales calls.

Jim encountered considerable difficulty in trying to attract someone to manage *The Advocate*. After repeated attempts to hire someone, he brought in a public relations staffer from the state capitol and assembled a small, separate sales staff for *The Advocate*. Looking back on this event, Jim observed that the new manager's

> success as a publisher of *The Advocate* was almost totally a product of our system. He was 31 years old and making somewhere around $10,000 a year. He had not accomplished anything really spectacular in his professional life, and we still took him. In the five years before he left the company, *The Advocate* went from zero to $500,000 in total billings. He left the company with

some cash from the sale of his stock to start a venture on his own which subsequently failed.

The Second Advocate—Debacle

The Village Advocate did so well the first year and cost so little to create that Jim and Sandy began thinking of branching out into other cities and eventually franchising the whole operation. Their pilot test of these ideas, which began only a year after the Chapel Hill shopper, was to start a second *Advocate* in another college town in North Carolina. The deal, a 50-50 joint venture between the company and a local partner, created a situation in which Jim and the other partner had equal management authority. The test was Heavner's first important failure, and he learned two lessons from it: do your homework and avoid dual-management situations.

First, Jim failed to attach enough importance to the strength of the local newspaper. As soon as the local paper management got wind of Jim's plans, they created their own shopper that Jim believed was produced below actual cost and that was, in his view, "against the law."

> I was supposed to bring the sales expertise to it and he was supposed to bring the local management to it. But we found that having two chief executive officers is worse than having none . . . you can't get a decision. It took us a year to decide to sue for relief. . . . I am convinced that if either of us had been in charge, the venture would have been a success. In fact, my partner and I remain close friends and he has become a very successful broadcasting executive in the region.
>
> . . . we told the guys at the paper, that if they would start charging a competitive price and if they would pay us $25,000, we'd drop the suit. They paid us $25,000, but by

that time the battle was already won. They had nudged us out. So we got out of it.

During this episode, Roger Jennings had been promoted from the position of WCHL sales manager to general manager of *The Village Advocate*. Under Roger, sales at *The Advocate* continued their upward climb. As Roger remembers:

> There was a philosophy in the early stages that we were all working together toward a common purpose; that the goals of the individuals were compatible with the corporate goals. You didn't worry too much about the appearance of things.
>
> In 1973, I left CHL to run *The Village Advocate*. It wasn't very prestigious. I was the sales manager at CHL, and *everyone* who knew anything about us assumed that someday Jim would step down, or step up, and I would be the manager of WCHL . . . that was sort of the natural order of things. But Jim and I got together and decided that the best career path for me would be to try to strike out in an expansive move. . . . So I waived my opportunity to manage WCHL and went over and ran *The Village Advocate* to learn that business.
>
> Well, that raised a lot of eyebrows. People wondered what had happened to me . . . had I gotten sidetracked, or demoted, or just what. And, in all honesty, that didn't bother me at all.

The Print Shops

The discovery of the Print Shop was another of Heavner's "marvelous accidents." He had taken a walk down Brattle Street in Harvard Square one afternoon while attending a seminar on sales management at the Harvard Business School in 1970. As soon as he walked in the store he recognized its potential in Chapel Hill. As Jim recalls,

> Two or three things caught my attention. One was instant dry mounting of prints. . . .

I'm looking at an easel that says "Dry mounting on styrofoam while you wait." I thought . . . "Um . . . very interesting. Instant gratification." Then I began to think, "McDonald's . . . um . . . interesting idea." The price was acceptable. The other thing that intrigued me was the way the merchandise was displayed. I had an idea that a lot of people would buy a lot of art, but they are intimidated by the idea of having to go in and display their lack of knowledge.

I wandered into the back room, and 30 minutes and two beers later the manager was showing me his books and telling me how to do one in North Carolina.

In 1973, when Chapel Hill's first and only shopping mall opened, the Print Shop was one of the most successful stores in it. Jim put in "a little training program" for the employees which emphasized both merchandizing and strategy. The demand for low cost art was high among university students and was stimulated by the rapid increase in new households in Chapel Hill.

As Jim explained, "We're not in the art business; we're in the business of making people happy with what they hang on the wall." But, the demand for more expensive frames was so great that Jim soon replaced the framing contractor with his own framing operation. Sandy also remarked that the Print Shop had a side benefit of putting WCHL in the shoes of a retailer. To him it was very helpful ". . . to open a retail business and have to sit back and wait for customers to come to you rather than you go to them. Selling like you do in broadcast advertising is just an entirely different ballgame."

The Programming Side

The programming side to Village Broadcasting consisted of the program director and the announcers, disc jockeys, copy writers, and support staff involved in planning, designing and operating the broadcasting activities of the station. Beginning with the founding of WCHL, the predominant strategy had been to be the training center for programming talent throughout the region. As Sandy explained:

> We knew that we were just a training station for the Carolinas. [We existed initially] because of our ability to use college talent at a very reasonable price. We could afford only to use that talent. We couldn't afford to keep them after they graduated; we didn't have any place for them to go.

Blessed with the strong radio, television, and motion pictures department at the University, located only a mile and a half away, WCHL management always found an abundant and inexpensive supply of talented and eager part-timers to meet the station's programming requirements. To obtain the most from these college students, Heavner adopted a policy of "helping them meet their goals, inside or outside the company." Because of the single-cell nature of the initial company, he attempted to compensate for the lack of advancement opportunities within WCHL by creating opportunities for programmers elsewhere in larger radio and television operations in the region.

Often when an employee from the programming side approached graduation, he or she would consult with Jim about career opportunities. Invariably, if the individual's commitment to WCHL had been high, Jim returned the company's commitment to the individual by locating attractive employment elsewhere. During the company's pre-expansion phase, many of the part-time announcers and news reporters moved from WCHL at graduation to become "anchor men" and "morning men" at larger stations in the region. Perhaps the best story, and the one still very much alive in the programming group, is the one told about Jim Lampley, a bright and innovative stringer in sports broadcasting.

Lampley developed an evening sports program that involved debates between coaches in the Atlantic Coast Conference on the eve of major contests. His style was engaging and he always seemed to ask the really interesting questions. The program became an overnight success. But, as with so many others, when Lampley reached graduation the growth in WCHL had not been sufficient to enable Heavner to offer him an appropriate opportunity within the company. So, as the story goes, Heavner wrote Roone Arledge, director of ABC Sports, and helped mount a campaign to get Lampley's name before the executives of ABC. Lampley has been a sportscaster in that national network ever since.

Throughout this early period the opportunity balance favored the sales side of the company. It was obvious to all that Jim had decided that future general managers were to be developed within the sales group. The sales force bonus system and career development program, which involved formal management training and intensive in-house coaching, reinforced this imbalance. The social climate of the late 1960s and early 1970s exacerbated it.

From the sales point of view, the social unrest and the questioning of authority in general, and the capitalist ethic in particular, made recruitment more difficult. On the programming side, however, these values and predispositions could not be screened, but were internalized within that part of the organization. WCHL became a microcosm of social unrest: money-oriented, upward-mobile sales people rode in uneasy harness with the artistic and stifled programmers.

Kay Allison, who arrived on this scene in 1972, described what she found:

> From the sales side, this was a place of great opportunity. There was the opportunity to sign on with a group of close-knit, aggressive, young people who had some pretty big ideas for themselves . . . that in growing with the company one might achieve riches and fame. . . . On the production side, you just think of individual conversations, of sniping at sales people because of their position in the company. If anybody stayed a year he or she was a vet!

This state of affairs persisted through the early 1970s. For instance, until 1974, Heavner kept in his desk what he referred to as a "People and Sales Growth" chart. It summarized key personnel additions and other important business events and linked them to estimates of how much each contributed to sales growth in the company during their first year of placement or occurence. The notes scribbled beside his ever-increasing sales curve are reproduced in Exhibit 2. Reviewing this period, Jim said,

> In the interest of accuracy, you'd have to say that while the sales thing was developing in a remarkably predictable way, the era of the 60s, my first decade there, was marked by a fairly high degree of job dissatisfaction in the programming area. On balance, we didn't have anybody that came out of there thinking he or she had worked for a very select boss.

Programming talent and motivation, as measured by the number of annual broadcasting awards captured by WCHL, waxed and waned with the evolution of the company. Awards were frequent when Heavner guided programming and during the period he still had time to be closely involved with program directors. But as expansion occurred, together with Jim's obvious devo-

---

Exhibit 2   "People and Sales Growth"*

	People	Growth
1967	Add Roger Jennings to WCHL (sales dept.)	+ $33,000 in WCHL sales
1968	Add George McCall to WCHL (sales dept.)	+ $15,000 in WCHL sales
1969	WCHL becomes a nighttime operation	+ $73,000 in WCHL sales
1970	Village Publications is created	+ $134,000 in Village Publications sales
1971	Add another person to WCHL (sales dept.)	+ $36,000 in WCHL sales
	Add two persons to Village Publications	+ $45,000 in Village Publications sales
1972	Add two more persons to WCHL (sales dept.)	+ $117,000 in WCHL sales
	Add Kay Allison to Village Publications	+ $81,000 in Village Publications sales
1973	Add Geiger to WCHL (sales dept.)	+ $97,000 in WCHL sales
	Transfer Jennings to head Village Publications	+ $102,000 in Village Publications sales
1974	Add one person to WCHL (sales dept.)	+ $60,000 in WCHL sales
(projected)	Add three persons to Village Publications	+ $124,000 in Village Publications sales

* Personal notes kept by Jim Heavner until mid-1974.

---

tion to the development of the "sales side," disenchantment among programmers resulted in less impressive broadcasting results.

Village Communications: The Lexington Venture

The fiasco with the out-of-town *Advocate* caused Jim and Sandy to consider a strategy shift. They knew they could run successful radio operations and the combined cash flows of WCHL and *The Village Advocate* now made it possible for them to consider broadcasting acquisitions. As Sandy explained, "We went back into the radio business because you can get rid of a radio station; everybody understands it." In fact, it was general knowledge in the industry that a radio station with no frills and with a poor location could be sold for about 2½ times annual revenues. Sandy and Jim believed this multiple would only go up with time because of the limited number of stations available.

This was 1973, a year in which Jim and Sandy had consulted an "estate planner" who, in turn, had informed them that their goals for the future were quite different. For instance, Sandy had a number of financial interests in the village that might benefit from less commitment to a high-leveraged broadcasting operation. Based on the discussions which followed, Sandy suggested that Jim assume a majority share in all future expansions.

That same year, Roger was sent out on a mission to find a suitable radio acquisition. After rejecting several possibilities, the company negotiated a package AM-FM combination in Lexington, Kentucky, that became Village Communications. Even with the enhanced cash flow, however, the company had to stretch with outside financing to acquire the new stations. Sandy took a one-third share and Jim took a two-thirds share. They decided to offer portions of their ownership to the managers they would select to run these ventures if they were successful.

Lexington was another Southern university town, only considerably larger than Chapel Hill. According to Jim, both he and Roger recognized that Lexington was going to be a challenge:

> Roger perceived, and I think correctly, that going to Lexington was going to be the most difficult, challenging assignment he'd ever make. We did not have experience in a market that size and we didn't have a lot of personnel. We had no conception at that time of how important it would be to take your own people, experienced people, and plug them into a turnaround operation.

Hindsight confirmed Roger's premonitions and revealed a number of other factors that both he and Jim found to be more important than anticipated. For instance, Lexington was a rated market, and the AM station had a very poor market rating. It also had an unfavorable dial location, at the end opposite all the popular radio competitors in Lexington. The FM station had a good sales record, but the AM station would require a major programming overhall that might cause its traditional clients to turn elsewhere. Then, too, Lexington was not the village.

Heavner sent two general managers to Village Communications, each to run his own station. Both were to occupy the same building and to share certain resources, including a common administrative staff. Roger Jennings took the AM station, which posed the greatest challenge. An individual who had successfully engineered a turnaround in one of the South's largest radio stations was brought in to run the FM operation that was already doing very well. Jim remembers that the FM manager frequently complained of "the bureaucracy" in his former organization; but only later did he realize that the new manager was going through a complete life change. After taking the summer off, the newcomer announced

to Jim that he was leaving his wife of over two decades. Within two months, one of Heavner's Chapel Hill employees had left her job and stock option to join the FM manager in his new life in Lexington. Jim continued, with obvious emotion,

> Roger and the [outsider] came into my office one day shortly before they left for Lexington and said that they had had a meeting and that they wanted me not to come to Lexington because they wanted all the troops to know they were the bosses, not me. Hmmm. The concern about the bureaucracy . . . being carried right through to the situation in Lexington! . . . Within weeks it became obvious that the operation was not successful. We were losing money.

In terms of revenues, Village Communications was half a success, half a failure. Advertising sales for the FM station took off smartly, but sales for the AM station continued to stagnate well below the more popular AM stations in Lexington. Moreover, monthly expenses were exceeding the joint budget for both operations by roughly 80 percent.

Personnelwise, the early operation of Village Communications was *a disaster*. According to Jim,

> Village Communications was totally unsuccessful in recruiting a single salesperson out in Lexington who could cut it for us. You know, we had zero failures among people we had recruited after we established our system at WCHL.

Even the sales and programming people sent from WCHL to Village Communications quickly became disenchanted and left. These individuals had been patiently coached and groomed in the home operation.

Jim fired the FM manager after the first six months of the Lexington venture, and gave

Roger responsibility for both operations with a mandate to "get the damned thing on budget!" Roger described the situation as follows:

> We went into Lexington just about as unprepared for that kind of venture as I think a company could be. We brought in a seasoned manager from another radio station, who went up there with me as co-manager, but even he really wasn't prepared. He was a great salesman . . but in many respects was totally incompatible with the way we want to run a company. The kinds of people that he was bringing on board were the kinds of people that I felt were not in the mold of what had been successful for us. They had a great deal of loyalty to him personally, but very little loyalty to our objectives as a company.
>
> Overall, I think we underestimated the severity of the problem. We went with too few resources in terms of our own kinds of people. We did not fully appreciate the technical and physical problems that we would encounter. We went too far away from home the first time. We probably went into a situation that, ideally, we shouldn't have until we had two to three other expansions under our belts. We went into a larger market than we were accustomed to, into a very head-on competitive situation.
>
> We took the attitude that if we put in a good radio service and gave people an alternative, and if we were aggressive and promotional, it would do the trick. But the listening habits were so engrained in people, and we started from such a zero point, that it became very frustrating to all of us very soon. We had anticipated going in there and, frankly, just turning the town around real fast.

Roger, whom Jim regarded as having "overidentified" with his staff, eventually was relieved of his duties as general manager of Village Communications. He was replaced by Peter Jorgenson, formerly sales manager at *The Village Advocate*. Looking back in 1978, Roger commented on the damage to his relationship with Jim the Lexington experience had caused:

> It destroyed the relationship . . . a toll was taken on both parties as a result of this experience. When you are the person charged with the performance of a new entity and it is not coming anywhere near producing at that level, especially when you are accustomed to calling your shots pretty well, it is a deflating experience.
>
> Both of us overreacted. I probably, in retrospect, had let the problems get in the way of solutions, and really felt the whole thing was just a tremendous mess. I also could see the other end; and there was no question in my mind that the home office was overreacting, because my point of view was that nobody had to tell me, or remind me, how bad things were. Nobody had to tell me what our obligations were. Nobody had to motivate me to try to do things to correct it. The problem was, and I still hold this view, that the old solutions just weren't adequate, that the people here—Jim is the embodiment of that—were calling for the old standard solutions that had worked in Chapel Hill.
>
> We're a great rah-rah, cheerleading kind of outfit, and I subscribe to that; but we had a situation there where we didn't have people who had come up through our ranks. We had outside, cynical, "show me," types. You know, "Don't tell me how great it's going to be. Show me, then I'll believe it."
>
> I felt that we were up there trying to crawl, and the kinds of sessions we would have when Jim would come to town were talking about how we were all going to run the marathon. All we were trying to do at that point was just crawl! And I felt there was a real mismatch in what was being said to the people and what they could hear at that point.

Enter Woodruff and Financial Controls

The first year of operation with Village Communications made it clear that better company-wide financial controls were needed. From Kay Allison's perspective,

> It was a major financial investment for us. The fact that it did not turn around immediately has made us more conscious of cost accounting and bottom lines and all those good things.

While Jim was proud of the company's successes in developing "people skills" among his potential general managers, he realized along with other company leaders that financial expertise was the company's weak spot. Thinking specifically about the Lexington situation, he said,

> Anybody that loses money as fast as we did needs somebody to count it! . . . George McCall [who became general manager of WCHL at the start-up of Village Communications] threatened either suicide or early retirement because we were having all kinds of problems. We were just outgrowing our system.

It was under these conditions, within a few months of the start-up of Village Communications, that Bob Woodruff was hired. Jim approached Arthur Anderson, the firm that had helped arrange the financing for the Lexington venture, to see if they could recommend someone to help him manage the company's increasingly complex internal accounting and control functions. Bob, a CPA with 10 years of experience at Arthur Andersen, was recommended.

Bob's primary role focused on managing the growing financial affairs of the company. He set up and refined budgeting on a divisional basis and was a key figure in the allocation and monthly review processes. In addition, he soon became the chief negotiator of company acquisitions and divestitures and the primary link between the company and financial institutions.

By this time, the company had four business divisions: Village Broadcasting (WCHL), Village Publishing, the Print Shop, and Village Communications. Bob and Jim decided that each division general manager would be accountable for division performance in terms of sales, budget and operating profit. As Jim described, annual goals were formulated by division managers using a bottoms-up approach based on the personal-development and performance goals of each subordinate. Each division manager would then meet with Jim and Bob to "negotiate." During this meeting, the figures would be "massaged." In addition, self-development and subordinate-development goals were reviewed; they were especially important for the general managers of WCHL and The Village Advocates. As Jim explains,

> I am willing to acknowledge that the company is always going to want more revenue than the troops are going to want to deliver. That's just the nature of the beast. I talk about expectations and they talk about goals.
>
> Bob and I have looked at everything and we've massaged the marketplace. Based on the assumptions that retail sales will increase by this amount, fueled by this much inflation; based on the expectations that our sales team will stay intact for the coming year, it is my feeling that it is reasonable for WCHL to expect this group of people that we've put together to have an X percent increase for the year, which might be 18 percent. Then, they go back and work with their people. They know if they come back to me with a plan that will get us more than

an 18 percent increase that I tend to be very generous in rewarding the achievement of that kind of goal.

Sandy spoke very highly of Bob and the systems he had helped Jim refine:

> Bob sure has been a life-saver. My knowledge in financing was very limited. . . . I had nowhere near the ability that Woodruff has. . . . He certainly has taken a load off of Jim . . . in being the intermediary between Jim and the managers of the various divisions.

From Jim's point of view:

> He's just great! He's a confident, right-hand man, manages a hard set of books, is an excellent negotiator, and has a comprehensive knowledge of tax law. He's conscientious to a fault. . . . Marvelous guy.

Turnaround in Programming

The lessons learned from Lexington also made it clear that well trained and coached company people were essential if new acquisitions were to become successful. The individuals affected the most by this turn-over in realization were the programmers. No longer was the policy of "tolerated turnover in programming" viable. Now it was important to build into the programming side the reward systems and developmental activities which had proved so successful for sales.

Jim now felt that it was a "cop-out" to ignore goal-setting in the programming area simply because tasks there were more difficult to quantify and link to company performance. "We pretty much did with Bob Holliday [current program director at Village Broadcasting and the only program director in the company to hold the rank of vice president] what I did with Roger Jennings."

From Holliday's perspective,

Life in programming and production has definitely changed dramatically since [I came aboard in] 1973. I think, necessarily, five years ago the company had a heavy bias toward sales people. The emphasis was on having a first-rate sales department and, regrettably, once in a while the programming people got run over. But I think those who survived can attest that it's much better today and those who've come back are always amazed at how different things are today.

Holliday indicated that the company was now keeping score in programming. Such things as the quality of air sound and being on budget were assessed regularly. For example, every Monday evening, Holliday has a staff meeting in which announcers bring their "skimmers" (a tape which telescopes a performer's air shift). Members of the group criticize each other's shows. Holliday also explained that he was hiring better people:

> We're more competitive in what we pay and we're more expansive in where we look for people. So, the announcers we hire now are better; they're more talented. They have more room for growth. As a result, they're going to feel better about where they work. . . . The salaries our top programmers are making now are virtually double what they were making five years ago. Programmers, in some cases, are making more than sales people.

When asked what his primary role was, Holliday replied,

> My biggest role is as a people-grower, and our biggest need, other than doing the best we can with the people we have, is to find new people and develop them.

New Businesses Division

Jim set up a New Businesses Division for Roger to run after he returned from Lexington. Roger was given some stock in these businesses and George McCall was moved from general manager of WCHL to work with him. Lee Hauser, who had trained in WCHL sales and was WCHL sales manager, was promoted to general manager of Village Broadcasting to replace McCall.

Over time, the excess printing capacity of *The Village Advocate* had spawned a number of small ventures. By 1976, the New Businesses Division contained: (1) Village Graphics, the artwork operation supporting the company's printing operations; (2) the Sports Network franchise; (3) University Directories, which published student directories for colleges and universities; and (4) *Triangle Pointer*, a regional tourist magazine.

The Sports Network served to expand audience identification with WCHL beyond the village community to the whole southeastern region of the United States. Moreover, sports broadcasting was something Jim Heavner liked to do personally. The other three divisions complemented the publishing activities of *The Village Advocate.*

By the end of 1978, Jim was planning to open another Print Shop in Durham. His second shop was a pilot to determine the feasibility of franchising the Print Shop concept on a regional and eventually a national basis. He felt that the low start-up cost and minimal management requirements of a Print Shop were keys to the franchising idea.

The Village Companies—1978

By 1978, the evolution of The Village Companies could be summarized as shown in Exhibit 1. Exhibit 3 reveals the pattern of sales growth for the company as a whole, and by major divisions, during this period. But more changes were just around the corner.

By late 1978, Jim had acquired the rights to two new stations in Wilmington, a resort city on the coast of North Carolina. The package involved AM and FM stations. In addition, he had acquired the right to purchase an FM station from Duke University, located less than 10 miles from WCHL. The station had lost money in recent years, and Duke wanted to sell it. But student listeners had appealed to the FCC for a denial of the transfer of license. This action was causing a delay in settlement. Nevertheless, Heavner was confident that he would be able to make the purchase in the coming weeks. This would give him both AM and FM capabilities in his home theatre of operations. Both Wilmington stations were scheduled to begin operations on January 1, 1979. The Duke station could begin operation soon thereafter.

Also in 1978, Jim had opened the second Print Shop in nearby Durham. Finally, construction had begun on both a new half-million-dollar printing facility, to be called Village Printing, and a new $750,000 home office building, both located in the greater Chapel Hill area.

It was now the first week in December of 1978. These additions would certainly cause changes in both the present organization chart (Exhibit 4) and financial statements (Exhibit 5 and 6) of The Village Companies.

Current Issues and Priorities

On the eve of the expansion into all these new ventures, key members representing different business divisions and functions within The Village Companies commented on what they believed were the major issues confronting their organization and the priorities Jim Heavner should be focusing on.

From McClamroch's perspective, Heavner's priorities should be to improve the fi-

Exhibit 3   **Annual Sales for The Village Companies: 1966–1977**

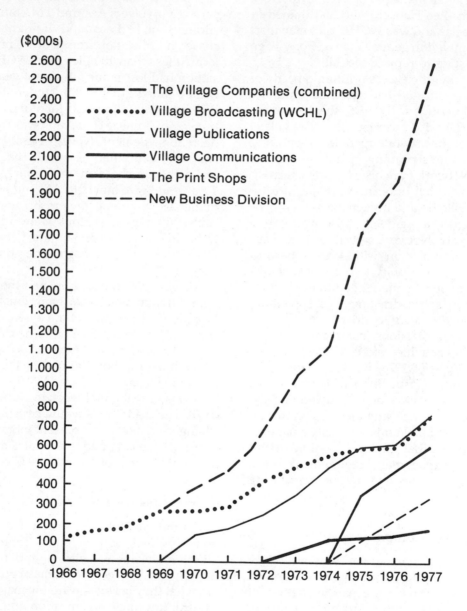

Exhibit 4   The Village Companies, Inc.—Organization Chart, December 1978

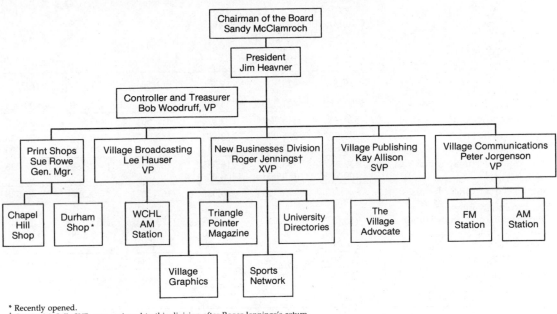

* Recently opened.
† George McCall, SVP, was assigned to this division after Roger Jennings's return.

nancial condition of the company and to "find the people to move into the expanding system." The two were closely tied. For example, on the financial issue, Sandy commented that

> financing is the prime thing—how we are going to continue to get the necessary monies needed to grow at the rate I think we have to to satisfy the personnel.

The other issue posed two requirements in Sandy's view. First, he believed that the base salaries of personnel were below average. Base salary increases, in the absence of promotions, amounted generally to cost-of-living adjustments. Real increases in earnings were obtained through promotions and through the annual bonus plan. For example, for sales personnel and general managers in divisions which met their annual goals, bonuses averaged 30 percent of base pay. Very little if any bonus was paid to personnel in divisions failing to meet their annual goals.

Second, Sandy recognized that the personnel requirements, especially those for middle managers, of this rapidly growing company could not be met by individuals developed in the home division alone. People would have to be brought in and they would have little appreciation of the central values of the core group that Sandy believed were critical in the company's great successes. He saw a major problem in assimilating these outsiders.

George McCall, a member of the core group and now senior vice president, observed that "there are an awful lot of stran-

Exhibit 5

THE VILLAGE COMPANIES
Combined Statement of Operations
1975, 1976, 1977

	WCHL			Village Communications		
	1975	1976	1977	1975	1976	1977
Sales	$591,821	$621,320	$735,764	$ 347,500	$ 473,500	$ 600,924
Total costs and expenses	324,743	318,722	389,575	455,564	393,558	463,879
Operating profit (loss)	233,807	276,206	318,884	(147,067)	10,512	71,536
Home office	94,620	92,380	102,549	20,100	20,100	24,000
Profit (loss) after home office	139,187	183,826	216,335	(167,167)	(9,588)	47,536
Officer bonuses	100,000	170,000	200,000	—	—	—
Profit (loss) after officer bonuses	39,187	13,826	16,335	(167,167)	(9,588)	47,536
Other income (expenses):						
Depreciation and amortization	(10,572)	(10,127)	(16,907)	(173,153)	(151,732)	(87,627)
Other	(6,869)	6,575	(8,330)	(96,331)	(96,429)	(133,697)
Income Taxes	(6,500)	(8,900)	(600)	—	—	—
Total	(23,941)	(12,452)	(25,837)	(269,484)	(248,161)	(221,324)
Net income (loss)	15,246	1,374	(9,502)	(436,651)	257,749	(173,788)

ers in the company now. I mean, we've grown so much that I don't know the names of some of these people!" He believed the major question confronting Jim Heavner should be "how do you hold onto good people?"

Because the company has been small, I believe we had a lot of strong personal friendships and love and respect for each other. And I think during those periods some people may have been oversold or bought a little bit more than they should have. . . .

. . . the idea emerged [in this company] that anytime you're expanding, you have to pay all your profits back in. Sandy and Jim do that. . . . In a sense Jim's saying, "I'm not the guy taking $250,000 out of this company. We're putting it all right back in." And I feel a bit lower paid than I probably should, but I think that's the reason for it.

. . . See, everything now is down the road; and somebody said, you know, "down the road we'll all be dead." I can wait 'til I'm 65 and the stock I have is projected to be worth maybe $300,000 or $400,000 . . . and, you know, at age 65, if I live that long, that will be a nice nest egg. But I don't think at 65 that's going to be anything that I can travel around the world with and not have anything to worry about. So the question is whether one should try to figure out a way to do something on one's own. We were all told we were going to get rich, but I think that truth is nobody gets rich working for someone else.

Bob Holliday, now vice president and program director at WCHL and the only long-time member from the programming side, identified the following problem which he thought should be Jim's number one priority: ". . . continuing to create a climate of growth for the people we now have." In terms of the opportunities at The

Village Advocate			Other Divisions			Combined		
1975	*1976*	*1977*	*1975*	*1976*	*1977*	*1975*	*1976*	*1977*
$603,738	$614,998	$766,492	$91,122	$201,941	$335,665	$1,634,270	$1,911,759	$2,438,845
483,670	505,593	616,594	59,145	151,377	243,608	1,323,122	1,369,250	1,713,656
109,016	93,040	140,213	31,977	50,564	83,707	227,733	430,322	614,340
52,200	60,000	66,000	—	—	39,487	166,920	172,480	232,036
56,816	33,040	74,213	31,977	50,564	44,220	60,813	257,842	382,304
76,000	66,000	90,000	—	—	—	176,000	236,000	290,000
(19,184)	(32,960)	(15,787)	31,977	50,564	44,220	(115,187)	21,842	92,304
(6,224)	(3,462)	(3,121)	—	—	—	(189,949)	(165,321)	(107,655)
13,443	7,728	(5,137)	—	—	5,688	(89,757)	(82,126)	(141,476)
(7,000)	(550)	(3,000)	—	—	—	(13,500)	(9,450)	(3,600)
219	3,716)	(11,258)	—	—	5,688	(293,206)	(256,987)	(252,731)
(18,965)	(29,244)	(27,045)	31,977	50,564	49,908	(408,393)	(235,055)	(160,427)

Village Companies, Holliday commented that,

Like so many of the people in the organization, the difference between how I got started and where I am now is night and day. Rarely have I seen so many individual situations that started so small become so big.

. . . I would have to say that for the short term none of the top managers have any problems . . . not getting into Roger's situation. . . . I do think that the challenge the corporate leaders must [deal with] five years from now is how to continue to meet the needs and expectations of people like Lee Hauser, George McCall, Peter Jorgenson, Kay Allison, ultimately me.

It might happen that we generate enough wealth to move into a bigger market and certainly that would be stimulating to people like Lee and Kay; but on the other hand we may have others who get into Roger's situation and say, "Well, it's been a great 10 years, but where can I go from here?" I think it's probably just a process of the organization maturing.

During this period in December, Kay Allison, who had moved from part-time sales assistant to senior vice president of Village Publishing in less than five years, reflected on how she came aboard and what the most pressing issues were for the company. Her first encounter with The Village Companies began when she responded to an *Advocate* ad for a part-time disc jockey at WCHL. She had just received her undergraduate degree in radio and television and was looking for a means to stay in Chapel Hill for the summer. She described her interviews for the job as follows:

I was amazed at how I was coming in to apply for a part-time job and was getting the sort of ninth degree about some things [such

Exhibit 6

THE VILLAGE COMPANIES
Balance Sheet*

	1975	1976	1977
Assets			
Current assets	$ 342,674	$ 376,442	$ 710,595
Receivables from affiliates	9,445	—	20,000
Receivables from stockholders	—	—	—
Property and equipment	244,406	230,503	300,626
Other assets	175,253	105,994	84,301
Total assets	$ 771,778	$ 712,939	$1,115,522
Liabilities and Stockholders' Investment			
Current liabilities	$ 379,328	$ 371,281	$ 781,014
Deferred revenue	13,144	20,658	67,624
Long-term notes	485,590	511,339	424,858
Payables to stockholders and affiliates	216,000	456,000	435,000
Stockholders' investment:			
Common stock	124,000	124,000	130,448
Capital paid in excess of par value	—	—	153,340
Retained earnings (deficit)	(446,284)	(641,339)	(801,762)
Less: treasury stock	—	75,000	75,000
Total stockholders' investment	$ 322,284	$(592,339)	$ (592,974)
Total liabilities and stockholders' investment	$ 771,778	$ 712,939	$1,115,522

* Contains only Village Broadcasting, Village Communications, and Village Publications.

as] "What are your goals in life?" So anyway, I talked with a number of people over the course of about two weeks trying to get a $1.65 an hour part-time job! And, you know, it was just getting ridiculous. But I was impressed and I think the seriousness with which they approached this process made me think more. But I mean not many people hire you for $1.65 an hour, which was minimum wage at the time, and make you believe that you are being interviewed to be chairman of the board!

The job that finally came agreed with Kay:

I found a pretty open atmosphere with a teaching environment and enjoyed very much doing a variety of things, and have said to people since that I think it was a perfect opportunity for me because, at $1.65 an hour, I wasn't too expensive to do anything. [Referring to McCall and Jennings] They came in and cheered in the afternoons or cried together or did whatever was appropriate based on the day's activities. And they were also doing a lot of very creative things.

. . . it was a 20 hour a week job, taking about 55 hours a week, and I was loving every minute of it. . . . I would punch out because I knew what their budget was for me and I would take the work home and do it anyway because I just wanted to do a good job and it's part of my compulsive nature. During that period a lot of times I would bump into Roger here working at night and we would end up talking about life and the meaning of work and a lot of things that I really needed to hear.

Kay missed the close personal relationships of those early days at WCHL, but obviously relished her present position as head of Village Publishing. She believed Jim's number one priority should be personnel development.

> We just don't have enough people to do what we're about to do, not enough experienced people. It's the whole middle manager thing. . . . We need some people who have fought the wars and whether they've won or lost have learned something and are able to go out and try again. . . . We just have really green people.

Jim's reflections on Kay's rise in the organization revealed his interpretation of the personnel development problem:

> When Kay arrived at WCHL, the only kind of coaching she needed was in the area of company procedures. . . . Even when Kay was working in her original job as a part-time go-fer, she had a special solution-oriented perspective that enabled you to send her on any assignment with great confidence. . . . When she could not come back with the prescribed solution, she could devise one on the scene in such a way as to leave her superiors an easy opportunity for final approval. . . . As a result, people working around Kay suddenly found many of her ideas in effect.
>
> Kay's development brings up an interesting question. We know that we can teach systems and instill many new values into a personnel development program, but can we instill an "entrepreneurial mind-set" into these people?

Even Bob Woodruff, the company's controller and treasurer, placed personnel ahead of financial position in his priorities. He believed Heavner's first priority should be to develop general managers "with the ability to stand alone and manage their operations more like entrepreneurs."

The departing Roger Jennings believed the company had changed too much. He regretted the loss of excitement and the sense of camaraderie he associated with the small, face-to-face character of the company's beginning. Roger thought Jim's number one priority should be,

> to try to reinstate some of the motivating forces for people who came in a few years ago. I think they are still valid and I believe the company runs a risk of alienating some members of the core group. . . . I think that with the caliber of people that we have, they deserve more . . . it would be beneficial to recognize the need for them to have more autonomy and more authority that would be commensurate with the responsibility with which they are charged. They have tremendous responsibilities and yet I'm not sure they are in a position to make the kind of commitments [their responsibilities require] . . . We have set up a lot of red tape for the purpose of simply making things difficult in the hope that if it is not important enough, you won't pursue it. I rebel at that. I like to think I'm a responsible enough person, and an intelligent enough person, and a mature enough person that I'm not going to bring insignificant things to somebody's attention anyhow.

Part of Roger's observations were a reflection of his resentment not of Bob Woodruff personally, but of Jim's decision to place Bob between him and members of the core group. But Roger had one additional piece of advice for Jim:

> although I think they have learned some things from Lexington, I think there is still a failure to understand the nature of that experience. I think they have seen the more visible signs of Lexington. I think they still have an inadequate understanding of what really goes on . . . the dynamics of a new operation, all of the things that are swirling under the surface there. And I think we are

still taking an approach of well, by golly, if we are just positive about this thing, it can all come out all right.

Finally, an officer of the bank financing The Village Companies' expansion program had its own opinions of the current strengths and weaknesses of the organization. Heavner had turned to this bank for financing when the bank the company had worked with through the years refused to extend enough credit to finance his expansion plans.

On the positive side, the banker had this to say.

> The strengths at WCHL are, number one, they have been in the business 25 years; number two, they are a community-oriented organization, probably as much so as any organization I've ever been around. But, for me, the largest asset they have is their people. Sandy McClamroch is just a super human being, and Jim Heavner is one of the most dynamic, sales-oriented people that you would ever run into. But, it goes right down the line. They have people that are so hyped-up over the company. They think they are the best, and they are the best as far as they and a lot of other people are concerned. And it is just the attitude, the people, the way they go about things. And a new bank in town never expects to land a business like this. But they have growing pains. They wanted to do some things that their other bank would not allow them to do.
>
> I think, also, something very important is [that] a lot of companies you run into, especially the smaller companies where there is control by just a few people, are selfish. They don't want to give any of the company away. Jim is willing to do this. He has told all of these people, the key people, "I want you to grow; I want you to make a lot of money because the more money you make the more money I'm going to make." And,

the stock plan, I think, has really gotten a lot of people fired up. You know, they stay fired up. It gives them a chance to own a piece of the company, and they are going to stay with it. There is no telling how much they could be worth one of these days as long as the company is doing well.

On the matter of current weaknesses, the banker had this to say about The Village Companies:

> as far as their weaknesses, any bank could tell you they don't like to see a deficit on a balance sheet. But it is the nature of the animal to have a tremendous cash flow. . . . As highly leveraged as they are, their cash flow is their lifeline. They have to watch that very, very carefully.

But the banker was feeling relatively secure. For one thing, he believed that Heavner,

> could sell just WCHL, the station itself, for $3 or $4 million, pay off everything they owed, have probably a couple of million dollars in cash, and still have everything else they have now . . . if they really got into a bad situation.

His confidence in the organization was bolstered also by the presence of Bob Woodruff. When asked how he viewed Heavner's decision to hire Woodruff, he replied,

> I think it is probably one of the smartest things they ever did. Jim is an idea man, and he's super. He's a go-go guy and he can sell. He comes up with some terrific ideas, but not all of them are good. But, Bob is a stabilizing force. He and Jim have a relationship where Jim bounces things off of Bob. Bob is a level-headed accountant. Now he's a go-go guy, too, but when it comes to hard, cold facts, unless it looks like it's going to fly, I don't think Bob is going to go along with it.

Heavner at the Dawn of His Most Ambitious Campaign

Jim was wrestling with these problems on the eve of his most ambitious expansion project. A lot was at stake, not to mention the years of personal sacrifice and the future prospects for Heavner himself.

1978 had been another growth year for Village Broadcasting, Village Publishing, the Print Shop, and the New Businesses Division. Lexington had finally broken even, but only because of the strong finish of the FM station. More important, the Lexington experience had been a real meat grinder, consuming and discarding much of the sales and programming talent Jim had so carefully trained and coached over the years in the Chapel Hill operations. Roger's definite departure in one month was, Jim hoped, the last vestige of that turmoil.

In recent years Jim had tried to encourage an "investment ethic" in his key employees. By now, they owned approximately 8 percent of the company. In some cases, he had guaranteed loans at the bank for them, much as Sandy had done for him a decade earlier, so that they could buy stock in The Village Companies. He and Sandy now had equal shares in this growing enterprise.

Scribbled on a pad on top of his desk were some notes he made the night before as he reflected on the immediate future of his expanding venture. Ten years from now Jim would be 49. By that time, he figured, if the company's growth trend of 25–30 percent per year continued, billings for The Village Companies would approach $50–60 million and his personal holdings would increase by a roughly proportional amount. But the notes he had made the night before were the things that captured his attention now. They read as follows:

"OUR IMMEDIATE FUTURE"

— <u>Uncertainty</u>

— Sandy possibly out

— If we win big in '79, it will produce leaders

— If not, think about: (a) divestiture
                          (b) recruitment
                          (c) long haul

— Opportunities   (a) broadcasting
                   (b) printing business
                   (c) Print Shop franchise

— Obstacles   (a) internal
               (b) leadership

— Great sales organization; questionable marketing organization

— I believe I have a "marketing mind;" do enough of the troops have one?

— Form of capitalization: no retained earnings to avoid taxes; poor balance sheets scare bankers.

— 1978 will be very, very strong except for the huge overexpenditure in Lexington's budget the first two quarters.

— Wilmington sales and programming strategy looks strong.

— Durham sales and programming strategy looks weak; no people; litigation; PR.

— Search for leadership.

Jim had to make a lot of important decisions in the next few weeks. Both personnel and organizational changes would be involved. And he wanted to make the kinds of decisions that not only would help him cope with his immediate organizational problems, but would contribute also to the longer term development of his expanding organization.

On the immediate scene, there were decisions regarding the departure of Roger Jennings, the fate of the Lexington venture, the start-up of new broadcasting operations, and the near-term completion of construction on the separate home office and printing facilities. He had to make decisions now regarding both personnel and organization design to accommodate these changes. He also wondered what changes would be required in the role he was to play in all of these developments.

But he was also concerned about the need to concentrate on issues related to the longer term development of his rapidly growing organization. For example, he was trying to determine what actions he should take to ensure that his company attracted, developed and retained people who had the entrepreneurial talent to sustain the growth and proliferation of the businesses of The Village Companies. And he felt that there was an important connection between the decisions he had to make right away and

these longer term concerns. Finally, he was trying to project himself into the future to discover what implications it held for his own role in The Village Companies.

* * * * *

THE JIM HEAVNER STORY (B)
Robert H. Miles

By the end of the first quarter of 1979, several of what Jim Heavner refers to as "marvelous accidents" had occurred. Together with his personnel and organizational rearrangements, they had helped him cope successfully with the immediate problems of starting up his new ventures.

First, the start-up of the Durham station had become gnarled in litigation and red tape owing to the appeals to the FCC of Duke University students who wanted to maintain control of the losing radio station. The management of The Village Companies relaxed, at least momentarily. For them the delay meant fewer immediate demands on their already overextended personnel resources and cash position. They knew it was only a matter of time before the station would be theirs, but they were in no mood to exert any pressure to speed up the process.

Second, Roger Jennings departed, but without the impact on the company's cash flow that had been anticipated. Instead of saddling the company with a heavy monthly payoff on his stock holdings, Roger received, after negotiations with Woodruff and Allison, a smaller cash transfer and the Village Graphics Company, which he acquired for $35,000. Moreover, the bank loaned the company the balance of their obligation to Roger which, in turn, was paid out to him upon settlement. According to Bob Woodruff, "From a cash flow perspective, it helped us because we were looking at a two-and-a-half-year payout to Roger, and now we've got a 10-year payout with [the bank]." Thus, Roger Jennings would be running his own show with Village Graphics and a small radio station in a nearby town he had purchased with the cash settlement.

Third, Heavner sold off the AM station in Lexington for the handsome sum of $800,000; a price significantly greater than the $250,000 he paid for it four years earlier. The transfer of ownership of the AM station was scheduled for March 1979. Village Communications was then consolidated around the successful FM station under the management of Peter Jorgenson, who had been trained initially in sales at *The Village Advocate* in Chapel Hill. His salesforce had been augmented by individuals also transferred from Chapel Hill; but by now Lexington people were developing strongly, according to Heavner.

Fourth, the Durham Print Shop was beginning to break even. Bob Woodruff was overseeing the combined Print Shop operations, and Sue Rowe, an experienced manager of the Chapel Hill store, was named general manager of the Print Shop Division. Jim and Bob were confident that with minimal additional time and effort the Durham Print Shop would become a valued contributor to the company's cash flow.

Fifth, in Wilmington, both AM and FM stations were kicked off according to schedule on January 1, 1979. Woodruff noted that the reception and acceptance of The Village Companies in Wilmington was much better than the experience in Lexington, Kentucky.

Lee Hauser, who had been a highly successful general manager of WCHL in Chapel Hill, was transferred to the top spot in charge of both Wilmington stations. Hauser was accompanied by his sales manager, David McGowan, and a solid core of WCHL sales personnel. Among those replacing the salespeople transferred from WCHL was Heavner's secretary.

George McCall, who had run WCHL during the early stage of the Lexington venture, returned to head Village Broadcasting, which now contained both WCHL and the Sports Network franchise.

Sixth, the New Businesses Division was abolished. Its remaining publishing activities together with *The Village Advocate* were consolidated under Kay Allison in Village Publishing.

Woodruff noted other changes in Jim's approach to the new Wilmington operation. For instance, Jim sent two people out to start up the Lexington operation. One was an outsider; the other was Roger Jennings, Jim's second-in-command. Each ran one of the Lexington stations with considerable initial autonomy from the home office. Most of the staff was drawn from the Lexington community.

Contrasting this approach to the one taken by Heavner in the new Wilmington venture, Woodruff observed (Heavner was not available in Chapel Hill for comment) that,

Wilmington is going very well. Jim is down there 60–70 percent of his time. I think this is the big difference between the Lexington operation and Wilmington. Jim is in there day-to-day . . . involved in everything. We're probably ahead of my projections.

In addition, Woodruff observed that Jim's absence from Chapel Hill may be having a positive impact on the development of managers there. In addition to overseeing the Wilmington start-up, Jim was commuting back to Chapel Hill to teach a course in sales management at the university's Department of Radio, Television, and Motion Pictures. For the first time, he was not available on a day-to-day basis to lend a hand or an idea to a struggling Chapel Hill manager.

Finally, all indicators at this time pointed to Sandy's departure from The Village Companies. Sandy, now in his mid-60s, desired

not to be involved in the company's future debt structure. So, both he and Jim had agreed on a long-term payout of Sandy's roughly $2 million in stock which would avoid an immediate cash drain on the company and permit minority stockholders to acquire greater ownership.

Jim also decided to formalize the bonus system for his general managers and sales people. Until now, bonuses were based on good faith remuneration for superior performance. Now, Jim was in the process of developing set bonuses for specific divisional performance levels. He hoped this new system would create a clearer perception among his key people of the shorter-term performance-reward contingencies in the company.

Jim hoped that these changes would help him maintain the 25–30 percent growth rate of The Village Companies.

Exhibit 1 The Village Companies, Inc.—Organization Chart, January 1, 1979

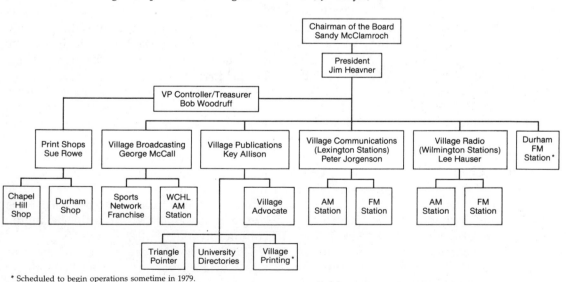

* Scheduled to begin operations sometime in 1979.

On the eve of his departure, Sandy reflected on what he believed to be Jim's greatest strength:

> I think Jim's real love is to teach people—to train them to be sales people and general managers. He loves this type of work. He saw that we had to have experienced managers to be able to expand.

CASE 2
PEOPLE EXPRESS
Debra Whitestone and Leonard A. Schlesinger

We're now the biggest air carrier in terms of departures at any New York airport. We've flown almost 3 million passengers and saved the flying public over one quarter of a billion dollars (not including the savings from fares reduced by other airlines trying to compete with us). We expect to see a $3 million profit this year. . . . We have a concept that works and is unique.

But with no growth horizon, people have been disempowered. We've started slowing down, getting sleepy. So, we've decided to set a new growth objective. Instead of adding 4 to 6 aircraft as we planned for this year, we are now thinking in terms of 12 or more new aircraft a year for the next few years.

With this announcement, Don Burr, founder, president and CEO of People Express airline, concluded the business portion of the company's third quarterly financial meeting of 1982, graciously received rousing applause from several hundred of his stockholder/managers there to hear about and celebrate the success of their young company, and signaled for the music to begin.

Origins and Brief History

People Express had been incorporated on April 7, 1980. In July of that year it had applied to the Civil Aeronautics Board (CAB) for permission to form a new airline to be based in the New York/Newark metropolitan area and dedicated to providing low-cost service in the eastern United States. Organized specifically to take advantage of provisions of the 1978 Airline Deregulation Act, People Express was the first airline to apply for certification since its passage. (The act, which was designed to stimulate competition, allowed greater flexibility in scheduling and pricing and lowered the barriers to new entrants.)

In applying to the CAB for a "determination of fitness and certification of public convenience and necessity," People Express committed itself to:

1. Provide "a broad new choice of flights" with high-frequency service.
2. Keep costs low by "extremely productive use of assets."
3. Offer "unrestricted deep discount price savings" through productivity gains.
4. Focus on several high-density eastern U.S. markets which had yet to reap the pricing benefits of deregulation.
5. Center operations in the densely populated New York/Newark metropolitan area with service at the underutilized, uncongested, highly accessible Newark International Airport.

The Civil Aeronautics Board was sufficiently impressed with this stated intent that it approved the application in three months (compared to the usual year or more). On October 24, 1980, People Express had its certificate to offer air passenger service between the New York/New Jersey area and 27 major cities in the eastern U.S.

Start-Up

People Express's managing officers proceeded to work round the clock for the next six months to turn their plans and ideas into a certificated operating airline. They raised money, leased a terminal, bought planes, recruited, trained, established routes and schedules, and prepared manuals to meet the FAA's fitness and safety standards. "We were here every night . . . from November until April when they [the Federal Aviation Administration, FAA] gave us our certificate. . . . It was hell" (Burr). People's operating certificate was granted April 24, 1981.

Operations Begin

Flight service began on April 30, with three planes flying between Newark and Buffalo, New York; Columbus, Ohio; and Norfolk, Virginia. By the following year, the company employed a work force of over 1,200, owned 17 airplanes, and had flown nearly 2 million passengers between the 13 cities it was servicing. People Express had grown faster than any other airline and most businesses. It had managed to survive a start-up year filled with environmental obstacles, a severe national economic recession, a strike of air traffic controllers, and bad winter weather—all of which had serious negative effects on air travel. By June 1982, though the airline industry in general was losing money, and though competition resulting from deregulation was intense, People had begun showing a profit. Exhibit 1 lists milestones in the growth of People Express.

In the spring and summer of 1982, People underwent an extensive review of its infrastructure, added resources to the recruitment function so as to fill a 200-person staffing shortfall, and modified and attempted to implement more systematically a gover-

Exhibit 1   Major Events

April 1980	—	Date of incorporation
May 1980	—	First external financing—Citicorp venture
October 1980	—	CAB Certificate awarded
November 1980	—	Initial public offering—$25.5 mm common
March 1981	—	First aircraft delivered
April 1981	—	First scheduled flight
August 1981	—	PATCO strike
October 1981	—	Florida service emphasized
January 1982	—	1 millionth passenger carried
March 1982	—	17th aircraft delivered
April 1982	—	Reported first quarterly operating profit
July 1982	—	Filed 1,500,000 shares of common stock

nance and communication system for which there had been little time during start-up. By the fall of 1982 three more planes were about to arrive and three more cities were scheduled to be opened for service.

Background and Precursors

Donald Burr had been president of Texas International Airlines (T.I.) before he left it to found People Express with a group of his colleagues. The airline business was a "hobby business" for Burr; his love of airplanes went back to his childhood and he began flying in college, where as president of the Stanford Flying Club he could get his flight instruction paid for. After receiving an MBA from the Harvard Business School in 1965 he went to work for National Aviation, a company specializing in airline investments, thus combining his affinity for aviation with his interest in finance. In 1971 he was elected president of National Aviation. While at National Aviation, Burr began a venture capital operation which involved him in the start-up of several companies, including one which aimed at taking advantage of the recently deregulated telecommunications industry.

Eighteen months later he decided he wanted to get into the "dirty fingernails" side of the airline business. He left Wall Street and joined Texas International Airlines as a director and chairman of the executive committee. In June 1973 he became executive vice president and in 1976 assumed the responsibilities of chief operations officer. Between 1973 and 1977, Texas International moved from a position close to bankruptcy to become a profitable business. Burr was largely credited in the media for managing the turnaround. In June 1979 he was made president of Texas International. Six months later, he resigned.

Looking for a new challenge, one option he considered at that time was starting a new airline. The day after Burr left T.I., Gerald Gitner, his VP of planning and marketing, and Melrose Dawsey, his own and the CEO's executive secretary at T.I., both submitted their resignations and joined Burr to incorporate People Express.

By the fall of 1980, 15 of Texas International's top managers and several more experienced staff from the ranks followed Burr to become part of the People Express management team and start-up crew. Some gave up their positions even before they knew where the new company would be based, how it would be financed, whether they would be able to acquire planes, or what their exact jobs would be. In spite of the personal and financial risks, the opportunity to start an airline from scratch, with people they liked and respected, was too good to pass up. It was an adventure, a chance to test themselves. Burr at 39 was the oldest of the officers. Even if People Express failed, they assumed that they could pick themselves up and start again.

According to Hap Paretti, former legal counsel and head of government relations at Texas International, who became the fifth managing officer at People Express,

> We weren't talking about my job description or what kind of a budget I would have. It was more, we're friends, we're starting a new airline, you're one of the people we'd like to have join us in starting the company . . . what you do will be determined by what your interests are. The idea of getting involved and letting my personality and talents come through to determine my job appealed to me. I'm not happy doing just one thing.

Bob McAdoo, People's managing officer in charge of finance, had been corporate comptroller at Texas International. For MacAdoo, joining People Express "was an easy decision, though I was having a good time at Texas International. . . . I happen to be a guy driven by things related to efficiency. This was a chance to build an airline that was the most efficient in the business."

Lori Dubose had become director of human resources at T.I.—the first female director there—within a year after being hired.

> When Burr called to offer me the "People" job he explained that we would all be working in different capacities. I'd get to learn operations, get stock—I didn't know anything about stock, never owned any. At 28 how could I pass it up?

She came even though she was married and her husband decided not to move with her to Newark.

Financing and Airplane Acquisition

To finance this adventure, Burr put up $355,000; Gitner put in $175,000; and the other managing officers came up with from $20,000 to $50,000 each. Burr secured an additional $200,000 from FNCB Capital Corporation, a subsidiary of Citicorp. The papers for the Citicorp money, People Express's first outside funds, were signed on May 8, 1980, Burr's 40th birthday. Subsequently, the investment firm of Hambrecht & Quist agreed to help raise additional start-up funds. Impressed with Burr's record and the quality of his management team, and aware of the opportunities created by airline deregulation, William Hambrecht agreed to Burr's suggestion of taking People Express public. (No other airline had ever gone public to raise start-up money.)

As soon as the CAB application was approved in October 1980, all eight managing officers went on the road explaining their business plan and concepts to potential investors throughout the country. They were able to sell over $24 million worth of stock—3 million shares at $8.50 per share.

The official plan stated in the CAB application had called for raising $4–$5 million, buying or leasing one to three planes, and hiring 200 or so people the first year. According to Hap Paretti, "We thought we'd start by leasing three little DC-9s, and flying them for a few years until we made enough money to buy a plane of our own." According to Burr, however, that plan reflected Gitner's more cautious approach and what most investors would tolerate at the beginning. Even with the additional money raised, Gitner thought they should buy at most 11 planes, but Burr's ideas were more expansive. From the beginning he wanted to start with a large number of planes so as to establish a presence in the industry quickly and support the company's overhead.

With cash in hand they were able to make a very attractive purchase from Lufthansa of an entire fleet of 17 Boeing 737s, all of which would be delivered totally remodeled and redecorated to People's specifications.

While other managing officers recalled being a bit stunned, Burr viewed the transaction as being "right on plan."

Burr's Personal Motivation and People's Philosophy

Government deregulation appeared to provide a "unique moment in history," and was one of several factors which motivated Burr to risk his personal earnings on starting a new airline. At least as important was his strong conviction that people were basically good and trustworthy, that they could be more effectively organized, and if properly trained, were likely to be creative and productive.

> I guess the single predominant reason that I cared about starting a new company was to try and develop a better way for people to work together . . . that's where the name People Express came from (as well as) the whole people focus and thrust. . . . It drives everything else that we do.
>
> Most organizations believe that humans are generally bad and you have to control them and watch them and make sure they work. At People Express, people are trusted to do a good job until they prove they definitely won't.

From its inception, therefore, People Express was seen as a chance for Burr and his management team to experiment with and demonstrate a "better" way of managing not just an airline but any business.

While Burr recognized that his stance was contrary to the majority of organized structures in the United States, he rejected any insinuation that he was optimistic or soft.

> I'm not a goody two-shoes person; I don't view myself as a social scientist, as a minister, as a do-gooder. I perceive myself as a hard-nosed businessman, whose ambitions and aspirations have to do with providing

goods and services to other people for a return.

In addition, however, he wanted PE to serve as a role model for other organizations, a concept which carried with it the desire to have an external impact and to contribute to the world's debate about "how the hell to do things well, with good purpose, good intent, and good results for everybody. To me, that's good business, a good way to live. It makes sense, it's logical, it's hopeful, so why not do [it]?"

Prior to starting service, Burr and the other managing officers spent a lot of time discussing their ideas about the "right" way to run an airline. Early on, they retained an outside management consultant to help them work together effectively as a management team and begin to articulate the principles to which they could commit themselves and their company. Over time, the principles evolved into a list of six "precepts," which were written down in December of 1981 and referred to continually from then on in devising and explaining company policies, hiring and training new recruits, structuring and assigning tasks. These precepts were: (1) service, commitment to growth of people; (2) best provider of air transportation; (3) highest quality of management; (4) role model for other airlines and other businesses; (5) simplicity; (6) maximization of profits.

From Burr's philosophy as well as these precepts and a myriad of how-to-do-it-right ideas, a set of strategies began to evolve. According to People's management consultant, the "path" theory was the modus operandi—management would see what route people took to get somewhere, then pave the paths that had been worn naturally to make them more visible.

Thus, by 1982, one could articulate fairly clearly a set of strategies that had become "the concept," the way things were done at People Express.

The People Express Concept: The Philosophy Operationalized

The People Express business concept was broken down and operationalized into three sets of strategies: marketing, cost, and people. (Over Burr's objections, the presentation prepared by investment company Morgan Stanley for PE investors began with the marketing and cost strategies rather than the people strategies.)

Marketing Strategy. Fundamental to People's initial marketing strategy was its view of air travel as a commodity product for which consumers had little or no brand loyalty. (See Exhibit 2 for a representative advertisement.) People Express defined its own version of that product as a basic, cut-rate, no-nonsense air trip. A People Express ticket entitled a passenger to an airplane seat on a safe trip between two airports, period. The marketing strategy was to build and maintain passenger volume by offering extremely low fares and frequent, dependable service on previously overpriced, underserviced routes. In keeping with this strategy, the following tactics were adopted:

1. *Very low fares*—On any given route, People's fares were substantially below the standard fares prevailing prior to P.E.'s announcement of service on that route. For instance, People entered the Newark-to-Pittsburgh market with a $19 fare in April 1982, when U.S. Air was charging $123 on that route. Typically, peak fares ran from 40 percent to 55 percent below the competition's standard fares and 65 percent to 75

Exhibit 2

SHOULD AN EXPERIENCED TRAVELER LIKE YOU FLY A NEW AIRLINE LIKE US?

Or phone in your reservation in advance with us and purchase your ticket right on the plane.

YOU AND YOUR LUGGAGE NEED NEVER BE SEPARATED.

Someone whose time is as valuable as yours has no intention of wasting it waiting for luggage. So instead of hassling you about carry-on luggage, we actually encourage you — by providing unusually spacious overhead and underseat areas. But if you have luggage you want us to handle, we're happy to do it for $3 a bag.

TASTEFUL BOEING 737's. WITHOUT THE INDIGESTION OF AIRLINE FOOD.

People Express flies the finest equipment in the air: Boeing 737's. Easy on your eyes...thanks to our clean, tasteful appointments. Easy on your weary bones ...thanks to our comfortable seats. And easy on your stomach ...because we don't serve airline food. Of course, if you're willing to spend a little of all that money you're saving, you can get a first rate beverage or snack on board.

Particularly a new airline, with the audacity to consistently charge two-thirds less than you're accustomed to paying.

For example, before we flew to Columbus, the standard air fare was $146. People Express charges $40 off peak and $65 peak. What's more, our price to Florida is just $75 off peak and $89 peak.

In short, People Express offers low prices every seat. Every flight. Every day.

And we always will.

But even if paying much less takes a little getting used to, you'll appreciate our other attributes. In no time flat.

OUR SCHEDULES ARE GEARED TO YOUR SCHEDULE.

Because we know how hectic your life can be, instead of the usual frequent excuses, we give you frequent flights — 98 non-stops each business day.

And, unlike any other major airline, People Express doesn't accept freight or mail. So you don't sit on a plane cooling your heels while mail bags and freight cartons are loaded and unloaded.

ALL OUR PEOPLE TREAT YOU AS ATTENTIVELY AS IF THEY OWNED THE AIRLINE. BECAUSE THEY DO.

At People Express, we don't offer jobs. We offer careers. From the person who welcomes you on the plane to the person who pilots the plane, each and every full time member of our staff owns an average of — amazing as it sounds — $13,000 of our stock. (And the stock of the company founders was not averaged in.)

The result quite simply, is the first airline where attitude is as important as altitude.

NON-STOP CHECK IN.

And to save a little more time and hassle, we've done away with another nemesis: the ticket counter. Purchase your ticket through your travel agent.

THE FASTEST MOVING AIRLINE IN THE WORLD.

People Express offers more flights out of convenient Newark Airport than any other airline.

And we've already flown over a million passengers.

After only ten months of operation.

Perhaps it was our attitude. Or our prices. Or our frequency to all ten cities.

But no other airline has come this far this fast. Which proves we've offered the public something it's been waiting for a long time...a better way to fly.

And nobody will appreciate us more than someone who has been around as much as you.

PEOPLExpress
FLY SMART

NEW YORK/NEWARK, BOSTON, WASHINGTON/BALTIMORE, SYRACUSE, BUFFALO, NORFOLK, COLUMBUS, JACKSONVILLE, SARASOTA, WEST PALM BEACH

Exhibit 2 (*concluded*)

percent below, during off-peak hours (after 6:00 P.M. and weekends).

2. *Convenient flight schedules*—For any route that its planes flew, People tried to offer the most frequent flight schedule. With low fares and frequent flights, People could broaden its market segment beyond those of established airlines to include passengers who would ordinarily have used other forms of transportation. In an effort to expand the size of the air travel market, People's ads announcing service in new cities were pitched to automobile drivers, bus riders, and even those who tended not to travel at all. People hoped to capture most of the increase as well as some share of the preexisting market for each route. ·

3. *Regionwide identity*—People set out to establish a formidable image in its first year as a major airline servicing the entire eastern U.S. Large established airlines could easily wage price wars and successfully compete with a new airline in any one city, but they would probably have to absorb some losses and would be hard pressed to mount such a campaign on several fronts at once.

4. *Pitch to "smart" air travelers*—In keeping with its product definition, People's ads sought to identify People Express not as exotic or delicious or entertaining, but as the smart travel choice for smart, thrifty, busy travelers. The ads were filled with consumer information, as well as information

about PE's smart people and policies. Unlike most airlines, for instance, every People Express plane had roomy overhead compartments for passengers' baggage, thereby saving them money, time, and the potential inconvenience of loss.

5. *Memorable positive atmosphere*—Burr's long-term marketing strategy, once the airline was off the ground financially, was to make flying with People Express the most pleasant and memorable travel experience possible. The goal was for passengers to arrive at their destination feeling very well served. Thus, People Express's ultimate marketing strategy was to staff every position with competent, sensitive, respectful, upbeat, high-energy people who would create a contagious positive atmosphere. The message to staff and customers alike was: "At People Express, attitude is as important as altitude."

Cost Structure. People's cost structure was not based on a clear-cut formula so much as on an attitude that encouraged the constant, critical examination of every aspect of the business. According to Bob McAdoo, the management team "literally looked for every possible way to do things more simply and efficiently." McAdoo could point to at least 15 or 20 factors he felt were important in keeping costs down while preserving safety and quality. "If you look for one or two key factors, you miss the point." Cost savings measures affecting every aspect of the business included the following:

1. *Aircraft*—Since fuel was the biggest single cost for an airline, People chose, redesigned, and deployed its aircraft with fuel efficiency in mind. Its twin-engine Boeing 737-100 planes were thought to be the most fuel-efficient planes for their mission in the industry. By eliminating first-class and gal-

ley sections, interior redesign increased the number of all coach-class seats from 90 to 118 per plane. Overhead racks were expanded to accommodate more carry-on baggage. The planes were redecorated to convey a modern image and reassure potential passengers that low fares did not mean sacrificing quality or safety.

P.E. scheduled these planes to squeeze the most possible flying time out of them, 10.36 hours per plane per day, compared with the industry average of 7.08 hours. Finally, plane maintenance work was done by other airlines on a contract basis, a practice seen as less expensive than hiring a maintenance staff.

2. *Low labor costs*—Labor is an airline's second biggest expense. Though salaries were generally competitive, and in some cases above industry norms, People's labor costs were relatively small. The belief was that if every employee was intelligent, well-trained, flexible, and motivated to work hard, fewer people (as much as one third fewer) would be needed than most airlines employed.

People kept its work force deliberately lean, and expected it to work hard. Each employee, carefully selected after an extensive screening process, received training in multiple functions (ticketing, reservations, ground operations, and so on) and was extensively cross-utilized, depending on where the company's needs were at any given time. If a bag needed to be carried to a plane, whoever was heading towards the plane would carry the bag. Thus, peaks and valleys could be handled efficiently. This was in sharp contrast with other airlines which hired people into one of a variety of distinct "classes in craft" (such as flight attendants, reservations, baggage), each of which had a fairly rigid job description, was represented by a different union, and therefore was precluded from being cross-utilized.

3. *In-house expertise and problem solving*—In addition to keeping the workforce small and challenged, cross-utilization and rotation were expected to add the benefits of a de facto ongoing quality and efficiency review. Problems could be identified and solutions and new efficiency measures could be continually invented if people were familiar with all aspects of the business and motivated to take management-like responsibility for improving their company.

The Paxtrac ticketing computer was commonly cited as a successful example of how P.E. tapped its reservoir of internal brain power rather than calling in outside consultants to solve a company problem. Many of P.E.'s longer routes were combinations of short-haul flights into and out of Newark. The existing ticketing system required a separate ticket for each leg of the trip, resulting in higher fares than P.E. wanted. Burr spotted the problem when he was flying one day (he tried to spend some time each month on board the planes or in the ground operations area). An ad hoc team of managers was sent off to a hotel in Florida for a week to solve the problem. They came up with a specially designed microprocessor ticketing machine with the flexibility to accommodate the company's marketing plans and fast enough (7 seconds per ticket versus 20 seconds) to enable on-board ticketing of larger passenger loads.

4. *Facilities*—Like its aircraft, People Express's work space was low cost and strictly functional. The main Newark terminal was located in the old North Terminal building, significantly cheaper to rent than space at the West and South terminals a mile away. People had no ticket counters. All ticketing was done either by travel agents in advance, or by customer service managers on board the planes once they were airbound. Corporate headquarters, located upstairs over the main terminal, had none of the luxurious trappings associated with a major airline. Offices were shared, few had carpeting, and decoration consisted primarily of People Express ads, sometimes blown up poster size, and an occasional framed print of an airplane.

5. *Reservations*—The reservations system was kept extremely simple, fast, and therefore inexpensive. There were no interline arrangements with other airlines for ticketing or baggage transfer; no assistance was offered with hotel or auto reservations in spite of the potential revenue leverage to be derived from such customer service. Thus, calls could be handled quickly by hundreds of easily trained temporary workers in several of the cities People served, using local lines (a WATS line would cost $8,000 per month) and simple equipment ($900 versus the standard $3,000 computer terminals).

6. *No "Freebies"*—Cost of convenience services were unbundled from basic transportation costs. People offered none of the usual airline "freebies." Neither snacks nor baggage handling, for example, were included in the price of a ticket, though such extras were available and could be purchased for an additional fee.

People. Burr told his managers repeatedly that it was People's people and its people policies that made the company unique and successful. "The people dimension is the value added to the commodity. Many investors still don't fully appreciate this point, but high commitment and participation, and maximum flexibility and massive creative productivity are the most important strategies in People Express.''

Structure and Policies

As People moved from a set of ideas to an operating business, People's managers took pains to design structures and develop policies consistent with the company's stated precepts and strategies. This resulted in an organization characterized by minimal hierarchy, rotation and cross-utilization, work teams, ownership, self-management, participation, compensation, selective hiring and recruitment, multipurpose training, and team building.

1. *Minimal hierarchy*—People's initial organizational structure consisted of only three formal levels of authority. At the top of the organization was the president/CEO and six managing officers, each of whom provided line as well as staff leadership for more than 1 of the 13 functional areas (see Exhibit 3 for a listing of functions).

Reporting to and working closely with the managing officers were eight general managers, each of whom provided day-to-day implementation and leadership in at least one functional area, as well as planning for and coordinating with other areas. People's managing officers and general managers worked hard at exemplifying the company's philosophy. They worked in teams, rotated out of their specialties as much as possible to take on line work, filling in at a gate or on a flight. Several had gone through the full "in-flight" training required of customer service managers. They shared office furniture and phones. Burr's office doubled as the all-purpose executive meeting room; if others were using it when he had an appointment, he would move down the hall and borrow someone else's empty space.

There were no executive assistants, secre-taries, or support staff of any kind. The managers themselves assumed the activities that such staff would ordinarily perform. Individuals, teams, and committees did their own typing, which kept written communications to a minimum. Everyone answered his or her own phone. (Both practices were seen as promoting direct communication as well as saving money.)

Beyond the top 15 officers, all remaining full-time employees were either flight managers, maintenance managers, or customer service managers. The titles indicated distinctions in qualifications and functional emphasis rather than organizational authority. *Flight managers* were pilots. Their primary responsibility was flying; but they also performed various other tasks, such as dispatching, scheduling, and safety checks, on a rotating basis or as needed. *Maintenance managers* were technicians who oversaw and facilitated maintenance of P.E.'s airplanes, equipment, and facilities by contract with other airlines' maintenance crews. In addition to monitoring and assuring the quality of the contracted work, maintenance managers were utilized to perform various staff jobs.

The vast majority of People's managers were *customer service managers*, generalists trained to perform all passenger-related tasks, such as security clearance, boarding, flight attending, ticketing, and food service, as well as some staff function activities (see Exhibit 3).

By and large, what few authority distinctions did exist were obscure and informal. Managing officers, general managers, and others with seniority (over one year) had more responsibility for giving direction, motivating, teaching, and perhaps coordinating, but *not* for supervising or managing in the traditional sense.

2. *Ownership, lifelong job security*—Every-

Exhibit 3 Organizational Structure, 11/82—Author's Rendition (CEO, president*—chairman of the board, Don Burr)

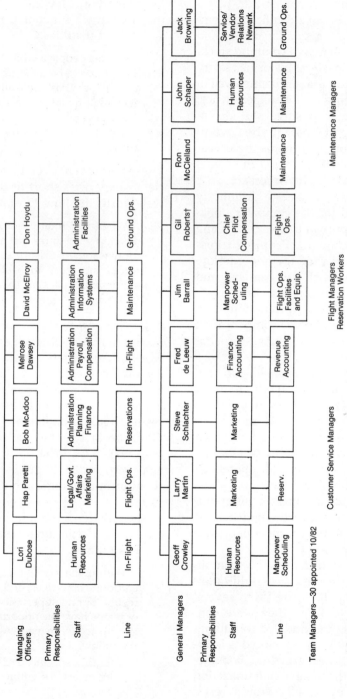

Managing Officers

Primary Responsibilities

Staff

Line

Lori Dubose	Hap Paretti	Bob McAdoo	Melrose Dawsey	David McElroy	Don Hoydu
Human Resources	Legal/Govt. Affairs Marketing	Administration Planning Finance	Administration Payroll, Compensation	Administration Information Systems	Administration Facilities
In-Flight	Flight Ops.	Reservations	In-Flight	Maintenance	Ground Ops.

General Managers

Primary Responsibilities

Staff

Line

Geoff Crowley	Larry Martin	Steve Schlachter	Fred de Leeuw	Jim Barrall	Gil Roberts†	Ron McClelland	John Schaper	Jack Browning
Human Resources	Marketing	Marketing	Finance Accounting	Manpower Scheduling	Chief Pilot Compensation		Human Resources	Service/ Vendor Relations Newark
Manpower Scheduling	Reserv.		Revenue Accounting	Flight Ops. Facilities and Equip.	Flight Ops.	Maintenance	Maintenance	Ground Ops.

Team Managers—30 appointed 10/82

Customer Service Managers   Flight Managers   Maintenance Managers
                                   Reservation Workers

* Original president, Gerald Gitner, resigned 3/82 and Burr assumed presidency.
† Gil Roberts appointed chief pilot 11/82.

one in a permanent position at P.E. was a shareholder, required as a condition of employment to buy, at a greatly discounted price, a number of shares of common stock, determined on the basis of his or her salary level. It was expected that each employee in keeping with being a manager/owner, would demonstrate a positive attitude towards work, and participate in the governance of the company. As managing officer Lori Dubose pointed out, "We'll fire someone only if it is (absolutely) necessary. . . . For instance, we won't tolerate dishonesty or willful disregard for the company's policies, but we don't punish people for making mistakes." In exchange, People Express promised the security of lifetime employment and opportunities for personal and professional growth through continuing education, cross-utilization, promotion from within the company, and compensation higher than other companies paid for similar skills and experience.

3. *Cross-utilization and rotation*—No one, regardless of work history, qualifications, or responsibility, was assigned to do the same job all the time. Everyone, including managing officers, was expected to be "cross-utilized" as needed and to rotate monthly between in-flight and ground operations and/or between line and staff functions. (The terms *line* and *staff* in P.E. differentiated tasks which were directly flight-related from those related to the business of operating the company.)

Seen by some as unnecessarily complicated and troublesome, cross-utilization and rotation was justified by PE in several ways. According to Burr, they were conceived primarily as methods of continuing education, aimed at keeping everyone interested, challenged, and growing. Bob McAdoo appreciated the flexible staff utilization capability which eventually would result

from everyone having broad exposure to the company's functions. Rotation did create some difficulties:

> It takes people a while to master each job. It might seem better to have an expert doing a given job. Cross-utilization also means you need high-quality people who are capable of doing several jobs. This in turn limits how fast you can recruit and how fast you can grow.

These were seen, even by McAdoo, the efficiency expert, as short-term inconveniences well worth the long-term payoff.

> When you rotate people often they don't develop procedures that are too complicated for newcomers to learn and master fast. This forces the work to be broken down into short simple packets, easily taught and easily learned.

4. *Self-Management*—People were expected to manage themselves and their own work in collaboration with their teams and coworkers. According to Jim Miller, coordinator of training, "We don't want to teach behaviors—we want to teach what the end result should look like and allow each individual to arrive at those results his or her own way. . . . When desired results aren't achieved, we try to guide people and assist them in improving the outcome of their efforts."

The written, though never formalized, guidelines regarding "self-management" read as follows:

> Within the context of our precepts and corporate objectives, and with leadership direction but no supervision, individuals and/or teams have the opportunity (and the obligation) to self-manage, which encompasses the following:
> — Setting specific, challenging, but realistic objectives within the organizational context.

— Monitoring and assessing the quantity/quality/timeliness of one's own performance ("how am I doing?") by gathering data and seeking input from other people.

— Inventing and executing activities to remedy performance problems that appear and exploiting opportunities for improved performance.

— Actively seeking the information, resources and/or assistance needed to achieve the performance objectives.

When it came time for performance reviews, each individual distributed forms to those six co-workers from whom feedback would be useful. Again, growth rather than policing was the objective.

5. *Work teams*—Dubose observed that "even with smart, self-managed people, one person can't have all the components to be the answer to every situation." People therefore had decided to organize its work force into small (3–4 person) work groups as an alternative to larger groups with supervisors. "If you don't want a hierarchical structure with 40 levels you have to have some way to manage the numbers of people we were anticipating." Teams were seen as promoting better problem solving and decision making as well as personal growth and learning.

Every customer service manager belonged to a self-chosen ongoing team with which he or she was assigned work by a lottery system on a monthly basis. Though monthly staff assignments were made individually according to interests, skills, and needs, staff work was expected to be performed in teams. This applied to flight managers and maintenance managers as well as customer service managers. Each team was to elect a liaison to communicate with other teams. Each staff function was managed by a team of coordinators, most of whom were members of the start-up team recruited from Texas International. Managing officers also worked in teams and rotated certain responsibilities to share the burden and the growth benefits of primary leadership.

6. *Governance, broad-based participation*—People's governance structure was designed with several objectives: policy development, problem solving, participation, and communication.

While Burr was the ultimate decision maker, top management decisions, including plans and policies, were to be made by management teams with the assistance of advisory councils. Each of the eight managing officers and eight general managers was responsible for at least one of the 13 functional areas (see Exhibit 3) and served on a management team for at least one other function. The 13 function-specific management teams were grouped into four umbrella staff committees: operations, people, marketing, and finance and administration. For each staff committee, composed of managing officers and general managers from the relevant functional areas, there was an advisory council made up of selected customer service managers, flight managers, and maintenance managers serving on relevant line and staff teams. The councils were intended to generate and review policy recommendations, but until August 1982 they followed no written guidelines. A study done by Yale University students, under the direction of Professor Richard Hackman, showed considerable confusion about their purposes (influencing, learning, solving, communicating issues) and role (advising versus making decisions).

To minimize duplication and maximize communication, each advisory council elected a member to sit on an overarching "coordinating council," which was to meet regularly with Don Burr (to transmit information to and from him and among the councils). These ongoing teams and councils were supplemented periodically by ad hoc committees and task forces which could be created at anyone's suggestion to solve a particular problem, conduct a study, and/or develop proposals.

In addition to maximizing productivity, all of the above practices, teams, and committees were seen as essential to promote personal growth and keep people interested in and challenged by their work.

7. *Compensation: high reward for expected high performance*—People's four-part compensation package was aimed at reinforcing its human resource strategy. Base salaries were determined strictly by job category on a relatively flat scale, ranging in 1981 from $17,000 for customer service managers to $48,000 for the managing officers and CEO. (Competitor airlines averaged only $17,600 for flight attendants after several years of service, but paid nearly double for managing officers and more than four times as much for their chief executives.)

Whereas most companies shared medical expenses with employees, People paid 100 percent of all medical and dental expenses. Life insurance, rather than being pegged to salary level, was $50,000 for everyone.

After one year with P.E. all managers' base salaries and benefits were augmented by three forms of potential earnings tied to the company's fortunes. There were two profit-sharing plans: (1) a dollar-for-dollar plan, based on quarterly profits and paid quarterly to full-time employees who had been with P.E. over one year; and (2) a plan based on annual profitability. The former was allocated proportionally, according to salary level and distributed incrementally. If profits were large, those at higher salary levels stood to receive larger bonuses, but only after all eligible managers had received

some reward. The sustained profits were distributed annually and in equal amounts to people in all categories. Together, earnings from these plans could total up to 50 percent or more of base salary. The aggregate amount of P.E.'s profit-sharing contributions after the second quarter of 1982 was $311,000.

Finally, P.E. awarded several stock option bonuses, one nearly every quarter, making it possible for managers who had worked at least half a year to purchase limited quantities of common stock at discounts ranging from 25 percent to 40 percent of market value. The company offered five-year interest-free promissory notes for the full amount of the stock purchase required of new employees, and for two thirds the amount of any optional purchase. As of July 1982, 651 employees, including the managing officers, held an aggregate 513,000 shares of common stock under a restricted stock purchase plan. Approximately 85 percent were held by employees other than managing officers and general managers. The total number of shares reserved under this plan was, at that time, 900,000.

8. *Selective hiring of the People Express "type"*—Given the extent and diversity of responsibilities People required of its people, Lori Dubose, managing officer in charge of the company's "people" as well as in-flight functions, believed firmly that it took a certain type of person to do well at People Express. Her recruiters, experienced CSMs themselves, looked for people who were bright, educated, well-groomed, mature, articulate, assertive, creative, energetic, conscientious, and hard-working. While they had to be capable of functioning independently and taking initiative, and it was desirable for them to be ambitious in terms of personal development, achievements, and wealth, it was also essential that

they be flexible, collaborative rather than competitive with co-workers, excellent team players, and comfortable with PE's horizontal structure. "If someone needed to be a vice president in order to be happy, we'd be concerned and might not hire them" (Miller).

Recruiting efforts for customer service managers were pitched deliberately to service professionals—nurses, social workers, teachers—with an interest in innovative management. No attempt was made to attract those with airline experience or interest per se (see Exhibit 4). Applicants who came from traditional airlines where "everyone memorized the union contract and knew you were only supposed to work x number of minutes and hours" were often ill-suited to People's style. They were not comfortable with its loose structure and broadly defined, constantly changing job assignments. They were not as flexible as People Express types.

The flight manager positions were somewhat easier to fill. Many pilots had been laid off by other airlines due to economic problems, and People Express had an abundant pool of applicants. All licensed pilots had already met certain intelligence and technical skill criteria, but not every qualified pilot was suited or even willing to be a People Express flight manager. Though flying time was strictly limited to the FAA's standard 30 hours per week (100/month, 1,000/year), and rules regarding pilot rest before flying were carefully followed, additional staff and management responsibilities could bring a flight manager's work week to anywhere from 50 to 70 hours.

Furthermore, FMs were expected to collaborate and share status with others, even nonpilots. In return for being flexible and egalitarian—traits which were typically somewhat in conflict with their previous training and job demands—pilots at P.E. were offered the opportunity to learn the business, diversify their skills and interests, and benefit from profit sharing and stock ownership, if and when the company succeeded.

9. *Recruitment process*—As many as 1,600 would-be CSMs had shown up in response to a recruitment ad. To cull out "good P.E. types" from such masses, Dubose and her start-up team, eight CSMs whom she recruited directly from T.I., designed a multistep screening process.

Applicants who qualified after two levels of tests and interviews with recruiters were granted a "broad interview" with at least one general manager and two other senior people who reviewed psychological profiles and character data. In a final review after a day-long orientation, selected candidates were invited to become trainees. One out of 100 CSM applicants was hired (see Exhibit 5 for a CSM profile).

In screening pilots, "the interview process was very stringent. Many people who were highly qualified were eliminated." Only one out of three flight manager applicants was hired.

10. *Training and team building*—The training program for CSMs lasted for five weeks, six days a week, without pay. At the end, candidates went through an in-flight emergency evacuation role-play and took exams for oral competency as well as written procedures. Those who tested at 90 or above were offered a position.

The training was designed to enable CSMs, many without airline experience, to perform multiple tasks and be knowledgeable about all aspects of an airline. Three full days were devoted to team building, aimed at developing trainees' self-awareness, communication skills, and sense of community. "We try to teach people to respect differ-

Exhibit 4

TEAMWORK TAKES ON A WHOLE NEW MEANING AT PEOPLExpress!

TOTAL PROFESSIONALISM

Customer Service Managers

PEOPLExpress has a whole new approach to running an airline! As a Customer Service Manager, you'll be a vital part of our management team, working in all areas from In-Flight Service, Ground Operations, and Reservations to staff support functions such as Marketing, Scheduling, Training, Recruiting, Accounting, and more.

This cross-utilization takes a lot of hard creative work—but it's the best way we know to achieve greater professionalism and productivity! Instead of doing just one limited job, you'll be involved in both line and staff activities—so you can learn the airline business fully. Faced with our variety of challenge, you'll develop and *use* all your decision-making skills. That's how bright people grow at PEOPLExpress...by finding simple creative solutions to complex problems...solutions that contribute to our productivity and growth...and *yours*.

Even better, your productivity can show a direct return. As a Customer Service Manager, you'll have the opportunity to participate in our unique STOCK PURCHASE PROGRAM (subject to legal requirements) and our profit-sharing plan.

If challenge stimulates you, if you really want to pursue management and growth,...and are willing to invest the time it takes to achieve TOTAL PROFESSIONALISM, joining PEOPLExpress could be the turning-point in your career (we're already one of the phenomenal success stories in the history of American business).

Our basic requirements are that, preferably, you've had previous business management experience—and that you be poised, personable, have some college education—and be between 5'2" and 6'4" with weight proportional.

If you would like to learn more about the opportunities available to you...

THE GRAND HYATT NEW YORK
Park Ave. at Grand Central Station, NYC

NO PHONE CALLS ACCEPTED
SATURDAY, APRIL 23, 1983
11 A.M. to 4 P.M.

PEOPLExpress

We are an Equal Opportunity Employer M/F

Exhibit 5   **Profile of a Customer Service Manager**

Look for candidates who:

1. Appear to pay special attention to personal grooming.
2. Are composed and free of tension.
3. Show self-confidence and self-assurance.
4. Express logically developed thoughts.
5. Ask intelligent questions; show good judgment.
6. Have goals; want to succeed and grow.
7. Have strong educational backgrounds, have substantial work experience, preferably in public contact.
8. Are very mature, self-starter with outgoing personality.
9. Appear to have self-discipline, good planner.
10. Are warm, but assertive personalities, enthusiastic, good listeners.

Appearance Guidelines

Well-groomed, attractive appearance.
Clean, tastefully worn, appropriate clothing.
Manicured, clean nails.
Reasonably clear complexion.
Hair neatly styled and clean.
Weight strictly in proportion to height.

No offensive body odor.
Good posture.
For women, makeup should be applied attractively and neatly.
Good teeth.

Above listed guidelines apply to everyone regardless of ethnic background, race, religion, sex, or age.

---

ences, to work effectively with others, to build synergy'' (Miller).

On the last team-building day everybody chose two or three others to start work with. These groups became work teams, People's basic organizational unit. Initially, according to Miller, these decisions tended to be based on personalities and many trainees were reluctant to choose their own work teams. They were afraid of hurting people's feelings or being hurt. Trainers would remind them that People Express gave them more freedom than they would get in most companies, more than they were used to, and that "freedom has its price . . . it means you've got to be direct and you've got to take responsibility" (Kramer).

Over time, trainers learned to emphasize skills over personalities as the basis of team composition and to distinguish work teams from friendship groups. Choosing a work team was a business decision.

Bottom Lines: Business Indicators

As of the second quarter of 1982, People was showing a $3 million net profit, one of only five airlines in the industry to show any profit at that time. In addition to short-term profitability, Burr and his people enjoyed pointing out that, by several other concrete indicators typically used to judge the health and competitive strength of an airline, their strategies were paying off and their innovative company was succeeding.

Marketing Payoff.   Over 3 million passengers had chosen to fly with People Express. The size of air passenger markets in cities serviced by People had increased since People's entrance. In some instances the increase had been immediate and dramatic, over 100 percent. Annual revenue rates were approaching $200 million.

Cost Containment.   Total costs per available seat-mile were the lowest of any major airline (5.2¢ compared to a 9.4¢ industry av-

Exhibit 6

PEOPLE EXPRESS
Statement of Operations

	From April 7, 1980, to March 31, 1981	Nine Months Ended December 31, 1981	Six Months Ended June 30, 1982 (Unaudited)
	(In thousands, except per share data)		
Operating revenues:			
Passenger	$ —	$37,046	$59,998
Baggage and other revenue, net	—	1,337	2,302
Total operating revenues	—	38,383	62,300
Operating expenses:			
Flying operations	—	3,464	4,240
Fuel and oil	—	16,410	22,238
Maintenance	21	2,131	3,693
Passenger service	—	1,785	2,676
Aircraft and traffic servicing	—	7,833	10,097
Promotion and sales	146	8,076	7,569
General and administrative	1,685	3,508	2,498
Depreciation and amortization of property and equipment	6	1,898	3,087
Amortization—restricted stock purchase plan	—	479	434
Total operating expenses	1,858	45,584	56,532
Income (loss) from operations	(1,858)	(7,201)	5,768
Interest:			
Interest income	1,420	1,909	763
Interest expense	14	3,913	5,510
Interest expense (income), net	(1,406)	2,004	4,747
Income (loss) before income taxes and extraordinary item	(452)	(9,205)	1,021
Provision for income taxes	—	—	(470)
Income (loss) before extraordinary item	(452)	(9,205)	551
Extraordinary item—utilization of net operating loss carryforward	—	—	470
Net income (loss)	$ (452)	$(9,205)	$ 1,021
Net income (loss) per common share:			
Income (loss) before extraordinary item	$ (.20)	$ (1.92)	$ .11
Extraordinary item	—	—	.09
Net income (loss) per common share	(.20)	(1.92)	.20
Weighted average number of common shares outstanding	2,299	4,805	5,046

erage). Fuel costs were ½–¾¢ per-seat-mile lower than other airlines.

Productivity. Aircraft productivity surpassed the industry average by 50 percent (10.36 hours/day/plane compared to 7.06). Employee productivity was 145 percent above the 1981 industry average (1.52 compared to 0.62 revenue passenger miles per employee) for a 600-mile average trip. Return on revenue was 15.3 percent, second only to, and a mere 0.9 percent below, Southwest—the country's most successful airline. (Exhibit 6 shows operating statements through June 1982, and Exhibit 7 presents industry comparative data on costs and productivity.)

Explanations of Success

How could a new little airline with a funny name like People Express become such a formidable force so fast in such difficult times? Burr was fond of posing this question with a semipuzzled expression on his face and answering with a twinkle in his eye! The precepts and policies represented by that "funny" name—People—had made the difference. To back up this assertion, Burr and the other managing officers gave examples of how the people factor was impacting directly on the company's bottom line.

Consumer research showed that, notwithstanding heavy investments in award-winning advertisements, the biggest source of People's success was word of mouth; average customer ratings of passenger courtesy and personal treatment on ground and on board were 4.7 out of 5.

Several journalists had passed on to readers their favorable impressions of People's service: "I have never flown on an airline whose help is so cheerful and interested in their work. This is an airline with verve and an upbeat spirit which rubs off on passengers." Others credited the commitment, creativity, and flexibility of People's people with the company's very survival through its several start-up hurdles and first-year crises.

Perhaps the biggest crisis was the PATCO strike, which occurred just months after P.E. began flying. While the air traffic controllers were on strike, the number of landing slots at major airports, including Newark, were drastically reduced. This made People's original hub-and-spoke short-haul route design unworkable. To overfly Newark and have planes land less frequently without reducing aircraft utilization, People Express took a chance on establishing some new, previously unserviced, longer routes between smaller, uncontrolled airports, such as Buffalo, New York, to Jacksonville, Florida. This solution was tantamount to starting a new airline, with several new Florida stations, new advertising, and new route scheduling arrangements. The costs were enormous. According to Hap Paretti:

> We could have run out of $25 million very quickly and there wouldn't be any People Express. The effort people made was astronomical, and it was certainly in their best interest to make that effort. Everybody recognized truly and sincerely that the air traffic controllers strike was a threat to their very existence. They rearranged their own schedules, worked extra days, really put the extra flying hours in, came in on their off days to do the staff functions, all things of that nature; people just really chipped in and did it and did a damned good job. So when we went into these markets from Buffalo to Florida, we could go in at $69. If we

Exhibit 7

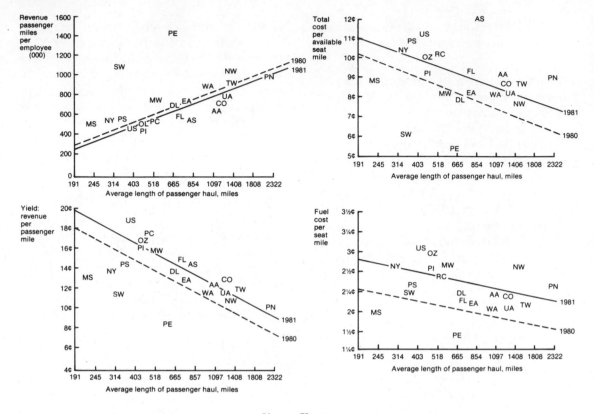

Key to Charts

Symbol	Airline	Symbol	Airline
AA	American	PN	Pan American
AS	Alaska	PS	Pacific Southwest
CO	Continental	PE	People Express
DL	Delta	PI	Piedmont
EA	Eastern	RC	Republic
FL	Frontier	SW	Southwest
MW	Midway	TW	Trans World
MS	Muse	WA	Western
NY	New York Air	UA	United
NW	Northwest Orient	US	USAir
OZ	Ozark		

All data have been drawn from calendar 1981 results, except People Express and Muse, for which the first quarter of 1982 is used in order to offer comparisons not influenced by the start-up of operations.

Notes:
— Total cost is operating cost plus interest expense net of capitalized interest and interest income.
— Yield represents passenger revenues divided by revenue passenger miles (RPM).
— Average length of passenger haul is plotted on a logarithmic scale.
— The average line in each graph is a least-squared linear regression curve, based on 16 carriers which evolved in the regulated environment. Southwest, People Express, New York Air, Muse, and Alaska were not used in the calculations to determine the average. The 16 carriers were assigned equal weightings in the average.

Source: Hambrecht and Quist, June 1982.

went in at $199 like everybody else we wouldn't have attracted one person. We could go in very low like that because we had a cost structure that allowed us to do that. That's where the people strategy, from a cost standpoint, resulted in our survival. If it wasn't there we'd be in the same situation many other carriers are today, hanging on by a toenail.

By way of comparison, New York Air, a nonunion airline started by others from Texas International around the same time as People Express with plenty of financial backing, economical planes—and a similar concept of low-cost, high-frequency service, but different people policies—was losing money.

The Human Dimensions: Positive Climate and Personal Growth

In addition to becoming a financially viable business, People Express had shown positive results in the sphere of personal growth, the number one objective of its "people strategy." High levels of employee satisfaction showed up in first-year surveys done by the University of Michigan. Less tangible but nevertheless striking were the nonverbal and anecdotal data. A cheerful, friendly, energetic atmosphere permeated the planes and passenger terminals as well as the private crew lounge and hallways of corporate headquarters. Questions about the company were almost invariably answered articulately, confidently, and enthusiastically. Stories of personal change, profit and learning were common:

Ted E., customer service manager:

I was a special education teacher making $12,000 a year, receiving little recognition, getting tired, looking for something else. I

started here at $17,000, already have received $600 in profit sharing, and will soon own about 800 shares of stock worth $12 on the open market, all bought at very reduced rates. [Two months after this statement the stock was worth $26 a share.]

Glenn G., customer service manager:

I was running a hotline and crisis program, then was assistant manager of a health food store before seeing the People Express recruitment ad in the newspaper and coming to check it out. I'm about to sell my car in order to take advantage of the current stock offer to employees.

Both Glenn and Ted had worked primarily in training but had also done "in-flight" and "ground-ops" jobs. They wanted more responsibilities, hoped to get them but even if they didn't get promoted soon they expected to continue learning from and enjoying their work.

Michael F., a flight captain:

I'm making $36,000. With my profit-sharing checks so far I've got $43,000 and on top of that I'll get sustained profit-sharing deals . . . I'm doing O.K. . . . Granted, at [another company] a captain might be making $110,000 working 10 days a month [but] they're not really worth it. [In other companies] the top people might make over $100,000 but they throw on 200 guys at the bottom so they can continue to make their salary. Is that fair? [Also, the seniority system would have kept Michael from being a captain at most other airlines.] We're radically different and I believe radically better.

Most pilots know very little about what's going on in their company. In a People flight manager position, the knowledge people gain in this ratty old building is incredible. It's a phenomenal opportunity. It's very stimulating and exciting. I never thought I would have this much fun.

The stories of People's start-up team members and officers were even more dramatic. Each had profited and diversified substantially in their two years with People.

Melrose Dawsey, Burr's secretary at Texas International, was a managing officer at People with primary responsibility for administration. She owned 40,000 shares of stock, purchased at $0.50 a share and worth, as of November 1982, over $20/share. For her own career development, she had also begun to assume some line management responsibilities in the in-flight area. In her spare time, she had earned her in-flight certification and had run the New York marathon (as had Burr).

Lori Dubose, the youngest officer, had come to People to head the personnel function. In addition, she had taken on primary responsibility for the "in-flight" function as well as assuming the de facto role of key translator and guide vis-à-vis the company's precepts. As others came to see the value and purpose of People's precepts and human resource policies, Dubose's status among the officers had also risen.

Jim Miller had been a flight attendant for a year and base manager of in-flight services for four years at Texas International. As part of Dubose's start-up team, he had been coordinator of training, played a key role in recruitment, and then took on added responsibility for management and organizational development as well.

Hap Paretti, who began as legal counsel and head of government relations, quickly became involved in all aspects of the marketing function, and then went on to head flight operations, a move he acknowledged was "a little out of the ordinary" since he didn't have a technical background as a pilot. He spoke for all of the officers in saying, "As a managing officer you're expected to think about virtually every major decision that comes up for review."

Many spoke of the more subtle aspects of their personal development. Hap Paretti enjoyed the challenge of motivating other people and "managing by example" so as to enhance the growth of others.

Geoff Crowley, general manager in charge of ground operations and manpower scheduling, talked of becoming "less competitive" and "less up-tight about winning alone" and more interested in working together with others to accomplish group and company goals.

The Downside of People's Growth and Strategies

People Express's growth rate and strategies were not without significant organizational, financial, and human costs. By Burr's own observation,

> I would say at best, we're operating at 50 percent of what we'd like to be operating at in terms of the environment for people to do the best in. So we're nowhere near accomplishing what we would really like to accomplish in that regard. [But] I think we're better off today than we ever have been. And I think we're gaining on the problem.

Chronic Understaffing

Lori Dubose saw the hiring rate as the most difficult aspect of the company's growth process, causing many other problems:

> If we could get enough people to staff adequately in all three areas of the company so that people got some staff and some line responsibility and would have some time for management development . . . I think things would be a lot different. [There's

been] constant pressure to hirc, hire, hire, and we just haven't gotten enough.

She was adamant, however, about not relaxing People's requirements.

When Dubose came to P.E. she expected to have to staff a company flying three planes, which would have required rapid hiring of perhaps 200–300 people. The purchase of the Lufthansa fleet meant five to six times as many staff were needed. Given the time consumed by the selective recruiting process, and the low percentage of hires, the staffing demands for supporting and launching 17 planes stretched People's people to the limit. The result was chronic understaffing even by People's own lean staffing standards.

As of November 1982, the 800 permanent "managers" were supplemented with over 400 temporaries, hired to handle telephone reservations, a function trained CSMs were originally expected to cover. Some of these "res" workers had been there a year or more, but still were not considered full-fledged People people, though many would have liked to be. They received little training, did not work in teams, own stock, receive profit-sharing bonuses, or participate in advisory councils. They were just starting to be invited to social activities. For a while those wishing to be considered for permanent CSM positions were required to leave their temporary jobs first, on the theory that any bad feelings from being rejected could be contagious and have a bad effect on morale. That policy was eventually seen as unfair, and dropped. Indeed, some managers saw the "res" area as a training ground for CSM applicants.

In August 1982 several MOs estimated that, aside from reservation workers, they were short by about 200 people, though the recruiting staff was working 10 to 12 hours daily, often six days a week, as they had since January 1981. This understaffing in turn created other difficulties, limiting profits, policy implementation, and development of the organization's infrastructure.

> If we had another 100 to 150 CSMs without adding an additional airplane, we could just go out and add probably another half a million to a million dollars a month to the bottom line of the company. . . . There is additional flying out there that we could do with these airplanes . . . we could generate a lot more money . . . almost double the profits of the company.   (MacAdoo)

The policy of job rotation, critical to keeping everyone challenged and motivated, had been only partially implemented. Initial plans called for universal monthly rotations, with 50 percent of almost everyone's time spent flying, 25 percent on ground line work, and another 25 percent in "staff functions." Due to staffing shortages, however, many people had been frozen in either line jobs without staff functions or vice versa. Some had become almost full-time coordinators or staff to a given function like recruiting and training, while others had done mostly line work and had little or no opportunity to do what they expected when they were hired as "managers." Since neither performance appraisal nor governance plans had been fully carried out, many felt inadequately recognized, guided, or involved.

There were also certain inherent human costs of People's people strategies. Rotating generalists were less knowledgeable and sometimes performed less efficiently than specialists on specific tasks. High commitment to the company plus expectations of flexibility in work hours could be costly in terms of individuals' personal and family lives. For many who were single and had moved to Newark to join People Express, there "was no outside life." As one customer service manager described it, "People Express is it . . . you kind of become socially retarded . . . and when you do find yourself in another social atmosphere it's kind of awkward."

For those who were married, the intense involvement and closeness with co-workers and with the company was sometimes threatening to family members who felt left out. Of the initial 15 officers, 3 had been divorced within a year and a half. The very fact of People's difference, in spite of the benefits, was seen by some as a source of stress; keeping the hierarchy to a minimum meant few titles and few promotions in the conventional sense.

> You might know personally that you're growing more than you would ever have an opportunity to grow anywhere else, but your title doesn't change, (which) doesn't mean that much to you but how does your family react?   (Magel)
>
> Even People's biggest strengths, the upbeat culture, the high-caliber performance, and positive attitude of the work force could be stressful. "It's not a competitive environment, it's highly challenging. Everybody's a star . . . but, you know," said one customer service manager, "maintaining a high positive attitude is enough to give you a heart attack."

High commitment and high ambition, together with rapid growth and understaffing, meant that most of People's managers were working long, hard hours and were under considerable stress. Said one CSM, "Nobody is ever scheduled for over 40 hours [a week], but I don't know anybody who works just 40 hours."

Dubose recognized that the situation had taken a toll on everybody's health. "I was never sick a day in my life until I worked for People Express, and in the last two years I've been sick constantly." Other managing officers, including Burr, had also been sick a lot, as had general managers. "And start-up team members—oh, my God! they've got ulcers, high blood pressure, allergies, a divorce . . . it's one thing after another . . . we've all been physically run down." She adds, however, "It's not required that we kill ourselves," asserting that personality traits and an emotionally rewarding workplace accounted for the long hours many worked.

Burr's stance on this issue was that there were no emotional or human costs of hard work. "Work is a very misunderstood, underrated idea. In fact human beings are prepared and can operate at levels far in excess of what they think they can do. If you let them think they're tired and ought to go on vacation for two years or so, they will."

By the fall of 1982, though people were still generally satisfied with their jobs and motivated by their stock ownership to make the company work, many of People's managers below the top level were not as satisfied or optimistic as they once were. A University of Michigan 18-month climate survey taken in September 1982 showed signs of declining morale since December 1981. "People are feeling frustrated in their work [and feel they can't raise questions], cross-utilization is not being well-received, management is viewed as less supportive and consultative, the total compensation package [including pay] is viewed less favorably. Clearly there is work to be done in several areas." (Exhibit 8 contains excerpts from the 1982 survey.) The report found significant differences in the perceptions of FMs and CSMs: flight managers were more

Exhibit 8   Excerpts from the 1982 Survey

Changes since the December 1981 Climate Survey:

In comparing the responses from the December 1981 and September 1982 surveys, the following significant changes have apparently taken place:*

— Getting help or advice about a work-related problem is not as easy.
— What is expected of people is not as clear.
— People are not being kept as well informed about the performance and plans of the airline.
— Satisfaction with work schedules has decreased.
— The number of perceived opportunities to exercise self-management is lower.
— The process used to create initial work teams is viewed less favorably.
— The work is generally perceived to be less challenging and involving.
— The overall quality of upper management is being questioned more.
— Fewer opportunities for personal growth and career development are apparent.
— People are not very comfortable about using the "open door" policy at People Express.
— People feel that their efforts have less of an influence on the price of People Express stock.
— The buying of discounted company stock is being perceived as less of a part of the pay program.
— The compensation package is thought to be less equitable, considering the work people do.
— People feel they have to work too hard to accomplish what is expected of them.
— The team concept at People Express is being questioned more.
— Officers and general managers are thought to be nonconsultative on important decisions.
— People Express is thought to be growing and expanding too fast.
— There is a stronger perception that asking questions about how the airline is managed may lead to trouble.

All of these changes are in a negative direction. Clearly, people are frustrated with the "climate" at People Express; morale and satisfaction are on the decline.

On the positive side, people's expectations of profiting financially were somewhat greater.

---

* Responses on many of these items were still quite positive in an absolute sense, though showing statistically significant decline from earlier studies.

---

skeptical of cross-utilization and more uncertain of what self-management meant; they felt most strongly that management was nonconsultative.

When questioned about such problems, those in leadership positions were adamant that both business and personal difficulties were short-term, and the costs were well worth the long-term benefits. They felt that virtually every problem was soluble over time with better self-management skills—

including time management and stress management, which everyone was being helped to develop—and with evolving improvements in organizational structure. Even those responsible for recruitment insisted, "The challenge is that it seems impossible and there's a way to do it" (Robinson).

I don't think the long-term effects on the individual are going to be disastrous because we are learning how to cope with it. And I think the short-term effects on the organization will not be real bad because I think we're trying to put in place all the structure modifications at the same time that we're continuing the growth. That makes it take longer to get the structure modifications on the road. Which isn't real good. But they'll get there. Long term, I think they will have a positive effect. I think. I wish I knew, for sure. (Dubose)

Within two months of the climate survey report, Dubose and others from the People advisory council made a video presentation to address many of the items raised in the report. For almost every major item a solution had been formulated.

In spite of all the new initiatives, each of which would entail considerable time and energy to implement, People's officers did not believe they should slow down the company's rate of growth while attending to internal problems. Their standard explanations were as follows:

> If you don't keep growing then the individual growth won't happen. People here have a very high level of expectation anyway, I mean unrealistic, I mean there's no way it's going to happen. They're not going to be general managers tomorrow; they're not going to learn each area of the airline by next month. But they all want to. And even a reasonable rate of growth isn't going to be attainable for the individual if we don't continue to grow as a company. And the momentum is with us now we're on a roll. If we lose the momentum now we might never be able to pick it up again. (Dubose)

Burr put it even more strongly:

> Now there are a lot of people who argue that you ought to slow down and take stock and that everything would be a whole lot nicer and easier and all that; I don't believe that. People get more fatigued and stressed when they don't have a lot to do. I really

believe that, and I think I have tested it. I think it's obvious as hell and I feel pretty strongly about it.

He was convinced that the decrease in energy and decline in morale evident even among the officers were not reason to slow down but to speed up. For himself, he had taken a lot of time to think about things in his early years and had only really begun to know what was important to him between his 35th and 40th years. Then he had entered what he hoped would be an enormous growth period, accelerating "between now and when I get senile. It's sensational what direction does. The beauty of the human condition is the magic people are capable of when there's direction. When there's no direction, you're not capable of much."

Approaching 1983, the big issue ahead for People Express, as Burr saw it, was not the speed or costs of growth. Rather, it was how he and People's other leaders would "keep in touch with what's important" and "not lose sight of their humanity."

CASE 3
PDI
Cliff Darden, John Davis, Wendy Vittori, David Fisher, and Jeffrey A. Sonnenfeld

The two consultants shifted uncomfortably in their chairs, sensing the futility of trying to resolve the issue. Alan Wolf continued:

> The people at HEW expect to see more of you, Dick. Your participation was critical in selling the study and frankly we can't duplicate your knowledge of the technical evaluations . . . Now, I know you're overcommitted *but* we were promised 12 hours a week

of your time on the study, and even that was a compromise!

Dick Harbour thought to himself, "We both know I can't put in that kind of time. . . ." Then he spoke:

> I'm 130 percent now and next week it becomes 150 percent. Something has to give and so far it's been the HEW project. The pressures on the other projects have been greater, Alan. Take the HUD project, for example. . . . It should let up soon and then you'll get more time.

"I think it would be helpful if you went to Eric Herr [vice president in charge of the HUD project] and asked to have some of your other commitments reduced." With this comment Alan felt that he had fulfilled his obligations as project manager.

"O.K., I'll talk to Eric," Dick said distantly.

Alan rose. "Good, I'll drop in tomorrow and maybe we can talk about some things you can be doing."

Dick nodded. His pleasant smile was still there, but inside he felt the pressure building. As the door closed, he turned his chair to the window. Cambridge streets were beginning to swell as commuters rushed home to beat the forecasted winter blizzard. The intersection down the street was jammed, and the snow was deepening. Dick was facing another late night at work and felt that he, too, was stuck in a frustrating jam.

Dick, a project manager, had received an angry call that day from one of his own clients at the Department of Housing and Urban Development (HUD). The client was threatening to cancel its contract with Dick's firm, Policy Development, Inc. (PDI), because PDI had been so "uncooperative." The contract was of great importance to both Dick and PDI. He was convinced that it was HUD expertise which would secure his promotion to vice president. Although he

had developed and sold the study, he needed to manage it successfully in order to be seriously considered for promotion next year.

He wondered how he could give more time. Last week he had worked 64 hours only by pledging to himself that he would keep his hours down. Yet, again this week, things seemed out of control. He had not been home for dinner one night, and was facing another weekend of work. Even worse, he had promised to spend the weekend in New York with his wife. Domestic problems were growing as her patience began to weaken. He resented what was happening to his life. He had always thought that the type of pressure he was experiencing now would diminish once he became a successful professional, but it only seemed to be getting worse and worse.

Company Background

PDI was founded in the fall of 1969 by the current president, Pat Guilfoyle, and the executive vice president, Rick Lesaar. The two had met each other at the Kennedy School of Government at Harvard while Pat was finishing a PhD in public policy. Rick had been working on his MBA at the Harvard Business School and was taking some courses in public policy. The two men were immediately impressed with each other's skills and, in the spring of Rick's second year, 1969, they agreed they would take an enterprising leap and start their own "think tank." PDI nearly collapsed in its first year but was revived in the winter of 1970 by two large government contracts, one from the Department of Health, Education, and Welfare (HEW) and the other from the National Institutes of Health (NIH). By 1973, PDI had become a profitable consulting firm and was enjoying continued growth. PDI growth trends are shown in Exhibit 1.

Exhibit 1   PDI Growth Trends

End of Year	No. of Professional Staff	No. of Support Staff	No. of Contracts	$ Contracts*	$ Profits*
1969†	3	1	1	37,000	−2,000
1970	7	2	4	268,000	−11,000
1971	17	4	7	723,000	39,000
1972	21	4	9	972,000	68,000
1973	39	8	20	1,940,000	155,200
1974	58	13	31	3,190,000	255,200
1975	70	15	43	4,209,000	357,000
1976	76	18	52	4,940,000	434,700
1977	83	20	61	5,810,000	447,400

* All amounts are expressed in current dollars.
† Only four months of work during 1969.

While Guilfoyle and Lesaar were both initially active in project research and consulting, by 1972 Guilfoyle began devoting himself to publicizing the research findings of PDI (with appearances before Congressional subcommittees, and speeches and journal and magazine articles) and Lesaar turned to managing PDI's internal affairs.

There were three other officers in the firm. Eric Herr joined PDI in 1971 with a good reputation in the health field and, in 1972, was made a vice president and given responsibility for directing all studies. Jerry Nagel also joined in 1971, straight from the University of Wisconsin, where he had earned a PhD in economics. Because of PDI's rapid growth, Nagel was quickly given responsibility for managing projects under Eric Herr's direction. He was promoted to vice president for the health policy area in 1975. Joe Kelly, PDI's most recent officer, was recently hired away from a competitor in 1974 and promoted to vice president in 1975 to direct studies in the health technology area.

The nature of the studies at PDI changed after 1969. Initially, PDI focused on health-related problems. Pat Guilfoyle had written

his thesis on the administration of a national health insurance plan and had gained an outstanding reputation in the health field. One consultant joked about PDI's reliance on health research: "Even up to a year ago we all joked that we should write 'A subsidiary of NIH' below our company name." While PDI had concentrated on health-policy studies, it had also hired consultants who were experts in health-care technology with the result that the firm began to get contracts from such clients as the American Medical Association (AMA) to study the applicability of certain health-care systems in different environments.

In 1975, in an attempt to diversify, Eric Herr led PDI to do work in the area of housing and urban development. So far, this study area had remained small, but Herr felt it held great promise for the firm:

A few years ago, I examined company growth. We were doing very well and still are. . . . But I knew we were too narrowly focused. I had ridden the crest of the last wave; I wanted to ride the crest of the next one. I've always been interested in the housing and urban development area, and now, with Carter's new urban policy, I know it was the right choice. HUD contracts will really grow in the years to come, and I have put PDI in line for some of them. The challenge now is to get *and control* the people to do those studies. He sighed, "Sometimes you've got to be stubborn . . ."

While the growth of the health-related contracts had fallen off slightly since the beginning of 1977, the urban development area was beginning to crystallize in 1978 and seemed poised for big growth.

Ownership, Compensation, and Organizational Structure

In 1978, Guilfoyle, then 38, owned 40 percent of PDI stock and Lesaar, 37, owned about 25 percent. The remainder of the stock was divided among the three other officers. Eric Herr, 36, held 20 percent. Jerry Nagel, 33, and Joe Kelly, 34, each had about 7 percent.

An officer's compensation package was composed of his fixed salary, an annual dividend declared on PDI stock, and a fixed percentage of the business that he developed. This last component was particularly important and could account for up to half of an officer's total income.

Lesaar had this to say about PDI's organizational structure:

> PDI is a matrix organization. The other vice presidents manage our projects and I handle administration such as scheduling, financial matters, career development, and the like [originally for all staff, but now he shared it somewhat with other officers—see below]. Project managers report to the officer-in-charge if they have a project-related problem, like a problem with a client or the budget. The project manager talks to the administrative officer concerning project assignments, scheduling of people or career development matters. Ideally, we want the project manager to resolve the day-to-day

project hassles so the officers can concentrate on business development.

On a given project, an individual would report to one vice president for external client relations (budget, schedule, and so on) and one vice president for administrative purposes (assignments, evaluation, and the like). Thus an individual consultant would report to possibly a different vice president (through the project manager for each project) for client relations, but only to one vice president for administrative or career-related issues. On the other hand, a project manager had to manage team members who may all report to different vice presidents for these administrative issues. Such administrative concerns were the assignment of researchers to projects, the monitoring of consultant progress, and the evaluation of consultant performance.

Originally, Rick Lasaar was responsible for the administrative and career overview of all the associates and research assistants. By 1976, however, he realized that he could no longer manage these administrative and career development issues for all the professional staff members. Early in 1977 his load was lightened by the reassignment of 18 of the then-25 senior associates to either Eric Herr, Jerry Nagel, or Joe Kelly, three other vice presidents.

These 25 senior associates had the potential to become officers of PDI (vice presidents) within two to three years and were often "adopted" by their administrative officers in a mentor-protégé relationship. The number of senior associates assigned to an officer was based on his projected contract volume for the coming year. As it worked in 1978, Herr projected the heaviest volume first and got his choice of senior associates. Nine senior associates were assigned to Herr, five to Nagel, and four to Kelly.

The project manager role at PDI was potentially both satisfying and frustrating. The project manager was responsible for budgets, work schedules, and report quality. Often, he or she had to manage others who were equal or superior to him or her in rank, and control over these individuals could be very weak. The project manager formally evaluated the performance of each participant on his or her project, but the individual's administrative officer could weight the evaluations in any way he or she chose.

Staff Development and Career Progression

An important element of resource management at PDI was managing the career development of the professional staff. Lesaar commented:

> Our professional staff is here because it wants experience with the variety of studies we offer. They are very bright and work *extremely* hard. Without variety they get bored . . . you can see it . . . something behind their eyes. It's up to us to make sure they get the variety they need and develop into consultants that can handle a range of problems.

The professional career ladder at PDI was fairly well defined. Depending on the entry level, the typical promotion path was as follows:

officer (i.e., vice president)

↑

senior associate

↑

associate

↑

research assistant

Those joining PDI with a BA and no work experience entered as research assistants.

They did the library searches, computer programming, and simple data analysis required in PDI work. Those entering with an advanced degree (PhD, MA, MS, or MBA), with little or no work experience, usually entered as associates. These staff members produced the analytical core of PDI studies; and when they had demonstrated promise of management talent, they were allowed to manage a study. After sufficient management experience, they were promoted to the senior associate level.

Most of the research assistants quit after a year or two to pursue graduate training, while some were promoted to associate. After a three-year period, associates were eligible to become senior associates. The requirements for promotion from senior associate to officer had just recently been articulated. The promotion policy was known as "up-or-out," and was a source of considerable stress. In the words of one consultant:

> I guess it's a little frightening once you reach the senior associate level. It's clear to everyone at that level that in order to become an officer you must be a solid project manager, which too often only means making a good profit, and you must be able to market and find projects for PDI. It's the last part that throws most people. We're not really exposed to client development work and developing business under an officer. If you can't develop your own area, you have to take business away from the officer to get promoted. The only way Jerry Nagel made it to VP was because Eric Herr founded the urban area, leaving health policy to him and health technology to Joe Kelly. For a long time no one had been here long enough to be affected, but four more guys are up for promotion this year. You see, we've been growing really fast. I don't think management has anticipated the implications of this policy.

Dick Harbour's Projects

Dick Harbour was assigned to four projects—labelled HUD, HEW, AMA, and Marketing (see Appendix 2; the project managers for each project are also shown). Dick was the manager on all his assigned projects except the HEW project, which was managed by Alan Wolf. As in Appendix 1, the project manager has one officer-in-charge guiding him on project problems, but sometimes there is more than one administrative officer with whom he must work on project assignment issues.

Dick's first assignment was for 50 percent of his time (20 hours a week) to manage a six-month $110,000 project for HUD. The task here involved the thorough investigation of a major piece of legislation to aid the cities. The Congress had already ratified Carter's urban program and HUD would have to administer it the following year when the law became effective. PDI had been chosen after a hard contract fight to look into all the various implications of the legislation in order to suggest administrative guidelines. The project represented a very large amount of business for PDI, and a great potential for future work from HUD and from each municipality participating in the HUD program. The composition of the HUD project team reflected the importance of this study. To provide the needed expertise, and to prepare for later project development which might grow out of this work, four senior associates and one highly valued associate were assigned to the HUD study. Dick had worked with all of them before, but never as their project manager.

Eric Herr was the officer-in-charge for the project. Except for Dick and another senior associate, all team members were administratively assigned to Rick Lesaar. Dick and

the other senior associates were assigned to Eric Herr.

Dick was also the project manager of a three-month $30,000 study of public implications of proposed medical technology innovations for the AMA (American Medical Association). He was assigned only 20 percent there. This project largely relied on past work by PDI and did not have great potential for business growth. For these reasons, the study provided an excellent training opportunity. Accordingly, PDI had assigned two brand-new associates and a new research assistant to the project. In addition, a very experienced associate, Andy Cooper, who was being considered for promotion to senior associate, acted as a quasi-project manager. Dick acted as the quasi-officer-in-charge, although he still reported to the actual OIC, Joe Kelly, on this study. All of the AMA team members, with the exception of Dick himself, were administratively assigned to Rick Lesaar.

Dick's third assignment was as a member of a study team where he and another member of that project, Ed Killory, were the only senior associates of the seven team members. Alan Wolf, the project manager, was an associate, being considered for promotion to senior associate. This $80,000 study was being conducted for HEW and looked into improving regional cooperation between health-care providers. It involved an investigation into present and projected health-care needs in various communities, present medical services, access, quality, and technological evaluations. It was considered a moderately profitable project with fair growth potential.

Jerry Nagel was the officer-in-charge of the project and was also the administrative officer for Ed Killory. Eric Herr was the administrative officer for Dick Harbour. The other five team members were administratively assigned to Rick Lesaar.

Although PDI had much experience in this area, they had nearly lost the contract because they were staffing it with junior personnel. Jerry Nagel saved the contract by negotiating with Eric Herr for 12 hours a week (30 percent) of Dick Harbour's time. Eric closed the deal by letting Nagel know that he owed him a favor in the future. The client wanted even more of Harbour's time, but had settled for the 12 hours per week.

Finally, Dick was expected to spend between one and two days a week marketing projects for the firm. This basically required being in Washington and making the rounds: presenting papers at conferences, making regular calls on clients, and, as Dick described it, "taking copious notes to make sure I don't forget to do anything." Although he was skilled in the health field, his assignment to Herr meant he worked to increase business in the urban area.

Dick Harbour's Background and Attitude toward the Projects

Dick Harbour had graduated from Berkeley in 1972 with a PhD in economics. His strong interest in public policy, in general, and health issues in particular, attracted him to PDI, and he joined in the summer of 1972. He soon gained valuable expertise in both the health policy field and the medical technology field. In 1975, however, when Eric Herr entered the urban development area, Dick, too, became interested in it.

> When Eric created this new area, he talked to me a lot. I was actually more familiar with certain aspects of it than he was. We both thought it would take off and I was getting tired of the health area. I needed a change, plus my greatest chance for a VP slot was to carve a niche out of the urban

area. It's wide open, and Eric can't master all of it.

> As for marketing, I like presenting papers. Like many people here, I almost went into teaching, and I like to think of myself as an academic. But the other stuff is less fun; it's an effort to market. I'm much better at research and consulting. But if I don't market a lot and land some big work, I'll be asked to leave. I guess it's necessary if the firm is to continue to grow, but the pressure on me is really great.

Of the four things he was working on, Dick was most excited about the HUD project and marketing projects for the firm. In addition, he viewed these as the two most important areas from the point of view of getting promoted.

The HEW Project

There were many points of view concerning this problem. Jerry Nagel, the OIC for the HEW project, had this to say:

> Sure, I'll tell you what's wrong. It started in February of '77 when some of the senior associates were assigned to the other VPs. Eric Herr (OIC for the HUD project) expected a mass of work to pour in, so he got most of the senior associates assigned to him. Well, Eric's work didn't materialize as fast as he thought it would, and I needed Dick on the HEW project—it was clear we would have lost it without him. No one at PDI can match Dick's ability to do technological evaluations; it will literally take two years to bring a beginning associate up to Dick's level, although some of our competitors have consultants nearly as competent as Dick. HEW, understandably, insisted on having Dick on the project team and now wants to see him at our meetings with them.

> But later, the HUD project came through and Dick was selected to be project manager. Now Dick wants the experience of running a big project in the urban area. He's run

a couple of big projects for me, but now he wants one in the urban area. I think he should concentrate on his strengths, which are clearly in the health field. Frankly, I think this move will hurt him, but that's for him to decide.

As for now, we need Dick's time. PDI has been facing some stiff competition from other firms in the health field. Health policy studies are still our bread and butter and, if we don't show our clients that we want to do superior work, they'll go to our competitors. If I lose just two or three contracts, PDI really suffers, people become idle, and my business sinks.

It's the job of Alan Wolf [project manager, HEW project] to get him to put in the time he promised us. I've talked with Dick also but all I can do is to encourage. The only one who can really discipline Dick is his administrative officer, and that's Eric [Herr].

Alan Wolf, the project manager, had this to say:

I knew my talk with Dick was only a ritual. It was my job to convince him to give us more, but I can't threaten anything. Besides, I can understand his motives. I'd probably do just what he's doing. So I went to the OIC—Jerry [Nagel]. But he can't do much, either. So I went to Eric [Herr] and got a couple of minutes, literally, to explain the situation. He said he'd talk to Dick about it. But he has no real incentive to change things. His bonus is based on the volume of business his area manages.

You know, if this project flops, it's my neck. We can't just hire a guy off the street to do what Dick can do. Our expertise here is learned only after a lot of time on the job. So, we need him.

Eric Herr also had his viewpoint:

I know the HEW project needs him, but they're exaggerating. Besides, Dick should move where he's going to benefit most, and that's in my area. He agrees. I'm sure he'll

free up the time to do a good job for Wolf and Nagel on the HEW thing.

Dick Harbour had this to say:

The problem with my project is the travel. It chews up so much time. My writing and basic research have to be done at night and on weekends. So I don't see my wife very often. I've cut back as far as I can on the AMA project and my marketing. If anything, I should increase my marketing. I want to work more in the urban area, but my expertise is still very valuable in the health area. I'm still being called by old clients to offer advice. The shortage of manpower around here is growing more and more acute. But recruiting is very time consuming. Besides, the lead time required to produce an "expert" here is about two years. We are way behind. Just to get Wolf and Nagel off my back, I'd be glad to give them more time now, but now there's this client hassle with HUD.

HUD Project

Dick had found the HUD client increasingly difficult to deal with, and he felt that a serious rift in this relationship could jeopardize his career at PDI. Even his afternoon call from the client had begun on an antagonistic tone:

Client: Hello, Dick? This is Bob Anderson.

Dick: Hi Bob, what's new?

Client: That's what I called to ask you.

Dick: Well, not much since yesterday. We're still waiting to get clearance from you to go around to the other federal agencies we need to speak with to move on to the next phase.

Client: What next phase?

Dick: The next phase of the research plan we agreed to last week.

Client: Dick, I said that I'd accept that plan as a draft for consideration. It is *not* a final plan.

Dick: Well, perhaps I was mistaken, but I . . .

Client: You *were* mistaken, and I hope these mistakes don't continue. We are the ones who pay for these mistakes. I've got to have a more detailed breakdown of what you hope to do before you guys fly down here from Cambridge and swarm all over Washington. I need to know who you're going to see, why, and when. Meetings of this sort can be sensitive. I thought you would have a greater appreciation for such work.

Dick: I'm sorry that you're not happy, Bob, and I'll see that we do a more detailed plan. I must add, though, that it is this labor which is costing you the most. I don't believe that you need this degree of detail. This is the fourth draft of what we thought would be a tentative outline of our checkpoints in the study.

Client: If you people spent some time down here now and then you'd have a better sense for what we need and not just what you like to do. I know you people are pretty sharp, but you're not doing much for me.

Dick: We are coming down there two days a week and have Harry down there full time.

Client: Harry is an inexperienced junior associate. If this is a low-priority project for PDI, perhaps it would be better for both parties if HUD finished this project with another firm.

Dick: Well, look, Bob, I'll reword the schedules tonight and get back to you tomorrow about putting more time in at your office. You've given us great office facilities to work with down there, and we'd like to take better advantage of your hospitality.

Client: Look, I'm not an insulted party hostess. I don't care if you find us hospitable. I'm just trying to get PDI to give this project the attention it deserves.

Dick knew that his team wouldn't be very cooperative about another rescheduling. As senior associates they, like Dick, had many other very high priority commitments, including projects that they, too, were managing. They resented being told that they owed Dick more time than they felt their other projects needed. One team member commented:

> Dick's a great guy, but this project is just not where it should be by now. He's trying so hard to keep control over all facets of this project that he won't let us specialize at all. We were brought on to this project because of our special expertise, but he won't give us the chance to use it. I think he's anxious to stay on top of all aspects of this study because it's so important to him and to PDI. He probably thinks it will look like he's lost control if we move off on our own into the areas we know more about than he does.

Another team member complained:

> Initially, I was really excited about this project, but now I just dread these trips to Washington. We don't do anything except try to hold the hands of this damn client. He hardly has any staff of his own and is new to HUD. I don't know how bright he is, but he sure is uncomfortable in his job. We never get very positive feedback. He is an old Army officer who believes in a lot of eyewash for inspections. He has thrown more red tape in our way than any other client I've ever worked with. All we do is pull things out of thin air right now because he won't let us research in the field yet. I don't think Dick should keep us all on the project in this phase. In fact, it looks to me as if he has the junior associate not even doing RA work, but secretarial work.

With the other team members aching to get off the HUD project, Dick felt even more pressure to put more of his own time into it.

The Future

Dick gazed out at the storm and reflected on his predicament. He knew that minor scheduling modifications of his own time and others would no longer solve the HUD problem, and yet any major shifts in allocation would change the timetable budget, and contract proposal. Major shifts might just further damage the client relationship and signal poor project management. Discussion of this in a full group meeting might show how committed people were to other projects, but he rarely got much vocal support in these meetings.

Dick was also concerned about the AMA project. PDI had provided no formal orientation program for the new associates and

Dick felt he should be more involved in their training. We also saw Andy working every weekend and worried about the amount of work he had delegated to him.

And, finally, he was facing the HEW problem. "If I'm so valuable around here," he thought, "why do I feel so awful?" He was the man in the middle and he was responsible for finding a solution, but how did all this happen? He wasn't sure, but he wondered if the problems he faced didn't stem from larger problems at PDI.

Appendix 1
Reporting Relationships on Project Y

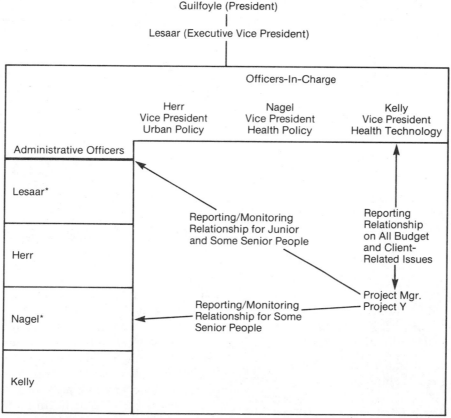

* Assigns researchers to projects, follows their work on project assignments, and evaluates their performance.

Appendix 2
Reporting Relationships for Dick Harbour's Projects

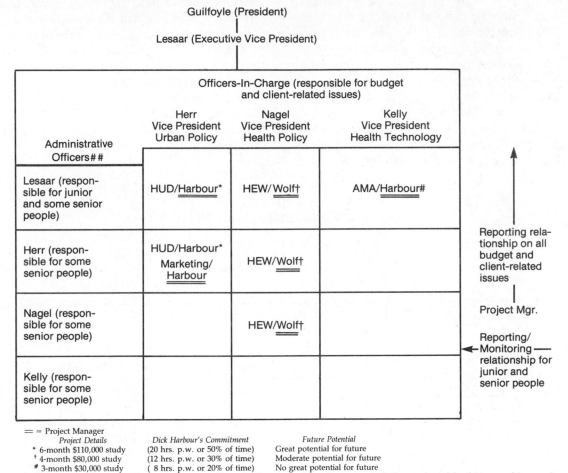

Guilfoyle (President)

Lesaar (Executive Vice President)

Officers-In-Charge (responsible for budget and client-related issues)			
Administrative Officers##	Herr Vice President Urban Policy	Nagel Vice President Health Policy	Kelly Vice President Health Technology
Lesaar (responsible for junior and some senior people)	HUD/Harbour*	HEW/Wolf†	AMA/Harbour#
Herr (responsible for some senior people)	HUD/Harbour* Marketing/ Harbour	HEW/Wolf†	
Nagel (responsible for some senior people)		HEW/Wolf†	
Kelly (responsible for some senior people)			

Reporting relationship on all budget and client-related issues

Project Mgr.

Reporting/ Monitoring relationship for junior and senior people

≡ = Project Manager

Project Details	*Dick Harbour's Commitment*	*Future Potential*
* 6-month $110,000 study	(20 hrs. p.w. or 50% of time)	Great potential for future
† 4-month $80,000 study	(12 hrs. p.w. or 30% of time)	Moderate potential for future
# 3-month $30,000 study	(8 hrs. p.w. or 20% of time)	No great potential for future

From the point of view of being administrative officers (looking after project assignments, scheduling people, and developing people's careers), Lesaar, Herr, Nagel, and Kelly were on the same level.

CASE 4
TRANSCOM, INC. (A)
James J. Dowd and
Jeffrey A. Sonnenfeld

President Dan Patterson had been in this situation before: should he accept this offer

to be acquired by a large multinational corporation, or should he reject it? Contemplating this decision, he thought of his duty to Transcom shareholders, of the needs of the firm, and of his own personal career goals. He also recalled his previous experience with acquisition, and considered those lessons carefully. But Rothborough-Heathcliffe wanted an answer tomorrow morning, and he had to decide tonight, Labor Day, September 4, 1982.

Dan Patterson

With a BSME from Cal Tech University and an MBA from Stanford, Patterson had established an impressive career in the management of high-technology, high-growth firms. In particular, by age 41, he had a reputation for success in managing turnaround situations—first with Computech Corporation and now with Transcom. In each case, Patterson restored the company's profitability and successfully managed its growth, so successfully, in fact, as to make the companies very attractive acquisition targets.

The Computech Acquisition. From 1973 until 1977, Patterson was president of Computech Corporation, a supplier of peripheral component equipment to the telecommunications industry. Computech had been in serious trouble when Patterson took over, but he succeeded in bringing the company back to profitability. In 1976, Computech made profits of $1.1 million on sales of $26.5 million. Essentially, it had been a company with ideas which was both ahead of its time for the market and which required managerial skills beyond those of its founders. Computech products were marketed abroad by Baderglen Computer Company, based in West Germany. Patterson remembered their relationship as one of confrontation characterized by difficult and sometimes hostile negotiations. In May of 1977, then, Patterson was greatly disturbed to find that Computech had been acquired by Baderglen without his having been consulted by the Computech board of directors. The offer to acquire had come to the board by one of the directors. Patterson resented what he viewed as this "back-door approach."

According to Patterson, it did not take long for problems to arise after the acquisition. Predictably, the greatest clash came in determining the autonomy of the new Baderglen subsidiary, and the decision-making authority of its president, Dan Patterson.

For example, Patterson understood that the formulation of strategic plans for Computech would remain the responsibility of Computech management. Baderglen moved quickly to exert corporate control, and soon assumed almost full responsibility for Computech's product policy. According to Patterson, suggestions from Computech employees for integrating the firm's product lines seemed to be summarily rejected by Baderglen simply because they had come from Computech people. Patterson viewed these actions as violations of what had been agreed to in the merger negotiations. Promises made had now been broken, and Patterson soon came to feel he could not trust the Baderglen management.

Finally, in a major disagreement on fundamental issues, Patterson took a final stand with the Baderglen board in November of 1977. He demanded that the board support his recommendation or he would resign. The board agreed to his resignation, which was submitted only six months after the combination had been announced.

Patterson's employment contract guaranteed him a salary from Baderglen for three years. Consequently, his search for a new position was not rushed; he took three months off to relax with his family. In January he sent out his résumé; in March he had narrowed his choices to three companies; on April 19, 1978, he became president of Transcom, Inc., a financially troubled high-technology firm hoping for a turnaround, located in Framingham, Massachusetts, two towns away from Computech.

Transcom

Founded in 1970 by two computer scientists and two telecommunications engineers, Transcom was one of the first independent companies to enter the renewed battleground in the telecommunications industry. Transcom soon developed equipment which challenged valuable turf of not only the giants in the telephone industry but also the key forces in the computer and document reproduction businesses. Firms like ATT, IBM, GTE, and Xerox scrambled to meet the threat imposed by Transcom's facsimile transmission and information processing equipment.

Transcom met with limited success in its early years, but nevertheless grew rapidly beyond the ability of the founders to manage it. After a substantial loss in 1975 and a break even year in 1976, the founders relinquished control. This was just when the company was making major advances with the use of microwave relays and satellite transmissions. Two left the company, and two remained, one as chairman of the board.

When Patterson took over, Transcom was close to bankruptcy. The vice president of finance came to his office shortly after his arrival and informed him that the company would be unable to meet its upcoming payroll. Patterson worked with Transcom's bank to resolve that problem, and through his personal efforts secured a loan of over a half-million dollars. He pushed hard on the company's receivables, and paid off the bank. With the immediate financial crisis over, Patterson turned to implement the other changes needed to bring Transcom back to permanent health.

His program focused on strengthening and expanding the company's sales and marketing organizations, on new product development, and on upgrading Transcom's other functional areas. Patterson realized also the importance of improving morale, and worked to instill a new spirit of optimism and enthusiasm among Transcom's employees.

As he began to implement his turnaround program, Patterson met with some resistance. Nonetheless, he remained committed to his plans, backed by the board's mandate to make any changes necessary to improve Transcom's performance. Within a few months, the vice president of finance resigned. Patterson replaced him with a former associate from Computech. As more turnover occurred, he continued to fill management positions with former Computech employees.

The most serious resistance to Patterson's changes came from the chairman of the board, one of Transcom's founders. Originally, these two were meant to work together to revive the company, but they soon found themselves in fundamental disagreement about the company's plans for the future. Believing that the situation had reached the point where working together was impossible, Patterson approached the board and demanded full and final management authority. The board stood behind him, and the chairman stepped down. He remained a director for one more year, and was not renominated at the end of his term.

Within two years, Transcom's prospects were dramatically improved: growth had been resumed at about the industry average, a broad product line had been developed, and sales efforts had been started abroad. Revenues and income were up and potential for growth in both seemed almost limitless. However, to pursue that growth, Transcom needed capital.

The Western Equipment Acquisition Offer

In July of 1980, plans had almost been finalized for a major stock offering when an unexpected development brought those plans to a halt. Western Equipment Company, owning over 20 percent of Transcom's stock, with two directors on its board, made an offer to purchase Transcom for about $90 million. The work on the stock offering stopped, and Patterson and Transcom's lawyers went to work investigating and considering the benefits of the proposed merger.

With the investigation completed, Patterson went home the weekend before the decision was due and thought the offer over. He decided to reject it. He walked into the board meeting on Monday morning and recommended against the combination, asking for the resignation of the two Western Equipment directors. Again Transcom's board stood squarely behind Patterson; the offer was rejected, the directors resigned, and Transcom went ahead with the stock offering.

Two weeks later, when the stock was offered for sale, the issue sold out in 25 minutes. From an initial sale price of $20 per share, the stock quickly rose in value to over $40 per share. Patterson felt that the market had proved him right: Transcom's 5.2 million shares now had a market value of over $200 million, more than double Western Equipment's offer.

Patterson said he rejected the Western Equipment offer for two reasons. The first and most important reason was price. But he also had a perception of Western Equipment as too tightly controlled, and too large

a company for him to feel comfortable with its operating style. A friend had told him it would take six months just to sort through Western Equipment's accounting system, and Patterson shuddered at the thought.

For its part, Western Equipment made out very well with its Transcom investment despite its rejected purchase offer. In October of 1980 it acquired Rapigraph, one of Transcom's small, but innovative, competitors. Under a consent decree from the Department of Justice, Western Equipment was required to dispose of its Transcom holdings. The subsequent offering yielded $40 million on Western Equipment's original investment of about $2 million. Rapigraph was acquired for about $90 million in what became a hostile takeover after initial deliberations between the two boards reached an impasse on price.

Transcom: June 1981

Now two years after that stock offering, Transcom found itself once again in need of capital. Sales had almost tripled since 1979, and projections for working capital needs had risen from $30 million to almost $100 million. If Transcom were to remain a full-line supplier, it would need large amounts of additional capital; otherwise, it would have to settle for small market niches and leave the largest shares in this booming market to the larger and new domestic competitors: GE, IBM, ATT, Xerox, Exxon, and a growing cast of Japanese and German competitors.

But the equity markets were extremely weak, with Transcom selling at about $21 per share. Patterson began to consider the possibility of merger. He was aware that in the growing trend toward acquisition, Transcom could become a target for unfriendly takeover. In addition to the Western Equipment offer, he had received several tentative inquiries about merger, but had always turned them down. But now, given Transcom's need for capital, and considering the possibility of hostile takeover, Patterson began to think about looking for a suitable parent.

Rothborough-Heathcliffe

At the top of the list of prospective suitors was Rothborough-Heathcliffe, Inc., a major international publishing house with 1981 revenues of $3.1 billion. Even before the Western Equipment offer, one of Transcom's directors whose partner sits on Rothborough-Heathcliffe's board suggested that Patterson speak with Lyman Heathcliffe III, Rothborough-Heathcliffe's chairman, about a possible merger. Patterson agreed to talk, but when asked for a rough estimate of the purchase price, responded with a half-serious demand for $50 per share. The discussions were discontinued.

But in the summer of 1981, that same director approached Patterson again. He suggested that, when next in New Jersey, to review Transcom's field services, Patterson might meet once again with Heathcliffe to talk acquisition. Patterson agreed.

In this second encounter, Heathcliffe was direct and honest: one way or another, he told Patterson, Rothborough-Heathcliffe would enter the telecommunications business. He explained that publishers must move to new forms of information transfer. Furthermore, he said that the company preferred to enter through acquisition, and had already investigated combinations with Transcom's competitors before deciding to pursue Transcom. He expressed a commitment to negotiate in good faith, and he encouraged Patterson to ask any questions, to

talk with Rothborough-Heathcliffe subsidiary managements, to do any research to find out all he needed to know about Rothborough-Heathcliffe.

Patterson's subsequent investigation revealed a great deal. Rothborough-Heathcliffe had been founded in 1919 by a prominent editor of a major New York City newspaper and the editor of a Philadelphia-based general-interest magazine. Their expansion from general-interest periodicals to trade periodicals and to scholarly publications in the 1920s was so successful that they dramatically enlarged their range of products in the 1940s. The tremendous surge of energy in industry and in academia following the Second World War, coupled with great advances in knowledge, led to new opportunities for those in the communications business. Rothborough-Heathcliffe was the first publisher to detect and respond to the emerging markets. Rothborough-Heathcliffe had always maintained a limited line of scholarly research and theory monographs. In the 1940s the book publishing effort rushed forward with full throttle as Rothborough-Heathcliffe created successful autonomous units for textbooks, trade books, scholarly books, and general-interest books.

While this maverick spirit enabled Rothborough-Heathcliffe to anticipate the information demands of the 1950s and the 1960s, by the late 1960s many in the industry felt that Rothborough-Heathcliffe had become a stodgy relic of an earlier age. In 1974, however, Lyman Heathcliffe III, an heir of one of the founders, began a successful effort at shaking the firm from its two decades of strategic lethargy. Rothborough-Heathcliffe received high marks by the investment community for its effort to grow from its reliance on book and magazine publishing. Its more recent acquisitions had brought it into the businesses of technical journal publishing, the collection of economic trend and performance data, and finally into corporate training seminars.

The dynamic changes of Rothborough-Heathcliffe had been driven by Lyman Heathcliffe. One senior vice president in the firm commented.

> Heathcliffe runs his firm like a Southern plantation owner. He speaks in homilies and analogies, and has the image of a beneficent paternal figure. On the other hand, he is also a workaholic with a penchant for detail. Finally, he is an ardent supporter of the human resources function, a firm believer in personnel programs' critical role in management.

Conflicting Picture — Under Heathcliffe, the firm was tightly controlled with centralized policies and procedures in personnel, financial control, and operations. Resulting efficiencies in operations along with generous awards programs had given employees and shareholders a renewed faith in the vitality of this enterprise. Turnover remained among the lowest in the industry and stock price one of the highest.

Patterson's Decision

Satisfied with the information from his research, Patterson agreed in June to begin serious negotiations with Rothborough-Heathcliffe. The first session was held in the last week of June, the second in July. Price was discussed for the first time in August. Patterson drew up a two-page list of demands and presented them to the Rothborough-Heathcliffe negotiators on Labor Day. These points were all accepted in principle; all that remained was for Patterson to decide to accept Rothborough's offer.

TRANSCOM, INC. (B)
James J. Dowd and
Jeffrey A. Sonnenfeld

On September 5, 1981, Dan Patterson accepted Rothborough's offer to acquire Transcom. At a price of $250 million, the tax-free deal would give two Rothborough shares for every three shares of Transcom stock. The merger agreement offered employment agreements to all of Transcom's senior executive officers, guaranteeing them up to two years' compensation if terminated without cause. *[Stock Option]* Patterson was guaranteed $200,000 per year for four years in the event of his termination, and was also tentatively granted (subject to Rothborough's stock option committee approval) an option to buy 20,000 shares of Rothborough at its fair market value.

After signing the letter of intent, Patterson left New Jersey and returned to Framingham to inform his management team. He called all the professionals at Transcom together for a company meeting, at which he told them what had been done, and why. Throughout the first few months of the implementation of the merger, Patterson continued to play a strong and visible personal role in ensuring the smooth integration of Transcom into its new corporate parent. *[stayed to help]*

Changes in Operations

With the acquisition of Transcom, Rothborough-Heathcliffe created a new group, Rothborough Heathcliffe Information Systems (RHIS). RHIS was commissioned to spearhead a new company-wide effort to reach electronically large institutions with information previously accessible only through publications. Various kinds of statistics, literature summaries, document retrieval, and reproduction systems were planned. The expanded use of satellite and microwave transmissions would be coupled with emerging technologies in computer graphics to better present information gathered by other Rothborough units.

Patterson was named the group vice president of this new arm of the business. RHIS was a confederation of previously unrelated businesses, such as a small computer-aided design unit, an economic forecast unit, a manufacturer of computer electrostatic printers, a training service unit, and Transcom. Patterson was assigned to report to Herbert Ginsbrook, senior vice president of operations, who planned to retire in two years. Heathcliffe's group staff included the functions of controller, personnel, legal services, and technological development. This unit would represent 14 percent of company revenues.

In taking this position, Patterson continued on as general manager of Transcom, until a replacement could be found. The choice of his successor was left to his own discretion. Candidates were a Transcom employee with 4 years' tenure and a Rothborough-Heathcliffe employee with 16 years' tenure. The leading internal candidate for Patterson's former position was Ed Walters, the vice president of operations at Transcom. Ed Walters commented on life under Rothborough-Heathcliffe six months after the merger:

> Rothborough is much more formal an organization than Transcom has ever been. Their penchant for standardization has resulted in many corporate forms, all of which must now pass through New Jersey. Transcom managers, as a result, perceive Rothborough as an incredible bureaucratic morass

which must be endured in order to get the capital needed for further growth. We view Transcom procedures as a game which must be played according to the rules in order to get what we want.

A director of microcopying services from another Rothborough division, who was also being considered for Patterson's old job, gave this somewhat different account:

> There is some concern here that the electronic media is out to overtake the printed media. The book and publishing people feel that they are not only losing status in the organization and prestige on the outside, but their very products are being gobbled up from supposedly sister divisions. They feel that the various joint projects being pushed from above are milking old Rothborough units as sources and giving the information to Transcom to disseminate.

Despite such sentiments, both Heathcliffe and Patterson agree that the improved packaging and delivery of information has already demonstrated that they can provide far better customer services than almost anyone in the business. Eventually, in fact, RHIS may be strengthened as a unit and reorganized around customer/business units to build on industry expertise.

Changes in Control Systems

According to Patterson, the imposition of Rothborough-Heathcliffe corporate controls was neither onerous nor traumatic for Transcom. One requirement was the monthly submission of a two-page report to corporate management, outlining the firm's financial results, opportunities, and problems. In addition, some procedures were formalized and Patterson was asked to inform the corporate planning staff of major moves in staffing or in operations. A monthly travel schedule had to be submitted to his superior, who also forwarded his travel plans to Patterson to ensure easy communication between the two. Patterson looked upon this activity as bothersome, but mildly amusing. Rothborough-Heathcliffe also required Transcom to begin developing long-range business plans, independent of those soon to emerge under RHIS, for corporate review and approval. Patterson saw this as a bit more confusing.

Changes in the Reward System

The merger-related changes which have had the greatest early impact on Transcom employees seemed to have been those which dealt with compensation and benefits. The first step after the merger was the slotting of Transcom jobs into Rothborough-Heathcliffe salary grades. Job descriptions were filled out at Transcom, evaluated at Rothborough-Heathcliffe, and graded. This was done in the first two months after the acquisition. The Transcom personnel director commented, "It was real hell then—we had never used carefully phrased job descriptions to match what people really did, we did what had to be done; it was a team."

The major difficulty entered with the examination and subsequent standardization of Transcom's incentive plans for top executives. With the grading complete, Rothborough-Heathcliffe made the announcement that all Transcom managers grade 26 and above were going to be admitted to the Rothborough-Heathcliffe Executive Incentive Plan. Ed Walters complained:

> This was touted as a big deal. The variable compensation at Rothborough-Heathcliffe took the form of both long-term and short-term compensation with higher-ups getting stock options, etc. On the other hand, Transcom's plan for its cash-oriented workforce was very different. This group has little interest in accumulating options for the future. They wanted cash bonuses.

As a result, the Transcom plan had been highly leveraged, with the base salary reflecting perhaps only 40 percent of total compensation and the variable target then, 60 percent, at most. Nonetheless, after much discussion, the Rothborough-Heathcliffe plan was implemented.

It was understood from the beginning that the plan involved deferred long-term compensation. What was not as clearly understood, however, was the meaning of the word "target," which was the basis of the bonus for exceeding the plan's targets. At the end of the first year, 1981, the problem was obvious. Transcom managers on the Rothborough-Heathcliffe Executive Incentive Plan would have done much better if they had remained on their old Transcom incentive plans. The Transcom plans, as in the past, were drawn up to have very difficult targets. When they were exceeded, it really was indicative of extraordinary performance and Transcom managers expected to be rewarded for that.

Unfortunately for these Transcom managers, Rothborough-Heathcliffe required senior management approval to reward performance which exceeded the plan. In this case, such approval was not granted. Patterson understood the subsequent disappointment and exclaimed, "We've been had, but we'll correct this for the future." Patterson was unsuccessful also, however, in securing senior-management approval for a proportionate increase in the bonus. He frequently heard complaints such as this one from the group vice president of textbooks:

> Transcom is like a spoiled child. The managers get very high salaries compared to grade-level counterparts in New Jersey. This is largely due to the incentive components of their compensation plans.

Patterson responded that he is in a different

industry than publishing and must pay celebrity wages or else he will lose his talent to competing high-technology firms. Following these senior-level negotiations, Patterson was able to simply remove his 30 top managers from the corporate plan. They are now compensated on a market plan quite similar to that of the Transcom sales force which, while worse than their old incentive plan, is still far better than the Rothborough-Heathcliffe plan.

Further problems developed in the salary administration area with the adoption of Rothborough-Heathcliffe's payroll cycle. Transcom had a semimonthly payroll, but Rothborough-Heathcliffe had a policy which dictated that, once one earns over $30,000, they go on a monthly schedule. The Transcom personnel director, Sarah Lerner, commented:

> On its face this was a small issue, but, given the education and quantitative bent of the Transcom employees, they soon figured out that, because of the change, they would be losing money, depending on when, in the year you convert. With the next conversion scheduled in two months, they estimated losses of several hundred dollars per employee. The phone calls came in fast and furiously. I have a good rapport, however, with my counterpart at Rothborough-Heathcliffe, who is a Transcom supporter, and we worked it out fine.

All the other rewards systems were rationalized at Transcom to bring them in line with Rothborough-Heathcliffe: profit sharing, shorter vacations, long-term disability, pensions, tuition aid, etc. The difficulty here was the differential appeal of these items to Rothborough-Heathcliffe employees who were long-service employees with an average age of 40 years old versus Transcom employees whose average was just under 30 years old. As a result the new cafete-

ria-style benefits plan involved a good deal more loss of cash for Transcom employees. They were not satisfied with the knowledge that they had traded off cash for a generous and sound pension plan. In response to such grumblings, Lyman Heathcliffe wrote in a memorandum to employees:

> We have one company here. Our integration effort must put us all on the same team. It is important that we cooperate across office doors, between floors, and between units. We have many collaborative projects in the works which require the sharing of ideas and energy. We also are redefining our businesses in ways which necessitate interunit transfers. If our employees are not all treated as equal players with the same set of rules, we will not have the needed flexibility for company and individual growth.

The Career Options Plan

As in other human resource areas, the notion of job rotations and transfers were common practice in Rothborough-Heathcliffe—and a foreign concept to Transcom employees. Rather than greet these interunit relocations with enthusiasm, Ed Walters explained that there was some reticence by Transcom workers:

> Here again is an example of Rothborough-Heathcliffe trying to standardize a human resource program in Transcom as it has been throughout the corporation, and here again problems were encountered because of the way Transcom had been operating previously.

> The career options program encourages and enables Rothborough-Heathcliffe employees to learn of and move to positions in other Rothborough-Heathcliffe units. The problem at Transcom began with the fact that, historically, raiding had been a problem among the groups within Transcom, and Patterson had laid down the law, "Thou shalt not raid." As a result, internal transfers

were simply not done within Transcom. Further, the extremely lean operating staffs at Transcom are not well suited to this type of employee mobility. In the profit-driven mentality at Transcom, managers are highly individualized in their approaches, in the face of intense internal competition for resources including staff. They are extremely lean in support staff especially, with professional exempt staff working 45–50 hours per week, and there is a lot of pressure from being understaffed. Each employee is a critical part of the operation, and managers are loath to lose one. The kind of mobility enjoyed in other Rothborough units is a luxury they can afford with large staffs; at Transcom it simply does not fit.

Requisitions for replacements, and the job-posting program's part in the process continue to be problems at Transcom. Where before the employment process was rapid and largely dependent on the hiring manager, now there are corporate requisitions to fill. Transcom has traditionally played its hiring process "close to the vest;" managers get printouts on financial results daily, and use these to react quickly to market downturns. A fall-off in revenues can only be met with a reduction in costs. So, for example, while a manager may budget a new hire for June, the organization will wait until May to see the financials before moving ahead to hire. Therefore, it is hopeless to get a requisition to New Jersey in advance for posting for other Rothborough-Heathcliffe employees when it is known that it will be months before the position is budgeted. The way the process really runs, a manager will say he wants to fill a position; the president will say, "Go ahead and look around, but let's wait until April and see how things look." So the manager begins to look without out a requisition, without informing Rothborough-Heathcliffe. If a good candidate is found, he or she will be hired. The news goes down to New Jersey that the position is already filled, and Rothborough-Heathcliffe gets angry.

In fact, the requisition itself, when filled, is never seen by the hiring manager. The "A-3 form," as it is called, is required by Rothborough for personnel changes but Transcom has retained its original, simpler form for internal use, and the personnel function at Transcom fills out the forms for corporate's purposes. In this way Transcom managers are kept free from the "bureaucratic jungle" and left to operate as informally, administratively, as possible. Thus, personnel at Transcom serves as a buffer between Rothborough and Transcom managers.

Career Pathing Brochure

Another corporate program, this was begun shortly after the job slotting was accomplished. Rothborough-Heathcliffe took the lead here, writing the "snazzy" brochure describing typical career paths for Transcom employees in several areas. The main problem mentioned by Transcom executives was the difficulty of describing a moving target. While the ladders describe the positions accurately, the positions changed so rapidly that the ladders became less useful as time passed. For example, the "consultant" position has recently been merged into educational services and is now a "trainer." The new practice concept for the organization means that jobs will be merged. While the brochure was correct then when produced, its value had decreased and it was largely obsolete in three months.

The Performance Appraisal Program

Professional staff had performance reviews for the 1981 calendar year performance in the first quarter of 1982. This was the first time ever for formal appraisal at Transcom. In September and October 1982, employees were trained in the use of the program. Walters described this as "a battle we lost." Nonetheless, despite some problems, he feels "anything is better than nothing" and says it is a good exercise, a candid and open exchange with good dialogue. On the other hand, it is very long, a lot of paperwork, which makes it less welcome in Transcom.

Reflection on the Acquisition

Twelve months after the agreement was signed, Patterson was pleased with the merger implementation thus far. He was convinced he had made the right decision from the standpoint of Transcom's shareholders, for the competitive position of the firm, for its management, and for his own personal career.

The changes made at Transcom resulted in no management turnover during the first 12 months. The new emphasis on formal controls and planning seemed to be perceived as welcome improvements in management systems; the changes in the reward systems seemed to be seen as proof that Rothborough-Heathcliffe "cares."

Patterson credited Rothborough-Heathcliffe management for the smooth integration thus far, saying their actions were consciously meant to minimize the career trauma of the acquisition. For example, he pointed to Rothborough's decision to leave Transcom's international structure and management positions unchanged. Realizing the personal significance of titles and reporting relationships to most executives, they saw no value in risking upsetting managers by changing titles to conform to corporate patterns. Patterson said that Rothborough knew that Transcom's true value was in the minds of its employees, and that this sensitivity to them was largely respon-

sible for bringing Transcom through the transition intact.

Comparing his two experiences with merger, Patterson offered these suggestions for acquiring companies: maintain open communications with acquired company managements, responding to all expressed concerns, even those which do not seem "real" to them. Furthermore, once the deal is made, he stressed the importance of living up to its terms. Personal integrity, he claimed, is the critical basis for trust between corporate and subsidiary managers, and without it, serious conflict is inevitable.

As for acquired companies, Patterson emphasized the importance of "looking before you leap." Managements should ask questions and back out immediately if there is a hint of a "con job." Face-to-face negotiation between managements is critical; according to Patterson, "back-door" negotiations will permanently damage relations between parent and subsidiary executives.

Concerns for the Future

In September 1982, Patterson, on his own initiative, changed the company sign outside Transcom's Framingham headquarters to read, "Transcom: A Rothborough-Heathcliffe Company." When the current supply runs out, he said, the same will be added to Transcom's business cards.

But Patterson, looking ahead to Transcom's future, expressed some doubts. From his own experience, and particularly in light of what he had seen at Computech, he asserted that there are actually two phases for an acquired company:

> The first phase is immediate—the turmoil resulting from uncertainty about the effects of the acquisition. The second phase follows in about a year, after the managers have understood the impact of the change. Some

people will discover that they cannot or will not adjust to the changed environment, and these people will slowly begin to leave the organization.

Patterson stated that Transcom had reached the second phase, and that some managers' résumés were "out on the streets" following the first year of Rothborough-Heathcliffe ownership. While there were no clear signs that a mass exodus would happen at Transcom, Patterson said, he would be watching carefully to see.

CASE 5
THE SPLIT*
By Nicholas Lemann†

Early in June of last year, the lawyers of Washington got in the mail a stiff cream-colored card on which was embossed, in a dignified black type, the following message:

> We are pleased to announce that
> having terminated our relationship with
> Jones, Day, Reavis & Pogue
> we will continue the practice of law
> under the name
> Crowell & Moring
> in our offices at
> 1100 Connecticut Avenue, N.W.

For months there had been talk on the streets that this was coming; there had even been brief stories in the newspapers, alluding to "conflicts of interest" that were driving the Jones, Day firm apart. Still! On the

* Reprinted from *The Washington Post Magazine*, March 23, 1980, by permission of the publisher. Copyright © 1980 by the Washington Post. All rights reserved.

† Nicholas Lemann is a staff writer for The Magazine. This article is based on dozens of not-for-quotation interviews with lawyers in Washington and Cleveland, including most of its principal subjects; on internal law firm documents; and on public sources. The conclusions drawn, however, are the author's.

back of that stiff card were the names of 53 lawyers, nearly two thirds of the firm. It was impossible to remember when a law firm had lost so many people at one time— maybe one never had.

The size of the defection accounted for the slightly cheeky tone of the message on the card, the "we will continue the practice of law . . . in our offices," implying that these lawyers who called themselves Crowell & Moring *were* Jones, Day, Reavis & Pogue, rather than some group of rebels. Their attitude seemed especially irreverent when you considered that the firm they were leaving was the sixth largest in the country, with 220 lawyers spread between a home office in Cleveland and branches in Washington and Los Angeles. The Washington office, with 80 lawyers, was the largest outpost here of an out-of-town firm.

It was also an old, eminent, established firm, commonly thought of as the best and most solid law firm west of the Hudson. It counted among its partners many men distinguished not only inside the profession but outside it too: Erwin Griswold, the former dean of the Harvard Law School and solicitor general; James Lynn, the former secretary of Housing and Urban Development and director of the Office of Management and Budget; H. Chapman Rose, the former under secretary of the Treasury; Seth Taft, of the Ohio Tafts; the list went on and on. Its clients were similarly respectable: General Motors, Westinghouse, Republic Steel, TRW, Eaton Corporation, Marathon Oil, Cleveland Trust and many others.

Like the divorce of a prominent clergyman, the rupture of a firm like Jones, Day might be taken as a signal that powerful forces of disharmony were present in a world with a reputation for being stately and secure. The lawyers who got the cream-colored card could only speculate, of course. The internal affairs of law firms were private and secret, not a proper subject of conversation even among close friends.

So even the lawyers of Washington did not know what the Jones, Day split was really all about. They didn't know the extent to which it was a signal of a wider splintering in Washington law practice, and of the growing bad feeling between the capital and the rest of the country. Nor did they know how much it had to do with one proud old man, who had built and ruled the Washington office of Jones, Day only to find himself, at the end of his career, being pressured by his partners in Cleveland and then, to his utter surprise, turned upon by the young lawyers in his own office in Washington.

I: The Gentleman

In 1912, in a town called Villisca in Iowa, someone murdered eight people with an axe. Four years later, in the town of Red Oak, the Villisca Ax Murder case came to trial. It was a big event in southwest Iowa. Important lawyers from the East were arguing the case, and a crowd gathered every day to hear them.

In the crowd was a 17-year-old boy named Welch Pogue, whose father, grandfather, and great-grandfather had been farmers in Iowa. The boy became fascinated by the case—so much so that he went to the courthouse in Red Oak every day after school to watch, and so much so that he decided he would one day leave the farm and become a lawyer himself.

Sixty years later, nearing 80, Welch Pogue was presiding over the Washington office of the law firm that bears his name: Jones, Day, Reavis & Pogue. He was a small, trim man, clear of eye, brisk of step, neat—all in all, beautifully preserved, with hardly a

wrinkle. Mr. Pogue often referred to people of whom he approved as gentlemen, in a way that made it clear that a central part of his vision of himself was that he, too, was a gentleman. He was known to disapprove of flashiness, of ostentation, of strong drink. When younger lawyers in the firm would gather, sometimes, late on Friday afternoons for a drink or two in someone's office, care was taken not to advertise it, because it was likely that Mr. Pogue would not fully approve.

Welch Pogue was of the opinion that the practice of law should be a gentleman's profession. Thus his practice was somewhat at odds with the public perception of the activities of the Washington lawyer. He did not ordinarily lobby on Capitol Hill. He did not throw his weight around at the White House. He did not peddle influence. It was his belief that that kind of work—political work—inevitably led to a lessening of a lawyer's respect in the community.

He did, it was true, practice mainly before the Civil Aeronautics Board, which he had chaired back in the 1940s. He had come to the CAB in 1938, leaving a career as a corporate finance lawyer with the Boston firm of Ropes & Gray because he had sensed that aviation was a growing field, and had quickly advanced at the board, becoming chairman in 1943. In 1946 he had left to go into private practice, and founded a firm called Pogue & Neal. But he saw aviation law as purely a technical field, not a political one, requiring primarily the ability to present complicated rate and route requests to the board.

Pogue was, in his restrained way, also a man of great pride and ambition, and he channeled these impulses into his law firm. Under his leadership, Pogue & Neal grew and prospered; but in the mid-60s Pogue became concerned that it had become too dependent on aviation, especially on the business of its biggest client, Eastern Air Lines. So in 1967 he arranged for Pogue & Neal to merge with the small Washington office of Jones, Day, which was then operating under the name of Jones, Day, Cockley & Reavis. The men in Jones, Day were fine lawyers, Pogue felt, and they were gentlemen, too; and coincidentally, Pogue's son Dick was building a fine career out in the main office in Cleveland. Partly as a sign that Pogue & Neal was not just joining Jones, Day—that, if anything, it was the other way around—the new merged firm in Washington was given a different name from the Cleveland firm—Reavis, Pogue, Neal & Rose.

This was the start of an odd relationship between the firm's offices in Washington and Cleveland. Both offices were run, unlike most law firms, by a single managing partner with absolute power: Pogue in Washington and Jack Reavis in Cleveland. In theory Reavis was Pogue's boss, but in practice Pogue was given a free rein to run his office. Besides the different names, the finances of Washington and Cleveland were largely separate, and Washington was allowed to do its own hiring. It seemed at first as if the two offices were independent of each other—a notion that would one day bring Pogue much pain, but that was off in the future. For now, the Washington office was Pogue's law firm, whose degree of greatness would be a reflection of his efforts.

It was partly for that reason that the Washington office began to expand, and in directions quite apart from the established practice of Cleveland. By and large, the business of Washington lawyers is helping large corporations deal with federal rules and regulations, most of which have been passed under the banner of reform and so-

cial justice. Washington lawyers who are liberals often champion these reforms and then help clients get around them; Washington lawyers who are conservatives (like most of the lawyers in Jones, Day) usually feel that they are misguided and a nuisance, but nonetheless find them a financial bonanza because they increase the need for legal services.

In the years following the merger of Jones, Day and Pogue & Neal, Washington lawyers were therefore fortunate to have in positions of influence Lyndon Johnson and Ralph Nader, who helped spawn the greatest wave of regulatory legislation since the New Deal. The more the government began to regulate businesses, the more new buildings sprang up along K and L streets to house lawyers and lobbyists. Suddenly corporations needed not just the old Washington standbys, tax and antitrust lawyers, but also occupational safety and health lawyers, equal employment opportunity lawyers and, more recently, environmental and energy lawyers.

So Welch Pogue's law firm began to grow very quickly. It hired not only young associates out of law school but also more than a dozen "lateral" partners from other firms or government agencies. Pogue's own practice grew when he gave up the Eastern account in 1972 for that of Pan American World Airways, a bigger client. By 1977, Pan Am was paying the firm $966,275 in annual legal fees, which accounted for the biggest single chunk of its total revenues of perhaps $10 million a year. Partners were making, on the average, well over $100,000 a year. And when the firm opened a Los Angeles office, it changed to a single name nationwide: Jones, Day, Reavis & Pogue. Welch Pogue now had his name on the sixth largest firm in America. He had also, by now, fully created all the elements—the growth, the independence from Cleveland, the specialized practice, the representation of Pan Am—of his own unpleasant fall from power.

On October 17, 1977, the Civil Aeronautics Board voted three to one to award a new route from Dallas/Fort Worth to London to Pan Am, Pogue's client, rejecting a competing bid to get the route by Braniff Airlines, which is based in Dallas. Like all international route awards, this one had to get President Carter's approval. Ordinarily that is a formality.

But on December 21, Carter overturned the CAB's decision and awarded the route to Braniff. Pan Am's chairman, William T. Seawell, immediately issued a statement saying he was "outraged" at Carter's decision, which he attributed to "the kind of political manipulation that the President promised would not characterize his administration."

By this, Seawell was presumably referring to the strong support the Texas congressional delegation had expressed to Carter for Braniff's getting the route, and to the letters from prominent citizens and chambers of commerce all over Texas. The White House insisted that the decision had been made on its merits, but by all accounts Seawell remained convinced that the decision had been a political one (he will not comment on the matter today) and acted on that conviction.

One evening during the time of Carter's decision, a 48-year-old lawyer named Berl Bernhard was invited to a meeting at the home of Averell Harriman to muster support for the Panama Canal treaties. Bernhard was a man whose ideas about Washington law practice were rather different from Welch Pogue's. He had been involved in politics for years—he managed Edmund Muskie's presidential campaign in 1972—and believed that the view that law-

yers should not make politics part of their practice was a narrow and unrealistic one. A lawyer's job in Washington was, in Bernhard's opinion, to look after all his clients' needs, and if that meant politics and lobbying, fine.

At the Harrimans' home that night, William T. Coleman, the former secretary of Transportation and a member of the Pan Am board, took Bernhard aside. The two men were old friends, having met when they both worked on a White House civil rights conference in the Johnson administration. Coleman asked Bernhard if he would be interested in taking over the Washington representation of Pan Am. Bernhard said he would.

The next week, Sol M. Linowitz, the negotiator of the canal treaties and another member of the Pan Am board and old friend of Bernhard's (Linowitz and Ed Muskie had been law school classmates at Cornell), called Bernhard and discussed the matter further. Bernhard talked to his partners about it. Seawell came down to Washington for more talks. On January 1, 1978, Pan Am officially switched its Washington legal account from the firm of Jones, Day, Reavis & Pogue to the firm of Verner, Liipfert, Bernhard & McPherson.

There was a nice irony, instructive about the ways of Washington, in the way the contact between Bernhard and Pan Am had been made. The hostess at the Harriman house that night, Pamela Harriman, was herself on the board of Braniff, the source of Pan Am's misery.

Mrs. Harriman, through a spokesman, declines to say whether she took part in Braniff's effort to get the Dallas-to-London route; but the point is that Pan Am's interests were being looked after at a party given by Pan Am's arch-rival, the primary purpose of which was to muster the support of

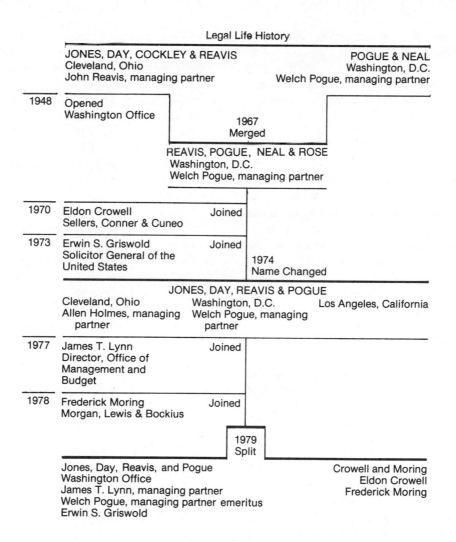

Legal Life History

JONES, DAY, COCKLEY & REAVIS
Cleveland, Ohio
John Reavis, managing partner

POGUE & NEAL
Washington, D.C.
Welch Pogue, managing partner

1948   Opened
Washington Office

1967
Merged

REAVIS, POGUE, NEAL & ROSE
Washington, D.C.
Welch Pogue, managing partner

1970   Eldon Crowell   Joined
Sellers, Conner & Cuneo

1973   Erwin S. Griswold   Joined
Solicitor General of the   1974
United States   Name Changed

JONES, DAY, REAVIS & POGUE
Cleveland, Ohio   Washington, D.C.   Los Angeles, California
Allen Holmes, managing   Welch Pogue, managing
       partner   partner

1977   James T. Lynn   Joined
Director, Office of
Management and
Budget

1978   Frederick Moring   Joined
Morgan, Lewis & Bockius

1979
Split

Jones, Day, Reavis, and Pogue   Crowell and Moring
Washington Office   Eldon Crowell
James T. Lynn, managing partner   Frederick Moring
Welch Pogue, managing partner emeritus
Erwin S. Griswold

people interested in Pan Am, people interested in Braniff, and many others, for a government policy. The ability of all those people to do business with one another transcended their connections of the moment to one or another private or public interest group; no doubt long after they had all switched jobs and clients, they would still be friends. It was a different world from that of the Cleveland lawyers in Jones, Day, with their single-minded lifelong devotion

to a few large clients. In Washington, lawyers moved from client to client and from government to private practice, and whether you were in the game was more important than which side you were on.

When Seawell broke the news that he was switching law firms to Welch Pogue, he said only that the relationship had not worked out as he had hoped. But Pogue knew perfectly well that Seawell had had his heart set on the Dallas-to-London route. He remained unshaken in his conviction that a lawyer should not attempt to exercise political clout; he had never held himself out as someone who would do that. Still, Pogue and his law firm in Washington had just lost their biggest client.

II: The Succession

As a practical matter, the loss of Pan Am was not a mortal threat to the Washington office of Jones, Day, Reavis & Pogue. It did mean, however, that Welch Pogue was no longer the biggest income-producer in the office, and there began to be more and more talk, in those early months of 1978, about who his successor as managing partner would be. After all, he would be 79 that fall.

Certainly one possibility was James Lynn, who had just finished his triumphal tour of Cabinet offices. Lynn was a short, no-nonsense, intelligent, garrulous man who had grown up and gone to college in Cleveland and had spent 18 years in the Cleveland office of Jones, Day before joining the Nixon administration. His ties to Cleveland and his prominent name were points in his favor. He was ambitious—what Washington lawyer wasn't?—but he had said when he came to the Washington office that he was not interested in management. That seemed to make his ascension to the managing partnership unlikely.

The other obvious candidate was Eldon Crowell, the head of the firm's government contracts department, who with the loss of Pan Am had become the biggest source of business in the office and for that reason alone a major figure. Crowell, whose friends called him by his childhood nickname, Took, was in his early 50s, and on first encounter he gave the impression of being a man of elegance and refinement. He dressed elegantly. He spoke elegantly. He

was a graduate of Princeton and of the University of Virginia Law School and on the whole he seemed to be cut from a more Eastern and sophisticated cloth than the Midwesterners who ran Jones, Day.

On the rare occasions when Crowell went to the Jones, Day Cleveland offices, they struck him as—well, *oaken* was the word that came to mind. They bespoke an entirely different way of life and set of beliefs from the bright, airy Washington offices, with their hallways full of modern art. The Cleveland lawyers were business lawyers, fighting arms of the large corporations they represented; whereas Crowell's lifeblood was his expertise in a Washington procedure, which he lent to a wide range of clients.

Crowell had started his legal career in 1951, when he joined the firm of Sellers, Conner & Cuneo, which under the direction of Gilbert Cuneo had become the leading government contracts firm in Washington. Cuneo's great stroke of good fortune as a lawyer had come in 1961, when Robert McNamara took over the Defense Department and announced that most Pentagon contracts would henceforth be awarded on a fixed-price basis, ending the cost-plus-fixed-fee arrangement that had prevailed during the Eisenhower years. The Defense Department wasn't going to guarantee contractors their profits any more.

What that often meant was that the big defense contractors would bid a low price in order to get a contract, and then litigate the agreed-upon price upward by claiming that the conditions on which the contract was based had changed. That was where Gilbert Cuneo came in.

As the 60s ended, the government moved away from fixed-price contracts; but by that time there were so many complicated contracts, so many claims and counter-claims, and so many disputes between prime contractors and subcontractors, that business for the contracts lawyers continued to boom. In 1970 Took Crowell and three other lawyers left Sellers, Conner, where Crowell had been second fiddle to Cuneo, and joined Jones, Day, where in contracts Crowell was the number one man. Since then he had done extremely well. Now, in 1978, he was the second most powerful, and arguably the single most important, partner in the entire Washington office.

It was a sign of Crowell's importance that he now had a role in the management of the firm, albeit a small one. He was one of five members of a Washington executive committee that Welch Pogue had appointed early in 1978, indicating perhaps that Pogue was now willing to share his power and even possibly to pass it on to the kind of management committee that most firms had. But Crowell would soon find out that the power of the Washington executive committee was less than it appeared to be.

One day in September Pogue called the members of the executive committee together and told them he was thinking of bringing two new partners into the Washington office: Jonathan Rose and Joe Sims, both young men in their 30s, well-credentialed, who had worked in the antitrust division of the Justice Department under Donald Baker, a former head of the division who had joined Jones, Day as a partner a few months before.

The members of the executive committee met and decided that was a bad idea, and they told Pogue they thought so. For one thing, there wasn't much existing antitrust business in the Washington office of Jones, Day, so for the time being Rose and Sims would have to be supported out of the other partners' earnings, which already were supporting Donald Baker. It didn't seem to be a

rational business move. But Allen Holmes, who by now had succeeded Jack Reavis as the managing partner in Cleveland, was an antitrust specialist, and so was Welch Pogue's son Dick, who was Holmes's heir apparent. It looked as if this might be their plan—as if Cleveland telling Washington who its partners would be. Not only that, when the committee met with Don Baker, it was clear that he thought the bringing in of Rose and Sims had been worked out long before. Evidently somebody had told him that—evidently someone in Cleveland, because Welch Pogue insisted that the decision was his to make and that he hadn't made it yet.

Pogue brought up the matter of Rose and Sims before the entire Washington partnership at a meeting one Friday in September. After he had explained the proposition, Baker and several others spoke in favor of it. Then the members of the executive committee spoke in opposition. It seemed to those who wanted to bring in Rose and Sims that Took Crowell and the others were being especially vocal and uncooperative about the whole thing. They seemed to be deeply suspicious of the Cleveland office, and to think of themselves as members of an entirely different law firm. They even had the bad taste to hint that, because Jon Rose was the son of a senior partner, Chapman Rose, nepotism was a more important factor than his first-rate qualifications in the move to bring him into the firm. They didn't recognize that there came a time, when men of quality were involved, to put aside local concerns and be team players.

The meeting ended inconclusively, as meetings at Jones, Day always did, because the final decision would rest with Pogue. But a few days later, after a trip to Cleveland, he announced that Rose and Sims would indeed be taken on. Washington would pay half their salaries, and Cleveland would pay half and provide them with plenty of business. This did not make the executive committee happy; to them, this still had a Cleveland scent.

And it also began to seem, in subtle ways, that Cleveland was not happy with the Washington executive committee. John Macleod, an earnest young partner who represented coal mines in safety proceedings, served on the executive committee, and assisted Pogue in management under the title of "assistant to the Washington managing partner," dealt fairly often with the Cleveland office. As the fall wore on, Macleod began to get the distinct feeling that the leadership there was displeased with the executive committee, and also felt more coolly toward him than it once had.

What he—and, for that matter, Crowell—didn't know was that the two managing partners, Welch Pogue and Allen Holmes, were in those months deciding who would replace Pogue. By the end of the year they had made up their minds. There would be a single managing partner, not a committee. It would not be Took Crowell. It would be Jim Lynn.

III: The Ouster

On Saturday evening, January 13, 1979, Mr. and Mrs. Eldon Crowell gave a dinner at the Chevy Chase Club for Robert W. Oliver. Oliver had worked for Pogue at the CAB back in the 1940s and had been the third member of Pogue & Neal. Now he was retiring.

It was a nice occasion. Some of Oliver's friends were there, and some of his partners, and some of his business associates. The men wore black tie and almost all of them made toasts to Oliver.

The first thing Monday morning, January 15, Welch Pogue's secretary called Crowell and said Mr. Pogue wanted to see him. When would be convenient? she asked. Ten-thirty, said Crowell.

At 10:30, Crowell went to Pogue's office. Pogue told him how nice he thought the party for Oliver had been. Then he got down to business. He said that the government contracts group had been an enormously successful operation. Because of its very success, Pogue said, it had created problems for the firm.

Therefore, said Pogue, the firm had made the decision that it would be in the best interests of the firm for Crowell and three other government contracts partners to leave.

Crowell was taken completely by surprise. How could one be too successful? Whose idea was this? He asked Pogue who was aware of this decision. Pogue mentioned several partners in Washington, and, of course, the Cleveland management.

Crowell said he wanted to talk to the other three partners in the government contracts group about it. Pogue said that would be fine. He asked Crowell to come back on Wednesday with his response, and not to tell anyone but those three men. He also handed Crowell a strange two-page memorandum, entitled "Points Discussed" and neither signed by nor addressed to anyone, which summarized what he had just said.

When he left Pogue's office, Crowell quickly discovered that the government contracts partners were scattered all over the country, and he went back and told Pogue he needed more time because he wanted to tell them all in person. Pogue said that would be fine.

In any event, by the end of the week everyone in the firm knew, and then all hell broke loose. Perhaps Pogue had not imagined that everyone would find out he wanted the government contracts partners to leave; certainly he had not imagined how upset everyone would be when the word got out.

Partners all over the firm, especially the younger ones, were in a state of great agitation. There were meetings, frantic phone calls to Cleveland, speculation—and behind it all was the idea that something outrageous had occurred. The biggest and most successful section of Jones, Day/Washington was being kicked out, without any consultation among the partnership. At best, it was a foolish business decision made unilaterally by Welch Pogue; at worst it was a case of lawyers in Cleveland—people not even in the Washington office—meddling in Washington affairs in the most divisive and financially foolish way possible. By now there were also rumors that Jim Lynn would succeed Pogue, and, while everyone liked and respected Lynn, his secret selection was yet another example of government from outside.

On Friday, several partners went to see Pogue to ask him to change his mind, and he refused. In the episode of Rose and Sims, most of the young partners had been mildly annoyed but had not really turned their ill will toward Pogue. Now things had changed; now they had lost their faith in Pogue's judgment and in his independence from Cleveland. It was sad, but it was true.

That weekend, several young partners went down to the office to try to figure out some organized response to the ouster of the government contracts group. They thought about sending a resolution to the Cleveland management, expressing the view that the ouster was unacceptable. But that would not be binding.

Then another idea began to emerge: they would fire Welch Pogue as managing partner.

There was a provision for this in the firm's partnership agreement. It said that if partners representing two thirds of the ownership shares in the Washington office voted to change the office's management, their votes would be binding.

If it were right that asking Crowell to leave had been Pogue's decision, as he insisted it was, then the only way to void that decision was to remove Pogue from the managing partnership. Of course, most people believed the ouster had really been more Cleveland's decision than Pogue's, but if that were so, firing Pogue would show Cleveland how angry everyone was. And what could Cleveland do in response, with a new management in place in Washington?

So the group in the office that weekend drafted a document. It was brief, just two paragraphs, bore the title, "Certification to Cleveland Managing Partner," and was attached to a regretful but firm cover letter from John Macleod. It announced the replacement of Welch Pogue by the five-member Washington executive committee.

On Monday and Tuesday, the document was drawn up and signed, and on Tuesday afternoon one of the signers, a young partner named Dick Mathias, was dispatched to Cleveland with a copy.

As soon as Mathias was gone, John Macleod went to Pogue's office and broke the news to him. It was obviously a difficult meeting, for Macleod as well as for Pogue; Macleod had been Pogue's assistant, and had come to think of himself as something of a confidant and protégé of the old man's.

It was all mercifully brief. Pogue said he had had a difficult day and preferred not to discuss this at length until later. Macleod had heard rumors that the people in Cleveland were saying that all this trouble was Washington's affair, and he guessed Pogue was disappointed that Cleveland wasn't backing him up more.

More than that, Pogue seemed to be ending his career by, intentionally or not, making an irrational move that was now backfiring in a way that would bring him great personal embarrassment. Why would he do such a thing? Perhaps it was for the sake of his son Dick, who would be taking over the management of Jones, Day in just a few years and who would have been greatly hampered in that role by the strong presence in Washington of Took Crowell. Perhaps it was to spare Jim Lynn the trouble of having to contend with a strong rival from the start of his tenure as managing partner. Perhaps, being near the end of his career and well aware that it was the *firm* and not just the Washington office that now bore his name and would live on no matter what happened to him now, he was loath to defy Allen Holmes. In any event, Macleod had the strong impression, although Pogue never said so, that Pogue felt his young assistant, and all the other young lawyers whose careers he had nurtured, had in the end betrayed him.

As for Pogue, he realized that this was not something he could fight, and so the best thing would be for him to hide his true feelings. He had had some practice at this, years before when he had been in college at the University of Nebraska and had spent his free time acting in a traveling student troupe. He would have to be an actor now.

So, on Friday, January 26, at a meeting of the Washington partnership, Welch Pogue resigned from the managing partnership, and Crowell gave a little talk, praising the great contributions of Pogue to the firm and explaining that now the time had come for a committee to take over.

It still remained for the new management to make its peace with Cleveland, so a com-

mittee on inter-office relations was formed, and it began to discuss the idea of the two managements getting together to talk. There were some difficulties in scheduling the meeting—difficulties that, in truth, had a mysterious edge to them, in that the Cleveland people seemed positively loath to talk about the agenda for the meeting at all—but after a few delays Cleveland called and proposed a definite time and place. They would all get together in Washington, at 8:00 o'clock on the morning of Wednesday, February 14, for a breakfast at the Metropolitan Club.

IV: The Massacre

Valentine's Day, 1979, was a cold, miserable day. The day before, 5.6 inches of snow had fallen on Washington, tying up traffic and closing schools. At the Metropolitan Club, a four-story brick edifice on I Street that exudes stolidity, the five members of the Washington executive committee sat down with the Cleveland managing partner, Allen Holmes, and several other lawyers from the Cleveland and Washington offices.

Eldon Crowell stood up and said that, on behalf of the new management of the Washington office of Jones, Day, Reavis & Pogue, he wanted to welcome the Cleveland management to Washington, and to express the hope that the two managements could work fruitfully together to resolve the differences of the past and move forward to even greater success in the future.

Then Allen Holmes got up. He was a big, white-haired man of 59, wearing black-framed glasses. He suffered periodically from attacks of a severe neurological disease called Guillain-Barre Syndrome that had left his arms and legs weak and spindly. During the attacks, each of which was more severe than the last, his lungs would collapse and his body would become completely paralyzed, and he would have to spend months in a hospital bed, breathing through a tube. He was, obviously, an extremely determined man, having risen to the leadership of the firm and to national prominence in the field of antitrust law. He had a first-rate mind. He particularly prided himself on his rationality, his powers of analysis, his resistance to illogic and emotionalism.

Holmes said that he saw matters somewhat differently from Crowell. As he was speaking, an eight-page memo from him was being placed in the mail slot of each of the partners in the Washington office, in a sealed envelope.

The memo explained that because so many large corporations were sending more and more of their legal business to their in-house counsels, which were far less expensive than law firms, the law firms had to become more competitive. They had to be able "to respond on what I would term a transactional basis to complex, wide-ranging litigation and other legal problems pertaining to a variety of corporate interests."

The "Government Contracts Group," the memo said, had been very successful, but its success had "created obstacles to the growth of our national practice." The group had clients that might be on the other side of litigation from Jones, Day's regular corporate clients.

It had an "individual possessory approach" toward its clients. It was not interested in building a national practice.

Therefore, Holmes wrote, "I regretfully conclude that the rapid growth of the Government Contracts Group has created an imbalance in our Washington office, a potential for conflicts in representation, and a philosophical dichotomy which have made the Group incompatible with the national

firm at which we have aimed. . . . Accordingly, I am opening discussions with the management of the Washington Office looking toward an open, amicable and negotiated settlement which will preserve those elements in Washington vital to our national practice."

There was no way around it. If the issue were to be forced, all the partners in Washington, Cleveland, and Los Angeles would decide it, and Holmes clearly had the votes. Crowell and his group and the new management were out.

To Allen Holmes, it was perfectly obvious that this would happen; in fact, as early as 1976 his analysis of the situation had led him to the conclusion that there would be a split one day. He had never considered letting the five-man committee run the office. Jones, Day was one law firm, and it had to be under the control of the managing partner in Cleveland. It had to be able to muster its forces quickly and efficiently, to handle the biggest and toughest corporate mergers and stock offerings and law suits without clearing everything through a lot of committees. It couldn't be a confederation of dukes who had to be consulted at every turn. Lately even young law students applying for jobs at Jones, Day/Washington had begun to say they were hearing that the office was a fine place to go if you were interested in government contracts, but that it did not really offer a well-rounded practice. In Holmes's mind, there was not the slightest question about what had to be done.

In point of fact, Washington had for years mystified Holmes. Just as every newspaper editor believes somewhere deep down that his Washington correspondent has gotten a little too close to the officials he covers, just as every chief executive officer believes his Washington vice president to be more a creature of Washington than of the corporation he works for, so Allen Holmes believed that Washington can be treacherous ground for lawyers. They begin to represent many different clients before a single agency, and soon they fall into the live and let live atmosphere of Washington. They know that if they push too hard for one client, they may lose the relationship with the agency that will permit them to represent other clients. The lawyers begin to tell their clients what the agency wants, rather than telling the agency what the client wants. They lose their sharp cutting edge.

V: The Split

A few diehards clung to the idea of making a new peace, but really it was clear after Valentine's Day that many more lawyers than the 15 or so who seemed to fall under Holmes's directive were going to leave the firm. The only question was who would go where. By the following weekend, Crowell and a few others were sitting down and working out rough estimates of the budget for the new firm they would start. Most of the partners—27 of 43—decided to leave Jones, Day. They were Washington lawyers; they had little interest in a national practice of the kind Holmes had in mind; and by now they were emotionally hostile to Holmes and the brusque management-from-afar that he represented. Such a man—a man who would summarily dismiss his own partners—was not someone you wanted to practice law with.

The ones who stayed were by and large the older partners (along, of course, with Rose and Sims) and those with closer ties to Cleveland and more traditional views about how a law firm should be run. The only older man that the group leaving had real hopes of luring away was Dean Erwin Griswold. The dean was perhaps the most prominent member of the firm. There was

already a building at Harvard named after him; he had argued 120 cases before the Supreme Court, more than anyone alive; and at 74, he had the kind of crusty, independent demeanor that seemed to signal that whichever side he was on was the right side. Nothing would legitimate the new firm so much as his presence.

There was some basis for thinking he might leave. He was known to have disapproved of the abrupt dismissal of Crowell in January and had flown to Cleveland to have a talk with Allen Holmes about it. He had been at the Valentine's Day breakfast and had been vocally surprised and upset at what Holmes had done there. The dean was primarily involved in litigating cases in the higher courts, and he worked mainly with the associates. So some of the associates who had worked with him most closely were dispatched to try to convince him to come with the new group.

But the dean was from Cleveland originally, had practiced briefly there as a young man, and still felt strong ties to the city. He also liked the idea of a national firm, and Welch Pogue and Chappie Rose were his old and dear friends. So, while it was true he had not entirely approved of the way the separation had been handled, he decided to stay.

Then there was the question of the associates, who did not bring business with them but did much of the firm's work and produced about three times as much income as they were paid. On Valentine's Day both groups had talked to the associates, and later each group had circulated a prospectus to them, explaining how it intended to practice law. They were valuable commodities.

On Sunday, February 18, Lionel Epstein, one of the partners who would be staying, had a party to which all of the associates were invited. Epstein was a man of independent wealth, and he lived in a large house with large grounds on Oregon Avenue, filled with his impressive collection of the works of Edvard Munch and other artists.

Allen Holmes and Dick Pogue were among those at the party, and they had personal chats with many of the associates. Then Holmes gave a little speech. He said the Washington office would continue to grow and prosper, that it would be a good place to work. One of the associates asked him why he had fired the government contracts group. Holmes said that that was past history, and he didn't want to relive it. To most of the associates, caught up as they were in the outrage at what Holmes had done, that wasn't the answer they were looking for. Besides, most of the partners they worked with would be leaving. In the end, 26 of them decided to leave Jones Day, and only 10 stayed.

After that, it was mostly details. All the paralegals and secretaries and copier operators had to decide whether to stay or leave. There were negotiations over the division of the firm's property, at which it was decided that those who were leaving would keep the law library and the firm's lease to the top four floors of 1100 Connecticut Avenue, since they represented a majority of the office, and that in return they would forfeit their pension rights. After some debate, the group that was leaving decided on the name of Crowell & Moring—it was short, and the inclusion of the name of Frederick Moring, an energy lawyer, would signify that they did not intend to be just a government contracts firm. For several months the two groups practiced in the same offices while Jones, Day looked for a new space; the receptionists answered the phone by saying simply "law offices." For the most part, everyone got along and tried not to bear ill will; after all, they were gentlemen.

June 1, 1979, was the day the partnership

officially dissolved and Crowell & Moring officially opened its doors. The day before that, one of the Crowell & Moring partners, Philip Fleming, decided to go around and shake the hand of every partner who would be staying with Jones, Day and say how much he had enjoyed practicing law together. Fleming was a lanky, gentle man who had served on the Washington executive committee but had tried hard to hold the firm together, and had been genuinely upset that it came apart.

When Fleming got to Welch Pogue's office, he said he had enjoyed it and that he was sorry it had worked out the way it had. He *was* sorry. He had worked for Pogue for 22 years, ever since he came to Pogue & Neal right out of law school. Pogue said he thought Fleming had always been fair. He said he appreciated that. And then the old man started to cry.

There was no real loser in the split, unless it was Pogue. Crowell & Moring has prospered, and has aggressively recruited new associates. Jones, Day, under Lynn's leadership, brought in several partners and associates from Cleveland to fill the gaps left after the split, and began hiring several more from outside. There is plenty of legal business in Washington to go around.

On November 19, 1979, Jones, Day moved into its new office, an expensive-looking suite with off-white walls, thick gray carpets, and chrome name plates outside every door. The next day, the lawyers of Washington got in the mail another stiff cream-colored card on which was embossed, in a dignified black type, the following message:

> Jones, Day, Reavis & Pogue
> announces that
> its Washington office
> has moved to
> 1735 Eye Street, N.W.

CASE 6
WESTON CORPORATION:
THE AMHERST PLANT
Pamela A. Posey and
Jeffrey A. Sonnenfeld

Tom Newton stared at the three sobbing older women who sat before him and wondered what he could possibly do for them. The women, Joan, Alice, and Martha, were each in their early 60s and had been employed at Amherst for more than 30 years. They were close friends, having worked in the same operations area for 25 years. A few days before, they had been transferred to new departments separate from each other. Joan was put on the night shift for light maintenance work; Alice was put on a machine operating job, which had always frightened her; and Martha was put on a complex automated process which would require training to operate. All three were not only upset about the collapse of their department, but were dismayed in their assignments and separation. They felt that with so many years of dedicated service to the plant they deserved better consideration than this. Tom realized that their complaints might be symptomatic of the larger problems facing him at Amherst.

After the women left, Tom gazed out the office window toward the hazy skyline of Williston, and wondered about the future of the Amherst plant, Weston Corporation's oldest manufacturing facility. He had been the general manager at Amherst for three years, and had become increasingly aware of the special problems confronting a workforce employed in a plant which technological change was making obsolete. During his time as general manager, Tom had

found himself caught in a bind between addressing the pressing operations problems created by new markets and technologies on one hand, and addressing the chronic personnel issues on the other.

The Amherst Plant

The Weston Corporation, a producer of heavy industrial equipment, was founded in 1911. Its Amherst plant, the flagship of its three national manufacturing facilities, was the original company headquarters and occupied 150 acres of rolling meadows on the western border of the city of Williston. Amherst itself had been designed as a company town, with housing, stores, and recreational facilities located within the perimeter of company land. In the early 1900s, most employees had lived in the company-owned housing adjacent to the three manufacturing buildings. Amherst was a self-contained social and recreational center.

The environment generated a close-knit plant culture, which continued to grow and develop into the 1920s and 1930s. Amherst in the 1920s was so popular that, in spite of the general economic boom which the country enjoyed, special connections and family ties were often necessary to secure employment there. Employee relations were good, the plant was safe and efficient, and the market was healthy and growing. By 1935, the Amherst plant employed nearly 30,000 workers.

Following World War II, the situation began to change. The wide accessibility of transportation and increased mobility of the population created shifts in residential patterns. Employees began to move away from company housing and into more distant suburban areas. They were drawn away from the social amenities that had always been offered by Amherst. The plant became a job site rather than a family and social center. Technological advances had generated change in the manufacturing processes for the equipment produced at Amherst; and in 1965, the Weston Corporation decided that the new technologies demanded newer, more efficient production facilities. By 1970, new plants had been constructed near St. Louis and Houston, and many of Amherst's operations had been transferred to these sites. Many young workers, too, transferred to the new plants.

Amherst, in 1981, retained its core manufacturing processes. Operations had been consolidated into one building where newer technologically advanced production equipment had been installed. The other two buildings were shut down and boarded up: employees felt that these would be allowed to fall into the same state of dilapidation that the once-vital family housing units had suffered. The reduction of physical space needs was accompanied by large layoffs, and the current workforce was composed of fewer than 5,000 employees. The workers who remained after the layoffs were those with greatest seniority, and the average age of the Amherst work force was now over 50. Many workers were on the same jobs they had performed two or three decades ago, yet were using different technologies in a vastly different world. Fully one third were over age 55.

The Workforce

The older workers who once found Amherst to be the social center of their lives now spoke with anger about the lack of appreciation management had shown them by pulling them away from comfortable jobs they had mastered and placing them in new jobs with vastly different operation methods. Many of the older managers had been downgraded in rank so they could be retained through layoffs. They felt that their career opportunities, in spite of long service and good performance reviews, had eroded seriously. Although the Amherst plant remained profitable (sales had increased steadily by 10 percent per year since 1972), many workers were convinced that the plant would soon be closed completely.

Tom Newton had challenged these feelings, arguing that Amherst was still and would remain a significant operation for Weston Corporation. He did, however, state that new market pressures and continually developing technological changes were forcing the company to adopt different operating policies and procedures.

The Current Situation

The current plant problems were provoked by a changeover from an outdated technology to a more advanced and mechanized production process. More layoffs were imminent, retraining was a necessity, and some shifting of personnel to more complex and demanding tasks would have to occur.

Production operations previously performed by small work teams were now completed by new equipment requiring only a single operator. Development of new training programs designed to provide workers with skills needed to operate the new equipment met with resistance. Not only was the technology different, but old well-established social relationships were being broken up to better meet the demands of the new processes. Union-plant relationships were still positive, but union rules precluded replacing those employees having seniority with younger workers more accustomed to the newer production methods.

Tom knew he had to devise a plan to meet the needs of his plant and the Weston Corporation, but was worried about the apparently insurmountable obstacles facing him as plant manager. He had to devise a training program for workers to teach them the new production processes; yet the workers requiring training were resistant to the changes which had caused such upheaval in their lives. Employee morale was at an all-time low, further complicating the situation he faced.

Tom wondered if he should bring the union in, but was concerned about setting a precedent for future decisions. He wondered if part of the answer lay in improved communications, yet knew that his management staff had already worked hard in this area.

Several days before, Tom had held a meeting with his employee development staff, and as he gazed out the window, he thought about the questions he had posed for them to consider.

> How do we develop programs to retrain workers into new technologies when those workers resist the technological and work environment changes that necessarily result? Training programs are critical, but what types are most appropriate? We cannot replace the workers: they have seniority and most are not ready to retire even if we offered it early. The corporate culture supports a philosophy of lifetime employment, but I have a responsibility to keep this plant profitable as well as to the employees. How can we design and implement training programs capable of meeting both objectives now?

CASE 7
WEYMOUTH STEEL CORPORATION
Linda McJ. Micheli and
Thomas J. C. Raymond

In the fall of 1979, Weymouth Steel Corporation found itself with both good news and

bad news to communicate to its salaried employees. The good news would affect all salaried employees, the bad news only some. When Chairman of the Board Carl Weymouth and his staff discussed the matter, they realized that they faced a familiar but difficult task in corporate communication—a task, moreover, that seemed to encourage reappraisal of some of Weymouth's traditional approaches to employee communication.

Good News And Bad News

The good news was that nearly all salaried employees would be receiving salary increases and improved benefits. Provisions for retirement, vacations, medical and dental care, life insurance, and stock ownership were liberalized or improved in a variety of ways. (Highlights of the changes can be found in Exhibit 1.) While some of the changes derived from provisions of the most recent union contract, others resulted from Weymouth's ongoing adjustment of salaries and benefits. Ordinarily, such changes were communicated to employees through personnel bulletins and regular issues of the appropriate Weymouth publications—*Metal News* for salaried employees, *The Open Hearth* for hourly employees.

The bad news was that the company anticipated that it would have to terminate a sizable number of its employees—salaried as well as hourly. Long recognized as a highly cyclical business, the steel industry was entering one of its periodic slumps. In addition, like all U.S. steelmakers, Weymouth was encountering increasingly stiff competition from overseas companies. In the next 18 months, Weymouth's business was likely to fall off 25 percent. At the same time, a variety of forces intensified the company's need for capital. To become more competitive with European and Japanese

Exhibit 1   **Highlights of 1979 Improvements in Salaried Employee Compensation**

Salaries

Management Roll Employees

Salary Increases.   In recognition of continuing levels of high performance and the need for individual extra effort, the company has decided that most eligible Management Roll employees in grades 9 and 10 may be given a salary increase effective October 1. This adjustment is discretionary and may vary based on performance but may not increase salaries beyond the new salary range maximums. Employees will be notified of their increases personally by their supervisors.

Employees hired on or after May 1, 1979, are not immediately eligible for this increase. Assuming acceptable performance, management, at its discretion, may authorize an increase any time after a minimum of six months service.

Performance Increase Supplements.   In addition to the salary increases, performance increase quotas for 1980 will be supplemented by an amount that reflects the Cost-of-Living Allowance rise forecasted from September 1979 to June 1980. Guidelines for granting performance salary increases have been modified to provide greater participation in the performance increase supplements. Within the next few weeks, you will receive details of the revised program from your staff vice president or division general manager.

Premium Payments—Seven-Day Operations.   Effective November 1, 1979, seven-day operations employees (except for those in steelmaking incentive operations) will be paid time and one-quarter for Sunday work. The new Sunday rate applies to hours that do not otherwise qualify for a greater overtime or holiday premium.

Supplemental Compensation Roll

Performance Increase Supplements.   Salary adjustments for Supplemental Compensation Roll employees will continue to reflect individual performance and contributions to the success of the company.

For 1980 the performance increase quotas will be supplemented by an amount that reflects the COLA rise from September 1979 to June 1980 (as for MR employees), and by the salary increase approved for employees in grades 9 and 10.

Vacations and Leaves

Employees in grades 9 and above will be eligible for eight "additional" vacation days in 1980, and nine each in 1981 and 1982. The first five of these days each year will be taken as vacation time. For employees below grade 13, the balance will be paid in lieu at year end unless management directs that time off be taken. Here is how vacation eligibility will look for grades 9–12:

Exhibit 1 (*continued*)

Years of Service	Regular Vacation Days	"Additional" Vacation Days				
		Time Off	Pay-in-Lieu		Total Days	
			1980	1981 & 1982	1980	1981 & 1982
1	15	5	3	4	23	24
10	20	5	3	4	28	29
20	25	5	3	4	33	34

For employees in grades 13 and above, the "additional" vacation days beyond five each year will be banked under the new vacation banking plan. Vacation eligibility for employees in grades 13 and above will be:

Years of Service	Regular Vacation Days	"Additional" Vacation Days				
		Time Off	Banked Days		Total Days	
			1980	1981 & 1982	1980	1981 & 1982
1	20	5	3	4	28	29
20	25	5	3	4	33	34

For employees in grades 13 and above, the first five "additional" days and the fifth week of regular vacation will be banked automatically if not taken by year end. No special request will be required. Employees in grades 9–12 (as well as General Salary Roll employees) may elect, if they wish, to have any time the company has directed be taken as pay-in-lieu banked instead.

Under the new vacation banking plan, banked days will be paid at retirement or other termination at the salary rate then in effect, but never less than 107 percent of the salary in effect at the time banking took place.

In addition to the liberal vacation provisions, 40 holidays have been announced for the next three years. Employees below grade 13 also will become eligible for a compensatory day in December of 1979, 1980, and 1981. This day will not apply to employees in grades 13 and above.

One change will be of particular interest to the small but growing number of employees whose spouses are also company salaried employees. If an employee is geographically transferred and the spouse must leave company employment because a suitable employment with the company is not available immediately in the new location, an unpaid leave of up to three years may be granted. This change allows the spouse a greater opportunity to maintain company service until reemployment is possible.

Disability Benefits

On January 1, 1981, employees in salary grades 9–12 will become eligible for disability benefits presently available only to employees in salary grades 13 and above. That means all employees in grades 9 and above will be eligible for:

Exhibit 1 (*continued*)

- Six months of full pay instead of three months.
- Twelve months of benefits at 60 percent of base salary after full pay has been exhausted, instead of 10 months.
- Thereafter, 50 percent of base salary will be paid until age 65 instead of being limited to a period equal to length of service. (Payments could extend beyond 65 if the employee became disabled after reaching age 63.)

Benefit Plan Eligibility

New Management Roll employees hired on or after October 1, 1979, will be eligible on date of hire for medical, disability, and life insurance benefits. Previously, eligibility for medical and disability benefits began the first day of the third month after hire and for life insurance the first day of the month after the month of hire.

Savings and Stock Investment Plan

A number of changes have been made to the Savings and Stock Investment Plan to make it more responsive to employee needs. Included in the changes are:

- *Earlier maturity*—Starting with the 1980 Class, vesting will occur on June 30 of the third year after a Class closes. Partial vesting on a monthly basis over the course of the third year will be eliminated. Distribution of assets will be made as soon as practicable after the Class is vested for those who elect to take their assets out of the plan.
- *Additional savings*—Employees who contribute 10 percent of their salary—the highest amount matched by company contributions—will be able to contribute up to another 5 percent. The amount above 10 percent will not be matched by the company. The extra 5 percent provides an opportunity to invest more, with tax-deferred accumulation of earnings. Earnings on these savings are not taxable while in the plan.
- *Income fund*—The Income Fund is extended as a regular investment option to all members of the plan. The fund had been limited to those 50 and older. All employee contributions may be invested in this option with principal and interest guaranteed by an insurance company.

The additional savings and Income Fund options become effective April 1, 1980.

Life Insurance

Important changes have been made to the employee-paid optional life insurance program. The insurance company has agreed to cut the cost to employees and to boost the coverage for spouses. For those in the program on October 1, 1979, no premium will be charged for the first three months of 1980. Then, effective April 1, 1980, premiums for most employees will be

Exhibit 1 (*continued*)

reduced significantly. The actual reduction will depend on the employee's age. There will be similar premium reductions for spouse coverage. Maximum allowable spouse coverage will be increased to $50,000 from $25,000 at the same time.

General Retirement Plan

Substantial improvements have been made in General Retirement Plan benefits effective October 1, 1979. Included are changes that improve benefits for employees who contribute to the plan, for people who will retire before age 65, and for present retirees. Other changes help consolidate and simplify plan provisions.

Minimum Benefit

Wide-ranging improvements boost the minimum benefit rate used to compute monthly benefits. The rate for each year of service for most salaried employees is increased immediately to $16.50, up from $11.50. Further increases will be made over the next three years to raise the rate to $18.95.

Contributory Benefit

Under the revised plan, benefits will be unreduced for retirement at age 62 and above. Before this change, contributory benefits were reduced before age 65. Smaller reduction factors will mean larger benefits for employees who retire early.

Greater benefits are available to employees who contribute to the plan. Contributory benefits for service before 1971 will be based on the average contributory salary for 1966–1970. Previously, the benefits for service before 1966 were based on the average for 1961 through 1965. The change applies to employees even if they haven't participated at all times eligible. Similar increases in the past have excluded these employees, making the improvement even more important for them.

Employee contributions to the General Retirement Plan are based on salary over a specified level. The present monthly level is $875. That will be increased to $1,050 in 1980, to $1,100 in 1981, and to $1,150 in 1982. The 1980 change will increase contributing members' take-home pay by about $6 per month. For most employees, the resulting reduction in the contributory retirement benefit for future years will be more than offset by the improved benefit resulting from increases in base salaries and increases in Social Security benefits.

Supplements

The plan provides supplements and temporary benefits to raise benefits for employees who retire early. One of these presently supplements the minimum monthly benefit to a total of

Exhibit 1 (*continued*)

$700 for people retiring before age 62 with at least 30 years of service. For retirements from October 1, 1979, the total has been increased to $800 and the amount will continue to increase during the next three years, reaching $935 on August 1, 1982. Similar improvements are made to the supplement payable to people retiring before age 62 with less than 30 years of service. Also, both supplements will no longer be reduced by the additional benefit paid contributing members. These changes will substantially increase benefits for those retiring before age 62. Supplements will no longer be paid after age 62 and the contributory temporary benefit has been eliminated.

Retiree Increases

Benefits for those already retired under the General Retirement Plan are improved substantially. The minimum benefit is increased. In addition, there are increases in the benefits relating to contributory membership that range from five to 40 percent, for employees who retired before October 1, 1978.

Health Care

Health care plans providing medical, dental and vision care benefits have been improved for employees, retirees, and dependents. Certain medical care that wasn't included before is covered now and maximum levels have been increased.

Medical

Not all improvements deal with usual medical problems. One change gives a surviving spouse assistance for some time after an employee's death. Previously, if the employee was not eligible for retirement, the spouse had to pay to continue medical care coverage. Effective October 1, 1979, if death should be from a work-related accident, medical plan coverage is paid by the company for life, or until the surviving spouse remarries. In addition, for non-work-related deaths, if survivor income benefits are payable, the company will pay for six months' coverage.

A number of new benefits are provided effective January 1, 1980—some simple, some complex—all important to someone. Some examples of the new benefits are:

- Certain reconstructive surgical procedures, including breast reconstruction following cancer surgery.
- Body CAT scans on approved equipment without deductibles or co-payment.
- Disposable syringes and needles for injection of insulin without deductibles.

Exhibit 1 (*concluded*)

Dental

Changes to the Dental Plan will help cut payments for dental care for employees and families. From October 1, 1979, the maximum benefit for work other than orthodontics will be increased to $1,000 from $750 for each plan-year—October 1 through September 30 of the following year.

The lifetime maximum benefit for expenses related to orthodontics will be increased to $800 from $650 on January 1, 1980. Also, X-rays, extractions, and oral surgery related to orthodontics will be covered on the same basis as all other similar work—90 percent of the usual, reasonable, and customary charges. Coverage now is 50 percent.

Exhibit 2   1978 Fact Sheet on Weymouth Steel Corporation

	Amounts (in millions)
Sales	$6,702
Net income	(307)
Total assets	6,973
Raw steel production	21.6 tons
Employees:	
Hourly	125,000
Salaried	25,000

firms, Weymouth needed to purchase and install new Concast processing machines and to construct modern rolling and hot strip mills. In addition, their plants needed to satisfy increasingly stringent federal antipollution standards. During the next five years, capital spending was expected to average $2 billion a year. Therefore, all areas of the company urgently needed to reduce costs.

In anticipation of this period of declining sales and increasing capital needs, Weymouth managers initiated several measures. They shut down several smaller and less-efficient mills and processing plants. They deferred some plant modernizations, particularly those not necessary to meet environmental regulations. They restricted the use of overtime and temporary salaried employees. They encouraged efforts to reduce purchasing and supply costs. They limited travel and related expenses; whenever possible, meetings were to be held in company facilities. Ultimately, they would have to reduce the number of salaried employees.

No exact figure was set, and the company hoped to keep the number as low as possible, but as many as 5,000 salaried positions might be affected. Half of these might be painlessly eliminated through normal attrition, early retirement, and transfers. Whenever possible, open positions that could not be filled by transferring present employees would be left unfilled. The company planned to stay in touch with colleges through career days and faculty contracts, but actual recruiting on campuses was cancelled for the balance of 1979. Nonetheless, when the painless methods were exhausted, 2,000 to 2,500 employees might have to be let go.

The Salaried Employee

Salaried employees at Weymouth encompassed 20 different pay grades, from file clerks to top management. Grades 1–10 included college trainees, maintenance workers, printing office employees, plant foremen, general foremen, plant superintendents, general engineers; grades 11 and up included the senior engineers and managers. It was assumed that the reductions would take place across the board; proportionally, no one grade would be significantly more affected than any other.

A salaried employee with one or more years of service would be eligible for a termination payment. He or she would also be paid for unused vacation for 1979 and any vacation accrued for 1980. Insurance coverage continued for one month after layoff and could be continued beyond one month by the former employee at reasonable rates. Unlike the hourly employees (25,000 of whom were laid off by October 31, as it turned out), salaried employees could not count on the improved supplemental employment benefits (SUB) that were available to members of the United Steelworkers of America. Between SUB and state unemployment compensation, a union member who was laid off could receive a substantial portion of his or her former base pay for up to two years, depending on length of service. Salaried employees had a much smaller cushion against the hardships of termination. Weymouth managers were well aware of this fact and planned to do what they could to assist former employees in their search for a new job.

How to Communicate the News?

Traditionally, the company made no general announcement of planned reductions of salaried employees, nor did it usually explain its reasons in any public forum. Employees were individually informed by their supervisors that their positions had been eliminated or that their services were no longer needed. James Harrison, VP for public affairs, had recommended that in such situations Weymouth should begin to take the initiative in openly communicating important information to its employees. Layoffs during the 1974–75 recession had been handled in the traditional way, Harrison pointed out, and the grapevine had exacerbated bad feeling. Instead of letting the press pick up a rumor about the layoffs, instead of letting the grapevine distort the reasons for the decision, he felt the company should go directly to its salaried employees with the full story. He urged that Weymouth explain the reasons for the decision and reassure all salaried employees that the company would do what it could to soften the blow.

When the matter was discussed by the staff, Harrison's view was generally accepted; but the decision to take the initiative raised several questions. Assuming that some special communication(s) should go out to the salaried employees, should the possibility of layoffs and the improvements in benefits be treated in the same document or in separate ones? How should the special communication(s) be coordinated with the regular channels—*Metal News* and *The Open Hearth*, personnel bulletins, and the like? Who should sign—Byron Miller, executive vice president; Samuel Bernstein, VP for personnel; or Weymouth himself?

The Staff Debate

These questions sparked considerable debate. Bernstein argued for one letter; Harrison felt two letters were needed. No matter how carefully explained, he argued, the two messages would seem inconsistent, or, at the very least, the good will generated by increased salaries and benefits would be immediately cancelled out by anxiety and resentment over the possibility of layoffs. Weymouth agreed with Bernstein that one letter would serve. However, he stressed that employees and the media should both be considered key audiences; perhaps a letter and a press release were in order.

The staff did not entirely agree on the emphasis of any letter or memo to the employees. Harrison felt that employees needed to be informed about the impact of the economic downturn in general and about the various measures the company was taking to reduce costs. He also urged that any special communication include a strong and explicit expression of concern for the employees who might be laid off. Weymouth questioned whether information about other cost-cutting measures ought to be included; to someone who was about to lose his or her job, restrictions on travel and overtime might seem trivial or irrelevant. Bernstein was wary of attempting to express the company's concern; he felt such sentiments were awkward to express and might seem condescending or hypocritical to some employees.

The staff also debated the origin and the audience(s) of the special communication(s). Some argued strongly for a "corporate" communiqué, signed by Weymouth. Others felt that Bernstein of personnel should sign. Some felt the company should discuss the impact of the economic slowdown with all its salaried employees, not just those actually laid off. Others urged that, in order to minimize anxiety, only those actually affected should be addressed. Everyone agreed that timing was important and that employees should know the company's plans before anything appeared in the press. They also recognized that both employees and the media were likely to have questions once these matters were openly discussed and that they needed to provide supervisors and others with answers—as far as was practicable.

Weymouth was leaving for Japan the next day, but he felt the time had come to act on the staff's discussions. Harrison agreed to draw up an action plan and draft the special communication(s) he deemed necessary.

CASE 8
WEBSTER INDUSTRIES (A)
R. Roosevelt Thomas, Jr.

On Friday, October 17, 1975, Bob Carter, a 32-year-old graduate of the Amos Tuck School, was observing his first anniversary as manufacturing manager in the Fabrics Division of Webster Industries. Except for 2 years spent earning his MBA, he had been with the company for 10 years and he was very satisfied with his Webster experiences. Before being selected for his current position, he had spent two years as a plant production superintendent, three years as a plant manager, and two as assistant to the president, Abe Webster. On a day that should have been one of celebration, Carter sat at home in a very somber mood and started on his third martini of the afternoon.

Earlier in the day Ike Davis, head of the Fabrics Division, had told Carter that Fabrics would have to reduce its personnel by 20 percent and that the manufacturing department, in particular, would have to make a cut of 15 percent at the managerial level. This meant that Carter would have to trim his 289 managers by 43 individuals. Davis's request stemmed from reduction plans presented to him by Abe Webster. Because Abe had set the following Friday as the deadline for the submission of termination lists, Davis wanted his top divisional managers to begin a review as a group on the preceding Wednesday of all proposed Fabrics separations. Davis concluded his conversation with Carter by listing the five guidelines that Abe Webster had provided:

1. No one with over 20 years of Webster service and 50 years of age should be terminated without a review by the president.
2. Since the last reduction (approximately one year before) had affected primarily hourly and weekly workers, this go-around was to focus on managerial levels.
3. Seniority was not to be a major determining factor as to who would be separated.
4. Early retirement should not be relied on as a mechanism for meeting reduction targets.
5. Blacks, women, and other minorities were not to be terminated more aggressively than other employees.

After speaking with Davis, Carter went home to ponder the situation.

Carter spent the afternoon in his den thinking about the task before him. He remembered the first time he had terminated an employee. Early in his career he had fired a secretary—it had taken him a week to muster enough courage to do it and a week to recover. Since that experience, however, he had found each successive termination increasingly easy. But never before had he been involved in releasing so many individuals at once, especially so many people with whom he had worked and developed social relations. Though he

had been in his present position for only a year and had no previous experience in the Fabrics Division, Carter knew most of his managers by name and considered several to be friends. Furthermore, he and his family dealt with many of these individuals and their families in various community and civic activities. In addition to the likelihood of having to recommend the termination of personal and family friends, Carter worried about the possibility of having to release employees with significant lengths of service. He knew that any person with over 10 years of Webster employment would be very surprised by termination. While pondering the possible consequences of the reductions, Carter became more and more anxious as he realized that he had few firm ideas on how the cuts should be made. The only certainty was that he must conform to Abe's guidelines.

General Information on Webster Industries

Location. Located on 17 acres of rolling red Georgia hills on the northern outskirts of Clearwater, Georgia, Webster's headquarters resembled a college campus with plantation-like buildings. Top management was housed in the refurbished "Big House" of the old Webster Plantation, while middle-level corporate managers were situated in a modern three-story office building that was known as the "Box." Built a thousand yards from the Big House, the modern structure appeared out of place in the plantation setting. The Big House and the Box were the heart of one of America's most successful textile companies.

Clearwater was unabashedly a company town. Of its population of about 35,000, one half of the employed residents worked for Webster, one third engaged in serious farming, and the remainder labored in several small factories around the town. Not only was Webster the dominant employer, Websterites held all important community positions. The company stressed community involvement and encouraged its people to accept civic responsibilities.

Because Webster attracted highly educated employees from a variety of places, Clearwater differed from the typical small, rural Georgia town. For example, Georgia educators ranked its school system ahead of Atlanta's. The town had experienced much success in attracting quality teachers by offering generous salary schedules and excellent facilities. Another unique feature of the town was a thriving set of cultural and entertainment events, from regular appearances by the Atlanta Symphony and various theater groups to exhibition games featuring Atlanta's professional athletic teams. As one Clearwaterite put it, "Clearwater is not your run-of-the-mill mill town."

Company History.   Colonel Jeremiah Webster, an officer in the Confederate army, founded the company after the Civil War. When the colonel retired from the operations, his youngest son assumed the leadership. He in turn was followed by his oldest male offspring, Mark Webster, who presided over the company from 1941 to 1960. Under Mark's tenure, Webster grew and branched into other fabric markets. By 1960 the company produced fibers for carpeting and for home and industrial furnishings. Sales rose from $150 million in 1941 to approximately $900 million in 1960. During this period Webster opened its first plants outside of Clearwater. Growth and geographical dispersion of operations greatly strained the company's management.

In the 1950s Mark Webster recognized his company's need for skilled management. Convinced of management's importance for the future of Webster, he set out to attract MBAs to his organization in 1955. Though trained as a lawyer, he had considerable respect for professional business education. This respect had been fostered by consulting relationships with professors from some of the leading national and regional business schools. Mark also encouraged his son, Abe, to attend the Wharton School.

After earning his MBA at Wharton, Abe served five experience years before assuming the presidency. Until that time, Webster's president had also served as chairman of the board of directors. After Abe's five years of experience, however, Mark decided to split the jobs. Abe became president and Mark concentrated on the chairmanship. Mark still kept regular hours, but emphasized that Abe was running the business. Under Abe the company continued to grow, primarily through diversification by acquisition of several small furniture and carpet manufacturers. Following these acquisitions, Webster's management adopted a divisional structure (see Figure 1). Despite its diversification, Webster was very much a

Figure 1   Webster Industries, Partial Corporate Organization Chart

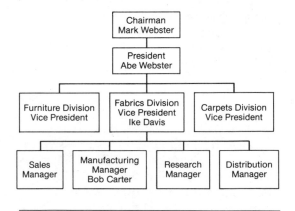

textile company. Of its 1974 sales of approximately $1.7 billion, 70 percent came from the Fabrics Division. The carpet and furniture lines each accounted for 15 percent.

The Fabrics Division's products were categorized as fibers for apparel, home furnishings, carpeting, and industrial furnishings. Organizationally, Fabrics had a functional structure of sales, manufacturing, distribution, and research. Within sales, the organization was by markets; the sales force was organized around the different fiber classifications. Comparable to sales, the manufacturing plants were

grouped by markets with three in apparel and two in each of the other areas. Each group reported to a production manager, who in turn reported to the assistant production superintendent, Cecil Stevens (see Figure 2).

Organizational Climate. Websterites described the company as a first-class place to work. Employees took great pride in the company's nationally known products and frequently remarked, "You can tell Webster fabrics from a mile away!" The organization consistently won industry awards for superior products, which were displayed in the

Figure 2 Fabrics Division Organization Chart

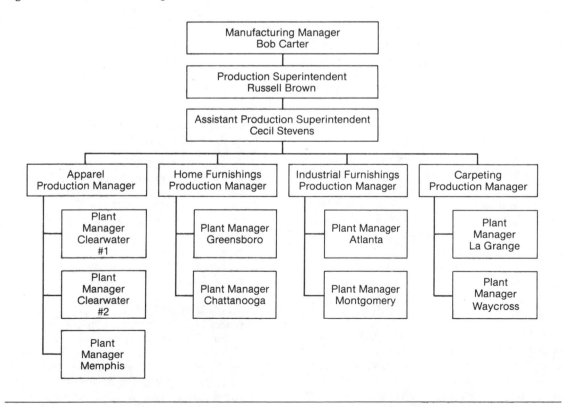

Big House lobby. Webster also maintained excellent relations with its employees.

Management spared little in its efforts to make work at Webster rewarding *and* productive. The organization's facilities and working conditions excelled those of its competitors. Webster's pay and fringe benefits systems offered attractive financial packages and served as models for several firms located throughout the country. Further, because of its rapid growth, Webster had been able to provide its people with challenging work and opportunities for advancement. The company pioneered in establishing a Human Resources Division, which performed the regular personnel functions along with a number of activities intended to facilitate the employees' growth and development. As part of its development projects, the Human Resources Division designed both a performance appraisal system (PAS) and an information system capable of tracking each employee's career and development. Top management gave the division much credit for the fact that no Webster plant was unionized.

Company officials also pointed to the firm's paternalistic culture as another factor contributing to good employee relations. They used the term *constructive paternalism* when describing the organization's attitudes and activities. For example, there were the annual company picnics, luncheons, dinners, and parties centered around special occasions. The employees' belief structure also reflected paternalism. Typically, the Webster employee believed, "If you make it through the 10th year, you can be reasonably assured that Webster always will have a place for you." Many employees expected this reciprocal agreement to hold even for individuals who had developed drinking and/or emotional problems. In more than one instance, Webster had kept an employee long after alcoholism had impaired his or her effectiveness, primarily because of top management's feelings that the person had no other place to go. Similarly, the company had paid the psychiatric bills of several employees rather than dismiss them as ineffective performers. Some viewed the open-door policies of the chairman and the president as another illustration of paternalism. All decisions could be appealed to the highest levels. A few managers expressed concern that employees with the appropriate connections had tended to use the open-door policies to secure undeserved promotions. Finally, the company on several occasions had financed the education of local youths—obviously with hopes that they would return to Clearwater and Webster, but with no strings attached. Two beneficiaries of this practice were the present Montgomery plant manager (Harvard B.A. and MBA) and the chief corporate counsel (Yale B.A. and J.D.). Neither had ever worked for any other organization than Webster.

Clearwaterites openly spoke of the firm's paternalism, as shown here in the words of one plant controller:

> There is a sense of family here. An expectation that if you are loyal to the company, it will be loyal to you. An expectation that if you have a problem, you can take it to Papa Webster [the company] and it will be at least seriously considered. Twelve years ago, a tornado came through and fiercely hit Clearwater. Those new houses you see along Webster Drive are a result of the company's generous response.
>
> I could go on and on. Fringe benefits also reflect how the company takes care of its people. The whole fringe benefits package is oriented toward taking care of the employee's family. We were the first to insure the education of a worker's children should he or she die. We continually up-

grade retirement benefits to offset inflation. The company's hiring and promotion practices are also paternalistic. The offspring of employees always have first shot—if they are qualified—at openings. Webster—along these same lines—promotes from within. Rare is the case of someone being hired from the outside for a top position. What more is there to say? Webster is a darn good company.

Webster's Employees. Webster's managerial employees came from several areas of the United States. Typically, they had received degrees from schools on the East Coast. The MBAs were from the top national and regional schools. Managers without MBAs had sophisticated technical training. The backgrounds of Webster's managers differed significantly from those of its typical plant laborers, who tended to come from the area around the plant and to have at least a high school diploma or at most an associate degree from a community college. Despite these differences, Webster had experienced little class conflict. Most attributed this harmony to the Human Resources Division, the many opportunities for advancement, and Webster's practice of having MBAs (especially those in manufacturing) spend some time in low-level plant positions.

Manufacturing in the Fabrics Division had 1,787 people located at headquarters and in nine plants. Of these, 289 served as managers. Managers worked either at corporate headquarters on the manufacturing manager's staff, or functioned in a managerial, supervisory, or staff capacity at one of the plants. The background of manufacturing managers was similar to that described above for Webster managers in general. Of the 289 managers, 160 lived in and around Clearwater.

Webster's Troubles

The symptoms that set off the alarm at Webster were second quarter earnings of less than 50 percent of 1974 earnings and a threatened cash position. The economy and Webster's sloppy growth habits contributed to each of these difficulties.

The economy, especially the slowdown in the construction industry, hit Webster's furniture and carpeting businesses hard. The softening of the demand for furniture and carpeting caused Webster's sales to decline from a 1973 peak of $2.1 billion. Simultaneously, inflation exerted upward pressure on costs. The dips in sales and earnings reduced Webster's cash flow considerably, so much so that money became extremely tight for the first time in 35 years. Though Mark and Abe Webster had expected the current earnings and cash troubles, they were unnerved by the extent of the problems. In addition to the troubled economy, the firm's phenomenal growth had complicated matters further.

The production manager in the largest Clearwater plant offered the following observations:

We grew too fast. We wanted diversification but were not ready to handle it. With the acquisitions of the 1960s we became a different company almost overnight. Truthfully, we definitely were not prepared to break the billion-dollar level in sales. We grew too fast to consolidate. Only now are we learning the basics of managing a multibusiness enterprise. Controls were poor, especially in some of the plants we acquired. Staffing was done sloppily, so we ended up with a lot of fat. Plus we were—in my opinion—lax in our evaluation of performance.

The economy and the problems of diversification combined to slow Webster's growth and to threaten its financial integrity.

Bob Carter's Evening

By 6:00 P.M. Carter began to overcome his initial shock and to realize that, while painful, the reduction was probably needed and probably best for the company. He had known for some time that his department had fat at the managerial levels. Just six months earlier he had sought to demote three individuals—including his second in command. In denying his recommendation, Ike Davis had told Carter, "These men have too much service to be treated as you have proposed." So Carter was stuck with them; at least that had been the case until then. Carter reasoned that one benefit of the reduction in force would be an opportunity to make some long-needed changes. He saw his task as that of making the best reductions possible in the least painful manner.

After dinner Carter returned to his den to address the issue of how to cut 43 individuals from his managerial payroll. Because of his relatively brief tenure, he wanted to consult at least one other individual. The logical choices were the number two and three persons in his hierarchy; however, Carter wanted to demote the production superintendent, Russell Brown, and to promote the assistant production superintendent, Cecil Stevens. He had been impressed with Stevens and had decided some time back that he should have Brown's job. The reduction presented an opportunity to make the change.

Carter concluded that Stevens should be involved initially and perhaps others later on some basis. At 8:30 P.M. he called Stevens, who lived four miles away, and asked him to come over to discuss the critical situation. Cecil arrived an hour later. Carter informed him of the reduction plans and of his intention to recommend him for promotion to production superintendent.

Stevens was both delighted by his promotion and shocked by the magnitude of the proposed separations. After relating details of his session with Davis, Carter asked Stevens to aid him in developing a strategy for determining the individuals to be released. Specifically, he requested that Stevens be prepared by Monday morning to identify and discuss issues that should be considered in formulating a reduction plan.

Carter and Stevens spent another 45 minutes discussing their perceptions of the company's situation and the need for the reduction. They also raised some questions about Webster's PAS. Stevens wondered how much weight should be given to performance ratings. Carter admitted that he had not gotten around to using PAS on a regular basis, but indicated that he would be interested in hearing Stevens's views of the system and its usage in the department. Stevens asked if they should consider inviting others to the session on Monday morning. After some discussion, they agreed to invite the production managers with the exception of the home furnishings manager, who was a likely candidate for demotion or termination. Carter and Stevens ended their meeting by agreeing on a timetable: Monday, 8:00 A.M.—develop strategy; Monday, 1:00 P.M.—begin to implement strategy; and Wednesday, 2:00 P.M.—present list to divisional managers.

The Monday Morning Meeting

On Monday morning Carter, Stevens, and three of the four production managers met as planned. Stevens began the meeting by presenting his thoughts on possible criteria for developing a termination list:

> The following represents my thinking on possible options open to use. I see five.
> The first is *seniority*. Though guidelines prohibit much use of this criterion, there are

a few individuals who might be receptive to offers of early retirement.

The second is *fairness*. Should this be a criterion? Operationally, I do not know what it means except that we would not do anything that would be perceived as grossly unfair. I do know, however, that our people will expect fairness.

The third is *fat*. The list would be determined by the elimination of "fat" or excess positions. This approach has legitimacy. The difficulty, however, is that some good people are in "fat" positions. The use of this criterion alone could result in a net quality-downgrading of manufacturing personnel.

The fourth is *performance*. The basic question here is, "How do we measure performance?" How much weight do we give to PAS data? Some individuals feel that the PAS data are hopelessly biased, because of the managers' tendency to give everyone good ratings. How much weight do we give to the personnel audit data?* If we were to give significant weight to the audit data, would we be compromising the future effectiveness of the auditor? When making field visits, the auditor not only gathers data on performance from managers but also talks to individuals about their careers and problems. Many employees have been very frank with the auditors. If we use audit data as input in making termination decisions, the employee may feel betrayed and become reluctant to trust the auditors in the future. This would be especially likely if managers tried to make the auditors scapegoats. I can hear a manager telling a terminated employee, "I wanted to keep you, but our auditor Jack had too strong a case against you."

Additionally, to what extent are we constrained by past practices? In the past, few managers have been diligent and responsi-

ble in talking with their people about performance; as a consequence, many employees are not aware of their relative standing with respect to performance. If these individuals are terminated, they will likely be shocked and feel that they have been treated unfairly. Can we fairly terminate on the basis of performance?

The fifth is *potential*. Again, the basic questions are around measurement and the weights to be given to PAS and audit data. How do we measure potential? How much weight do we give to PAS data? Audit data? Should we terminate an individual with little potential but capable of doing his or her present job fully satisfactorily? I am thinking about one plant controller in particular. He is an excellent assistant plant controller, but he does not have the potential to advance further. Would he be a candidate?

I consider this large reduction to be a one-shot deal. As such, the reduction represents a beautiful crisis opportunity to make moves that would be difficult under normal circumstances. We can seize the opportunity not only to meet our termination target but also to upgrade our department. Other divisions are releasing competent people. Some will be better than those that we will propose to keep. This means that we could upgrade by reducing a larger number than our target, and then hiring replacements from our sister divisions' terminations. For example, our target is 43. If after meeting this target we identified 5 available individuals who were better than persons we were planning to keep, we could terminate 48 and hire the 5 former employees of the other divisions. However, if we are to seize this opportunity, we will have to develop sound ways of evaluating performance and potential

A lively discussion of PAS and the personnel audit followed Stevens's remarks. During these deliberations the group relied heavily on Stevens's memorandum on performance appraisal at Webster (see Exhibit 1).

---

* Personnel auditors from the Human Resources Division visited each manager at least once a year to discuss his or her employees' performances. During these discussions they obtained a performance rating for each employee. This process was separate from Webster's performance appraisal system (PAS).

Exhibit 1 Memorandum

TO: Bob Carter

FROM: Cecil Stevens

RE: Performance Appraisal at Webster

DATE: October 20, 1975

Since leaving your home on Friday evening, I have had an opportunity to talk with a number of individuals. Specifically, I saw Ed Johnson, the designer of our PAS system, at the club and had a good conversation; talked with Jack Bryant, our personnel auditor, about his work with the division; and spent two hours after church discussing the reduction with the manufacturing managers of the other divisions. Immediately below are my impressions of PAS and also the personnel audit function of the Human Resources Division.

Performance Appraisal System (PAS)

Bob, PAS was designed three years ago and has been used primarily on a voluntary basis. My discussion of the system is based primarily on conversations with its designer, Ed Johnson.

Purpose

The system is intended to help the manager act as a:

- manager responsible for attaining organizational goals,
- judge responsible for evaluating individual performance and making decisions about salary and promotability,
- helper responsible for developing subordinates.

One problem in the past has been a failure to recognize the three roles cited above, or a tendency to emphasize one over the others. PAS is based on the assumption that each role is equally important and is intended to help the manager do justice to each.

Components

PAS components are three in number: Management By Objectives (MBO), a developmental review, and an evaluation and salary review:

Exhibit 1   (*continued*)

MBO.   This component focuses on results and is intended to help the manager realize organizational goals. Though each manager is expected to adapt MBO to his or her situation, there are typically six steps.

1. *Identification of Objectives.*   Here, objectives are identified and prioritized. Also, review periods are set.
2. *Establishment of Measurement Criteria.*   The basic question here is, "What monetary measures, percentages, and/or other numbers will be used to measure the achievement of objectives?" For example, if we in manufacturing were to establish "greater production effectiveness" as one of our objectives, we would have to decide how to measure the extent of achievement. Total unit costs? Total direct labor unit costs? Total production?
3. *Planning.*   Plans are made for achieving the identified objectives. What is to be done? Who is to do it? When is it to be done? How is it to be done?
4. *Execution.*   Plans are implemented.
5. *Measure.*   Secure actual monetary figures, percentages, and/or other numbers so that results may be reviewed.
6. *Review Results.*   Compare actual measurements to plan. The frequency of measurements and review will depend on the number of review points within a year. Typically, the entire MBO cycle is repeated once a year, with intermittent reviews in between.

MBO is essentially a system for identifying what is to be done and ensuring that it is done. As such, MBO has a major weakness in terms of the managerial role: It does not aid the manager in observing, evaluating or improving the behavior of subordinates. If the manager is to help his employees improve their behavior, he will need a behavior-oriented tool. The developmental review was designed to meet this need.

The Developmental Review.   As indicated above, the review is intended to help the manager observe, analyze, and improve subordinate behavior. There are three subcomponents: the Performance Description Questionnaire, the Performance Profile, and the Developmental Interview.

1. *Performance Description Questionnaire.*   The questionnaire contains 70 behavioral statements, each describing a behavior determined through research to be indicative of effectiveness. Supervisors are asked to rate the extent to which the subordinate exhibits the behavior described. The 70 behavioral statements are grouped into a smaller number of dimensions such as openness to influence, priority setting, formal communications, organizational perspective, decisiveness, delegation/participation, support for company, unit productivity, and conflict resolution. The manager is asked to complete a questionnaire for each subordinate. He or she is asked to indicate on a six-point rating scale how descriptive the statement is of the employ-

---

Exhibit 1 (*continued*)

ee's actual behavior. Also, under each statement is space for the recording of any critical incidents supporting the manager's judgment. (See *Attachment 1.*) The performance profile is produced by computer from the questionnaire data.

2. *Performance Profile.* The profile is intended to serve as a tool to help managers discriminate among a subordinate's performances on a number of performance dimensions. An individual's profile shows net strengths or weakness for each dimension in terms of the person's own average. The profile line represents the average of the employee's ratings on all performance dimensions. The number and location of X's show the extent to which the employee's score for a particular dimension is below or above his or her average for all dimensions. Dimensions with X's to the left of the profile line are those where the individual is relatively weak (compared to his or her average). Dimensions with X's to the right are those where the subordinate is relatively strong. The number of X's indicates the extent of the weakness or strength. (See *Attachment 2.*) The tool is designed to facilitate analysis of a subordinate's performance and is not valid theoretically for comparison of individuals.

3. *Developmental Interview.* The purposes of the developmental interview are to provide the subordinate with a performance analysis based on the performance questionnaire and profile, to identify areas of weaknesses, and to translate these weaknesses into an appropriate developmental program. Tools are available to help the manager and subordinate in designing developmental plans.

The reasoning behind the design of the Developmental Review was a hope that the Performance Description Questionnaire and Profile would help the manager and his subordinates distinguish development from MBO and evaluation, and thereby reduce subordinate defensiveness that typically characterizes feedback sessions where developmental and evaluative issues are handled simultaneously.

Evaluation and Salary Review. This review is separate from the MBO and developmental reviews. Its basis is a form which asks the manager to rate the employee's overall performance and his or her potential. (See *Attachment 3.*) The overall rating should reflect the MBO sessions and the Developmental Review data and interview. In short, the two other components of PAS provide important inputs for the Evaluation Review. Possible overall ratings are unsatisfactory, fair, fully satisfactory, excellent and outstanding.

Once the overall rating has been given, the salary matrix may be used as a *guide* in determining recommendations for salary adjustments. The matrix approach is straightforward and used by several organizations. Under this method salary adjustments are a function of the subordinate's rating and the relative standing of the employee's salary within his or her pay range. (See *Attachment 4.*)

Exhibit 1 (*continued*)

Usage of PAS

Bob, as I indicated earlier, the system has been used on a voluntary basis so far. In the corporation as a whole, the usage rate is 29 percent; in manufacturing it is 40 percent. The only group using it 100 percent is Fabrics' sales force.

The Personnel Audit

In addition to PAS the Human Resources Division is also responsible for conducting the personnel audit. The purposes of the audit are to secure performance data that will facilitate corporate manpower planning, to encourage and improve communications between superiors and subordinates, and to provide career development counseling. There is a potential conflict among the purposes in that the auditor is required to perform both evaluative and counseling roles. Some individuals who "pour out their souls" to the auditors are unaware of their evaluative function.

Our auditor, as you know, is Jack Bryant. At least once a year Jack visits each manager and talks about their subordinates. He also talks with subordinates about their development and their perceptions of where they stand. Where there are discrepancies between a subordinate's perception and what his or her manager has said, Jack works with the manager in developing a plan for correcting the employee's misperceptions. Jack, however, has no enforcement power; consequently, some managers fail to give accurate—if any—feedback to their employees. The audit has been very successful in securing information for the central corporate data bank, but has had somewhat less success in getting managers to be honest with subordinates. Though individual employees may see their central file, few avail themselves of the opportunity; consequently, many subordinates remain in the dark as to how they are actually perceived by their bosses. I, however, understand that a computer-based system capable of providing each employee with performance data has been designed and implemented below managerial levels. Reportedly, the system annually provides each employee with a printout showing—among other things—performance ratings and career history. April 1, 1976, is the target date for full implementation in the managerial ranks.

Currently, the form used by the auditors asks for a rating of the individual's performance and potential. There also are sections dealing with the employee's strengths and weaknesses and the manager's recommendations for future reassignments. (See *Attachment 5*.)

I have checked with Jack, and he has assured me that there are audit ratings on file for at least 97 percent of our personnel.

Bob, hopefully these remarks on PAS and the personnel audit will stimulate discussion leading to an appropriate reduction plan.

Exhibit 1   (*continued*)

Attachment 1

Sample Items from Performance Description Questionnaire

1. Involves subordinates in decision-making process _____
2. Makes a special effort to explain Webster policies to subordinates _____
3. Molds a cohesive work group _____
4. Fails to follow up on work assignments given to others _____
5. Works closely with subordinates who lack motivation _____

6. Selects and places qualified personnel _____
7. His or her subordinates accomplish a large amount of work _____
8. Objects to ideas before explained _____
9. Is accurate in his work _____
10. Gives poor presentations _____

Ratings

Number	Definition
1	Strongly Agree
2	Agree
3	Somewhat Agree
4	Somewhat Disagree
5	Disagree
6	Strongly Disagree

Attachment 2

Sample Profile Interpretations

Dimension		A		B		C	
1. Openness to Influence	xx		xxxxx			xx	
2. Priority Setting		xx		xxx			xxxxxx
3. Formal Communications		xx		xxx	xxxxxx		
4. Organizational Perspective	xx		xxxxxxxxxx			xx	
5. Decisiveness		xx		xx		xx	
6. Delegation/Participation	xx			xx	xxxxxx		
7. Support for Company		xx	xx				xxxxxx
8. Unit Productivity	xx			xxx	xx		
9. Conflict Resolution		xx	xx		xx		
10. Team Building	xx			xxx	xx		
11. Control		xx		xx		xxx	

A. Implication is that manager is well-balanced *dimensionally*.

B. Implication is that this manager has one *very* significantly weak *dimension*, another relatively weak *dimension*, contrasted to the remaining favorably balanced *dimensions*.

C. Implication is that this manager has two relatively weak dimensions, two relatively strong *dimensions*, with remaining *dimensions* relatively balanced.

CAUTION: Remember that you are only comparing the individual to himself and *NOT* with other people. IF an individual is "well-balanced dimensionally," it means there is not much difference between what he does best and what he does the poorest; it does *not* necessarily mean he is a "well-balanced manager."

Exhibit 1   (*continued*)

Attachment 3

Detach and Send To: Private

Position Preference   Date _____
Employee Name _____   Employee Number _____
Division _____   Location _____
Position _____   Supervisor _____

Supervisor and subordinate develop *together*. Indicate below subsequent positions for your subordinate *that you both can agree* are realistic, appropriate, and interesting. Specify both functional area (e.g., Sales, Personnel, etc.) and, whenever possible, type of job.

Order of Preference for Next Jobs:
  Short Term   *Long Term* (within next 5 years)
    First Choice: First Choice:
    Second Choice: Second Choice:

> *Supervisor's Summary:* Supervisor fills in by himself *after* the developmental interview. The subordinate should be shown these ratings after the supervisor has coordinated the rating with the *second* level supervisor.

A. *Change of Status:* Indicate by your choice of the statements below (check one) the change of status you recommend for this person during the next twelve months.

_____ Should be separated as soon as possible. (SEP)

_____ Should be reassigned to position with a decreased responsibility. (DEM)

_____ Should be reassigned to a position with a similar level of responsibility. (LAT)

_____ Need more experience before reassignment can be considered. (EXP)

_____ Should be reassigned to a position with more responsibility. (RDY)

_____ Should remain in present position. (STA)

B. *Career Potential:* Based on current knowledge, indicate in the spaces below (check one) the level this person has the greatest probability of achieving. Note: Potential ratings do *NOT* imply a person's readiness for promotion now.

_____ Potential Division Manager or equivalent. [must be Group 50 or above.] (BLUE)

_____ Potential to higher supervisory/managerial level. (GREEN)

_____ Potential is best utilized within a specialty or as an individual performer. (BROWN)

_____ Good performer; no indication to date of potential for a higher level. (YELLOW)

_____ Questionable performance. (RED)

C. *Overall Job Performance* during the past 6–12 months may be characterized as: (check scale)

Unsatisfactory	Fair	Satisfactory	Excellent	Outstanding

D. *Comments:*

Endorsement of Second Level Supervisor
_____ I agree with all of the above recommendations.
_____ I disagree with some (or all) of the above recommendations and would make the following recommendations:

_____
                        Signature

Exhibit 1 (*continued*)

Attachment 4

Salary Matrix

Comparative Ratio	Outstanding	Excellent	Fully Satisfactory	Fair	Poor
1.20 (max.) – 1.10	6%	4%	2%	—	—
1.10 – 1.00	8%	6%	4%	—	—
1.00 – .90	10%	8%	6%	—	—
.90 – .80 (min.)	12%	10%	8%	6%	—

Ratings

Note: Comparative ratio equals actual salary divided by the midpoint of the individual's salary range. Salary adjustment was a function of the individual's ratio and rating. An employee with an .85 ratio and a rating of excellent would receive an adjustment of 10 percent.

Attachment 5

Employee Name _____ Supervisor _____ Date _____

Performance   *Potential*

1 2 3 4 5 NR (Circle One)   (Circle One) 1 2 3 4 5 NR

Comments: (Supervisor should define significant strengths and weaknesses [development needs] and accomplishments.)

Change of Status: (for the next 12 months) (Check One)

1. _____ Should be separated as soon as possible (termination).

2. _____ Should be reassigned to a position of decreased responsibility (demotion).   Which function(s) (comment) _____

3. _____ Should be reassigned to a position with a similar level of responsibility (lateral move).   Which function(s) (comment) _____

4. _____ Needs more experience before reassignment can be considered (not ready).   Which function(s) (comment) _____

5. _____ Should be reassigned to a position of more responsibility (promotion).   Which function(s) (comment) _____

6. _____ Will probably remain in present position indefinitely (leveled).

Exhibit 1 (*concluded*)

Performance

Number	Definition
5	Outstanding
4	Excellent
3	Fully Satisfactory
2	Fair
1	Unsatisfactory

Potential

Color	Number	Definition
Blue	5	Potential division manager or equivalent (for individuals currently at the "A" payroll level).
Green	4	Potential to higher supervisory position.
Brown	3	Potential is best utilized within a specialty or as an individual performer.
Yellow	2	Good performer; no indication to date of potential for a higher level.
Red	1	Questionable performer.

WEBSTER INDUSTRIES (B)
R. Roosevelt Thomas, Jr.

In October 1975 Webster Industries found it necessary to reduce its managerial personnel by 20 percent. Bob Carter, manufacturing manager of the company's Fabrics Division, was charged with making a 15 percent reduction in his department.[1] This case describes how that reduction was accomplished and its impact upon the department.

The Process

Bob Carter described the sequence of events as they occurred on Monday, October 20, 1975:

> After discussing Cecil Stevens's memorandum on performance appraisal, we formulated our approach. This was around noon. We broke for lunch before beginning implementation of our plans. During lunch someone remarked that Production Superintendent Russell Brown, who was scheduled to be demoted, had the longest managerial tenure in the department and probably would be able to provide invaluable input.

> We all agreed that Russ was an example of the Peter Principle, that he had been an excellent plant manager before being promoted to production superintendent. We decided to offer him a demotion to a plant manager position. After lunch I made the offer to Russ who—to my surprise—expressed shock *and* relief. It was as if he had wanted the burden lifted. Russ also agreed to participate in our deliberations.

[1] "Webster Industries (A)," HBS Case Services No. 476–110, contains background data, a description of Carter's reaction to his assignment, and Stevens's memorandum.

I guess you can describe what we did later in four steps: (1) reorganization, (2) staffing of new organization, (3) a second review of personnel, and (4) an upgrading review. We decided that we would do what was best for the business. Our thinking was centered around three basic questions: What are our departmental objectives and tasks? How do we have to go about accomplishing these objectives and tasks? What positions are needed to accomplish these tasks and objectives? Based on our answers to these questions, we reorganized the department. Among other actions, this involved the clos-

ing of one apparel plant and the elimination of the home furnishings production manager position. The home furnishings plants were made the responsibility of the industrial furnishings production manager [see Figures 1 and 2].

After the reorganization, we wanted to staff the positions with the *best* possible people. Here, we called in Jack Bryant and his audit data. He served as a useful check on our perceptions. Typically, an individual's name would come up and we would all voice our opinions. It was a time of truth telling. I feel that the input was realistic and

Figure 1   *Old* Fabrics Division Organization Chart

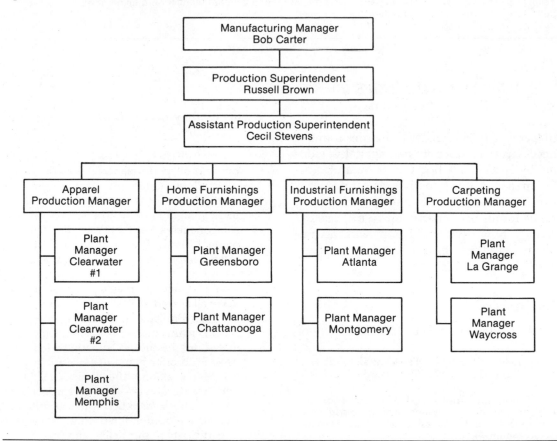

Figure 2   *New* Fabrics Division Organization Chart

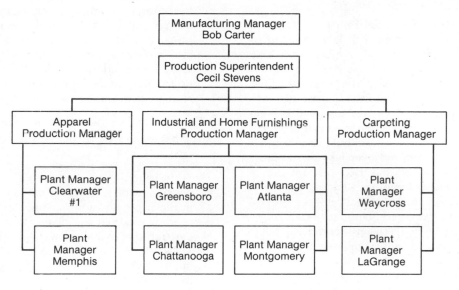

fair. Where our perceptions did not jibe with his audit data, Jack would quickly let us know. Between the audit data and our comments, I think we got some good assessments. PAS [Performance Appraisal System] data, where available, was thrown in by Jack; however, little weight was given to it. We just did not trust it.

During the staffing the basic issue was, Who is the best person for this position? Decisions were based on assessments of individuals' performance *and* potential. It is difficult for me to say which received the greater weight. What was clear, however, was that an individual with both performance and potential was better off than one with either of the two. After staffing the positions, the excess employees were our prime candidates for separation. We referred to this as our excess list.

The excess list was reviewed. We wanted to make certain to the extent possible that we did not release anyone better than the people we were keeping. Again, Jack was

very helpful. We did make several changes, especially where an excess individual was broad enough to qualify for more than one position. At this point our tentative list was 5 over our reduction guideline of 43.

Before finalizing the list I asked Jack to learn who was available from the other divisions. From Jack's list we identified seven people superior to individuals we were proposing to retain. We added to our reduction list accordingly and made offers to the seven former employees of our sister divisions. Our final list was composed of 55 names.

Because of our long working hours—until 10:00 P.M. on Monday and Tuesday nights— I was able to present our list at 2:00 P.M. on Wednesday to the other divisional managers. They disagreed with 3 of our recommendations; consequently, our final list was down to 53. In addition, six individuals were demoted to the weekly payroll.

I am finding it difficult to describe the trauma we experienced. What I have told you sounds too cold. It does not capture the intense sensitivity we had to human pain and suffering. One case in particular comes to mind.

We terminated a plant engineer, Ray Pearson, who had been with Webster 23 years and was 52 years old. He had three children—one of whom was just entering law school. Though his performance had been unsatisfactory for at least the last 10 years, he was not given any negative feedback until the fall of 1974. Concerned that he would be paying for the sins of his past managers, we really agonized over his case. Because we all knew Ray and had worked with him in various community settings, we found our decision to be especially difficult. But we had no other choice, he simply was not performing. Abe [Webster's president] reluctantly agreed with our action. Unfortunately, Ray's case was not unique.

The community has been very understanding of the company's position. Generally, the feeling is that Webster did the right thing. Abe did a good job of presenting our case. Drastic action was required to preserve our financial integrity.

Attitudes toward the Process

The attitude of the top manufacturing managers was that the process had not been perfect, but had been done as well as possible, "given human frailties." Cecil Stevens, the new production superintendent remarked:

We did the best we could under the circumstances. I would have liked more time; I did not like the "rush-rush" atmosphere. We let some *good* people go. My guess is that 75 percent of those released were at least satisfactory employees. My misgivings about the process have been somewhat mitigated by the success that some former employees have experienced in getting new jobs at significantly higher pay.

When put in a situation like we were, one

eventually begins to play God. And even to believe eventually that he is God. During the process a feeling of doing the right thing had prevailed. After all, God does not make mistakes. After the fact, however, we realized that we were still mortals and that mortal decisions had been made. Nevertheless, I do feel that the department is much, much stronger than before. We came out of it well.

The apparel production manager who participated in the process offered these thoughts:

My belief in the rightness of the macro-decision made it easier for me to participate in the micro-decision making. My greatest concern was that too many people had to pay for the mistakes of their managers. These employees either had no business being in their positions, or no inkling of their relative standing in terms of performance and potential. Also, there were too many instances of individuals having been retained long after they had ceased to be effective. All of this represented poor management of performance.

Impact of the Reduction in Force

The most frequently cited impact was the shattering of the Webster belief structure. Bob Carter considered this shattering to be a very important point:

The Webster employee had been laboring under the assumption that "if I make it past my 10th year and remain loyal to the company, the company will take care of me." This was the basic premise of the belief structure that was shattered by the large reduction.

A belief structure is what you believe even in the absence of supporting evidence. It is what keeps you going. And it is necessary—just to get out of bed each morning. Our task as managers is to foster the development of a replacement that will be supportive of the company. We want to reinforce those beliefs supportive of the company and discourage those that would be dysfunctional.

If we were to encourage the belief that loyal individuals will be safe for life, we would be dishonest—for this simply is not true. It cannot be true. Loyalty is important and will be returned in kind, but it is not all encompassing. Employees cannot expect absolute loyalty; neither can the company. To do so would be destructive and incongruent with business realities.

In addition to the loyalty belief, the expectation of continuous, unparalleled growth was shattered. To me this is not disastrous. For this expectation to have continued to prosper would have been destructive. We now must work toward a realistic and functional belief structure.

A production engineer and a quality control specialist were among those commenting on the effects of this shattering experience.

Production engineer. Whatever the company had with its employees before the reduction rift is gone. Consider my case. I looked around and saw men and women with twice my years of service being dismissed, men and women with children entering college and graduate school, men and women with all kinds of advanced degrees, men and women who never had worked for any other company. My conclusion? It could happen to me! My sheer sense of loyalty to the corporation used to make me do things beyond the call of duty. The loyalty I had has been greatly reduced. I am gravely concerned for my family and myself. When I reach 45 or 50, the company may kick me out. I saw good people with years of service go out the door. This signaled to me that Webster is no longer a "cradle to the grave" organization. I would like to feel reasonably comfortable that if I am doing a good job, I am safe. I would like some assurance that if I should peak out after a good career, I will be

working here as long as I am doing my job well. The reduction did not give me that assurance. I saw the dismissal of individuals who had leveled off, *but who were doing fully satisfactory work in their position.* Does this company have a place for a good, solid performing, "peaked-out," middle-aged employee? I once thought it did, but now I am no longer certain.

Quality control specialist. The reduction has resulted in growing uncertainty, anxiety, and cynicism. Morale is low. Webster gave the individuals who survived no hope of promotions and, indeed, demoted several managers. On top of this, the company established a salary freeze. Those of us who remain are concerned that the company will not admit its mistakes. For example, in several cases Webster dismissed the wrong people but refused to rehire them. There is also a general belief—rightly or wrongly—that everybody terminated got more money in their new jobs. Many survivors are now beginning to wonder just how well off they are here at Webster. Cynicism toward personnel policies and practices is unbelievably high. A sign reading "Up your MBO and all that" was placed on one of the bulletin boards.

Most of the manufacturing managerial personnel agreed with Carter that the reduction and the shattering of the belief structure were positive factors. One plant manager in particular saw the shattering of the belief structure as beneficial:

I think maybe many of us were getting too comfortable. I am really a firm believer that an employee should not get too secure, but ought to always be a little afraid of losing his or her job. Employees should never get *too* comfortable—either because of seniority or performance. This holds for everybody! Security leads to performance below potential. I've seen it happen. People start arriving late in the morning and leaving early in the evening. Of course, uncertainty should not be carried to the extreme. A person should not have to come to work uncertain as to whether he or she will have a job at the day's end. However, some uncertainty is definitely in order.

The most frequent question asked by terminated employees was, "Why me?" This was especially true if he or she had a record of good performance or had received few formal appraisals. In several instances, separated employees reportedly were told in essence, "There was a meeting and your name came up on the list. I'm sorry, but I do not know any more." What most disturbed those terminated was their inability to place the dismissals in a performance context. Unable to relate their separation to poor performance, many concluded that other factors were involved—for example, politics, membership in the right groups, or the ability to keep selling oneself.

Reportedly, wives felt betrayed by the dismissals of their husbands. One manager commented: "Wives were much more bitter than their separated husbands. A typical reaction was, 'Here we go again. After all you have done for the company, this [separation] is the thanks you get. And this is the thanks I get for being a camp follower.'"

Despite their puzzlement over the reduction decision-making process, terminated employees and their families were happy with the services provided by the Human Resources Division. In effect, the division became an outplacement center offering a number of services: training in the writing of résumés; circulation of job information; arrangement of carpools to Atlanta for visits with regional and national recruiters; and location of facilities for headhunters who wanted to recruit in Clearwater. Most of the released employees gave Webster an "A" in the area of "services rendered after termination." One individual reported, "I got more

from personnel after I was separated than when I was employed."

Performance Appraisal

The common denominator underlying the various reactions to the reduction in force was a strong feeling that "something had to be done about performance appraisal." This sentiment was pervasive at all levels of the organization. Abe Webster spoke on the topic at the monthly meeting of divisional vice presidents:

> The fact that many individuals terminated did not know where they stood in their managers' eyes reflected poor managerial practice. My position is that every Webster employee has a right to know where he or she stands and to be helped in his or her development. Managers must develop the capability of telling the employee "how it is." If he or she is doing well, the manager should communicate his satisfaction. Similarly, if the individual is doing poorly, the manager should make it known. The employee should be told, "If you do not do (a)—(b)—(c)— and (d)—, you will be asked to leave." We owe it to our people—especially the young people we bring on board—to give them honest and clear feedback and assistance.

Mark Webster, chairman of the company's board, concurred with his son Abe except that he believed the individual should always be given hope, so that he or she would remain motivated. Abe was in agreement with the psychology of his father's perspective, but he thought that it could lead to some poor decisions. He felt that motivational considerations should be handled separately from the feedback process. His position was, "the truth should be told."

There was some opinion at Webster that managerial resistance to PAS stemmed from concerns about its design. In particular, some complained about tying salary to performance ratings. The contention was that this link encouraged managers to play games in order to get top salary adjustments for their people. On the other hand, the Human Resources Division staff argued that each manager was allotted a certain amount for salary adjustments in total and was expected to adhere to his or her allotment. Consequently, the opportunity for playing games was considerably reduced.

Another complaint was that the system was so complex that it often was misused. One example cited was the Performance Profile. Reports were plentiful that the profile, though not designed for comparative purposes, was being used to rank employees.

Jasper Calhoun, a personnel auditor who was involved in the designing of PAS, believed the problem to be external to the system:

> Our managers simply are not cold-blooded enough. . . . [*pause*] I guess *objective* is a better word than *cold-blooded*. Right? . . . [*pause*] In any event our managers are not objective enough to tell an individual how he or she is doing. We're going to have to squeeze the managers to get them to use PAS. Our young people deserve to be told how they are doing and how they can improve.

> We need a monitoring system that will insure usage. Monitoring could be done by keeping track of each manager's percentage of completions and the extent to which he or she follows through on recommendations from the Human Resources Division. The monitoring system also could be used to track the promotions process to insure that promotions are based on appraisals. To work, the monitoring system must have *teeth*! There should be some punishment for failure to use PAS.

The danger of such a monitoring system is that the manager will feel so controlled that PAS will be viewed more as an imposition from above than as a potentially useful tool. I firmly believe that PAS—like any performance appraisal system—is a necessary tool for fulfillment of managerial responsibility.

Carter's New Task

Approximately two weeks after the reduction, Ike Davis—head of the Fabrics Division—approached Carter about attaining 100 percent utilization of PAS. Davis informed Carter that the Human Resources Division was soliciting suggestions as to how full utilization might be realized. Reportedly, they were open to recommendations on design changes and implementation strategy. Davis wanted Carter to represent the Fabrics Division at an off-site brainstorming session the following week. The purpose of the meeting would be to formulate an implementation plan for PAS.

READING 1
EVOLUTION AND REVOLUTION AS ORGANIZATIONS GROW*
A Company's Past Has Clues for Management That Are Critical to Future Success
Larry E. Greiner

Foreword

This author maintains that growing organizations move through five distinguishable phases of development, each of which contains a relatively calm period of growth that

Author's note: This article is part of a continuing project on organization development with my colleague, Professor Louis B. Barnes, and sponsored by the Division of Research, Harvard Business School.

ends with a management crisis. He argues, moreover, that since each phase is strongly influenced by the previous one, a management with a sense of its own organization's history can anticipate and prepare for the next developmental crisis. This article provides a prescription for appropriate management action in each of the five phases, and it shows how companies can turn organizational crises into opportunities for future growth.

Mr. Greiner is Associate Professor of Organizational Behavior at the Harvard Business School and is the author of several previous HBR articles on organization development.

A small research company chooses too complicated and formalized an organization structure for its young age and limited size. It flounders in rigidity and bureaucracy for several years and is finally acquired by a larger company.

Key executives of a retail store chain hold on to an organization structure long after it has served its purpose, because their power is derived from this structure. The company eventually goes into bankruptcy.

A large bank disciplines a "rebellious" manager who is blamed for current control problems, when the underlying cause is centralized procedures that are holding back expansion into new markets. Many younger managers subsequently leave the bank, competition moves in, and profits are still declining.

The problems of these companies, like those of many others, are rooted more in past decisions than in present events or outside market dynamics. Historical forces do indeed shape the future growth of organizations. Yet management, in its haste to grow, often overlooks such critical developmental questions as: Where has our organization been? Where is it now? And what do the answers to these questions mean for where we are going? Instead, its gaze is fixed outward toward the environment and the future—as if more precise market projections will provide a new organizational identity.

Companies fail to see that many clues to their future success lie within their own organizations and their evolving states of development. Moreover, the inability of management to understand its organization development problems can result in a company becoming "frozen" in its present stage of evolution or, ultimately, in failure, regardless of market opportunities.

My position in this article is that the future of an organization may be less determined by outside forces than it is by the organization's history. In stressing the force of history on an organization, I have drawn from the legacies of European psychologists (their thesis being that individual behavior is determined primarily by previous events and experiences, not by what lies ahead). Extending this analogy of individual development to the problems of organization development, I shall discuss a series of developmental phases through which growing companies tend to pass. But, first, let me provide two definitions:

1. The term *evolution* is used to describe prolonged periods of growth where no major upheaval occurs in organization practices.

2. The term *revolution* is used to describe those periods of substantial turmoil in organization life.

As a company progresses through developmental phases, each evolutionary period creates its own revolution. For instance, centralized practices eventually lead to demands for decentralization. Moreover, the nature of management's solution to each revolutionary period determines whether a company will move forward into its next stage of evolutionary growth. As I shall show later, there are at least five phases of organization development, each characterized by both an evolution and a revolution.

Key Forces in Development

During the past few years a small amount of research knowledge about the phases of organization development has been building. Some of this research is very quantitative, such as time-series analyses that reveal patterns of economic performance over time.[1] The majority of studies, however, are case-oriented and use company records and interviews to reconstruct a rich picture of corporate development.[2] Yet both types of research tend to be heavily empirical without attempting more generalized statements about the overall process of development.

A notable exception is the historical work of Alfred D. Chandler, Jr., in his book *Strategy and Structure*.[3] This study depicts four very broad and general phases in the lives of four large U.S. companies. It proposes that outside market opportunities determine a company's strategy, which in turn determines the company's organization structure. This thesis has a valid ring for the four companies examined by Chandler, largely because they developed in a time of explosive markets and technological advances. But more recent evidence suggests that organization structure may be less mal-

leable than Chandler assumed; in fact, structure can play a critical role in influencing corporate strategy. It is this reverse emphasis on how organization structure affects future growth which is highlighted in the model presented in this article.

From an analysis of recent studies,[4] five key dimensions emerge as essential for building a model of organization development:

1. Age of the organization.
2. Size of the organization.
3. Stages of evolution.
4. Stages of revolution.
5. Growth rate of the industry.

I shall describe each of these elements separately, but first note their combined effect as illustrated in Exhibit 1. Note especially how each dimension influences the other over time; when all five elements begin to interact, a more complete and dynamic picture of organizational growth emerges.

After describing these dimensions and their interconnections, I shall discuss each evolutionary/revolutionary phase of development and show (*a*) how each stage of evolution breeds its own revolution, and (*b*) how management solutions to each revolution determine the next stage of evolution.

Age of the Organization. The most obvious and essential dimension for any model of development is the life span of an organi-

---

[1] See, for example, William H. Starbuck, "Organizational Metamorphosis," in *Promising Research Directions*, edited by R. W. Millman and M. P. Hottenstein (Tempe, Ariz.: Academy of Management, 1968), p. 113.

[2] See, for example, the *Grangesberg* case series, prepared by C. Roland Christensen and Bruce R. Scott, Case Clearing House, Harvard Business School.

[3] *Strategy and Structure: Chapters in the History of the American Industrial Enterprise* (Cambridge, Mass.: M.I.T. Press, 1962).

[4] I have drawn on many sources for evidence: (*a*) numerous cases collected at the Harvard Business School; (*b*) *Organization Growth and Development*, edited by William H. Starbuck (Middlesex, England: Penguin Books, Ltd., 1971), where several studies are cited; and (*c*) articles published in journals, such as Lawrence E. Fouraker and John M. Stopford, "Organization Structure and the Multinational Strategy," *Administrative Science Quarterly*, vol. 13, no. 1, 1968, p. 47; and Malcolm S. Salter, "Management Appraisal and Reward Systems," *Journal of Business Policy*, vol. 1, no. 4, 1971.

Exhibit 1   **Model of Organization Development**

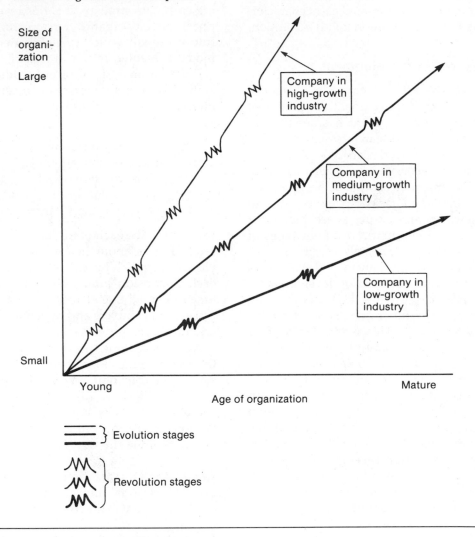

zation (represented as the horizontal axis in Exhibit 1). All historical studies gather data from various points in time and then make comparisons. From these observations, it is evident that the same organization practices are not maintained throughout a long time span. This makes a most basic point: management problems and principles are rooted

in time. The concept of decentralization, for example, can have meaning for describing corporate practices at one time period but loses its descriptive power at another.

The passage of time also contributes to the institutionalization of managerial attitudes. As a result, employee behavior becomes not only more predictable but also more difficult to change when attitudes are outdated.

Size of the Organization.   This dimension is depicted as the vertical axis in Exhibit 1. A company's problems and solutions tend to change markedly as the number of employees and sales volume increase. Thus, time is not the only determinant of structure; in fact, organizations that do not grow in size can retain many of the same management issues and practices over lengthy periods. In addition to increased size, however, problems of coordination and communication magnify, new functions emerge, levels in the management hierarchy multiply, and jobs become more interrelated.

Stages of Evolution.   As both age and size increase, another phenomenon becomes evident: the prolonged growth that I have termed the evolutionary period. Most growing organizations do not expand for two years and then retreat for one year; rather, those that survive a crisis usually enjoy four to eight years of continuous growth without a major economic setback or severe internal disruption. The term evolution seems appropriate for describing these quieter periods because only modest adjustments appear necessary for maintaining growth under the same overall pattern of management.

Stages of Revolution.   Smooth evolution is not inevitable; it cannot be assumed that organization growth is linear. *Fortune*'s "500" list, for example, has had significant turnover during the last 50 years. Thus we find evidence from numerous case histories which reveals periods of substantial turbulence spaced between smoother periods of evolution.

I have termed these turbulent times the periods of revolution because they typically exhibit a serious upheaval of management practices. Traditional management practices, which were appropriate for a smaller size and earlier time, are brought under scrutiny by frustrated top managers and disillusioned lower-level managers. During such periods of crisis, a number of companies fail—those unable to abandon past practices and effect major organization changes are likely either to fold or to level off in their growth rates.

The critical task for management in each revolutionary period is to find a new set of organization practices that will become the basis for managing the next period of evolutionary growth. Interestingly enough, these new practices eventually sow their own seeds of decay and lead to another period of revolution. Companies therefore experience the irony of seeing a major solution in one time period become a major problem at a latter date.

Growth Rate of the Industry.   The speed at which an organization experiences phases of evolution and revolution is closely related to the market environment of its industry. For example, a company in a rapidly expanding market will have to add employees rapidly; hence, the need for new organization structures to accommodate large staff increases is accelerated. While evolutionary periods tend to be relatively short in fast-growing industries, much longer evolutionary periods occur in mature or slowly growing industries.

Evolution can also be prolonged, and revolutions delayed, when profits come easily. For instance, companies that make grievous errors in a rewarding industry can still look good on their profit and loss statements; thus they can avoid a change in management practices for a longer period. The aerospace industry in its infancy is an example. Yet revolutionary periods still occur, as one did in aerospace when profit opportunities began to dry up. Revolutions seem to be much more severe and difficult to resolve when the market environment is poor.

Phases of Growth

With the foregoing framework in mind, let us now examine in depth the five specific phases of evolution and revolution. As shown in Exhibit 2, each evolutionary period is characterized by the dominant *management style* used to achieve growth, while each revolutionary period is characterized by the dominant *management problem* that must be solved before growth can continue. The patterns presented in Exhibit 2 seem to be typical for companies in industries with moderate growth over a long time period; companies in faster growing industries tend to experience all five phases more rapidly, while those in slower growing industries

Exhibit 2   **The Five Phases of Growth**

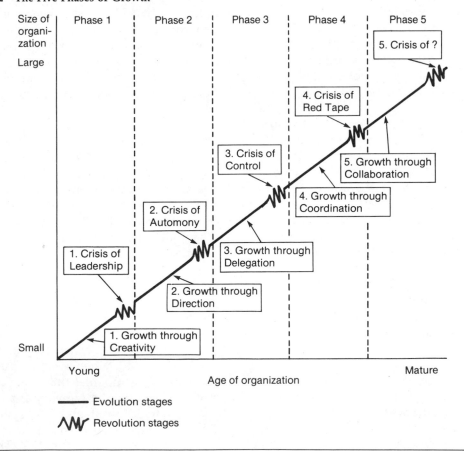

— Evolution stages

⋀⋁⋀ Revolution stages

encounter only two or three phases over many years.

It is important to note that *each phase is both an effect of the previous phase and a cause for the next phase.* For example, the evolutionary management style in Phase 3 of the exhibit is "delegation," which grows out of, and becomes the solution to, demands for greater "autonomy" in the preceding Phase 2 revolution. The style of delegation used in Phase 3, however, eventually provokes a major revolutionary crisis that is characterized by attempts to regain control over the diversity created through increased delegation.

The principal implication of each phase is that management actions are narrowly prescribed if growth is to occur. For example, a company experiencing an autonomy crisis in Phase 2 cannot return to directive management for a solution—it must adopt a new style of delegation in order to move ahead.

Phase 1: Creativity. . .

In the birth stage of an organization, the emphasis is on creating both a product and a market. Here are the characteristics of the period of creative evolution:

• The company's founders are usually technically or entrepreneurially oriented, and they disdain management activities; their physical and mental energies are absorbed entirely in making and selling a new product.

• Communication among employees is frequent and informal.

• Long hours of work are rewarded by modest salaries and the promise of ownership benefits.

• Control of activities comes from immediate marketplace feedback; the management acts as the customers react.

. . . The Leadership Crisis. All of the foregoing individualistic and creative activities are essential for the company to get off the ground. But therein lies the problem. As the company grows, larger production runs require knowledge about the efficiencies of manufacturing. Increased numbers of employees cannot be managed exclusively through informal communication; new employees are not motivated by an intense dedication to the product or organization. Additional capital must be secured, and new accounting procedures are needed for financial control.

Thus the founders find themselves burdened with unwanted management responsibilities. So they long for the "good old days," still trying to act as they did in the past. And conflicts between the harried leaders grow more intense.

At this point a crisis of leadership occurs, which is the onset of the first revolution. Who is to lead the company out of confusion and solve the managerial problems confronting it? Quite obviously, a strong manager is needed who has the necessary knowledge and skill to introduce new business techniques. But this is easier said than done. The founders often hate to step aside even though they are probably temperamentally unsuited to be managers. So here is the first critical developmental choice—to locate and install a strong business manager who is acceptable to the founders and who can pull the organization together.

Phase 2: Direction . . .

Those companies that survive the first phase by installing a capable business manager usually embark on a period of sustained growth under able and directive leadership. Here are the characteristics of this evolutionary period:

• A functional organization structure is introduced to separate manufacturing from marketing activities, and job assignments become more specialized.

• Accounting systems for inventory and purchasing are introduced.

• Incentives, budgets, and work standards are adopted.

• Communication becomes more formal and impersonal as a hierarchy of titles and positions builds.

• The new manager and his key supervisors take most of the responsibility for instituting direction, while lower-level supervisors are treated more as functional specialists than as autonomous decision-making managers.

. . . **The Autonomy Crisis.** Although the new directive techniques channel employee energy more efficiently into growth, they eventually become inappropriate for controlling a larger, more diverse and complex organization. Lower-level employees find themselves restricted by a cumbersome and centralized hierarchy. They have come to possess more direct knowledge about markets and machinery than do the leaders at the top; consequently, they feel torn between following procedures and taking initiative on their own.

Thus the second revolution is imminent as a crisis develops from demands for greater autonomy on the part of lower-level managers. The solution adopted by most companies is to move toward greater delegation. Yet it is difficult for top managers who were previously successful at being directive to give up responsibility. Moreover, lower-level managers are not accustomed to making decisions for themselves. As a result, numerous companies flounder during this revolutionary period, adhering to centralized methods while lower-level employees grow more disenchanted and leave the organization.

Phase 3: Delegation . . .

The next era of growth evolves from the successful application of a decentralized organization structure. It exhibits these characteristics:

• Much greater responsibility is given to the managers of plants and market territories.

• Profit centers and bonuses are used to stimulate motivation.

• The top executives at headquarters restrain themselves to managing by exception, based on periodic reports from the field.

• Management often concentrates on making new acquisitions which can be lined up beside other decentralized units.

• Communication from the top is infrequent, usually by correspondence, telephone, or brief visits to field locations.

The delegation stage proves useful for gaining expansion through heightened motivation at lower levels. Decentralized managers with greater authority and incentive are able to penetrate larger markets, respond faster to customers, and develop new products.

. . . **The Control Crisis.** A serious problem eventually evolves, however, as top executives sense that they are losing control over a highly diversified field operation. Autonomous field managers prefer to run their own shows without coordinating plans, money, technology, and manpower with the rest of the organization. Freedom breeds a parochial attitude.

Hence, the Phase 3 revolution is under way when top management seeks to regain control over the total company. Some top managements attempt to return to centralized management, which usually fails because of the vast scope of operations. Those companies that move ahead find a new solution in the use of special coordination techniques.

Phase 4: Coordination . . .

During this phase, the evolutionary period is characterized by the use of formal systems for achieving greater coordination and by top executives taking responsibility for the initiation and administration of these new systems. For example:

• Decentralized units are merged into product groups.
• Formal planning procedures are established and intensively reviewed.
• Numerous staff personnel are hired and located at headquarters to initiate companywide programs of control and review for line managers.
• Capital expenditures are carefully weighed and parceled out across the organization.
• Each product group is treated as an investment center where return on invested capital is an important criterion used in allocating funds.
• Certain technical functions, such as data processing, are centralized at headquarters, while daily operating decisions remain decentralized.
• Stock options and companywide profit sharing are used to encourage identity with the firm as a whole.

All of these new coordination systems prove useful for achieving growth through more efficient allocation of a company's limited resources. They prompt field managers to look beyond the needs of their local units.

While these managers still have much decision-making responsibility, they learn to justify their actions more carefully to a "watchdog" audience at headquarters.

. . . The Red-Tape Crisis. But a lack of confidence gradually builds between line and staff, and between headquarters and the field. The proliferation of systems and programs begins to exceed its utility; a red-tape crisis is created. Line managers, for example, increasingly resent heavy staff direction from those who are not familiar with local conditions. Staff people, on the other hand, complain about uncooperative and uninformed line managers. Together both groups criticize the bureaucratic paper system that has evolved. Procedures take precedence over problem solving, and innovation is dampened. In short, the organization has become too large and complex to be managed through formal programs and rigid systems. The Phase 4 revolution is under way.

Phase 5: Collaboration . . .

The last observable phase in previous studies emphasizes strong interpersonal collaboration in an attempt to overcome the red-tape crisis. Where Phase 4 was managed more through formal systems and procedures, Phase 5 emphasizes greater spontaneity in management action through teams and the skillful confrontation of interpersonal differences. Social control and self-discipline take over from formal control. This transition is especially difficult for those experts who created the old systems as well as for those line managers who relied on formal methods for answers.

The Phase 5 evolution, then, builds around a more flexible and behavioral approach to management. Here are its characteristics:

- The focus is on solving problems quickly through team action.
- Teams are combined across functions for task-group activity.
- Headquarters staff experts are reduced in number, reassigned, and combined in interdisciplinary teams to consult with, not to direct, field units.
- A matrix-type structure is frequently used to assemble the right teams for the appropriate problems.
- Previous formal systems are simplified and combined into single multipurpose systems.
- Conferences of key managers are held frequently to focus on major problem issues.
- Educational programs are utilized to train managers in behavioral skills for achieving better teamwork and conflict resolution.
- Real-time information systems are integrated into daily decision making.
- Economic rewards are geared more to team performance than to individual achievement.
- Experiments in new practices are encouraged throughout the organization.

. . . The ? Crisis.   What will be the revolution in response to this stage of evolution? Many large U.S. companies are now in the Phase 5 evolutionary stage, so the answers are critical. While there is little clear evidence, I imagine the revolution will center around the "psychological saturation" of employees who grow emotionally and physically exhausted by the intensity of teamwork and the heavy pressure for innovative solutions.

My hunch is that the Phase 5 revolution will be solved through new structures and programs that allow employees to periodically rest, reflect, and revitalize themselves. We may even see companies with dual organization structures: a "habit" structure for getting the daily work done, and a "reflective" structure for stimulating perspective and personal enrichment. Employees could then move back and forth between the two structures as their energies are dissipated and refueled.

One European organization has implemented just such a structure. Five reflective groups have been established outside the regular structure for the purpose of continuously evaluating five task activities basic to the organization. They report directly to the managing director, although their reports are made public throughout the organization. Membership in each group includes all levels and functions, and employees are rotated through these groups on a six-month basis.

Other concrete examples now in practice include providing sabbaticals for employees, moving managers in and out of "hot spot" jobs, establishing a four-day workweek, assuring job security, building physical facilities for relaxation *during* the working day, making jobs more interchangeable, creating an extra team on the assembly line so that one team is always off for reeducation, and switching to longer vacations and more flexible working hours.

The Chinese practice of requiring executives to spend time periodically on lower-level jobs may also be worth a nonideological evaluation. For too long U.S. management has assumed that career progress should be equated with an upward path toward title, salary, and power. Could it be that some vice presidents of marketing might just long for, and even benefit from, temporary duty in the field sales organization?

Implications of History

Let me now summarize some important implications for practicing managers. First, the main features of this discussion are depicted in Exhibit 3, which shows the specific management actions that characterize each growth phase. These actions are also the solutions which ended each preceding revolutionary period.

In one sense, I hope that many readers will react to my model by calling it obvious and natural for depicting the growth of an organization. To me this type of reaction is a useful test of the model's validity.

Exhibit 3   Organization Practices during Evolution in the Five Phases of Growth

	PHASE 1	PHASE 2	PHASE 3	PHASE 4	PHASE 5
MANAGEMENT FOCUS	Make & sell	Efficiency of operations	Expansion of market	Consolidation of organization	Problem solving & innovation
ORGANIZATION STRUCTURE	Informal	Centralized & functional	Decentralized & geographical	Line-staff & product groups	Matrix of teams
TOP MANAGEMENT STYLE	Individualistic & entrepreneurial	Directive	Delegative	Watchdog	Participative
CONTROL SYSTEM	Market results	Standards & cost centers	Reports & profit centers	Plans & investment centers	Mutual goal setting
MANAGEMENT REWARD EMPHASIS	Ownership	Salary & merit increases	Individual bonus	Profit sharing & stock options	Team bonus

---

But at a more reflective level I imagine some of these reactions are more hindsight than foresight. Those experienced managers who have been through a developmental sequence can empathize with it now, but how did they react when in the middle of a stage of evolution or revolution? They can probably recall the limits of their own developmental understanding at that time. Perhaps they resisted desirable changes or were even swept emotionally into a revolution without being able to propose constructive solutions. So let me offer some explicit guidelines for managers of growing organizations to keep in mind.

Know where you are in the developmental sequence.

Every organization and its component parts are at different stages of development. The task of top management is to be aware of these stages; otherwise, it may not recognize when the time for change has come, or it may act to impose the wrong solution.

Top leaders should be ready to work with the flow of the tide rather than against it; yet they should be cautious, since it is tempting to skip phases out of impatience. Each phase results in certain strengths and learning experiences in the organization that will be essential for success in subsequent phases. A child prodigy, for example, may be able to read like a teenager, but he cannot behave like one until he ages through a sequence of experiences.

I also doubt that managers can or should act to avoid revolutions. Rather, these periods of tension provide the pressure, ideas, and awareness that afford a platform for change and the introduction of new practices.

Recognize the limited range of solutions.

In each revolutionary stage it becomes evident that this stage can be ended only by certain specific solutions; moreover, these solutions are different from those which were applied to the problems of the preceding revolution. Too often it is tempting to choose solutions that were tried before, which makes it impossible for a new phase of growth to evolve.

Management must be prepared to dismantle current structures before the revolutionary stage becomes too turbulent. Top managers, realizing that their own managerial styles are no longer appropriate, may even have to take themselves out of leadership positions. A good Phase 2 manager facing Phase 3 might be wise to find another Phase 2 organization that better fits his talents, either outside the company or with one of its newer subsidiaries.

Finally, evolution is not an automatic affair; it is a contest for survival. To move ahead, companies must consciously introduce planned structures that not only are solutions to a current crisis but also are fitted to the *next* phase of growth. This requires considerable self-awareness on the part of top management, as well as great interpersonal skill in persuading other managers that change is needed.

Realize that solutions breed new problems.

Managers often fail to realize that organizational solutions create problems for the future (i.e., a decision to delegate eventually causes a problem of control). Historical actions are very much determinants of what happens to the company at a much later date.

An awareness of this effect should help managers to evaluate company problems with greater historical understanding instead of "pinning the blame" on the current development. Better yet, managers should be in a position to *predict* future problems, and thereby to prepare solutions and coping strategies before a revolution gets out of hand.

A management that is aware of the problems ahead could well decide *not* to grow. Top managers may, for instance, prefer to retain the informal practices of a small company, knowing that this way of life is inherent in the organization's limited size, not in their congenial personalities. If they choose to grow, they may do themselves out of a job and a way of life they enjoy.

And what about the managements of very large organizations? Can they find new solutions for continued phases of evolution? Or are they reaching a stage where the government will act to break them up because they are too large.

Concluding Note

Clearly, there is still much to learn about processes of development in organizations. The phases outlined here are only five in number and are still only approximations. Researchers are just beginning to study the specific developmental problems of structure, control, rewards, and management style in different industries and in a variety of cultures.

One should not, however, wait for conclusive evidence before educating managers to think and act from a developmental perspective. The critical dimension of time has been missing for too long from our management theories and practices. The intriguing paradox is that by learning more about history we may do a better job in the future.

READING 2
PROBLEMS OF HUMAN RESOURCE MANAGEMENT IN RAPIDLY GROWING COMPANIES*
John Kotter and Vijay Sathe

Rapid growth companies—that is, companies that grow at an average rate greater than 20 percent per year (in number of employees) for at least four or five years in a row—are of considerable importance to managers, investors, and the public at large. They offer managers an exciting place to work and significant career advancement opportunities. It is not uncommon to find young managers in top spots in these companies. They offer the investor the chance for a much greater than average financial return. It boggles the mind to think how much money was made by those who bought large blocks of IBM, Polaroid, or Xerox stock around 1950. And rapid growth companies offer the public at large a significant source of expanding employment. Just a few rapidly growing companies in the

same geographic region can sometimes make the difference between a stagnant economy with high unemployment and a robust economy with low unemployment.

Those interested in rapid-growth companies would agree that most of them share a common key to their success—their high rate of growth is sustained by virtue of their position of leadership in a rapidly expanding production/market area. This leadership position is typically achieved and maintained via the aggressive marketing of new and technically sophisticated goods or services. Through good fortune or shrewd calculation, these companies tend to be at the right place, at the right time, with the right set of capabilities.

People interested in rapid-growth companies seem to be much less aware of the fact that most of these firms share at least one other important pattern in common. These companies tend to experience similar human resource problems.[1] These problems are important because the way in which managers deal with them typically determines whether or not the company will be able to sustain its rapid growth over time.

In this article we will first identify the common problems that seem to plague rapid growth companies, and then discuss solutions that some of the more successful ones have used to deal with them. This article is based on our experiences with 12 companies that have grown on the average at 40 percent per year for five or more years.

------

[1] Two recent articles deal with some of this subject. One is based on a study of five small (100–200 employees) but rapidly growing firms: George Strauss, "Adolescence in Organizational Growth," *Organizational Dynamics*, Spring 1974. The other is based on the experience of one rapidly growing firm: William George, "Task Teams for Rapid Growth," *Harvard Business Review*, March–April 1977.

Problems Caused by the Need for Rapid Decisions

The president of one rapidly growing firm told us the following story, which highlights one of the problems created by rapid growth:

> I was having lunch with an acquaintance of mine who is the president of a company that is about twice our current size. His firm has been growing at between 5 and 7 percent per year for the last 10 years. I was telling him about some of the decisions I had made during the previous two weeks and some of the decisions I had to make in the upcoming week. At one point he stopped me and said something like, "You know, you make as many important business decisions in a month as I do in a year." And while he may be exaggerating a bit, I think he's basically right. Since we grow at about 5 percent per month, I end up making decisions in a month that he gets nearly a year to make.

The speed with which decisions must be made in rapid-growth companies puts a strain on management that many people simply cannot cope with. Many of us intellectually and emotionally need more time to make decisions than is available in such situations. We need time to get relevant information, to analyze that information, to identify alternative decisions, and to select a decision. Especially when the decision stakes are high, many people need time to emotionally come to grips with their intellectual choice. For some managers, this needed time runs into, months or even years.

The required decision-making speed in rapid-growth companies also places the organizational structure under stress. The need for quick new product design, development, manufacturing, and marketing decisions, which is characteristic of these companies, requires a rapid flow of information across departmental lines and close cross-functional coordination. The traditional functional structure is not designed to cope with these requirements. It is best equipped to handle a more stable set of tasks. When it is small, a rapidly growing company can achieve the necessary cross-functional coordination because of the flexibility afforded by its small size. As it grows, however, the traditional functional structure will start to cause problems for a rapid-growth company. Decisions will begin to "fall between the cracks." Decisions will not be made. And certain activities will get "bogged down" because the structure cannot cope with the rapidly changing environment.

The need for rapid decisions has a similar impact on informal structure and culture. The informal relationships among individuals and groups in organizations almost always include some distrust, suspicion, bad feelings, and misunderstandings. All of these factors impede smooth information flow, effective collaboration, and rapid decision making. When a company is small, these relationships can be managed so as not to undermine effective decision making. But growth makes such management more difficult because the number of relationships to be managed increases more rapidly than the number of employees.

Problems Caused by Rapidly Expanding Job Demands

Similar organization positions in companies of very different size obviously place quite different demands on the incumbents. The job of the chief financial officer in a $10 million company, for example, is significantly different from that of the person holding the same position in a $150 million company. Internal reporting and control, data processing, financial planning, annual budgeting, and internal auditing all would probably be a significant part of the responsibilities of the chief financial officer of the larger company. Most, if not all, of these functions would probably be absent in the smaller company. Since a rapid-growth company's annual sales could grow from $10 million to $150 million in just a few years, the chief financial officer's job in such a company could change dramatically in a relatively short time period. Some people can adjust to such a change. Many cannot.

Peter Drucker has said that one of the biggest impediments to successful growth is the inability of key managers to change their attitudes and behavior to fit the changing needs of the organization.[2] And while Drucker is talking about all growth situations, we believe this is especially true in high growth situations.

The problem of people not being able to change as rapidly as their jobs typically creates two more problems. First, it often leads to a shouting match between various levels of management regarding questions of delegation and development. For example:

- A middle-level manager: The biggest problem we have in this company is top management's unwillingness to delegate more. My boss is still making the same kinds of decisions in the same ways he did five years ago. But the company today is three times as large as it was then. He should be doing other things today and delegating many of those decisions to me.

- A top manager: Our biggest problem today is somehow getting middle management to the point where they can handle their ever increasing responsibilities. I'm still making some decisions that I should not be making. But I have no qualified person

beneath me to whom I can delegate those decisions.

- A middle-level manager: Top management says that we are not ready to handle more delegation. But how are we ever going to get ready if they don't allow us to make some of those decisions. Sure we would probably make a few errors, but we would learn a lot in the process.

- A top manager: We can't afford mistakes around here. We cannot take chances with the record of success we have had here.

People's inability to grow and change as quickly as their jobs creates a second problem related to unmet career expectations. Managers often join rapid-growth companies for the advancement opportunities. But many of these companies find it necessary to fill between 10 and 50 percent of their non-entry-level openings from the outside because people with the necessary experience are not being developed as rapidly as needed within the company. When an ambitious person sees numerous higher-level jobs filled from the outside, he or she often becomes frustrated.

Finally, people's inability to grow with job demands can place key managers in difficult, guilt-eliciting positions. The following story has been repeated to us in varying forms literally dozens of times:

Jerry was my fourth employee. I hired him in 1966 to be my first full time salesman. He worked long hours for us and got two key contracts that saved the company in 1967.

When we hired our seventh salesman, I made Jerry sales manager. And in 1971, I made him vice president for sales. Today, in 1977, we have revenues of 25 million on a yearly basis, the marketing department has nearly 100 employees, and Jerry is way over his head.

In retrospect, I should never have made him vice president of sales in 1971. But he

---

[2] Peter Drucker, *The Practice of Management* (New York: Harper & Row, 1954), pp. 246–52.

expected the title change since I had just made my engineering manager the vice president of engineering. And I didn't want to hurt his feelings or make him think I didn't fully appreciate the loyalty and long hours he had given the company.

Today his inability to manage his department is hurting us severely, but I have delayed moving him for months. I know I have to act soon. But god, it's hard. I really think that as much as I love my wife, throwing her out of the house would not be as emotionally demanding.

Problems Caused by Large Recruiting and Training Demands

Perhaps the most obvious problems faced by fast-growing companies are recruiting and training. Fast growth requires the recruitment, selection, and assimilation of large numbers of people. And for most rapidly growing companies, satisfying this need at an affordable cost is difficult.

The slow-growing company in a mature industry can often satisfy its hiring needs by waiting for the right people to walk in the door. It can satisfy its assimilation needs by osmosis; the relatively few new people learn the ropes from those they interact with.

Rapidly growing companies, however, cannot rely on such a passive stance. Such firms often have to hire five to ten times as many people each year as do slow-growing companies of equal size. They are forced to aggressively seek out possible employees. Because they are often in new industries or have new products or services, they may need somewhat atypical combinations of talents, which makes recruiting even more difficult. As a result, the typical high-growth company spends considerable time and energy in recruitment and selection of new employees, but is still unable to hire

people as quickly as required. A personnel officer in one such company told us:

I go through a hundred resumes a day. So do other people here, including some line managers. Our whole department is constantly involved in recruiting and hiring. And that's not necessarily good, because we neglect other duties like training and organizational development duties. But even though we are so focused on just recruiting, we still do not bring people in as quickly as many of our line managers want. To get the kind of engineers we need, for example, it usually takes us six months. In the company I worked for 10 years ago, which wasn't growing very fast at all, six months for hiring was fine. Here it's not. Our engineering vice president says the strain we put on his department by hiring so slowly is enormous.

Assimilating and training new employees is equally difficult in rapid-growth firms. Unlike the situation in a slow growth company, the new employees are seldom put in a group where they are surrounded by "old-timers" who can informally teach them the job, the company's goals and values, and the structure and procedures. It is quite possible that the average seniority of the people they interact with is a year or less. This situation can cause a number of problems, such as those described by one company president:

Our new recruits out of college can sometimes get lost in here. We had one last year that nearly cost us a $100,000 order because he was not trained or being supervised closely.

The people we hire with 10 to 20 years of prior experience can cause another type of problem. They bring with them a whole set of ideas about corporate goals, personnel philosophy, how to do things, and the like which sometimes are quite different from our own. In their cases, we not only have to teach them our ways, we have to get them to unlearn what we consider "bad habits."

The difficulty of achieving quick assimilation is particularly important because of its crucial role in rapidly growing companies. When only 2 or 3 percent of the employees are relatively new, it really doesn't matter much if they are not fully on board for six months to a year. However, when 20 to 50 percent of the employees are relatively new, how quickly they get on board matters a great deal.

Problems Caused by Constant Change

"Change is inevitable in a situation like ours," one president of a rapidly growing company told us, "and it's a fact of life we just have to learn to accept and live with. But that's easier said than done."

Rapid-growth situations tend to be full of uncertainty and ambiguity caused by constantly changing employees, job demands, structures, systems, products, and markets. And uncertainty can create problems. It is not possible, for example, to do career planning, as in a more stable and certain environment. It is very difficult to devise clear rules and procedures to help guide people's actions. Some individuals like this type of an environment, but many do not. If there are too many employees of the latter type in a high-growth situation, the strain they feel will affect organizational performance.

Constant change also means perpetual loss of the familiar, including aspects of it that were valued, and the constant need for readjustment. Psychological research shows that loss and readjustment cause stress, even on people who like change because of the challenge or the material rewards associ-

ated with it. And stress, beyond a point, creates its own problems. As one executive in a rapid-growth firm told us:

> Lots of people around here are on edge. The stress sometimes shows in their work, and in their marriages. The divorce rate in our management group is considerably above the national average.

Finally, change usually creates the need for even more change to keep the organization in balance. Increased revenues require more employees, which require more recruiting and training. Increased size eventually requires new systems to be developed, which often requires more specialists to be hired and trained. And all of these activities consume resources, which tend to be scarce in high-growth situations.

Problems Caused by a Constant Strain on Resources

Rarely are high-growth companies such a "sure bet" in the long run that investors are willing to run up operating losses in the short run. As such, the stockholders or the corporate management of these companies typically expect them to turn in at least a modest profit every year. But profit generation can be incredibly difficult, for two major reasons. First, because of constant change, these companies cannot realize the efficiencies that are possible in more stable situations. Second, rapid-growth firms typically have to plan for and operate in business environments that are always larger than their current financial resources. As the controller of one company so aptly put it:

> We are currently doing planning and development as if we were a $100 million a year company, which we will be in two years. In

terms of sales orders and manufacturing capacity, we are operating like a $50 million a year company. But the money we are putting in the bank as a result of deliveries is equivalent to yearly sales of about $35 million.

Financial analysts are familiar with this paradox—companies experiencing a substantial revenue growth are frequently cash starved. What is often overlooked, however, is that the simultaneous strain on the company's human resources is often equally or more severe.

It is not uncommon for managers and professionals in high-growth companies to complain of being "burned out," and of being unfairly compensated relative to their contributions:

- We never have enough people. Everybody works 60 to 80 hours a week. After a while it really gets to you, especially since the pay isn't that great.
- I joined the company in 1973, which means I've been here for 10 years! [From an interview in 1977.]
- My wife keeps asking me why I haven't gotten much larger bonuses. Given my contribution to the company and its success, she has a good point.

The relentless resource strain also means that people do not have the time to do anything but what is required immediately. Important activities that are not cloaked in urgency tend to fall by the wayside. Thus, the tasks of assimilation, training, and development of the ever-growing numbers of employees typically receive the short shrift from line managers who are constantly preoccupied with more pressing matters. These tasks also are often ignored by personnel people who are fully occupied with the more urgent demands of recruitment and hiring, and with routine but necessary functions, such as employee benefits and payroll. Tasks associated with the design and implementation of new information, control, and operating systems are also easily ignored. And planning of all types gets neglected.

Interaction Effects

The problems already described are difficult in themselves. If unattended, however, these problems can interact to produce a vicious circle in which the situation can get completely out of hand (see Figure 1). The following detailed case history illustrates what can happen:

Three years ago a company we are familiar with was highly effective and growing rapidly. The ability of the professional and managerial employees and the flexibility possible because of its small size enabled the firm to develop and market new products rapidly. As the company grew, so did the job demands. Some people grew with their jobs, but others began to strain under the ever-growing number of responsibilities. Most, however, were satisfied and highly motivated because the company was achieving its objectives in ways that could clearly be related to their own efforts. There was a personnel manager but no formal human resource function. However, human resource problems were generally handled effectively on a personal basis by top management.

As the company's growth continued, a point was reached at which there was a clear need for considerable human resource development activity. Although many persons were being promoted, an equally large number were being brought in from the outside to fill high-level openings. Those not promoted were skeptical when told they were passed over because they lacked the necessary experience. They felt they deserved a

Figure 1   The Consequences of Unattended Human Resource Problems in Rapid-Growth Companies

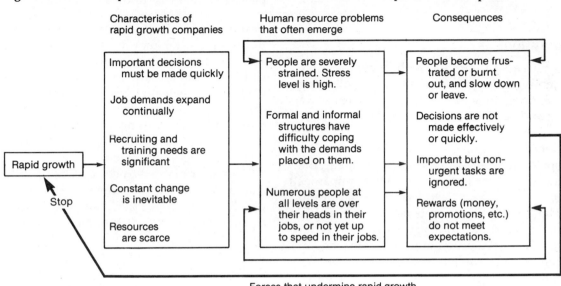

chance and could learn quickly if given the opportunity. Top managers, however, were unwilling to take chances with those who, in their opinion, were not yet ready for promotion. At one point consideration was given to establishing a human resource function to aid in the assimilation of the ever-growing number of newcomers and to help in the training and career development of all employees, particularly those not promoted. Given the demands on the company's resources that this entailed, however, the plan was "temporarily" shelved.

The situation remained as described for about one year. Those affected waited to see what action management would take. When it appeared that there would be no major change in the handling of these problems, some employees that management considered to be valuable but unpromotable began to leave. Others wondered why they were

putting in such long hours without any promotion. They began to cut back their contribution to a level they perceived as equitable with the recognition and rewards received.

The turnover and diminution of effort predictably hurt the company's performance and resulted in a greater strain on its financial and human resources. The high turnover meant that even more people had to be hired from the outside. This, in turn, led to further problems of assimilation, on the one hand, and more frustration for those not receiving promotion, on the other. Turnover continued to increase, and performance fell dramatically. The company was trapped in a vicious circle.

Today this firm's rate of growth has dropped to 12 percent per year. Profitability remains poor. Morale is low. Competition has moved in and the initial momentum has been lost. A new president has taken over recently and is in the process of deciding how best to get the company fired up again.

Solutions

Successful rapid-growth companies we know rely on some or all of the following solutions to cope with the problems we have described.

Recruiting, Selection, and Training. Despite the short-run problems related, the more successful rapid-growth companies tend to be very selective in their hiring. They screen large numbers of people, sometimes hundreds for each opening, in order to hire a large percentage of people who: (a) can perform the job without a great deal of training—as a result, they do not hire large numbers of people right out of college; (b) have obvious potential for growth; (c) like volatile environments; (d) are willing to work long hours; (e) are flexible; (f) have philosophies and personalities consistent with the company "culture."

To keep the cost of finding these types of people within bounds, a number of firms actively encourage their employees to do informal recruiting and screening whenever they can. As one human resource person told us:

> You can always spot our people at cocktail parties. They will have some guy pinned in the corner while they get information about him or while they try to sell him on the company.

To help get these people assimilated, the more successful rapid-growth firms often hold one- to three-day orientation sessions. These sessions are typically run by line executives—not staff personnel people—who outline the company's history, philosophy, strategy, structure, and compensation system. In one firm, the chief executive officer plays a central role in these sessions.[3]

Team or Matrix Structures, and Team Building. After they have reached a certain size, most successful rapid-growth companies adopt an organizational structure that relies heavily on teams or a matrix.[4] Unlike most traditional structures, these types of organizational arrangements are capable of successfully handling a volatile, rapid decision-making environment.

Team and matrix structures can be difficult to implement, however. They completely undermine the "authority must equal responsibility" dictum that most managers follow. The resulting ambiguity can be frustrating and difficult to live with. This is probably why some rapid-growth companies try to do without these structures despite the fact that they are needed.

To help make their team or matrix structure work, successful rapid-growth companies usually rely on team building activities.[5] With the aid of outside consultants or experts within their human resource department, they periodically have managers in natural work teams (which might involve people within or across departments) go away from the firm for a few days to clear up any problems that are hampering the group's effectiveness. Team building activities help members maintain good working relationships despite the ambiguity inher-

---

[3] For a more detailed description of this type of orientation session, see John P. Kotter, "The Psychological Contract: Managing the Joining Up Process," *California Management Review,* Spring 1973, pp. 91–99.

[4] See George, "Task Teams . . . ," and William Goggin, "How the Multidimensional Structure Works at Dow Corning," *Harvard Business Review,* January–February 1974.

[5] For a further description of team building, see Shel Davis, "Building More Effective Teams," *Innovations,* 1970, pp. 32–41.

ent in the organizational structure and assist in increasing a work team's ability to make effective decisions quickly.

Managing the Culture. All of the more successful rapid-growth companies we have encountered emphasize the importance of creating and maintaining a certain type of informal company culture. The characteristics of this culture include a shared belief in openness, a shared sense of what the company is and where it is going, a clearly perceived commitment to employee welfare, and norms supporting flexibility and change.

To help keep information flowing efficiently and accurately, an atmosphere of open doors, unlocked desks, and approachability is usually encouraged. "We want no secrets around here," one person told us, "and we work hard to convince people that we mean it."

People we have talked to sometimes refer to their company's "philosophy" or their company's "religion." To create this shared sense of goals and values, one firm spent considerable time and energy communicating a new corporate strategy to virtually all employees. The president of another firm had actually written a paper, which was widely circulated in the firm, on the company's philosophy. Such a shared vision, he believes, helps bind people together and helps coordinate their actions without the need for more formal rules, procedures, and structures.

The employees in the successful rapid growth companies we know of generally believed that the company really cared about its people. As one person put it:

> One of the reasons I've worked as hard as I have and feel as strongly as I do about the company is because I know it really cares about me and others.

This belief is created through many different kinds of actions. In two of these firms, job openings are always posted and insiders are always considered before hiring someone from the outside. In another company, people are given time off whenever the long hours seem to be affecting them physically.

Finally, the culture in these companies tends to be supportive of flexibility and change. This is fostered by the words and deeds of top people. One CEO, for example, has told groups of employees on numerous occasions that he is not sure he will be the right person for the CEO job in four to five years: "If I'm not, so be it. I'll find a more appropriate replacement for myself and try to contribute here in some other way."

Planning. Successful rapid-growth companies manage to find the time to do organizational and human resource planning. Being aware of the potential problems described in this article, their leaders periodically look into the future and modify current decisions if they see important problems developing. They recognize that change is inevitable and try to plan for it. They work to project human resource needs so as to keep staffing demands consistent with available resources.

This type of planning activity does not have to be time-consuming. The key to its success is largely attitudinal; that is, if managers understand the problems of rapid growth and anticipate their potential negative impact, they can devise various means of overcoming them.

Organizing and Staffing the "Personnel" Functions. Because of the potential severity of human resource problems in rapid growth firms, the more successful companies generally have a full-time, formally designated human resource function. The less successful ones seem to resist this. Instead, they cling to the more traditional role of the personnel function—recruitment, hiring, fringe benefits, and so forth.

Even when quite small ($30 million per year in revenues for manufacturing firms), successful rapid-growth companies typically have a head of human resources who is unusually talented and well paid in light of the company's size. This person generally reports directly to the president and often has a very close informal relationship with the president. Because of this relationship and the person's own competence, the human resource function is perceived as powerful and important in these companies.

In many of the more successful firms, the human resource function is also staffed below the director with a very capable group of people.

Organizationally, these people are often deployed such that each of the other departments in the company has one or more human resource personnel assigned to it. Each of these staff people then works closely with the assigned department to recruit and train people, to run team-building sessions, to help manage the culture, to plan, and to help people both understand and adjust to the inevitable stresses and strains.

Being Sensitive and Tough at the Top. The top managers of successful rapid-growth companies tend to be unusually sensitive to human resource problems and are willing to deal with them with toughness if necessary.

Without a high level of sensitivity to potential organizational and human resource problems, top management will tend either to ignore them or to relegate them to a low order of priority. And toughness is needed to deal with tasks that can be unusually unpleasant. An example is the frequent need

to replace or reassign individuals (including those at the very highest levels) whose jobs have outgrown them. Another example is the willingness to do battle with a corporate management group that may be unfamiliar with, and hence insensitive to, the special challenges and needs of human resource management in a rapidly growing company.

One of the more impressive examples of sensitivity and toughness we have seen was when a CEO replaced himself, long before retirement, with an outsider. He sensed that he was no longer appropriate for the job and that no one who reported to him could handle it then or in the foreseeable future. So he hired an outsider and explained his actions at length to a number of disappointed insiders.

There is no question that it takes a very capable group of people, and one that can absorb a lot of physical and emotional strain, to manage a high-growth company successfully. To maintain its record of success, the management of such a company needs to understand, anticipate, and overcome the problems described in this article. An awareness of the solutions used by companies that have successfully sustained high growth over long periods of time should help in devising remedies that best fit a particular situation.

READING 3
BALANCING THE
PROFESSIONAL SERVICE FIRM*
David H. Maister

The topic of managing professional service firms (including law, consulting, investment banking, accountancy, architecture, engineering, and others) has been relatively neglected by management researchers. With the exception of some primarily sociological literature and some work dealing with topics in firm administration, little attention has been given to the special problems of the professional service firm (PSF).[1] Yet in recent years large (if not giant) PSFs have emerged in most of the professional service industries.[2] The neglect of the PSF in the management literature is unfortunate, since it is generally considered that these firms differ in significant ways from most organizations, and face their own particular set of management problems.

The professional service firm is the ultimate embodiment of that familiar phrase "our assets are our people." Frequently, a PSF tends to sell to its clients the services of particular individuals (or a team of such individuals) more than the services of the firm. Professional services usually involve a high degree of interaction with the client, together with a high degree of customization. Both of these characteristics demand

that the firm attract (and retain) highly skilled individuals. The PSF, therefore, competes in two markets simultaneously: The "output" market for its services and the "input" market for its productive resources—the professional workforce. It is the need to balance the often conflicting demands and constraints imposed by these two markets that constitutes the special challenge for managers of the professional service firm.[3]

This article explores the interaction of these forces inside the professional service firm, and examines some of the major variables that firm management can attempt to manipulate in order to bring these forces into balance. The framework employed for this examination is shown in Figure 1, which illustrates the proposition that balancing the demands of the two markets is accomplished through the firm's economic and organizational structures. All four of these elements—the two markets and the two structures—are tightly interrelated. By examining each in turn, we shall attempt to identify the major variables which form the links shown in Figure 1. First, the article will examine the typical organizational structure of the firm; second, it will explore the economic structure and its relation to other elements. It shall then consider the market for professional labor, and finally discuss the market for the firm's services. As we shall see, successful PSF management is a question of balance among the four elements of Figure 1.

---

[1] For an early review of sociological literature, see: H. M. Vollmer and D. L. Mills, *Professionalization* (Englewood Cliffs, N.J.: Prentice-Hall, 1966); J. E. Sorensen and T. L. Sorensen, "The Conflict of Professionals in Bureaucratic Organizations," *Administrative Science Quarterly*, March 1974, pp. 98–106.

Discussion of firm administration is found in: A. Wilson, *The Marketing of Professional Services* (London: McGraw-Hill, 1972); R. E. Sibson, *Managing Professional Services Enterprises* (New York: Pitman Publishing, 1971); H. E. McDonald and T. L. Stromberger, "Cost Control for the Professional Service Firm," *Harvard Business Review*, January–February 1969.

[2] A number of the Big-8 accounting firms now have over 1,200 partners and more than 20,000 employees. Large law firms employ over 250 professionals and some architectural firms employ over 400 professionals. The largest consulting firms collect over $100 million in fees annually, and the largest advertising agencies generate $250 million and more per year. The Big-8 firms alone constitute a $4 billion industry. The advertising business exceeds this figure, and even consulting has grown to nearly $2 billion.

[3] Other organizations (such as manufacturing firms) also face the challenge of balancing the requirements of the markets for output and labor force. However, the professional service firm has had to face this issue more explicitly than other organizations. As the U.S. workforce becomes more "professionalized," more and more organizations will confront the issues addressed in this article. See E. Ginzberg, "The Professionalization of the U.S. Labor Force," *Scientific American*, March 1979.

Figure 1   Framework for Analyzing the PSF

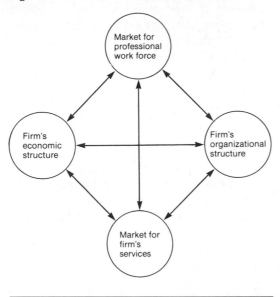

Figure 2   The Professional Pyramid

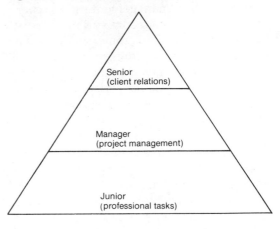

The Organizational Structure of the PSF

The archetypal structure of the professional service firm is an organization containing three professional levels which serve as a normal or expected career path. In a consulting organization, these levels might be labeled junior consultant, manager, and vice president. In a CPA firm they might be referred to as staff accountant, manager, and partner. Law firms tend to have only two levels, associate and partner, although there is an increasing tendency in large law firms to formally recognize what has long been an informal distinction between junior and senior partners. Whatever the precise structure, nearly all PSFs have the pyramid form shown in Figure 2.

There is nothing magical about the common occurrence of *three* levels (a greater or lesser number may be found), but it is instructive to consider other organizations that have this pattern. One example is the university which has assistant professors, associate professors, and full professors. These ranks may be signs of status as well as function (reminding us of another three-level status structure: the common people, the peerage, and royalty). Another analogy is found in the organization of the medieval craftsman's shop which had apprentices, journeymen, and master craftsmen. Indeed, the early years of an individual's association with a PSF are usually viewed as an apprenticeship: the senior craftsmen repay the hard work and assistance of the juniors by teaching them their craft.

Project Team Structure.   What determines the shape or architecture of the organization—the relative mix of juniors, managers, and seniors that the organization requires? Fundamentally, this depends on the nature of the professional services that the firm provides, and how these services are delivered. Because of their customized nature, most professional activities are organized on a project basis: the professional service firms are the job shops of the service sector.

The project nature of the work means that there are basically three major activities in the delivery of professional services: client relations, project management, and the performance of the detailed professional tasks.

In most PSFs, primary responsibility for these three tasks is allocated to the three levels of the organization: seniors (partners or vice presidents) are responsible for client relations; managers, for the day-to-day supervision and coordination of projects; and juniors, for the many technical tasks necessary to complete the study. In the vernacular, the three levels are "the finders, the minders, and the grinders" of the business.[4] Naturally, such an allocation of tasks need not (indeed, should not) be as rigid as this suggests. In a well-run PSF, juniors are increasingly given "manager" tasks to perform (in order to test their competence and worthiness to be promoted to the manager level), and managers are gradually given tasks that enable them to develop client-relations skills to prepare for promotion to the senior level.[5] Nevertheless, it is still mean-

ingful to talk of "senior tasks," "manager tasks," and "junior tasks."

Capacity Planning. The required shape of the PSF is thus primarily influenced by the mix of client relations, project management, and professional tasks involved in the firm's projects. If the PSF is a job shop, then its professional staff members are its "machines" (productive resources). As with any job shop, a balance must be established between the types of work performed and the number of different types of "machines" (people) that are required. The PSF is a "factory," and the firm must plan its capacity. This planning process is illustrated by the experience of Firm X (see Table 1).

While Firm X engages in a variety of projects, there nevertheless exists an average or typical project which requires 50 percent of a senior's time, 100 percent of a manager's time, and the full-time efforts of three juniors. This average mix of senior, manager, and junior work we shall call Firm X's project team structure. No one is expected to bill 100 percent of his or her available time. However, if the firm is to meet its economic goals, seniors and managers must be able to bill 75 percent of their time and juniors 90 percent.[6]

---

[4] This characterization is, of course, simplified. Additional "levels" or functions can be identified at both the top and bottom of the pyramid. To the top we can add those individuals responsible for managing the *firm* (rather than managing projects). At the bottom of the pyramid lie both "nonprofessional" support staff and trainees.

[5] Client relations involves a great deal more than marketing and selling. (Indeed, it may exclude these.) Two primary characteristics of client relations should be noted: diagnosis and process. To the extent that the service delivered is a customized one (and I take this to be one of the defining characteristics of a professional service), then the first client relations task that must be performed is determining precisely *what* needs to be done. Tasks may subsequently be performed by more junior staff members, but a key component of the professional's added value is in the diagnosis. The second aspect of the client relations task that deserves identification is the *process* of client interaction. Clients of professional service firms seek not only the solution to a technical problem that falls within the professional's expertise, but also look for advice, reassurance, support, and involvement. In general a professional service project is not something to be "taken away, fixed,

and returned to the client." Rather, the client seeks a process of interaction with the professional. This, as much as the disposition of the technical problem, constitutes the added value that the professional provides. Decisions on the level and nature of the interactive process are a critical management variable in positioning the PSF against its competitors.

[6] While relative workloads have an influence on professionals' choice of firms to work for, no judgment is being made here as to the relative weight given to this factor compared to other influences. It should be noted, however, that workloads cannot only be too high, they can also be too low. Professionals, along with other types of workers, appear to "flourish" under conditions of high pressure and challenge. Overcoming such pressures can be a major source of professional satisfaction.

Table 1 Capacity Planning at Firm X

Average Project Requirements	Target Utilization*	Required Staff For 6 Projects	For 12 Projects
50% of senior's time	0.75	4	8
100% of manager's time	0.75	8	16
300% of junior's time	0.90	20	40

* Percentage of total available time that firm aims to bill clients.

Firm X currently has four seniors. If it is to meet the target of 75 percent billed senior time, available senior time will be 4 × 75 percent, or the equivalent of three seniors working full time. This implies six projects if the typical project requires 50 percent of a senior's time. With six projects the firm needs the equivalent of six full-time managers, according to the project team structure. At 75 percent target utilization, the firm must have (6/0.75) or eight managers. Similarly, at 3 juniors per project, the firm needs 18 full-time juniors; or at a 90 percent billing target, 20 juniors. Simple calculations such as these show that with eight seniors, the firm would need 16 managers and 40 juniors. The proportions remain constant: one senior to every two managers to every five juniors. Unless there is a change in either the project team structure or the target utilization, the firm must keep these ratios constant as it grows.

This example illustrates that there are two primary influences on the organizational structure of the PSF: the mix of project types and the target utilization. By choosing the mix of project types, the firm implicitly chooses a project team structure which, combined with the utilization figures required by the firm's economics, can be used to *specify* the required shape of the organization.[7]

The Economics of the PSF

Most professional service firms are partnerships; some are corporations. Regardless of the precise form, however, certain regularities in the economic structure are observable. For example, since most PSFs have few fixed assets, they only require capital to fund accounts receivable and other working capital items. Consequently, the vast majority of revenues are disbursed in the form of

---

[7] It may be felt that, for some PSFs, it is hard to identify a "typical" project in order to perform this capacity planning analysis. For many firms that take this view, this means that such calculations are infrequently performed, if ever. However, the difficulty appears greater than it is. In fact, any job shop operation (whether in the manufacturing or service sector) faces the same problem in this regard: a varying and unpredictable mix of jobs, each of which requires different amounts of time from the different productive resources (machines or professionals) in the "factory." In the typical industrial job shop, this problem is overcome by grouping the different products (services) into "families" with similar time demands on different machines. It is then possible either to forecast the mix of family types (and plan to adjust capacity available) or, having established the mix of projects that can be handled, to "sell" to a predesignated mix. There is little reason why the PSF cannot engage in a similarly structured type of analysis, forecasting, and planning at this aggregated level.

salaries, bonuses, and net partnership profits. A typical division of revenues might be 33 percent for professional salaries, 33 percent for support staff and overhead, and 33 percent for senior (or shareholder) salary compensation. However, in some PSFs, partnership salary and profits might rise to 50 percent or more, usually corresponding to lower support staff and overhead costs.

Generating Revenues. If revenues are typically disbursed in this way, how are they generated? Table 2 shows the relevant data for Firm X, a typical operation. The relevant variable is, of course, the billing rate—the hourly charge to clients for the services of individuals at different levels of the hierarchy. The ratio between the lowest and highest rates at Firm X is over 2 to 1; in some firms it can exceed 3 or 4 to 1. The final column of Table 2 shows the basic revenue structure of the PSF. Juniors' billings account for 49 percent of the revenues of the firm, and seniors' billings account for 20 percent.

When we examine the relative compensation levels of the different groups (Table 3), we discover that the juniors, who bill 49 percent of the firm's total billings, receive 30.6 percent of total professional compensation. The seniors, who bill 20.4 percent of the dollars, receive 38.8 percent of the com-

Table 2   **Revenues of Firm X**

	Number	Available Hours*	Target Utilization	Target Billed Hours	Hourly Billing Rate	Revenues
Seniors	4	8,000	75%	6,000	$100	$0.60M
Managers	8	16,000	75	12,000	75	0.90M
Juniors	20	40,000	90	36,000	40	1.44M
					Firm total	$2.94M

* Based on 2,000 available hours per individual.

Table 3   **Economics of Firm X**

		Revenues		Compensation		
	Number	Generated	Percent of Total	Annual Individual	Firm Total	Percent of Total
Seniors	4	$0.60M	20.4%	$190K*	$0.76M	38.8%
Managers	8	0.90M	30.6	75K	0.60M	30.6
Juniors	20	1.44M	49.0	30K	0.60M	30.6
		$2.94M	100.0%		$1.96M	100.0%
Support staff and overhead (at 33% of revenues)					$0.98M	
					$2.94M	

* Includes partnership profits.

pensation. This imbalance is central to the economics of the PSF. The "rewards of partnership" come only in part from the high rates that top professionals can charge their clients. Partners' rewards are also derived, in large part, from the firm's ability, through its project team structure, to *leverage* the professional skills of the seniors with the efforts of juniors. As the managing senior of a top consulting firm observed, "How is it that a young MBA, straight from graduate school, can give advice to top corporate officers?" The answer lies in the synergy of the PSF's project team. Acting independently, the juniors could not "bill out" the results of their efforts at the rates that can be charged by the PSF. The firm can obtain higher rates for the juniors' efforts because they are combined with the expertise and guidance of the seniors.

The successful leveraging of top professionals is at the heart of the success of the PSF. While the services of a PSF are generally not as highly price sensitive as other business enterprises, most PSF industries are increasingly facing price competition, particularly as rapidly rising professional salaries raise the overall cost of professional services. For the client what usually matters is the total budget for the project. By controlling its project team structure and suitably leveraging high-cost seniors with low-cost juniors, the firm can lower its *effective* hourly rate and stay competitive (or, in a price-insensitive market, increase partnership profits).

The Billing Multiple. It is also instructive to compare the net weighted billing rate to compensation levels within the firm. This (conventional) calculation is known as the billing multiple, and is calculated (for either the firm or an individual) as the billing rate per hour divided by the total compensation per hour. As illustrated in Table 4 billing

Table 4 Billing Multiple

	Compensation		Hourly Billing Rate	Billing Multiple
	Average Annual	Average Hourly		
Seniors	$190K	$95	$100	1.1
Managers	75K	37.50	80	2.1
Juniors	30K	15	40	2.7
		Weighted average billing multiple		2.4

multiples may vary across levels, but the average multiple for most firms is between 2.5 and 4.

The appropriate billing multiple that the firm can achieve will, of course, be influenced by the added value that the firm provides and by the relative supply and demand conditions for the firm's services. The market for the firm's services will determine the fees it can command for a given project. The firm's costs will be determined by its ability to deliver the service with a "profitable" mix of junior, manager, and senior time. If the firm uses the same project team structure as its competitors and thus must pay similar salaries, then it will achieve only the "standard" industry multiple. However, if it can find a way to deliver the service with a higher proportion of juniors to seniors, it will be able to achieve lower costs and hence a higher multiple. The project team structure of the firm is, therefore, an important component of firm profitability.

The billing multiple is intimately related to the breakeven economics of the firm. If total professional salaries are taken as an amount $Y, and support staff and overhead cost approximate, say, an equivalent amount $Y, then breakeven will be attained when the firm bills $2Y. This could be attained by charging clients a multiple of 2 for professional services, but only if all available time was billed out. If the firm wishes to break even at 50 percent target utilization (a common figure in many PSFs), then the required net billing multiple will be 4.

Compensation. At Firm X, the middle-level professionals (the managers) receive as their share of total professional compensation an amount proportional to their share of billings. This is not coincidental, but a reflection of fundamental forces of supply and demand in the labor market. As we have noted, juniors in a PSF correspond to apprentices: they are learning their craft. While the firm may obtain a "surplus value" for their services, the juniors could not obtain this for themselves independently. However, since managers have learned their craft, numerous career opportunities outside the PSF are available to them. Many professionals leave voluntarily at this time, even though the firm wishes to retain them. It is important, therefore, that middle-level professional rewards inside the firm reflect the earning capacity of these managers.

Some firms have made major tactical errors in this regard by undercompensating middle-level professionals. In order to prevent this, the PSF needs to monitor routinely all voluntary turnover, and to examine the salaries and positions obtained to use as a guide for compensation system adjustments. The "external value" problem (whereby experienced junior and middle-level professionals can obtain more on the outside than on the inside of the PSF) is more common in some industries than in others. For example, career opportunities exist for middle-level professionals from consulting firms to join industrial corporations at senior executive levels. This accounts for most voluntary turnover in consulting, although some individuals (particularly junior professionals) leave to join other consulting firms. In contrast, out-

side opportunities for lawyers are limited, since relatively few positions are available in industry (although the trend toward in-house counsel may change this). Lawyers that "don't make partner" at prestigious law firms tend to join smaller law firms or set up individual practices. A number of PSFs are increasingly using deferred compensation plans to manage the middle-level "external value" problem. Such practices are known as "golden handcuffs."

The PSF and the Market for Professional Labor

One of the key characteristics of the PSF is that the three levels (junior, manager, senior) constitute a well-defined career path. Individuals joining the organization normally begin at the bottom, with strong expectations of progressing through the organization at some pace agreed to (explicitly or implicitly) in advance. While this pace may not be a rigid one ("up or out in X years"), both the individual and the organization usually share strong expectations about what constitutes a reasonable period of time. Individuals that are not promoted within this period will seek greener pastures elsewhere, either by their own choice or career ambitions or at the strong suggestion of those who do not consider them promotable. Intermediate levels in the hierarchy are not considered by the individual or the organization as career positions. It is this characteristic, perhaps more than any other, that distinguishes the PSF from other types of organizations.[8]

---

[8] These comments neglect, of course, the issues of "lateral hires" (the hiring of mid-career professionals) and the attempts of some PSFs to establish career positions at less than partner level. These are valid topics of concern, but they exceed the scope of this article. It should be noted, however, that, at the present time, both lateral hires and mid-level career positions are departures from the norm in most PSF industries.

Promotion Policy. While there are many considerations that attract young professionals to a particular firm, career opportunities within the firm usually play a large role. Two dimensions of this rate of progress are important: the normal amount of time spent at each level before being considered for promotion and the "odds of making it" (the proportion promoted). These promotion policy variables perform an important screening function. Not all young professionals are able to develop the managerial and client-relations skills required at the higher levels. While good recruiting procedures may reduce the degree of screening required through the promotion process, they can rarely eliminate the need for the promotion process to serve this important function. The "risk of not making it" also serves the firm by placing pressure on junior personnel to work hard and succeed. This pressure can be an important motivating tool in light of the discretion which many PSF professionals have over their working schedules.

An Example: Firm X. In order to explore the relationship between promotion policy and organizational structure, we shall again consider Firm X. According to this firm's promotion policies, a junior requires four years to acquire the expertise and experience to perform the manager function. Firm X expects to promote 80 percent of its candidates for manager, since a lower percentage would be insufficient to attract new juniors, and a higher percentage would imply that insufficient screening was taking place (i.e., that there was no room for "hiring mistakes"). Although promotion from manager to senior should also take four years, on average only 50 percent of candidates develop the critical client-relations skills that Firm X requires for promotion.

Given this knowledge of Firm X's promotion policy and (since it takes four years to "make senior") assuming that two of its eight managers are in their final year as manager, we can trace the firm's evolution over time. If Firm X abides by its policy to promote 50 percent of candidates for senior positions, then only one manager will be promoted to senior. The nonpromoted candidate will usually leave the firm, whether by firm policy or a personal decision. Counting both those promoted and those leaving, the number of managers has been reduced by two and the number of seniors increased by one. Since the firm now has five seniors, it requires 10 managers. However, it only has six (eight minus two) managers remaining, and it therefore must seek four new managers from among its juniors. Of the 20 in the firm, one quarter (or five) will be in their final year as junior. Since Firm X's policy is to promote 80 percent at this level, it will promote four out of the five to fill the four available manager slots. It may reasonably be assumed that like the rejected manager, the fifth junior will leave the firm. Firm X now has 15 juniors left. However, with five seniors and 10 managers, the firm requires 25 juniors and, therefore, must hire 10.

This evolution will continue over time as illustrated in Table 5. By year 5, the four managers that were promoted from junior to manager in year 1 will be ready to be considered for promotion to senior. If promotion opportunities are to be maintained, then two managers (50 percent) will be promoted and two will leave the firm, creating a total of 10 seniors. This, of course, will be the first year in which the firm promotes two individuals rather than the one per year that has been the norm for the last four years. This shift can be troublesome for firms that have developed well-established norms. However, if Firm X were to abide by

Table 5   Firm X Grows

	0	1	2	3	4	5	6	7	8	9	10 . . .
						Year					
Seniors	4	5	6	7	8	10	12	14	16	20	24 . . .
Managers	8	10	12	14	16	20	24	28	32	40	48 . . .
Juniors	20	25	30	35	40	50	60	70	80	100	120 . . .
Total	32	40	48	56	64	80	96	112	128	160	192 . . .
New hires		10	10	10	10	20	20	20	20	40	40
Resignations		2	2	2	2	4	4	4	4	8	8
Annual percent growth in staff		25	20	17	14	25	20	17	14	25	20

100%   100%

its norms and continue to promote one manager per year, it would erode the promotion incentive so critical to the successful operation of the PSF. Assuming then that Firm X has 10 seniors in year 5, it will require 20 managers. Of the 16 managers in the firm the previous year, 4 have been promoted or have left and, therefore, eight juniors must be promoted. Fortunately (but not fortuitously), the 10 juniors hired in year 1 are ready to be considered for promotion. The expected 80 percent target may be maintained.

Target Growth Rate.   We have arrived at these staffing levels solely by considering the interaction of the PSF's organizational structure with its promotion incentives (career opportunities). It is the interaction of these two forces that determines a target (or required) growth rate for the firm. As Table 5 shows, Firm X must double in size every four years in order to preserve its promotion incentives. If it grows more slowly than this, then either much of the firm's incentive will be eliminated, or the firm will grow into an "unbalanced factory" (too many seniors and not enough juniors), which will

have a deleterious effect upon its economic structure.

Accommodating Rapid Growth.   If the firm attempts to grow *faster* than the target rate it will either have to promote a higher proportion of juniors or have to promote them more quickly. Without corresponding adjustments, this could have a significant adverse impact on the quality of services that the firm provides.

What adjustments can be made to allow faster growth? Basically, there are four strategies. First, the firm can devote more attention and resources to its hiring process so that a higher proportion of juniors can be routinely promoted to managers. (In effect, this shifts the quality-of-personnel screen from the promotion system to the hiring system, where it is often more difficult and speculative). Second, the firm can attempt to hasten the "apprenticeship" process through more formal training and professional development programs, rather than the "learn by example" and mentoring relationships commonly found in smaller firms and those growing at a more leisurely pace. In fact, it is the rate of growth, rather than the size of the firm, which necessitates formal development programs.[9] Even a large firm can usually afford to continue mentoring and experiential learning if it is close to its target growth rate. However, since these procedures are decentralized and often "hidden" from the administrators of the firm, they can easily be neglected during periods of excessive growth. This, of course, compounds the problem: at the very time that the firm needs its junior and middle-level personnel to progress rapidly, the seniors are "swamped" with business and easily distracted from their recruiting, training, and mentoring tasks.

The third mechanism that the firm can adopt to accelerate its target growth rate is to make use of "lateral hires": bringing in experienced professionals at other than the junior level. In most PSFs, this strategy is avoided because of its adverse effect upon the morale of junior personnel, who tend to view such actions as reducing their own chances for promotion. Even if these have been accelerated by the fast growth rate, juniors will still tend to feel that they have been less than fairly dealt with.

Modifying the project team structure is the final strategy for accommodating rapid growth without throwing out of balance the relationships between organizational structure, promotion incentives, and economic structure. In effect, the firm would alter the mix of senior, manager, and junior time devoted to a project. This strategy will be discussed in a later section.

Turnover.   We have seen that the organizational structure and the promotion system together determine a target (or required) growth rate. An alternative way of stating this relationship is that, given a growth rate and an organizational structure, the resulting promotion incentives can be determined.[10] For example, suppose that we had constructed Table 5 by specifying the growth rate and the project team structure. We would then have discovered that we could afford to promote only four out of five juniors and one out of two managers. We would also have discovered a "built-in" or target turnover rate averaging over 4 percent (two resignations per year for the first four years while the average number of nonsenior staff was 45.5).[11]

In most PSF industries, one or more firms can be identified that have a high target rate of turnover (or alternatively, choose to grow at less than their optimal rate). Yet individuals routinely join these organizations knowing that the odds of "making it" are very low. Such "churning" strategies have some clear disadvantages *and* benefits for the PSF itself. One of the benefits is that the

---

[9] Speeding the development of individuals so that the firm can grow faster is, of course, not the only role for formal training programs. They can also be a device to allow the firm to hire less (initially) qualified and hence lower wage individuals, thereby reducing its cost for juniors.

[10] In practice, many PSFs look at this relationship in a different way. Rather than the "supply-driven" growth implied by our discussion here, many firms adopt a "demand-driven" approach, accepting (within reasonable limits) whatever growth rate the market offers them. In essence, such firms "manage to the backlog," hiring and laying off staff according to the size of work booked but not yet undertaken. This is a perfectly reasonable strategy as long as the implications of such policies on promotion incentives are well understood, and the market for professional labor allows such policies to be maintained. Some firms have sacrificed their reputation in the labor market through such policies, adversely affecting their long-run viability.

[11] This, of course, does not predict the firm's actual turnover experience (which can be as high as 20 to 25 percent in some PSFs). Rather, we are considering here the turnover that the firm requires to keep itself in balance. While it may be able, through its promotion system, to ensure that the actual rate does not get too low, it may have to use other devices to ensure that the actual turnover rate does not get too high through too many people quitting.

firm's partners (or shareholders) can routinely earn the surplus value of the juniors without having to repay them in the form of promotion. The high turnover rate also allows a significant degree of screening so that only the "best" stay in the organization. Not surprisingly, firms following this strategy tend to be among the most prestigious in their industry.

This last comment gives us a clue as to why such firms are able to maintain this strategy over time. For many recruits, the experience, training, and association with a prestigious firm compensate for poor promotion opportunities. Young professionals view a short period of time at such a firm as a form of "post-postgraduate" degree, and often leave for prime positions they could not have achieved (as quickly) by another route. Indeed, most of the prestigious PSFs following this strategy not only encourage this, but also provide active "outplacement" assistance. Apart from the beneficial effects that such activities provide in recruiting the next generation of juniors, such "alumni/ ae" are often the source of future business for the PSF when they recommend that their corporate employers hire their old firm (which they know and understand) over other competitors. The ability to place ex-staff in prestigious positions is one of the prerequisites of a successful churning strategy. (An exception might be those PSF industries where legal requirements, such as professional certification, necessitate that juniors spend time in a firm. However, even there the prestigious firms provide active outplacement assistance.)

The Market for the Firm's Services

The final element in our model is the market for the firm's services. We have already explored some of the ways in which this market is linked to the firm's economic structure (through the billing rates the firm charges) and to the organizational structure (through the project team structure and target growth rate).

We still must add to our model one of the most basic linkages in the dynamics of the PSF: the direct link between the market for professional labor and the market for the firm's services. The key variable that links these two markets is the quality of professional labor that the firm requires and can attract. Earlier, when we considered the factors that attract professionals to a given PSF, we omitted a major variable that often enters into the decision process: the types of projects undertaken by the firm. Top professionals are likely to be attracted to the firm that engages in exciting or challenging projects, or that provides opportunities for professional fulfillment and development. In turn, firms engaged in such projects *need* to attract the best professionals. It is, therefore, necessary to consider different types of professional service activity.

Project Types.   While there are many dimensions which may distinguish one type of professional service activity from another, one in particular is crucial: the degree of customization required in the delivery of the service. To explore this, we will characterize professional service projects into three types: "Brains," "Grey Hair," and "Procedure."

In the first type (Brains), the client's problem is likely to be extremely complex, perhaps at the forefront of professional or technical knowledge. The PSF that targets this market will be attempting to sell its services on the basis of the high professional craft of its staff. In essence, this firm's appeal to its market is "hire us because we're smart." The key elements of this type of professional service are creativity, innovation, and the pioneering of new approaches, concepts, or techniques—in effect, new solutions to new problems.

Grey Hair projects may require highly customized "output," but they usually involve a lesser degree of innovation and creativity than a Brains project. The general nature of the problem is familiar, and the activities necessary to complete the project may be similar to those performed on other projects. Clients with Grey Hair problems seek out PSFs with experience in their particular type of problem. The PSF sells its knowledge, its experience, and its judgment. In effect, it is saying: "Hire us because we have been through this before. We have practice in solving this type of problem."

The third type of project (Procedure) usually involves a well-recognized and familiar type of problem, at least within the professional community. While some customization is still required, the steps necessary to accomplish this are somewhat programmatic. Although clients may have the ability and resources to perform the work itself, they may turn to the PSF because it can perform the service more efficiently; because it is an outsider; or because the clients' staff capabilities may be employed better elsewhere. In essence, the PSF is selling its procedures, its efficiency, and its availability: "Hire us because we know how to do this and can deliver it effectively."

Project Team Structure.   One of the most significant differences between the three types of projects is the project team structure required to deliver the firm's services. Brains projects are usually denoted by an extreme job-shop operation, involving highly skilled and highly paid professionals. Few procedures are routinizable: each

project is a "one-off." Accordingly, the opportunities for leveraging the top professionals with juniors are relatively limited. Even though such projects may involve significant data collection and analysis (usually done by juniors), even these activities cannot be clearly specified in advance and require the involvement of at least middle-level (project management) professionals on a continuous basis. Consequently, the ratio of junior time to middle-level and senior time on Brains projects tends to be low. The project team structure of a firm with a high proportion of Brains projects will tend to have a relatively low emphasis on juniors, with a corresponding impact on the shape of the organization.

Since the problems to be addressed in Grey Hair projects are somewhat familiar, some of the tasks to be performed (particularly the early ones) are known in advance and can be specified and delegated. More juniors can be employed to accomplish these tasks, which are then assembled and jointly evaluated at some middle stage of the process. Unlike the "pure job-shop" nature of Brains projects, the appropriate process to create and deliver a Grey Hair project more closely resembles a disconnected assembly line.

Procedure projects usually involve the highest proportion of junior time relative to senior time, and hence imply a different organizational shape for firms that specialize in such projects. The problems to be addressed in such projects, and the steps necessary to complete the analysis, diagnosis, and conclusions, are usually sufficiently well established so that they can be easily delegated to junior staff (with supervision). Whereas in Grey Hair projects senior or middle-level staff must evaluate the results of one stage of the project before deciding how to proceed, in Procedure projects the range of possible outcomes for some steps may be so well known that the appropriate responses can be "programmed." The operating procedure takes on even more of the characteristics of an assembly line.

While the three categories described are only points along a spectrum of project types, it is a simple task in any PSF industry to identify types of problems that fit these categories. The choice that the firm makes in its mix of project types is one of the most important variables available to balance the firm. As we have shown, this choice determines the firm's project team structure, thereby influencing significantly the economic and organizational structures of the firm.

Conclusions: Balancing the Professional Service Firm

Figure 3 summarizes our review of the four major elements involved in balancing the PSF and the major variables linking these elements. What may we conclude from this review? Our discussion has shown that the four elements are, indeed, tightly linked. The firm cannot change one element without making corresponding changes in one or more of the other three. The interrelationships illustrated in Figure 3 can be explored and planned in a formal way, thus providing PSF managers with a methodology for exploring the current, and more importantly, the future balance of their firms. It is also significant that most of the variables we have discussed can be expressed quantitatively. The analyses for Firm X, therefore, can be easily replicated for other firms.

How should such planning begin? Figure 3 is a closed diagram with no starting point and no ending point. This form of presentation is used to illustrate that all four ele-

Figure 3   Balancing the PSF

ments must be integrated, and that planning for each element must be conducted iteratively until the elements are in balance. While many firms routinely project their future economic and organizational structures, the key to successful balance is to integrate these two analyses and to test them against the actual markets for labor and the firm's services.

In performing these balance analyses, the firm must distinguish between the "levers" (variables that it controls) and the "rocks" (variables substantially constrained by the forces of the market). This distinction is not always an easy one to make. Billing rates and compensation rates are clearly more similar to rocks than levers. However, career and promotion opportunities may be more "rocklike" than many firms may acknowledge. As a prime source of attracting professionals, decisions in this area may be substantially constrained. In contrast, the firm's growth rate, which is often considered a variable "given" to the firm by the market, should be considered as a management-controlled variable. As we have seen, the growth rate chosen by the firm has significant impacts on all aspects of the firm. Thus, rather than accepting whatever growth rate the market currently offers, the firm may wish to consider the impacts of different rates on all aspects of its operations before selecting its target growth rate.

Perhaps the most significant management variable is the mix of projects undertaken and the implications this has for the project team structure. This variable is a significant force in influencing the economics of the firm, its organizational structure, and both markets. The project team structure as defined in this article (i.e., the *average* or typical proportion of time required from professionals at different levels) has not been a variable that is routinely monitored by PSF management. However, as we have shown, its role in balancing the firm is critical.

It is possible, and not uncommon, for the firm's project team structure to change over time. If it is possible to deliver the firm's services with a greater proportion of juniors, this will reduce the costs of the project. Competition in the market will, over time, require the firm to seek lower costs for projects, thus creating opportunities for more juniors to be used on projects that required a high proportion of senior time in the past. Projects that, in the past, had Brains or Grey Hair characteristics may be accomplished as Procedure projects in future years.[12]

When considering new projects to undertake, it is usually more profitable for the firm to engage in a project similar to one recently performed for a previous client. The knowledge, expertise, and basic approaches to the problem that were developed (often through significant personal and financial investment) can be capitalized upon by applying them to a similar or related problem. Frequently, the second project can be billed out to the client at a similar (or only slightly lower) rate, since the client perceives (and receives) something equally custom-tailored: the solution to his or her problem. However, the savings in PSF costs in delivering this customization are not *all* shared with the client (if, indeed, any are). The firm thus makes its most money by "leading the market": selling a service with reproducible, standardizable elements as a fully customized service at a fully customized price.

Unfortunately, even before the market catches up and refuses to bear the fully customized price, the firm may encounter an internal behavior problem. While it is in the best interest of the *firm* to undertake similar or repetitive engagements, often this does not coincide with the desires of the *individuals* involved. Apart from any reasons of status, financial rewards, or fulfillment derived from serving the clients' needs, most individuals join PSFs to experience the professional challenge and variety and to avoid routine and repetition. While individuals may be content to undertake a similar project for the second or third time, they will not be for the fourth, sixth, or eighth. Yet it is in the interest of the firm (particularly if the market has not yet caught up) to take advantage of the experience and expertise that it has acquired. One solution, of course, is to convert the past experience and expertise of the individual into the expertise of the firm by accepting a similar project,

---

[12] This argument suggests that there is a "life-cycle" to professional "products" in the same way that such cycles exist for tangible products.

but utilizing a greater proportion of juniors on it. Besides requiring a lesser commitment of time from the experienced seniors, this device serves to train the juniors.

For all these reasons, we might suspect that the proportion of juniors to seniors required by the firm *in a particular practice area* will tend to increase over time. If this is allowed to proceed without corresponding adjustments in the range of practice areas, the project team structure of the firm will be altered, causing significant impacts on the economics and organization of the firm. The dangers of failing to monitor the project team structure are thus clearly revealed. Examples of this failure abound in many PSF industries. One consulting firm that learned how to increasingly utilize junior professionals began to aggressively hire new junior staff. After a reasonable period of time for the promotion decision, the firm realized that, at its current growth rate, it could not promote its "normal" proportion of promotion candidates: it did not need as many partners and managers in relation to the number of juniors it now had. Morale and productivity in the junior ranks suffered. An investment banking firm discovered that, over a period of years, it had so increased its range of analyses and services in advising clients that more juniors were needed on projects. Successfully integrating this new project team structure required major changes in the firm's administrative procedures, particularly in its human resource and professional development activities.

Because the issues involved are so large and complex, we cannot explore here how to successfully manage a shift in project team structure or how to avoid making such a shift. However, like the changes in other variables discussed in this article, changes in this variable will require a reexamination of all the elements in Figure 3. Successful PSF management is a question of balance.

READING 4
WHAT "MERGED" EMPLOYEES NEED TO KNOW*
J. Gerald Simmons

When the word went forth that White Weld & Company was being acquired by Merrill Lynch & Company, there was no small amount of panic in the White Weld ranks. According to a Merrill Lynch personnel executive, many staff members quit their jobs immediately, not even staying around long enough to find out about severance pay. "While it was inevitable that there would be a great deal of consolidation," he said, "they did not consider that plans called for many of them to be asked to stay on."

That kind of reaction to the news that one's company has been taken over is understandable, on one level. No one enjoys having his working world turned upside down or facing the uncertainties of a new chain of command. But in the current climate, with mergers and acquisitions coming thick and fast, it is important that employees develop a more reasoned and logical response pattern.

My experience indicates that the majority of middle-to-top management is psychologically unprepared for the realities of a merger. Far too many executives, for example, unlike those who left White Weld, are inclined to be complacent, telling themselves that the up-coming merger will not affect their status. It seems that the more successful the man, the stronger his sense

---

* Copyright © 1978 by the New York Times Company. Reprinted by permission from the *New York Times*, November 12, 1978.

of security, confidence, and self-esteem—and the less likely he is to imagine that his talents will not be needed. Yet the fact is that the higher one is in the company hierarchy, the more vulnerable one is in time of merger.

The central concern of an executive of an acquired company, of course, is over what his new bosses intend to do. What are their plans for the company? What are their management techniques and policies? With answers to those questions, the executive can make an educated guess as to what his future will be.

To be sure, it is not always easy to get the facts. For instance, the head of a corporate empire divesting unwanted subsidiaries candidly says that he is not about to bandy information about. "When the morale of a unit's management, and its customers, can be maintained, the sale of the business is greatly facilitated," he says. Another chief executive officer adds that, in an acquisition, "we try to move quietly and quickly. With panic, the best people, who know they can locate elsewhere, tend to bolt and we are not always left with the best or the brightest."

Such attitudes notwithstanding, it is possible for executives to set up criteria for "second-guessing" the acquiring company. Here is a list of some of the questions to ask:

• Is your company being acquired because of its management talent? If the acquiring company is weak on management, specifically weak in the area where your expertise is strong, it's a safe bet that your talent will be of value and that you'll be expected to stay.

• Is your division of the company attractive to the new parent, or does your company's appeal lie elsewhere? If you are a key executive in a profit center of importance to new management, you will probably be on the new owner's list of key people.

• Will the management structure be significantly changed under the new owners? If the answer is yes, you'll have to do some hard-nosed self-appraisal. If you are a manager within a functionally centralized company, and it is reorganized into divisional profit centers, you will have to ask yourself whether your talent will still be needed.

• Many corporations today are undergoing a process of un-diversifying—of getting out of businesses that fall outside their main areas of expertise and that they have been unable to operate profitably. If your division is being spun off, you need to find out why. How much does the answer reflect upon your own performance as a manager? If the corporation is simply abandoning a business that falls outside its main areas of expertise, improved support from the new parent could give your own performance additional gloss. But if your division has had profitability problems for other reasons, the acquiring company could well attempt to rectify them by installing its own management team.

• If your company was acquired for non-management reasons—plant and facilities or distribution capabilities—were you in a key operational role? If so, you stand an excellent chance of being asked to remain. Your chances of remaining with the company are good if you have specialized knowledge, the right "connections" in your business, or have a key position in the creation or maintenance of a particular manufacturing facility, marketing, or distribution system. This is particularly true if the acquisition is a move toward diversification on the part of the acquirer.

• What is the compensation scale of the acquiring company? If your own present salary is high in relation to theirs—particularly as compared to the new chief executive or your counterpart—your position may very well be in jeopardy. On the other hand, if your industry is relatively unknown to the acquiring company and your salary is in line with the industry average, you should make certain the new management understands this. And if your salary is higher than the industry average because of special qualities that you bring to the position, be sure that the facts are brought to their attention.

• Is your expertise in service areas such as law, administration, finance, public relations, or personnel? If so, it makes you particularly vulnerable, because of the likely duplication of those functions within the acquiring company. If you are an executive in these areas, chances are really slim that there will be a spot for you when the new management takes over.

• How do you appraise public knowledge of your own attitudes toward the merger or acquisition? If you were vociferously against the takeover, it's unlikely that you will be very popular with the new management.

• Are you in a staff position? Then selling yourself to the new management won't be easy. Staff executives are most vulnerable unless you can develop some special leverage. An analysis of the functions of each staff person in the acquiring company might enable you to find an appropriate slot for yourself or even to create one. But it's not easy.

If in doubt about any of these early warning signals, keep in mind one sure guideline: Remember that your bargaining power with the acquiring company will, in all probability, reflect to an important degree your marketability on the outside. If you

don't have a clear idea of what that is, you would do well to find out—merger or no merger.

READING 5
CANADA'S GOOD EXAMPLE WITH DISPLACED WORKERS*
William L. Batt, Jr.

In the spring of 1982, when Outboard Marine closed its Galesburg lawnmower plant, 800 workers lost their jobs, and this west central Illinois community of 35,000 suffered a disaster. The jobless rate went from 14 percent to 17 percent. Other signs of a town in distress—a decrease in population and a sharp increase in personal bankruptcy, divorce, and child and spouse abuse—are still evident in Galesburg.

A few months later, General Tire closed Akron's last tire plant. The former tire-making center now has 35,000 jobless workers. Bob Smith, who had been a tire builder in the Seiberling plant outside Akron before it closed two years ago, told a *New York Times* reporter of some of the side effects of plant closings on people in his hometown: "I'd say 80 percent of the guys I worked with still aren't working. Some of them went South but came back. Some of them are getting trained for jobs that aren't there, like jobs for auto mechanics. Some got divorced and just left." Some even committed suicide. Last year, one young friend of Smith's shot his wife and then, amid the litter of unpaid bills, himself.

Once laid off when a plant closes, workers have a hard time finding jobs. A Cornell University study of Mahwah, New Jersey,

* Copyright 1983 by the President and Fellows of Harvard College; all rights reserved. Reprinted by permission of the *Harvard Business Review*, July–August, 1983.

Ford workers found that 18 months after that factory closed, 56 percent had still not found work.[1]

A *Wall Street Journal* reporter wrote from Seattle that Boeing's reduction of the work force by 8,000 workers since 1980 (and its threatened reduction by 8,000 to 10,000 more) has punished the town severely.

"We're talking to many more people who are depressed either because they've been laid off or because they're anxious for their jobs," said Mrs. Lyn Schroeder of a telephone crisis line for counseling and referral. Calls are up 50 percent for alcoholism, drug abuse, marital stress, and threatened suicide. "We had six suicides in progress on New Year's Eve," she reported. At the same time, government cutbacks have forced her to reduce her paid staff from 25 to 16.

Rockford, Illinois, has the nation's heaviest unemployment rate—19.1 percent. Public aid administrator Scherri Hall told the *Washington Post* about the particularly devastating effect on middle-aged men who had prospered working in factories, bought homes and cars, and then found themselves jobless and unable to find work: "We're having repeated cases of men—women, too, but especially men—breaking down in the intake center, crying or swearing, because they have to come to our office. There is more wife abuse and child abuse, more alcoholism and severe depression, which is affecting the children; they run away."

Plant closings leave a wide swath of community, family, and individual disasters in their wake. Dr. M. Harvey Brenner of Johns Hopkins University, testifying before Congress's Joint Economic Committee in 1976, pointed out that, for every one percentage point rise in unemployment, 4.3 percent more men and 2.3 percent more women enter mental hospitals; 4.1 percent more people commit suicide; 5.7 percent more are murdered; 4 percent more wind up in state prisons; and over a six-year period, 1.9 percent more people die from heart disease, cirrhosis of the liver, and other stress-related ailments. The 1970 recession, which caused a 1.4 percent rise in joblessness, can be linked to 51,570 deaths between 1970 and 1975. Since the present recession is more severe, its results may well be much worse. Unfortunately, Galesburg, Rockford, Akron, Mahwah, and Seattle are not isolated cases.

Canada Provides a Model

Despite the high degree of suffering that plant closings cause, in almost all major layoffs in this country employees are largely on their own when it comes to finding new jobs.[2] This is not the case across our northern border. In Canada, companies, unions, and workers facing factory closings can call the Manpower Consultative Service (MCS), part of Employment and Immigration Canada, for help. The service works very simply, effectively, and fast.

The Disston Story.   In July 1979, Disston Canada decided to close its Acton, Ontario, plant and consolidate manufacturing at its Montreal site. The 110 hourly and 20 salaried employees in Acton were going to lose their jobs. At the request of the company

---

[1] Quoted in "Shock Is Long-lasting for Workers Shelved by Factory Shutdowns," by Thomas E. O'Boyle, *The Wall Street Journal*, June 24, 1982.

[2] Studies indicate that only about one in seven gets help in finding a new job from the state employment service. See Harold L. Sheppard, Louis A. Ferman, and Seymour Faber, *Too Old to Work—Too Young to Retire: A Case Study of a Permanent Plant Shutdown* (Washington, D.C.: U.S. Government Printing Office, 1960).

and Local 8603 of the Steelworkers Union, MCS had, within weeks of the decision to close, helped both sides establish and fund their Manpower Adjustment Committee. The committee's mission was to help all workers requesting assistance find new jobs before the plant gates closed in November—some four months later. Of the 130 employees, 101 sought help; by November, 90 had found other suitable positions.

The production and personnel managers represented the company on the joint labor-management committee, and the union president and secretary-treasurer spoke for the union. Salaried nonunion employees chose their own representative. An MCS officer acted as adviser, while the committee itself, after reviewing credentials, selected an outside third party—Jack Hemmings—as chairman. The company and the provincial and the federal governments shared the committee's expenses for workers' time at its nine meetings, for disbursements for travel and office supplies, and for remuneration of the chairman.

In late November 1979, just when the Manpower Adjustment Committee was winding down, a group from the U.S. Department of Labor, the U.S. Department of Commerce, and the Steelworkers Union concerned about plant closings spent two days observing the Disston plant and other Canadian cases firsthand. (The Iron and Steel Institute was invited but could not attend.) I talked with Enar Nilsson, Disston's production manager, with Bob Lauzon, the parent company's personnel manager, with Steelworkers officers Ken Swan and Gerry Ashley, and with Earl Goodman of MCS.

Both management and labor members explained to me how the committee went about its work. First, they signed a standard agreement setting the parameters of the committee and spelling out its funding. Next, they held an organizing meeting and made a one-page survey of the skills, hobbies, and willingness to move of each worker electing to participate.

The company, the union, the third-party chairman, and the provincial job service then went about determining demand for their workers. The company used its networks among the local business community, its suppliers, and its customers. The union contributed its knowledge of what shops were hiring in the industry. The job service had its job orders and area labor market information to draw on. The chairman had knowledge of and contacts with other employers.

Over the 20 years of experience they've had with this approach, the Canadians have found that combined efforts like this, directly involving the company and the union, who know these workers best, prove far more productive in uncovering jobs than do the impersonal and overworked job service offices.

Disston Canada gave workers paid time off to go on job interviews and to talk to interested employers who made visits to see workers on the job. The company also made sure that employees who accepted job offers before their separation did not lose their severance pay. In his research into the effects on both workers and managers of a Pittsburgh Plate Glass paint plant closing in Detroit back in 1963, Dr. Sidney Cobb discovered the importance of this last point. Anyone who wants to understand viscerally what a plant shutdown means to the people affected and to learn more about Cobb's work should read Alfred Slote's *Termination: The Closing at Baker Plant*. Cobb found that making severance pay conditional on a worker's remaining until a plant closes deters initiative to seek a job before the axe falls. The best jobs generally go to those who get into the job market first.[3]

The committee chairman's job at the Disston closing was to preside at meetings and see that assignments were made and carried out, to engage intensively in job development and encourage other members to do so as well, and to keep records of the people placed. Jack Hemmings wound down the committee when it completed its job and made a final report specifying what had happened to every laid-off worker.

Such detailed reporting offers a refreshing contrast to what happens in the United States. As a general rule here, no one knows what has happened to the displaced people—not the company, not the union, not the employment service, not anyone. Nor does anyone appear to care enough to find out. In 1980, plant manager C. J. Stone at U.S. Steel's Torrance, California, site made many efforts to outplace steelworkers when that mill closed, leaving 600 jobless. But management had no idea how effective its efforts were. As one top manager explained, "We must assume they've gotten a job when they stop coming to the personnel office to sign up for supplemental unemployment benefits."

In Canada, workers can also receive retraining and 50 percent of their moving expenses, which apply even to jobs in the same company. The MCS representative connects workers whose skills do not match job market demands with retraining programs that the provincial government offers.

The Canadian emphasis is on helping workers find new jobs as expeditiously as possible, not on subsidizing extended unemployment. On this side of the border, we depend mainly on unemployment insurance and supplemental unemployment benefits. Essential as they are for income maintenance, these programs are simply not designed or adequately funded to cope with the needs of workers and their families hit by plant closings and permanent layoffs. They were meant to tide over workers planning to return to existing jobs after temporary layoffs.

Two other points struck me when observing the Disston experience. First, the advance notice of several months that provincial law requires gives the committee time to implement an effective outplacement program. Second, the MCS program provides a prompt, responsive, uncomplicated, and voluntary format that pools everyone's efforts in this direction and ensures that the limited time available is used well.

Disston's experience is not an isolated case. A. L. Cobb, who, with Allan Jacques, oversees the MCS program for Employment and Immigration Canada, spoke in January 1981 to a plant closings seminar cosponsored by the U.S. Department of Labor and the White House. Cobb reported that in 1980 alone, 365 company and worker groups signed agreements similar to Disston's and the Steelworkers' that affected 200,000 workers. The Manpower Adjustment Committees lasted an average of one year. Two thirds of the workers participating obtained almost immediate employment.

Although the typical closing involves between 500 and 600 employees, the Canadians have had experience with large layoffs as well. A. L. Cobb brought with him to the plant closings seminar a UAW–Ford–MCS team. They reported their experience of using the Manpower Adjustment Committee

---

[3] Alfred Slote, *Termination: The Closing at Baker Plant* (Indianapolis: Bobbs-Merrill, 1969); now distributed by the Institute for Social Research, University of Michigan, Ann Arbor, Mich. 48106, p. 330.

approach in a major layoff of 2,000 workers at Ford Canada's Oakville, Ontario, plant in May 1980. Their program was similar to Disston's except that it set up separate committees for hourly and salaried employees, which met for the eight months it took to complete their mission. Despite a serious downturn in the economy, of those seeking help, 94 percent received jobs. The company and the federal and the provincial governments split the $60,000 cost of the program. The diversity of industry in the Hamilton–Toronto labor market area was a big contributor to the committee's success.

The company and the union agreed on five reasons for starting the program:

1. To give employees assistance in securing alternative employment.

2. To allay the fears of employees still at work by demonstrating that they could expect positive assistance if further layoffs became necessary.

3. To relieve the impact of mass unemployment on the community.

4. To project a favorable image to the public by accepting responsibility for assisting employees.

5. To lessen the drain on supplemental unemployment benefits.

The government gave two reasons for its involvement:

1. To relieve serious unemployment in the area.

2. To lessen unemployment insurance costs by providing alternative employment:[4]

Other Countries' Experience

Canada is not alone. Western European countries and Japan all have standard procedures for handling plant closings and permanent layoffs that are light-years ahead of the United States in their concern for the affected workers and communities. In 1978, a group of us from the automakers', steelworkers', and machinists' unions, the U.S. Department of Labor, and the U.S. Department of Commerce visited Sweden, Germany, and England to see such programs firsthand.

The emphasis in these countries' programs is also on reemployment and retraining rather than on providing financial support in unemployment. The most comprehensive outplacement efforts go on in Sweden, where by law a company must give advance notice of a closing, the amount of time ahead depending on the size of the closing or layoff. With strong company, union, and community support, the Regional Labor Market Board takes primary responsibility for outplacement. Immediately after the company announces the expected closing, the board establishes job-finding centers at the facility that link up with a nationwide computerized job vacancy identification system.

Companies across the country are required to list all vacancies with the National Labor Market Board, a government agency largely run by a joint labor-management board of directors. Federal funds for moving and retraining are available, as are industrial development subsidies for communities.

We saw how all this works in Vikmanshyttan, a small steel-making village in central Sweden. In 1976, Stora Kopparberg, the only employer in Vikmanshyttan, closed its 500-year-old steel mill. The Regional Labor Market Board, the company, the union, and the community leaders agreed on a plan. Through intensive industrial development efforts, the coalition recruited nine small

[4] See Robert B. and William S. McKersie, *Plant Closings: What Can Be Learned from Best Practice* (Washington, D.C.: U.S. Department of Labor, 1982); available from the U.S. Government Printing Office.

companies to locate in former mill buildings. One was a small business that was to produce a new product developed by former steelworkers. With assistance from Labor Market Board subsidies, the companies provided new jobs for Stora's 440 workers. The city built roads to serve the new plants.

During the transition time, Stora Kopparberg employed the workers to rehabilitate the old mill structures for their new users and to rebuild the road system. During the same time, some workers attended a nearby Regional Labor Market Board vocational training center to acquire new skills, and some worked on loan for a while for the forestry agency. Although the workers were still employed by Stora Kopparberg, the Labor Market Board subsidized 75 percent of their wages for the two- to three-year period this lifesaving effort took.

In Germany, also, the law requires a warning. Before it can close a plant, a company and its works council must draw up and agree on a "social plan" that spells out a course of action for every affected worker. For some, the plan may involve simple outplacement in similar jobs. For others, it may mean retraining. It may even mean moving to another city. Implementation is largely a company responsibility, but large government subsidies are available. In 1981, displaced workers averaged only two weeks' idle time before they received other jobs or started retraining programs.

How Would It Work in the United States?

Although it is far less comprehensive than either the Swedish or the German plan, the Canadian approach should prove more acceptable to Americans. Except for the required advance notice, it is completely

voluntary. It uses the cooperative labor-management committee approach with which we have extensive experience in this country. It depends far less on government and more on the private sector, and it is far less costly.

What are the chances of replicating a simple, effective system like Canada's in the United States? Through legislation, not good. Plant-closing legislation has become a bitter bone of contention in both Congress and state legislatures. Management and labor have lined up on opposite sides of the barricades. This development is a sure precursor to stalemate. Senator Orrin Hatch of Utah, chairman of the Senate Committee on Labor and Human Resources, has introduced a bill on worker readjustment in plant closings—S.2650—that incorporates parts of the Canadian approach, including an ingenious provision for voluntary advance notice; but knowledgeable observers give it little chance of passing.

The Job Training and Partnership Act, however, which addresses a part of the problem by authorizing in Title III limited funds for retraining displaced workers, has passed and is scheduled to go into effect on October 1. It authorizes limited funds for job-search training, job clubs, and skill training. These are to be administered locally by management-dominated private industry councils, or PICs. So companies and unions desiring to establish joint outplacement committees now have a source of matching funds previously unavailable. It is a new tool to work with, but the initiative to use it is still theirs.

Legislative aid or the lack of it should not be an excuse, however, for progressively minded managements and unions not to improve on today's crude, jerry-built, cut-and-run plant-closing practices. Companies like Dana Corporation, Brown and Williamson, and International Silver offer good examples of how to improve plant closing. All three participated in the Labor Department's January 1981 plant closings seminar. The unions involved in these cases were the UAW, the Machinists, the Bakery and Confectionery Workers, the Rubber Workers, and the Steelworkers. Dana Corporation, one of the nation's leading automotive parts manufacturers, headquartered in Toledo, has come as close to replicating the Canadian model as any U.S. company. At the seminar a management-labor team reported on the closing of Dana's Edgerton, Wisconsin, factory in 1980.

The Dana Model.   With the oil embargo of 1973 and 1974 and the gasoline shortage of 1979, the demand for front axles for vans and trucks evaporated. Dana decided it had to close the Edgerton plant, a nine-year-old, 900,000 square-foot facility with a young, productive labor force. In addition to offering preferential hiring and relocation assistance (which were of little use because 30 percent of Dana's employees nationwide were then on layoff), severance pay, supplemental unemployment insurance (though the fund was then just about exhausted), and extended health insurance (perquisites all negotiated with the UAW), Dana developed an outplacement training program and a job search center. At a previous shutdown at Ecorse, Michigan, Dana had used a Detroit consulting firm to handle the closing. At the time several of Dana's trainees went through the course as well. At Edgerton, the Dana trainees handled the closing themselves through their "Dana University," a training center at Dana's Toledo headquarters.

In the 18-hour course, the Dana workers undertook a skills inventory, practiced résumé writing, and listened to motivating speakers. The course also included sessions on communication skills, financial planning, and retirement planning. Most important to the success of the program was the job center that Dana had set up with the help of the union and the Wisconsin Job Service. At the Washington seminar, Dana's Phil Murphy reported that "we allocated a section of our offices and gave it to the people and said, 'Here are desks, here are reference materials, here are papers from all over the country, and here are bulletin boards for job notices and success stores. Here is the job service microfiche equipment, here are telephones. Use them!' We placed no restrictions on anybody. We didn't want people to call Europe, but they could call all over the country. I had one person calling me in Toledo trying out his telephone technique."

Ron Sanderson, president of the local UAW, found both the course and the center helpful: "It gave us a good self-image and boosted our morale. I think when you get down in the dumps, you need something to pick you up. It did a good job. We worked under the buddy system, which was a good feature. In other words, we teamed up with one or two other people and made sure that we used the service provided for us. We used the telephone to make calls to prospective employers. We used the microfiche setup to find out which areas of the country or state were looking for certain types of workers.

"The other key thing was that this service was provided in the plant. It was an atmosphere that we were used to. To go down to Job Service, especially the one in Janesville, where you have 5,000 or 6,000 laid-off people, wasn't helpful—you can imagine how congested an office like that gets. So being able to go into our old plant and utilize the services right there was a big help to us."

Dana also made an aggressive job development effort. According to Jerry Ward, Dana's industrial relations manager, "We went through the list of employers in Wisconsin, looking for all of those that would have machine operations similar to ours. We came up with 2,740 in the state of Wisconsin and another 500 in the four northern countries of Illinois. We mailed letters to 3,250 employers, including a list of all the people, listed by various skills and categories, who had gone on our job search program. There was a total of 15 pages in that letter. The response was astounding, and the requests were tremendous. It proved again that only about 30 percent of available jobs are listed or advertised. I worked through Job Service employer committees and invited various employers to go through our plant, to see that our worker was more qualified than a guy who's putting a nut or a bolt on."

In addition, for one year following the factory's closing, Dana maintained an office in the area to assist employees with problems and to handle medical exams.

Under Dana's preferential hiring program, other Dana plants hired a number of employees. If the employees were qualified to do the work, they were eligible for relocation assistance of up to two months' pay. Dana offered other jobs to 29 percent of Edgerton's salaried employees and to 20 percent of the hourly workers. Other companies gave jobs to 112 former Edgerton employees. This reemployment effort is continuing. For example, when a small warehouse opened in Fogelsville, Pennsylvania, the manager determined that Dana people would fill all 33 jobs. Workers came from not only Edgerton but also Athens, Georgia; Havana, Illinois; Toledo, Ohio; and Reading, Pottstown, and Berwick, Pennsylvania.

A survey of the 250 employees who elected to use the job search program indicated that 86 percent of the hourly and 95 percent of the salaried employees found jobs; 38 percent of the hourly and 59 percent of the salaried employees took less than six months to find work, the balance longer. But as the recession deepened, not all kept their jobs—months after the plant closed, only 63 percent of the hourly and 88 percent of the salaried workers reported still having work.

Other exemplary shutdown experiences reported at the January 1981 plant closing seminar were Brown and Williamson in Louisville with the Baker, Confectorionery, and Tobacco Workers and Machinists; the International Silver Company with the Steelworkers in Meriden, Connecticut; Empire-Detroit Steel with the Steelworkers in Portsmouth, Ohio; and Lee Tire (a Goodyear subsidiary) with the Rubber Workers in Conshohocken, Pennsylvania. These companies and unions have demonstrated convincingly that, working together, management and labor can help workers and their families weather plant closings and speed the transition to new jobs.

Experience Teaches

A model program drawing on these experiences should focus primarily on reemployment in new jobs, with income support to bridge the gap. It should include the best features of Canada's Manpower Consultative Service plus the U.S. innovations of self-directed job search and job clubs. It should also include half-day briefings by community agencies spelling out for affected families the resources their towns provide, such as unemployment insurance, food stamps, and welfare, and how to obtain them. The best model here is the Illinois AFL-CIO's program that the AFL-CIO's Human Resources Development Institute in Washington has recently replicated and made available nationally.

In addition to the financial safety net that exists in the master agreement or that should be negotiated when closing is announced (continuation of hospitalization insurance until reemployment should be high on this list), a responsible program should include at least the following nine features:

1. *Advance notice.* Because legislation to provide advance notice has long been stymied in Congress and numerous state legislatures, workers will probably only hear of their plants' shutdowns as a result of collective bargaining or enlightened management practice. I first learned about outrageously mismanaged shutdowns in the anthracite area of Pennsylvania. My instructor was a hard coal mine in Coaldale. I was secretary of labor and industry in Governor George Leader's reform cabinet in the late 1950s, when a mine management there announced on Friday that the following Monday the mine would be closed permanently, throwing 2,000 miners out of jobs. We rushed a team in to expedite registration for unemployment insurance and job search, but the total absence of notice made any intelligent effort at planning or programming hopeless.

Shortly after that, U.S. Steel closed a captive soft coal mine in Fayette County at the opposite corner of Pennsylvania. Alerted by the company well beforehand, I visited the vice president for coal production and the Steelworkers Union in Pittsburgh, and we agreed on a tripartite outplacement effort. This advance notice from a responsible management gave us time—to arrange with the company for office space at the mine head; to centralize state, company, and union resources for taking unemployment insurance claims; to prepare job develop-

ment, counseling, testing, and outplacement programs.

Even today, a generation later, companies like our Coaldale anthracite mine often close with no advance notice. Robert McKersie and Robert Aronson, in their excellent study of three plant closings in New York State, relate how with no advance notice at all the GAF Corporation reduced its Binghamton operations by 1,100 workers in 1977. Not only did this precipitate action magnify the traumatic effect on the workers, their families, and the community, it also left no time for planning and implementing an orderly outplacement effort.[5]

Recognition of the need for planning time is nothing new. In their classic 1966 book, *Strategies for Displaced Workers*, George Shultz and Arnold Weber described their experience as third-party helpers to the Armour Company, and the Meat Cutter's Union, representing thousands of workers dislocated by the closing of Armour plants throughout the Midwest. They concluded that six months' or preferably a year's advance notice was "a procedural prerequisite for constructive action. It gives the various organizations some time to organize their programs and permits employees to adjust their own plans as well as to consider the various available options with care."[6]

Recently several unions have succeeded in getting advance notice provisions into their master contracts. The Steelworkers' contract stipulates three months and the Rubber Workers' six. Although last-ditch efforts to keep Uniroyal Rubber plants open

---

[5] See Robert B. McKersie and Robert Aronson, *Economic Consequences of Plant Shutdowns in New York State* (Ithaca, N.Y.: Cornell University, New York State School of Industrial and Labor Relations, 1980), p. 16.

[6] See George P. Shultz and Arnold R. Weber, *Strategies for Displaced Workers* (New York: Harper & Row, 1966), p. 190.

in Massachusetts and Michigan failed, most reports agree that these advance notice provisions are proving their worth. Advance notice of two scheduled closings of U.S. Steel's structural steel mills at Ambridge and Shiffler in western Pennsylvania did leave time for negotiating contract modifications that kept the plants open.

When they closed their Louisville facility, Brown and Williamson provided more than two years' notice. As Carroll Teague, labor relations vice president, explained, "This gradual phase-out has allowed affected employees to make required job transition in a more orderly, less emotionally disturbing manner. It has provided for a staggered influx of new workers into general job markets and thus reduced community unemployment burdens and minimized competition between workers who once stood side by side. Senior employees had the option to leave the company earlier than junior employees to enhance their chances of finding suitable jobs elsewhere."

2. *Joint labor-management outplacement committees.* The 20 years of Canadian experimentation with joint committees provide hundreds of cases that U.S. companies and unions can use as examples for setting up similar joint efforts. In nonunion plants the employees can choose the worker members, and, as in the case of Dana at Edgerton, the committee can arrange for employment service participation. As in Canada, the committee's main role would be to see that everyone requesting outplacement help got it and that before the plant gates closed as many as possible were placed in acceptable jobs.

3. *Job search training.* Our model committee would take on an added function that the Canadians haven't tried—job-search training. Dana at Edgerton taught this skill, as have increasing numbers of U.S. manu-

facturers, such as Lee Tire at Conshohocken, Firestone at six of its closed plants, General Electric at Ontario, California, and Crucible at Midland, Pennsylvania. Managements, union, and workers agree that such training is generally helpful, although the success rate, of course, heavily depends on the labor market.

4. *Job clubs.* Close on the heels of going through the job search training, a worker should join a job club. Job clubs are an exciting innovation in social engineering that Nathan Azrin, in southern Illinois, Albert Cullen and Joseph Fischer in Cambridge, Massachusetts, and Charles Hoffman in San Diego have pioneered with backing from the U.S. Labor Department's Work Incentive Program.

Few experiences in life are as isolating as looking for a job. The job club helps combat that isolation. It is a place where workers can put into practice the techniques they have learned in job-search training. Working together in small groups, reinforcing each other's efforts, they use the buddy system. The job club should be located in a convenient place and equipped with telephones, desks, industrial directories, Yellow Pages, and want ad sections from Sunday papers serving nearby cities and selected growing labor markets. At its Ontario plant, GE converted the recreation center just across from the plant gate into a retraining and outplacement center and job club. In Midland, Pennsylvania, workers used the basement of the Steelworkers' Union Hall, which Crucible had outfitted with surplus partitions.

5. *Aggressive job development.* Job development works best when the company takes the leading role, as Dana did in Edgerton and Disston and Ford did in Ontario. The company has contacts with suppliers through its purchasing department, with customers through its salespeople, and with the business community generally. A company simply cannot leave this task to state employment services. They lack the access to other employers that a company has, they have other clienteles to serve, and, despite almost unprecedented demand for their services, they are losing staff because of state budget cuts.

6. *Skill training.* Most displaced workers do not undertake training in a new skill or occupation. One study of a Midwestern plant closure in the 1960s showed that almost two thirds of the workers laid off were making no effort to obtain retraining, although it was cost-free.

Another study in 1974 of a British steel plant revealed that only 20 percent were taking advantage of retraining. Participation was higher among the younger and already higher skilled. Interest in retraining appeared to decline with advancing years.[7]

At the Downriver Project in Wayne County, Michigan, in 1982, about 25 percent of the workers laid off in plant closings sought and obtained skill training. Experience indicates that retraining will provide an answer for only a minority of the county's displaced workers.

For that minority, there are some resources available now that we have not had before. In addition to the 50 percent matching funds in Title III of the Job Training and Development Act, which participating states will somehow have to find money to match, there are innovative retraining programs emerging in collective bargaining. The largest is the UAW-Ford Employee Development and Training Program, which provides not only retraining for active em-

ployees but also retraining, job-search, and placement assistance for laid-off employees. It is now being used to assist Ford workers laid off in Ford's Milpitas, California, and Sheffield, Alabama, plant closings.

Jones & Laughlin and the Steelworkers have established a program in Midland, Pennsylvania, to retrain former Crucible Steel Company workers, who used to make steel at the plant J&L has recently bought. J&L also plans to offer job search and skill training to interested unemployed citizens of this and neighboring communities.

7. *Qualified company personnel to help out.* For almost a year after the Edgerton plant closed, Dana kept a skeleton personnel staff to provide counseling, job development, and other assistance to laid-off workers. To fill these roles, Gerald Newmin, president of International Silver, recruited Robert Treloar, a talented salesman and himself a casualty of the closing. Treloar received his training in outplacement skills through a consulting service.

8. *Third parties.* Most of the companies in our sample got help from outside consultants. When a shutdown occurs, it is often a first for the company, the union, and the community. Someone who has been through it all several times before can be a great help. Managements report that the savings in unemployment insurance taxes and supplementary unemployment benefits offset the costs many times over.

When Empire-Detroit Steel closed its gates, the Portsmouth, Ohio, CETA, under Dick Bussa, was the catalyst for organizing an innovative migration effort. David Brown and Meredith Associates helped International Silver. Lee Tire used Tom Jackson's Career Development Team from New York.

9. *Industrial development.* The January 1981 conferees reported little about their ef-

---

[7] See Jaclyn Rundle and Richard R. Deblassie, "Unemployment in the Postindustrial Age: Counseling Redundant Workers," *Journal of Employment Counseling,* December 1981, p. 186.

forts to help the communities they left replace the lost jobs. Dana did report that it
had sold its plant to Caterpillar Tractor
Company, which planned to employ 300
people by 1983. Because of the recession,
plans have been slow to develop. Caterpillar now employs 49 in Edgerton; 30 of
these new jobs have gone to former Dana
workers.

With little thought for the effect on the
community or former employees, companies leaving a community usually turn over
their redundant plants to their corporate industrial real estate people or to an industrial
realtor to dispose of for top dollar. I recall
two cases in which state and federal agencies intervened to tilt the scales in the public
interest direction and companies proved
cooperative. In 1960, when Ford closed its
old Chester, Pennsylvania, factory, it had
two purchase offers. The higher bid was
from Scott Paper, which wanted to use the
plant for warehousing, and the other was
from Reynolds Metals, which wanted to use
it for manufacturing.

At the suggestion of Governor David
Lawrence, I asked Ford's management if
there was any way that it could keep the
plant in manufacturing because of the large
number of jobs that that would create. Ford
agreed to offer Reynolds the opportunity to
match the higher bid, which Reynolds
promptly took. Just last year, Reynolds
closed the plant, but in the meantime Chester had had 20 years of further employment.

When in the early 1960s GE closed its
plant in the Mohawk Valley village of
Clyde, New York, Clyde's enterprising con-
gressman, Frank Horton, invited top executives to his Capitol Hill office to explore with
a group of us from the Area Redevelopment
Administration (ARA) what could save
Clyde from the crippling blow of losing its
major employer. What evolved was a plan

whereby GE denoted the plant to a local development corporation set up for this purpose. GE also helped Clyde find a supplier
located in Cleveland to purchase it. Clyde
then used the proceeds from the sale to develop an industrial park on adjacent land
and to bring in other employers. The ARA
helped out with loans and grants for sewer
and water lines. The town ended up with
more jobs and more diversification than it
had had before GE closed the plant. Also,
diversification meant that the community
would be immune to the cyclical feast and
famine that plagues one-industry communities.

Two of the most comprehensive cases of
developing industry through plant closings
occurred in Britain and France. Through a
subsidiary established for this purpose, British Steel Corporation provides financial and
technical assistance and inexpensive space
to all sizes of enterprises—from multinationals to two-man machine shops—that
will manufacture in former steel mills or
new plants specially constructed on old mill
properties. Rhone-Poulenc, France's largest
chemical manufacturer, not only provides
this opportunity but also provides equity financing and sometimes enters partnerships
with companies locating in their redundant
facilities.

Worker ownership is still another alternative. In 1981, GM helped the workers at its
Hyatt Bearing plant in Clark, New Jersey,
buy and operate the facility. General Motors
provided $100 million in orders for several
years. South Bend Lathe in Indiana, the Library Bureau in Herkimer, New York, and
Rath Packing Company in Davenport,
Iowa, are other plant closing examples
where this alternative has proved a lifesaver
for the community.

In all these cases, the Commerce Department's Economic Development Administra-

tion, ARA's successor, provided critical financing. If Congress implements proposed budget cuts in which this most useful agency is scheduled for liquidation, EDA's assistance will come to an end. Although they are often more restricted than EDA's grants, as of now Urban Development Action Grants are still available from the Department of Housing and Urban Development.

If the Canadians Can, Why Can't We?

There is no mystery about what needs to be done when plants close: help displaced workers find new jobs. Existing management presenting new products or services, using the same workers with new skills, is one alternative. A new management, producing the same product with the same labor force and skill, is another. Worker ownership is a third. Where the plant cannot be saved, a joint labor-management committee with an effective outsider as chairman and the mission of helping find new jobs for their displaced workers before the factory doors shut is still another.

No one model will fit every situation, just as no one shoe will fit every foot. But men of goodwill from both management and union—combining their knowledge of people and labor markets—can, in a spirit of cooperation rather than confrontation, design and implement programs to fill the fearful, wasteful, and senseless vacuum that workers face today.

From Ontario, California, to Ontario, Canada, from Wisconsin on the Great Lakes to Alabama on the Gulf of Mexico, there is a wealth of experience to draw on. Concerned public officials can act as catalysts, but if an effective job is to be done, managements and unions of the plants closing down must take the lead. After all, who knows these workers better and who should feel a greater sense of responsibility for their welfare than the companies they have worked for and the unions they have belonged to?

Career Systems in the Societal Context

Introduction

It is widely accepted that various human resource practices will affect the productivity of workers and their satisfaction with their work lives. In the last four chapters, however, we have seen that the dynamics of a company's career system explain those human resource practices which determine the organization's very membership. Decisions concerning who is hired, how they are attracted, who is trained, who is promoted into positions of power, who is retained, and who is released are interrelated considerations which shape the fundamental nature of the firm. The types of individuals selected, developed, and placed in influential roles will directly influence current and future business practices. Previously we have considered the interaction of the career system with the dynamics of individual life histories and the dynamics of company life histories. In this final chapter, we will consider the interaction of company career systems and the dynamics of the external social context.

Company career practices affect which community members will be provided with work opportunities and the quality of those opportunities. Employment needs and experiences at times will vary by ethnicity, race, sex, religion, age, and geographic region. In addition to such well-established differences in social background, which are more ascriptive in nature, employment needs and interests will vary through voluntarily selected identities, such as through lifestyle (e.g., dual career, urban/rural) or through personal values (e.g., whistle-blowers).

These various social segments express their interests by using formal institutions and informal pressure vehicles to influence the firm's decision making about corporate career policies. Such levers of stakeholder influence include: the courts, legislation, trade union representation, community-interest groups, and direct employee feedback through grievances and requests as well as indirect feedback through morale and performance. The societal control levers listed above vary in usage depending upon the issue. Some issues may be concerned with directing the external human resource impact of company career practices, such as plant closings, discriminatory hiring, and technologically displaced workers. Other issues may be focused upon the internal human resource implications of company career practices, such as the disinterest of many dual-career families in making traditional sacrifices in hours and travel, or the disillusionment and crushed motivation in the wake of aspirations frustrated by the "baby boom's" demographic chokehold on opportunity. Those issues with substantial externally oriented implications will be expressed more frequently through formal institutional levers, while those issues with internally oriented implications will be expressed more frequently through informal company complaint channels. The company's career system must be sensitive and responsive to both sets of societal influences on firm practices. We shall look briefly at examples of how these societal concerns are registered upon several key components of the career system.

Recruitment and Selection

Perhaps the most blatant form of confrontation between corporate career practices and societal employment concerns is in recruitment and selection processes. Once human resource needs are identified by the firm, the company begins its staffing effort by gathering a pool of appropriate candidates. The definition of which background qualities are truly job relevant and which are merely reflections of ancient prejudices against various races, ethnic groups, religions, as well as those which reflect biases against women and older workers, is the element of the career system most open to societal challenge. For centuries employers have hung out signs cautioning that one or another race, ethnic group, religion, or the like "need not apply." The target of the discrimination would vary by era and by region, but the exclusion of outsiders and the preservation of a social order through stratification of social class led to limited career opportunities for many groups. Employers have served as fundamental vehicles for maintaining the status quo. Thus, it is not surprising that employers themselves would become ready targets of efforts to produce social change by expanding employment opportunities.

Some firms have consistently been sensitive to changing social mores and have consistently worked to enhance the implicit fairness of their employment practices in advance of outside challenge. As a result, such companies as IBM, General Electric, Procter & Gamble, and Johnson & Johnson, among many others, have established admirable reputations as responsible, progressive employers. Such reputations certainly serve as recruiting assets as well as valuable support for the firm's broader philosophical missions. The daily headlines of our newspapers, however, remind us that, regardless of the benefits enjoyed by such employers, and regardless of the legislation designed to protect equal opportunity regardless of race, sex, religion, ethnicity, or age, insensitive employers persist. They become engulfed in costly litigation as well as costly attacks on the reputation of the firm.[1] Even the more subtle forms of selection discrimination cause difficulty for firms today. For example, a very large and prominent international management consulting firm was challenged on its long-standing practice of not hiring women for its European and Asian offices through its campus recruitment campaign. The firm quietly responded to the challenges, stating that its clients would not accept the advice of women. The competitors of this consulting firm quickly seized the opportunity to point out how

---

[1] R. D. Arvey, *Fairness in Selecting Employees* (Reading, Mass.: Addison-Wesley Publishing, 1979).

many women were successfully employed as professionals in these same lands. This firm found itself suddenly unable to attract most of its first-choice candidates, particularly among women, and several campuses threatened to revoke privileges for on-campus access to students through school facilities.

Another highly subtle form of discrimination entering the process of recruitment and selection is one which is based more in unconscious prejudice than in overt and intentional discrimination. Such hidden bias is readily evidenced through biases in the interview stage of selection. The effects of race and sex have been found to have the effect of "self-fulfilling prophecies" in selection, in that the expectations of recruiters may color how they interpret what they hear. Tougher questions, heightened tensions between applicants and recruiters, and mistaken comprehension of what each party is saying are all examples of certain emotional blockages to effective communication in the selection process. Interviewers are unconsciously affected by the race of an applicant, the attractiveness of an applicant, their regional accent or dialect, and so on.[2] Interviewers must be trained to be alert to their own prejudices so that such prejudices can be controlled.

Promotions and Assignments

Unfortunately, these difficulties with the corporate career system do not end with hir-

ing. Once employed, inequities in career development may continue. For example, the increase in the number of blacks in management in administrative positions has been small (4 percent in 1972 and 5 percent in 1978).[3] A large-scale study of career development difficulties for blacks and other minorities in U.S. corporations uncovered a cluster of career blockages labeled "neoracism" and a cluster of career blockages labeled "institutional racism." While neoracism referred to the overt denial of opportunity to minorities, institutional racism referred to much more subtle difficulties.[4] These include such factors as: (1) the need for minority group members to demonstrate that their performance is better than that of whites and not merely as good as that of whites; (2) the lack of role models; (3) the exclusion from informal friendships and off-the-job social life where valuable tips, mentoring, and information is exchanged; (4) the difficulty of relocation due to the dangers of being transferred to hostile communities; and (5) the restraint on advancement opportunities which result from supervisors' fear of losing the minority group employees who allow that supervisor to easily meet affirmative action compliance standards.

Many other factors, such as the different types of career motivation and work values, have been suggested by researchers to be further difficult considerations. Several studies, for example, have identified apparent gaps between aspirations for upward mobility (blacks in managerial positions tending to score higher than whites) and

[2] Christopher Orpen, "The Effects of Race of Applicant and Type of Job on Hiring Decisions," *The Journal of Social Psychology* 118 (1982), pp. 279–80; Robert L. Dipboye, "Self-Fulfilling Prophecies in the Selection-Recruitment Interview," *Academy of Management Review* 7 (1982), pp. 579–86; Terry A. Beehr and David C. Gilmore, "Applicant Attractiveness as a Perceived Job-Relevant Variable in Selection of Management Train-

ees," *Academy of Management Journal* 25, no. 3 (1982), pp. 607–17.

[3] U.S. Bureau of the Census, *Statistical Abstracts of the United States: 1979* (Washington, D.C., 1979), p. 417.

[4] J. P. Fernandez, *Racism and Sexism in Corporate Life* (Lexington, Mass.: Lexington Books, 1981).

motivation for task accomplishment (blacks tending not to score as high).[5] It has been suggested by researchers into the treatment of minorities at work that the special developmental concerns place an increased emphasis on the need for formal career-planning activities. Although senior management may resist the loss of control which they have over the informal career planning, a more formal approach would provide specific benefits. There would be a more equitable distribution of career information and a more fairly applied system for career planning that did not tie a minority-group manager's future to a given boss.[6]

Women also experience substantial barriers to career advancement. Most obviously, studies and frequent lawsuits identify both differences in starting salaries and in unequal pay for comparable work throughout a career.[7] One particular study of men and women MBA alumni of the Columbia Business School found that, after 10 years, women were making only 80 percent of the men's salaries. The differences were not explained by such commonly held notions as women's marital status, child-rearing responsibilities, career values, or prior leadership experience.[8] A large study of readers of

the *Harvard Business Review* found that men and women differed dramatically in their explanation about the causes of the earnings gap. Women tended to attribute the salary gap to biases in organizational selection and compensation, while men tended to blame women for having chosen lower-paying jobs and dead-ended positions.[9] Large-scale studies of women, particularly of those in jobs which have not traditionally been open to women, have found that women tend not to be taken seriously about a commitment to a professional career.[10] This has been demonstrated in the assignment to: dead-ended analyst-type jobs, jobs which do not control major chunks of company resources, and jobs with little line authority regardless of the hierarchical level of the title.

In addition to these more standard forms of discrimination are the ways women's careers suffer merely because they look and act differently from men.[11] Many men in positions of authority find it difficult to learn to accept women as work peers. While sexual harassment at work is not a new problem for women, it is a new social issue for firms to address.[12] As increasing numbers of men and women begin to work together as peers and as professionals, they must learn forms of interaction which intelligently anticipate

[5] A. Howard and D. W. Bray, "Today's Young Managers: They Can Do It, But Will They?", *The Wharton Magazine* 5 (1981), pp. 23–28; J. J. Kirkpatrick, "Occupational Aspirations, Opportunities, and Barriers," in *Comparative Studies of Blacks and Whites in the United States*, eds. K. S. Miller and R. M. Dreger, (New York: Seminar Press, 1973), pp. 357–74.

[6] J. P. Fernandez, *Racism and Sexism in Corporate Life* (Lexington, Mass.: Lexington Books, 1981), p. 265.

[7] S. A. Stumpf, M. Greller, and R. Freedman, "Equal Employment Opportunity Regulation and Change in Compensation Practices," *Journal of Applied Behavioral Science* 16 (1980), pp. 29–40; R. D. Arvey, *Fairness in Selecting Employees* (Reading, Mass.: Addison-Wesley Publishing, 1979).

[8] Mary Anne Devanna, "Wage Differences Between Male and Female MBAs: The First Decade," *The Career Development Bulletin* 3, no. 1 (1982), pp. 5–8.

[9] Benson Rosen, Sara Rynes, and Thomas A. Mahoney, "Compensation, Jobs, and Gender," *Harvard Business Review*, July–August 1983, pp. 170–90.

[10] Phyllis Wallace, *Women in the Workplace* (Boston: Auburn House, 1981); Margaret Hennig and Anne Jardim, *The Managerial Woman* (Garden City, N.Y.: Doubleday, 1976).

[11] M. C. White, G. L. DeSanctis, and M. D. Crino, "A Critical Review of Female Performance, Performance Training, and Organizational Initiatives Designed to Aid Women in Work-Role Environment," *Personnel Psychology* 34 (1981), pp. 227–48; J. R. Terborg, "Women in Management: A Research Review," *Journal of Applied Psychology* 62 (1977), pp. 647–64.

[12] Marilynn B. Brewer and Richard A. Berk, "Beyond Nine to Five: Introduction," *Journal of Social Issues* 38, no. 4 (1982), pp. 1–4.

sexual tensions. With costly litigation and damage to morale threatened, some firms have begun programs to help managers learn to work with each other, regardless of sex, in periods of stress and close interaction, while still respecting personal dignity and professional boundaries. Certainly, human nature requires that affection and even romance can develop through work relationships. Corporate career systems, however, must be sensitized to one-sided advances and persistent intimidation of one party by another where work conditions, advancement, and job security are jeopardized.

Increasing numbers of women at work also raise another challenge for companies' career systems. Firms must now develop ways of holding onto talented people who are members of dual-career families. A firm's ability to relocate and a firm's ease in making extreme and sudden demands for extended work days are being curtailed. New policies for relocation assistance and for developmental patterns of job assignments must be considered.[13] Long-distance marriages may add a special challenge to a firm's commitment to respect the career dedication of a woman manager. Frequently, firms will erroneously conclude that the man's career is still the dominant one in the family and offer promotions with that bias in mind.

Training and Education

While training and education are often used in prejudicial ways which intentionally or inadvertently favor the enrichment and em-

powering of white males, the greatest beneficiaries of training dollars appear to be workers in transition from early to mid-career. Those in their later career stages tend to be denied opportunities for development. A 1983 study by researchers for the National Institute of Education found that workers between the ages of 25 and 34 receive the greatest investments in formal company-sponsored training and those over the age of 55 received the least of any age group.[14] This bias was confirmed in a study of readers of the *Harvard Business Reveiw* which identified another self-prophetic tendency.[15] This is that managers tend to conclude that the older workers offer less to a firm, because they are soon to become obsolete and leave, and thus they are denied opportunity for needed development. This has become a major concern not merely because of the great increase in wrenching age discrimination law suits but also because of the deteriorating effect on the fabric of the company's morale to have many fearful older employees. The fears are prompted by the dramatic shift in workplace demographics, by sudden explosive changes in the technologies of work, and by radically altered concepts of product markets and the very definition of many industrial boundaries.[16]

---

[13] Francine S. Hall and Douglas T. Hall, *The Two-Career Couple* (Reading, Mass.: Addison-Wesley Publishing, 1979).

[14] Robert Zemsky, *Training's Benchmarks: A Statistical Sketch of Employer-Provided Training and Education: 1969–1981* (Philadelphia: Higher Education Finance Research Institute, University of Pennsylvania, June 1983).

[15] Benson Rosen and Thomas H. Jerdee, "Too Old or Not Too Old," *Harvard Business Review*, November–December 1977, p. 105.

[16] Jeffrey A. Sonnenfeld, "Dealing With the Aging Work Force," *Harvard Business Review*, November–December 1978; Margaret Yao, "Managers' Miseries: Middle-Aged Officials Find New Group Hit by Slump: Themselves," *The Wall Street Journal*, September 1, 1982; Earl C. Gottschalk, Jr., "Blocked Paths: Promotions Grow Few as 'Baby Boom' Group Eyes Managers' Jobs," *The Wall Street Journal*, October 22, 1981.

The baby boom which began in 1946 and which peaked in 1964 is surging forward towards mid-career. The mid-career workforce is growing at two times the rate of the civilian labor force. The traditional plateauing in career advancement and the customary disillusionment at mid-life are bound to catch up and hit companies in epidemic proportions. As these forceful but unhappy workers demand more from their jobs, the older workforce will continue to suffer lost opportunities. In financial services, training has become a key competitive tool to meet changes in the nature of the business; but the emphasis has been on the younger worker, thereby making the bulk of the current workforce feel even more like endangered species.[17]

In addition to these age tensions, the training and educational activities of firms have been challenged by other expanded demands for the firm to act as an educator. The new, complex social agenda requires firms to address such wide-ranging educational needs as Private Industry Councils, which assist; (a) "the hard-core unemployed," (b) displaced workers due to technological change, (c) the jobless due to foreign competition, and the need to assist people at mid-life to make career changes. Many firms must decide how much of a social burden they feel is incumbent upon them to address as responsible corporate citizens, how much of the educational needs they can address alone, and finally where the needs of society and the needs of a private employer diverge. The better that firms deliver career-related services, the more society will shift from other institutions and look to employers.

Organizational Exit

In turning to organizational exit, we again revisit the earlier forms of discrimination. Just as hiring decides who becomes a member, firing decides who remains a member. Consequently race, sex, age, etc., resurface as issues. The intergenerational tensions mentioned in the previous section merely heighten what has been a long-standing societal bias against older workers. Programs which encourage early retirements involve implicit judgments favoring youth over age to avoid layoffs or to make available more opportunities for advancement. This assumption against age, however, is not always in the interests of the firm or of the workers. Firms frequently lose their most valuable players in such expensive buyouts, and individuals often find that trying to locate work late in life is quite difficult. Even more disturbing are the actual firings of late-career workers to allow younger workers to continue working. Multimillion-dollar lawsuits have recently been handed down against firms for such practices.[18]

Another new trend affecting organizational exit has to do with changing social mores. Even workers without contracts and workers without the protection of unions are finding that courts are providing protection from many types of abusive dismissals. These workers, frequently managers, are considered "employees-at-will," but managerial discretion has been challenged in prominent court cases across the nation whereby the right to free speech has been invoked to protect whistleblowers and others wishing to speak out in ways that may smack of disloyalty and dissent. The

---

[17] John Helyar, "Banks Training Workers to Market a New Wave of Financial Services," *The Wall Street Journal*, July 20, 1983.

[18] Arnold H. Lubasch, "Con Edison Settles Age Bias Case; Home Insurance Loses Similar Suit," *New York Times*, December 16, 1982.

employer's right to fire may be limited by implicit contract providing grievance procedures and the right of redress. Increasingly, society has come to appreciate the contribution of corporate insiders in bringing dangerous executive wrong-doing to the attention of authorities.[19]

Finally, a last major societal challenge to employer career systems concerns plant closings. This corporate event generally results in the suffering of shock and great hardship. Rather than fighting for punitive litigation against employers who do not provide advance notification and assistance to those towns enduring such hardship, advocates of employer responsibility for the community impact of plant closings have tried new approaches which recognize the financial distress and need for confidentiality of companies who must also weather these hardships. The new approaches emphasize collaborative efforts at job search and retraining among firms and public institutions.[20]

The Cases

The first case, Manchild in the Mainstream, is an extremely powerful and provocative presentation of one man's view of black life in corporate America. He speaks eloquently but often harshly and profanely about his experience, with abusive reference to other groups, such as women and gays. The anger of this person is insightful, but unsettling to the reader.

The next case, Betsy Morgan, describes a difficult attempt by a bank executive to manage her sexually abusive boss while on

a foreign assignment. The (A) case sets up her dilemma while the (B) case asks whether her response was appropriate and adequate.

The case entitled Frieda Mae Jones involves both sexual and racial issues. The case provides us with a view of a black couple at home discussing a problem in Freida Mae's assignment pattern at work.

The next case, The Vermont Decision, presents the career conflict and challenge to both the family members and the employers of a dual-career couple. The middle-aged couple must deal with the resolution of a job change which will separate the two, both senior executives, by 3,000 miles.

The Tony Santino case presents us with some insight into an individual wrestling with pressing family problems, the illegal activities of unethical bosses, and his own strong personal convictions. Tony is being pressured into accepting the responsibility of violating the law and his personal value, but he is worried about the financial and personal consequences of taking a career risk given an already checkered employment history.

The last case, Who Will Make Money in the 1980s?, describes the impact of demographics on an individual's career progress.

The Readings

The first reading, "Institutional Barriers: What Keeps Women out of the Executive Suite?" by Cynthia Fuchs Epstein, discusses changing trends in the employment of women, the control of deviance, and types of exclusionary practices which women feel.

The article "Sexual Harassment: Some See It, Some Don't," by Eliza Collins and Timothy Blodgett presents a survey of *Harvard Business Review* readers that reveals a

---

[19] David W. Ewing, "Your Right to Fire," *Harvard Business Review*, March–April 1983, p. 38.

[20] "Plant Shutdowns: States Take A New Tack," *Business Week*, October 24, 1983, pp. 72–76.

vast difference in the definition and diagnosis of the problem.

The article "Dual Careers" by Hall and Hall discusses how both firms and couples can prepare themselves for the conflicting needs of couples and companies in managing the spillover of home life and work life.

The article by Jeffrey Sonnenfeld and Paul Lawrence, "Why Do Companies Succumb to Price-Fixing," looks at how companies inadvertently encourage illegal behavior by employees.

The *Business Week* article entitled "Armor for Whistle-Blowers" describes changing protection for employee free speech.

The piece by David Ewing, "Challenges of Perceived Illegality and Waste," provides some case examples of contested employee dismissals.

The *Business Week* article entitled "America's New Immobile Society" profiles the ways firms are responding to the challenge dual-career couples present to established procedures.

Finally, the article by Jeffrey Sonnenfeld, "Dealing with the Aging Workforce," explores many of the myths associated with age and performance and discusses ways employers can get better use out of workers at all ages.

CASE 1
MANCHILD IN THE MAINSTREAM*
George Davis and Glegg Watson

Willis Thornton did not like the title of David Halberstam's 1972 bestseller, *The Best and the Brightest*, which was about the brilliant young men who came to Washington

* "Manchild in the Mainstream," from *Black Life in Corporate America* by George Davis and Glegg Watson. Copyright © 1982 by George Davis and Glegg Watson. Reprinted by permission of Doubleday & Company, Inc.

during the Kennedy presidency to run the country. He simply did not like anyone being called "best" and "brightest" until they had done something to prove that they were better and brighter than he.

Even before the black man Henry Aaron broke the home run record of the white man Babe Ruth, he had refused to acknowledge Babe Ruth as the home run king, because Babe Ruth had done nothing to prove that he was better than Josh Gibson, the legendary black home run hitter who lived at the same time as Ruth but was prohibited from playing major-league baseball. How can anyone claim to be the best at any particular thing until he wins the honor in free and open competition? History had proven that white men were best at seizing power, but were they really best at all the other functions that simply accrued to them because they held power?

This is the kind of thing that Willis Thornton brooded over while he was almost flunking out of Cardozo Vocational High School in Washington, D.C. His mother and teachers agreed that he had absolutely no sense of direction and almost no motivation. His father had nothing to say because no one knew where his father was. Willis was just another surly black boy until the civil rights movement came along. It was only then that he began to live.

He went South to join any marches, sit-ins, pray-ins, freedom rides, demonstrations, rallies, and boycotts he could find. He enrolled in college in North Carolina simply to be where the action was. He still flunked quite a few courses but he read all of the black books he could get his hands on: *Black Rage, Black Power, Black Thought, Black Judgement, Black Thunder, Black Uprisings, Black Worker, Black Is, Black Like Me, Black Man's Burden, Black Boy, Black Cargo, Black Music, Black Rebellion.*

He read Fanon and Camus and Sartre and Malraux. He began calling himself an existentialist and wearing a beret. He was part true believer and part con man. He was not deep enough in the movement to rise to the top of it, and he was not interested enough in college to keep from getting booted out.

He moved back to Washington at about the time that Martin Luther King, Jr., was bringing the racial struggle to the doorsteps of the White House. Willis managed to get into Howard University somehow, and he stayed on the fringes of the kind of activity that had done so much to awaken his intellect.

He did volunteer work for the Peace and Freedom Party, which in turn brought him into contact with many influential white people. He had never known great numbers of whites before. He was surprised to discover that they liked him and he liked them. He enjoyed arguing with them about some of the ideas that his new reading had set to burning in his brain.

One of the influential whites he met arranged for him to get into Harvard on a special program, and he, being ever the opportunist, decided that after Harvard College he wanted to go to Harvard Business School in order to try his hand at something he still called "bidness."

Before Willis Thornton went away to the freedom movement, he had been affectionately known to his friends as Nightmare.

Nightmare is now earning a high five figures as a corporate manager of marketing for a company in the *Fortune* "Top 100." He is proof that a good manager does not have to come from a single kind of ideal background, that indeed a good manager does not have to be a single kind of standardized character type.

At 36 he is more successful than most of his white contemporaries. His immediate supervisor, a marketing vice president, who does not know him as Nightmare, calls him William, thinks he is an excellent corporate manager and a great "team player."

Nightmare loves his job. So far racial problems have not been so large that he could not overcome them, but he knows that continued advancement is more problematic. "I don't fool myself. The higher you go the more important race becomes. Above me everything is white." There are four blacks in the organization who are higher than Nightmare. Three of these are not in decision-making positions, however, they are in staff jobs, and the other, a black vice president, has, in Nightmare's words, been pretending to be white so long that you can't even count him as a "brother."

Nightmare does not argue that his background is in any way similar to the backgrounds of the white managers and directors who are climbing the ladder with him. He rejects, however, the idea that his background represents the kind of "mark of oppression" described in the book of the same name by Abram Kardiner and Lionel Ovesey.

"I browsed through that shit up at the B-school, man," he said, waving his hands in disgust at the idea that "the Negro has no possible basis for a healthy self-esteem and every possible incentive for self-hatred." He was equally unimpressed by the assertion that the basic black personality is a "caricature of the corresponding white personality, because the Negro must adapt to the same culture, must accept the same social goals, but without the ability to achieve them."

Kardiner and Ovesey go on to name a group of pathological traits they say must characterize the life of the Negro: a conviction of unlovability, a sense of helplessness (fate control), uncontrolled hostility and a weak ego structure. "I have been that in my life, but I have never been only that. Never. You do come up under a lot of stress, but if you survive it you've also developed, along the way, some very healthy and effective coping mechanisms. For example, I can deal with uncertainty better than most white cats. I'm used to it. I can function under stress better. I can deal with crisis better, and I'm better motivated because I know what it is to live at Fourteenth and Chapin Street and I'll work like hell to keep from going back," he said.

Nightmare admitted that managers raised as middle-class whites have certain advantages, too. "They are more standardized and therefore fit in with each other better. They are less prone to emotional extremes, more cooperative with each other, and compromise more easily with each other," he said. "This is what the corporation needs, what the corporation will always need. There are black managers who provide this as well as white ones, but there are other talents that it needs when the status is not quo—out here in the flux, out here in this confusion, you need more dudes like me. Dudes who can shoot on the run, who can think on the go, who are not bound down by a sense of how things have always been, who don't have to stop the action in order to analyze it, who can look for opportunities and seize them, who are hungrier and tougher."

He spoke rapidly, saying that he firmly believed that white people and black people are different. Raised as he was raised, it was not surprising that he would think so. "The question is, Must difference always imply superiority/inferiority? Can we really be a multicultural society which takes advantage of the proclivities of all of its people, or must we all either standardize and become alike or else be judged to be inferior and pushed back out into the margins of the economy? We all want to give our best to the country.

"In some ways it's all rhetorical because we are going to become a multicultural soci-

ety. There is no choice, just as we are going to become—let me find a good word—a society that is controlled by two sexes.

"The only decision to make is, Is this going to be accomplished begrudgingly, in a way that will make America a second-rate culture because of the destructive animosity that exists between its people, or will it be accomplished progressively, making us the first multinational country?" he said, smiling. "I don't know."

He smiled, knowing that whether the listener believed it or not, there was something irresistible about his con. It had the ring of truth. It promised something to everyone. All they had to do was see things his way.

He said that he talked to the president of his company just as he was talking to the interviewer. He pulled no punches, and this was one of the reasons why the president liked him. "The only problem is the president has a reputation for avoiding tough decisions. Bringing a black man into senior management will involve some tough politics. I'm not sure he can face up to them, even though I think he's been grooming me for senior management."

Nightmare is certainly not a typical black male manager, but he is typical of a certain kind of black American male. As a manager he is an exception because he came out of the deepest jungle of our statistics on social pathology.

He believes that there are ways that America can benefit by using blacks like him. Because of their lives in the ghetto, they have lost something, but "white boys have also lost something by living in suburbia. They've lost some will, they've lost some heart. The blacks who have survived what I have survived have a contribution to make—one that cannot be found anywhere else in America. In order to win, America is going to have to use everything it's got," he whispered, smiling, feeling that his time was finally coming.

"Just as I said, the president of the company is afraid. He's not afraid of me. He is, understandably, afraid of what would happen if he forced me down the throats of senior management. He knows I can do the job. Senior management knows I can do the job. There's just a lot of fear that has to be overcome."

Several black male managers agreed with Nightmare's point of view as they assessed their own chances of making the breakthrough. They knew that some people from the black middle class had made breakthroughs. They had gotten important mainstream jobs in the mainstream.

But no black had made the big breakthrough, and Nightmare felt that it would be someone like him who would finally become the first black president or chairman of the board of a *Fortune* 500 company. He felt that America would soon be desperate enough to give him a chance.

Nightmare considers himself a black black, and by black he is not referring to the fact that his complexion is very dark, he is referring to his attitude and his orientation. He is referring to where he came from and to the fact that he is not ashamed nor willing to give up who he is. "Do you succeed, really succeed, by imitating white men, or by being yourself and waiting for the white men to become comfortable with who you really are?"

In this Nightmare was speaking about something that has only a little to do with style and diction—outward manifestations of what men like Nightmare hold on to in order to hold on to some more essential parts of themselves. "If Henry Kissinger can make it in America, speaking as he does, why do I have to start speaking like Walter Cronkite in order to be trusted in that inner circle of power? Am I not more fully American than Henry Kissinger? And I just may have some other qualities that he doesn't.

Nightmare is a student of the modern corporation. He owns more than 50 books on corporate management and he has read all of them, he said in his Manhattan apartment one evening. He looked tired. Part of his dark belly shone beneath a shrunken T-shirt.

He said that he has used books to transform himself, which is what the black manager has to do. "Read everything you can get your hands on about the way they function," he said. The book that struck him like lightning, in the same way that Fanon's books struck him during the 60s, was Michael Maccoby's *The Gamesman*.

This book, he explained, as he pointed into the air periodically with two fingers, did not transform him as the writings of Fanon had transformed him. He had already been in the process of transformation when the book was published. He took it down off his bookshelf, which also held an expensive-looking turntable and stereo amplifier. The book simply froze "the darting, scattered fragments of my life so that I could really see them for the first time. That book was an eye-opener," he said.

"You're not going to understand why I lined over what I did. That's why I don't let people read my books," he said. There were notes in the margins of some of the pages. Some sections were heavily highlighted. Pale-yellow lines totally covered the black type on one page.

> The modern gamesman is best defined as a person who loves change and wants to influence its course. He likes to take calculated risks and is fascinated by techniques and new methods. He sees a developing

project, human relations, and his own career in terms of options and possibilities.

In the margin alongside this passage Nightmare had written:

> He must see the possible positive benefits in everything that is required of him to do.

Farther down the page another passage was lined out with the same yellow felt pen:

> He is cooperative but competitive, detached and playful but compulsively driven to succeed; a team player but a would-be superstar; a team leader but often a rebel against bureaucratic hierarchy; fair and unprejudiced but contemptuous of weakness; tough and dominating but not destructive.

It was apparent that Nightmare was talking rapidly to keep from having too many of his lined passages read. On another page he had highlighted:

> The gamesmen's yearnings for autonomy and their fear of being controlled contribute to a common mid-career uneasiness.

In the margin beside this passage he had written:

> Make sure you have an alternate path when this uneasiness comes. The uneasiness will be increased if progress has been retarded by racism.

"This was a natural evolution for me," Nightmare said. "In the streets as a teenager, I was a little slickster. Then I started to believe, during the 60s, and I got hurt really bad. I thought I was going to go crazy. Then I got into Harvard because I was clever—I could do the job, but that wasn't the point— it was never in the cards for a guy like me to get into Harvard and then into the B-school. This whole damn thing has been a game. That's the only thing down here on earth right now, is a goddamn game. This shit

isn't real. This shit isn't about nothing that's real. It's a game, and I'm a player."

He took his copy of *The Gamesman* back and slid it into its place on the shelf. He differed from the gamesman because he had fierce loyalties to those he had developed personal relationships with, including the president of his company, whom he calls a "very decent cat with a good heart." In addition to fiercer loyalties he explained that he also had some deeper obsession.

"I am obsessed with winning. I want to win not simply for me and my own advancement but I want to win for my team, my company, my country. Everybody." He said he was also obsessed with the image of his own integrity. "I will never betray you," he said. "If we are together. If I give my word, I will never betray you." He leaned forward, pressing his case.

He seemed different from the gamesman because there seemed to be something more solid at his core. He seemed more passionate and therefore less opportunistic.

The irony of the lives of men with boyhoods like his is that for all the freedom that the streets offered, there were still rituals— rituals of manhood, rituals of personhood— that promoted values that left them more tradition-bound than men and women raised in liberal, extremely permissive homes.

Emotionally they were very much like those right-wing Republicans who are their own main adversaries in the fight to sway the liberal middle. The biggest evidence of this is in the way Nightmare complained about the excessive tolerance in a liberal city like New York. He had a habit of saying, "We're in our last days. Sodom and Gomorrah didn't have anything that New York City doesn't have right now." Regardless of constitutional guarantees, he said that the police and the fire department should burn down all of those porno places and peep shows. "If anyone ever dragged a kid of mine into child pornography, there wouldn't be a trial. I would pay the guy a visit and one way or another the shit would stop."

He argued that gay people are just morally lazy or morally weak. "They need to be kicked in their behinds and someone needs to grab them in their goddamned chests and told to either go out and find a woman or else take the ugliness back in the closet where it belongs. Unless someone does this, we're in our last days. This motherfucker"—he pointed to the ground under the building where he lived, he pointed to America—"this motherfucker is coming down."

Like a right-wing Republican he longed for "the good old days." Yet, because he was black, he couldn't just long for the past. There had been too much degradation in his personal and racial past. He wanted the future to be as the past should have been.

"I don't think that it will be true of our children. My kids will go to school with white kids. They will be raised with white kids and so there won't be a great deal of differences. All kids will gain something from the strengths of other traditions. Then people will be differentiated by individual talents and temperaments and not by race."

But something didn't ring true about his worried optimism. Statistics seem to say that white kids and black kids are not being raised together, that there are people who would let the public schools of this country go to hell before they allowed this to happen.

A few well-to-do blacks would be able to get their children into predominantly white public and private schools; but the majority of black kids will still go to neglected public schools, and find themselves growing up without the skills they need to take their places in the economic order.

We talked to Nightmare again at an outdoor café for the next session of the interview. It was apparent that he was glad to be out in sloppy gray shorts and no socks, strolling in the sun down Columbus Avenue. The interview seemed to justify his taking time away from corporate affairs in order to look at his life—itself a corporate affair.

"Most cats who go to Wharton or Harvard trade in their old lives and become imitation white boys. I'm a believer in the idea that people function best when they can be close to their natural selves on a job, when they don't have to transform themselves by imitation. I've been lucky enough, or smart enough, to be in company situations which allowed me to be that. I would say lucky because I've always worked for some fairly secure white dudes who weren't threatened by the fact that I didn't imitate them. What I did in B-school is refine my stuff, not give it up. I smoothed it out so I could fit in. I learned the vocabulary of la-di-da so I could hide behind words when I had to, but behind that façade of words I'm using my street sense. I'm kicking ass the way I know how.

"This company is loose, so I can use what I mastered in the street. I can be a con man, or I can kick ass, corporately, to get the results," Nightmare said. He admitted that had he been in any other company he would have been fired by now.

In corporate America it seems that the newer, rapidly growing high-technology companies that are "marketing-driven" are, in his word, loose. Their phenomenal growth over a very short time has created within them a different internal environment from the older companies in, for example, the public utilities field, in steel, and the automobile industry.

He said that the world had gotten really fucked up and it was no wonder that people were fucked up. He admitted that he had done something that most blacks needed to do but couldn't because they were too tradition-bound: "There's a stigma among black dudes about going to see a shrink—a psychiatrist. It looks like a sign of weakness. My problem is that I didn't go to see one early enough because I was in the middle of a sustained nervous breakdown. You've heard of walking pneumonia, well I had been having a walking nervous breakdown for a good part of my adult life. So I finally went to see this big black dude who was a psychiatrist. I needed someone to give me some objective data on me. This dude came off the streets just like I did. He had studied in Germany and so he had the academic shit down, but he hadn't lost his basic blackness and so he didn't come at me from the point of view that I was sick or crazy.

"He just gave me a reading of myself. He explained the things in my background that made me what I am. See, that's why you can't go to a regular white shrink. He has a white standard and he can't help you to deal with where you're coming from because he doesn't know where you're coming from.

"I met this psychiatrist at a party and we were trying to hit on the same woman. I got hostile and he got hostile and so some of the people there had to cool us out. And this motherfucker gave me his business card and told me anytime I wanted to kick his ass then give him a call—'If I ain't home leave a message on my answering machine, faggot.'

"See how ridiculous this all is: I pulled out my business card and told him if he thought he could kick my ass then give me a call and if I wasn't in the office 'leave a message with my secretary, you big punk.'

"Anyway, I saw on the card that he was a psychiatrist and I had this brother working for me who was having some trouble. This brother was freaking out. The white people were getting to him and so I called the shrink and asked would he meet me and this brother for a drink without saying that he was a shrink—just say he was a friend of mine. We were going to talk to this brother and help him cope. So that's how I got to know the shrink. After that we used to go out for drinks and the shrink would give me a reading. I mean, I never went into his office and stretched out on his couch or any of that phony shit.

"He told me that one of the things that might hold me back on my job is a weak or brittle ego structure—yeah! yeah! yeah!—he said, really. For example, he said, 'I bet you have a hard time taking instructions. You always want to do things your way. You take instructions because you got to, but it burns you inside. And you have a very hard time taking criticism because whenever someone criticizes anything you do, you feel that they are criticizing you. You personalize everything, he told me.

" 'A corporation is a team,' he told me, 'and you are an individualist. That's natural, coming from your background. Everything you've ever gotten in life you've gotten it for yourself, and the only person you could honestly thank for ever helping you is your mother, who brought you onto this ball of dirt. After that it's been you, you, you.'

"We talked about his background too, which made it cool since he wasn't putting me in the position of being a sicky and he being the almighty doctor. I didn't pay him, either, but I did get him some consulting work with the company because he was a hip dude. He ran some classes for black managers. The white cat I was working for accepted the fact that he would be better for some of the black employee problems, better than a white shrink.

"Anyway, we would just go out and rap until all hours of the night. Some people might have thought we were weird because we were always together and we would turn down dates with women just so we could talk about black male things—see, that right there is very different for black males. We are never, ever, really deep and honest with each other.

"He told me a lot of stuff, man. How I had had to become egocentric in order to survive all the shit that was trying to destroy my ego and destroy me [to not be victimized by the "mark of oppression"]. I had to believe in me. I had to trust me. Now this helped me up to a certain point; but as I moved up in the corporation this was a liability, I wasn't alone anymore.

"My loneliness made me a workaholic. It gave me a very dictatorial management style. It made me very suspicious of other people, especially white people, and so it made it difficult for me to accept help. He told me I had difficulty delegating responsibility. Now this cat was telling me all these true things about me and he had never seen me on the job.

"So I learned of some stuff that is in black backgrounds, especially black male backgrounds, that put them at a disadvantage in a corporation. This was a heavy cat, man. He had done a lot of consulting with the U.S. army and so he knew his shit." Nightmare paused to hear a reaction to what he was saying.

"He told me that to some extent I believed in 'fate control,' that I believe that a person's destiny was not controlled by himself but was controlled by fate, and this gave me a slight touch of come-si, come-sa, which meant I was more inclined to accept and adjust to things rather than try to make them better.

"He told me some fantastic things. He even interpreted my dreams. Just before I was to get this promotion and big raise, I used to have these dreams about being shot, or about being killed in an automobile accident or dying in a plane crash. He told me that black people are very often like that when they're on the verge of success. They are so fatalistic that they fear that something will happen to rob them of the success. It was amazing. I had never been able to get that close to another man before, without feeling, as I said, that some fag was coming out in me.

"I didn't agree with everything he said, though. I mean, he said that the fact that I loved to buy expensive shoes and suits was a manifestation of an insecure ego. I don't believe that. I think this is a manifestation of a little bit of the peacock in the black man, which should be in all men. It's also the black man's desire to have an individualized style. Blacks like to be individualized, whites like to be standardized—they used to anyway. Now they are seeing that too much standardization destroys creativity and personality, while blacks are discovering that too much individuality destroys organization and cooperation.

"We discussed the idea that in the urban black male's background there is also often some gang experience, so he has been used to blending into an organization. He has had experience following a leader, but the leader always had to be somebody he respects.

"But very often in the corporation the

leader, his boss, is not someone he respects, because he doesn't respect the process by which the boss came to be the boss. He has become the boss without winning the right to be the boss. He might have gotten to be the boss because he kissed someone's ass, or he married the daughter of the chairman of the board, or because he had a Nordic appearance. This is what I mean: who is best and who is brightest?

"The competition has to be open and fair. Then if I get beaten I can truly respect the person who has beaten me because, first of all, I can learn something from that person that will aid my growth. But look at the other side: Suppose you know this white cat who, when you were coming up together, you outsold him, you outperformed him. You went into his territory after him and did a better job. Yet here he is sitting in the boss's chair telling you what to do. You have to listen to him because of the structure, but you don't respect him. The whole deal is fraudulent and so you lose respect for the entire system. This is what has happened in America: too many people have spotted the fraud. I mean, Watergate, what was that?

"That's why it's hard to get people motivated. That's the problem with productivity, and this has nothing to do with color. White people too have seen the fraud and so it's very hard for them to really believe in the system."

Nightmare looked out at the variety of pretty girls passing along the avenue. He commented on them. He didn't agree with those black male managers who felt that sexual jealousy and sexual competition are at the basis of much of the tension between the white men who run corporations and the black men who want to get the chance to run them.

He is reminded that there is a school of psychologists who say that subconsciously all male competition is for the attention of the female of the species, women's liberation notwithstanding. Does this mean that the white man does not want the black man to advance for fear that this would make the black man more attractive to women of both races?

"I know what you're saying, but I think this is bullshit. I can't believe that a white man sits at his desk and thinks like this. This might have been true a long time ago, but there's every evidence that during the 60s the white man would rather give you a white woman than to have you take some real power off to where he didn't have one of his women watching it.

"I think that the sexual thing only clouds the issue," Nightmare said, displaying annoyed impatience with the opinions of other black male managers who felt that this sexual thing was too deep in Western history for it not to play an important part in a mixed sexual and racial environment today. "People don't care that much about sex these days," Nightmare said. "The question is survival."

His feeling was that sex had been so organized and bureaucratized, like so much else in modern life, that much of the passion had gone out of it. So there could not be much passion in the sexual competition between white and black men anymore. "It's power and money, nothing else."

Even the vocabulary of sex, he argued vigorously, is corporate rather than erotic. "A love affair is called a relationship. People get together to fulfill needs. A lush word like lust has been replaced by a computer pip like horny." He laughed cynically.

In such a brave new world, he argued passionately, it seems absurd to talk about the white man not wanting the black man to have white women. But not all the black men we talked to agreed.

"It's subsurface," another manager had said earlier, "but it's still there. For one thing the guys who run corporations came up during the 50s and it's like a religion to them. They're not comfortable with racial mixing on a sociosexual level. You can't tell me they are, and you can't tell me this doesn't influence the way they think.

"You also have to remember that when you talk about corporate life, you're talking about every little town in America. You're not just talking about busy people in cities, but you're talking about the 'redneck' who worked his way up, who has a daughter going to integrated schools and a wife who may not be appealing to him, or he may not be appealing to.

"The race/sex thing is too deep in history to say it has disappeared just because people are struggling to become high corporate dingdongs." This manager subscribed to the idea that the sexual tension between black and white men is still strong enough to put black men at a disadvantage in any sexual environment that white men control.

"Sure it's a problem," said a black secretary. "They especially don't like to see a black manager in a position of authority over a white woman. I remember there was this brother in our section who went out and hired a pretty blond secretary. You should have seen how all the white men in the section watched him—like hawks. Every time he came out of his office to speak to her some of them would stop what they were doing and listen, and God! you could see them squirming when she went into his office and closed the door.

"They tried everything," the secretary said. "They tried to talk her into quitting. They used to make jokes about it to make the entire thing ugly. Pretty soon the girl did quit and the black guy got transferred."

The part of America's nightmare that includes a black man is, more often than not, a sexual nightmare. This, no doubt, is the reason why some of the black men we interviewed wondered if the emphasis on sexual harassment in corporate America will be used against them. By mid-1981 sexual harrassment ranked along with declining worker productivity as the hot issue in many major corporations. It brought out the paranoia in more than one black male manager we interviewed. It brought out caution in others and resentment in more than a few.

Sexual harassment was bound to come up as a major issue because so many women were moving into the labor force, especially into high-mobility jobs where they depended on the fairness or the favor of men to determine how rapidly they would rise.

Some women have used sexual attraction and favors to get what they wanted—or thought they deserved—from men for as long as there have been men and women. Some men have used superior social or economic positions to extract sexual delights from women in circumstances too numerous to mention. The extremes in each case have been outright prostitution and outright rape. Between these extremes are the shaded variations that make the problem so complex. Corporations are right to be concerned, because a tone has to be set that will make the workplace as fair as possible for both men and women.

Errors are going to be made that will affect many people's careers. As we will see later, black men have good reason to fear that many of these errors will have negative effects on their already fragile corporate lives.

"You know there aren't going to be many sexual-harassment charges filed by black women against white men. I think that even if you do have a lot of mixing between white men and black women it's done under conditions where both of them, but especially the black woman, have too much to lose to risk filing charges," said a black female who has a white lover in the company she works for. "I think a few people know we're close, and a few people actually suspect that we are going together, but it's not a public thing," she said.

This woman lives 45 miles from her job and there is very little chance that anyone who works with her would ever see who her visitors were. "I'd rather keep my business to myself," she said. "I started dating white guys in North Carolina, actually, and then when I came up to the Midwest region I dated a few black guys in the company and then I found this one man that I liked and he was white and so he and I have been friends for about seven months now."

It is likely that there will be even fewer sexual-harassment charges filed by black women against black men. Most black managers do not have enough corporate power to really harass in any heavy way. Whatever happens between them is usually handled privately.

Most cases of harassment will, undoubtedly, involve white women and white men. This is true because of numbers and the power of white men in corporate America, and the willingness of white women to file such charges. "Between these two groups there are the greatest number of possibilities," said a young white salesman who said he didn't have enough power to harass anyone, either. We interviewed him with a black salesman in a northern Virginia suburb of Washington, D.C.

The black salesman added that there were several secretaries in his office that he wouldn't mind harassing. They laughed, but there was no way of knowing how serious either one of them was. "I'll give you a switch on that," the black salesman said. "There was this guy in the office they called Lance, a white guy, and they called him Lance because he tried to lance every good-looking woman he could find. He was a young good-looking dude and he was supervisor for all of the customer service reps, who were mostly female. The men who worked for him turned him in for sexual harassment because the good-looking women were getting all the promotions."

A black female social scientist, who is a professor and human resources consultant, said: "Black men have the most to lose in this because they justify any white fear that social contact will mean sexual contact. It doesn't matter that white men and black women have been doing it for generations. For the black man it can be deadly." She had set up her consulting company when she learned that major corporations were beating the bushes to find experts who could help them with their human resource problems. She said that one corporation alone had enough problems to keep a good consultant in business for years. "Black men disregard the vulnerability of their positions and do take on white women who work for them as lovers. Now these women might be jockeying for promotions or they might not be. It might just be a matter of mutual thrills, but it really angers black women, who are experiencing a shortage of males in the first place. Black women get angry but they don't try to turn the brothers in, in most cases, because they like to see black men advancing in the corporations. So the black woman just looks at him as a fool and handles her rage internally—even in cases when the white woman gets promoted ahead of her by a black supervisor who has a touch of vanilla fever," she said, laughing.

"But I think this is going to end. I think that black women are going to stop handling the entire matter on an emotional level and they are going to start looking at it more as a matter of unfair career competition. These are women who have begun to see things in career terms rather than racial terms, but you'd be surprised how difficult this transition is and how few of us have actually made it—the transition from group-mindedness to individual-mindedness and career-mindedness."

She went on to explain, with a mixture of regret and self-mockery in her voice, how she and other women have tried to maintain commitments to something larger than their own careers. She explained that if women give in to this kind of selfishness then everybody in America will be pursuing "self" and there will be no keepers of the hearth. She laughed at how lonely life can be for the keeper.

"Another interesting case is one I had to investigate in California last year. This black guy was making it with a white woman who reported to him. They had a heavy thing that everyone knew about. This black guy was up for a promotion and he was competing with two white guys for this promotion. One of the white guys went to the white woman who was going with the brother and told her that she either make a charge of sexual harassment or he would expose the entire situation and get her fired.

"She panicked and made the charges because she felt that her career was really in jeopardy; but their affair had been so open that she couldn't make the charges stick, so both of them lost out. She was transferred out of the branch and the brother was not given the promotion. His career is dead-ended.

"Then there have been several false charges of sexual harassment lodged by white women against black men. There is a significant fear among black men that this sexual harassment thing will be unfairly used against them. Corporate America has always been very political, but this sexual thing is complicating the politics even more; you'd be surprised."

Black men sense that their image in America's eye is not totally negative. They know that lurking below the surface is an image similar to that which Norman Podhoretz partially revealed in his 1963 essay "My Negro Problem—And Ours." Podhoretz wrote:

> just as in childhood I envied Negroes for what seemed to me their superior masculinity, so I envy them today for what seems to me their superior physical grace and beauty. I have come to value physical grace very highly, and I am now capable of aching with all my being when I watch a Negro couple on the dance floor, or a Negro playing baseball or basketball. They are on the kind of terms with their own bodies that I should like to be on with mine, and for that precious quality they seem blessed to me.

In *Soul on Ice*, Eldridge Cleaver discusses how those white men who concede "the body" to the black man will forever deny that he also has a mind that equals theirs, for to make this concession would be to give the black man a two-to-one victory.

More pertinent to our discussion, however, is another passage from *Soul on Ice*:

> The Class Society has a built-in bias, which tends to perpetuate the social system. The Omnipotent Administrators, wishing to preserve what they perceive as their superior position and way of life, have, from a class point of view and also on an individual

level, a negative reaction toward any influence in the society that tends to increase the number of males qualified to fulfill the functions of administration. When it comes to anything that will better the lot of those beneath him, the Omnipotent Administrator starts with a basic "anti" reflex. Any liberality he might show is an indication of the extent to which he has suppressed his "anti" reflex, and is itself a part of his lust for omnipotence. His liberality is, in fact, charity.

"Okay, okay, okay, okay," Nightmare said after our long discussion of sexual harassment and its various effects on black and white careers. "I admit that. I used to date a lot of them. They were easier to get along with. They didn't hassle me as much. I was getting hassled on my job and I didn't want to be hassled on my off-duty time, so I started dating white women.

"I was making good money and so if I wanted to run down to Barbados to relax, it was better for me to take a white woman. If I had taken a black woman she'd have considered me a marriage candidate. She'd have been negotiating with me to make a commitment, and she'd have been uptight about her morals and about what I thought of her. She'd have tried to act marriageable and I wanted someone to act free and loose for some hot fun in the sun.

"The white woman, she doesn't want to marry you. She just wants to have some fun like you. It's easier. She can give herself without feeling demeaned because the bottom line is she's still white and you're her social inferior and she doesn't have to get into a status battle. To her you're still an M&M, not the chocolate candy by that name. An M&M is a Madison Avenue Mandingo.

"For a long time I found white women easier. I didn't have to approach them or woo them. They approached me and wooed me. That's what I needed at the time. But then I got tired of that and I swung back across the line, but I found it hard to get into sisters because there was always so much tension between us.

"So what I tried to do was to find a black female psychiatrist I could talk to like I talked to the other psychiatrist; but when I went to this one black woman, she couldn't deal with me on a conversational level. She kept trying to set herself up as a mother-confessor to the prodigal son.

"She was very directive, and superformal. I think her education went to her head. I got less understanding out of her than I did out of this white Ph.D. psychologist I was fucking up at the B-school.

"You know," Nightmare said, "if you want to talk about what might work on the white man's mind even more, I'll tell you something that occurred to me when I was reading the book *Games Mother Never Taught You.*

"A fact that might work on his mind more is that black men are the Sunday gladiators of the American Republic. The football field is the coliseum and the action is piped into American homes by TV with these gladiators earning all this big money to be symbols of masculinity for the civilization," he continued.

In the book that he referred to, author Betty Lehan Harragan attempted to analyze this situation:

> It is no accident that 80 percent of the businessmen who comprise today's chief executive officers told *Fortune* magazine some years ago that football was their favorite spectator sport. . . . College textbooks often introduce business management subjects to inexperienced students by using the illustration of a football platoon. . . . Top management in business feels an intense affinity to

the head coach of a football team; their problems seem almost identical. . . . Sports metaphors abound in business talk, as might be expected.

To illustrate her point Harragan shows these parallels:

Back-up team or bench strength: Full complement of trained, duplicate players who sit on the sideline bench prepared to enter the game at any moment to replace players who are hurt, tired, or otherwise removed. In management, the upper three levels of hierarchy contain several strong executives who are fully trained to take over the top job at any time. By extension, smart supervisors move to train subordinates for their jobs to pave the way for their own advancement to higher levels. Considered a sign of a well-managed company or department.

Coach: The boss. The unquestioned decision maker for the team. Not a player. One whose job is to motivate and help players perform well together. A current fad in management training, as in "the best manager considers himself a coach."

Disqualified player: One who has been ousted from the game as a penalty for a personal foul. The severest penalty for prohibited acts traceable to loss of emotional control under stress, as illegally tripping or hitting another player in anger. Significantly, women "disqualified" from management are usually described as "emotionally unsuited."

End run: Moving around the lightly defended ends of the line to avoid massed opposition in the center, as when women create new jobs for themselves rather than competing with men for an existing "man's" job.

Huddle: Get together with selected co-workers before a meeting to devise ways to get one's point across against opposition; make a deal with collaborators who stand to benefit from cooperation. Literally, the team get-together before each play on the field when quarterback gives secret signals that tell each

player where to position himself, what to do, to facilitate the play.

Jock: A male professional athlete; a thoroughgoing competitive team sportsman. The "jocko mentality" pervades highly competitive, nonregulated industries.

Monday morning quarterback: A pejorative term describing player or spectator who delights in explaining how something "should have been done," or "How I would have done it." An after-the-fact analyzer who points out the obvious—that something should have been done differently since the attempted move failed.

Punt: A quick kick of the ball in desperate circumstances when it's necessary to get out of an untenable position. A gamble against great odds.

Quarterback: A key player who calls the signals, i.e. tells other players what to do, and how. Absolute authority figure on the field as delegate of coach.

Tackle the job: Approach a task with single-minded concentration, as "Let's break the back on this." Overused cliché supposed to rev up team players.

"You see what I'm saying," Nightmare said. "If football is the metaphor for corporate competition, how does the white man feel about the fact that black men, who are only 10 percent of the American male population, make up 75 percent of the superstars in football and about 35 percent of all professional football players?

"I think this works on his mind in subtle ways more than the sexual thing, but I don't think it's all negative—the way it works on his mind. I think it makes him curious. See, Vince Lombardi is the patron saint of CEOs, the master coach. But I think one of these guys is going to be like Hank Stram, when he was coach of the Kansas City Chiefs, in the AFL. Remember? The AFL was the *other* league. The NFL had all the great teams and all the great players.

"Secretly Hank Stram began drafting all these niggers, picking them up from Grambling and Southern while the NFL was bidding for the talent from Notre Dame and Michigan State.

"Hey, it's a documented fact. Then they started having interleague games and Hank Stram turned all these niggers loose on the NFL's glory boys. The niggers killed them. Check the record. Check out the Super Bowls. The NFL was never recovered.

"Corporate life is like it was with baseball before Jackie Robinson. You're going to get a crazy Branch Rickey-type white boy as a CEO, who is going to come out of the dugout in a losing cause and signal for a bad black dude like Cliff Alexander, or me. He's going to say: "I don't care if I get booed. I don't care if they make threats on my life. I'll tough this one out. I want to win and I'm going to field the best player."

Nightmare leaned back, pleased with himself, pleased that he had been able to get a lot of things out of himself. He is not a typical black male manager, nor has his life been usual. It seems instead to be the hyperbole which expresses the essence of many men's struggle to find and maintain a sense of self in the corporation.

CASE 2
BETSY MORGAN (A)
Arthur N. Turner

Betsy Morgan had to admit to herself that she was very excited as her plane circled for a landing at the International airport in Lagos, Nigeria. It was October 1976 and Betsy was about to undertake an assignment

which she knew could go a long way toward establishing her career with the United Bank. Betsy had been assigned as the economic analyst and trade development officer in the bank's major West African office. She felt well prepared for the assignment, and believed her success in it would enable her to overcome the disadvantages which had resulted from her first overseas assignment with the bank.

Partly to settle her nerves, she mused about that earlier assignment. After going through the bank's orientation and training program in New York, she had been assigned as the junior economic officer in the largest bank branch in Latin America. She had been given some language training and had approached that assignment with great anticipation. After all, she had been graduated less than one year earlier at age 22 from a prestigious Midwestern university, where she had achieved a double major. (She recalled that it had almost been a triple major.) At 23, she had been nearly the first member of her college class to land a professional job, and felt very good about it. She was also the first female member of her family to take up a professional position.

However, that first assignment had quickly turned sour. She had found herself working for a traditional-minded overseas bank officer who openly expressed his belief that women should be either secretaries or loyal, dependent wives supporting the bank's mission both at home and overseas. She had felt, almost from the day she arrived, that the branch manager was prejudiced against her because she was a woman, and had not provided her with the kinds of growth opportunities she felt she needed. Betsy felt that he never fully accepted her as a professional. He would often treat her as he had been accustomed to treating dependent wives and secretaries.

For example, for months he tried to persuade Betsy to attend the bi-weekly luncheons which were held for bankers' wives throughout the international community. Also, it was many months before Betsy found herself situated in a suitable office, whereas male officers assigned to similar duties got an office immediately upon arrival. The situation had been made more complicated by the fact that Betsy's written evaluations by her branch manager were uniformly unflattering, and by the time she left after two years in Latin America, she believed her future at the bank was dim.

Upon reassignment to New York, however, Betsy discovered that there was a grievance mechanism within the bank which permitted the filing of sex discrimination complaints. With some help from more senior women in the bank, Betsy devoted considerable time and effort to filing—and ultimately winning—her grievance against the branch manager.

The result of Betsy winning the grievance was that the bank began training her for a second overseas post which represented a significant increase in responsibility over her first post. In its letter acknowledging settlement of the grievance, the bank's director of personnel told Betsy specifically that she was fully reinstated and that her record would be annotated to include the results of the grievance proceeding, which were very favorable to Betsy. For her part, Betsy Morgan felt completely vindicated. So she was approaching her new assignment in Lagos full of optimism and determination that nothing would get in the way of her success in her new job.

Her disappointment at the end of her tour in Lagos could not have been more complete. After that two-year tour was over, she said: "My experiences and those of the other professional women and dependent wives assigned to the bank's branch in Lagos during the period 1976–1978 constituted sexual harassment in the sense that the behavior of the branch manager, David Brown, had the effect of substantially interferring with our work performance and creating an intimidating, hostile and defensive working environment." How did this happen?

In the Lagos branch, Betsy was economic analyst and trade development officer. She was in charge of a small unit, and supervised a commercial assistant of Nigerian nationality and, during her summers in Lagos, an intern from the bank's central intern program. In effect, Betsy was David Brown's second in command, and in his absence she was the chief substantive officer for the Lagos branch.

However, Betsy commented that "David would introduce me as 'his daughter,' 'his friend,' or as 'someone whose skills he was trying to develop' when I met professional contracts." She added that "I felt this form of introduction left government and business associates either ignorant of my position with the bank or, at the very least, doubtful of my authority and abilities. It made it difficult for me to be taken seriously by those with whom I had to deal as a professional. And following such introductions by the branch manager, it always took time for me to reestablish my professional stature.

"For instance, at one point the Nigerian government bought over $5 million worth of tractors and earth movers from a major U.S. firm with the help of our export-import bank financing. I had assisted in some of the financial arrangements, and to celebrate closing the deal, the Nigerians hosted a dinner. They invited David Brown, but he had a prior commitment and asked me to represent him. I did. Mr. Brown, however, stopped by for drinks before dinner, and while he was there made a big deal of having sent 'a girl' since he couldn't stay for the entire occasion. He went on at great length to point out the fact that one girl was not enough to go around for all the men in attendance. I had been made to feel as if I were to strip and pop out of a cake. Then he left, and despite the role I had played in helping the Nigerians obtain financing for the farm equipment, I was treated as a bit of fluff for the rest of the evening."

When asked about other incidents she perceived as sexual harassment, Betsy provided the following examples:

One of the most unpleasant experiences I had in Lagos occurred almost immediately after I arrived. David Brown and I, together with most of the other bank officials in Lagos, were at a social gathering one evening. As we were driving home in David's car, he stopped to let all the others out at various points. He asked if I would like a quick drink at his place before he took me home. I felt social etiquette demanded that I agree. When we sat down and David had served me a drink, he seated himself nearby and I soon found his hand on my knee. I brushed it off. Later he moved over to sit next to me and slipped his arm around my shoulders. I got up to leave. But before I could get out the door, he grabbed me and kissed me several times directly on the lips. I finally broke free and ran, flustered, from his house, and took a taxi home.

A month or so after I arrived in Lagos, David Brown developed the habit of stopping by my office the first thing each morning for a kiss. He would come bounding in and stand next to my chair. I would rise, as I felt I should, and extend my hand to shake his. But he would grab my hand and pull me toward him for a kiss. After several mornings of this experience I began shutting my door. He was not deterred. He came in anyway and continued to kiss me. I then began

to arrive early enough to open my safe, spread work out on my desk, and then go hide in the ladies' room until after the branch manager had gone into his own office.

On another occasion, as a favor to friends and contacts in the American embassy, I agreed to help in the planning for the first U.S. naval ship visit in several years. Mr. Brown took an active interest in the project. In addition to all the normal duties related to facilitating such a visit, I was instructed to find out where the local whorehouses were located, so the sailors might be informed. When Mr. Brown first directed me to do this, I refused. However, he continued to pester me. Even after refusing and explaining that I felt such inquiries were improper, since prostitution was illegal in Nigeria, he continued to hound me. The following year the whole episode was, unfortunately, repeated.

She continued, "Even after the initial shock of the branch manager's physical advances had worn off, I found myself occasionally being harassed by him. One day after I had been in Lagos about six months, he came up and patted me on the back, seemingly to congratulate me for a job I felt I had done well. Instead he said, 'Oh, you're wearing a bra!' On another occasion, he had reached just inside the edge of my sleeveless top and pulled my bra strap down from my shoulder.

I was by no means the only victim of the branch manager's roving hands and mouth. I recall that one day, while his secretary was sitting at her desk typing, Mr. Brown stole up behind her and snapped her bra; and at a Christmas-Eve party at my home in 1976, he reached through another secretary's dress and snapped the elastic at the waist of her underpants. A year or so later I saw him doing the same thing to another woman.

Betsy said that the incidents she related had either happened to her, were witnessed by her, or were reported to her by the victims. "I participated in many informal gripe sessions which served to defuse the frustration and anger of the women of the bank. One reason we put up with David Brown's antics was that we knew that a regular bank inspection team would be coming soon. We raised Mr. Brown's conduct with the inspectors several times during their visit to Lagos. The inspectors agreed with us about the seriousness of the problem and about its adverse effect on the work and morale of what was, after all, supposed to be an important branch of the bank's West African operations."

She continued by admitting that "Even though we had heard that the head of the inspection team was an old friend of Mr. Brown, we believed that the inspectors would have to take account of the extraordinary sexual harassment to which the manager was subjecting the female members of his staff and the wives of his male staff members." She added that "I personally felt particularly strongly that the inspectors would take prompt remedial steps because of my positive experience in fighting and winning my earlier grievance against my first branch manager. All the bank's female staff individually and collectively met with the inspectors and complained to them in excruciating detail about Mr. Brown's behavior. The inspectors also spoke with him privately before they left Lagos. The effect of their conversation with him was apparent, for about two months. During that period David Brown left us alone.

However, to our great disappointment, we soon learned that the inspectors had failed to take any of the formal or institutional steps available to them regarding David Brown's behavior. In effect, they appeared to cover up and condone the sexual

harassment to which he was subjecting us. Also, there was no written record of Mr. Brown's misconduct, and so no one in New York could be charged with following up to make sure that he modified his behavior. And as for Mr. Brown himself, after determining that there was nothing on his record and after he received orders transferring him in the normal course of events to a better position in the New York headquarters, he picked up where he had left off before.

In fact, I sometimes thought his behavior deteriorated after the dust from the inspectors' visit had settled down. One example will suffice. Midway through my tour in Lagos I had become engaged to another bank officer who was serving in the Arab world at the time. My fiancé and I had planned to meet for our vacation in France. I asked the branch manager's permission to be absent for a period of two weeks for this vacation period. Mr. Brown replied, with half of the bank's staff in Lagos listening, "If he wants to f— you that badly, let him come here." You can imagine the mortification I felt.

It was obviously not easy for Betsy to recount these incidents. She felt humiliated, infuriated, enraged, and helpless in remote Lagos. She commented that without having lived abroad it may be difficult for people to understand the oppressive sense of helplessness and isolation that staff members feel when they are subjected to any kind of harassment or disagreeable behavior by a superior of the organization they represent.

Betsy wondered what to do next.

BETSY MORGAN (B)
Arthur N. Turner

Betsy Morgan still works for United Bank. She is now assigned to the bank's New York headquarters. Betsy said she had been un-decided when she left Lagos about what course of action she should follow. "I have been wrestling with the question of whether to file another grievance against my super-visor. My reluctance is based on two major factors. First, I had fought the good fight once already. I had won, and overall the gains had outweighed the losses. But to stand up and be counted a second time might label me a troublemaker and put an end to my career. I enjoy what I am doing and feel that I am very good at it. Secondly, I would be asked to recount in detail inci-dents of sexual harassment, a nasty, un-pleasant, and an emotionally charged sub-ject. This is a subject that women, including myself, are reluctant to talk about because somehow the victim always seems to end up guilty of being a victim.

> Additionally, David Brown now occupies a sensitive position in New York, where he could very easily have a significant effect on my future career. And he certainly does not shy away from acknowledging our joint ser-vice overseas. When he sees me, he fre-quently comments that, "I made her what she is today."

In thinking about her case, Betsy wonders if she did the right thing. She has decided to remain with the bank, at least for the near future, and give it one more try. She did not file any kind of grievance on her return from Lagos.

Still, she wonders, even three years later, how people will react when they read about her case. Could they understand her des-perate sense of confusion, shame, humilia-tion, and anger as she left Lagos? Would they appreciate the pressures she placed upon herself to succeed in a career never attempted by another member of her fam-ily? Would they judge her too harshly?

CASE 3
FREIDA MAE JONES
Martin R. Moser

Freida Mae Jones was born in her grand-mother's farm house in Georgia on June 1, 1949. She was the sixth of George and Ella Jones's 10 children. The Joneses moved to New York City in 1953 because they felt that the educational and career opportunities for their children would be better in the North than in rural Georgia. With the help of some cousins, they settled in a five-room apart-ment in the Bronx. George got a job as a janitor at Lincoln Memorial Hospital and Ella did part-time housekeeping work in a nearby neighborhood. The Joneses were conservative and strict parents. They kept a close watch on their children's activities, de-manding them to be home at a certain hour, and having them account for all of their ac-tivities outside of the home. The Joneses be-lieved that since they were black, that their children would have to perform better than their peers and be better behaved in order to succeed in the world. They both believed that their children's education would be the most important ingredient in their lives as adults.

Freida entered Memorial High School in September 1963, a racially integrated public school. Seventy percent of the student body were Caucasian, 20 percent black, and 10 percent Hispanic. About 60 percent of the graduates went on to college. Of this 60 per-cent, 4 percent were black and Hispanic and all were male. In January 1966, Freida was in the middle of her senior year at Memorial and was academically the top-rated student in her class. As required by school regula-tions, Freida met with her guidance counselor to discuss her plans upon graduation. It was suggested to her that she consider obtaining training in a "practical" field, such as housekeeping, cooking, sewing, and the like, so she would be able to find employment upon her graduation.

George and Ella Jones were furious when Frieda told them what the guidance counselor had said to her. "Don't they see what they are doing. Frieda is the top-rated student in her whole class and they are telling her to become a manual worker. She showed that she has a fine mind and can work better than any of her classmates and still she is told not to become anybody in this world. It's really not any different in the North than back home in Georgia, except that they don't try to hide it down South. They want her to throw away her fine mind because she is a black girl and not a white boy. I'm going to go up to her school tomorrow and talk to the principal."

As a result of her visit to the principal of Memorial High School, her daughter was assisted in applying to 10 fine Eastern colleges, all of whom offered her full four-year scholarships. In September 1966, Frieda entered Werbley College, an exclusive and private women's college located in Massachusetts. Majoring in history, Frieda graduated in 1970 summa cum laude. She decided to return to New York to teach grade school in the city's public school system. Frieda was unable to obtain a full-time position, so she substituted. She also enrolled as a part-time student in Columbia University's Graduate School of Education. In 1975 she had attained her master of arts degree in teaching (MAT) from Columbia, but could not find a permanent teaching job. New York City was laying off teachers and had instituted a hiring freeze due to the city's financial problems.

Feeling very frustrated about her future as a teacher, Frieda decided to get an MBA.

She thought that there was much more opportunity in the business world than in the educational world. Freida enrolled in Churchill Business School's MBA program. Churchill was a small but prestigious business school located in upstate New York.

Freida completed her MBA in 1977 and accepted an entry-level position at the Industrialist World Bank of Boston in a fast-track management development program. It was a three-year program which gave her exposure to all facets of bank operations, from telling to loan training to operations managing. She was moved to different branch offices throughout New England. Upon completion of the program she was assigned as an assistant manager for branch operations in the West Springfield branch office.

During her second year in Boston, Freida met James Walker, a black doctoral student in business administration at the University of Massachusetts. Her assignment in West Springfield precipitated their decision to get married. They originally anticipated that they would marry when James finished his school work and he would move to Boston. Instead, he could pursue a job in the Springfield–Hartford area. Her assignment to West Springfield allowed them to be together without interfering with either of their careers.

Freida was the first black, as well as the first woman, to hold an executive position in the West Springfield branch office. Throughout her training program Freida felt somewhat uneasy, although she did very well. There were six other blacks in the training program, five men and one woman. She found support and comfort in being able to share her feelings with them, especially relating to racial issues. The group of six spent much of their free time together. Freida had hoped that she would be located near one or more of the group when she went out into the "real world." She felt that, although she was able to share her feelings about work with James, he did not have the full appreciation or understanding of her co-workers. The nearest person from the group was located 100 miles away.

Freida's boss at the bank was Stan Luboda, a 55-year-old native New Englander. Freida felt that he treated her differently than the other people. He was always trying to help her and took a lot of time (too much according to Freida) in explaining things to her. Freida felt that he was treating her like a child, and not as an intelligent and able professional.

"I'm really getting frustrated and angry about what is happening at the bank," Freida said to her husband. "The people don't even realize it, but their prejudice comes through all of the time. I feel like I have got to fight all of the time just to start off even. Luboda is giving Paul Cohen more responsibility than me, and we both started at the same time with the same amount of training. He's getting out with the customers alone and Luboda has accompanied me to each meeting I've had with a customer."

"I run into the same kind of stuff at school," said James. "The people don't even know that they are doing it. The other day I met with a professor who is on my dissertation committee. I've know and worked with the guy for over three years. He said that there was something that he wanted to talk with me about but couldn't find the memo he was looking for. So I asked him what it was about. He said that the records office sent him a memo about me being out of school during the spring semester and that I needed to sign some forms as soon as he could find them. He had me confused with Martin Jordan, another black student. Then he realized that it

wasn't me, but Jordan, who he was looking for. All I could think about was how we all probably look alike to him. I was angry. Maybe it was an honest mistake on his part, but whenever something like that happens, and it happens often, it really gets me angry."

"Something like that happened to me with Luboda's secretary," said Freida. "I was using the copy machine, and she was talking to somebody in the hall. She had just gotten a haircut and was saying how her hair was like Freida's, short and kinky, and that she would have to talk to me about how to take care of it. My back was to her, and it's a good thing. I just bit my lip and went on with my business. Maybe she was trying to be cute, because I know that she saw me standing there. But comments like that are not cute, they are racist."

"I don't know what to do," said James. "I just try to keep things in perspective, and unless people are interfering with my progress I try to let it slide. I only have so much energy and it doesn't make any sense to waste it on people who don't matter. But that doesn't make it any easier to function in a racist environment. People don't realize that they are being racist. But a lot of times their expectations of black people or women, or whatever, is different because of skin color or gender. In other words, they expect you to be different, although if you ask them they would say that they don't. In fact, they would be highly offended if you implied that they were being racist or sexist. They don't see themselves that way."

"Luboda is interfering with my progress," said Freida. "The kinds of experiences I have now will have a direct bearing on my career advancement in the future. And if decisions are being made because I am black or a woman, then they are racially and sexually biased. It's the same kind of attitude that the guidance counselor had when I was in high school, although not as blatant."

In September 1980, Frieda decided to talk to Luboda about his treatment of her. She met with him in his office. "Mr. Luboda, there is something that I would like to discuss with you, and I feel a little uncomfortable in doing so because I'm not sure how you will respond to what I am going to say."

"I want you to feel that you can trust me," said Luboda. "I am anxious to help you in any way that I can."

"I feel like you are treating me differently than you treat the other people around here," said Freida. "I feel like you are overcautious with me, that you are always trying to help me do things, and never let me do anything on my own."

"I always try to help the new people around here," answered Luboda. "I'm not treating you any different than I treat any other new person. I think that you are being a little too sensitive. Do you think that I treat you differently because you are black?"

"The thought had occurred to me," said Freida. "Paul Cohen started here the same time that I did and he has much more responsibility than I do." Cohen had started at the bank at the same time as Freida and completed the management training program with Freida. Cohen was already handling accounts on his own, and Freida had not been given that responsibility yet.

"Freida, I know that you are not a naive person," said Luboda. "You know the way the world works. There are some things which need to be taken more slowly than others. There are some assignments which Cohen has been given more responsibility than you, and there are some assignments which you are given more responsibility than Cohen. I try to put you where you do the most good."

"What you are saying is that Cohen gets the more visible customer-contact assignments and I get the behind-the-scenes running of the operations assignments," said Freida. "I'm not naive, but I'm also not stupid, either. Your decisions are unfair. Cohen's career will advance much quicker than mine because of the assignments that he gets and that I don't."

"Freida what you are saying is not true," said Luboda. "Your career will not be hurt because you are getting different responsibilities than Cohen. You both need the different kinds of experiences you are getting. And you have to face the reality of the banking business. We are in a conservative business. When we talk to customers we need to gain their confidence, and we put the best people for the job in the positions to achieve that end. If we don't get their confidence they can go right down the street to our competitors and do business with them. Their services are no different than ours. It's a competitive business and you need to use every edge you have. It's going to take a while for people to change some of their attitudes about who they borrow money from, or where they put their money. I can't change the way people feel. I am running a business, but believe me I won't make any decisions that are detrimental for you or for the bank. There is an important place for you here at the bank. But you have to use your skills to the best advantage of the bank as well as your career."

"So what you are saying is that all things being equal, except my gender and my race, that Cohen will get different treatment than me in terms of assignments," said Freida.

"You're making it sound like I am making a racist and sexist decision," said Luboda. "I'm making a business decision utilizing the resources at my disposal and the market situation in which I must operate. You know exactly what I am talking about. What would you do if you were in my position?"

CASE 4
THE VERMONT DECISION
Emily Stein and Michael Beer

In September 1977, Diane, 45 years old, director of marketing at the Hanson Company in Manhattan, came to Harvard to attend the Advanced Management Program (AMP). Her husband Bill, 47 years old, formerly in marketing himself, had been job hunting for the past six months. Just before Diane left for Harvard Bill received an offer to become vice president, marketing, at the Scottsfield Corporation in Los Angeles. In October, Diane and Bill spent a weekend together in Vermont and made the decision for Bill to take the job and move to the West Coast. In December, Diane and Bill had mixed feelings about their decision. They discussed their concerns at length.

Background

Diane: I've been with Hanson now, in line marketing for 13 years. It wasn't easy at the beginning. For the first five years, as a matter of fact, there was a lot of resistance from a lot of people. Those were difficult times. I had to make a living; I had a child to support. I never really made a conscious decision to have a career. I was raised like every other girl in my generation. My goals were to be married and have babies. I went to college with those ideas. I did what I had to to get by, managed fairly well, had a very

good time and met someone. Once we got married I did work but only to support us while my husband was in medical school. As things worked out, our marriage broke up and I was left with a child to support. There I was with no money at all. I needed work and found a job in public relations for a large food corporation. I didn't need a lot of experience for that job. All I needed was to be friendly and fairly attractive. I had those qualifications.

When I think back on it I was pretty brazen in those days. I convinced the corporation that public relations meant more than just one charity bazaar a year and that they ought to do some advertising. I can't believe it now, but I had the gall to write and place ads. I didn't know what I was doing. I just did it. It worked out well and, before long the company had given me a quarter-million-dollar advertising budget. At about that time the president of the company asked me if I would be interested in taking charge of public relations for their entire restaurant division. There were 40 altogether and, up until that point, I had been working on only 10 or 11. The opportunity excited me, but corporate headquarters and the job were in Cincinnati and I wanted to be in New York. At that time my grandparents and parents were in the East and they were a lot of help with my daughter. They babysat weekends and would stay with her if she was sick. Generally, the family was a great support system for Robin, my daughter, and for me.

Being in the East was very important to me so I didn't take the job. I was just as well because, although I didn't know it specifically, I had been growing professionally out of public relations and into marketing. I'm not sure I even knew what it was called then but my interests were definitely becoming crystalized. I began to interview in New York, "where the action was." For three months I stood in unemployment lines, talked to companies, advertising agencies, or anyone who would listen. The longer I talked, the more convinced I became that marketing was my area. During that period I interviewed with Hanson. The time was right for me. They were beginning to experiment with the idea of hiring, training, and developing women. I qualified and at 32 years old began my career.

I got into it quickly, liked it, and was good at it. I spent the first few years proving myself. It was difficult to gain acceptance from some of the men I had to work with. My immediate supervisors were no problem. But the salesmen and the manufacturing men made it very hard for me to accomplish things. I was lowest on the ladder and a woman. Those characteristics brought out a great deal of resistance, silent and vocal. I remember questions like "what right have you got to earn a living when a man should or could have this job." At that point I would very clearly explain my position. I was, in fact, the sole source of support for myself and my daughter. There were other kinds of resistance, too. I had some difficulties involving unwanted and inappropriate overtures from men. Every time I turned someone down I worried if my career was in jeopardy.

In retrospect, it was a struggle to get where I am today professionally and attitudinally as well. I am appalled, for instance, at the way I used to react to promotions. I always worked very hard and, as it turned out, was responsible for some very important marketing successes. I made decisions which resulted in new brands and changes in product lines. I was producing, had accomplishments to prove it, and was promoted consistently. The first few times I was promoted I felt so grateful. I remember calling the president and thanking him for doing such a nice thing for a woman. I was capable and deserved those promotions but felt grateful.

Things have changed since I first started. I don't find resistance any more, at least none at Hanson. I've been around now for nearly 15 years and am known around the company and in the field. I do have a good reputation but it took time and effort to build.

Looking back on it now, it's gratifying to know I've had a child, a career and a marriage. I was lucky in a way, though. I was able to carry everything off successfully because I was in a position to attack one piece of the "life puzzle" at a time. I didn't try to establish a career, family, and marriage all at once between the ages of 25 and 30. In my case, a child came first. In the early years when Robin was very young, I was just earning a living to support us. I had to do that, did, and launched her. I absorbed that part first. My career came next. I worked very hard at that for years. In the last five years I've been working very hard at my marriage. But I've been able to work on each aspect separately and then add on one more major piece. I think the timing could be faster than the way it happened to turn out for me; but I think it's important not to delude yourself into thinking you can do it all at once because each of those things takes time, interest, and energy. You must have enough to go around for the mastering of mothering, career, and marriage. Each is a separate and important task.

My marriage is very important to me. I'm married to a very special man. A lot of my ability to continue to be successful at work and be married at the same time has been due to the support my husband has given me. He is absolutely terrific.

He really understands who I am, why I do what I do, what motivates me. He cares about that, he supports it. I don't mean he props me up, he simply understands and accepts me. That makes an enormous amount possible. We respect each other, I think that's what marriage is about. We fought very hard for our marriage, which is an important thing, too. Because we each came from other marriages and from some disappointment and some feelings of failure, and so forth, I wasn't sure we were going to make it for a few years there. We worked very hard at learning how to be married, and how to really give and take with each other, learning how to fight, learning how to love, learning how to break the walls down, learning how to do a lot of things. We really worked at it and I'm very glad for it.

Bill: I met Diane about seven years ago. I was 39 then. About that time my whole life became explosive. Everything I had been used to fell apart at once. It was really a classic story. I was a guy in the middle of a 15-year-old marriage; I had three marvelous kids. I had a great reputation in marketing in New York. I was really living in one straight-line way. If someone had said to me, "Bill, are you happy?" I would have said, "Amen. I'm as happy as I can be." Suddenly, though, without realizing it I wasn't happy at all. I don't know exactly how it began but I found myself reevaluating my life and I didn't like at all what I was. Then Diane came into it. We hit a nerve in each other instantly. That lead to my divorce and, in turn, our marriage a couple of years later.

When my personal reevaluation and crisis began I left marketing and went to work to manage a small family-held business in New Jersey, the Ellis Company. The timing was really right for me there. The family wanted to let go somewhat and, for the first time, brought in outside management. It was a great experience for me. For a long time I had fantasized about managing a business and my fantasies worked out quite well. As a matter of fact, I couldn't do any thing wrong there. I earned a lot of money for the company. I was very good, as good as I thought I'd be in that kind of situation. People enjoyed working with me in that role, and I enjoyed working with them. Despite the success, personal and for the company, the situation ended terribly. I got fired! Without going into all the ins and outs, the family got resentful because with their bonus system a couple of outside people (non-family) made a lot of money out of their business.

Anyway, I was fired and not long after that went to work as a manager for the Loomis Corporation in Connecticut. Specifically, I was running a small group of recreational businesses that the parent corporation had acquired. That was in late 1971 or early

1972. Diane and I were married about three or four months after I had taken the Loomis job. We subsequently bought a house in New Canaan, Connecticut. On December 17 of this year we will have our fifth wedding anniversary. As I look back on it, that business venture was personally growthful. I had a lot of autonomy there. At the same time, however, it was a bit suicidal. Because it was an acquisition program and because it was a small piece of a very big corporation, I guess I knew that it was really only a matter of time before that group of small businesses would be sold.

Diane: Bill really felt that the small companies were really not compatible with the parent corporation. He recommended they be sold.

Bill: It was ironic, I told the corporation to sell and at the same time sold myself out of a job. I wasn't very concerned at that point. About that time Diane and I were really beginning to pull our marriage together. At first things were not easy for us. We were trying to sell each other on our own values, I think. We were spending a lot of time with a psychiatrist; I was sleeping in the living room and we kicked and screamed at each other. At any rate, we finally managed to accept and respect our differences and, as a result, know each other well and feel terrific about the relationship. We worked very conscientiously at having this marriage last.

The Problem

Diane: Actually the problems we are faced with now have nothing to do with our relationship. We know that's important to both of us. The issue really was that at the delicate age of 46 Bill began to look for a new job. He was confident that his past experience, which was exciting for him, would qualify him for something even more exciting. That wasn't really the case.

Bill: I guess I was naive but I really thought that my experience at Loomis was so superb and I was so successful that I would be in demand. I was sure that I'd be able to step out into the world, wave my hands, and the world would come beating down my door. Well, the world wasn't waiting despite my good credentials.

Diane: In fact, the job-searching process became very frustrating. There just were not that many alternatives.

Bill: Looking for work was a very frustrating process. It was slow and painful to realize that I wasn't as salable as I thought I was. It became scarey as hell. Somewhere in the middle of the summer, after looking for months, for some unknown reason, I began to feel better about the whole thing. The process was still painful but somehow I began to trust myself as I never have before. I found myself giving myself credit for skills and savvy.

Diane: Although the looking time was awful we both agreed that he shouldn't settle.

Bill: Somewhere in the middle or end of the summer the Scottsfield situation came up. We were sitting out in the backyard and the phone rang. Someone said it was California calling. When I got to the phone it was the Scottsfield guy. I listened and talked and when I got off the phone I thought to myself, "I'd have to be crazy to consider California." Diane, God bless her, was the one who said, "You can't afford not to consider this." Soon after that I spoke with their vice president of industrial relations in New York and came away liking him. As it turned out the president of Scottsfield was in New York then, too. I met with him and we just sort of accidentally chatted for a few minutes. I liked him, too. That night I came home and thought, "Gee, what do I do now?" I really hadn't been prepared for feeling good about the company or the offer. To make a long story short, I went to California several weeks later to talk with the president again and meet other people. I went out there fully prepared to find a big, structured, cumbersome company loaded with people with whom I'd be incompatible. This was really the beginning of what turned out to be a

major dilemma. I liked and admired the people and the environment enormously. They were not out of the corporate mold. There was a bit of maverick running through a lot of them. While it was part of a big conglomerate, the company was really quite autonomous. I guess I was impressed because it was the big leagues. While I hadn't really realized it, several years earlier, I had stepped out of the big leagues. With Scottsfield, I had the opportunity to get back into them. I didn't know what the hell to do. I liked those guys. I liked the environment and I was increasingly persuaded by the fact that they knew who I was and what I was. They had adequately sized up their needs and were really actively looking for me. It was the ingredient that had been missing all through the past months of talking to people and looking for jobs.

The interview process continued and Diane came out and joined me, saw the situation, and drove around. We both thought, "Oh, my God, Southern California." Diane was very helpful then. She forced me to keep my eyes open, she listened to me, and questioned me to make me think. I wasn't totally sure of what I was saying or thinking. On the one hand, I said, "No way in the world could I be in California; the kids are back East, Diane has a career in New York; why the hell would I want to live in California." On the other hand, I was saying, "Boy, does it feel good to see an environment where my talent is recognized and I feel as if I can operate successfully." When we came back from California and Diane was headed for Harvard I had an offer in my pocket. There was a lot of money involved and it was a desirable position.

Diane: We really had a very big dilemma in front of us. It was not going to be an easy decision. There were a multitude of factors involved. Not only am I here with my career in the East, but Bill has three children by his previous marriage. He's very close to his kids. His oldest daughter is off at college but the two boys are at home and he attends all their football games. As a matter of fact, he's the kind that takes movies of the Saturday afternoon football games; he's deeply involved in their lives. This was a decision that involved a lot more than just us. About that time I think he had an offer in the East. It would have been a decent situation. The real struggle then revolved around whether or not he would settle for a pretty good job, pretty decent salary, probably even a company presidency, but not in the big leagues. We weren't sure whether that was a good move at this point in his life. He still wanted to do something more important. As I said, the idea of settling was just not acceptable. Mostly because he had spent over a year looking and had had his ego pretty badly battered. It was very important for him to reestablish himself, and a mediocre job wouldn't have been satisfying.

We had a very tough year. I will say, though, that during that frustrating time he was marvelously strong. He didn't drink, do something crazy, or get violently depressed. Our marriage was a support for him; the kids were a support. His running and tennis activities were a support. He was doing healthy things to deal with the feelings of being continually rejected. He got those feelings being interviewed. Talking and laying himself on the line day in and day out. During that time, I think, he learned he was no longer perceived as a big success in the eyes of the world. Perhaps he would have decided to stay in the East if he did not need to reestablish and reaffirm himself so badly. He's really very good. He did need another chance to accomplish something big. Anyway during the year of looking we made a rule about the whole job situation. The rule was that we had to keep talking about it. Even though it was difficult, we had to keep in touch with what was going on. That got very hard to do because when I'm working and I'm coming home with working problems, my success is sort of evident. I was getting all kinds of good positive feedback

and was about to go off to AMP at Harvard. On the other hand, Bill's days were spent getting turned down on telephones, going through tough interviews, and having to bare his soul time after time. We really were coming from two totally different places. That was difficult. We'd lose the ability to communicate and then we'd have to work at getting it together again.

In July, when we were facing no paycheck for the first time, the California call came. I had a really funny feeling about that phone call then. We later discovered that we both had the same sense that this was the big one. At that point I was about to go off to Harvard. Right before Harvard I flew to California with Bill to meet with the people out there. I went to see it because they wanted me to have some sense of where he would be. They were very smart. They were very considerate of my problem and my position and were very high on him. Whatever he kind of asked for, they gave him. They really made it very hard for him to turn it down. They were sensitive to us, though. They said to Bill, "We understand the situation but we really want you to come with us." They worked very hard at convincing him to go. I guess there comes a point when you can't say no.

The Decision Process

Diane: In September I went off to Harvard. Our talking rule really went into effect.

Bill: We went through weeks of nonstop talking.

Diane: The phone calls were really flying and you said anything you felt because you wanted to make sure that you were considering every piece of input possible. We decided that we would take the first break I would have from the AMP program and go away for a long weekend. We went to Vermont to see the foliage and make our decision. It was on October 10–12, I think and that's exactly what we did.

Bill: Again, it was nonstop talking.

Diane: It was funny. Bill sat down and his words said, "I'm not going to do it." What I heard was he wanted to do it. I said that. I told him, "You're saying one thing but what I hear is another thing."

Bill: I seesawed back and forth between how the hell can I do it, to how can I not do it. We walked around and looked at the situation from every way possible. One really important issue emerged for me. It was at the core of all my concern. I realized, frankly, that I was 47 years old and, no matter how good I thought I was or how good a lot of people told me I was, I was very close to 50. By 50, unless you are in a good situation or are famous you're damn close to a big nothing. I've seen some very good people in that kind of situation and I knew desperately I didn't want to be there. I couldn't imagine myself in that place, didn't see myself as that kind of animal. I guess I thought I was too good for that. I don't mean that in a conceited way, I mean that I saw 50 as a hell of a threat. I was scared that if I didn't find something that made real long-term sense, I would be in very serious trouble.

Scottsfield represented some very good and rare opportunities. It was likely that I'd never have another one like it. I hadn't seen one before, and it wasn't because I hadn't looked hard enough. I had. I'd seen big corporations, though, where you molded yourself to them. At that point in my life I couldn't see living that way.

Diane: We spent two days considering the effect on our marriage, whether our marriage could stand the distance, and whether the children could get on. We worked so hard for the marriage that the idea of jeopardizing it was very hairy. People at Hanson know people at Scottsfield. The minute Bill made a decision to go to California, people in my company would know. As a result I worried about my career, too. Was Bill's being on the West Coast signaling that my career on the East Coast was dead? I didn't know how Hanson would handle that. One thing I

knew was that I would never give up my career. I worked much too hard to get where I am and I value my financial independence. There are only one or two women in line marketing in an industry like this at my level. I am probably viewed as an enigma to some of our friends. There are women I know, my age, who think there's no question that if your husband is on the West Coast you follow him and settle for a lesser job if it comes to that or be stubborn and stay in the East and lose him. I won't give up the kind of job I have and I won't give up Bill. When I get to the point of thinking that that is an either or situation, I can get pretty panicky. I suppose it is possible that at some point in my career I will move, but that didn't even come up over our weekend. Bill never said, "Well, now dear, you'll just pack up and follow me." And, I never said to him, "Of course, do whatever you want, I'll paddle along behind you." We spent time trying to talk through what the job in California would mean to us, what it would mean to both careers, and we tried to reconcile those things. We made the decision after all that talking.

The Decision

Bill: Yes, we came out of the Vermont weekend with what we call the Vermont decision. The result of the weekend: Yes, we had to do it. On the way up to Vermont I had only halfway decided that I would not do it. However, what came out in those two or three days of nonstop talking was the realization that I would be nowhere if I said no. What were my alternatives? After the weekend we knew that we really had to do it for my future, my sense of self-identity, and for helping reestablish my sense of self-importance.

We knew the problems, though. We knew that my being 3,000 miles away from Diane and my two sons was an absolute negative. There was a problem with lifestyle, too. We really had begun to put some roots down in

Connecticut. We had good friends, really good friends, and were a part of our community. I was involved in the Y and stuff. Actually, when you think about it, there were an enormous amount of negatives. There were a whole lot of positives in the East—my kids, my roots, my lifestyle, and my marriage. The incredible thing is, that with all the negatives both the kids and Diane agreed that the most important factor of all was for me to have the chance to reestablish my sense of self-worth. It's unbelievable that with all the negatives we made the decision for me to take the job.

Diane: There were some qualifiers, however. Although we decided yes, we knew that we could only tolerate that situation for a limited time period. I know that there are married people who both have careers, who live apart for 10 or 20 years. That wasn't acceptable for us. We put a time limit on it. Bill has one year to decide what he wants to do long term, and I have another year after that. It is unbelievable to be in this situation. I keep thinking that, if it had not taken Bill so long to find something, we would never have made a decision to live on separate coasts. It really wasn't easy.

Bill: It isn't easy now. We put a lot of effort into deciding. In Vermont we really tried to explore all the pros and cons of the situation so we wouldn't be going into it with our eyes closed. We came to an agreement that the answer was simply not precise. We didn't know how we would get together again. We know now that we'll move back together, somehow.

Diane: There are several alternatives. Either he has to hit the track at about 60 miles an hour out there to establish that he's good, bad, or indifferent. If he does very well there, he may know that that's what he's going to be. If that happens, and he decides that he likes California and we would be happy living there, then it will be up to me to try to find a way to get out to the West Coast.

Bill: Already Scottsfield has been actively working to help Diane find something.

Diane: I've already had one interview. I can't trade down, though. I can't go be a product manager for somebody. I just can't even imagine doing that. My concern is that there are so few women in line marketing that, although someone might like to have me as their consumer affairs director, hiring a woman in marketing or even as a general manager is very problematic. I don't know how real that is and I haven't tested it. I have to find that out.

Bill: We are really not thinking at that too seriously now. We both agree that we don't want things to happen too soon. We don't want to burn our bridges in the East. If this doesn't work out but we've both ended up in California that would be disastrous.

Diane: Another alternative is if he does very well, and after a period of time says to the parent corporation, "Look, I've done my damnedest, you knew we had a problem. I want to go back East to one of your four companies there. If you won't do it for me I'll quit or something." He wouldn't say it as a threat, just in a manner of exploring possibilities. The third alternative is that we find out that the pressure of being apart is too great and we are both willing to make a compromise and do something like go into business for ourselves.

Bill: Maybe that is a viable choice. Maybe it's time now for "the Pound Ridge Nursery." Maybe I can do now what I have never been able to do before and tell my ex-wife, "You've got to live on less money." It may, in fact, be the time to consciously make the decision for a real lifestyle change. I don't know what will happen, but I know that when we make a decision it will be a conscious and deliberate one. We want to decide having considered ramifications. We don't want to choose out of desperation.

Diane: I think we have, and people, in general, react to that need which is pressing us the most greatly.

We made the decision for Bill to go to the West Coast, and I say we made it because it was very much a joint decision; we made it because he wanted to reestablish himself and because I wanted him to. I wanted that for him. I wanted for him to feel that way about himself. That was the most pressing need then. We are probably at the age where we should begin to settle down. At the moment, though, we have some reestablishing and reaffirming to do.

Living with the Decision—One Month after Vermont

Diane: It hasn't been very long but I can see my pressing needs changing. The most pressing need, I predict, is going to become being together. Then the need will be to figure out how to do that and, whatever it takes, we'll do that. Anyway, for now, it's been logically planned out. Over the next six weeks, because of holidays and vacation, we'll be together quite frequently. We negotiated all that at the beginning so that there was no question about it. From then on, it's going to get very rough. Bill will probably attempt to get home every other weekend on the Red Eye and I will attempt to get out about once a month. They've given him about a dozen plane tickets. Cross-country travel is not inexpensive so the ticket deal is super. It means, too, that Bill has gotten back to working and living in the kind of world he's used to. As a matter of fact, he's traded up. In addition to the tickets, they've given him an apartment. We should be set with the traveling then for six or nine months. After that, when we pay for it ourselves it will begin to get expensive. It's really a very expensive proposition because another part of our plan is for me to stay in the house, to keep it running, and to keep the roots planted until we know where we're going. That's an expensive decision, though, because it's an expensive house to run. The alternative was that I should take an apart-

ment in New York and Bill would have one in California. We weren't ready for that. It may come to that, but that is not where we are now. Where we are now is for me to maintain the homestead and see what happens. A cross-country marriage can become expensive, though. I want him to be comfortable and I want to be comfortable, too. We both have children in college and, I think, a year from now money will become a problem. It will be a problem if we haven't, if I haven't, gotten to the coast by then. Right now there are no problems other than adjusting.

Hanson reacted very well initially and have been supportive of me since. I contacted them within 24 hours after the decision had been made. I didn't want it appearing in the press and have all hell breaking loose. I went down to see them and talk with them. They knew that Bill was looking for a job so it was not something that came out of the blue. I think as men, both president of the company and my boss, who is general manager of the division, could empathize very well with why Bill made the decision he made. They said they're viewing our situation as a very real human problem and suggested I relax, finish AMP, then come back and do my thing. They said I'm terrific and that's it. I'm not sure whether this has put any doubts in the back of their minds as to how long I'll be around.

I like my spot at Hanson, though, I have a great line job. I'm afraid I couldn't get this thing elsewhere. That may be my own lack of confidence. I guess the real test will be if I decide to try for something else. I just don't know.

Bill: There are a lot of possibilities but we don't want to make any decision now. I want the time and need the time to get recognition and have success in the big leagues. We can also use the time to carefully consider what is best for us. At this point, however, we've been into the situation for four weeks. The geography is a pain in the butt, no question about it. I must admit, I'm fighting California a bit, too. I'm not sure how I feel about the Southern California West Coast environment. Workwise things have been stupendous. I just happen to have hit it at a point in time where the track has been incredibly fast. In the past month I've had opportunities to really make a mark. I've hit it like gang busters.

Diane: We both know our most pressing need has been for you to reestablish yourself and put yourself in a position to grow and regain your self-respect. We made a decision that is allowing you to do that. Now, as we talk, it becomes even more apparent that the most pressing need is quickly becoming for you and for me to figure out a way to get together again. It may be a lot sooner than we planned. I am beginning to try to figure out how I can get to the West Coast, what my routes are for doing that. Very soon we will have to assess your standing there, to figure out whether or not you've hit it right so that you can have some bargaining power to get back East in a year or two.

Bill: I think you are right about the need. However, it is good to have all the other things in place. With me working and you working we are both functioning as productive individuals. Now our heads and guts feel good. Coming from that position, it will be easier to make other decisions. We have options now, or will have. We'll be able to solve it.

Diane: Right now, though, I'm also thinking that since I've spent these past few months at AMP that I may need and want a change. I may be anxious to do some things I can't do at Hanson. Maybe it would be a good idea to make a change now, whether it's on the East or West Coast. I just want to be careful that I don't move to the West Coast out of desperation.

Bill: The Vermont decision says that won't happen.

Diane: Oh, I know that, but I'm just reminding myself. Whatever I do next must be right for me. The concern I have is that our solution

and rationale sounds so ideal, as though neither one of us is ever going to have to make a trade-off. It's possible that one of us might have to and that's something we haven't considered. I might just have to make a trade-off to get this marriage together again and move to the West Coast.

Bill: That's possible. It makes me uncomfortable but I guess it's possible. You know, it's also a real possibility that there are good opportunities for you in California. They may be less obvious than those here in the East, but, the West Coast could be good for both of us. It wouldn't make sense to make a conscious job compromise, though. Maybe it wouldn't make sense not to after awhile. Maybe we just won't be able to live this way for very long.

Diane: I feel like I can give it a year or two. I think we'll need that time to decide if we want to uproot and move to Southern California. It really isn't only a question of how well you do, it's also if you and I could be happy there.

Bill: That's something to consider but the real cruncher question is, how can we walk away from a hell of a lot of money there. If we decide to do something entirely new, how do we give up both paychecks. I don't know. Do you?

Diane: No. All I know is that it seems that the seeds of confusion and loneliness are already beginning to sprout. That's something, perhaps, you didn't anticipate when you said we could last for a year and see each other every other weekend.

Bill: That's true. I must say the whole thing hit me as pretty ridiculous and as a shock when I began looking for an apartment out there. For the past couple of weeks everytime I've looked at one I say, "What the hell am I looking for a bachelor apartment in Los Angeles for? Every root I have is 3,000 miles away." I think it will hit us harder and sooner than we thought it would.

Diane: We've both been too busy to have the reality of the situation hit us. You've been working like crazy and I've been very involved in this AMP program. It will be a different story when I get to our house in Connecticut and I'm alone. I'm concerned that I will build up resentment at having the house, the lousy weather, that commute. I can almost predict the resentment and I wonder if I will deal with it well, or what.

Bill: Tune in tomorrow!

Diane: Don't you see a risk for you? That you'll work like hell and try to bury all this?

Bill: I don't think it's a risk really. I will work hard but I'm also working at not blocking any of my feelings. In fact, you know we've both gotten up at three in the morning on opposite coasts, called each other and yelled about what a dumb decision it was. But you know why we had to do this. We had some very important reasons, and as long as the reasons make sense then we'll stick with it.

Diane: I think there is a risk in that you may be willing to put in a lot of hours at work but if you are miserable you won't be very productive.

Bill: I guess there is a risk.

Diane: You bet there is a risk. I'm telling you I could get very lonely. I can picture going home on a train at night, arrive in New Canaan at 6:30 with snow and ice and cold, get myself home to the mailbox and walk into an empty house night after night after night, weekend after weekend.

Bill: Now come on—

Diane: It's true. And, it's going to be absolutely terrible. It's going to be as terrible as your going back to the Disneyland Hotel and wondering whether you'll have Chinese or Mexican food.

Bill: Well, I think we have to remember why we're doing this. Maybe on the next go-round our priorities will be different but this was right for now.

Diane: Needs change. I don't know what my needs will be a month from now and what will come next. When people ask me what next? I say nothing. Actually, doing nothing is the hardest thing to do. I have to go back

to Hanson and do well. I will have to cope with this decision and not react by grabbing at a solution that isn't there. I don't want to force a solution. I do think that sheer emotional pressure could distort things, though. There are a few rules we are going to have to remember very carefully. One is, being with any other mate is off-limits. That's not even to be considered. That may be old-fashioned but that's our solution. That doesn't mean we can't have escorts—dear, old, or mutual friends to go to dinner with. But that's it. We've made a conscious decision not to flirt with what could be a pretty easy support system. You know a simple dinner date can lead to a lot more when you are lonely. So that's off-limits. It's very important to make explicit what we feel and not hide things.

I'm trying to figure out what I can do to develop some support systems for myself. Maybe tennis or exercise class. I'm not sure yet but you and I will both be looking for outlets. We will need people to talk to.

Bill: Yes, one other rule is to really try to constantly communicate with each other. We each have the responsibility to write, call, unload, and bitch about things that bother, or worry, or get us angry.

Diane: In other words don't smooth. We have to keep confronting. Another rule is not to joke when it's not funny. I used to tease you about taking up with the president of GE. You used to tease me about this exotic girl you had in the closet. Well, we called a halt to that.

Bill: You may tease about it but what's really behind it is that you're scared it may happen. We've had to eliminate humor that's not humor.

Diane: Also, we have to "up-front" about needing reassurance. If I need it I hope I'll be able to say, "My God, I'm lonely and I need comforting."

Bill: We are going to try our damndest to practice these rules. I think our relationship is too good and too important for both of us to let go of it. I hope we can carry it off. I don't know whether we'll end up owning the

Pound Ridge Nursery, running a consulting business God knows where, both working in California, or both working in New York. I just know we will put it together because we will not permit it to fall apart.

Diane: We have worked so hard at understanding each other, examining the situation, and staying in touch that I hope we don't blow it. That would be a real shame!

CASE 5
TONY SANTINO (A)
Jeffrey A. Sonnenfeld

Tony Santino closed the door of his office and related his career predicament:

> I'm being set up as a patsy to take the blame for a clear-cut violation of the Robinson-Patman Act and I'm not sure what to do. The risk of prosecution may not be high, but I find the whole thing to be personally abhorrent to the way I want to conduct business. In class discussions at business school, I always joined the voices demanding truth, justice, and the American way. But it's so easy to make compromises when you're outside of the comfortable safety of the classroom. I feel like I'm prostituting myself, but I've got a lot of financial, family, and personal career pressures to contend with. There are no medals for making ethical stands out here. It's easy to say that I should quit, but how do you time such a thing in my circumstances.

Tony spoke these words in late September. He joined his present employer, Evansco Precision Pressings, the preceding January. Evansco was a small 40-year-old manufacturer of special-order industrial products. The company's primary customers were equipment suppliers to pro-

ducers in the oil, automobile, and aerospace industries. As the director of marketing at Evansco, Tony was bothered about some company pricing actions taken under his auspices. Tony questioned the legality of a new price list and was suspicious of the behavior of his superiors regarding the matter. A week in advance of the public distribution of this internally controversial price list, Tony began to solicit the advice of friends.

Work History

Following high school, Tony received a 1A draft classification and enrolled in the U.S. Navy. He earned the rank of lieutenant during his subsequent 10 years of service. While in the service, Tony completed his BA degree, attended flight school, flew over 70 missions in Vietnam, and served embassy assignments around the world.

On Tony's return to civilian life, he entered the Harvard Business School. Although soft-spoken in the classroom, he was a good student who frequently led class discussions in novel directions. His folksy warmth and humor made him quite popular among his classmates.

Tony's first job out of business school was with a large, well-established aerospace company. Tony was enthusiastically recruited by a dynamic director of manufacturing who was seeking to hire a cadre of bright, experienced MBAs. All of these candidates were offered generous starting salaries. Tony was impressed by the personal style and the business savvy of this ambitious company official. Furthermore, he liked the area where the company was located. Finally, he was impressed by the caliber of the four other MBAs who had joined the company. Tony accepted the firm's offer and felt confident that he was making a sound decision.

Shortly after his arrival, Tony was promoted to department manager of manufacturing, engineering, and planning. In this position Tony had a wide range of business unit responsibilities and 150 subordinates. He worked closely with the director, Eric Hoffman, who hired him, and Eric continued to serve as Tony's mentor. After two years, however, Eric abruptly left the firm, as the surprise fallout from a battle between himself and a rival vice president. The new victorious vice president, Jim Stevens, launched an overt power-play to fold Eric's division into his own operations and he followed through on his plans immediately after Eric Hoffman's departure. All of Eric's protégés found they were no longer on the fast track.

Thus Tony was reassigned in what he termed ". . . the effort to squeeze out Eric's boys." He was given marketing responsibilities which involved research and analysis for NASA, a major customer. Following one study, Tony received an award for distinguished service. Tony then uncovered what he thought were some extraordinarily large cost overcharges to the federal government. Tony was shocked to find that such large overcharges had been intentionally applied. When he questioned his superiors regarding this matter, Tony was abruptly told to forget it. Several of his peers gave the same advice, suggesting that such shady practices were unofficially recognized norms for business dealings.

During this period, Tony had been summoned by Jim Stevens to meet for a private discussion. Tony was told that Jim, unlike Eric, ". . . didn't go for overeducated prima donnas" and that ". . . there is no longer any such thing as a fast track around here . . . all you guys will be spending some time in the trenches unless you decide to clean out your desks and take off." Various agreements that Tony had made with Eric were withdrawn by Jim, and Tony and his other MBA colleagues realized that they had been detrimentally affected by the political crossfire. By the end of the third year after graduation from business school, all had secured jobs in other firms.

Tony's search for a new position was not easy. At age 37, his lack of a private-sector track record seemed to be a liability for entry-level management. After several months of searching, Tony discovered what appeared to him to be an ideal job. The company, Evansco, was located near his home in a neighboring community outside Los Angeles. Evansco was quite small but quite profitable, with sales of $15 million. Evansco had been in business for close to 40 years as a manufacturer of industrial products which were critical, but inexpensive, components of production equipment used in resource extraction machinery and automotive parts fabrication. Tony was interviewed for the position of director of marketing by the president, Reinhold von Rehstung. Reinhold explained to Tony that, because of the personal and professional disputes between Reinhold and his vice president of sales and marketing, Reinhold no longer wanted to be as dependent on that individual for marketing expertise. Tony had heard that this vice president was unhappy and was beginning to look for work elsewhere. Given the possible career advancement, the convenience of the location, and the chance to try the atmosphere of a small company, Tony felt that Evansco was just the place to begin his second job.

Soon after he started in at Evansco, however, Tony began to feel like a "marriage counselor" in his mediation between the vice president of sales and marketing, Wolf Gorman, and Reinhold, the president. Both Wolf and Reinhold were strong-willed individuals in their late 30s (much younger than many of their employees). What distressed Tony even more than being put in such an uncomfortable position was the fact that he came to understand much of what Reinhold had termed ". . . the problem with Wolf" was in effect the president's problem in understanding marketing concepts. Tony came to see Reinhold as a technically brilliant individual with terrible interpersonal skills. Furthermore, Tony frequently agreed with the spirit of many of Wolf's approaches. Tony found that he himself had felt frustrated by "Reinhold's doctrinaire accountant's view of the world." Tony complained:

> This president is an archetypical CPA type. He's real detail-oriented. Big things just aren't taken care of. In my job I'm looking at the strategic issues involved in placing our products, but all he cares about is the neatness and exactness of figures. He doesn't like to look to the future or to appreciate the back-slapping nature of our present customer relations. All my plans must be prepared on an accountant's cross sheets. Once Reinhold gets these spread sheets he studies them only to audit the numbers.

Meanwhile, Tony was far from a welcome colleague in the eyes of Wolf. He often felt so caught between the conflicting commands of Reinhold and Wolf that he began to feel less like a counselor and more ". . . like a whipping boy." One such time where Tony felt trapped was when Wolf encouraged him to do some analysis of their competitors' strengths. Reinhold did not want Tony to spend time on such an activity. Wolf, however, so insisted on this investigation of competitor activity that he ordered Tony to approach these other firms pretending to be an executive recruiter with the covert mission of extracting confidential information. Tony at first protested; but remembering his recent difficult job search

and the fact that his request was only after one month on the job, he reluctantly performed the task. He actually ". . . came to enjoy the masquerade" when he saw how successful he was at uncovering this information.

After completing some preliminary analysis of the competition, Tony reported back to Wolf and Reinhold that there had been a dramatic change in the structure of the market. Tony had found that the customary practice in the industry had been to practice de facto price fixing by maintaining prices parallel to those published in the price lists of Standard Pressed Products. Standard was the market leader with 40 percent of the market. Evansco, which was number four in sales in the industry, along with the six other major producers had set prices based on this well-circulated Standard Products price list. Since the products were so important, but insignificant in price to the customers, items valued at 15¢ could sell as high as $15. This generous margin for the manufacturers was easily maintained in the past, but with the decline of the automobile industry and the doldrums affecting the general economy, demand had dropped by 50 percent. Such conditions readily tugged at the loyalties to the old informal cartel. Tony had discovered that the shakeout was just beginning as the fifth-largest competitor had just caught up with Evansco's sales by dropping prices a full 40 percent.

Tony was particularly surprised when he found that this other company, Palomar-Pelos, was actually able to cut price this much without losing money because of their reinvestment in new technology over the past few years. While other companies in this industry were skimming off the rich profits of the past and distributing these gains to owners and management, Palomar-Pelos was investing this money in the business.

As a result, Palomar had a formidable advantage to the extent that its business growth was limited only by its own production capacity and the degree of laziness of engineering departments of potential customers. More specifically, Palomar was readily gathering virtually all the new business while its competitors were surviving largely through their old customers. Evansco's customers then were unlikely to bother to shift to Palomar because these customers' own engineering departments did not consider the purchase large enough to bother to run new certification tests on Palomar's cheaper products.

Tony wondered how long this situation would last before other competitors began to explore and adapt new technologies. When he brought this to the attention of Reinhold and Wolf, Reinhold responded, saying,

> Look, Tony, I like sending out a quality product at a quality price. I don't want to put out a shlock, low-grade piece. I wouldn't take pride in competing on price. I like our image, the Mercedes this business allows me to drive, and the customers we have.

When Tony explained that he felt that such a way of thinking was difficult when selling such undifferentiated commodity-type products, Wolf interrupted stating,

> Well, Tony, we may not be able to reinvest now, but we can do the next best thing. We can offer our more price-sensitive customers the same line with a different name but at a much cheaper price.

Tony was shocked at the suggestion and asked if Wolf was suggesting that Evansco discriminate against its old customers. Wolf answered stating, "Hey, we're just trying to meet competition." Tony then stated tersely, "Say, guys, we had better be careful about that kind of stuff. That, to my way of thinking, sounds like a clear-cut violation of the Robinson-Patman Act." At that point Tony noticed Wolf's eyes look back at Reinhold, who had then rejoined the discussion stating, "Tony, try to calm down. I think Wolf's onto something here. You shouldn't be so negative. We've been a little concerned about your attitude lately." Tony now felt that he been frozen out of the team because of a rare degree of consensus between Wolf and Reinhold.

Nonetheless, Tony left the president's office feeling very unenthusiastic about the proposed scheme. When he stopped back in Wolf's office at the end of the day, he asked Wolf how Evansco would have the technical specifications to fake this new product line, and Wolf explained that Tony would have to go to R&D engineers in Evansco and have them just change the composition figures on the old products. Tony asked how this scheme would be kept from the old customers. Wolf then said that he and Reinhold felt that the old customers would not mind but, just so no one was offended, the reorder clerks in Evansco would have a long list appear on their CRT screens which indicated what companies were not to hear of the new line.

Tony went home that night and talked over the plan with Helen, his wife. They agreed that it might make sense to update his résumé. Tony then began to try to renew contacts in Southern California industry for job leads. Meanwhile, he continued to protest the proposal as he began the preliminary stages of the fraud. His arguments about the questionable ethics, and the legal risks were dismissed by Reinhold and Wolf with their explanation that "Tony, you just don't understand. You are too new. This is how things are done in this sort of a business."

Tony was surprised to find confirmation of this description of industry norms from the Evansco research and development engineers from whom he had to attain forged lab test results. They complied promptly but stated that this was a disturbing practice. One of these two engineers, who were both in their 60s, complained,

> Tony, I know you're just caught in the middle, but I've been around here 39 years and have never gotten to like these things any better. This is professional disgrace. We should try to *make* something new rather than to try to *fake* something new.

Tony wondered if he would encounter such reluctance from his sales managers. When one called inquiring about the rumored new products, he asked Tony,

> Hey, what's the story on the new 1700s? I've heard that they're just the 1400s with a new name. Since when do we have the capabilities to make these specs?

Tony tried to maintain the ruse but felt too embarrassed to carry it out. He later recalled,

> I couldn't lie to the guy. I just told him: "Yeah, well how's the weather in Cleveland these days?" He chuckled back and said: "Okay, I understand. Don't worry, I won't say anything to the guys. It's fine with us if we can get a wider line to sell."

The sales managers' probing convinced Tony that the scheme was as transparent as it was dishonest. At another joint meeting with Reinhold and Wolf he asked about the risk of detection. They again responded with annoyance, claiming that this was the customary practice within the industry. Tony suggested that some old customers might realize that the two products were the same and order the cheaper-priced ones.

Wolf countered by informing Tony that old customers would not even know about the "new" products. Furthermore, Wolf argued, that even if the engineers at an old customer did hear about a new set of products, they would not want to bother investing the effort to run certification tests on such a small item given their more pressing larger purchases.

Tony was still bothered by this plan for three months. He told his superiors that they ". . . needed to bite the bullet and reinvest to be cost competitive," but was soundly rebuffed. At a recent meeting with an outside consultant, an industrial marketing professor from a large local university, Tony raised his concern. The purpose of the consultant's visit was to advise the company on some broader strategic issues and Tony's superiors looked on in horror as Tony began to ask about the Robinson-Patman violation. The consultant then turned to Tony with a smile and said as he shook his head, "Tony, grow up—the jails aren't big enough to hold all the folks who do this sort of thing." He later commented to Tony in private: "You know, sometimes it's better to be employed than right."

Tony then turned to a local lawyer for advice. The lawyer, who was also his next-door neighbor, told Tony:

> Relax, small businesses are known for this sort of stuff. Furthermore, the Department of Justice and the Federal Trade Commission are hardly in a position now to sniff this stuff out, anyhow.

Much to Tony's dismay, this advice was now supported by Tony's wife, a CPA by profession. She suggested that:

> You don't have a stable work history, you've been looking and found nothing, and, on top of it all, you don't get medals any more for being a hero.

Tony sat back and wondered about this advice and his own convictions. He told a friend in confidence:

> I'm not so sure what to do any more. I still think I know what's the right thing to do, but with all this outside, these other voices telling me to go ahead and sign the price list, maybe I'm just making a mountain out of a molehill. Yet, I remember reading an article which quoted a professor on the mushrooming nature of small ethical concession. Maybe I compromised myself through the executive headhunter intrigue and I've already lost credibility to call for righteousness and cleanliness. I may learn to rationalize other wrong acts. I already feel like a bit of a prostitute. That's not the way I want to do business. If I leave, how do I leave? Do I call the authorities? How do I explain my short job tenure again to any potential employer without carrying a hero sign to the interview? I don't even know if I'll have any interviews around this area.

This conversation took place with barely a week remaining before the cover letter and price list had to be mailed to reach customers in advance of product certification tests and purchasing.

TONY SANTINO (B)
Jeffrey A. Sonnenfeld

Tony Santino, a 37-year-old director of marketing at a small industrial products firm, was worried about his role in this firm's potential violation of the Robinson-Patman Act. He consulted three people: his wife, a lawyer, and a professor of industrial marketing, all of whom agreed that the pro-

posed act was illegal, but all told him the risk was insignificant. His superiors, the company president and the vice president of sales and marketing, had insisted that Tony sign the cover sheet of a price list which was going to be made available only to certain customers. The company's old customers were not to know about the existence of some "new" products because they were identical to old products which sold at a far higher price under a different name. The rationale was to allow this company, Evansco Precision Pressings, to meet the prices of one of its competitors in the battle for new business without having to lower the price of less-sensitive old customers. The deception involved lab technicians, phone-order clerks, and the company sales force.

Tony resolved not to sign the price list. The support for this action came from former classmates from his MBA years. He had not talked to several of these old friends in years but was determined to find some support for his reluctance. He encountered peers who had resolved similar sorts of ethical dilemmas who could appreciate his distress. Eventually, Tony asked his secretary to retype the cover letter to the price list to allow instead for the signature of his superior, the vice president of sales and marketing. Along with this letter draft he sent a note which stated, "After a good deal of consideration, I feel that the announcement of new products would never come from a director. Something this momentous should come from a vice president to avoid arousing suspicion."

Tony was both surprised and relieved when his superior agreed with this reasoning and signed the letter. However, the vice president then asked Tony to present the new products at the upcoming retreat for the sales force at a nearby resort. The purpose of this address was to pitch the value of the fake products and suggest ways to sell their uniqueness. He had to make the address in a week and wondered if he should "get sick" or just go ahead and make the presentation.

CASE 6
WHO WILL MAKE MONEY IN THE 80s?*
Chris Welles

So you think brains, aggressiveness, and ambition are all you need to make money in the 80s? Forget it. By all predictions, we're in for a decade a lot rougher, economically speaking, than the one we've just been through. At least until we find some way out of our energy dilemma, the outlook is for more or less continual bouts of inflation and recession—an economic atmosphere hardly conducive to piling up a big net worth. We wish we had some surefire investment ideas to help you get through the 80s. But we don't. And considering the record of most investment advisers, we doubt anybody else does, either. But we do have some ideas about your career and the amount of money you'll be able to make at your job. And we feel confident about these ideas because the job market, unlike the capricious stock market, is shaped by long-term fundamental forces that are reasonably subject to accurate predictions. To be specific: We know that due to the "baby boom," the postwar birthrate surge, the number of people in the labor force between the ages of 25 and 44 will jump by more than 50 percent between 1975 and 1990. We

know that these individuals, by and large, have been or are being well educated, that they have lofty success expectations, and that they are aiming for high-status managerial and professional jobs. Consequently, we can be quite certain that as a group they—and perhaps you, if you're among them—are going to encounter traumatic career troubles. There will be, in short, too many aspirants and not enough jobs of the sort they're looking for. And the worse the economy, the fewer these jobs.

To give you an idea of what it's going to be like to be a member of the baby boom, or what demographers call the bulge cohort, we offer, beginning shortly, the unpleasant tale of a prototypical middle manager of a large conglomerate, circa 1986. The way Harold ends up dealing with his problems is, we admit, rather rash. To help you, if you are part of the bulge cohort, to avoid Harold's fate, we follow Harold's story with some solutions and alternatives. A few eminent authorities tell what they would have advised Harold to do, and charts provide ballpark estimates of the future earnings of individuals starting out this year in several representative jobs.

We offer herewith, based on gleanings from authoritative sources, our own considered advice on how to play the job market of the 80s.

1. *If you're extremely bright and capable, you have a good chance to make a great deal of money in a managerial or professional occupation.*

Large corporations especially have become much more flexible in their compensation policies, owing partly to the problematic economy, and are more willing to pay for top talent. "The standard deviation of salaries has grown," says Albert P. Hegyi, president of the Association of MBA Executives. "The fittest will get much greater rewards." But there is a catch. "We're moving into a very high-reward but high-risk environment," says Louis J. Brindisi, Jr., a compensation specialist with the management consulting firm of Booz, Allen & Hamilton. "Because the pay packages are so large, there isn't much toleration of failure."

2. *If you're extremely bright and capable but want big rewards without big risks, stay away from big corporations.*

Consider such smaller and more entrepreneurial concerns as investment banking houses, management consulting firms, and law firms. In contrast to the practice of many corporations, advancement at these concerns is determined by a structured weeding process based mainly on ability. If you are good enough, you will survive the various cuts and, within 5 or 10 years, make partner. As a partner you can expect, as our charts indicate, a salary well into the six figures, especially at the major big-city firms. Senior corporation executives, of course, can make much more, but they are often bounced out of their jobs. Life as a partner is less stressful and hazardous. The chances that you will be asked to leave for reasons less serious than knifing another partner over lunch at the Four Seasons are very slim.

3. *If you're less than extremely bright and capable, such as just plain bright and capable, don't plan on a high-level professional or managerial job.*

The experience of Harold, who had a lot going for him but who unfortunately wasn't among the creme de la creme, is instructive. The struggle among the less-talented bulge group members for advancement, most labor experts predict, will be fierce. According to recent studies by the Congressional Office of Technology Assessment and the Bureau of Health Manpower, even the market for doctors—historically the profession most characterized by shortages—will be saturated by 1990.

4. *Don't get caught in the "cobweb feedback system."*

This is an academic term for the cyclicality that perennially afflicts the job market. "We have a tremendously responsive market for jobs because young people are very, very sensitive to market conditions," says Harvard labor economist Richard B. Freeman. Cycles are particularly severe in fields chosen mainly for their vocational potential, such as engineering. At the moment, engineering is going through a boom phase. Predictably, freshman classes at engineering schools have grown by 50 percent over the past few years. Most experts foresee an inevitable bust by the mid-80s. Like an astute stock market investor, the job market player entering college or preparing to change his career must be something of a contrarian. He should focus his energies not on what is hot now but on what will be hot five years down the road, when he finishes his education.

5. *Look into computer science.*

If any field resists booms and busts during the 80s, this will be it. Says Edmund F. Nolan, a compensation expert at the CPA firm Coopers & Lybrand, "Experts have been predicting an oversupply of computer people since the 60s. But it hasn't happened. During the 80s, we see even more pervasive demand. It just keeps exploding." The growth of computer usage is so steep and the pace of technological change so rapid, adds Leonard M. Lewis, Nolan's associate, that "the educational system just can't keep up." Computer science salaries, as our charts show, don't approach those in fast-track professional and managerial careers. But because the competition for jobs will be sharply reduced, there will be much less risk of failure. According to one estimate, the 12,000 to 14,000 new bachelors of computer science this year were able to take their pick among some 55,000 available jobs.

6. *Don't look into the glamour fields.*

A good rule of thumb is: The more allure attached to a particular pursuit, the fewer the opportunities and, except for the big stars, the lower the salaries. Peripheral media fields, such as public relations and technical writing, will offer somewhat better prospects. As for newspaper reporting, the number of job openings during the 80s is expected to be only one quarter of the number of journalism-degree recipients. In the performing arts, if the past is any guide, you'll be lucky to survive. A recent survey of professional screen and stage actors and actresses showed that 75 percent earned less than $2,500 a year from acting. Only 3 percent had made it sufficiently into the big time to make more than $25,000.

7. *If you're unsure about your brainpower, your best future may lie in your hands.*

Management consultant Felix Kaufmann foresees a desperate shortage of skilled craftsmen and technicians, such as mechanics and electricians, that will intensify over the coming decade. These jobs, of course, lack the prestige and status of white-collar managerial jobs—which is precisely the reason they are eschewed by the highly educated bulge cohort. But there are compensations: note the charts. If you start out this year as a plumber's apprentice, you'll make only $10,500 your first year, compared with $30,000 for a fast-track MBA. But look at 1990. The plumber, now a journeyman, will be picking up $39,270 (in 1980 dollars). The fast-track MBA will find himself being rewarded for his survival of probably exhausting and bitter promotional battles with only a few thousand dollars a year more in salary than the man who comes to fix his sink. For

a lot of people in the 80s, status is going to have to be its own reward.

It Is the Mid-80s. Harold Has Just Been Scratched from the Fast Track. He Has Done Everything Right. Why Is Everything Going Wrong?

Now worn and tattered, the clippings had been carried tucked neatly in Harold's billfold for six years. Back in his office after what had turned out to be an extremely upsetting lunch, Harold extracted and unfolded them. Glaring for a moment at the boldface headlines, he slammed his fist on the top of his desk and slowly shook his head. Harold had cut out the articles during his last year at Harvard's Graduate School of Business Administration. They seemed a reaffirmation of his considerable confidence that he was not only on the fast track but at the head of the pack. Ever since he had first looked up at New York City's skyscrapers as an eighth-grader and learned who lived in them, he had wanted to run a large corporation. Closely counseled by his father, a corporate vice president, Harold prepared for his career with meticulous care. Exeter. Princeton, cum laude in history. Three years at the investment banking firm of Morgan Stanley & Company in the mergers and acquisitions department. (Work experience before business school was regarded as a valuable résumé listing.) Marriage to a socially prominent Radcliffe graduate and prospective lawyer. Then the Harvard business school, where he specialized in strategic corporate planning.

Friends in the executive-search business assured him that planning had become the inside lane of the fast track. Traditionally, chief executives rose up through line jobs: manufacturing in the postwar years, sales and marketing during the booming 50s and

60s. In the more economically complex 70s, staff people, particularly finance executives and lawyers, began moving to the forefront. During the even more arduous and uncertain inflation- and recession-ridden 80s, he was told, planners would be moving into executive suites in droves. "Everybody else is getting too specialized," one recruiter said. "The planners are into the big picture. They know about everything." To meet the anticipated demand, many of the best business schools in the late 70s offered more strategic planning courses.

In early 1980, his last year at Harvard, Harold scheduled interviews with nearly two dozen corporations. But he focused most of his attention on the large management consulting firms, such as Booz, Allen & Hamilton, the Boston Consulting Group, and McKinsey & Company. They paid the highest starting salaries to MBA graduates because they, unlike other employers, could put new MBAs immediately to work using their B-school analytical methods doing studies for clients.

Harold knew that although starting salaries paid by the largest consulting firms—often $40,000 or more—always received a lot of press attention, only a tiny fraction of the graduating MBAs were so fortunate. Booz, Allen, for instance, typically hired only 50 of the more than 1,000 MBAs interviewed. The market for MBAs, though, was sharply segmented. While many MBAs from lesser schools would be lucky to be hired by a firm in the *Fortune* 1,000, graduates from the top schools, such as Harvard, Stanford, Columbia, the Sloan School at MIT, Amos Tuck at Dartmouth, and Wharton at the University of Pennsylvania, were still being enthusiastically courted. Harold, who was in the top third of his class, never worried. Sure enough, from several gener-

ous offers, Harold chose McKinsey for $41,000 a year.

Management consulting, Harold was also aware, is an up-or-out profession. Only a fraction—sometimes less than 10 percent—of the new MBAs at the major firms last the six or seven years it takes to make partner and collect partners' typically lofty six-figure compensation. Associates must pass several critical hurdles. At McKinsey, the first cut comes after a careful assessment of the associate's performance at the end of the second year. Harold survived. But one day in early 1983, during an ostensibly casual drink at the Harvard Club, a McKinsey partner suggested to him that perhaps he might consider some other career alternatives.

Harold was mildly discouraged. But he had never regarded making partner at McKinsey as anything more than an interim goal anyway. Many MBAs never even considered trying for partner. Like many of his classmates, Harold had been preparing for his departure from McKinsey almost from the first day he arrived. During assignments, he took care to befriend strategically situated executives at the most promising client companies and to nourish those relationships over lunch, dinner, or golf. A few offhand but well-placed remarks from Harold that he might be receptive elicited several attractive offers. Less than two months after the Harvard Club drink, Harold accepted a $52,000 offer (in 1980 dollars) to join the 15-person planning staff of International Dynamics, Inc., a $7-billion consumer-products conglomerate.

Harold remembered vividly his first morning at IDI, a bright, clear day in May 1983, just over three years ago. From his roomy office on the 44th floor of the new IDI Building on midtown Manhattan's now-fashionable West Side, it seemed to him he could see all the way to his home in Short Hills, New Jersey. Like all new skyscrapers, the IDI Building was elaborately energy-efficient, and Harold was able to open his window to let in some fresh air. Ceremoniously, he took the clippings from his billfold and looked at the headlines. "Still on that old fast track," he said aloud with an unconcealed grin.

Reflecting on those three years, Harold was hard-pressed to determine just when it had begun. Perhaps as early as the end of his first year. But, probably because he had never believed his career advancement could be halted, he hadn't noticed anything amiss until last fall. He was somewhat concerned, of course, when he received merit raises at the end of his first and second years that did not even match the rise in the cost of living. But his superiors had seemed encouraging and satisfied with his work. There had been no portentous conversations at the Harvard Club. He kept very busy, often working late into the evening. There were always meetings to attend, studies to be conducted, memoranda to write.

But he gradually came to realize that his reports weren't very widely circulated, and he was unsure whether anyone was really reading them. His comments at meetings were listened to politely, but he was unsure whether anybody was really remembering them. He didn't seem to be having much effect on what was going on at IDI. Maybe no effect at all. The evidence was mounting that, for reasons he couldn't fathom, he had been detoured off the main track and onto a siding.

Over lunch today he had brought the matter up with his close friend Brian, a 1980 Stanford MBA who had come to IDI a year before Harold.

"They're keeping us in reserve," Brian said matter-of-factly.

"What do you mean?"

"It's the bulge. There are so many qualified middle management types like us that big companies like IDI, who can afford to, like to keep a lot of us around."

"Why?"

"Just in case they need us. If there's a big increase in sales. For peak loads. So they can have more people to choose from." Brian sounded a little impatient.

"How long will we have to wait?"

Brian shrugged. "Who knows? Maybe forever. Maybe this is as far as we're ever going to get."

Harold was a sufficiently astute student of the job market to know all about the bulge. It was generated by the dramatic postwar baby boom, roughly from the late 40s to the late 50s, when births jumped to as high as four million annually from the two-million level that had prevailed during the so-called birth dearth of the 30s. By the early 80s, this demographic surge was inundating the job market. The number of people in the prime workforce age bracket of 25 to 44 was projected to grow from 39 million in 1975 to 60.5 million in 1990, a 55 percent increase that was twice the projected growth of the civilian labor force as a whole.

That by itself meant plenty of trouble for Harold's generation. But several other developments had vastly exacerbated the impact of the bulge. The bulge group members were far better educated than their predecessors. After World War II, education became a national passion. From their early days in grade school, these children were told by authority figures—parents, teachers, guidance counselors, community leaders, government officials—that a college degree was the best ticket to economic success, social status, and the good life generally. Numerous government programs helped finance a rapid expansion in educational facilities and lowered the economic barriers to college attendance. During the 50s and 60s, the number of bachelor's degrees granted nearly doubled, and postgraduate degrees more than tripled. With the company booming, the degree holders were able to find work easily.

By the early 70s, when Harold was at Princeton, the educational system had gotten out of control. It was producing twice as many graduates as it had during the 60s and far too many for the now-weakening economy to absorb. PhDs were widely reported to be pumping gas and tending bar.

The worst glut, though, was in academia, where many of the advanced-degree holders had sought jobs. Having expanded rapidly to accommodate the bulge students, the educational institutions had become, as Columbia Graduate School of Business labor expert Eli Ginzberg put it, "tremendous consumers of their own trained manpower." After the bulge students graduated, though, the institutions were forced into retrenchment.

Authority figures now advised bulge graduates, most of whom had majored in liberal arts, to pursue professional and other vocational degrees in order to take advantage of abundant opportunities in the business world. The output of lawyers and doctors soon accelerated. But most dramatic was the increase in business-school graduates, from 21,000 a year in 1970 to more than 50,000 in 1980.

The supply of aspirant corporate executives was swelled even further by unprecedented numbers of women and, to a lesser degree, minorities. During the 70s, the number of women in graduate school increased five times as fast as the number of men to nearly 45 percent of the total enrollment. The share of MBAs granted to women jumped from 3.9 percent in 1972 to 19 percent in 1980. Nearly 23 percent of Harold's graduating class were women, as were 28 percent of his wife's graduating class at Harvard Law School. Women now made up 30 percent of IDI's planning staff.

As the supply of highly qualified corporate executives seeking advancement grew, demand leveled off. Recurring bouts of energy shortages, inflationary surges, and recessionary troughs throughout the early 80s had reduced real economic growth to a crawl. Even the richest concerns, such as IDI, who could afford to keep reserves of middle managers, kept their highly paid senior executive ranks lean. The men occupying those ranks, meanwhile, were hanging onto their jobs, often well into their 70s. Rising life expectancy and the shrinkage of retirement pensions due to inflation had reduced their incentive to retire. And since the abolition of mandatory retirement age requirements, they did not have to.

Boards of directors were in no hurry to see them leave. By the mid 80s, the notion had faded that staff positions, such as planning, were the fastest track to the top. And corporations were losing much of their respect for the MBA credential. Simply that somebody had done well playing with case studies at Harvard or mapping long-range strategies on a planning staff, corporations decided, didn't necessarily mean he or she could handle real-world crises in a problematical economy. There was a resurgence of enthusiasm for more experienced line executives with "track records" who were "street smart." Managers in their 60s with an impressive string of turnarounds became the hottest commodities on the executive job market. Only a few bulge middle managers were able to break into upper management.

Growing supply and shrinking demand were having an inescapable effect on bulge cohort salaries. The salary advantage of college graduates over nongraduates had been shrinking since 1969. But now few bulge executives' salaries were even keeping up with inflation. Many were suffering a substantial loss of purchasing power.

Even more discouraging was a phenomenon known to compensation experts as compression. The bulge group had been followed by another demographic reversal that had produced the so-called baby bust cohort. While the number of workers in the 25-to-45 age category was projected to increase 55 percent between 1975 and 1990, the number in the 16-to-24 age group was projected to *decrease* by 6 percent. By the mid-80s, the onetime glut of entry-level workers had turned into a shortage. Starting salaries were rising so quickly that many newly hired baby busters were making more than baby boomers with five or six years' experience.

Most of these developments were a boon to corporate shareholders. Because middle-level salaries were compressed, corporations could slow the growth of their personnel costs. Because their workforce was the best educated in history, they were able to make major gains in productivity. And because they had more middle managers to choose from, they could obtain enormously capable individuals for senior posts.

The consequences for bulge managers themselves were much less pleasant. Labor market experts, in fact, had been warning of the grim effects of the bulge for years. In 1979, in a study for the Work In America Institute, Richard B. Freeman, a Harvard economist with the National Bureau of Economic Research, predicted a "fierce competition for promotions, coupled with substantial career disappointment" and "major personnel and labor-relations problems." The same year, Carnegie-Mellon University economist Arnold Weber foresaw "increased tension and potential conflict among the various groups in the labor force." Tension and conflict had already become abundantly manifest at large companies likt IDI. Male members of the bulge group, of course, were warring with one another. But other antagonisms were even more intense. Men were very upset about the elevation of growing numbers of women to positions traditionally reserved for them. Pre-70s sexism returned with a vengeance. Intergenerational conflicts raged as well. Bulge members complained bitterly about the high starting salaries being paid to younger baby bust executives. And they exerted pressure on older and—as bulge people continually pointed out—less-educated senior executives to stop blocking the way and retire. At some companies, middle managers staged job actions and even formed labor unions to obtain wage increases and promotions.

Political infighting, of course, has always been a staple of organizational life. Yet the generally muted hostilities and circumspect rivalries Harold had observed at client companies during his McKinsey days were now often erupting into open confrontations and shouting matches. It was not uncommon for an angry executive to take a swing at another.

Corporations sought to subdue that tensions. Aided by a new breed of "human resource" consultants, they attempted to deemphasize progress up the hierarchy as the chief criterion of career success. They downplayed the celebratory trappings, such as cocktail parties and effusive public announcements, that normally attended promotions. They reduced some of the high-office perquisites, such as extra secretaries, limousines, and first-class air travel. To alleviate the boredom and improve the morale of languishing middle managers, they instituted retraining programs, educational sabbaticals, nonpromotional incentive systems, flexible working hours, and mechanisms for horizontal transfer to a new division or plant as a promotional substitute for vertical movement.

These tactics were not without effect. But most of the bulge group, especially the most capable and ambitious members, found them unsatisfying. Perhaps the major reason was what management expert Peter F. Drucker had foreseen in 1979 as the "huge and widening gap" between the gloomy realties of the job market and the bulge group's lofty expectations. Their expectations, Drucker pointed out, were shaped by the extraordinary career successes of many older siblings and friends who were fortunate enough to have been born just when the birth dearth began to turn into the baby boom. Due to the manpower shortage and the economic expansion of the 50s and 60s, there had been a great demand for corporate executives and, as a result, a marked shift toward faster tracks of advancement and the elevation of younger managers. Members of this cohort, Drucker wrote, "were sucked into high positions at a fast clip. It used to take 25 years in a 'respectable' bank to become assistant vice president; in the late 60s and early 70s one reached the position in three or four years."

Bulge group members, especially after having invested so much time and money in their education, anticipated equally prompt ascension of the corporate ladder. A reveal-

ing 1980 study by *Fortune* of a group of fast-track 25-year-olds—Harold's contemporaries—found them ambitious, impatient, unabashedly materialistic, completely preoccupied with their careers, and "phenomenally confident of their native abilities, maybe more so than any previous group of business beginners." "To them," *Fortune* reported, "being second best is anathema."

Like so many of the best-qualified bulge managers, Harold had always believed that the dire predictions of the traumas his cohort would have to endure did not apply to him. The middle-management crunch, Harold always thought, would be a problem only for those of lesser abilities, education, and attainments, who had never expected to make it very far and who were used to squabbling over the scraps. Harold was among the elite. Not only was he very bright and well brought up, but he was Exeter/Princeton/Morgan Stanley/Harvard. He had made all the right moves. If you had Harold's credentials, you never had to worry. There was always room. Good times and bad, you pretty much got whatever you wanted. Maybe not chief executive officer, of course. But something much better than the humiliating siding, the team of reserve players, to which Harold had found himself perhaps terminally consigned.

"You and me, Harold, we're not dummies," Brian had said today as they finished lunch. "I mean, we're pretty damn good at what we do. That used to be enough. Now you have to be brilliant to get anywhere. You have to be a goddamn genius."

Brian had meant to be consoling. He had seen the effect of their discussion on Harold's face. But Brian's words hit Harold like a shot. Harold always knew he wasn't brilliant. After all, how many people are? But nobody had warned him that everything he was and everything he had done wasn't enough. It wasn't, Harold kept saying to himself over and over, *fair*.

Harold cancelled his meetings and told his secretary to hold his calls. Throughout the afternoon and into the early evening, he sat at his desk. On a yellow legal pad, in his characteristically methodical way, he sketched out his options.

He could transfer to a smaller company. Yet the bulge problem persisted throughout the corporate world. Brian, who obviously had been thinking about this for some time, had told him that most companies didn't maintain reserve middle managers, as IDI did. They simply weren't hiring any but the most standout people for middle-management positions. Harold had heard, as well, of the bull market in older line executives with track records and the bear market in younger people with staff backgrounds. He wondered about his marketability. He wondered if there was any market for him at all. Maybe he was much more fortunate to have the IDI job than he had thought.

He could become an entrepreneur. Harold knew several MBAs who had left corporate jobs to start new ventures. Was that a viable option for him? The risks and the failure rate were very high. Even if he could come up with a good idea and sufficient financing—not easy tasks—he doubted he had the stomach for such a gamble. And he had spent a decade developing and honing the skills he needed to function as a team player, to manage a large and complex corporation. How relevant would any of that be to the highly individualistic task of shepherding a tiny start-up?

Another possibility was switching careers. What else was he interested in? Harold remembered being tempted after Princeton by a technological career, especially in computer science or engineering, though his only acquaintance with these

fields had been an undergraduate physics course. Career journals during the 70s were filled with discussions of the acute shortage of engineers and their soaring starting salaries.

Yet, as Harold knew from several engineering friends, the market for science and engineering specialties was even more cyclical than the job market in general and had been rent by numerous booms and busts. Booms typically attract an oversupply of trained specialists; busts generate an undersupply. By the mid-80s, due in part to a huge influx of women, the engineering boom of the late 70s and early 80s was becoming a bust much like that of the early 70s. Even the perennial high demand for computer scientists was easing.

Harold could, perhaps, enroll in an engineering or computer-science school in anticipation of an early 90s boom. Law school and medical school were also options, though at the moment a growing oversupply of bulge doctors and lawyers was developing.

Harold considered the prospect of writing off his long career preparation, relinquishing his current salary and corporate status, and enduring the substantial costs and other hardships of another 5 to 10 years of preparation for a new career. Just thinking about it enervated and depressed him. It was too late for such a change.

Other fields were less subject to supply/demand gyrations. In some, long-standing labor shortages were becoming severe. There was a great demand for janitors, dishwashers, waiters, salesclerks, hospital orderlies, and menial workers in similar dead-end service jobs. Among the reasons were the small supply of baby bust teenagers and the eschewal by women and minorities of their traditional labor-market roles. Too many people wanted "good" jobs and were unwilling to accept "bad" jobs, for work was no longer just work but the primary means of self-definition.

Demand was nearly as great for highly skilled manual workers such as mechanics, carpenters, plumbers, machinists, machinery repairmen, and service technicians. Wages for many blue-collar jobs were higher than those for many white-collar jobs and had been rising faster. Harold knew of plumbers and carpenters whose income even approached his.

Harold could become a plumber much faster than he could become a doctor. But he just couldn't picture himself as a plumber. People might not be reading his memos, but he was still an accepted member of the white-collar managerial elite. Maybe some plumbers earned as much money. But they were still his inferiors. There was a chasmal gulf in class and status between him and them that Harold didn't think he could ever cross, even if he wanted to. What would his father say? What would his wife, now a partner at a Wall Street law firm, say? What would his two young sons tell their friends?

More and more of Harold's contemporaries were coming up with a much simpler solution to the dilemma. Brian, Harold learned today, was one of them.

"It took me a while to get used to the idea, I have to admit," Brian said over dessert. "You have to look at yourself in some very different ways. It's not an easy process. But I'm convinced now it's the only answer for me. What you have to do is stop thinking that working at IDI—stop thinking that your *career*—is the most important thing in the world."

"Then what is?" Harold asked.

"A lot of things. I go home earlier now. I spend more time with the kids. I talk to my wife. And I'm doing things like, would you believe, building a harpsichord. Then I'm going to learn how to play the harpsichord. I'm loving it."

"That's a cop-out. It's a surrender." Harold's voice was stern.

"Don't be so dramatic," Brian said. "Listen, I'm not quitting IDI. I still put in a good day's work. I'm just not bucking for CEO. You know what I mean? Who really wants the hassle of that job, anyway? I know I don't. It's not worth it."

Harold didn't say anything. What could he say? But he felt an overpowering contempt for Brian. Brian, like him, had spent years planning and striving and expecting and hoping. Now he was just throwing in the old towel. Harold was shocked. Rationalizing failure was no solution. But what was?

Harold put down his pencil and looked out at the lighted city.

He reflected on what a waste his life had been. Thousands of dollars and a dozen years had been wasted preparing him to do nothing. What a goddamned waste.

And it wasn't fair. He had done what everybody told him he needed to do. He had done everything right. It had always worked before. But he had ended up in a job where he did nothing, contributed nothing, meant nothing. He was worth nothing, going nowhere, couldn't do anything else.

He was at a dead end. He had no future.

It wasn't fair.

Harold rapidly tore the clippings into tiny fragments. More deliberately, he got up and walked over to the open window.

What Should Harold Do?

Harold has a lot of growing up to do. Where did he get the idea that life should be fair? Life isn't fair. He should face facts: a staff job is not a line job. It's difficult to prove yourself. He must exercise patience, stay with the job, and if a line position opens up, go for it. He should ask for a job in an acquired company or in another division. He should negotiate himself out of strategic planning, which may be intellectually satisfying but is loaded with bright people.

—Myles Mace, professor emeritus,
Harvard Graduate School
of Business Administration

Harold has exceptional experience, and he's very attractive in the marketplace. I have no doubt he could do *much* better. He should select a company that would use his expertise to its advantage, a small- to medium-size operation. When choosing a company, he should look at the average age of the people. If they are older than 50, he should stay away.

—Richard Ferry, executive vice
president, Korn/Ferry International
(executive recruiters)

Don't jump, Harold! Harold is spoiled, uniquely spoiled. Harold doesn't know how lucky he is. He realized at 33 what many of his contemporaries realize at 40—that he took the wrong path. He should do one of several things: (1) He could sit down with IDI management and say, "Look, I've worked hard; I'm a good commodity. Put me somewhere I can use my skills." (2) If he doesn't want to "lose face" with IDI, Harold can go to a company that is just getting started. New companies are always looking for people with good educational and work backgrounds. He can end up making good and having a stake in the company. (3) If Harold feels he doesn't have the guts or the talent needed to do (1) or (2), he can go back to being a consultant. This is happening a lot in Harold's age bracket. Strategic planning is a hell of a fertile field. (4) If he feels he's inept and on the wrong track with private enterprise, he can go to Washington and work for the government. It would be better than just hanging around IDI. If Harold is as short-sighted as he sounds, he doesn't deserve his education.

—Robert W. Lear,
executive in residence,
Columbia Graduate School of Business

Harold is obviously not a fellow who takes risks, and great success just doesn't come to people who don't take risks. The street-smart people are coming up and replacing the Harolds of the world. Harold's a loser. He should become a good washing machine repairman.

—Abraham Gitlow, dean, New York
University College of Business

READING 1
INSTITUTIONAL BARRIERS: WHAT KEEPS WOMEN OUT OF THE EXECUTIVE SUITE?*
Cynthia Fuchs Epstein†

A movie of some years ago called *Barbarella* had a haunting scene in which the heroine, marooned in a wasteland, sees in the distance a horde of automated dolls, lovely, wide-eyed, long-haired dolls, the kind little girls have long cherished. But as Barbarella moves close to these creatures, she is dismayed and terrified to see that their mouths open and shut like those of puppets, emitting shrill sounds and revealing teeth that are steel traps, sharp and pointed.

This to me seems to symbolize current reality. Whether women ask for equality softly or firmly, the male gatekeepers, and some established women as well, often hear only shrill and piercing sounds. Requests are heard as demands. Demands seem to imply violence. This response is by no means universal but it predominates. It prolongs the resistance to women's participation in spheres long dominated by men, and reflects the continued cultural conflict between the norms specifying womanly or ladylike behavior and the norms specifying

competent business and professional behavior.

Both our perceptions of behavior and our expectations as to proper behavior shape present conditions. Women newcomers to business and the professions still face age-old prejudices and cultural biases that define their roles and their potential contributions. These stereotypes intrude on their social and business relations with men and make assimilation difficult.[1]

Of primary importance are those informal structures of interaction in the business and professional world that affect and are affected by women's behavior. Informal behavior is institutionalized at least as thoroughly as the formal modes of interaction depicted on organizational charts, and it is probably more important to analyze informal interaction. The closer one gets to the top, the more commonly are decision-making judgments and rewards determined by subjective criteria; "understandings" rather than rules govern behavior, and personal qualifications are judged against a range of attributes not immediately relevant functionally to the job at hand. These factors have always been important, but they may become even more important as legal strictures forbid the exclusion of women and others once rejected categorically.

A.   Trends in the Status of Women

Before considering the informal modes of institutional exclusion of women, we may review women's position, cross-culturally over the years, as it bears on these issues.

* From *Bringing Women into Management*, by F. E. Gordon and M. H. Strober, eds. Copyright © 1975 by McGraw-Hill, Inc. Reprinted with permission of McGraw-Hill Book Company.

† I would like to acknowledge the invisible structure of the reasoning in this paper which, in part, relies on a number of concepts developed by Robert K. Merton in *Social Theory and Social Structure* (Chicago: Free Press, 1957). Among those which I immediately identify are those of the power of relative and absolute numbers in the dynamics of social groups; the emergence of a notion of deviance on the part of those whose status sets are inconsistent with the pattern most frequently seen; the unintended consequences of intent; and the self-fulfilling prophecy. Similarly, I am indebted to the perspective offered by Erving Goffman on the presentation of the self.

[1] Lawrence C. Hackamack and Alan B. Solid, "The Woman Executive: There Is Still Ample Room for Progress," *Business Horizons*, April 1972, pp. 89–93; and Benson Rosen and Thomas H. Jerdee, "Sex Stereotyping in the Executive Suite," *Harvard Business Review*, March–April 1973, pp. 45–58.

Perhaps the factor that best determines what may be women's work is not the nature of the work performed nor the burden it may create mentally or physically, but rather the symbolic significance of the work and whether or not it is considered important, honorable, and desirable. The greater the social desirability of a type of work, the less likely it is that women are identified with it. All societies seem to prefer *men* in the jobs most valued. Even where women constitute a majority among personnel of an occupation, such as in schoolteaching, librarianship, or textile work, men seem to have a disproportionately greater chance to be in the top administration of the field. This is true even in Soviet medicine, where men, although a minority of the profession, hold the top professorships and hospital administration posts.[2] In all cultures, women are at best tolerated in the most desired fields, and the few found there are regarded as having special and idiosyncratic traits that justify the anomaly.[3] This rationalizing impedes women's integration into top jobs even when few formal obstacles exist.

Although today we assume widespread changes in the position of women, there have probably been fewer significant changes than media publicity indicates. The 1970 census showed percentage increases for women in male-dominated professions and occupations not unlike those of the previous two decades. Women lawyers rose from 2.4 percent of the profession in 1940 to 3.5 percent in 1960 and 4.9 percent in 1970, a minimal increase in light of the enormous emphasis on women's liberation during the 60s. In medicine, women moved from 6.5 percent of their profession in 1960 to 9.3 percent in 1970, but women were only 8.5 percent of all medical students that same year.[4] Presumably those percentages have increased since the 1970 census.

But some of the statistics point the other way. In manufacturing industries the percentage of managers dropped from 7.1 percent women in 1960 to 6.3 percent in 1970.[5] This was below the 6.4 percent listed in 1950, when the status of women was relatively lower than during the previous two decades and when the proportion of women dropped in all career-oriented spheres of life. It was a period characterized by Jessie Bernard as the time of the "motherhood mania."

There are few reliable statistics about women's opportunities for promotion in publishing, banking, commerce, or the public utilities. When the statistics are at hand, it will then be necessary to look beyond the new titles to the actual roles being filled.[6] Visibility is a central problem for women in business and the other male-dominated professional activities. Certain jobs are less visible than others, and those in the former don't get as much credit as they would otherwise. Women tend to get the jobs that are actually and symbolically less visible—*actually*, because they do not have contact with clients and with the market, and *symbolically*, because the jobs they have are not defined as crucial.

One further complication is that even where women are given higher-level administrative jobs, these do not lead to top-management posts, but rather are on ancil-

---

[2] Norton T. Dodge, *Women in the Soviet Economy* (Baltimore: Johns Hopkins, 1966).

[3] Eleanor Brantley Schwartz, "The Sex Barrier in Business," *Atlanta Economic Review*, June 1971, p. 6.

[4] "The Economic Role of Women," *Economic Report of the President* (Washington, D.C., 1973).

[5] Ibid., p. 101.

[6] Burton G. Malkiel and Judith A. Malkiel, "Male-Female Pay Differentials in Professional Employment," *American Economic Review*, September 1973, pp. 693–705.

lary routes that may be dead ends. A women may be called a vice president or special assistant to the president, but be assigned to administrate an affirmative action plan or asked to recruit women personnel. Such activity is rarely viewed as more than peripheral to the goals of the firm and is unlikely to lead to the top. Today the diverging of women to alternative routes may occur at a higher level than before, but the ultimate consequences are the same.

1. Characteristics of Women in Top Management.

There are still so few women executives that certain tantalizing questions must go unanswered: e.g., Are there "self-made" women in the same sense that some men are seen as self-made? A study attempted by the Harvard Business School in the late 60s had to be abandoned for lack of sufficient subjects. In 1966 the British Political and Economic Planning organization (PEP) sponsored a study of women in managerial jobs in government service, the British Broadcasting Corporation, and two large companies. The team of researchers, headed by Michael Fogarty and Rhona and Robert Rapoport, reported on their work in two volumes published in 1971 called *Women in Top Jobs* and *Sex, Career and Family*.[7] They found that women who rose to the top of these organizations did so largely because of chance, the wartime diversion of manpower, or the death of a relative. It was clear that the women who assumed directorship roles under these conditions would not have sought them, nor been offered them, under normal circumstances.

In the United States in 1971 Margaret Hennig[8] studied 25 women presidents and vice presidents of medium-to-large nationally recognized business firms, out of a specially selected sample of 100 women who then held such posts. Most were widows or daughters of men who had led these firms or women who had other ties with a man in command. *Fortune*, in an article on the 10 top-paid women in the United States, reported a similar situation that serves to underline the importance of affectional or kinship ties in determining women's success.[9]

Why should this be so? In a world where the door is barred to women, only a few get in totally uninvited, most of them because of special circumstances. Friendship and kinship provide an alternative opportunity structure, paralleling a system of protégé-ship by which men gain entrance to the inner circles. As intimates of the mighty, women have access to the information *any* aspirant needs to mount the ladder of success. But the route of marriage or friendship has never been a true alternative opportunity structure. It is a testament to the subtle skills of the gatekeepers that the underlying disapproval elicited by this kind of alternative route serves as a social control mechanism to ensure that women, already denied recourse to the male stratagem, cannot truly succeed by the only stratagem open to them.[10]

---

[7] Michael Fogarty, Rhona Rapoport, and Robert Rapoport, *Women in Top Jobs: Four Studies in Achievement* and *Sex, Career, and Family*, prepared jointly by Political and Economic Planning (PEP) and the Tavistock Institute (London: G. Allen, 1971).

[8] Margaret Marie Hennig, "Career Development for Women Executives," unpublished doctoral dissertation, Harvard University, Cambridge, Mass., 1971.

[9] Wyndham Robertson, "Ten Highest Ranking Women in Big Business," *Fortune*, April 1973, pp. 80–89.

[10] Cynthia Fuchs Epstein, "Bringing Women In: Rewards, Punishments, and the Structure of Achievement," *Annals of the New York Academy of Sciences*, March 1973, pp. 62–70.

For women, the costs of using a particularistic route are high and the profits are always contingent. Positions won by being tied to one man are nontransferable. Until a woman has proven herself, she is in a poor bargaining position for title or money. Her competence is always under scrutiny, and many women can prove their talent only after the death of a husband, if they succeed to his position.

2. Mechanisms of Exclusion. Not only is competition keen for the pinnacles, but active mechanisms thin the ranks of the competitors. Women, like other groups who have potential talent and ability, have been kept out of the pool of eligibles in science, law, and other male-dominated professions. A certain evenness of resistance to the inclusion of women is apparent in these spheres long dominated by men. Women have not had access to the same reward structure that men have, and this is as much a cause of their low participation and productivity in the professions as is the discrimination that bars them.[11]

In some ways the exclusion of women may have been more effective than the barring of other groups because women, unlike the other groups, have had an initial acculturation to values of the ruling elites. They have grown up with men, learned their manners, been educated in their schools, and been exposed to the same circuitry of contacts. But the Radcliffe sisters of Harvard brothers and their other Ivy League counterparts, classes of 1940, 1950, and 1960 (which produced the heads of our corporations, the rulers of our country), somehow

were tracked into careers, not usually called careers, as adjuncts to their husbands.

Careers in corporate and government life have typically been so demanding that men have needed able wives to entertain, soothe, make contacts, and offer ballast. Most top careers, in fact, have been cooperative efforts, but husbands hold the titles and power and their wives serve as statusless, unpaid partners.[12] As corporations institutionalized the 12-hour day for their executives and developed a set of expectations that a man's family be at the call of the corporation, both the single man and the man whose wife who has an independent life have been hampered in the climb to power. The woman executive is likewise handicapped. Given the norms of family life in America, she could hardly be expected to make the same demands on her husband that the husband can make on his wife.

When it was inconceivable for women to be on the same path as men, alternative routes to the top were suggested. As secretaries or gal Fridays, serving men, supposedly they would learn the ropes. Actually some did, and realized too late that it was not know-how alone that would give them promotions; it was knowledge acquired in specified settings and according to certain rules. Women who insisted they be given the same chances as men were seen as immodest and pushy, lacking in the very qualities of charm and grace that made women nice to have around. The female recruit entered the world of work with a built-in bias, with a different set of experiences, without a peer group, to face a situation where she would be damned if she did and damned if

[11] Cynthia Fuchs Epstein, "Structuring Success for Women: Guidelines for Gatekeepers," *Journal of the National Association of Women Deans and Counselors*, Fall 1973, pp. 34–42.

[12] Cynthia Fuchs Epstein, "Law Partners and Marital Partners: Strains and Solutions in the Dual-Career Family Enterprise," *Human Relations*, December 1971, pp. 549–64.

she didn't perform well. The British study of women directors indicated that colleagues saw them as "dragons" if they were authoritative, or as "nice mice" if they were mild in demeanor.

3. Problems of Identification.

Some of the structures within the occupations are becoming more clearly recognized today as being instrumental in making women feel uncomfortable and unwanted.

The business world has for a long time considered women executives to be such a rarity that clients and colleagues could only react with surprise or disbelief. Most men assumed that any woman at a business meeting was a secretary. A woman executive often had to announce who she was, had no implicit status, and had difficulty exerting authority. Imagine a male executive who could *always* expect to be mistaken for the salesman or the filing clerk, and would have to identify himself and hope he would be treated with respect. Men in positions of authority expect that others will know their power. In fact, they know that the more power they have, the less they need to announce it. Lesser men can lean on the image of power, emulating the model member of upper corporation management in classic gray flannel suit with vest, and assume an air of detached authority. For women there has been no comparable model.

Ironically, as types of authority loosen and the male executive tends to be more approachable and informal, women may face greater ambiguity in defining their roles than before. One may call the boss "Bill" rather than "Mr. Jones" and still not upset the power structure, because it is clear who stands in authority. But calling the boss "Jane" rather than "Ms. Hastings" may easily produce a patronizing and comradely ambience in which lines of power, difficult to read swiftly between men and women in the clearest of circumstances, are misunderstood.

B. Consequences of the Numbers of Women in Top Positions

We must also consider the relevance of numbers and ratios in interaction. When women in management are few in number, they feel excluded and often become estranged. They say they are not really considered to be part of the organization in a true membership sense, but interlopers. Women's minority position in management is institutionalized by rules guaranteeing a tiny quota. When there is only one woman in the executive suite, it is awkward for her; she has no peer group, no referent for her behavior.[13] And it is awkward for her male colleagues, who perceive her as a lone intruder to their all-male bastion. It is essential to create a critical mass in management, a large enough proportion of women to make their presence a matter of course rather than a phenomenon.

1. Informal Interaction.

Numbers and ratios are significant in establishing the all-important norms of informal social interaction, a process that is of utmost importance in top-management circles. Consider the key informal contacts made over lunch, or the easy camaraderie of the bar. A male colleague might feel awkward asking a woman business associate to have a drink, and vice versa. One man to one woman suggests an overture to a specifically social relationship, and the combination of three men and one

---

[13] Eleanor Brantley Schwartz and James J. Rago, Jr., "Beyond Tokenism: Women as True Corporate Peers: Can Organization Cope with Male Executives Who Resist Working with Women as Peers?" *Business Horizons*, December 1973, pp. 69–76.

woman may seem awkward to the woman who might feel like an intruder on their "man talk"; but if there were four men and two women, or three men, then the informal social relations intertwined with business would not have a sexual overtone. In other contexts where no arbitrary rules limit the normal exchanges between men and women, work proceeds smoothly. The mere presence of women does not disrupt the structure, and the men don't feel diminished.

The consequences of a social pattern that distinguishes between men and women in terms of membership, dining rooms, dining tables, or mere access may be more injurious then the degradation suffered by those who are wholly excluded. When women cannot mingle easily with men as colleagues in the informal settings where business gets done, they cannot become fully prepared to exercise influence. When women expect and are given full participation in the formal and informal structures of their occupations at every level, including the top one, they can be included as equals and be let in on the silent rules of the game along with the males.

2. The Reward-Punishment System. With this model of membership a woman would be prepared to make a contribution on her own. She would have to become, as they say, her own "man." She would have to know that her performance will face the same tests as those of men and that on the same criteria she will succeed or fail. This model would not shelter or hide women in invisible positions. It would convince them that if they contribute, they will rise in rank and increase in visibility and be paid and respected accordingly; if they fail, it is not because they are women but because their performance has been found wanting. And

as they rise, the standards will become higher, as with men. When men are clearly at the top, the driving motivation for them ceases to be the expectation of greater rewards—more money or even more rank—but the need (gradually internalized over time) to *continue to achieve*. Few women have so far been exposed to this conditioning.

3. Processes in the Creation of Criteria for Competence. We are concerned about the way in which business roles are institutionalized so that only *certain* people are seen as appropriate partners in normal interaction. Denial of access to the structure in which competence is created has perpetuated the exclusion of women from top posts. Those who are not admitted or who are not *admissible* to inner circles are denied what is perhaps the most crucial learning of their trade. This is most obvious in the case of professions. Top surgeons learn their special skills not when they are in medical school, but when they are selected to be residents with the finest physicians in their specialty. Top lawyers start as apprentices to the senior partners in the large firms. The process is comparable in business, where most skills are not objectively learned but are rather the product of intelligence, diplomacy, knowhow, and "know-who." Information about who is the best producer of an item and what kind of pricing is possible is passed on to protégés, who are also introduced to top people.

Our social conditioning encourages us to think of persons of only a certain age or sex or race as being able to understand tasks or to carry them out. Women have not been thought of as business executives, and younger men too have often been discriminated against, simply because they seemed too young to hold a job of responsibility and did not fit the mold. Discrimination is not always directed at the *classic* underdog, but it works against any group that does not fit the stereotype. We may not pity the young man because we expect he will *ultimately* get the position for which he might be fit now. We think he is too young partially because we know that older people do not like to be commanded by the young. But he is also handicapped by our stereotypes about how many years a person should devote to each stage of his career. These expectations are defined by how it has always been done. We also have views about the amount of time any particular task ought to take and how long the workday ought to be for a "committed" person. On all sides we are encumbered by expectations that are operationalized as coercive rules. They are rationalized as logical, but a closer look shows that they are based on unchallenged assumptions and reflect the status quo. These assumptions typically favor the class of persons in command and make others seem to be the "wrong" persons for the job, whoever they are and whatever the job may be.

4. Style, Self, and the Aura of Competence. We must be concerned about the difficulty of objective evaluation of competence. Psychological and sociological studies make clear the impact of "labeling," the process by which a person is called competent or incompetent, appropriate or inappropriate, good or bad. The label defines the self-image that in turn shapes the behavior. A person who is seen as a "go-getter" likely to succeed will work harder than the person who is perceived as inept and unable to accomplish a goal or a dream.

The more we study people who are ostensibly "self-made," the more we see that what really made them is not only their idiosyncratic set of talents but also the framework in which they lived, the opportunities available to them, and the role of persons important in their lives in the formation of a self-image that facilitated career attainments.

Gatekeepers are often so committed to stereotypes that they are incapable of seeing talent or emerging competence because the package in which it is presented is so unexpected. If we do not listen to the brilliant woman because we don't expect bright ideas to come in a female form, we won't hear her contributions. And when, after a while, she falls silent because no one listens, the initial stereotype is confirmed and reinforced.[14] There are, of course, exceptions to this pattern, but again our stereotypes get in the way.

Women in politics say that because Bella Abzug is aggressive and forthright in her personal style, her congressional colleagues find it embarrassing to interact with her and they try to avoid her as much as possible. It is clear that many male politicians assume an aggressive personal style that is not only tolerated but defined as consistent with leadership. The woman, however, is caught in a morass of conflicting expectations and may be damned whatever style she chooses.

An increase in the numbers of women in male settings will doubtless change current attitudes that accept a greater range of styles for men than for women. Then any one woman's personal style would be less attributable to all women, and each would be accepted as an individual, as is any man. Enough women would be visible at one time to make clear the lack of homogeneity. This has already been demonstrated to

---

[14] Matina Horner, "Toward an Understanding of Achievement Related Conflicts in Women," *Journal of Social Issues*, 1972, pp. 157–76.

some degree in formerly male bastions, such as business and law schools, that now admit substantial percentages of women students. Male students and teachers are accepting women and judging them according to the same standards as men. Men in business and professions do not necessarily intend to discriminate. We all tend to define what we see most often as normal. The world in which they work is mostly male, and that is the most comfortable and natural way for them. Probably few are even aware that women are excluded or made to feel unwanted, although in certain cases the possibility of bad intentions cannot be ignored.

Exclusionary consequences can flow from good motives as well as bad. Some men really do think they are helping a woman by being sensitive to her family responsibilities and not asking her to do the extra work that might be just what she needs to prove her talents and perhaps get a promotion. This paternalism deprives women of the right to decide independently and thereby to learn. No single answer will fit all women, and each must choose her own priorities in life and be free to act accordingly.

5. Culture and the Structure of Motivation. What is unique about the situation of women today is that almost everyone is to blame, including women themselves, who have joined the conspiracy by accepting the idea that they must monitor their ambitions and goals in terms of what everybody else expects of them—including their husbands, children, fathers, or bosses. Our culture expects and encourages women to hold back, not to "go for broke": not to sacrifice family savings or the immediate comfort of the family in service of long-range goals. But this is exactly what is expected of a man

who is an entrepreneur or struggling professional. Clearly, motivational structures are not alike for men and women.[15]

While both his private and professional lives combine to encourage the man to put his best into his work, and promise him rewards for doing so, the woman's private life—the home and community—tends to undermine her work goals, presenting challenges to her right to work and outright hostility. Community values will often condemn her career goals as antisocial and an abandonment of husband and children. In her professional life, her colleagues often question her ability and the extent and depth of her commitment. On the basis of an incomplete assessment of her own accomplishments she may form a negative self-image that she then extends, somewhat defensively, to characterize women more generally. These women often stifle their desire for self-fulfillment or deflect it in other directions, some of them destructive to the husbands and children through whom they try to live vicariously.

C. Change and Resistance to Change in the Status of Women

Things can change, and there is evidence that they are changing. My findings[16] in studying women in elite positions in business and the professions show that the old homily "Nothing succeeds like success" is well grounded in fact. It is a self-fulfilling prophecy not unlike the labeling discussed

---

[15] Cynthia Fuchs Epstein, *Women's Place: Options and Limits in Professional Careers* (Berkeley: University of California Press, 1970).

[16] Cynthia Fuchs Epstein, "Encountering the Male Establishment: Sex-Status Limits on Women's Careers in the Professions," *American Journal of Sociology*, May 1970, pp. 965–82.

above. Yet I believe that the idea of opening the doors to women somehow, whether for traditional, cultural, or psychological reasons, seems a basic threat that will always stand in the way of truly equal opportunities in management for both sexes.

These fears are not groundless; they stem from women's obvious potential. It is certainly true that women, who constitute such a large proportion of the educated, could take over quite a few men's jobs tomorrow if they were so inclined and if they were given the opportunity. Yet it must be possible to devise work structures in which we can upgrade *all* jobs, provide reward incentives for all, and define competition from the bottom to the top in terms of sheer creative talent, ambition, and drive.

The search continues for specific structural solutions to these problems. These cannot succeed without a simultaneous concern with the attitudes that are created early in life in the home and in school, for changing attitudes and changing structure go hand in hand. We may change work conditions more easily than attitudes, but no situation is hopeless. The large law firms that have employed women and have even made them senior partners find that clients accept the judgment of the firm as to who will serve them well. Further, no firm has reported suffering a financial loss or a diminution of prestige for doing so.

At General Motors, once directives were handed down from top management to expedite the affirmative action program demanded by the government, GM's middle managers not only went along but often found good reasons for changing the old practices. Everyone, it seems, became interested in the success of the plan.

The American Telephone & Telegraph Company now has a vice president who is mobilizing a task force of bright managers to rethink job sequences, job criteria, and job segmentation. They are going beyond the thinking lodged in commonplace notions about how things have been done. Of course, such innovations will have many consequences beyond simply assimilating women.

Women have generally been deprived of the charisma of the halo effect of title and rank. When officers of business concerns give women the same deference as well as accoutrements of office given men, women will be more at ease in assuming command. When firms back women executives with the expectations that they will do well and let their subordinates know it, women will measure up to these expectations. But the institution must feel it has a stake in the person and vice versa. Job commitment and high performance cannot develop when women sense that the promises held out to them are empty, or tokens intended primarily to pacify the demands of EEOC. Women have long permitted themselves to accept a bad bargain, but today more and more they are insisting on a fair price, the market price, for their services.

READING 2
SEXUAL HARASSMENT . . .
SOME SEE IT . . . SOME WON'T*
Eliza G. C. Collins and
Timothy B. Blodgett†

"This entire subject is a perfect example of a minor special interest group's ability to blow up any

* Copyright 1981 by the President and Fellows of Harvard College; all rights reserved. Reprinted by permission of the *Harvard Business Review*, March–April 1981.

† *Authors' note:* We thank Grace L. Mastalli, Linda Bose Lord, and Mary Rowe for their help and encouragement and thank the respondents to the survey for their thoughtful comments and opinions.

'issue' to a level of importance which in no way relates to the reality of the world in which we live and work.''—A 38-year-old plant manager (male) for a large manufacturer of industrial goods.

"A vice president of the company where I worked made overt advances following a company banquet. This included stroking my buttocks and continually rubbing himself against me. At one point he got me alone—away from the group—and put his hand down my dress. I finally managed to get rid of him. For several weeks afterward he kept calling me at work. When I talked to my supervisor about it, his only reaction was amusement. A few months later, my supervisor started making advances. When I found another job, I left. It's much better where I am now.''—A 27-year-old computer specialist (female) in a large public utility.

"In my own circumstances, sexual harassment included jokes about my anatomy, off-color remarks, sly innuendo in front of customers—in short, turning everything and anything into a sexual reference was an almost daily occurrence. I have just left this company [a big chemical manufacturer] partially for this reason.''—A 34-year-old first-level manager in environmental engineering (female) for a large producer of industrial goods.

"I'm baffled by this issue. I used to believe it was a subject that was being exaggerated by paranoid women and sensational journalists. Now I think the problem is real but somewhat overdrawn. My impression is that my own company is relatively free of sexual harassment. But I don't know the facts.''—A 53-year-old senior vice president (male) of a medium-sized financial institution.

Is sexual harassment a manufactured issue? Is it widespread? Should it concern top management? To try to answer these and other questions, the editors of *Harvard Business Review* and *Redbook* magazine surveyed 7,408 HBR subscribers (1,846, or nearly 25

percent, of whom responded) in the United States. (See the ruled insert for a complete description of how the survey was conducted.)

Our major findings are:

• Sexual harassment is seen as an issue of power. In four out of six situations that we described to readers, they rate a supervisor's behavior as considerably more serious and threatening than the same action by a co-worker.

• Men and women generally agree in theory on what sexual harassment is but disagree on how often it occurs. Nearly two thirds of the men, compared with about half the women surveyed, agree (or partly agree) with the statement, "The amount of sexual harassment at work is greatly exaggerated."

• Top management appears isolated from occurrences of harassment, and middle-level managers are somewhat less aware of misconduct than lower-level managers.

• Most respondents favor company policies against harassment, but few organizations have any policies to address it. For example, 29 percent of respondents work in companies where top executives have issued statements to employees disapproving of sexual misconduct, but 73 percent favor such statements.

• In general, most see the Equal Employment Opportunity Commission (EEOC) guidelines issued in 1980 as reasonable and necessary and agree that they will not be difficult to follow. But the returns show that the mildest and most pervasive forms, such as innuendo and dirty jokes—to many women the most obnoxious forms—are harder to prove and often impractical to take action on, even though the guidelines cover them.

Survey Approach

This survey, conducted jointly by *Redbook* magazine and HBR, aimed to measure opinions on and awareness of the issue of sexual harassment in the workplace. We mailed a questionnaire to 7,408 HBR subscribers in the United States and tabulated 1,846 replies, a 24.9 percent response. (A further 234 completed questionnaires were returned after the cut-off date and could not be included.)

To serve as a benchmark for respondents and give them a certain amount of information as a starting point, we listed the EEOC guidelines on sexual harassment in the introduction to the questionnaire.

We divided the survey into three sections. In the first, to elicit definitions and attitudes we offered readers 11 statements and asked whether they agreed with them or not. We also listed 14 comments that have been made about the behavior of men toward women at work and asked whether the behavior described constituted sexual harassment and whether people had heard of or observed this behavior in their organizations.

In the second section, we described four vignettes and asked what action to take. The third set of questions concerned EEOC guidelines and company policies, and the fourth section was statistical.

In the first section we split the sample in half to get at differing attitudes that might not otherwise be revealed. Of the 14 comments on behavior, 8 differed between the white and colored forms. The four vignettes in the second section were also worded differently between the two forms.

In examining the data, we discovered a certain amount of conditioning. In the eight split-sample statements on behavior, the aggressor in the colored form was always a supervisor, while in the white form he was a co-worker. In the other six questions in the group that were the same in both forms, those who returned the colored questionnaires were more likely to term an action harassment than those who returned the white ones.

We excluded all non-U.S. subscribers (22 percent of HBR's total number of subscribers) from the sample because we wanted to probe the issue from a strictly American viewpoint. We also skewed the sample another way: to ensure a representative response from women, we mailed a questionnaire to virtually every female subscriber, for a male/female ratio of 68 percent to 32 percent. This bias resulted in a response of 52 percent male and 44 percent female (and 45 percent who gave no indication of gender)—compared with HBR's U.S. subscriber proportion of 93 percent male and 7 percent female.

The administrative levels of the survey group broke down as follows: top management, 24 percent; middle management, 33 percent; lower management, 34 percent; and other, 7 percent. Nearly three quarters of the group were in the 25 to 45 age bracket. The breakdown was: under 25, 3 percent; 25 to 35, 42 percent; 36 to 45, 32 percent; 46 to 55, 15 percent; 56 to 65, 6 percent; and over 65, less than 1 percent; 1 percent did not answer.

The salaries of about one quarter of the group fell into the $20,000 to $29,999 range, another one quarter in the $30,000 to $39,999 range, while 11 percent earned less than $20,000, and 6 percent more than $100,000. Some 49 percent held graduate degrees and 35 percent, college degrees.

The sizes of the organizations for which the individuals worked were spread widely, the most significant categories being 1,000 to 9,999 employees (23 percent), more than 20,000 (16 percent), and under 50 (13 percent).

On average, the survey group was at a lower management level than our U.S. subscribers overall. Respondents were generally younger and earned less but were about as well educated. We ascribe the differences between respondents and HBR's subscriber group to the fact that our sample was skewed to include more women, who have not reached the higher echelons of U.S. corporations in great numbers.

• Most respondents think sexual harassment can be a very serious matter. Ten percent report they have heard of or observed a situation as extreme as the following in their organizations: "Mr. X has asked me to have sex with him. I refused, but now I learn that he's given me a poor evaluation."

Regardless of the perceived seriousness of the problem, however, the findings cannot reveal how pervasive sexual harassment is. Obviously, those who were most interested or involved completed the questionnaire; we do not know about the experiences of others who did not answer or who were not included in the survey.

• Finally, many people—nearly one out of three—took the time to write about their concerns and uncertainties regarding this issue. In their comments, many women despair of gaining top management's understanding of how harassment damages them.

Until recently, consciousness of sexual harassment has been low. But people have become aware of it as more women have arrived at levels of authority in the workplace, feminist groups have focused attention on rape and other violence against women, and students have felt freer to report perceived abuse by professors. (Although the survey was designed to investigate mainly women's experiences, we recognize—and the answers to the questionnaire make clear—that harassment of men by women and homosexual harassment do occur, also with distressing consequences to the victims.)

In the last five years, other studies have also shown that sexual misconduct is a big problem. For example, in a recently published survey of federal employees, 42 percent of 694,000 women and 15 percent of 1,168,000 men said they had experienced some form of harassment.[1]

In November 1980, the EEOC adopted its final guidelines for employers to deal with the problem. The new guidelines define sexual harassment as "unwelcome sexual advances, requests for sexual favors, and other verbal or physical conduct of a sexual nature" that take place under any of the following circumstances:

1. When submission to the sexual advance is a condition of keeping or getting a job, whether expressed in explicit or implicit terms.

2. When a supervisor or boss makes a personnel decision based on an employee's submission to or rejection of sexual advances.

3. When sexual conduct unreasonably interferes with a person's work performance or creates an intimidating, hostile, or offensive work environment.

According to the EEOC, employers have "an affirmative duty" to prevent and eliminate sexual abuse. Additionally, the guidelines make the employer responsible for misbehavior by supervisory personnel, their assistants, coworkers, or outside personnel. (See the Appendix for the legal issues.)

Top managers, middle and lower-level managers, women, and men do not always agree on what constitutes harassment or

---

[1] Merit Systems Protection Board Report on Sexual Harassment in the Federal Workplace, given before the Subcommittee on Investigations, Committee on the Post Office and Civil Service, U.S. House of Representatives, September 1980. See also Frank J. Till, "Sexual Harassment: A Report on the Sexual Harassment of Students," National Advisory Council on Women's Educational Programs, U.S. Department of Education, August 1980; Catherine A. MacKinnon, *Sexual Harassment of Working Women* (New Haven: Yale University Press, 1979); and Claire Safran, "What Men Do to Women on the Job," *Redbook*, November 1976, p. 149.

even whether it is prevalent. But because so many perceive it as a problem, and because the EEOC has issued guidelines and raised the prospect of stepped-up litigation by employees, top management of for-profit and nonprofit organizations clearly should pay attention to the issue.

In this article we explore what some of our readers think sexual harassment is and how much they think it occurs in their organizations. In doing so, we report what they think about the EEOC guidelines, company policies, and, more personally, how they feel when harassed.

What Is It & How Much?

"I attended a meeting of department heads (only two women were classified as department heads). There, 40- to 45-year-old men—department heads and elected officials—were tossing a prophylactic back and forth, with the usual comments accompanying the tosses. I don't know if this show was for the benefit of the two women present or if they just found out what the item was used for. We tried to ignore their behavior. Another department head suggested they pay attention and grow up." (female)

"Constant 'small' examples show lack of awareness, such as from a boss: 'You deserve a pat on the fanny for a good job.'" (female)

"I have heard much 'joking' about sex in regard to women's bodies in the office. I have seen this going on for years. Since it is supposedly said in jest, it is apparently supposed to be ignored. But most of the female employees get very uncomfortable when these remarks are made. The men enjoy every minute of it and it seems to amuse them even more if the women get embarrassed. This has happened in one-

on-one situations and in group situations." (female)

"There is a great deal of fondness in my company, particularly my division, but I'm confident it does not include the necessary element of harassment, i.e., indebtedness. Maybe I'm naive. Better yet, maybe my businesslike deportment prevents any encouragement of innuendos or allows me to be 'one of the boys.' There is an unusually high comfort level among the men and women in our company. I attribute most of that to the age of the group (30 to 35) and the fact that they've been brought up in a more aware time." (female)

"I have supervised many women and have found them very sensitive especially to biases of their male bosses. Many times their sensitivity is more acute than my own—that is, I saw nothing obvious but they were quite sure of the bias. As a result, I am unsure whether accusations of sexual bias are not just disguises of—or poorly stated initial reactions to—some other underlying management problem (or perception)." (male)

Not surprisingly, respondents to our survey agree about which extreme situations constitute sexual harassment but differ over the more ambiguous cases. For instance, 87 percent think that the following statement definitely indicates abuse: "I have been having an affair with the head of my division. Now I've told him I want to break it off, but he says I will lose out on the promotion I've been expecting." (Exhibit 1 shows the 4 instances of 14 we described that most people think constitute misconduct.)

Opinions on these extreme cases differ little between men and women and between top and lower-level management. For example, 89 percent of the men and 92 percent of the women think the first statement in Ex-

Exhibit 1 Views on Extreme Behavior by Percent of Total Respondents: 1,846*

	Not Harassment	Possibly Harassment	Sexual Harassment	Don't Know	Heard of or Observed in Company	Not Heard of or Observed in Company
A. "I can't seem to go in and out of my boss's office without being patted or pinched."	1%	8%	90%	1%	14%	83%
B. "Mr. X has told me that it would be good for my career if we went out together. I guess that means it would be bad for my career if I said no."	2	17	79	2	12	85
C. "Mr. X has asked me to have sex with him. I refused, but now I learn that he's given me a poor evaluation."	1	20	78	1	10	87
D. "I have been having an affair with the head of my division. Now I've told him I want to break it off, but he says I will lose out on the promotion I've been expecting."	4	7	87	2	7	90

* In some cases, throughout the exhibits, not all people answered all questions.

Exhibit 2   Views on Less Extreme Behavior According to Supervisor/Co-worker Split Sample

	Not Harassment	Possibly Harassment	Sexual Harassment	Don't Know	Heard of or Observed in Company	Not Heard of or Observed in Company
A. "Whenever I go into the office, my supervisor (a man I work with) eyes me up and down, making me feel uncomfortable."	20% (26)	60% (54)	16% (15)	4% (4)	61% (71)	37% (27)
B. "My supervisor (A man I work with) starts each day with a sexual remark. He insists it's an innocent social comment."	5 (10)	46 (49)	44 (37)	4 (4)	35 (45)	63 (53)
C. "Often in meetings my supervisor (a man I work with) continually glances at me."	62 (65)	26 (26)	1 (2)	10 (6)	50 (61)	47 (36)
D. "Every time we meet, my supervisor (a man I work with) kisses me on the cheek."	4 (17)	43 (47)	46 (20)	7 (10)	11 (18)	86 (79)
E. "My supervisor (A man I work with) asked me out on a date. Although I refused, he continues to ask me."	10 (33)	39 (41)	48 (20)	4 (5)	26 (42)	71 (56)
F. "My supervisor (A man I work with) puts his hand on my arm when making a point."	43 (46)	44 (42)	3 (4)	10 (9)	59 (63)	36 (33)

hibit 1 is harassment ("I can't seem to go in and out of my boss's office without being patted or pinched"). Nearly 87 percent of top management and 91 percent of lower-level management also think it is.

In other, less extreme situations, however, people are less certain about the interpretation but still consider the behavior quite offensive (see Exhibit 2). An average of 40 percent say the situation where a man starts each day with a sexual remark and insists it's an innocent social comment is harassment; an average of 48 percent say it is possibly; 8 percent say it is not; and 4 percent don't know. According to many readers, a situation where a man often puts his hand on a woman's arm when making a point is even more innocent (see Exhibit 2).

The perceived seriousness of the harassment seems to depend on who is making the advance, the degree of interpreted intent, and the victim's perception of the consequences. The amount the victim appears to suffer, however, does not necessarily vary with the perceived seriousness. In many comments, for instance, the writers seemed more vexed by persistent low-level misbehavior, which, although covered by EEOC guidelines, is impractical to do something about and is often harder to prove than more extreme forms.

A 26-year-old female market research analyst for an industrial goods manufacturer wrote: "It is not easy for a smart woman to avoid sexual harassment. Case in point—a male in our DP department continually makes comments and gestures to me. I reacted at first by being 'cool and silent.' When this did not have any effect, I requested that he stop, as I found it offensive. I must deal with this person professionally, and I feel that our relationship has been hindered. We both found each other's actions and reactions offensive."

Harassment is not, of course, limited to the office. Wrote a 30-year-old male foundry materials manager for an industrial goods producer: "When secretaries walk through the shop, there are whistles and catcalls. However, management has not seen this as a problem. It does not interfere with promotion or pay, but I find it an offensive situation."

To test whether a supervisor's behavior is seen as more threatening and serious than a co-worker's, the survey included a split sample in which we asked readers' opinions of statements made by female employees about male co-workers and supervisors (see Exhibit 2). For example, the colored survey form, sent to half the subscribers pooled, stated, "Whenever I go into the office, my supervisor eyes me up and down, making me feel uncomfortable." On the white form, which was sent to the other half, "my supervisor" became "a man I work with" (Exhibit 2, part A the white form data appears in parentheses).

In four of these six less extreme cases, a higher percentage view the supervisor's behavior as worse than the co-worker's. Quite clearly, the perceived seriousness of the action correlates with the power of the person making the advances. (The two situations where the co-worker is seen as more blameworthy—continually glancing at the woman, part C, and putting a hand on her arm when making a point, part F—are rather ambiguous, and the behavior is certainly less threatening in relation to work but more repugnant because it constitutes unwanted intimacy.)

Many people commented on how power influences perceptions of harassment. As one reader put it, "The indebtedness increases the harassment's potency." Some of our male readers were very aware of the implications of power differences: "There is a male code of silence regarding harassment of females that has to be broken, particularly in the area of male 'power' figures and females without power," said the 38-year-old male vice president of marketing in a large insurance company. "Either too many men never recover from being high school jocks or they understand that corporate power can be a new way to be attractive. Having suffered through both lessons, I feel free to comment."

The power phenomenon is not necessarily restricted to men, either. "The more power people have, the more able they are to let go of their inhibitions and act on their desires," testified a 36-year-old government administrator. "As a woman manager, I must admit to temptation! It is when the overtures are unwanted, persistent, and *power* based that they are unhealthy organizationally."

In five of the six split-sample cases, more women than men consider the behavior offensive, whether the statement is about a supervisor or a co-worker. For instance, in the situation where the man eyes the woman up and down (Exhibit 2, part A), 24 percent of all women, compared with 8 percent of all men, think it is harassment. (Since it was not possible to include all the survey data in the exhibits, here and in a few other instances, the data have been extrapolated.)

In the remaining split-sample case—where the man kisses the woman every time they meet (part D)—somewhat more men than women, proportionately, rate the action objectionable whether by a supervisor or a fellow worker. Perhaps women are often more conscious of social formalities and tend to accept this kind of behavior from supervisors, whereas men are more likely to consider it merely an encounter between the sexes.

In response to two other statements that

were more conventionally social—where the man often offers to drive the woman home and where the married man and the woman have dinner together and go to a nightclub while on a business trip—slightly more men than women also think these are possibly harassment.

Additionally, as all the split-sample responses in this section testify, top managers say that the behavior by supervisors is more blameworthy than the same behavior by co-workers.

Answers to the split sample clearly demonstrate that the power relationship implicitly carries a coercive threat. But what about co-workers? Why do only a third of top managers who completed the white form think that being greeted each day with a sexual remark from a co-worker is harassment? (The white form data appears in parentheses.)

Throughout the survey we found answers that could be explained only by a "that's the way men are" assessment on the part of both men and women—resignation or acceptance bred of recurring experience. Perhaps the more one sees behavior like that we described, the less one is stirred to call it misconduct.

How Much?

Except for the incident where the man kisses the woman on the cheek every time they meet (Exhibit 2, part D), all the situations in Exhibit 2 have been heard of or seen by many people. For example, an average of one third say that they have heard of or observed persistent requests for a date by men in their organizations.

The four activities our sample considers the most objectionable (Exhibit 1) they have seen or heard of the least. Understandably, these are the least likely to occur, be detected, or be admitted to.

In general, of those who have knowledge of certain sexual behavior in their organizations, a higher proportion assert that such behavior is not harassment. For example, 10 percent of the people who have seen or heard of someone starting each day with a sexual remark say it is not harassment, compared with 5 percent of those who haven't heard of or seen such behavior.

The spread appears greater when we look at the co-worker/supervisor split sample. In cases where the supervisor makes the advance, people are much more likely to call it harassment when they have no knowledge of its occurrence in their own organizations. (Does familiarity breed contempt?) In all these cases, however, interpretation of intent may cloud the statistics.

The most striking finding on the question of how much abuse actually takes place is the difference in perception between men and women and between high-level and lower-level management. (Because most high-level managers in our survey were men and more lower-level managers were women, the two sets of responses often parallel each other.) The answers to the statement, "The amount of sexual harassment at work is greatly exaggerated," are:

	Agree or Partly Agree	Disagree or Partly Disagree
Top management	63%	22%
Middle management	52	30
Lower-level management	44	40
Women	32%	52%
Men	66	17

In most instances substantial differences appear in men's and women's perceptions of how frequently sexual harassment occurs.

For example, one third of the men, but a full half of the women, have witnessed or heard of a case where the man starts each day with a sexual remark that he insists is an innocent social comment (Exhibit 2, part B).

How can we explain the differences in viewpoint? Sexual harassment may not take place when male managers are around to observe it; and even if it does, they may not "see" it as women do. Consider this account from a 30-year-old female project leader in the finance department of a large company: "Not a day passes without my boss either sharing a particularly lewd joke with me or asking me what I did with my boyfriend the night before—complete with leers and smirks. My requests for him to cease have fallen on deaf ears; he seems to enjoy my discomfort and chides me for being a 'poor sport.' Prior to my divorce he was totally inoffensive."

That such an attitude on the part of male managers is discouraging for women is evident from many comments we received. Typical was this remark from a 32-year-old financial officer in a small company: "I was the victim of harassment and it was a miserable experience. When I voiced complaints to my so-called feminist male boss and male colleagues, I was made to feel crazy, dirty—as if I were the troublemaker." Another woman wrote, "Sexual harassment eats away at the core of a woman's being, destroys self-confidence, and can contribute to a lowered feeling of self-worth."

Even though men generally agree in the abstract with women about what harassment is, the gap in perception of what actually happens is real and significant. From the comments in the returns, a visitor from another planet might conclude that men and women work in separate organizations.

One factor that may help explain the difference in perception is social conditioning.

For example, 44 percent of the women view the statement about the man who starts each day with a sexual remark (Exhibit 2, part B) as only "possibly" misconduct. "Many incidents go unnoticed by both parties because of conditioning," wrote a 30-year-old female radio station manager. "Men are 'expected' to do such things, women are 'expected' to have to cope with that type of behavior." Perhaps some women, accustomed to accept such incidents as a price of survival in the business world, have lost sensitivity. They, as well as men, suffer from sexual astigmatism.

One reader, a 30-year-old female vice president of marketing in a large financial institution, wrote, "Senior people are the wrong people to ask about such behavior because they may not know much. The 'little people' are afraid to complain." The survey corroborates her observation, perhaps because the "little people" are afraid of exposure, embarrassment, and retribution.

In extreme cases, higher-level executives report that they are generally unaware of what's going on. Perhaps one of the worst examples of abuse in our survey is epitomized by Exhibit 1, part C—where the man gives the woman a poor evaluation because she refuses to have sex with him. Ten percent of all respondents have heard of or observed this situation. The response by management level breaks down this way: top management, 5 percent; middle management, 9 percent; lower-level management, 13 percent; persons other than managers (a small number), 19 percent.

As in other situations, more women than men testify to knowledge of the situation described in Exhibit 1, part C—16 percent against 5 percent. Whether conditioning, denial, or lack of awareness explains these disparities, the gap in perception between different levels of management and be-

tween men and women poses a serious problem for policymakers.

What Would You Do?

"Men in my company are not penalized for sexual encounters with co-workers, whereas women are. You feel [helpless] trying to confront silent accusations and using the company complaint channels where the men you talk to share a common, somewhat negative philosophy about women." (female)

"I have worked successfully in good positions all my life. Since I was both attractive and smart, [the problem] was always the boss. I either had to learn to say no graciously, or lose every good job I got. I find that a woman must defend herself every day, and I don't believe you can find rules for the top men. The world is made of men and women who either get along or don't. If they do get along, the men invariably try to have a physical attachment I think it's inborn in a man." (female)

"I was in an elevator along with the president and some other men. One man made a dirty comment, and the president came back with a remark telling this employee to keep his locker room comments to the locker room and not make them around any women in the firm." (female)

The problem of disparities in perception appears throughout the survey. To probe differing attitudes, we sent two different versions of four vignettes in our split-sample questionnaire. In one we asked readers to say what they would do as managers in these situations; in the other, what typical managers would do (see Exhibit 3). One can draw many conclusions from the answers, but three disparities in perception stand

Exhibit 3   Split-Sample Responses to Four Vignettes*

	Male	Female	Top Management	Middle Management	Lower Management	Other
Number responding, colored form	489	412	245	332	289	62
(white form)	(470)	(391)	(192)	(277)	(347)	(61)

A. The president of a company walks into the office of his sales manager to congratulate him on setting a new record in sales. When he enters the office, he finds the sales manager standing very close to his secretary, who looks upset and flustered. When the president and sales manager are alone, what do you think the president would do—if he were typical of company presidents you have known or heard about? (If you were the president, what would you do when you were alone with the sales manager?)

	Male	Female	Top Management	Middle Management	Lower Management	Other
a. He (I) would do nothing, not knowing what had happened.	33%	30%	30%	33%	32%	35%
	(30)	(25)	(27)	(30)	(29)	(15)
b. He (I) would do nothing, not wanting to confront the sales manager on a personal matter such as this.	13	36	20	24	26	29
	(1)	(1)	(1)	(1)	(1)	(1)
c. He (I) would suggest to the sales manager that even the appearance of sexual behavior was unwise.	47	3	42	39	37	27
	(61)	(66)	(63)	(61)	(63)	(77)
d. He (I) would express strong disapproval to the sales manager.	4	2	4	3	2	3
	(4)	(4)	(4)	(5)	(3)	(3)
e. He (I) would tell the sales manager that if such behavior continued, it would have an adverse effect on his career.	2	3	3	1	2	3
	(2)	(3)	(4)	(1)	(3)	(2)

B. Two middle-level male executives (A senior executive and a junior executive) enter an elevator. One of them (The junior executive) turns to the other occupant, a female employee, and makes a suggestive remark about her body. Then he winks in amusement at his companion (the senior executive). If the companion (senior executive) were typical of those in your company, what would his response be?

	Male	Female	Top Management	Middle Management	Lower Management	Other
a. He would share the first executive's amusement.	14%	41%	17%	25%	33%	36%
	(7)	(23)	(6)	(12)	(20)	(18)
b. He would feel neutral, believing that if the woman objects, it's up to her to say so.	19	21	21	25	18	36
	(9)	(17)	(13)	(13)	(13)	(13)
c. He would remain silent because it's an embarrassing issue to raise.	23	21	24	22	19	24
	(7)	(14)	(8)	(10)	(12)	(10)
d. He would indicate disapproval by his coolness or aloofness.	22	8	17	15	16	11
	(30)	(20)	(26)	(26)	(24)	(30)
e. He would express disapproval within the woman's hearing.	4	5	6	4	2	7
	(8)	(6)	(9)	(7)	(7)	(8)
f. He would express disapproval when he and the other executive were alone.	17	5	16	10	12	8
	(37)	(18)	(37)	(30)	(24)	(21)

* Throughout the four sections of this exhibit, in order to determine readers' intuitive responses to the vignettes, we did not include as an option the correct legal approach—starting a full investigation in each situation depicted.

Exhibit 3 (*concluded*)

C. A female executive earning $40,000 a year is one of the most promising executives of either sex in her insurance company. She complains to the executive vice president in charge of her division (A secretary complains to the vice president in charge of her division) that her boss has been making unwelcome and persistent sexual advances to her. The vice president has reason to believe her even though, in a private talk, her boss insists that the woman has mistaken his "innocent" remarks and gestures. If you were the executive vice president, what would you do?

		Male	Female	Top Management	Middle Management	Lower Management	Other
a.	I would wonder about the woman's ability to handle interpersonal relationships.	4% (1)	2% (1)	4% (1)	3% (1)	3% (1)	3% (2)
b.	I would advise the woman on how she might better deal with such behavior.	20 (12)	20 (11)	15 (14)	23 (13)	20 (9)	18 (10)
c.	I would offer the woman a transfer to another division.	2 (9)	4 (5)	2 (6)	3 (8)	4 (9)	3 (3)
d.	I would express my strong disapproval to the boss.	25 (29)	16 (21)	23 (27)	21 (27)	18 (25)	13 (26)
e.	I would inform the boss that if such behavior continued, it could have an adverse effect on his career.	45 (48)	56 (60)	52 (53)	47 (49)	52 (55)	58 (59)
f.	I would discreetly arrange a transfer for the boss.	3 (1)	3 (2)	3 (1)	3 (1)	4 (1)	3 (0)

D. A female (male) executive with a large manufacturing company has been the object of persistent sexual advances from the male (female) vice president of a major customer. She (He) has tried to discourage these advances tactfully, but in the course of negotiating a new contract, the customer has suggested that she (he) might lose the contract if she (he) were not "friendlier." The woman (man) discusses the problem with the head of her (his) division. What do you think the typical division head would do?†

		Male	Female	Top Management	Middle Management	Lower Management	Other
a.	Offer to transfer the woman (man) from the account.	23% (15)	35% (18)	27% (16)	24% (16)	30% (18)	42% (21)
b.	Encourage the woman (man) to parry the advances without offending the client.	21 (28)	32 (36)	23 (26)	26 (35)	25 (33)	36 (34)
c.	Encourage the woman (man) to be tactful but firm, regardless of the consequences.	45 (33)	28 (26)	43 (35)	38 (29)	34 (28)	31 (25)
d.	Send a team to future negotiations with the client.	33 (24)	30 (33)	36 (27)	29 (29)	32 (27)	34 (31)
e.	Indicate disapproval to the client.	7 (1)	3 (2)	4 (1)	6 (2)	6 (1)	6 (0)
f.	Other	6 (9)	4 (9)	7 (7)	6 (7)	6 (8)	2 (7)
g.	Don't know.	2 (6)	4 (9)	3 (5)	3 (6)	4 (10)	2 (8)

† Respondents were not limited to a single choice.

out: (1) the differential treatment men and women employees receive after an unwanted advance, (2) how women should handle themselves, and (3) how responsible managers ought to act in the workplace.

Perceived Differential Treatment

The responses to the vignettes show that men and women hold very different opinions on how top managers will act in an ambiguous situation. Their opinions also differ depending on whether the victim is a female or male executive, a female executive or secretary, and on who is making the advance.

For example, in the first vignette a company president walks into his sales manager's office and finds him standing near his secretary, who looks upset and flustered (Exhibit 3, part A). On the colored questionnaire we asked what the typical president would do, and on the white form we asked what "you" would do. Nearly two thirds of the women who filled out the colored form believed that the typical president would do nothing—being unaware of what happened or unwilling to confront the sales manager on a personal matter—while fewer than half the men voted this way. (The white form data appears in parentheses.)

In thinking that the typical president would do nothing, most of the women chose avoidance of confrontation as the motivation, while most men selected ignorance as the reason for inactivity. Women, it seems, tend to think that male executives take an uninvolved stance even when they know what is happening (and even when it is addressed in the guidelines). "Unless women make an issue of harassment, management will be more than willing to bury their collective heads and say they have no

problem," wrote a 31-year-old female manager of training and development in a petrochemical services company.

This assumption by women of how male executives will behave reveals itself in another vignette. We described a scene in an elevator where a male executive makes a remark about a female occupant's body to another male executive (Exhibit 3, part B). In the white form one man was senior; in the colored form the two executives were peers.

Of the women who answered the colored questionnaire, 41 percent asserted that the second executive, the peer, would share the first's amusement, while only 14 percent of the men chose this option. On the white form, 23 percent of the women decided that the senior executive would join in the joke, while only 7 percent of the men said that he would find the remark amusing. Instead, 37 percent of the men who filled out the white form asking them what the senior executive would do said he would express verbal disapproval when alone with the other executive (option f). In contrast, the prime choice of men who returned the colored form asking what the peer executive would do was option c, where he would remain silent.

Given the same facts, men and women expect vastly different reactions from senior executives and even from two peer males together. On both forms, "share the joke" received more votes from women than any other choice. Here is a representative view from a 32-year-old female manager of customer services in a large insurance company: "Our CEO thinks sexual innuendo, risqué jokes, and flirtations are a natural part of male-female relationships inside and outside the office."

We wonder whether the disparity in perception stems from women's cynicism or from their realism. Are things really as bad as women think? Are the men who answered our questions realistic or are they unaware?

In another vignette, we asked readers who got the white forms to say what they would do if confronted by a female secretary complaining about unwanted advances from a boss (Exhibit 3, part C). In the colored form, a woman executive complained.

The responses to this vignette clearly show that women take harassment more seriously than men. In the case of the secretary, almost two thirds of the female respondents voted to inform the boss that if his behavior continues, it will harm his career—while only 48 percent of the men selected that action. (In response to a question about the impact of harassment on the workplace, 75 percent of the women had "quitting or firing" as one choice, while 62 percent of the men selected that severe outcome.)

The responses to this vignette also reveal perceived differential treatment of executive women and secretaries. Women disapprove of the activity slightly more when the victim is a secretary (40 percent) than when she is an executive (36 percent). One quarter of all our respondents would express their disapproval to the secretary's boss, while one fifth would do so on behalf of the executive. If secretaries are unprotected, executive women are even more so, although more respondents say they would give advice on how to deal with the behavior to executives than to secretaries (11 percent to 6 percent).

Whatever the sources of this difference, it crops up again. In another vignette, the white form featured a male executive and the colored form a female, receiving unwanted advances from a client of the opposite sex. When asked to rate what the typical division head would do, the male and female respondents differ sharply in their answers (see Exhibit 3, part D).

In both variants, most male readers assume that the typical manager would advise the executive—whether male or female—to handle the client with tact, regardless of the consequences. Most women, on the other hand (perhaps reasoning that the typical division head would regard the client as more important than the employee), believe that the boss would encourage the male executive to parry the advances and, most important, would offer to transfer the female from the account before doing anything else.

If we look at the order of options that our female respondents think a typical division manager would choose in the case of a woman executive, we see a discouraging picture of how much support women think management will give them in the face of sexual harassment. Rather than buttress them with a team (their next-to-last choice), back them regardless of the consequences, or encourage them to parry the advance, women assume that the division managers would want to transfer them. Whether women fear this most as the outcome or base their opinions on personal experience, their perceptions of how management would act should ring alarms for top officers.

What Can a Woman Handle?

Do men and women hold different views on how women should or can deal with sexual advances? Women disagree among themselves here. Some think that women, to survive in the business world, have to handle whatever comes their way. A 43-year-old female office manager in a small transportation company wrote: "Women should stop feeling sorry or deprived, trying to play both sides to get the career they want, and act more like business people—as men do. Furthermore, the so-called liberated women are probably the ones who are causing this commotion after all. It would be better for everyone if women would start acting more like people."

Other women think that harassment within organizations is too much for any person to handle alone. The following comment by a 34-year-old administrative assistant in an average-sized consumer services company is representative of many made by women: "In every incident in my organization, every woman has been fired, encouraged to resign or transfer, or demoted. Never has a man been in any way disciplined or punished for sexual harassment. Even when a complaint is won, the work situation continues to be uncomfortable. It is far easier to change jobs."

We asked our readers whether "a smart woman employee ought to have no trouble handling an unwanted sexual approach." Fifty-nine percent of the women disagree or partly disagree and the same proportion of men agree or partly agree. Men seem to think that women can overcome sexual overtures through tact, as in the vignettes of the female executive with the client (Exhibit 3, part D) and the female executive and the secretary who complain about their bosses' advances (part C). In other words, it's her problem. That fewer women chose sanctions against the two female executives' bosses than against the secretary's boss indicates that some women think female executives *should* be able to or can handle more.

Most women are less sure that they can deal with an unwanted sexual approach and, in fact, they wonder whether *anything* they do would make them safe from such behavior in the workplace. A full 78 percent of them disagree with the statement, "If a woman dresses and behaves properly, she will not be the target of unwanted sexual approaches at work."

The same proportion of women, however, agree or partly agree with the statement, "Women can and often do use their sexual attractiveness to their own advantage" (compared with 86 percent of the men). As one woman who is a 55-year-old supervisor in a large financial institution noted: "Although I do not side with sexual harassment from *any* source at the office, many young women invite this sort of response by their behavior and the type of clothing they wear. Whether it is intentional makes little difference. When dealing with the human factor, you (male or female) should know what can happen and avoid it on the job."

Although we cannot assume that the opposite of the statement—"If a woman dresses and behaves properly, she will not be the target of unwanted sexual approaches at work"—is true, the strong female disagreement with it indicates that women feel vulnerable on the issue. If they cannot avoid unwanted advances themselves, what is the manager's duty here? What do our respondents and the top managers among them think about managerial responsibility?

How Much Can a Manager Know?

In dealing with the ambiguity in part A of Exhibit 3—where the company president finds the sales manager standing very close to his secretary, who looks upset and flustered—63 percent of high-level managers who answered the white form said they would "suggest to the sales manager that even the appearance of sexual behavior was unwise." On the colored form, 42 percent indicated that the typical president would choose that option. However, 30 percent of this latter group feel that the typical president would do nothing because they think the executive would be ignorant of the facts or their importance—or of the EEOC guidelines.

Although top managers are convinced that they themselves *would* do something, apparently many people see real problems for most presidents in reacting to the ambiguity. Also, most think top managers are in no position to know about misconduct if it occurs; half of them disagree with the statement, "A good manager will know if it's happening in his or her department." Not surprisingly, lower-level managers and women are in even greater disagreement (56 percent for both groups).

The 27 percent of top managers filling out the white form who pleaded ignorance about part A of Exhibit 3 by marking option a—doing nothing, not knowing what had happened—were playing it very safe considering that they also had option c—suggesting to the sales manager that even the appearance of sexual behavior was unwise. This situation may or may not be harassment, but it should be confronted regardless.

Do women and lower-ranking managers—who may have heard of and observed much more sexual harassment than men and upper-level managers—really know how difficult it is for top managers to be aware of the problem? Does high-level management deceive itself about the difficulty of detecting abusive behavior? Are top managers aware mainly of the grosser forms and less knowledgeable about the daily "accepted" forms that annoy our female readers?

In part D of Exhibit 3, in which the executive faces unwanted advances from the client, top managers' first choice (43 percent) was a tactful response, when a woman is the object of the advances. Lower-level managers also selected tact first (34 percent)

but spread themselves much more evenly among the other options.

Given that two thirds of high-level executives agree or partly agree that the reported amount of sexual harassment at work is greatly exaggerated, it might follow that for the *perceived* seriousness of the problem, "tact" would be a sufficient response. But since so many of our women respondents think tact is insufficient, what can a manager do? Will the new EEOC guidelines solve the problem? Should company policies and procedures address directly the subtler, varied, and more covert forms of misconduct that (although covered by the guidelines) are difficult to take action on or prove? If so, which policies would work?

EEOC Guidelines & Company Policies

"The guidelines will be hard to implement because of 41,000 years of habit." (male)

"We have several store managers involved with women and harassment issues. We have a company policy which allows managers who find the need to transfer to another unit. Counseling is available. We don't want to lose people, but if a harassment charge is proven correct, we terminate that management person. Within the last year we have had to terminate three managers for harassment. Interestingly, the problem continues to plague us. Heart-to-heart, man-to-man talks, policy statements, and a proven corporate response have been no visible deterrent." (male)

"I do not know of a significant incident of sexual harassment at the company recently. The issue came up at seminars on male-female relationships run by the company in January and February 1980—much to the surprise of most males attending (including me). The general issue was problems of atmosphere—sexual remarks, innuendo, etc. As a result, management took a clear position on proper behavior at a series of meetings of all management personnel. I believe the situation has improved, but is is not the type of problem that is ever going to be solved by one action or policy." (male)

"This is a middle-western conservative work force, stable, with little turnover, and closely managed [20,000-plus employees]. Any individual having a problem could quickly and easily get support through peer relationships or by contacting another manager. Any manager demonstrating such immaturity and insecurity would immediately find his career declining and would be told the reason. This would be done without publicity." (male)

"Women would have to be brought under a new and stricter dress code." (male)

As one might expect, the degree to which people see the EEOC rules as reasonable and necessary correlates closely with the degree to which they think sexual misbehavior is a problem at work. Exhibit 4 shows opinions on the guidelines.

In their comments many respondents maintain that, while the guidelines are reasonable in theory, it is unreasonable to expect much success in implementing them. These people consider them vague and unworkable because so much male-female interaction is ambiguous, private, and varied.

A 31-year-old man who manages special projects in a small trade association observed: "Too much of whatever harassment and/or sexual activity that occurs between employees is subject to interpretation. While employees who are clearly harassing

others can be disciplined, I suspect that clear-cut cases will be hard to identify or prove."

Consistent with their perception of the seriousness of the problem, most male managers (68 percent) think the guidelines will be "not difficult" to implement. Others expressed concern that the guidelines will "become a crutch for disgruntled employees." Asserted a 35-year-old advertising promotion manager for a very large manufacturer of consumer goods, "It could be used as a smoke screen to defend against legitimate performance reviews."

Unforgettable Quotes

"My department is financial, rather staid. The creative side of the business might well be rife with cases of sexual harassment." (female)

"I married a subordinate. I believe there was no coercion involved." (male)

"Have not had any experience in this area. Too busy working." (male)

"I have never been harassed but I would welcome the opportunity." (anonymous)

"I filled this out with my personnel manager, who is a female (and I harassed her to give me the answers I wanted)." (male)

"I know of no such incidents; two of our top four managers are active churchgoers." (male)

"I am very nearsighted, so when I look at someone (male or female) I give the appearance of staring or ogling. What do I do?" (male)

A number of the men agree with a 44-year-old CEO who declared that his bank

Exhibit 4   Opinions on whether the EEOC Guidelines Are Reasonable and Necessary and whether They Will Be Difficult to Adjust to

	Highly Reasonable, Very Necessary	Reasonable, Necessary	Reasonable, Unnecessary	Unreasonable, Very Unnecessary	Not Difficult
Total	15%	57%	16%	7%	63%
Male	5	51	27	11	68
Female	27	64	4	2	58
Top management	9	44	27	14	69
Middle management	13	59	17	6	64
Lower management	19	62	11	4	61

could "take care of misconduct without government snoopervision." Even more men (and a few women) expressed sentiments like the following from the 40-year-old personnel director of a large health care enterprise: "The guidelines are procedurally okay, but people are reluctant to change deep-seated, culturally reinforced attitudes."

Replies to a question on company policies again show how lack of experience with them, as much as experience, affects opinions on the issue. For instance, although 68 percent of the men and 58 percent of the women think the EEOC guidelines will not be difficult to implement, few work for companies that have any rules governing harassment. As Exhibit 5 shows, a significant gap also exists between what most people favor as policy and what their organizations actually have. (Implementing such rules can sometimes mitigate corporate liability but is not an absolute defense as far as individual liability is concerned.)

The policies listed in Exhibit 5 received substantial support, except for the management statement disapproving of office flirtations. The lukewarm reception for this is consistent with the concern, expressed by younger people particularly, over legislation against love affairs and condemnation

of camaraderie. Elsewhere, some 20 percent of the sample expressed neutrality, rather than agreement or disagreement, on the statement, "A little flirtation makes the workday more interesting." The 51-year-old male vice president of a large company wrote, "I do not favor any legislative attempts to interfere with natural female-male forms of communication. Vive la différence!"

Judging from many comments, smaller organizations rely more on peer pressure and informal controls to deal with misbehavior. Since such organizations, in general, do not suffer from the impersonal atmosphere of those with thousands of workers, they perhaps feel less need for written and formally enunciated rules. (Whether they ought to is another issue.) Wrote the male president of a professional service firm with fewer than 50 employees, "We wouldn't tolerate sexual harassment any more than we would lying or theft. However, we don't have formal procedures for dealing with any of these forms of misconduct."

That many companies fail to communicate to employees the directives they do have is clear from the responses. And we found a significant difference in men's and women's opinions as to whether their com-

Exhibit 5   Opinions on Company Policies

		Do You Favor This Policy?	Does Your Company Have This Policy?
A.	A management statement to all employees disapproving of sexual harassment.	73%	29%
B.	A management statement disapproving of office flirtations, even when mutual.	28	9
C.	Developing appropriate sanctions for sexual harassers.	68	17
D.	Orientation programs to make all new employees aware of company policy on sexual behavior at work.	59	13
E.	Developing materials—employee manuals, films, and so forth—to make all employees aware of this issue.	44	8
F.	A management directive that asks each department head to take responsibility for preventing sexual harassment in his or her department.	68	16

panies even have certain policies. The difference is described in the following table (the letters refer to the list in Exhibit 5).

	Percent of Respondents Who Say Their Company Has This Policy	
Policy	Men	Women
A	33%	25%
C	20	14
D	15	11
F	19	14

Why this difference? Do respondents really understand whether the policy exists, or have some answered according to their perception of whether the policy is working? Women, who are predominantly in the lower echelons of organizations, may not know what company policy is—especially the sanctions developed for sexual harassers (policy A) and management directives asking department heads to take responsibility for preventing harassment (policy F). And managers may just assume that the policies exist or are working.

Which policies and approaches work? Which really promote an understanding of harassment, its damaging effects on employees, and its divisiveness? And which support women and men in their stands against such abuse? Here are respondents' suggestions:

• Make known, in a firm but subdued manner, the chief executive's attitude about sexual misconduct.

• Install an all-purpose procedure, bypassing any union channels, that allows people to voice their concerns—including complaints of harassment—confidentially.

• Hold in-house consciousness-raising seminars to inform managers of the consequences of misbehavior.

• Assign responsibility for cases of harassment to a high-level person—a vice president or assistant to the chief executive. This person should be seen to have the ear and respect of senior management and have credibility in other issues as well.

• Foster strong peer relationships among women employees.

• Encourage women to confront harassers by letter, after a confidential consultation with an appropriate officer of the company.

The last suggestion is clearly crucial because no enunciated or implied policies, however firmly and evenly applied, can be effective unless victims attack the problem themselves. Also, the situations are so varied that they need individual responses. Sometimes harassment calls for forthright action, such as that recommended by the 56-year-old female treasurer of a small manufacturer of industrial goods: "I have been in the work force for 40 years and find that the female visual and verbal attitude of 'hands off' works. When I was an airline stewardess in 1946, I perfected a devastating hands-off look that still works today. 'Develop the look' is my advice to my daughters and employees."

At other times, a casual confrontation is more appropriate and effective. A 33-year-old woman, the general manager of a management consulting firm, wrote, "My boss has a habit of making sexual innuendos and jokes to female managers. We have not filed a complaint but have instead raised his consciousness. We immediately offer to take him up on his suggestion. I've said, 'Okay,

let's get on with it if you're that hot to trot.' He is generally a good guy and this embarrasses him and improves his behavior."

Numbers of men indicate that they don't know "where the line is"—don't know when a joke that is funny to them is offensive to women. They believe it is up to women to tell men when a remark is not funny. In our opinion, by failing to take action right away, the woman risks letting the harasser think that it is welcome. Before women feel safe enough to speak up, however, managers must promote a supportive atmosphere through enforced company policies that make clear what behavior is not permitted.

A Complex Problem

"A lot of women hesitate to report sexual harassment because women: (1) don't think they'll be believed; (2) will be punished by smaller raises or cruddy jobs; (3) will be ostracized by male and female employees; (4) will be accused of inviting the advance; (5) have guilt feelings that perhaps it was invited subconsciously; (6) fear publicity; (7) are unsure exactly what is harassment and what is just interaction of people." (female)

The problem is not just an artificiality created by the numbers and the varying responses to our probing; it is real. We give the last word to the 37-year-old director of communications for a large financial institution. She wrote:

"Sexual harassment is corporate rape and, as with rape on the streets, many people see the victim as responsible. Most of the time the victim who complains falls under suspicion and is thought of as 'dingy.'

"Our company has a formal complaint

system that allows employees to take problems to the chairman of the board without retribution. This procedure should be adequate to deal with complaints of sexual harassment, but it is not. It puts the burden of action on the victim, forcing her to complain and continue complaining until something is done.

"Always the 'real world' issue surfaces. Women can't expect protection from confrontations that are offensive to them in one way or another. Can we hope to achieve in the workplace what we have never been able to achieve anywhere else in society? Women have to take responsibility for managing the conflicts in their lives. Most of us do.

"Something that occurred in my office illustrates the problem for women and managers. A male employee who worked for me recently resigned his position. After he left, four women came forward and complained about his sexual overtures, which included statements about his ability to help them in their jobs. One of the women reported directly to him. All four had handled the situation deftly themselves.

"The story points up a serious issue. If no one complains how can management know? Here I sit, a female executive appalled by the idea of sexual harassment, while a male manager who reported to me was practicing it. (All of this is complicated, of course, by the fact that what one woman thinks is sexual harassment, another may never notice.)

"Some evidence exists that the situation is changing but, regardless, I think it is extremely difficult for a man to understand the demanding nature of sexual harassment to a woman and to investigate it objectively. Men don't understand what it is, and I find this to be true without exception. It is hard to recognize something as negative when it has been part of your own way of thinking, and harassment has survived in corporate locker room attitudes for a long time.

"A man's view will always be colored by the way he behaves toward women and what he finds acceptable. . . . I do not mean to malign the motives of men, but simply to say they cannot understand what they have never experienced or been educated about. The more we women educate them, the better they'll be able to deal with this subject."

Appendix: The Legal Context

by Grace L. Mastalli*

The law provides a variety of means by which victims of sexual harassment in the workplace can seek redress through legal action against their employers, directly against the harassers, or (as is often the case) against both.

Title VII

The primary basis for action against employers is Title VII of the 1964 Civil Rights Act (as amended), which prohibits discrimination on the basis of sex in employment and provides the

---

* Grace L. Mastalli, a lawyer, is senior associate of the Law and Public Management Program, National Institute of Education. She is also a member of the employment discrimination committee of the Women's Legal Defense Fund.

legal authority for the final interpretive guidelines on sexual harassment issued by the EEOC.[1] The final guidelines provide that:

"Unwelcome sexual advances, requests for sexual favors, and other verbal or physical conduct of a sexual nature constitute sexual harassment when (1) submission to such conduct is made either explicitly or implicitly a term or condition of an individual's employment, (2) submission to or rejection of such conduct by an individual is used as the basis for employment decisions affecting such individual, or (3) such conduct has the purpose or effect of unreasonably interfering with an individual's work performance or creating an intimidating, hostile, or offensive working environment."

The guidelines impose absolute liability on employers for the acts of supervisors regardless of whether the conduct was known to, or authorized or forbidden by, the particular employer.

The standard of employer liability for the acts of coworkers is somewhat less stringent. An employer is responsible for such acts if the employer knew, or should have known, of the conduct in question—unless the employer can demonstrate that it took immediate and appropriate action to correct the problem on learning of it.

Similarly, under the guidelines an employer may be liable for acts in the workplace committed by nonemployees if the employer knew, or should have known, of the conduct and failed to take appropriate corrective action. Moreover, a controversial section of the guidelines states that an employer may be held liable for sex discrimination against qualified third parties who have been denied opportunities or benefits granted to another who provided sexual favors to a mutual supervisor.

In addition to establishing standards for imposing liability, the guidelines make employers responsible for developing programs to prevent sexual misconduct in the workplace. The elements of an adequate prevention program are not specified, but they would probably include the adoption and dissemination of a strong policy statement prohibiting sexual harassment, presentation of the subject in employee training materials and orientation sessions, and development and publication of procedures for handling complaints in the organization—including a range of sanctions and remedies and information about employee rights.

Under the guidelines, an employer must also thoroughly investigate all complaints alleging sexual harassment and all instances potentially constituting harassment that come to the employer's attention through means other than formal complaints. Following an investigation, an employer is required to take immediate and appropriate corrective action to remedy any illegality detected and prevent its recurrence. Failure to do so constitutes a violation of Title VII as interpreted by the EEOC.

Although the guidelines in and of themselves lack the force of law, the courts accorded them some weight while they were still in interim form, and courts are likely to rely on them substantially in the future. In fact, to a large extent the guidelines only restate and amplify the evolving line of Title VII cases establishing employer liability for the sexual harassment of employees by other employees. For example, in a leading Title VII case on the issue of employer liability, *Miller v. Bank of America,* the U.S. Court of Appeals for the Ninth Circuit held an employer to be liable for the sexually harassing acts of its supervisors, even if the company has a policy prohibiting such conduct and even if the victim did not formally notify the employer of the problem.[2]

This is also the standard articulated by the guidelines. However, in the provisions concerning any conduct that is offensive, conduct by coworkers and nonemployees, and third-party rights in

---

[1] "Guidelines on Discrimination on the Basis of Sex" (Washington, D.C.: Equal Employment Opportunity Commission, November 10, 1980).

[2] 600 F.2d 211 (1979).

the guidelines, the EEOC went beyond what the courts had established as harassment constituting sex discrimination under Title VII. Pending further litigation, it is difficult to assess whether the courts will adopt or qualify the EEOC's broad assignment of liability for and liberal definition of sexual harassment. However, in what may be a bellwether case, the guidelines recently received significant support from the U.S. Court of Appeals in Washington, D.C. In January 1981, the court ruled in effect that sexual harassment in and of itself is a violation of Title VII. The court said that the law does not require the victim to prove she resisted harassment and was penalized for the resistance. According to the decision in *Bundy* v. *Jackson*, employers are liable for sexual harassment in the workplace because it creates an offensive "discriminatory environment" by "poisoning the atmosphere of employment."

(Incidentally, employer reliance on the guidelines provides a defense to charges of discrimination where the acts of alleged discrimination were taken in reliance on the EEOC's interpretation.)

Civil suits

Victims of sexual harassment are not limited to a Title VII cause of action; they may combine the sex discrimination claim with other civil charges against an employer in order to obtain a more extensive remedy and/or damages. Common law doctrines on assault, battery, and intentional infliction of distress—as well as actions for breach of contract—may be used to establish employer liability for sexual harassment in some circumstances where the elements of a *prima facie* Title VII case may be lacking.

The wide range of compensatory relief, including damages, available through common law actions, combined with what may be more easily met standards of proof, has encouraged victims of employment-related harassment to seek recovery directly from their harassers and, under the tort law doctrine of *respondeat superior*, to hold employers liable for the misconduct of their workers. (*Respondeat superior* is the theory that an employer is liable for all the acts of an employee committed "within the scope of employment.")

Case law suggests that the courts may broadly construe what constitutes "the scope of employment" in order to establish employer liability for acts of sexual harassment. In such cases, however, some damages could be mitigated by the existence of a strong employer-sponsored harassment prevention program.

Sexual harassment that results in the wrongful dismissal of the victim and economic loss may also provide the basis for a suit against the employer for interference with an employment contract or breach of contract. In such cases an employer may be liable for back pay and conceivably even for damages awarded for mental suffering that the harassment causes. (As a rule, courts do not award damages for mental suffering in breach of contract actions unless the breach is of such a kind that serious emotional disturbance is to be expected or likely.)

Similarly, although litigation of this issue is not complete, employers may be subject to liability for breach of contract involving sexual harassment in instances where the victim is unable to demonstrate the degree of harm required under tort law.

Criminal actions

An extreme instance of sexual harassment in the workplace may also constitute a criminal offense—ranging from criminal assault and battery to self-exposure to rape or other sexual assault—and may subject the perpetrator to prosecution. The nature of such actions varies with state jurisdiction but normally would not involve employer liability. Under certain circumstances and in some jurisdictions, however, employers may be subject to civil liability related to such criminal actions for failing to provide a safe and secure work environment.

Summary

The combination of Title VII, as broadly construed by the EEOC, and the availability of a wide range of other civil actions provides a multitude of ways to establish employer liability for sexual harassment in the workplace. The courts can fashion remedies involving substantial victim compensation for harassment without making a finding of discrimination. Moreover, the flexibility afforded by this combination means that one or more claims against the employer could emerge from the factual circumstances surrounding almost any charge of work-related sexual harassment.

The employer's sole protection against liability is prevention of harassment. In those cases where prevention proves impossible, the employer's actions will, at least under common law, help limit damages.

READING 3
DUAL CAREERS—HOW DO COUPLES AND COMPANIES COPE WITH THE PROBLEMS?*
Francine S. Hall and Douglas T. Hall

Two years ago, a personnel vice president for one of the world's largest international banks was asked, "What does your bank do about dual-career couples?" "Nothing," was the reply. "That's their problem."

A few months later a female officer in this bank with the potential to go all the way to the top married a male officer with whom she had lived for several years. The bank had a nepotism rule that forbade two people in the same family to be officers, and this young, highly valued couple was in clear violation of this policy. (Ironically, as long as they were living together, everything was fine so far as the bank was concerned.) Therefore, one of them had to leave. But whom? The couple decided the woman (who was the more highly rated of the pair) should go. But the bank had been under suit by a women's group for sex discrimination in higher management positions, and

the loss of this woman was costly indeed. As a result of this policy, the bank's nepotism rule was relaxed to permit relatives to be officers, so long as one would not be in a supervisory relationship over the other.

For reasons such as this, today the question of who is responsible for dealing with dual careers elicits a different response from that of the personnel vice president above. Most firms, uncertain about *what* to do, still know they have to do something about employees in dual-career families. As one executive put it, "We're losing some damn good people!"

Increasing numbers of two-career couples have changed the composition, values, and mobility patterns of the workforce. (By "two-career couple" we mean a couple, either married or living together, who are both employed.) The consequence of dual-career couples is that traditional personnel policies and practices are no longer adequate to meet the changing needs and problems presented by many employees.

In this paper we will attempt to show how companies can begin to deal with these needs and problems. We will address four issues:

1. What are the typical characteristics and conflicts of couples at different life/career stages?

* Reprinted, by permission of the publisher, from *Organizational Dynamics*, Spring 1978, pp. 57–77. © 1978 by AMACOM, a division of American Management Associations. All rights reserved.

2. What is the impact of career couples on the organization?

3. What are the necessary ingredients for managing two careers?

4. How can companies develop an effective strategy for dealing with the two-career couple?

Much of our learning to date comes from group interviews and workshops during the last two years with more than 300 people from Chicago, New York, and Washington.

Where couple careers conflict, the loss is not always the one you might expect. In a Chicago bank a rising young man resigned after the birth of a first child so his wife could resume *her* highly successful career. Since bank policy did not allow him to take a leave of absence, the bank had to let him go.

Among employees remaining with their companies there are other problems. At the management level one of the biggest problems presented by the two-career couple is refusal to relocate. The traditional pattern of corporate advancement through mobility is facing greater resistance than ever before. According to a study conducted by the New York firm of Gilbert Tweed Associates, one in three executives can't or won't relocate because it would interfere with the careers or studies of their spouses.

At lower levels the issues are different but no less problematic. Scheduling, overtime, and transferring people to different shifts often meet with similar resistance. Behind the resistance we find conflicts with the spouse's job and the demands of managing two careers while sharing home and family roles.

Why the Trend?

Behind the increase in dual-career couples are two social phenomena: a rapid increase in the number of (married) women in the workforce and a shift in values. People are moving away from the traditional success ethic and toward a "quality of life" ethic. Two incomes may be an economic necessity for many couples, but it is also the key to liberation and new life/career choices.

According to the latest statistics, more than half of all mothers with children under the age of three are in the workforce. Based on Labor Department statistics, we find that 57.7 percent of all working women are married and living with employed spouses. This represents more than 46 million employed men and women (out of 98 million people in the American workforce) who are part of two-career couples.

Indeed, the economic significance of the two-career couple is reflected in Peter Drucker's claim that working wives are the reason consumers aren't "behaving" properly. (During the last few "recessionlike" years, while unemployment and economic uncertainty were high, spending on luxury items such as Cadillac Sevilles, chartered vacation travel, and large homes hit record levels.) Drucker explains this economic paradox as follows (*The Wall Street Journal*, December 1, 1976):

> The husband is still considered the breadwinner, and his income is used for normal household purposes. The wife's income averages 60 percent of the husband's, and is used for "extras." Her money provides the margin for a bigger house, the luxury car, the expensive vacation. But the household spending pattern, based on the husband's income, remains sensitive to consumer confidence and to expectations about job security and income.

Most demographers agree that the influx of women into the workforce can be attributed to at least three forces: economic necessity; search for personal fulfillment outside the home; and technological improvements in the kitchen as well as the bedroom. With the annual rate of inflation for the basic necessities of food, shelter, energy, and health 44 percent greater than the rate of inflation for nonnecessities, a second income is essential in many homes. Women who once worked only until the couple could save a down payment or have a baby now continue working to meet mortgage payments and clothe the kids.

For many other couples, however, the end is not money but professional growth, advancement, and recognition. Meeting these goals takes a heavy commitment of time and energy, and organizational demands may conflict with home/work and personal/family roles.

For some couples, the combined income derived from two working partners brings the security that allows them to pursue what Douglas Hall refers to as the "protean career," a career directed by the person rather than the company and whose driving force is self-fulfillment. Traditionally, in the "organizational career," career tracks, moves, and choices were dictated by corporate needs, opportunities, and policies. Today, many people are exercising more personal choice in making career decisions. They may turn down a promotion or resign from a job that is unsatisfying or incongruent with personal goals and family member needs. For some people, it represents an opportunity to get off the treadmill. For others, it offers the choice of never getting on.

Whether a couple is motivated by economic need or personal and professional fulfillment, organizations are preparing for a new breed of employee. We find this employee to be one who faces conflicts with which he or she is usually unprepared to cope.

The personal issues faced by the dual-career couple, however, are not separate from the career issues each faces as a member of an organization. Our research has found that personal and company concerns interact on how the organization can and will function in the future. Corporate efforts to select, recruit, develop, train, relocate, and promote are all directly affected. To understand how organizations can cope with these problems, let us first consider some typical two-career couples. We are finding that the issues raised by dual careers are different from couples in different career stages. Therefore, we will examine some couples who are representative of their respective career stages.

Early Career Stages

Profile I. A Couple at Entry. Anne and Mark never thought much about getting a job. The key to a successful career seemed to be getting an MBA. After a year into their program at Northwestern they decided to get married—and panic! Alone, each knew he or she had tremendous potential on the job market and could pick the best offer from among many. As a couple, they wondered if they would be a liability to each other and to a company. They dreaded facing corporate recruiters and wondered if they would ever find jobs together.

However, Anne and Mark were not alone. When they realized that other couples in the program were equally concerned and unprepared, they organized a problem-solving session and "brainstormed" a number of practical ideas. Since Anne's major was more specialized and Mark's (accounting) gave him great mobility, their strategy was to go where her opportunities were the best, knowing that he would be able to locate almost anywhere. They eventually had several good options to choose from and are now off to a good start with major companies.

Profile II. Advancing Careers. Bob and Barbara brought us a different problem. After finishing their degrees, both landed jobs with firms headquartered in the Southwest. He is in a management training program with an oil company. She holds a staff position in the personnel department of a large national service organization. Given that dual-career couples are a relatively recent phenomenon, problems at early career stages tend to catch them unprepared. They have to worry about each of them entering the job market and about conflicts that arise as they follow their separate career paths. They have been in their jobs for a year. Today, Barbara is pregnant and Bob faces the prospect of a field assignment lasting at least a year. "Barb plans to continue her career," he told us. "Her career is very important to her. It's important to me. She shouldn't *have* to give it up."

Barb's chances to advance in her company are good if she stays in the city they live in now, but Bob knows his advancement is tied to moving through a variety of assignments in different locations. Had he and Barb planned how they would handle this? Had he talked to anyone in his company about his concerns? The answer to both questions was "No!" He was worried that his concern about their two careers would be interpreted as a lack of personal ambition and an unwillingness to make personal sacrifices for his own career.

Common Characteristics. Although these two couples are at slightly different career stages, they share many similarities. They also share the characteristics of many pro-

fessional couples we have counseled who are in early career stages. What are these early career characteristics? Typically, these characteristics often include:

1. *Similar career stage needs.* For both partners, the need to develop skills and contacts and gain broad experience in the firm often means traveling, relocations, long hours, and a high degree of job involvement. For each the job is top priority.

2. *Conflicting career path alternatives.* The best opportunity for each, in terms of advancing his or her career, may mean locating or moving in different directions geographically.

3. *High degree of commitment to career goals.* Both partners usually have a drive to make it. Because of this, they understand the other's commitment to career. That doesn't lessen the intensity of their own commitment, however.

4. *Lack of preparation.* Most couples seem to possess little information about managing two careers or what lies ahead if they plan to have a family. Many have no plans and haven't thought through what they will do if faced with a conflict, a crisis, or a baby.

5. *Lack of experience in conflict resolution.* For many people, the conflict over a first job or relocation is their first experience in working on problems together. Their problem-solving skills may be rigid, and they often perceive the situation in terms of "my career versus yours."

6. *Fear or reluctance to approach the company.* Many couples are afraid to discuss their problems with a boss or superior in the firm for fear it will reflect negatively on them and their chances. They tend to see company policies as rigid (whether or not they actually are) and to accept corporate alternatives as "givens" without testing their assumptions.

7. *Personal flexibility*. When pushed, most young couples seem willing to explore life alternatives that fall out of the traditional way of managing a family or marriage. Living apart, long-distance commuting, "taking turns," and so on, are viewed as viable, if not always desirable, ways of taking care of both partners' needs over time.

Mid-Career Stages

What about the couple at mid-career? Its crises are no less acute, just different.

Profile III. Established versus Delayed Career Needs. Jerry and Pat decided to follow his career opportunities, since his degree put him in a visible and high-demand position. After a couple of moves, during which she took jobs out of her field, they had a baby and settled into a city they both loved. He was a rising young star, and she was still trying to patch together odd jobs. When the organization he had left offered both of them jobs in their fields, his present employer panicked. Even though Jerry wanted to stay where he was, the job offer also had a new twist—*spouse bargaining*. Turning down the offer would mean turning off his wife's chances to pursue a career in her field at last. According to Jerry, it was "Pat's turn."

Unlike the couples described above, however, Jerry and Pat went to his employer with the problem, a clear set of goals, and an acceptable solution—helping Pat to find a position in the area. His employer, not wanting to lose him, was relieved to be asked to help—and did. He contacted several local organizations and put Pat in touch with employers who were able to use her skills on a part-time basis. In the end, Pat had two local offers, and the couple stayed. Interviewing them later, we found that Pat felt an increased loyalty to Jerry's employer because of his efforts.

Profile IV. Two Established Careers and a Family. For Mary and John the problem was different. As assistant regional commissioner of a government bureau, she was comfortably settled with three children and a successful husband. But their career problems, according to her, went "way back." He had left a job in one location to join her and get married, then went back to school. Along the way, she had turned down offers in the auto industry as well as a commissioner's job because the location wouldn't offer John much opportunity in his field. As Mary put it, "If the place had no opportunities for him, I wouldn't even consider it." Meanwhile, he regularly turned down jobs in small towns that wouldn't be near the large cities that might offer her a government transfer. When he returned to school again to work on an MBA, he jokingly told her. "Now you're grounded for two years."

A year later she was approached about a commissionership in Washington. They agreed that she should pursue the opportunity, and she eventually got the offer. John had told his wife that he would be willing to stay to finish his program and then join her later. When she got the offer, "He went into a tailspin. He thought it was the end of the marriage—that I'd get all caught up in my job in Washington and lose touch with the family." Mary turned down the Washington job. Now that John has finished his MBA, he is looking for a new position, and Mary has again responded to opportunities elsewhere. She laughed at this point in the interview. "This time . . . whoever gets there first, wins."

Profile V. Multiple Careers. Ron's family problem was not two careers but several. When presented with the opportunity to move up and back to the Detroit headquarters of his auto firm, he turned it down. Not only was his wife happily settled, but his two remaining children at home were pursuing successful careers at local schools. One, a high school student, was the local drama star at a school with one of the finest programs in the country. Rather than sacrifice his family's careers, he compromised his own. Two years later, the company came back with the same offer. By this time, his son was graduating and going to college. Ron and his wife were ready to accept the move and, as she put it, "become corporate gypsies one more time."

For couples like these, mid-career also means mid-life. It is a time when family concerns take priority over one's own career. Corporations find themselves on a collision course, running head on into the established needs of spouses and children.

Common Characteristics. What are the typical traits of the mid-career couple? Our interviews have developed the following profile:

1. *Career stage needs conflict with life family needs.* In most cases, there are more than two people to think about. A spouse's career may be established beyond the point of mobility and relocation is viewed as traumatic.

2. *Alternative career paths viewed as viable.* Mid-career couples are more likely to ignore the typical career-path alternatives where they conflict, and to view saying no or forgoing one's own needs as legitimate. The company's expectations are not always central; the family's needs are.

3. *Clear couple and family goals and priorities.* People seem to have developed a sense of what is important in life and what isn't. Their goals have crystallized, and factors such as location may be as important as salary. Decisions and plans seem to be made within the parameters of family/couple goals rather than in terms of individual opportunities.

4. *Commitment to the unit.* Couples at this point seem to view themselves as a "unit" or a family. Their careers are no longer individual pursuits but are seen as a "package" or a collective, interactive arrangement. The individual is no longer committed to his or her own career alone. The commitment is now to the family.

5. *Better prepared to plan and cope.* Couples at mid-career have more experience in solving problems, planning together, and making decisions. They also possess more information about themselves, their values, their needs, their organizations, and their career options in general. They usually have fairly well-developed coping mechanisms and ways of handling conflicts.

6. *Less reluctant to approach company.* They are likely to share career concerns with the company and to approach people in the firm in an attempt to find a solution. They feel established within the company and do not see their personal or family career conflicts as a reflection on them as valuable employees.

7. *Acceptance of family as "given," career as flexible.* Career constraints are now viewed as manageable (perhaps because they are more willing to compromise). Children and established-spouse career needs are often viewed as fixed. Thus, at mid-career, personal flexibility seems to decrease while career decision flexibility increases. People are more willing to compromise themselves and the company, less willing to compromise their family.

In the examples we have given, all the couples have had viable career options backed by a strong relationship. Many of the couples we have worked with, however, present a different pattern. Take Donald and Marge, for example.

Profile VI. Mid-Career Crises versus Spouse Career Needs. After many years in Washington, Donald found himself out of a job. Marge, on the other hand, had finally established herself as a successful photographer with a strong local following. For Donald, the options were elsewhere. He accepted a position in the South, planning for Marge and the children to follow if it worked out. The job didn't turn out to be what he expected, and he realized that local living arrangements wouldn't be acceptable for his family. He quit.

When we met Donald, he was still unemployed and the couple was trying to figure out what he should do and where his many years of service in the government would be marketable. They had agreed that a large Eastern city was what they wanted. For Donald, now in his 40s, the options were not opening up. But for Marge, who had followed him around the world for many years, if she was going to have a career, it was now or never.

Donald is typical of many men faced with the necessity or desire to change jobs, career fields, and companies. Often we find that the husband's mid-career crisis coincides with the wife's reentry into the labor market. Like the early career couples, they face competing career-path needs. In most cases, however, the couple is characterized by years of "giving" on the part of the wife.

Now liberated from caring for children and realizing an awareness of their own needs, many women are unwilling to compromise—one more time. Thus we find couples on the verge of a divorce after 20 years of marriage when faced with the prospect of managing two careers for the first time at mid-life. Their old relationship, built around meeting the needs of the husband's career, cannot accommodate the wife's needs, too. She either gives up on the marriage or gives up on her needs and bows out

as "the little woman behind the successful man."

In one humorous incident we witnessed, a wife sent printed announcements to the guests who would be attending an annual reception given by her husband. The purpose? To tell them that after years of standing at his side in the receiving line she would *not* be there this year. She was proud to announce that they were getting a divorce and that she didn't have to hostess one more reception for *his* business.

While this may seem extreme, it highlights just one of the changes that working women have made on the career-related activities of spouses. Social entertaining is down, particularly at home, while the need to pitch in and help out at home is increasing. Men who used to excuse themselves from a meeting to get to a community fundraising dinner are now leaving the office to cook dinner.

For some couples, the crisis arises because the husband cannot accommodate to his wife's new work role. This was the case with Karen. As part of a blue-collar family, she found that her promotion to supervisor in a manufacturing plant was more than her husband could take. He didn't mind the fact that she could run and repair machines weighing several tons. It was when he found his wife having to go back to the plant at odd hours to deal with a problem or going out for a beer "with the boys" that their marriage faced a crisis and, ultimately, a divorce. As some companies are finding, women are willing and eager to accept nontraditional roles; their husbands are not.

Ingredients for Managing Two Careers

How do couples and corporations cope? In our interviews we have been able to identify several factors that contribute to the successful management of two careers. Many of our findings reinforce the importance of career competencies in what Donald Super calls "vocational maturity," the "readiness to cope effectively with the developmental tasks of one's life stage in relation to other people in the same life stage." What he is saying is that different life and career stages are accompanied by different conflicts, tasks, and decisions. The couple has to be able to meet these and to deal with them at each stage. Mature coping varies with life and career stage. In particular, there seem to be four critical factors in successful dual-career relationships, as identified by Rhona and Robert Rapoport in their study of British couples. Let us consider each in turn: mutual commitment to both careers; flexibility; coping mechanisms; and energy and time management.

Mutual Commitment to Both Careers. Couples who are able to sustain their relationships and their careers are people who share a mutual commitment to work and to the other's need and right to pursue a career. Ben, for example, likes to brag that his wife is a stockbroker. According to Sally, "He is very proud of the fact and enjoys pulling me into his business contacts. I enhance his position at work."

In many cases, the couple's self-concept is built around themselves as a working team. Sid and Cathy are an example. "Sid is eager to introduce me to his clients and business associates. His career is enhanced by our husband-wife team, which is unheard of in our business. Sid likes to use the phrase, 'Two heads are better than one.' " The partner's career is often viewed as an integral part of that partner as a person. Thus we find successful two-career couples much more likely to refer to each other by name— rather than as "my husband" or "my

wife"—and to identify or define each other in terms of what he or she does.

On the corporate side, commitment to a spouse's career is a new phenomenon. Although we have not measured corporate commitment to date, we find evidence that companies who are committed to helping couples resolve career conflicts have generally benefited. According to one personnel executive, "If we commit ourselves to helping them, we can usually count on two people who will be highly committed to staying with our organization. Not only do we keep good people, but a positive attitude toward the company is reinforced."

Flexibility. Two types of flexibility seem to be associated with successful career couples—personal flexibility and flexibility in the job. On the personal side, we find that the willingness and ability to shift gears, revise plans, try new ways of doing things, and consider alternatives all lead to greater adaptability to coping with couple problems.

The flexibility the job provides, however, is equally and oftentimes more important, with a payoff to both the career and the relationship. Many of the couples we interviewed had at least one spouse with a high-autonomy job. Libby and Sam are a good example. When he finished his tour of duty in the army, she, a nurse, took a job with a VA hospital to support him while he went to school. Both knew he could accept a job almost anywhere and she could follow. After he graduated, he accepted a position with a well-known hotel chain. She was easily able to transfer to the local VA hospital. Both knew that this may be the first of many such moves, but that he can stay with the chain and she can pursue her own career without leaving the VA system.

To the corporate recruiter, a flexible spouse is viewed as a definite asset. One recruiter we know beamed recently about the gold mine he had found: a top-notch woman M.B.A. with a C.P.A. spouse ". . . who is willing to hang his shingle anywhere."

For couples like these, flexibility removes the potential conflict between career-path choices. Autonomy within the job itself, however, has other advantages that contribute to coping with home/job conflicts. Thus the hourly employee who is bound to a set schedule and a time clock may have to call in sick when his children have a school holiday. Professors (in high-autonomy positions) bring their kids to the office.

Coping Mechanisms.   For the viable career couple, coping mechanisms are essential. Interestingly, we have found that no single type of coping or coping mechanism is necessarily better than another. The important thing is that the couple has worked out some means of coping with various conflicting demands. In our own case, two careers and two children presented the need to cope with child care. At different times we have used part-time help, live-in help, and day care centers. All have worked well, depending on the age of the children and the demands of our career schedules in relation to each other. The outside help, however, was the necessary mechanism. After a while, we referred to the babysitter or day-care center as "the glue in our lives."

One couple we know, both staff writers for major publications, drew up a premarital contract stating that they would cope with transfer by "taking turns." When the wife was offered a move to New York she turned it down because she didn't like the city. Is it his turn now? They aren't sure. Realizing that their contract didn't specify things like that, they are now renegotiating their agree-

ment. We asked if they would recommend a contract and they laughed—all too aware that specific conflicts are difficult to anticipate and resolve in advance. "The contract doesn't define the marriage," she replied. "It's the relationship that defines a contract."

Contracts aside, the process of working together on resolving conflicts seems to be the key. For most two-career couples, a relationship that revolves around cooperation and collaboration seems to produce both coping mechanisms and satisfaction with the arrangement. One couple we know appeared for a while to have a rather lopsided arrangement when it came to sharing domestic roles. Queried about this, the wife quickly defended her husband's contributions to the two-career marriage. She provided more domestic support, but she was quick to point out that he gave her much more emotional support. He acted as the sounding board for working through frustrations at the office. This was as necessary a coping mechanism in their two-career lives as getting the laundry done.

In one research study we found that people tend to use three distinct styles of coping with conflicts between different roles. The first, which we called *role redefinition*, involves negotiating with your role senders to change the role and make it more compatible with other responsibilities and interests. Some ways of restructuring your roles include:

• Simply agreeing with role senders that you will not be able to engage in certain activities. (For example, in our community, a hotbed of volunteerism, we are both known as "spot-jobbers." We will accept specific, one-shot volunteer jobs, but we will not accept continuing positions.)

• Enlisting assistance in role activities from other family members or from people outside the family (for example, cleaning or babysitting help).

• Engaging in collaborative problem solving with role senders (boss, spouse, children).

• Integrating careers by working with the spouse or working in related fields (so that the two careers become more like one). Lotte Bailyn refers to this method of coping as "linking up."

Not surprisingly, these activities, which in effect reduce role conflicts by stopping them where they originate—in the environment—are associated with high levels of satisfaction and happiness in the people we studied. They are proactive, collaborative responses to role conflicts, and integrate the careers:

> Most important to me has been the rewarding experience of working with my husband. Observing him in his executive capacity, besides as a father and husband, I have come to understand him and appreciate him even more. (I also understand why his business trips are necessary and why he is working so late. . . .)

The second style of coping was *personal reorientation*, changing one's own attitudes about various roles and doing what was personally seen as most important. Some examples are:

• Establishing priorities. ("A child with a high fever takes precedence over school obligations. A child with sniffles does not. A very important social engagement—especially one that is business related—precedes the tennis.")

• Partitioning and separating roles. Devoting full attention to a given role when in it and not thinking about other roles (for example, "not bringing my work home, so home can be devoted to family and their needs").

• Ignoring or overlooking less important role expectations (for example, dusting).

• Rotating attention from one role to another as demands arise. Letting one role slide a bit if another needs more attention at the time.

• Seeing self-fulfillment and personal interests as a valid source of role demands. ("I chose leisure occupations to balance responsibilities—piano and organ playing, singing for release from being tied down when children are small.")

This style of coping means changing yourself rather than the family or work environment, although personal reorientation may be a necessary step to take before you can accomplish real role redefinition; you need to be relatively unconflicted about what you expect of yourself before you can change other people's expectations of you. Personal reorientation was not significantly related to satisfaction and happiness.

A third style of response to role demands is what we called *reactive role behavior*. This approach involved implicitly accepting all role demands as given and finding ways to meet them. Examples are:

• Planning, scheduling, and organizing better.

• Working harder to meet all role demands. (As one expert on women's roles and role conflict said in frustration, "After years of research, I've concluded that the only answer to a career and a family is, learn to get by on less sleep!")

• Using no conscious strategy. Let problems take care of themselves. This reactive behavior, in contrast to role redefinition, is a passive response to role conflict. Not surprisingly, people who used this style reported very low levels of satisfaction and happiness.

Most companies today are less prepared to cope than couples are. Their experiences with career couples are only beginning to accumulate and the rigidity of company policies frequently makes it impossible to react with speed. In some companies the response to couple conflicts can be classified as either "noncoping" or "control." In one energy company, for example, noncoping has resulted in losing good people to competitors. Saddled with a policy that states employees are to be fired if they turn down a transfer and an average rate of 15 moves in a person's career, personnel administrators admit that the company isn't prepared for the two-career couple. They are now rethinking the wisdom of the policy and the necessity for frequent moves.

The control syndrome reflects just the opposite approach. Rather than relax or reverse policies, some companies are making new ones in anticipation of conflicts—usually conflicts of interest. Thus couples may be required to sign a statement that they will not discuss or divulge business information at home, lest the spouse use it to his or her employer's advantage.

Energy and Time Management. Two factors related to effective coping are the amount of energy a couple is willing to expend to "make it work" and the ways in which the couple handles time. In most cases, we find that people view working on the relationship and managing their respective roles as a legitimate and, in fact, top-priority task. Television watching may be forgone in favor of time spent together talking about how to get through the next week. Cocktails and after-dinner coffee become times for problem solving rather than idle chitchat. The laundry gets folded over the 11 o'clock news, and the spaghetti sauce may be stirred during a phone call to the baby-sitter.

Most working couples "pare their lives,"

finding time only for essential activities that are of top priority. One husband we talked to recently pointed up the value of time and the fact that he rarely has any to himself after putting in a workday, doing the shopping, coaching his daughter's ball team, and meeting a heavy schedule of work-related social obligations, a requirement in his job. "My family asked me what I wanted for Christmas," he told us. "And I told them that the thing I wanted more than anything else was just a day to myself with no one—absolutely no one—making any demands of me."

Career Competencies. Developing career competencies is as important to managing two careers as the characteristics of the relationship or the job are. The basic skills required for managing one career seem even more important when managing two.

Self-Assessment. Most vocational and career counselors agree that getting in touch with yourself—your strengths, weaknesses, and values—is the first step in managing a career. Among couples, we find that the ability to sort out values and to assess where they are and what they have (or don't have) going differentiates many floundering couples from those who succeed.

Many corporations invest huge amounts of money in managerial assessment centers and psychological testing facilities. Rarely in the past have companies helped people assess their career values in relation to their spouses.

Getting Vocational Information. We find the need for information about career demands and opportunities is critical, especially at early career stages. Young people frequently accept jobs on the basis of very little information about what will be expected of them in the future, what the typical pattern of movement in the organization is, or what alternatives might be open if they can't or won't follow the typical track.

Goal Setting. As we noted earlier in our examples, mature couples typically have clearly defined goals; younger couples do not. Yet, in terms of managing two careers and resolving conflicts, it behooves both the company and the couple to identify career goals clearly. In our illustration of Bob and Barbara, she knew exactly where she wanted to go. She wanted to remain in her staff function in the short run and move up in the personnel department.

Was Bob's goal as clear-cut? He wanted to stay with the company and ultimately wind up settled back in corporate headquarters. Between the couple stood the possibility of several field assignments. "What are the company's goals?" we asked. "What is the purpose of the field assignment?" Bill described the assignment in multipurpose terms: to provide experience with a technical plant facility and its people, to develop contacts in the field that would prove useful later in sales, and to gain supervisory experience. We asked why the assignment had to be a year in the field. "Well," he replied, "it probably takes five to six months to get to know a plant and, besides, that's the way it has always been done."

The interview intrigued us. The case was a classic example of couple and companies assuming they are a win/lost situation. Either Bob and others like him take the assignment while the spouse gives up her job, or she keeps her job and keeps him at home, affecting his career mobility within his firm.

To get around the conflict, both the couple and the company need to focus first on their goals and second on alternative strategies for reaching them. Are the com-

pany's goals really incompatible with those of the employee and the employee's spouse? Does the situation have to be viewed in either/or terms?

When we presented the problem to a class of MBAs, they seized on the opportunity to find a solution and began to redesign the training program as well as the couple's (temporary) lifestyle. The "give" had to be on both sides. Bob and Barb didn't have to be together seven days a week to be happy or successful, they concluded. But neither did the company need Bob warming a chair in Oklahoma for the next 360 days to develop his potential to move up.

What we wound up with was a list of alternatives ranging from a fleet of Lear jets transporting company couples to a system of team management in the field that would allow couples to work staggered schedules alternating between the plant and headquarters. Both we and the class concluded that the key was to find an alternative that fit the goals of the people and the training program. All too often, couples and corporations try to work within a single, fixed alternative rather than try to generate new ways to get themselves or their people where they need to be.

Planning. The fourth competency is planning, preferably in advance. Sue and Mike are typical of the successful couple. "We try to foresee any major problems or decisions and discuss them early in the game. Everything else falls into place on a day-to-day basis."

Young couples, we find, may not plan. "How will you and Barb react," we asked Bob, "when the assignment finally comes?" "I don't know," he replied. We suggested that he and Barb begin to plan now, to prepare for the inevitable. We strongly suggest planning to the MBAs with whom we work.

One of the strengths of planning, we find, is that couples, in developing alternatives for handling their problems, generate solutions for the company as well.

To prepare entry-level employees, we have our students generate a list of all the questions they fear (about their two-career status) from a recruiter. Then we ask them to generate a list of concerns—questions they want to ask to elicit more information about the job in relation to their own couple conflicts. Last, we have them practice ways to raise these issues themselves during the interview. What we find is that the interviewee's planning also benefits the recruiter. Because the recruiter often cannot ask certain questions, he or she is relieved to have the applicant bring the couple's situation out into the open. Both parties wind up with valid information and do not have to act on (often false) assumptions.

Problem Solving.   The final skill that couples and companies need is problem solving—developing and exploring many alternative means for getting around couple conflicts. To be effective at this, we find, both sides have to suspend judgment, stop making assumptions, and think flexibly.

In the seminars we run, we find that the *ability* to engage in problem solving is not the issue. Faced with the necessity, most people can brainstorm an endless list of solutions. The issue is that many couples and corporations don't turn their creative thinking to developing alternative ways of meeting the couple problem. When a situation arises, they aren't prepared to cope.

The Impact of Couple Conflicts on Organizations

What does all this mean for companies? To find an answer, we surveyed 35 organizations based in Chicago. In our interviews, we found at least 10 different ways in which couples impact on the personnel function of organizations:

1. *Recruiting.* Recruiters are becoming increasingly sensitive to the role of the spouse in career decisions. They are seeking ways to identify the people who are part of career couples and who have a high likelihood of accepting an offer and staying with the company.

2. *Scheduling.* The need for flexibility has made scheduling and schedule changes more of a problem. Scheduling vacation time and work hours is also affected as more employees seek "off" time to coincide with children's school schedules and day-care center hours.

3. *Transfers and relocation.* This is probably the area of greatest impact and poses the biggest problem for large companies. Refusal to relocate may mean the company must dip into the pool and send less qualified people into a new assignment. Those who refuse to relocate may be fired or quit, entailing high replacement and training costs.

4. *Promotions.* Many couples are less eager for promotion opportunities, regardless of whether they involve a geographic move or not. Many two-career people have aspirations for more free time, less work pressure, and fewer responsibilities. With two incomes the pay differentials may not compensate sufficiently to make promotions worthwhile.

5. *Travel.* People are less willing or able to travel in two-career couples where family demands are high. People seem to "burn out" faster in high-travel occupations such as public accounting, sales, and consulting.

6. *Benefits.* The need for benefit program revision is growing. Both men and women are seeking maternity leaves or leaves without pay to accommodate spouse and family demands. Life insurance has become more important as people accommodate to a standard of living based on two incomes. "Personal days" are another benefit that couples seek and use with greater frequency.

7. *Conflicts of interest.* Employees with spouses in the same professions—such as advertising, banking, accounting, consulting, law, or publishing—or working for competing firms may represent a potential liability or security risk. In the same firm, one spouse may have information that is not normally available to the part of the organization in which the other spouse works. Corporate policies dealing with these conflicts have not yet been developed in most companies.

8. *Career development.* The most significant change that couples have had on career programs is in the area of "career pathing," or the design of developmental tracks through which to move people. This is closely linked to the relocation effect. Many firms are finding the need to redesign training programs with limited geographic mobility in mind.

9. *Deadwood.* The combination of resistance to relocation, lower aspirations, unwillingness to travel, and other drawbacks of this kind presents a potential problem of deadwood among high-potential recruits who would otherwise develop and advance.

10. *Career bargaining.* A newly emerging trend is for couples to bargain for considerations that result directly from the career of the spouse. Examples are assurances of being sent to a particular location, assistance in finding a new position for the spouse, and subsidies until the spouse obtains a position.

Overall, we find that all the changes re-flect the need for more flexibility among couples and companies. Rigid policies are giving way to case-by-case exceptions, which are bound to give way in time to major shifts in policies as more couples enter the workforce.

Developing a Company Strategy. How can companies cope with the issues raised by the dual-career couple? The most effective way, we find, is to help the couple to cope. An effective program should have the following characteristics:

• Flexible career-development tracks and experiences.

• Skill development in coping with conflict and life/career management.

• Spouse involvement in career planning, decision making, and problem solving.

• Support services for career couples.

What are the components of an effective program? The following seem to be the most important.

Dual-career audit. When we surveyed Chicago area administrators recently, the number one suggestion was to "recognize the problem." Often, this is only done after a potential problem turns into a crisis. How can you identify the company's couple needs? The most direct way is through an employee survey, preferably one that is built into the regular career audit. What should you be looking for? Here are some sample areas to cover:

• How many employees are presently in a two-career situation and how many probably will be in the next few years?

• How many people interviewed on campus for starting positions are part of two-career families?

• How does your employee population break down in terms of life/career stage, organization level, location, and function? In other words, where are your dual-career employees?

• What conflicts do they have or may they have if they remain?

• How do they perceive company policy, career tracks, support, and opportunities in relation to their own careers?

• In what areas are they most and least competent to manage careers?

Special recruiting techniques. Three techniques should be considered. The first is the *preselection job preview for couples.* By giving both partners a realistic picture of the company, the job, and the typical career advancement track in terms of hours, travel, and so on, the program helps eliminate potentially bad couple/company fits. The second technique is *dual recruiting*—seeking husband-wife teams at the hiring end. The third technique is *couple counseling and orientation* immediately after selection but before placement. The company would help the couple to identify potential conflicts and begin to plan their coping mechanisms.

Many personnel departments are beginning to identify potential placement possibilities for spouses outside of their organizations. Thus, in recruiting one person, they may informally try, at least, to help the spouse find a job by making names of employers in the area available or by circulating the spouse's résumé to friends in the personnel departments of other companies. Few companies actually promise to find the spouse a job, but there is an increase in informal efforts to help.

Revision of career development and transfer policies. The first step is to identify the goals of your career-development program. Next, examine these goals against existing programs and policies, noting problem areas that may conflict with couple careers. Relocation is the most common problem. Consider whether the goals of the program can

be achieved without geographical transfer. The following alternatives may •be possible:

• Can field experience be simulated in local training through cases, simulations, or the use of videotaping or other devices?

• Can familiarity with certain facilities, products, and processes be learned in new ways (such as temporary assignments; say, two or three months)?

• Can shorter workweeks or staggered schedules be set up to allow couples to commute more easily?

• Can more training moves and tracks be developed within limited geographical areas?

• What are some of the ways company contacts can be developed without relocation?

In most cases, both training programs and career tracks are based on historical patterns and both are rarely subjected to critical examination. People are developed on the basis of how long it has taken other people to move up or the typical jobs other people have moved through on their way up. A new approach, instituted at Sears, Roebuck, has identified career tracks based on a skills analysis. What skills does a person need to advance? How long does it take to acquire these? In what range of positions can these skills be developed?

Revision of nepotism policies. In many major firms, former nepotism rules are being changed to allow companies to hire spouses. Typically, the policy is that relatives may be employed by the company, but persons may not supervise a relative or be involved in his or her salary, performance, or promotion evaluations.

Assistance for couples in career management. The packaged career materials on the market today, although good in many cases, are geared to individual career planning. In our seminars, we have found that couple planning is critical, even if the focus is on one partner's career. (This is also true, we find, in the single-career family.) Even if one spouse is not in the workforce, he or she may be planning to go back to school or reenter the job market. These decisions are not independent of the working spouse. Similarly, decisions one working spouse may have to make with regard to advancement in the firm could be affected by his or her spouse's career opportunities.

The part of the career management process for which corporate help is critical is in providing information to the couple to help them assess their opportunities, choices, potential conflicts, and developmental needs. The company cannot set goals for the couple, but it can provide programs to help couples develop their career competencies and acquire the information they need. Thus the company's role is helping people to learn the *process* of managing two careers by providing seminars, workshops, and training materials. Although the use of seminars is fairly new, at least one insurance company in Boston has begun to underwrite employee participation in the belief that help in managing the conflicts between work and family will enable employees to perform better.

There are several other ways the company can assist couples with career management:

1. *Developing family and spouse opportunities for company involvement.* Many working couples find that their empathy and willingness to compromise increase with their understanding of the partner's or parent's job and job-related responsibilities. One company sponsors days when family members are invited to "work along-side" a parent to see firsthand what the job involves. Others have used films to orient families to what the company and the parent do. Company-sponsored social events often provide an opportunity for family members to meet co-workers and develop supportive relationships. One major oil company found it difficult to transfer personnel to Saudi Arabia and keep them there. After instituting orientation sessions for husband and wife and asking them to decide *together* whether to accept the transfer, there was a great reduction in the number of people who returned before completing their tour of duty.

2. *Training couples in career coping and problem solving.* Over the past year we have developed several programs for developing couple skills in career coping and problem solving. One, for example, helps couples understand career and life roles and the various techniques for managing role conflict. Another revolves around typical two-career decisions and problems. Using cases, we have been able to help couples anticipate some of the problems they will encounter and then plan a strategy for solving these problems. The more skills the couple has, the less of a problem the dual-career situation creates for the company.

3. *Setting up support structures for transfers and relocation.* Where it is necessary to transfer and relocate personnel, the availability of special services and support may make the difference between whether the target employee accepts or not and be a contributing factor in how quickly the spouse and family adjust. Some of the services helpful to two-career families are:

- Helping to find the spouse a job.
- Locating day-care or child-care arrangements.
- Assisting in selling and buying homes.
- Assisting in getting advance information about the new community during a transfer and helping the couple to become integrated into the community.

• Helping couples to develop strategies for planning and coping with transfers in advance (before either one has been offered a transfer). Specialized relocation companies (for example, Relo and the Relocation Council) are already providing these services on a consulting basis to corporations. The Union Oil Company has reported several cases of successful relocation for couples within their firm. In some of these, one spouse was promoted and the administrative services department helped find an opening in the corporation for the other. In one case, the company granted a leave of absence to an employee to search for a job after her spouse was transferred. For the most part, these success stories reflect a case-by-case approach.

4. *Providing local support services.* In addition to those already mentioned, the two biggest day-to-day needs of the dual-career family still seem to be flexibility and child/home-care services. We do not necessarily advocate company-sponsored day-care centers, but company clout can be wielded in many communities to advance the needs of working parents and their children. Lunch programs, after-school centers and sport programs, and facilities for children of working parents on school holidays are all needs many communities have yet to meet.

5. *Providing couple counseling.* At many points in the process of goal setting, planning, and problem solving, couples need a third party to help them sort out their priorities and resolve conflicts. There are many people who can be used to provide this help, ranging from in-house counselors to outside resource people who are available in your area.

Training of supervisors in career counseling skills. Probably the best source of counsel—if not for the couple, then at least for the employee—is the skilled supervisor. Unfor-tunately, most supervisors have little training in career management, the areas of working parents (especially women), and conflict resolution. Yet they are the ones most directly affected on a day-to-day basis with the conflicts that work/home roles present to an employee.

What can you do to train supervisors?

• Provide seminars for supervisors to alert them to the typical dual-career conflicts that may come up.

• Develop their third-party skills in counseling, coaching, and listening.

• Provide simulations in handling employee problems caused by spouse and family needs.

Setting up of interorganizational cooperative arrangements. The most helpful resources a company can have in managing two-career relocations are contacts in other companies and organizations. These provide a base for helping the spouse relocate. These contacts are often used informally by personnel managers, but there is a growing need in many companies for a more systematic network of cooperation.

Providing flexible work environments. More within the grasp of the company, however, are policies regarding working hours and days off. Flexible working hours is probably the single most effective technique companies have instituted to meet working parents' needs. The establishment of family emergency days or "personal days" is another. Some companies, such as research and consulting firms, allow employees to work at home when necessary to do "think work," write reports, and accomplish other tasks for which the office may be too distracting.

Evaluating the effectiveness of the program. The final component is measuring the effects of your efforts against bottom-line-related results and costs. To do this, we suggest that you first establish goals and criteria based on current turnover, problem incidents, days lost, and so on, as well as on the basis of your initial or annual dual-career audit results. The evaluation design should *precede* the program design so that baseline data will be recorded and interventions measured.

Conclusion

In this paper we have attempted to highlight the issues associated with an emerging corporate phenomenon: the dual-career couple. In an earlier paper (*Organizational Dynamics*, Summer 1976), we referred to the dual-career employee as a ''corporate time bomb,'' because the impact will be greatest about five years from now, when the dual-career employee (now mainly at entry level) will be in a more responsible, critical position, will be starting a family, and will be facing various relocation opportunities and pressures. As professional and management employees move from early career positions into mid-career, they will become less willing to sacrifice family and personal needs to corporate requirements. To cope successfully with these stresses, couples will need to develop coping mechanisms, flexibility, and a mutual commitment to each other's careers and to invest large amounts of time and energy. With more married women and couples entering the workforce, companies will experience greater difficulties in recruiting, scheduling, and transferring professional personnel. Problems regarding travel, benefits, conflicts of interest, and career pathing are also sure to grow.

Companies are just becoming aware that there are problems. They admit the problems exist, but feel that the problems belong to the employee, not to them. When they do react, it is on a case-by-case basis. Few actual programs for dual-career employees have been developed. Orientation programs for the spouse are the most frequent action taken to date.

Other recommended company actions include auditing dual-careers; revising development, transfer, and nepotism policies; providing assistance to couples in dual-career management; training supervisors in counseling and coaching skills; providing intercompany cooperation; and providing more flexible work environments. Most of these necessary steps are not unique to dual-career issues; they are important in any program to develop and utilize human talents more effectively. The dual career is just one more manifestation of a new corporate phenomenon: more employees are coming to see their work lives as protean careers. As Douglas Hall said in *Careers in Organizations*:

> The protean career is a process which the person, not the organization, is managing. It consists of all of the person's varied experiences in education, training, work in several organizations, changes in occupational field, etc. The protean career is *not* what happens to the person in any one organization. The protean person's own personal career choices and search for self-fulfillment are the unifying or integrative elements in his or her life. The criterion of success is internal (psychological success), not external. In short, the protean career is shaped more by the individual than by the organization and may be redirected from time to time to meet the needs of the person (p. 201).

Like it or not, this increasing desire for self-direction in one's career is a fact to which organizations will have to adapt. Some companies may try to resist this trend by selecting more passive or easily socialized people. In our opinion, this is a short-term solution with very high long-term costs (increasing corporate rigidity). The other corporate response, which makes a lot more sense to us, is to develop more flexible management policies and practices so that the potential for growth and creativity of the protean employee is not only tolerated but utilized for increased corporate, as well as personal, success.

READING 4
ARMOR FOR
WHISTLE-BLOWERS*
Business Week

When Ray Palmateer, a foreman in International Harvester Company's tractor works in East Moline, Illinois, reported in 1977 to undercover police that a fellow employee offered to sell him stolen tools (not the property of IH), he may have expected a pat on the back from his employer. Instead, IH fired him as a troublemaker. Now "whistle-blower" Palmateer, who had worked 16 years for IH, is proving that he can make more trouble for the company outside than in. Last April he won a major ruling from the Illinois Supreme Court permitting him to sue IH for "retaliatory discharge." The court has just denied a petition by the company for a rehearing, setting the stage for the trial Palmateer has sought for the past four years.

Palmateer's case is one of a number of signs, including a law that has recently taken effect in Michigan, that the concept of whistle-blowing is gaining firm legal ground. Usually scorned by the corporate community, the whistle-blower, these developments suggest, will be increasingly

freer in the next few years to expose corporate wrongdoing.

Ill-Defined Policy

The Illinois decision is notable because it considerably broadens a fairly narrow exception to the general rule, honored in most states until recent years, that an employee could be fired "at will"—that is, the employer could discharge a worker for any or even no reason at all. During the 1970s, however, a number of state supreme courts ruled that an employee may recover damages if fired for refusing an employer's demand that he violate a law. For example, the California Supreme Court last year permitted a suit against Atlantic Richfield Company by an employee who charged that he was fired for refusing to fix prices. State legislatures, too, have been busy protecting workers who seek to establish their rights or carry out civic duties. Since 1978 some 20 states have passed laws barring the discharge of employees who do such things as serve on juries or file workers' compensation claims.

But Palmateer's actions fell into none of these categories. Instead, he claimed that he was fired in violation of an ill-defined "public policy." In addition to reporting a possible felony to the police, Palmateer contends that he had agreed to gather more evidence to implicate the suspect and that he would have testified at a criminal trial. Although no law requires anyone to ferret out crime, the Illinois court said that "public policy nevertheless favors citizen crime-fighters."

IH took the position that such a public policy is much too broad. The company argued that the theft could involve a $2 screwdriver and that it should be permitted to discharge a "managerial employee who recklessly and precipitously resorts to the

---

* Reprinted from the July 6, 1981, issue of Business Week by special permission. © 1981 by Mc-Graw Hill, Inc.

criminal justice system to handle such a personnel problem." The court responded that "the magnitude of the crime is not the issue. . . . IH's business judgment, no matter how sound, cannot override" the legislature's decision that minor thefts can still be prosecuted.

IH's lawyer, Stuart R. Lefstein of Rock Island, Illinois, asserts that the court's ruling gives birth to a "pernicious doctrine." It means, he says, that "with the burden on the employer, who may not always be sure what a 'clearly mandated public policy' is, all kinds of things that should be settled peacefully and forgotten" might not be. "If two employees get into a fistfight, even if they want to bury the hatchet later, a third employee could go to the police and report a possible crime. This ruling stirs up a hornet's nest of problems which could be chaotic."

Palmateer's attorney, Gerald J. Meehan, disagrees. He argues that the ruling "requires employers to be a little more careful in handling discharges." But, he adds, "a company that documents its actions and is prudent has nothing to worry about."

Power to the Courts

The state legislature of Michigan, in a nearly unanimous bipartisan vote, decided to short-circuit the case-by-case judicial approach by enacting tough rules to protect other workers in Palmateer's straits. The Whistle-blowers' Protection Act, which took effect on March 31 [1981], is the first such statute in the country, although California, New Jersey, and New York are preparing similar legislation. The Michigan act makes it illegal for an employer to discharge or threaten a worker or to discriminate in salary, benefits, privileges, or location of employment because an employee has reported a violation of law or regulation to any public body. The law covers both state and private employees. Courts are empowered to order reinstatement on the job, along with seniority, back wages, damages, and even, in appropriate cases, all costs of the litigation.

Alan F. Westin, professor of public law and government at Columbia University and an authority on employee rights, predicts that statutes and judicial decisions designed to aid the whistle-blower will proliferate in the near future for two reasons. The first is that companies traditionally shun mechanisms that could deal internally with the concerns of whistle-blowers. "The corporate structure does not respond well when criticism is made of clearly illegal practices," says Westin, author of *Whistle Blowing! Loyalty and Dissent in the Corporation*. Some companies, however, including IBM, Xerox, Citibank, and Allied Corporation, have created sophisticated management systems that are set up to listen and respond to such complaints.

Whistle-blowing statutes will spread also because they give "more regulatory bang for the buck," Westin says. No governmental regulatory system is required to ferret out or monitor corporate practices under such a law. In this sense, Westin claims, the legal impetus complements the new political winds in Washington.

Indeed, a study of whistle-blowing in the federal service, just released by the Merit Systems Protection Board, is being avidly read in the capital. Its findings—that numerous federal employees are aware of fraud and abuse in federal agencies and departments but are afraid to come forward—is ideologically attuned to last fall's campaign rhetoric and could well prompt Congress to enact whistle-blowing legislation in the near future.

READING 5
WHY DO COMPANIES SUCCUMB TO PRICE FIXING?*
Jeffrey Sonnenfeld and
Paul R. Lawrence

Down the centuries social analysts have frequently charged, "Laws are like spiderwebs, which may catch small flies but let wasps and hornets break through." As more and more corporations have been caught in the web of price-fixing laws, however, this charge has lost its punch. Senior business managers in industries that have never before known these problems, as well as previous offenders, are probably more concerned now about their corporate exposure to being indicted and convicted of price fixing than they were in any other recent period.

The reasons are not hard to find. As federal agencies, the courts, and Congress respond to the heightened post-Watergate expectations of the public, the law enforcement net has been substantially strengthened.[1] Instead of hearing protests over the legal immunity granted to the large and powerful, one now hears the anguish coming from the reverse direction. One can regularly read about prominent individuals and organizations that are overwhelmed by the stiff penalties they have incurred for behavior which may have been customary business practice in the past but which now violates social and legal standards.[2]

---

[1] "Carter Trust Busters," *Newsweek*, September 26, 1977.

[2] United States v. Park 421 U.S. Court 658 (1975); Tony McAdams and Robert C. Miljus, "Growing Criminal Liability of Executives," HBR March–April 1977, p. 36.

The costs of violating price-fixing laws are very high: lawyers' fees, government fines, poor morale, damaged public image, civil suits, and now prison terms. Justice Department statistics indicate that 60 percent of antitrust felons are sentenced to prison terms.[3] Thus, for very pragmatic reasons as well as for personal convictions, America's top executives are searching for fail-safe ways of meeting legal requirements. While top executives strongly complain about increasing government interference, they also acknowledge, "We operate through a license from society which can be revoked whenever we violate the terms of the license."

Executives in large decentralized organizations, however, find it increasingly difficult to carry through on their intentions. The considerable time and money corporations spend developing positive public images can be wasted by the careless actions of just one or two lower level employees. At the same time that organization size and complexity increase, top executives find that the law imposes on them additional responsibility for the business practices of their subordinates.

Executives tremble over what may be going on in the field despite their internal directives and public declarations. One CEO well expressed the frustration common to executives in convicted companies:

"We've tried hard to stress that collusion is illegal. We point out that anticompetitive practices hurt the company's ethical standards, public image, internal morale, and earnings. Yet we wind up in trouble continually. When we try to find out why employees got involved, they have the gall to say that they 'were only looking out for the best

---

[3] Timothy D. Schellhardt, "Price-Fixing Charges Rise in Industry Despite Convictions," *The Wall Street Journal*, May 4, 1978, p. 31.

interests of the company.' They seem to think that the company message is for everyone else but them. You begin to wonder about the intelligence of these people. Either they don't listen or they're just plain stupid."

Some executives we interviewed in researching this article believe with the CEO quoted that their employees who collude in price fixing are just not listening or are plain stupid. In our view it is less likely that the employees are deaf or stupid than that many well-meaning, ethical top managers simply are not getting their message down the line to loyal alert employees.

To better understand this lack of communication as well as other forces contributing to employees committing unlawful acts, we thought that it would be enlightening to look at the unfortunate experience of the forest products and paper industry in the midst of antitrust litigation. Looking just at antitrust cases in 1977, one can see that the paper industry was hit with separate prosecutions for price fixing in consumer paper, fine paper and stationery, multiwall bags, shopping bags, labels, corrugated containers, and folding cartons. In early 1978, over 100 suits have been filed against the industry.

In addition, a U.S. grand jury has been gathering information on competitive practices in the industry at large—which many suspect is part of a probe into industry collusion to restrain supply.[4] In fact, *The Wall Street Journal* recently stated that the paper industry is gaining the reputation as the "nation's biggest price fixer."[5]

The folding-box litigation has, by far, been the most damaging (see the ruled insert on page 897). The Justice Department has described this case as the largest price-fixing one since 1960. It is hard to understand how socially responsible companies could ever have found themselves in such a nightmarish situation. To find out, we discussed the various pressures and conditions in this industry with 40 senior, division, and middle-level executives. Our investigation concentrated on the predicament of the large forest products companies that derive about 4 percent or 5 percent of their total company sales from folding-carton revenues.

The shock for those companies, with strong, well-publicized ethical positions, is perhaps most severe. In case the reader is skeptical, our interviews with the senior people in these companies left us without a shred of doubt about the sincerity and completeness of their personal commitment to legal compliance. In fact, the top people we spoke to in the major forest products companies desperately want to know how and why they got on the wrong side of the law so that they can be sure it never happens again.

How It Can Happen

Before we discuss the factors that create a price-fixing prone industry and organization, we would like to point out that the various problematic situations that contributed to this unhappy end are certainly not unique to the paper industry. One can easily draw parallels between the paper industry's difficulties and the situations leading

---

[4] "13 Paper Concerns Face Price Fixing Charges," *New York Times*, December 23, 1977, p. D5; "Two Paper Firms are Convicted in Price-Fixing," *The Wall Street Journal*, November 27, 1977, p. 3; "Indictment Cites 14 Paper Makers for Price-Fixing," *The Wall Street Journal*, January 26, 1978, p. 3; Morris S. Thompson, "Aides of Box-Making Concerns Sentenced to Prison, Fined in Price-Fixing Case," *The Wall Street Journal*, December 1, 1976, p. 4.

[5] Schellhardt, "Price-Fixing Charges Rise," p. 1.

to price fixing in other very different industries. For such a comparison, we will at times glance at the 1960 electrical contractors' conspiracy. We hope, too, that no one will read this article without reflecting on his or her own company's situation.

Price-Fixing-Prone Industry. Many economists would consider the folding-carton industry to be one of the least likely to spawn a price-fixing conspiracy. The industry's very diffuse structure is the complete antithesis of the tight-knit oligopoly, which, economists tell us, breeds collusion. Of the over 450 box-making companies, the larger ones control only from 5 percent to 7 percent of the market; only one company controls near 10 percent.

With this number of companies, one would think that the rivalry among them would be so intense that it would preclude any mutual understandings and tacit agreements. Yet companies representing 70 percent of the $1.5 billion in annual industry sales were convicted.

In fact, the number of companies in the industry is one of the factors that tempted some business men to abandon the rugged competitor role and adopt "a more statesmanlike attitude toward competitors," as one executive euphemistically puts it. The market was, simply, badly crowded. Other pressures toward collusion were the job-order nature of the business and the fact that the products were undifferentiated.

Crowded and Mature Market. In the late 1950s and early 1960s, as the expansion of prepackaged and frozen foods kept the market growing at about 7 percent a year, the folding-carton business attracted new entrants. With low barriers to entry, competitors of all sizes saw this area as a great opportunity. Traditionally dominated by small family-run box-making shops, the industry became attractive to very large forest products companies, which integrated forward. These large companies first supplied the paperboard for box making, and then began to compete with their customers further down the line in making the actual boxes themselves.

The tendency toward overcapacity in paperboard production tempted these large paper companies to look on folding boxes as a way to unload excesses. Some blamed the softening of the box market on this attitude, claiming that "the big companies did not care about box prices because they were making their profit back at the paperboard mill."

Also harmful to the market in the intervening years was the halt of supermarket expansion as well as the growth of the use of substitute containers, such as plastics, which eroded the market share for paper containers. The industry is now very mature and has even suffered revenue as well as profit declines.

These declines place great pressure on middle level managers who are keenly aware that the constant use of existing capital equipment is the way to drive down unit costs. One general manager commented:

"Large volume is important because we didn't make the investment in more efficient equipment we should have years ago. We could have brought on more sophisticated equipment and been more efficient in the use of labor and style of production. However, we can't get the money now. Too much was invested in the paperboard mills and nothing in folding-carton plants. Financial analysts look at these past bad investments and the bad earnings here and refuse to look on this industry with a favorable eye. It's a bad cycle we're caught in."

Some say a shakeout is long overdue;

others complain about vicious customers. Some managers in folding-box companies complain of the predatory influence of the large companies they supply. One division manager stated:

"This sector has been ripped off by big customers for a long time. Anything this industry has done has been more in defense than offense. Business is really dwindling, and we are even more dependent on pleasing the big customers we depend on. You really can't do a profitable business with a customer buying $30 million from one carton manufacturer. They will destroy you. . . . No one here is making much in this industry anymore. Now the pressures are not to make more money but to keep from going under. Price discussions between competitors are important just to keep from going broke. Our customers should be investigated instead."

When a manager feels his or her division's survival is in question, the corporation's standards of business conduct are apt to be sacrificed. In the 1960 electrical contractors case the issue was also survival. A convicted General Electric division vice president explained:

"I think we understood it was against the law. . . . The moral issue didn't seem to be important at that time . . . it was a period of trying to obtain stability, to put an umbrella over the smaller manufacturers . . . I've seen the situation change, primarily due to overcapacity, to almost a situation where people thought it was a survival measure. . . ."[6]

Job-Order Nature of Business.   In the folding-box industry cost-cutting practices are also hampered by the nature of the produc-

tion process. Boxes are generally manufactured for short job orders. One general manager said:

"Those guys up in headquarters think making boxes is like making paper, but papermaking is just following recipes. No two boxes are the same for us. Even with soap boxes, there are diverse product specifications."

Each of these jobs is costed and priced individually. Since each order is custom made, the pricing decisions are made frequently and at low levels of the organization. One salesman illustrated how a job-order business exposes a company to low-level price collusion:

"Every order is a negotiation, even when we've got a contract. Dialogue on prices is always on your mind. Any time I've met with a competitor, whether at a trade association meeting or in a customer's waiting room, one of us will eventually crack a smile and say, 'You son of a bitch, you're cutting my prices again. . . .' Sometimes things go on from there and sometimes they don't. I think our company has been stupidly naive. It is impossible not to have talked price at some time."

Undifferentiated Products.   Finally, while job specifications vary greatly between orders, the skills and equipment are fairly undifferentiated between companies. Several executives we interviewed concur with the following statement from one vice president:

"Part of the problem is that we're not competing with a unique article here. Our bags and boxes aren't really any better or worse than those of our competitors. You don't really go out and sell the product. Salespeople don't have any special product to sell. The only way to get a buyer is to sell at a lower price. Thus competitors may

---

[6] John Herling, *The Great Price Conspiracy* (Washington, D.C.: Luce, 1962), p. 241.

think that the only way to make it is to get together and fix prices."

With such factors as a crowded and mature market, declining demand, difficulty in cutting costs, and no company product differentiation, it is not surprising that profits have been bad. Lately, folding-carton profits, at best, have been running between 3 percent and 6 percent of sales. Several companies have folding-carton divisions that have not seen a real profit in years. Just in the period of time in which we conducted this research, three large box makers announced they were either selling out or closing up.

Collusion may then take place despite economists' doubts that it will succeed and despite company statements that legal compliance is mandated.[7] When we try to empathize with someone fighting for the survival of a sick business, we realize that the problem may be greater than employees that don't listen or are just plain stupid. Perhaps these people really believe that they are committed to the company's best interests. We heard one convicted executive explain in a quivering voice:

"The unhealthy state which characterizes this industry has of course afflicted this company as well. We're not vicious enemies in this industry, but rather people in similar binds. I've always thought of myself as an honorable citizen. We didn't do these things for our own behalf. It was presumably done for the betterment of the company."

It seems that the recognition of common goals can be shared within a large group of diverse competitors as well as within a close-knit oligopoly. Certainly not all industries face such adverse conditions. But many other industries face some combination of these circumstances, and management complacency in the face of these conditions could be very costly.

Price-Fixing-Prone Organization. Our interviews clearly reveal that not all the factors contributing to price fixing come from the industry, economic, and technical factors we have considered. Some come directly from the companies themselves and the subculture of the industry; some are built into personnel pricing, sales, and legal staff practices.

Culture of the Business. In the electrical contractors conspiracy, there were strong pressures to enforce the anticompetitive norms. A GE vice president describing the type of coercion placed on an executive who resisted the norms of collusion stated, "We worked him over pretty hard, and I did, too; I admit it." One GE executive who was a target of this pressure from his colleagues committed suicide.[8] In one recent folding-box case, some executives threatened others with physical violence if they resisted raising prices.[9]

Executives in the paper industry point out that people in the folding-carton business are not necessarily evil but are just people who have worked in a system with a history of very different ground rules. A convicted executive claimed that price fixing was common practice in his business:

"Price agreements between competitors was a way of life. Our ethics were not out of line with what was being done in this com-

---

[7] W. Bruce Erickson, "Price Fixing Conspiracies, Their Long Term Impact," *Journal of Industrial Economics*, March 1976, p. 200; Almarin Phillips, *Market Structure, Organization and Performance* (Cambridge, Mass.: Harvard University Press, 1962). The belief is that as the number of companies increases, the probability of mutual understanding and anticompetitive agreement will decrease.

[8] Herling, *The Great Price Conspiracy*, p. 249.

[9] Schellhardt, "Price-Fixing Charges Rise," p. 1.

pany and, in fact, in this industry for a long time. I've been in this industry for 32 years, and this situation was not just a passing incident. That's just the way I was brought up in the business, right or wrong."

Another factor encouraging price fixing arises when a company with one culture acquires another with a quite different one. In several companies convicted of price fixing, senior executives acknowledge that rapid vertical integration brought their forest products companies into secondary converting businesses, which were little and poorly integrated.[10] One division vice president of a convicted company conceded:

"Our folding-carton units were like a bunch of geographic 'left outs.' The geographic separation was fantastic. The 15 individual plants were poorly coordinated and poorly managed. We just came along with our acquisition drive and then sent top-management attention elsewhere."

The parent companies often naively assumed that business practice and ethics in the two companies would automatically be congruent even if there were no common heritage. As an illustration of the sort of side practices that may come with a business acquisition, the management of one large forest products company learned to its shock that the box-making company it had just acquired had been running a house of prostitution as a customer service for years. One vice president stated:

"The guys at the core of this conspiracy were acquired people from acquired companies and not part of our culture. That is just not the way we do business. Questions of ethics were never raised. We assumed that people do business ethically at our com-

pany. Apparently that was a simple-minded assumption."

Personnel Practices. On top of any other influences, the personnel practices used in many companies seemed actually to encourage people to engage in price fixing.[11] In a number of the companies convicted, management almost exclusively appraised individual performance on the basis of profits and volume. And not only advancement but also bonuses and commissions, which often exceeded 50 percent of base salary, were dependent on these measures. A division manager spelled out these practices:

"In the folding-carton division, our local salesmen have all been compensated with a base salary and a commission. Some bonus programs account for 60 percent of someone's compensation. People have been evaluated on the basis of profit and how forcefully they can execute a price increase. Thus, if he does this by price agreement with competitors, he'll build profit and price credits and get a reward."

So, instead of seeing the top people explicitly and officially acknowledge the difficult industry conditions, many of the lower officials see only strong pressures and inducements to "get the numbers no matter what." As one executive of a convicted company sadly acknowledged, "We've definitely run into some problems from jam-

---

[10] The recent acquisition spree may exacerbate this problem. See "The Great Takeover Binge," *Business Week*, November 14, 1977, p. 176.

[11] Gilbert Geis, "White Collar Crime: The Heavy Electrical Equipment Anti-trust Case in 1961," in *Criminal Behavior Systems: A Typology*, eds. Marshall B. Clinard and Richard Quinrey (New York: Holt, Rinehart & Winston, 1967), p. 150. Here it is explained that structural factors are major contributing elements to criminal behavior. Executives who were uncooperative with price-fixing training were transferred by the company. These issues are more fully discussed in: Laura Shill Schrager and James J. Short, Jr., "Toward a Sociology of Organizational Crime," presented at the American Sociological Association meeting, Chicago, August 1977.

ming our corporate targets down every-one's throats."

It is not surprising that junior managers perceive such company-induced pressure as conveying top-management's intent. One sales manager explained that any other corporate messages that came down from other company executives were only from ". . . staff guys and were not related to my evaluation and advancement. If it is known that the operating chief of your area wants business conducted in a certain way, it seems that is what really counts."

One chief executive officer who spent a lot of time thinking over his company's involvement in the recent conspiracy summed up the effect of these kinds of pressures:

"I think we are particularly vulnerable where we have a salesman with two kids, plenty of financial demands, and a concern over the security of his job. There is a certain amount of looseness to a new set of rules. He may accept questionable practices feeling that he may just not know the system. There are no specific procedures for him to follow other than what other salesmen tell him.

"At the same time, he is in an industry where the acceptance for his product and the level of profitability are clearly dropping. Finally, we add to his pressures by letting him know who will take his job from him if he doesn't get good price and volume levels. I guess this will bring a lot of soul-searching out of an individual."

Pricing Decisions. Another area that caused vulnerability in companies convicted of price fixing was their decentralized price-setting mechanism. A GE division manager jailed for price fixing made this point before a senate subcommittee 15 years ago:

"I think decentralization exposed the flanks a great deal more. It made the expo-sure greater. . . . It has put more pressure on the manager because he has complete responsibility in a smaller organization. Yes, I think decentralization has certainly contributed to the forces that tend to make [conspiracies] a reality."[12]

Descriptions of this earlier conspiracy indicate that the job-order nature of this equipment business increased the frequency of these decisions and the degree of competitor contact.

In the paper industry, we found that senior managers assumed pricing was done as it was for commodity products, where any changes were large, rare, and received top-management attention. The prices for folding boxes, however, like other job-order business, are heavily influenced by very junior managers and salespeople. This was true even though a general manager was nominally held responsible for pricing. Because managers made pricing decisions frequently, the number of diffuse influences on these decisions is great. As a result, one salesman explained:

"Everyone gets his nose into pricing issues. You're nothing unless you get into the pricing mechanism. There are maybe 10 guys that can get involved in every decision, including clerks, plant managers, cost estimators, and salespeople. Yeah, the responsibility rests ultimately with the general manager but that's horseshit! Everyone wants a piece of the action and an awful lot of people get their hands into prices unnecessarily."

Thus people can get involved in pricing issues for status reasons alone and can be tempted to use their influence to impress and help friends in other companies. It is

---

[12] "Administered Prices," Hearings Before the Subcommittee on Anti-trust and Monopoly of the Committee on the Judiciary, U.S. Senate, April 12 to May 2, 1961, p. 17065.

also clear that the more decentralized pricing decisions become, the more difficult it will be for top managers to control collusion.

Trade Associations.   Over two centuries ago, Adam Smith, the dean of free market economics, warned:

"People of the same trade seldom meet together, even for merriment and diversion, but the conversation ends in a conspiracy against the public, or in some contrivance to raise prices."[13]

In keeping with this prediction, a sales manager of a convicted paper company complained that industry trade association activities can directly contribute to a company's involvement in conspiracy:

"You must limit the occasion of sin. You can't put yourself in a position of contact with competitors. I've dropped contact with personal friends in competing companies since this prosecution started, and I should have dropped such contacts sooner. I don't go to industry meetings at all. Now, finally, this whole company frowns on industry bullshit!"

Though many executives will not now talk to old friends in competitive companies, some general managers disagree with these assessments. They feel that there may be truth to the suspicion that these trade meetings give an opportunity for price fixing, but as one manager argued:

"Just the same, these associations have a great value, and it's too bad to see them in trouble. A lot of lobbying relevant to the industry happens there. Perhaps participation has been too liberal . . . it's just a big party."

Virtually all the senior managers surveyed agree "that it's hard to talk about the costs of production without discussing prices." An executive at one of the relatively uninvolved companies proudly stated that his company has sharply curtailed the number of company employees participating in trade association meetings:

"I think that trade associations have some value, but the risks are fairly high. We've cut back dramatically and now only one or two people per division attend the meetings. The trade meetings are limited to the top people. Some second echelon employees just loved to go to these meetings and take their wives. They wanted to be entertained. I've always believed that familiarity breeds attempt. For each point on the asset side, trade associations have two points on the liability side."

Similarly, executives in the electrical contractors case condemned the collusionary influence at the trade association meetings. In 1960, a GE vice president stated to a congressional committee:

"The way I feel about it now, sir, the way my company . . . has been damaged, the way my associates and their personal careers have been damaged and destroyed, the way my family and myself have been suffering, if I see a competitor on one side of the street, I will walk on the other side, sir."[14]

Corporate Legal Staff.   Several corporate lawyers reluctantly acknowledge that their performance was related to their company's convictions. While in many companies antitrust memoranda and periodic legal lectures became more frequent after the landmark 1960 electrical contractors conspiracy, legal departments in the paper companies still tended to react to problems rather than to anticipate them. The corporate counsel at

---

[13] Adam Smith, *The Wealth of Nations.*

[14] "Administered Prices," p. 16663.

one of the convicted paper companies explained:

"In the past, we practiced what we thought was our proper role, and that was to respond to legal questions. We sometimes did big group things like lectures, but we never sat down to talk the subject through with small groups of managers."

Similarly, another vice president of legal affairs conceded that, although his department is quite heavily involved in antitrust education now, "We've only really become anticipatory since the folding-carton case."

Thus the lawyers did not serve as a source for legal advice to avoid problems but allowed people to navigate to the brink of prosecution. A division manager in one of the convicted companies summed this up by giving his impression of the performance of the legal division:

"I can tell you that the lawyers here are a damned smart bunch of guys who can get you out of trouble once you've gotten into it. But we sure need more of an active force."

How to Avoid It

We have examined both the industry and the company factors that contributed to one industry's being so badly caught up in price fixing. It is time to take stock of the implications of our inquiry for managers who are resolved to avoid such traumatic experiences. How should managers respond to this predicament? The lessons are, in fact, fairly easy to perceive but at times very difficult to put into practice.

It is obvious but not trivial to say that managers in competing companies who would be fail-safe should move to the opposite poles from each and every one of the contributing factors we have identified.

(The Exhibit lists these factors and their opposites.) But, of course, recognizing danger signs provides no more than a start toward solving the problem. Which factors are relatively controllable and which are not? What specific practices have we identified in our study that were helpful? What ideas and concepts can be useful in achieving compliance?

Managing the Market Conditions. Certainly very little in the market environment is under management's direct control. One may conclude that the conditions of the folding-carton industry are sufficiently hostile that a company would be justified in leaving the business entirely. Since four large companies have left the business over the past year, obviously some involved executives have reached that very conclusion. In our interviews, senior managers at one forest products company expressed sheer relief at being "liberated."

Those who have remained are striving for cost control and product differentiation to allow for longer runs and greater pricing freedom. Only a few have as yet succeeded in this effort. Many executives complain that their company could never remove itself from the brutal paper carton market unless top management made a really major commitment to a new strategy. Most are unable to free themselves from the tradition of trying to be all things to all people. A vice president of legal affairs in one convicted company pointed to the superficial nature of some attempts to affect the market and shows how they can backfire:

"Everyone here is competing for the same sales. We wanted to somehow differentiate ourselves, so through the 1950s and the early 1960s we developed over 300 minor patents. These patents weren't really worth the time, but that was the way we competed then. Customers would insist that at least one other box maker be licensed under the patent so they wouldn't be so dependent on one supplier. That's how we then got involved in pricing discussions. When discussing royalties, prices became important issues."

A sales manager of one of the convicted companies reported that the larger companies did seriously try to segment the market into areas such as frozen food, beverages, cosmetics, and so forth.

But, said this manager, "Some independents would just continue to treat their businesses like general printing shops, and the large companies could never organize the market." Such a market allocation could, of course, still violate antitrust legislation.

Only a handful of companies seems to have succeeded in a product differentiation strategy. But the fact that a few have is not insignificant, and we will return to this point later.

Managing the Company Culture. As we talked to executives in the forest products industry, we of course asked about their experience with management methods that could help control the price-fixing problem. One of the consistent and early points that came up was the example set for the company by the behavior of top management. We found one of the most frequent approaches senior management uses to encourage legal compliance is to cite its record in regard to social responsibility.

Psychological research on obedience,[15] business research on employee morality,

and common sense all indicate that the behavior of those in authority serves as important role models to others.[16] Unless top management projects consistent and sincere company commitment, operating practices will not change.

This commitment, however, is a necessary but not a sufficient factor to ensure compliance. The major forest products companies where we interviewed have a long-standing reputation for the expression of public interest commitment by senior executives. Each company has its own internal maxim for, "We believe that ethics start at the front office." Unfortunately, these statements tend to stop here as well. A vice president of a convicted paper company explained:

"When we were small enough and in a stable environment, people all knew each other by first names. We could communicate informally, and we were successful in molding behavior through modeling. People could resolve gray areas of decision making by reflecting on how their superiors would handle such an issue. But, with our very explosive growth of the last decade and a half, this old approach has become problematic. Can we still communicate corporate standards to a lot of people in the same way we communicated to a few?"

A number of companies are actively developing some promising ways to go beyond the example of the front office.

General Management Signals. Some executives talked very explicitly about the prob-

---

[15] Stanley Milgrim, *Obedience to Authority: An Experimental View* (New York: Harper & Row, 1974).

[16] Raymond Baumhart, *An Honest Profit* (New York: Holt, Rinehart & Winston, 1968). This survey, based on 1,710 subscribers responding to an HBR poll, found most subordinates ultimately accept the values of chief executives. See also Archie B. Carrol, "Managerial Ethics: A Post Watergate View," *Business Horizons*, April 1975, p. 75.

lem of changing the culture of a problem division. Having been burned in the past, the financial vice president of a convicted company has adopted a preventive approach. He has communicated new acquisition criteria to his investment brokers. He is now at least as interested in information about a company's ethical practices as in its financial performance. One chief executive officer said that he and his top managers learned the hard way from troubles soon after making an acquisition. He felt that retraining management is helpful:

"Managing these disparate cultures in the face of institutional transition is difficult. You have to change the self-perpetuating norms. Given our hard-charging acquisition policy, maintaining our corporate beliefs is hard. We have to move in and go with the old management still in place. Managing newly acquired divisions is like trying to raise adopted kids. An adopted child after age five may still need his new parents to teach him when to go to bed and when to get up."

Some companies find that just as training acquired personnel is helpful to reorient business practices, training salesmen to sell product features rather than to sell for price alone also helps change practices. If a company manages to develop special mechanical packaging systems, special graphic design abilities, or some other means of differentiation, salesmen must be given the knowledge needed to sell these features. Well-trained salesmen can often find ways to compete in terms of special delivery services, inventory aids, and design suggestions. As one sales manager put it, "Only lazy sales managers rely on commissions to get their salesmen to sell."

Another tool of general management is the evaluation and rewards system. The companies that were least involved in the price-fixing conspiracy compensate their sales forces on straight salary and evaluate on the basis of volume rather than of price level or profit. Several companies convicted of price fixing have now adopted this method and are in the process of learning to evaluate people along broader dimensions.

Price Decision Procedures.   One of the factors contributing to price fixing we cited

---

Exhibit   Danger and Safety Zones of the Factors Contributing to Price Fixing

Industry characteristics:

Danger zone	Safety zone
Overcapacity	Undercapacity
Undifferentiated products	Differentiated products
Frequent job-order pricing	Infrequent commodity pricing
Contact with competitors	No contact with competitors
Large, price-sensitive customers	Small, price-insensitive customers

Company characteristics:

Danger zone	Safety zone
Collusion culture	Top-management modeling and training
High rewards for profits	Multidimensional rewards
Decentralized pricing decisions	Centralized pricing decisions
Widespread trade association participation	Constrained trade association participation
Reactive legal staff	Anticipatory legal staff
Loose, general ethical rules	Specific ethical codes with auditing

previously was the practice in some of the companies studied of allowing specific price decisions to be influenced by salespeople and others below the general management level. In effect, because of bonus and commission arrangements, junior people were acting almost as profit center managers. Since these were the same people who might well see their competitors' sales representatives in the customers' waiting rooms, the scene for illegal action was set.

Some managers in the companies we studied have been reviewing their practices in this regard and making tighter definitions of who can legitimately take part in pricing decisions. It takes careful analysis of the multiple sources of relevant information concerning prices as well as an explicit commitment procedure to make such rules both workable and prudent.

Code of Ethics.   Attempts to move beyond top-level role modeling have led some executives to prepare codes of ethics on company business practices. In some companies this document circulates only at top levels and, again, the word seems to have trouble getting down the line. Even those documents that were sent to all employees seemed to have been broadly written, toothless versions of the golden rule. One company tried to get more commitment by requiring employees to sign and return a pledge. A senior vice president in this company complained that even though a copy of a law is also sent along:

"This stuff isn't all that valuable. In the first place you're only sending the employee what the law says and you're not telling him or her anything new. Second, it's not signed in blood! You haven't committed him to any behavior; he just recognizes that he has to sign the card to work."

An employee convicted of price fixing agreed with these comments and questioned the view that price fixers can be helped by ethical statements:

"A code of ethics doesn't do anything. I thought I had morals. I still think I do. I didn't understand the laws . . . not morals. What might to me be an ethical practice might have been interpreted differently by a legal scholar. The golden rule might be consistent with both views."

For codes to really work, substantial specificity is important. One executive said his company's method was successful because the code was tied in with an employee's daily routine:

"There is a code of business conduct here. To really make it meaningful, you have to get past the stage of endorsing motherhood and deal with the specific problems of policy in the different functional areas. We wrote up 20 pages on just purchasing issues."

Auditing for Compliance.   Once these more specific codes of business conduct are distributed, top managers may want more than a signed statement in return. Individuals can be held responsible if they have been informed on how to act in certain gray areas. The company can show its commitment to the code by checking to see that it is respected and by then disciplining violators.

Several companies are developing ways to implement internal policing. Some executives think that audits could hold people responsible for unusual pricing successes as well as for failures.[17] Market conditions, product specifications, and factory schedul-

[17] William D. Hartley, "More Firms Now Stress In-House Auditing, But It's Old Hat at GE . . . Staff Doesn't Spare Top Brass Keeping Antitrust Vigil," *The Wall Street Journal,* August 22, 1977, p. 75.

ing could be coded, put on tables, and compared to prices. High variations could be investigated. One division vice president also plans to audit expense accounts to see that competitor contact is minimized.

Legal Training.   As we noted earlier, executives in the convicted paper companies acknowledge that the lack of contact between them and company lawyers makes it hard to apply the law. Direct contact between operating managers and members of the legal staff seemed to be less frequent in the companies that were more heavily involved in the conspiracy. There are at least three barriers that the legal division must overcome in order to take this more anticipatory stance.

The first barrier is a negative image. As advisers, lawyers must accept being seen as holier-than-thou naysayers. One general manager complained:

"I'm very critical of legal people in big corporations. Most corporate counsel is negative on any level of risk. They say don't take chances in new areas, when we should. They tell us not to sue, when we should. They don't want us to cause any waves because it's easier for them. If it were up to them, they'd say don't even get out in the market."

This statement indicates how important it is for operating managers to understand the legal constraints on their plans and for the lawyers to be sensitive to the pressures of operating managers. Senior management must take the initiative to legitimize both perspectives.

The second barrier, limited interaction, is a problem for lawyers when they play the detective role, which they must at times. In one convicted company we often heard comments such as:

"Lawyers only come around when they're invited. That's only when we're in trouble. We could really use a lot more of a missionary effort from the legal department with more frequent visits."

Lawyers also complain that meeting people at infrequent lectures and formal visits rarely gives them the information that they seek.

Part of this problem is owing not only to the frequency of the visit, but also to the level of the people visited. At many companies lawyers often meet with only top-level managers who are expected to spread the word through the organization. Unfortunately, the word rarely reaches the people in an organization who are the most vulnerable and who need to hear it most. One convicted sales manager explained:

"If you want to face facts, we never got any indication from above that what we were doing was wrong. I was never asked to attend any of the lectures our legal division gave. I guess only the general managers did. If any applicable information had ever been passed down to me or if there had been any support to ask questions from above, I don't know what I would have done. You can bet that, at the least, I would have begun to ask some questions."

The third barrier, boredom, stems from the educator role that the corporate counsel must assume. One lawyer in one of the convicted companies complained, "We really don't know how to teach this stuff without sending people off to the coffeepot." Another lawyer complained that only now, because the costs of prosecution have been so severe, are people starting to listen.

Some companies have developed successful legal programs by fostering very close contact between the general managers and the legal division. In one such program there are two lawyers who specialize in traveling around and meeting the general managers. The chief legal counsel added:

"Any whistle blowing probably comes through the lawyers. This style of communication is essential in getting the point across. We try to be serious and sincere. Also the approach is important. A lot of smart legal departments used to start off with the first line of vice presidents and work up in their education program. However, these people often think that they're smarter than the lawyer or else they may not have very good communication with their subordinates, so we try to get close to the danger line. If nothing happens in five years, they say we're paranoid, but with top management support we can continue."

Thus even a successful program has problems of its own. If it works, people may not believe it was needed in the first place.[18]

Executives in another company, which was not involved in the conspiracy, agree with the need to tailor a program to the danger line of the organization. Outside counsel is extensively involved on two levels. First, attorneys meet with each salesman on a one-on-one basis. The lawyer digs up expense reports and other files and grills the salesman. This same procedure is then repeated at group and general manager meetings.

At the general manager and vice president levels, the legal staff puts on a simulated grand jury inquiry. In these dramatizations even the president sits on the witness stand to defend himself on the basis

---

[18] These sorts of frustrations are frequently heard in legal conferences, for example, see Allen D. Choka, "The Role of Corporate Counsel," presentation at the Eighth Annual Corporate Counsel Institute, Northwestern School of Law, October 8 and 9, 1969.

Costs of Ambiguous Policies

In late 1976, a federal judge imposed fines, probation, or jail terms on 47 of 48 executives in 22 companies charged with and found guilty of price-fixing violations in the folding-carton industry. In terms of the numbers of defendants, this case was the largest price-fixing one since 1964.

Of those convicted, 15, including chief executive officers, were sentenced to brief prison terms, from 5 to 60 days, and were individually fined as much as $35,000. Of the remaining executives, 17 were fined from $500 to $30,000 and placed on probation. The remaining 15 executives were fined between $100 and $2,500. The 22 companies were initially fined $50,000 each, the maximum fine for a misdemeanor violation. The maximum fine now for a felony violation of antitrust law is $2 million for each violating company.

Following these criminal convictions, the companies faced 45 civil suits filed by customers seeking damages for alleged overcharges. Over the past two years, many of these same companies have been inundated with charges of criminal price fixing involving felony and misdemeanor violations in virtually every one of the converting ends of the business. One chief executive officer reported that his folding-carton division's past five years' earnings had been surpassed by just the legal fees involved in this case. The cost to image and company morale is incalculable.

---

of documents prepared by his vice presidents. There is a great deal of tension surrounding these mock trials. The president of this company cited this trial as:

". . . one of the most important ways we've sought to keep the organization sensitive to legal issues. We identify several hundred people with point-of-sales exposure and talk to a large percentage of that group. We're trying to get the lawyers to prepare a dossier and challenge each of these people. This confessional situation is a very intensive experience.''

This procedure helps management spot problems so it can clear up misunderstandings before they become more serious. The possible interpretations of employee words and actions are made very clear. The president said that this sort of investigation on top of the usual lectures is needed to bring the message across:

"We've had attorneys giving their fire and brimstone talks to large groups for 10 to 15 years, and we have simply concluded that isn't strong enough medicine for this ailment. Our experiences in other parts of the company convinced us that this thoroughness is vital.''

Several members of this same company told us that they feel more comfortable discussing these issues with outside counsel, as this plan provides. They prefer speaking to someone who represents broader legal expertise and who is not immediately tied in with the corporate hierarchy and internal pressure. The interrogation by a fresh outsider seems to bring more reality to the investigation.

Most of the managers in the company believe that communication with counsel is protected by attorney-client privilege, but recent court decisions suggest that should the interests of the corporation differ from those of any executives, it is the corporation, in the name of the shareholders, not management, which really has the right of attorney-client privilege. Unless shareholders abdicate this right, management cannot be categorically protected in such communi-

cation.[19] The use of safeguarded channels of communication, however, whether they be lawyers or general ombudsmen, is important for individuals trapped by the questionable practices of superiors.[20]

Professional Pride

Many industries share the exposures to price fixing we have highlighted. And the problems of ensuring compliance increase in complexity as the list of contributing factors grows. Our review of the specific compliance methods that are being used in the forest products companies with the better records provides a good start toward the development of a fail-safe approach. In our interviews we were also searching for a promising general approach—perhaps a philosophy of management—that could infuse a company and serve as an antibody to thoughts of price collusion.

We believe we did find such a condition in one company. The evidence we saw was largely indirect, but it can probably best be characterized as professional pride. This company is one of the handful that is largely successful in developing a differentiated set of products. It is no accident. Even in the face of all the industry difficulties we have cited there exists a very strong belief that ''if we're not smart enough to make reasonable profits without resorting to any form of price fixing, we'll simply get out of the business.''

This belief is translated at the individual level into ''I'd rather quit than stoop to get-

[19] Howard E. O'Leary, Jr., ''Criminal Antitrust and the Corporate Executive,'' *American Bar Association Journal*, October 1977, p. 1389; ''Attorneys Privilege,'' *U.S. Law Week, Bureau of National Affairs*, February 28, 1978, *46*, p. 2435.

[20] Helen Dudar, ''The Price of Blowing the Whistle,'' *New York Times Magazine*, October 30, 1977, p. 41.

ting my results that way." In effect, this company's executives are making an old-fashioned distinction between clean, earned profits and rigged, dirty profits. It is literally unthinkable for them to want to make money the latter way. They have too much self-esteem.

Although executives and salespeople in this company widely share the strong code of behavior, it is not clear exactly how it has been disseminated throughout the organization. The best evidence is that when top managers emphasize professional pride and the distinction between clean and dirty profits, the commitment to achieve profits through legal means is clearly driven down the line. Such emphasis cuts out ambiguous signals that lead to junior people second-guessing top management's intentions.

> There is no way to success
> in our art but to take
> off your coat, grind paint,
> and work like a digger on
> the railroad, all day
> and every day.
>
> —Emerson, *Conduct of Life: Power*

READING 6
CHALLENGES OF PERCEIVED ILLEGALITY AND WASTE*
David W. Ewing

Statistically, most complaints and allegations of management inefficiency or illegality must be off the mark. They reflect frustration and envy more often than accurate, disinterested perception. Nevertheless,

___
* Excerpt from *Do It My Way—Or You're Fired! Employee Rights and the Changing Role of Management Prerogatives*, by David W. Ewing, pp. 51–67. Copyright © 1983 by David W. Ewing, John Wiley & Sons Publishers. Reprinted by permission of John Wiley & Sons, Inc.

since an important minority of these complaints do come from subordinates with first-hand knowledge, the trend is in favor of giving the complainant some standing at the expense of the superior's traditional prerogative. This trend is the result of the efforts of several groups of people.

The *American public*, as indicated earlier, is sympathetic to the right of a critic to sound off if the criticism is substantial. Whether this sympathy springs from compassion for the underdog, chronic suspiciousness of top management, a belief in the principle of civil liberties, or some combination of these motives, no one knows for sure. In any case, the majority of Americans believe that a true whistleblower deserves some kind of a break—at least, until proved wrong. A case in point is James Morrissey, the white-haired retired seaman who for many years has been blowing the whistle on leaders of his union, the National Maritime Union. When Morrissey has charged union leaders such as Joseph Curran and Shannon Wall with raiding the union till for personal benefit, battled them in court, and spoken out against them in the press, in many quarters he has been hailed as a hero. Clyde Summers, a University of Pennsylvania law professor and specialist in labor law, probably echoes the majority sentiment when he asserts that rebels like Morrissey help to keep the union bureaucracy from going completely sour.[1] Morrissey has succeeded in getting more national attention than most dissidents, of course, but the same generous reservoir of public sympathy that he has drawn from has nourished thousands of other rank-and-file rebels.

Employees generally give a dissident the benefit of a doubt if his or her criticisms are

___
[1] *The Wall Street Journal,* July 13, 1981, p. 1.

not self-serving. Although the dissident may be given a wide berth by employees who fear that bosses will find them guilty by association, and in some cases may even be threatened physically by fellow workers (as in Morrissey's case, for example), he or she usually has the sympa'hy of other workers. Dissidents fortunate enough to have unique status or prestige may have almost instant credibility. For instance, Robert M. Stronach, who in the 1970s blew the whistle repeatedly on his employer of 34 years, Narragansett Electric Company, was a vice president in the organization and, because of his status, was believed by almost everyone.

Many *courts* are tending to be sympathetic to employee critics of management waste and impropriety, as the *Tameny, McNulty,* and *O'Sullivan* cases already mentioned illustrate. To elaborate on the last, Frances E. O'Sullivan was a hospital nurse who, when asked to perform catheterizations, refused on the ground that she was not properly trained to do so. When she was dismissed, she took the doctors and the hospital to court for breach of contract. In court, the defendants pleaded that she had no right to sue because she was an employee at will, but the Superior Court of New Jersey broke from tradition and held that she had indeed stated a valid cause of action. Since both the public interest and the law (i.e., the Medical Practice Act of New Jersey, forbidding catheterizations by unlicensed nurses and physicians) were involved, the judges thought that an exception to the traditional common-law rule should be made.[2]

It must be emphasized again, however, that such holes in the common-law dike are still small, management's prerogative remains strong, and the inside critic of illegal-

ity or inefficiency has a heavy burden of proof. A case in point is *Martin* v. *Platt*.[3] In 1974 two employees of Magnavox reported to the president that a vice president was soliciting and receiving kickbacks from suppliers. The two whistleblowers were sacked. Whether their allegations were sound was a question the Indiana Court of Appeals did not bother with, for it felt that the boss's prerogative to fire for any reason or no reason should not be disputed. Though that case probably would have gone the other way in a number of other states, and might even go the other way in Indiana today, it is a reminder that the old rule still has some standing.

In addition, *labor arbitrators* customarily protect union members who speak out against perceived illegality and inefficiency. This protection is far from being automatic, however. For example, an arbitrator is not likely to rescue an employee who vindictively bad-mouths management in public, speaks so vehemently in the shop that worker morale is threatened, or in other ways appears to abuse the freedom.

Finally, *chief executives* are becoming more sympathetic to the employee critic of waste and wrongdoing. They believe that such an attitude may serve the cause of employee morale as well as help to keep superiors on their toes. Impressive statements of this philosophy have appeared in magazines like the *Harvard Business Review, Dun's,* and *Personnel Administration.* One may wonder why it has taken so long for chief executives to take this stance. The answer probably is that they used to believe that top-down pressure on managers and supervisors was enough to assure honesty and efficiency. Once upon a time it may have been.

In *King John* Shakespeare has his hero ob-

---

[2] *O'Sullivan* v. *Mallon et al.,* 390 A.2d 149 (1978).

[3] *Martin* v. *Platt,* 386 NE.2d 1026 (1979).

serve, "How oft the sight of means to do ill deeds makes ill deeds done." Most smart executives can see ways to cut corners here and there, or make an end run around this law or that regulation, and the temptation indeed may be irresistible. What will block it? As we shall see in the following two accounts, one involving a bank and the other a state agency, the only thing that stands between the perpetrator and success may be an observant subordinate.

The Case of the Beleaguered Banker

Banking was not John C. Harless's first choice of a career, partly because he may have believed he lacked sufficient education for advancement.[4] After graduation from high school in Rivesville, West Virginia, he attended Fairmont State College for one semester, then went to Cleveland for a year and worked as an apprentice machinist. Giving up on that career idea, he returned to Rivesville and, after holding various construction and sales jobs, went to Fairmont and took a position in a small loan company that was willing to educate him in retail credit financing. He learned on the job, he went to seminars, and he took courses offered by the National Retail Credit Association. After five years, he was promoted into management.

Shortly after this promotion, he made two fateful contacts: a vice president of the bank across the street, the First National Bank in Fairmont, and a director of that bank, a man who also happened to be a county judge. These two contacts led to a job offer in the bank, which he accepted.

Happily, Harless began learning all he could about a new world of deposits, loans,

[4] The data for this account are drawn from court records, local newspaper articles, and an interview with John Harless.

interest rates, service charges, federal and state regulations, and organization. He wanted to learn everything he could, and First National helped him. It sponsored his attendance at seminars of the American Institute of Banking. It paid his expenses to attend a course on computer operations conducted by IBM in Pittsburgh. He was promoted to office manager of the consumer credit department. And then, as he continued to learn and benefit and win the respect of the bank's staff, it sent him to a three-year resident program in banking at the University of Virginia in Charlottesville. The bank officer who recommended him for the university program was vice president Aubrey B. Wilson.

It was Harless's habit to observe and question. For some time he had suspected that the bank was overcharging certain customers and that his mentor Wilson was involved. However, he himself was not directly involved, and for obvious reasons he didn't want to go out of his way to force the issue. Unhappily, in June 1975 Wilson put an end to his innocence. It appeared to him that Wilson had succumbed to "the sight of means to do ill deeds." According to testimony in court later on, the vice president was authorizing the illegal withholding of part of the rebate due customers who had prepaid an installment loan, calling the sum a service charge. It was illegal, Wilson admitted, but he wanted Harless to do it anyway. Harless says that Wilson told him, "Add $50 or $100 to the charge, whatever you think you can get away with."

Harless protested. He talked to other employees of the bank. He returned to Wilson with a reply that forced the senior officer's hand. "I'll do it only if you give me written authorization," Harless said. He knew, as Wilson knew, that a written order was out of the question. Late that June, Wilson fired the manager whom he himself had recommended and in whom First National had spent so much training money and effort. Harless's halcyon days at the bank were over.

However, a week later, Harless received a letter from Wilson telling him to return to work on July 3. What accounted for Wilson's change of heart? Harless thinks the letter was sent under pressure from members of the board. Harless also believes that a board member had reminded Wilson that one officer of the bank could not unilaterally fire another officer—that only the board itself could fire an officer.

But none of this made Wilson happy about the reinstatement. The dismissal, he told Harless, would be treated as a one-week suspension without pay. He also told Harless that he had the backing of the board in the overcharging practice. If you complain again, Wilson told him, you'll be fired for good.

Back in harness, Harless was once again the workhorse that the bank wanted, but not the servile subordinate that Wilson wanted. The illegal overcharging was continuing, and Harless went in September to J. Harper Meredith, the county judge with whom he had become acquainted while at the small loan company. In the judge's chambers he reported that Wilson was trying to force him to overcharge customers. (In court later, Meredith denied this conversation.) Harless says that Meredith promised to look into the matter and, if the illegal practice existed, to stop it. But shortly thereafter, says Harless, the judge called him to report that an auditor could find only trifling overcharges. Harless says he argued that this was not the case. He had verified accounts showing larger overcharges, he told the judge.

Shortly after this, according to the court record, telltale documents began to disappear. Harless believes that Wilson instructed certain employees to get rid of records showing illegal overcharges and withholding of proper rebates. In court later on, Wilson denied giving such an instruction. Someone gave it, however, and Harless was able to rescue some of the incriminating records from trash cans.

Apparently this purging of the files continued for several months, which suggests that there were quite a few incriminating documents to be gotten rid of. In court four years later, Beverly Daniels, an employee who got fired presumably for knowing too much, testified that files were thrown away at Wilson's direction as late as December. After the purging, the files were put downstairs in the bank building where, like Bluebeard's corpses, they would remain silent forever.

Of more immediate concern to Harless than the files was his demotion. In October, soon after his talk with Judge Meredith, he was told that he would no longer serve as office manager but would work as a clerk in the Federal Housing Administration department of the bank. In his harassment of Harless, Wilson was indefatigable, Harless recalls:

> I was transferred to the FHA department to do clerical duties such as type FHA reports, type loan agreements, and do various other types of clerical duties and reports. Every chance Mr. Wilson got when we were alone, he kept reminding me how he had the power to ruin my career and see that I was never able to obtain a job in any other bank or to advance in First National Bank. Mr. Wilson would call employee meetings. Everyone was to attend but me. He would advise the employees not to talk or associate

with me during or after working hours. As though to keep ridiculing me, Mr. Wilson would continuously pass around memos to all the employees to remind them that if he should have to leave the office for any reason, I was not in charge. He advised them not to go to me with their problems or to obtain any approvals from me on their work. In February of 1976, Mr. Wilson saw one of the young women who worked at the office with my wife and me at one of the local shopping malls, and the following day he dismissed her.

The hazing of Harless continued into the winter, spring, and summer of 1976. Early in the summer, however, he took another action that would bolster his cause; he retained a local attorney to help him. The attorney, Ross Maruka, went to Judge Meredith with a list of about a dozen accounts of egregious overcharging. But the months dragged on, and in October Harless still had received no response from the board or any relief from Wilson's harassment.

Now he decided to get in touch with a local federal bank examiner. At their meeting he disclosed numbers, dates, and then hard facts about the overcharging. Soon the examiner, reporting the evidence to the comptroller's office, was sent to First National to verify the allegations. After investigating, he told Harless that his allegations were essentially correct and that the overcharging was serious. Auditors from the Pittsburgh office of Ernst & Ernst came in and made a long list of overcharged accounts. The bank made some 441 refunds, Harless says, but not all of the customers on the list got their due.

On November 1, both Harless and Wilson were summoned to the boardroom by a committee of officers who had been appointed to investigate the illegal practices.

At this session one of the directors said that the committee realized that overcharging had indeed been going on and would be stopped.

Wilson now admitted the overcharges, but protested that he didn't know they were illegal. Judge Meredith answered that ignorance of the law was no excuse, and instructed Wilson not to come to board meetings (a privilege Wilson had enjoyed in the past) and not to try to fire Harless. Harless was reinstated as manager of the consumer credit department, and the judge told him to inform the executive vice president right away if Wilson caused him any more grief.

For a few minutes, Harless was happy with everything. But when he returned to his office, Wilson threatened to get even with him. Back in his old job, Harless found the people in his department helpful and friendly. Only Wilson seemed to want to hassle him.

Around the middle of November, two federal bank examiners appeared. They had been assigned to investigate the illegal practices. In a couple of weeks, two officers of the bank, executive vice president Patrick L. Schulte and auditor Charles E. Hawkins, began a series of interviews with various employees to dig up as much evidence as possible. When they came to Harless, they emphasized that the interview was confidential—their main purpose was to find out about refunds still due. Harless disclosed all he knew. He had retrieved some of the records thrown into the wastebaskets and garbage cans, he said. They asked if he could produce them. Yes, he guessed he could. He gave the incriminating records to Hawkins.

On December 30, Harless was called to Schulte's office and told he was fired. Harless asked why. The board had decided that no reason should be given, the executive vice president answered. Even after Harless's attorney contacted the board and the bank's attorney, no reason was ever given orally. However, a couple of years later Harless's lawyer, then David L. Solomon, told reporter Peggy Edwards, who faithfully reported the many twists and turns of Harless's story in the *Fairmont Times–West Virginian*, that the minutes of the board meeting noted the dismissal decision was based on "personal possession of bank records and supplying false and misleading information to regulatory agencies."

What must have happened is that the directors who wanted to oust Harless were briefed by legal counsel and told that it was quite unnecessary to offer a reason for firing him. Indeed, the law made it undesirable to do so in a case like this, counsel might have explained. Perhaps counsel quoted the often cited rule of the U.S. Supreme Court's decision in 1884 in *Payne* v. *Western & A.R.R. Railroad*—employers "may dismiss their employees at will . . . for good cause, for no cause, or even for cause morally wrong, without thereby being guilty of legal wrong." One can imagine a scene something like this:

Director: What we really want to fire him for is causing a hell of a lot of trouble, to say nothing of the money he's cost us.

Counsel: I realize that.

Director: To be blunt, he's a pain in the neck.

Counsel: You don't have to explain.

Director (with dollar-thin smile): You mean to tell me we don't have to give a reason?

Counsel: That's essentially correct.

Director (with unbelieving smile): Not to Johnny himself?

Counsel: That's right.

Director (more smile): Not to the bank staff or the press?

Counsel: That's right, sir.

Director (beaming): Not even to the bank examiners?

Counsel: To no one, no reason at all.

So Harless was on the streets looking for work. When he applied for unemployment pay, the reason he gave for getting sacked was that he had refused to engage in illegal overcharging and had reported the wayward practice to the feds. This statement was sent to First National and in due course it was returned without being disputed. So he was at least able to start drawing jobless pay without having to hassle for it.

"After contacting nearly every bank in a three-county area, and being treated very rudely by them," Harless says, "I gave up and went to work for Consolidated Coal as a laborer in a deep coal mine. In April of 1977, several of the banks I had applied to advised me that Mr. Wilson had contacted them before I had ever applied for a job, and advised them that I was a troublemaker."

In court two years later, an officer of a bank in Morgantown testified that he had been called by Wilson and told that Harless was nothing but a troublemaker. However, Wilson has denied such a conversation.

The hazards in Harless's way multiplied. In *The Merchant of Venice*, Shakespeare writes: "You take my house, when you do take the prop / That doth sustain my house; you take my life, / When you do take the means whereby I live." Although Harless was able to hold on to both his house and his life, the months that followed his discharge took a heavy toll. "He could not sleep, eat, he wouldn't associate with his family," his lawyer was to report later on. "For nine months he was broken in spirit and body."

But he got help from family and friends. Some help also came from his old friends at the bank, who kept him informed about goings-on there. Fear of losing their jobs kept them from seeing him publicly, however—perhaps they remembered the swift dispatching of the young employee seen with the Harlesses at a shopping mall some time earlier. Also, they would not sign depositions for him confirming the practice of overcharging.

Although hampered in his efforts to find a satisfactory job and vindication, Harless was not handcuffed. He possessed an important advantage, and he made the most of it: his case was based not on his opinion against the bank's, or his judgment against Wilson's, but on hard, factual, often quantitative evidence. The fact that he could recite numbers, names, dates, and places could not fail to impress interviewers. His break came at a bank in Morgantown. It was Central National Bank, a newly chartered bank scheduled to open its doors in the fall of 1977. Since it did not have a track record, as Harless puts it, it had a hard time luring qualified people from secure jobs in banks with standing. Nor could it pay generous salaries. Of course, none of these disadvantages bothered Harless.

Back when he had been with the small loan firm, he had gotten to know one of Central National's directors. That helped his cause. Another director of Central National happened to have been a victim of First National's illegal overcharging. He met several times with the directors and explained in detail what had happened at First National. He assured them that he had not blown the whistle without first discussing the problem with the First National board and trying to solve it quietly inside the bank.

Central National hired Harless in September as second man in charge, with the title of cashier. Like a tenacious ghost, however,

Wilson continued even then to haunt him. Various directors of Central National, says Harless, told him that Wilson had called them to say what a troublemaker he was and to predict he wouldn't be able to handle the job. But these last-ditch efforts at revenge failed, and on July 1, 1978, Harless was promoted to chief executive officer.

In the meantime, however, Harless was head to head with First National on a different front. In the spring of 1977, about four months after being fired, Harless sued the bank, Schulte, and Wilson for $1,250,000. As presented by his attorneys David Solomon, a former prosecutor for Monongalia County, and Morgantown lawyer S. J. Angotti, his case alleged that he had been maliciously fired and blackballed for objecting to illegal overcharging practices; he sought $750,000 in compensatory damages and $500,000 in punitive damages. The action came before Marion County circuit court judge Fred L. Fox II. Judge Fox ruled against Harless, on the basis that an employee at will has no cause of action against an employer for arbitrary dismissal. However, Fox sent the case to the West Virginia Supreme Court of Appeals for review, and the high court agreed to hear it.

In July 1978, Justice Thomas Miller, speaking for the Supreme Court, ruled that Harless was entitled to recover damages in a trial. Although acknowledging the long-standing rule, Miller pointed out that public policy was firmly on Harless's side. In a case like Harless's, he said, the old rule needed to be reformed. "Where the employer's motivation for discharge contravenes some substantial public policy principle," he ruled, "then the employer may be liable to the employee for damages occasioned by the discharge."[5]

---

[5] *Harless* v. *First National Bank in Fairmont*, 246 SE Reporter 2d 270, 275 (1978).

So in September 1979, the case was tried before Judge Fox (who, incidentally, shared the Sixteenth Judicial Circuit with Chief Judge J. Harper Meredith, the director of First National) and a jury. Bitterly fought, the trial brought Harless face to face with those who had hamstrung him at First National, including Wilson and Schulte (the latter was relieved of being a defendant, however). Wilson testified that Harless's allegations were spurious. It was Harless who was in the wrong, Wilson claimed—for trying to protect a guilty employee. When he tried to correct the troublemaker, Wilson claimed that he was berated and told to get off the plaintiff's back. He "would sit at his desk. He wouldn't do anything unless he was told to. He stared off into space. He had a chip on his shoulder." Thus testified the vice president. As for the allegations that Wilson had ordered illegal overcharging, the vice president called them ridiculous, and he further denied ordering the destruction of incriminating records.

Harless, on the other hand, kept hammering away with fact after fact and number after number, many of them confirmed by the actions of the accounting firm, the bank examiners, and witnesses.

On September 20, 1979, after four hours of deliberation, the jury returned a verdict for Harless and awarded him $125,000 in compensatory and punitive damages. Significantly, Wilson was tagged with a larger share of this amount than the bank was. The jury ordered Wilson to pay $10,000 for the act of firing Harless, $40,000 for "outrageous conduct causing emotional distress," and $25,000 for the blackballing.

What is the lesson of the Harless case for managers? It does not say that you are no longer free to manage as your predecessors could years ago. It does not say that you are no longer free to dispatch a troublemaker. It only says that you cannot manage with abandon. You had better look out if the real troublemaker, from a legal standpoint, is yourself or your colleagues. The courts and the public want you to manage efficiently and make a profit. However, in an ever larger number of states (though by no means every one) judges and legislators do not want you to manage at the expense of the law, and if you try to make an end run by getting rid of conscientious objectors or muzzling them by intimidation, the judges will not take your side.

"We Invited You into Our House, and You Took an Axe to the Furniture"

With no axe to grind, though with youthful idealism, Michael Nelson entered Barbara Sugarman's house on July 21, 1975.[6] Of course, it was not a house in the literal sense; it was the Office of Volunteer Services of Georgia's Department of Human Resources. Sugarman was the official head of the household, created a few years earlier by the governor of Georgia at the time, Jimmy Carter. In converting a number of old departments into "divisions," Carter had had to build a new bureaucratic level. On this level were erected units like the Office of Volunteer Services.

Nelson entered with enthusiasm. He was going to help the government clean up poverty and misery. A graduate of the college of William and Mary who had gone on to earn a master's degree in political science at Johns Hopkins, he had been influenced by what he calls the "moralistic tone" of the campuses in the late 1960s and early 1970s.

[6] The data for this account are drawn from Michael Nelson's article, "Whistle-Blowing in Carter Country," *Johns Hopkins Magazine*, November 1976, and an interview.

"I wasn't involved in the student Left," he says, "but everyone in college then learned to regard politics in terms of good guys and bad guys." Though his salary was as low as his ideals were high, this didn't bother him. With no family responsibilities, he could live on $2,500 a year—and besides, it was just for a year that he was visiting.

Working out of an air-conditioned office in suburban Augusta, Nelson encountered some people who reinforced his idealism. For example, he worked with two dedicated state officials, one a volunteer coordinator for regional institutions for the retarded, the other the head of the local regional mental health center. In addition, in Barbara Sugarman, the boss, he saw an executive who was extraordinarily persuasive and winning when dealing with other state officials, though he perceived that her household staff was less than enthusiastic about her.

Sugarman would describe how she had gotten to know Rosalynn Carter, taken her around to different mental hospitals, and gotten her seriously interested in mental health, a cause she would support when the Jimmy Carters moved to the White House. Sugarman was the first head of the Office of Volunteer Services, and later on she would be promoted to a government position in Washington.

Nevertheless, Nelson soon became disillusioned. "It did not take long for me to realize that what I was doing had about as much to do with fighting poverty as that chair you are sitting in," he says. He wrote in his alumni magazine, "I was the quintessential paper-shuffling, pencil-pushing bureaucrat. I worked in an office with other paper-shuffling, pencil-pushing bureaucrats. All except the boss. He did not have anything useful to do either, but he had so many friends in the state capital that he did not have to pretend to." It was like a house where everyone is so busy reading and passing notes back and forth that nobody gets dinner on or tends the leak in the roof.

Of course, he didn't work inside all the time. Carrying the imposing title of Area Volunteer Resources Coordinator, his assignment was to drive around a seven-county area, visit local welfare offices, encourage them to use volunteers, and send weekly reports to Atlanta. But he didn't find these visits very useful, either.

"On a typical day I would drive out to, say, Lincolnton, a Plains-style metropolis, to 'confer' with John Ludwig, the head of the local welfare office. 'John,' I would say, 'why don't you use some volunteers here?'

" 'Because I don't need 'em, Mike,' he would tell me. 'I got too much paid help already.'

"Then on to antebellum Washington [Georgia]. 'Mrs. Beckum,' I would ask, 'how about using some volunteers here in your office?'

" 'Why I already do, Mike. We've got old Mr. Pollard, he drives the children to clinic, and Betsy Blanchard,' and so on.

"After a few weeks of this it began to sink in: what I was doing—and I did it fairly well, I was told—served no useful purpose at all! If local DHR offices needed volunteers, they went out and did the one thing most likely to startle an Atlanta planner out of his shoes—got them all by themselves. If they did not have any use for volunteers, they were not about to go get some just because I came around. I was the living, breathing embodiment of fat in government. If I owned a briefcase, the only thing I would have thought worth putting in it was a peanut butter and jelly sandwich."

Nelson began looking around for a transfer. Finding an opening in the Georgia Legal Services Program, a worthwhile federal–state program assisted by the national Volunteers in Service to America (VISTA) program, he packed his suitcases and left the Sugarman household.

At Legal Services, where he represented Medicaid clients, the problem was just the opposite of the problem at Volunteer Services. Though inexpensive medical aid for the poor was much needed, cutbacks were being planned because of pressure from the governor's mansion to economize. Since Nelson's work occasionally brought him into contact with high officials in the Department of Human Resources, he was able to complain about the proposed cutbacks at the policy level. The officials retorted that there was no money in the budget. No state agency was improving itself, they said.

No agency? Well, in fact, there was one— the Office of Volunteer Services. It was getting a big boost in funding—specifically, more than a doubling of its appropriation, from $220,000 to $470,000.

Nelson could hardly believe it. Legal Services, which really helped the poor and didn't have enough, was getting cut back, but Volunteer Services, his old organization that accomplished nothing, was getting an enormous increase! He knew that Sugarman was intensely loyal to Jim Parham, commissioner of the Department of Human Resources (also, a protégé of Jimmy Carter), and he knew that Parham reciprocated that loyalty—but this was a little much: Could government be so perverse? He recognized it could be inefficient. He realized it could bog down in red tape. But he was not prepared to find it so "off-the-wall crazy"! This was like deciding to add a new wing to an 18-room house where an old couple sat rocking all day, and taking space off a two-room house across the street where 18 people lived.

Nelson decided to sit down, analyze why the Office of Volunteer Services shouldn't

get an increase, and send his written analysis to a half-dozen key legislators. It was January 1976—late in the cycle to be doing this. Ordinarily, in fact, it would have been too late, for Sugarman's bonanza had been made a part of Governor George Busbee's fiscal program and had cleared the Georgia legislature's appropriations committee. However, Nelson knew that the legislators were frantic to hold the line on the budget, and for that reason they just might listen to him.

In his analysis, Nelson pointed out that Volunteer Services was hampered by poor staff morale, clogged with paperwork, dishonest (it forged data in its performance reports), poorly administered, and poorly conceived. He advised the legislators to check around for themselves.

It was too late to discuss his letter first with his old boss Sugarman or with Commissioner Parham. Such a discussion wouldn't have done any good, he believed—as Zorba the Greek said, "You can knock forever on a deaf man's door." But he sent copies of the letter to Sugarman and Parham.

This letter was a precocious and risky step, and Nelson knew it. For one who had lived in Sugarman's house, and who still lived in Parham's house, it was the worst type of table manners. He would be classified with the Goops described in Gelett Burgess's poem:

> The Goops they lick their fingers
>   And the Goops they lick their knives;
> They spill their broth on the tablecloth;
>   Oh, they lead untidy lives.

Only in this case he was spilling the broth not only on the table cloth but all over the floor of the legislature.

None of the risks deterred Nelson. Once

the idea came to mind, he says he just sat down and began drafting the letter. "I'm a person who believes that often you should follow your impulses," he explains, "because I don't believe most impulses are impulses at all. I think they tend to be what comes forth from a lot of sifting and sorting of information in the back of your mind." Besides, he says, he didn't have very much to lose. His salary wasn't substantial enough to be important. Also, his commitment was for only one year. Finally, he wasn't constrained by the need for a regular paycheck to pay the bills and fulfill family obligations—the kind of pressure that gives many employees a powerful incentive to be "good" houseguests when they see wrongdoing that should be reported.

Reaction to his letter from the capitol was swift. Chairman Joe Frank Harris of the House Appropriations Committee directed his staff to contact Nelson for more details. Nelson sent them a point-by-point critique of the annual report that Volunteer Services had sent to the governor; his critique showed, among other things, that the numbers had been grossly inflated under orders from the top. The official report was so bad that it didn't even disguise this chicanery very well—Nelson had little trouble pointing it out. He confined his remarks to the financial reporting and wrote in terms of costs and benefits; he didn't volunteer a lot of seamy information that he had acquired from Volunteer Services staff about matters that had been swept under the beds and rugs.

Reaction to his letter from the heads of the agency house also was swift. They hit the roof. They told the solons, according to one Nelson confidante, that his critique was "absolute and outright garbage." (Apparently this was mild language by top officials' standards. When Nelson wrote his story for *Johns Hopkins Magazine* a year later, Parham sent the magazine editor a letter that attacked Nelson so intemperately that it could not be printed. As Nelson remembers the essence of the letter, it warned that, though the young whistleblower might picture himself as a David fighting Goliath, he was really a Judas.)

But the timing was just right. The legislators were searching everywhere for places to make cuts in the budget. And Nelson had credibility. He had worked in the Office of Volunteer Services; he also had a fine academic background. The letter not only got to the right people at the right time in just the right stage of the budget proceedings, but it also came from the right source.

On February 10, Harris and other legislative leaders met with Governor Busbee. They persuaded him to remove the entire budget increase for Volunteer Services. They also persuaded him to launch a long-term study of whether this agency should be funded at any level.

Nelson's letter had been sensationally successful: Many veteran legislature watchers will tell you they've never seen a simple one-stroke coup produce such quick and decisive results.

So Nelson and his friends celebrated. However, the jubilation was short-lived. Parham called Nelson's new boss at Legal Services, John Cromartie. He also called the head of VISTA. Angrily Parham demanded that they throw Nelson out.

Obediently Cromartie called Nelson. "I have to fire you," he said. "Parham says he won't support Legal Services if I don't fire you, and we can't get along without his support."

Nelson went out and walked the streets of Atlanta for several hours. What should he do? He decided to go to Parham and plead his case. He called Parham's office.

Parham said to come over. When Nelson got there, Parham shook his hand and asked him to sit down—"not warmly, but politely," Nelson recalls. Nelson told him he knew how angry he was, and said he supposed that if he were in Parham's position he'd be angry, too. But the work he was doing for Legal Services was useful work, Nelson said. Telling Cromartie to fire him was not going to do Parham or anybody any good.

First, Parham denied that he had threatened to withdraw his support from Legal Services if Cromartie wouldn't fire Nelson. Then Parham said, "I feel that we have invited you into our house, and you took an axe to the furniture."

Nelson felt stunned by this unusually frank expression of the bureaucratic mind. Was he hearing things? It wasn't Parham's house, or Cromartie's, or Sugarman's, or any other state official's. It was the *taxpayer's* house.

However, as the old saying goes, "Your boss may not be right, but he's the boss." And so Nelson was evicted. It was like the old story of the father who points his wayward daughter into the night and commands, "Don't darken my doorway again." Then and there, pleading does her no good.

But there was a possible solution—VISTA's appeal process for aggrieved employees. Nelson decided to try it. He learned that it involved half a dozen stages or layers and a lot of letter-writing and discussion. In his first official consultation, an informal talk, the official's main effort seemed to be to get him to resign quietly. It was tempting to do so. But no, Nelson said to himself, he wasn't going to give up that easily. Next began the written communications part. He found that there were complicated rules concerning when an aggrieved employee had to file, what the nature of the

written complaint must be, and so on. Fortunately, one of his telephone calls to Washington, D.C., brought him into contact with a helpful woman in one of the employee relations offices there. Deciding Nelson had a case, she gave him encouragement and careful advice. She told him how to avoid missing the filing deadline, how to make sure the appeal went to the right person and address, whether to certify or register the letter, and so on. "There were a lot of technicalities on which they were hoping to trip me up in the appeals process," Nelson remembers. "She guided me through it, and without her I don't know what would have happened."

As he negotiated one stage and level after another, the state was bringing charges against him. One was that he had violated VISTA's prohibition about moonlighting; he had written a piece for the Op-Ed page of the *New York Times* on the subject of the New Jersey Turnpike and had been paid $150 for it. This was an impermissible violation of the house rules, the bureaucrats pointed out. Another charge—this one vague and worded in the most general terms—was that Nelson had acted in a manner detrimental to VISTA.

The hearing examiner dismissed the moonlighting charge as trivial. He dismissed the second charge as unsupported.

About a week before Nelson's year was up, he was informed that he had won his appeal. The good news was sent begrudgingly, however, and had he been a long-term employee it might not have come to him at all. The hearing examiner had recommended to the regional director in Atlanta, Paul Jones, that Nelson be reinstated. The director wrote Nelson that he didn't agree with the decision but that, since Nelson had only a week to go, he would let it slide.

Following his eventful year in Georgia,

Nelson moved to Washington, D.C., and became an editor of the *Washington Monthly*. After earning his doctorate at Johns Hopkins in 1978, he went to Vanderbilt University as assistant professor of political science. Reflecting on the general problem of government employees who want to speak out, he observes:

> "Whistleblowing" is an all too rare phenomenon in American bureaucracy. The disincentives are powerful. A bureaucrat who "goes public" to expose waste or malfeasance has few legal protections against dismissal. Even if not actually fired, his on-the-job effectiveness will surely be destroyed beyond repair. He becomes, after all, the "traitor" who "took an axe to the furniture." It is a rare and courageous person who would risk all this for the sake of principle.
>
> Yet clearly our system requires the kind of information about how bureaucracy operates that only insiders can provide. Executive agencies now spend more than a third of our gross national product every year, and employ one sixth of our work force. As scholars from Max Weber to Francis Rourke have pointed out, their very size, complexity, and power make them all but impossible for elected officials to penetrate and control. Unless "whistleblowers" can bring problems to lawmakers' attention when they arise inside agencies, democracy inevitably breaks down.

Nelson believes that his own experience points to a good way to cope with the problem. Student interns, visiting academics, "dollar-a-year men," and short-term, low-salary volunteer workers like himself have little to lose by speaking out, he argues. They could be looked to as watchdogs, as observers who get a good chance to see from the inside what is going on. They would not serve as "spies" for the public for they would not be *expected* to report wrongdoing. But once acquiring a conviction that

wrongdoing exists, they would not have personal reasons *not* to speak out. Though the bureaucracy might see them as malcontents, they would not feel in jeopardy.

Of course, as Nelson points out, there is a danger in such an approach. People with nothing to lose may "sound off at every real and imagined shortcoming and cause chaos in government." But he doesn't see this possibility as a serious one: "People who intern initially have, as I did, a favorable orientation to their agency." In addition, the burden of proof falls on the whistleblower, not on the officials impugned. "Surely the greater danger," he says, "lies in a runaway bureaucracy whose errors go unchecked because those inside it are cowed into silence."

READING 7
AMERICA'S NEW IMMOBILE SOCIETY*
Business Week

It is midsummer [1981], the peak season of the United States' annual relocation rite—a costly and nerve-racking exercise in perpetual motion in which one out of five Americans traditionally has moved each year. But this summer there are fewer "For Sale" signs on front lawns and fewer moving vans on the roads. Almost unnoticed, a historic shift is under way: America's celebrated "mobile society" is putting down roots.

After a quarter century in which 20 percent of the population changed addresses each year, the percentage is dropping. It fell to 17.7 percent in the last Census Bureau study in 1976 and is continuing to decline, according to census officials, who will ana-

---

* Reprinted from the July 27, 1981, issue of *Business Week* by special permission, © 1981 by McGraw-Hill, Inc.

lyze 1981 figures more precisely next year. Larry H. Long, the bureau's chief migration specialist, says the U.S. "is very unlikely to return to the mobility of the 1950s and 1960s." That easy mobility—which had been both evidence and a cause of the nation's freewheeling ways and innovative economy—has ended.

Dealing with the effects of this change will be one of the top challenges of the 1980s for U.S. industry. "We've got a real crunch coming," warns John F. Veiga, a University of Connecticut management professor. How industry responds could alter traditional ways of doing business—and living—in the U.S. as well as determine the fates of individual companies. At the least, the companies will face major problems in recruiting, training, motivating, and promoting employees, especially managers and professionals, who henceforth will remain in one spot for long periods. Moreover, declining mobility will decentralize the U.S. economy as companies build new, electronically linked plants near untapped labor sources, to the increasing detriment of the cities.

Evidence that Americans are staying put is as close as the next house or office. Tied down by dual-career marriages, housing costs, inflation, and a growing emphasis on leisure and community activities—the "quality of life"—workers are resisting relocation. At the same time, soaring moving costs are making U.S. companies less eager to transfer their employees. Specifically, many corporations are deciding that frequent moves to broaden the horizons of bright young managers are wasteful as well as disruptive.

That Americans are moving less may come as a surprise in light of the highly publicized migration from the Frostbelt to the Sunbelt in the 1970s. Some 3 million people made that move—a large number, to be sure, but only about 1.3 percent of the U.S. population and spread over 10 years. Some continue to move, including blacks returning to the South. However, the mass of Americans have remained in place, and that includes Sunbelt residents, who have halted the previous exodus from their region.

Money Is Not Enough

Robert B. Frost is one American who will not be relocating this summer despite an enticing opportunity. Avionics manager of Boeing Company's Military Airplane Division in Seattle, Frost was courted by a Los Angeles aerospace company that offered him a 30 percent raise, $25,000 to ease him into a new house, and a moorage for his sailboat. But Frost, 42, decided that the offer paled beside his 7¾ percent mortgage in Seattle, his wife's nursing job, and the more pleasant sailing on Puget Sound. "The incentives companies are offering to move just aren't enough to offset things like that," he says.

Norton Company feels the pinch of such attitudes. The big abrasives manufacturer, based in Worcester, Massachusetts, is getting refusals from one third of the employees it asks to relocate among its 120 plants. A few years ago the rate was only half that high, says Donald R. Melville, Norton's chief executive.

Georgia-Pacific Corporation faces a similar problem. It is moving its headquarters from Portland, Oregon, to Atlanta and had hoped that 400 executives and professionals—of the headquarters workforce of 700—would follow. Although it gave the employees three years to prepare and offered 8.5 percent long-term mortgages to buy homes—which are significantly cheaper in Atlanta—the company has persuaded only

250 to pull up stakes. The remaining 150 preferred to relinquish good jobs rather than relocate.

In other cases, high moving costs are causing companies to accept and even encourage employee immobility. The Employee Relocation Council, a Washington (D.C.) research group for 750 big companies, figures that its members' average cost of moving a homeowning employee has tripled in the last five years, to $30,000. Moving someone to an expensive area such as California or New York can cost three times his salary, as First National Bank of Chicago discovered to its chagrin. Merrill Lynch Relocation Management, Inc., figures that corporate-sponsored moves have declined by 25 percent in the U.S. over the past two years. Bell System Telephone Company, for example, which transferred 17,000 employees in 1979, slashed the number to 13,500 last year.

The most dramatic switch has come at International Business Machines, where frequent moves have been so ingrained in the culture that wags claim the company's initials stand for "I've Been Moved." Prodded by both the national atmosphere of employee resistance and corporate doubts about the efficiency of map-hopping, IBM is cutting the percentage of its 200,000-person work force that it moves each year to less than 3 percent, from 5 percent in the mid-1970s. And the company hopes to reduce the figure further next year "if we demonstrate we can run the business effectively with fewer transfers," says Walton E. Burdick, vice-president of personnel.

Where IBM formerly relocated one employee to fill a branch manager's opening and another employee to develop skills for future responsibilities, the company now seeks to have one move serve both purposes. "We try to make sure that there truly is a business need" for every transfer, says Burdick. Under the new rules, no worker can be "invited" to relocate more than once in two years or three times in 10 years; previously there were no limits. And while Burdick claims that refusing a move was never officially a black mark on an employee's career, the new transfer policy formally bans such attitudes.

IBM is only the most conspicuous of the companies that have changed their ways. It is hard to find a company that has not reduced transfers—willingly or not—or a headhunter who cannot relate a dozen stories about job candidates who refused to move. Although a few demographers wonder if staying put may be simply a temporary result of high inflation and a weak economy—akin to the big drop in mobility that the U.S. experienced during the Depression—there are persuasive reasons to believe that America's roots are deepening permanently.

Probably the chief reason is the proliferation of two-career families. In 1979 they represented 52 percent of U.S. marriages, up from 46.6 percent just four years earlier, and most experts predict that the number will continue to rise rapidly. But the statistics tell only part of the story: Far more working wives have serious careers today, not merely jobs that are easy to start and stop. Such couples are much harder to uproot than are single-breadwinner families. Moreover, thanks to the women's movement, even jobless wives carry more weight in family decision-making, claims James S. Manuso, a psychologist and planner with Equitable Life Assurance Society in New York City. Nonworking wives, who depend more on community ties than do their job-oriented husbands, "are less willing to grin and bear" frequent moving than they used to be, Manuso says.

What it cost to move a manager from Chicago to San Francisco

Here is what First National Bank of Chicago paid recently to move a mid-level manager earning $37,600 a year with a wife and two children

Housing-related costs, paid in full for two years, 75% the third year, 50% the fourth year:

	Years	
Housing cost differential (increases in market value, property tax, commuting costs, and utilities)	First	$ 7,700
	Second	7,700
	Third	5,775
	Fourth	3,850
Mortgage interest-rate differential	First	8,500
	Second	8,500
	Third	6,375
	Fourth	4,250
Payment covering income tax on differentials	First	7,400
	Second	7,400
	Third	5,500
	Fourth	3,750
	Subtotal....	$ 76,700

Low-rate loan partially covering downpayment on home	$ 1,900
Pre-move housing search by employee and wife	3,100
Selling costs on former home	15,400
Shipment of household goods	10,000
Final travel and temporary living expenses	4,500
One month's salary for incidental expenses	3,133
Total....	$114,733

Data: First National Bank of Chicago

Another factor favoring immobility is that the average age of the population is rising. In addition, the projected slower growth rate of the nation's economy means that there will be fewer opportunities for job-switching. Various legislative changes also encourage stability: no-growth laws, rent control, fat unemployment benefits, and plant-closure regulations.

Finally, there is the "lifestyle" issue—a hard factor to measure but crucial. "Nowadays a manager will decide he just plain likes it where he is," says Pearl Meyer, executive vice president of Handy Associates Inc., a New York City–based management consulting firm. "He likes the town, he likes the fishing, he likes coaching Little League, and it's all worth more to him than bigger bucks or a bigger job." L. Clinton Hoch, executive vice president of Fantus Co., the relocation arm of Dun & Bradstreet Corp., blames the "now generation" of the 1960s for demanding instant lifestyle gratification once jobs are secured. "We've lost the former loyalties of corporate life," he says.

For the United States as a whole, the mobility crunch will speed the economic decentralization set in motion by the revolution in data communications and the economy's growing orientation toward service and high technology. If people cannot or will not move to jobs, many jobs will move to them. Electronics companies, which regard product transportation as a minor concern, have already set up satellite operations in rural areas to tap resident work forces. Now other industries are likely to follow the electronics companies' suit.

A Lockheed Corp. task force is currently looking at sites in the Midwest and East for engineering and technical centers where locally hired personnel could work on space programs via computer hookups with the company's Sunnyvale (Calif.) Missiles & Space Division. "You don't have to work right next door anymore," says Louis J. Barnard, Lockheed's personnel director. Neither do executives have to occupy offices in the same building to discuss problems and come to decisions. Teleconferencing which uses closed-circuit TV to permit face-to-face discussion among executives in widely scattered offices, is becoming a corporate substitute.

Heading for "the Boonies"

The mobility dilemma—employees who resist moving and employers who find it too expensive to move them—does offer some potential benefits. Corporations may enjoy a new depth of experience in their ranks, perhaps similar to that in Japanese companies. And the situation could force companies to improve the quality of their career-planning programs, since transfers can no longer take the place of thorough training. But a disturbing trend also is surfacing. Recruiting firms around the U.S. say their clients increasingly reject top job candidates who would have to move, preferring to hire less experienced local people. In San Francisco, a Schlage Lock Co. executive admits that the company plans to promote a sales-

man to a high-level marketing job partly because he lives where the opening is, even though other Schlage employees "are probably more qualified."

The bulk of Americans who are moving to new areas are heading for small towns—where costs are lower, air is cleaner, and outdoor recreation is nearby—in such states as Wisconsin, North Carolina, Oregon, and New Hampshire. Employers are following. "People want to live in the boonies," says Kenneth L. Capen, corporate personnel manager of Hewlett-Packard Company. Based in Palo Alto, California, H-P has built plants in such smaller towns as Greeley, Colorado.

The 1970s, in fact, were the first decade in U.S. history that saw more people move to rural areas than away from them, reversing 200 years of farm-to-city migration. "We used to apologize" for being based in Orrville, Ohio (population 8,000), says Bruce E. Fike, corporate personnel director of J.M. Smucker Company. "But suddenly it's an advantage."

The trend is bad news for U.S. cities and for the minorities who are being left behind in growing concentrations. Lacking easily marketable skills, the inner-city poor will be an increasing drain on urban welfare budgets that are shrinking because of declining economic bases. Michigan has had to borrow $1 billion in federal funds to pay unemployment benefits, largely for Detroit auto workers who refuse to move elsewhere, and the state still faces a $113 million deficit this year. America's new small-town roots may also mean that "a lot of large downtown office buildings now under construction will become white elephants" in a few years, says Richard C. Carlson, a senior policy analyst at SRI International, a research organization in Menlo Park, California. Many large companies, led by the insurance industry, have been leaving skeleton staffs at big city offices and moving larger operations to distant towns.

The reduction in mobility is greatest among those groups that have been most willing to move in the past: educated professional and managerial people. Blue-collar workers never have been particularly mobile; employers, as a rule, do not transfer them, and those who head out on their own drop to the bottom of union seniority lists. Although Texas newspapers have been hot sellers in Detroit, where laid-off auto workers pore over the want ads, the scant evidence available indicates that wage-earners still resist moving. If anything, their resistance may now be stronger than ever because housing costs and the two-job marriage affect these workers at least as much as they affect supervisors.

Recent efforts by Midwest companies to find jobs elsewhere for laid-off workers have fizzled. About 600 Youngstown (Ohio) steelworkers have been offered jobs requiring relocation since 1978, but fewer than 200 accepted. Goodyear Tire & Rubber Company, which under a 1976 contract must give laid-off employees priority in openings at its other unionized plants, says few have been willing to transfer. Many who did relocate soon quit and returned "home" to Ohio, Goodyear adds. Tom Martin, a 27-year-old Detroit auto worker who lost his job at Chrysler Corporation last November, notes that nonmovable unemployment benefits give him no financial incentive to leave Michigan for at least a year. Sunbelt states, where jobs are more plentiful, "don't pay as well on any type of social program," Martin says.

San Francisco-based Bechtel, Inc., complains of a shortage of skilled construction workers. "They just don't move like they used to," says Hugh B. Wallace, manager of labor relations. He blames richer unemployment benefits, in part. Says George Sternlieb, director of Rutgers University's Center for Urban Policy Research in Piscataway, New Jersey: "Like it or lump it, the U.S. is slowly freezing its mobility" through seniority rules, termination pay, unemployment compensation, and welfare payments.

"Badge of Honor"

Such problems may intensify arguments for a national welfare system to even out local differences in benefits and to permit the labor market, rather than a patchwork of state legislation, to govern workers' decisions. Midwesterners without jobs "need to be able to move," says John E. Pearson, chief financial officer of 3D/International, a Houston engineering company. "If not, there is a serious threat to productivity at both ends. The more restrictions there are to moving, the more the economy stays out of whack." However, the chances of low-benefit states or the present Administration backing such a notion are minimal.

Troublesome as the issue of the immobile blue-collar worker may be, it is the totally new problem of the immobile manager, technician, and professional that most concerns U.S. companies these days. Whether the immobility results from the individual's or the employer's wishes, it confronts companies with an array of managerial and psychological problems that are particularly ticklish in a culture that has viewed frequent transfers as evidence of "fast-track" career success. Keeping on the move has been "a badge of honor" in corporate America, says Robert E. Coleman, chairman of Riegel Textile Corporation in Greenville, South Carolina.

Many companies are trying to change such attitudes, which can make managers feel left behind and can hurt their job performance when transfers decline. A new study by the University of Connecticut's John Veiga offers some ammunition. Examining 6,300 job changes by middle managers over the past 20 years, Veiga found that a large percentage of frequently moving managers who thought they were on a fast track were actually stuck on a treadmill of lateral moves. That is costly for the employer, not only because the expense of moving such people around has soared, but also because transfers can hurt productivity.

Crown Zellerbach Corporation figures that it takes three to six months before a transferred employee settles fully into his new job. The company recently decreed a new moving policy typical of the kind that is rapidly becoming the norm for companies that have gone into shock over moving costs. Transfers that do not involve a genuine promotion are now outlawed unless approved by top management. "We've got to get the message across that moving every year or two isn't the game anymore and staying put doesn't jeopardize your career," says Ray Brooks, a company personnel officer.

Declining mobility poses especially difficult problems for companies that have used transfers as a management-development tool. In the past, General Electric Company routinely packed off promising young managers for six-month stints at four different plants over two years. But employee reluctance to move—which GE first detected five years ago and which, it says, has been growing ever since—prompted the company to set up one-stop, rotational training programs at its larger facilities so that trainees can stay put. GE says the new system has cut turnover and costs. Lockheed, Crown Zellerbach, and other companies are similarly rejiggering training.

Weakened Loyalty?

A number of management experts fear that employees who are allowed to put down roots in a community will lose a sense of corporate identity, loyalty, and job worth. They argue that creating a feeling of "corporate community" by tearing down geographical ties had been a major motive—albeit an unconscious one in most cases—for the musical-chairs moving policies of such companies as Shell Oil Company and IBM.

Finding substitute ways of strengthening the corporate culture will be crucial in a less mobile America. Julien Phillips, a San Francisco partner of management consultants McKinsey & Company, suggests that companies hold frequent conferences and training sessions to bring together far-flung employees and also award prizes liberally. Veiga of the University of Connecticut is pushing a variant of the honors that Japanese companies often bestow on valued senior workers. U.S. companies, he says, should create "senior advisory" slots to reward and motivate managers whose geographical ties make further promotions difficult.

The temporary training move, with a preplanned return to home base, is rapidly becoming a substitute for the open-ended mobility of yore at many corporations. Prudential Insurance Company sends regional computer staffers to learn the ropes for two years at its Roseland (N.J.) headquarters. The employee rents out his home, with Prudential picking up any differences in out-of-pocket costs.

In an attempt to isolate problems early, some companies are assigning employees to mobile or nonmobile pools, often from the day they are hired. Stouffer Corporation is considering speeding up its management-training transfers, identifying talented recent college graduates more quickly, with an eye to moving them before immobility sets in.

With relocation costs so high, employers want to make sure that transferred families make successful moves. More and more, that means helping spouses find jobs. In a number of cities, companies are forming "spouse employment networks" that trade information on jobs that might suit the wives of transferred employees—or the husbands, since women now account for about 8 percent of the principal transferees in corporate moves, according to one relocation expert. Some 175 companies in New York, New Jersey, and Connecticut use dual-career job banks developed by Home Buyers Assistance Corporation, a Westport (Conn.) company specializing in relocating executives. Client companies list job specialties in which they typically recruit, and a computer sends them appropriate resumes of transferred spouses.

Relocation costs have jumped partly because of inflation and partly because companies have been forced to sweeten their transfer packages to persuade employees to move. Payments covering the difference between an employee's old and new mortgage costs have caused the biggest increase. Typically, companies pay them for three years, after which the employee must absorb the full impact of the more expensive mortgage himself—unless he moves elsewhere under a new corporate mortgage umbrella. Merrill Lynch Relocation, in a survey of 605 major companies, found that 61 percent paid a mortgage-interest differential allowance in 1980, compared with only 27 percent just the year before.

Keeping Costs Down

Decentralization, especially to rural areas, offers expanding companies an attractive way out of the relocation-cost spiral. Although mortgage interest rates are not lower in smaller towns, home prices and thus the size of mortgages are.

Moreover, there is less need to transfer people because operations can be started where labor is available. Hewlett-Packard, which has set up plants in 18 locations around the U.S., splits off just a small cadre of executives from one facility to take over the newest one and hires the rest of the staff on the spot.

IBM has spread itself across the map for years, but the company is now giving greater autonomy to its regional branches in an effort to combat the restlessness and dead-end feelings that immobility can foster. Fremont General Insurance Company, which previously based all its employees at its Los Angeles headquarters, five years ago split into 10 regional offices in four Western states, where 80 percent of its 1,300 employees now work. The motive was strictly to get closer to customers. But a happy side effect is that turnover has been cut in half. President James A. McIntyre believes that this happened in great part because decentralization created more independent managerial jobs to which employees could aspire. However, when the company has wanted to transfer people among its branches, "it's shocking to see the turndown rate," McIntyre says.

The odds are high that such rejection rates are here to stay. "People are not nearly as flexible as they used to be," says Jay R. Elliot, 41, personnel manager for Intel Corporation's California operations. Elliot has watched Intel employees put down roots, and he has seen the same phenomenon in his own life. He joined Intel's Santa Clara headquarters last year after quitting a job as personnel manager of IBM's big complex in nearby San Jose, where he had spent 14 years. He left IBM because his boss had made it clear that Elliot's further career advancement required a move to corporate headquarters in Armonk, New York—and Elliot simply could not bring himself to leave California.

READING 8
DEALING WITH THE
AGING WORKFORCE*
Jeffrey A. Sonnenfeld

The extension of mandatory retirement to age 70, signed into U.S. law last April, has caught most organizations off-guard and has surfaced latent fears about the general age drift in the workforce. Management experts and journalists over the last year or so have become quite vocal in their prophecies about the changing complexion of the work force.

We used to hear predictions about the "greening of America." Now we hear references to impending problems resulting from the "graying of America," as the country belatedly awakens to the composite effects of demographic trends, improvements in life expectancy, and changes in social legislation. Executives are being warned to anticipate changes in employee performance and attitudes, performance appraisals, retirement incentives, training programs, blocked career paths, union insurance pen-

sions, and affirmative action goals, among other worrisome issues.

Business managers have been the target of superficial and conflicting admonitions appearing in the press. As the chief executive of a leading paper company recently complained to me, "At first we were interested in the warnings. Now, they all say the same things. We hear all the fire alarms being sounded, but no one suggests where we should send the engines."

The needs of a very different workforce overshadow many of the other issues of the 1980s for which managers must prepare their organizations. Just as other organizational activities must adapt to a changing environment, human resource planning dictates a major overhaul in recruitment, development, job structure, incentives, and performance appraisal. Thus management attention should now be focused on specific problems in mid- and late-career planning.

It is hard enough to comprehend the individual aging process without at the same time assessing the effects of an entire population growing older. If Congress and President Carter had not extended the work years, leaders of America's organizations would still have had to face troublesome human resource changes.

As a consequence of the 43 million babies born in the years immediately following World War II, a middle-aged bulge is forming and eventually the 35-to-45-year-old age group will increase by 80 percent. By the year 2030, this group will be crossing the infamous bridge to 65, increasing the relative size of that population from 12 percent of all Americans to 17 percent, a jump from 31 million to 52 million people.[1]

[1] U.S. Bureau of the Census, "Current Population Reports," Series P-25, no. 61, "*Projections of the Population of the United States, 1975 to 2050*" (Washington, D.C.: U.S. Government Printing Office, 1975).

Some labor analysts point out that even those Department of Labor statistics are conservative, for likely changes downward in the mortality rate due to advanced medical treatment are not reflected in the predictions. Today, the average life expectancy is about age 73, which is 10 years longer than the years of life expected at birth in the 1950s.

On examining the rate of this change, one sees that the size of the preretirement population, between the ages of 62 and 64, will not be affected dramatically until the year 2000. Until that time, this group will expand at an annual rate of 7.6 percent above 1975 figures. Between 2000 and 2010, however, it will grow by 48 percent. For one to assume, however, that there are at least 22 years before major problems arise would be incorrect. This population bulge will be moving through several critical career phases before reaching the preretirement years.

One should pause and reflect on how, in just the next 10 years, the population bulge will be lodged in the "mid-life crisis" age. This added strain will magnify the traditional work and nonwork problems associated with the sense of limited opportunity at that age. Even sooner, the decline in youth population, which is currently causing the consolidation of secondary schools, will shift the balance of power and the approach in company recruitment.

As a consequence, a dwindling young workforce will make it more difficult to fill entry-level positions. Already there are predictions about shortages in blue-collar occupations by the mid-1980s.[2] It is not at all too soon for managers to start investigating their company demographics.

On top of the foregoing, the recent legislation on extending mandatory retirement further heightens the concern about job performance in the later years. Sooner than even the advocates of this legislation dreamed, business managers find themselves faced with contemplating the implications of long-tenured senior employees.

The immediate impact of this legislation depends, of course, on how older workers respond to the opportunity to remain on the job. Many companies are looking at the well-publicized trend toward earlier retirement, and concluding that this trend will counteract the effects of extended tenure possibilities. Labor force participation rates are dropping for workers age 55 and older and for those age 60 and over.

A retirement expert on the National Industrial Conference Board, a business research organization, said, "People want to retire while they are still young and healthy enough to enjoy the activities of their choice."[3] Another Conference Board researcher reported that these younger retirees are interested in education, in traveling, and in spending more and more money on themselves.[4]

Also, Victor M. Zin, director of employee benefits at General Motors, commented, "There used to be a stigma to going out. He was over the hill, but now it's a looked-for status. Those retirement parties, they used to be sad affairs. They are darn happy affairs now. The peer pressure is for early retirement."[5]

Research suggests, however, that such a trend reflects worker income, education, job

[2] Neal H. Rosenthal, "The United States Economy in 1985: Projected Changes in Occupations," *Monthly Labor Review*, December 1973, p. 18.

[3] Jerry Flint, "Early Retirement Is Growing in U.S.," *New York Times*, July 10, 1977.

[4] Jerry Flint, "Businessmen Fear Problems from Later Age for Retirement," *New York Times*, October 2, 1977.

[5] Ibid.

conditions, and retirement security. Dissatisfied workers and those with better pension plans seem to be more likely to opt out earlier. The experience of Sears, Roebuck and Polaroid, and several insurance companies which have already introduced flexible retirement, shows that at least 50 percent of those workers reaching age 65 remain on the job. In contrast, only 7 percent of auto workers take advantage of the opportunity to continue past age 65.

Gerontologists also do not support an early retirement trend. They cite the greater political activity of older Americans, the increasing average age of nursing home occupants, and a 1974 Harris Poll survey of retirees over 65 who claimed they would still work if they had not been forced out.[6] Such a reversed trend might be strengthened as age 65 becomes early retirement and workers see extended career opportunities.

Mid-Career Considerations

With the projection of middle-aged workers shortly comprising a large part of the workforce, and with greater numbers of older people a certainty later on, executives have good reason to be interested in relationships between age and performance.

Important age and performance considerations are manifest in younger workers well before they ever become established members of the "gray work force." In looking across the occupations of those in their mid-30s to mid-40s, one sees career drops in performance and morale, along with higher rates of turnover. There has also traditionally been higher mobility in these mid-life years as well.

Longitudinal career studies tracking people over 10-year intervals for the past three decades show that, despite growing barriers to employment in certain occupations, there has been an outstanding peak in job mobility for those in their mid-30s to mid-40s. This mobility may vary somewhat across occupations because of exceptionally high turnover rates in some jobs such as sales and service.

Candidates for second careers tend to be in their 40s and report a perceived discrepancy between personal aspirations and current opportunities for achievement and promotion. This gap widens as the opportunity for advancement decreases and results in major career frustration.

Occupational Stagnation. A survey of over 1,000 middle-aged men in managerial and professional positions found that five out of every six respondents endured a period of severe frustration and trauma which began in their early 30s. Work performance, emotional stability, and physical health were seriously affected. The study also found that one out of every six middle-aged workers never fully recovered from traumatic realizations that their sense of eternal youth had been replaced by physical deterioration and greater sensitivity to the inevitability of death. The loss of spirit led to lowered goals and diminished self-expectations.

Psychologist Erik Erikson first brought academic attention to this mid-career crisis, characterizing it as the locus of a conflict between feelings of "generativity versus stagnation,"[7] The middle-aged worker senses that new starts in life are coming to an end.

---

[6] "The Graying of America," *Newsweek*, February 28, 1977, p. 50.

[7] Erik Erikson, *Childhood and Society* (New York: W. W. Norton, 1963).

Gerontologist Bernice Neugarten, reporting on her research that indicated a new perspective on "time" appears in the mid-to-late 30s, commented:

"Life is restructured in terms of time-left-to-live rather than time-since-birth. Not only the reversal in directionality, but the awareness that time is finite is a particularly conspicuous feature of middle age. Thus 'you hear so much about deaths that seem premature—that's one of the changes that come over you over the years. Young fellows never give it a thought. . . .' The recognition that there is 'only so much time left' was a frequent theme . . . those things don't quite penetrate when you're in your 20s and you think that life is all ahead of you."[8]

Harvard psychiatrist George E. Vaillant likens this period to the stresses of adolescence and rebellion against authority and structure. His original clinical research tracks people through 40 years of life, and provides a valuable in-depth analysis of adult development. Vaillant feels that, by 40, people "put aside the preconceptions and the narrow establishment aims of their 30s and begin once again to feel gangly and uncertain about themselves. But always, such transitional periods in life provide a means of seizing one more change and finding a new solution to instinctive or interpersonal needs."[9]

From his clinical studies of people progressing through their middle years, Yale psychologist Daniel Levinson argues, "This is not an extended adolescence, but a highly formative, evolving phase of adult life." He found that, while a smooth transition is indeed possible, more often dramatic chaos is likely to characterize mid-life transition. One's former life structure (e.g., occupation, marital life) suddenly seems inappropriate and new choices must be made.

According to Levinson, "If these choices are congruent with his dreams, values, talents, and possibilities, they provide the basis for a relatively satisfactory life structure. If the choices are poorly made and the new structure seriously flawed, however, he will pay a heavy price in the next period."[10]

Regardless of the causes of this stressful period, several events in society indicate that the symptoms will soon spread in epidemic proportions:

First, those persons reaching the mid-career period in the next 10 years will have achieved far higher educational levels and associated higher aspirations than ever experienced by this group previously. By 1980, one out of four workers will have a college degree.

Second, the pattern of occupational growth suggests increasingly insufficient opportunities for advancement in a narrower occupational hierarchy. Unfavorable predictions of future needs through 1985 by the Bureau of Labor Statistics confirm the cause for distress. Professional positions will remain scarce, and the expanded demands of the 1960s for engineers, scientists, and teachers, which influenced so many young people to undertake higher education, will remain history. Clerical, sales, service, and operative workers are expected to be in demand.

Third, the size of the postwar baby boom means intense competition for whatever opportunities do exist. This competitiveness is due to the bulk of the population being at

[8] Bernice Neugarten, *Middle Age and Aging* (Chicago: University of Chicago Press, 1968), p. 97.

[9] George E. Vaillant, *Adaptation to Life* (Boston: Little Brown, 1977), p. 193.

[10] Daniel J. Levinson, "The Mid-Life Transition: A Period in Adult Psychosocial Development," *Psychiatry* 40 (1977), p. 104.

the same career point rather than being more evenly distributed.

Finally, the new legislation on mandatory retirement threatens to further limit opportunities for advancement.

Organizations should prepare now for the inevitable frustrations of career stagnation in the middle years. Already there are individual and organized complaints from those who say that somehow society has cheated them. After investing valuable years in expensive higher education, following glowing promises held out by society, graduates are entering a stagnant labor market. In many cases, academic degrees have become excess baggage to those recipients who are forced to enter the labor market at inappropriate levels.

Many research studies have warned about the growing expectations for self-fulfillment in work. Poor physical health, mental maladjustment, and social disenchantment are consequences of status conflict.

Some social analysts have suggested that anarchistic tendencies of the terrorists in Italy and other parts of Europe are expressions of rage against betrayal by the social order. The fury that burned college buildings in this country in the last decade may strike again in the coming decade, as that generation reacts in frustration to limited opportunities and a sense of defeat.

Stereotyped Perception. One of the fears of businessmen is that they will no longer be able to ease out older workers. Much of the initial reaction to the recognition of a graying work force has been to try to figure out new ways of "weeding out the deadwood." Pension inducements, less generous and "more realistic" performance appraisals, and other rationalizations for eliminating older, less desirable workers are being developed.

Who should be the target of those designs? Columnist William L. Safire has echoed the fears of many businessmen who link age to performance.

". . . old people get older and usually less productive, and they ought to retire so that business can be better managed and more economically served. We should treat the elderly with respect which does not require treating them as if they were not old. If politicians start inventing 'rights' that cut down productivity, they infringe on the consumer's right to a product at the lowest cost."[11]

The Later Years

It is important to explore how much factual evidence there is to support the stereotyping and the prejudices that link age with senility, incompetence, and lack of worth in the labor market. Age 65 was an arbitrarily selected cutoff age used by New Deal planners who looked back historically to Bismark's social welfare system in 19th century Germany.

Certainly, one does not have to look hard to find the elderly among the greatest contributors to current society. The list is long of older citizens who have made major contributions in all fields including the arts, industry, science, and government, and who continue to be worthy and inspiring members of our society.

Age-Related Change. Physiological changes are most pronounced and most identified with old age, but vary markedly in degree between individuals of the same age. It is not clear what changes are actually a result of aging and what can be attributed

---

[11] William L. Safire, "The Codgerdoggle," *New York Times*, September 3, 1977, p. 29.

to life-styles. Researchers indicate, however, that after age 50 life-style becomes a less influential factor in physiological change than aging itself.

Among age-related changes are declines in the sensory processes, particularly vision, failures in the immunity system that lead to cardiovascular and kidney problems, and degenerative diseases such as rheumatoid arthritis. While 85 percent of those workers over 65 suffer from chronic diseases, these are not sudden afflictions. Hence 75 percent of those 60 to 64 years old suffer from these diseases, many of which can be controlled by modern medical treatment. The major effects of these diseases are loss of strength in fighting off invaders and loss of mobility.

Reaction time seems to be affected by the increase in random brain activity, or "neural noise," which distracts the brain from responding to the proper neural signals. A fall in the signal-to-noise ratio would lead to a slower performance and increased likelihood of error. To correct for this possibility of error, performance is delayed to permit time to gain greater certainty. Research on cognitive abilities shows that older people are more scrupulous in the use of decision criteria before responding or forming associations required for decision making. Older people are less likely to use mnemonic or "bridging" mechanisms to link similar concepts. They require a 75 percent chance of certainty before committing themselves, while younger people will take far greater risks.[12]

When time pressure is not a relevant factor, the performance of older people tends to be as good, if not better, than that of younger people. In self-paced tests and in self-paced learning situations, older people do not have to make speed versus accuracy trade-offs and, consequently, their performance is higher.

Learning is also inhibited by the lowered signal-to-noise ratio since it interferes with memory. Most of the learning difficulties of older people stem from acquisition and recall rather than from retention. This relates to the two-step process of memory involving an initial introduction and a later retention period. That is, older people have a harder time holding information in short-term memory, awaiting long-term storage, due to neural noise. This is the same sort of problem older people have with recall.

However, once the information reaches long-term storage, it can be retained. The process of inputting the information, and retrieving it, can become blocked for intervals of time. Cognition is perhaps the most important difficulty of older workers and relates to problem solving, decision making, and general learning ability. Training in appropriate mental techniques can overcome many of these short-term memory blockages.

Similarly, intelligence tests often have age biases built in with the inherent speed versus accuracy trade-off. Recent researchers have tried to avoid such a bias and have found problem solving, number facility, and verbal comprehension to be unaffected by age. The ability to find and apply general rules to problem solving are more related to an individual's flexibility and education than to age.

Work Attitude. Research studies on all sectors of the American workforce have found that age and job satisfaction seemed to bear positive relationships, but it has become apparent that it is hard to consider job

---

[12] For an example of research on cognitive abilities, see A. T. Welford, "Thirty Years of Psychological Research on Age and Work," *Journal of Occupational Psychology* 49 (1976), p. 129.

satisfaction without considering what aspects of the work experience are important to the individual.[13] Organizations must carefully consider the type of satisfaction which they are measuring, and try to determine how both the more productive and less productive workers in different age groups vary. Perhaps the types of incentives built into a company's rewards package may encourage the less productive, rather than the more productive, older workers to remain with the company.

Along the same line, increasing monetary benefits but not expanding opportunities for job variety would be a serious mistake if the desired workers are more interested in personal growth and achievement than in financial incentives. Mastery and achievement are closely related to job satisfaction. As such, the need for mastery, or recognized accomplishment, becomes increasingly important.

Thus sudden change in job structure and social networks can be threatening to older workers. Their niche in society is defined largely by their contribution in the workplace. The job presents friendship, routine, a sense of worth, and identity. Obsolescence and job change are major fears of older workers.

Job Performance. In reviewing studies of performance by occupation for different age groups, it is important to be aware of biases built into the performance appraisals themselves. On top of this, cross-sectional studies of different age groups are also viewing different individuals. It is quite possible that selection factors in older populations ex-

plain much of the difference between older and younger populations. In other words, the older workers staying on the job may be different somehow in their skills or interests in that they have managed to remain on the same job.

Looking first at *managers,* one once again sees the manifestation of the tendency toward caution with age. Victor H. Vroom and Bernd Pahl found a relationship between age and risk taking and also between age and the value placed on risk.[14] They studied 1,484 managers, age 22 to 58, from 200 corporations and used a choice-dilemma questionnaire. It seemed that the older managers were less willing to take risks and had a lower estimate of the value of risk in general.

These findings are supported by another study on determinants of managerial information processing and decision-making performance; 79 male first-line managers with ages ranging from 23 to 57 years (a median of 40 years) were measured by the Personnel Decision Simulation Questionnaire.[15] Older decision makers tended to take longer to reach decisions even when the influence of prior decision-making experience was removed.

However, the older managers were better able to accurately appraise the value of the new information. Hesitancy about risk taking was also supported in this study; older decision makers were less confident in their decisions.

Another study focusing on task-oriented groups also found that older group mem-

---

[13] See, for example, John W. Hunt and Peter N. Saul, "The Relationship of Age, Tenure, and Job Satisfaction in Males and Females," *Academy of Management Journal* 20, 1975, p. 690; also, Bonnie Carroll, "Job Satisfaction," *Industrial Gerontology* 4 (Winter 1970).

[14] Victor H. Vroom and Bernd Pahl, "Age and Risk-Taking Among Managers," *Journal of Applied Psychology* 12 (1971), p. 22.

[15] Ronald N. Taylor, "Age and Experience as Determinants of Managerial Information Processing and Decision-Making Performance," *Academy of Management Journal* 18 (1975), p. 602.

bers once again sought to minimize risk by seeking more reliable direction.[16] Younger members were more willing to shift authority within the group and to make better use of the experience of others. In this way, younger members of the group were more flexible and more tolerant.

Studies of professionals generally concentrate on *scientists* and *engineers.* Perhaps this is because their output is so easy to measure (e.g., publications, patents). Such studies have found bimodal distributions of innovativeness as a function of age. That is to say, there were two peaks of productivity separated by 10-year intervals in research laboratories compared with development laboratories. The first peak in research laboratories occurred by age 40, and the second peak did not appear until age 50. In the development laboratories, the first peak occurred around age 45 to 50, and the second appeared around age 55 to 60.[17] These studies tracked contribution longitudinally over a person's career.

Wider studies of scholarship and artistic contribution revealed a similar first peak at about age 40 and a second peak in the late 50s. Looking more broadly at productivity, it is clear that creative activity was lowest for the 21- to 50-year-old group and generally increased with age.[18] It is also a fact, however, that younger scholars and scientists

have a more difficult time achieving recognition in the journal networks than do their senior colleagues.

Older people seem to have achieved superior standing among *sales workers* as well and to have remained higher performers. Reports from insurance companies, auto dealers, and large department stores suggest that age is an asset, if a factor at all, in performance.

In a large study of sales clerks in two major Canadian department stores, performance improved with age and experience, the actual peak performance of the sales clerks being about age 55.[19] In several organizations, particularly high technology companies, however, morale plummeted corresponding to length of service. These latter organizations may have used sales as a traditional entry position for managerial development. Those employees remaining on the job over 10 years began to perceive frustration in their personal goals of managerial advancement.

Age has had surprisingly little effect on *manual workers*. In several studies, performance seemed to remain fully steady through age 50, peaking slightly in the 30s. The decline in productivity in the 50s never seemed to drop more than 10 percent from peak performance. Attendance was not significantly affected, and the separation rate (quits, layoffs, discharges) was high for those under age 25 and very low for those over 45.[20]

These findings may not only indicate

---

[16] Ross A. Webber, "The Relation of Group Performance to Age of Members in Homogeneous Groups," *Academy of Management Journal* 17 (1974), p. 570.

[17] Ronald C. Pelz, "The Creative Years in Research Environments," Industrial and Electrical Engineering, Transaction of the Professional Technical Group on Engineering Management, 1964. EM-11, p. 23, as referenced in L. W. Porter, *"Summary of the Literature on Personnel Obsolescence,"* Conference on Personnel Obsolescence, Dallas, Stanford Research Institute and Texas Instruments, June 21–23, 1966.

[18] Wayne Dennis, "Creative Productivity Between the Ages of 20 and 80 Years," *Journal of Gerontology* 21 (1966), p. 1.

[19] *"Age and Performance in Retail Trades,"* Ottawa, Canadian Department of Labor, 1959, as referenced in Carol H. Kelleher and Daniel A. Quirk, "Age Functional Capacity and Work: An Annotated Bibliography," *Industrial Gerontology* 19 (1973), p. 80.

[20] U.S. Department of Labor, *The Older American Worker*, Report to the Secretary of Labor, title 5, sec. 715 of the Civil Rights Act of 1964 (Washington, D.C.: U.S. Government Printing Office, June 1965).

greater reliability among older workers, but also suggest that those who have remained on the job are, in some way, the most competent. Such a sorting out of abilities may not take place equally well across all industries. While tenure among factory workers within industries is reduced with age, absenteeism rates in heavy industry and construction do increase with age. This may be a more evident consequence of mismatches between job demands and physical abilities.

Finally, the high variation of manual labor performance within age groups, compared with the variation between age groups, suggests that individual differences are much more important than age group differences. The need to evaluate potential on an individual basis, and not by age group, has been convincingly established in these studies.

Considerable variation within age groups is found in studies on *clerical workers* as well. A study of 6,000 government and private industry office workers found no significant difference in output by age. Older workers had a steadier rate of work and were equally accurate. Researchers in many studies found that older clerical workers, both male and female, generally had attendance records equal to that of other workers, as well as lower rates of turnover.[21]

Corporate Experience. Many well-publicized reports identify particular companies in various parts of the country which have never adopted mandatory retirement poli-

cies yet have continued to be profitable and efficient with workers well into their 70s and 80s. For example, Thomas Greenwood, president of Globe Dye works in Philadelphia, who has retained workers hired by his grandfather, commented, "As long as a man can produce, he can keep his job."[22] The 87-year-old president of Ferle, Inc., a small company owned by General Foods, which employs workers whose average age is 71, commented, "Older people are steadier, accustomed to the working discipline."[23] Sales workers at Macy's department stores in New York have never had to conform to a mandatory retirement age, and have demonstrated no apparent decline in performance attributable directly to age.

Banker's Life and Casualty Company proudly points to its tradition of open-ended employment, retaining top executives, clerks, and secretaries through their late 60s, 70s, and 80s. Of the 3,500 workers in Banker's home office, 3.5 percent are over 65 years of age. Some have been regular members of the Banker's workforce, while others have come after being forced into retirement from other companies. The company reports that older workers show more wisdom, are more helpful and thorough, and perform their duties with fewer personality clashes. Studies on absenteeism at Banker's Life and Casualty show that those over 65 have impressive attendance records.

Large companies that have changed to flexible retirement plans in recent years have had similar satisfactory performance reports. U.S. Steel has permitted more than 153,000 nonoffice employees to continue working as long as they can maintain satis-

---

[21] See, for example, U.S. Department of Labor, Bureau of Labor Statistics, *Comparative Job Performance by Age: Office Workers*, Bulletin No. 1273 (Washington, D.C.: U.S. Government Printing Office, 1960); and U.S. Department of Labor, Bureau of Labor Statistics, *Comparative Performance by Age: Large Plants in the Men's Footwear and Household Furniture Industries*, Bulletin No. 1223 (Washington, D.C.: U.S. Government Printing Office, 1957).

[22] J. L. Moore, "Unretiring Workers, to These Employees, the Boss is a Kid," *The Wall Street Journal*, December 7, 1977.

[23] S. Terry Atlas and Michael Rees, "Old Folks at Work," *Newsweek*, September 26, 1977, p. 64.

factory levels of performance and can pass medical examinations.

Polaroid has found that those employees who choose to remain on the job after age 65 tend to be better performers. Company retirement spokesman, Joe Perkins, explained, "If you like to work, you're usually a good worker." He added that attendance is also exemplary as older workers ". . . often apologize for having missed work one day, three years ago because of a cold. There is a fantastic social aspect as people look forward to coming to work." No one is shifted between jobs at Polaroid unless the worker requests a change. Even among older workers whose jobs entail heavy physical demands high performance is maintained.

Performance Appraisal. Generally the companies just mentioned have not had to deal with older workers who remain on the job despite poor performance. There is no guarantee that workers will always be able or willing to perform well, and to relinquish their jobs when they are no longer capable of fulfilling the job requirements. Even if both the company and the individual want to continue their relationship, it is not always possible to effectively match an employee's skills with the company's job opportunities.

This need to identify differences between more and less productive older workers is a difficult distinction to make with current performance measurement techniques. The process must be objective, consistent, and based on criteria that are uniformly applied and which will endure court challenges. Arthur C. Prine, Jr., vice president of R.R. Donnelley & Sons Company, recently explained, "As soon as you pick and choose, you'll scare a lot of people when they are most sensitive. I just dread the thought of

calling someone and saying, 'You've worked for 45 years and have done a wonderful job, but you've been slipping and you must retire.' "[24]

Instead of carrying less productive older workers near retirement on the payroll, employers may begin to weed them out earlier in an effort to deter age-discrimination charges. Richard R. Shinn, president of Metropolitan Life, forecasts that "employers are going to make decisions earlier in careers if it appears that someone is going to be a problem as time goes on."[25]

Thus predictions of future performance will be important criteria in performance appraisal. Even the use of formal standard evaluations does not eliminate age bias or avoid self-fulfilling prophecies which prejudice the evaluation process.

Such a bias was shown in a recent poll of managers. A 1977 questionnaire of HBR readers concluded that "age stereotypes clearly influence managerial decisions."[26] HBR readers perceived older workers as more rigid and resistant to change and thus recommended transferring them out rather than helping them overcome a problem. The respondents preferred to retain but not retrain obsolete older employees and showed a tendency to withhold promotions from older workers compared with identically qualified younger workers.

Part of this discrimination problem is that many companies consider an employee's potential to be an important element in his evaluation. As mentioned in the section on basic abilities, chronological age never has been a valid means of measuring a worker's

[24] Irwin Ross, "Retirement at Seventy a New Trauma for Management," *Fortune*, May 8, 1978, p. 108.

[25] Ibid.

[26] Benson Rosen and Thomas H. Jerdee, "Too Old or Not Too Old," *Harvard Business Review*, November–December 1977, p. 105.

potential and now is illegal under the Age Discrimination Employment Act. The strength of various faculties may slightly correlate with age in certain regards, but there is no categorical proof that age has an effect on capabilities. Individuals vary greatly, and useful measures of potential must recognize such differences.

One of the best known functional measures was the GULHEMP system designed by Leon F. Koyl, physician from DeHaviland Aircraft.[27] This system had two dimensions, the first being a physical-mental profile and the second a job-demand profile. Workers were examined on seven factors of general physique, upper extremities, lower extremities, hearing, eyesight, mental features, and personality attributes. These individual factors were plotted on a graph and superimposed on similarly graphed job task profiles. Individuals were then viewed in relation to the job profiles available. While successful in its pilot experience, this federally supported project was not seen as a high-priority government expenditure. Thus the project in functional age measurement was terminated.

Functional measures, however, are not the answer to the performance appraisal question. While they can provide the quantifiable "expert" criteria companies might need for age-discrimination suits, their strength lies in largely assessing the potentials of physical labor. The sensitive areas in performance appraisal are evaluations of the more nebulous factors.

Ratings of "mental abilities" and "personality attributes," which were the poorest factors on the GULHEMP scale, are the most sensitive areas in the appraisal process, and the only truly relevant dimensions

[27] Leon F. Koyl and Pamela M. Hanson, *Age, Physical Ability and Work Potential* (New York: National Council on the Aging, 1969).

in most white-collar and managerial jobs. Some consulting firms have been assessing the important elements of successful job performance, appraising corporate personnel, and establishing appropriate organizational recruitment and development programs.

What Managers Can Do

How can companies resolve the kinds of frustration expressed at the beginning of this article by the chief executive of the paper company? Where can they send the fire engines? It is far easier to read about social trends than to perceive ways of preparing for them. It is clear that America's work force is graying. Older workers will tend toward caution, will experience far greater levels of frustration, and will show signs of age individually at very different rates.

However, companies are not fated for stodginess. In this section let us look at six priorities for managers to consider in preparing for the impending dramatic change in their own internal environments:

1. *Age profile.* It has been demonstrated that age per se does not necessarily indicate anything significant about worker performance. Instead, executives should look at the age distribution across jobs in the organization, as compared with performance measures, to see what career paths might conceivably open in the organizations in the future and what past performance measures have indicated about those holding these positions.

2. *Job performance requirements.* Companies should then more precisely define the types of abilities and skills needed for various posts. A clear understanding of job specifications for all levels of the organization is necessary to plan for proper employee selection, job design, and avoidance of age-discrimination suits. For example, jobs may be designed for self-pacing, may require periodic updating, or may necessitate staffing by people with certain relevant physical strengths.

Several companies have looked at the skills needed in various jobs from the chief executive down to reenlisted older and even retired workers who have the needed experience and judgment. For example, as Robert P. Ewing, president of Banker's Life and Casualty, stated, "Our company sets performance standards for each job and these standards are the criteria for employment. Age doesn't count. Getting the job done does."

Such an approach requires careful assessment of needed job competence where traits, motives, knowledge, and skills are all evaluated. When this information is considered in relation to the magnitude and direction of planned company growth, future manpower needs can be predicted. Obsolete job positions can be forecast and workers retrained in advance. Necessary experience cannot be gained overnight, and development programs should be coordinated with precise company manpower needs.

3. *Performance appraisal.* Corresponding with improved job analyses, companies must improve their analyses of individual performance as well. Age biases are reflected in both the evaluation format and the attitudes of managers. Management development programs should be aware of the need to correct these biases. Both Banker's Life and Polaroid have teams that audit the appraisals of older workers to check for unfair evaluations. These units have also been used to redress general age prejudice in the workplace.

Companies need a realistic understanding of current workforce capabilities for effective human resource planning. A company cannot adjust its development, selection, and job training strategies appropriately without knowing the current strengths and weaknesses of its workers. Additionally, potential courtroom challenges on staffing and reward procedures necessitate evidence of solid decision criteria.

4. *Workforce interest surveys.* Once management acquires a clearer vision of the company's human resource needs, and what basic abilities its workers have, it must then determine what the current workers want. If management decides that it wants to selectively encourage certain types of workers to continue with the organization while encouraging turnover of other types, it must next determine what effects different incentives will have on each group.

In addition, management must be well aware of workers' desires and values so that it can anticipate and prepare for morale drops. Understanding workforce aspirations is essential in reducing the harmful organizational and personal consequences of mid-career plateauing. For example, companies might offer counseling programs to those who frequently but unsuccessfully seek job changes, or might consider making alterations in the prevailing company culture and in the norms which link competence and mobility.

5. *Education and counseling.* Management may discover that its workers are also confronted with a variety of concerns regarding the direction of their lives after terminating current employment. Counseling on retirement and second-career development are becoming increasingly common to assist workers in adjusting to the major social disengagement following retirement.

IBM now offers tuition rebates for courses on any topic of interest to workers within three years of retirement, and continuing into retirement. Subject matter need not have any relation to one's job and many workers include courses in preparation for second careers (learning new skills, professions, and small business management).

Counseling is also important to address problems of the workforce which remains on the job. Career planning to avoid mid-career plateauing, and training programs to reduce obsolescence, must be developed by each company. The educational programs must reflect the special learning needs of older workers. Self-paced learning, for example, is often highly effective. Older workers can learn new tricks, but they need to be taught differently.

6. *Job structure.* A better understanding of basic job requirements and employee abilities and interests may indicate a need to restructure jobs. Such restructuring cannot be done, however, until management knows what the core job tasks are in the organization and what types of changes should be instituted. Alternatives to traditional work patterns should be explored jointly with the workforce. Some union leaders have expressed reservations about part-time workers whom they fear may threaten the power of organized labor. Management, too, wonders about its ability to manage part-time workers. Some part-time workers have found that they "lack clout and responsibility" in their jobs in small companies.

Management may have more flexibility than anticipated in changing conditions like work-pace, the length or timing of the workday, leaves of absence, and challenges on the job. With a tightened reward structure for older workers, satisfaction with the job may shift increasingly to intrinsic features of one's current job.

America's workforce is aging, but America's organizations are not doomed to hardening of the arteries. Older workers still have much to offer but organizations must look at certain policies to ensure that their human resources continue to be most effectively used. Organizations must be alert to changing workforce needs and flexible in responding to meet those needs.

Index of Cases

Index

This book has been set in 10 and 9 point Palatino, leaded 2 points. Chapter numbers are 30 point and chapter titles are 24 point Palatino Bold. The size of the type page is 35 by 47 picas.